The Corsini Encyclopedia *of* Psychology

The Corsini

Encyclopedia *of*

Psychology

FOURTH EDITION

Volume 1

Edited by

Irving B. Weiner
W. Edward Craighead

WILEY

John Wiley & Sons, Inc.

This book is printed on acid-free paper. ⊗

Copyright © 2010 by John Wiley & Sons, Inc. All rights reserved.

Published by John Wiley & Sons, Inc., Hoboken, New Jersey.
Published simultaneously in Canada.

No part of this publication may be reproduced, stored in a retrieval system, or transmitted in
any form or by any means, electronic, mechanical, photocopying, recording, scanning, or
otherwise, except as permitted under Section 107 or 108 of the 1976 United States Copyright
Act, without either the prior written permission of the Publisher, or authorization through
payment of the appropriate per-copy fee to the Copyright Clearance Center, Inc., 222
Rosewood Drive, Danvers, MA 01923, (978) 750-8400, fax (978) 646-8600, or on the web at
www.copyright.com. Requests to the Publisher for permission should be addressed to the
Permissions Department, John Wiley & Sons, Inc., 111 River Street, Hoboken, NJ 07030, (201)
748-6011, fax (201) 748-6008.

Limit of Liability/Disclaimer of Warranty: While the publisher and author have used their
best efforts in preparing this book, they make no representations or warranties with respect to
the accuracy or completeness of the contents of this book and specifically disclaim any implied
warranties of merchantability or fitness for a particular purpose. No warranty may be created
or extended by sales representatives or written sales materials. The advice and strategies
contained herein may not be suitable for your situation. You should consult with a professional
where appropriate. Neither the publisher nor author shall be liable for any loss of profit or any
other commercial damages, including but not limited to special, incidental, consequential, or
other damages.

This publication is designed to provide accurate and authoritative information in regard to the
subject matter covered. It is sold with the understanding that the publisher is not engaged in
rendering professional services. If legal, accounting, medical, psychological, or any other
expert assistance is required, the services of a competent professional person should be sought.

Designations used by companies to distinguish their products are often claimed as
trademarks. In all instances where John Wiley & Sons, Inc. is aware of a claim, the product
names appear in initial capital or all capital letters. Readers, however, should contact the
appropriate companies for more complete information regarding trademarks and registration.

For general information on our other products and services, please contact our Customer Care
Department within the United States at (800) 762-2974, outside the United States at (317)
572-3993 or fax (317) 572-4002.

Wiley also publishes its books in a variety of electronic formats. Some content that appears in
print may not be available in electronic books. For more information about Wiley products,
visit our website at www.wiley.com.

Library of Congress Cataloging-in-Publication Data:

The Corsini encyclopedia of psychology / edited by Irving B.
Weiner, W. Edward Craighead.—4th ed.
     v. cm.
  Rev. ed. of: The Corsini encyclopedia of psychology and behavioral science.
3rd ed. New York : Wiley, c2001.
  Includes bibliographical references and index.
  ISBN 978-0-470-17024-3 (cloth, set)
  ISBN 978-0-470-17025-0 (cloth, Volume 1)
  1. Psychology—Encyclopedias. I. Weiner, Irving B. II. Craighead, W. Edward.   III.
Corsini encyclopedia of psychology and behavioral science.
  BF31.E52 2010
  150.3—dc22

                    2009031719

Printed in the United States of America

10 9 8 7 6 5 4 3 2 1

PREFACE

The fourth edition of the *Corsini Encyclopedia of Psychology* contains entries whose utility has endured through several editions and entirely new entries written for this first edition of the twenty-first century. The selected previous entries have been updated to reflect recent conceptualizations and research findings; the new entries, which constitute approximately half of the articles, were commissioned to broaden the coverage of the encyclopedia and to capture a full range of contemporary topics in psychology. For readers previously unfamiliar with a particular topic, related articles are intended to be an informative source of what is most important for them to know about it; for readers already knowledgeable about a topic, articles related to it are intended to provide useful, concise summaries of current knowledge.

Numerous features of the encyclopedia are designed to help readers gain information about topics of interest to them. Most entries are referenced to relevant publications in the psychological literature and include suggested additional readings and cross-references to other articles in the encyclopedia on similar or related topics. Many topics are discussed in more than one entry, to provide additional facts about the topic and identify different ways of looking at it. Along with articles on substantive topics in psychology, this fourth edition of the encyclopedia includes detailed biographies of 63 of the most distinguished persons in the history of psychology. Supplementing these biographies is a special alphabetized section in Volume 4 consisting of brief biographies of 543 other important contributors to psychological theory and research.

Among other special topics, the encyclopedia features entries on the history and current status of psychology in various countries from around the world in which there are active communities of psychologists; numerous articles describing the activities and functions of the major psychological and mental health organizations and societies; and attention to topics of psychological significance in related fields of social work and medicine, with a particular emphasis on psychiatry. With further respect to the breadth of coverage in the encyclopedia, the areas in which numerous specific articles appear include the following:

- Child, adolescent, adult, midlife, and late-life development
- Cognitive, affective, and sensory functions
- Cross-cultural psychology
- Forensic psychology
- Industrial and organizational psychology
- Mental and psychological disorders listed in the DSM, the PDM, and the ICD
- Neuroscience and the biological bases of behavior
- Language and linguistic processes
- Personality processes and interpersonal relationships
- Psychological therapies and psychosocial interventions
- Psychopharmacological treatment methods
- Psychological and neuropsychological assessment methods
- Social and environmental influences on behavior
- Statistical procedures and research methods

After selecting the topics for inclusion in this fourth edition, the editors set about to identify and recruit individuals whose scholarly background and professional experience would enable them to give inquiring readers clear and accurate information about topics of their interest. We believe that we were highly successful in this effort, and we are grateful to the approximately 1,200 authors who contributed articles to these four volumes. We appreciate their knowledge, their literacy, and their tolerance of our editing their work to achieve a consistent format across the large number of articles in the four volumes.

An undertaking of this magnitude involves the cooperation and collaboration of a many of individuals in addition to its authors. We would like first of all to express our gratitude to Patricia Rossi, Wiley Executive Editor in Psychology, who brought us together to work on this project. She has been a wonderful editor, leading and supporting us throughout this process beginning with our first meeting to discuss the encyclopedia, what we would include, and the development and implementation of a plan to bring the publication of the encyclopedia to fruition. It is hard to imagine a better editor with whom one could work. For their essential roles in the preparation and production of the encyclopedia, we would like to thank as well Wiley staff members Kim Nir, Senior Production Editor; Kathleen DeChants, Senior Editorial Assistant; and Ester Mallach, Administrative Assistant.

We are especially grateful to Jennifer Moore for her many activities associated with the production of these volumes. She found addresses (especially e-mail addresses), retyped articles, located missing references for articles, and was generally extremely helpful in our completion of the manuscript. We would also like to express our appreciation to Rebecca Suffness and Ava Madoff, who helped with various aspects of the development of the manuscript.

Finally, we would like to thank four librarians who reviewed our plan for the new edition and provided valuable advice concerning its format and content: Barbara Glendenning of the University of California Berkeley Library; Sally Speller of the New York Public Library; Bruce Stoffel of the Milner Library at Illinois State University; and Michael Yonezawa of the University of Calfornia Riverside Library.

Irving B. Weiner, Tampa, FL
W. Edward Craighead, Atlanta, GA
June, 2009

HOW TO USE THIS ENCYCLOPEDIA

Welcome to this fourth edition of the *Corsini Encyclopedia of Psychology*. Like its predecessors, the fourth edition is organized into four distinct parts. Each of the four volumes begins with frontmatter that includes the entire list of entries for all four volumes and a complete list of the contributing authors and their affiliations. The second part of each volume consists of the actual entries, listed in alphabetical order. Included among these alphabetized entries are biographies of 63 of the most important figures in the history of psychology. Alphabetized entries constitute most of Volumes 1 though 3 and some of Volume 4. As a third part of the encyclopedia, Volume 4 contains a section of brief biographies for 543 other important contributors to psychological theory, research, and practice. Finally, Volume 4 concludes with an Author Index and a Subject Index for the entire four-volume set.

Readers looking for information on a particular topic should first check the list of entries in the frontmatter to see if there is an article on that topic. If so, the article can be found in its alphabetical location. If not, the next place to look is the Subject Index in Volume 4. If the topic is mentioned in the encyclopedia, the Subject Index will identify the particular pages on which the topic is discussed. Readers looking for information about a particular person should also first check the list of entries to see if the person is one of the distinguished individuals for whom there is a biography among the alphabetized entries. If not, the next place to look is the section of Brief Biographies in Volume 4. Should the person not appear in either of these locations, the searcher should turn to the Author Index. If the person is mentioned anywhere in the encyclopedia, the author index will identify the pages on which this mention occurs. In most instances in which persons are mentioned in an article, some of their publications are included in a list of references accompanying the article.

An important additional source for locating information is in the cross-referencing that appears at the end of most entries. The following cross-references listed with five selected entries illustrate this guide to further information and also speak to the breadth of coverage in the encyclopedia:

Central Nervous System (See also Brain; Neuroscience; Parasympathetic Nervous System; Sympathetic Nervous System)

Cognitive Development (See also Emotional Development; Intellectual Development; Social Cognitive Development)

Major Depressive Disorder (See also Antidepressant Medications; Depression; Depressive Personality Disorder)

Multivariate Methods (See also Analysis of Covariance; Analysis of Variance; Factor Analysis; Multiple Correlation)

Psychotherapy (See also Counseling; Current Psychotherapies; Psychotherapy Research; Psychotherapy Training)

Each of the cross-references accompanying an article has cross-references of its own to related articles. By pursuing the trail of cross-references related to a topic, readers can maximize the amount of information they can get from the encyclopedia.

CORSINI ENCYCLOPEDIA ENTRIES

CONTRIBUTORS

Norman Abeles, Michigan State University

Jonathan S. Abramowitz, University of North Carolina at Chapel Hill

Lyn Y. Abramson, University of Wisconsin-Madison

Philip A. Ackerman, Georgia Institute of Technology

Thomas G. Adams, University of Arkansas

Wayne Adams, George Fox University, Newburg, OR

Howard Adelman, University of California, Los Angeles

Bernard W. Agranoff, University of Michigan

Muninder K. Ahluwalia, Montclair State University

Leona S. Aiken, Arizona State University

Peter Alahi, University of Illinois College of Medicine, Peoria

Anne Marie Albano, Columbia University College of Physicians and Surgeons

John A. Albertini, Rochester Institute of Technology

Amelia Aldao, Yale University

Mark D. Alicke, Ohio University

Daniel N. Allen, University of Nevada Las Vegas

Lauren B. Alloy, Temple University

Carolyn J. Anderson, University of Illinois, Urbana-Champaign

Corey Anderson, Pacific University

Keelah D. Andrews, Wheaton College

Hymie Anisman, Carleton University

Heinz L. Ansbacher, University of Vermont

Martin M. Antony, Ryerson University, Toronto, Canada

Steven J. Anzalone, State University of New York at Binghamton

Robert P. Archer, Eastern Virginia Medical School

Ruben Ardila, National University of Columbia

Eirikur Orn Arnarson, Landspitali University Hospital, Reykjavik, Iceland

Mark Arnoff, University at Albany, SUNY

Jane Ashby, University of Massachusetts Amherst

Gord, J. G. Asmundson, University of Regina, Canada

John A. Astin, California Pacific Medical Center, San Francisco, CA

Martha Augoustinos, University of Adelaide, Australia

Tatjana Ave, University of Chicago

Oksana Babenko, University of Alberta, Canada

Michael Babyak, Duke University Medical Center

Bahador Bahram, University College London, United Kingdom

Clark Baim, Birmingham Institute of Psychodrama, Birmingham, UK

Tatiana N. Balachova, University of Oklahoma Health Sciences Center

Scott A. Baldwin, Brigham Young University

Michael Bambery, University of Detroit Mercy

Albert Bandura, Stanford University

Marie T. Banich, University of Colorado at Boulder

Steven C. Bank, Center for Forensic Psychiatry, Ann Arbor, MI

Jacques P. Barber, University of Pennsylvania

Daniel Barbiero, US National Academy of Sciences

John A. Bargh, Yale University

Blanche Barnes, Mumbai, India

Sean Barns, Binghamton University

Barnaby B. Barratt, Prescott, AZ

Rowland P. Barrett, Warren Alpert Medical School of Brown University

Tammy D. Barry, University of Southern Mississippi

Jennifer L. Bass, The Kinsey Institute, Bloomington, IN

David S. Batey, University of Alabama School of Medicine

C. Daniel Batson, University of Kansas

Steven H. R. Beach, University of Georgia

Theodore P. Beauchaine, University of Washington

Eric Beauregard, Simon Fraser University

Robert B. Bechtel, University of Arizona

Judith S. Beck, Beck Institute for Cognitive Therapy and Research and University of Pennsylvania

Carolyn Black Becker, Trinity University

Deborah C. Beidel, University of Central Florida

Bernard C. Beins, Ithaca College

Mark Beitel, Yale University School of Medicine

Genevieve Belleville, University of Quebec at Montreal, Canada

J. B. Bennett, Texas Christian University

Shannon Bennett, University of California, Los Angeles

Yossef S. Ben-Porath, Kent State University

Gary G. Benston, Ohio State University

Peter M. Bentler, University of California, Los Angeles

Tanya N. Beran, University of Calgary, CA

Stanley Berent, University of Michigan

Kathleen Stassen Berger, Bronx Community College, City University of New York

Arjan Berkeljon, Brigham Young University

Gregory S. Berns, Emory University School of Medicine

Jane Holmes Bernstein, Children's Hospital Boston and Harvard Medical School

David T. R. Berry, University of Kentucky

Michael D. Berzonsky, State University of New York at Cortland

Jeffrey L. Binder, Argosy University/Atlanta

Andri S. Bjornsson, University of Colorado at Boulder

Danielle Black, Northwestern University

Donald W. Black, University of Iowa Roy J. and Lucille A. Carr College of Medicine

Alberto Blanco-Campal, University College Dublin, Ireland

Ricardo D. Blasco, University of Barcelona, Spain

Sidney Bloch, University of Melbourne, Australia

Deborah Blum, University of Wisconsin-Madison

Mark S. Blum, University of Iowa

Anthony F. Bogaert, Brock University, St. Catharines, Canada

G. Anne Bogat, Michigan State University

Johan J. Bolhuis, Utrecht University, The Netherlands

Trevor G. Bond, James Cook University, Australia

Mark W. Bondi, Veterans Administration San Diego Healthcare System and University of California, San Diego

C. Alan Boneau, George Mason University

Hale Bolak Boratav, Istanbul Bilgi University, Turkey

John G. Borkowski, University of Notre Dame

Robert F. Bornstein, Adelphi University

James F. Boswell, Pennsylvania State University

Lyle E. Bourne, Jr., University of Colorado

James N. Bow, Hawthorn Center, Northville, MI

Christopher R. Bowie, Queen's University, Kingston, ON, Canada

Elza Boycheva, Binghamton University

Michelle J. Boyd, Tufts University

Virginia Brabender, Widener University

Paul Bracke, Mountain View, CA

Rom Brafman, Palo Alto, CA

David Brang, University of California, San Diego

Gary G. Brannigan, State University of New York-Plattsburg

Ann D. Branstetter, Missouri State University

Myron L. Braunstein, University of California, Irvine

Jeremy W. Bray, RTI International, Research Triangle Park, NC

Alisha Breetz, American University

Britton W. Brewer, Springfield College

K. Robert Bridges, Pennsylvania State University at New Kensington

Sara K. Bridges, University of Memphis

Arthur P. Brief, University of Utah

John Briere, University of Southern California

Nicholas E. Brink, Coburn, PA University of Colorado

Martin Brodwin, California State University, Los Angeles

Arline L. Bronzaft, City University of New York

Sarah Brookhart, Association for Psychological Science

Alisha L. Brosse, University of Colorado at Boulder

Ronald T. Brown, Temple University

Sheldon S. Brown, North Shore Community College, Danvers, MA

Caroline B. Brown, University of North Carolina at Chapel Hill

Patricia Brownell, Fordham University Graduate School of Social Service

Timothy J. Bruce, University of Illinois College of Medicine, Peoria

Martin Brüne, University of Bochum, Bochum, Germany

Silvina Brussino, National University of Córdoba, Córdoba, Argentina

Angela Bryan, University of New Mexico

Sue A. Buckley, University of Portsmouth, United Kingdom

Kristen A. Burgess, Emory University School of Medicine

M. Michele Burnette, Columbia, SC

Brenda Bursch, David Geffen School of Medicine at UCLA

William Buskist, Auburn University

James N. Butcher, University of Minnesota

Barbara M. Byrne, University of Ottawa, Canada

James P. Byrnes, Temple University

Desiree Caban, Columbia University

John T. Cacioppo, University of Chicago

David J. Cain, Alliant International University, San Diego

Lawrence G. Calhoun, University of North Carolina Charlotte

Amanda W. Calkins, Boston University

Jennifer L. Callahan, University of North Texas

Joseph Cambray, Massachusetts General Hospital, Harvard Medical School

Jenna Cambria, University of Maryland

Jonathan M. Campbell, University of Georgia

Keith Campbell, University of Georgia

Larry D. Campeau, Clarkson University School of Business

Caroline Campion, Tulane University School of Medicine

Tyrone Cannon, University of California, Los Angeles

Claudio Cantalupo, Clemson University

E. J. Capaldi, Purdue University

Rudolf N. Cardinal, University of Cambridge, United Kingdom

Bernardo Carducci, Indiana University Southeast

Leeanne Carey, National Stroke Research Institute, Melbourne, Australia

Jon Carlson, Governors State University

Laura A. Carlson, University of Notre Dame

Malique L. Carr, Pacific Graduate School of Psychology

Sonia Carrillo, University of the Andes, Bogotá, Columbia

Rachel Casas, University of Iowa College of Medicine

Margaret J. Cason, University of Texas at Austin

Wendy J. Caspar, University of Texas at Arlington

Louis G. Castonguay, Pennsylvania State University

Yoojin Chae, University of California, Davis

Kate Chapman, Pennsylvania State University

Stephanie G. Chapman, University of Houston

Susan T. Charles, University of California, Irvine

Cary Cherniss, Rutgers University

Allan Cheyne, University of Waterloo, Canada

Jean Lau Chin, Adelphi University

Jinsoo Chin, University of Michigan

Nehrika Chowli, University of Washington

Joan C. Chrisler, Connecticut College

Shawn E. Christ, University of Missouri-Columbia

Edward R. Christophersen, Children's Mercy Hospitals and Clinics, Kansas City, KS

Charles Clifton, Jr., University of Massachusetts Amherst

W. Glenn Clingempeel, Fayetteville State University

Sam V. Cochran, University of Iowa

Rosemary Cogan, Texas Tech University

Adam B. Cohen, Arizona State University

Barry H. Cohen, New York University

Karen R. Cohen, Canadian Psychological Association

Lisa J. Cohen, Beth Israel Medical Center and Albert Einstein College of Medicine

Taya R. Cohen, Northwestern University

P. T. Cohen-Kettenis, VU University Medical Center, Amsterdam, The Netherlands

Theodore Coladarci, University of Maine

Raymond J. Colello, Virginia Commonwealth University

Frank L. Collins, Jr., University of North Texas

Lillian, Comas-Diaz, Transcultural Mental Health Institute, Washington, DC

David J. Y. Combs, University of Kentucky

Jessica L. Combs, University of Kentucky

Jonathan Comer, Columbia University

Mary Connell, Fort Worth, TX

Daniel F. Connor, University of Connecticut School of Medicine

Michael J. Constatino, Pennsylvania State University

Frederick L. Coolidge, University of Colorado at Colorado Springs

Steven H. Cooper, Harvard Medical School

Stewart Cooper, Valparaiso University

Tori Sacha Cordiano, Case Western Reserve University

David Cordy, University of Iowa College of Medicine

Stanley Coren, University of British Columbia, Canada

Dave Corey, Portland Oregon Police Bureau

Erminio Costa, University of Illinois, Chicago

Stefany Coxe, University of Arizona

Robert J. Craig, Roosevelt University

Benjamin H. Craighead, Salisbury Pediatrics, Salisbury, NC

Margaret C. Craighead, Emory University School of Medicine

W. Edward Craighead, Emory University School of Medicine

Phebe Cramer, Williams College

Michelle G. Craske, University of California, Los Angeles

Candice E. Crerand, Children's Hospital of Philadelphia

Mario Cristancho, University of Pennsylvania School of Medicine

Pilar Cristancho, University of Pennsylvania School of Medicine

Thomas S. Critchfield, Illinois State University

Paul Crits-Christoph, University of Pennsylvania

Katherine B. Crocker, John College, City University of New York

Jessica M. Cronce, Yale University

Julio Eduardo Cruz, University of the Andes, Bogotá, Columbia

Pim Cuijpers, VU University of Amsterdam, The Netherlands

E. Mark Cummings, University of Notre Dame

David Yun Dai, University at Albany, State University of New York

Melita Daley, University of California, Los Angeles

J. P. Das, University of Alberta, Canada

William Davidson II, Michigan State University

Joanne Davila, SUNY Stony Brook

Samuel B. Day, Indiana University

Edward L. Deci, University of Rochester

Gregory DeClue, Sarasota, FL

Patricia J. Deldin, University of Michigan

Patricia R. DeLucia, Texas Tech University

Heath A. Demaree, Case Western Reserve University

Florence L. Denmark, Pace University

M. Ray Denny, Michigan State University

Brendan E. Depue, University of Colorado at Boulder

Leonard R. Derogatis, Sheppard Pratt Hospital and Johns Hopkins University School of Medicine

Paula S. Derry, Paula Derry Enterprises in Health Psychology, Baltimore, MD

Sreedhari D. Desai, University of Utah

Esther Devall, New Mexico State University

Donald A. Dewsbury, University of Florida

Lisa J. Diamond, University of Utah

Milton Diamond, University of Hawaii

Andreas Dick-Niederhauser, University Psychiatry Service, Berne, Switzerland

Adele Diederich, Jacobs University Bremen, Germany

Marc J. Diener, Argosy University, Washington, DC

Volker Dietz, University Hospital Balgrist, Zurich, Switzerland

Nicholas DiFonzo, Rochester Institute of Technology

Raymond A. DiGiuseppe, St. Johns University

Sona Dimidjian, University of Colorado, Boulder

Beth Doll, University of Nebraska Lincoln

Lorah H. Dom, Cincinnati Children's Hospital Medical Center

Aila K. Dommestrup, University of Georgia

John W. Donahue, University of Massachusetts

M. Brent Donnellan, Michigan State University

William I. Dorfman, Nova Southeastern University

William F. Doverspike, Atlanta, GA

Peter W. Dowrick, University of Hawai'i at Manoa

David J. A. Dozois, University of Western Ontario, Canada

Peter A. Drake, DePaul University

Michelle Drefs, University of Calgary, Canada

Clifford J. Drew, University of Utah

Eric Y. Drogin, Harvard Medical School

Dan Du, Tufts University

Rand A. Dublin, Hofstra University

David Dunning, Cornell University

Francis T. Durso, Georgia Institute of Technology

Donald G. Dutton, University of British Columbia, Canada

Joel A. Dvoskin, University of Arizona College of Medicine

Lutz H. Ecksenberger, German Institute for International Educational Research and Johann Wolfgang Goethe University, Frankfort, Germany

Barry A. Edelstein, West Virginia University

Louisa Egan, Yale University

Howard Eichenbaum, Boston University

Steven M. Elias, New Mexico State University

David Elkind, Tufts University

Brigitte Elle, Roskilde University, Roskilde, Denmark

Robert W. Elliott, Aerospace Health Institute, Los Angeles, CA

Roger E. Enfield , West Central Georgia Regional Hospital, Columbus, GA

Jan B. Engelmann, Emory University School of Medicine

Alyssa M. Epstein, University of California, Los Angeles

Jane Epstein, Weill College of Medicine at Cornell University

Franz Etping, University of Florida

Sean Esbjorn-Hargens, John F. Kennedy University, Pleasant Hill, CA

Chris Evans, Nottingham University, United Kingdom

David R. Evans, University of Western Ontario, Canada

Sara W. Feldstein Ewing, University of New Mexico

Carol Falender, University of California, Los Angeles

Jeanne M. Fama, Harvard University Medical School

Qijuan Fang, University of Hawaii at Manoa

Richard F. Farmer, Oregon Research Institute

Jaelyn, R. Farris, University of Notre Dame

Greg A. Febbraro, Counseling for Growth and Change, L.C., Windsor Heights, IA

Laurie Beth Feldman, University at Albany, SUNY

Eva Dreikers Ferguson, Southern Illinois University Edwardsville

Shantel Fernandez, Medical University of South Carolina

Joseph R. Ferarri, Drake University

F. Richard Ferraro, University of North Dakota

Seymour Feshbach, University of California, Los Angeles

Chelsea E. Fiduccia, University of North Texas

Dustin Fife, University of Oklahoma

Ione Fine, University of Washington

Stephen Finn, Center for Therapeutic Assessment, Austin, TX

Michael B. First, Columbia University

Constance T. Fischer, Duquesne University

Kurt W. Fischer, Harvard University

Kelly S. Flanagan, Wheaton College

Debra A. Fleischman, Rush University Medical Center, Chicago

Gordon L. Flett, York University, Canada

Peter Fonagy, University College London, United Kingdom

Rex Forehand, University of Vermont

Joseph P. Forgas, University of New South Wales, Australia

Blaine J. Fowers, University of Miami

Carol A. Fowler, University of Connecticut

Marcel G. Fox, Beck Institute for Cognitive Therapy and Research, Bala Cynwynd, PA

Lisa A. Fraleigh, University of Connecticut School of Medicine

Norah Frederickson, University College London, United Kingdom

Carolyn R. Freeman, McGill University, Canada

Fred Friedberg, Stony Brook University

Harris Friedman, University of Florida

Regan E. Friend, University of Kentucky

W. Otto Friesen, University of Virginia

Irene Hanson Frieze, University of Pittsburgh

Rober H. Friis, California State University Long Beach

Patrick C. Friman, Boys Town, NE

Randy O. Frost, Smith College

Daniel Fulford, University of Miami

K. W. M. Fulford, University of Warwick Medical School and

St. Cross College, Oxford, United Kingdom

Wyndol Furman, University of Denver

Karina Royer Gagnier, York University, Toronto, Canada

Rodolfo Galindo, University of California, Merced

David A. Gallo, University of Chicago

Howard N. Garb, Lackland Air Force Base, Texas

Steven J. Garlow, Emory University School of Medicine

Gareth Gaskell, University of York, York, United Kingdom

Marisa Gauger, University of Nevada, Las Vegas

Kurt F. Geisinger, University of Nebraska-Lincoln

Pamela A. Geller, Drexel University

Charles J. Gelso, University of Maryland, College Park

Carol George, Mills College

Mark S. George, Medical University of South Carolina

Melissa R. George, University of Notre Dame

Kenneth J. Gergen, Swarthmore College

Andrew R. Getzfeld, New Jersey City University

Mary Beth Connolly Gibbons, University of Pennsylvania

Uwe Gielen, St. Francis College, Brooklyn, NY

Howard Giles, University of California, Santa Barbara

Charles F. Gillespie, Emory University School of Medicine

Marika Ginsburg-Block, University of Delaware

Richard G. T. Gipps, University of Warwick Medical School, United Kingdom

Todd A. Girard, Ryerson University, Toronto, Canada

James T. Gire, Virginia Military Institute

Thomas A. Glass, Honolulu, Hawaii

David Gleaves, University of Canterbury, New Zealand

Peter Glick, Lawrence University, Appleton, WI

Laraine Masters Glidden, St. Mary's College of Maryland

Lisa Hagen Glynn, University of New Mexico

Juan Carlos Godoy, National University of Córdoba, Córdoba, Argentina

Maurice Godwin, St. Augustine's College, Raleigh, NC

Hillel Goelman, University of British Columbia, Canada

Jerry Gold, Adelphi University

Peter B. Goldblum, Pacific Graduate School of Psychology

Charles Golden, Nova Southeastern University

Marvin R. Goldfried, Stony Brook University

Tina R. Goldstein, University of Pittsburgh

Robert L. Goldstone, Indiana University

Reginald Golledge, University of California Santa Barbara

Juliya Golubovich, Michigan State University

Emily E. Good, Pennsylvania State University

Jeffrey L. Goodi, Uniformed Service of the Health Sciences

Madeline S. Goodkind, University of California, Berkeley

Gail S. Goodman, University of California, Davis

Amanda Gordon, Sydney, Australia

Robert M. Gordon, Allentown, PA

Bernard S. Gorman, Nassau Community College, SUNY and Hofstra University

William Graebner, State University of New York, Fredonia

James W. Grau, Texas A & M University

Melanie Greenaway, Emory University College of Medicine

Lauren M. Greenberg, Drexel University

Martin S. Greenberg, University of Pittsburgh

William A. Greene, Eastern Washington University, Spokane

Shelly F. Greenfield, Harvard Medical School and McLean Hospital

Gregoire, Jacques Gregoire, Catholic University of Louvain, Belgium

Robert Gregory, SUNY Upstate Medical University

Robert J. Gregory, Wheaton College, IL

Bruce Greyson, University of Virginia Health System

Tiffany M. Griffin, University of Michigan

Vladas Griskevicius, University of Minnesota

Robert J. Grissom, San Francisco State University

Marc Grosjean, Leibniz Research Centre for Working Environment and Human Factors, Dortmund, Germany

James J. Gross, Stanford University

Gary Groth Marnat, Pacifica Graduate Institute, Carpinteria, CA

Corey L. Guenther, Ohio University

Bernard Guerin, University of South Australia, Australia

R. E. Gutierrez, Drake University

Russell Haber, University of South Carolina

Michael N. Haderlie, University of Nevada Las Vegas

William K. Hahn, University of Tennessee, Knoxville

William E. Haley, University of Wisconsin-Milwaukee

Judy E. Hall, National Register of Health Service Providers in Psychology

Mark B. Hamner, Medical University of South Carolina

Gregory R. Hancock, University of Maryland, College Park

Leonard Handler, University of Tennessee

Jo-Ida Hansen, University of Minnesota

Rochelle F. Hanson, Medical University of South Carolina

Lisa A. Harlow, University of Rhode Island

Robert J. Harnish, Pennsylvania State University at New Kensington

Robert G. Harper, Baylor College of Medicine

Anton H. Hart, William Alanson White Institute

Stephen D. Hart, Simon Fraser University, Canada

Chrisopher B. Harte, University of Texas at Austin

Glenn Hartelius, California Institute of Integral Studies

Abby B. Harvey, Temple University

Allison Harvey, University of California, Berkeley

Philip Harvey, Emory University School of Medicine

Nadia T. Hasan, University of Akron

David B. Hatfield, Developmental Behavioral Health, Colorado Springs, CO

Elaine Hatfield. University of Hawaii

Louise Hawkley, University of Chicago

Steven C. Hayes, University of Nevada

N. A. Haynie, Honolulu, HI

Alice F. Healy, University of Colorado

Bridget A. Hearon, Boston University

Pamela Heaton, University of London, United Kingdom

Monica Hedges, University of Southern California

Elaine M. Heiby, University of Hawaii at Manoa

Kathleen M. Heide, University of South Florida

Nicole Heilbrun, University of North Carolina at Chapel Hill

Deborah Heiser, State Society on Aging of New York

Janet E. Helms, Boston College

Lynne Henderson, Shyness Institute, Palo Alto, CA

Scott W. Henggeler, Family Service Research Center, Charleston, SC

James M. Hepburn, Waynesburg University

Gregory M. Herek, University of California, Davis

Hubert J. M. Hermans, Radboud University, Nijmegen, The Netherlands

Adriana Hermida, Emory University School of Medicine

Laura Hernandez-Guzman, National Autonomous University of Mexico

Edwin L. Herr, Pennsylvania State University

M. Sandy Hershcovis, University of Manitoba, Canada

Allen K. Hess, Auburn University at Montgomery

Herbert Heuer, University of Dortmund, Germany

Paul L. Hewitt, University of British Columbia, Canada

Richard E. Heyman, Stony Brook University

Ernest R. Hilgard, Stanford University

Thomas T. Hills, Indiana University

Stephen P.Hinshaw, University of California, Berkeley

Stephen C. Hirtle, University of Pittsburgh

Christine Hitchcock, University of British Columbia, Canada

CONTRIBUTORS

Kristin Hitchcock, Northwestern University

Julian Hochberg, Columbia University

Ralph Hoffman, Yale University

Thomas P. Hogan, University of Scranton

Ronald R. Holden, Queens University, Canada

Lori L. Holt, Carnegie Mellon University

Ryan Holt, California State University at San Bernardino

Phan Y. Hong, University of Wisconsin Oshkosh

Audrey Honig, Los Angeles Count Sheriff's Department

Burt Hopkins, Seattle University

Adam O. Horvath, Simon Fraser University, Canada

Arthur C. Houts, University of Memphis

Robert H. Howland, University of Pittsburgh School of Medicine

Wayne D. Hoyer, University of Texas, Austin

Jeanette Hsu, Veterans Affairs Palo Alto Health System

Charles H. Huber, New Mexico State University

Samuel Hubley, University of Colorado, Boulder

Daniel A. Hughes, Lebanon, PA

Bradley E. Huitema, Western Michigan University

Olivia Y. Hung, Emory University School of Medicine

Scott J. Hunter, University of Chicago

Steven K. Huprich, Eastern Michigan University

Jena Huston, Argosy University, Phoenix, AZ

Kent Hutchison, University of New Mexico

Pamela Hyde, New Zealand Psychological Society, New Zealand

William G. Iacono, University of Minnesota

James R. Iberg, The Focusing Institute, Chicago, IL

Kaori Idemaru, University of Oregon

Stephen S. Ilardi, University of Kansas

Aubrey Immelman, St. John's University, MN

Mary Helen Immordino-Yang, University of Southern California

Rick Ingram, University of Kansas

Kathleen C. Insell, University of Arizona

Thomas R. Insel, National Institute of Mental Health

David Irwin, Drexel University College of Medicine

James S. Jackson, University of Michigan

Russell E. Jackson, California State University at San Marcos

Safia C. Jackson, University of Washington

Frederick M. Jacobsen, Transcultural Mental Health Institute, Washington, DC

Jacob Jacoby, New York University

Jack James, National University of Ireland, Galway, Ireland

Leonard A. Jason, DePaul University

Sharon Rae Jenkins, University of North Texas

Arthur R. Jensen, University of California, Berkeley

David W. Johnson, University of Minnesota

Deborah F. Johnson, University of Southern Maine

James H. Johnson, University of Florida

Kathryn Johnson, Arizona State University

Roger T. Johnson, University of Minnesota

Sheri L. Johnson, University of Miami

Susan K. Johnson, University of North Carolina-Charlotte

Keith S. Jones, Texas Tech University

Staci Jordan, University of Denver

Anthony S. Joyce, University of Alberta, Canada

Julia I. Juechter, Georgia State University

Barbara J. Juhasz, Wesleyan University

Robert M. Julien, Oregon Health Sciences University

James W. Kalat, North Carolina State University

Thomas Kalpakoglou, Institute of Behaviour Research and Therapy, Athens, Greece

Randy W. Kamphaus, Georgia State University

Jan H. Kamphuis, University of Amsterdam, The Netherlands

Anil Kanjee, Human Sciences Research Council, South Africa

Frank R. Kardes, University of Cincinnati

Georgia Karutzos, RTI International, Triangle Research Park, NC

Nadine J. Kaslow, Emory University

Marina Katz, San Diego, CA

Alan S. Kaufman, Yale University School of Medicine

James C. Kaufman, California State University at San Bernardino

Margaret M. Keane, Wellesley College

Terence M. Keane, Boston University School of Medicine

Christopher A. Kearney, University of Nevada, Las Vegas

Pamela K. Keel, University of Iowa

Michael Keesler, Drexel University and Villanova University School of Law

W. Gregory Keilin, University of Texas at Austin

Ken Kelley, University of Notre Dame

Francis D. Kelly, Greenfield, MA

Joan B. Kelly, Corte Madera, CA

Mary E. Kelley, Emory University

John A. Kenard, Temple University

Carrie Hill Kennedy, Kennedy Naval Aerospace Medical Institute, Pensacola, FL

Ray D. Kent, University of Wisconsin

Roy M. Kern, Vytautus Magnus University, Lithuania

Roy P. C. Kessels, Radboud Unversity Nijmegen, The Netherlands

Ronald C. Kessler, Harvard Medical School

Corey L. M. Keyes, Emory University

Kathryn Kidd, Colorado State University

John F. Kihlstrom, University of California, Berkeley

Bruce A. Kimball, USDA/APHIS/NWRC and Monell Chemical Senses Center, Philadelphia, PA

Gregory A. Kimble, Duke University

Douglas Kimmel, City College, City University of New York

Bruce M. King, Clemson University

Cheryl A. King, University of Michigan

D. Brett King, University of Colorado at Boulder

Roger E. Kirk, Baylor University

Ryo Kitado, Queens University, CA

Karen Strom Kitchener, University of Denver

Elena Klaw, San Jose State University

Daniel L. Klein, Stony Brook University

Dena A. Klein, Albert Einstein College of Medicine

Peggy J. Kleinplatz, University of Ottawa, Canada

E. David Klonsky, Stony Brook University

Tracy A. Knight, Western Illinois University

Kenneth A. Kobak, MedAvante Research Institute, Hamilton, NJ

Carolynn S. Kohn, University of the Pacific

George F. Koob, Scripps Research Institute, La Jolla, CA

Sander L. Koole, VU University, Amsterdam, The Netherlands

Mary P.Koss, University of Arizona

Beth A. Kotchick, Loyola College in Maryland

Chrystyna D. Kouros, University of Notre Dame

Margaret Bull Kovera, John Jay College, City University of New York

Robin M. Kowalski, Clemson University

Eileen M. Kranz, Brandeis University

Alan Kraut, Association for Psychological Science

Dennis L. Krebs, Simon Fraser University, Canada

Tina Kretschmer, University of Sussex, United Kingdom

Ann M. Kring, University of California, Berkeley

Stanley Krippner, Saybrook Graduate School, San Francisco, CA

Radhika Krishnamurthy, Florida Institute of Technology

Joachim I. Krueger, Brown University

Robert F. Krueger, Washington University at St. Louis

Romana C. Krycak, University of Missouri-Kansas City

Kathryn Kuehnle, University of South Florida

G. Tarcan Kumkale, Koc University, Istanbul, Turkey

Robert G. Kunzendorf, University of Massachusetts-Lowell

Jung Kwak, University of Wisconsin-Milwaukee

Virginia S. Y. Kwan, Princeton University

Margie E. Lachman, Brandeis University

Michael Lambert, Brigham Young University

Dominque Lamy, Tel Aviv University, Israel

Frank J. Landy, Baruch College, City University of New York

Brittany Lannert, Michigan State University

Molly Larsen, Emory University

Randy J. Larsen, Washington University

Daniel K. Lapsley, University of Notre Dame

Leah Lavelle, University of Chicago

Michael Lavin, Washington, DC

Patrick F. Lavin, Chattanooga, TN

Foluso M. Williams Lawal-Solarin, Emory University

Jay Lebow, Northwestern University

Susan J. Lederman, Queen's University, Kingston, Canada

Courtland C. Lee, University of Maryland at College Park

Erica D. Marshall Lee, Emory University

Sandra R. Leiblum, Robert Wood Johnson Medical School, University of Medicine and Dentistry New Jersey

Martin Leichtman, Leawood, KS

Jacqueline P. Leighton, University of Alberta, Canada

Michael P. Leiter, Acadia University, Nova Scotia, Canada

Larry M. Leitner, Miami University

Alison P. Lenton, University of Edinburgh, Scotland, United Kingodm

Frederick T. L. Leong, Michigan State University

Richard M. Lerner, Tufts University

David Lester, Richard Stockton College, Pamona, NJ

Richard Lettieri, New Center for Psychoanalysis, Los Angeles, CA

L. Stan Leung, University of Western Ontario, Canada

Ronald F. Levant, University of Akron

Allan Levey, Emory University College of Medicine

Karen Z. H. Li, Concordia University, Montreal

Norman P. Li, University of Texas at Austin

Shu-Chen Li, Max Planck Institute for Human Development, Berlin, Germany

Ting-Kai Li, National Institute on Alcohol Abuse and Alcoholism, NIH, Bethesda MD

Peter A. Lichtenberg, Wayne University

Scott O. Lillienfeld, Emory University

Geoff Lindsay, University of Warwick, Coventry, United Kingdom

Roderick C. Lindsay, Queens University, Ontario Canada

Marsha M. Linehan, University of Washington

Carol F. Lippa, Drexel University College of Medicine

Mark D. Litt, University of Connecticut

Roderick J. Little, University of Michigan

John E. Lochman, University of Alabama

John C. Loehlin, University of Texas at Austin

Jeffrey M. Lohr, University of Arkansas

Richard G. Lomax, Ohio State University

Jeffrey D. Long, University of Minnesota

Julie R. Lonoff, Miami University

David Loomis, California State University at San Bernardino

Christopher M. Lootens, University of North Carolina at Greensboro

Jeffrey P. Lorberbaum, Medical University of South Carolina

William R. Lovallo, VA Medical Center and University of Oklahoma Health Sciences Center

Tamara Penix Loverich, Eastern Michigan University

Kristen Lowell, University of North Dakota

Rodney L. Lowman, Lake Superior State University

Sara E. Lowmaster, Texas A&M University

James K. Luiselli, May Institute, Randolph MA

Katarina Lukatela, Brown University Medical School

Ralph W. Lundin, Wheaton, IL

Robert W. Lundin, The University of the South

Desiree Q. Luong, San Jose State University

Steven Jay Lynn, Binghamton University

Shelley M. MacDermind, Purdue University

William M. Mace, Trinity College, Hartford CT

Armando Machado, University of Minho, Portugal

Maya Machunsky, University of Marburg, Germany

Colin M. MacLeod, University of Waterloo, Canada

Joshua W. Madsen, VA San Diego Healthcare System

Jeffrey J. Magnavita, University of Hartford

Brittain L. Mahaffey, University of North Carolina at Chapel Hill

Robert Malgady, Touro College, New York, NY

Jill Malik, Stony Brook University

Thomas E. Malloy, Rhode Island College

Tina Malti, University of Zurich, Switzerland

Valerie Malzer, University of Chicago

Rachel Manber, Stanford University School of Medicine

Jon K. Maner, Florida State University

Jamal K. Mansour, Queens University, Ontario Canada

Amy Jo Marcano-Reik, University of Iowa

Stephanie C. Marcello, University Medicine and Dentistry of New Jersey

Stephen Maren, University of Michigan

Richard S. Marken, University of California at Los Angeles

G. Alan Marlatt, University of Washington

Ronald R. Martin, University of Regina, Canada

Steve Martino, Yale University School of Medicine

Ana P. G. Martins, Purdue University

Melvin H. Marx, N. Hutchinson Island, FL

Joseph D. Matarazzo, Oregon Health Science University

Kenneth B. Matheny, Georgia State University

Nancy Mather, University of Arizona

David Matteo, Drexel University

Brian P. Max, Boston University School of Medicine

Molly Maxfield, University of Colorado at Colorado Springs

Ryan K. May, Marietta College

Richard E. Mayer, University of California, Santa Barbara

Dan Mayton, Lewis-Clark State College

Randi E. McCabe, McMaster University, Hamilton, Ontario, Canada

Robert McCaffrey, State University of New York at Albany

Barry McCarthy, American University

Elizabeth McCauley, University of Washington and Seattle Children's Hospital

Brook McClintic, University of Colorado at Boulder

Allyn McConkey-Russell, Duke University Medical Center

Bridget L. McConnell, State University of New York at Binghamton

Christine McCormick, University of Massachusetts-Amherst

Barbara S. McCrady, University of New Mexico

Robert R. McCrae, National Institute on Aging

James P. McCullough, Jr., Virginia Commonwealth University

Janet L. McDonald, Louisiana State University

Kate L. McDonald, University of Arizona

William M. McDonald, Emory University School of Medicine

Lata M. McGinn, Albert Einstein College of Medicine, Yeshiva University

Eleanor McGlinchey, University of California, Berkeley

F. Dudley McGlynn, Auburn University

Robert E. McGrath, Fairleigh Dickinson University

Ian McGregor, York University, Toronto, Canada

Laura Gale McKee, University of Vermont

John Paul McKinney, Michigan State University

Kathleen McKinney, University of Wyoming

Patrick E. McNight, George Mason University

Kaitlyn McLachlan, Simon Fraser University, Canada

Richard J. McNally, Harvard University

Neil McNaughton, University of Otago, Dunedin, New Zealand

Kateri McRae, Stanford University

Paul W. McReynolds, University of Nevada, Reno

Stephanie K. Meador, Developmental Behavioral Health, Colorado Springs, CO

Heide Meeke, Pacific University

J. Reid Meloy, University of California, San Diego

Ronald Melzack, McGill University, Canada

Dana Menard, University of Ottawa, Canada

Tamar Mendelson, Johns Hopkins Bloomberg School of Public Health

Jorge Mendoza, University of Oklahoma

Douglas S. Mennin, Yale University

Andrew J. Menzel, Florida State University

Jessie Menzel, University of South Florida

Peter F. Merenda, University of Rhode Island

Stanley B. Messer, Rutgers University

Cindy M. Meston, University of Texas at Austin

Lotte Meteyard, University College London, United Kingdom

Alicia E. Meuret, Southern Methodist University

Andrew M. Meyers, University of Memphis

Kristina D. Micheva, Stanford University School of Medicine

Jesse B. Milby, University of Alabama at Birmingham

Alec L. Miller, Albert Einstein College of Medicine

Andrew H. Miller, Emory University School of Medicine

Carlin J. Miller, University of Windsor, Canada

Catherine Miller, Pacific University

Gloria Miller, University of Denver

Joshua D. Miller, University of Georgia

Mark W. Miller, Boston University School of Medicine

Ralph I. Miller, State University of New York at Binghamton

Cindy Miller-Perrin, Pepperdine University

Glenn W. Milligan, The Ohio State University

Theodore Millon, Institute for Advanced Studies in Personology and Psychopathology, Port Jervis, NY

Jon Mills, International Federation for Psychoanalytic Education

Michael Mingroni, Newark, DE

Hamid Mirsalimi, Argosy University, Atlanta

Victor Molinari, University of South Florida

Ivan Molton, University of Washington

Alexandra Monesson, University of Massachusetts, Amherst

Myriam Mongrain, York University, Toronto, Canada

Timothy E. Moore, York University, Toronto, Canada

Nilly Mor, Hebrew University of Jerusalem, Israel

Marlene M. Moretti, Simon Fraser University, Canada

Leslie C. Morey, Texas A&M University

George A. Morgan, Colorado State University

Robert D. Morgan, Texas Tech University

Charles M. Morin, Laval University, Canada

John W. Morin, Center for Offender Rehabilitation and Education, Fort Lauderdale, FL

Daniel G. Morrow, University of Illinois at Urbana-Champaign

Ezequiel Morsella, San Francisco State University and University of California, San Francisco

Susan M. Mosher, Boston University School of Medicine and Department of Veterans Affairs Healthcare System, Boston Campus

Christohper J. Mruk, Bowling Green State University

Paul M. Muchinsky, University of North Carolina at Greensboro

Kim T. Mueser, Dartmouth Medical School

Michael J. Mullard, Pacifica Graduate Institute, Carpinteria, CA

Ricardo F. Munoz, University of California, San Francisco

Anjana Muralidharan, Emory University

Nancy L. Murdock, University of Missouri-Kansas City

Kevin R. Murphy, Pennsylvania State University

Frank B. Murray, University of Delaware

Lisa M. Nackers, University of Florida

Raymond Nairn, New Zealand Psychological Society, New Zealand

James S. Nairne, Purdue University

Julius Najab, George Mason University

Urs M. Nater, University of Zurich, Switzerland

Francis A. Nealon, Rice Diet Program, Durham, NC

Becca Neel, Arizona State University

Sonya Negriff, Cincinnati Children's Hospital Medical Center

Robert A. Neimeyer, University of Memphis

Rosemery O. Nelson-Gray, University of North Carolina at Greensboro

Cory F. Newman, University of Pennsylvania School of Medicine

Thomas C. Neylan, University of California, San Francisco

Arthur M. Nezu, Drexel University

Christine Maguth Nezu, Drexel University

Michael E. R. Nicholls, University of Melbourne, Australia

Pekka Niemi, University of Turku, Finland

Gil G. Noam, Harvard University and McLean Hospital

Pedro J. Nobre, University of Tras-os-Montes e Alto, Douro, Portugal

Samuel S. Norberg, Pennsylvania State University

Jacob N. Norris, Texas Christian University

Brian A. Nosek, University of Virginia

Raymond W. Novaco, University of California, Irvine

Jack Novick, Michigan Psychoanalytic Institute

Kerry Kelly Novick, Michigan Psychoanalytic Institute

David Nussbaum, University of Toronto Scarborough, Canada

Amy K. Nuthall, University of Colorado at Boulder

Michael S. Nystul, New Mexico State University

William H. O'Brien, Bowling Green State University

Lynn E. O'Connor, Wright Institute and University of California, Berkeley

William T. O'Donohue, University of Nevada, Reno

Daniel O'Leary, Stony Brook University

Thomas Oakland, University of Florida

Carmen Oemig, Bowling Green State University

Christin, M. Ogle, University of California, Davis

Sumie Okazaki, University of Illinois at Urbana-Champaign

Piotr Oles, John Paul II Catholic University of Lublin, Lublin, Poland

Kristina R. Olson, Yale University

Eyitayo Onifade, Michigan State University

Jeanne Ellis Ormrod, University of Northern Colorado and University of New Hampshire

Pamela Orpinas, University of Georgia

Ingrid Osbuth, Simon Fraser University, Canada

Marlene, Boston University School of Medicine and Department of Veterans Affairs Healthcare System, Boston Campus

Frank Oswald, University of Heidelberg, Germany

Michael W. Otto, Boston University

Randy K. Otto, University of South Florida

Willis F. Overton, Temple University

Timothy J. Ozechowski, Oregon Research Institute

Steven R. Pacynski, SRCD Research Associate

David C. Palmer, Smith Colleege

Edward L. Palmer, Davidson College

Josefa N. S. Pandeirada, University of Santiago, Portugal

Joyce S. Pang, Nonyang Technological University, Singapore

Mauricio R. Papine, Texas Christian University

Kenneth I. Pargament, Bowling Green State University

Bernadette Park, University of Colorado

Martin Parker, Northwestern University

Fayth Parks, Georgia Southern University

Christopher J. Patrick, University of Minnesota

Diane T. V. Pawluk, Virginia Commonwealth University

Joshua W. Payen, University of North Texas

Joseph J. Pear, University of Manitoba, Canada

Mary Jo Peebles, Bethesda, MD

Daniel Perlman, University of North Carolina Greensboro

Michael G. Perri, University of Florida

Melissa Peskin, University of Pennsylvania

Christopher Peterson, University of Michigan

Jean Sunde Peterson, Purdue University

John Petrila, University of South Florida

Charles S. Peyser, University of the South.

Bruce E. Pfeiffer, University of New Hampshire

Daniel Philip, University of North Florida

Sheridan Phillips, University of Maryland School of Medicine

John Piacentini, University of California, Los Angeles

Jennifer R. Piazza, University of California, Irvine

Wade E. Pickren, Ryerson University, Toronto, Canada

Ralph L. Piedmont, Loyola College in Maryland

Alison Pike, University of Sussex, United Kingdom

Aaron L. Pincus, Pennsylvania State University

Nancy A. Piotrowski, Capella University

William Piper, University of British Columbia, Canada

Thomas G. Plante, Santa Clara University and Stanford University School of Medicine

Ingrid Plath, German Institute for International Educational Research, Frankfort, Germany

John Porcerelli, Wayne State University School of Medicine

Amir Poreh, Cleveland State University

Nicole Porter, DePaul University

Bruno Poucet, Universite de Provence, Marseille, France

Daniel J. Povinelli, University of Louisiana

Michael J. Power, University of Edinburgh, Scotland, United Kingdom

Judith Preissle, University of Georgia

Jose M. Preito, University of Madrid, Spain

George P. Prigatano, St. Joseph's Hospital and Medical Center, Phoenix, AZ

Mitchell J. Prinstein, University of North Carolina at Chapel Hill

Jerilynn C. Prior, University of British Columbia, Canada

Robert W. Proctor, Purdue University

Dennis Proffitt, University of Virginia

Jean Proulx, University of Montreal

Aina Puce, West Virginia University School of Medicine

Tom Pyszczynski, University of Colorado at Colorado Springs

Sara Honn Qualls, University of Colorado at Colorado Springs

Naomi L. Quenk, Analytical Psychology, Ltd., Albuquerque, NM

James Campbell Quick, University of Texas at Arlington

Mark Quigg, University of Virginia

Karen S. Quigley, Department of Veterans Affairs New Jersey Healthcare System, East Orange, NJ and New Jersey Medical School, University of Medicine and Dentistry of New Jersey

Christine A. Rabinek, University of Michigan

Nosheen K. Rahman, Punjab University, Lahore, Pakistan

Joseph S. Raiker, University of Central Florida

Adrian Raine, University of Pennsylvania

Charles Raison, Emory University School of Medicine

Leo Rangell, University of California, Los Angeles

Mark D. Rapport, University of Central Florida

Richard L. Rapson, University of Hawaii

June Rathbone, University College London, England

William J. Ray, Pennsylvania State University

Tenko Raykov, Michigan State University

Keith Rayner, University of California, San Diego

Robert J. Reese, University of Kentucky

William C. Reeves, Centers for Disease Control and Prevention, Atlanta, GA

Lynn P. Rehm, University of Houston

Holly A. Reich, Wheaton College

Tara C. Reich, University of Manitoba, Canada

Charles S. Reichardt, University of Denver

Scott, A. Reid, University of California, Santa Barbara

Jost Reinecke, University of Bielefeld, Germany

Harry T. Reis, University of Rochester

Sally M. Reis, University of Connecticut

Joseph Renzulli, University of Connecticut

Gilbert Reyes, Fielding Graduate University, Santa Barbara, CA

Cecil R. Reynolds, Texas A&M University

William M. Reynolds, Humboldt State University, Arcata, CA

Soo Hyun Rhee, University of Colorado-Boulder

George R. Rhodes, Ola Hou Clinic, Aiea, HI

David C. S. Richard, Rollins College

Jodie Richardson, McGill University

Margaret W. Riddle, University of Denver

Cedar Riener, University of Virginia

Christopher L. Ringwalt, Pacific Institute for Research and Evaluation, Chapel Hill, NC

Evan F. Risko, University of British Columbia, Canada

Lorie A. Ritschel, Emory University School of Medicine

Rostyslaw W. Robak, Pace University

Gary J. Robertson, Tampa, FL

Richard W., University of California, Davis

George H. Robinson, University of North Alabama

Jennifer L. Robinson, University of Texas Health Sciences Center at San Antonio

Kathryn A. Roecklin, University of Vermont

Karin Roelofs, Leiden University, The Netherlands

Lizabeth Roemer, University of Massachusetts, Boston

Ronald Roesch, Simon Fraser University, Canada

Roger Roffman, University of Washington

Richard Rogers, University of North Texas

Kelly J. Rohan, University of Vermont

Michael J. Rohrbaugh, University of Arizona

George Ronan, Central Michigan University

Elsa Ronningstam, Harvard University Medical School

Steven P. Roose, New York State Psychiatric Institute, Columbia University

Robert Rosenthal, University of California, Riverside, and Harvard University

Alan M. Rosenwasser, University of Maine

David H. Rosmarin, Bowling Green State University

William H. Ross, University of Wisconsin at La Crosse

Joseph S. Rossi, University of Rhode Island

Barbara Olasov Rothbaum, Emory University School of Medicine

Donald K. Routh, Florida Gulf Coast University

Linda Rubin, Texas Women's University

Jerry W. Rudy, University of Colorado, Boulder

Michael G. Rumsey, U.S. Army Research Institute for the Behavioral and Social Sciences, Arlington, VA

Sandra W. Russ, Case Western Reserve University

Alexandra Rutherford, York University, Canada

Bret R. Rutherford, New York State Psychiatric Institute, Columbia University

Richard M. Ryan, University of Rochester

Jeremy Safran, New School for Social Research

Donald H. Saklofske, University of Calgary, Canada

Morgan T. Sammons, National Register of Health Service Providers in Psychology

Trond Sand, University of Science and Technology and Trondheim University Hospital, Norway

William C. Sanderson, Hofstra University

Jerome Sanes, Alpert Medical School of Brown University

Craig Santerre, VA Puget Sound Health Care System, Seattle Division

Craig Santree, VA Puget Sound Health Care System, Seattle Division

Edward P. Sarafino, College of New Jersey

David B. Sarwer, University of Pennsylvania School of Medicine

William I. Sauser, Jr., Auburn University

Lisa M. Savage, State University of New York at Binghamton

Victoria Savalei, University of California, Los Angeles

Mark L. Savickas, Northeastern Ohio Universities College of Medicine

Douglas J. Scaturo, State University of New York Upstate Medical University and Syracuse VA Medical Center

E. Warner Schaie, Pennsylvania State University

Marcia J., Scherer, University of Rochester Medical Center

Dawn M. Schiehser, Veterans Administration San Diego Healthcare System and University of California, San Diego

Elizabeth A. Schilling, University of Connecticut Health Center

Lindsay J. Schipper, University of Kentucky

Kelly Schloredt, University of Washington and Seattle Children's Hospital

Karen B. Schmaling, University of North Carolina at Charlotte

Frank L. Schmidt, University of Iowa

Klaus Schmidtke, University Hospital Freiburg, Germany

Neal Schmitt, Michigan State University

Kirk J. Schneider, Center for Existential Therapy, San Francisco, CA

Michael E. Schoeny, Institute for Juvenile Research and University of Illinois at Chicago

Joseph E. Schumacher, University of Alabama School of Medicine

Julie A. Schumacher, University of Mississippi Medical Center

Dale H. Schunk, University of North Carolina at Greensboro

Alexander J. Schut, Pennsylvania State University

Alan Schwartz, University of Illinois at Chicago

Eliezer Schwartz, Argosy University Chicago

Jonathan P. Schwartz, University of Houston

Marlene B. Schwartz, Yale University

Stephanie Schwartz, Association for Behavioral and Cognitive Therapies, New York, NY

Julie B. Schweitzer, University of California Davis School of Medicine

Lisa S. Scott, University of Massachusetts, Amherst

Gretchen B. Sechrist, University at Buffalo, State University of New York

Daniel L. Segal, University of Colorado at Colorado Springs

Lauren S. Seifert, Malone College

Stephen Seligman, University of California, San Francisco

Edward P. Serafino, College of New Jersey

Ilene A. Serlin, San Francisco, CA

Michael C. Seto, Center for Addiction and Mental Health and University of Toronto, Canada

William R. Shadish, University of California, Merced

Anne Shaffer, University of Minnesota

David L. Shapiro, Nova Southeastern University

Deane H. Shapiro, University of California School of Medicine, Irvine

Francine Shapiro, Mental Research Institute, Palo Alto, CA

Johanna Shapiro, University of California School of Medicine, Irvine

Josh D. Shapiro, University of California, San Diego

Kenneth J. Shapiro, Animals and Society Institute, Washington Grove, MD

Shauna L. Shapiro, Santa Clara University

Brian A. Sharpless, University of Pennsylvania

Richard J. Shavelson, Stanford University

Erin S. Sheets, Brown University Medical School and Butler Hospital

Anees A. Sheikh. Marquette University

Kenneth J. Sher, University of Missouri

Lonnie R. Sherrod, Fordham University

Alissa Sherry, University of Texas at Austin

Stephanie A. Shields, Pennsylvania State University

Robert Shilkret, Mount Holyoke College

Merton A. Shill, University of Michigan

Varda Shoham, University of Arizona

Lauren B. Shumaker, University of Denver

Kristin Shutts, Harvard University

Jerome Siegel, University of California, Los Angeles

Judith P. Siegel, Silver School of Social Work at New York University

David Silbersweig, Weill College of Medicine at Cornell University

Francisco J. Silva, University of Redlands

Doris K. Silverman, New York, NY

Wendy K. Silverman, Florida International University

Louise Silvern, University of Colorado at Boulder

Marshall L. Silverstein, Long Island University

Steven M. Silverstein, University Medicine and Dentistry of New Jersey

Amy M. Smith Slep, Stony Brook University

Frank L. Small, University of Washington

Colin Tucker Smith, University of Virginia

Gregory T. Smith, University of Kentucky

J. Allegra Smith, University of Colorado

Jeffrey K. Smith, University of Otago, New Zealand

Lisa F. Smith, University of Otago, New Zealand

Nathan Grant Smith, McGill University, Canada

Richard H. Smith, University of Kentucky

Ronald E. Smith, University of Washington

Myriam J. Sollman, University of Kentucky

Roger M. Solomon, Buffalo Center for Trauma and Loss, Buffalo, NY

Subhash R. Sonnad, Western Michigan University

Peter W. Sorenson, University of Minnesota

Elizabeth Soucar, Penndel Mental Health Center, Penndel, CA

Susan C. South, Purdue University

Marion Spengler, Saarland University, Saarbrucken, Germany

Dante Spetter, Tufts University

Eric P. Spiegel, James A. Haley VAMC, Tampa, FL

Charles D. Spielberger, University of South Florida

Robert Spies, Buros Institute of Mental Measurements

Frank M. Spinath, Saarland University, Saarbrucken, Germany

Philip Spinhoven, Leiden University, The Netherlands

Bonnie Spring, Northwestern University

Jayne E. Stake, University of Missouri—St. Louis

Jayne M. Standley, Florida State University

Ursula J. Staudinger, Jacobs University, Bremen, Germany

Jeffrey T. Steedle, Council for Aid to Education, New York, NY

Timothy A. Steenburgh, Indiana Wesleyan University

Rebecca Y. Steer, Emory University

Dana Steidtmann, University of Kansas

Axel Steiger, Max Planck Institute of Psychiatry, Munich, Germany

Howard Steiger, McGill University

Emily Stein, Weill College of Medicine at Cornell University

Jennifer Steinberg, Cognitive and Behavioral Consultants of Westchester, White Plains, NY

Melissa K. Stern, University of Florida

Robert M. Stern, Pennsylvania State University

Michael J. Stevens, Illinois State University

Paul Stey, University of Notre Dame

Timothy R. Stickle, University of Vermont

John M. Stokes, Pace University

Stephen Strack, U.S. Department of Veterans Affairs, Los Angeles, CA

David L. Streiner, University of Toronto, Canada

George Stricker, Argosy University Washington

Natalie Stroupe, University of Kansas

Margaret L. Stubbs, Chatham University, Pittsburgh, PA

Sally J. Styles, Yale University

Peter Suedfeld, University of British Columbia, Canada

Alan Sugarman, University of California, San Diego

Jeff Sugarman, Simon Fraser University, Canada

Jennifer A. Sullivan, Duke University Medical Center

Norman D. Sundberg, University of Oregon

Elizabeth Susman, Pennsylvania State University

Lisa A. Suzuki, New York University

Harvey A. Swadlow, Brown University Medical School

Robert A. Sweet, University of Pittsburgh and VA Pittsburgh Healthcare System

Derek D. Szafranski, University of the Pacific

Brian J. Taber, Oakland University

Raymond Chip Tafrate, Central Connecticut State University

Harold Takooshian, Fordham University

Rebecca L. Tamas, University of Louisville School of Medicine

Junko Tanaka-Matsumi, Kansei Gakuin University, Japan

Sombat Tapanya, Chiang Mai University, Thailand

Steven Taylor, University of British Columbia

Richard G. Tedeschi, University of North Carolina Charlotte

Hedwig Teglasi, University of Maryland

Howard Tennen, University of Connecticut

Lois E. Tetrick, George Mason University

Timothy J. Teyler, Washington State University

Michael E. Thase, University of Pennsylvania School of Medicine

Ryan Thibodeau, St. John Fisher College, Rochester, NY

Jay C. Thomas, Pacific University

J. Kevin Thompson, University of South Florida

Scott M. Thompson, University of Maryland

Travis Thompson, University of Minnesota School of Medicine

B. Michael Thorne, Mississippi State University

Shira Tibon, Bar-Ilan University and Academic College of Tel-Aviv, Yaffo, Israel

Jane G. Tillman, The Austen Riggs Center, Stockbridge, MA

Michael Tobia, Temple University

James Toch, State University of New York at Albany

Patrick H. Tolan, Institute for Juvenile Research and University of Illinois at Chicago

David F. Tolin, Institute of Living, Hartford, CT and Yale University School of Medicine

Jessica L. Tracy, University of British Columbia, Canada

Daniel Tranel, University of Iowa College of Medicine

Michael Treanor, University of Massachusetts, Boston

Warren W. Tryon, Fordham University

Ivy F. Tso, University of Michigan

William T. Tsushima, Straub Clinic and Hospital, Honolulu, HI

Larissa Tsvetkova, St. Petersburg State University, St. Petersburg, Russia

Jane Tucker, New York University

Denis C. Turk, University of Washington

Dio Turner II, University of Nevada, Las Vegas

Rachael Unger, Towson University

Annmarie Urso, State University of New York College at Geneseo

Uma Vaidyanathan, University of Minnesota

Mary M. Valmas, Boston University School of Medicine and Department of Veterans Affairs Healthcare System, Boston Campus

Henk T. van der Molen, Erasmus University Rotterdam, The Netherlands

Judy L. Van Raalte, Springfield College

Rodney D. Vanderploeg, James A. Haley VAMC, Tampa, FL and University of South Florida

Susan M. VanScoyoc, University of Phoenix

Myrna V. Vashcenko, Tufts University

Ruut Veenhoven, Erasmus University Rotterdam, The Netherlands

Beth A. Venzke, Concordia University-Chicago

Mieke Verfaellie, Boston University School of Medicine and VA Boston Healthcare System

Philip E. Vernon, University of Calgary, Canada

Ian Verstegen, Philadelphia, PA

Ryan P. Vetreno, State University of New York at Binghamton

Donald J. Viglione, Alliant International University, San Diego, CA

Penny S. Visser, University of Chicago

Jennifer E. Vitale, Hampden-Sydney College, Hampden-Sydney, VA

Ladislav Volicer, University of South Florida

Nora D. Volkow, National Institute on Drug Abuse

Jennifer Vonk, University of Louisiana

Kim-Phuong, L. Vu, California State University, Long Beach

Paul L. Wachtel, City College and CUNY Graduate Center

Nicholas J. Wade, University of Dundee, Scotland, United Kingdom

Harriet Wadeson, University of Illinois at Chicago

Hans-Werner Wahl, University of Heidelberg, Germany

Howard Wainer, National Board of Medical Examiners

Deward E. Walker, Jr., University of Colorado at Boulder

Elaine F. Walker, Emory University

Stephanie Wallio, VA Connecticut Health Care System and University of Kansas

Roger Walsh, University of California College of Medicine, Irvine

Michael R. Walther, University of Wisconsin-Milwaukee

Alvin Wang, University of Central Florida

Philip S. Wang, National Institute of Mental Health Care Policy

William H. Watson, University of Rochester School of Medicine and Dentistry

Adam Waytz, University of Chicago

Stanley Wearden, West Virginia University

Danny Wedding, University of Missouri-Columbia School of Medicine

Bernard Weiner, University of California, Los Angeles

Karen Colby Weiner, Southfield, Michigan

Irving B. Weiner, University of South Florida

Daniel Weisholtz, Weill College of Medicine at Cornell University

Daniel J. West, Pennsylvania State University

Myrna M. Weissman, College of Physicians and Surgeons and Mailman School of Public Health, Columbia University

Julie C. Weitlauf, Veterans Affairs Palo Alto Health Care System and Stanford University School of Medicine

Barbara J. Wendling, University of Arizona

Kathryn R. Wentzel, University of Maryland, College Park

Michael Wertheimer, University of Colorado at Boulder

Donald Wertlieb, Tufts University

Hans Westmeyer, Free University of Berlin, Germany

Michael G. Wheaton, University of North Carolina at Chapel Hill

Mark E. Wheeler, University of Pittsburgh

Mark A. Whisman, University of Colorado at Boulder

Stephen G. White, University of California, San Francisco

Thomas W. White, Training and Counseling Services, Shawnee Mission, KS

Thomas A. Widiger, University of Kentucky

Donald E. Wiger, Elmo, MN

Allan Wigfield, University of Maryland

Ken Wilber, Integral Institute, Boulder, CO

Sabine Wilhelm, Harvard University Medical School

Douglas A. Williams, University of Winnipeg

Paul Williams, Queens University Belfast, Northern Ireland

Rebecca B. Williamson, The Hague, The Netherlands

Hillary D. Wilson, University of Washington

Janelle Wilson, University of Minnesota Duluth

Michael Windle, Emory University

Idee Winfield, College of Charleston

David L. Wolitzky, New York University

Nina Wong, University of Central Florida

Margaret T. T. Wong-Riley, Medical College of Wisconsin

Diana S. Woodruff-Pak, Temple University

Douglas W. Woods, University of Wisconsin-Milwaukee

Robert F. Woolfolk, Rutgers University

J. Brooke Wright, Wheaton College

Jesse H. Wright, University of Louisville School of Medicine

Li-Tzy-Wu, Duke University Medical Center

Robert E. Wubbolding, Center for Reality Therapy, Cincinnati, OH

Yufang Yang, Chinese Academy of Sciences, Beijing, China

William A. Yost, Arizona State University

Larry J. Young, Emory University School of Medicine

Adam Zagelbaum, Sonoma State University

Patricia A. Zapf, John Jay College of Criminal Justice, City University of New York

Tamika C. H. Zapolski, University of Kentucky

Charles H. Zeanah, Tulane University School of Medicine

Moshe Zeidner, University of Haifa, Israel

Elias A. Zerhouni, National Institutes of Health

Eric A. Zillmer, Drexel University

Philip Zimbardo, Stanford University

Grégoire Zimmerman, University of University of Lausanne, Switzerland

Marvin Zuckerman, University of Delaware

Ofer Zur, Zur Institute, Sonoma, CA

A

ABA AND ABAB DESIGNS

Single-case designs are often used to assess the effects of an intervention. The designs usually focus on one participant who is observed numerous times. Large-sample designs, by comparison, use many participants who are observed only a few times. The simplest single-case design is the AB design. The letter A denotes a baseline phase during which no intervention is in effect; the letter B denotes the intervention phase. The baseline phase serves three purposes. It provides data about a participant's performance prior to instituting an intervention, it provides a basis for predicting a participant's future performance in the absence of an intervention, and it indicates the normal variability in the participant's performance.

The results of AB designs are often presented by means of a graph in which the horizontal axis represents successive observations during the two phases and the vertical axis represents a measure of the participant's performance. Any difference between the A and B phases in the average level of the data points or change in the trend of the data points is attributed to the intervention. The special issues involved in the statistical analysis of single-subject designs are discussed by Kazdin (1984).

Unfortunately the AB design is subject to a number of threats to internal validity, that is, threats to correctly concluding that the intervention is, in fact, responsible for changes in performance. The most serious threats are history, instability, and instrumentation. For example, if a participant's performance changes during the B phase, it is always possible that some unknown variable coincided with the application of the intervention and is responsible for the changes. In order to rule out this possibility, researchers can reintroduce the A phase in which the intervention is withdrawn. The resulting design is called an ABA design. If, when the intervention is withdrawn, the participant's performance returns to or resembles the baseline level, a researcher can be reasonably confident that the intervention and not some other unknown variable was responsible for the changes.

There is a problem with the ABA design: the experiment ends with the baseline phase. As a result, the participant is denied the full benefits of the intervention. This can raise ethical and moral issues. These issues clearly arise in clinical and educational settings where the intervention is designed to reduce an unacceptable behavior or increase a desirable behavior. The solution to this problem is to reintroduce the B phase following the second A phase so that the experiment ends with the intervention phase. The design is called an ABAB design. In addition to solving the ethical and moral issues associated with the ABA design, the ABAB has an added benefit. Internal validity is enhanced because the researcher can monitor three transition cycles: from A to B, from B to A, and from A to B.

REFERENCE

Kazdin, A. E. (1984). Statistical analyses for single-case experimental designs. In D. H. Barlow & M. Hersen (Eds.) *Single case experimental designs* (2nd ed.). New York: Pergamon Press.

SUGGESTED READINGS

Hayes, S. C. (1992). Single case experimental design and empirical clinical practice. In A. E. Kazdin (Ed.) *Methodological issues & strategies in clinical research*. Washington, DC: American Psychological Association.

Barlow, D. H., & M. Hersen (Eds.). *Single case experimental designs* (2nd ed.). New York: Pergamon Press.

ROGER E. KIRK
Baylor University

See also: **Time-Series Analysis**

ABILITY TESTS (See Aptitude Testing)

ABNORMAL PSYCHOLOGY

A number of laypeople will be more than happy to say that they know when someone is suffering from mental illness and that they know abnormal behavior when they see it. They purport to be experts on abnormal psychology, with the ability to recognize and perhaps even diagnose abnormality in their fellow human beings. Of course, many of these individuals are incorrect. Here is an example.

You live in an apartment building in a large city. One fine spring day, you hear a man outside singing (in a very loud voice) an aria. You look out the window and watch him walking down the street, singing in his operatic tenor, loud enough for everyone to hear. This man is well-dressed in a work uniform, appears well coiffed, and is not really interacting with other people. The aria fades as he continues down the street. You detect nothing unusual in his behavior except for the fact that he was singing and doing so rather loudly. Some people were obviously annoyed; some even crossed the street to avoid him (Getzfeld, 2006).

Would this man's behavior be considered abnormal? Is his behavior considered dangerous to himself or to others? Perhaps he is just a happy individual, willing to share his voice with the rest of the neighborhood. Perhaps he is what Weeks and James (1995) call an eccentric. Eccentrics have odd or unusual habits, but they are not mentally ill.

Generally speaking, psychologists define abnormal behavior by using three perspectives. First, the statistical frequency perspective labels behavior as abnormal if it occurs rarely or infrequently in relation to the behavior of the general population. This perspective looks at the individual's behavior and sees if it matches up with the behaviors of the general population. For example, while most people get depressed at some point during the year, most people do not get so depressed that they cannot leave the house because they are so weakened from the depression; or even get out of bed regularly. The opera singer might fit into this category, since people rarely or infrequently sing loudly on the street, especially opera.

Social norms define behavior as abnormal if the behavior deviates greatly from accepted social standards, values, or norms. Norms are spoken and unspoken rules for proper conduct. These are established by a society over time and, of course, are subject to changes over time. Thus, is the opera singer a deviant based on this perspective? Would it be easier to evaluate him if he were walking around half-naked or if he had not showered for a week?

Finally, the maladaptive perspective views behavior as abnormal if it interferes with the individual's ability to function in life or in society. For example, based on this perspective, one would ask is the singing man able to work, take care of himself, and have normal social interactions?

As can be seen, one key feature needed when defining abnormal or normal behavior is the need for as much information as possible before making a diagnosis. It should also be quite clear that determining whether behavior is abnormal or not is a difficult process indeed. In fact, there is not one criterion that completely defines abnormal behavior. As in many areas of applied psychology, many factors are involved. Thus, where does the opera singer fit into this equation?

More information about him might help to clear up the picture. This gentleman goes to work every day in a uniform. In fact, he is a building superintendent who has a hobby of singing arias. In his opinion, he has a wonderful voice, and he desires to share it with others. He knows he will never sing at the Met, but for him music is about

making people happy and spreading his good will. Thus, he sings as he walks to work in the morning and when coming back from lunch. He has held jobs for 12 years and, from his perspective, no one really complains about his singing. If they do, he just sings louder! Is this man's behavior abnormal based on the aforementioned perspectives?

It is difficult to clearly define abnormal behavior. To help diagnose, one must also look at factors such as duration, age of onset, and the intensity of the behavior(s). In fact, abnormal behavior has been difficult to define since ancient times. Since the groundwork has never been laid, let us examine the history of abnormal behavior and how such behavior was treated before considering some other issues.

The history of abnormal psychology dates back hundreds if not thousands of years. Stone Age civilizations evidently believed that serious mental illness or abnormal behavior was due to being possessed by evil spirits. Archaeological finds have discovered skulls that have holes borne into them. This process was called trepanation (or trephining): A small instrument (a trephine) was used to bore holes in the skull, the idea being that the holes would allow the evil spirits to leave the "possessed" person. Many believe that the goal was in fact to exterminate the individual. Perhaps these were the first examples of mistreatment of mentally ill individuals. In later societies, exorcisms were performed, usually by a shaman or priest. This was a noninvasive way to drive out the evil spirits in the possessed individual. Exorcisms, although rare, are still performed today. Millon (2004) noted that in Ancient Persia (now Iran) from 900 to 600 B.C.E., all mental as well as physical disorders were considered to be the devil's work.

Views on abnormal behavior were significantly advanced by Hippocrates (460–377 B.C.E.), the father of modern medicine. He viewed abnormal behavior—and illnesses in general—as having internal causes and, therefore, having biological etiologies. Hippocrates did not believe that the devil was responsible for physical and mental illnesses. Hippocrates's prescriptions for the ill included rest, proper diet, sobriety, and exercise, many prescriptions that are still used today.

During the Middle Ages (approximately the fifth to the fifteenth century), the view that demons were causing mental illnesses in certain people once again became popular, and the ancient Greek and Roman views that saw physiological causes of such behaviors lost favor. Plagues were common during these times, and exorcisms reemerged as a form of "treatment" for mental illnesses.

During the Renaissance (around 1400–1700 A.D.), the treatment of the mentally ill improved significantly. The mentally ill were seen as having "sick" minds that needed to be treated along with their bodies. During the fifteenth and sixteenth centuries, asylums were created for the purpose of providing housing for the mentally ill. During this time, the mentally ill were referred to as lunatics; persons with mental retardation were called idiots. The care provided to them was minimal, and their plights did not provoke much attention. Even though the name "asylum" connotes bad feelings and scenes of patient abuse today, this was not the connotation at their founding. The sole purpose of asylums was to treat the mentally ill in a humane fashion, and founders of these asylums believed that society should be responsible for the treatment of the mentally ill (Grob, 1994). Unfortunately, the asylums soon became overcrowded, and the treatment in them soon turned to punishment and torture in order to manage behavior. Reforms in mental health treatment really did not occur until the nineteenth and twentieth centuries.

During the nineteenth century, two people made particularly important contributions to the mental health reform movement. Philippe Pinel (1745–1826) advocated that the mentally ill be treated with sympathy, compassion, and empathy. Dorothea Dix (1802–1887) helped establish many state mental hospitals in the United States during a nationwide campaign to reform treatments of the mentally ill. She was directly responsible for laws that aimed to reform treatment of this population.

Many significant changes occurred during the late nineteenth and twentieth centuries. Emil Kraepelin (1856–1926) was indirectly responsible for laying the foundation for what would become the psychiatric diagnostic system. Like Hippocrates, he also believed in the concept that physical factors were responsible for mental illnesses.

In 1897, the sexually transmitted disease syphilis was discovered by von Kraft-Ebing (1840–1902). This was important because syphilis sufferers demonstrated delusions of grandeur, which can be a sign of a mental illness. Thus, there was medical evidence that physical illnesses could mimic symptoms of mental illnesses and, more importantly, that physiological factors were somehow involved with some, if not all, of the mental disorders known at that time.

For many psychologists the most important figure began his work in the 1890s in Vienna. Sigmund Freud (1856–1939) was initially a researcher who was studying the reproductive systems of eels. Josef Breuer (1842–1925), another Viennese physician, treated patients who suffered from hysteria, which literally means "wandering uterus." However, upon examining these patients with hysteria, Breuer discovered that they had no physical symptoms. Breuer found that some patient's symptoms eased or disappeared once they discussed the past with him in a safe environment, without censure, and while under hypnosis. Breuer discussed these ideas with Freud, who expanded on them and created psychoanalytic theory, thus leading to an entire movement that is still popular today.

During the 1920s and 1930s, somatic treatments for the mentally ill became widely popular due in part to the legacy of Samuel Woodward, the first superintendent at the Massachusetts Lunatic Asylum in 1833. Woodward claimed that mental illnesses could be cured just like many physical illnesses and that moral indiscretions by individuals were partly to blame for their condition. These ideas led to the widespread use of lobotomies, in which the frontal lobe's nerve fibers are severed and thereby separated it from the rest of the brain. Other common somatic treatment methods included insulin shock therapy (inducing a coma in an individual) and fever therapy (inducing a fever in the individual by injecting blood infected with malaria). All of these treatments were used for a number of years with little or no success.

The field of abnormal psychology reached two major milestones in the early 1950s. Henry Laborit (1914–1955) introduced chlorpromazine (generally known as Thorazine) for the treatment of schizophrenic disorders. Initially this medication was used to tranquilize surgical patients, but Laborit noticed that chlorpromazine managed to calm patients without putting them to sleep. This led to its widespread use for the treatment of schizophrenic disorders. A second landmark in the helping professions was the publication of the *Diagnostic and Statistical Manual of Mental Disorders* (*DSM*) in 1952. This manual contained about 60 different disorders and was based on theories of abnormal psychology. However, the *DSM* and *DSM-II* (1968) were considered to have many limitations; arguably the main limitation was that the concepts had not been scientifically tested. In addition, all of the disorders listed were considered to be reactions to events occurring within the individual's environment, and there was really no distinction between abnormal and normal behavior. In effect, everyone was considered to be abnormal to a certain degree, depending on the severity of their condition.

When the *DSM-III* was published in 1980, the psychoanalytic basis for the *DSM*s was abandoned, and the diagnostic criteria were now based on the medical model and on clinical symptoms, not on theories. The five-part multiaxial system was also introduced. The *DSM* was revised twice more until the current *DSM-IV-TR* was published (American Psychiatric Association [APA], 2000). This volume is heavily research-based and includes much information about the etiologies of all the disorders. The next revision (*DSM-V*) is scheduled to come out in 2011 or 2012.

Abnormal psychology research is somewhat complicated because experiments are conducted on human beings who have some kind of mental illness. Sometimes the most difficult aspect of this research is gaining cooperation from the subject. For example, many individuals with anorexia nervosa are in denial about the seriousness of their problem (Bruch, 2001) and may therefore not agree to be research subjects because they see nothing wrong with them.

Generally researchers will use one of three experimental designs to investigate mental illness. First there is the case study, sometimes called the N = 1 design. This method is an in-depth look at the individual being studied over a certain period of time. Case studies often cannot be generalized to the population as a whole, because the results really only apply to the person under investigation. There are also single- and double-blind studies, sometimes using placebos (e.g., sugar pills that look identical to real medication but are medically inert). In a single-blind design, the experimenters know which group is receiving the actual treatment and which group is the control or placebo, group (the group that receives a presumably inactive treatment). In a double-blind study, even the experimenters do not know who is getting the active treatment and who is getting the placebo treatment.

The best designs usually are double-blind, and they are designed to answer the following kinds of questions: How significant a factor is the environment in the etiology of the mental illness under investigation? What role, if any, do genes play? How successful is the method of therapy being investigated for treating the mental illness in question? Although on the surface these seem relatively simple to answer, they are quite difficult. Psychologists need to find results that are statistically valid and reliable. Not only is research interested in etiological factors, research is also conducted to gain more statistical information about mental illness such as prevalence, racial and ethnic data, gender and age-related information, to name a few. In addition, research is conducted to measure the efficacy of therapy and specific treatment modalities, including medications. Although it is difficult to "prove" that therapy works outside of a controlled experimental setting, research has supported one idea in abnormal psychology; namely, there is no single causal factor for any of the mental illnesses. Stemming from this idea is the notion that no single causal factor works alone without influencing other factors. That is, one thinks a certain thought, the body reacts by demonstrating behaviors, neurotransmitters go to work, and one engages other people as needed.

As for the future of abnormal psychology, the overriding goal in abnormal psychology is to find therapeutic modalities that work best and most effectively for each disorder listed in the *DSM-IV-TR* (APA, 2000; Nathan & Gorman, 2002). This goal clashes with those of insurance companies that demand quick fixes in the fewest sessions possible. The field needs to come to an agreement so the patient's best interests are served. The field also has to determine the proper place for psychotropic medications.

Although medications do not solve all problems, they have been proven necessary in treating some mental illnesses, and they have and will continue to save lives (Getzfeld, 2006; Bezchlibnyk-Butler, Jeffries, & Virani, 2007). Until rather recently, it was widely believed that medication and psychotherapy should not be used together and were mutually incompatible (Gabbard & Kay, 2001). However, this combination has now become common in clinical practices and is not generally considered unusual or incompatible (Thase & Jindal, 2004). Two related issues that remain under investigation include (1) administering medications to children and adolescents because of potential suicide risks (Hammad, Laughten, & Racoosin, 2006;

Olfson, Marcus, & Schaffer, 2006); and, (2) how lithium, which is used to treat bipolar disorder, actually works and why (Goodwin & Jamison, 2007).

One important aspect with which the field continually struggles is education, specifically, educating the public at large about the prevalence and nature of mental illness. Some, perhaps many, think of mental illness as being best represented by Charles Manson, Jeffrey Dahmer, and Jigsaw (of the "Saw" movies), for example, who are extreme individuals rather than the norm. Psychology still needs to get the message out that mental illness affects people from all backgrounds, relatives as well as the stranger down the block.

The debate over medication continues in the field, and it does not appear as though it will be resolved any time soon. Some of the issues researchers are exploring include whether psychologists should have prescribing privileges; whether children and adolescents should be medicated; and whether medications are overused because of pressure from family members, pharmaceutical companies, and insurance companies. Related to this is the apparent increase in autistic disorder and bipolar disorder in children. Research has substantiated that the mercury preservation thimerosal, especially present in the Measles/Mumps/Rubella vaccine prior to 2001, has little to no cause and effect relationship with the onset of autism (Schechter & Grether, 2008). Therefore, researchers have yet to discover the causes of this series of disorders, which continue to baffle the field, including finding overwhelming effective ways to treat these disorders.

In sum, abnormal psychology has many questions that remain unanswered and many unresolved conflicts. Medications and treatment modalities continue to evolve and advance, but the core nature of mental illness has remained unchanged, at least since Hippocrates' time. Simply, mental illness has no singular cause, but the origins seem to have biological bases, with the environment and other factors playing significant roles. In many ways, we have come full circle since Hippocrates' time, so perhaps we would be wise to heed his ideas.

REFERENCES

American Psychiatric Association (2000). *Diagnostic and statistical manual of mental disorders* (4th ed., text rev.). Washington, DC: Author.

Bezchlibnyk-Butler, K. Z., Jeffries, J. J., & Virani, A. S. (2007). *Clinical handbook of psychotropic drugs.* Cambridge, MA: Hogrefe & Huber.

Bruch, H. (2001). *The golden cage: The enigma of anorexia nervosa.* Cambridge, MA: Harvard University Press.

Gabbard, G. O., & Kay, J. K. (2001). The fate of integrated treatment: Whatever happened to the biopsychosocial psychiatrist? *American Journal of Psychiatry, 158,* 1956–1963.

Getzfeld, A. R. (2006). *Essentials of abnormal psychology.* Hoboken, NJ: John Wiley & Sons.

Goodwin. F. K., & Jamiso, K. R. (Eds.). (2007). *Manic-depressive illness: Bipolar disorders and recurrent depression* (2nd ed.). New York: Oxford University Press.

Grob, G. (1994). *The mad among us: A history of the care of America's mentally ill.* New York: Free Press.

Hammad, T., Laughren, T., & Racoosin, J. (2006). Suicidiality in pediatric patients treated with antidepressant drugs. *Archives of General Psychiatry, 63,* 332–339.

Millon, T. (2004). *Masters of the mind.* Hoboken, NJ: John Wiley & Sons.

Nathan, P. E., & Gorman, J. M. (Eds.). (2004). *A guide to treatments that work* (2nd ed.). New York: Oxford University Press.

Olfson, M., Marcus, S., & Schaffer, D. (2006). Antidepressant drug therapy and suicide in severely depressed children and adolescents. *Archives of General Psychiatry, 63,* 865–872.

Schechter, R., & Grether, J. K. (2008). Continuing increases in autism reported to California's developmental services system. *Archives of General Psychiatry, 65,* 19–24.

Thase, M. E., & Jindal, R. E. (2004). Combining psychotherapy and pharmacotherapy for the treatment of mental disorders. In M. J. Lambert (2004), Bergin and Garfield's *Handbook of psychotherapy and behavior change* (pp. 743–766). New York: John Wiley & Sons.

Weeks, D., & James, J. (1995). *Eccentrics: A study of sanity and strangeness.* New York: Villard.

SUGGESTED READINGS

Allport, G. W. (1965). *Letters from Jenny.* New York: Harcourt Brace Jovanovich.

Craighead, W. E., Miklowitz, D. J., & Craighead, L. W. (2008). *Psychopathology: History, diagnosis, and empirical foundations.* New York: John Wiley & Sons.

Nathan, J. (2004). *The secret life of the lonely doll: The search for Dare Wright.* New York: Picador.

ANDREW R. GETZFELD
New Jersey City University

See also: Abnormality; Emotional Disturbances; Psychopathology

ABNORMALITY

From time immemorial, societies have consistently classified a small minority of people in their midst as psychologically "abnormal." The classic research of Jane Murphy (1976) demonstrates that people in non-Western cultures, such as the Yorubas of Nigeria and the Yupic-speaking Eskimos of Alaska, readily recognize certain behaviors as abnormal. Moreover, many of these behaviors, such as talking to oneself, are similar to those regarded as abnormal in Western society. Murphy's findings suggest that the concept of abnormality is not entirely culturally relative, and that individuals in disparate cultures often label comparable behaviors as abnormal.

Nevertheless, these observations leave unanswered a crucial question: What is abnormality? Put somewhat differently, what implicit criterion or criteria do individuals use to identify abnormality? Surprisingly, a conclusive answer to this question remains elusive. In this entry we examine several conceptualizations of abnormality and their strengths and weaknesses. All of these conceptualizations strive to provide a definition of abnormality that encompasses both physical and mental disorders, although most place principal emphasis on the latter.

The first and most radical conception examined here is that abnormality is entirely a function of subjective societal values. According to this *subjective values* model, which has been championed by Thomas Szasz (1960), abnormal conditions are those deemed by society to be undesirable in some way. Although this model touches on an important truth, namely that many or most abnormal conditions are perceived as undesirable, it does not explain why many socially disapproved behaviors, such as rudeness, laziness, and even most forms of racism, are perceived as undesirable but not strictly pathological. A comprehensive definition of abnormality seems to involve more than subjective values.

Advocates of a *statistical* approach, such as Sir Henry Cohen (1981), posit that abnormality can be defined as statistical deviation from a norm. Thus, any behavior that is rare in the population is abnormal. Appealing in its simplicity as this conceptualization appears, it suffers from several weaknesses. First, the cutoff points for abnormality are scientifically arbitrary. Should abnormality be defined as the uppermost 1% of population, the uppermost 3%, or some other figure? Second, a statistical approach offers no guidance regarding which dimensions are relevant to psychopathology. As a consequence, it erroneously classifies high levels of certain socially desirable dimensions, such as creativity, intelligence, and altruism, as abnormal. Third, a statistical approach erroneously classifies all common conditions as normal. For example, it implies that the bubonic plague (Black Death), which killed approximately one-third of Europe's population in the fourteenth century, was not abnormal because it was widespread.

Other theorists, such as F. Kraupl Taylor (1971), have embraced the pragmatic position that abnormality is nothing more than the set of conditions that professionals treat. According to this parsimonious "disorder as whatever professionals treat" view, psychologically abnormal conditions are those that elicit intervention from mental health professionals. Although this view avoids many of the conceptual pitfalls of other definitions, it fails to explain why many conditions treated by professionals, such as pregnancy, a misshapen nose corrected by plastic surgery, and marital conflict, are not by themselves regarded as pathological.

Advocates of a *subjective discomfort* model maintain that abnormal conditions are those that produce suffering in affected individuals. It is undeniable that many psychopathological conditions, such as major depressive disorder and obsessive-compulsive disorder, produce considerable subjective distress. Nevertheless, several other conditions, such as psychopathy (a condition characterized by guiltlessness, callousness, and dishonesty) and the manic phase of bipolar disorder (a condition characterized by extreme levels of elation, energy, and grandiosity), are often associated with little or no subjective distress among affected individuals, although they sometimes cause distress among those close to them. Moreover, like the statistical model, the subjective discomfort model offers no guidance concerning what cutoffs should be used to define abnormality. How much discomfort is required for a condition to be pathological?

Most of the aforementioned definitions focus largely or entirely on subjective judgments concerning the presence of abnormality. In contrast, proponents of a *biological model*, such as R. E. Kendell (1975), contend that abnormality should be defined by strictly biological and presumably objective criteria, particularly those derived from evolutionary theory. For example, Kendell argued that abnormal conditions are marked by a reduced life span, reduced biological fitness (the capacity of an organism to transmit its genes to future generations), or both. Despite its potentially greater scientific rigor relative to other models, a biological model is subject to numerous counterexamples. For example, being a soldier in a war tends to reduce one's longevity but is not a disorder; priesthood (which results in having no children) tends to reduce one's fitness but is similarly not a disorder. Moreover, a biological model falls prey to the same problem of arbitrary cutoffs that bedevils the statistical model: How much below average must life span or fitness be for a condition to be regarded as abnormal?

Whereas some of the preceding conceptualizations of abnormality primarily invoke social criteria, such as value judgments, others primarily invoke biological criteria. Jerome Wakefield (1992) suggested that the correct definition of abnormality requires both social and biological criteria. Specifically, he posited that all abnormal conditions are *harmful dysfunctions*. The *harm* component of Wakefield's conceptualization refers to social values regarding a condition's undesirability, whereas the "dysfunction" component refers to the failure of a system to function as "designed" by natural selection. Panic disorder is abnormal, according to Wakefield, because (a) it is viewed by society as harmful; and (b) the fear system was not evolutionarily designed to respond with intense anxiety in the absence of objective danger.

Wakefield's analysis is a significant advance in the conceptualization of abnormality, because it distinguishes those features of abnormality that are socially constructed from those that are scientifically based. Moreover, his analysis may help to distinguish from largely expected reactions to life circumstances from genuine mental disorders. As Allan Horwitz and Wakefield (2007) argued, some conditions, such as extreme sadness triggered by life events (e.g., divorce, loss of a job) are presently classified as depressions even though they often do not reflect true psychological dysfunctions.

Nevertheless, Wakefield's analysis may have its shortcomings. It assumes that all mental disorders involve breakdowns of evolved psychological or physiological systems. Yet some disorders, such as anxiety disorders, may be extreme cases of evolved defensive reactions to perceived threats. For example, as David Barlow (2002) observed, panic disorder may reflect "false alarms," that is, extreme fear reactions that are evolutionarily adaptive but expressed in situations that do not pose direct threats to the organism. In addition, Wakefield's analysis may be difficult to apply in practice because of the lack of a clear-cut distinction between adaptive function and dysfunction. The functioning of many psychological systems, such as the human systems for anxious and depressed mood, may be distributed continuously with no unambiguous dividing line between normality and abnormality.

In response to the difficulties with earlier efforts to provide an adequate definition of abnormality, some authors, such as David Rosenhan and Martin Seligman (1995) and Scott Lilienfeld and Lori Marino (1995), have proposed a *family resemblance* model of abnormality. According to this model, the concept of abnormality cannot be defined explicitly, because abnormality is an inherently fuzzy concept with unclear boundaries. Instead, conditions perceived as abnormal share a loosely related set of characteristics, including statistical rarity, maladaptiveness, impairment, need for treatment, and perceived dysfunction.

The family resemblance view implies that all efforts to construct a clear-cut definition of abnormality are doomed to failure. Moreover, according to this view, disagreements concerning whether certain conditions, such as attention-deficit/hyperactivity disorder or alcohol dependence (alcoholism), are truly "mental disorders" are probably inevitable, because there are no strictly defining criteria for abnormality. At the same time, this view implies that there will often be substantial consensus regarding whether many or even most conditions are abnormal, because individuals rely on largely overlapping features when identifying abnormality.

REFERENCES

Barlow, D. H. (2002). *Anxiety and its disorders: The nature and treatment of anxiety and panic* (2nd ed.). New York: Guilford Publications.

Cohen, H. (1981). The evolution of the concept of disease. In A. Caplan, H. Engelhardt, & J. McCarthy (Eds.), *Concepts of health and disease: Interdisciplinary perspectives* (pp. 209–220). Reading, MA: Addison-Wesley.

Horwitz, A. V., & Wakefield, J. C. (2007). *The loss of sadness: How psychiatry is transforming normal sorrow into depressive disorder.* New York: Oxford University Press.

Kendell, R. E. (1975). The concept of disease and its implications for psychiatry. *British Journal of Psychiatry, 127,* 305–315.

Kraupl Taylor, F. (1971). A logical analysis of the medico-psychological concept of disease. Psychological Medicine, *1,* 356–364.

Lilienfeld, S. O., & Marino, L. (1995). Mental disorder as a Roschian concept: A critique of Wakefield's "harmful dysfunction" analysis. *Journal of Abnormal Psychology, 104,* 411–420.

Rosenhan, D., & Seligman, M. (1995). *Abnormal psychology* (3rd ed.). New York: Norton.

Szasz, T. S. (1960). The myth of mental illness. *American Psychologist, 15,* 113–118.

Wakefield, J. C. (1992). The concept of mental disorder: On the boundary between biological facts and social values. *American Psychologist, 47,* 373–388.

SUGGESTED READINGS

Ghaemi, S. N. (2003). *The concepts of psychiatry: A pluralistic approach to the concepts of mind and mental illness.* Baltimore, MD: Johns Hopkins University Press.

Gorenstein, E. E. (1992). *The science of mental illness.* San Diego: Academic Press.

Spitzer, R. J., & Klein, D. F. (Eds.). (1978). *Critical issues in psychiatric diagnosis.* New York: Raven Press.

Scott O. Lilienfeld
Emory University

See also: **Psychopathology**

ABORTION COUNSELING

Induced abortion is the deliberate termination of a pregnancy and is subcategorized into therapeutic and elective. *Therapeutic abortion* is performed following medical advisement in order to save the life of the pregnant woman, preserve the woman's physical or mental health, prevent the birth of a child with a congenital disorder that would be fatal or associated with significant morbidity, or selectively reduce the number of fetuses to lessen health risks associated with multiple conceptions. *Elective abortion* is the termination of a pregnancy performed for any other reason.

The types of procedures employed are essentially determined by timing. During the 1st trimester (when 90% of abortions occur), options include surgical abortion or medical (nonsurgical) abortion—where women have greater involvement in the process. Suction Aspiration (or suction curettage or vacuum aspiration) is the surgical procedure utilized between 6 and 12 weeks gestation. Medical abortions, using Methotrexate and Misoprostol (MTX) or Mifepristone and Misoprostol (also referred to as RU-486, the abortion pill and Mifeprex), are performed up to 7 weeks or 7 to 9 weeks gestation, respectively. During the 2nd and 3rd trimesters, only surgical procedures can be utilized; dilation and curettage (D&C) (13 to 15 weeks) and dilation and evacuation (D&E) (15 to 21 weeks) are typically used, whereas induction abortion is used rarely. Dilation and extraction (D&X) (or intrauterine cranial decompression), which is performed after 21 weeks, is not permitted in the United States as per the *Partial-Birth Abortion Ban Act of 2003,* except under certain circumstances.

Approximately 22% of the 205 million annual pregnancies worldwide end in induced abortion (Sedgh et al., 2007). In 2003, 26 of every 1,000 women of childbearing age (15–44) were estimated to have had an induced abortion in developed countries (versus 29 of every 1,000 in developing countries). In places where abortion is legal, it is generally safe and utilizes the procedures indicated above.

Abortion is one of the most commonly performed gynecological procedures in the United States, with CDC and Guttmacher Institute estimates of 839,226 legal elective abortions voluntarily reported in 2004 and more comprehensive estimates suggesting approximately 1.2 million. Of those, 17.4% were less than 19 years of age, 32.8% were 20–24 years, and the majority were white (54.1%, versus 38.2% black, and 7.7% other), non-Hispanic (78.5% versus 21.5%), and unmarried (82.8%). Approximately half of all pregnancies to American women, excluding those ending in miscarriage, are unintended, and 4 in 10 of these are terminated by abortion (Finer, L. B. et al., 2006). Forty-three percent of all U.S. women will have had at least one induced abortion by the time they are 45 years of age.

Counseling Issues

Therapeutic abortion. After the woman and her partner have been informed of the medical circumstances prompting the recommendation of therapeutic abortion, pre-abortion counseling involves discussion of options that require decision making. The primary decision may be whether to take action (e.g., induce labor), as opposed to allowing the pregnancy and birth to follow its natural course despite the risks of perinatal morbidity and mortality. This discussion includes the types of procedures that are available given the woman's medical condition and the stage of the pregnancy. That such pregnancies may be planned, wanted, and possibly difficult to achieve in the first place may exacerbate feelings of uncertainty, grief, and despair as parents struggle with decision making. Religious and ethical concerns can arise in counseling. Following therapeutic abortion, genetic and grief counseling can lessen the severity of the grief reaction.

Elective abortion. With up to half of all pregnancies in the United States unanticipated, pre-abortion counseling may focus first on decision making—that is, helping the woman to choose whether to continue the pregnancy and raise the child or to authorize an adoption or other parenting arrangement, or to choose elective abortion. (Online resources, such as pregnancyoptions.info, also exist). Counseling may help women evaluate their reasons for considering abortion. For example, an unanticipated pregnancy can result in disruption of academic, career, or other life plans and can present a financial burden. Pregnancies that occur in the context of domestic violence or as a result of rape or incest may not be desired. If the woman is unmarried or there is a lack of a committed partner, the pregnancy can result in social stigma, as well as relationship dissolution and strained relationships with family and community (e.g., friends, religious affiliates).

Adolescent women also must confront their perceived maturity and readiness for parenthood, hindered social development, and also possible isolation from family or family discord because of the pregnancy. A woman's religious orientation and attitude toward abortion, as well as that of her partner and family (and associated pressure), can contribute to decision-making challenges and may be discussed in pre-abortion counseling. Depending on the entity providing the counseling, there may be a specific purpose/agenda. Every state requires patients to provide informed consent before a medical procedure is conducted, but in some cases the provision of information under the guise of required "counseling" can be irrelevant or misleading (Richardson & Nash, 2006). In addition to counseling on procedure options, pre-abortion contraception counseling also may be provided and has been found to improve the correct use of contraception in the short-term post-abortion (Schunmann & Glasier, 2006).

An elective abortion itself does not necessitate post-abortion counseling. A range of emotions may be experienced following elective abortion, with distress generally greatest prior to abortion as opposed to after its occurrence. Methodologically sound reviews of the scientific literature (Boonstra et al., 2006) substantiate, and the American Psychological Association and American Psychiatric Association recognize, that although post-abortion responses can involve feelings of sadness, anxiety, guilt, or regret, most women are not at risk for developing severe negative psychological reactions. Lack of social support, coerced decision making, and greater ambivalence regarding the pregnancy and the meaning of abortion may contribute to negative reactions, as can preexisting circumstances (e.g., poverty, prior mental health problems). Feelings of relief and other positive responses also are observed, particularly among those who perceive support from their partner and family for the termination of an unwanted pregnancy.

Given that women's experiences are unique to their particular life situations, life values, moral and religious beliefs, age, and the time since the abortion, the focus of post-abortion counseling can be very individualized. Although a variety of approaches may be helpful, no specific protocols have been published. In general, post-abortion counseling helps women identify and articulate the emotions they are experiencing, as well as how other aspects of their life may be impacting or impacted by their experience. There may be a focus on enhancing and activating adaptive coping behaviors. To assist with personal resolution, women may be encouraged to engage in some type of spiritual ritual or other activity (e.g., writing a letter, burying a memento, gestalt dialog with the fetus) in order to "say good-bye." Such online self-help and referral sites as 4exhale.org and heartsite.com also are available.

Spontaneous Abortion

Spontaneous abortion, or miscarriage, involves the spontaneous termination of an intrauterine pregnancy before 27 completed weeks of gestation and results in fetal death. Miscarriage occurs in approximately 12%–15% of clinically recognized pregnancies, but because many pregnancies end before even the woman recognizes she is pregnant, some estimates indicate that there may be as many as 45%–50% of all pregnancies. This amounts to approximately 500,000 to 650,000 miscarriages annually in the United States. Risk appears to vary substantially by age: 9% for women aged 20–24 years, but 75% for women older than 45 years. The U.S. rate of stillbirth, defined as late fetal death with a fetus weighing more than 500 grams, is 6–7 deaths per 1,000 live births, amounting to 26,000 to 30,000 annually. Risk factors that have been established or speculated in one or more studies can be broadly classified as environmental or biological (e.g., chromosomal abnormalities).

Counseling Issues

Pregnancy loss constitutes an unanticipated and sometimes physically painful event that involves an "ambiguous death" not recognized by many social and legal definitions. Since the loss often remains unknown to all but a woman's most intimate confidants and her healthcare providers, the grieving process may be further compounded by limited social support, by feelings associated with the loss of a potential child, and by comments from others that appear to minimize her individual loss (e.g., "You can get pregnant again"). Psychologically, miscarriage may produce fears and doubts about procreative competence, as well as sadness, distress, anger, guilt, and self-reproach. Controlled research has established that miscarriage is a risk factor for depressive symptoms, minor depressive disorder, and major depressive disorder in the six months after loss (Klier, Geller, & Ritsher, 2002). Women also may be anxious about immediate medical symptoms, possible underlying genetic or medical factors that may have contributed to the loss, or their ability to carry a subsequent pregnancy to term. Controlled research demonstrates that anxiety symptoms may be elevated and sustained for at least four months after miscarriage and that miscarriage increases risk for a recurrent episode of obsessive-compulsive disorder, and posttraumatic stress disorder (Geller, Kerns, & Klier, 2004).

A goal of post-loss counseling is to validate the death and legitimize feelings of grief. Counseling typically focuses on symptom reduction and grief management, but also may address coping resources and psychosocial factors such as women's relationships with their partners and children, as well as attachment to future children.

REFERENCES

Boonstra, H., Gold, R. B., Richards, C., & Finer, L. B. (2006). *Abortion in Women's Lives.* New York: Guttmacher Institute.

Finer, L. B., & Henshaw, S. K. (2006). Disparities in rates of unintended pregnancy in the United States, 1994 and 2001. *Perspectives on Sexual and Reproductive Health, 38,* 90–96.

Geller, P. A., Kerns, D., & Klier, C. M. (2004). Anxiety following miscarriage and the subsequent pregnancy: A review of the literature and future directions. *Journal of Psychosomatic Research, 56,* 35–45.

Klier, C. M., Geller, P. A., & Ritsher, J. B. (2002). Affective disorders in the aftermath of miscarriage: A comprehensive review. *Archives of Women's Mental Health, 5,* 129–149.

Richardson, C. T., & Nash, E. (2006). Misinformed consent: The medical accuracy of state-developed abortion counseling materials. *Guttmacher Policy Review, 9*(4). Retrieved February 20, 2008, from http://www.guttmacher.org/pubs/gpr/09/4/gpr090406.html.

Schunmann, C., & Glasier, A. (2006). Specialist contraceptive counseling and provision after termination of pregnancy improves uptake of long-acting methods but does not prevent repeat abortion: A randomized trial. *Human Reproduction, 21,* 2296–2303.

Sedgh, G., Henshaw, S., Singh, S., Ahman, E., & Shah, I. H. (2007). Induced abortion: Rates and trends worldwide. *Lancet, 370,* 1338–1345.

SUGGESTED READINGS

Breitbart, V. (2000). Counseling for medical abortion. *American Journal of Obstetrics and Gynecology, 183*(2 supplement), S26–33.

Ely, G. E. (2007). The abortion counseling experience: A discussion of patient narratives and recommendations for best practices. *Best Practices in Mental Health, 3*(2), 62–74.

Limbo, R. K., & Wheeler, S. R. (2003). *When a baby dies: A handbook for healing and helping.* La Crosse, WI: Bereavement Services.

Rubin, L., & Russo, N.F. (2004). Abortion and mental health: What therapists need to know. *Women & Therapy, 27*(3/4), 69–90.

PAMELA A. GELLER
Drexel University

See also: **Counseling**

ABREACTION

In mental health, abreaction has come to mean an intense emotional release or discharge in an involuntary, vivid, sensory reliving or re-experiencing, of an event that was originally neurobiologically overwhelming (i.e., "traumatic") and thus could not be remembered (or forgotten) in normal ways. Abreaction has its origins in psychoanalytic theory, but because it taps essential principles of emotional functioning, memory, and mind-body interaction, aspects of it are blended into diverse modalities across theoretical orientations. Originally, abreaction was viewed as curative in itself, believed to be healing through the discharging of excessive, dysregulating emotions thought to be the cause of dysfunctional symptoms.

Beliefs about the curative elements in abreaction derive from notions both ancient and pervasive across cultures and fields of inquiry, including philosophy, medicine, and religion. The historical belief that disease or disharmony is the result of the accretion of toxins, often thought to result as punishment for the crossing of sociocultural taboos (e.g., plague viewed as punishment for sin; mental illness seen as evidence of character weakness), and that restoration of health or harmony requires purgation of the toxins, resulting in purification or cleanliness, recurs so frequently across centuries that one could theorize an aspect of biological or phylogenetic imperative or truth contributing to the maintenance of this notion over millennia.

Whether considering medical treatments ranging from bloodletting to purgative cathartics; chelation therapy, expectorants, or steam showers; religious rituals ranging from blood sacrifice to purification from baptismal waters; or social solutions ranging from scapegoating (derived from ancient Hebrew practices) to saunas; or the catharsis of theater or reality television, we are dealing with the abiding belief that purging the body and mind of toxins, through ejection or release, restores health. Equally abiding has been the observation that the calming effects of purgation tend to be short-lived, and crises of toxic eruptions recur. One response to this observation has been to prescribe repeated treatments of purgation. Another has been to augment purgation with structure-building that prevents or diminishes recurrences. This is no different in the field of mental health.

In mental health, intense emotional releases, reaching epileptic-like proportion, were described in the 1700s in response to Mesmer's treatment of psychological distress using the energy of magnetized rods. Following these seizure-like experiences (named "une crise"), patients were exhausted, then calm, and then emerged cured of presenting symptoms. These episodes of physical and emotional dyscontrol were not unlike those seen during religious exorcisms of earlier and simultaneous periods, viewed in these latter contexts as indicative of demons exiting the person's body/soul, releasing the person of symptoms of madness.

The term *abreaction*, to describe such emotional releases, was first utilized by Breuer and Freud (1893). However, contrary to popular understanding, Breuer and Freud did not prescribe spontaneous emotional reliving of traumatic events as curative. Their understanding of trauma, and the therapeutic action of abreaction, was more sophisticated and nuanced than that. Breuer and Freud used the term abreaction to name the full emotional and motoric response to a traumatic event required to adequately relieve a person of being repetitively and unpredictably assailed by the trauma's original, unmitigated emotional intensity.

Breuer and Freud described that, without adequate abreaction, a person is plagued with persisting "freshness" (p. 9) of emotions of the original event, that come with "hallucinatory vividness," as well as a lack of control over access to, or freedom from, the memory. Adequate abreaction can be blocked during trauma because action is prevented by social circumstances or because the intensity or quality of the stimulated emotions is paralyzing. Without adequate abreaction, traumas cannot be disposed of through normal means of associations. Instead, splits, or disruptions in continuity (disconnects) occur among multiple aspects of consciousness.

The result is that a person cannot adequately forget (or intentionally remember) by utilizing the normal means of memory storage. Instead, an "attack" (p. 16) of hysteria (spontaneous abreaction or flashback) occurs in place of memory. Treatment, as proposed by Breuer and Freud, consisted of utilizing hypnosis, and in later years, free association, to access the sensory-emotional flashback, and then help the patient adequately reconnect the sensory experience with words in order to effect an "adequate" abreaction, or full response, that, they believed, could lay the traumatic memory to rest by discharging the original emotion and reconnecting the experience to the associational processes necessary for normal memory storage.

Subsequent clinicians' interpretations of Breuer's and Freud's work, perhaps misled by Breuer's and Freud's use of the word "cathartic" as well as primed by the millennia-old belief in the efficacy of purgation, misconstrued their description of abreaction as an endorsement of discharge through re-exposure to the original traumatic event, missing their emphasis on integration of disconnected associational processes and adequate, full response to the trauma. It was this misconstruction of the term abreaction that has endured as its definition. As a result of this misconstruction, clinicians during subsequent decades have rediscovered, lost, and rediscovered again the fact that abreaction as uncontrolled reliving not only does not heal; it can cause harm by lowering the threshold for subsequent uncontrolled flashbacks, bathing the brain in noxious chemicals, and even affecting brain structural development and neuronal cell death (e.g., van der Kolk, 1996).

Current clinical understanding of the therapeutic place for abreaction has been elaborated upon and expanded by advances in both infant development research and neuroscience (Porges, 1996; Schore, 2001). The splintering of aspects of experience ("dissociation") is now seen as the central disruptive element in trauma, capable of interfering with not only adequate affect regulation, but also with capacity for trust, confidence in reality testing, a sense of continuity of self, and the experience of enlivenment and spontaneity in life. Integrating the neurobiologically-based, trauma-induced disconnections—between sensory and verbal aspects of experience, between experiences of oneself inside differing emotions ("self states"), between permitted and prohibited perceptions of others—has become the focus of trauma therapy (van der Hart & Brown, 1992).

Abreaction is no longer pursued as a purifying cathartic (sometimes chemically or therapeutically induced as it was during World War II and post-Vietnam). If it is pursued (i.e., in modalities such as exposure therapy or EMDR), it is done so in a carefully dosed way, only after structures within the patient have been built or strengthened—structures allowing for sustaining trust, maintaining reality testing, and restabilizing in the face of disruption. In most trauma treatment modalities, abreaction is not pursued; it is understood as inevitable, and when it occurs, the therapist works actively and rapidly to utilize the access abreaction provides to sensory-motor aspects of traumatic memories as an opportunity for integrating disconnections. Sometimes the goal is to use higher cortical understanding, mediated by language, to override conditioned responses. Other times, the goal is a more ambitious rewiring of the conditioned amygdala reactivity, the rigidly repetitive neuro-associational pathways, and the toxic neurochemical responses through mindful and paced experimentation with new behaviors and activities that allow for exposure to new environmental responses and thus new neuropsychological responses.

REFERENCES

Breuer, J., & Freud, S. (1893). On the psychical mechanism of hysterical phenomena: Preliminary communication. In J. Strachey, *The standard edition of the complete psychological works of Sigmund Freud* (Vol. II, pp. 3–17). London: Hogarth Press, 1955.

Porges, S. W. (1996). Physiological regulation in high-risk infants: A model for assessment and potential intervention. *Development and Psychopathology, 8*, 43–58.

Schore, A. (2001). The effects of a secure attachment relationship on right brain development, affect regulation, and infant mental health (I). *Infant Mental Health Journal, 22*, 7–66.

Van der Hart, O., & Brown, P. (1992). Abreaction re-evaluated. *Dissociation 5*(3), 127–140.

Van der Kolk, B. (1996). The body keeps the score: Approaches to the psychobiology of posttraumatic stress disorder. In B. van der Kolk, A. McFarlane, & L. Weisaeth (Eds.), *Traumatic stress: The effects of overwhelming experience on mind, body, and society* (pp. 214–241). New York: Guilford Press.

MARY JO PEEBLES
Bethesda, MD

See also: Catharsis; Emotions

ABSENT-MINDEDNESS (See Attention Lapses)

ACADEMIC ACHIEVEMENT

Academic achievement has been an important societal topic for many years. In the years following World War II, schools educated increasing numbers of students. To optimize achievement, teachers geared their lessons to students' ability levels. The advent of the space age further elevated the importance of achievement, especially in mathematics and science. In the 1960s there was greater emphasis on disadvantaged children and on making school more relevant and less threatening. But declining achievement by the 1970s produced higher standards and greater accountability. The publication of *A Nation at Risk* (National Commission on Excellence in Education, 1983) led educators to improve teaching quality, curriculum requirements, and achievement standards.

Currently the *No Child Left Behind Act of 2001* (U.S. Department of Education, 2002) requires testing of children in reading and mathematics. Results often show high percentages of students not meeting minimums. Schools are accountable for students' achievement. All students are expected to master basic skills to be successful in college and the workforce.

Definition and Assessment

Achievement is "Task-oriented behavior that allows the individual's performance to be evaluated according to some internally or externally imposed criterion, that involves the individual in competing with others, or that otherwise involves some standard of excellence" (Spence & Helmreich, 1983, p. 12). *Academic achievement* is achievement in an academic domain such as reading, mathematics, science, and social studies.

Academic achievement reflects a student's learning, but learning and achievement are not synonymous in meaning. Achievement is assessed by behavior—oral, written, performance. It is assumed that achievement reflects underlying learning, but students may not display (achieve) all that they have learned for various reasons (e.g., illness, low motivation).

There also is no automatic relationship between achievement and ability (e.g., verbal, spatial). Students with similar abilities do not achieve at similar levels (Zimmerman, 2000). Dweck's (2006) research in fields such as education, business, and parenting, shows that achievement depends on people believing that their abilities can be improved through effort and persistence.

School achievement is assessed by tests, quizzes, oral responses, projects, papers, and performances (e.g., correctly demonstrating laboratory procedures). A distinction is made between formative and summative evaluation (Ercikan, 2006). Formative evaluation takes place during learning and is used by teachers to determine what students have learned and where improvement is needed. Summative evaluation occurs at the end of units or courses and often serves as the basis for grades.

Influences on Academic Achievement

Theory and research support the idea that several variables can influence academic achievement (Table 1). These variables are grouped in three categories: personal, social/cultural, contextual.

Personal

Students differ in their abilities to learn academic content. Students with learning disabilities, for example, often have difficulty acquiring reading and mathematical skills. But achievement depends on more than ability because high, average, and low achievers are found across all ability levels. Students' knowledge and skills affect their achievement, as do their prior experiences. Those with more experience taking tests and working on group projects should perform better on tests and group projects, respectively, than students with limited experience. Motivation is an internal process that instigates and sustains goal-directed behavior (Schunk, Pintrich, & Meece, 2008). Some important motivational variables are students' self-efficacy (perceived capabilities), academic goals, and the value they place on achievement. Self-regulation refers to the process whereby students activate and sustain behaviors, cognitions, and affects systematically oriented toward attaining their learning goals (Zimmerman, 2000). Students with better self-regulatory skills (e.g., planning, monitoring, self-evaluating) achieve at higher levels.

Social/Cultural

Socioeconomic status (SES) often is implicated as an influence on achievement, but SES is a descriptive variable that includes a family's capital or resources: financial/material, human/nonmaterial, social. Higher SES families have greater capital, provide computers and educational materials for their children, use their social

Table 1. Influences on Academic Achievement

Personal	Social/Cultural	Contextual
Abilities	Socioeconomic Status	Instruction
Knowledge and Skills Family		Teacher Support
Prior Experiences	Cultural Norms	Formative Evaluation
Motivation	Community Models	School/Classroom Culture
Self-Regulation	Peer Groups	Feelings of Relatedness

connections to secure opportunities, and stress academic achievement. Some cultural norms also may be influential. In mathematics, Asian American and White American students tend to outperform African American and Hispanic American students (Byrnes, 1996). Achievement can be affected by communities. Where education levels are higher there are more models for students to emulate. Peer groups are important. High school students who associate with higher-achieving peers achieve better than students who start high school comparable to them but associate with lower-achieving peers (Steinberg, Brown, & Dornbusch, 1996).

Contextual

Academic achievement is affected by the quality of instruction. Achievement benefits from teachers who teach skills and strategies and raise students' self-efficacy. Teacher support is critical because teachers who provide needed academic support promote students' learning. Teachers who use formative evaluation to plan their lessons should raise achievement more than those who rely only on summative evaluation. The culture of the school and classroom can affect achievement; some learning environments stress achievement more than others. Students' feelings of relatedness to the school are important (Ryan & Powelson, 1991). Many students who drop out of school feel isolated. Feelings of relatedness contribute to motivation and learning.

Improving Academic Achievement

Although there is no clear strategy for raising student achievement, theory and research provide some guidance.

Ensure that students learn skills and strategies they need to be successful. Most school learning is oriented toward basic skills, and all students should be able to acquire these. Students benefit from high expectations, sound instruction, and positive support.

Teach self-regulation. Self-regulation includes strategies such as setting goals, monitoring and evaluating progress, and seeking help when needed. These actions promote learning and achievement.

Address student motivation. Students motivated to learn achieve more. Motivation will be high when students set learning goals, feel efficacious about attaining them, and are interested in (value) the learning.

Use models. Models teach skills and build students' self-efficacy for learning. Using as models successful peers whom students view as similar to themselves can motivate observers to learn.

Use formative evaluation. Formative evaluation aids in lesson planning and conveys to students their progress in learning. This teacher support motivates students to learn and achieve.

Academic achievement is important for educators, parents, students, and policy makers. There are multiple influences on achievement, many of which can be modified to raise achievement. Improving student achievement can help to reduce school dropout rates and prepare students well for their futures.

REFERENCES

Byrnes, J. P. (1996). Cognitive development and learning in instructional contexts. Boston: Allyn & Bacon.

Dweck, C. S. (2006). Mindset: The new psychology of success. New York: Random House.

Ercikan, K. (2006). Developments in assessment of student learning. In P. A. Alexander & P. H. Winne (Eds.), Handbook of educational psychology (2nd ed., pp. 929–952). Mahwah, NJ: Lawrence Erlbaum.

Ryan, R. M., & Powelson, C. L. (1991). Autonomy and relatedness as fundamental to motivation and education. Journal of Experimental Education, *60*, 49–66.

Schunk, D. H., Pintrich, P. R., & Meece, J. L. (2008). Motivation in education: Theory, research, and applications 3rd ed.). Upper Saddle River, NJ: Merrill/Prentice Hall.

Spence, J. T., & Helmreich, R. L. (1983). Achievement-related motives and behaviors. In J. T. Spence (Ed.), Achievement and achievement motives: Psychological and sociological approaches (pp. 7–74). San Francisco: Freeman.

Steinberg, L., Brown, B. B., & Dornbusch, S. M. (1996). Beyond the classroom: Why school reform has failed and what parents need to do. New York: Simon & Schuster.

U. S. Department of Education. (2002). No Child Left Behind Act of 2001. Public Law 107-110, 115 Stat. 1425 (2002).

Zimmerman, B. J. (2000). Attaining self-regulation: A social cognitive perspective. In M. Boekaerts, P. R. Pintrich, & M. Zeidner (Eds.), Handbook of self-regulation (pp. 13–39). San Diego: Academic Press.

SUGGESTED READINGS

Borkowski, J. G., & Thorpe, P. K. (1994). Self-regulation and motivation: A life-span perspective on underachievement. In D. H. Schunk & B. J. Zimmerman (Eds.), *Self-regulation of learning and performance: Issues and educational applications* (pp. 45–73). Hillsdale, NJ: Lawrence Erlbaum.

Spence, J. T. (Ed.). (1983). *Achievement and achievement motives: Psychological and sociological approaches.* San Francisco: Freeman.

Zimmerman, B. J. (2001). Theories of self-regulated learning and academic achievement: On overview and analysis. In B. J. Zimmerman & D. H. Schunk (Eds.), *Self-regulated learning and academic achievement: Theoretical perspectives* (2nd ed., pp. 1–37). Mahwah, NJ: Lawrence Erlbaum.

DALE H. SCHUNK
University of North Carolina at Greensboro

See also: Learning Disabilities; Motivation; Self-Monitoring

ACADEMIC SKILL DISORDER (See Learning Disabilities)

ACCULTURATION

Acculturation is commonly understood as a process of change that results from prolonged cultural contact. The anthropologists Redfield, Linton, and Herskovits (1936) defined acculturation as "those phenomena which result when groups of individuals having different cultures come into continuous firsthand contact, with subsequent changes in the original culture patterns of either or both groups" (p. 149). The modern concept of acculturation traces its disciplinary roots to anthropology and sociology, where scholars sought to understand the effects of cultural contacts arising from various forms of colonization, immigration, and modernization taking place during the nineteenth and twentieth centuries.

Acculturation became a central construct in cross-cultural psychology and ethnic minority psychology in the late twentieth century as scholars sought to understand the psychological experiences of immigrants and ethnic minorities, both of whom face the task of negotiating the sometimes competing demands of their heritage culture and the dominant or host culture. Psychological acculturation is thought to involve changes in several domains of behavior, values, preferences, and cultural identity. Furthermore, research has demonstrated that acculturation is most likely not a linear, unidirectional process in which an acculturating individual starts out as a monocultural person identified with a heritage culture and is presumed to undergo a change process toward becoming a monocultural person identified with the new

or dominant culture. Such a unidirectional model of acculturation implies that the movement toward host culture orientation is accompanied simultaneously by a movement away from heritage culture orientation.

Of the various contemporary acculturation theories that have been put forth in psychology, Berry's (1980) bidimensional model of acculturation has garnered the most attention. This conceptual model posits that each individual holds a relative preference for maintaining one's heritage culture and a relative preference for participating in the second culture. These two attitudinal dimensions are thought to interact to produce four acculturation strategies. Assimilation strategy results from the individual seeking interaction and participation in the second culture but not wishing to maintain heritage culture participation and identity. Integration strategy (sometimes referred to as biculturalism) results from individuals wishing to maintain both their heritage cultural identity and participation as well as participating in the second culture. Separation strategy describes individuals who value their heritage culture maintenance and do not wish to participate in the second culture. Finally, the marginalization strategy describes individuals who have relatively little interest or the capacity neither to maintain their heritage culture nor to participate in the second culture.

By positing the possibility of various forms of acculturation, including integration or biculturalism, Berry's and other similar bidimensional models of acculturation hold much conceptual appeal. However, debates abound with respect to empirical support for this bidimensional model. Critics have raised concerns regarding its lack of attention to contextual factors (such as ideologies and policies of the dominant cultural group toward minorities and immigrants), lack of consistent and reliable assessment methods, and simplification of a complex process into four typologies. Acculturation remains a vibrant theoretical and research topic in psychology.

REFERENCES

Berry, J. W. (1980). Acculturation as varieties of adaptation. In A. Padilla (Ed.), *Acculturation: Theory, models, and findings* (pp. 9–25). Boulder, CO: Westview.

Redfield, R., Linton, R., & Herskovits, M. (1936). Memorandum on the study of acculturation. *American Anthropologist, 38,* 149–152.

SUGGESTED READING

Chun, K. M., Organista, P. B., & Marin, G. (Eds.). (2003). *Acculturation: Advances in theory, measurement, and applied research.* Washington, DC: American Psychological Association.

SUMIE OKAZAKI
University of Illinois at Urbana-Champaign

See also: **Cross-Cultural Psychology**

ACHIEVEMENT MOTIVATION

Motivational psychologists study what moves people to act and why people think and do what they do (Weiner, 1992). Motivation energizes and directs actions, and so it has great relevance to many important developmental outcomes such as school achievement, performance in other activity areas, and overall mental health. Fundamentally, motivational theorists and researchers work to understand the motivational predictors of choice, persistence, and effort (Wigfield, Eccles, Schiefele, Roeser, & Davis-Kean, 2006). Achievement motivation refers more specifically to motivation relevant to performance on tasks in which there are criteria to judge success or failure. Examples of these kinds of tasks are school activities, work activities, and competitive sport activities. In all such activities competence is a crucial part of motivation to achieve. Motivation in all forms is most directly observable in the level of energy in individual's behaviors.

Historically, drives, needs, and reinforcements were proposed as the primary sources of motivation (Weiner, 1992). Much current theory and research on motivation can be characterized as having a social cognitive emphasis and so focuses on individuals' beliefs, values, and goals as primary influences on motivation (Wigfield et al., 2006), although needs are still prevalent in some models. Major theories of motivation emphasize different aspects of these beliefs, values, and goals. Some theories focus primarily on competence-related beliefs, including perceived self-efficacy, perceptions of control, and other competence-related beliefs. Others focus on purposes or aims that individuals pursue; goal theories are the primary example. Expectancy-value theories integrate these two sets of constructs as ways of explaining individuals' performance on different activities and choices of which to do. Self-determination theorists emphasize the role of basic psychological needs (competence, relatedness, autonomy) and also the importance of intrinsic motivation, or an individual's sense of internal control over their task.

Development of Motivation

There are important changes in children's beliefs, values, and goals as they grow up. Many children begin school with positive competence beliefs, strong interest in school and other activities, and a focus on mastery and improvement. Young children's beliefs and interest are relatively general. Children's competence beliefs and values concerning many school subjects decline as they go through school. Their beliefs, values, and goals also become more differentiated and variable across different activities, such that they can form complex patterns. These variables also relate more closely both to children's performance in and out of school and choice of activities to do (Wigfield et al., 2006). Through adolescence and adulthood, beliefs, values, and goals continue to be further differentiated across

activity areas and continue to influence the choices individuals make about which activities to do. These beliefs, values, and goals also become relatively stale during adolescence although they can change based on the pattern of experiences of success and failure.

There are also important individual and group differences in the development of motivation. Gender differences in children's beliefs, values, and goals often mirror cultural stereotypes about which activities are more or less appropriate for boys and girls to do, although these differences often narrow as children go through adolescence (Wigfield et al., 2006). Racial and ethnic differences in motivation are complex and can interact with gender. Further research on ethnic differences in motivation is a strong priority for future research.

Impact of Socialization Agents

Parents can support students' motivation by their provision of mastery experiences, the ways they react to children's successes and failures and their support of student's autonomy in doing different activities. When parents react too strongly to children's failures, focus too much on children's competence rather than effort, and exert too much control over their children, negative motivational patterns can develop, even in the early childhood years (Dweck, 2002).

Recent work on motivation emphasizes the importance of contextual influences on motivation (Turner & Patrick, 2008). Teachers and schools' instructional practices can enhance students' motivation when the work they do is meaningful, they have some control over their own learning, and feedback about how they are doing focuses on the importance of effort and improvement rather than ability. The increase in high-stakes testing likely has negative influences on many students' motivation, particularly those doing poorly on the tests (Deci & Ryan, 2002).

New Directions in Motivation Research

Although social cognitive models and their focus on beliefs, values, and goals remain important, there is increasing interest on unconscious motivational processes along with the impact of the social cognitive variables on motivation (Schultheiss & Brunstein, 2005). Such work is prevalent in social psychology, but is beginning to emerge in developmental and educational psychology as well. As just noted, there is increasing interest in the complex interactions of the individual and the contexts in which individuals study and work on motivational and achievement outcomes (Turner & Patrick, 2008). Motivation clearly is not only a characteristic of the individual, but also greatly influences the kinds of contexts they experience. These experiences greatly influence the development trajectories of individuals' motivation. Finally, researchers are increasingly interested in the neurobiological underpinnings of different aspects of motivation, and fMRI studies will become more prevalent in the field in the coming years.

REFERENCES

Deci, E. L., & Ryan, R. M. (2002). The paradox of achievement: The harder you push, the worse it gets. In J. Aronson (Ed.), *Improving academic achievement: Impact of psychological factors on education* (pp. 61–87). San Diego: Academic Press.

Dweck, C. S. (2002). Messages that motivate: How praise molds students' beliefs, motivation, and performance (in surprising ways). In J. Aronson (Ed.), *Improving academic achievement: Impact of psychological factors on education* (pp. 37–60). San Diego: Academic Press.

Schultheiss, O. C., & Brunstein, J. C. (2005). An implicit motive perspective on competence. In A. J. Elliot & C. S. Dweck (Eds.), *Handbook of competence and motivation* (pp. 31–51). New York: Guilford Press.

Turner, C. J., & Patrick, H. (2008). How does motivation develop and why does it change? Reframing motivation research. *Educational Psychologist, 43*, 119–131.

Weiner, B. (1992). *Human motivation: Metaphors, theories, and research.* Newbury Park, CA: Sage.

Wigfield, A., Eccles, J. S., Schiefele, U., Roeser, R. W., & Davis-Kean, P. (2006). Development of achievement motivation. In W. Damon (Series Ed.) & N. Eisenberg (Vol. Ed.), *Handbook of child psychology* (Vol. 3, pp. 933–1002). Hoboken, NJ: John Wiley & Sons.

SUGGESTED READINGS

Eccles, J. S., & Wigfield, A. (2002). Motivational beliefs, values, and goals. *Annual Review of Psychology, 53*, 109–132.

Pintrich, P. R. (2003). A motivational science perspective on the role of student motivation in learning and teaching contexts. *Journal of Educational Psychology, 95*, 667–686.

ALLAN WIGFIELD
JENNA CAMBRIA
University of Maryland

See also: Academic Achievement; Achievement Need

ACHIEVEMENT NEED

Achievement Need (*n*Ach) is a recurrent concern to excel or to do better at a task for the intrinsic satisfaction of doing better. It is measured using nondeclarative measures such as the Thematic Apperception Test (TAT), or more commonly using the Picture Story Exercise (PSE; McClelland, Koestner, & Weinberger, 1989). McClelland, Atkinson, Clark, and Lowell (1953) created the content-coding system for *n*Ach that includes major coding subcategories for the presence of a wish, need, or goal related to competition with a standard of excellence, for positive emotional reaction after a successful achievement outcome, and for reference to a unique accomplishment.

People motivated by *n*Ach display four characteristic modes of behavior. First, they have a preference for moderately challenging tasks, set moderately difficult goals, and work harder when the chances of succeeding are only moderately great (Atkinson, 1957). This is the most consistent finding associated with *n*Ach, and it has been related to such outcomes as career aspirations and distances chosen during a ring-toss game. Atkinson provided a formula for explaining the moderate risk-taking behavior typical of people who are high in achievement need. The formula states that the tendency to approach tasks is a joint function of the amount of achievement motive, one's probability of succeeding at the task, and the incentive provided by succeeding at the task (Tendency = Motive × Probability × Incentive). Since probabilities of success are presumed to be inversely related to incentives of success, a moderately difficult task with moderate levels of probability and incentive would be most attractive to those motivated by *n*Ach.

Second, people motivated by *n*Ach have a need for autonomous and independent goal setting. They compete for personal accomplishment through their own efforts, and thus they are uninterested in taking part in activities such as gambling that rely on luck and chance. Consequently, achievement motivated individuals also avoid interacting with committees and in other situations in which they have to undertake goals that have been dictated by others or in which performance is used not as a measure of personal accomplishment but in order to obtain external incentives such as money or time off (McClelland, 1987).

Third, people motivated by *n*Ach have a preference for engaging in activities in which there is consistent, immediate, and concrete feedback (French, 1958). Activities such as academic work where another person (such as the teacher) determines the degree of progress and accomplishment but does not provide immediate and direct feedback are less motivationally satisfying.

Finally, high *n*Ach people possess a greater degree of innovativeness than other people and research their environment with more initiative and concern for variety (McClelland, 1987). They may do so by traveling more, trying out new things, and engaging in more entrepreneurial activities.

Several criterion variables related to executive success and economic achievement have been positively correlated with high *n*Ach. With respect to executive success, McClelland and others have reported a consistent positive relationship between *n*Ach and managerial and organizational effectiveness (e.g., McClelland & Boyatzis, 1982). However, Spangler and House (1991) pointed out that the *n*Ach need to have personal control over one's goals has negative implications for performance in high-level leadership positions in nontechnical positions. In a study of 39 elected American presidents, they found that *n*Ach is negatively related to the president taking direct presidential action while in office, as in entering into war, avoiding war, or making decisions that have major worldly impact.

As for economic achievement, McClelland (1961) provided cross-cultural evidence that higher societal levels of achievement need would lead to greater numbers of entrepreneurs, which in turn produces more national economic growth. However, McClelland's proposal has received mixed support from subsequent studies. Some researchers have found that, although *n*Ach does correlate with later economic development, the effects are smaller than those originally reported by McClelland, and others have found negative or even nonsignificant correlations (e.g., Mazur & Rosa, 1977).

There has been some limited research on whether and how *n*Ach can be cultivated. It is assumed to be developed through parenting experiences in which parents expect a higher standard of excellence while simultaneously providing positive reinforcers for successfully reaching challenging but developmentally appropriate goals (Rosen & D'Andrade, 1959). Based on the logic that the more clearly a person conceptualizes the cognitive and behavioral associative network defining a motive, the more likely the person is to develop that motive, McClelland and Winter (1971) educated Indian, Mexican, and American executives and businessmen on components of achievement motive coding systems. In the Indian and U.S. samples, they found that the achievement training generally produced greater business and industrial activity levels.

The expression of *n*Ach is affected to some extent by gender roles. A study of elite well-educated women in the 1960s found that *n*Ach declines in the years immediately after college graduation, because these women are in a phase of life when establishing one's home and family is a major concern, thus dampening their desire for personal accomplishment; however, women with high *n*Ach were the most likely to reenter full-time employment in the years after their family life has been established (Baruch, 1967).

It is generally acknowledged that TAT/PSE measures and questionnaire measures of *n*Ach capture different types of motivation and predict different types of outcomes. TAT/PSE scores are significantly correlated with industrial and agricultural output, career success, and other similar outcomes that have intrinsic or task-related incentives, whereas questionnaire scores are significantly correlated with grades and other similar outcomes that have extrinsic incentives or carry social-evaluative implications (McClelland, Koestner, & Weinberger, 1989). However, scores on implicit and explicit measures of *n*Ach become more congruent if a person has greater private body

consciousness, is low in self-monitoring, and has a high preference for consistency (Thrash, Elliot, & Schultheiss, 2007).

A distinction has also traditionally been made between the active, approach-oriented aspects of *n*Ach—also named hope of success—and the anxiety-based, avoidant tendencies of fear of failure. However, research on this approach-avoidance distinction has been inconsistent at best, because of the lack of an experimentally derived and easily-accessible nondeclarative measure of hope of success and fear of failure.

REFERENCES

Atkinson, J. W. (1957). Motivational determinants of risk-taking behavior. *Psychological Review, 64,* 359.

Baruch, R. (1967). The achievement motive in women: Implications for career development. *Journal of Personality and Social Psychology, 5*(3), 260–267.

French, E. G. (1958). Effects of the interaction of motivation and feedback on task performance. In J. W. Atkinson (Ed.), *Motives in fantasy, action, and society*. Princeton, NJ: Van Nostrand.

Mazur, A., & Rosa, E. (1977). An empirical test of McClelland's "achieving society" theory. *Social Forces, 55*(3), 769–774.

McClelland, D. C. (1961). *The achieving society*. Princeton, NJ: Van Nostrand.

McClelland, D. C. (1987). *Human motivation*. Cambridge: Cambridge University Press.

McClelland, D. C., Atkinson, J. W., Clark, R. A., & Lowell, E. L. (1953). *The achievement motive*. East Norwalk, CT: Appleton-Century-Crofts.

McClelland, D. C., & Boyatzis, R. E. (1982). Leadership motive pattern and long-term success in management. *Journal of Applied Psychology, 67,* 737–743.

McClelland, D. C., Koestner, R., & Weinberger, J. (1989). How do self-attributed and implicit motives differ? *Psychological Review, 96*(4), 690–702.

McClelland, D. C., & Winter, D. G. (1971). *Motivating economic achievement*. New York: Free Press.

Rosen, B. C., & D'Andrade, R. (1959). The psychosocial origins of achievement motivation. *Sociometry, 22,* 185–218.

Spangler, W. D., & House, R. J. (1991). Presidential effectiveness and the leadership motive profile. *Journal of Personality and Social Psychology, 60*(3), 439–455.

Thrash, T. M., Elliot, A. J., & Schultheiss, O. C. (2007). Methodological and dispositional predictors of congruence between implicit and explicit need for achievement. *Personality and Social Psychology Bulletin, 33,* 961–974.

SUGGESTED READINGS

Heckhausen, H. (1991). *Motivation and action* (pp. 199–243). Berlin: Springer.

Schultheiss, O. C., & Brunstein, J. C. (2005). An implicit motive perspective on competence. In A. J. Elliot & C. S. Dweck (Eds.), *Handbook of competence and motivation* (pp. 31–51). New York: Guilford Press.

JOYCE S. PANG
Nanyang Technological University, Singapore

See also: Achievement Motivation; Underachievement

ACQUIRED DRIVES

One of the raging controversies in the history of psychology once centered on the aspect of the nature-nurture issue, which asks whether motives are inborn or learned. Some psychologists, of whom William McDougall was the most important, took the instinctivist position that motives are inborn, unlearned, universal within species, and—at least to a degree—continuous between species. Other psychologists, for whom John B. Watkins was the most important spokesman, argued that motives are acquired through learning and therefore differ from individual to individual, culture to culture, and species to species. As occurred generally with the nature-nurture issue, the intensity of this controversy has lessened with time. It is now clear that all motives are a joint product of biological and environmental forces. If the question is asked at all, it is in terms of the relative importance of these two contributions.

Certain motives, sometimes called *primary drives*, are chiefly biological. Hunger, thirst, pain avoidance, and sex are examples. Even in these cases, however, experience plays a part. Rhythms of feeding and drinking, sensitivity to pain, and preferences in sexual partners are all influenced in this way. Other motives, sometimes called *secondary* or *acquired drives*, are determined primarily by experience, as for instance fears, affection for parents, drug addictions, and functionally autonomous habits such as miserliness. These examples show something of the variety of acquired drives. They also suggest that different acquired drives may depend on forms of learning that differ at least superficially.

Acquisition of Fear

One of the forms of learning just referred to is *classical conditioning*. Experimental evidence that some motives are acquired as the result of this process dates at least to the famous study of Watson and Rayner, who conditioned the boy "little Albert" to fear a white rat. The rat (CS) was shown to the child, simultaneously with a loud and unpleasant sound (US) produced by the striking of a steel bar behind the child's head. The sound caused the child to cry (UR). After a few repetitions, Albert cried at the sight of the rat (CR), and this fear generalized to other furry objects such as a fur neckpiece or a Santa Claus mask. Attempts to repeat the Watson and Rayner study were not always successful, and Valentine made the cogent point that fears might be much more easily conditioned to furry objects such as a caterpillar or a rat than to others such as a pair of opera glasses. In spite of these criticisms, the impact of the Watson and Rayner study on the history of psychology was considerable. It indicated that reactions once thought to be instinctive were more properly seen as the result of learning.

Affectional Responses

The young of many species come to treat the first large, moving, noisy object they see as if it were a parent. In most cases this object is in fact a parent, but the process of *imprinting*, as it is called, may produce such attachments to other species and even inanimate objects.

Various lines of evidence indicate that an essential component of imprinted reactions is motivational. The hatchlings of precocial birds, if imprinted on any object, stay near that object and will climb over obstacles to get near it; further, they make distress calls in its absence. The process of learning involved in imprinting bears a strong resemblance to classical conditioning.

Social Techniques

Literature in the area of acquired motivation suggests that some motives may be acquired by a process that is akin to instrumental learning. E. C. Tolman has given us an account that is fairly representative. Figure 1 summarizes his view, which holds that in infancy the individual has only a set of biological drives. Inevitably these drives are subjected to frustration, and new techniques are developed to satisfy them. Whatever techniques lead to relief from frustration are learned, and they become characteristic of the individual's repertory of responses to the world. As Tolman's drive-conversion diagram (Figure 1) also suggests, these first primitive adjustments achieved by the individual are not adequate to deal with all situations. They are too frustrated, with the result that new learning occurs and the individual's reactions to the world are modified further.

It should be noted that, so far in this account, nothing has been said about motives. Yet a glance at Figure 1 will reveal that several of the social techniques are ones that we often describe in motivational terms. Aggression, hostility, social approval, loyalty, identification, and self-punishment are all terms that probably occur more often in psychological literature in the context of motive than in that of habit. This suggests that there must be

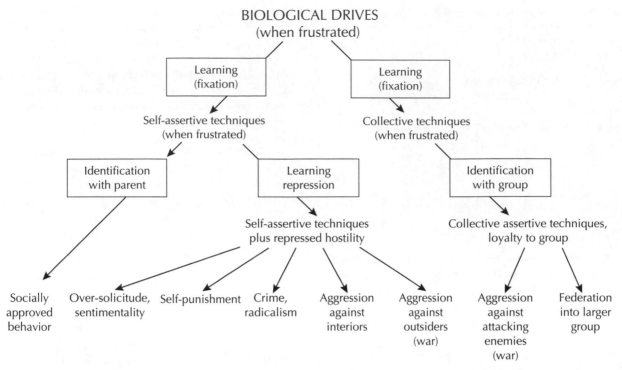

Figure 1. Tolman's drive-conversion diagram.
Source: Figure adapted from G. A. Kimble (1961). Based on E. C. Tomlin (1942).

some sense in which habits are, or can become, motives. Gordon Allport once suggested in an article that such is the case, and he offered the concept of functional autonomy, whereby well-established habits become ends in themselves—that is, motives. It should be noted, however, that functional autonomy does not explain such effects; it only describes them.

Addictions

Addictions to tobacco, alcohol, and other substances are of special interest because they dramatize certain features of the psychology of acquired motivation. The motivational power of the addictions is obvious: Lives have been devoted to, and even lost to activities performed to support an addiction. Established addictions no doubt represent a change in the physiology of the addicted person, probably a change in how certain neurotransmitters function. But at the same time, addictions are clearly acquired. This testifies to the power that experience may sometimes have over biological processes.

The mechanism of learning an addiction appears to be a two-stage process. In the first stage, the future addict experiments with the addictive substance out of curiosity or a yielding to peer pressure, or for some other reasons that soon becomes irrelevant. In the case of some drugs, like the opiates, only a few such encounters are required to leave the individual with a powerful craving after the initial euphoria produced by the drug wears off. The only ways to relieve this craving are either painful

waiting for the craving to subside or taking more of the substance in question. People who become addicted choose the latter alternative, thus beginning the vicious circle: drug—euphoria—agonized craving—drug again. In abstract terms, the learning process appears to be of the operant or instrumental variety, with the relief from craving and the agony of abstinence playing a greater role than the positively reinforcing euphoric experience initiated by the drug.

Motivation and Emotion

The literature on the various acquired drives and drugs provides a particularly straightforward way of making a methodological point. Although common speech and some psychological theories make a distinction between motives and emotions, it is clear that these terms refer to different aspects of the same process. *Motivation* refers to the power of an acquired drive to promote certain kinds of behavior, chiefly those of reaching certain goals—being near a parent, relief from fear, achieving certain social goals, or avoiding withdrawal symptoms. *Emotion* refers to the subjective experience associated with the arousal of these states.

These points are all very nicely integrated in R. L. Solomon's opponent-process theory of emotion. The essential ideas in this theory are the following: (1) the conditions that arouse a motivational/emotional state (State A) also call out a more sluggishly acting opposed state (State B); (2) State B is a "slave" state, which occurs as an inevitable accompaniment of State A; (3) termination of the original emotional circumstances leaves State B as the individual's dominating emotional state; and (4) State B, but not State A, increases with use and decreases with disuse.

Solomon and others have applied this opponent-process theory to many different motivational/emotional reactions. The application provides a rich account of the details of such behavior and a means of understanding the changes in such reactions after many arousals of the emotion. In opiate addiction, for instance, at first the effect of the drug (State A) is a feeling of euphoria, a "rush"; when the drug wears off, its aftereffect (State B) is craving. With continued usage and the strengthening of State B, the effect of the drug is less intense and is often described as a feeling of contentment. Its aftereffect is now much more intense—an excruciatingly painful set of withdrawal symptoms. Similar accounts are put forward for other emotional experiences.

GREGORY A. KIMBLE
Duke University

See also: Pavlovian Conditioning

ACTING OUT

The term "acting out" has been used to label behavior in a variety of contexts, ranging from preschools and kindergartens (to describe kids such as Johnny, who has decimated a prized collection of stuffed animals, and thrown them about) to psychological treatment settings (with regard to patients like Mildred, who has punched her therapist in the nose after he offered her a particularly insightful interpretation). The concept is most extensively in vogue, however, in organizations that deal with criminal offenders or persons who have been diagnosed as having mental health problems.

"Acting out" as a process denotes a deficit or a lapse in the exercise of appropriate self-control. As an adjective applied to another person's behavior (never one's own,) "acting out" carries a pejorative connotation, in that it implies (1) that the person has failed to keep in check particularly unsavory feelings, or primitive impulses that most people would not overtly express; and (2) that the person has provided evidence of deficits in his or her upbringing or failure to assimilate the most elementary norms of civilized conduct. Acting-out behavior is also deemed to be both destructive and self-destructive—not a testimonial to the inception of a promising career.

In the world of the theater, acting out connotes dramatic behaviors whereby actors convey inner conflicts or private feelings to an audience. Such activity calls for considerable acumen, and for special thespian skills, and it is undertaken deliberately. By contrast, spontaneous acting out—such as during psychological treatment, involves the revelation of inner conflicts without conscious intent or awareness. Patients like Mildred can thus communicate information against their own best judgments, surfacing emotions they may not be ready to face, or enacting experiences they may not be ready to discuss. Such junctures are variously reacted to by therapists. Wolberg (1977) points out that

> There are some psychotherapists who take the view that acting-out can serve a useful purpose in some patients. That it may be growth-inducing and, particularly where basic problems originated in the preverbal stage, constitute a preliminary step toward gaining insight. Consequently, they tend to encourage and even to stimulate acting-out. Other therapists, however, regard acting-out as always detrimental to therapeutic progress since it drains off the tension that should be employed for a requisite understanding and working through of conflicts. (p. 619)

Ideally, psychotherapy provides a safe venue for the expression of volatile emotions. In his therapeutic play sessions, Johnny (or Bobby) can thus be permitted to be quite destructive, and even to disembowel an occasional stuffed bear (assuming that his parents are willing to pay for its replacement). There are, however, limits to what Johnny or Bobby would be licensed to enact as play. Johnny would not be allowed to assault his therapist, though he might be encouraged to kill the therapist in effigy (Dorfman, 1951, p. 258). Such violence by proxy can paradoxically promote closer relatedness, because once the child has expressed his violent resentment, he may feel free to become more amiable, and to ultimately become more amenable to treatment. For example

Therapist: I am all gone now?
Bob: You're dead. I killed you.
Therapist: I am killed.
Bob: You're all washed up.
Therapist: I am very, very dead?
Bob: You sure are. (*Suddenly, he smiles.*) I'll have you a game of catch now.
Therapist: You want to play with me now? Ok. (p. 260)

Acting-out behavior is expressive behavior. By releasing feelings, it serves to reduce tension when a person feels frustrated or under stress. The result, unfortunately, can feel threatening to observers caught in the wake of the behavior, who are not likely to make allowances for the function the behavior serves. Some who come to see themselves as targets of acting-out behavior are likely to demonstrate resentment or assertively express displeasure. Behavioral sequences that follow in such situations can become cyclical chain reactions. Angry responses by bystanders can contribute to the stressed person's stress, producing an escalation of his acting-out behavior, which may invite further responses from those who feel affronted by the behavior.

In institutional settings, the cycle tends to be exacerbated by structural constraints. Acting-out behavior invariably violates institutional rules, and rule-transgressions eventuate in punishments meted out by institutional staff. Unsurprisingly, punishments by staff are experienced as stressful by those being punished, which can give impetus to further acting-out behavior. Occasionally, a point is reached in punitive cycles where staff members who have been functioning as sources of stress get to experience stress themselves, and are goaded into engaging in acting-out behavior of their own.

Some people demonstrate a redundant propensity for acting out (Toch & Adams, 2002). There are individuals who appear to explode with rage at the slightest provocation. Others present themselves as perpetually helpless victims of preemptive impulses, or advertise ineluctable chips on their shoulder. There are persons who are known for low boiling points or for hair-trigger sensitivity to perceived affronts. Others are renowned for picking fights or for richly earned reputations for unpredictable craziness.

The latter reputations, on the face of it, are not calculated to earn admiration, but they do inspire fear, which in some circles is a vehicle for acquiring status. In groups that are composed of self-styled tough and formidable delinquents, acting-out behavior can make the individual a role model for peers who aspire to replicate his intimidating ferocity. Acting out in groups of less seasoned delinquents can be emotionally contagious when the atmosphere is volatile. In this regard Redl and Wineman (1951) have observed that

> The mere fact that a youngster sees one of his less relaxed contemporaries throwing things around, banging his fork against the plate ferociously, jumping up and crawling under bed and table, may in itself suddenly set loose behavior in him of which he really hadn't thought until that very minute. In short, it seems as though sometimes behavior will "spread" and become "infectious" by the very lure its visualization implies. (p. 87)

Particularly among preadolescents, impulse-release and tension-reducing behavior lends itself to being emulated. This fact makes acting out a group phenomenon as well as a manifestation of individual misconduct—and both permutations are understandably apt to be of continuing concern to psychologists and educators.

REFERENCES

Dorfman, E. (1951). Play therapy. In Rogers, C. R., *Client-centered therapy: Its current practice, implications and theory*. Boston: Houghton Mifflin Company, pp. 235–277.

Wolberg, L. R. (1977). *The technique of psychotherapy (3rd ed.)*. New York: Grune & Stratton.

SUGGESTED READINGS

Redl, F., & Wineman, D. (1951). *Children who hate: The disorganization and breakdown of behavior controls*. Glencoe: The Free Press.

Toch, H., & Adams, K. (2002). *Acting out: Maladaptive behavior in confinement*. Washington, DC: American Psychological Association (APA Books).

Hans Toch
State University of New York
at Albany

See also: **Conduct Disorder; Juvenile Delinquency**

ACTION SELECTION

Action selection, also known as response selection, refers to how people determine specific actions to perform and, as studied in choice-reaction tasks, to processes involved in deciding which response to make to a presented stimulus. Action selection is considered to be distinct from perception and from the processes involved in the execution of movements to carry out the actions. F. C. Donders (1869/1968) was among the earliest researchers to study action selection in his investigations of the temporal properties of information processing. Recent years have witnessed an expansion of interest in action-selection phenomena, since the linking of perception and cognition to action is fundamental to all behavior.

Stimulus-Response Uncertainty and the Hick-Hyman Law

Contemporary research on action selection can be dated to the early 1950s when W. E. Hick and R. Hyman reported studies showing a lawful increase in reaction time as event uncertainty increased. The Hick-Hyman law is based on information theory, for which the amount information in bits (binary digits) is $\log_2$ of the number of alternatives. According to the Hick-Hyman law, reaction time is a linearly increasing function of the amount of information transmitted by the performer, which is essentially the information provided by a stimulus that can be determined from knowing the response. For equally likely stimuli, each with a unique response, the information transmitted is $\log_2$ of the number of alternative stimuli if no errors are made. The amount of information transmitted will be less if stimuli occur with different frequencies and if errors are made, resulting in shorter reaction times. Researchers quickly rejected information theory, with its emphasis on binary decisions, as providing an adequate explanation of the processing underlying the Hick-Hyman law.

Usher and McLelland (2001) developed a model that attributes the Hick-Hyman law to accumulation of information in competing decision units for each stimulus-response alternative. In this model, when a stimulus occurs, information starts accumulating in the respective decision units, with the response corresponding to a particular unit selected when its threshold is reached. Because the accumulation process is noisy, each additional decision unit provides another opportunity for an incorrect response to be selected. To prevent the error rate from increasing dramatically as uncertainty increases, people set the decision-unit criteria at higher levels, lengthening reaction time.

Stimulus-Response Compatibility

Also in the early 1950s, P. A. Fitts and colleagues reported the first investigations of stimulus-response compatibility effects, which are thought to provide relatively pure measures of action selection. Compatibility effects are differences in reaction time and accuracy as a function of the relation between stimulus and response sets or the mapping of members of the stimulus set to members of the response set (Proctor & Vu, 2006). Spatial compatibility effects are most widely known and investigated. Performance is better: when the spatial arrangement of stimuli matches the spatial arrangement of responses; and, when each stimulus is mapped to its spatially corresponding response. However, compatibility effects occur whenever there is similarity, or overlap, between the dimensions of the stimulus and response sets. This similarity does not have to be physical, as it does for spatial locations; but it can also be conceptual (e.g., the words "LEFT"–"RIGHT" mapped to left–right keypresses yield a compatibility effect). Moreover, a third form of similarity, structural, affects performance in a variety of situations for which there is no physical or conceptual similarity. Structural similarity may be of ordered relations (e.g., numbers 1–4 mapped to a left-to-right ordering of response keys) or of the polarities of codes for binary classifications (Proctor & Cho, 2006).

Compatibility effects are among the most reliably obtained phenomena in psychology, and they are resistant to practice. Their magnitude often decreases over the first few hundred trials, but the effects typically remain sizeable across extended practice (Dutta & Proctor, 1992). The benefit for a spatially compatible mapping is reduced and often eliminated, though, only for situations in which compatible and incompatible stimulus-response mappings are intermixed (Proctor & Vu, 2002). This benefit is also eliminated when a task for which location is relevant is intermixed with a task of the type described next, for

which stimulus location is relevant and another stimulus dimension relevant.

The Simon Effect

The concept that spatial compatibility effects occur when stimulus location is irrelevant was first demonstrated by J. R. Simon in the 1960s. For example, when red and green stimuli are presented in left and right locations and participants are to make a left keypress to red and right keypress to green, responses are faster when the stimulus location corresponds with the response assigned to the color than when it does not. The term *Simon effect* is used nowadays with reference to these correspondence effects. The Simon effect has attracted considerable interest since the mid-1990s because it illustrates that action selection is influenced by stimulus properties that are not part of the action goals (Hommel & Prinz, 1997). The effect is related to the more familiar Stroop color-naming effect with the major difference being that the Simon effect can be attributed more directly to action selection since similarity exists only between the irrelevant stimulus-location dimension and the response-location dimension.

Most accounts of compatibility and Simon effects attribute them to two action-selection routes (Hommel & Prinz, 1997). One route is automatic and response activation is presumed to occur through it by way of long-term stimulus-response associations. A stimulus will produce activation of its corresponding response via this route, providing the basis for the Simon effect. The second route is intentional, and it is presumed to involve short-term associations implemented to perform the instructed task. This route is a major factor in compatibility effects obtained for relevant stimulus-response mappings.

Attributing the Simon effect to automatic activation suggests that the effect should be difficult to override. Yet, it is not (Proctor & Vu, 2002). When the response keys are labeled so that the relevant stimulus dimension can be mapped incompatibly to the responses (e.g., press the green key to the red stimulus), the Simon effect reverses to favor the noncorresponding response. Likewise, when trials of a Simon task are intermixed task with trials for a task in which stimulus locations are mapped incompatibly to responses, the Simon effect reverses to favor the noncorresponding responses. Even more surprising, fewer than 100 practice trials with an incompatible spatial mapping can eliminate or reverse the Simon effect in a subsequent transfer session, even after a one-week delay. Thus, the "short-term" associations established for one task persist to influence performance of a later task for which they are inapplicable.

The codes on which action selection is performed in spatial compatibility and Simon tasks are thought to be predominantly spatial. One of the clearest demonstrations of spatial coding is that the effects remain relatively unaltered if the hands are crossed such that a right key is operated by the left hand and a left key by the right hand (Wallace, 1971). Thus, anatomical factors such as the mapping of stimuli to hands are of secondary importance. Moreover, the spatial coding of actions does not necessarily involve the location of the responding effector. If each hand holds a stick that is crossed to press the key on the opposite side, the stimulus-key relation determines the compatibility effect. If the goal of the action is to produce an effect (e.g., turning on a light) to the left or right, the relation between the stimulus and the action effect is crucial rather than that between the stimulus and the key pressed by the hand to produce the action effect.

Dual-Task Performance

Limitations in dual-task performance are usually attributed to action selection. When two tasks must be performed, the response for the second task is slowed when its stimulus occurs within a few hundred milliseconds after onset of the first task's stimulus. This phenomenon, known as the psychological refractory period effect (Pashler, 1994), has been attributed to a response-selection bottleneck. Considerable research effort is currently being devoted to whether this bottleneck is part of the cognitive strategic or architecture, and whether the capacity for response selection can be divided between tasks or must be devoted to one task at a time. An additional issue concerns conditions under which the bottleneck may be bypassed. Several recent studies have demonstrated cross-task effects between tasks similar to the Simon effect, suggesting that at least some cross-task activation of response information occurs.

In conclusion, spatial compatibility, Simon effects, and related phenomena may seem at first glance to be of limited relevance to most psychologists. However, such effects reflect fundamental cognitive processes that come into play in a variety of situations. For example, Simon effects have been used in recent years to study activation of emotional information (the affective Simon effect), of specific actions afforded by objects, and of mental representations of numbers. They have been used to investigate effects of aging across the lifespan and various other individual differences in processing. With the recent advent of the "embodied cognition" view, which ascribes meaning and thought to action, compatibility effects of various types have moved to center stage in psychology.

REFERENCES

Donders, F. C. (1868/1969). On the speed of mental processes. In W. G. Koster (Ed.), *Acta Psychologica, 30, Attention and Performance II* (pp. 412–431). Amsterdam: North-Holland.

Dutta, A., & Proctor, R. W. (1992). Persistence of stimulus-response compatibility effects with extended practice. *Journal of Experimental Psychology: Learning, Memory, and Cognition, 18*, 801–809.

Hommel, B., & Prinz, W. (Eds.). (1997). *Theoretical issues in stimulus-response compatibility*. Amsterdam: North-Holland.

Pashler, H. (1994). Dual-task interference in simple tasks: Data and theory. *Psychological Bulletin, 16*, 220–224.

Proctor, R. W., & Cho, Y. S. (2006). Polarity correspondence: A general principle for performance of speeded binary classification tasks. *Psychological Bulletin, 132*, 416–442.

Proctor, R. W., & Vu, K.-P. L. (2002a). Eliminating, magnifying, and reversing spatial compatibility effects with mixed location-relevant and irrelevant trials. In W. Prinz and B. Hommel (Eds.), *Common mechanisms in perception and action: Attention and performance Vol. XIX* (pp. 443–473). Oxford: Oxford University Press.

Proctor, R. W., & Vu, K.-P. L. (2006). *Stimulus-response compatibility principles: Data, theory, and application*. Boca Raton, FL: CRC Press.

Usher, M., & McClelland, J. L. (2001). The time course of perceptual choice: The leaky, competing accumulator model. *Psychological Review, 108*, 550–592.

Wallace, R. J. (1971). S-R compatibility and the idea of a response code. *Journal of Experimental Psychology, 88*, 354–360.

SUGGESTED READINGS

Hommel, B., Müsseler, J., Aschersleben, G., & Prinz, W. (2001). The theory of event-coding (TEC): A framework for perception and action planning. *Behavioral and Brain Sciences, 24*, 849–878.

Proctor, R. W., & Vu, K.-P. L. (2003). Action selection. In A. F. Healy & R. W. Proctor (Eds.), *Experimental psychology* (pp. 293–316). Volume 4 in I. B. Weiner (Editor-in-Chief) *Handbook of psychology*. New York: John Wiley & Sons.

Proctor, R. W., & Vu, K.-P. L. (2006). Selection and control of action. In G. Salvendy (Ed.), *Handbook of human factors and ergonomics* (3rd ed., pp. 89–110). Hoboken, NJ: John Wiley & Sons.

ROBERT W. PROCTOR
Purdue University

KIM-PHUONG L. VU
California State University, Long Beach

ACTUALIZATION

The general common meaning of actualization is moving from potential into reality–actuality. Actualization is broadly valued in American culture, as is evident in the saying that anyone can become president, and in a recent army advertisement campaign urging potential recruits to "Be all that you can be." In American psychology, self-actualization has come to refer to a person's bringing into reality his or her own potential for a richly fulfilling, open, and appreciative life. In most recent times, actualization is more explicitly coming to include moving beyond self to identifying with humanity, nature, and the cosmos.

Within American psychology, actualization is most closely associated with humanistic psychology, especially with Carl Rogers' (1902–1987) position that humans are growth-oriented (1951, 1961), and with Abraham Maslow's (1908–1970) conception of self-actualization (1954, 1971). The psychologists who founded what became known as humanistic psychology were critical of the prevailing assumptions and foci of 1940s psychology. At that time the major psychological theories were strict behaviorism and drive- and aggression-oriented psychoanalysis; both were reductive and deterministic. Psychology was primarily university-based and concerned with being a science in the manner of the successful natural sciences. Academic psychology rarely addressed consciousness, choice, health, or possibility. Into the 1950s and 1960s (and residually into our twenty-first century), educational and clinical psychology emphasized classi-fication; psychology and psychiatry further emphasized identification and treatment of deficiency and disease.

Humanistic psychology came into being to address aspects of being human that were not being addressed by mainstream psychology. Eventually Maslow named the diverse efforts to develop alternative views to determin-istic psychoanalysis and behaviorism as "the third force." Much of this force also became known as the human potential movement, which encouraged people to pursue positive human values such as joy, love, commitment, hope, interpersonal connection, and service to others. In significant respects, humanistic psychology has served as a forerunner to contemporary "positive psychology."

Parallel to and sometimes overlapping the earlier humanistic movement, there was a popular "humanistic" movement that opposed not so much deterministic psy-chological theories and practices as the restrictions of the 1950s and 1960s culture. This was largely a self-centered, counterculture movement, not a psychological movement.

Rogers proposed that humans have a basic tendency to strive toward being fully functioning, to actualize their full potential. He described this process as requiring courage, but as often attended by joy as well as by pain and heartbreak. The process is continuous, not a completed achievement. Rogers described his approach to counseling and psychotherapy as "nondirective"—limited to provid-ing the conditions that allowed the person to strive. Later he referred to the approach as "person-centered" and "client-centered," stressing the importance of recog-nizing the person's worth, perceived world, and potential to grow. In this approach, the counselor empathically but matter-of-factly speaks back what the client has said, with no effort at interpreting or directing. In turn, the client fur-ther clarifies and deepens his or her own understanding. The client discovers contradictions among beliefs, affect, and behavior and, without direction from the counselor,

strives toward a coherent grasp. This striving promotes growth, and the counselor's nonjudgmental "unconditional positive regard" allows the client's understandings to deepen in an integrated way.

Rogers viewed maladjustment as inconsistencies in one's self-concept, maintained through ignoring relevant sensations and feelings. Providing a respectful, calm, accepting presence allows people to recognize fuller per-spectives and to allow themselves to grow toward inte-grated functioning. Fully functioning persons continually strive to be open to possibility and to avoid distortion. They trust their judgment and dare to be creative. These persons are open to their own needs and seek to balance them. Beyond therapy, Rogers extended his approach to the field of education and developed a learner-centered model that stressed "the freedom to learn." In his later years, Rogers applied his approach to group, national, and international conflict, promoting individual empowerment and social change.

Maslow was one of the few nontherapist humanistic writers. He was primarily university-based and a major theorist of humanistic psychology. He founded the Asso-ciation of Humanistic Psychology and its journal, the *Journal of Humanistic Psychology,* as well as the *Journal of Transpersonal Psychology.* Although he was trained as an experimental psychologist, his work was observational and theoretical. He is best known within psychology and by the public for having described the characteristics of well-known people who were emotionally healthy and achieving and whom he regarded as self-actualized, for example, Abraham Lincoln, Eleanor Roosevelt, and Albert Schweitzer.

He found that such persons were self-aware and attuned to their inner impulses and made choices to improve and to change. They also were diligent problem-solvers, both practically and creatively. They were not particularly culturally constrained, and often were seen as detached, although they also maintained close personal ties. They were nonjudgmental and accepting. They often were closely attuned to and deeply appreciative of simple social or natural events. More than most people, they were open to and changed by peak experiences, often in nature, in which their sense of self was transcended as they found themselves in holistic relation to humans in general, to other species, to nature, and to the cosmos. These transcendent experiences often moved these people to further their commitments.

Maslow found that self-actualizing people of course were not actualized in every moment. Moreover, actual-ization was not an achieved status; rather, these people repeatedly answered the call toward growth. Maslow extended his work into business management models that hold an optimistic view of human nature (e.g., Eupsychian management and Theory Z). Contemporary times have extended self-actualization to include identification with humanity, nature, and all that is, particularly through pursuing humanistic values, service, deep ecology, and mediation practices.

REFERENCES

Maslow, A. H. (1954). *Motivation and personality*. New York: Harper & Row.

Maslow, A. H. (1971). *The farther reaches of human nature*. New York: Viking Press.

Rogers, C. R. (1951). *Client-centered therapy: Its current practice, implications, and theory*. London: Constable.

Rogers, C. R. (1961). *On becoming a person: A therapist's view of psychotherapy*. London: Constable.

SUGGESTED READINGS

Hart, T., Nelson, P. L., & Puhakka, K. (Eds.) (2000). *Transpersonal knowing: Exploring the horizon of consciousness*. Albany: State University of New York Press.

Wertz, F. W. (Ed.). 1994. *The humanistic movement: Recovering the person in psychology*. Lakeworth, FL: Gardner.

CONSTANCE T. FISCHER
Duquesne University

See also: Client-Centered Therapy; Humanistic Psychotherapies

ACTUARIAL PREDICTION (See Statistical Prediction)

ADAPTIVE TESTING (See Computerized Adaptive Testing)

ADDICTION

Addiction is a term widely used to indicate any type of excessive repetitive involvement with an activity or substance, and colloquially it is applied as readily to exercise, eating chocolate, and computer gaming as to alcohol, methamphetamine, or heroin use. Such broad use of the term detracts from its technical value, and thus in this entry *addiction* will be used to refer only to substance use disorders.

Problematic substance use can be described by two distinct patterns—Abuse and Dependence (American Psychiatric Association, 2000). Abuse refers to life problems from substance use: Use in situations that are physically dangerous, use interfering with occupational roles (e.g., work or school) or with family and other social relationships, or use resulting in legal difficulties. By contrast, Dependence includes physiological, behavioral, and psychological components. Physiological aspects of dependence may include tolerance (the need for increasing amounts of the substance to attain the same behavioral and subjective effects) or withdrawal (a physical syndrome activated by cessation from or cutting down on use of the substance). Behavioral components include using larger amounts of the substance over longer periods of time than intended; spending excessive amounts of time obtaining, using, and recovering from the substance; or using instead of engaging in other recreational and social pursuits. Psychological components include continued use despite knowledge of medical or psychological conditions caused or exacerbated by substance use, and desires or actual attempts to reduce or cease use of the substance.

Use of alcohol, other sedative/hypnotic/anxiolytic drugs, cocaine, other stimulants, opioids, cannabis, hallucinogens, inhalants, or nicotine all can lead to Substance Abuse or Dependence. A withdrawal syndrome can be associated with all except for cannabis, hallucinogens, and inhalants. Note that legality and addictiveness are not interchangeable; some illegal substances are not considered physically addictive and many legal substances are addictive.

Epidemiology

Regular use of alcohol is common among adults in the United States (67% lifetime prevalence), unlike regular use of illicit drugs (just 16%). Similarly, Alcohol Abuse and Dependence are relatively common (a lifetime prevalence of 42% for men and 29.5% for women; Hasin, Stinson, & Ogborn, 2007), whereas illicit-drug abuse or dependence are less common (13.9% of men and 7.2% of women; Compton, Thomas, & Stinson, 2007). Nicotine dependence remains prevalent as well: 23.9% of men and 18.0% of women smoked cigarettes in 2007 (Centers for Disease Control, 2007). After alcohol and nicotine, the most common drug of abuse or dependence is cannabis, followed by prescription drugs, cocaine, amphetamines, hallucinogens, opioids, and sedatives.

Etiology

The causes of addiction are complex and involve an interplay among three dimensions—the biological, the psychological, and the social. The relative importance of each dimension varies with the specific substance of abuse and with the individual user. In general, individuals vary in their genetic vulnerability to develop dependence on any substance, and this vulnerability interacts with their physiological make-up, psychological characteristics, social environment, and access to the substance.

Substance use disorders run in families, and research has attempted to distinguish genetic from familial aspects of etiology. Both twin and adoption studies suggest a heritable component to Alcohol Dependence. With other drugs, some studies suggest genetic elements, such as evidence of common drug preferences in monozygotic twins and increased risk for drug dependence in families. Candidate genes have been associated with increased vulnerability to specific substance use disorders, but evidence to date suggests that multiple genes interact to increase risk, and there is no single gene that determines whether a person develops an addiction. The majority of offspring from families with a substance use disorder do not develop problems, and the majority of those with a substance use disorder do not have a clear family history.

Genetic vulnerability is expressed through specific physiological and psychological vulnerabilities. For example, individuals vary in the forms of specific enzymes (isozymes) that break down alcohol in the body; some forms of these isozymes increase susceptibility to developing dependence on alcohol, and other forms are protective. Neurochemical research points to differences in sensitivity to dopamine or to deficiencies in GABA. Psychologically, vulnerable individuals often have inherited a temperament that is high in sensation seeking, low in harm avoidance, and low in reward dependence that makes them more susceptible to substance use.

Exposure to alcohol or drugs also leads to changes at the cellular or molecular level that may contribute to the development or maintenance of dependence. A number of different neuronal changes have been suggested as causing Alcohol Dependence, including changes in neuronal membranes, changes in the excitability and function of nerve cells mediated through the calcium and GABA receptor/chloride channels, changes in the activity of excitatory neurotransmitter systems, and changes in second messenger systems (see Moak & Anton in McCrady & Epstein, 1999). Research on opioid dependence has failed to find changes in opioid receptors associated with addiction. However, at the subcellular level, chronic exposure to opioids has been demonstrated to lead to long-term changes in specific G protein subunits (see Stine & Kosten in McCrady & Epstein, 1999).

Psychological research also has demonstrated the importance of interactions between the individual and environment. Repeated exposure to drug use situations can lead to conditioned physiological responses to the situations that are similar to physiological responses to the actual drug. The development of strong positive expectancies about the effects of certain drugs can also contribute to continued use. Individuals with substance use disorders also show deficiencies in self-control in that they have difficulties inhibiting behavior or making decisions that favor long-term over short-term rewards. However, it is not clear whether these tendencies are a cause or consequence of substance use. Individuals may use substances to enhance positive moods as well as to cope with negative emotions, and those with other psychological problems are at particularly high risk for the development of substance use disorders as well.

Alcohol and drug use occurs in a social context. Introduction to alcohol and drug use most commonly occurs with either peers or family members. Individuals who are at high risk for using drugs and for other problem behaviors often join with peers of a similarly high risk level and these peer groups then may influence those within the group to use or experiment with substances and other high-risk behaviors. Adolescents are less likely to develop alcohol or drug problems if they come from families that provide consistent and fair discipline, spend time together on a regular basis, and have a positive religious orientation.

Prevention

Prevention of addiction has taken many forms, including broad-brush prevention programs in schools (e.g., DARE); prevention targeted at specific populations (e.g., pregnant women); and environmentally focused interventions that change laws and policies, decrease access to the substance, and increase penalties (e.g., raising tobacco taxes, restricting alcohol sales near college campuses, and installing mandatory ignition-interlock devices following DUI). Some individually and environmentally focused interventions have been successful in preventing or delaying the onset of use, decreasing use among those already using, and decreasing harmful consequences to using individuals or to others. Motivational enhancement, social-norms feedback, and behavior-modification approaches are consistently effective; however, education-only, morality, and fear-based programs are often ineffective.

Treatment

Treatment efforts include both psychological and pharmacological approaches. Several psychological therapies are effective in the treatment of Substance Abuse or Dependence. Brief, motivationally focused interventions are effective for individuals with milder problems, and they also may enhance treatment outcomes when combined with ongoing treatments. Cognitive-behavioral therapies—including community reinforcement treatment, relapse prevention, social skills training, and behavioral couples therapy—are well-supported for treating Alcohol Dependence (Miller & Wilbourne, 2002). Interventions effective in treating illicit-drug dependence include family therapy and community reinforcement approaches (Copello et al., 2005), as well as contingency management programs (Prendergast et al., 2006). Treatments to facilitate involvement with mutual-help groups (e.g., Alcoholics Anonymous) are also effective (Miller & Wilbourne, 2002), and continued active participation in those groups correlates with better outcomes.

Aside from medications for withdrawal, there are few effective pharmacotherapies to treat substance-use disorders. Naltrexone, acamprosate, and disulfiram are supported for treating alcohol dependence, and a long-acting injectable form of naltrexone is now available. Methadone and buprenorphine have strong evidence of effectiveness in the treatment of opioid dependence (see Barber & O'Brien in McCrady & Epstein, 1999). Nicotine replacement products (delivered by transdermal patch, gum, sublingual tablet, lozenge, nasal spray, or inhaler) are effective in the initial phases of treatment for nicotine dependence, and bupropion is effective for longer-term pharmacotherapy. Nortriptyline and clonidine are recommended for patients who are unable to use nicotine replacement products or bupropion, and the tranquilizer buspirone might also help smokers to reduce withdrawal-related anxiety (Cofta-Woerpel et al., 2006). The newer drug varenicline has produced favorable quit rates over placebo or bupropion and its effectiveness looks promising (Gonzales et al., 2006).

The term *addiction* is overused, but it is useful in referring to a range of substance use problems. Etiology of these problems is complex, with multiple biological, psychological, and social factors contributing. Prevention is possible, and a number of effective treatments are available.

REFERENCES

American Psychiatric Association. (2000). *Diagnostic and statistical manual of mental disorders* (4th ed., text revision). Washington, DC: American Psychiatric Association.

Centers for Disease Control and Prevention. (2007). Adult cigarette smoking in the United States: Current estimates. Retrieved March 3, 2008, from http://www.cdc.gov/tobacco/data_statistics/Factsheets/adult_cig_smoking.htm.

Cofta-Woerpel, L., Wright, K. L., & Wetter, D. W. (2006). Smoking cessation 1: Pharmacological treatments. *Behavioral Medicine*, *32*(2), 47–56.

Compton, W. M., Thomas, Y. F., & Stinson, F. S. (2007). Prevalence, correlates, disability, and comorbidity of DSM-IV drug abuse and dependence in the United States: Results from the National Epidemiologic Survey on Alcohol and Related Conditions. *Archives of General Psychiatry*, *64*, 566–576.

Copello, A. G., Velleman, R. D. B., & Templeton, L. J. (2005). Family interventions in the treatment of alcohol and drug problems. *Drug and Alcohol Review*, *24*(4), 369–385.

Gonzales, D., Rennard, S. I., Nides, M., Oncken, C., Azoulay, S., Billing, C. B., et al. (2006). Varenicline, an alpha4beta2 nicotinic acetylcholine receptor partial agonist, vs. sustained-release bupropion and placebo for smoking cessation: A randomized controlled trial. *Journal of the American Medical Association*, *296*(1), 47–55.

Hasin, D. S., Stinson, F. S., & Ogburn, E. (2007). Prevalence, correlates, disability, and comorbidity of DSM-IV alcohol abuse and dependence in the United States: Results from the National Epidemiologic Survey on Alcohol and Related Conditions. *Archives of General Psychiatry*, *64*, 830–842.

Miller, W. R., & Wilbourne, P. L. (2002). Mesa Grande: A methodological analysis of clinical trials of treatment for alcohol use disorders. *Addiction*, *97*, 265–277.

Prendergast, M., Podus, D., Finney, J., Greenwell, L., & Roll, J. (2006). Contingency management for treatment of substance use disorders: A meta-analysis. *Addiction*, *101*(11), 1546–1560.

SUGGESTED READINGS

McCrady, B. S., & Epstein, E. E. (1999). *Addictions: A comprehensive guidebook*. New York: Oxford University Press.

Miller, W. R., Walters, S. T., & Bennett, M. E. (2001). How effective is alcoholism treatment in the United States *Journal of Studies on Alcohol*, *62*, 211–220.

BARBARA S. MCCRADY
LISA HAGEN GLYNN
University of New Mexico

See also: Drug Addiction; Food Addiction; Gambling Addiction

ADHD (See Attention-Deficit/Hyperactivity Disorder)

ADJUSTMENT DISORDER

When individuals, regardless of their age, are subjected to a significant psychosocial stressor, two possible outcomes are likely—in one instance the person is not significantly affected by the stressor and proceeds on with their life without indication of perceptible problem. In the other possible scenario, the individual experiences a negative reaction to the stressor. Herein, at some point the person begins to exhibit behavioral, mood, or emotional symptoms, the person is then described as manifesting an adjustment disorder, and there is then the need to initiate change in order to restore even functioning. It is important to emphasize that adjustment disorders differ from acute stress disorders in that the latter represent reactions to extraordinary traumatic stressors (i.e., life-threatening events).

The diagnosis of adjustment disorder in children, adolescents, and adults is not without debate and controversy regarding diagnostic specificity and prevalence. It has been referred to as a "waste-basket" diagnosis (Fard et al., 1979), so vague as to not be helpful, and deemed unstable as a diagnostic entity (Greenberg et al, 1995). This reflects some recent commentary questioning the utility of the diagnosis. A major reason why critics are skeptical about the classification relates to the variability in diagnosis with respect to children (Newcorn & Strain, 1992) as well as adults (Strain, Smith, & Hammer, 1998). Casey et al.

(2001) draw attention to the debate around the utility of the diagnosis and urge continued research with sensitivity to tightening diagnostic specificity in relation to symptoms and areas of dysfunction.

Although critics have questioned the reliability and validity of this diagnosis, there are other positions. These assertions are countered by several studies that report adequate construct and predictive validity (Andresen, Hoenk, & Synder, 1990; Kovacs, Ho, & Pollack, 1995). Finally, the diagnosis is often cited as too frequently employed in order to meet the treatment criteria demanded by managed care (Pomerantz & Segrist, 2006). However, an interesting counter position suggests that this diagnosis may actually be employed less frequently because clinicians are more inclined to diagnosis children with more severe disorders in order to receive reimbursement (Harpez-Rotem & Rosenheck, 2004).

These controversies notwithstanding, the diagnosis is widely employed with standardized criteria used to inform diagnostic decisions. Determining whether an individual is exhibiting symptoms suggesting an adjustment disorder sees most clinicians referencing the five criteria outlined by the American Psychiatric Association (i.e., American Psychiatric Association, 2000).

- By definition an adjustment disorder occurs within three months of a significant external stressor and may not persist for longer than six months; after this it either dissipates or becomes a more ingrained problem and may now meet the criteria for a significant emotional disorder or syndrome.

- The distress exceeds what would normally be expected as a reasonable response to the stressor, and there may be indication of significant social or occupational/academic impairment.

- The disturbance does not meet the criteria for another specific Axis I diagnosis and is also not a flare-up of an already diagnosed Axis I disorder.

- The symptoms are not a bereavement reaction and finally, once the stressor or its effects on the person have attenuated or terminated.

- The symptoms do not persist for more than an additional six months. An important exception can occur if the person is experiencing a chronic stressor (e.g., an abusive foster parent) or to a stressor whose ramifications and impact may endure (e.g., a difficult and financially disabling divorce).

The DSM-IV-TR classification system delineates six specific variations of adjustment disorder reflected in Table 1.

A recently developed alternative to the DSM-IV-TR classification system, the Psychodynamic Diagnostic Manual (PDM) (i.e., PDM Task Force, 2006), expands DSM-IV criteria by including reference to how adjustment disorders influence internal experiences: affective states,

Table 1. DSM-IV-TR Classification of Adjustment Disorders

Adjustment Disorder
With Anxiety
With Depressed Mood
With Mixed Symptoms of Anxiety and Depression
With Disturbance of Conduct
With Mixed Disturbance of Emotions and Conduct
Unspecified

cognitive patterns, somatic states, and relationship patterns. Thus, this paradigm adds more breadth and depth to the DSM-IV diagnostic composite, offering a developmental psychoanalytic theoretical perspective in describing adjustment disorders.

The remaining sections will illustrate brief clinical vignettes of adjustment disorders in children, adolescents, young and older adults in order to provide the reader with illustrative clinical examples.

Adjustment Disorders in Children

Certain environmental events may trigger adjustment disorders in young children. For example, the child who at age 5 is expected to make a major developmental transition (i.e., leaving home and attending school) experiences separation problems when he or she enters school—symptoms of nocturnal enuresis, nightmares, and diffuse fears—are cited by parents. The situation persists for several weeks but suddenly abates and the child now trundles off to school without any of the aforementioned problematic symptoms. Another youngster in the same class also exhibits a very similar constellation of symptoms but, unlike his classmate, after three months continues to demonstrate significant separation issues not only in relation to school but with respect to home as well—he refuses to let his parents go out for an evening without tantrums and desperate pleas they stay home. The problems continue past the six-month point and the clinical situation, first an apparent adjustment disorder, now moves into another realm suggesting that this child is manifesting symptomatology consistent with DSM-IV-TR diagnosis of Separation Anxiety Disorder.

Adjustment Disorders in Adolescence

Adjustment disorders in adolescents may also be triggered by separation demands. College mental health services are familiar with late adolescence adjustment disorders as these occur with considerable frequency in the first college year. This initial adjustment is a challenge for many students who have to confront an array of novel situations—a separation from all that is familiar and predictable. For the majority of students the multiple challenges (i.e., separation from family and friends, adjusting to less structure in many instances, and the academic demands) are confronted and handled, but for some, significant problems may arise.

Consider the case of a young woman who begins to attend a large state university located in a major urban area where she has no ties or connections (not at all an unusual occurrence) and who comes from a tight-knit, small rural community. She feels overwhelmed by academic and social pressures (e.g., roommates who are not welcoming, large and impersonal classes, requests to party and date) and she becomes distraught, wondering if she would have better off attending a local community college. She has difficulty sleeping and suffers from loss of appetite; she stays in her room or seeks solace in the school library because she finds it unpleasant to be with roommates. She experiences self-doubt about her abilities, has difficulty budgeting her time, meeting deadlines and staying focused. Frequent calls to her parents and attendance at a group in her dormitory for incoming first year students help her to stay afloat. Discussions with the residence counselor provide opportunities to obtain additional support and reassurance. By the end of the first semester she is sleeping better, has joined some campus organizations, and is finding that the first round of papers and examinations can be managed. Her symptoms are ameliorating and a follow-up interview sees her doing well.

Adjustment Disorders in Young Adulthood

Young adulthood brings new developmental and phase-specific demands to the table. Leaving home, entering the world of work, entering into and sustaining intimate ties, beginning a family, obtaining specialized training and/or higher education, entering the armed forces would cover most of the late adolescence/early adult transitions and tasks that might be confronted. And again, what is routine and ordinary for one person may see another individual momentarily derailed and overwhelmed to the point where a cluster of symptoms are manifest, suggesting an adjustment disorder.

A young father suddenly begins to experience heart palpitations, gastrointestinal distress, and fears that he will contract a fatal illness and die. He has trouble sleeping, experiences early-morning wakening, and has episodic thoughts he will harm his wife or infant daughter. At work he has trouble concentrating and focusing. He seeks assistance through the Employee Assistance Program where he experiences almost total symptom relief after being instructed in cognitive-behavioral interventions designed to target his obsessive, ego-dystonic thoughts, and after being advised that his fears about being up to the task of being a new father are juxtaposed against the fact that his own father was often unavailable because of work demands and personal problems. His ability to understand how unresolved and conflicted feelings about his own father were activated by his becoming a father was

an important connection that served to help him place matters in a more understandable perspective.

Adjustment Disorders in Older Adults

Older adults, middle-aged, and those more senior are particularly susceptible to adjustment reactions precipitated by real and imagined loss not involving bereavement. More specifically, the theme of loss may naturally involve physical attributes and skills that are of course inevitable but exceedingly difficult for some individuals to accept. Loss may intertwine with identity and self-regard issues.

Consider an individual, recently retired, who has spent the majority of his career in one setting (e.g., a civil servant, career military personnel, a teacher) who now is acutely aware of the loss of camaraderie, self-worth, and security. For some, this phase of life hurdle is easily forded and the person moves on; for others, there is the emergence of anxiety, depression, and loneliness, a sudden confrontation with an existential type of loss. It is quite expected that the types of losses that increasingly confront one in the later years call for taking stock, and may momentarily derail some people. For those who temporarily languish, mourn the loss of what might have been, and are unable to move on (i.e., become symptomatic), then the initial concern, if the requisite amount of time has passed, would be to suggest the person is exhibiting an adjustment disorder.

The aforementioned clinical examples depict different types of adjustment disorders that usually resolve with minimal clinical intervention. To reiterate, an adjustment disorder may be construed as a reasonable response to an identifiable stressor. It suggests external or internal factors have coalesced to momentarily derail the person, resulting in the development of symptoms, dictating the need to initiate corrective measures so that emotional homeostasis is restored.

REFERENCES

American Psychiatric Association (2000). *Diagnostic and statistical manual of mental disorders* (4th ed.) Washington, DC: Author.

Andresen, N., & Hoenk, P. (1982). The predictive value of adjustment disorders: A follow-up study. *American Journal of Psychiatry, 139*, 584–590.

Casey, P., Dowrick, C., & Wilkinson, G. (2001). Adjustment disorders: Fault line in the psychiatric glossary. *The British Journal of Psychiatry, 179*, 479–481.

Fard, F., Hudgens, R., & Welner, A. (1979). Undiagnosed psychiatric illness in adolescents: A prospective and seven year follow-up. *Archives of General Psychiatry, 35*, 279–281.

Greenberg, W., Rosenfeld, D., & Ortega, E. (1995). Adjustment disorders as an admission diagnosis. *American Journal of Psychiatry, 152*, 459–461.

Harpez-Rotem, I., & Rosenheck, R. (2004). Changes in outpatient psychiatric diagnosis in privately insured children and adolescents from 1995 to 2000. *Child Psychiatry and Human Development, 34*, 329–340.

Kovacs, M., Ho, V., & Pollock, M. (1995). Criterion and predictive validity of the diagnosis of adjustment disorder: A prospective study of youths with new onset insulin dependent diabetes mellitus. *American Journal of Psychiatry, 152*, 525–528.

Newcorn, J., & Strain, J. (1992). Adjustment disorder in children and adolescents. *Journal of the American Academy of Child and Adolescent Psychiatry, 31*, 318–326.

PDM Task Force. (2006). *Psychodynamic diagnostic manual.* Silver Spring, MD: Alliance of Psychoanalytic Organizations.

Pomerantz, A., & Segrist, D. (2006). The influence of payment method on psychologists' diagnostic decisions regarding minimally impaired clients. *Ethics & Behavior, 16*, 253–263.

Strain, J., Smith, G., & Hammer, J. (1998). Adjustment disorder: A multisite study of its utilization and interventions in the consultation-liaison psychiatry setting. *General Hospital Psychiatry, 20*, 139–149.

SUGGESTED READINGS

Beiser, M. (1996). Adjustment disorders in DSM-IV: Cultural considerations. In J. Mezzich, A. Kleinman, H. Fabrega, & D. Parron (Eds.), *Culture and psychiatric diagnosis. A DSM-IV Perspective* (pp. 215–226). Washington, DC: American Psychiatric Press.

Woolston, J. (1988). Theoretical considerations of the adjustment disorders. *Journal of the American Academy of Child and Adolescent Psychiatry, 27*, 280–287.

FRANCIS D. KELLY
Greenfield, MA

ADLER, ALFRED (1871–1937)

Alfred Adler founded the school of Individual Psychology, a theory of personality and psychopathology, as well as a method of psychotherapy. Based on the concepts of the unit, goal striving, and active participation of the individual, it is a humanistic view of psychology rather than a mechanistic drive psychology. It stresses cognitive rather than unconscious processes. Adler accepted being called "father of the inferiority complex."

Adler graduated from Vienna Medical School in 1895 and became a general practitioner. He soon wrote articles on public health issues, in line with his early interest in the social democratic movement. In 1902, he and three others were invited by Freud for weekly discussions of problems of neurosis. From these meetings the Vienna Psychoanalytic Society developed; Adler became its president in 1910.

In 1911, Adler resigned from the society to form the Society for Free Psychoanalytic Research, soon afterward renamed the Society for Individual Psychology. He objected primarily to what became known as Freud's metapsychology, then essentially limited to mechanistic concepts of libido and repression. Adler sought a conception of neurosis "only in psychological terms, or terms of cultural psychology." In this quest he published in 1907 his *Study of Organ Inferiority and Its Physical Compensation,* broadening the biological foundation from sex to the entire organism. In 1908, he wrote a paper on the aggression drive, which he identified as a drive to prevail, thus replacing sex as the primary drive. Then in 1910 he wrote a paper identifying a feeling of inferiority and masculine protest as overcompensation and replaced the concept of drive altogether with one value. Masculine protest, in its original sense, was shortly afterward replaced by a striving power aimed at gaining superiority. Adler saw the individual in its unity and goal orientation operating as if according to a self-created plan, later called lifestyle. Drives, feelings, emotions, memory, and the unconscious are all processes that are subordinated to the life style.

In 1912, Adler presented his new psychology in *The Neurotic Constitution.* It contained most of his main concepts, except that of social interest. This last concept, in 1918, became, along with striving for overcoming inferiority feelings, Adler's most important concept—the criterion for mental health. In cases of psychopathology, which Adler called failures in life, the aptitude for social interest is not adequately developed. Such persons are striving on the socially useless side for personal power over others, versus the healthy, socially useful striving for overcoming general difficulties. The psychotherapist raises the patient's self-esteem through encouragement, demonstrates the patient's mistakes to the patient, and strengthens his or her social interest. Thus, the therapist works for a cognitive reorganization and more socially useful behavior. In particular, early recollections and birth-order position, as well as dreams, are used to give the patient an understanding of his or her lifestyle.

During the 1920s Adler became largely interested in prevention. This included child-guidance training of teachers at the Vienna Pedagogical Institute where Adler had his first academic appointment, the establishment of numerous child-guidance centers in public schools, and adult education courses that resulted in his popular book, *Understanding Human Nature.* From 1926 on, Adler visited the United States regularly, lecturing to a wide range of audiences. He was a successful speaker, attracting up to 2000 listeners per lecture. In 1932, he became a professor of medical psychology at Long Island Medical College and in 1934, he settled permanently in New York City.

In the personal realm he married Raissa Timofejevna Epstein, a radical student from a highly privileged Jewish family in Moscow. During the course of their marriage, she worked with Adler at several different times. They had four children, three girls and a boy, of whom the second child, Alexandra, and the third, Kurt, became Adlerian psychiatrists. Alfred Adler died of a heart attack on May 28, 1937, in Aberdeen, Scotland.

Regarding Adler's work there is a paradox: His concepts have been generally validated and have entered most personality theories, including psychoanalysis in particular, yet this has remained largely unrecognized. However, Adlerian tradition is being continued by the North American Society of Adlerian Psychology, which publishes both a newsletter and the quarterly *Individual Psychology*, and holds regular meetings and sponsors workshops. There are Adlerian training institutes as well as scores of local organizations, family education centers, and study groups, for which the groundwork was done chiefly by Rudolf Dreikurs (1897–1972). Abroad, Adlerian societies exist in numerous countries, the largest being in West Germany, which publishes the quarterly *Zeitschrift fur Individualpsychologie*. An International Association for Individual Psychology holds congresses every three years. Affiliated with it is the International Committee for Adlerian Summer Schools and Institutes, which constructs a yearly two-week institute in various countries.

REFERENCES

Adler, A. (1927). *Understanding human nature*. New York: Greenberg.

Adler, A. (1929). *The practice and theory of individual psychology*. London: Routledge & Kegan Paul.

Adler, A. (1930). *The neurotic constitution: Outlines of a comparative individualistic psychology and psychotherapy*. New York: Dodd, Mead and Company.

HEINZ L. ANSBACHER
University of Vermont

ADMISSIBILITY OF EXPERT TESTIMONY

The first test for the admissibility of expert testimony occurred in 1923 in a case entitled *Frye v. United States* (293 F 1013, 1923). Although this case dealt with the admissibility of the polygraph in court, it has been used in a much wider context to decide the admissibility of any proffered or proposed expert testimony. It is described as a general acceptability theory. That is, if the theory, methodology, or conclusion that is being "proffered" or offered as expert testimony is "generally accepted" within the relevant scientific field, it is deemed to meet the criteria for acceptability. Reliability, in other words, is determined by general acceptability. One of the problems with the *Frye* standard is that it did not define what "generally acceptable" meant. Subsequent commentary by various legal scholars has described general acceptability as referring to acceptance by "a substantial majority of the relevant scientific discipline," but once again the term "substantial majority" was not defined. In a similar manner, the "relevant scientific discipline" was not well-defined either.

One of the other major problems that the *Frye* standard encountered was that the criterion of general acceptability left no room for the admissibility of a well-validated but innovative or new technique. Let us assume that a particular scientist has done extensive work validating a new scientific procedure. No matter how extensive the validity studies are, under a *Frye* standard it could not be admitted into evidence unless it is also well-known and well-accepted in the scientific community. A good example of this shortcoming occurred during the trial of John Hinckley Jr., the attempted assassin of President Reagan, when some of the proffered expert testimony the defense wanted admitted had to do with a neuropsychiatrist's diagnosis of Hinckley as schizophrenic based on what was then a new technique of brain imaging studies. This work was very well-validated from a scientific point of view; however, because the idea of abnormal brain chemistry in schizophrenic persons was not generally accepted in the scientific community in 1981, the testimony was ruled inadmissible. Had that testimony been proffered in the present day and age, when this technique is well-accepted, it would certainly be admitted into evidence.

1975 Federal Rules of Evidence

In 1975, the Federal Rules of Evidence were adopted by the U.S. Federal Court system. The rules had special sections (Rules 702 through 705) to assist the Court with criteria for the admissibility of expert testimony. The Federal Rules of Evidence have been incorporated into the evidence codes in many states, so that some of them now have either an exact replica or words closely approximating them as the basis for their own rules of evidence. These relevant sections for the present discussion dealt with what was called "scientific, technical or other specialized knowledge." These Rules of Evidence stated that if such scientific, technical, or other specialized knowledge would be of assistance to the triers of fact (i.e., judges or juries) and out of the "ken" or knowledge base of the ordinary layperson, then an expert who was qualified by knowledge, skill, education, experience, and training could render an opinion.

It is important to note that these Federal Rules of Evidence deal with broader information than merely the scientific, for it talks about the possible introduction into expert testimony of technical or specialized knowledge also. This becomes a particularly critical issue when the admissibility of social science evidence (such as psychology) is debated. Is psychology scientific, is it technical knowledge, or is it some other kind of specialized knowledge? How this question is answered leads to different answers regarding admissibility.

The second important phrase in the Rules I is the one stating that the material should be "of assistance to the trier of fact." This may seem somewhat paradoxical. Why would we be discussing material at all if it were not of assistance to the trier of fact? What is meant here is that the knowledge proposed by the expert witness must not be something already known by the average person. In other words, it must add something new to the knowledge base of the layperson or provide some information to challenge misinformation that the trier of fact could be expected to deduce from common sense.

Rule 703 discusses the criteria required for the methodology on which experts base their opinion. It indicates that the methodology used by the expert must be of the sort "reasonably relied upon by other experts in the same field." One of the problems with this aspect of the Federal Rules of Evidence is that the phrase "reasonably relied upon" was not defined, leaving it to the courts to figure out if a method is scientific or not.

Daubert, Kumho, and Relevant Case Law

In actual practice, following the introduction of these Federal Rules of Evidence, courts used some informal combination of the *Frye* standard and the Federal Rules of Evidence to determine admissibility of expert testimony until 1993, when the U. S. Supreme Court, in deciding a case called *Daubert*, dramatically altered the standards of admissibility of expert testimony in Federal Courts. In *Daubert v. Merrell Dow Pharmaceuticals* (509 U.S. 579, 113 S.Ct. 2786, 1993), a case concerning whether a particular medication caused birth defects, the attorneys for the plaintiff wanted to introduce expert testimony by a biochemist who reanalyzed the prior medication tests (called trials) and found that the trials that had declared the medication was safe were not done properly. The trial court ruled that the testimony was inadmissible, finding the reanalysis of the prior trials to be "junk science" because the biochemist had used a new methodology that was not generally acceptable and therefore failed to meet the *Frye* standard.

The U. S. Supreme Court, in a majority opinion authored by Justice Blackmun, described the *Frye* standard as too austere, not allowing for innovation and creativity, and suggested using the Federal Rules of Evidence with some important modifications for judges to test for the scientific reliability of a proposed expert's opinion. These new standards are now called the *Daubert* standards and have been adopted by a number of different states, and in 2001 they were incorporated into the newly revised Federal Rules of Evidence. The reasoning behind this Supreme Court decision was to give judges more guidance in how to make these difficult admissibility decisions. An important point to be noted is that Justice Blackmun restricted the analysis in the case only to scientific evidence, because that was the nature of the evidence being considered in the *Daubert* case. The implication of Justice Blackmun's comment was that the criteria he was proposing would be applicable only to scientific testimony and that technical or other specialized information could well be judged by other criteria. Nevertheless, many people misinterpreted *Daubert* as requiring the application of certain standards useful in judging scientific evidence to all kinds of expert testimony.

Justice Blackmun also noted that the criteria to be outlined were suggested guidelines and were not "dispositive"; that is, these were guidelines that the judge, as "gatekeeper," would utilize to determine the admissibility of expert scientific testimony. Some legal scholars believe that the *Daubert* decision gives judges more power to decide what expert to admit and whom to keep out of the court, whereas others see *Daubert* only as a guide to the decision-making power judges always had under *Frye* and the Federal Rules of Evidence.

The following criteria suggested by Blackmun appear to be an elaboration of the undefined "reasonable reliance" discussed in Federal Rule of Evidence 702: (1) the hypothesis to which the matter pertains is testable; (2) the procedure has been tested; (3) the procedure has a known error rate; (4) the procedure has been published; (5) the procedure has been peer reviewed; and (6) the procedure is generally accepted by the scientific community.

As already noted, there was a good deal of discussion following the handing down of the *Daubert* decision, not only among legal scholars but also among mental health professionals wondering exactly where expert psychological testimony would fall. It takes only a moment's reflection to realize that much of what clinical forensic examiners do in their evaluations may not have testable hypotheses or known error rates. What, for instance, is the testable hypothesis in a child custody evaluation? How does one determine the "known error rate" of a clinical interview? Does it have to do with whether or not the judge or jury agrees with the proposed testimony? These are all issues that appear to separate clinical forensic evaluations from the kinds of criteria enumerated in the *Daubert* case if they are strictly followed, rather than just used as guidelines as Blackmun suggested.

Many courts adopted this rather narrow interpretation of *Daubert*, which resulted in the exclusion of a large body of expert testimony that could not be "scientifically validated." On the other hand, more clinically oriented individuals were of the opinion that the narrowly construed *Daubert* criteria would keep a great deal of valuable clinical material out of consideration in the courts. How one conceptualizes psychology is a critical issue. Is psychology a science? It is technical knowledge? Or, is it specialized knowledge? These questions were debated by psychologists in a very heated manner for a good number of years following the *Daubert* decision.

Further clarification appeared to come in 1999 in the case of *Kumho Tire v. Carmichael* (526 U.S. 137, 119 S.Ct.

1167, 1999). In this case, which dealt with proffered expert testimony of a "tire expert," the trial court ruled as inadmissible the expert's testimony, because he had not conducted any controlled scientific experiments. The expert had, on the other hand, based his opinion on 30 years of experience, rather than on empirical studies. On appeal, the Court of Appeals for the Eleventh Circuit reversed the trial court, indicating that the *Daubert* criteria should be applicable only to scientific testimony and not to "experience-based testimony."

When the case reached the U. S. Supreme Court, however, the court ruled that *Daubert* should apply to all proposed expert testimony, but that it should be interpreted flexibly, and that the six criteria enumerated earlier were only guidelines and were not intended to be taken as rigidly excluding different kinds of expert testimony. In fact, the Supreme Court went on to state that the important issues were "relevance and reliability" and that it was at the discretion of the trial judge to determine how relevance and reliability could be determined. This ruling essentially reopened the area for clinical forensic psychological expertise, since a judge did not have to rely only on those six factors. *Kumho* was important because it made the admissibility of expert testimony far more flexible and far more at the discretion of the individual trial judge than *Daubert*.

2000 Federal Rules of Evidence

More recently, Rule 702 of the Federal Rules of Evidence was modified and adopted in December 2000. The modifications did not replace Rule 702, but supplemented it with two additional criteria: (1) the testimony must be based on sufficient facts or data, and (2) the testimony derives from reliable principles and methods.

The first part of the new modification is important for mental health professionals, because it parallels very closely what appears in various codes of ethics: we make diagnoses, draw conclusions, and give recommendations only when there are sufficient data to support them. The second part of the modification, calling for the testimony to derive from reliable principles and methods, is apparently another attempt to discourage the use of invalidated or unreliable methods. To meet this part of the criteria, the proposed expert witnesses must demonstrate that they have applied the principles and methods reliably to the facts of the case. In other words, experts must be aware of what are the appropriate scientific psychology procedures and demonstrate that they have reached their conclusions by using the proper procedures and have utilized them in an acceptable manner.

Clinical forensic psychologists need to show that the methods by which they have performed evaluations meet the psychological standards. This may include use of standardized tests for which there are reliability and validity measures as well as standard errors written in the manuals. It may also include utilizing textbooks that describe clinical examinations using mental status exams, standard clinical interview techniques, and various ways of assessing samples of behavior. Many clinical forensic psychologists have begun using structured interviews to meet these standards. Including tests that measure the over-reporting or under-reporting of symptoms of mental illness may be another way to demonstrate the careful methodology that was used before coming to an opinion.

DAVID L. SHAPIRO
Nova Southeastern University

See also: **Confidentiality and Legal Privilege; Forensic Psychology**

ADOLESCENT DEPRESSION

Depression during the adolescent years is a major public health problem. While somewhat rare in childhood, the rate of depressive disorders escalates over five-fold in the adolescent years, moving from a 12-month prevalence of less than 3% in the sixth- to ninth-grade years to a prevalence of 17% during the eighteenth year of life (Hankin, Abramson, Moffitt, Silva, McGee, & Angell, 1998). Whereas rates of depression increase during this period for both boys and girls, by mid to late adolescence, depressed females outnumber depressed males by a ratio of 2:1 (Hankin et al., 1998). It is estimated that 20% of young people will have at least one episode of clinical depression by age 18, and 65% will experience transient or less severe depressive symptoms (Lewinsohn, Hops, Roberts, Seeley, & Andrews, 1993).

Adolescent depression compromises the process of development by interfering with academic and social functioning, and it represents a risk factor for both substance use and suicide. Moreover, the sequelae of adolescent depression include a host of later psychosocial deficits, including poor global and adaptive functioning, academic and occupational impairment, disrupted interpersonal relationships, early childbearing, reduced life satisfaction, and substance abuse/dependence (Fergusson & Woodward, 2002; Glied & Pine, 2002; Lewinsohn, Rhode, Seeley, Klein, & Gotlib, 2003).

Clinical Presentation

Clinical depression as seen in adolescents is characterized by depressed mood and/or loss of interest in activities as well as related symptoms such as sleep difficulties, appetite changes, a sense of hopelessness, increased aches and pains, loss of self-esteem, difficulties with concentration, and thoughts of death and dying, sometimes with active suicidal plans. Many adolescents express their depressed mood via extreme irritability. Given that brief periods of low mood are common, the presence of a clinically significant depression should be considered when multiple depressive symptoms are present at the same time, persist for a period of at least two weeks, and are associated with significant impairment in the adolescent's functioning. Impairment can be observed if a teen's depressed mood, loss of interest in activities, and/or irritability interfere with his/her ability to participate in activities, go to school regularly and keep up with school work, or if they lead his/her teachers, parents, and/or friends to become upset with him/her. Parents, teachers, and primary care providers should offer support and monitor transient periods of low mood, while keeping a watchful eye out for a clustering and persistence of symptoms, especially when they are associated with a decline in functioning and social participation.

In some young people, episodes of clinical depression can last for many months and can interfere significantly with the adolescent's ability to keep up in school and remain active with friends. Adolescent depression is also associated with a high recurrence rate, with up to 69% of depressed adolescents experiencing a relapse within two to five years.

Causal Models

Current research suggests that, rather than a single specific pathway, depression arises from the convergence of a number of risk factors. Biological vulnerability is one of these factors: Children whose parents have had significant depression are at increased risk for depression as well as other behavioral and emotional problems. Children may inherit a genetic risk for depression or temperamental qualities such as sensitivity to negative emotions, or they may learn depressive coping styles modeled by their parents. Recent research on genetic risk factors has focused on the serotonin transporter (SERT) gene, a transmembrane protein that facilitates reuptake of serotonin. The SERT gene, located on 17q, contains a well-described insertion/deletion polymorphism (5-HTTLPR) in the promoter region. Research following a group of youth through adolescence and into early adult life found that individuals who carry one or two copies of the short (s) allele of the SERT gene are significantly more likely than those homozygous for the long (l) allele to experience depression following exposure to life stressors (Caspi et al., 2003).

Significant stressful life events are also considered a key element in triggering depression. Vulnerability to depression may be greater in adolescents who respond when exposed to stressful life events with a depressive or negative way of thinking that leads them to view themselves, the world, and their future in a negative manner. This is

frequently described as seeing "the glass as half empty," while others can look at the same situation and see the possibilities—"the glass as half full." Many times individuals with a "depressive" cognitive style may come to see all failures as due to their own inherent faults but any success as pure chance or a fluke (Cole et al., 2008). This is called a negative attributional style. For adolescents, stressful events frequently include parental separation or divorce, moves, or exposure to abuse or neglect, with more recent attention given to the role of bullying, sexual harassment, and social pressures around physical presentation. Antidotes for depression include increased social support and social activity as well as teaching skills needed to manage stress.

Intervention Approaches

Although initial efforts to prevent the onset of depression in at-risk young people and to treat depression in children and adolescents were promising, concerns about how best to treat adolescent depression have emerged more recently. There is support for both pharmacological and psychosocial interventions for depressed youth, but the efficacy data suggest that a significant subset of teens do not respond to these interventions and, of those who do respond, many experience a relapse of symptoms within one year (Brent, et al., 2008). Many adolescents are resistant to taking medications, and serious concerns have been raised regarding the potential increased risk of suicide in youth using antidepressant medication (Newman, 2004).

Two structured psychotherapeutic approaches have shown promise in the treatment of youth who are clinically depressed. Cognitive behavioral therapy (CBT) is a 12 to 16 week individual treatment approach that focuses on teaching teens how to identify and then challenge (change) negative thought patterns as well as how to increase participation in pleasant events and improve stress management and social support. Interpersonal psychotherapy (IPT), another brief treatment (12 weeks), stresses the importance of the youth's social relationships and conceptualizes depression as occurring when a young person is in the midst of a change in social role (i.e. the adolescent transition) or does not have the social skills or social support to maintain a sense of well-being. Initial studies of this approach indicate success in improving overall social function, which may in turn lead to a decrease in depressed mood. Recent reports suggest more modest effects associated with these psychotherapeutic approaches (Goodyer et al., 2007; March et al., 2004; Weisz, McCarty, & Valeri, 2006), which underscores the need for further development of innovative treatment options for depressed adolescents.

In the context of these precautions, the current approach recommended is combined treatment. Many care providers begin with a trial of psychotherapy and add pharmacotherapy as an additional component when sleep disturbance and/or recurrent worries are present or when a teen's depressed mood is so severe that it interferes with his/her ability to engage in psychotherapy. Prozac is generally recommended as the first choice medication, as it is FDA approved for use with youth and has proven efficacy for use with youth with Major Depressive Disorder (Simon, 2006). Care recommendations include the need for careful evaluation to assure that depression is the core problem and to identify co-occurring problems that may also need attention. Adolescents and their families must be warned about the potential risk of increasing suicidal ideation and in some cases aggressive behaviors as they begin both pharmaco- and psychotherapy. Plans need to be established for managing suicidal behavior should it arise, including attention to alternative coping strategies for the young person, safety proofing the home environment (i.e. securing medications and firearms), and regular follow-up with active outreach.

REFERENCES

Birmaher, B., Brent, D. A., Kolko, D., Baugher, M., Bridge, J., Holder, D., Iyengar, S., & Ulloa, R. E. (2000). Clinical outcomes after short-term psychotherapy for adolescents with major depressive disorder. *Archives of General Psychiatry, 57*, 29–36.

Brent, D., Emslie, G., Clarke, G., Wagner, K. D., Asarnow, J. R., Keller, M., et al. (2008). Switching to another SSRI or to venlafaxine with or without cognitive behavioral therapy for adolescents with SSRI-resistant depression: The TORDIA randomized controlled trial. *Journal of the American Medical Association, 299*, 901–913.

Caspi, A., Sugden, K., Moffitt, T. E., Taylor, A., Craig, I. W., Harrington, H., et al. (2003). Influence of life stress on depression: Moderation by a polymorphism in the 5-HTT gene. *Science, 301*, 386–389.

Cole, D. A., Ciesla, J. A., Dallaire, D. H., Jacquez, F. M., Pineda, A. Q., LaGrange, B., et al. (2008). Emergence of attributional style and its relation to depressive symptoms. *Journal of Abnormal Psychology, 117*, 16–31.

Fergusson, D. M., & Woodward, L. J. (2002). Mental health, educational, and social role outcomes of adolescents with depression. *Archives of General Psychiatry, 59*, 225–231.

Glied, S., & Pine, D. S. (2002). Consequences and correlates of adolescent depression. *Archives of Pediatric Adolescent Medicine, 156*, 1009–1014.

Goodyer, I., Dubicka, B., Wilkinson, P., Kelvin, R., Roberts, C., Byford, S., et al. (2007). Selective serotonin reuptake inhibitors (SSRIs) and routine specialist care with and without cognitive behaviour therapy in adolescents with major depression: Randomised controlled trial. *British Medical Journal, 335*, 142.

Hankin, B. L., Abramson, L. Y., Moffitt, T. E., Silva, P. A., McGee, R., & Angell, K. E. (1998). Development of depression from preadolescence to young adulthood: Emerging gender differences in a 10-year longitudinal study. *Journal of Abnormal Psychology, 107*, 128–40.

Lewinsohn, P. M., Hops, H., Roberts, R. E., Seeley, J. R., & Andrews, J. A.. (1993). Adolescent psychopathology: I.
Prevalence and incidence of depression and other DSM III-R disorders in high school students. *Journal of Abnormal Psychology, 102*, 133–144.

Lewinsohn, P. M., Rohde, P., Seeley, J. R., Klein, D. N., & Gotlib, I. H. (2003). Psychosocial functioning of young adults who have experienced and recovered from major depressive disorder during adolescence. *Journal of Abnormal Psychology, 112*, 353–363.

March, J., Silva, S., Petrycki, S., Curry, J., Wells, K., Fairbank, J., et al. (2004). Fluoxetine, cognitive-behavioral therapy, and their combination for adolescents with depression: Treatment for Adolescents with Depression Study (TADS) randomized controlled trial. *Journal of the American Medical Association, 292*, 807–820.

Newman, T. B. (2004). A black-box warning for antidepressants in children? *New England Journal of Medicine, 351*, 1595–1598.

Weisz, J. R., McCarty, C. A., & Valeri, S. M. (2006). Effects of psychotherapy for depression in children and adolescents: A meta-analysis. *Psychological Bulletin, 132*, 132–149.

ELIZABETH MCCAULEY
KELLY SCHLOREDT
University of Washington / Seattle Children's Hospital

See also: **Depression; Lifespan Depression; Mood Disorders**

ADOLESCENT DEVELOPMENT

Adolescence may be defined as the period in life when most of a person's biological, cognitive, psychological, and social characteristics are changing in an interrelated manner from what is considered childlike to what is considered adultlike. When most of one's characteristics are in this state of change, one is an adolescent.

Three Phases of the Scientific Study of Adolescence

Historically, the scientific study of adolescent development can be described as occurring in three overlapping phases (Lerner & Steinberg, 2004). The first phase was initiated by the work of G. Stanley Hall (1904), who conceptualized adolescent development from a deficit perspective. Adolescence was portrayed as a period marked by what Hall regarded as evolutionary-based and therefore inevitable "storm and stress." Although other major theorists during this phase in the study of adolescence (e.g., Erikson, 1959; Anna Freud, 1969) described adolescence in different terms, they accepted Hall's biologically based, deficit conception of this period.

A characteristic of the second phase in the development of this field was a focus on research about adolescent transitions. This work provided evidence that there are multiple pathways through this period of life—only a minority of which can be characterized as reflecting deficits or "storm and stress." These findings elicited an interest in diversity within adolescence, as well as a concern with developmental plasticity (the potential for systematic variation in the structure and function of behavior) across this and other periods of life.

These interests ushered in the third and current phase in the study of adolescence, which is framed by a focus on developmental systems models. These conceptions involve the study across development of bidirectional, individual-context relations (represented as individual ↔ context relations) (Lerner, 2002). Moreover, the individual is seen as constituted by multiple levels of structural organization (e.g., genes, tissues, organ systems) and of multiple functional systems (e.g., physiology, cognition, emotion, motivation, and behavior), that are all reciprocally linked to multiple levels of the ecology of human development (e.g., families, communities, culture, the physical setting, and history).

In this third phase, these systems models guide research and application, and involve collaborative efforts among researchers and practitioners. As a key sample case of the scholarship involved within this third phase of the development of the field, we may point to research and applications associated with the Positive Youth Development (PYD) perspective.

Studying and Promoting Positive Youth Development

Developmental systems models emphasize that plasticity derives from variations within and across people in individual ↔ context relations across life. Adolescence is a transitory period, during which an individual is experiencing a considerable amount of change in regard to his or her individual and contextual domains. These multiple transitions include changes in the self (e.g., pubertal, cognitive, and emotional changes), family, peer groups, and institutions (e.g., in many societies, youth make transitions from elementary schools to middle schools). Although all adolescents experience these shifts, there are individual differences in the timing, speed, and outcomes of these transitions. As such, diversity becomes a core, substantive focus of developmental analysis and, because of plasticity, researchers and practitioners can be optimistic that combinations of individuals and contexts can be found to optimize development among diverse people.

Within the adolescent period, the ideas of plasticity and diversity have been used to understand how the well-being of adolescents can be fostered by maximizing the alignment of their strengths (e.g., their potential for change) with the developmental assets within their ecological context (e.g., home, school, and community). Such assets, conceived of as resources needed for the growth of a healthy, thriving, young person, may involve support from adults (e.g., parents, teachers, or mentors), effective out-of-school time activities (e.g., 4-H, Boys & Girls Clubs, Big Brothers/Big Sisters, YMCA, or Scouting), and opportunities for young people and adults to work together on valued community activities (e.g., food drives, school boards, or community service projects).

Positive Youth Development (PYD) is believed to occur as a consequence of this alignment between individual strengths and ecological assets, and has been conceptualized as involving several latent variables referred to as the Five Cs (Competence, Confidence, Connection, Character, and Caring). If an adolescent acquires these qualities across time, then he/she is "thriving" and on a path toward positive adulthood, where a sixth "C" arises, Contribution—defined by contributions to self, family, community, and institutions of civil society. The 4-H Study of Positive Youth Development has found that higher levels of the Five Cs are associated within and across the early adolescent years (e.g., grades 5 through 8) with higher scores for Contribution and lower scores for externalizing and internalizing problems (e.g., Lerner et al., 2005).

As evidenced by the research on PYD that has burgeoned across the third and current phase in the study of adolescence, current models of this developmental period stand in marked contrast with earlier descriptions of this period as one of "storm and stress." Adolescence is not a period of biologically inevitable problems or distress. Instead, it is a time of life involving enormous changes in the young person and opportunities to enhance the course of development among *all* youth. Simply, the potential for change in the course of development across an individual's life is a fundamental strength of human development, and certainly of adolescent development.

Accordingly, the current status of the field of adolescence provides an opportunity for researchers, practitioners, and policy makers to capitalize on the strengths of young people and the resources of their contexts to promote more positive development among the diverse youth of the world. As such, the cutting edge of current scholarship in the study of adolescence is to understand how research and applications (i.e., programs and policies) can mutually inform each other and serve both the advancement of science and the enhancement of the lives of youth.

REFERENCES

Erikson, E. H. (1959). Identity and the life cycle. *Psychological Issues, 1*, 50–100.

Freud, A. (1969). Adolescence as a developmental disturbance. In G. Caplan & S. Lebovier (Eds.), *Adolescence* (pp. 5–10). New York: Basic Books.

Hall, G. S. (1904). *Adolescence: Its psychology and its relations to physiology, anthropology, sociology, sex, crime, religion, and education* (Vols. 1 & 2). New York: Appleton.

Lerner, R. M. (2002). *Concepts and theories of human development* (3rd ed.). Mahwah, NJ: Lawrence Erlbaum Associates.

Lerner, R. M., Lerner, J. V., Almerigi, J., Theokas, C., Phelps, E., Gestsdottir, S., Naudeau, S., Jelicic, H., Alberts, A. E.,

Ma, L., Smith, L. M., Bobek, D. L., Richman-Raphael, D., Simpson, I., Christiansen, E. D., & von Eye, A. (2005). Positive youth development, participation in community youth development programs, and community contributions of fifth grade adolescents: Findings from the first wave of the 4-H Study of Positive Youth Development. *Journal of Early Adolescence*, 25(1), 17–71.

Lerner, R. M., & Steinberg, L. (Eds.). (2004). *Handbook of adolescent psychology* (2nd ed.). Hoboken, NJ: John Wiley & Sons.

SUGGESTED READINGS

King, P. E., Dowling, E. M., Mueller, R. A., White, K., Schultz, W., Osborn, P., Dickerson, E., Bobek, D. L., Lerner, R. M., Benson, P. L., & Scales, P. C. (2005). Thriving in Adolescence: The voices of youth-serving practitioners, parents, and early and late adolescents. *Journal of Early Adolescence*, 25(1), 94–112.

Lerner, R. M., & Spanier, G. B. (1980). A dynamic interactional view of child and family development. In R. M. Lerner & G. B. Spanier (Eds.), *Child influences on marital and family interaction: A life-span perspective* (pp. 1–20). New York: Academic Press.

Lerner, R. M. (2004). Diversity in individual ← → context relations as the basis for positive development across the life span: A developmental systems perspective for theory, research, and application. *Research in Human Development*, 1(4), 327–346.

RICHARD M. LERNER
MICHELLE J. BOYD
DAN DU
Tufts University

See also: Cognitive Development; Emotional Development; Personality Development

ADULT INTELLECTUAL DEVELOPMENT

Why do some individuals retain their behavioral competence well into advanced old age, whereas others show early decline? This question has long been a central topic in the psychology of adult development and aging. Five central questions and relevant research findings address this issue: (1) Does intelligence change uniformly through adulthood or are there different life-course ability patterns? (2) At what age is there a reliably detectable decrement in ability, and what is the magnitude of that decrement? (3) What are the patterns of generational differences, and what are their magnitudes? (4) What accounts for individual differences in age-related changes in adulthood; and (5) Can cognitive decline in old age be reversed?

The Measurement of Adult Intelligence

Most large-scale studies of adult intelligence conducted during the past few decades have used either the Wechsler Adult Intelligence Scale (WAIS; Wechsler, 1939), one of its derivatives, or a derivative of Thurstone's (1935) work on the primary mental abilities. Findings of these studies differ markedly, however, depending on whether age comparisons have been made cross-sectionally or whether the same individuals have been followed longitudinally over time.

Differential Patterns of Change

There is no uniform pattern of age-related changes across all intellectual abilities. Studies of overall intellectual ability (IQ) are therefore insufficient to monitor age changes and age differences in intellectual functioning for either individuals or groups. Age-difference work with the WAIS suggests that verbal abilities are maintained well, whereas performance tests show early age differences favoring younger adults (Matarazzo, 1972). Longitudinal data on the WAIS also show high levels of stability of verbal behavior into advanced old age, while performance scores begin to decline in midlife. Studies of Primary Mental Abilities indicate that active or fluid abilities tend to decline earlier than passive or crystallized abilities. These findings are complicated by ability, gender, ability-by-age, and ability-by-cohort interactions. For example, women tend to decline earlier in the active abilities, whereas men decline sooner on crystallized abilities. Although fluid abilities begin to decline earlier, crystallized abilities appear to show steeper decrement once the late 70s are reached.

Age Level and Magnitude of Age-Related Intellectual Decline

Cross-sectional studies with the WAIS suggest that significant age differences favoring young adults can be found by the 30s for performance tests and by the 60s for verbal tests. These differences, however, confound cohort effects in education and health status. By contrast, in longitudinal studies, reliably replicable average age decrements in intellectual abilities are rarely found before age 60 but are observed for all intellectual functions at least by age 74. Analyses of individual differences in intellectual change, however, demonstrate that even at age 81 less than half of all observed individuals showed reliable decremental change over the preceding seven years. An example of trajectories for six abilities taken from the Seattle Longitudinal Study (Schaie, 2005) is provided in Figure 1.

Generational Differences

The existence of generational (cohort) differences in intellectual abilities has been conclusively demonstrated. Almost linear positive cohort shifts have been observed for inductive reasoning, with more spasmodic positive shifts for verbal ability and spatial orientation. A curvilinear

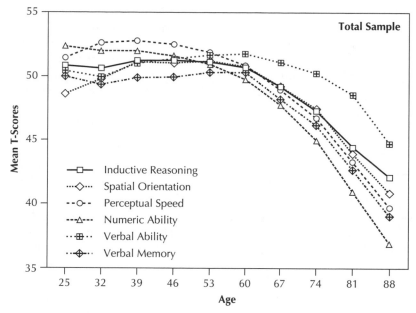

Figure 1. Longitudinal age changes in adulthood on six latent intellectual abilities. From K. W. Schaie, 2005.

cohort pattern has been found for number skills, which reach a peak for birth cohorts in the 1920s and then follow a largely negative slope. A similar curvilinear cohort pattern also has been observed for word fluency. As a consequence, cross-sectional studies of intellectual aging underestimate age changes before age 60 for abilities with negative cohort gradients and overestimate age changes for abilities with positive cohort gradients.

Individual Differences in Age-Related Change in Adulthood

Individual differences are large at all ages, such that substantial overlap among samples can be found from young adulthood into the mid-70s (Schaie, 2005). Very few individuals decline on all or most abilities. Indeed, maintaining functioning of one or more abilities is common for most individuals well into advanced old age. A number of factors account for individual differences in decline, some of which have been shown to be amenable to experimental intervention. Predictors of favorable cognitive aging include (1) absence of cardiovascular and other chronic diseases; (2) favorable environment as indicated by high SES; (3) involvement in a complex and intellectually stimulating environment; (4) flexible personality style at midlife; (5) high cognitive status of spouse; and (6) maintaining one's level of perceptual processing speed.

Reversibility of Cognitive Decline

Present understanding of individual differences in cognitive decline suggests that unless neurological pathology is present, cognitive interventions may serve to prevent known intellectual decline and reduce cohort differences in individuals who have remained stable in their own performance over time but have become disadvantaged compared with younger peers. The effectiveness of cognitive interventions has been demonstrated in various laboratory studies as well as in a recent major clinical trial (Willis et al., 2007). Cognitive decline in many older people may well be the result of disuse of specific skills and can be reversed by appropriate training regimens. In two studies, approximately 66% of the experimental subjects showed significant improvement, and about 40% of those who had declined significantly over 14 years were returned to the pre-decline level (Schaie, 2005).

REFERENCES

Matarazzo, J. D. (1972). *Wechsler's measurement and appraisal of intelligence.* Baltimore, MD: Williams & Wilkins.

Schaie, K. W. (2005). *Developmental influences on adult intelligence: The Seattle longitudinal study.* New York: Oxford University Press.

Thurstone, L. L. (1935). *Vectors of mind: Multiple-factor analysis for the isolation of primary traits.* Chicago: University of Chicago Press.

Wechsler, D. (1939). *The measurement of adult intelligence.* Baltimore, MD: Williams & Wilkins.

Willis, S. L., Tennstedt, S. L., Marsiske, M., Ball, K., Elias, J., Koepke, K. M. et al. (2006). Long terms effects of cognitive training on everyday functional outcomes in older adults. *Journal of the American Medical Association, 296*(23), 2805–2814.

K. Warner Schaie
Pennsylvania State University

See also: Aging and Intelligence; Primary Mental Abilities

ADULTHOOD AND AGING

People are inherently social beings. Although this need for social relationships is observed in people of all ages, the structure and relative importance placed on various members of the social network changes across the lifespan. The convoy model of social relations discusses both the stability and changes that occur in social network composition over time. According to the convoy model, an individual moves through life embedded within a network of people who provide aid, assistance, and support, as well as serve as a secure attachment base from which the individual may explore his or her world. The size of this network is posited to change predictably across the lifespan to reflect shifting social roles and family composition. These changes follow a curvilinear pattern, with numbers of close relationships lowest in early childhood, increasing throughout early and middle adulthood, and then decreasing in later adulthood (see review by Antonucci, Akiyama, & Takahashi, 2004).

The age-related reduction in social network size is one of the most reliable findings in social gerontology. Although shifting roles and changes in family composition may, in part, be responsible for decreases in social network size, socioemotional selectivity theory posits that this age-related shift is the result of a developmental process of social selection that begins early in adulthood. According to this theory, people actively reduce the number of peripheral partners with whom they interact, but retain the same number of emotionally close social partners across the life-span, a pattern documented across ethnically diverse groups of Americans and in cross-cultural samples (see review by Charles & Carstenson, 2007).

People Comprising the Social Network

Social networks consist of both friends and family members. Friendships comprise various types of associations, from casual relationships to more intimate, collaborative, and enduring bonds. Friends serve as confidants, model coping strategies, enhance self-esteem, and buffer stressful life events. Despite the finding that the number of peripheral relationships decrease with age, older adults still maintain a small number of acquaintances in their social networks. For older adults, these casual friendships provide companionship that contributes to well-being and lower levels of loneliness (see review by Rook, Mavandadi, Sorkin, & Zettel, 2007).

In contrast to the decreases in number of casual acquaintances with age, the number of intimate social partners remains relatively stable in late life. In addition, reported satisfaction with family members increases with age (see review by Charles & Carstensen, 2007). Compared with younger adults, older adults report more intense positive emotional experiences with family members, equally as intense positive emotional experiences with established friends, and less intense positive emotional experiences with new friends, which may reflect the value placed on these different social partners.

Turning to familial relationships, connections with siblings are enduring relationships that are related to emotional well-being. In addition, the marital tie is also important to overall well-being, but reports of satisfaction vary over time. Relational satisfaction for people who are married or in a long-term partnership decreases over time. People whose marriages survive into old age, however, report high levels of marital happiness and contentment. Although they report that difficult times occurred in their marriage, they attribute their marriage's longevity to strong levels of mutual commitment and friendship (e.g., Henry, Berg, Smith, & Florsheim, 2007).

The parent-child bond is also a source of satisfaction for parents of all ages. Research by Karen Fingerman reveals that middle-aged mothers enjoy watching their daughters enter adulthood, and report greater investment in these relationships than do their adult daughters. Relationships between parents and children are, by and large, marked by reciprocity, with both generations reporting high levels of shared emotional and instrumental support. This reciprocity extends across the lifespan, where time investment with children earlier in life predicts the social support provided by these adult children when the parents reach old age (Silverstein, Conroy, Wang, Giarusso, & Bengtson, 2002).

The extant work on family ties may not necessarily capture the changes in family structure currently observed in the United States. The majority of research examining family ties has focused predominantly on the insular traditional family group of children and parents, but the definition of family is changing. With greater life expectancy, intergenerational connections will become more important to family members to fulfill emotional and practical needs. In addition, higher rates of divorce and remarriage introduce understudied unions that will also influence social networks of older adults. Moreover, non European-American family systems often include extended kin networks, and the importance of these family members has been relatively ignored in the literature.

The Importance of Social Connection for Health and Well-Being

The structure of the social network shifts across the life span; yet, regardless of age, social connections are necessary for mental and physical well-being. Among older adults, having meaningful relations is associated with better immune profiles, improved cardiovascular indices such as lower blood pressure and decreased cardiovascular reactivity, faster recovery from illness, lower chances of illness relapse, and lower risk of mortality compared to those with poor social support indices (see review by Rook et al., 2007). In fact, the effects of low perceived social support in later life may be even more detrimental to physical health when it occurs in an older, more physically vulnerable system. The influence of social ties extends to cognitive outcomes as well. Higher levels of cognitive functioning are associated with higher levels of social support and greater social integration, whereas social disengagement is associated with greater cognitive decline (e.g., Beland, Zunzunegui, Alvarado, Otero, & del Ser, 2005).

The Negative Side of Social Relationships

Despite the positive outcomes associated with social relationships, negative consequences also can occur. Older adults report fewer interpersonal conflicts than do younger adults, but these negative exchanges have stronger associations with affective and physical well-being than do positive social exchanges. For example, stable high levels of negative social interactions across time are also associated with poorer self-rated health, a greater number of chronic health conditions, and a greater incidence of functional limitations (Newsom, Mahan, Rook, & Krause, 2008).

One source of interpersonal stress that increases in prevalence with age is the strain associated with spousal caregiving. Spousal caregiving for a spouse with dementia is a situation marked by unpredictability, loss of control, and higher levels of distress (Schulz & Beach, 1999). The role of spousal caregiver demands emotional and physical stamina and takes its toll in both of these domains. With the exception of a minority of adults who experience increases in their sense of purpose and life satisfaction, most caregivers experience decreases in well-being. Rates of depression and anxiety are higher among caregivers than the general population, and physical complaints often increase with the added physical and emotional strain of caregiving (Schulz & Beach, 1999).

Social processes are critical at every age and by no means diminish in importance across the adult life span; over time, the number of social partners may decrease, but the meaning of close friends and family members becomes even more central to the daily lives of older men and women. Most social relationships are positive, yet interpersonal conflict and strain sometimes occurs, and this conflict is strongly tied to affective distress. These social relationships, which comprise sources of both joy and strain, remain strongly related to physical and affective well-being across the adult life span.

REFERENCES

Antonucci, T. C., Akiyama, H., & Takahashi, K. (2004). Attachment and close relationships across the life span. *Attachment & Human Development*, 6, 353–370.

Beland, F., Zunzunegui, M. V., Alvarado, B., Otero, A., & del Ser, T. (2005). Trajectories of cognitive decline and social relations. *Journals of Gerontology: Psychological Sciences and Social Sciences*, 60, 320–330.

Charles, S. T., & Carstensen, L. L. (2007). Emotion regulation and aging. In J. J. Gross (Ed.), *Handbook of Emotion Regulation* (pp. 307–327). New York: Guilford Press.

Henry, N. J. M., Berg, C. A., Smith, T. W., & Florsheim, P. (2007). Positive and negative characteristics of marital satisfaction and their association with marital satisfaction in middle-aged and older couples. *Psychology and Aging*, 22, 428–441.

Newsom, J. T., Mahan, T. L., Rook, K. S., & Krause, N. (2008). Stable negative social exchanges and health. *Health Psychology*, 27, 78–86.

Rook, K. S., Mavandadi, S., Sorkin, D. H., & Zettel, L. A. (2007). Optimizing social relationships as a resource for health and well-being in later life. In C. M. Aldwin, C. L. Park, & Spiro, A. III (Eds.), *Psychology of aging and health*. New York: Guilford.

Schulz, R., & Beach, S. R. (1999). Caregiving as a risk factor for mortality: The Caregiver Health Effects Study. *JAMA: The Journal of the American Medical Association*, 282, 2215–2219.

Silverstein, M., Conroy, S., Wang H., Giarrusso, R, & Bengtson, V. L. (2001). Reciprocity in parent-child relations over the adult life course. *Journal of Gerontology: Social Sciences*, 57, S3–S13.

Susan T. Charles
Jennifer R. Piazza
University of California, Irvine

See also: **Geropsychology; Human Development**

ADVERTISING PSYCHOLOGY

Consumer psychologists utilize psychological concepts to understand, influence, and predict consumer behavior. Of these concepts, the study of attitude formation and change are of particular interest. Marketers use a wide variety of advertisements to attempt to persuade consumers to buy their products and services. These "ads" can be classified in terms of the type of attitude they are designed to change and in terms of consumers' regulatory focus (Kardes, 2005). People regulate themselves or control their behavior by focusing on information that is most relevant to their goals.

An attitude is an evaluative judgment that consumers form about people, objects, and issues. It consists of two main components: direction (e.g., good or bad, positive or negative) and extremity (e.g., slightly good, somewhat good, fairly good, very good, extremely good) (Kardes, 2002). There are four major types of attitudes based on the functions they serve: knowledge, value expression, ego defense, and adjustment (Kardes, 2005). Attitude function theory suggests that, to be effective, a persuasion strategy must match consumers' attitude function (Katz, 1960). Research has demonstrated that persuasive messages receive more attention and are considered more carefully when persuasion techniques match attitude functions (Petty & Wegener, 1998).

There are two major types of regulatory focus: (a) a promotion focus or concern about achieving a desirable end state; and (b) a prevention focus or concern about an undesirable end state (Higgins, 1998). Regulatory focus theory suggests that personality traits and situations jointly influence whether people are more concerned about achieving their hopes, wishes, and ideal end states (a promotion focus). For maximal effectiveness, advertising techniques should match both consumers' attitude function and regulatory focus. Combining attitude function theory and regulatory focus theory results in eight distinct categories of advertisements related to consumer motives and goals. These categories are summarized in Table 1.

Attitudes that serve a knowledge function summarize large amounts of information to provide consumers with an organized, meaningful, and stable perception of the world. Attitudes serving this function simplify consumer decision making by integrating information into a single overall evaluation. Once the overall evaluation is formed, it is no longer necessary to evaluate the relative benefits and costs of all relevant decision options each time we are faced with a decision. Even deciding what to eat at McDonald's would be remarkably difficult and time-consuming: The benefits (e.g., taste, aroma, satiating properties, appearance) and cost (e.g., price, calories, messiness) of each and every item on the menu would need to be evaluated each and every time a consumer walks into a McDonald's restaurant. The best way to change attitudes that serve knowledge function is to focus on facts and arguments and to anticipate how consumers will use these facts and arguments while thinking and reasoning about an advertisement. In general, knowledge appeals work best for complex products with a large number of attributes.

Promotion-focused knowledge ads rely on strong arguments in the form of factual, logical, and comparative ads to encourage consumers to form favorable brand attitudes

that are held with a high degree of certainty and confidence. These types of appeals provide meaningful information about specific features and uses of products relative to achieving a desired end state. Prevention-focused knowledge appeals use ambiguity, uncertainty, and confusion to reduce resistance to persuasion. Good examples of these types of ads are mystery (teaser) ads, surprise ads, and confusion (disruption) ads. These types of ads gain consumer attention and encourage open-mindedness through building curiosity and interest, introducing a surprising piece of information, or creating confusion. Open-minded consumers are more likely to try new brands that they have never used before. Further, Kardes et al. (2007) demonstrated that confusing consumers with a disruptive message and then reducing ambiguity by reframing the message increases persuasion.

Knowledge appeals involve the use of strong arguments provided by the advertiser and careful thinking on the part of the consumer. These are hallmarks of the central route to persuasion, which involves carefully thinking about information that is relevant (or central) to the merits of a product (Petty et al., 2005). The other appeals to be discussed (value expression, ego defense, adjustment) often involve simple cues provided by the advertiser and relatively little thinking on the part of the consumer. That is, the other appeals often involve the peripheral route to persuasion in which consumers rely on a simple cue (e.g., brand new reputation, likeable spokesperson, cute babies or animals, music, mood) to form an attitude quickly and easily (Petty et al., 2005).

Attitudes that serve a value-expressive function help us to communicate our traits, preferences, and interests to others, thereby aiding in social interactions. As consumers, we express ourselves through attitudes toward products and services. Ads that appeal to the value-expressive function work best for products that are used publicly. Promotion-focused value-expressive appeals emphasize the attainment of positive self-expression. For example, preferring conservative clothes reflect conservative attitudes and lifestyles, whereas preferring daring clothes reflect daring attitudes and lifestyles. If we want to appear sophisticated, we may express favorable attitudes about goods like Dom Perignon champagne, Rolex watches, and BMWs. If we want to express our patriotism, we may buy only American-made products. If we want to express our concern for the environment, we may purchase environmentally friendly ("green") goods. Consumers who are highly concerned with projecting positive self-images are highly susceptible to image appeals and celebrity advertising. These types of ads utilize attractive actors and celebrities that consumers wish to emulate. Surprisingly, consumers continue to believe that celebrities really like the products they endorse even when they are reminded that celebrities are paid handsomely for their endorsements (Cronley, Houghton, Goddard, & Kardes, 1998).

Table 1. Types of Advertisements

Attitude Function	Promotion-Focused Ads	Prevention-Focused Ads
Knowledge	Factual Logical Comparative	Mystery Surprise Confusion
Value Expression	Image Celebrity	Nerd Alerts
Ego Defense	Authority Figures Experts	Fear
Adjustment	Pleasure	Pain

Source: Adapted from Kardes (2005)

Prevention-focused value-expressive appeals emphasize avoiding a negative image. These types of ads utilize unattractive actors and celebrities that are portrayed in a socially negative fashion using an ineffective competing brand. These poor, sad, physically unattractive actors may wear thick glasses and ugly clothes, display unintelligent facial expressions and use products that are completely ineffective (e.g., cooking utensils that fall apart during use, cleaning products that do not remove any type of stain). These types of ads are referred to as nerd alert ads. One way of not emulating unattractive or undesirable people is to not use the products they use. Consistent with the implications of attitude function theory, image-conscious teens are more influenced by nerds and cool kids than by boring facts, figures, and statistics (knowledge appeals) about the negative effects of tobacco, drugs, and alcohol (Herr, Kardes, & Kim, 1991).

Attitudes that serve an ego-defense function bolster our self-esteem and help us feel better about ourselves. These attitudes help people deal with frustration, emotional conflict, and threats to our ego. Religious and political beliefs typically fit in this category, and, consequently, religious and political beliefs are rarely swayed by facts and figures (knowledge appeals), image (value-expressive appeals), or hedonic concerns (adjustment appeals). Attitudes toward protection devises such as security systems (for homes and cars), insurance policies, retirement policies, guns, condoms, medicines, and other health-related products are also influenced primarily by ego-defensive appeals. These appeals involve the use of Freudian defense mechanisms like wishful thinking (good things will happen to you and bad things will not), denial (refusing to believe what you do not want to believe), repression (forgetting things you do not want to think about), and projection (seeing your flaws and weaknesses in others). Freudian defense mechanisms help people to feel safe from real or imagined threats and to feel superior to real or imagined groups (e.g., stereotypes) (Amodio & Devine, 2005). Ego-defense ads are most effective when targeted toward insecure consumers.

Promotion-focused ego-defense ads use trusted authority figures (e.g., political and religious leaders) and experts (e.g., doctors, lawyers, and scientists) to help consumers feel safe and secure from real or imagined threats. Advertisements often utilize character actors, stereotypic attire and behavior, and specific settings and props to give the impression of authority or expertise. For example, a careful placement of an impressively large bookshelf filled with scholarly books behind a politician, a lawyer, or a banker can make the person look more intelligent (Cialdini & Sagarin, 2005). Prevention-focused ego-defense ads use fear appeals to make consumers feel threatened. Fear is a powerful emotion that is useful in motivating consumers to buy products that make them feel more safe and secure. For fear appeals to work, consumers must believe that

they are capable of changing their behavior; if they do not believe they are capable, they give up prematurely.

Attitudes that serve an adjustment function help consumers to gain immediate rewards and avoid immediate pain. The pleasure/pain principle can be very motivating and persuasive to consumers. Consumers buy products simply because the product tastes good or feels good and consumers avoid some products simply because the products taste bad or feel bad. Complex arguments and logical thinking (knowledge appeals), the image of consumers who use this type of product (value-expressive appeals), and concerns about safety or self-esteem (ego-defensive appeals) are largely irrelevant for these types of goods.

Promotion-focused adjustment ads emphasize benefits (e.g., simple pleasures, incentives) to encourage consumers to buy the advertised brand. Simple benefits, such as saving money and feeling good, are often emphasized in promotion-focused ads. These types of appeals work for both hedonic and utilitarian products. Hedonic products, especially "guilty pleasures," include high-calorie foods and beverages, comfortable but ugly clothing, and entertainment products that no one wants to admit they like. Shavitt (1990) further demonstrated that promotion-focused adjustment appeals are persuasive for utilitarian products like air conditioners. Air conditioners serve a specific utilitarian purpose: to keep consumers cool and comfortable (pleasure). Prevention-focused adjustment ads emphasize cost (e.g., pain, loss, regret) to encourage consumers to avoid competing brands and purchase the advertised brand. Products like pain relievers, antacids, and laxatives are advertised most effectively using this type of appeal. These products do not promote good health or longevity, but they make unpleasant symptoms such as pain and discomfort go away.

In summary, when consumers see or hear an advertisement that uses a persuasive technique that fails to match the function of their attitudes toward the advertised brand, consumers pay little or no attention to the ad. On the other hand, when consumers see or hear an ad that uses a technique that matches the function of their attitudes and their regulatory focus, consumers attend to the ad more carefully and think about the implications of the advertiser's message, and this increases ad effectiveness.

REFERENCES

Amodio, D. M., & Devine, P. G. (2005). Changing prejudice: The effects of persuasion on implicit and explicit forms of race bias. In T. C. Brock & M. C. Green (Eds.), *Persuasion: Psychological insights and perspectives* (2nd ed., pp. 249–280). Thousand Oaks, CA: Sage.

Cialdini, R. B., & Sagarin, B. J. (2005). Principles of interpersonal influence. In T. C. Brock & M. C. Green (Eds.), *Persuasion:*

Psychological insights and perspectives (2nd ed., pp. 143–169). Thousand Oaks, CA: Sage.

Cronley, M. L., Houghton, D. C., Goddard, P., & Kardes, F. R. (1998). Endorsing products for the money: The role of the correspondence bias in celebrity advertising. *Advances in Consumer Research, 26,* 627–631.

Herr, P. M., Kardes, F. R., & Kim, J. (1991). Effects of word-of-mouth and product-attribute information on persuasion: An accessibility-diagnosticity perspective. *Journal of Consumer Research, 17,* 454–462.

Higgins, E. T. (1998). Promotion and prevention: Regulatory focus as a motivational principle. In M. P. Zanna (Ed.), *Advances in experimental social psychology* (pp. 1–46). San Diego, CA: Academic Press.

Kardes, Frank R. (2002), Consumer behavior and managerial decision making, Upper Saddle River, NJ: Prentice Hall.

Kardes, F. R. (2005). The psychology of advertising. In T. C. Brock & M. C. Green (Eds.), *Persuasion: Psychological insights and perspectives* (2nd ed., pp. 281–303). Thousand Oaks, CA: Sage.

Kardes, F. R., Fennis, B. M., Hirt, E. R., Tormala, Z. L., & Bullington, B. (2007). The role of the need for cognitive closure in the effectiveness of the disrupt-then-reframe influence technique. *Journal of Consumer Research, 34*(3), 377–385.

Katz, D. (1960). The functional approach to the study of attitudes. *Public Opinion Quarterly, 24,* 163–204.

Petty, R. E., & Wegener, D. T. (1998). Matching versus mismatching attitude functions: Implications for scrutiny of persuasive messages. *Personality and Social Psychology Bulletin, 24,* 227–240.

Petty, R. E., Cacioppo, J. T., Strathman, A. J., & Priester, J. R. (2005). To think or not to think: Exploring two routes to persuasion. In T. C. Brock & M. C. Green (Eds.), *Persuasion: Psychological insights and perspectives* (2nd ed., pp. 81–116). Thousand Oaks, CA: Sage.

Shavitt, S. (1990). The role of attitude objects in attitude functions. *Journal of Experimental Social Psychology, 26,* 124–148.

SUGGESTED READINGS

Crano, W. D., & Prislin, R. (2006). Attitudes and persuasion. *Annual Review of Psychology, 57,* 345–374.

Kardes, F. R. (2005). The psychology of advertising. In T. C. Brock & M. C. Green (Eds.), *Persuasion: Psychological insights and perspectives* (2nd ed., pp. 281–303). Thousand Oaks, CA: Sage.

Petty, R. E., Cacioppo, J. T., Strathman, A. J., & Priester, J. R. (2005). To think or not to think: Exploring two routes to persuasion. In T. C. Brock & M. C. Green (Eds.), *Persuasion: Psychological insights and perspectives* (2nd ed., pp. 81–116). Thousand Oaks, CA: Sage.

BRUCE E. PFEIFFER
University of New Hampshire

FRANK R. KARDES
University of Cincinnati

AESTHETICS

Aesthetics is the study of how human beings react in sensory and emotional fashion to the things we encounter in life, especially as being appealing or not appealing. Is a person beautiful? Is this dessert delicious? Is that work of art particularly moving? Researchers who study taste or beauty in humans are engaged in work in aesthetics, but in recent years the field has focused more on how people react to works of art, broadly defined (fine arts, music, architecture, film, and so on). Although the field evolved from and still has close ties to philosophy, aesthetics from the perspective of how people actually perceive and react to works of art can be seen as a logical branch of the study of psychology. This is sometimes referred to as the psychology of aesthetics or empirical aesthetics, to differentiate it from its philosophical cousin. This line is not always clear, however, and some scholars, notably Dewey, move with facility between philosophy and psychology. Aesthetics can be contrasted to the related term, art, in that aesthetics concerns the reception of stimuli rather than their production.

The question arises as to whether aesthetics is more properly considered to be the study of beauty or the study of art? Clearly one can see beauty in objects that are not art (e.g., the things of nature), and equally clearly, not all art would be classified as beautiful. So, what is this field about? It is probably most accurate to say that the field evolved from contemplation of things beautiful and pleasing to encompass art very broadly defined, without losing its original interests in things that appeal to our senses. The psychological approach to exploring these issues involves empirical study and the generation of models and theories based in psychology to explain and understand what we experience in life. Thus, aesthetics from a psychological perspective is the study of all things beautiful whether art or not, and all things art whether beautiful or not.

History of the Field

It is almost always possible to trace the origins of a scientific discipline to antiquity, and aesthetics is no exception. We can see a concern for aesthetics in ancient biblical, Chinese, Islamic, Talmudic, and philosophical writings. Plato, Aristotle, Confucius, Hegel, Schopenhauer, Kant, Marx, and Freud all wrote about aesthetics. It is not surprising that the great thinkers have contemplated the issue of what is art and what is beautiful. Art is universal, and it follows logically that the perception of art and beauty are universal as well. Thus, an interest in how humans perceive beauty and art can be seen to be almost as natural, indeed inextricably entwined, with art itself. It would not be possible in this discussion to mention all the notable figures in the field of aesthetics, so we concentrate on three essential scholars.

Gustav Fechner

Just as psychology grew out of philosophy in general, so did the psychology of aesthetics grow out of philosophical approaches to aesthetics. And so a logical place to begin looking at the history of aesthetics from a psychological perspective would be with one of the founders of the field of psychology, Gustav Fechner. In the 1870s, Fechner took the prevailing philosophical approaches to aesthetics and turned them literally upside down (Fechner, 1978). He argued that philosophical approaches to aesthetics took a top-down approach, beginning by defining beauty from philosophical principles and then working toward a theory of aesthetics from that starting point. Fechner took a bottom-up approach by trying to determine the basic aspects and conditions of how and why people like things. His goal was to supplant Aristotelian and Kantian theories by building a theory up from these basic understandings (Allesch, 2001).

Fechner's methodological approach helped to develop the entire field of experimental psychology. He developed three complementary approaches to measuring aesthetic preference: (1) choice, in which the participant chooses a preferred object or rank orders more than two objects; (2) production, in which the participant modifies an object until a preferred state is obtained; and (3) constant stimuli (or single stimuli), in which a response is given to a single object (as contrasted with the choice approach). These methods are still used in a wide variety of sub-disciplines within psychology.

Daniel Berlyne

It would be an overstatement to say that the psychology of aesthetics basically remained dormant from the time of Fechner to the work of Daniel Berlyne in the 1950s, but one might say the field experienced a renaissance through Berlyne's efforts, summarized in *Art and Visual Perception: The Psychology of the Creative Eye* (Berlyne, 1971). Working from a psychobiological perspective, Berlyne was particularly interested in the arousal that objects produced in individuals. Although this presentation greatly simplifies his theory, his basic argument was that arousal was strongly influenced by the complexity and novelty of an object. Furthermore, humans typically find a moderate level of arousal to be most pleasing. Berlyne's model also included variables such as the meaning of the object and its intensity, ambiguity, brightness, and size. Recent research in the psychology of aesthetics (e.g., Martindale, 1991) has questioned Berlyne's model; philosophical approaches to aesthetics have questioned whether Berlyne was actually asking the most important questions.

Rudolf Arnheim

In *Art and Visual Perception,* along with other seminal works, Rudolph Arnheim (1971) brought Gestalt psychology to the study of aesthetics, in particular to painting and film. Arnheim emphasized the importance of the individual who is viewing a work of art, the relationship of the parts to the whole of artistic creation, working from the whole to the parts, and what he termed *the power of the center* in art. His approach focused on how viewers bring together what he called forces or fields that influence the perception of a work. Arnheim (1971) argued that vision is "not a mechanical recording of elements but rather the apprehension of significant structural patterns" (p. 6). Arnheim's model is less concerned with the culture or context of a work of art than its structural aspects and how the viewer responds to them. An excellent summary of Arnheim's contributions to aesthetics can be found in Cupchik (2007).

Aesthetics Research Today

The field of the psychology of aesthetics, although small in the overall structure of the discipline of psychology, is nonetheless thriving today. Some areas of research focus on those issues first discussed in work by Berlyne, Arnheim, and other pioneers, while others are asking new and different questions. For example, Locher, Gray, and Nodine (1996) have used experimental approaches and eye movement cameras to examine issues related to balance, symmetry, and the center of artistic works. Based on extensive interviews with more than 300 individuals, Parsons (1987) presented a cognitive-developmental perspective on how people experience aesthetic encounters. Leder, Belke, Oeberst, and Augustin (2004) have developed an information-processing model of the process through which people make sense out of abstract art. These and other research paradigms exemplify the vibrancy of the field of the psychology of aesthetics as it exists today.

REFERENCES

Allesch, C. G. (2001). *Fechner's aesthetics–a provocation?* Lecture given at the symposium in honour of Gustav Fechner's 200th anniversary, Leipzig, 19–20 Oct. 2001.

Arnheim, R. (1971). *Art and visual perception.* Berkeley: University of California Press. (Original work published 1954.)

Berlyne, D. E. (1971). *Aesthetics and psychobiology.* New York: Appleton-Century-Crofts.

Cupchik, G. C. (2007). A critical reflection on Arnheim's gestalt theory of aesthetics. *Psychology of Aesthetics, Creativity, and the Arts, 1,* 16–24.

Fechner, G. T. (1978). *Vorschule der Ästhetik* (Nachdruck d. 2. Ausg. Leipzig 1925), 2 Bde. in 1 Bd.; beigebunden: *Zur experimentalen Aesthetik* (Nachdruck d. Ausgabe Leipzig 1871). Hildesheim: Olms.

Leder, H., Belke, B., Oeberst, A., & Augustin, D. (2004). A model of aesthetic appreciation and aesthetic judgments. *British Journal of Psychology, 95,* 489–508.

Locher, P., Gray, S., & Nodine, C. (1996). The structural frame-work of pictorial balance. *Perception 25*, 1419–1436.

Martindale, C. G. (1988). Aesthetics, psychobiology, and cognition. In F. Farley & R. Neperud (Eds.), *The Foundations of Aesthetics, Art, and Art Education* (pp. 7–42). New York: Praeger.

Parsons, M. J. (1987). *How we understand art: A cognitive developmental account of aesthetic experience*. Cambridge: Cambridge University Press.

SUGGESTED READINGS

Dewey, J. (1934). *Art as experience*. New York: Penguin Putman Inc.

Locher, P., Martindale, C., Dorfman, L., Petrov, V., & Leontiev, D. (Eds.). (2006). *New directions in aesthetics, creativity, and the psychology of art*. Amityville, NY: Baywood.

LISA F. SMITH
JEFFREY K. SMITH
University of Otago, New Zealand

See also: Society for the Psychology of Aesthetics, Creativity, and the Arts

AFFECT (See Emotions)

AFFECTIVE DEVELOPMENT

Affect, as a feature or type of behavior, and hence a focus of psychology, is one of the least understood and most challenging problems in the field. "Affect" relates to and/or encompasses a wide range of concepts and phenomena including feelings, emotions, moods, motivation, and certain drives and instincts. It is often used as a synonym of "emotion"; however, others have used it to describe external manifestations of emotion or mood. Anger, joy, fear, laughter, sadness, anxiety, pride, love, hate, and so on—are all so central to human experience, yet so little understood by psychology. Theorists and researchers have approached affect in numerous ways, often using idiosyncratic, contradictory, or mutually exclusive conceptualizations and operational definitions, thus resulting in confusion and limited progress in our understanding of affect or any of these other related or synonymous constructs.

The psychology of *affective development* seeks to describe, map, and explain the processes, continuities, and changes in the experience, differentiation, and expression of affect over the life course. Traditionally, affective development has been placed in dichotomy, or even counterpoint, with cognitive development, reflecting an age-old concern with mind-body dualism, thinking versus feeling. Much of the current discussion centers around the interaction or mutual influence of emotion, cognition, and behavior.

Emotions play an important role in the lives of people. As a state of feeling, emotions have physiological and cognitive components. Various stimuli trigger a physiological response (e.g., as evidenced by heart-rate measures or fMRI indices) referred to as arousal. The individual's cognitive appraisal of the event includes assessing the personal relevance of the arousing stimuli, as well as coping options available to the individual, thus determining the emotion aroused (see Lazarus & Folkman, 1987; Smith & Lazarus, 1993). Individuals differ as to the intensity of their affective responsiveness across specific emotion categories (Larsen & Diener, 1987), which suggests that temperament plays an important role in people's affectivity. Aside from affective experience, affect regulation has received increasing attention from researchers across several disciplines. Affect regulation refers to maintaining self-control in the face of highly arousing stimuli. The ability to regulate affect is a mechanism that underlies mood and anxiety disorders; it is sometimes referred to as the affective illnesses.

Models of affective development vary in the degree to which they emphasize biological elements or socialization elements. Traditional Freudian and Eriksonian theories of psychosexual and psychosocial development present stage theories of affective development. Piaget noted a parallel system of the development of affectivity but emphasized cognitive features of development. Darwinian and ethological models are especially interested in unlearned complex behavior; they often posit central nervous system specificity, as well as correspondence between stimulus or elicitors and an individual's affective response. Socialization models emphasize learning processes, especially in the infant-caregiver attachment and interaction as well as situational or environmental influences on the affective experience or expression. Reliance on one or the other model type, of course, influences the manner in which affective development is understood or studied. For instance, biological researchers might be more likely to measure electrophysiological responsiveness or neurophysiological correlates of specific emotions, whereas socialization researchers might be more interested in observing the quality of parent-child attachment and separation reactions over time. It is likely that integration of multiple models and perspectives will be essential to furthering our understanding of affective development. Indeed, such comprehensive and integrative bio-ecological approaches are evident in current theories of affective development such as Sroufe's organizational perspective, Tomkins and Izard's differential emotions theory, and Davidson's affective neuroscience.

Humans learn to regulate emotions in infancy. A growing number of studies (e.g., Gunnar et al., 2006) show compelling evidence for the need to consider both biological and contextual elements of affective development. The basic neural mechanisms of emotions develop in the context of caregiver-child relationships. Infants and their caregivers interactively co-construct the environment needed for maturation of a control system in the right brain of the infant, which plays a key role in emotional development (Schore, 2001). Infants are equipped to play a primitive role in their own regulation (e.g., by sending "signals" of distress), however they are not capable of self-regulation, only "co-regulation," which requires ample assistance from caregivers (Sroufe, 2000). In daily exchanges of signals with responsive caregivers, children learn to turn extreme emotional reactions into more regulated emotions and maintain calm levels of arousal (Greenspan & Shanker, 2004). The infant's growing ability to regulate emotions, in turn, affects the caregiver's emotional state and the ability to provide continuous stimulation and emotionally appropriate sensations.

A divergence from narrow models affords a far more inclusive and nonlinear approach to studying affective development. Recognizing the capacity of both the child and the environment for self-organizing, inherent in the notion of the transactional (circular) nature of person-context interactions allows us to look at the neurobiology of affective development, *temperament*, cognitive development, parent-child relations in mutually interactive nonlinear ways. While traditional inquiry emphasized the development and impact of negative affects such as depression and anxiety, recent focus on processes involving positive affects—joy, hope, contentment, interest, excitement—promise a more complete and useful emergent understanding.

REFERENCES

Greenspan, S. I., & Shanker, S. (2004). *The first idea: How symbols, language and intelligence devolved from our primate ancestors to modern humans.* Boston: Da Capo Press, Perseus Books.

Gunnar, M. R., Fisher, P. A., & The Early Experience, Stress, and Prevention Science Network. (2006). Bringing basic research on early experience and stress neurobiology to bear on preventive intervention research on neglected and maltreated children. *Development and Psychopathology, 18,* 651–677.

Larsen, R., & Diener, E. (1987). Affect intensity as an individual difference characteristic: A review. *Journal of Research in Personality, 21,* 1–39.

Lazarus, R. S., & Folkman, S. (1987). Transactional theory and research on emotions and coping. *European Journal of Personality, 1,* 141–170.

Schore, A. N. (2001). Effects of a secure attachment relationship on right brain development, affect regulation, and infant mental health. *Infant Mental Health Journal, 22*(1– 2), 7–66.

Schultz, D., Izard, C., & Bear, G. (2003). Children's emotional processing: Relations to emotionality and aggression. *Development & Psychopathology, 16,* 371–387.

Smith, C. A., & Lazarus, R. S. (1993). Appraisal components, core relational themes, and the emotions, *Cognition and Emotion, 7,* 233–269.

Sroufe, L. A. (2000). Early relationships and the development of children. *Infant Mental Health Journal, 21*(1–2), 67–74.

SUGGESTED READINGS

Bradley, S. J. (2000). *Affect regulation and the development of psychopathology.* New York: Guilford Press.

Davidson, R., Klaus Rainer Scherer, K., & Goldsmith, H. (Eds). (2003). *Handbook of affective sciences.* NY: Oxford University

Griffiths, P. E. (1997). *What emotions really are: The problem of psychological categories.* Chicago: University of Chicago Press.

LaFreniere, P. J. (2000). *Emotional development: A biosocial perspective.* New York: Wadsworth.

DONALD WERTLIEB
MYRNA V. VASHCHENKO
DANTE SPETTER
Tufts University

See also: Emotional Development

AFFECTIVE DISORDER (See Mood Disorders)

AFFILIATION NEED

Theorists of personality and social psychology have long speculated about the processes involved in motivating individuals toward relationships with others. In the 1930s Henry Murray (1893–1988) and his multidisciplinary team at Harvard University studied the personality traits of 51 young men and produced one of the first major systematic studies of human personality. Stemming from this research was the landmark *Explorations in Personality* (Murray, 1938), which cataloged more than 20 human motives or "needs," one of which was the need for affiliation (*n*Aff). Murray's research program in personality formed the basis for several early personality tests, including the Thematic Apperception Test (TAT; Morgan & Murray, 1935), which assesses a dimension of need affiliation.

Out of his list of human motivation, Murray identified affiliation motivation as being the tendency to "form friendships and associations; to greet, join, and live with others; to co-operate and converse sociably with others; to love; to join groups" (Murray, 1938, p. 83). Murray believed that affiliation motivation was related to other social needs, and he grouped need for affiliation with three other social affect needs—rejection, nurturance, and succorance (the seeking out of emotional support). In this regard, Murray saw need for affiliation being strongly related to the needs for nurturance and succorance, whereas need for rejection was the "flip side" or alterego form of affiliative need.

McClelland (1951, 1953), along with his team of research assistants, drew on Murray's list of motives in developing his acquired needs theory (also referred to as the three-need theory or the learned-needs theory). In this theory, McClelland proposed that human needs are acquired over time and shaped by our individual early life experiences and our particular cultural background. A key premise of this theory is that most human motivation comprises three dominant needs: (1) the need for achievement (nAch); (2) the need for power (nPow); and (3) the need for affiliation (nAff). McClelland proposed that the importance of each of these three needs varies from individual to individual, and that the level of people's motivation and effectiveness in different situations such as work and family life will differ depending upon their personal need orientation.

McClelland asserted further that individuals with high-power needs are motivated to either control others or to influence social and organizational situations, whereas individuals with high-achievement needs are characterized by a desire to do well and achieve. In contrast, individuals high in affiliative need desire to feel related to others in positive ways. Highly affiliative individuals wish to maintain others' affections and are motivated to seek out interpersonal relationships and friendships. In work environments, highly affiliative individuals generally feel rewarded by being involved in work that involves a high level of interaction with others. In this regard, they tend to be employees who are successful in the fields of human service and in work that involves teamwork and group collaboration.

In terms of measurement, McClelland used a version of the TAT to investigate the saliency of power, achievement, and affiliative needs in individuals. While he focused particularly on developing scoring techniques for assessment of achievement need, Shipley and Veroff (1952) developed a reliable system for scoring need affiliation.

Based on the early work of Murray (1938) and McClelland (1951, 1953) and his colleagues, among others, Hill (1987) further developed the concept of need for affiliation by specifying four different incentive motivators that can serve to move individuals towards affiliative behavior with others. These motivators include (1) positive stimulation, or the ability of affiliation to provide opportunities for enjoyable affective and cognitive stimulation; (2) attention or praise, which offers the possibility of enhancement of feelings of self-worth and importance; (3) social comparison, which allows for the reduction of ambiguity about one's personal position through comparison with others; and (4) emotional support or sympathy, which offers the potential for reduction of negative feelings through social contact. Using factor analysis, Hill designed the Interpersonal Orientation Scale (IOS), which was the first personality measure designed to assess these four underlying dimensions of motivation for affiliation.

Based on his own work, as well as the earlier work of Shipley and Veroff (1952), Hill (1987) proposed that the reason certain individuals are more highly affiliative than others is because they have a heightened sensitivity toward the availability of these four types of social rewards and because they also experience highly positive emotional reactions to these rewards. Hill also found that the types of affiliative behavior people engage in may be expected to change depending on the type of rewards offered across different social situations. For example, individuals are generally more likely to report a motivation to engage with others in a party situation for the rewards of positive social stimulation, whereas they tend to seek out positive attention and recognition in a work-project situation.

REFERENCES

Hill, C. A. (1987). Affiliation motivation: People who need people … but in different ways. *Journal of Personality and Social Psychology, 52*(5), 1008–1018.

McClelland, D. C. (1951). *Personality*. New York: William Sloane Associates.

McClelland, D. C., Atkinson, J. W., Clark, R. A., & Lowell, E. L. (1953). *The achievement motive*. Princeton: Van Nostrand.

Morgan, C. D., & Murray, H. A. (1935). A method for investigating fantasies: The Thematic Apperception Test. *Archives of Neurology and Psychiatry, 34*, 289–306.

Murray, H. A. (1938). *Explorations in personality*. New York: Oxford University Press.

Shipley, T., & Veroff, J. (1952). A projective measure of need for affiliation. *Journal of Experimental Psychology, 43*(5), 349–356.

Stephanie G. Chapman
Jonathan P. Schwartz
University of Houston

See also: **Achievement Need; Altruism**

AGE REGRESSION

Age regression, as a clinical hypnotic technique, leads clients in trance back through time to re-experience past events from their lives. Clinically, hypnotic age regression has been useful in uncovering information important to therapy. Classically, this technique has been used to uncover earlier traumatic experiences with the belief that the catharsis of reliving the experience is healing. Other therapies such as psychoanalysis also find the examination of earlier life experiences useful, but when hypnotic age regression is used, the emotions of the experience can be relived more vividly and efficiently.

Age regression has also been used in uncovering memories for use in forensic investigations and testimony. Such uncovered information may be of use at times, but the veracity of these recovered memories is rightfully questioned, and the recovery techniques must be used with extreme care to avoid any leading suggestions.

In the clinical setting, a client comes to therapy with specific complaints, symptoms, or problems. Sometimes, as therapy progresses, issues arise related to experiences earlier in life. Sometimes memories may be vague and need to be uncovered or clarified in order to be faced more directly. The veracity of these memories may not be certain, yet the emotional and somatic experiences they elicit are significant. At other times, clients' emotional or somatic complaints may not seem to be related to anything specific in their past and are described with unknown etiology. In each of these situations the use of age regression will likely facilitate greater understanding.

Hypnotic age regression is performed by first inducing a hypnotic trance in the client or subject. Many techniques of trance induction can be found in numerous books on hypnosis (e.g., Hammond, 1990). After a basic trance has been induced, the language to induce age regression includes such phrases as, "As you go back through time, watch the years go by, watch the events of your life, places, people, situations pass by . . . " If the issue of concern is already known to be a specific earlier life experience, the suggestion is made that the client go back to that specific time. If the past situation is not specifically known, age regression is used in conjunction with the technique of the affect or somatic bridge (Watkins, 1992, p. 60–64). The bridge is an affective or somatic complaint as described by the client in psychotherapy. As trance induction proceeds, the suggestion is added that the client carry back through time the emotion or somatic complaint, for example, the client's symptoms of anxiety or heartburn. Ideomotor signaling (Hammond, 1990, p. 518) is also useful in this situation, in which the client is instructed to lift a finger to signal to the therapist when something relevant or important is experienced during the regression.

The client is then asked to describe the experience and is led by the therapist's questions to elaborate on the experience while remaining in trance. Often this experience leads to an abreactive emotional release. These procedures are often referred to as analytical hypnotherapy or hypnoanalysis (Barnett, 1981; Watkins, 1992). Without such an emotional release, the suggestion may be made that the client go further back in time, while again using the affect bridge. Depending upon the nature of what is uncovered, comparing three or more past experiences may reveal a pattern of behavior or cognition that makes the experiences significant.

Sometimes anxiety or fear is experienced when a severe trauma is hypnotically re-experienced. If such fear or anxiety is severe, having defined earlier in therapy a safe place to which the client can retreat is useful, but initially offering a cautionary suggestion that the client will face only that which he or she is emotionally ready to face generally diminishes such anxiety. Hypnotically re-experiencing traumatic experiences may not always be cathartic but may intensify the trauma, especially when the client does not have available alternative or healthier behaviors or responses to the trauma. Besides first uncovering the traumatic experience(s) and second, supporting the emotions released by the experience, two additional steps in the therapeutic process may be necessary. Brink (2002, pp. 158–160) identifies the third step: While considering the traumatic experience, the client can be asked to answer the question "What do I need?" For example, what is needed from an abusive parent could be stated "I need my father to be gentle and patient with me. I need him to understand that I am only a child," or, "I need a strong mother who can protect me." The client is encouraged to identify as many such positive alternatives and phrases as possible. The fourth step (pp. 160–161) is then to lead the client to practice filling this need for others in his or her life by being gentle, patient, and strong.

Although cognitive behavior therapists tend to deny the importance of early life experiences and unconscious processes, these techniques of hypnotic age regression can be very useful in cognitive therapy (Brink, 2004–2005, pp. 281–292; Zarren & Eimer, 2002, pp. 227–231). Several reasons seem evident as to why a memory is forgotten. It may be suppressed because of the pain of the trauma. The experience may have been preverbal and experienced only emotionally without a cognitive component, or it may have been denied as important by a parental figure and thus denied by the client through learning. Yet the memory is retained at an unconscious level. For example, while in trance one client recalled that when his father came into the room when he, as a young boy, was playing with pots and pans from the kitchen cupboard, the father "sighed." This "sigh," a sign that communicated disappointment, disgust, or a lack of approval, led the child as a young adult to feel inadequate and eventually to fail in college. Only in therapy were words finally put to this young man's feelings. As the memory is uncovered and words are put to it, these cognitions may be modified, and such modification can be greatly facilitated through the therapeutic techniques described above.

REFERENCES

Barnett, E. A. (1981). *Analytical hypnotherapy: Principles and practice.* Kingston, ON, Canada: Junica.

Brink, N. E. (2002). *Grendel and his mother: Healing the traumas of childhood through dreams, imagery and hypnosis.* Amityville, NY: Baywood.

Brink, N. E. (2004–2005). Using emotions, hypnosis, and the past to increase the effectiveness of cognitive-behavior therapy. *Imagination, Cognition and Personality, 24,* 281–292.

Hammond, D. C. (Ed.). (1990). *Handbook of hypnotic suggestions and metaphors*. New York: Norton & Co.

Watkins, J. G. (1992). *Hypnoanalytic techniques: The practice of clinical hypnosis*, Vol. II. New York: Irvington.

Zarren, J. I., & Eimer, B. N. (2002). Brief cognitive hypnosis: Facilitating the change of dysfunctional behavior. New York: Springer.

Nicholas E. Brink
Coburn, PA

See also: Abreaction; Recovered Memories; Trauma Psychology

AGGRESSION

The most widely accepted definitions of aggression define it as behavior that is intended to injure another individual, physically or psychologically. Within this definition, a number of important subtypes are identified. First, a distinction is made between hostile or reactive aggression, which is aggression arising from feelings of anger or hostility, and instrumental aggression, which is aggression that arises in service of goal attainment (e.g., armed robbery).

Second, physical aggression and relational aggression can be differentiated. Relational aggression is characterized by the use of verbal acts (including gossip and taunts) and social exclusion to cause psychological harm. Females engage in relational aggression at higher rates than they engage in physical aggression. However, the overall gender difference in relational aggression is small. Many males also exhibit relational aggression.

A third distinction can be made between interpersonal aggression and institutional aggression (e.g., war, genocide). Although this is an interesting and potentially useful distinction, most aggression research focuses on interpersonal aggression.

Given this heterogeneity in defining aggression, summarizing rates of aggression is a difficult task. The most readily available data are for criminal-level violence. According to the United Nations Statistics Division, the worldwide homicide rates per 100,000 inhabitants in 1996 ranged from 0.3 in Guyana to 80 in Colombia. Other violent criminal offenses can also be considered. In 2005, the U.S. Bureau of Justice Statistics recorded 15,495 occurrences of murder and nonnegligent manslaughter (5.9 per 100,000 inhabitants) and 791,988 cases of aggravated assault (301.6 per 100,000 inhabitants). These statistics help to clarify the scope of violent interpersonal aggression, but they do not provide any information regarding noncriminal or unreported aggression.

Studies show that aggressive behavior is exhibited across the life span. Studies of children age 12–18 months show that approximately half of children's interpersonal exchanges can be defined as conflict-based or disruptive. For most children, levels of physical aggression decrease over time, although a minority demonstrate consistently high levels of physical aggression throughout childhood. This decrease in physical aggression appears to be greater for girls than for boys (Côté, Vaillancourt, & Barker, 2007). Indirect aggression follows a different pattern, appearing in low rates consistently throughout childhood for the majority of children and increasing over the course of childhood for a minority of children.

Data tend to show a gender disparity in physical aggression, although there may be specific situations in which women are as aggressive as or more aggressive than men. Meta-analysis of physical aggression research reveals a gender difference that is moderate in size ($d = .5$). A smaller effect size is found for gender differences in verbal aggression ($d = .09$) (Archer, 2004). In the United States between 1961 and 1999, 85% to 91% of homicides were committed by males. These data are consistent with homicide data across several countries (e.g., Canada, England, and Australia). However, research on domestic violence has shown that there may not be a significant gender difference in the number of physically aggressive acts committed within a relationship (Straus & Ramirez, 2007). This research also showed that when only one partner in the relationship engaged in aggression, it was twice as likely to be the female partner.

Regional differences in rates of aggression also exist. Homicide rates vary widely across the globe. Even within a single country, differences in aggression may emerge between regions. In the southern United States, rates of homicide, self-reported violence, and executions are all higher than in the northern United States.

Factors that influence group and individual variation in aggression can be identified at the biological, sociological, and psychological levels. There appears to be a genetic vulnerability to aggression. Studies of childhood and juvenile antisocial behavior have shown higher concordance rates for self-reported aggressiveness, delinquency, and conduct disorder symptoms for identical (monozygotic) than for nonidentical (dizygotic) twins, suggesting a significant contribution of genetics (Carey, 1996). In studies of adult antisocial behavior, the findings have been similar. Adoption studies also suggest that the adopted-out children of mothers and fathers with a criminal conviction are more likely to have an arrest or conviction than the adopted-out children of noncriminal mothers and fathers.

Biological approaches to aggression focus on the role of the hormone testosterone. Testosterone is present in higher levels in males than in females, it is tied to masculine physical development, and it is associated with masculine-typed social behaviors, including aggressiveness. Consistent with this association, Dabbs (2000) and colleagues have found that prison inmates with higher testosterone levels commit more violent crimes, on average, than inmates with lower testosterone levels. Further, in nonincarcerated samples, higher testosterone levels are associated with higher rates of delinquency, a greater history of violent behaviors, and more trouble with the law. Finally, individuals given increasing doses of testosterone, either as part of an experiment or as the result of medical sex-change procedures, show associated increases in aggressive behavior.

According to evolutionary psychology theories, human aggression results from the competition for mates. Specifically, males compete—often aggressively—for status and resources as a means of improving their reproductive odds. Consistent with this proposal, males tend to show higher levels of aggression at those ages when competition for mates is most important (i.e., late teens and early 20s).

Sociological theories also emphasize motivations for status and dominance as explanations for aggressive behavior. According to this approach, aggression is a tool that individuals use to gain resources and status when poverty or deprivation has limited other options (Hovland & Sears, 1940). Consistent with this proposal, Dabbs (2000) and colleagues have shown that although high testosterone levels are strongly associated with aggressive behavior among low-status men, among men of higher status, testosterone levels do not reliably relate to adult antisocial behavior.

Regional differences in aggression in the United States are also explained on the basis of status and dominance theories. According to Cohen and Nisbett (1997), the differences in aggression between the northern and southern States reflect the presence of a southern "culture of honor," wherein perceived disrespect must be answered with aggression. Such aggression is meant to preserve social status. In support of this model, it has been shown that homicide rates are higher in the South only for cases involving argument or insult (i.e., homicides committed in the course of a robbery are not elevated). In an experimental situation, southern participants who were insulted showed higher levels of anger and higher levels of testosterone following the insult than northern participants. The proposal that perceived disrespect will increase the likelihood of aggressive behavior is also consistent with work by Dodge (1986) and colleagues showing that children with severe conduct problems are more likely than other children to view an ambiguous provocation as an act of hostility and to retaliate aggressively.

This latter finding emphasizes the role of social information processing in aggression. The social information processing approach emphasizes the role of aggressive schemas and scripts in aggression and proposes that aggression is more common when nonaggressive responses are less well learned, less accessible, and viewed as less likely to be effective. The cognitive-neoassociation theory (Berkowitz, 1993) focuses on the importance of the accessibility of aggressive cognitions. According to this model, anything in the environment that increases the accessibility of aggressive thoughts will increase the likelihood of aggressive behavior. Consistent with this theory, the presence of a weapon has been shown to significantly increase the likelihood that research participants will engage in aggressive retaliation against an individual who has angered them.

Social psychological research has also provided evidence for a link between exposure to media violence and aggressive behavior. Correlational studies reveal an association between exposure to violent media in childhood and criminal (including violent) behavior in adulthood. This relationship has also been demonstrated in the laboratory, where exposure to violent media (film clips and video game play) results in short-term increases in aggression. These effects are strongest when the viewer identifies with the aggressor portrayed in the clip and when the aggression is portrayed as justified.

Other situational factors can increase aggression. Heat is correlated with aggression. There are higher rates of violent (but not nonviolent) crime in cities with hotter climates, and rates of violence tend to peak in summer months. This effect of heat may exemplify a broader category of causal factors. Any situation that increases discomfort may increase the likelihood of aggression. For example, individuals are also more likely to aggress when exposed to physical pain, hunger, overcrowding, noxious smells, and insults.

Personality theorists account for differences in aggression at the trait level. For example, the psychopathic personality, which is characterized by callousness, lack of empathy, fearlessness, and impulsivity, is also associated with elevated rates of both instrumental and hostile aggression (Hare, 2003). Given the heterogeneity of aggressive behavior, it is unlikely that any single perspective will address all forms of aggression. Thus, prevention and treatment efforts must be developed at the biological, sociological, and psychological levels.

REFERENCES

Archer, J. (2004). Sex difference in aggression in real-world settings: A meta-analytic review. *Review of General Psychology, 8,* 291–322.

Berkowitz, L. (1993). *Aggression.* New York: McGraw-Hill.

Carey, G. (1996). Family and genetic epidemiology of aggressive and antisocial behavior. In D. Stoff and R. Cairns (Eds.), *Aggression and violence: Genetic, neurobiological, and biosocial perspectives.* Mahwah, NJ: Lawrence Erlbaum.

Catalano, R., Dooley, D., Novavco, R., Wilson, G., & Hough R. (1993). Using ECA survey data to examine the effect of job layoffs on violent behavior. *Hospital and Community Psychiatry, 44,* 874–878.

Cohen, D., & Nisbett, R. E. (1997). Field experiments examining the culture of honor: The role of institutions in perpetuating norms about violence. *Personality and Social Psychology Bulletin*, *23*, 1188–1199.

Côté, S. M., Vaillancourt, T., & Barker, E. D. (2007). The joint development of physical and indirect aggression: Predictors of continuity and change during childhood. *Development and Psychopathology, 19*, 37–55.

Dabbs, J. M. Jr. (2000). *Heroes, rogues, and lovers: Testosterone and behavior*. New York: McGraw-Hill.

Dodge, K. A. (1986). A social information processing model of social competence in children. In M. Perlmutter (Ed.), *Minnesota symposium on child psychology* (Vol. 18, pp. 77–125). Hillsdale, NJ: Lawrence Erlbaum.

Hare, R. D. (2003). *Manual for the Hare Psychopathy Checklist-Revised* (2nd ed.). Toronto, Ontario, Canada: Multi-Health Systems.

Hovland, C. I., & Sears, R. R. (1940). Minor studies of aggression: Correlations of lynchings with economic indices. *Journal of Psychology, 9*, 301–310.

Straus, M. A., & Ramirez, I. L. (2007). Gender symmetry in prevalence, severity, and chronicity of physical aggression against dating partners by university students in Mexico and USA. *Aggressive Behavior, 33*, 281–290.

SUGGESTED READINGS

Bandura, A. (1973). *Aggression: A social learning analysis*. Englewood Cliffs, NJ: Prentice-Hall.

Hare, R. D. (1993). *Without conscience: The disturbing world of the psychopaths among us*. New York: Guilford Press.

JENNIFER E. VITALE
Hampden-Sydney College, VA

See also: Anger

AGING AND INTELLIGENCE

Phenomena of aging effects on intellectual and cognitive functioning are investigated by research approaches at the psychometric, information-processing, and biological levels. Evidence from these approaches complements each other and should be considered conjointly for a comprehensive overview of aging and intelligence. Recent neurocomputational approaches help to integrate theory and data across these levels.

The Behavioral Psychometric Approach

Extant psychometric data on aging and intelligence indicate three major phenomena. First, intellectual aging is multifaceted. Multifactorial models of intelligence (e.g., the Cattell-Horn *Gf-Gc theory* or the dual-process model of lifespan intellectual development) suggest that abilities in

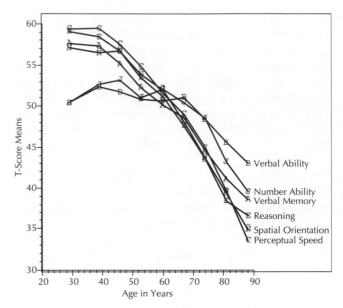

Figure 1. Cross-sectional age gradients in six primary mental abilities (N = 1628). Abilities were assessed with three to four different tests, and are scaled in a T-score metric. (Data source based on Schaie & Willis, 1993; figure adapted from Lindenberger & Baltes, 1994).

the fluid-mechanics (*Gf*) domain, reflecting an individual's capacity for problem solving, information organization, and concentration, are more biology-based. In contrast, abilities in the crystallized-pragmatic (*Gc*) domain reflect the acquisition and use of culture-based information (see Baltes, Staudinger, & Lindenberger, 1999, for review). Figure 1 shows that cross-sectional age gradients of primary mental abilities in the fluid-mechanics domain (i.e., verbal memory, reasoning, spatial orientation, and perceptual speed) decline linearly beginning in the 40s. However, abilities in the crystallized-pragmatics domain (i.e., verbal and numeric abilities) remain stable up to the 60s or 70s (Schaie & Willis, 1993).

Second, cross-sectional age differences are generally more pronounced than longitudinal age changes. While modest cross-sectional negative age differences are found by the 40s for some and by the 60s for most abilities, moderate longitudinal negative age changes in most abilities are usually not evident until the mid-70s or early 80s (e.g., Schaie, 1996). Discrepancies between cross-sectional and longitudinal age gradients are due to cohort effects, practice effects, and selective attrition in longitudinal studies (see Baltes & Mayer, 1998; Lindenberger & Baltes, 1994, for reviews). After controlling for cohort and historical time effects, discrepancies between cross-sectional age differences and longitudinal age changes are reduced (Schaie, 1996).

Third, aging contracts the factor space of intellectual abilities. Ample cross-sectional data show that correlations among subscales are generally larger in older samples, indicating an increasing degree of ability dedifferentiation

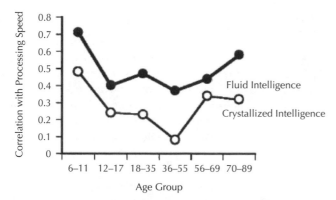

Figure 2. Less differentiated intelligence structure at both ends of the lifespan (adapted from Li et al., 2004).

(see Figure 2; see Li, Lindenberger, Hommel, Aschersleben, Prinz, & Baltes, 2004 for recent findings and historical review). Furthermore, ability dedifferentiation generalizes beyond the intellectual domain. A series of recent studies using simple measures of sensory acuity, contrast sensitivity, and muscle strength report an increase in the sensory-cognitive correlation with advancing age in age-heterogeneous samples. The strengthening of the sensory-cognitive link in old age has been interpreted as an indication of general neurological decline affecting both domains of functioning. The nature of the sensory-cognitive link is, however, still under debate. A few recent studies have taken an experimental, instead of a correlational, approach to study the sensory-cognitive link. Findings from experimental dual-task studies suggest that as people grow older, they seem to allocate an increasing amount of attention to tasks that require maintaining balance in an upright posture or walking (e.g., see Li & Lindenberger, 2002, for a review).

The Behavioral Information-Processing Approach

In formulating theories of intelligence, researchers have examined several information-processing mechanisms or resources that may mediate age-related differences in intelligence. A common hypothesis of cognitive aging is that aging constrains general cognitive resources (*GCRs*). Three related types of GCRs—working memory, processing speed, and executive control functions—have been investigated most extensively in relation to the fluid-mechanics domain of intelligence.

Working Memory. Working memory (WM) refers to the ability to simultaneously hold information in immediate memory while transforming the same or other information. Associated with higher-level cognition, WM is involved in language processing, problem solving, and concurrent task performance. Age-related declines in WM performance have been well documented. Furthermore, large-scale studies show that a substantial portion of age-related variance in *Gf* abilities is shared with age-related differences in WM (see Craik & Salthouse, 2007, for a review).

Processing Speed. Age-related intellectual declines have biological underpinnings such as neuronal slowing, which lead to the slowing of basic cognitive operations and exacerbated effects in complex tasks. Correlational analyses show that the observed age-associated variance in *Gf* abilities is greatly reduced or eliminated after controlling for individual differences in processing speed (see Craik & Salthouse, 2007, for reviews). In addition to slowed information processing, trial-to-trial reaction time variability, an indicator of processing fluctuation (e.g., Li et al., 2004), increases during aging.

Executive Control Functions. It has also been proposed that aging impairs executive control functions such as selective attention, dividing attention across concurrent tasks, and task switching (Verhaeghen & Cerella, 2002). Nested within this category are general accounts of age-related decline in attention and inhibitory processes, leading to greater interference and difficulty in suppressing previously relevant information and habitual responses. Measures of interference proneness have accounted for significant proportions of age-related variance in cognitive performance (see Craik & Salthouse, 2007, for review). More recent work implicates the anterior cingulate cortex in conflict monitoring situations (e.g., overcoming competing sources of information) and in outcome evaluation (e.g., negative feedback, error detection), thus providing a neuroanatomical account of a variety of executive functions (e.g., Botvinick, Cohen, & Carter, 2004). Taken together, strong theoretical and empirical links appear to exist among all three GCRs, which may be best conceptualized as basic mechanisms (e.g., speed, conflict monitoring) nested within more complex cognitive functions (WM).

The Cognitive and Computational Neuroscience Approaches

Recent developments in cognitive neuroscience have motivated researchers to investigate functional relationships between aging deficits in basic cognitive mechanisms and their biological underpinnings (see Figure 3). The biological correlates of aging effects on intelligence examined so far involve molecular and neuronal mechanisms.

Molecular Correlates. ApoE is a plasma protein involved in cholesterol transportation. There is recent consensus that the ε4 variant of ApoE is a risk factor for developing Alzheimer's disease. It may also relate to milder forms of nonclinical cognitive impairment (see Deary et al., 2004, for a review).

Neuronal Correlates. Besides anatomical changes (Raz et al., 2005), there is consensus that during the course of normal aging the concentration of neurotransmitters—for instance, dopamine in the frontal cortex, striatum, and basal ganglia—decreases by 5–10% in each decade of life. Functional relationships between aging-related deficits in the dopaminergic system and age-related decrements

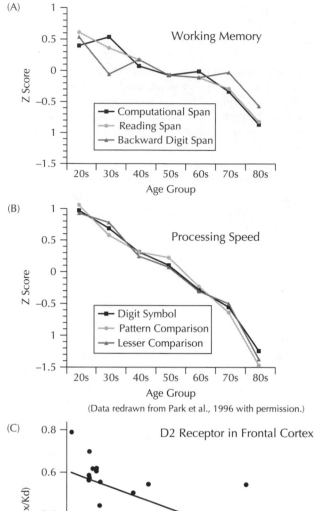

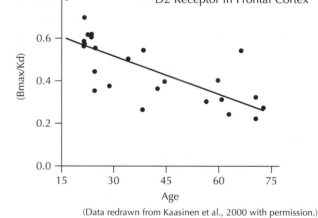

(Data redrawn from Park et al., 1996 with permission.)

(Data redrawn from Kaasinen et al., 2000 with permission.)

Figure 3. Aging-related declines in information processing and neurotransmitter density. Negative adult age differences in working memory (A), processing speed (B), and dopamine D2-like receptor availability in the frontal cortex. (Data source based on Park et al., 1996, and Kaasinen et al., 2000; figure adapted from Li, Lindenberger, & Sikström, 2001).

in various aspects of information processing have also been documented. For instance, the density of dopamine receptors in the nigrostriatum associates negatively with reaction time (RT) and positively with RT variance. Other studies have demonstrated that aging-related decline in WM function is, in part, due to attenuated dopaminergic function (e.g., Bäckman et al., 2006, for a review).

Emerging Research Trends

Research on aging and intelligence has traditionally been investigated with the above three approaches. During the last decade, much effort has been devoted towards cross-level integrations of these approaches. For instance, recent neurocomputational approaches provide computational explications for linking aging-related decline in neuromodulation and cognitive deficits. Simulations show that declines in dopaminergic modulation could be related to reduced neural information processing fidelity, cortical representation distinctiveness, and various aspects of cognitive aging deficits. Other models relate deficits in dopamine modulation more specifically to aging effects on memory context representation and maintenance, and on error processing (see Li et al., 2001, for a review). Functional neuroimaging experiments in combination with individual difference approaches are also now more commonly applied to understanding the relations between cognitive and brain aging (Cabeza, Nyberg, & Park, 2005).

Furthermore, another new development is to consider the aging neurocognitive system as an embodied brain that is situated in the environmental and sociocultual context (see Baltes, Reuter-Lorenz, & Rösler, 2006, for a review). As such, within-person variability as indicators of the fidelity (e.g., Li et al., 2004) of information processing as well as cognitive intervention studies for tapping into the reserve of neurocognitive plasticity are the foci of vibrant areas of new research (Kramer & Erickson, 2007; Nyberg et al., 2003). Furthermore, studies that directly compare and contrast patterns of senescence and maturation to understand the shared and distinct mechanisms of cognitive aging and child cognitive development are also very much a part of the current research trends (e.g., Brehmer, S.-C. Li, Müller, von Oertzen, & Lindenberger, 2007; Bialystok & Craik, 2006; Figure 4).

In conclusion, psychometric studies conducted since the 1920s indicate that intellectual aging is not a unitary process. Culture-based intelligence is maintained into the 70s; whereas biology-based intellectual abilities begin declining in the 40s. There is growing interest in understanding cognitive and neurobiological mechanisms that may underlie age-related declines in *Gf* abilities. At the information-processing level, factors such as working memory, processing speed, and executive control processes, are correlated with age differences in intelligence. Furthermore, there is emerging consensus that the prefrontal cortex and its supporting neuromodulation mechanisms underlie such cognitive functions. At present, the cross-level link from brain aging to intellectual aging continues to be refined and expanded. Emerging research investigates reciprocal co-constructive dynamics between social-culturally based environmental interventions and neurobiological processes in order to harvest the

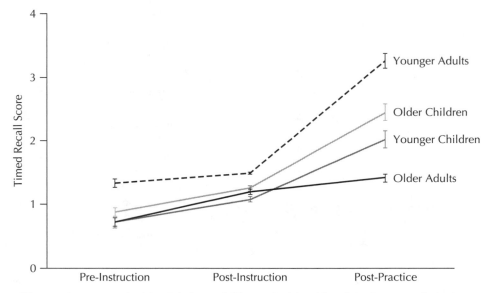

Figure 4. Lifespan age differences in memory plasticity. Relative to children and adults, older adults show more limited memory plasticity (adapted from Brehmer et al., 2007).

benefit of still available cognitive and brain plasticity in old age.

REFERENCES

Bäckman, L., Nyberg, L., Lindenberger, U., Li, S.-C., Farde, L. (2006). The correlative triad among aging, dopamine, and cognition: Current status and future prospects. *Neuroscience & Biobehavioral Reviews*, 30, 791–807.

Baltes, P. B., & Mayer, U. (1998). *The Berlin aging study*. Cambridge, UK: Cambridge University Press.

Baltes, P. B., Staudinger, U., & Lindenberger, U. (1999). Lifespan psychology: Theory and application to intellectual functioning. *Annual Review of Psychology*, 40, 471–507.

Bialystok, F., & Craik, F. I. M. (2006). (Eds.). *Lifespan cognition: Mechanisms of change*. New York: Oxford University Press.

Botvinick, M. M., Cohen, J. D., & Carter, C. S. (2004). Conflict monitoring and anterior cingulated cortex: An update. *Trends in Cognitive Sciences*, 8, 539–546.

Brehmer, Y., Li, S.-C., Müller, V., von Oertzn, T., & Lindenberger, U. (2007). Memory plasticity across the life span: Uncovering children's latent potential. *Developmental Psychology*, 43, 465–478.

Deary, I. J., et al. (2004). Searching for genetic influences on normal cognitive aging. *Trends in Cognitive Sciences*, 8, 178–184.

Kaasinen, V., et al. (2000). Age-related dopamine D2/D3 receptor loss in extrastriatal regions of human brain. *Neurobiology of Aging*, 21, 683–688.

Kramer, A. F., & Erickson, K. I. (2007). Capitalizing on cortical plasticity: Influence of physical activity on cognition and brain function. *Trends in Cognitive Sciences*, 11, 342–348.

Li, K. Z. H., & Lindenberger, U. (2002). Relation between aging sensory/sensorimotor and cognitive functions. *Neuroscience & Biobehavioral Reviews*, 26, 777–783.

Li, S.-C., Lindenberger, U., & Sikström, S. (2001). Aging cognition: From Neuromodulation to representation. *Trends in Cognitive Sciences*, 5, 479–486.

Li, S.-C., Lindenberger, U., Hommel, B., Aschersleben, G., Prinz, W., & Baltes, P. B. (2004). Transformations in the couplings among intellectual abilities and constituent cognitive processes across the lifespan. *Psychological Science*, 15, 155–163.

Lindenberger, U., & Baltes, P. B. (1994). Aging and intelligence. In R. J. Sternberg (Ed.), *Encyclopedia of human intelligence* (Vol. 1, pp. 52–66). New York: Macmillan.

Nyberg, L., Sandblom, J., Jones, S., Stigsdotter Neely, A., Petersson, K. M., Ingvar, M., et al. (2003). Neural correlates of training-related improvement in adulthood and aging. *Proceedings of National Academy of Sciences USA*, 100, 13728–13733.

Park, D. C., et al. (1996). Mediators of long-term memory performance across the lifespan. *Psychology and Aging*, 4, 621–637.

Raz, N., Lindenberger, U., Rodrigue, K. M., Kennedy, K. M., Head, D. Williamson, A., Dahle, C., Gerstorf, D., & Acker, J. D. (2005). Regional brain changes in aging healthy adults: General trends, individual differences, and modifiers. *Cerebral Cortex*, 15, 1676–1689.

Schaie, K. W. (1996). *Intellectual Development in Adulthood: The Seattle Longitudinal Study*. Cambridge, UK: Cambridge University Press.

Schaie, K. W., & Willis, S. L. (1993). Age differences in patterns of psychometric intelligence in adulthood: Generalizability within and across domains. *Psychology and Aging*, 8, 44–55.

SUGGESTED READINGS

Baltes, P. B., Reuter-Lorenz, P. A., & Rösler, F. (Eds.). (2006). *Lifespan development and the brain: The perspective of biocultural co-construction*. New York: Cambridge University Press.

Cabeza, R., Nyberg, L., & Park, D. (Eds.). (2005). *Cognitive neuroscience of aging: Linking cognitive and cerebral aging*. Oxford: Oxford University Press.

Craik, F. I. M., & Salthouse, T. A. (2007). *The handbook of aging and cognition* (3rd ed.). Mahwah, NJ: Lawrence Erlbaum.

SHU-CHEN LI
*Max Planck Institute for Human Development,
Berlin, Germany*

KAREN Z. H. LI
Concordia University, Montreal, Canada

See also: **Aging, Physiological and Behavioral Concomitants of; Geriatric Psychology; Intelligence**

AGING, PHYSIOLOGICAL AND BEHAVIORAL CONCOMITANTS OF

Aging is accompanied by many physiological changes, with behavioral and psychological concomitants. To illustrate, we describe selected age-related physiological changes in two sensory systems (vision and hearing) and in the cardiovascular and musculoskeletal systems, and we review the resulting effects of these changes on behavioral and psychological phenomena. Readers should note that many of these changes are not inevitable consequences of aging.

Hearing

Approximately one of every three adults between the ages of 65 and 75 has a hearing loss, and approximately 40–50% of adults aged 75 and older have a hearing loss (National Institute on Deafness and Other Communication Disorders, 2008). Aging leads to histological, electrophysiological, and molecular changes in the structures involved in hearing. Age-related hearing loss, presbycusis, occurs gradually and usually involves loss of hearing for the higher frequencies. Causes of presbycusis may include changes in the blood supply (e.g., diabetes, hypertension, cardiovascular disease), repeated exposure to loud noises, loss of hair cells, side effects of medications (e.g., aspirin, antibiotics), and abnormalities of the outer and/or middle ear (NIDCD, 2008).

There are several potential consequences of presbycusis. First, older adults may experience difficulty hearing high-frequency sounds (e.g., children's and women's voices, squeaking brakes). Second, older adults may have difficulty hearing speech embedded in background noise (e.g., in conversations in loud environments). Third, older adults may have more difficulty recognizing consonant sounds of shorter durations at lower decibel levels. Therefore, when conversing, older adults may ask speakers to talk louder.

Similarly, older adults may increase the volume on radios or television sets. Fourth, older adults may experience more difficulty hearing rapidly presented speech with a low degree of context. Therefore, whenever novel information is orally presented rapidly (e.g., messages over public announcement systems), older adults may miss important details. Fifth, older adults may experience difficulty hearing and understanding speech that lacks normal fluctuations in tone and rhythm (e.g., hearing unwavering speech or undifferentiated computer-generated speech).

The behavioral and psychological consequences of hearing impairment can be significant. Individuals may participate in fewer leisure activities and become more socially isolated. They may become irritated with their hearing impairment and the speech characteristics that interfere with auditory perception. Individuals may experience depression, or paranoia. The paranoia may arise from individuals believing that others are speaking about them, perceiving others as "mumbling" or speaking softly to purposefully exclude the older listener.

Vision

Several age-related changes occur in the visual system that can have psychological and behavioral consequences. First, older adults require more light to see because of the increased density and opacity of their lenses, and the decreased number of photo receptors (Whitbourne, 2002). Second, older adults are more likely to experience glare when viewing bright objects, due to the scattering of light within the lens resulting from the increased density. Third, older adults are more likely to experience difficulty with accommodation due to the increased lens density and loss in flexibility of the eye capsule. Fourth, depth perception decreases with age, caused by the increased density of the lens. Fifth, age-related problems with color discrimination are caused by the increased yellowing of the lens and pigmentation of the vitreous humor. Finally, an age-related decrease in the visual field can be caused by macular degeneration. Age-related macular degeneration is the most common cause of blindness and vision impairment in older adults in the United States, with over 1.6 million having advanced macular degeneration (National Eye Institute, 2002).

The behavioral consequences of impaired vision can be quite significant. The increased difficulty in seeing objects in reduced light and greater susceptibility to glare can lead individuals to increasingly restrict their evening driving and walking. These vision changes can also lead to increased accidents and falls resulting from failure to see hazardous objects, and diminished self-esteem resulting from such accidents and restrictions incurred from low vision. Changes in color perception can create difficulties in correctly matching clothing and facial makeup, and sometimes cause others to question the individual's aesthetic sensibilities (Whitbourne, 2002). These changes also can diminish one's understanding of color-coded information and diminish one's appreciation of artwork, movies, and scenery. The diminished visual acuity can lead to difficulty reading, watching television, recognizing friends, and learning and remembering the distinctive features of the faces of new acquaintances. Finally, the embarrassment associated with these problems can lead to increased social isolation and decreased social activities.

Cardiovascular and Respiratory System

Age-related changes in the cardiovascular and respiratory systems can have significant behavioral and psychological consequences. However, not all older adults experience the same levels of decline of these systems. Exercise, disease, and genetic predisposition are important, in addition to the effects of aging, in the determination of cardiorespiratory fitness.

Aging is associated with reduced elasticity and compliance of the aorta and arteries, resulting in higher systolic arterial pressure, increased resistance to left ventricular ejection, and subsequent left ventricular hypertrophy and interstitial fibrosis (Mangoni & Jackson, 2004). The left ventricle takes longer to fill and relax. Heart rate decreases with age, and heart rate response is reduced during exercise. The sensitivity of the heart to neural stimulation, which controls the timing and rate of heart contractions, decreases with age. Aging results in structural changes of the lungs (e.g., decreased elastic recoil and increased rigidity of chest wall) that limit lung capacity and the efficiency of the gas exchange.

The consequences of cardiovascular and respiratory changes may include a decreased ability to cope with physical stress. The older adult may become more easily fatigued and experience shortness of breath more quickly compared to younger adults. Consequently, the older adult may become fearful of activities associated with physical exertion. Likewise, older adults may demonstrate frustration with the limitations associated with cardiovascular and respiratory changes and become more fearful of activities that cause physical exertion, and therefore pursue activities that are more sedentary. All of these limitations can also lead to lowered self-esteem.

Musculoskeletal System

Age-related musculoskeletal changes have important implications for the daily lives of older adults. Muscle mass decreases with age and can lead to increased weakness. Muscle endurance also diminishes with age. Bone mass and porosity decreases, increasing susceptibility to fractures. The joint cartilage also degenerates with age, resulting in increased joint pain and stiffening. Musculoskeletal changes can be reduced (e.g., increased muscle strength and endurance) in both younger and older adults via exercise.

Age-related musculoskeletal changes may result in older adults restricting movements and being less willing to undertake physically demanding tasks. Older adults may become more easily fatigued and more cautious in their movements, particularly on slippery surfaces. They may experience difficulty climbing stairs or rising from a sitting position. Fear of falling may develop because of leg weakness or fear of breaking bones when ambulating. These musculoskeletal changes may restrict participation in enjoyable and leisure activities and diminish self-esteem. The chronic pain sometimes associated with musculoskeletal changes can also lead to depression.

In summary, numerous changes occur in the aging body that can have substantial behavioral and psychological effects. Fortunately, the human body exhibits amazing resilience, accommodation, and adaptation to the aging process.

REFERENCES

Mangoni, A. A., & Jackson, S. H. D. (2004). Age-related changes in pharmacokinetics and pharmacodynamics: Basic principles and practical applications. *British Journal of Clinical Pharmacology, 57,* 6–14.

National Institute on Deafness and Other Communication Disorders. (2008). Retrieved February 28, 2008, from http://www.nidcd.nih.gov/health/hearing/presbycusis.asp.

National Eye Institute. (2002). Retrieved February 28, 2008, from http://www.nei.nih.gov/news/pressreleases/032002.asp.

Whitbourne, S. K. (2002). *The aging individual: Physical and psychological perspectives* (2nd ed.). New York: Springer.

BARRY A. EDELSTEIN
West Virginia University

JEFFREY L. GOODIE
Uniformed Service University of the Health Sciences

RONALD R. MARTIN
University of Regina, Canada

See also: **Aging and Intelligence; Geropsychology; Late-Life Forgetting**

AGORAPHOBIA

Although the Greek word agoraphobia means fear of large open spaces, our current conceptualization of agoraphobia is far more situationally encompassing. The term was introduced by Westphal in 1871 in a case series of four men who presented with fears of large open spaces (Boyd & Crump, 1991). In the fourth edition of the American

Table 1. Common Situations that are Feared in Agoraphobia

Being home alone
Crowded places
Grocery stores, shops, large stores, and shopping malls
Traveling on buses, airplanes or trains
Driving in heavy traffic, on highways, through tunnels, or over
  bridges
Waiting in line
Movie theaters and arenas
Restaurants
Talking walks
Wide open spaces such as parks
Enclosed places such as elevators or small rooms
Public places
Traveling away from home

Psychiatric Association's (APA) *Diagnostic and Statistical Manual of Mental Disorders* (APA, 2000) agoraphobia is defined as anxiety about, or avoidance of, situations where help may not be available or where it may be difficult or embarrassing to escape the situation in the event of panic-like symptoms or a full-blown panic attack. Patterns of agoraphobic avoidance are variable with levels of avoidance ranging from just a few situations to an extensive range of situations. Commonly feared situations are listed in Table 1.

Individuals with moderate to severe agoraphobia often report having a "safe zone" or specific geographic area within which they feel comfortable. Traveling outside of this safe zone is either completely avoided, particularly if unaccompanied, or else endured with significant distress. In the most severe cases, the individual is housebound. Individuals with agoraphobia also vary in their reliance on safety cues, which are used to reduce anxiety in a specific situation. Examples of safety cues may include the presence of a familiar person, carrying a cell phone, medication or water bottle, and sitting in a seat that is close to a door or exit.

Descriptive Characteristics of Agoraphobia

Agoraphobia is not a specific disorder in its own right but occurs within the context of either panic disorder with agoraphobia or agoraphobia without history of panic disorder. The lifetime prevalence rates of these two disorders is 1.1% and 0.8%, respectively (Kessler et al., 2006). The presence of agoraphobia is more common in women than men and has been associated with increased role impairment, greater panic disorder symptom severity, and increased comorbidity with other Axis I disorders compared to panic disorder without agoraphobia (Kessler et al., 2006).

Treatment of Agoraphobia

Evidenced-based treatments for agoraphobia include both cognitive behavior therapy (CBT) and pharmacotherapy, based on randomized controlled trials conducted in individuals with panic disorder with agoraphobia. Effective medication treatments include selective serotonin reuptake inhibitors (SSRIs), tricyclic antidepressants, other antidepressants (e.g., venlafaxine), and high-potency benzodiazepines. CBT approaches target agoraphobic avoidance through the use of gradual, systematic exposure to feared situations (*in vivo* exposure), exposure to feared physical sensations such as shortness of breath, palpitations, dizziness, and feelings of unreality (interoceptive exposure), and cognitive restructuring of catastrophic beliefs regarding feared physical sensations and feared situations.

REFERENCES

American Psychiatric Association. (2000). *Diagnostic and statistical manual of mental disorders*, 4th ed., text revision. Washington, DC: Author.

Boyd, J. H., & Crump, T. (1991). Westphal's agoraphobia. *Journal of Anxiety Disorders, 5*, 77–86.

Kessler, R. C., Chiu, W. T., Jin, R., Ruscio, A. M., Shear, K., & Walters, E. E. (2006). The epidemiology of panic attacks, panic disorder, and agoraphobia in the National Comorbidity Survey Replication. *Archives of General Psychiatry, 63*, 415–424.

SUGGESTED READINGS

Hazlett-Stevens, H. (2006). Agoraphobia. In J. E. Fisher and W. T. O'Donohue (Eds.), *Practitioner's guide to evidence-based psychotherapy* (pp. 24–34). New York, NY: Springer Science and Business Media.

Kessler, R. C., Chiu, W. T., Jin, R., Ruscio, A. M., Shear, K., & Walters, E. E. (2006). The epidemiology of panic attacks, panic disorder, and agoraphobia in the National Comorbidity Survey Replication. *Archives of General Psychiatry, 63*, 415–424.

McCabe, R. E., & Antony, M. M. (2005). Panic disorder and agoraphobia. In M. M. Antony, D. Roth Ledley, and R. G. Heimberg (Eds.), *Improving outcomes and preventing relapse in cognitive-behavioral therapy* (pp. 1–37). New York, NY: Guilford Press.

RANDI E. MCCABE
McMaster University, Hamilton, ON

AINSWORTH, MARY D. SALTER (1913–1999)

Mary Ainsworth received a B.A., M.A., and Ph.D. (1939) from the University of Toronto. She was appointed Assistant Professor at University of Toronto (1946), Professor at Johns Hopkins University (1963), Commonwealth Professor at University of Virginia (1975), and was an Emeritus Professor after 1984. Ainsworth devoted a lifetime of research to the study of infant-mother relationships. She introduced a 20-minute, controlled laboratory technique called the "strange situation," which provides a widely used measure of child-mother attachment.

At London's Tavistock Clinic, under John Bowlby's direction, she investigated the effects on personality of infant-mother separation (1950). This was the beginning of a 40-year productive scholarly association with Bowlby. They established a new field of scientific study by means of Bowlby's ethological theories of attachment, separation, and loss as well as Ainsworth's empirical longitudinal studies from home visits using the strange situation technique.

Ainsworth wrote numerous scientific articles and books. She also extended her research into attachment beyond infancy by examining other affectional bonds throughout the life cycle. Ainsworth was cited as one of the outstanding "Models of achievement . . . of eminent women in psychology" (O'Connell & Russo, 1983) and received the American Psychological Association award for Distinguished Scientific Contribution (1989) and its award for Distinguished Professional Contributions to Knowledge (1987), and she was elected a fellow of the American Academy of Arts and Sciences (1992).

REFERENCES

Ainsworth, M. D. S., & Bowlby, J. (1965). *Child care and the growth of love*. London: Penguin Books.

Ainsworth, M. D. S. (1978). *Patterns of attachment: A psychological study of the strange situation*. Hillsdale, NJ: Lawrence Erlbaum.

SHELDON S. BROWN
*North Shore Community College,
Danvers, MA*

AKATHISIA

The term *akathisia* (literally "not to sit") was introduced by the Bohemian neuropsychiatrist Lad Haskovec in 1901 (Haskovec, 1901). Akathisia represents a complex psychomotor syndrome, comprising a subjective (emotional) and an objective (motor) component (Sachdev, 1995; Iqbal, Lambert, & Masand, 2007). The subjective symptoms of akathisia include inner restlessness, urge to move (tasikinesia), inability to remain still, general unease, discomfort, inability to relax, poor concentration, dysphoria, anxiety, fear, terror, rage, suicidal ideation, and aggressive thoughts.

The objective signs of akathisia include several in the sitting position and several in the standing position. In the sitting position, these are fidgetiness of arms and hands;

face rubbing; rubbing, caressing, or shaking of arms or hands; rubbing or massaging of legs; tapping or picking on clothes; crossing and uncrossing of arms; crossing and uncrossing of legs; swinging or kicking crossed legs; toe tapping; frequently squirming in chair and straightening motions; and rocking or twisting of the body. In the standing position, these are marching in place; changing stance; flexing and extending knees; rocking from foot to foot; and pacing and repetitive walking.

Subjectively distressing inner restlessness and repetitive movements of the legs are the most frequently observed signs and symptoms. These signs and symptoms predominantly emerge when the patient is requested to sit or stand still in one spot, with there being some relief when lying down or walking around. As none of the signs and symptoms is pathognomonic for akathisia, it can be extremely difficult to distinguish akathisia from other causes of restlessness as well as from other movement disorders (Sachdev 1995; Weiden, 2007). Other possible causes of restlessness include psychotic agitation, anxiety, agitation due to affective disorder, drug withdrawal syndromes, antipsychotic-induced dysphoric mood, and agitation due to organic disorders (e.g., dementia, hypoglycemia). Other movement disorders from which akathisia may be difficult to distinguish include restless-legs syndrome, tardive dyskinesia, steriotypies, tremor, myoclonus, and restless repetitive movements due to organic disorder (e.g., pacing in dementia, hyperactivity in Tourette's syndrome or ADHD).

Prevalence of Akathisia and Clinical Relevance

Even though akathisia was first mentioned in postencephalitic parkinsonism and in idiopathic Parkinson's disease long before antipsychotic drugs became available, akathisia is nowadays mostly associated with the administration of antipsychotic drugs (Iqbal et al., 2007). The first generation of antipsychotic substances (FGA) are much more likely to produce akathisia compared to second-generation antipsychotics (SGA), due to the higher affinity of the former to block dopamine D2 receptors (Van Putten, May, & Marder, 1984; Iqbal et al., 2007).

However, this does not mean that SGA are free of producing extrapyramidal side effects, including akathisia. Depending on their affinity to pre- and postsynaptic dopamine receptors, the SGAs may well cause akathisia in clinically relevant numbers (Pierre, 2005; Weiden, 2007). Many clinicians also tend to disregard the fact that antiemetic drugs can produce akathisia dose-dependently, which may be of considerable importance for the treatment of cancer patients (Kawanishi et al., 2007). Moreover, agents targeting serotonin receptors are also suspected of causing an akathisia-like syndrome (Sachdev, 1995).In psychiatric populations akathisia is of specific clinical relevance because it may complicate the treatment by aggravating noncompliance or impulsivity, which can

Table 1. Subtypes of Drug-Induced Akathisia (Modified after Sachdev, 1995)

Acute akathisia: Onset within six weeks after initiation of treatment, dose increment, or change of drug-type; concurrent medication not decreased or discontinued.

Chronic akathisia: Symptoms persist for over three months; specify acute, tardive, or withdrawal onset.

Tardive akathisia: Onset at least three months after initiation of treatment, dose increment, or change of drug-type; no dose increment or change of drug within six weeks prior to onset; concurrent medication not decreased or discontinued.

Withdrawal akathisia: Onset within six weeks after discontinuing or marked reduction of dose; prior to onset, duration of treatment at least three months; concurrent medication not decreased or discontinued.

Pseudoakathisia: Typical objective symptoms without subjective distress.

---

include assaultive or suicidal behaviors (Van Putten, 1975). Moreover, akathisia is sometimes mistaken as psychotic agitation or can be overlooked, particularly because the focus of undesirable effects of antipsychotic treatment has shifted to metabolic problems and weight gain associated with the administration of SGA (Weiden, 2007).

Akathisia generally has an acute beginning within hours or days after initiation of antipsychotic treatment. High initial dosages and rapid dose increment are predisposing factors to produce acute akathisia (Iqbal et al., 2007). Other subtypes of akathisia have been described according to the time of onset during antipsychotic treatment with more ambiguous risk factors (see Table 1).

When taking a chronic course, subjective distress may decrease, and the movement patterns may look more like stereotypies, suggesting an overlap with tardive dyskinesia (Sachdev, 1995).

Pathophysiological Mechanisms and Clinical Management of Akathisia

The pathophysiology of akathisia is not entirely understood. Akathisia may best be viewed as resulting from the interaction of dopaminergic neurones with noradrenergic, serotonergic, cholinergic, GABAergic, glutamatergic, and opioid systems in mesolimbic and mesocortical pathways, where dopamine antagonism is assumed to play the most important role in producing the syndrome (Sachdev, 1995; Iqbal et al., 2007).

One of the most relevant problems in clinical practice is that clinicians may fail to recognize akathisia (Weiden, 2007). Establishing an early diagnosis is critical, however, due not only to the possible complications associated with akathisia but also to the impending dilemma of insufficient or delayed treatment response. Thus, preventive measures such as choosing the lowest effective dose of antipsychotics, and stepwise increment of dose are

warranted (Sachdev, 1995). Moreover, a routine clinical check for extrapyramidal side effects is recommended for which several clinically useful rating scales have become available (details in Sachdev, 1995).

If akathisia is present, stopping the offending drug or at least reducing the dose is considered to be the best option (Sachdev, 1995; Iqbal et al., 2007). However, in highly agitated patients, waiting for a spontaneous wearing-off may be impracticable. Anticholinergic drugs, beta-adrenergic drugs, and benzodiazepines are effective for acute treatment, yet response rates are variable. If onset of akathisia is less acute, change of antipsychotic class or administration of modern agents is proposed. Treating chronic or tardive akathisia has often been problematic (Sachdev, 1995), but is now rarely seen in patients on SGA.

REFERENCES

Haskovec, L. (1901). L'akathisie. *Revue Neurologique, 9,* 1107–1109.

Iqbal, N., Lambert, T., & Masand, P. (2007). Akathisia: Problem of history or concern today. *CNS Spectrum, 12,* 1–13.

Kawanishi, C., Onishi, H., Kato, D., Kishida, I., Furuno, T., Wada, M., & Hirayasu, Y. (2007). Unexpectedly high prevalence of akathisia in cancer patients. *Palliative Support and Care, 5,* 351–354.

Pierre, J. M. (2006). Extrapyramidal symptoms with atypical antipsychotics. *Drug Safety, 28,* 191–208.

Sachdev, P. (1995). *Akathisia and restless legs.* New York: Cambridge University Press.

Van Putten, T. (1975). The many faces of akathisia. *Comprehensive Psychiatry, 16,* 43–47.

Van Putten, T., May, P. R. A., & Marder, S. R. (1984). Akathisia with haloperidol and thiothixene. *Archives of General Psychiatry, 41,* 1036–1039.

Weiden, P. J. (2007). EPS profiles: The atypical antipsychotics are not all the same. *Journal of Psychiatric Practice, 13,* 13–24.

MARTIN BRÜNE
University of Bochum, Bochum, Germany

See also: Motor Control

ALCOHOL USE DISORDERS

Within the *Diagnostic and Statistical Manual of Mental Disorders* (DSM-IV-TR; American Psychiatric Association, 2000), alcohol use disorders (AUDs) can be subdivided into two major diagnoses: alcohol abuse and alcohol dependence. *Alcohol abuse* refers to a pathological pattern of drinking marked by one or more of four domains of problems—specifically recurrent using of alcohol in physically hazardous situations, legal problems, problems in fulfilling role obligations, and interpersonal problems. *Alcohol dependence* refers to a presumed more severe condition marked by three or more of seven criteria—tolerance, withdrawal, impaired control of drinking, inability to cut down or abstain, a great deal of time spent drinking or recovering from alcohol's effects, important activities given up because of drinking, and drinking despite knowledge that it is having adverse effects on one's mental and/or physical health.

Although the abuse/dependence distinction has its roots in earlier taxonomies that distinguish the alcohol dependence syndrome from alcohol-related consequences, it has been coming under increasing criticism on several grounds. Statistically, for example, abuse symptoms such as legal problems are very rare and thus psychometrically "severe," whereas some dependence symptoms such as tolerance are common and psychometrically "mild." Individuals with just one or two dependence symptoms are diagnostic "orphans" who do not qualify for an AUD diagnosis. In addition, a challenge has been raised to the categorical approach to diagnosis as opposed to a dimensional approach (Martin, Chung, & Langenbucher, 2008). Despite these problems, however, alcohol abuse and alcohol dependence continue to be the major diagnostic categories for classifying alcohol-related mental disorders.

Epidemiology

AUDs are among the most prevalent mental disorders in the general population of the United States, with nationally representative samples of the adult population showing that 8.5% of adults meet criteria for having had an AUD in the past 12 months (4.7% for abuse, 3.8% for dependence) and 30.3% over their lifetime (17.8% for abuse, 12.5% for dependence; Hasin, Stinson, Ogburn, & Grant, 2007). These overall statistics obscure the fact that the distribution of these disorders varies widely in demographically defined subpopulations. Specifically, men meet criteria for AUDs much more frequently than women in the United States and most other countries. Moreover, the prevalence varies dramatically over the life course, with the peak risk for onset for the disorder occurring in the late teen years and the peak 12-month prevalence occurring at about age 21. Of note, however, the average age for entrance into treatment and the average age of patients in treatment are approximately 10 to 15 years later in life (Weisner, Matzger, Tam, & Schmidt, 2002).

Comorbidity

AUDs frequently co-occur with other mental disorders including anxiety disorders, mood disorders, psychotic disorders, other substance use disorders (i.e., drug use disorder and tobacco dependence), and personality disorders (especially antisocial personality disorder and borderline personality disorder) (Kessler, Chiu, Demler, & Walters, 2005; Sher et al., 1999). Depending on the nature of the co-occurring disorder, the AUD might have an onset prior to, at approximately the same time as, or subsequent to the other disorder. The temporal ordering of the onsets of AUDs and co-occurring disorders have sometimes led experts to distinguish between primary AUDs (those having an onset prior to the co-occurring condition) or secondary AUDs (those having an onset subsequent to the co-occurring condition).

However, in practice it is often difficult to stage sequence onsets. Moreover, even when onsets can be confidently ordered, it is usually difficult to determine whether the so-called primary condition has caused the secondary condition, whether some third factor (e.g., personality traits such as neuroticism) have contributed to the onset of both disorders, or whether these two disorders are co-occurring by chance (since both AUDs and many of its frequent comorbidities are relatively common). This is not to say that there are no clear-cut examples of alcohol dependence being secondary to another disorder. It is a reasonable supposition to say that, when an AUD only occurs during the context of a manic episode in a person with bipolar disorder (and a "normal" drinker at other times), that the AUD is secondary to the bipolar disorder. It is also the case that extended periods of alcohol consumption can induce short-term mental disorders, called alcohol-induced disorders (e.g., a mood or anxiety disorder; Schuckit, 2006) that will remit after a period of abstinence. Thus, in assessing an individual with both an AUD and a co-occurring mental disorder, it is important to determine whether the co-occurring condition only occurs during periods of heavy drinking and its immediate aftermath.

Etiological Factors

Systematic research over the past 50 years has documented a number of factors that contribute to the development of AUDs. Although these factors are conceptually distinct, it is important to highlight that they may overlap and involve related processes.

Genetics

In the 1970s and 1980s, twin and adoption studies clearly documented that a substantial amount of the risk for AUDs can be attributed to genetic factors. More recently, molecular genetic studies have begun identifying specific genes associated with risk for AUDs (Dick & Foroud, 2003). One class of genes that have been identified is related to individual differences in how a drinker metabolizes alcohol. There are two major metabolizing enzymes: (1) alcohol dehydrogenase (ADH), which breaks down alcohol into acetaldehyde, and (2) aldehyde dehydrogenase (ALDH), which breaks down alcohol into acetate and water. The immediate metabolite of alcohol, acetaldehyde, is toxic and causes flushing (turning the skin red) and feelings of discomfort. Because acetaldehyde is rapidly metabolized by ALDH, it usually does not build up in the body. Consequently, most people do not experience this aversive reaction. However, in Asian populations, there is considerable variation in the genes that code for both ADH and ALDH. One of these variants of ADH is associated with rapid metabolism of alcohol into acetaldehyde, and one of these variants is associated with slow metabolism of acetaldehyde (and therefore flushing and discomfort). Individuals with these variants of ADH and ALDH genes are much less likely to drink and develop an AUD (Luczak, Glatt, & Wall, 2006).

However, most of the genetic influence in North Americans of European descent appears attributable to other and, at present, largely unknown genetic factors. Several genes have now been identified in multiple studies that are associated with the major neurotransmitter systems in the brain, such as GABA, dopamine, and serotonin. The large-scale genome-wide association studies now being conducted in populations worldwide will provide a clearer view of the specific nature of genetic influence.

Personality

Although there clearly is no single "alcoholic personality," a number of prospective studies have demonstrated that major personality traits such as neuroticism (i.e., negative emotionality), impulsivity, and sensation-seeking are associated with risk for alcoholism. Moreover, a number of studies have documented the intervening processes between broad-based dispositional tendencies and drinking outcomes. Specifically, different personality traits appear to be associated with risk for AUDs for different reasons.

For example, individuals with high levels of neuroticism tend to drink to cope with negative emotions; individuals with sensation-seeking tendencies who are also high in impulsivity tend to drink to "enhance" their current state (e.g., "get buzzed"). While both the coping and enhancement pathways can lead to AUDs, they appear to do so in somewhat different ways. For the enhancement pathway, risk for AUDs (or related problems) appears to be completely explained by their higher levels of consumption. For the coping pathway, the amount of alcohol consumed does not appear to fully explain the increased risk, which suggests that, when individuals drink to cope, they are doing it in ways that tend to magnify risk behind pure drinking levels, perhaps by drinking at inappropriate times or in hazardous situations (Sher et al., 1999).

Social Influence Processes

Most individuals begin drinking in adolescence, and the strongest correlate of drinking in this age group is the level of peer-group drinking. Peer drinking norms appear to be a potent risk factor and to have a causal influence in socializing individuals into drinking. However, as individuals progress through adolescence and into adulthood, the selection of specific peer groups and social settings appears to become increasingly important. Thus, with respect to drinking, social influence works both ways: Individuals are influenced by their peer group but are also active selectors and creators of their peer groups, not just passive recipients of peer influence (Borsari & Carey, 2001).

The Macro Environment

In the United States, indeed throughout the world, there is considerable variation in the rates of drinking and AUDs. Although genetic factors may play some role in this (e.g., the previously mentioned genotypic variation in ALDH genes in Asians), without question the larger influence comes from cultural and religious factors surrounding how alcohol use and drunken comportment are viewed and the policies that governmental entities put into place to control the sale and distribution of alcoholic beverages and alcohol-related behavior. There is now little doubt that controlling the price and distribution of alcohol affects consumption levels and rates of AUDs. Thus, although national prohibition in the United States from 1919 to 1933 is widely regarded as a social failure, it was not a failure from the standpoint of reducing alcohol consumption and alcohol-related diseases (Dills & Miron, 2004). Consequently, when we consider etiological risk factors at the individual (e.g., genetics, personality) level or the near-environment (e.g., peer group) level, it needs to be in the context of the larger, sociocultural policy environment in which these are embedded.

Treatment

A variety of treatments for AUDs currently exist. These treatments range from brief interventions by physicians or other health providers intended to motivate behavior change to outpatient treatment (either weekly or intensive) using a range of cognitive behavioral techniques, marital and family therapy approaches, and group treatment approaches (both professionally led and consisting of self-help groups like Alcoholics Anonymous), and they also include day hospital and inpatient residential treatments that typically involve a variety of approaches. Although treatment generally has been believed to be moderately effective, there is no clear evidence for the superiority of one treatment approach over another and little evidence that certain patients are particularly likely to benefit more from one treatment than another. Additionally, alcohol dependence is often a chronic, relapsing disorder, and many individuals who recover from alcohol dependence relapse after a period of abstinence.

There is an increasing number of medications that are being used to treat AUDs. Disulfiram has been approved for more than 50 years by the FDA and acts by blocking ALDH (the effects of which were noted previously) and leading to an aversive reaction when alcohol is consumed. Although it has not been found to be effective by itself, it is often used as part of multicomponent interventions (e.g., behavioral contracting). Two additional drugs, naltrexone (which blocks opiate receptors in the brain) and acamprosate (which acts on glutamate receptors in the brain) have been FDA approved in the past 15 years, and other drugs (e.g., topiramate) have been empirically supported to have salutary effects on alcohol dependence. A number of existing medications and novel drugs are being evaluated to expand the range of drug treatment options for AUDs (Berglund et al., 2003).

REFERENCES

American Psychiatric Association (2000). *Diagnostic and statistical manual of mental disorders* (4th ed., text rev.). Washington, DC: Author.

Berglund, M., Thelender, S., Salaspuro, M., Franck, J., Andreasson, S., & Ojehagen, A. (2003). Treatment of alcohol abuse: An evidence-based review. *Alcoholism: Clinical and Experimental Research, 27,* 1645–1656.

Borsari, B., & Carey, K. B. (2001). Peer influences on college drinking: A review of the research. *Journal of Substance Abuse, 13,* 391–424.

Dick, D. M., & Foroud, T. (2003). Candidate genes for alcohol dependence: A review of genetic evidence from human studies. *Alcoholism: Clinical and Experimental Research, 27,* 868–879.

Dills, A. K., & Miron, J. A. (2004). Alcohol prohibition and cirrhosis. *American Law and Economics Review, 6,* 285–318.

Hasin, D. S., Stinson, F. S., Ogburn, E., & Grant, B. F. (2007). Prevalence, correlates, disability, and co-morbidity of DSM-IV alcohol abuse and dependence in the United States. *Archives of General Psychiatry, 64,* 830–842.

Kessler, R. C., Chiu, W. T., Demler, O., & Walters, E. E. (2005). Prevalence, severity, and comorbidity in the National Comorbidity Survey Replication. *Archives of General Psychiatry, 62,* 617–627.

Luczak, S. E., Glatt, S. J., & Wall, T. L. (2006). Meta-analysis of ALDH2 and ADH1B with alcohol dependence in Asians. *Psychological Bulletin, 132,* 607–621.

Martin, C. S., Chung, T., & Langenbucher, J. W. (2008). How should we revise diagnostic criteria for substance use disorders in the DSM-V? *Journal of Abnormal Psychology, 117,* 561–575.

Schuckit, M. A. (2006). Co-morbidity between substance use disorders and psychiatric conditions. *Addiction, 101*(Suppl. 1), 76–88.

Sher, K. J., Trull, T. J., Bartholow, B., & Vieth, A. (1999). Personality and alcoholism: Issues, methods, and etiological processes. In H. Blane and K. Leonard (Eds.), *Psychological theories of drinking and alcoholism* (2nd ed., pp. 55–105. New York: Guilford Press.

Weisner, C., Matzger, H., Tam, T., & Schmidt, L. (2002). Who goes to alcohol and drug treatment? Understanding utilization within the context of insurance. *Journal of Studies on Alcohol, 63,* 673–682.

SUGGESTED READINGS

Erickson, C. K. (2007). *The science of addiction: From neurobiology to treatment.* New York: W.W. Norton.

Leonard, K. E., & Blane, H. T. (Eds.). (1999). *Psychological theories of drinking and alcoholism* (2nd ed.). New York: Guilford Press.

Sher, K. J., Grekin, E., & Williams, N. (2005). The development of alcohol problems. *Annual Review of Clinical Psychology, 1,* 493–523.

KENNETH J. SHER
University of Missouri

See also: Addiction; Antabuse and Other Drugs for Treating Alcoholism

ALEXIA/DYSLEXIA

In an increasingly literate world, the inability to read is a significant disability that may affect academic success, employment, and self-concept. Because widespread literacy is a relatively recent historical development, it should not be surprising that it was only about 100 years ago that the first case of alexia or "word blindness" was described. By definition, the term *alexia* describes a condition in which reading ability is lost as a result of some neurological insult, such as head injury or stroke. With alexia, it is assumed that the individual had adequate reading achievement prior to the neurological insult, and therefore, the disability is not developmental in nature.

The term *dyslexia* refers to an inborn or congenital inability to learn to read. The term rose out of the medical literature and is not completely accepted by many educators who work with children with reading problems. Many educators or psychologists prefer the terms *developmental reading disorder* or *reading disability*, because these terms avoid the implication that the etiology of the reading disorder is due to neurological deficits. Consequently, the term *dyslexia* is most appropriate when it describes a severe reading disorder presumed to be neurological in origin. Although prevalence estimates vary across studies, the incidence of dyslexia has been estimated at approximately 7% of the school-aged population (Shaywitz, Morris, & Shaywitz, 2008).

There is significant and ongoing controversy in the research and clinical communities about the definition of dyslexia. There are two competing definitions. One definition is based on significant discrepancy between reading achievement and a measure of general cognitive ability or intellectual functioning. The second is a cut-score model, wherein any individual with reading achievement scores below a minimum criterion is diagnosed with dyslexia. Related to the latter model is the response-to-treatment (RTI) movement, wherein children are made eligible for special education services under the label of learning disabilities based on the outcome of highly focused intervention. This definition of reading disability has become widely accepted and is the basis for the provision of special education services to many children in the United States.

The biological bases of dyslexia have gained significant research attention since the early 1990s. Many researchers have targeted the left hemisphere's perisylvian region, or the area surrounding the Sylvan fissure on the lateral surface of the cortex (Phinney, Pennington, Olson, Filley, & Filipek, 2007). Symmetry or rightward asymmetry in the length or volume of the planum temporale has been associated with dyslexia. Subtle differences in perisylvian morphology have also been noted in some individuals with dyslexia. Recent studies using diffusion tensor imaging have documented disturbances in the white matter tracts in the perisylvian region. Many of the studies of the biological basis of dyslexia were founded on early work by Geschwind and Galaburda documenting polymicrogyri and heterotopias in this region in postmortem studies of individuals known to have dyslexia.

Although significant research attention has been focused on the biological bases of dyslexia, it is not entirely clear why brains with perisylvian atypicalities are more likely to be found in individuals with dyslexia. The symmetry or reduced asymmetry noted in these brains may result from neuronal migrations errors or poor pruning of redundant pathways. Because the individual has fewer functionally connected cells, those that are functional may be less able to compensate for these atypicalities.

Although research findings have largely focused on the perisylvian region, there have been a limited number of studies that have documented neurological abnormalities in other areas of the brain (Peterson, McGrath, Smith, & Pennington, 2007). For example, there are studies showing reduced leftward asymmetry of the inferior frontal gyrus, with abnormal activation patterns in this same area, associated with dyslexia. Other studies have shown atypicalities in structure and/or function in the cerebellum and the corpus callosum.

Reading is a complex cognitive task that combines numerous skills, including attention, memory, phonological processing, and rapid naming. Consequently, any findings related to individual chromosomal involvement in the development of dyslexia might actually pertain to language tasks in general. Despite this caveat, research has implicated a number of quantitative trait loci (QTLs)

and candidate genes involved in dyslexia (Peterson et al., 2007). Frequently cited studies suggest the involvement of the following QTLs: 1p34-p36, 2p11-16, 3p12-q13, 6p21.3-22, 15q15-21, 18p11, and Xq27.3. Candidate gene research has been somewhat more equivocal, but several possible genes have been implicated, including DYX1C1, DCDC2, K1AA0319, and ROBO1.

Although there is significant evidence to support genetic involvement in dyslexia, environmental factors also play a role. Behavioral genetics research has suggested that slightly more than 50% of the variance in reading performance is the result of the differences in genetic heritability. Thus, environmental factors clearly have a role in dyslexia. Factors identified as contributing to reading difficulties include reading exposure, socioeconomic status, parental education, and home literacy environment (Harlaar, Dale, & Plomin, 2007).

Although research supports the involvement of genetics and differences in the brain as being risk factors for the dyslexia, these studies do not answer questions about the underlying cognitive processes that are involved in reading and that are aberrant in dyslexia. Research on dyslexia suggests that phonological processing and orthographic coding are two cognitive processes that play significant roles in reading ability and dyslexia (Boets, Wouters, van Wieringen, De Smedt, & Ghesquiere, in press). Furthermore, these processes interact with each other and other cognitive processes to promote reading acquisition.

Phonological processing allows an individual to hear and manipulate individual sounds in spoken language. Although there are only 26 letters in the English language, there are 44 phonemes. Phonological processing is part of the larger skill of auditory perception and discrimination, but it is involved only with sounds used in speech. Rather than being one unitary skill demonstrable in a single behavior, phonological processing is actually a group of skills, including letter-sound association, rhyming, blending, segmenting, and sound replacement. Phonological processing skills are developing in children before they enter school, and these early skills appear to predict future reading achievement. Furthermore, these skills continue to develop as children learn to read, such that the relationship between phonological processing and reading is symbiotic. Research with dyslexic children suggests that phonological deficits may be the core deficits impeding their reading acquisition (Vukovic & Siegel, 2006). Furthermore, there is evidence to suggest that these skills are influenced by genetics and underlying brain structures in the perisylvian region.

Orthographic processing is a second and related area of research investigation (King, Lombardino, & Ahmed, 2005). It involves the interpretation of abstract representation, specifically series of letters that form words during the reading process. Orthographic processing is most closely related to sight word reading, in which the individual does not use decoding strategies to read words but rather recognizes the entire word on sight. It appears to be influenced mostly by environmental factors, rather than genetic heritability. Findings from these studies suggest that individuals with dyslexia, as children and into adulthood, are significantly slower and less accurate than individuals without dyslexia across orthographic tasks.

Numerous studies suggest a strong link between dyslexia and comorbid disorders. Specifically, there is significant evidence for high rates of dyslexia's comorbidity with Attention-deficit/Hyperactivity Disorder (ADHD) and specific language impairment (Willcutt, Pennington, Olson, Chhabildas, & Hulslander, 2005). Studies suggest that these comorbidities may be the result of underlying shared risk factors or reciprocal interaction between overlapping skills. Findings are more equivocal for a link with dyslexia and internalizing disorders, such as depressive and anxiety disorders (Miller, Hynd, & Miller, 2005). Although there are anecdotal reports for other comorbidities, empirical data has not generally supported these hypotheses.

Intervention for dyslexia typically consists of remediation and compensation strategies. When children are diagnosed with dyslexia during the early school years, the emphasis is on teaching them phonetic skills to improve their decoding ability and teaching them to recognize sight words to increase reading speed. The results of these reading intervention programs, including Reading Recovery and Reading First, are not universally good. For many but not all children, their reading improves and shows normal developmental outcomes, such as employment and, in some cases, higher-level education. For those individuals who do not develop adequate reading ability by adolescence and adulthood, the emphasis changes to include compensatory strategies. As adults, dyslexic individuals typically have access to books on tape and other compensatory approaches. Individuals who do not develop adequate literacy skills by the time they leave school face difficulties with further training, employment, and functional outcomes.

REFERENCES

Boets, B., Wouters, J., van Wieringen, A., De Smedt, B., & Ghesquiere, P. (In press). Modeling relations between sensory processing, speech perception, orthographic and phonological ability, and literacy achievement. *Brain and Language*.

Harlaar, N., Dale, P. S., & Plomin, R. (2007). Reading exposure: A (largely) environmental risk factor with environmentally-mediated effects on reading performance in the primary school years. *Journal of Child Psychology and Psychiatry, 48*, 1192–1199.

King, W. M., Lombardino, L. L., & Ahmed, S. (2005). Accuracy and speed of orthographic processing in persons with developmental dyslexia. *Perceptual and Motor Skills, 101*, 95–107.

Miller, C. J., Hynd, G. W., & Miller, S. R. (2005). Children with dyslexia: Not necessarily at risk for elevated internalizing symptoms. *Reading and Writing, 18*, 425–436.

Peterson, R. L., McGrath, L. M., Smith, S. D., & Pennington, B. F. (2007). Neuropsychology and genetics of speech, language, and literacy disorders. *Pediatric Clinics of North America, 54*, 543–561.

Phinney, E., Pennington, B. F., Olson, R., Filley, C. M., & Filipek, P. A. (2007). Brain structure correlates of component reading processes: Implications for reading disability. *Cortex, 43*, 777–791.

Shaywitz, S. E., Morris, R., & Shaywitz, B. A. (2008). The education of dyslexic children from childhood to young adulthood. *Annual Review of Psychology, 59*, 451–475.

Vukovic, R. K., & Siegel, L. S. (2006). The double-deficit hypothesis: A comprehensive analysis of the evidence. *Journal of Learning Disabilities, 39*, 25–47.

Willcutt, E. G., Pennington, B. F., Olson, R. K., Chhabildas, N., & Hulslander, J. (2005). Neuropsychological analyses of comorbidity between reading disability and attention deficit hyperactivity disorder: In search of the common deficit. *Developmental Neuropsychology, 27*, 35–78.

SUGGESTED READINGS

Beaton, A. (2004). *Dyslexia, reading, and the brain: A sourcebook for psychological and biological research*. New York: Psychology Press.

Fletcher, J. M., Lyon, G. R., Fuchs, L. S., & Barnes, M. A. (2007). *Learning disabilities: From identification to intervention*. New York: Guilford Press.

Shaywitz, S. (2003). *Overcoming dyslexia: A new and complete science-based program for reading problems at any level*. New York: Random House.

Swanson, H. L., Harris, K. R., & Graham, S. (2003). *Handbook of learning disabilities*. New York: Guilford Press.

CARLIN J. MILLER
University of Windsor

See also: **Learning Disabilities; Reading Disability**

ALEXITHYMIA

All individuals experience emotions and feelings, two terms that are often used interchangeably in everyday language. However, contemporary specialists in the area of affect concur that emotions are multifaceted phenomena characterized by more or less coordinated changes in three components: a cognitive-experiential component (subjective conscious experience, such as feeling happy), a behavioral-expressive component (characteristic overt expression, such as frowning), and a physiological component (autonomic arousal, such an increase in heart rate or blood pressure). With particular respect to the cognitive component, people differ considerably in the degree to which they pay attention to their emotional experiences, as well as in their abilities to differentiate between their feelings and share them with others. The alexithymia construct has been proposed to account for this variability.

The concept of alexithymia—which means, literally, "without word for emotions" (from the Greek *a* for "lack," *lexis* for "word," and *thymos* for "emotion")—is based on observations of psychosomatic patients and was first proposed in the early 1970s by Sifneos (1973). Alexithymia is characterized by a cluster of cognitive and affective features that includes difficulty in identifying and expressing feelings, a striking paucity of fantasies, difficulty in distinguishing between feelings and physical sensations, and a cognitive style that is utilitarian and externally oriented (closely related to the *pensée opératoire* of the French psychoanalysts Marty and de M'Uzan). In combination, these characteristics are conceptualized as a deficit in the cognitive processing and regulation of emotional states, which in turn provides potential explanations to account for individual differences in vulnerability to various mental health and physical problems.

First studied in classical psychosomatic or somatic disorders, alexithymia is known today as a personality trait that is normally distributed in the general population, and a high level of alexithymia is considered a risk factor for a variety of common medical and psychiatric disorders. A leading theory holds that the limited cognitive processing and subjective awareness of emotion in alexithymia lead to an amplification of somatic sensations and an increased emotional response at the physiological level accompanying emotional arousal, thereby producing vulnerability to the development of disorders (Taylor, Bagby, & Parker, 1997). On the one hand, misinterpretation of the bodily sensations could foster functional somatic complaints and lead to hypochondria or other types of somatoform disorder. On the other hand, individuals could alternatively alleviate unpleasant somatic tension through uncontrollable and possibly violent behaviors, such as substance abuse, eating disorders, or antisocial conduct. In addition, sustained or hyperphysiological arousal could also contribute to the development of certain types of somatic disorder (e.g., essential hypertension, inflammatory bowel disease, or functional gastrointestinal disorders).

The validity of alexithymia has for a long time been supported mainly by correlational and measurement-based research. Some studies have examined, in particular, the relationships between alexithymia and basic dimensions of personality. As expected, alexithymia overlaps with various dimensions of the Five-Factor Model (it correlates positively with Neuroticism and negatively with Openness to Experience and Extraversion), with Cloninger's psychobiological model of personality, and with such other personality dimensions as external locus of control and irrational beliefs. Globally, these results indicate that alexithymia (1) constitutes a unique cluster of traits across several dimensions of personality and (2) is a cognitive

state of externally oriented thinking associated with emotional instability and limited ability to cope with stressful situations (Zimmermann, Rossier, Meyer de Stadelhofen, & Gaillard, 2005).

Recently, the validity of alexithymia as a personality trait is receiving increasing support from experimental laboratory research. For example, there is some evidence from psychophysiological studies (e.g., Luminet, Rimé, Bagby, & Taylor, 2004) that failure to regulate distressing emotions through cognitive processes can result in prolonged states of sympathetic nervous system arousal that could potentially alter the body's autonomic, endocrine, and/or immune systems. With reference to neurobiological models, a structural cerebral deficit was hypothesized in alexithymia as early as the end of the 1970s. Most of the early research in this area suggested that alexithymia results from a dysfunction either in interhemispheric communication or in the right cerebral hemisphere. Evidence from modern imaging techniques that make it possible to observe brain functions during the elicitation and processing of emotional states has shown that reduced activities in the cingulate cortex might play an important role in alexithymic disturbances (Allen, 2005).

Although of interest, such neurobiological findings do not provide information about the sources of variations in the patterns of neural activity that are associated with alexithymia. It is reasonable to hypothesize that the etiology of alexithymia is determined by a complex interaction of some genetically induced neurobiological deviations and certain childhood rearing conditions or other environmental circumstances. The results from a large population-based sample of twins suggest that alexithymia is influenced primarily by genetic and nonshared environmental factors and to a lesser extent by shared familial factors (Jørgensen, Zachariae, Skytthe, & Kyvik, 2007). Nevertheless, there is some evidence in the literature that attachment experiences in early childhood play a central role in the development of emotion regulation, and these findings support the likelihood that attachment quality may play an essential role in the intergenerational transmission of alexithymia.

A few clinical and empirical studies have suggested further that alexithymia in adulthood may be associated with the parenting style of the caregivers, climate in the family, and experiences of sexual and physical abuse during childhood. This possibility has been partially confirmed in a study of relationships between alexithymia, perceived parenting, and physical and sexual abuse in a clinical population (Kooiman et al., 2004). However, these associations are fairly modest and do not support the idea that parental care and physical or sexual abuse during childhood exert a strong influence on the development of alexithymia (Kooiman et al., 2004). Other possibly significant factors include relationships with people other than parents who also play an important role in the emotional development of children, such as their siblings, peers, and teachers.

Clinically, the original observations of the 1970s indicate that people who are high in alexithymia respond poorly to traditional psychotherapies. Alexithymic clients can be expected to have difficulty with identifying and describing to their therapist the nature of their internal experience, thereby limiting their ability to participate effectively in psychotherapy and respond to it. Researchers have begun to focus attention on the impact of pretreatment alexithymia on the prognosis in psychological and somatic treatments. On the whole, empirical findings do confirm that alexithymia predicts relatively poor treatment outcomes. For example, Ogrodniczuk, Piper, and Joyce (2004) found that alexithymia—and particularly the difficulty in identifying feelings—is predictive of residual symptoms in patients with major depression who respond to short-term psychotherapy.

Interestingly, findings from a companion study of the same group of patients suggested that negative reactions on the part of the therapist to alexithymic patients mediates the relationship between alexithymia and outcome (Ogrodniczuk, Piper, & Joyce, 2005). Finally, although alexithymia has been considered a relatively stable personality trait, some clinical reports and preliminary empirical results suggest that modified psychotherapeutic techniques (e.g., art therapy, hypnosis, meditation), applied mainly in a group setting, can contribute to the alteration of the alexithymic characteristics.

More than 30 years after its introduction and despite criticisms of it, the alexithymia construct continues to give rise to a growing body of research and interest. In the course of becoming more widely known, it has been examined from different perspectives, including personality psychology, cognitive psychology, developmental psychology, clinical psychology, psychophysiology, and neurobiology. Currently integrated into the wide field of affective sciences, the extensive literature on the concept of alexithymia adds to our understanding of human emotions, emotion regulation, and the etiology of somatic and psychological disorders.

REFERENCES

Allen, A. (2005). Feelings you can't imagine: Toward a cognitive neuroscience of alexithymia. *Trends in Cognitive Sciences, 9*(12), 553–555.

Jørgensen, M. M., Zachariae, R., Skytthe, A., & Kyvik, K. (2007). Genetic and environmental factors in alexithymia: A population-based study of 8,785 Danish twin pairs. *Psychotherapy and Psychosomatics, 76*, 369–375.

Kooiman, C. G., Vellinga, S. V., Spinhoven, P., Draijer, N., Trijsburg, R. W., & Rooijmans, H. G. M. (2004). Childhood adversities as risk factors for alexithymia and other aspects of affect dysregulation in adulthood. *Psychotherapy and Psychosomatics, 73*, 107–116.

Luminet, O., Rimé, B., Bagby, M. R., & Taylor, G. J. (2004). A multimodal investigation of emotional responding in alexithymia. *Cognition and Emotion, 18*(5), 741–766.

Ogrodniczuk, J. S., Piper, W. E., & Joyce, A. S. (2004). Alexithymia as a predictor of residual symptoms in depressed patients who respond to short-term psychotherapy. *American Journal of Psychotherapy, 58*(2), 150–161.

Ogrodniczuk, J. S., Piper, W. E., & Joyce, A. S. (2005). The negative effect of alexithymia on outcome of group therapy for complicated grief: What role might the therapist play? *Comprehensive Psychiatry, 46*, 206–213.

Sifneos, P. E. (1973). The prevalence of "alexithymic" characteristics in psychosomatic patients. *Psychotherapy and Psychosomatics, 22*, 255–262.

Taylor, G. J., Bagby, M. R., & Parker, J. D. A. (1997). *Disorders of affect regulation: Alexithymia in medical and psychiatric illness.* Cambridge, UK: Cambridge University Press.

Zimmermann, G., Rossier, J., Meyer de Stadelhofen, F., & Gaillard, F. (2005). Alexithymia assessment and relations with dimensions of personality. *European Journal of Psychological Assessment, 21*(1), 23–33.

SUGGESTED READINGS

Lumley, M. A., Neely, L. C, & Burger, A. J. (2007). The assessment of alexithymia in medical settings: Implications for understanding and treating health problems. *Journal of Personality Assessment, 89*, 230–246.

Taylor, G. J., & Bagby, M. R. (2004). New trends in alexithymia research. *Psychotherapy and Psychosomatics, 73*, 68–77.

GRÉGOIRE ZIMMERMANN
University of Lausanne, Switzerland

See also: **Emotion Regulation; Somatoform Disorders**

ALL-OR-NONE LAW

The major parts of a neuron or nerve cell include the dendrites, the cell body, and the axon, which is a single, relatively long process extending away from the cell body. The neuron typically receives information from neighboring neurons through chemical substances called neurotransmitters that are released near the dendrites and cell body. The neuron may relay this information to other neurons by the nerve impulse, which is a characteristic of the axon.

The axon generally operates according to the all-or-none law, which states that transmission of a nerve impulse occurs either all the way or not at all. If the changes that produce the nerve impulse—that is, the movement of positively charged sodium ions—cause a certain threshold level to be reached, then the impulse (also called the action potential or spike potential) is conducted at a constant level from its origin to the end of the axon.

Thus, axonal transmission is independent of the intensity of the stimulus that produces it. As long as the stimulus causes enough ionic movement to exceed a threshold, the nerve impulse occurs all the way, without decreasing as it travels the length of the axon. A mild stimulus that surpasses the threshold produces the same nerve impulse as an intense stimulus.

Stimulus intensity is coded by the rate of generation of action potentials, not by whether they occur, and also by the number of neurons activated in a given area. The greater the intensity of a stimulus, the more neurons are activated and the more rapidly they generate action potentials. A neuron's action potentials are analogous to signals from a telegraph key; a neuron cannot send bigger or faster action potentials any more than a telegraph operator can send bigger or faster signals with the telegraph key.

The all-or-none concept applies to other tissue as well, and the principle was first demonstrated in 1871 in heart muscle by American physiologist Henry P. Bowditch. In 1902, English physiologist F. Gotch discovered evidence for an all-or-none effect in nerves, but the effect was not convincingly proven until Edgar Douglas Adrian's work, for which he received a Nobel Prize in physiology in 1932. Adrian's research was preceded by studies performed by K. Lucas, who actually named the all-or-none law in a 1909 article.

SUGGESTED READINGS

Kandel, E. R., Schwartz, J. H., & Jessell, T. M. (2000). *Principles of neural science* (4th ed.). New York: McGraw-Hill.

Klein, S. B., & Thorne, B. M. (2007). *Biological psychology*. New York: Worth.

B. Michael Thorne
Mississippi State University

ALLPORT, GORDON WILLARD (1897–1967)

Gordon Willard Allport grew up in the Midwest and earned his bachelor's, master's, and doctoral degrees (1922) at Harvard University. His Ph.D. thesis foreshadowed his life's work, because it dealt with the psychology of personality and assessment. For two years he traveled and studied in Turkey, Germany, and England. He returned to Harvard to serve as an instructor from 1924 to 1926; he was then appointed Assistant Professor of Psychology at Dartmouth College in 1927. He came back to Harvard in 1930 and remained on the Harvard faculty until his retirement, serving for several years as chairman of the psychology department. He was president of the American Psychological Association in 1939 and received numerous honorary doctorates. His outstanding position in the psychology of personality attracted many students who have held posts of distinction in American and other universities.

He regarded personality as the natural subject matter of psychology and believed that other standard topics, such as human learning, could not be studied adequately without taking into account the self or ego who wanted to learn. His approach was eclectic, drawing on a wide variety of sources, including McDougall's theory of motives and experimental and social psychodynamic theories. However, he was strongly opposed to Freudian views of the unconscious; his position was much closer to that of Adler. He rejected any reductionist theory that attributed human behavior to innate instincts, childhood conditioning, or repressed complexes. Personality is an organized whole, not a bundle of habits and fixations. It is present now, and it looks to the future rather than to the past. Thus, in his book *Becoming* (1955) he argued that the self can make choices and to some extent influence the development of its own personality. A fundamental part in personality growth is played by what Allport called the functional autonomy of motives, i.e., the emergence of new motivation systems. For example, a son may take up medicine because his father is a doctor; but gradually his interests develop and medicine becomes a goal in its own right, independent of the initial drive.

Allport was not given to extreme views. He avoided writing dogmatically or provocatively and preferred courtesy to controversy. He could aptly be called one of the first humanists in psychology, but he did not allow his humanitarian sentiments to interfere with scientific integrity and logical thinking in his writings. He realized, however, that there is a fundamental contradiction between scientific and intuitive views of man. These are referred to as the nomothetic and idiographic standpoints. The nomothetist tries to arrive at general laws that apply to all human kind, and one's procedures are based on accurate measurements of behavior. Inevitably this involves fragmentation of the individual into measurable variables. But the idiographic view sees each particular individual as a unique whole and relies largely on intuitive understanding. Allport believed that the two should be combined. Nomothetic characteristics can be measured, for example, by personality questionnaires that measure extraversion, dominance, anxiety, etc. Idiographic description must be based on case study data, or inferred from personal documents such as diaries or imaginative writing. He rejected the usefulness of projective techniques for understanding normal people as distinct from neurotics. He himself did devise certain tests of personality traits, attitudes, and values, but saw little point in factorial studies of personality.

Allport's personality theory put him at odds with the vast majority of American psychologists, who were behavioristic empiricists. Nevertheless, he was widely respected for his ideas. He dealt with the bewildering complexity of personality by posting personality traits as the basic units or components. A trait is a generalized type of behavior that characterizes each individual and distinguishes that person from others. It is a real and causal neuropsychic structure, not merely biosocial—that is, derived from the impressions of people who observe the individual. This concept has been attacked by later writers who point out the frequent inconsistency, rather than the generality, of people's behaviors in different situations. Unfortunately, Allport did not live long enough to answer such critics as Walter Mischel, who regarded personal behavior as determined more by the situation than by internal traits. But he did allow for the uniqueness of each individual personality by distinguishing common traits—variables that occur in different strengths in all persons—from unique traits or personal dispositions peculiar to the particular person.

Although Allport's main work was the development of a comprehensive theory of personality, he had wide-ranging interests, including eidetic imagery, religion, social attitudes, rumor, and radio. The book that probably has the greatest practical and social value was his analysis of *The Nature of Prejudice* (1954). His major work was *Pattern and Growth in Personality*.

The following citation was presented when Allport was awarded the Gold Medal of the American Psychological Foundation in 1963: "To Gordon Willard Allport, outstanding teacher and scholar. He has brought warmth, wit, humanistic knowledge, and rigorous inquiry to the study of human individuality and social process."

REFERENCES

Allport, G. W. (1955). *Becoming: Basic considerations for a psychology of personality*. Clinton, Mass: Yale University Press.

Allport, G. W. (1960). *Pattern and growth in personality*. New York: Holt, Rinehart, and Winston.

Allport, G. W. (1968). *The person in psychology: Selected essays*. Boston: Beacon.

Philip E. Vernon
University of Calgary, Canada

ALLPORT-VERNON STUDY OF VALUES

The Allport-Vernon Study of Values (SOV) is one of the earliest, theoretically well-grounded questionnaires measuring personal values on the basis of declared behavioral preferences. The SOV was first published in 1931 by G. W. Allport and P. E. Vernon (1931) and later revised in 1970 by Allport, Vernon, and G. Lindzey (1970). It is a psychological tool designed to measure personal preferences of six types of values: theoretical, economic, aesthetic, social, political, and religious. The method is rooted in a philosophy of values by E. Spranger, who postulated six ideal types of people corresponding to their most important and general beliefs, ways of thinking, and preferred patterns of living. Each one is oriented toward a basic value: (1) Theoretical: truth; (2) Economic: usefulness; (3) Aesthetic: harmony and beauty; (4) Social: love for people; (5) Political: power and leadership; (6) Religious: unity or moral excellence. The idea was developed by G. W. Allport (1961), who argued that personal philosophy of life related to values is a core feature of personality implying direction of motivation, future goals, and current choices.

The psychological meaning of the six value orientations are assessed by the SOV as follows: (1) Theoretical: dominant value is discovery of truth with interests that are empirical, critical, and rational; (2) Economic: dominant value is usefulness with a tendency to be practical, seeing unapplied knowledge as being wasteful; (3) Aesthetic: dominant value is form and harmony, with interests in the artistic side of life, and a tendency toward individualism and self-sufficiency; (4) Social: dominant value is the altruistic and philanthropic love of others with a tendency to be kind, sympathetic, and unselfish; (5) Political: dominant value is power with a tendency to desire power, influence, and renown, and with likelihood of becoming a leader of society; (6) Religious: dominant value is unity with a tendency to seek to comprehend the cosmos as a whole, attempt to relate it to themselves, and embrace its totality (Lublinski, Schmidt, & Benbow, 1996, p. 445).

The SOV contains six scales corresponding to the aforementioned types of values. The method is designed to measure basic preferences, so it concerns alternative forms of activity introduced as behavioral scenarios and related to different values. The answers, which imply a choice, cover potential and realistic everyday experiences. The method consists of 45 questions across two sections with different formats of questions and answers. Part I consists of 30 questions with two alternative answers concerning preferences; respondents indicate their preferences by distributing three points between two answers (giving 3 and 0, or 2 and 1). Part II contains 15 questions with four possible answers concerning choice of preferable activity; respondents rank these possibilities from the most preferred (4) to the least preferred (1), so they distribute 10 points (according to pattern 4-3-2-1). Examples of the items: Part I. 4. Assuming that you have sufficient ability, would you prefer to be (1) a banker; (2) a politician. Part II. 13. To what extent do the following famous persons interest you: (1) Mother Theresa; (2) General Colin Powell; (3) Bill Gates; (4) Marie Curie.

Each value enters into comparisons with the others 20 times all together, 10 times in each part of the method. A total score for a given value is the sum obtained in two parts. Total score in each scale of the SOV ranges from 10 to 70. The method is ipsative, so a choice of one value is more preferred than another at the expense of this second value—which fits the nature of the valuing process, implying a choice and preference of one goal directed behavior over another. The sum of scores in all six scales is always 240.

For almost 50 years the SOV was one of the most cited questionnaires of personality. Since the 1980s the method was cited more rarely, due to (1) decreased interest of values in the field of personality; (2) development of new simple tools for direct measurement of preferences in the field of social psychology; and (3) archaic content of the SOV and dated language. In 1995 R. E. Kopelman, J. L. Rovenport, and M. Guan (2003) revised the SOV, updating language, modifying behavioral indices of values according to current culture, and broadening the concept of religiosity. They modified 15 items by replacing dated pronouns, including gender-inclusive wording, by broadening examples of religiosity originated from different religions, and by updating cultural conventions through incorporation of current referents and mores.

The comparison of mean scores in the original and revised versions of the method does not reveal any significant differences. Correlation between old and updated scales were also pretty high (mean coefficient was $r = 0, 74$). Internal consistency of the scales is also similar and acceptable with the following Cronbach alpha scores for revised scales: Theoretical $(0, 59)$, Economic $(0, 72)$, Aesthetic $(0, 68)$, Social $(0, 66)$, Political $(0, 55)$, and Religious $(0, 80)$. The revised version is substantially and psychometrically equivalent to the original one. The greatest advantage of the SOV is the diagnostic validity of the scale. In comparison to the Rokeach Value Survey (RVS), which is based on values ranking, and the Schwartz Value Survey (SVS), which is based on values rating, the SOV is based on an indirect assessment of values, through a choice between behavioral scenarios so it concerns preferred not preferable values. Moreover, the validity of the types of values was confirmed by different personal meanings as well as patterns of feelings obtained for the six notions of values (Hermans & Oles, 1994). A unique study about intellectually gifted adolescents, repeated 20 years later, showed 20-year relative stability of the SOV. This stability was comparable to the stability of personality traits, which confirms importance of value preferences as crucial personality feature (Lublinski, Schmidt, & Benbow, 1996).

According to the authors of the SOV, the six types of values are equal in that each may underlie a personal philosophy of life or may be connected to personality maturity. However, empirical results brought inspiring conclusions. There are some gender differences. Aesthetic, Social, and Religious values are preferred by females, whereas Theoretical, Economic, and Political values are preferred by males. A common and core feature of the former is communion, while that of the latter is agency. Intercorrelations of the scales have found a negative correlation between Religious, Social, and Aesthetic values and Economic and Political values. Such a structure of intercorrelations brings indirect support for a philosophical division of higher or final values and instrumental values with one exception: theoretical values represented by truth belong to higher values according to a philosophical standpoint (Lublinski, Schmidt, & Benbow, 1996).

Summing up, the psychometric properties of the SOV are acceptable, and the method has been used in scientific research as well as for psychological counseling, occupational and educational guidance, and psychoeducational purposes. The method can also be used in career planning, measurement of vocational interest, and assessment of individual preferences of style of life.

REFERENCES

Allport, G. W., & Vernon, P. E. (1931). *Study of values: Manual.* Boston, MA: Houghton Mifflin.

Allport, G. W., Vernon, P. E., & Lindzey, G. (1970). *Study of values* (Revised 3rd ed.). Chicago: Riverside Publishing.

Hermans, H. J. M., & Oles, P. (1994). The personal meaning of values in a rapidly changing society. *Journal of Social Psychology, 134,* 569–579.

Kopelman, R. E., Prottas, D. J., & Tatum, L. G. (2004). Comparison of four measures of values: Their relative usefulness in graduate education advisement. *North American Journal of Psychology, 6,* 205–218.

Kopelman, R. E., Rovenport, J. L., & Guan, M. (2003). The study of values: Construction of the fourth edition. *Journal of Vocational Behavior, 62,* 203–220.

Lublinski, D., Schmidt, D. B., & Benbow, C. P. (1996). A 20-year stability analysis of the study of values for intellectually gifted individuals from adolescence to adulthood. *Journal of Applied Psychology, 81,* 443–451.

SUGGESTED READINGS

Allport, G. W. (1961). *Pattern and growth in personality.* New York: Holt, Rinehart and Winston.

Braithwaite, V. A., & Scott, W. A. (1991). Values. In: J. P. Robinson, P. R. Shaver, & L. S. Wrightsman (Eds.), *Measures of personality and social psychological attitudes* (pp. 661–753). San Diego, CA: Academic Press.

Oles, P. K., & Hermans, H. J. M. (2003). Values assessment. W: R. Fernández-Ballesteros (Ed.), *The Encyclopedia of Psychological Assessment* (Vol. 2, s. 1082–1088). London: Sage Publications.

PIOTR K. OLES
*John Paul II Catholic University of Lublin
Lublin, Poland*

HUBERT J. M. HERMANS
Nijmegen, The Netherlands

See also: **Career Counseling; Vocational Counseling**

ALPHA COEFFICIENT (See Coefficient Alpha)

ALPHA RHYTHMS

Ensembles of synchronously active cortical neurons generate electromagnetic field potentials that can be measured by electroencephalography (EEG) or magnetoencephalography (MEG). The alpha frequency band is defined to be between 8 and 13 Hz (Berger, 1929). The classical alpha rhythm is prominent at electrodes overlying the occipital (visual) cortex and to a lesser extent over the posterior temporal and parietal areas. Alpha rhythm occurs in a condition of relaxed wakefulness with eyes closed. The alpha rhythm disappears gradually during drowsiness, and different types of alpha activity appear in rapid eye movement (REM) sleep.

Blind children do not develop the alpha rhythm. The alpha frequency matures and reaches the approximate average values of 8 Hz at age 3 years, 9 Hz at age 9 years and 10 Hz at age 15 years. The interindividual variability is quite large. About 6% to 10 % of healthy subjects have "low voltage alpha activity," below 20 μV. Consistent amplitude asymmetries exceeding 2:1 are usually considered to be abnormal. Alpha variant rhythms with frequency of half or double the normal frequency may occur in some healthy subjects (Markand, 1990).

Alpha rhythm peak frequency correlates with cerebral blood flow and metabolism, and low frequency is found in metabolic, infectious, and degenerative disorders, including dementia of the Alzheimer's type. Unilateral slowing or loss of alpha rhythm occurs in the presence of traumatic, neoplastic, infectious, or vascular lesions of one occipital lobe. Abnormal "alpha coma pattern" occurs in some comatose patients. The outcome is variable, depending on the underlying condition, but it is most often poor.

Other physiological rhythms within the alpha frequency band are the mu rhythm (9–11 Hz) recorded over the sensorimotor cortex and the tau rhythm (Hari, 1999). Mu may be the only routinely recorded alpha-band rhythm in EEG of infants and small children. In order to see the proper alpha rhythm, passive eye closure or recording in darkness should be performed.

Subdural and intracortical recordings, as well as source localization studies, have shown that the alpha rhythm has multiple generators within the cerebral cortex. Although early studies suggested that the alpha rhythm was driven by feedback inhibition of thalamic relé cells, more recent studies suggest that both cortico-cortical and thalamo-cortical connections are of importance. It has been suggested that both intrinsic membrane ion channel properties and local neuron network properties determine rhythmic behavior (Lopes da Silva, 1991). Recent studies have identified specific thalamocortical neurons with high-threshold burst properties that seem to drive the classical alpha rhythm in dogs and cats (Hughes & Crunelli, 2005). Alpha phase and rhythmicity may indeed play an important part in attention, memory and consciousness (Palva & Palva, 2007).

The coherence-function has become a popular tool because it reveals information about functional connectivity between different parts of the brain during various tasks and states (Gevins, 1995). Volume conduction and the EEG-reference montage must be considered during interpretation. Event-related desynchronization (ERD) of central and occipital alpha rhythms represents activation of those cortical areas that are active in vision, motor preparation, or selective attention (Pfurtscheller, Stancák, & Neuper, 1996). Event-related alpha-oscillations in visual and auditory cortex following visual and auditory stimuli respectively have been described (Basar, Basar-Eroglu, Karakas, & Schürmann, 1999). Conflicting results have been published regarding the possible relationship between alpha frequency and cognitive performance (Markand, 1990; Klimesch, 1999). The proposed relationship between depression and frontal alpha asymmetry has been challenged (Debener et al., 2000).

Considerable progress has been made toward a better understanding of the basic mechanisms behind alpha rhythms and brain function during recent years. Data regarding alpha coherence seems to challenge the concept that cognitive events only are associated with gamma (30–100 Hz) activity (Nunez, Wingeier, & Silberstein, 2001). High-resolution EEG and MEG combined with mathematical methods and magnetic resonance imaging are exciting tools for human brain research.

REFERENCES

Basar E., Basar-Eroglu, C., Karakas, S., & Schürmann, M. (1999). Are cognitive processes manifested in event-related gamma, alpha, theta and delta oscillations in the EEG? *Neuroscience Letters, 259*, 165–168.

Berger H. Über das elektroenkephalogramm des Menschen. I. (1929). *Archives of Psychiatric Nervenkr, 87*, 527–570.

Debener, S., Beauducel, A., Nessler, D., Brocke, B., Heilemann, H., & Kayser, J. (2000). Is resting anterior EEG alpha asymmetry a trait marker for depression? Findings for healthy adults and clinically depressed patients. *Neuropsychobiology, 41*, 31–37.

Gevins, A., Leong, H., Smith, M. E., Le, J., & Du, R. (1995). Mapping cognitive brain function with modern high-resolution electroencephalography. *Trends Neuroscience, 18*, 429–436.

Hari, R. (1999). Magnetoencephalography as a tool of clinical neurophysiology. In: Niedermeyer, E., da Silva, F. H. (Eds.). *Electroencephalography: Basic principles, clinical applications and related fields.* (4th ed.). (pp. 1107–1134). Baltimore: Lippincott Williams & Wilkins.

Hughes, S. W., & Crunelli, V. (2005). Thalamic mechanisms of EEG alpha rhythms and their pathological implications. *Neuroscientist, 11*, 357–372.

Klimesch, W. (1999). EEG alpha and theta oscillations reflect cognitive and memory performance: A review and analysis. *Brain Research Reviews*, 169–195.

Lopes da Silva, F. (1991). Neural mechanisms underlying brain waves: from neural membranes to networks. *Electroencephalography and Clinical Neurophysiology*, 7, 81–93.

Markand, O. N. (1990). Alpha rhythms. *Journal of Clinical Neurophysiology*, 7, 163–189.

Nunez, P. L., Wingeier, B. M., & Silberstein, R. B. (2001). Spatial-temporal structures of human alpha rhythms: Theory, microcurrent sources, multiscale measurements, and global binding of local networks. *Human Brain Mapping*, 13, 125–164.

Palva, S., Palva, J. M. (2007). New vistas for α-frequency band oscillations. *Trends Neuroscience*, 30, 150–158.

Pfurtscheller, G., Stancák, Jr. A., & Neuper, Ch. (1996). Event-related synchronization (ERS) in the alpha band—an electrophysiological correlate of cortical idling: A review. *International Journal of Psychophysiology*, 24, 39–46.

SUGGESTED READINGS

Niedermeyer, E. (1999). The normal EEG in the waking adult. In: Niedermeyer, E., da Silva, F. H. (Eds.). *Electroencephalography: Basic principles, clinical applications and related fields.* (4th ed.). (pp. 149–173). Baltimore: Lippincott Williams & Wilkins.

Steriade, M., Gloor P., Llinas, R. R., Lopes da Silva, F., & Mesulam, M. M. (1990). Basic mechanisms of cerebral rhythmic activities. *Electroencephalography and Clinical Neurophysiology*, 76, 481–508.

TROND SAND
Norwegian University of Science and Technology and Trondheim University Hospital, Norway

See also: **Electroencephalography; Magnetic Resonance Imaging**

ALTRUISM

Altruism refers to a specific form of motivation for benefiting another. Some biologists, economists, and psychologists speak of altruism as a form of behavior (e.g., costly helping or helping with no external reward). However, such use fails to consider the motivation for the behavior, which has historically been crucial for altruism.

Comte (1851/1875) coined the term altruism in juxtaposition to egoism, and, soon thereafter, it became prominent in philosophy. To the degree that one's ultimate goal in benefiting another is to increase the other's welfare, the motivation is altruistic. To the degree that the ultimate goal is to increase one's own welfare, with increasing the other's welfare being an instrumental means to reach this goal, the motivation is egoistic. Accordingly, altruism may be defined as a motivational state with the ultimate goal of increasing another's welfare. Egoism may be defined as a motivational state with the ultimate goal of increasing one's own welfare. In these definitions, "ultimate goal" refers to a state one is seeking in a given situation, not to a metaphysical first for final cause. A person can have multiple ultimate goals, so altruistic and egoistic motives can co-occur.

Dictionary definitions of altruism reflect this motivational focus. They typically define altruism as "unselfish concern for the welfare of others" (e.g., *Webster's*, 1990). However, for scientific use it seems best to avoid the term "unselfish" for two reasons. First, unselfish has clear evaluative connotations because of its juxtaposition to selfish, a term that implies undue or immoral attention to one's own welfare. Altruism, as defined, is not necessarily moral; indeed, it may lead one to violate one's own moral standards if doing so increases the welfare of the other toward whom one is altruistically motivated (see Batson, Kline, Highberger, & Shaw, 1995). Second, to speak of "unselfish concern" can lead to the assumption that self-sacrifice or net cost to self is a necessary component of altruism. This is not the case. Increasing the other's welfare, not decreasing one's own, is the focus of altruism.

Over the past 50 years, the term altruism has been widely used in biology, where it has at times been suggested that altruism is contrary to natural selection and therefore cannot exist. Making a useful distinction, Sober and Wilson (1998) point out that these biologists are referring to evolutionary altruism—behavior by one organism that reduces its reproductive fitness relative to the reproductive fitness of others. Evolutionary altruism is quite different from what is normally meant by altruism as just defined, which Sober and Wilson call psychological altruism. The existence of psychological altruism does not depend on the existence of evolutionary altruism.

The Egoism-Altruism Debate

Clearly, humans devote much time and energy to helping others. Is this evidence of psychological altruism? Most proponents of altruism say, not necessarily. Proponents of universal egoism go further. They say, necessarily not—that everything we do, no matter how noble and beneficial to others, is directed toward the ultimate goal of self-benefit. They point out that even when helping involves material or physical cost, we may benefit by getting social and self-rewards (praise, esteem) and avoiding social and self-punishment (censure, guilt). Proponents of altruism do not deny these self-benefits, nor do they deny that the motivation for helping is often egoistic. However, they claim that at least some of us, to some degree, under some circumstances, help with an ultimate goal of benefiting the person in need. They point out that even though we get self-benefits from helping, these benefits may not be the reason we helped. Rather than an ultimate goal, the self-benefits may be unintended consequences.

Helping another person—even at great cost to oneself—may be altruistically motivated, egoistically motivated, or both. To know which it is, we must determine whether benefit to the other is (1) an ultimate goal and any self-benefits are unintended consequences (altruism) or (2) an instrumental means to reach the ultimate goal of benefiting oneself (egoism). To do this, we first need to identify a likely source of altruistic motivation.

The Empathy-Altruism Hypothesis

In both earlier philosophical writings and in more recent psychological work, the most frequently mentioned likely source of psychological altruism is an other-oriented emotional reaction to seeing another person in need. This emotional reaction has variously been called compassion, empathy, empathic concern, pity, sympathy, and tenderness. It is other-oriented in the sense that it involves feeling for the other—feeling sorry for, distressed for, concerned for the other. We can also feel direct, self-oriented sorrow, distress, or concern when we are faced with a distressing situation, including seeing someone in need. The direct distress experienced at witnessing another person in distress—sometimes called "personal distress"—is distinct from other-oriented empathic concern for that person (Batson, 1991). To use the same terms for both other-oriented and self-oriented emotional reactions to seeing another in distress invites confusion. The relevant psychological distinction must be based not on whether terms like "sad" or "distressed" are used but on whose welfare is the focus of the emotional response—the other person's welfare or one's own.

The proposal that empathic concern felt for someone in need produces altruistic motivation to relieve that need has been called the empathy-altruism hypothesis (Batson, 1991). In the past several decades, more than 30 experiments have tested this hypothesis against various egoistic alternatives (see Batson, 1991, for a partial review and Batson, in preparation, for a more complete review). Although still controversial, results have been remarkably supportive of the empathy-altruism hypothesis, suggesting that psychological altruism—motivation with the ultimate goal of increasing another's welfare—is within the motivational repertoire of most humans.

REFERENCES

Batson, C. D. (1991). *The altruism question: Toward a social-psychological answer*. Hillsdale, NJ: Lawrence Erlbaum.

Batson, C. D. (In press). *Altruism in humans*. New York: Oxford University Press.

Batson, C. D., Klein, T. R., Highberger, L., & Shaw, L. L. (1995). Immorality from empathy-induced altruism: When compassion and justice conflict. *Journal of Personality and Social Psychology, 68*, 1042–1054.

Comte, I. A. (1875). *System of positive polity* (Vol. 1). London: Longmans, Green & Co.

Sober, E., & Wilson, D. S. (1998). *Unto others: The evolution and psychology of unselfish behavior*. Cambridge, MA: Harvard University Press.

Webster's desk dictionary of the English language (1990). New York: Portland House.

C. Daniel Batson
University of Kansas

See also: **Affiliation Need; Morality; Prosocial Behavior**

ALZHEIMER'S DISEASE

Alzheimer's disease (AD) is a progressive neurodegenerative disease, affecting memory, intellectual functions, and behavior. The prevalence of Alzheimer's disease is increasing with the growing percentage of the population over age 65. Two to three percent of those aged 65–69 have AD. This percentage doubles every five years until almost 1 out of 2 or 3 individuals over the age of 85 are reported to have AD (Kukull et al., 2002). Approximately 14–16 million persons are expected to have AD in the United States alone by mid-century.

The clinical presentation of AD usually begins with memory loss, which slowly worsens over years and progresses to include impairment in additional cognitive domains such as language, executive function, or visuospatial skills. Early on in AD when memory loss is the only issue, or the cognitive difficulties do not yet significantly impair daily functioning, many of these individuals will be classified as having Mild Cognitive Impairment. While still a controversial topic, many view Mild Cognitive Impairment as a transition stage between normal aging and Alzheimer's disease.

In the early stages of AD, there is frequent repetition of stories/questions, misplacing of belongings, geographic disorientation, dysnomia, and difficulty managing finances or handling complex tasks. Sleep disturbances, depression, psychosis (hallucinations and paranoia), and other neuropsychiatric problems commonly evolve as the disease progresses. Assistance is eventually needed for dressing, bathing, meals, and other activities. Individuals often become lost in familiar surroundings and have reduced comprehension. Late stages often bring agitation and aggression, profound cognitive impairment, and loss of control of bodily functions. These disabilities often lead to institutionalization, increased risk of decubitus ulcers, aspiration pneumonia, and urosepsis from indwelling catheters.

Diagnosis of AD is based on the clinical features and the exclusion of other etiologies. Two commonly used diagnostic criteria are listed in Table 1. Confirmation of

Table 1. Current Diagnostic Criteria for Alzheimer's Disease

NINCDS-ADRDA Criteria for Probable Alzheimer's Disease (McKhann et al., 1984)

A. Include the following:
  1. Dementia established by clinical examination and documented by the Mini-Mental Test, Blessed Dementia Scale, or some similar examination, and confirmed by neuropsychological tests.
  2. Deficits in two or more areas of cognition.
  3. Progressive worsening of memory and other cognitive functions.
  4. No disturbance of consciousness.
  5. Onset between ages 40 and 90, most often after age 65.
  6. Absence of systemic disorders or other brain diseases that in and of themselves could account for the progressive deficits in memory and cognition.
B. The diagnosis is supported by the following:
  1. Progressive deterioration of specific cognitive functions, such as language (aphasia), motor skills (apraxia), and perception (agnosia).
  2. Impaired activities of daily living and altered patterns of behavior.
  3. Family history of similar disorders, especially if confirmed neurohistopathologically.

DSM-IV Criteria for Dementia of the Alzheimer's Type

A. The development of multiple cognitive deficits manifested by both:
  1. memory impairment (impaired ability to learn new information or to recall previously learned information) and
  2. one (or more) of the following cognitive disturbances:
     a. aphasia (language disturbance)
     b. apraxia (impaired ability to carry out motor activities despite intact motor function)
     c. agnosia (failure to recognize or identify objects despite intact sensory function)
     d. disturbance in executive functioning (i.e., planning, organizing, sequencing, abstracting)
B. The cognitive deficits in Criteria A1 and A2 each cause significant impairment in social or occupational functioning and represent a decline from a previous level of functioning.
C. The course is characterized by gradual onset and continuing cognitive decline.
D. The cognitive deficits in Criteria A1 and A2 are not due to any of the following:
  1. other central nervous system conditions that cause progressive deficits in memory and cognition (e.g., cerebrovascular disease, Parkinson's disease, Huntington's disease, subdural hematoma, normal pressure hydrocephalus, brain tumor)
  2. systemic conditions that are known to cause dementia (e.g., hypothyroidism, vitamin B12 or folic acid deficiency, hypercalcemia, neurosyphilis, HIV infection)
  3. substance induced conditions
E. The deficits do not occur exclusively during the course of a delirium.
F. The disturbance is not better accounted for by another Axis I disorder (e.g., Major Depressive Disorder, Schizophrenia)

Table 2. Disease Processes that Should be Considered in the Differential Diagnosis of Dementia and their Principle Method of Evaluation

Treatable causes of dementia, which must be excluded primarily by serologic studies:
  Hypothyroidism
  Vitamin B12 deficiency
  Folate deficiency
  Neurosyphilis
  Hypercalcemia
  Hypo- or hypernatremia
  Renal dysfunction
  Liver dysfunction
  Chronic drug intoxication
  HIV infection

Treatable causes of dementia, which must be excluded primarily by neuroimaging studies:
  Normal pressure hydrocephalus
  Subdural hematoma
  Multi-infarct dementia
  Subcortical arteriosclerotic encephalopathy (Binswanger's disease)
  Space occupying lesions (tumor, abscess, etc.)
  Demyelinating diseases (multiple sclerosis, PML)

Other causes of dementia, which may be excluded by EEG:
  Subclinical seizures
  Creutzfeld-Jakob disease (CSF 14-3-3 protein also diagnostic)

Other causes of dementia, which must be excluded primarily by clinical features:
  Pseudodementia (depression)
  Pick's disease and Frontotemporal dementias
  Parkinson's disease
  Progressive Supranuclear Palsy
  Diffuse Lewy Body disease
  Cortical-basal-ganglionic degeneration
  Huntington's disease

cognitive impairment is important. Common screening tools for dementia include the Mini-Mental State Exam (Folstein & Folstein, 1975), the Dementia Rating Scale, 2nd edition (Jurica, Leitten, & Mattis, 2001), and a clock-drawing test. Often, more detailed neuropsychological testing is needed to confirm the cognitive difficulties associated with AD and to differentiate AD from normal aging and other types of dementia.

Laboratory testing is important in the evaluation of cognitively impaired individuals to identify reversible causes of dementia (Table 2). Blood tests evaluate metabolic, hormonal, and nutritional derangements. Neuroimaging is essential to detect subdural hematomas, hydrocephalus, stroke, and space occupying lesions. Noncontrast CT or MRI are suitable for most cases. PET and SPECT scanning of patients with AD characteristically reveal hypometabolism in the parietotemporal region, even in preclinical individuals at high genetic risk for disease. However, these studies are expensive and are not widely available. They are most useful when attempting to discriminate AD from other neurodegenerative conditions that show distinct regional patterns of hypometabolism. Measurement of Barcode of Life Data (BOLD) response in mesial temporal lobe structures using functional MRI have been shown to be sensitive to detecting early AD in some individuals (Wierenga and Bondi, 2007). *In vivo* PET imagining using the Pittsburgh Compound B has also shown promise in visualizing Alzheimer's pathology (Klunk, Engler, and Nordberg, 2004). Currently, neuroimaging alone is not diagnostic of AD. That being said, imaging research is evolving rapidly, promising more sensitive and specific tools for future clinical use.

The pathology of AD involves the degeneration of neurons in select cortical regions and ascending brainstem systems, including the cholinergic basal forebrain. These regions exhibit pathological hallmarks of the disease, including neurofibrillary tangles within neurons and extracellular senile plaques containing $A\beta40$ and $A\beta42$. There are other pathological changes, however, including synaptic and neuronal loss, vascular changes, granulovacuolar degeneration, alterations to endosomal/lysosomal systems, and inflammation and oxidative stress (Terry, 1994).

Genetic research has provided key insights into the biology of AD. Early onset familial AD is linked to autosomal dominant mutations in the β amyloid precursor protein (APP), presenilin 1, and presenilin 2 (Hardy & Selkoe, 2002). Late onset familial and sporadic AD risk is associated with Apo E. Increased amounts of $A\beta42$, derived from APP and resulting from mutations in APP and presenilins alike, may enhance $A\beta$ aggregation. Apo E genotype influences AD susceptibility, perhaps via increased $A\beta$ deposition. Numerous studies confirm that the $\epsilon4$ allele increases AD risk and decreases age of onset (e.g., Farrer et al., 1997). Genetic testing for Apo E and presenilin is commercially available but its role in AD diagnosis is often misunderstood. Apo E genotyping is not indicated for AD diagnostic testing, and adds little to the sensitivity and specificity of clinical judgment. Presenilin testing should only be performed with appropriate genetic counseling.

Current pharmacological therapies for AD are primarily based on augmenting the central cholinergic system (Doody, 2001). Available acetylcholinesterase inhibitor drugs have similar efficacy. Donepezil, rivastigmine, and galantamine have been shown to be effective in several large double-blind placebo-controlled clinical trials. Many patients may not show immediate clinical benefit, but over time (e.g., 6–12 months), tend to show less decline than untreated subjects. These drugs have efficacy for cognitive symptoms as well as for behavioral problems, they delay the need for institutionalization, and also reduce the overall economic burden. Memantine, an N-methyl-D-aspartate receptor antagonist, also has proven efficacy and is approved for late-stage AD in the United States.

Epidemiological studies have provided indirect evidence that other medications are associated with AD risk, including estrogen, nonsteroidal anti-inflammatory drugs, statins (NSAIDS), folic acid, and vitamin supplementation (e.g., Kukull & Bowen, 2002). However, prospective clinical studies are essential to determine if these treatments are effective and safe. Unfortunately, prospective double-blind studies have failed to show efficacy of estrogen replacement or NSAIDs; further study is necessary. Vitamin E, an antioxidant, which appeared to delay progression of the disease, was frequently prescribed in the past; however, this practice has declined after evidence arose of increased risk of mortality in large clinical trials (Miller et al, 2005). Until safety and efficacy issues are addressed with prospective studies, precautions against use of any unproven agents for AD should be heeded because of the risk of serious adverse events.

Health and environmental factors have also been found in epidemiology studies to relate to Alzheimer's risk (Qui, DeRonchi, & Fratiglioni, 2007). Specifically, high blood pressure, high cholesterol, and obesity in middle adult hood; diabetes; excessive alcohol intake, and cigarette smoking all have been related to a higher risk of AD. Lifestyle and social factors such as low education, reduced social network, lower engagement in mentally stimulating activity, and sedentary lifestyle have been linked to higher risk of AD. As with the medication and supplement links mentioned above, prospective studies into the benefits of altering these environmental/health factors have not yet been carried out.

Nonpharmacological or behavioral therapies for improving memory and cognition in AD have shown mixed results of effectiveness (Clare, Woods, Moniz Cook, Orrell, & Spector, 2003). The most support exists for spaced retrieval techniques and enriching the meaningfulness and organization of information to be learned and remembered. Research into these techniques, however, often fail to provide randomized trials, and the results are not found to be lasting or generalize beyond the specific task the individual was trained on. When the behavioral therapy focuses on compensation strategies for memory loss rather than attempts to "rebuild" memory, some success has been reported. As examples, placing an individual's name on the door of their nursing home room or providing them with personal notebooks with nursing home schedules and pictures of staff and loved ones have demonstrated some effectiveness (e.g., Bourgeois et al., 1997). Psychologists can also play an important role with families or in nursing care facilities by formulating and implementing behavioral management plans when behavioral problems arise in individuals with AD.

Finally, psychotherapy and education are often needed as families come to terms with a patient's changing abilities, experience the grief associated with perceived loss, and to provide more effective care. While the diagnosis may be perceived by some as catastrophic news, education and contact with community support such as the Alzheimer's Association and others may help lessen the anxiety and fear of the unknown, and enable individuals to function better and longer within their families and in their own homes.

REFERENCES

Bourgeois, M. S., Burgio, L. D., Schulz, R., Beach, S., & Palmer, B. (1997). Modifying repetitive verbalizations of community-dwelling patients with AD. *Gerontologist*, *37*, 30–39.

Clare, L., Woods, R. T., Moniz Cook, E. D., Orell, M., & Spector, A. (2005). Cognitive rehabilitation and cognitive training for early stage Alzheimer's disease and vascular dementia. *The Cochrane Database of Systematic Reviews*, *1*.

Doody, R. S., et al. (2001). Practice parameter: management of dementia (an evidence-based review). Report of the Quality Standards Subcommittee of the American Academy of Neurology. *Neurology*, *56*(9), 1154–1166.

Farrer, L. A., et al. (1997). Effects of age, sex, and ethnicity on the association between apolipoprotein E genotype and Alzheimer disease. A meta-analysis. APOE and Alzheimer Disease Meta Analysis Consortium. *Journal of the American Medical Association*, *278*(16), 1349–1356.

Folstein, M. F., Folstein, S. E., & McHugh, P. R. (1975). "Mini-mental state": A practical method for grading the cognitive state of patients for the clinician. *Journal of Psychiatric Research*, *12*, 189–198.

Hardy, J., & Selkoe, D. J. (2002). The amyloid hypothesis of Alzheimer's disease: progress and problems on the road to therapeutics. *Science*, *297*(5580), 353–356.

Jurica, P. J., Leitten, C. L., & Mattis, S. (2001). *Dementia rating scale-2: Professional manual*. Lutz, FL: Psychological Assessment Resources, Inc.

Klunk, W. E., Engler, H., Nordberg, A., et al. (2004). Imaging brain amyloid in Alzheimer's disease with Pittsburgh compound-B. *Annals of Neurology*, *55*, 306–19.

Kukull, W. A., & Bowen, J. D. (2002). Dementia epidemiology. *Medical Clinics of North America*, *86*(3), 573–590.

Kukull, W. A., Higdon, R., Bowen, J. D., McCormick, W. C., Teri, L, Schellenberg, G. D. et al., (2002). Dementia and Alzheimer disease incidence: A prospective cohort study. *Archives of Neurology*, *59*, 1737–1746.

McKhann, G., Drachman, D., Folstin, M., Katzman, R., Price, D. & Stedlan, E. M. (1984). Clinical diagnosis of Alzheimer's disease: Report of the NINCDS-ADRDA work group under the auspices of the Department of Health and Human Services Task Force on Alzheimer's disease. *Neurology*, *34*, 939–944.

Miller, E. R., Pastor-Barriuso, R., Dalal, D., Reimersma, R. A., Appel, L. J., & Guallar, E. (2005). Meta-analysis: High-dosage vitamin E supplementation may increase all-cause mortality. *Annals of Internal Medicine*, *142*, 37–46.

Qui, C., DeRonchi, D., & Fratiglioni, L. (2007). The epidemiology of the dementias: An update. *Current Opinion in Psychiatry*, *20*, 380–385.

Small, G. W., et al., (1995). Apolipoprotein E type 4 allele and cerebral glucose metabolism in relatives at risk for familial Alzheimer disease. *Journal of the American Medical Association*, *273*, 942–947.

Terry, R. D. (1994). Neuropathological changes in Alzheimer disease. *Progressive Brain Research*, *101*, 383–390.

Wierenga, C. E., & Bondi, M. W. (2007). Use of functional magnetic resonance imaging in the early identification of Alzheimer's disease. *Neuropsychology Review*, *17*, 127–143.

SUGGESTED READINGS

Cooke, D. D., et al. (2001). Psychosocial interventions for caregivers of people with dementia: A systematic review. *Aging Mental Health*, *5*(2), 120–135.

Cummings, J. L., & Cole, G. (2002). Alzheimer disease. *Journal of the American Medical Association*, *287*(18), 2335–2338.

Knopman, D. S., et al. (2001). Practice parameter: Diagnosis of dementia (an evidence-based review). Report of the quality standards subcommittee of the American Academy of Neurology. *Neurology*, *56*(9), 1143–1153.

Petersen, R. C., Smith, G. E., Waring, S. C., Ivnik, R. J., Tangalos, E. G., & Kokmen, E. (1999). Mild cognitive impairment: Clinical characterization and outcome. *Archives of Neurology*, *56*, 303–308.

MELANIE GREENAWAY
ALLAN LEVEY
Emory University

See also: Late-Life Forgetting; Memory Functions

AMBIVALENCE

The quest for unified thought is a consistent theme in philosophical and psychological traditions. Ancient Greeks from Pythagoras to Plato equated optimal well-being with absence of psychological conflict. Plato famously depicted virtue as arising from reason's skill at harnessing the potentially opposing "horses" of the will (spiritual versus sensual). Classic psychological theory and research on ambivalence emphasizes the neuroses that can arise from being of two minds and feeling torn between opposing inclinations. For example, Freud claimed that ambivalent feelings about sex or aggression caused neurotic feelings and reactions, and his contemporary, Eugen Bleuler, extended this view to position ambivalence as the primary basis for mental disorders.

As Freud's psychoanalytic ideas evolved, neoanalytic theorists increasingly emphasized ambivalence about the self as a key cause of unhappiness and dysfunctional behavior. In Erik Erikson's developmental theory, earnest and unambivalent identity commitment is the basis for adult maturity. In contrast, Karen Horney described the neurotically ambivalent tendency to focus defensively on a proudly idealized view of self as a means of masking awareness of a despised self. Carl Jung, who had been Bleuler's assistant, similarly noted that some people over-identify with a socially acceptable persona as a way to mask socially unacceptable shadow aspects of self. Carl Rogers' influential client-centered theory contended that psychosis results when the idealized self becomes morbidly disparate from the real self. Each of these views is grounded in Freud's very early, general observation that people repress unfavorable self-views by a defense mechanism that came to be known as reaction formation. Freud observed that repression was usually accomplished by immersing oneself in excessively intense, reactive thoughts about oneself that oppose the unwanted thoughts. As such, reaction formation can be a way of coping with ambivalent impulses and self-views. These classic theories share a common assumption that ambivalence about the self is highly aversive. Why should it be so?

At around the same time as these classic clinical theories of ambivalence were being developed, early laboratory investigations of motivational ambivalence were underway. Pavlov (1927) found that experimentally induced motivational ambivalence caused his dogs to have extreme reactions. In one study, for example, he conditioned his hungry dogs reliably to associate a painful electric shock to a specific leg site with the onset of food. Accordingly, when the shock was applied to that site, dogs had been conditioned to ignore the pain and eagerly focus on the expectation of food, drooling in confident anticipation. If the shock was applied to a different leg site, however, the shock introduced motivational ambivalence about whether to eagerly approach food or avoid the painful shock. In response to this kind of motivational conflict, the dogs howled, frothed, struggled, bit off their experimental apparatus, and became uncooperative and incapable of learning for the rest of the day.

At around the same time, Kurt Lewin conducted related research with toddlers to provide experimental evidence for Freud's views on the consequences of motivational ambivalence. He induced (and coined the term) approach-avoidance conflict in toddlers by motivating them to approach a goal that became compromised by danger just before goal completion. At that very approach-goal/ avoid-danger moment, like Pavlov's ambivalent dogs, the toddlers reacted with tantrums and became stubborn and unruly.

Contemporary research on the neuroscience of goal conflict provides a deeper understanding of why motivational ambivalence should be so distressing. Behavioral, pharmacological, and brain lesion studies have identified an evolutionarily old module in the brains of humans and other vertebrates—the behavioral inhibition system—that releases anxiety when individuals are confronted with ambivalent situations that arouse approach-avoidance conflicts (Gray & McNaughton, 2000). The anxiety is adaptive because it motivates the animal to disengage from the conflicted goal and scan for a more tenable alternative. For humans, this module has neural projections to and from the prefrontal cortex. This means that, for humans, even merely ambivalent thoughts can activate the anxiety of the behavioral inhibition system.

Lewin's student, Leon Festinger, popularized this insight with his work on the aversive arousal associated with "non-fitting cognitions," which he referred to as cognitive dissonance. According to Festinger (1957), an aversive motivational state of cognitive dissonance is aroused when individuals find themselves confronted with ambivalent attitudes about an attitude object. Performing a clearly boring task with little justification, then being subtly tricked into freely recommending it to another person as fun creates ambivalent feelings about a task. Ambivalent thoughts about a boring task and one's apparently positive attitude toward it leads to discomfort and defensive distortions that are aimed at unifying one's apparently ambivalent orientation toward the task (Festinger & Carlsmith, 1959). In another study Festinger and colleagues observed the despair of doomsday cult members who had been devoted to their cult, but who then experienced the dissonance of seeing that the world did not end on the day that their cult-leader had predicted. To cope with the resulting ambivalence, cult-members became all the more extremely committed to the cult, and they explained away the failed prophecy with dubious rationalizations.

Contemporary social psychological research on ambivalence focuses on the psychological consequences and discomfort of holding simultaneously favorable and unfavorable attitudes about an attitude object. One consequence is referred to as ambivalence amplification (Bell & Esses, 1997). This refers to the tendency to avoid ambivalence by cleaving to one-sided views. The tendency toward ambivalence amplification resembles the Freudian defense mechanism of reaction formation. It relieves distress because distress is experienced to the extent that an individual holds strong and equally strong views that have opposing valences. For example, one would experience distress to the extent that one strongly valued both the favorable aspects of capital punishment (e.g., perceived justice) as well as the unfavorable aspects (e.g., discomfort at the idea of hurting another human). The mathematical formula that best predicts the amount of felt discomfort is the square of the valence of the weaker of the ambivalent elements divided by the stronger of the ambivalent elements (Newby-Clark, McGregor, & Zanna, 2002). This formula helps clarify one of the reasons that extreme reactions to ambivalence are rewarding for individuals. Amplifying an extreme position in either direction increases the denominator of the ambivalence formula and accordingly decreases distress.

A further contributor to the discomfort of ambivalent thoughts is the extent to which the opposing thoughts are simultaneously accessible to awareness (Newby-Clark, McGregor, & Zanna, 2002). Discomfort is particularly high, for example, when both strong negative and positive thoughts about capital punishment come to mind equally quickly. This simultaneous accessibility finding further helps explain why people tend to react to ambivalence by strongly identifying with extremely one-sided views. Such extreme identifications may help commit the self to one side of the cognitive conflict, and self-relevant thoughts are particularly accessible to awareness. Accordingly, extremism may decrease simultaneous accessibility of conflicting elements by making the self-related element come to mind much more quickly than the opposing element.

REFERENCES

Bell, D. W., & Esses, V. M. (1997). Ambivalence and response amplification toward native peoples. *Journal of Applied Social Psychology, 27,* 1063–1084.

Festinger, L. (1957). *A theory of cognitive dissonance.* Evanston, IL: Row, Peterson and Company.

Festinger, L., & Carlsmith, J. M. (1959). Cognitive consequences of forced compliance. *Journal of Abnormal and Social Psychology, 58,* 203–210.

Gray, J. A., & McNaughton, N. (2000). *The neuropsychology of anxiety: An enquiry into the functions of the septo-hippocampal system.* New York: Oxford University Press.

Newby-Clark, I. R., McGregor, I., & Zanna, M. P. (2002). Thinking and caring about cognitive inconsistency: When and for whom does attitudinal ambivalence feel uncomfortable? *Journal of Personality and Social Psychology, 82,* 157–166.

Pavlov, I. P. (1927). Conditioned reflexes: An investigation of the physiological activity of the cerebral cortex: (G. V. Anrep, Trans.). In (Vol. Lectures 17 and 18): http://psychclassics .yorku.ca/Pavlov/.

SUGGESTED READING

Harmon-Jones, E., & Mills, J. (1999). *Cognitive dissonance: Progress on a pivotal theory in social psychology.* Washington, DC: American Psychological Association.

IAN MCGREGOR
York University, Ontario, Canada

See also: **Behavioral Inhibition; Cognitive Dissonance; Conflict Resolution**

AMBULATORY ASSESSMENT

Ambulatory assessment can be defined as the use of computer-assisted methodology for self-reports, behavior records, or physiological measurements, while the assessee undergoes normal daily activities. Ambulatory assessment is characterized by the following features: the recording takes place in real-life situations; computer-assisted methodology is widely used; and the assessor attempts to minimize method-dependent reactivity and strives to achieve a high degree of ecological validity. Ambulatory assessment has outstanding practical utility for various objectives such as monitoring and self-monitoring, screening, classification and selection, clinical diagnosis, and evaluation. It can be applied in various areas of psychology and other behavioral sciences, and there already are many successful applications in psychophysiology, personality psychology, health psychology, and clinical psychology. For more detailed information see Fahrenberg and Myrtek (1996, 2001) or the Web site of the European Network for Ambulatory Assessment (http://www.ambulatory-assessment.org).

Precursors of Ambulatory Assessment

Ambulatory assessment is not a completely new development. Self-monitoring procedures, electronic diaries, systematic behavior observation devices, and computer-assisted testing, to name only a few elements of the broad spectrum of methods applied in ambulatory assessment, have been with us for several decades. But the ambulatory assessment approach brought these diverse and often separate developments together and is on its way to becoming an influential movement in the field of psychological assessment that challenges traditional ideas, methods, and procedures (see Westmeyer, 2007).

Advantages of Ambulatory Assessment

It is still common practice in psychological assessment to assess a person's experience or behavior by applying questionnaires in a test laboratory or some other specifically designed situation that is far away and very different from the various contexts in which the experience or behavior of interest actually occurs. Therefore, traditional questionnaires have limited ecological validity and can assess the respective experience or behavior only retrospectively, whereas an ambulatory assessment procedure assesses that experience or behavior at the time and place of its actual occurrence. Such an assessment strategy has important advantages, because it avoids most of the errors and distortions characteristic of retrospective reports that rely on recall. Hufford, Shiffman, Paty, and Stone (2001), among others, mention incomplete and imperfect encoding, biased retrieval, and inadequate aggregation of information about events as well-documented sources of inaccuracy of retrospective recall.

Modes of Data Collection

There are two different types of data collection in ambulatory assessment: the event-controlled (or event–contingent) and the time-controlled (or time–contingent) mode. In the event-controlled mode, the subject must self-monitor the occurrence of certain events and perform an assessment whenever they occur. Examples are the self-observation and self-registration of target behaviors by a patient or the recording of the intensity of anxiety experienced by a person whenever confronted with fear-arousing stimuli. In the time-controlled mode, the subject has to follow a time-sampling schedule. Whenever the subject gets, in accord with the schedule, a signal by a prompting device (e.g., a handheld computer), he or she has to perform an assessment. Examples are the signal-contingent application of a computer-assisted self-report instrument to assess mood states and daily health following a variable time-interval schedule or the monitoring of blood pressure in hypertensive individuals at fixed time intervals. For more examples see Fahrenberg and Myrtek (2001) and Stone, Shiffman, Atienza, and Nebeling (2007).

Devices, Instruments, and Programs

The practice of ambulatory assessment depends heavily on the availability of suitable devices to record assessment data and programs for analyzing these data. For psychophysiological ambulatory assessment, one can choose between various recording and analyzing systems. There are specialized and multipurpose devices that assess a vast range of physiological parameters as, for example, blood pressure, skin or body temperature, and data from EEG, ECG, or EMG. Ambulatory assessment of experience and behavior makes use in most cases of handheld computers for which various software packages are available to assess, for example, personality variables, mood states, state of health, problem behaviors, or situational variables. For a state-of-the-art overview of available hardware and software solutions see Ebner-Priemer and Kubiak (2007). Appropriate methods for analyzing monitoring data may go well beyond what is common knowledge in the methodology of psychology. One example is circular statistics, a field of statistics that is well known in biology but unfamiliar to most psychological researchers. Under certain circumstances, it can be used as a superior alternative to traditional time-series analyses (Kubiak & Jonas, 2007).

Related Approaches

Apart from the ambulatory assessment movement, there is another group of researchers who pursue very similar goals but use other terms. Hufford, Shiffman, Paty, and Stone (2001) prefer the term Ecological Momentary Assessment (EMA). They are primarily interested in gathering self-reported health information in real time in the real world. EMA focuses on the collection of data on momentary states in the real world with a high degree of temporal resolution. This enables researchers to avoid the biases of retrospective recall, to achieve a high degree of ecological validity, and to analyze dynamic processes over time. In their most recent book, Stone et al. (2007) put EMA in the context of a more comprehensive *science of real-time data capture* (RTDC). "RTDC" and "ambulatory assessment" are terms with basically identical meanings, whereas EMA with its emphasis on self-reports can be conceived of as one of the three branches of ambulatory assessment. The other two branches focus on behavior records and physiological measurements, respectively.

Prospects

As far as behavior records and psychophysiological measurements are concerned, there is no real alternative to ambulatory assessment procedures, if one is interested in ecologically valid data. Therefore, we will see increasing applications of these procedures in, for example, health care, telemedicine, ergonomics, and occupational psychophysiology. But it is also to be expected that a growing number of researchers will be convinced by the obvious advantages that concurrent self-reports offer over traditional retrospective self-reports. This will foster the dissemination of this branch of ambulatory assessment, even if these data collection strategies are much more expensive and time-consuming than the simple application of traditional questionnaires to a large number of persons.

REFERENCES

Ebner-Priemer, U. W., & Kubiak, T. (2007). Psychological and psychophysiological ambulatory monitoring: A review on hardware and software solutions. *European Journal of Psychological Assessment, 23*, 214–226.

Fahrenberg, J., & Myrtek, M. (Eds.). (1996). *Ambulatory assessment*. Göttingen: Hogrefe & Huber Publishers.

Fahrenberg, J., & Myrtek, M. (Eds.). (2001). *Progress in ambulatory assessment*. Göttingen: Hogrefe & Huber Publishers.

Hufford, M. R., Shiffman, S., Paty, J., & Stone, A. A. (2001). Ecological momentary assessment: Real-world, real-time measurement of patient experience. In J. Fahrenberg, & M. Myrtek (Eds.), *Progress in ambulatory assessment* (pp. 69–92). Göttingen: Hogrefe & Huber Publishers.

Kubiak, T., & Jonas, C. (2007). Applying circular statistics to the analysis of monitoring data: Patterns of social interactions and mood. *European Journal of Psychological Assessment, 23*, 227–237.

Stone, A. A., Shiffman, S., Atienza, A. A. & Nebeling, L. (Eds.). (2007). *The science of real-time data capture: Self-reports in health research*. New York: Oxford University Press.

Westmeyer, H. (Ed.). (2007). Advances in the methodology of ambulatory assessment. Special Issue of *European Journal of Psychological Assessment, 23*, Number 4.

HANS WESTMEYER
Free University of Berlin, Germany

AMERICAN BOARD OF PROFESSIONAL PSYCHOLOGY

The American Board of Professional Psychology (ABPP; http://www.abpp.org) was originally established as the American Board of Professional Examiners in Psychology (ABEPP) in 1947. This followed recognition by the American Psychological Association (APA) of a need for assessing competency in professional psychology (Brent, Packard, & Goldberg, 1999). APA provided some initial funding for the establishment of the ABPP. Brent et al. (1999) provide a thorough history of ABPP through the late 1990s, and they detail the organizational evolution of ABPP.

Initially, the ABPP comprised two specialty areas: Clinical Psychology and Counseling Psychology. As of 2008, 13 specialty boards represent the following specialty areas: Cinical Child and Adolescent Psychology; Clinical Health Psychology; Clinical Neuropsychology; Clinical Psychology; Cognitive and Behavioral Psychology; Counseling Psychology; Couples and Family Psychology; Forensic Psychology; Group Psychology; Organizational and Business Consulting Psychology; Psychoanalysis in Psychology; Rehabilitation Psychology; and School Psychology.

Each specialty board is a member board of the ABPP, maintains its own governance, and it is responsible for establishing the ABPP definition of the specialty and its competencies, reviewing applicants, and examining candidates. Specialty boards may have an Academy that provides information about its specialty board certification process, continuing education, and other related specialty-specific activities. ABPP boards are individually subject to comparison with ABPP and non-ABPP boards. Quality and standards are reviewed within and across the ABPP boards on a regular basis.

Psychologists who become board certified may benefit professionally in a variety of ways. ABPP board certification is expected of psychologists joining the faculty of many universities and medical centers. Psychologists who are board certified through the ABPP may be eligible for pay increases and/or other benefits within the Department of Veterans Affairs, other governmental agencies, universities, hospitals and medical centers. ABPP board certification also facilitates mobility for psychologists who desire to relocate with many states recognizing ABPP in their licensing acts.

ABPP is an active participant, formal liaison, and/or observer to numerous national and international organizations. Examples within APA are the Committee for the Advancement of Professional Psychology (CAPP), Board of Professional Affairs (BPA), Board of Educational Affairs (BEA), and the Taxonomy Work Group. ABPP is a member organization of the Council of Credentialing Organizations in Professional Psychology (CCOPP) and has a liaison relationship with the Association of States and Provincial Psychology Boards (ASPPB) and the Council of Specialties in Professional Psychology (COS). Through these, ABPP is engaged in intra- and interorganizational quality improvement efforts. Within this context, ABPP continues to focus on the issues of *competency* and *competency assessment*. These are considered a vital part of ABPP's commitment to consumer protection and improving professional psychology.

ABPP has a long tradition of setting the standard for board certification within psychology. ABPP's ranking scope, multiple boards, and active relationships with other professional psychology organizations has led to its wide recognition and acceptance within the field of psychology.

REFERENCE

Brent, R. J., Packard, R. E., & Goldberg, R. W. (1999). The American Board of Professional Psychology, 1947 to 1997: A historical perspective. *Professional Psychology: Research and Practice 30*(1), 65–73.

DAVID R. COX
American Board of Professional Psychology

AMERICAN PSYCHOLOGICAL ASSOCIATION

In July 1892, G. Stanley Hall (1844–1924) met with a small group of men to discuss the possibility of organizing a psychological association. Hall and the group elected 31 individuals, including themselves, to membership, naming Hall as the first president. In organizing a disciplinary society, psychologists were following the lead of new scholarly and scientific disciplines like physiology, political science, and history. This was the time in America's history when many of the disciplines were establishing their identity and defining themselves. This was part of a reorganization of American knowledge production, reflecting a division of intellectual labor similar to the division of manufactory labor. Like its fellow disciplines, the new psychology grew and prospered as it responded to the needs of American society.

American higher education was reorganized in the last quarter of the nineteenth century, with the development of graduate education similar to the German university approach. Psychology, like the other new disciplines, soon developed advanced degrees providing credentials that served to validate the discipline's members as experts in their special field. This occurred in parallel with the progressive movement in politics, which called for a more efficient and less corrupt social order. The synergism of these two developments, specialized expertise and rationalized government, helped create the demand for trained personnel to fill the new professional niches created by the demands for a more efficient society. Psychology was one of the most successful of the new disciplines in making itself useful for the social management of an increasingly complex and diversified society.

The first meeting of the new American Psychological Association (APA) was held in December, 1892, at the University of Pennsylvania. The basic governance of the APA at this time consisted of a small Council with an Executive Committee. This plan remained in effect until the reorganization of APA during World War II.

Membership growth of the APA was modest over the first 50 years of its existence. From 31 members in 1892, there were 125 members in 1899, 308 in 1916, 530 in 1930, and 664 in 1940. In 1926 a new class of nonvoting membership was formed, the Associate class, and by 1940 the number of Associate members in APA had grown to 2,079. Many of these associates were individuals who were doing practical or applied work in psychology and also belonged to one of the applied associations that emerged at this time. Realizing that the growth of applied psychology represented a potential threat to its preeminence, the leaders of APA sought to reorganize the Association during World War II. Under this reorganization plan, the APA merged with other psychological organizations and created divisions to represent special fields of interest. There were initially 17 divisions (19 were proposed). The result was an association that was much more broadly based than previously and that was organized around an increasingly diffuse conceptualization of psychology. Now the Association's scope included professional practice and the promotion of human welfare, as well as the practice of the science of psychology. This flexibility in scope has remained to the present time, as new challenges and demands have arisen.

Psychology boomed after the end of World War II, with the greatest increase in membership coming between 1945 and 1970. This was due to intense interest in the field, especially in the domains of clinical and applied psychology and particularly among returning servicemen, many of whom saw the great need for better psychological services firsthand during the war. Institutional and structural factors that facilitated this growth included the GI Bill, the new Veterans Administration Clinical Psychology training program, and the creation of the National Institute of Mental Health. For the first time, psychology was a field of both science and practice that was richly funded for training and research. This was, as one scholar termed it, the Golden Age of Psychology. The rapid and incredible growth in APA's membership reflected this trend, as membership grew from 4,183 members in 1945 to 30,839 in 1970, an increase of 630%: By comparison, from 1970 to 2000, APA membership grew to 88,500, with an additional 70,500 affiliates.

Part of what facilitated this growth was the new divisional structure of the APA that grew out of the reorganization plan during World War II. Now members could join a special interest group within APA and find other like-minded members. Of course, this also facilitated the fractionation of psychology and pushed the field away from any sense of unity that it may have held prior to the war. Nineteen divisions were approved in 1944, with the two most numerous being clinical and personnel (now counseling). This reflected the sectional structure of the American Association of Applied Psychology (AAAP), which had emerged in 1937 as the chief rival to the APA and had been the chief reason for the reorganization. Because the Psychometric Society (Division 4) decided not to join, and after Division 11, Abnormal Psychology and Psychotherapy, merged with Division 12, Clinical Psychology, the number of active divisions was reduced to 17.

Growth in the number of divisions was slow until the 1960s, with only three more being added, in part because many of the older members, then in leadership positions, were quite resistant to increasing the number of divisions. From 1960 to 2007, 34 more divisions were formed to bring the total to 54. Many of the newer divisions reflect the growth of particular practice areas, such as Division 50, Addictions. However, there has also been growth in special interest areas that belie any simple science/practice dichotomy, including the Society for the Psychology of Women (Division 35), the Society for the History of Psychology (Division 26), International Psychology (Division 52), Media Psychology (Division 46), and the Society for the Psychological Study of Men and Masculinity (Division 51).

The effect on APA governance of the divisional structure and the growth of state and provincial psychological organizations has been marked. As mentioned, prior to World War II, APA's governance structure was a small Council with an Executive Committee. Since the reorganization and the end of the war, the Council of Representatives has grown in number to accommodate representation from each Division and from state and provincial psychological associations, thus making governance somewhat unwieldy. Various plans have been tried over the years to ensure a voice for each of the areas and interest groups in psychology on the Council, and it remains a dynamic situation. One governance result of the growth of professional psychology, especially clinical and counseling psychology, has been the increase in the representation of professional interests, such as licensing and specialization, in the deliberations of the Council. At times, this has led to tension between the representatives of psychological science and those whose main commitment is to advancing professional practice. In historical retrospect, it seems clear that this tension was inherent in the reorganization of APA, as the Association reflected developments in the field.

As a membership organization, APA has often been perceived as inadequately representing one or more of its constituencies. It has been the case, more often than not, that the resulting tension was resolved and the unhappy parties remained within the association. However, there have also been more serious disagreements that have resulted in new organizations being formed. In the late 1950s, a group of experimental psychologists grew unhappy with what they perceived as APA's drift from scientific psychology. By the end of 1959, this group had formed the Psychonomic Society in order, they asserted, to foster psychology as a science without a need to attend to professional issues. The Psychonomic Society remains a viable and valuable organization of scientists to the present moment; many of its members remained APA members, as well. A more serious division occurred in the mid- to late 1980s, as tensions between those who wanted APA to remain a primarily scientific organization and those who sought a greater emphasis by the association on professional practice rose to a boil. A proposed reorganization plan was defeated by a vote of the membership, and almost immediately thereafter a large group of dissident psychological scientists, including some former APA presidents, left the APA to form what is now the Association for Psychological Science (APS). Still, after a period of struggle, both organizations are strong, stable representatives of psychology, with many psychologists belonging to both associations.

One result of the split that led to the formation of APS is that professional interests have grown stronger within APA. Even so, APA has maintained a commitment to the promotion of psychological science. Internally, in the APA Central Office, this commitment is represented by the Science Directorate. Since the late 1980s, the Central Office has been reorganized to better represent the diverse constituencies of the membership. Beginning with the formation of the Practice Directorate in the late 1980s, other Directorates were formed in the hope that the interests of all the membership would be better represented. As of 2008, there are in addition to the Practice Directorate the Education, Science, and Public Interest Directorates. From a historical perspective, it is too soon to determine whether this approach represents an advance for the Association or a further balkanization of the field.

APA remains the world's largest membership organization of psychologists. It has a fascinating past, marked by growth, conflict, and increasing diversification.

SUGGESTED READINGS

Dewsbury, D. A. (1997). On the evolution of divisions. *American Psychologist, 52,* 733–741.

Evans, R. B., Sexton, V. S., & Cadwallader, T. C. (Eds.), *The American Psychological Association: A historical perspective*. Washington, DC: American Psychological Association.

Fernberger, S. W. (1932). The American Psychological Association: A historical summary, 1892–1930. *Psychological Bulletin, 29,* 1–89.

Guthrie, R. V. (1998). *Even the rat was white: A historical view of psychology.* Boston: Allyn & Bacon.

Pickren, W. E., & Schneider, S. F. (Eds.). (2005). *Psychology and the National Institute of Mental Health: A historical analysis of science, practice, and policy.* Washington, DC: APA Books.

WADE E. PICKREN
Ryerson University, Canada

AMERICAN PSYCHOLOGICAL ASSOCIATION CODE OF ETHICS

The American Psychological Association (APA) promulgated the first Code of Ethics for psychologists in 1953. This publication, however, had been preceded by a committee devoted to ethical concerns that had been formed in 1938, and was based on the work of a committee organized in 1947 (Canter, Bennett, Jones, & Nagy, 1994). The formalization and codification of ethical standards was a response to the increasing professionalization of psychology, a development that began during World War II.

The first Code of Ethics (American Psychological Association, 1953) was developed using an empirical, critical-incident methodology (Hobbs, 1948) that had been unprecedented among associations. Rather than using an a priori method to determine ethical principles, the membership of the association was surveyed and asked to report incidents in which a decision had been made with ethical implications, including a discussion of the ethical issues involved. This material then formed the basis for many drafts of the first Code of Ethics, each of which was distributed to the membership for commentary before the final version was adopted.

Since the introduction of the original Code of Ethics, revisions, either minor or major, have been adopted a great many times. These changes, regardless of scope, serve to keep the Code current and to respond to new issues, to changing views on traditional issues, and to legal imperatives that influence ethical behavior. Thus, it would be correct to describe the Code of Ethics as a living document and, as such, it is clear that it embraces an approach to ethics that is influenced by current events rather than based on universal ethical principles. In each revision, the Code of Ethics contains a set of ethical principles (or standards) without the inclusion of illustrative incidents.

The Code of Ethics in force presently was published in 2003 (American Psychological Association, 2002). Although the critical-incident methodology was not employed, the revision was informed by the history of ethical complaints that had been filed, so that an empirical basis was built in to the revision process. The alterations in the Code took 11 years after the publication of the 1992 Code (American Psychological Association, 1992), and involved many iterations involving the membership of APA, the Ethics Committee, the Revision Comments Subcommittee, and finally the Council of Representatives of APA. The document that was produced was intended to be accessible to psychologists and to consumers of psychological services, and to provide guidelines that would increase the quality of psychological services and also reduce the risk of harm to the consumers.

The Code of Ethics of a professional association is enforceable only with regard to members of the association, but it also forms the basis of the conception of ethics by many State Boards, who themselves are asked to make judgments of the professional conduct of licensed professionals. In addition, it is the foundation of the instruction in ethics that is mandated by accreditation for students in psychology. Thus, the influence of the Code is far broader than its scope of enforceability. Similarly, the maximum penalty that can be exacted for a serious violation of the Code is expulsion from the organization, but this expulsion is publicly noted, other relevant groups are informed (and may take independent action), and there are implications for matters such as insurability, so that the penalty is much more severe than simple expulsion by itself.

The 2003 Code of Ethics has two major sections, as well as introductory material that includes clarification that the Code applies only to psychologists' work-related activities, a point reiterated in the first enforceable standard. The first section of the Code consists of five General Principles. These Principles are aspirational rather than enforceable, but they can be used to interpret the enforceable standards that follow. The Principles represent standards for ethical behavior, as opposed to the areas of function that were embodied in the previous Code. The principles are Beneficence and Nonmaleficence, Fidelity and Responsibility, Integrity, Justice, and Respect for People's Rights and Dignity. The approach to ethics embodied herein is called principle-based ethics and refers to general principles that should guide moral behavior. There are no set and agreed upon set of principles, but the ones in this document are among those that have been suggested in the ethics literature (Kitchener, 2000). The Principles are operationalized in the more specific standards that make up the largest portion of the document.

The Ethical Standards are the specific and directly enforceable translation of the General Principles. There are a total of 89 standards, but they are most easily summarized by referring to the 10 sections that contain them. The first section, Resolving Ethical Issues, indicates the affirmative responsibility of psychologists to be familiar with and to help to uphold the ethical standards of the discipline. It indicates, among other things, that when the Code conflicts with the law, the psychologist may, but not must, act in conformity with the law, and must attempt to resolve the conflict consistent with the Code.

The second standard concerns Competence, emphasizing the need for psychologists to maintain competence and to practice within the areas of competence, informed by the most current knowledge base. Human Relations is concerned with the avoidance of exploitative relationships of many different types. Privacy and Confidentiality goes beyond the clinical activities of psychologists and indicates the nature of confidentiality and how it can be established and honored. Advertising and Other Public Standards has become more permissive since rulings of the Federal Trade Commission indicated the illegality of banning professional advertising. Standard six concerns Record Keeping and Fees, indicating the need to maintain proper records and to make fees clear and fair. Education and Training is specific to educational sites and discusses the design of training programs and the treatment of students. Research and Publication, along with several of the previous Standards, makes clear that the Code of Ethics is not restricted in its scope to professional practice, but is intended to be applicable to the activities of all psychologists.

Standard nine, Assessment, is predominantly, but not exclusively, applicable to clinical activities. It ranges from test construction to the use and basis of psychological tests. Finally, the last standard concerns Therapy and may be the area of major concern to most practitioners. It concerns the practice and delivery of therapeutic services, including all modalities, and includes the prohibition of sexual relationships with patients. It is only through the commitment of the individual psychologist to the Code of Ethics that psychology can progress toward a firm foundation in ethical and responsible conduct.

REFERENCES

American Psychological Association. (1953). *Ethical standards of psychologists.* Washington, DC: Author.

American Psychological Association. (1992). Ethical principles of psychologists and code of conduct. *American Psychologist, 47,* 1597–1611.

American Psychological Association. (2002). Ethical principles of psychologists and code of conduct. *American Psychologist, 57,* 1060–1073.

Canter, M. B., Bennett, B. E., Jones, S. E., & Nagy, T. F. (1994). *Ethics for psychologists: A commentary on the APA ethics code.* Washington, DC: American Psychological Association.

Hobbs, N. (1948). The development of a code of ethical standards for psychology. *American Psychologist, 3,* 80–84.

Kitchener, K. S. (2000). *Foundations of ethical practice, research, and teaching.* Mahwah, NJ: Lawrence Erlbaum.

GEORGE STRICKER
Argosy University

See also: **Ethical Issues in Psychology; Ethical Treatment of Animals**

AMERICAN PSYCHOLOGICAL ASSOCIATION OF GRADUATE STUDENTS

The American Psychological Association of Graduate Students (APAGS) is a continuing committee within the American Psychological Association (APA) that advocates for the unique needs and concerns of graduate students. APAGS consists of approximately 40,000 student affiliate members and is one of the largest constituency groups within the APA. APAGS is the largest group of organized psychology graduate students in the world (APAGS, 2008).

History

APAGS was founded in 1988 by two Canadian graduate students, Scott Mesh and David Pilon. Scott and David worked with then APA CEO, Raymond Fowler, to persuade the APA Council of Representatives to approve the formation of the APAGS Committee. This was the first successful attempt to create an organization within the APA to address the unique needs and concerns of graduate students. The new committee provided a much needed home for psychology graduates students within APA.

APAGS continues to grow and advance its influence and advocacy efforts on behalf of graduate students. For instance, APAGS liaisons with key boards and committees both within and affiliated with the APA, including the Committee for the Advancement of Professional Practice, the Board of Scientific Affairs, the Board of Educational Affairs, the Board of Professional Affairs, the Association of Psychology Postdoctoral and Internship Centers (APPIC), and many others (APAGS, 2008). APAGS has representation on the APA Committee on Accreditation, the APA Board of Directors, the APA Council of Representatives, and the Psychology Executives Roundtable (APAGS, 2008). APAGS currently holds voting privileges on the APA Committee on Accreditation and the APA Council of Representatives, and it is in the process of advocating for the APAGS membership on the APA Board of Directors to become a voting position. These relationships and representations demonstrate APAGS' integration and advocacy efforts within and outside of APA. This year marks APAGS' 20th anniversary of representing, advocating, and addressing the needs of psychology graduate students.

Mission and Purpose

APAGS is the voice of psychology students within the APA and community at large. The mission of APAGS is (1) to promote high standards in the research, teaching, and practice of psychology, (2) to represent and facilitate information exchange between all graduate study specialties of psychology, (3) to promote graduate student leadership development, and (4) to establish and maintain channels of communication between APAGS and schools, universities, training centers, institutions, and other members of the psychological community (APAGS, 2008). This mission helps to guide the work and goals of the APAGS committee.

Membership Composition

APAGS members include all graduate student affiliate members of the APA and any undergraduate students who elect to upgrade their membership to APAGS status for an additional fee. Members enjoy a host of benefits that include (1) subscriptions to the *American Psychologist*, the *Monitor on Psychology*, and the APAGS magazine, *gradPSYCH*; (2) a $10 credit for subscriptions to APA journals; (3) the right to purchase access to APA's online databases like PsycINFO; (4) access to listservs targeted to a variety of student interests; (5) internship and career resources; (6) scholarship and award eligibility; and (7) access to professional liability insurance (APAGS, 2008).

Members also receive access to information resources created by and for graduate students, such as the APAGS Practice Resource Guide; the APAGS Resource Guide for Lesbian, Gay, Bisexual, and Transgender Individuals; the APAGS Survival Guide for Ethnic Minority Graduate Students; Resource Guide for Psychology Graduate Students with Disabilities; the Networking Guide for Students within State, Provincial, and Territorial Psychological Associations; and the Mentoring, Balance and Self-Care—Especially for Women: A Collection of Articles and Resources (APAGS, 2008).

APAGS Governance Structure

Members who choose to run for elected office or apply for an appointed subcommittee position are able to become involved in APAGS governance. The APAGS governance comprises nine officers elected by APAGS members and five specialized subcommittees. The volunteer work is supported by an associate executive director and professional staff at the APA headquarters in Washington, D.C. The elected positions are the Chair, the Past-Chair, the Chair-Elect, and six Members at Large who focus on the specific areas of practice, science, education, diversity, communications, and membership. The APAGS governance structure is modeled after the structure of the APA governance system.

In addition, APAGS has four subcommittees: the Committee on Ethnic Minority Affairs (CEMA), the Advocacy Coordinating Team (ACT), the Committee on Lesbian, Gay, Bisexual, and Transgender Concerns (CLGBTC), and the Convention Committee (APAGS, 2008). CEMA represents and advocates for the perspectives and concerns of ethnic minority graduate students within the discipline of psychology. ACT is composed of psychology graduate students who primarily engage in legislative advocacy work on behalf of the science and profession of psychology (APAGS, 2008). ACT members promote the welfare of graduate students and the profession by engaging in legislative advocacy efforts. CLGBTC facilitates communication among gay, lesbian, bisexual, and transgender graduate students in psychology and it helps to educate psychologists, faculty, and students of the concerns and needs of lesbian, gay, bisexual, and transgender students. The APAGS Convention Committee works with APAGS staff to plan student programs and events for the annual APA Convention, which provides APAGS members with the opportunity to present their research, ideas, and work at the annual convention (APAGS, 2008).

Activities

APAGS governance members and staff work collaboratively to create and distribute information on education and training issues, legislative positions and developments, and current and future directions within the field through printed resources and the APAGS web site (APAGS, 2008). APAGS also provides opportunities for graduate students in the form of scholarships and awards, members support, resource development, leadership opportunities, and special convention programming. Further information about APAGS is available on its web site at http://www.apa.org/apags/.

REFERENCE

American Psychological Association of Graduate Students. (2008, September). *About APAGS.* Retrieved September 1, 2008, from http://www.apa.org/apags/about.html.

Nadia T. Hasan
University of Akron

AMERICAN PSYCHOLOGY-LAW SOCIETY

The American Psychology-Law Society (APLS), which is Division 41 of the American Psychological Association (APA), is a professional organization dedicated to the advancement of scholarship, education, public service, and practice in the field of psychology and law. The Society was founded in 1969 by several APA members, including Eric Dreikurs and Jay Ziskin, who had specific interests in psychology and law. Ziskin became the first president of APLS. The goals of the original members included advancing the professional practice of psychology in the legal field, using research to improve the quality of psychological expert testimony to the courts, and developing a community for researchers interested in the application of psychological methods and theory to the legal context (Grisso, 1991; Fulero, 1999). Most of the original members of the Society were trained in clinical psychology and were academicians or clinical practitioners (Grisso, 1991). Early members of the Society were interested in issues such as expert testimony, competency to stand trial, the insanity defense, jury decision making, and eyewitness testimony (Fulero, 1999). APLS established a conference in 1974. These conferences began as biennial meetings and became annual meetings in 2002.

In a separate organizational process, an APA committee convened in 1979 with the goal of forming a division to represent APA members interested in psychology and law (Grisso, 1991; Fulero, 1999). Division 41 of the APA was founded in 1981 with John Monahan serving as the first president. The APLS merged with Division 41 in 1984.

Although the Society and APA Division 41 are now a merged entity, APLS also remains a freestanding organization. APA membership is not required for membership in APLS. As of 2008, APLS has 1,955 registered members who are also members of APA, 409 members who are not APA members, and 731 student members. The Society's membership is diverse and includes academicians, clinical practitioners, attorneys, clinical researchers, scientists, and policy advocates (Fulero, 1999).

The Society and its members have made important contributions to the field of psychology and law. These include collaborating with APA on *amicus curie* briefs to provide guidance to the courts on psychological issues and developing ethical guidelines, currently undergoing revision, for the practice of forensic psychology (Committee on Ethical Guidelines for Forensic Psychologists, 1991). The Society's Scientific Review Paper Committee commissions scholars to review the research on a particular issue and provide recommendations for best practices in the area. The first of these review papers concerned the literature on eyewitness identifications (Wells et al., 1998) and the paper currently in preparation reviews the psychological literature on interrogation practices and the risk of false confessions.

The Society's official journal, *Law and Human Behavior*, was founded in 1977 and currently is published bimonthly. The Society also publishes an online newsletter three times per year. APLS formerly published a book series, *Perspectives in Law and Psychology*, with Kluwer Academic/Plenum Press, but since 2005 has partnered with Oxford University Press to produce a book series, with offerings addressing issues such as trial consulting, the death penalty, and psychological injuries. The web site for APLS is http://www.ap-ls.org. Current initiatives in the Society are to increase the diversity of the membership, to provide increased support to early career psychologists, and to maintain unity in the organization despite the diverse professional and research interests of APLS members.

REFERENCES

Committee on Ethical Guidelines for Forensic Psychologists. (1991). Specialty guidelines for forensic psychologists. *Law and Human Behavior, 15,* 655–665.

Fulero, S. M. (1999). A history of Division 41 (American Psychology-Law Society): A rock and roll odyssey. In D. Dewsbury (Ed.), *Unification through division: Histories of the divisions of the American Psychological Association, Vol. IV* (pp. 109–127). Washington, DC: American Psychological Association.

Grisso, T. (1991). A developmental history of the American Psychology-Law Society. *Law and Human Behavior, 15,* 213–231.

Technical Working Group for Eyewitness Evidence. (1999). *Eyewitness evidence: A guide for law enforcement* (NCJ 178240). National Institute of Justice, U.S. Department of Justice.

Wells, G. L., Small, M., Penrod, S., Malpass, R. S., Fulero, S. M., & Brimacombe, C. A. E. (1998). Eyewitness identification procedures: Recommendations for lineups and photo spreads. *Law and Human Behavior, 22,* 1–39.

CAROLINE B. CROCKER
MARGARET BULL KOVERA
John Jay College, City University of New York

AMERICAN PSYCHOSOMATIC SOCIETY

Founded in 1942, the American Psychosomatic Society (APS) was one of the first medical societies to be dedicated to the integration of biology, psychology, and social factors in medicine. This integration grew out of an understanding that the state of the mind could influence the health of the body, as shown by twentieth-century physiologists, including Walter Cannon. Psychosomatic concepts also grew out of observations by psychoanalysts of patients who had physical symptoms that were not explained by purely medical causes. Drawing upon these insights, the APS was formed through the work of a New York Academy of Medicine committee headed by Dr. Helen Flanders Dunbar, a pioneer trained in medicine and religion, who compiled a bibliography of the "psychosomatic" medical literature, published in 1935 as "Emotions and Bodily Changes." In 1936, the Josiah Macy, Jr., Foundation began financial support for psychosomatic studies and, along with the National Health Council in 1939, underwrote the publication of a new journal, *Psychosomatic Medicine.* The APS was subsequently formed as a medical society and held its first Annual Meeting in New York in 1942.

The current mission of the APS remains focused on understanding health in relation to biological, psychological, and social factors. The APS has remained focused on problems of long-standing interest, including the bidirectional relationships between the mind and the body. The ultimate goal of this scientific work is to develop improvements in health and in medical care for patients.

The APS currently has approximately 900 members from 40 countries. APS membership is drawn from students and professionals in medicine, psychology, epidemiology, and other health-related disciplines. The Annual Meeting is held each spring and provides members and nonmembers with a forum to exchange recent research findings and to obtain specialized training in clinical and scientific topics bearing on psychosomatic questions. APS has an active student mentorship program at the Annual Meeting to promote contacts among scientists and professionals and professionals in training. Special programs are also available to assist persons from developing countries to attend meetings and develop contacts with members of APS.

The APS maintains a web site (http://www.psychosomatic.org) to disseminate information on membership and on events such as the Annual Meeting. The Society continues to publish its journal *Psychosomatic Medicine* nine times a year (http://www.psychosomaticmedicine.org) and also a quarterly newsletter.

SUGGESTED READINGS

Dunbar, H. F. (1935). *Emotions and bodily changes.* New York: University of Columbia Press.

Levenson, D. (1994). *Mind, body, and medicine.* Philadelphia, PA: Williams & Wilkins.

Powell, Robert C. Healing and wholeness: Helen Flanders Dunbar (1902–1959) and an extra-medical origin of the American psychosomatic movement, 1906–1936. (PhD dissertation, Duke University, 1974).

WILLIAM R. LOVALLO
VA Medical Center and University of Oklahoma Health Sciences Center

AMNESIA

Our current understanding of amnesia owes much to the study of the patient HM, who in 1953, at the age of 26, underwent bilateral removal of structures in the medial temporal lobe (MTL) for treatment of intractable epilepsy. The surgery was largely successful in controlling his seizures, and it did not affect his sense of personal identity, his general fund of knowledge, or his social skills, but it left him with a global amnesia—he had a profound impairment in the ability to form new memories for events and information that he encountered after his surgery (Corkin, 1984). Thus, for example, he could not remember the plot of a movie he saw recently, could not recall what he ate at his last meal, and could not recognize the names or faces of new acquaintances. In the laboratory, HM showed profound impairments in recalling or recognizing recently presented lists of words, pictures, and other stimuli. He also showed impaired recall of events prior to his surgery, but could retrieve memories from his early life, prior to about age 16. With insights gleaned from studies of HM and subsequently from other amnesic individuals, we have achieved a more complete understanding not only of the amnesic syndrome, but also of the functional and neural architecture of normal human memory.

The cardinal feature of the amnesic syndrome is an impairment in new learning (anterograde amnesia), and this deficit is accompanied by a more variable impairment in the ability to retrieve memories formed prior to the onset of illness (retrograde amnesia). Amnesia occurs in the context of relatively preserved general intelligence and other cognitive abilities. Immediate or short-term memory is intact in amnesia. For example, an amnesic individual can hold in mind the current topic of conversation; can repeat a brief sequence of letters or numbers; and can address a new acquaintance by name upon initial introduction. After any distraction or delay, however, whether for minutes, days, or weeks, memory for this information is impaired. Thus, the anterograde memory impairment in amnesia characteristically affects long-term memory, rather than immediate or short-term memory.

Although amnesia can have a psychogenic origin, we focus here on organic amnesia, which results from structural brain damage. The impairment is typically associated with lesions of structures in the MTL (including the hippocampus and the adjacent entorhinal, perirhinal, and parahippocampal cortices), the diencephalon, and the basal forebrain. Amnesia has a variety of etiologies, including herpes simplex encephalitis, anoxia, Wernicke-Korsakoff syndrome, and cerebrovascular accidents (O'Connor, Verfaellie, & Cermak, 1995).

Anterograde Memory in Amnesia

The anterograde memory deficit in amnesia cuts across all types of materials (e.g., verbal and visuospatial) and perceptual modalities (e.g, auditory, visual), and it includes personally experienced events (episodic memory) as well as impersonal facts and concepts (semantic memory). One of the most important insights to emerge from studies of amnesia, however, is that the impairment is not uniform across all forms of long-term memory. For example, whereas amnesic patients show deficits on "explicit" or "declarative" memory tasks, which require deliberate reference to a prior experience, they often show normal performance on "implicit" or "nondeclarative" memory tasks, which do not require deliberate reference to a prior

experience, but in which memory for that experience is "implicit" in task performance.

Examples of preserved implicit memory effects in amnesia include classical eyeblink conditioning (learning to make an eyeblink in response to a tone if that tone was previously paired with an air-puff to the eye); skill learning (improved task performance with practice); and repetition priming (improved accuracy in identifying perceptually degraded words or pictures as a result of recent exposure to those stimuli). These findings suggest that, whereas explicit memory processes depend on neural circuits that are damaged in amnesia, implicit memory processes depend on neural circuits (e.g., in the cerebellum, the basal ganglia, or the neocortex) that are spared in amnesia (Gabrieli, 1998).

Even within the domain of explicit memory, not all forms of memory appear to be equally impaired in amnesia. For example, there is evidence in amnesia that memory for associations between items (e.g., remembering that the word "sample" was paired with the word "carriage" in a recently presented list) is more impaired than is memory for single items (e.g., remembering that the word "carriage" appeared in a recently presented list) (Giovanello, Verfaellie, & Keane, 2003). This behavioral finding accords well with theories that assign to the hippocampus a critical role in binding together unrelated items in memory.

Another differential impairment in amnesia is revealed when one considers two qualitatively distinct processes that support explicit memory: recollection and familiarity. Recollection refers to intentional retrieval of the content of a prior experience, whereas familiarity refers to an ease of stimulus processing that creates the sense that one has encountered that stimulus previously. By way of illustration, if one has recently made a new acquaintance, one might recollect (i.e., intentionally retrieve) that person's name upon encountering that person again, or one might experience a sense of familiarity (ease of recognition) that confirms that one has indeed met this person before. There is some evidence to suggest that recollection is more impaired than familiarity in amnesia (Yonelinas et al., 2002). For example, some patients with damage limited to the hippocampus show impaired performance when asked to recall a recent event (a task that requires recollection), but show intact performance when asked to recognize whether a particular item was present in that event (a task that may be based on a sense of familiarity with that item).

Patients with more extensive MTL lesions show explicit memory impairments that are evident both in recall and in recognition tasks, but that are more severe in the former than in the latter instance, consistent with a greater deficit in recollection than in familiarity. Findings such as these have led to the view that recollection is mediated by the hippocampus (which is typically severely compromised in amnesia), and familiarity depends upon extra-hippocampal MTL regions such as the perirhinal cortex that are more variably and less severely compromised in amnesia (Brown & Aggleton, 2001). This issue is controversial, however, because some amnesic patients—even those with damage restricted to the hippocampus—have shown equivalent impairments in recollection and familiarity (Manns, Hopkins, Reed, Kitchener, & Squire, 2003) supporting the alternative view that all MTL regions contribute equally to these two explicit memory processes.

Retrograde Memory in Amnesia

A classic finding in amnesia is that the retrograde memory impairment is temporally limited, such that very remote memories are spared, whereas memories from the time period closer to the onset of amnesia are compromised. This observation gave rise to an influential theory positing that the MTL is engaged in the consolidation (stabilization) of long-term memories (Squire, Cohen, & Nadel, 1984). Once the consolidation process is complete, memories no longer depend on the hippocampus, but are supported by neocortical brain regions that are not damaged in amnesia. This view provides a straightforward account of the pattern of retrograde memory loss in amnesia: Very remote memories are intact because they had already been consolidated in neocortex at the onset of amnesia, and more recent memories are lost because they were in the process of consolidation at the time of onset. By extension, the formation of new memories after the onset of amnesia is impaired due to the absence of a consolidation mechanism.

Recent studies, however, have called into question the view that very remote memories are entirely spared in amnesia. Although it seems clear that remote memory for semantic information (facts and concepts) is intact in amnesia, there is growing evidence that remote memory for episodic (autobiographical) information may be compromised. Detailed examinations of the quality and number of remote autobiographical memories in amnesia have revealed that there may be impairments that extend back in time for decades prior to the onset of amnesia. Such temporally extensive remote memory impairments cannot be explained easily by a consolidation view, because consolidation is unlikely to operate over such a lengthy time frame.

An alternative to consolidation theory known as the multiple memory trace view proposes that the hippocampus is engaged each time an autobiographical memory is retrieved (regardless of the age of that memory), and that each such retrieval establishes a novel memory trace in the hippocampus (Moscovitch, Nadel, Winocur, Gilboa, & Rosenbaum, 2006). By this view, autobiographical memories never become independent of the hippocampus and consequently are compromised in amnesia regardless of how remote they are. The degree of impairment may be smaller for very remote memories, because such memories have presumably been retrieved on numerous occasions over time, and are therefore associated with larger number of hippocampal traces and more resistant to partial hippocampal damage.

In summary, amnesia is a circumscribed memory impairment characterized by severe impairments in anterograde memory and more variable or limited impairments in retrograde memory. The functional impact of such deficits on activities of daily life is profound. In this context, the relative preservation of some forms of long-term memory (implicit memory, familiarity) takes on clinical importance, as these areas of preserved function may form the basis for the development of compensatory strategies or rehabilitative approaches in amnesia.

REFERENCES

Brown, M. W., & Aggleton, J. P. (2001). Recognition memory: What are the roles of the perirhinal cortex and hippocampus? *Nature Reviews Neuroscience, 2,* 51–61.

Corkin, S. (1984). Lasting consequences of bilateral medial temporal lobectomy: Clinical course and experimental findings in H. M. *Seminars in Neurology, 4*(2), 249–259.

Gabrieli, J. D. E. (1998). Cognitive neuroscience of human memory. *Annual Review of Psychology, 49,* 87–115.

Giovanello, K. S., Verfaellie, M., & Keane, M. M. (2003). Disproportionate deficit in associative recognition relative to item recognition in global amnesia. *Cognitive, Affective, and Behavioral Neuroscience, 3,* 186–194.

Manns, J. R., Hopkins, R. O., Reed, J. M., Kitchener, E. G., & Squire, L. R. (2003). Recognition memory and the human hippocampus. *Neuron, 37,* 171–180.

Moscovitch, M., Nadel, L., Winocur, G., Gilboa, A., & Rosenbaum, R. S. (2006). The cognitive neuroscience of remote episodic, semantic and spatial memory. *Current Opinion in Neurobiology, 16,* 179–190.

O'Connor, M., Verfaellie, M., & Cermak, L. S. (1995). Clinical differentiation of amnesic subtypes. In A. D. Baddeley, B. A. Wilson & F. N. Watts (Eds.), *Handbook of memory disorders* (pp. 53–80). Oxford, UK: John Wiley & Sons.

Squire, L. R., Cohen, N. J., & Nadel, L. (1984). The medial temporal region and memory consolidation: A new hypothesis. In H. Weingartner & E. S. Parker (Eds.), *Memory consolidation: Psychobiology of cognition* (pp. 185–210). Hillsdale, NJ: Lawrence Erlbaum.

Yonelinas, A. P., Kroll, N. E. A., Quamme, J. R., Lazzara, M. M., Sauve, M.-J., Widaman, K. F., et al. (2002). Effects of extensive temporal lobe damage or mild hypoxia on recollection and familiarity. *Nature Neuroscience, 5,* 1236–1241.

SUGGESTED READINGS

Hassabis, D., Kumaran, D., Vann, S. D., & Maguire, E. A. (2007). Patients with hippocampal amnesia cannot imagine new experiences. *Proceedings of the National Academy of Sciences, 104,* 1726–1731.

Tulving, E. (2002). Episodic memory: From mind to brain. *Annual Review of Psychology, 53,* 1–25.

Verfaellie, M., & Keane, M. M. (2002). Impaired and preserved memory processes in amnesia. In L. R. Squire & D. L. Schacter (Eds.), *Neuropsychology of memory* (3rd ed., pp. 35–46). New York: Guilford Press.

MARGARET M. KEANE
Wellesley College

MIEKE VERFAELLIE
*Boston University School of Medicine
and VA Boston Healthcare System*

See also: **Declarative Memory; Hippocampus; Memory Functions**

AMYGDALA

The amygdala is a collection of anatomically and functionally distinct nuclei buried deep within the temporal lobes of the brain. It has long been appreciated that the amygdala has a critical role in emotion and emotional memory. For instance, work in the 1930s by Kluver and Bucy revealed striking changes in the emotional responses of monkeys after temporal lobe lesions that included the amygdala (Kluver & Bucy, 1937). These changes in emotion were later shown to be reproduced by amygdala damage alone and linked to deficits in assigning emotional significance to biologically relevant stimuli (Weiskrantz, 1956). Indeed, humans with amygdala damage show similar deficits in emotional processing. For example, patient S.M., who has a rare illness that caused selective and complete bilateral damage to her amygdala, is impaired in recognizing facial expressions of emotion, particularly fear. Furthermore, when presented with fear-inducing stimuli, such as a movie clip, S.M. is unable to produce normal emotional responses, although she can explain that most people would feel afraid when watching these clips (Adolphs et al., 1999). Consistent with this, normal subjects who view facial expressions of fear exhibit increased regional cerebral blood flow in the amygdala.

One of the most fruitful behavioral paradigms for exploring the role of the amygdala in emotion is Pavlovian fear conditioning. In this form of learning, animals or humans are presented with an innocuous conditioned stimulus (CS), such as a tone, that is paired with an aversive unconditioned stimulus (US), such as a mild electric shock. After one or more pairings the subject learns that the CS predicts the US. As a consequence, CS presentations alone elicit a conditioned fear response (CR), which includes increases in heart rate, arterial blood pressure,

hypoalgesia, potentiated acoustic startle, stress hormone release, and freezing behavior.

Many years of work have identified the amygdala as a candidate region in which fear memories are encoded and stored (Davis & Whalen, 2001; LeDoux, 2000; Maren, 2001). Within the amygdala there are two sub-regions that contribute to fear learning and the expression of learned fear responses. The basolateral amygdala complex (BLA; consisting of the lateral, basolateral, and basomedial nuclei) is where the CS and US information converge and become associated (yielding the fear memory), and the central nucleus of the amygdala (CEA) translates this information into behavioral fear responses. In support of this, many studies have shown that damage to either the BLA or CEA prevent acquisition and/or expression of fear memories. However, rats with pretraining BLA lesions can acquire fear CRs if given sufficient training. This suggests that another brain area is involved in forming fear associations in the absence of the BLA. Recent studies have pointed to the CEA in the acquisition and consolidation of fear memories and suggest that the CEA may mediate fear in the absence of the BLA (Zimmerman et al., 2007).

The amygdala is also involved in a different form of aversive learning, known as instrumental avoidance. In this task, animals are able to prevent the occurrence of an aversive US by making a particular behavioral response to the CS. For example, rats can be readily trained to jump from one side of a rectangular alley to the other side to avoid a footshock. Rats with damage to the BLA are unable to learn that performing a specific response will turn off the aversive US, but they are still capable of displaying unconditioned fear responses. In addition damage to the CEA does impair conditioned freezing responses, as seen in Pavlovian fear conditioning, however some CRs like conditioned avoidance responses persist with CEA damage (Aggleton, 2000).

The amygdala also encodes aversive experiences involving interoceptive stimuli. Conditioned taste aversion (CTA) occurs when an animal feels sick after eating a particular food. The animal forms an association between the taste of the food and sickness. Therefore, in the future the animal will avoid consuming that particular food in the hopes of avoiding illness. In this paradigm, like other forms of aversive learning, the amygdala is important for acquiring taste information, evaluating the hedonic properties of taste, associating taste and malaise, and expressing CTA. Specifically, the BLA is primarily involved in forming associations between the taste CS and the malaise-inducing US (Aggleton, 2000).

Animal models have shown that the amygdala is not only involved in aversive emotional processing, but also plays a role in appetitive conditioning. In these tasks, CSs gain motivational significance through their association with a positive reward, such as food. Although the amygdala is involved in both aversive and appetitive learning the role of the amygdala may differ between these two learning paradigms. The amygdala is not necessary for animals to learn that a CS predicts a food US, however the BLA is necessary for the CS to gain access to the current value of a specific US with which it has been associated. For example, BLA lesions impair conditioned reinforcement, second-order conditioning, and US devaluation, all of which depend on the CS gaining access to the value of the US with which it has been paired (Holland & Gallagher, 2004).

On the other hand, the CEA appears to encode Pavlovian stimulus-response associations (S-R) that do not incorporate motivational values about the US and produces conditioned motivational responses (Aggleton, 2000; Murray, 2007). Forms of learning mediated by S-R associations that are disrupted by CEA lesions, but not BLA lesions, include conditioned suppression, conditioned locomotor approach, autoshaping, and Pavlovian-instrumental-transfer (Aggleton, 2000; Holland & Gallagher, 2004; Murray, 2007). In addition to its role in mediating S-R associations, the CEA is also important for increasing attentional performance when there is a shift from a predictive relationship between stimuli to a surprising relationship, but not when the predictive relationship is consistent. Rats with CEA lesions do not show effects of increased attentional performance and in fact display deficits in learning (Holland & Gallagher, 1999).

Although the role of the amygdala in emotional learning and memory has been well established in animal models for both aversive and appetitive learning, most studies in humans have largely concluded that the amygdala is involved in processing negative emotions, such as fear. However, there is emerging evidence that amygdala activity is also important for processing positive affect (Hamann et al., 2002; Murray, 2007). In one study human subjects were presented with positive, negative, and neutral emotional photographs during positron emission tomography (PET) scanning. Activity within the amygdala was greater when subjects were viewing positive and negative stimuli than neutral stimuli. Activation of the amygydala in response to positive emotional stimuli may reflect its role in other aspects of positive emotion demonstrated in rodent models, such as reward prediction, attentional processing, and goal-directed behaviors (Aggleton, 2000).

Whereas human studies support the view that the amygdala is important in negative and perhaps positive emotional processing, studies in non-human primates have shown that the amygdala is also necessary for social cognition. Recent neuroimaging data indicate that the amygdala integrated information about faces, such as facial expressions, postures, and gestures, in order to choose and adjust appropriate behavioral responses based on the current emotional and social context of a specific situation. Not only does the amygdala regulate social behavior, but it is also essential for regulating sexual behavior. Specifically, the medial amygdala in rodents has been to shown to control sexually dimorphic behaviors through connections with the medial hypothalamus. Lesions of the medial amygdala in rats abolish male-typical mating behavior, while most female sexual behaviors are spared (Aggleton, 2000). Moreover, amygdala activation accompanies orgasm in humans.

A major factor in determining how the amygdala contributes to different behavioral processes and responses is reflected in its connections with other brain structures (Aggleton, 2000). For example, the amygdala has projections to the brainstem that control the expression of fear responses, as well as areas of the cortex that are believed to mediate cognitive aspects of emotional processing, such as the experience of fear. In addition, amygdala connections with the prefrontal cortex are important for encoding predictive value of cues and the motivational properties of associated outcomes in order to guide goal-directed behavior. Projections from the BLA to the ventral striatum are important for processing incentive value of the Pavlovian CSs in instrumental learning tasks. CEA-dependent learning is primarily modulated by its connections with the mesolimbic and nigrostriatal dopaminergic pathways. Furthermore, the CEA has connections with cholinergic cells within the nucleus basalis and substantia innominata that mediate increased attentional processing during learning. In general, during learning the role of the amygdala is to mediate associative representations between the emotional significance and sensory properties of stimuli, which is used to help guide appropriate behavioral responses to emotional relevant cues. In this sense, the amygdala is a key emotional interface in the brain that endows sensory stimuli and the behavioral responses they generate with affective valence and value.

REFERENCES

Adolphs, R., Russell, J. A., & Tranel, D. (1999). A role for the human amygdala in recognizing emotional arousal from unpleasant stimuli. *Psychological Science, 10*, 167–171.

Aggleton, J. P. (2000). *The amygdala: A functional analysis.* New York: Oxford University Press.

Davis, M., & Whalen, P. J. (2001). The amygdala: Vigilance and emotion. *Molecular Psychiatry, 6*(1), 13–34.

Hamann, S. B., Ely, T. D., Hoffman, J. M., & Kilts, C. D. (2002). Ecstasy and agony: Activation of the human amygdala in positive and negative emotion. *Psychological Science, 13*(2), 135–141.

Holland, P. C., & Gallagher, M. (1999). Amygdala circuitry in attentional and representational processes. *Trends in Cognitive Sciences, 3*(2), 65–73.

Holland, P. C., & Gallagher, M. (2004). Amygdala-frontal interactions and reward expectancy. *Current Opinion in Neurobiology, 14*(2), 148–155.

Kluver, H., & Bucy, P. C. (1937). "Psychic blindness" and other symptoms following bilateral temporal lobectomy in rhesus monkeys. *American Journal of Physiology, 119*, 352–353.

LeDoux, J. E. (2000). Emotion circuits in the brain. *Annual Review of Neuroscience, 23*, 155–184.

Maren, S. (2001). Neurobiology of Pavlovian fear conditioning. *Annual Review of Neuroscience, 24*(1), 897–931.

Murray, E. A. (2007). The amygdala, reward and emotion. *Trends in Cognitive Sciences, 11*(11), 489–497.

Weiskrantz, L. (1956). Behavioral changes associated with ablation of the amygdaloid complex in monkeys. *Journal of Comparative Physiology, 49*(4), 381–391.

Zimmerman, J. M., Rabinak, C. A., McLachlan, I. G., & Maren, S. (2007). The central nucleus of the amygdala is essential for acquiring and expressing conditional fear after overtraining. *Learning and Memory, 14*(9), 634–644.

SUGGESTED READING

Phelps, E. A., & LeDoux, J. E. (2005). Contributions of the amygdala to emotion processing: From animal models to human behavior. *Neuron, 48*(2), 175–187.

CHRISTINE A. RABINAK
STEPHEN MAREN
University of Michigan

See also: Emotions; Instrumental Conditioning; Pavlovian Conditioning

ANAL STAGE (See Psychosexual Stages)

ANALOG RESEARCH METHODS

Analog research measures phenomena of interest through an emulation of real-life events. "Analog" is derived from the same root as "analogy"—an analog is like something else. What is measured or studied in analog research is a stand-in for the actual behavior or phenomenon of interest.

Research methods in psychology exist on a continuum of naturalism. Naturalism is a key element in making inferences about the external validity of a study's methods. External validity is the extent to which findings using particular ways of measuring a phenomenon (i.e., "operationalizations"), particular settings to study the phenomenon, or particular sample can be applied to operationalizations, settings, and people more generally. The external validity of methods range from high (e.g., observations of behaviors of interest in settings in which they occur) to low (e.g., extremely artificial, but more easily seen or measured; behaviors that are a stand-in for the true behavior of interest).

On one end of the naturalism continuum is "simulation research," in which participants role play or imagine themselves in certain situations that are of interest to the researcher. On the other end of the continuum is naturalistic research in which no constraint is put on the participants; the researcher observers the target behavior, or patterns of behavior, in the setting in which it usually occurs. Analog research falls between simulation and naturalistic research; researchers simulate a real-world, naturalistic setting while controlling for extraneous variables.

Analogs are used as a hypothesis-testing tool for three purposes: (1) to observe otherwise difficult to observe behaviors; (2) to isolate the determinants of behavior; and (3) to observe qualities of social interaction that unfold over time (although naturalistic observation might be preferable because observers would not need to guess about how comparable the behaviors were to those in real life situations). The first two purposes require controlled experimentation, necessitating the use of simulation or analog designs. For the third purpose, analog designs are often preferable to naturalistic observation because they allow the observer to "stack the deck" to make it more likely that the behaviors and behavioral patterns of interest will occur when the assessor can see them.

Types of Studies Using Analog Methods

Studies that use analogs can be roughly divided into (1) those that study the effects of specific settings, events, or behavioral stimuli on individuals' behavior; and (2) those that observe behaviors in quasi-naturalistic social situations. The goals of the first type of study are to manipulate the setting and test individual differences in response; that is, the situation is set and variations in individuals' behavior are observed. This type of study is common in developmental psychology (e.g., visual cliff experiments; Gibson & Walk, 1960), social psychology (e.g., prosocial behavior experiments, emotion regulation experiments), and clinical psychology (e.g., social anxiety assessment; Roberts & Hope, 2001). An example of this type of design is the cold pressor task, an analog used in pain studies (e.g., Burns, Bruehl, & Caceres, 2004). In this task, participants are instructed to keep a hand in ice water until they can no longer endure doing so. The cold pressor task can be used in a variety of laboratory experiments that look to target the participant's pain tolerance or reaction to stressors.

The use of confederates often serves as an analog for research on prosocial behavior, social support, or group bias (e.g., Darley & Latane, 1968). Confederates help to create more generalizable and naturalistic settings, and, at the same time, researchers are able to highly control and manipulate participants' behaviors. For example, researchers use confederates to study how manipulation of the confederate's behavior interacts with participant's task compliance, social affiliation, problem solving behaviors, and recall of an event.

The second type of analog study—sometimes referred to as analog behavioral observation (ABO; Heyman & Slep, 2004)—addresses quasi-naturalistic observation of behavior. The setting is designed to be similar to those that occur in the natural environment, and the researcher may use a protocol to elicit behavior for that situation. For example, in ABO studies of couples' communication (e.g., Heyman, 2001), researchers typically bring couples into the lab and give both partners questionnaires (or interviews) to find out what the biggest areas of conflict between them are. The observer then brings them into a room (equipped with cameras and microphones) and asks them to discuss a problem and try to resolve it as they might at home. They are then left alone for 10 to 15 minutes as the video records. This process is often repeated for additional conflicts or for similarly constructed social support tasks.

ABO is used mostly as a convenience. The goal of such assessment is typically to understand behavior and its determinants in situations in which participants influence each other while interacting (e.g., groups, families, and couples). Understanding generalizable factors that promote or maintain problem behaviors in such systems typically requires more naturalistic approaches than those used in controlled, manipulated situation studies.

In summary, the use of analogs can be a good theory-testing tool because, depending on exactly how it is employed, it minimizes the need for inferences to assess behavior. It can facilitate formal or informal analysis of cause and effect, it can provide the assessor with experimental control of situational factors, it can facilitate the observation of otherwise unobservable behaviors, and it can provide an additional source of useful information in a multimodal strategy (e.g., questionnaires, interviews, observation). Finally, because researchers can set up a situation that increases the probability that behaviors of interest will occur during the observation period, the use of analogs can be high in research efficiency. Like any tool, however, usefulness of analogs depends on its match to the resources and needs of the person considering using it. The conditional nature of validity may make it difficult to generalize observed behavior to the broad variety of real world settings; and the less naturalistic the analog, the more nagging the concerns about external validity (i.e., applicability to real-world situations).

REFERENCES

Burns, J., Bruehl, S., & Caceres, C. (2004). Anger management style, blood pressure reactivity, and acute pain sensitivity: Evidence for "Trait × Situation" models. *Annals of Behavioral Medicine, 27*, 195–204.

Darley, J. M., & Latané, B. (1968). Bystander intervention in emergencies: Diffusion of responsibility. *Journal of Personality and Social Psychology, 8*, 377–383.

Gibson, E., & Walk, R. (1960). The "visual cliff." *Scientific American, 202*, 64–71.

Heyman, R. E. (2001). Observation of couple conflicts: Clinical assessment applications, stubborn truths, and shaky foundations. *Psychological Assessment, 13*, 5–35.

Heyman, R. E., & Slep, A. M. S. (2004). Analogue behavioral observation. In M. Hersen (Ed.) & E. M. Heiby & S. N. Haynes (Vol. Eds.), *Comprehensive handbook of psychological assessment: Vol. 3. Behavioral assessment* (pp. 162–180). Hoboken, NJ: John Wiley & Sons.

Roberts, M. W., & Hope, D.A. (2001). Clinic observations of structured parent-child interaction designed to evaluate externalizing disorders. *Psychological Assessment, 13*, 46–58.

SUGGESTED READINGS

Bakeman, R., & Gottman, J. M. (1997). *Observing interaction: An introduction to sequential analysis* (2nd Ed.). New York: Cambridge University Press.

Haynes, S. N., & O'Brien, W. H. (2000). *Principles and practice of behavioral assessment.* New York: Kluwer.

RICHARD E. HEYMAN
JILL MALIK
AMY M. SMITH SLEP
Stony Brook University, State University of New York

See also: **Behavioral Observation**

ANALYSIS OF COVARIANCE

Analysis of covariance (ANCOVA) is a statistical method that may be viewed as an extension of analysis of variance (ANOVA) when, in addition to one or more factors (discrete explanatory variables, typically group membership), it is required to account for possible differences due to a continuous variable(s), usually called covariate(s) or concomitant variable(s). The latter variable(s) co-varies with a dependent variable under consideration (response, outcome), and it is of interest to examine whether group differences on the latter may be related to group differences on the covariate(s). Typically, a covariate is highly correlated with a response variable; that is, the covariate contains information about the response variable and therefore possibly also about group differences on the outcome measure(s). Empirical settings in which ANCOVA is appropriate usually have at least one categorical factor and one or more continuous covariates.

Oftentimes in applications, evaluation of effects—such as main effects and interactions—occur in ANCOVA after a dependent variable is adjusted for potential preexisting group differences associated with the covariate(s) (Raykov & Marcoulides, 2008). The latter is commonly measured at the beginning of the study, for example, before the administration of a treatment, therapy, or intervention or the start of a program. In such settings, the formal ANCOVA question is whether the groups would differ on the dependent variable(s) if they were equivalent on the covariate(s) to begin with. In those circumstances, an application of ANCOVA (under its specific assumptions, to be mentioned) aims to increase sensitivity, that is, to enhance the power of the tests of main effects and interactions by reducing the error term of the pertinent F-test statistics (F-ratios). In addition, ANCOVA permits the researcher to adjust the group means on a response variable to what they would have been if all subjects had scored the same on the covariate(s) in the first instance. Moreover, ANCOVA may also be applied after multiple analysis of variance (MANOVA) for the purpose of what is referred to as step-down analysis.

Another common application of ANCOVA is in non-experimental situations in which, for various reasons, it is not possible to randomly assign the study participants to groups; for example, one cannot randomly assign patients to income level, gender, or education. In a case such as this, ANCOVA may be used to statistically make the studied groups somewhat more statistically comparable; however, it should be noted that the method cannot, in general, completely account for the lack of random assignment of subjects to groups. There could be other group differences on the outcome that are not related to the covariate(s) being considered, or the latter could be related in a nonlinear way to the response(s). Thus, ANCOVA cannot guarantee adjustment of prior existing differences between groups. Further, although ANCOVA is a method for statistical adjustment of groups, no conclusions about causality can be made from its results, because such an after-the-fact procedure cannot be a substitute for running an experiment (Maxwell & Delaney, 2004).

A third type of ANCOVA application is made in situations in which one is concerned with assessing the contribution of various dependent variables to significant group differences that have been found in a MANOVA. Then ANCOVA may be used to account for the linear impact of a subset of dependent variables upon group differences on the remaining outcome(s). This is achieved by using ANCOVA with covariates being some of the outcome variables from that MANOVA.

From a statistical viewpoint, the ANCOVA null hypothesis is

$$H_{0,\text{ANCOVA}}: \mu_{1,a} = \mu_{2,a} = \ldots = \mu_{g,a},$$

where the subindex "a" stands for "adjusted" (i.e., resulting after accounting for the linear relationship of covariates upon dependent variables), and g is the number of groups in a given study (g > 1). This hypothesis is distinct from the null hypothesis of ANOVA,

$$H_{0,\text{ANOVA}}: \mu_1 = \mu_2 = \ldots = \mu_g,$$

where only the unadjusted group differences are of interest (i.e., the differences between the unadjusted means across groups or, in other words, the differences in group means before the ANCOVA adjustment is made). Conversely, group differences without the adjustment, which are of concern in ANOVA, are not really of interest in ANCOVA. Using the general linear model form (GLM; Timm, 2002) for the dependent measures, $\underline{y}$,

$$\underline{y} = X\underline{b} + \underline{\varepsilon}, \tag{1}$$

holds, where the individual predictor values are contained in the matrix X (at times referred to also as "design" matrix), $\underline{b}$ is a vector comprising pertinent unknown parameters, and, as usual, the error vector $\underline{\varepsilon}$ is assumed unrelated with the predictors and multinormally distributed, that is as $N_n(0, \sigma^2 I_n)$ (n denoting sample size); no assumptions are made in Equation (1) about the predictors, so they could be group membership and/or continuous variables. In a factorial design setting with additional continuous covariates, the GLM can be postulated as

$$\underline{y} = X_{(1)}\underline{b}_{(1)} + X_{(2)}\underline{b}_{(2)} + \underline{\varepsilon}, \tag{2}$$

where the matrix $X_{(1)}$ encompasses the individual data on all categorical predictors, the matrix $X_{(2)}$ that data on all continuous predictors (i.e., covariates), and the vectors $\underline{b}_{(1)}$ and $\underline{b}_{(2)}$ are the regression coefficients associated correspondingly with the categorical and continuous predictors. Equation (2) is readily re-expressed in the form of (1) as follows:

$$\underline{y} = [X_{(1)}X_{(2)}] \begin{bmatrix} \underline{b}_{(1)} \\ \underline{b}_{(2)} \end{bmatrix} + \underline{\varepsilon} = X\underline{b} + \underline{\varepsilon}, \tag{3}$$

where for compactness the notation $X = [X_{(1)} | X_{(2)}]$ is used for the set of individual scores on all predictors. Equation (3) may be viewed as representing the ANCOVA model, which is thus a special case of the GLM. Hence, all statistical methods available within the GLM framework can be utilized in an application of ANCOVA.

A "classical" application of ANCOVA occurs in the context of a pretest/posttest design (repeated measure design with two occasions). An alternative then to ANCOVA with pretest being the covariate, is to conduct ANOVA on the "gain" scores, that is, the difference between posttest and pretest scores. The ANCOVA approach is generally preferable to the difference score analysis because the ANOVA procedure underlying the latter is in fact based on the strong assumption of unit slope in the regression of posttest upon pretest (Maxwell & Delaney, 2004). Only when this population assumption is fulfilled, which will likely be infrequently the case in empirical research, using ANOVA on difference scores will be a more sensible approach to follow. This is because one will then not need to use sample information in order to evaluate this slope parameter as one would have to do if the above ANCOVA procedure were followed. However, because this assumption is frequently violated, that ANOVA method for change scores is typically going to be less powerful than the ANCOVA one, owing to the fact that the former method's application is tantamount to making the assumption of unitary posttest-on-pretest regression population slope. This assumption therefore generally misrepresents the underlying model (e.g., Maxwell & Delany, 2004).

Because ANCOVA is carried out formally within the framework of ANOVA, all the assumptions of ANOVA are also assumptions of ANCOVA (Huitema, 1980). The credibility of ANCOVA results also depends on additional assumptions: (1) the covariate(s) being perfectly measured; (2) the regression of the dependent variable on independent one(s) is linear and with the same slope(s) in all involved groups (often referred to as regression homogeneity; techniques generally known as hierarchical linear modeling and structural equation modeling allow different group-specific or random slopes); and (3) that there is no treatment by covariate interaction. Mild violations of assumption are not likely to have a profound effect upon the ANCOVA results. Assumption generally cannot be met in many behavioral and social studies that typically involve variables (covariates) measured with considerable error. In practical terms, one may "replace" this assumption with the requirement that whenever variables are to be used as covariates, they should exhibit high reliability (e.g., at least above .80 but preferably closer to or above .90). Otherwise, use of an alternative methodology, such as structural equation modeling, can be recommended; these procedures have also been developed to deal with such fallible predictors/covariates (Raykov & Marcoulides, 2006).

REFERENCES

Huitema, B. J. (1980). *Analysis of covariance*. New York: John Wiley & Sons.

Maxwell, S. E., & Delaney, H. D. (2004). *Designing experiments and analyzing data*. (2nd ed.). Mahwah, NJ: Lawrence Erlbaum.

Raykov, T., & Marcoulides, G. A. (2006). *A first course in structural equation modeling* (2nd ed.). Mahwah, NJ: Lawrence Erlbaum.

Raykov, T., & Marcoulides, G. A. (2008). *An introduction to applied multivariate analysis*. New York: Taylor & Francis.

Timm, N. H. (2002). *Applied multivariate analysis*. New York: Springer.

TENKO RAYKOV
Michigan State University

See also: Analysis of Variance; Multivariate Methods

ANALYSIS OF VARIANCE

Analysis of variance (ANOVA) was initially developed by R. A. Fisher, beginning around 1918, and had early applications in agriculture. It is now a dominant and powerful statistical technique used extensively in psychology. In ANOVA, a dependent variable is predicted by a mathematical model comprising one or more predictor variables, which may be categorical (factors) or quantitative and continuous (covariates; regressors). The model's best prediction is calculated by minimizing the sum of the squared residuals (errors, or deviations from the model's prediction). Having done this, the proportion of variance in the dependent variable accounted for by each predictor is assessed statistically, testing the null hypotheses that the mean of the dependent variable does not vary with the predictor(s); good predictors account for a large proportion of the variance, compared to unpredicted (error) variance, and poor predictors account for a small proportion. ANOVA allows the effects of predictors to be assessed in isolation, but it also allows the assessment of interactions between predictors (effects of one predictor that depend on the values of other predictors).

Assumptions

ANOVA assumes (1) that for each condition represented by a combination of predictor values, the dependent variable is normally distributed about the mean for that condition, or equivalently that error is normally distributed in each condition; (2) that the variance is the same in all such conditions and is the same as the residual variance (known as the homogeneity of variance assumption); and (3) that the model accounts for all systematic influences on the data, such that the residual variability represents random error, and all errors or observations in each condition are independent of each other. Checking these assumptions involves consideration of the experimental design, exploratory data analysis prior to ANOVA, and analysis of the residuals afterward. Sometimes, the suitability of data for ANOVA may be improved by appropriate *transformations* prior to analysis. Additional homogeneity-of-variance assumptions applying to ANOVA include *within-subjects factors*, which is discussed later.

Logic of One-Way ANOVA

The basic logic of ANOVA is simply illustrated using a single categorical predictor (single-factor or one-way ANOVA). Suppose A is a factor that can take one of k values (representing, for example, k different experimental treatments), and n values of the dependent variable Y have been sampled for each of the conditions $A1 \ldots Ak$ (giving nk observations in total). The null hypothesis is that the dependent variable Y has the same mean for each of $A1 \ldots Ak$, that is, that A has no effect on the mean of Y. ANOVA calculates a mean square for the predictor (MSA) and an error mean square (MSerror) and then compares them.

Mean Square for the Predictor

If the null hypothesis is true, then the k samples have been drawn from the same population, and by the Central Limit Theorem, the variance of the k sample means is an estimator of σ_e^2/n, where σ_e^2 is the population (and error) variance, so n times the variance of the sample means estimates σ_e^2. However, if the null hypothesis is false, the sample means have come from populations with different means, and n times the variance of the k sample means will exceed this value. The sum of squared deviations (abbreviated to *sum of squares*; SS) of each condition's mean from the grand mean ($\overline{Y}$) is calculated for the predictor, summing across all observations (in this example, $SS_A = \sum_{i=1...k} \sum_{j=1...n} [\overline{Y}_{A_i} - \overline{Y}]^2 = \sum_{i=1...k} n[\overline{Y}_{A_i} - \overline{Y}]^2$), and divided by the *degrees of freedom* (df) for the predictor (in this example, $df_A = k - 1$) to give the *mean square* (MS) for the predictor ($MS_A = SS_A/df_A$). If the null hypothesis is true, then the expected value of this number, $E(MS_A)$, is the error variance σ_e^2. If the null hypothesis is false, then the expected mean square will exceed σ_e^2, as it will contain contributions from the non-zero effect that A is having on Y.

Mean Square for Error

Whether or not the null hypothesis is true, the sample variances $S_{A_1}^2 \dots S_{A_k}^2$ estimate the corresponding population variances $\sigma_{A_1}^2 \dots \sigma_{A_k}^2$ and, by the homogeneity of variance assumption, also estimate the error variance σ_e^2. An estimate of σ_e^2 is therefore obtainable from the sample variances $S_{A_1}^2 \dots S_{A_k}^2$. The sum of squared deviations of each observation from its group mean—that is, the summed squared residual deviations after the prediction has been made—is calculated (in this example, $SS_{error} = \sum_{i=1...k} \sum_{j=1...n} [Y_{i,j} - \overline{Y}_{A_i}]^2$) and divided by the error degrees of freedom (in this example, $df_{error} = df_{total} - df_A = [nk - 1] - [k - 1] = k[n - 1]$) to give $MS_{error} = SS_{error}/df_{error}$. Whether the null hypothesis is true or not, $E(MS_{error}) = \sigma_e^2$.

F Test

Comparison of MS_A to MS_{error} thus allows assessment of the null hypothesis. The ratio $F = MS_A/MS_{error}$ is assessed using an F test with (df_A, df_{error}) degrees of freedom. From the observed value of F, a p value may be calculated (the probability of obtaining an F this large or greater, given the null hypothesis). In conventional approaches, a sufficiently large F and small p leads to the rejection of the null hypothesis.

Interactions, Main Effects, and Simple Effects

When multiple factors are used in analysis, a key feature of ANOVA is its ability to test for interactions between factors, meaning effects of one factor that depend on the value or level of other factor(s). The terminology will be illustrated in the abstract, temporarily ignoring important statistical caveats such as homogeneity of variance. Suppose the maximum speeds of many scrap cars are analyzed using two factors: E (levels: E_0 engine broken, E_1 engine intact) and F (levels: F_0 no fuel, F_1 fuel present). There will be a main effect of Engine: on average, ignoring everything else, E_1 cars go faster than E_0 cars. Similarly, there will be a main effect of Fuel: ignoring everything else, cars go faster with fuel than without. Since speeds will be high in the E_1F_1 condition and very low otherwise, there will also be an interaction, meaning that the effect of Engine depends on the level of the Fuel factor, and vice versa (the effect of a working engine depends on whether there is fuel; the effect of fuel depends on whether there is a working engine).

One can also speak of simple effects: for example, the simple effect of Fuel at the E_1 level is large (fuel makes intact cars go), whereas the simple effect of Fuel factor at the E_0 level is small (fuel makes no difference to broken cars). Likewise, the Engine factor will have a large simple effect at F_1 but a small simple effect at F_0. Main effects may be irrelevant in the presence of an interaction, since they gloss over known interrelationships between the factors. ANOVA results are conventionally reported in the form shown in Table 1.

Post-Hoc Analysis of Interactions and Multilevel Factors

Effects of interest in an ANOVA that are found to be significant are frequently analyzed further. Interactions may be followed up by analyzing their component parts, for example, by restricting the analysis to a subset of the data (such as by examining simple effects or simpler component interactions within a complex interaction). Likewise, significant main effects of interest may require further analysis. For example, if a three-level factor A is found to have an effect, then the null hypothesis $\mu_{A_1} = \mu_{A_2} = \mu_{A_3}$ is rejected, but the experimenter may still have an interest in which of $\mu_{A_1} \neq \mu_{A_2} = \mu_{A_3}$, $\mu_{A_1} = \mu_{A_2} \neq \mu_{A_3}$, and $\mu_{A_1} \neq \mu_{A_2} \neq \mu_{A_3}$ is the case. A range of *post hoc* tests is available for this purpose. The most important feature of such tests is that they involve the potential for multiple comparisons and thus have the potential to inflate the Type I error rate, particularly as the number of levels of the factor increases. Appropriate tests control the maximum Type I error rate for a whole 'family' of comparisons.

Table 1. ANOVA of Fictional Data, Showing Conventional Table Style as Might Be Produced by Statistical Software

In general, a factor with k levels has $(k-1)$ degrees of freedom (df). A linear predictor has 1 df, as does a linear contrast. An interaction $A \times B$, where A has a df and B has b df, has ab df. In this example, there are two factors, each with two levels each. If there are N observations of the dependent variable in total, the total df is $(N-1)$. In this example, $N = 24$. The total line is not always shown. MS total is the variance of the dependent variable; SS is the sum of squares; MS is the mean square.

Term	DF	SS	MS	F	p
A	1	2,795.04	2,795.04	17.738	0.0004289
B	1	1,650.04	1,650.04	10.472	0.0041415
A × B	1	2,147.04	2,147.04	13.626	0.0014463
Residual (error)	20	3,151.50	157.57		
Total	23	9,743.62	423.64		

ANOVA as a General Linear Model (GLM)

More generally, each observed value of Y can be modeled as a sum of predictors each multiplied by a regression coefficient (b), plus error not accounted for by the prediction (e):

$$\begin{bmatrix} y_1 \\ y_2 \\ \dots \\ y_n \end{bmatrix} = \begin{bmatrix} 1 & X_{1,1} & X_{1,2} & X1,\dots & X_{1,p} \\ 1 & X_{2,1} & X_{2,2} & X2,\dots & X_{2,p} \\ 1 & X_{\dots,1} & X_{\dots,2} & X\dots,\dots & X_{\dots,p} \\ 1 & X_{n,1} & X_{n,2} & Xn,\dots & X_{n,p} \end{bmatrix} \times \begin{bmatrix} b_0 \\ b_1 \\ b_2 \\ \dots \\ b_p \end{bmatrix}$$
$$+ \begin{bmatrix} e_1 \\ e_2 \\ \dots \\ e_n \end{bmatrix}$$

In matrix notation, this may be written:

$$Y = Xb + e$$

Here, Y is a matrix containing values of the dependent variable. X is the *design matrix*, containing columns for p predictors plus a column of ones to represent the additional predictor of the 'overall mean' of Y. Each row of X encodes the predictors and which levels of those predictors (for categorical predictors), or values of the predictors (for continuous predictors), apply to a given value of Y. Appropriate choice of a design matrix allows arbitrary designs including factors with multiple levels, combinations of categorical and continuous predictors, and interactions to be encoded. The matrix b contains coefficients (in this example, b_0 is the value of the overall Y mean, $\overline{Y}$), and e contains errors. This equation may be solved for b so as to minimize the summed squared residuals $(\sum e^2)$. Having done so, $SS_{error} = \sum_{i=1\dots n} e_i^2$, $SS_{total} = SS_Y = \sum_{i=1\dots n}(y_i - \overline{Y})$, and $SS_{model} = SS_{total} - SS_{error}$. The proportion of the variance in Y accounted for by the overall model is given by $R^2 = SS_{model}/SS_{total}$. The contribution of any given predictor may be assessed by comparing the predictive value of a 'full' model, containing all predictors, to a 'reduced' model containing all predictors except the one of interest:

$$F\left(df_{model[full]} - df_{model[reduced]}, df_{error[full]}\right)$$
$$= \frac{\left(SS_{model[full]} - SS_{model[reduced]}\right)}{\div \left(df_{model[full]} - df_{model[reduced]}\right)}{SS_{error[full]} \div df_{error[full]}}$$

or, to make clear the equivalence to the logic discussed above,

$$F\left(df_{predictor}, df_{error[full]}\right)$$
$$= \frac{SS_{predictor} \div df_{predictor}}{SS_{error[full]} \div df_{error[full]}} = \frac{MS_{predictor}}{MS_{error[full]}}$$

Effect sizes for individual predictors may be calculated in terms of R^2 (the proportion of variance in Y explained) or in terms of b (the change in Y for a given change in the predictor).

Viewing ANOVA in terms of a GLM makes its relationship to other well-known analytical techniques clear. For example, ANOVA with a single two-level factor is equivalent to a two-group t test; ANOVA with a single continuous predictor is equivalent to linear regression (Figure 1c); and so on. GLMs also subsume techniques such as analysis of covariance (ANCOVA) and multiple and polynomial regression and can be extended to multiple dependent variables (multivariate ANOVA or MANOVA). General linear models may also be extended to dependent variables with non-normal (e.g., binomial) distributions via the generalized linear model.

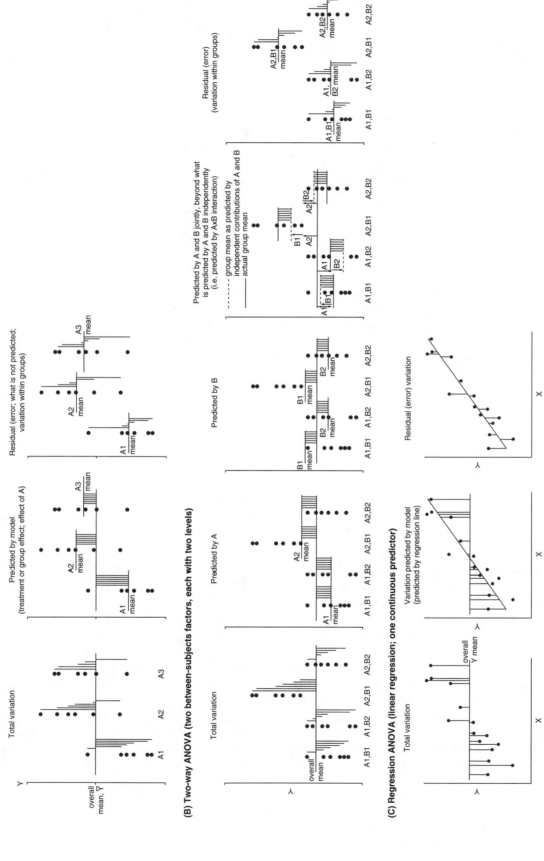

Figure 1. Illustration of simple ANOVA types. (A) One-way ANOVA, illustrated with a dependent variable Y and a single factor A having three levels ($A1$, $A2$, $A3$). In all figures, vertical lines indicate deviations that are squared and added to give a sum of squares (SS). The total sum of squares of Y (the summed squared deviation of each point from the grand mean; left panel) is divided into a component predicted by the factor A (the summed squared deviations of the A subgroup means from the grand mean, for each point; middle panel) plus residual or error variation (the summed squared deviation of each point from the prediction made using A; right panel). The SS are additive: $SS_{total} = SS_A + SS_{error}$. When SS_A and SS_{error} have been divided by their corresponding degrees of freedom (the number of independent pieces of information associated with the estimate), they may be compared statistically: if SS_A/df_A is large compared to SS_{error}/df_{error}, then A is a good predictor. (B) Two-way ANOVA. Here, two factors A and B are used, each with two levels. From left to right, panels illustrate the calculation of SS_{total}, SS_A, SS_B, the interaction term $SS_{A \times B}$, and SS_{error}. As before, the SS are additive ($SS_{total} = SS_A + SS_B + SS_{A \times B} + SS_{error}$) if the predictors are not correlated (see text). (C) Regression ANOVA, in which Y is predicted by a single continuous variable X. As before, the total SS (left panel) may be divided into a component predicted by the model (middle panel) and residual or error variation (right panel).

95

Contrasts and Trend Analysis

GLMs may also be used to perform *contrasts* to ask specific questions of the data. In this technique, a linear combination of weighted means is created that will have a value of zero under a given null hypothesis. For example, if a factor has 7 levels, one for each day of the week, then the linear contrast

$$L = 0.2\mu_{\text{Mon}} + 0.2\mu_{\text{Tue}} + 0.2\mu_{\text{Wed}} + 0.2\mu_{\text{Thu}}$$
$$+ 0.2\mu_{\text{Fri}} - 0.5\mu_{\text{Sat}} - 0.5\mu_{\text{Sun}}$$

(where μ_{day} indicates the day mean) may be used as a test of the null hypothesis that the dependent variable is equal on weekdays and weekends. In a GLM, these weights are encoded in a contrast matrix L. After solving $Y = Xb + e$, the contrast is calculated as $L = Lb$ and assessed statistically to test the null hypothesis $L = 0$.

Trend analysis involves the use of contrasts to ask questions about categorical predictors (factors) that may be treated quantitatively. For example, if subjects' reaction times are tested with visual stimuli of length 9 cm, 11 cm, 13 cm, and 15 cm, then it may be valid to treat the lengths as categories (do reaction times to the lengths differ?) and quantitatively (is there a linear or quadratic component to the relationship between reaction time and stimulus length?).

Correlations between Predictors and Unbalanced Designs

When an ANOVA design contains multiple predictors that are uncorrelated, assessment of their effects is relatively easy. However, it may be that predictors are themselves correlated. This may be because the predictors are correlated in the real world (for example, if age and blood pressure are used to predict some dependent variable, and blood pressure tends to rise with age). However, it may also occur if there are different sample sizes for different combinations of predictors. For example, if there are two factors, A (levels A_1 and A_2) and B (levels B_1 and B_2), then a *balanced* design would have the same number of observations of the dependent variable for each of the combinations $A_1B_1, A_1B_2, A_2B_1, A_2B_2$. If these numbers are unequal, the design is *unbalanced*, and this causes correlation between A and B. This problem also occurs in *incomplete factorial* designs, in which the dependent variable is not measured for all combinations of factors.

Whatever the reason for correlation between predictors, this causes a problem of interpreting their effects on the dependent variable (Figure 2). There are various approaches to this problem, and the best approach depends on the class of hypothesis preferred on theoretical grounds (do some predictors take precedence over others?) and on whether the design is unbalanced or incomplete.

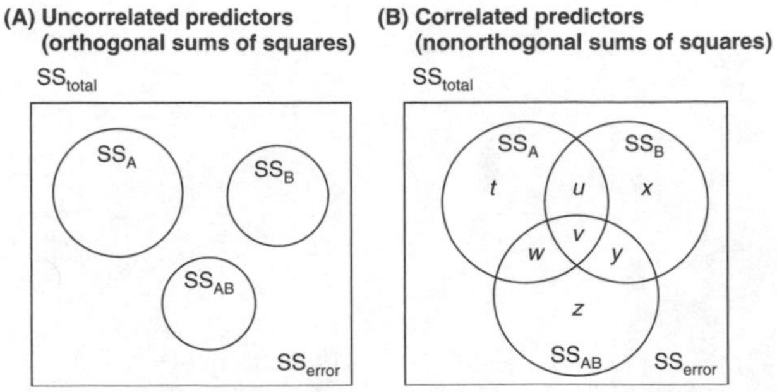

Figure 2. Assessing the effects of correlated predictors. Suppose a dependent variable Y is analyzed by two-way ANOVA, with predictors A, B, and their interaction ($A \times B$ or AB). The total variability in Y is represented by the sum of squares (SS) of Y, also written SS_{total} or SS_Y. This may be partitioned into SS attributable to A, to B, to the interaction AB, and to variability not predicted by the model (SS_{error}). (A) If the predictors are uncorrelated, then the SS are orthogonal, and are additive: $SS_{\text{total}} = SS_A + SS_B + SS_{AB} + SS_{\text{error}}$. ANOVA calculations are straightforward. (B) If the predictors are correlated, then the SS are not additive. There are various options for assessing the contribution of the predictors. For example, one possibility is to assess the contribution of each predictor over and above the contribution of all others; thus, the contribution used to assess the effect of A would be t, that for B would be x, and that for AB would be z (often termed 'marginal,' 'orthogonal,' or 'Type III' SS). A second possibility is to adjust the main effects for each other (i.e. not to include any portion of the variance that overlaps with other main effects), but not for the interaction (so SS_A is $t + w$, SS_B is $x + y$, and SS_{AB} is z, often known as 'hierarchical' or 'Type II' SS). Stated more generally, this approach adjusts terms for all other terms except higher-order terms that involve the same predictors. Alternatively, if there are reasons to treat the predictors as a hierarchy with A taking precedence, then one could assess the contribution of A ($t + u + v + w$), to assess the contribution of B above this ($x + y$), and then to assess the contribution of the interaction above these (z) (often termed 'sequential' or 'Type I' SS). These and other approaches to this problem have different advantages and disadvantages according to the type of design being analyzed. In practice, unless the sequential approach is desired, Type III SS are often used but the best approach is debated. All represent ways of comparing pairs of models of the data, as described in the text, to assess whether the difference between the models is significant; the experimental hypotheses determine the comparisons to be made.

Fixed and Random Effects

Up to this point, it has been assumed that factors have been *fixed effects*, meaning that the levels of the factor exhaust the population of interest and represent all possible values the experimenters would want to generalize their results to analytically; the *sampling fraction* (number of levels used ÷ number of levels in the population of interest) is 1. A simple example is sex: having studied male and female humans, all possible sexes have been studied. Experimental factors are usually fixed effects. It is also possible to consider *random effects*, in which the levels in the analysis are only a small, randomly selected sample from an infinite population of possible levels (sampling fraction = 0). For example, if an agronomist wanted to study the effect of fertilizers on wheat growth, it might be impractical to study all known varieties of wheat, so four might be selected at random to be representative of wheat in general. Wheat variety would then represent a random factor.

The most common random effect in psychology is that of subjects. When subjects are selected for an experiment, they are typically selected at random in the expectation that they are representative of a wider population. Thus, in psychology, discussion of fixed and random effects overlaps with consideration of between-subjects and within-subjects designs, discussed below. An ANOVA model incorporating both fixed and random effects is called a *mixed-effects model*.

With random effects, not only is the dependent variable a random variable as usual, but so is a predictor, and this modifies the analysis. It does not affect the partitioning of SS, but it affects the $E(MS)$ values, and thus the choice of error terms on which F ratios are based. Regardless of the model, testing an effect in an ANOVA requires comparison of the MS for the effect with the MS for an error term where $E(MS_{effect}) = E(MS_{error})$ if the effect size is zero, and $E(MS_{effect}) > E(MS_{error})$ if the effect size is non-zero. In fixed-effects models, the error term is the 'overall' residual unaccounted for by the full model; in random-effects models, this is not always the case, and sometimes the calculation of an error term is computationally complex.

Within-Subject and between-Subject Predictors, and More Complex Designs

Psychological experiments may be conducted with *between-subjects* factors, in which each subject is measured at just one level of the factor, or *within-subjects* factors, in which each subject is measured at every level of the factor, or a mixture. Within-subjects designs (also known as *repeated measures* designs) allow considerable power, since an individual at one time is likely to be similar to the same individual at other times, reducing variability. The main disadvantage is the sensitivity of within-subjects designs to *order effects*.

In a simple within-subjects design, a group of subjects might be measured on three doses of a drug each (within-subjects factor: D). It would be necessary to counterbalance the testing order of the dose to avoid order effects such as improvement due to practice, or decline due to fatigue, or lingering or learned effects of a previous dose. Having done so, then variability between observations may be due to differences between subjects (S), or to differences between observations within one subject; this latter variability may be due to D, or intra-subject error variability (which might also include variability due to subjects' responding differently to the different doses, written $D \times S$).

For a design involving both between- and within-subjects factors, suppose old subjects and young subjects are tested on three doses of a drug each. Age (A) is a between-subjects factor and dose (D) is a within-subjects factor. In this example, variability between subjects may be due to A, or to differences between subjects within age groups, often written S/A ('subjects within A') and thought of as the between-subjects error. Variability of observations *within* individual subjects may be due to D, or to a $D \times A$ interaction, or within-subject error that includes the possibility of subjects responding differently to the different doses (which, since subjects can only be measured within an age group, is written $D \times S/A$). This partitioning of total variability may be accomplished for SS and df and analyzed accordingly, with the caveat that as subject (S) represents a random factor, calculation of an appropriate error term may sometimes be complex, as described above.

Within-subjects designs also carry an additional assumption: that of *sphericity*, or homogeneity of variance of difference scores. For example, if subjects are measured at three levels of a within-subjects factor U, then three sets of difference scores can be calculated: $(U_1 - U_2)$, $(U_1 - U_3)$, and $(U_2 - U_3)$. Sphericity is the assumption that the variances of these three difference scores are the same. Violations of this assumption can inflate the Type I error rate. Violations may be tested for directly using Mauchly's test, but this may be over-conservative. Approaches to this problem include (1) using an F test as usual but correcting the df to allow for the extent of violation, such as with the Huynh–Feldt or Greenhouse–Geisser corrections; (2) transformation of the data to improve the fit to the assumptions, if this is possible and meaningful; (3) using MANOVA, which does not require sphericity; and (4) testing planned contrasts of interest, which have 1 df each and therefore cannot violate the assumption.

ANOVA designs may have arbitrary numbers of between- and within-subjects factors. In these designs, 'Subject' defines a type of relatedness between observations. More complex designs, involving multiple levels of 'relatedness,' are possible and indeed commonly reflect real-world experiments. For example, suppose schoolchildren (S) each perform four tests of four levels of difficulty (factor D). These children are taught in class groups (G), and sets of groups are taught according to different teaching methods (T). In this example, D is said to be *crossed* with S (since all subjects perform in all difficulty conditions), but S is *nested* within G (any given subject is only a member of one group), and groups are nested within T. This model may be written $DS/G/T$, and is an example of a *hierarchical* design involving two types of 'relatedness.' Such designs allow the analytical model to reflect correlations in the real world—such as observations that come from the same subject being likely to be more similar to each other than to randomly selected observations, or observations that come from different subjects who are in the same group being likely to be more similar to each other than to randomly selected observations. Ensuring a correct design is part of satisfying the assumption that the ANOVA model accounts for all systematic influences on the data.

REFERENCE

Cardinal, R. N., & Aitken, M. R. F. (2006). *ANOVA for the behavioral sciences researcher*. Mahwah, NJ: Lawrence Erlbaum.

Fisher, R. A. (1918). The correlation between relatives on the supposition of Mendelian inheritance. *Transactions of the Royal Society of Edinburgh, 52*, 399–433.

Fisher, R. A. (1925). *Statistical methods for research workers*. Edinburgh: Oliver & Boyd.

Howell, D. C. (2007). *Statistical methods for psychology*, 6th ed. Belmont, CA: Thomson/Wadsworth.

Langsrud, Ø. (2003). ANOVA for unbalanced data: Use type II instead of type III sums of squares. *Statistics and Computing, 13*, 163–167.

Maxwell, S. E., & Delaney, H. D. (2003). *Designing experiments and analyzing data: A model comparison perspective*. Mahwah, NJ: Lawrence Erlbaum.

Myers, J. L., & Well, A. D. (2003). *Research design and statistical analysis*, second edition. Mahwah, NJ: Lawrence Erlbaum.

StatSoft (2008). *Electronic Statistics Textbook*. Tulsa, OK: StatSoft. http://www.statsoft.com/textbook/stathome.html.

Verrill, S. (2001). Rolling your own: linear model hypothesis testing and power calculations via the singular value decomposition. *Statistical Computing and Statistical Graphics Newsletter, 12*(1), 15–18.

RUDOLF N. CARDINAL
*University of Cambridge,
United Kingdom*

ANALYTICAL PSYCHOLOGY

Analytical Psychology is the name Swiss psychiatrist Carl Gustav Jung (1875–1961) gave to his theoretical and methodological approach to the psychology of the unconscious, following his break with Freud and classical psychoanalysis in 1913. Unlike psychoanalysis, analytical psychology does not regard the structure of the unconscious as limited to contents that were initially a part of consciousness. Although not denying the psychoanalytic view that the unconscious includes contents that were once conscious, it holds that the unconscious also includes contents not yet capable of becoming conscious (i.e., symptoms) and contents incapable of ever becoming fully conscious (i.e., the symbolic manifestation of the archetypes of the collective unconscious).

Moreover, analytical psychology maintains that the dynamics at issue in the formation of the unconscious are not exhausted by repression. Analytical psychology does not contest either the psychoanalytic account of the felt incompatibility between conscious and preconscious (as well as unconscious) contents, or the consequent mechanism of repression resulting in the dissociation of the latter contents from consciousness. However, it maintains that an additional dynamic, rooted in the inability of consciousness to apperceive psychic contents, also results in psychic contents having a subliminal and therefore an unconscious status. Apperception is defined by analytical psychology as the psychic process whereby new contents are assimilated into consciousness on the basis of their similarity to the contents already existing in consciousness.

Attitude Types and the Four Functions of Consciousness

Analytical psychology diverges from psychoanalysis in its theory of the qualitative factors at issue in the blocking of psychic contents whose energy is sufficient for conscious entrance from entering consciousness. According to analytical psychology, in addition to psychoanalytic theoretical formulation of this qualitative factor in terms of conflicts between the so-called ego instincts and sexually charged libido, there are also qualitative factors that involve the apperceptive conflict between the two basic attitudes that govern the flow of psychic energy (introversion and extroversion) and the apperceptive conflict between the four basic functions of consciousness—thinking, feeling, sensation, and intuition.

Theory of Complexes

The analytical psychology theory of complexes is rooted in comprehending apperception as the psychic process by which a new content is articulated with similar, already existing contents in such a way that it becomes understood, apprehended, and clear. As such, apperception is the "bridge" that connects the already existing constellated contents with the new one. According to analytical psychology, apperception is either active or passive. When apperception is active, the bridge between the already existing and new contents is fashioned by the association of similar contents. When apperception is passive, the conditions are lacking for an associative bridge based on the similarity of the already existing contents and new contents. This has as its result the "dissociation" between the former and latter contents that, paradoxically, functions apperceptively to link the two. The paradoxically apperceptive apprehension of new contents that occurs in dissociation manifests these contents as symptoms.

The absence of an associative link between ego-consciousness and unconscious contents (i.e., the symptoms) in passive apperception does not preclude for analytical psychology the existence of associations with respect to the latter contents. Rather, the theory of complexes maintains that the existence of associations that refer psychic contents to other such dissociated contents, and therefore not to the ego, can be both observed and investigated. By the term "complex," analytical psychology understands the loose association of passively apperceived contents, which lack an associative link to ego-consciousness.

Personal and Collective Unconscious

Analytical psychology understands the personal character of the associations yielded by the symptomatic (i.e., dissociated) images of the complex to provide evidence for a "personal unconscious." It understands the transpersonal character of those associations yielded by the symptomatic images that refer not to ego consciousness but to other images, to provide evidence for a "collective unconscious." The methodical unfolding of the transpersonal context of the associations at issue in the collective unconscious involves what analytical psychology calls the "amplification" of the associations of images that refer not to ego consciousness, but to other images. Speaking of this method, Jung writes, "I adopt the method of the philologist, which is far from being free association, and apply a logical principle which is called *amplification*. It is simply the seeking of parallels" (Jung, 1935/1970). Proceeding in this manner, the initial appearance of associated images is guided by "parallel material" drawn from dreams, literature, myth, religion, and art. The point of departure for the amplification of associations is always the question, "How does the thing appear?" The guidance provided by the parallel material with respect to the initially appearing associated images functions to facilitate a conscious propensity to assimilate, and therefore to apperceive actively, hints or fragments of lightly toned unconscious complexes and, by associating them with parallel elements, to elaborate them in a clearly visual form.

Archetypes and Individuation

Analytical psychology unfolds a topology of the collective associative designs, termed *archetypes*, which surround the nucleus of the complex. The most basic archetypes identified by analytical psychology include the persona (the socially accepted mask assumed by the ego); the shadow (the undeveloped and therefore infantile aspects of the ego); the anima and animus (counter-sexual images in men and women, respectively, which apperceptively link their personal unconscious to the collective unconscious); and the self (the transpersonal basis of the ego and therefore of the conscious personality). The therapeutic goal of analytical psychology is the self-conscious differentiation of ego-consciousness from the various archetypes that become constellated in the course of the life of an individual. The process of striving to realize this goal is termed *individuation*. The crucial role of the analytical distinction between ego-consciousness and the archetypal contents of the collective unconscious in the process of individuation is signaled in the name Jung gave to his psychology in order to distinguish it from psychoanalysis: analytical psychology.

SUGGESTED READINGS

Jung, C. G. (1970a). *Two essays on analytical psychology*. Princeton: Princeton University Press. (Original work published in 1917)

Jung, C. G. (1970b). *Analytic psychology: Its theory and practice*. New York: Vintage Books. (Original work published in 1935)

Jung, C. G. (1976). *Psychological types*. Princeton: Princeton University Press. (Original work published in 1920)

BURT HOPKINS
Seattle University

See also: Archetypes

ANASTASI, ANNE (1908–2001)

Anne Anastasi is most closely associated with the development of differential psychology. She received her B.A. from Barnard and her Ph.D. from Columbia University, the latter at the age of 21. Although her long-standing plan had been to specialize in mathematics, a course using Pillsbury's *Essentials of Psychology* as the text aroused her interest in differential psychology. Then a course with Harry L. Hollingworth and an article by Charles Spearman clinched matters, the latter convincing her that psychology and mathematics could be combined. Her Columbia professors included Henry E. Garret (her dissertation advisor), Albert T. Poffenberger, Carl J. Warden, and Robert S. Woodworth, as well as visiting professors Richard M. Elliot and Clark L. Hull. Through her husband, John P. Folely Jr., who majored in psychology at Indiana University, she was exposed to the ideas of J. Robert Kantor. To all these influences she attributed her generalist orientation and her firm commitment to psychology as an objective science.

Anastasi taught at Barnard, Queens College (CUNY), and Fordham University. Her major books include *Differential Psychology, Fields of Applied Psychology,* and *Psychological Testing.* Her research centered chiefly on factor analysis and traits, problems of test construction, and the interpretation of test scores with special reference to the role of cultural factors in individual and group differences. Active in association affairs throughout her professional life, Anastasi was president of the American Psychological Association in 1972, the first woman to be elected to this office in 50 years. The holder of several honorary degrees, she received many awards including the APA Distinguished Scientific Award for the Application of Psychology (1981), the American Psychological Foundation Gold Medal (1984), and the National Medal of Science from the President of the United States (1987).

REFERENCES

Anastasi, A. (1979). *Fields of applied psychology*. New York: McGraw Hill.

Anastasi, A. (1997). *Psychological testing*. Upper Saddle River, NJ: Prentice-Hall.

STAFF

ANGER

Aristotle, Seneca, Darwin, and Ekman, a modern emotion theorist, have considered anger as one of the basic human emotions. Psychologists often use the term anger interchangeably with other terms like aggression, hostility, hate, and irritability. This usage has led to many confusing definitions and theories of anger, as well as numerous misconceptions. The resulting confusion has impeded our efforts to integrate anger research findings into a viable understanding of anger. Anger is of great concern, because it often precedes aggression, conflict, and violence.

We define anger as a subjectively experienced emotion with high sympathetic autonomic arousal. It is elicited by the perception of a threat to one's physical well being, property, present or future resources, self-image, social status or image as projected to one's group, maintenance of social rules that regulate daily life, or comfort. Anger is an enduring emotion, and it may persist well after a threat has passed. Anger is associated with attributions, evaluations, and the gathering of information that emphasizes the externalization of blame. Anger motivates a response of antagonism to thwart, drive off, retaliate against, attack, seek retribution, or control the source of the perceived threat. People communicate anger through facial or postural gestures, vocal inflections, aversive verbalizations, and aggressive behavior. One's choice of strategies to communicate anger varies with social roles, learning history, and environmental contingencies.

Several types of thoughts arouse anger. The perception of threat to high, unstable self-esteem often elicits anger. Anger includes an experience of high self-efficacy, or greater power or potency than the eliciting threat. This experience is counter to the common notion that anger is associated with low self-esteem (Baumeister, Bushman, & Campbell, 2000). Often, angry people believe that others do not hold them in the same esteem as they hold themselves. Anger can also be triggered by the perception of injustice, a grievance, or blameworthiness, whereby people perceive others as responsible for the events that preceded their anger. When people experience anger, they hold a hostile attribution of intent, or the belief that bad things occurred because others have purposely tried to do them harm. Resentment, the belief that one has had a worse life than others, is a common thought in those with high trait anger. Anger has been linked to impulsivity, usually in association with aggression. Aggression associated with anger has been called affective, impulsive aggression. Recent research suggests that the cognitive process of rumination is also associated with anger. It appears that people often ruminate about perceived anger triggers for some time. Rumination may tax a person's self-control skills and lead to impulsive aggression.

Because anger generates justification, moral certitude, righteousness, a sense of power, and low motivation for change, people feel little desire to change or control their experience of anger. The only basic emotion that people desire to change less is joy. Theorists have described emotions as motivating either approach behaviors, in which one seeks to get close to the eliciting stimuli, or avoidant behaviors, in which one avoids or withdraws from the eliciting stimuli. Anger produces a strong tendency to approach rather than to avoid the eliciting stimuli. Only joy surpasses anger in this approach tendency (Scherer & Wallbott, 1994). Anger is the only negative emotion to motivate approach behaviors. As a clinical problem, anger resembles addiction with respect to this approach motive. Anger and addictive substances provide short-term positive experiences, but they often lead to long-term negative consequences.

Anger generates several motives in people attempting to cope with threats (DiGiuseppe & Tafrate, 2006). One motive is a desire to resolve the problem that triggered the anger. However, the most common angry motive is revenge, the desire to punish or produce reciprocity with the transgressor. Revenge has been a common theme in literature over the last three millennia. Homer's *Iliad* and Shakespeare's *Hamlet* are among the famous works on revenge. Anger produces a desire to control the environment. This can lead to a secondary dysfunctional motive to coerce others to comply with one's wishes. Anger also motivates a desire to remove or reduce the physiological arousal caused by one's anger, which we call tension reduction. This motive is the only avoidant motive of anger.

Anger elicits greater variability of behavioral expression than other basic emotions (Deffenbacher, Oeting, Lynch, & Morris, 1996). The most adaptive behavior triggered by anger is assertiveness or conflict resolution. Other common reactions include immediate aggressive reactions such as physically assaulting people; physically assaulting objects by throwing, slamming, hitting, or banging them; and negative verbal expression such as noisy arguments, intimidating or threatening comments, and cynical or sarcastic outbursts. Anger is the second most verbally expressive of all human emotions, after joy. Anger elicits stronger paralinguistic changes in a person's voice than any other emotion (Scherer & Wallbott, 1994). Anger can provoke deliberate, premeditated aggression, such as the secretive destruction of property. Alternatively, one can socially isolate the target of one's anger by encouraging others to stay away from the target. In addition, anger can lead to passive aggression, which is the failure to help or complete tasks, resulting in the blocking of goals or well-being of the target. People often fail to express their anger and ruminate internally about the transgressions done against them. Psychologists refer to this as anger-in. Anger-in can lead to many medical problems.

Although anger is a normal emotion that leads to adaptive behavior, in excess it can also become a clinical problem. Dysfunctional anger frequently leads to aggression, child abuse, domestic violence, and physical or verbal assaults. Clients seek mental health services for anger problems just as often as they do for depression and anxiety disorders. Excessive anger can lead to harmful and dysfunctional consequences. Anger has been associated with many illnesses, including heart disease and chronic pain. Anger has also been associated with medication noncompliance and delayed healing of wounds. Anger can impede sexual functioning and destroy interpersonal relationships. Anger negatively affects marital relations, judgment, and goal attainment. Anger expressed by a family member toward a seriously mentally ill client is one of main elements that lead to relapse of serious mental illness. Excessive anger increases the chances that one will be involved with the criminal justice system and may lead to lower income.

The Roman philosopher Seneca in 50 A.D. was the first to recognize that anger could be a disorder. He referred to anger as *brevis furor*, or temporary madness. Anger has not been identified as an independent disorder in today's classification schemes, because it is assumed to be highly related to other disorders. Historically, psychologists identified a strong association between anger and depression. This came from Freud's proposal that depression was anger turned inward. The relation between anger and depression is very complex. Depression correlates more with the construct of anger-in and less with the outward expression of anger. Anger and depression both represent emotional parts of our social dominance system. Anger is the expression of dominance, whereas depression is the expression of submission. Thus, they are opposite ends of the dominance/submission social hierarchy and display system.

As people shift between dominant and submissive roles, their emotions may shift between anger and depression. Anger is more closely related to anxiety than to depression. Both anger and anxiety are part of the flight/fight system. Both emotions are triggered by the primary appraisal of the presence of a threat. A secondary appraisal of coping resources determines which emotion is experienced. If people perceive the threat as stronger than they are, they experience anxiety. If they experience the threat as weaker than they are, they experience anger.

Despite the association between excessive anger and harmful and dysfunctional outcomes, there are as previously noted no diagnostic categories that represent anger

disorders, either in the current fourth edition of the *Diagnostic and Statistical Manual of Mental Disorders* (DSM-IV-TR) or the tenth edition of the World Health Organization's *International Code of Diseases* (ICD). Several authors have proposed criteria for including an anger disorders category in the next edition of the DSM.

Effective treatments exist for disturbed anger in adults, adolescents, and children. The most strongly supported anger treatments include behavioral techniques such as relaxation, exposure to anger provoking stimuli, learning new responses to anger triggers, and rehearsal of new positive behaviors to resolve conflict. Cognitive techniques that have also received research support include cognitive restructuring that targets negative automatic thoughts, dysfunctional thoughts, irrational beliefs, hostile attributions, and inadequate social problem solving skills. No research has yet appeared to support the effectiveness of psychodynamic, family-systems, gestalt therapy, or client-centered treatments for dysfunctional anger. The effective anger treatments are about a third to a half as successful as our most effective treatments for depression and anxiety disorders. Presently, we cannot treat anger as successfully as we treat other emotional problems.

REFERENCES

Averill, J. R. (1982). *Anger and aggression: An essay on emotion.* New York: Springer.

Baumeister, R. F., Bushman, B. J., & Campbell, W. K. (2000). Self-esteem, narcissism, and aggression: Does violence result from low self-esteem or from threatened egotism? *Current Directions in Psychological Science, 9*(1), 26–29.

Deffenbacher, J., Oetting, E., Lynch, R., & Morris, C. (1996). The expression of emotion and its consequences. *Behaviour Research and Therapy, 34*(7), 575–590.

DiGiuseppe, R. A., & Tafrate, R. C. (2006). *Understanding anger disorders.* New York: Oxford University Press.

Scherer, K. R., & Wallbott, H. G. (1994). Evidence for the universality and cultural variation of differential emotional response patterns. *Journal of Personality and Social Psychology. 67*(1), 55–65.

RAYMOND A. DIGIUSEPPE
St. John's University

RAYMOND CHIP TAFRATE
Central Connecticut State University

See also: **Aggression; Emotions**

ANGER MANAGEMENT

Anger control has been a vexing issue that has been addressed in disparate ways by great thinkers across historical periods and by social scientists, clinicians, and community caretakers alike. It has been a societal agenda since classical philosophers grappled with the regulation of inner life and the enhancement of virtue. Anger is the prototype of the view of emotions as passions that seize the personality, disturb judgment, alter bodily conditions, and imperil behavior. While anger's troublesome facets and by-products are generally acknowledged, its personal and social value remains. Humans are hard-wired for anger because of its survival functions. There can be no sensible thoughts to negate it, much as the Stoics and the Victorians tried. Nevertheless, the aggression-producing, harm-doing capacity of anger is unmistakable, and so is its potential to adversely affect prudent thought, core relationships, work performance, and physical well-being. These problem conditions, however, are not derivative of anger *per se*, but result instead from anger being dysregulated, that is, its activation, expression, and experience occurring without appropriate controls.

Anger is a turbulent emotion that is ubiquitous in everyday life, yet it is also a feature of a wide range of psychiatrically classified disorders, including impulse control dysfunctions, mood disorders, many personality disorders, and schizophrenia, especially paranoid schizophrenia. Anger has long been recognized as a feature of clinical conditions that result from trauma, such as dissociative disorders, brain-damage syndromes, and, especially, post-traumatic stress disorder. Anger also appears in mental state disturbances produced by general medical conditions, such as dementia, substance abuse disorders, and neurological dysfunctions resulting from perinatal difficulties.

The term *anger management* was first used by Novaco (1975) to designate a cognitive-behavioral therapy (CBT) for chronic anger problems that was experimentally evaluated for its efficacy. Since then, anger management has become a rubric for a variety of interventions, as well as a part of common parlance. The term is, in a sense, a workplace metaphor, in that anger might be managed like a troublesome problem on the shop floor or, alternatively, as a crucial resource or asset not to be squandered by unnecessary activation and expenditure. Anger management programs are now marketed commodities.

In the psychotherapeutic context, three levels of intervention can be distinguished: (1) general clinical care for anger, (2) psycho-educational anger management, and (3) CBT anger treatment. General clinical care for anger identifies it as a clinical need and addresses it through counseling, psychotherapeutic, and psychopharmacological provisions, including client education, support groups, and eclectic treatments, without an intervention structure. The psycho-educational variant employs a CBT structure, delivered in group format, as occurs in court-referred or school-based programs, in prisons, and in general public workshops. Such programs typically follow a topical sequence that covers situational activators ("triggers"), how thoughts and beliefs influence anger, self-observation, various relaxation techniques, problem solving and conflict resolutions strategies, and other coping skills, such as calming self-statements, effective communication, and appropriate assertiveness. The length of these programs typically ranges from about 3 to 15 sessions.

CBT anger treatment is distinguished as a relatively high level of intervention by virtue of its theoretical grounding, its assessment and case-formulation basis, and its systematization, complexity, and depth of therapeutic approach. It is best provided as an individual therapy and may require a preparatory phase to facilitate treatment engagement. Increased depth is associated with thoroughness of assessment, attention to client core needs, individual tailoring, specialized techniques, and clinical coordination and supervision. A specialized form of CBT anger treatment follows a "stress-inoculation" approach that involves therapist-guided and -graded exposure to provocation stimuli as a way of facilitating anger control. This occurs "in vitro" through imaginal and role-play provocations in the clinic and "in vivo" through planned testing of coping skills in anger-inducing situations, as established by a hierarchy of provocation scenarios collaboratively constructed by client and therapist.

Cognitive Behavioral Therapy for Anger

The central therapeutic goal of CBT for anger is augmenting self-regulatory capacity. The aim is to minimize anger frequency, reactivity, intensity, and duration and to moderate anger expression. This is an adjunctive treatment for a targeted clinical problem that seeks to remedy the emotional turbulence associated with subjective distress, detriments to personal relationships, health impairments, and manifold harmful consequences of aggressive behavior. The main components are cognitive restructuring, arousal reduction, and enhancement of behavioral skills.

People with serious anger problems are often ambivalent about engaging in treatment, largely due to the value ascribed to anger in dealing with life's adversities. Because of the instrumentality of anger and aggression, the personal costs incurred by anger routines may go unrecognized; because of anger's being embedded in long-standing psychological distress, there is inertia to overcome in motivating change efforts. Getting leverage for therapeutic change can be elusive, particularly when treatment referrals entail some element of coercion. This is a salient issue in forensic settings, where clients are guarded about self-disclosure, and accessing anger in these settings is not straightforward. A preparatory phase may be required to foster engagement, develop core competencies (emotion identification, self-monitoring, skills in communication, and arousal reduction), and build trust in the therapist.

Core Principles and Treatment Provisions

A central perspective is that anger is produced by the self-appraised meaning of events and resources for dealing with them, rather than by objective properties of events. Sometimes anger occurs as a fast-triggered, reflexive response, while other times it results from deliberate attention, extended search, and conscious review. Anger activation is intrinsically linked to perceptions of threat and injustice. Treatment targets the way people process information, remember their experiences, and cognitively orient themselves to situations of stress or challenge.

Anger, as an engagement of the organism's survival systems in response to threat, involves interplay of cognitive, physiological, and behavioral components. Cognitive factors include knowledge structures (expectations, beliefs, and appraisal processes) that are schematically organized as mental representations about environment-behavior relationships and that entail rules governing threatening situations. Arousal or physiological factors include activation in the cardiovascular, endocrine, and limbic systems and tension in the skeletal musculature. Anger is affected by hormone levels (neurotransmitters), low stimulus thresholds for arousal activation, and diminished inhibitory control. Neurobiological mechanisms involve the amygdala, prefrontal cortex, and serotonin. Behavioral factors include conditioned and observationally learned repertoires of anger-expressive behavior, not only aggression but also avoidance. Implicit in the cognitive labeling of anger is an inclination to act antagonistically toward the source of the provocation. However, an avoidant behavioral style, as in some personality and psychosomatic disorders, can foment anger by leaving provocation unchanged or exacerbated.

CBT anger treatment targets enduring change in cognitive, arousal, and behavioral systems, achieved through changing valuations of anger and augmenting self-monitoring capacity. Addressing anger as grounded and embedded in aversive and often traumatic life experiences entails the evocation of distressed emotions, such as fear, sadness, and shame, as well as anger. Therapeutic work centrally involves the learning of new modes of responding to cues previously evocative of anger in the context of relating to the therapist, and this work periodically elicits negative sentiment within the therapist to the sometimes frustrating, resistive, and unappreciative behavior of the client. The treatment can be delivered in a protocol of about 12–15 sessions (see Taylor & Novaco, 2005) or in modular form (see Kassinove & Tafrate, 2002).

The Stress Inoculation Approach

The specialized form of CBT for anger involves (1) client education about anger, stress, and aggression; (2) self-monitoring of anger frequency, intensity, duration, and situational triggers; (3) construction of a provocation hierarchy, created from self-monitoring data and used for practice and testing of coping skills; (4) arousal reduction techniques of progressive muscle relaxation, breathing-focused relaxation, and guided imagery training; (5) cognitive restructuring of anger schemas by altering attentional focus, modifying appraisals, and using self-instruction; (6) training behavioral coping skills in communication, diplomacy, respectful assertiveness, and strategic withdrawal, as modeled and rehearsed with the therapist; and (7) practicing the cognitive, arousal regulatory, and behavioral coping skills while visualizing and role playing progressively more intense anger-arousing scenes from the personal provocation hierarchy. Thus, a key feature is therapist-guided progressive exposure to anger provocation, in conjunction with which anger regulatory skills are acquired (see Taylor & Novaco, 2005).

Research Base

There is convergent evidence that CBT for anger produces therapeutic gains. Several meta-analytic reviews of treatment efficacy have found medium effect sizes for various CBT interventions, indicating that the large majority of those treated were improved compared to those in control conditions (Del Vecchio & O'Leary, 2004; DiGuiseppe & Tafrate, 2003; Sukhodolsky, Kassinove, & Gorman, 2004). Many of the randomized control studies captured by meta-analyses have not involved seriously disordered patients. Nevertheless, there have been positive outcomes in controlled studies with such patients, two examples of which are a study by Chemtob, Novaco, Hamada, and Gross (1997) with Vietnam veterans having severe posttraumatic stress disorder and intense, recurrent post-war anger and aggressive behavior and a study by Taylor and Novaco (2005) with forensic patients having intellectual disabilities and co-morbid disorders. Meta-analytic reviews do not include case studies and multiple baseline studies with clinical populations, for whom CBT stress inoculation for anger has produced treatment gains, including for a hospitalized depressed patient, child-abusing parents, a chronically aggressive patient, an emotionally disturbed boy, a brain-damaged patient, mentally handicapped patients, adolescents in residential treatment, and hospitalized forensic patients (see Taylor & Novaco, 2005).

REFERENCES

Chemtob, C. M., Novaco, R. W., Hamada, R., & Gross, D. (1997). Cognitive-behavioral treatment for severe anger in posttraumatic stress disorder. *Journal of Consulting and Clinical Psychology, 65,* 184–189.

Del Vecchio, T., & O'Leary, K. D. (2004). Effectiveness of anger treatments for specific anger problems: A meta-analytic review. *Clinical Psychology Review, 24,* 15–34.

DiGuiseppe, R., & Tafrate, R. C. (2003). Anger treatments for adults: A meta-analytic review. *Clinical Psychology: Science and Practice, 10,* 70–84.

Kassinove, H., & Tafrate, R. C. (2002). *Anger management: The complete treatment guidebook for practitioners.* Atascadero, CA: Impact.

Novaco, R. W. (1975). *Anger control: The development and evaluation of an experimental treatment.* Lexington, MA: D. C. Heath.

Sukhodolsky, D. G., Kassinove, H., & Gorman, B. S. (2004). Cognitive-behavior therapy for anger in children and adolescents: A meta-analysis. *Aggression and Violent Behavior, 9,* 247–269.

Taylor, J. L., & Novaco, R. W. (2005). *Anger treatment for people with developmental disabilities: A theory, evidence, and manual based approach.* London: John Wiley & Sons, 2005.

SUGGESTED READINGS

Averill, J. R. (1982). *Anger and aggression: An essay on emotion.* New York: Springer Verlag.

DiGuiseppe, R., & Tafrate, R. C. (2007). *Understanding anger disorders.* New York: Oxford University Press.

Howells, K., & Day, A. (2003). Readiness for anger management: Clinical and theoretical issues. *Clinical Psychology Review, 23,* 319–337.

Novaco, R. W. (2007). Anger dysregulation: Its assessment and treatment. In T. A. Cavell & K. T. Malcolm (Eds.), *Anger, aggression, and interventions for interpersonal violence* (pp. 3–54). Mahwah, NJ: Lawrence Erlbaum.

RAYMOND W. NOVACO
University of California, Irvine

ANIMAL COGNITION

Animal cognition is a broad term that includes a diverse array of phenomena. Consider some examples. Can apes learn language? Are selective attention and rehearsal involved in learning and cognition? Do animals use tools? Do animals form categories? Can animals abstract rules embodied in a series of items? As a final example, can animals organize lower order items in a higher order chunk, as for example, humans do when organizing letters of the alphabet into a word?

How is cognition to be distinguished from other psychological processes? There are several answers. According to one, cognition involves complex information processing, as for example, when an animal travels over a broad area in search of prey. Cognition is often said to involve the representation of events, as when an animal forms a memory of some past event or anticipates a future one. Some see various cognitive activities, tool use, spatial learning, and the like as governed by a single general problem solving mechanism. Others suggest that cognitive capacities are best considered as modular. The modular view suggests that cognitive capacities are domain-specific adaptations to environmental demands.

For example, a species that ranges far and wide in search of prey may have better spatial learning abilities than one that does not. Some suggest that cognition involves flexibility and adaptability in contrast with simple learning abilities that are more rigid and inflexible. According to this view, in order to suggest that some activity involves cognition it must be shown that it cannot be explained in terms of simpler learning principles. Honig (1998), however, has suggested that there is no set of agreed-on criteria that distinguish the cognitive from the non-cognitive.

Cognition versus Associationism

It often happens that some cognitive explanation of some phenomenon has a rival associative one. For example, consider a series of items A-B-C-D ... consisting of food rewards that become progressively smaller over trials. Hungry animals learn such series as indicated by progressively weaker responding over the series. Two ways to explain this behavior are that animals have abstracted the rule governing the series, that is, each food item is smaller than the prior one, or animals have learned a series of associations, that is, item A signals item B, B signals C, and so on.

Another example is Pavlovian conditioning. In this procedure a stimulus such as a tone, called the conditioned stimulus (CS), may occur shortly before a biological significant stimulus such as food, called the unconditioned stimulus (US). Learning is said to occur when salivation that is elicited by the US occurs to the CS. A common explanation of such learning is that an association is formed between the CS and the US. The view that the cognitive and associative explanations are mutually exclusive in simpler forms of learning, such as Pavlovian conditioning, may be questioned for three major reasons.

First, it has been suggested, particularly in older treatments, that Pavlovian conditioning is simple, reflexive learning. But here is what one of the leading theorists in the area of Pavlovian conditioning, Robert Rescorla, said of his research:

> Pavlovian conditioning has historically been viewed as the most mechanistic and least cognitive of learning processes. Although it has often been used as an explanatory device to account for apparently cognitive aspects of complex behavior, Pavlovian conditioning has itself been less frequently described in cognitive terms. It is the contention of this paper that such a description can potentially encourage novel and interesting experimentation. (1978, p. 15)

So "simple associations" may themselves involve a greater degree of cognition than some may suppose.

A second reason is that CS-US associations in Pavlovian conditioning have been said by a variety of theorists to depend upon processes that are widely regarded as cognitive, such as attention to the CS, rehearsing the CS and the US together, remembering the CS when the US occurs, and organizing separately presented CS-US trials in a chunk (see Martins, Miller, & Capaldi, 2008).

Finally, many of the associations formed in Pavlovian conditioning are complex and may be said to involve cognition. Consider a single example: An association between a CS and a US may be formed even when a CS is presented and terminated long before the US itself is presented. Some representation of the CS clearly survives the temporal interval separating it from the US.

Some Popular Areas of Cognition

It is not possible in the space allotted here to discuss all the individual areas of study in animal cognition. By considering some of the more popular ones, in combination with earlier remarks, a reasonable idea of animal cognition may be provided.

Language

Language in apes was examined initially by attempts to get them to form words. However, they cannot do so for physical limitations. Two other attempts were to get chimpanzees to press symbols for words and to have them learn American sign language. The animals learned many symbols and signs and, according to some, combined the symbols and words into sentences, giving evidence of language. This conclusion encountered considerable opposition. The major criticism was that the animals were simply learning a series of associations of the sort described earlier, that is, A signals B, B signals C, and so forth. These attacks were successful in that various production methods (producing a gesture, etc.) were replaced by comprehension techniques. A bonobo (close relative of the chimpanzee) named Kanzi learned to understand many words presented singly or in a sentence. Kanzi's understanding of sentences was about equal to that of a three-year-old child named Alia. Beyond three years of age, Alia surpassed Kanzi.

Serial Learning

As we have seen, serial learning has been said to involve cognition in the form of rule learning. Evidence has also been presented that animals can organize items of a series into chunks (see e.g., Martins et al., 2008). Thus, even if language-trained animals learned associations rather than true language, they could be said to be employing cognition.

Transitive Inference

An animal may be said to form a transitive inference if it grasps some relation exhibited by a series of items. For example, if Harry is older than Mary and Mary is older than Peter, then it follows that Harry is older than Peter. There are several ways to investigate transitive inference in animals. A popular one is to provide the animal with a five-item series of the form $A > B > C > D > E$. After mastering the series, the animal may be tested with the items B and D presented together for the first time. Note that these two items have this in common: Each is smaller than the preceding item and larger than the following item. If in a test the animal provides evidence that it knows $B > D$, a basis exists for suggesting that an inference has been formed. Several associative models, differing among themselves, are capable of explaining why the animal knows $B > D$.

Categorization

In a series of investigations, pigeons were shown a number of slides, some containing various kinds of trees, others nontrees. The bird was reinforced for pecking the tree slides but not for pecking nontrees. The pigeon quickly discriminated between the two types of slides, pecking the tree slides but not the others. Subsequently, slides used in the learning phase were replaced by new tree and nontree slides the pigeons had not previously seen. The birds responded appropriately to the new slides. Category learning of this sort has been investigated in connection with a great variety of other categories. On the basis of such data it may be claimed that birds form concepts. Others suggest that concepts involve language and thus birds lack concepts.

Spatial Learning

Animals have to get from one place in space to another for many purposes—to find food, a mate, and so forth—and they do so using a variety of mechanisms. Dead reckoning is one: an internal sense of the direction and distance of its nest from the current position. Or they may orient to landmarks. Animals may also use the sun as a compass. Relevant to present purposes we may ask, do animals have cognitive maps or a device that represents direction and distance among objects or locations? The ability of animals to get around may not involve maps according to some. Rather, animals form memories of local views of the environment associatively linked by memories of movements that take them from one place to another.

Timing and Counting

Timing and counting are often treated together because according to certain models they are accomplished in the same way (Shettleworth, 1998). There can be little doubt that animals are adept at timing. They time intervals well and can judge time accurately when they both stop and start their "clocks." It seems clear that animals have some ability to count or enumerate events whether they are presented simultaneously or successively. Essentially, timing and counting methods are variants of discrimination learning. For example, following a two-second tone response A will be rewarded and following an eight-second tone response B will be rewarded. Some have suggested that animals' numerical ability may extend beyond counting or the simple enumeration of items, to addition, subtraction, multiplication and division. In the area of counting animals have been shown to exhibit cross-model transfer. For example, animals trained to count auditory stimuli can transfer to counting the same number of visual stimuli.

REFERENCES

Honig, W. K. (1998). Cognition in animals. In G. Greenberg & M. M. Haraway (Eds.), *Comparative psychology*. New York: Garland.

Martins, A. P. G., Miller, R. M., & Capaldi, E. J. (2008). Memories and anticipations control responding by rats (*Rattus norvegicus*) in a Pavlovian procedure. *Animal Cognition, 11*, 59–66.

Rescorla, R. A. (1978). Some implications of a cognitive perspective on Pavlovian conditioning. In S. H. Hulse, H. Fowler, & W. K. Honig (Eds.), *Cognitive processes in animal behavior* (pp. 15–50). Hillsdale, NJ: Lawrence Erlbaum.

Shettleworth, S. (1998). *Cognition, evolution, and behavior*. New York: Oxford University Press.

SUGGESTED READINGS

Greenberg, G., & Haraway, M. M. (Eds.). (1998). *Comparative psychology*. New York: Garland.

Wasserman, E., & Zentall, T. (Eds.). (2006). *Comparative cognition*. New York: Oxford University Press.

E. J. CAPALDI
ANA P. G. MARTINS
Purdue University

See also: Animal Intelligence; Animal Learning and Behavior

ANIMAL INTELLIGENCE

The study of animal intelligence has been addressed by ethologists, biologists, psychologists, anthropologists, neurologists, zoologists, and ecologists, among others, each guided by different theoretical perspectives. Representatives from each field have thus defined intelligence in different ways. The resulting disparate theoretical definitions have, not surprisingly, led to distinct operational definitions, encouraging strikingly different methodological approaches to the study of intelligent behavior in animals. Two broad approaches can be identified. Researchers studying animals in the field (e.g., ethologists, biologists, behavioral ecologists) have tended to focus on questions of how animals adapt to and solve ecological problems, whereas those studying animals in captive environments (e.g., psychologists) have focused on questions of generalized learning and memory and concept formation.

Questions of adaptation examine how perceptual and cognitive skills such as attention, memory, and decision making assist the animal's everyday functioning. For instance, how do those skills allow the animal to find food and mates, maintain and defend a territory, and fend off predators? Studies in this tradition have tended to examine species-specific behaviors rather than looking for generalized perceptual or cognitive abilities. Of importance is what typical members of a given species do under the average living conditions they have evolved to face, not what the limits of a species' capacities might be, or what a single individual might do under extraordinary circumstances.

Researchers concerned with questions of adaptation might take a comparative approach and examine, for example, whether species of birds who must cache or store their food over harsh winter months exhibit more advanced spatial memory skills relative to species who live in climates where their preferred food is abundant year-round, or who do not cache. Ethologists and behavioral ecologists study behaviors that are already within a species' behavioral repertoire and ask whether it makes evolutionary sense for a given skill to have evolved under the conditions in which that species naturally lives. With this approach, animals are typically not presented with problems they would not face in their natural environments.

When animal intelligence is framed in evolutionary terms (e.g., abilities that allow organisms to cope with their environments), then all animal behavior is intelligent, for all species are uniquely adapted for the environments they inhabit. Perhaps by that measure, one might consider the most intelligent species the ones that adapt to the broadest range of environments, or that are able to adapt most quickly to environmental changes, or even those who can change the environment to suit their needs. This latter definition might be deemed anthropocentric, as it certainly encapsulates an ability quite advanced in our own species. No other species transforms its environment or adapts to so many environments quite as readily as humans. Although many species of insects exist in a multitude of habitats, only humans have proven capable of advanced technological inventions such as equipment that allows us to breathe under water or in outer space.

Thus psychologists, who tend to focus on questions of what it is that makes humans unique, especially in terms of their cognition, have conceptualized intelligence in a different manner. They have tended to define intelligence as the ability of an individual to generalize learning beyond the specific conditions under which an event or object was encountered to events or objects that can only be imagined, or that might be encountered in the future, thereby allowing an individual to exhibit a high degree of transfer of learning from one situation to the next. Thus, transfer tests with novel stimuli have become acid tests of intelligent behavior in different domains for comparative psychologists. In this tradition, animals are frequently presented with objects that are foreign to them and asked what they can infer about the function or purpose of the object in order to demonstrate their intelligence. This approach takes an animal out of the context in which its abilities were evolutionarily sculpted and into one in which it might demonstrate, for example, insightful, inferential, or analogical reasoning, allowing researchers to distinguish intelligent from instinctive behavior.

Psychologists have also relied on learning sets. Do animals learn how to learn? That is, do they learn rules about learning or strategies for learning that transcend the particular stimuli they are learning about? For example, when learning a categorization task, they learn not only that particular stimuli such as food items must be grouped together and responded to in a certain way, but they also learn a more general rule: to figure out what the category is for any given stimulus set.

In contrast to field studies, laboratory studies are often directed at searching for a single instance of a behavior that would demonstrate a particular ability. Indeed, in some psychological traditions, only one member of the species needs to demonstrate a given ability in order for that ability to be deemed within the grasp of that species. For instance, Premack's chimpanzee, Sarah, single-handedly contributed to the notion that chimpanzees might be capable of reasoning about mental states (Premack & Woodruff, 1978) or that only language or token-trained chimpanzees might be capable of analogical reasoning (Premack, 1983). There are many instances of individuals who stand alone among their species, exhibiting extraordinary feats of intelligence that have yet to be replicated (e.g., Rico the Border Collie, Alex the African grey parrot, Betty the New Caledonian crow, Koko the gorilla, Chantek the orangutan, Washoe the chimpanzee, Kanzi the bonobo). Single instances of innovation, such as cultural learning and other instances of social learning, might be important for this conceptualization of intelligence as well.

More recently, researchers have attempted to bridge the gap and form multidisciplinary collaborations, taking the best of both theoretical and methodological approaches. Under this approach, researchers are guided to observe what an animal does in its own environment, to understand the contexts in which a behavior naturally occurs, and then to use laboratory tests to rigorously test

hypotheses about how and why specific behaviors may have evolved, the underlying mental/neural architecture supporting the behavior, and how those behaviors might be altered under varying conditions. Those behaviors that are flexible and malleable will allow an individual to adjust and adapt to an ever-changing, unpredictable environment—which is a useful operational definition of intelligence. By combining the traditional approaches, it is possible to ask what animals actually do in their own environments and what they are capable of learning when taken out of those comfort zones. Thus, both approaches can be integrated where feasible to promote the best understanding of what it is that makes behavior adaptive.

REFERENCES

Premack, D. (1983). The codes of man and beasts. *The Behavioral and Brain Sciences, 6*, 125–167.

Premack, D., & Woodruff, G. (1978). Does the chimpanzee have a theory of mind? *Behavioral and Brain Sciences, 4*, 515–526.

SUGGESTED READINGS

Shettleworth, Sara, J. (1998). *Cognition, evolution and behavior*. New York: Oxford University Press.

Tomasello, M., & Call, J. (1997). *Primate cognition*. Oxford, UK: Oxford University Press.

JENNIFER VONK
DANIEL J. POVINELLI
University of Louisiana

See also: **Animal Cognition; Animal Learning and Behavior; Comparative Psychology**

ANIMAL LEARNING AND BEHAVIOR

The study of animal learning and behavior has a rich tradition within the field of psychology. While learning has many definitions across fields, a useful framework for animal learning is defining it as a process in which behaviors are modified as a result of experience, provided that the change in behavior cannot be attributed to innate response tendencies, rapid change of stimuli (Domjan, 2006), developmental maturation, or temporary state factors (such as fatigue; see Runyon, 1977).

There are a number of reasons why animal models are beneficial for studying learning, even for those whose interest lies solely in the study of human psychology. Animal studies allow for the use of methods that, due to ethical considerations, are not accessible for use with humans, such as single-cell recordings from individual neurons in the brain. In addition, the use of animals permits greater control over the external environment. Environmental factors can often confound evidence of learning, and animals can be reared in environments that permit these factors to be carefully manipulated or controlled, such as the extreme case in which animals may be reared in isolation in order to test whether a particular cognitive feature or behavior relies on social learning. Finally, animal models may also provide an advantage in that they can provide simpler systems for studying behavior, again minimizing potential confounding variables inherent in the study of more complex systems.

Historical Views

Early philosophers, such as Aristotle, posited that animals are similar to humans in many respects, but lack the ability to reason (Pellegrin, 1986). Over the ensuing centuries, many positions on animal cognition were articulated, often influenced by religious beliefs about divine hierarchical ordering. One of the most influential early philosophical positions on animal behavior was espoused by Rene Descartes (1596–1650), whose theory of mind-body dualism was predicated on the notion that humans are capable of voluntary and involuntary behaviors, whereas animals are capable of only involuntary behaviors. This view held sway for roughly 200 years, until Charles Darwin (1809–1882) wrote a series of books positing that phylogenetic continuity across species was not only morphological, but also psychological (Darwin, 1871). Darwin's continuity hypothesis paved the way for modern psychological studies of animal behavior (see Roberts, 1998, for review).

Initially, Darwin and George Romanes (1848–1894), a close friend and author of *Animal Intelligence* (1882), used anecdotal evidence to support the argument for continuity. This method was challenged in the early twentieth century by C. Lloyd Morgan (1852–1936), who introduced a principle known as *Morgan's Canon* (1906). Morgan's Canon asserted that in interpreting behavior, one must exhaust simpler behavioral explanations before invoking the involvement of more complex behaviors. The articulation of this principle coincided with the Clever Hans affair, in which a then-famous horse named Hans was posited to possess human-like intelligence until the hoax was debunked by Oskar Pfungst (1847–1933), who found that Hans's behavior was guided by very simple behavioral associations. These developments, along with the emergence of influential researchers like Ivan Pavlov and Edward Thorndike paved the way for more carefully controlled and systematic studies of animal behavior.

In the early twentieth century, Pavlov and Thorndike began pioneering work on classical conditioning and associative learning, with the underlying theory that the mechanisms responsible for changes in animal behavior had analogues in humans. Pavlov (1849–1936), a Nobel-prize winning physiologist and surgeon, developed the concept of the conditioned reflex. During his research on the physiology of the digestive system in dogs, Pavlov noticed that if he paired the sound of a bell with the presentation of food, the dogs would begin to salivate when hearing the bell alone. This discovery paved the way for a rich theoretical framework, classical conditioning (see below), that is still studied today. Thorndike (1874–1949) was a harsh critic of using anecdotal evidence and is often credited as being the first researcher to bring the study of animal learning into the laboratory. Thorndike's Law of Effect postulated that behaviors that lead to satisfying outcomes are more likely to be repeated, whereas behaviors that lead to less desirable outcomes are less likely to reoccur. Thus, rewards are likely to strengthen stimulus-response (S-R) connections. Thorndike's work on instrumental conditioning set the stage for future behaviorists like B. F. Skinner, who also focused on the reinforcing properties of the environment.

The study of animal learning thrived in the Behaviorist era in psychology that began in the early twentieth century and predominated for roughly 60 years. The central tenet of behaviorism was manifest in J. B. Watson's (1878–1958) paper entitled "Psychology as the Behaviorist Views It" (Watson, 1913). Watson emphasized the importance of learning in psychology, eschewing mentalistic terms while emphasizing the importance of studying behavior. This view was later adopted and expanded by B. F. Skinner (1904–1990), considered to be the founder of radical behaviorism, a school of thought seeking to understand behavior strictly in terms of environmental histories of reinforcement consequences. Skinner extended the behaviorist doctrine to encompass inner physiological experiences as well, a critical deviation from other theoretical behaviorist accounts. Skinner's work on operant conditioning has had a tremendous impact on the field of psychology in research and in clinical applications, extending to the development of behavioral modification techniques.

During the Behaviorist era, most researchers shunned any serious consideration of internal mechanisms, except for two notable psychologists, Edward Tolman (1886–1959) and Clark Hull (1884–1952). Tolman and Hull were amenable to the idea of internal mechanisms mediating stimulus-response (S-R) models. For example, Tolman (1948) believed that stimuli were not connected in a one-to-one fashion with outgoing responses, but rather were elaborated into an internal cognitive map, which in turn determined the responses that would be produced. Tolman's behaviorism focused on the *molar* analysis, asserting the relevant unit for behavior study consisted of an entire action, as opposed to the molecular level favored by many behaviorists who focus on the smaller behavioral components (such as single muscle contractions) that produce more complex behaviors.

Tolman's approach to animal learning foreshadowed later theoretical positions, as the cognitive revolution of the 1960s and 1970s emphasized internal mental processes as central to the field of psychology. In fact, one of the enduring major debates in the description of animal learning and behavior is the extent to which cognitive mechanisms are thought to mediate observed behaviors. Behavioral approaches (consistent with Watson, Thorndike, Skinner, and others) focus on the relationship between observed behaviors and environmental events. In contrast, cognitive approaches posit that behavior is mediated by intervening internal variables (consistent with Tolman, Hull, and others).

Theoretical Orientations

The field of animal learning and behavior encompasses a wide variety of theoretical orientations that differ in their underlying assumptions and interests. Nobel laureate ethologist Nikolaas Tinbergen (1907–1988) proposed a broad framework to examine animal behavior that is useful for illustrating the different levels of analysis. Tinbergen (1952) proposed that in order to truly understand a behavior, four questions must be answered. Two questions pertain to the proximate mechanisms of behavior (i.e., addressing how the behavior is instantiated in the individual organism) and two questions pertain to the ultimate mechanisms (i.e., addressing why the behavior evolved in that species). The proximate level questions concern (1) The mechanisms underlying the behavior: What are the neural, physiological and psychological mechanisms involved in the expression of the behavior? and (2) The ontogeny (development) of that behavior: How does the behavior change with age and what experiences are necessary for its expression? To what extent is the behavior genetically encoded? The ultimate level questions concern (1) The phylogenetic (evolutionary) history of the trait. How does the behavior compare with behaviors observed in related species or in species facing similar selective pressures? and (2) The function (adaptation) of the behavior: How does the behavior impact survival and reproduction (fitness consequences)? Comparative psychologists have traditionally been interested in the proximate level questions, whereas ethologists have been more interested in the ultimate level questions.

Psychologists studying animal learning and behavior have typically adopted an anthropocentric approach (see Shettleworth, 1998) that is based on the notion that all species share a core set of underlying mechanisms that guide behavior. Accordingly, the study of learning in rats or pigeons can provide direct insights into fundamental principles applicable to human behavior. This general process approach (see Domjan, 2006) asserts that a limited system governed by a few basic principles can account for a wide variety of observable behaviors. Pavlov's classical conditioning and Skinner's operant learning theories fall squarely in this tradition, as the study of these learning mechanisms were meant to illustrate general principles and rules of learning that apply to behavior across all species. The anthropocentric approach, then, can be characterized as elucidating the proximate mechanisms underlying learning and behavior of all species.

In contrast to the anthropocentric approach, the biological approach (Shettleworth, 1998) to the study of animal learning and behavior (also termed the comparative approach; Domjan, 2006) is characterized by principles of evolutionary biology, focusing on the extent to which behaviors represent adaptive specializations shaped by natural selection to increase survival or fitness (i.e., ultimate mechanisms). Rather than emphasizing similarities across species, the biological approach to learning seeks behavioral differences across species that may be explained by differences in environmental selective pressures. A recent trend in research on animal learning and behavior has been an effort to incorporate both proximate and ultimate levels of analysis by synthesizing the anthropocentric and biological approaches. These efforts are characterized by studying the underlying mechanisms used by animals to resolve ecologically relevant challenges, thereby framing learning in the context of evolution.

Methodological Considerations

Many of the early theories and claims about animal learning and behavior were fueled by anecdotes. As mentioned above, even Darwin used an anecdotal approach in support of his continuity theory. After heavy criticism from Morgan, Thorndike, and others, the study of animal learning moved into the laboratory, where external variables could be better controlled. In the laboratory, numerous methods have been implemented, and here we review a small subset that represents some of the major classes of research.

Classical Conditioning

A common example of classical conditioning can be demonstrated with Pavolv's dogs. When he paired auditory sounds with the presentation of food (which naturally induced salivation), the sounds became conditioned such that their presentation alone could induce salivation. Classical conditioning studies typically involve taking a neutral stimulus (i.e., a stimulus that does not naturally evoke the conditioned response) and pairing it with an unconditioned stimulus (US) that elicits an unconditioned response (UR). The neutral stimulus becomes a conditioned stimulus (CS) through this pairing and will begin to elicit a conditioned response (CR) after a number of pairings. In the example above, the auditory sound was the neutral stimulus, which prior to conditioning did not elicit a salivating response. When it was paired with the food (the US), which naturally elicits salivation (the UR), the sounds became conditioned (the CS) such that their presentation alone could induce salivation (the CR).

Instrumental and Operant Conditioning

Unlike classical conditioning, instrumental and operant conditioning are predicated on the modification of behaviors by environmental consequences. The idea behind both instrumental and operant conditioning is that organisms engage in behaviors whose outcomes either lead to an increase in the frequency of the behavior (reinforcement) or a decrease in the behavior (punishment). When the environmental consequence for a given behavior is inconsequential, then the behavior will undergo extinction, the reduction of the reinforced response. There are two varieties of reinforcers and punishers, positive and negative. Positive refers to the additive effects (e.g., receiving a pellet for pressing a lever increases the behavior and is therefore considered to be a positive reinforcer) whereas negative effects are subtractive (e.g., the removal of an aversive stimuli as a result of a behavior will lead to an increase in the behavior, hence it is negative reinforcement).

Untrained Methods

Another type of research conducted with animals examines the fundamental computational abilities of various species, employing methodologies that involve no explicit training or associations. For example, habituation-discrimination experiments (also commonly used in field studies) expose participants to a particular stimulus until they no longer respond to it (habituation) and then are exposed to a new stimulus and the response is measured. If the participant responds, then it is evidence that the participant has detected a meaningful difference between the familiarization stimuli and the test stimulus. An advantage to employing untrained methods is that they can be employed with both human infants and nonhumans, thus allowing for a more straightforward comparison of cross-species similarities and differences (Weiss & Newport, 2006).

REFERENCES

Darwin, C. (1871). *The descent of man, and selection in relation to sex.* London: John Murray.

Domjan, M. (2006). *The principles of learning and behavior: Active learning edition.* Belmont, CA: Thomson/Wadsworth.

Morgan, C. L. (1906). *An introduction to comparative psychology.* London: Walter Scott.

Pellegrin, P. (1986). *Aristotle's classification of animals: Biology and the conceptual unity of the Aristotelian corpus.* Berkeley: University of California Press.

Roberts, W. A. (1998). *Principles of animal cognition.* Boston: McGraw-Hill.

Romanes, G. J. (1882). *Animal intelligence.* London: Kegan Paul, Trench, & Co.

Runyon, K. (1977). *Consumer behavior and the practice of marketing.* Columbus, OH: Charles E. Merrill.

Shettleworth, S. J. (1998). *Cognition, evolution, and behavior.* New York: Oxford University Press.

Tolman, E. (1948). *Cognitive maps in rats and men.* Psychological Review, *55*, 189–208.

Tinbergen, N. (1952). *Derived activities: Their causation, biological significance, origin, and emancipation during evolution.* Quarterly Review of Biology, *27*, 1–32.

Watson, J. B. (1913). *Psychology as the behaviorist views it.* Psychological Review, *20*, 158–177.

Weiss, D. J., & Newport, E. (2006) *Mechanisms underlying language acquisition: Benefits from a comparative approach.* Infancy *9*(2), 241–257.

SUGGESTED READING

Alcock, J. (2001). *Animal behavior: An evolutionary approach.* Sunderland, MA: Sinauer.

DANIEL J. WEISS
KATE CHAPMAN
Pennsylvania State University

See also: **Comparative Psychology; Ethology; Operant Conditioning; Pavlovian Conditioning**

ANOMIC APHASIA

Anomic aphasia is a very disabling disorder that results from acquired brain dysfunction (typically stroke, traumatic brain injury, or temporal lobe resection). Patients with anomic aphasia manifest an isolated deficit in their ability to name things like concrete entities (named by nouns), actions (named by verbs), or spatial relationships (named by prepositions). Defective naming, also known as anomia, is a frequent part of the symptom complex that characterizes patients with aphasia (Goodglass & Wingfield, 1997; Tranel & Anderson, 1999), where aphasia refers to disturbances of the comprehension and formulation of verbal messages caused by acquired damage to language-related brain structures (typically in the left hemisphere).

Anomia is also a common experience among people with Alzheimer's disease, epilepsy, and several other neurological disorders. However, when anomia occurs as an isolated manifestation of acquired brain dysfunction in the absence of additional symptoms of aphasia and other cognitive dysfunction, the designation of "anomic aphasia" applies. Some of the common aphasia syndromes, such as Wernicke's aphasia and conduction aphasia, tend to gradually resolve into a picture of anomic aphasia as the patient recovers.

It is sometimes assumed that naming ability and recognition are one and the same process. However, knowing what something is (its meaning, sometimes termed *semantics* or *recognition*) is distinct from knowing what something is called (referred to as *naming* or *lexical retrieval*). In fact, naming and recognition have partially distinct neural mechanisms (Damasio et al., 2004), which helps explain why patients with anomic aphasia have lost the ability to retrieve names of things, but they have not lost the ability to recognize what things are. Thus, even when they cannot name things, anomic aphasics can usually produce accurate descriptions of those things, or indicate by gestures that they have intact conceptual knowledge.

For example, when shown a picture of a camel, the patient may say, "That is an animal that has humps on its back, lives in the desert, and can go for a long time without water." Or when shown a picture of Bill Clinton, the patient may say, "That guy was a president; had an affair, had a southern accent." A related phenomenon known as "tip-of-the-tongue" state occurs fairly frequently in the realm of normal experience. Under conditions of fatigue, distraction, or in connection with normal aging, normal individuals sometimes experience the inability to retrieve a particular name even though they know perfectly well what it is that they are attempting to name (Burke et al., 1991). It is especially common for normal individuals to have trouble retrieving proper names (i.e., names denoting unique entities such as persons and places). In addition, anomia sometimes occurs in the course of normal verbal discourse such as when one is speaking and suddenly cannot retrieve the name for a particular concept that is part of the intended utterance.

The vast majority of current knowledge regarding the neural underpinnings of word retrieval and most theoretical accounts of this process are heavily tied to the visual modality. However, anomia can occur in connection with any sensory modality—for example, when attempting to name a picture of something, a sound, a smell, or something that is felt by the hand. Nevertheless, most researchers utilize "visual confrontation naming" paradigms to test for and investigate anomia, a method that involves presenting participants with pictures, line drawings, or actual objects and then asking them to provide a name for each item. This format is also the standard paradigm for assessing naming ability in patients with brain injuries. In fact, one such visual confrontation naming test, the Boston Naming Test (BNT) (Kaplan, Goodglass, & Weintraub, 1983), is the eighth most commonly used test among neuropsychologists in the United States (Camara, Nathan, & Puente, 2000). Tests of naming ability for the other sensory modalities have primarily been used in research investigations rather than clinical settings.

The classic aphasia syndromes, including Broca's ("nonfluent") and Wernicke's ("fluent") aphasia, are typically associated with brain damage in the vicinity of the sylvian fissure of the left hemisphere of the brain. Although anomia is typically characteristic of these syndromes, it is usually only one of many more serious and severe symptoms of language impairment. Cases of pure anomic aphasia, in which severe naming defects are manifested in the absence of more global symptoms of aphasia, are primarily associated with damage to structures in the left hemisphere that are outside the classic language regions. Specifically, anomic aphasia is most often caused by damage to the left anterior temporal lobe, to the inferior and lateral aspect of the left temporal lobe, or to the left occipitotemporal junction.

Interestingly, scientific investigations of patients with anomic aphasia have revealed a number of intriguing associations between specific brain structures and specific types of naming abilities (Damasio & Tranel, 1993; H. Damasio et al., 1996, 2004; Tranel et al., 2001). Studies in normal subjects, using functional neuroimaging procedures (positron emission tomography, functional magnetic resonance imaging) have corroborated several of these findings (Grabowski et al., 2001; Martin et al., 1995, 1996).

The evidence from this research indicates that the neural correlates of naming ability may be category-specific. For example, naming of proper nouns has been associated with the temporal polar region in the anterior left temporal lobe. Immediately behind the temporal pole, in the inferior and lateral aspect of the temporal lobe, is a region that has been associated with the retrieval of names for animals. And further back, in the vicinity of the temporal-occipital junction, is a region that has been associated with the retrieval of names for tools. These associations may appear arbitrary or even bizarre, but there are principled accounts of why the human brain may be organized in such a fashion (Dell et al., 1997; H. Damasio et al., 1996, 2004; Saffran & Sholl, 1999).

For example, factors such as whether an entity is unique (e.g., Tom Hanks) or nonunique (e.g., a screwdriver), whether it is living (e.g., a pig) or nonliving (e.g., a hammer), whether it is manipulable (e.g., a wrench) or nonmanipulable (e.g., a giraffe), or whether it makes a distinctive sound (e.g., a rooster) or not (e.g., a thimble), are important in determining which neural structures will be used in the mapping and retrieval of knowledge for entities, including their names (H. Damasio et al., 2004). Interestingly, the modality in which a stimulus is perceived may not make much difference: for example, retrieving the name "rooster" when confronted with a picture of a rooster, or when confronted with the characteristic sound of a rooster, appears to depend on the same left temporal lobe region (Tranel et al., 2005).

There are also intriguing distinctions between words that come from different grammatical categories, such as nouns versus verbs. Although the brain regions that are important for retrieving both types of words are primarily lateralized to the left hemisphere, the specific regions involved in the lexical retrieval of nouns is partially separate from those that are important for retrieving verbs. For example, the retrieval of nouns is related to structures in the left temporal lobe. The retrieval of verbs, by contrast, is related to structures in the left frontal operculum (in front of the Rolandic sulcus). Interestingly, some studies have suggested that noun-verb homophones—e.g., words like "hammer" or "duck," which are used frequently as either nouns or verbs—are retrieved by the brain system that fits the context in which the word is being used. Thus, if "hammer" is being used as a noun, the temporal lobe system will be used, but if "hammer" is being used as a verb, the frontal lobe system will be used (Tranel et al., 2005). Again, such dissociations may appear rather curious on the surface, but there are compelling explanations of why the brain has organized knowledge in different regions to subserve words from different grammatical categories (Damasio & Tranel, 1993; Tranel et al., 2001).

Naming defects are characteristic of a variety of neurological disorders and conditions; however, pure cases of anomic aphasia are rare. Severe naming impairments unaccompanied by other speech or linguistic deficits occur far less frequently than most of the "classic" aphasia syndromes. Nonetheless, patients with anomic aphasia have provided a unique opportunity to learn how the brain operates the processes associated with word retrieval, and how different brain structures are specialized for different types of words and different categories of entities. Thus, while anomic aphasia is important as a clinical disorder, its especial interest lies in the realm of scientific study of how the human brain operates language processes. This, in turn, can help inform rehabilitation efforts aimed at patients with acquired disturbances of naming. However, to date, most studies investigating the neural correlates of naming ability have focused on cases of anomic aphasia in monolingual speakers. Given the fact that bilingual and multilingual speakers greatly outnumber the population of monolingual speakers in the world, future research would benefit greatly from case studies of multilingual speakers who have acquired anomic aphasia.

REFERENCES

Burke, D. M., MacKay, D. G., Worthley, J. S., & Wade, E. (1991). On the tip of the tongue: What causes word-finding failures in young and older adults? *Journal of Memory and Language, 30,* 542–579.

Camara, W. J., Nathan, J. S., & Puente, A. E. (2000). Psychological test usage: Implications in professional psychology. *Professional Psychology: Research and Practice, 31,* 141–154.

Damasio, A. R., & Tranel, D. (1993). Nouns and verbs are retrieved with differently distributed neural systems. *Proceedings of the National Academy of Sciences, 90,* 4957–4960.

Damasio, H., Grabowski, T. J., Tranel, D., Hichwa, R., & Damasio, A. (1996). A neural basis for lexical retrieval. *Nature, 380,* 499–505.

Damasio, H., Tranel, D., Grabowski, T. J., Adolphs, R., & Damasio, A. R. (2004). Neural systems behind word and concept retrieval. *Cognition, 92,* 179–229.

Dell, G. S., Schwartz, M. F., Martin, N., Saffran, E. M., & Gagnon, D. A. (1997). Lexical access in aphasic and nonaphasic speakers. *Psychological Review, 104,* 801–838.

Goodglass, H., & Wingfield, A. (Eds.) (1997). *Anomia: Neuroanatomical and cognitive correlates.* New York: Academic Press.

Grabowski, T. J., Damasio, H., Tranel, D., Ponto, L. L. B., Hichwa, R. D., & Damasio, A. R. (2001). A role for left temporal pole in the retrieval of words for unique entities. *Human Brain Mapping, 13,* 199–212.

Kaplan, E., Goodglass, H., & Weintraub, S. (1983). Boston Naming Test. Philadelphia: Lee & Febiger.

Levelt, W. J. M., Roelofs, A., & Meyer, A. S. (1999). A theory of lexical access in speech production. *Behavioral and Brain Sciences, 22,* 1–75.

Martin, A., Haxby, J. V., Lalonde, F. M., Wiggs, C. L., & Ungerleider, L. G. (1995). Discrete cortical regions associated with knowledge of color and knowledge of action. *Science, 270,* 102–105.

Martin, A., Wiggs, C. L., Ungerleider, L. G., & Haxby, J. V. (1996). Neural correlates of category-specific knowledge. *Nature, 379,* 649–652.

Saffran, E. M., & Sholl, A. (1999). Clues to the functional and neural architecture of word meaning. In C. M. Brown & P. Hagoort (Eds.), *The neurocognition of language* (pp. 241–272). New York: Oxford University Press.

Tranel, D., Adolphs, R., Damasio, H., & Damasio, A. R. (2001). A neural basis for the retrieval of words for actions. *Cognitive Neuropsychology, 18,* 655–670.

Tranel, D., & Anderson, S. (1999). Syndromes of aphasia. In Fabbro, F. (Ed.), *Concise encyclopedia of language pathology* (pp. 305–319). Oxford, UK: Elsevier Science Limited.

Tranel, D., Damasio, H., & Damasio, A. R. (1997). A neural basis for the retrieval of conceptual knowledge. *Neuropsychologia, 35,* 1319–1327.

Tranel, D., Damasio, H., Eichhorn, G. R., Grabowski, T. J., Ponto, L. L. B., & Hichwa, R. D. (2003). Neural correlates of naming animals from their characteristic sounds. *Neuropsychologia, 41,* 847–854.

Tranel, D., Martin, C., Damasio, H., Grabowski, T., & Hichwa, R. (2005). Effects of noun-verb homonymy on the neural correlates of naming concrete entities and actions. *Brain and Language, 92,* 288–299.

RACHEL CASAS
DANIEL TRANEL
University of Iowa College of Medicine

See also: Conduction Aphasia; Language Comprehension; Speech Production

ANOREXIA NERVOSA

Anorexia nervosa is a mental disorder defined by deliberate self-starvation resulting in body weight below a minimum level necessary for health. In current diagnostic systems, such as the *Diagnostic and Statistical Manual of Mental Disorders* (DSM-IV-TR; American Psychiatric Association [APA], 2000), additional features include an intense fear of gaining weight or becoming fat, misperception or undue influence of weight or shape on self evaluation or denial of the seriousness of low weight, and, in postmenarcheal females, loss of three consecutive menstrual cycles. Of note, no definition provides a single threshold by which to evaluate low weight. In the DSM-IV-TR, weight less than 85% of that expected is provided as an example for diagnosis.

The term "anorexia nervosa" was introduced into the medical literature in 1874 by William Gull (1874). However, a self-starvation syndrome that predominantly affects adolescent and young adult females has been described in various accounts for centuries (see Keel & Klump, 2003). Several features have remained constant over time, including refusal to eat enough food to maintain a minimally healthy weight, denial of severity of the illness, and the increased risk of death due to starvation. Other features, such as fear of gaining weight or becoming fat, appear to be modern additions to the syndrome that may be absent in patients from non-Western cultures (Keel & Klump, 2003). Such historical and epidemiological patterns raise questions regarding the core features of the illness, suggesting that motivations for self-starvation may be ascribed *post hoc* and represent explanations for behaviors for which the cause remains largely unknown.

Epidemiology

In modern industrialized cultures, approximately 1 in 200 females develop anorexia nervosa over the course of their lifetimes, representing a lifetime prevalence rate of 0.5% in women (APA, 2000). Anorexia nervosa is significantly more common in women than men, with a ratio of approximately 10 female patients for every 1 male patient (APA, 2000). Further, the number of new cases per 100,000 individuals per year (or the 1-year incidence) has increased over recent decades (Keel & Klump, 2003). The onset of anorexia nervosa is most likely to occur during mid- to late adolescence.

Risk Factors for Developing Anorexia Nervosa

Lay explanations for anorexia nervosa often focus on the societal idealization of thinness. This explanation appears to account for the gender difference in risk for developing the disorder and increased incidence of the illness over recent decades. However, like any complex form of mental illness, anorexia nervosa is likely to be caused by a combination of biological, psychological, and social factors. The relative contributions of factors may vary on a case-by-case basis. Thus, it is possible for an individual's illness to result from societal pressures to emulate the thin ideal. However, given the pervasiveness of the thin ideal in modern Western cultures and the relative rarity of anorexia nervosa in the general population of women, it is clear that social factors alone are unlikely to account for the majority of cases.

Biological Risk Factors

Studies of identical and fraternal twins have identified the likely contribution of genes to the development of anorexia nervosa. Specifically, the risk of developing anorexia nervosa is higher when an individual has a genetically identical (monozygotic) twin affected with the disorder than when an individual has a fraternal (dizygotic) twin with the disorder (Becker, Keel, Anderson-Frye, & Thomas, 2004). Investigations of the actual genetic make-up of individuals with anorexia nervosa have suggested that they are more likely to have a specific form of a gene that codes for a type of serotonin receptor (Becker et al., 2004). Serotonin is a brain chemical (also called a neurotransmitter) that influences what signals are transmitted throughout the brain and body. Serotonin plays an important role in regulating appetite, mood, and self-regulation of behavior. Serotonin receptors influence how signals are received and processed for this chemical. Thus, finding an association between a gene that codes for a type of serotonin receptor and the presence of anorexia nervosa may help to explain why these individuals are vulnerable to develop the disorder.

Psychological Risk Factors

In her seminal book, *The Golden Cage*, Hilde Bruch (1978) provided a description of patients with anorexia nervosa based on her own observations and information from parents about circumstances and events preceding the onset of the illness. Girls who developed anorexia nervosa were described as striving towards perfection, concerned with controlling their own impulses in order to obtain approval from others, and prone to anxiety. These girls were also characterized by difficulties in differentiating internal states, such as feeling hungry versus feeling sad or tired. This description has withstood the test of time and can be seen in very early descriptions of patients and historical accounts of fasting girls that predate the introduction of anorexia nervosa into the medical literature (Keel & Klump, 2003). In addition, longitudinal studies have shown that individuals with higher levels of perfectionism are at increased risk for developing an anorexic syndrome later in life (Keel, 2005).

Social Risk Factors

As already described, anorexia nervosa has been defined in modern diagnostic systems by a fear of gaining weight or becoming fat, misperception of weight or shape, and undue influence of weight or shape on self-evaluation (APA, 2000). These features appear to be an extension of societal messages regarding the dangers of being overweight and importance of being thin in terms of being happy, healthy, loved, and respected (Becker et al., 2004). Numerous studies have demonstrated the stigmatization of being overweight and obese among children, adolescents, and adults, and numerous studies have demonstrated that individuals prefer thinner figures in themselves, friends, and potential partners (Keel, 2005). A social context that glorifies thinness and denigrates fatness may contribute to an adolescent's decision to go on a weight-loss diet. Once weight loss is initiated, social reinforcement may combine with psychological and biological risk factors in the ultimate development of anorexia nervosa.

Treatment

For adolescents with anorexia nervosa, a family-based treatment has demonstrated efficacy (Keel & Haedt, 2008). This treatment differs from traditional family therapies in which the family is viewed as the patient and treatment is designed to alter pathological family processes. In the family-based treatment for anorexia nervosa, family members are recruited as members of the treatment team in order to provide a home environment for adolescent children that encourages eating and weight gain. This intervention has proven superior to alternative treatments in independent randomized controlled treatment trials (Keel & Haedt, 2008). A striking problem in the field of eating disorders is the lack of evidenced based treatment for adults with anorexia nervosa (Bulik, Berkman, Brownley, Sedway, & Lohr, 2007).

Course and Outcome

As described in the DSM-IV-TR (APA, 2000), course and outcome are variable in anorexia nervosa. Community-based studies have indicated that individuals who meet criteria for anorexia nervosa may recover after a relatively brief period of illness, and this may be particularly likely for those with an early age of onset (Steinhausen, 2002). However, samples followed from clinical settings provide a more sober picture of course and outcome, with fewer than half of patients recovering, a third improving, and 20% remaining chronically ill more than a decade after diagnosis (Steinhausen, 2002). Particularly alarming, anorexia nervosa is associated with one of the highest risks for premature death of any mental disorder (Keel, 2005), with a 10-fold increase in death during early to mid-life compared to matched individuals without the

disorder. Primary causes of death include the physical consequences of starvation and suicide. Based on the lack of evidence-based treatments for anorexia nervosa in adults, the chronicity of the illness in a substantial subset of patients, and the elevated risk of death, anorexia nervosa represents a very serious form of mental illness.

REFERENCES

American Psychiatric Association. (2000). *Diagnostic and Statistical Manual of Mental Disorders* (4th ed., text rev.). Washington DC: Author.

Becker, A. E., Keel, P., Anderson-Frye, E. P., & Thomas, J. J. (2004). Genes and/or jeans?: Genetic and socio-cultural contributions to risk for eating disorders. *Journal of Addictive Diseases, 23*, 81–103.

Bruch, H. (1978). *The golden cage: The enigma of anorexia nervosa.* Cambridge, MA: Harvard University Press.

Bulik, C. M., Berkman, N. D., Brownley, K. A., Sedway, J. A., & Lohr, K. N. (2007). Anorexia nervosa treatment: A systematic review of randomized controlled trials. *International Journal of Eating Disorders, 40*, 310–320.

Gull, W. W. (1874). Anorexia Nervosa (apepsia hysterica, anorexia hysterica). *Transaction of the Clinical Society of London, 7*, 22–28.

Keel, P. K., & Klump, K. L. (2003). Are eating disorders culture-bound syndromes? Implications for conceptualizing their genetic bases. *Psychological Bulletin, 129*, 747–769.

Keel, P. K. (2005). *Eating Disorders.* Upper Saddle River, NJ: Pearson Prentice Hall.

Keel, P. K., & Haedt, A. (2008). Evidence-based psychosocial treatments for eating problems and eating disorders. *Journal of Clinical Child and Adolescent Psychology, 37*, 39–61.

Steinhausen, H. C. (2002). The outcome of anorexia nervosa in the 20th century. *American Journal of Psychiatry, 159*, 1284–1293.

PAMELA K. KEEL
University of Iowa

See also: **Bulimia Nervosa; Eating Disorders**

ANTABUSE AND OTHER DRUGS FOR TREATING ALCOHOLISM

Antabuse (disulfiram), a drug used as a supplementary therapy for alcoholism, was originally used in the manufacture of rubber. When the chemical got into the air in one factory and settled on the workers' skin, many developed dermatitis. If they inhaled it, they discovered that they could no longer tolerate alcohol. Beginning in the 1940s, therapists tried using the drug as a therapy for alcoholism, on the theory that alcoholics who drank alcohol after taking Antabuse would experience unpleasant effects and thereby learn an aversion to alcohol.

Ethanol (ethyl alcohol) is metabolized in the liver by the enzyme alcohol dehydrogenase into acetaldehyde, which is a toxic chemical. Acetaldehyde is then metabolized by the enzyme aldehyde dehydrogenase (also known as aldehyde NAD-oxidoreductase) into acetate (acetic acid), which is a source of energy. Antabuse and a similar drug, Temposil (calcium carbimide), bind to the copper ion of acetaldehyde dehydrogenase and thereby inactivate it. Consequently, after someone drinks ethanol, it is converted as usual to acetaldehyde, but the acetaldehyde then accumulates instead of being converted to acetate. Symptoms of acetaldehyde accumulation include flushing of the face, increased heart rate, hypotension, nausea and vomiting, headache, abdominal pain, and labored breathing. People using Antabuse are advised to take a pill daily. They are warned that drinking alcohol within a day or two after taking a pill can cause severe illness, and drinking alcohol even within a week can produce unpleasant consequences. They need to avoid even using shampoos containing alcohol, because of the danger of skin rashes. Furthermore, Antabuse interacts with other drugs someone may be taking, sometimes producing toxic effects.

People with certain genes produce lower than average amounts of the enzyme aldehyde dehydrogenase. If they drink large amounts of alcohol, they experience symptoms similar to, though milder than, those associated with Antabuse. More than a third of Chinese and Japanese people have low amounts of this enzyme, and partly because of this lack, alcohol abuse has historically been less common in China and Japan than in most other countries (Luczak, Glatt, & Wall, 2006).

Many sources state that Antabuse is not significantly more effective than a placebo, citing a study by Fuller and Roth (1979). That criticism is misleading, however. In that study, people in one group were correctly told that they were taking a placebo and those in another group were given placebos but intentionally misinformed that they were taking Antabuse. The group who believed they were taking Antabuse fared about the same as people actually taking Antabuse: About one-fourth of the individuals abstained completely throughout the year. Both of these groups did far better than the group who knew they were taking a placebo, who unsurprisingly continued drinking heavily. In other words, taking Antabuse, or believing one is taking Antabuse, is an effective deterrent to drinking and a useful adjunct to a decision not to drink. The pharmacological properties of Antabuse are irrelevant to someone who does not consume alcohol, except insofar as they maintain the threat of harm in case of relapse. Someone who takes Antabuse, also relapses, and therefore becomes sick is unfortunately more likely to quit Antabuse than to quit alcohol.

One review of 24 studies concluded that Antabuse on the average decreases the number of drinking days and the total consumption of alcohol, but does not significantly increase the probability of remaining abstinent long-term (Hughes & Cook, 1997). The problem in evaluating the effectiveness of Antabuse is the high frequency of noncompliance. Many alcoholics who begin with good intentions quit taking the pills or take them sporadically. When therapists have taken measures to increase compliance, such as having someone's friend or relative supervise the daily pill-taking, the results have been more encouraging (Azrin, Sisson, Meyers, & Godley, 1982). One possibility is to develop an implant that would provide sustained release in controlled quantities (Hughes & Cook, 1997).

Another drug approved in the United States for use against alcoholism is naltrexone, which blocks opioid receptors in the brain. Alcohol indirectly activates opioid pathways, which have rewarding effects. Naltrexone decreases cravings for alcohol and the subjective reward value of alcohol (Swift, 1999). On the average, people taking naltrexone drink less alcohol per week than those taking a placebo, although their probability of complete abstention is not significantly greater (Morris, Hopwood, Whelan, Gardiner, & Drummond, 2001). As with Antabuse, a major limitation is that many people quit taking the drug.

The third drug approved by the U.S. Food and Drug Administration, acamprosate (Campral), has been reported to increase the probability of abstinence for a year or more (Whitworth & Fischer, 1996). Alcohol facilitates binding of the neurotransmitter GABA to its receptors, and inhibits the neurotransmitter glutamate. When an alcohol abuser abstains from alcohol, the result is a rebound hyperactivity of glutamate, causing nervousness and distress. Acamprosate evidently reduces the glutamate hyperactivity, and therefore decreases the withdrawal effects and the associated craving. Acamprosate is recommended for preventing relapses when people are already abstaining. It appears to be ineffective for people who are still drinking (Chick, Howlett, Morgan, & Ritson, 2000).

The drug tiapride, used in parts of Europe, blocks dopamine receptors (Swift, 1999). Dopamine activity is critical for nearly all types of reinforcement, so although blocking it may have potential for decreasing alcoholism, it runs the risk of decreasing other motivations as well.

Topiramate (an antiepileptic drug) and ondansetron (an antinausea drug) are sometimes prescribed "off-label" for alcoholism, without approval by the Food and Drug Administration. Both of these drugs have shown encouraging results in very limited testing.

For all of these drugs used against alcoholism, the problem is compliance. Many alcoholics have mixed feelings about quitting alcohol and decreasing their own cravings, and at various times many of them quit taking the drugs. In short, any of these drugs can be a useful supplement to other forms of treatment, but none is a substitute for the alcoholic's own wish to abstain.

REFERENCE

Azrin, N. H., Sisson, R. W., Meyers, R., & Godley, M. (1982). Alcoholism treatment by disulfiram and community reinforcement therapy. *Journal of Behavior Therapy and Experimental Psychiatry*, *13*, 105–112.

Chick, J., Howlett, H., Morgan, M. Y., & Ritson, B. (2000). United Kingdom Multicentre Acamprosate Study (UKMAS): A 6-month prospective study of acamprosate versus placebo in preventing relapse after withdrawal from alcohol. *Alcohol and Alcoholism*, *35*, 176–187.

Fuller, R. K., & Roth, H. P. (1979). Disulfiram for the treatment of alcoholism: An evaluation in 128 men. *Annals of Internal Medicine*, *90*, 901–904.

Hughes, J. C., & Cook, C. C. H. (1997). The efficacy of disulfiram: A review of outcome studies. *Addiction*, *92*, 381–395.

Luczak, S. E., Glatt, S. J., & Wall, T. L. (2006). Meta-analysis of *ALDH2* and *ADHIB* with alcohol dependence in Asians. *Psychological Bulletin*, *132*, 607–621.

Morris, P. L. P., Hopwood, M., Whelan, G., Gardiner, J., & Drummond, E. (2001). Naltrexone for alcohol dependence: A randomized control trial. *Addiction*, *96*, 1565–1573.

Swift, R. M. (1999). Medications and alcohol craving. *Alcohol Research & Health*, *23*, 207–213.

Whitworth, A. B., & Fischer, F. (1996). Comparison of acamprosate and placebo in long-term treatment of alcohol dependence. *Lancet*, *347*, 1438–1442.

SUGGESTED READINGS

Collins, G. B., McAllister, M. S., & Adury, K. (2006). Drug adjuncts for treating alcohol dependence. *Cleveland Clinic Journal of Medicine*, *73*, 641–656.

Lingford-Hughes, A. R., Welch, S., & Nutt, D. J. (2004). Evidence-based guidelines for the pharmacological management of substance misuse, addiction and comorbidity: Recommendations from the British Association for Psychopharmacology. *Journal of Psychopharmacology*, *18*, 293–335.

JAMES W. KALAT
North Carolina State University

See also: Alcohol Use Disorders

ANTHROPOLOGY

Anthropology is an outgrowth of the sixteenth-, seventeenth-, and eighteenth-century European discoveries of the remains of ancient civilizations and fossil ancestors, as well as European encounters with contemporary cultures that differed greatly from those of Europe. The need to explain, understand, and deal with these discoveries as a means of better understanding their own cultures gave rise to anthropology as an academic and museum discipline. It was not until the late nineteenth and early twentieth centuries, however, that a coherent intellectual structure emerged for the discipline. In the United States Franz Boas, of Columbia University, helped combine four subfields into what we now see in most major United States university departments of anthropology: cultural anthropology, archaeology, anthropological linguistics, and physical (biological) anthropology. Together, research in these four subfields has achieved a broad coverage of human biological and cultural evolution in its study of the world's cultures, past and present, which is the most distinguishing feature of anthropology. The concept of culture has become the unifying theoretical framework that allows the subdisciplines of the field to interact in research and teaching.

Cultural anthropology deals with the description and analysis of the forms and styles of human social life. One subdiscipline of anthropology, ethnography, systematically describes societies and cultures. Another subdiscipline, ethnology, is the closely related theoretical comparison of these descriptions, which provides the basis for broad-based cultural generalizations.

Archaeology and its systematic excavation of the interred remains of the past reveal sequences of social and cultural adaptations and evolution under diverse natural and cultural conditions. Archaeology makes substantial contributions to the study of man in its quest to understand prehistory and in its investigation of the full cultural record of mankind. Anthropological linguistics provides yet another essential perspective with its investigation of world languages. A major objective of this field is reconstructing historical changes that have led to the formation of contemporary languages and families of languages. In a more fundamental sense, anthropological linguistics is concerned with the nature of language and its functions in human and prehuman cultures. Anthropological linguistics is also concerned with the relationships between the evolution of language and the evolution of cultures. Finally, anthropological linguistics is essential for the cultural anthropologist seeking to understand and to write heretofore unwritten languages.

The subfield of physical (biological) anthropology concentrates on man's prehuman origins and takes into account both genetically and culturally determined aspects of human beings. Physical anthropology seeks to identify the processes of human evolution by studying the fossil remains of ancient human and prehuman species and by describing and analyzing the distribution of hereditary variations among contemporary populations increasingly by means of genetic research. The emergence of biological anthropology as a main adjunct of forensic investigation has involved more biological anthropologists, a specialization that continues to grow within the framework of biological anthropology. The uses of biological anthropology in identifying military casualties has been yet another specialization at least since World War II.

The Relevance of Anthropology as a Discipline

Anthropology does not achieve its general and fundamental significance by organizing the data of other disciplines or by synthesizing higher-level theories from the other disciplines' concepts and principles. Anthropologists are interested in the facts and theories of other disciplines that apply to the study of man. Certainly there are many collaborative efforts and fruitful exchanges between anthropologists and biologists, psychologists, sociologists, social psychologists, geologists, historians, and economists, as well as with scholars in the humanities. Cultural anthropology also shares a broad concern with postmodernism, the arts, and theoretical concerns of other social sciences.

It should also be noted that, as research and publications accumulate in each of the four subfields of anthropology, fewer and fewer anthropologists are masters of the entire discipline. In fact, anthropologists increasingly find themselves working not only with fellow anthropologists, but also with members of entirely different scientific and humanistic disciplines. For example, cultural anthropologists interested in the relationships between cultural practices and the natural environment must study the principles of ecology. Physical anthropologists studying the relationships between human and protohuman fossils may, because of the importance of teeth in the fossil record, become more familiar with dentistry journals than with journals devoted to ethnography or linguistics. Cultural anthropologists who focus on the relationships between culture and an individual's personality are sometimes more at home professionally with psychologists than with archaeologists in their own university departments. Additionally, anthropology makes great contributions to museums, and many anthropologists spend their careers as museologists. In general it may be said that the working links between anthropological specialties and other disciplines are quite pragmatic. Ongoing specialization requires branching out in many directions in response to research opportunities, scholarly interests, and new discoveries and research techniques.

An important feature of anthropology as a discipline is that its scope is panhuman in its theoretical foundation. It is systematically and uncompromisingly diachronic and comparative in its insistence that the proper study of man can only be undertaken successfully through a general study of mankind. The anthropological impulse is, first and foremost, to insist that conclusions based on the study of one particular human group or civilization be checked against the evidence gleaned from other groups under both similar and different conditions. In this way the relevance of anthropology transcends the interests of American, Western, or any other culture. In anthropological perspective, all civilizations are particular, local, and evanescent; thus, anthropology opposes the ethnocentrism of those who would have themselves and none other represent humanity, stand at the pinnacle of progress, or be chosen by God or history to fashion the world in their own image.

Because of its diachronic and comparative perspectives, anthropology holds the key to answering the recurring fundamental questions of contemporary relevance to humanity. It lies peculiarly within the province of anthropology to contextualize the place of man's animal heritage in modern society, to define what is distinctively human about humans, and to differentiate between cultural and noncultural reasons for conditions such as competition, conflict, and war. Anthropological facts and concepts are essential to understanding the origins of social inequality, racism, exploitation, poverty, underdevelopment, and other human problems. Of decisive importance to the entire anthropological enterprise is the question of the nature and significance of human racial variation. Because of its combination of biological, archaeological, linguistic, and cultural perspectives, general anthropology is uniquely suited to address this problem.

In addition to its basic research mission, anthropology has become an applied science with applications in most areas of contemporary life. Techniques of applied anthropology may now be seen in problem solving activities across the spectrum of virtually all cultural and biological domains. Applied anthropologists in the United States alone number in the thousands and are employed as professionals and scientists in government (e.g., the State Department and Department of Defense), business (e.g., General Motors), health, education, and various other fields. Increasingly, anthropologists are employed by the CIA, FBI, ATF, and in the administration of prisons, because of the expanding ethnic groups that must be considered in the activities of such agencies. It is now predicted that half of all graduating doctorates in anthropology will pursue nonacademic careers. Many will join the emerging local practitioner organizations (LPOs) that have emerged in various parts of the U.S. and Canada and identify with these organizations rather than with academic departments of anthropology.

Underlying all of anthropology's other contributions to the sciences, humanities, and society is its abiding search for the causes of social and cultural differences and similarities in the family of man. This enduring quest to understand both the biological and cultural nature of mankind in a diachronic and comparative framework continues to distinguish anthropology as an essential and vital component of a sound education for the modern world.

SUGGESTED READINGS

Harris, M. (1979). *Cultural materialism: The struggle for a science of culture.* New York: Random House.

Moore, A. (1998). *Cultural anthropology: The field study of human beings,* (2nd ed.). San Diego, CA: Colgate Press.

Van Willigen, J. (1993). *Applied anthropology: An introduction*, (Revised ed.). Westport, CT: Bergin and Garvey.

DEWARD E. WALKER
University of Colorado at Boulder

ANTHROPOMORPHISM

Anthropomorphism is the attribution of humanlike characteristics to real or imagined nonhuman agents. The word anthropomorphism derives from Greek and, literally translated, means humanlike (*ánthrōpos*) in shape or form (*morphos*). In our daily lives, we do not have different languages to describe humans versus nonhumans. Therefore, humanlike characteristics are often used in a metaphorical sense to facilitate understanding (Lakoff & Johnson, 1980). For example, we might say our car refuses to start, but this does not require that we actually think the car has ill intentions. Nevertheless, anthropomorphism may have important psychological and social ramifications. In some cases, anthropomorphic agents may be thought of as actual persons in the lives of those for whom they are real. These personified agents may be deemed to have rights, responsibilities, or the potential for social interactions.

In psychology, Heider and Simmel (1944) were the first to demonstrate that humans are not the only targets perceived to be agents; people are ready to attribute intentional behavior even to bouncing balls or geometric figures in nonrandom motion. Not until recently have social psychologists documented that anthropomorphism runs the entire continuum, from merely imagining faces in the clouds to believing that they really do possess human characteristics. People anthropomorphize a range of targets from robots and apes to deities and household pets.

When we anthropomorphize something, what exactly are we doing? Are a pet dog and a computer equally humanlike? According to Loughnan and Haslam (2007), we have at least two ways of seeing something as humanlike. First, we can think of ways that humans are unlike other creatures, such as in the ability to be polite or organized. Such characteristics fall into a conceptualization of what is uniquely human. When we perceive rudeness in the automated voice on the telephone that refuses to direct us to a service representative, we are ascribing characteristics to the voice that are unique to humans—the ability to be (im)polite. In other interactions with nonhumans we may perceive characteristics such as curiosity or sociability that, although not unique to humans, are seen as prototypically human. Unlike uniquely human traits, these "human nature" traits tell us about the perceived essence of what it means to be human, but not about the boundary between the nonhuman and the human. When

we think of our own pet as being curious, for example, we are thinking along this human nature dimension.

It is important to note that some scholars distinguish anthropomorphism from several closely related ways of thinking about nonhuman beings. In theology, Islam and Judaism hold the position that God is absolutely unique without corporeal form or human attributes. Immaterial entities may be thought of as merely anthropopathic; that is, having the feelings and mental states of a human but not a human form. In other cultures, inanimate material entities may be perceived as being alive or having a spirit, but certainly not a human shape (e.g., rocks, fire, or celestial objects). These beliefs are more commonly described as animism. Finally, totems, demons, and certain Hindu gods are often zoomorphic, having the mental and emotional attributes of humans but the bodies or heads of animals.

Why Do People Anthropomorphize?

Ordinary social cognitions seem to play a significant role in anthropomorphic thinking. For example, by the age of five, children from every culture develop the understanding that other humans have thoughts, feelings, and beliefs that are different from their own. Humans may perceive the mental states of nonhumans using this same cognitive process. In this respect, anthropomorphism is a natural phenomenon that piggybacks on other social cognitions.

Some anthropologists and evolutionary psychologists have argued that humans have evolved to beware of a camouflaged predator in the bush, to identify human forms and faces, or to perceive the intentions of potential friends or foe. These self-protective adaptations may cause us to be over-vigilant in our detection of agency. Thus, in a better-safe-than-sorry strategy, humans often and easily attribute intentionality or causality to invisible agents (Boyer, 2001). After viewing a horror movie, we may be more inclined to imagine a ghost or a burglar, rather than a tree branch, tapping on the window at night.

Some situations induce more anthropomorphism than others. Recent studies show that both chronic loneliness and temporary feelings of rejection can increase anthropomorphic thinking (Epley, Waytz, & Cacioppo, 2007). Like the shipwrecked fellow in the movie *Castaway* (played by Tom Hanks), almost any entity will do when we desperately need to establish social connections—even a volleyball.

Another situation in which people anthropomorphize is when we want to make sense of our surroundings. In doing this, we use ourselves as a referent, inferring our own mental and emotional characteristics. Theoretically, the greater our need to explain, and the less familiar we are with an entity in our environment, the more likely we are to think of it in humanlike terms (Epley et al., 2007). Thus, anthropomorphism is used to understand and anticipate the behavior of nonhuman agents or to infer the mental states of non-human agents from knowledge of the self.

Further, some nonhuman agents, including pets, are more likely to be targets of anthropomorphism than others. Recently, Kwan, Gosling, and John (2008) examined whether dog owners project their own personality characteristics onto their dogs. Interestingly, they found that people who think that they are intelligent, creative, and imaginative also see these qualities in their dogs, suggesting that pets serve as a medium to allow their human owners to have favorable self-views. These studies and others illustrate the adaptive value of anthropomorphism.

REFERENCES

Boyer, P. (2001). *Religion explained: The evolutionary origins of religious thought*. New York: Basic Books.

Epley, N., Waytz, A., & Cacioppo, J. T. (2007). On seeing human: A three-factor theory of anthropomorphism. *Psychological Review*, 864–886.

Heider, F., & Simmel, M. (1944). An experimental study of apparent behavior. *The American Journal of Psychology*, 57, 243–259.

Kwan, V. S. Y., Gosling, S. D., & John, O. P. (2008). Anthropomorphism as a special case of social perception: A cross-species comparative approach and a new empirical paradigm. *Social Cognition*, 26, 129–142.

Lakoff, G., & Johnson, M. (1980). *Metaphors we live by*. Chicago: University of Chicago Press.

Loughnan, S., & Haslam, N. (2007). Animals and androids: Implicit associations between social categories and nonhumans. *Psychological Science*, 116–121.

SUGGESTED READINGS

Guthrie, S. (1993). *Faces in the clouds: A new theory of religion*. New York: Oxford University Press.

Kwan, V. S. Y., & Fiske, S. T. (2008). Missing links in social cognition: The continuum from nonhuman agents to dehumanized humans. *Social Cognition*, 26, 125–128.

Virginia S. Y. Kwan
Princeton University

Kathryn Johnson
Becca Neel
Adam B. Cohen
Arizona State University

See also: **Interpersonal Perception**

ANTIANXIETY MEDICATIONS

Classically, antianxiety medications (anxiolytics) have all been medicines referred to as sedative-hypnotic drugs or central nervous system (CNS) depressants. These medicines affect neurons so that the functioning of the brain is depressed, resulting in a behavioral state of calm, relaxation, disinhibition, drowsiness, sleep, and coma as doses of drug increased. These agents were classically ingested to ease anxiety, tension, and agitation and to induce a soporific state. Behaviorally, what was observed was a dose-related state of increasing intoxication with release from inhibitions, sedation, sleep, unconsciousness, general anesthesia, coma, and eventually death from respiratory and cardiac depression. Increasing cognitive and psychomotor impairments were induced as the dose of any anxiolytics was increased. The classic (and certainly first) of these CNS depressants used to treat anxiety was ethyl alcohol (ethanol). Certainly ethanol as a CNS depressant is not a specific treatment for anxiety, despite hundreds of years of use for this disorder. Neither ethanol nor any other CNS depressant is useful in relieving pain (they do not have specific analgesic actions), nor do they possess antidepressant actions (they actually make depression worse). However, until recently, these CNS depressants were treatments of choice for treating anxiety disorders.

Perhaps the first class of medicines used to treat anxiety were low doses of the barbiturates (introduced in the 1920s), with higher doses causing sleep, coma, and even death in overdosage. In the 1950s, variants such as meprobamate (Equanil) and carisoprodol (Soma) were marketed. Then, in 1960, the benzodiazepines (Librium and Valium being the earliest) were introduced as "specific" sedative-anxiolytics. Compared with alcohol and the barbiturates, the benzodiazepines had a lesser capacity to produce potentially fatal CNS depression. Because of this improved margin of safety, the benzodiazepines replaced the barbiturates for the treatment of anxiety. In the 1990s, we began a new era in the treatment of anxiety disorders. This began with the introduction of specific serotonin antidepressants (all of which have anxiolytic properties as well as antidepressant actions). In addition, medications of certain other classes (e.g., certain anticonvulsant mood stabilizers and certain "atypical" antipsychotic medicines) are now being noted to have clinically useful anxiolytic actions, especially in the treatment of anxiety disorders that are resistant to the serotonin antidepressant/anxiolytics.

One might well ask why this move away from benzodiazepines as anxiolytics to serotonin antidepressant/anxiolytics, anticonvulsants, and antipsychotics. First, the benzodiazepines are depressants (rather than antidepressants), are capable of inducing drug dependency, and cause clinically important impairments in psychomotor and cognitive functioning. Occasionally, the benzodiazepines are used to induce amnesia (such as for the performance of invasive medical procedures) and occasionally for the short-term treatment of severe anxiety disorders. Socially, sedative-hypnotic drugs (including alcohol) are used as drugs of abuse to induce a state of diminished awareness, diminished capacity, and intoxication.

All CNS depressants, including alcohol, diminish environmental awareness, reduce response to sensory stimulation, depress cognitive functioning, decrease spontaneity, and reduce physical activity. Higher doses produce increasing drowsiness, lethargy, clouding of consciousness with amnesia, hypnosis, and unconsciousness. Because sedative drugs can produce amnesia ("blackout") in people who may be otherwise awake, some (including alcohol) have been implicated as "date rape" drugs. In addition, one CNS depressant will potentiate the effects of any other CNS depressant. For example, alcohol exaggerates the depression induced by benzodiazepines, and benzodiazepines intensify the impairment of driving ability in a person who has been drinking alcohol. The depressant effects of sedative drugs are thus additive, and frequently they are supra-additive. They also potentiate the psychomotor impairments caused by marijuana. This interaction between any two or more sedatives (including marijuana) is often unpredictable and unexpected, and it can lead to dangerous or even fatal consequences. Depressant drugs should not be used in combination, especially if one of the drugs is ethyl alcohol.

All the CNS sedative-hypnotic agents carry the risk of inducing physiological and psychological dependence. *Physiological dependence* is characterized by the occurrence of withdrawal signs and symptoms when the drug is not taken. Signs and symptoms range from sleep disturbances (rebound insomnia, for example) to life-threatening withdrawal convulsions. *Psychological dependence* follows from the positive reinforcement effects of the drugs.

Benzodiazepines

Benzodiazepines have anxiolytic (antianxiety), sedative, anticonvulsant, amnesic, and relaxant properties. Soon after their introduction, they became the most widely used class of psychotherapeutic drugs, and the term *anxiolytic* became synonymous with *benzodiazepine*. Diazepam (Valium) and chlordiazepoxide (Librium) are the classic benzodiazepines. Alprazolam (Xanax), clonazepam (Klonopin), and lorazepam (Ativan) are other commonly prescribed benzodiazepines. Fifteen benzodiazepine derivatives are currently available in the United States, and still more are available in other countries. They differ from each other mainly in their pharmacokinetic parameters and by the routes through which they are administered. One major pharmacokinetic difference is the metabolic half-life of each medicine, which is the number of hours it takes one-half of a dosage to be metabolized, and then one-half of the remaining half, and so on. Five or six half-lives are necessary to eliminate the drug from the body nearly totally (Julien, 2008, p. 30). Of the benzodiazepines commercially available in the United States, 12 are available in dosage forms intended only for oral ingestion; two (diazepam and lorazepam) are available for both oral use and use by injection; and one (midazolam [Versed]) is available only in injectable formulation.

Benzodiazepines are generally not utilized for treating chronic anxiety or for treating depression. They should be avoided in situations requiring fine motor or cognitive skills or mental alertness or in situations where alcohol or other CNS depressants are used. They should be used only with great caution in young persons, who need cognitive ability for school success, and in the elderly, in whom these medicines can produce or intensify dementia.

One possible indication for benzodiazepine therapy is for the short-term treatment of anxiety that is so debilitating that the patient's life-style, work, and interpersonal relationships are severely hampered. A benzodiazepine may alleviate the symptoms of nervousness and psychological distress without necessarily blocking the physiological correlates accompanying the state of anxiety. Usually, resolution of the psychological distress is accompanied by amelioration of the physiological symptoms. Benzodiazepines are generally not utilized for chronic anxiety or for treating depression. They should be avoided in situations requiring fine motor or cognitive skills or mental alertness or in situations where alcohol or other CNS depressants are used. They should be used only with great caution in the elderly, in children, or adolescents, and in anyone with a history of drug misuse or ongoing abuse.

Panic attacks and phobias can be treated with benzodiazepines such as *alprazolam* (Xanax), although their efficacy is less than that of the serotonin-type antidepressants, which are actually more specific anxiolytics. Moreover, unlike with the benzodiazepines, cessation of use of serotonin antidepressant/anxiolytics is not accompanied by rebound increases in anxiety, impaired psychomotor performance, impaired learning and cognition, reduced alertness, and the potential for dependence and abuse (Arkowitz & Lilienfeld, 2007).

Serotonin Antidepressant/Anxiolytics

Six serotonin antidepressant/anxiolytics are currently available: fluoxetine (Prozac), paroxetine (Paxil), sertraline (Zoloft), fluvoxamine (Luvox), citalopram (Celexa), and escitalopram (Lexapro). These drugs are all potent blockers of the presynaptic transporter for serotonin reuptake. They do not block postsynaptic serotonin receptors of any subtype. Therefore, the primary acute neuronal effect of serotonin antidepressant/anxiolytics is to make more serotonin available in the synaptic cleft, which activates all of the many postsynaptic receptors for serotonin. This results in both the antidepressant and anxiolytic actions of these drugs as well as their side effects. The latter include serotonin toxicity (nausea, insomnia, anxiety, agitation, sexual dysfunction, and the production of a serotonin syndrome in higher doses) as well as a "serotonin withdrawal syndrome" upon withdrawal from the medicine. This syndrome is characterized by many symptoms that can include disorientation, confusion, hypomania, agitation, restlessness, symptoms resembling a case of severe flu, and a sensation of electrical shocks (headaches and sensory changes in the arms and legs). Of recent concern is the appearance of these symptoms occurring in newborn infants of mothers who take these medicines during pregnancy.

Approved therapeutic indications for serotonin antidepressant/anxiolytics therapy with serotonin antidepressant/anxiolytics include major depression, dysthymia, and all of the anxiety disorders (panic disorder, obsessive-compulsive disorder, generalized anxiety disorder, post-traumatic stress disorder, and phobic disorder). Additional detail on specific serotonin antidepressant/anxiolytics can be found in the text by Julien (2008, chapter 7). More recently recognized is the fact that the expected therapeutic responses are very often less than desired. For example, treatment of severe cases of posttraumatic stress disorder (PTSD) often necessitates therapy beyond use of a serotonin antidepressant/anxiolytic. In these instances, psychological therapies and adjunct medications are often needed. Two classes of these adjunct medications are discussed next.

Anticonvulsant Mood Stabilizers

Pregabalin (Lyrica) and gabapentin (Neurontin) have shown early onset of action and short-term and long-term efficacy in patients with generalized anxiety disorder (GAD), demonstrating efficacy equal to that exerted by the serotonin anxiolytics. They also are equivalent to paroxetine (Paxil) in significantly reducing anxiety and depressive symptoms and improved sleep quality and overall functioning in comorbid anxiety and depression. In addition, topiramate (Topamax), lamotrigine (Lamictal), pregabalin, and gabapentin have all been found useful for the treatment of PTSD. These mood stabilizers decrease nightmares and flashbacks and improve sleep quality in the majority of persons with severe, resistant PTSD episodes. They are also effective in treating persons with social phobias and severe panic disorder.

Interestingly, these same anticonvulsant mood stabilizers have value in treating persons with aggressive disorders, in whom they can ameliorate their anxiety, irritability, and anger, and reduce the tempestuousness and the impulsive aggressiveness of their relationships. They can be useful in persons diagnosed with intermittent explosive disorder, PTSD, or Cluster B personality disorders (borderline, antisocial, histrionic, and narcissistic disorders). In these instances, they can treat symptoms such as verbal assault and assault against objects, impulsive aggression, and irritability and reduce the global severity of such symptoms.

Finally, some of these anticonvulsant mood stabilizers possess important pain-relieving (analgesic) properties, which makes them especially useful when pain occurs in conjunction with anxiety, depression, and anger. Gabapentin and pregabalin are widely used for this purpose.

"Atypical" Antipsychotics

The use of newer atypical antipsychotic agents in treating anxiety disorders has rapidly increased in the last few years. Examples of such agents include olanzapine (Zyprexa), risperidone (Risperdol), ziprasidone (Geodon), quetiapine (Seroquel), and aripiprazole (Abilify) (Julien, 2008, chapter 9). In treating combat-related PTSD in persons either unresponsive or partially responsive to antidepressants, for example, these medicines can reduce symptoms of hyperarousal, reexperiencing, avoidance, nightmares, sleep disturbances, and flashbacks. They are also useful for persons with PTSD that results in domestic violence or sexual abuse. They also effectively augment the clinical response of patients with obsessive-compulsive disorder who are treatment-refractory to antidepressants. Other anxiety disorders that have been responsive to these atypical antipsychotics, as either monotherapy or an add-on, include social anxiety disorder, generalized anxiety disorder, and panic disorder (Gao et al, 2006).

In summary, we are currently experiencing a rapid progression from treating "anxiety" with sedative-depressants that are dependency-producing and cognitive inhibitors to more sophisticated treatment with serotonin antidepressant/anxiolytics, often in combination with a mood stabilizer and/or an atypical antipsychotic drug. Such medicines and combinations address anxiety, depression, anger, aggressiveness, explosiveness, and sleep disturbances that often complicate treatment of "simple" anxiety.

REFERENCES

Arkowitz, H., & Lilienfeld, S. O. (2007). A pill to fix your ills? *Scientific American Mind 18*(1): 80–81.

Gao, K., Muzina, D., Gajwani, P., & Calabrese, J. R. (2006).Efficacy of typical and atypical antipsychotics for primary and comorbid anxiety symptoms or disorders: A review. *Journal of Clinical Psychiatry 67*:1327–1340.

Julien, R. M. (2008). A primer of drug action,11th ed. New York: Worth Publishers.

ROBERT M. JULIEN
Oregon Health Sciences University

See also: **Antidepressant Medications; Mood Stabilizing Medications**

ANTICONVULSANT MEDICATIONS

Anticonvulsant medications, also known as antiepileptic drugs, are a pharmacologically diverse class of medications so named for their common efficacy in the prevention of seizures. Historically, seizures were referred to as convulsions and known colloquially as "spells" or "fits." Epilepsy is a general term used to describe the collection of diseases characterized by chronically recurrent seizures of any etiology. Prior to the advent of anticonvulsant medications and modern surgical therapy, patients with epilepsy were subjected to treatments such as bleeding, cupping, trephination, herbal remedies, and exorcism that were ineffective and often harmful.

In pathophysiological terms, seizures are discrete periods of paroxysmal brain dysfunction characterized by abnormally elevated and synchronous (e.g. "epileptiform") firing patterns of groups of cerebral neurons resulting in altered motor function and/or altered consciousness. Seizures are diagnostically classified by the anatomical extent of epileptiform neural activity that causes the event. Partial seizures are characterized by epileptiform neural activity confined to a particular region of one cerebral hemisphere during an event, whereas generalized seizures involve both hemispheres during an event.

Pharmacological Mechanisms of Anticonvulsants

In the most general sense, anticonvulsant medications suppress epileptiform neural activity and are thought to prevent epileptic seizures by dampening neural excitation and promoting neural inhibition. Individual anticonvulsant medications accomplish this through a diverse collection of pharmacological mechanisms that include attenuated release of the excitatory neurotransmitter, glutamate; enhanced synthesis and release of the inhibitory neurotransmitter, γ-amino butyric acid (GABA); reduced activity of presynaptic and voltage-gated sodium channels; and reduced activity of presynaptic calcium ion channels. It is important to remember that the aforementioned pharmacological effects, as well as other effects not listed, are the most proximal effects of anticonvulsants, and that the downstream physiological and genomic effects of anticonvulsants, both within individual neurons and at the level of neural ensembles and systems, that result in seizure prophylaxis remain obscure.

Despite uncertainty about the precise biological mechanisms of seizure prophylaxis, preclinical research using animal models and clinical research conducted with epileptic patients has resulted in the identification of fundamental differences between anticonvulsants with respect to their efficacy in the treatment of partial and/or generalized seizures (White, 1997). An important outgrowth of this work has been the development of animal models to screen candidate anticonvulsant compounds for both their efficacy and their spectrum of activity with regard to seizure prophylaxis. One of the most extensive methods used for this purpose is measuring the efficacy of a candidate anticonvulsant in the prevention of experimentally induced seizures in laboratory animals.

Experimentally induced seizures fall into one of two categories: (1) seizures induced by the maximal electroshock method; and (2) seizures induced by the administration of a chemical convulsant, typically pentylenetetrazole. Anticonvulsants that are effective in the prevention of maximal electroshock seizures in animal models are generally very effective in the prophylaxis of partial seizure disorders in humans. Conversely, anticonvulsants that are effective in the prevention of convulsant-induced seizures in animal models are usually effective in the prophylaxis of generalized seizure disorders in humans.

In contrast to what is known about the pharmacological mechanisms of anticonvulsants as they relate to the treatment of epilepsy, considerably less is understood about the means by which anticonvulsants are efficacious in the treatment of psychiatric illness. The explanatory power of preclinical *in vitro* or animal models that directly inform our understanding of the pathophysiology of psychiatric illness at a high level of specificity or which provide a highly predictive and biologically based rationale for the treatment of psychiatric illness with anticonvulsants remains limited.

Clinical Considerations in the Use of Anticonvulsants

In addition to their central role in the treatment of epilepsy, anticonvulsants are also used extensively in the treatment of other neurological diseases, including migraine headaches and neuropathic pain syndromes (e.g., trigeminal neuralgia, post-herpetic neuralgia, diabetic polyneuropathy, phantom limb syndrome). Anticonvulsants have also come to occupy a major place in the therapeutic armamentarium of clinical psychiatry as well. The successful treatment of patients with bipolar disorder using the anticonvulsant carbamazepine made available an additional medication option for bipolar patients who were unable to tolerate lithium or were clinically unresponsive to it (Post, Uhde, Putnam, Ballenger, & Berrettini, 1982). Over time, the effective treatment of bipolar patients with carbamazepine provided the impetus for the subsequent successful investigation of the efficacy of other anticonvulsants, most notably valproic acid and lamotrigine, in the treatment of bipolar disorder. More recently, anticonvulsants have also been used to assist in the treatment of alcohol withdrawal; binge eating in bulimic and obese patients; impulsive aggression in patients with head injuries, dementia, or developmental disorders; and explosive anger in patients with post-traumatic stress disorder.

Anticonvulsants are often quite literally life-saving and life-changing medications for patients with epilepsy or bipolar disorder as well as other clinical conditions. However, their effective and safe use requires vigilance on the part of both physician and patient. As a medication class, anticonvulsants are extraordinarily heterogeneous with respect to their individual patterns of drug interactions (Perucca, 2006), cognitive and physical side effect profiles (Loring, Marino, & Meador, 2007; Reynolds, Sisk, & Rasgon, 2007), risk for idiosyncratic adverse events (Zaccara, Franciotta, & Perucca, 2007), teratogenic potential as applied to risk for developmental delay (Meador, Baker, Cohen, Gaily, & Westerveld, 2007), and structural malformation (Meador, Pennell, Harden, Gordon, Tomson et al., 2008) in children exposed to anticonvulsants during gestation.

Treatment-emergent side effects and risk for teratogenicity or adverse events accompanying the use of anticonvulsants may be minimized through anticipation and avoidance of drug interactions, preference for monotherapy to polypharmacy whenever possible, avoidance of rapid escalation or discontinuation of anticonvulsants except in emergencies, careful assessment of contraceptive practice, exclusion of pregnancy, and prescription of folic acid prior to starting anticonvulsants in any woman of reproductive age. Effective communication with the patient as well as other consulting physicians, a strong therapeutic alliance with the patient, appreciation of psychosocial factors affecting response to the medication, and patient education about medication-associated risks and side effects partnered with careful monitoring of the patient by the physician is central to optimal treatment.

REFERENCES

Loring, D. W., Marino, S., & Meador, K. J. (2007). Neuropsychological and behavioral effects of antiepileptic drugs. *Neuropsychology Reviews, 17*, 413–425.

Meador, K. J., Baker, G., Cohen, M. J., Gaily, E., & Westerveld, M. (2007). Cognitive/behavioral teratogenic effects of antiepileptic drugs. *Epilepsy & Behavior, 11*, 292–302.

Meador, K. J., Pennell, P. B., Harden, C. L., Gordon, J. C., Tomson, T., & Kaplan, P. W., et al.; HOPE Work Group. (2008). Pregnancy registries in epilepsy: consensus statement on health outcomes. *Neurology, 71*, 1109–1117.

Perucca, E. (2006). Clinically relevant drug interactions with antiepileptic drugs. *British Journal of Clinical Pharmacology, 61*, 246–255.

Post, R. M., Uhde, T. W., Putnam, F. W., Ballenger, J. C., & Berrettini, W. H. (1982). Kindling and carbamazepine in affective illness. *The Journal of Nervous and Mental Disease, 170*, 717–731.

Reynolds, M. F., Sisk, E. C., & Rasgon, N. L. (2007). Valproate and neuroendocrine changes in women treated for epilepsy

and bipolar disorder: A review. *Current Medicinal Chemistry, 14*, 2799–2812.

White, H. S. (1997). Clinical significance of animal seizure models and mechanism of action studies of potential antiepileptic drugs. *Epilepsia, 38*, Suppl. 1, S9–S17.

Zaccara, G., Franciotta, D., & Perucca, E. (2007). Idiosyncratic adverse reactions to antiepileptic drugs. *Epilepsia, 48*, 1223–1244.

CHARLES F. GILLESPIE
Emory University School of Medicine

See also: **Convulsants; Epilepsy**

ANTIDEPRESSANT MEDICATIONS

The observation that the induction of seizure activity was useful in the treatment of psychiatric illness (Fink, 2001) was initially appreciated in asylum patients treated with convulsion-inducing chemical agents such as camphor and metrazole and then later with insulin. The subsequent development of electrical methods of seizure induction and technical refinements to its application resulted in modern electroconvulsive therapy (ECT), the prototypic brain stimulation treatment and one of the most extensively validated treatments for depression.

Since the initial observations of the antidepressant effects of convulsion-inducing compounds on depressed patients, clinical options for the biological treatment of depression have grown extensively. The serendipitous discovery of the first antidepressants, the monoamine oxidase inhibitors (MAOI), during the course of drug treatment for tuberculosis, led over time to additional empirically validated antidepressant medications (Slattery, Hudson, & Nutt, 2004).

At present, medication is the most common biological treatment employed for depression. A number of classes of antidepressant medications exist, based on either structure or function, that are used for the treatment of unipolar depression and, in some circumstances, bipolar depression as well (Nemeroff, 2007). These include the monoamine oxidase inhibitors (MAOIs; e.g., phenelzine, tranylcypromine, selegiline), tricyclic antidepressants (TCAs; e.g., imipramine, desipramine, clomipramine, amitriptyline, nortriptyline), selective serotonin reuptake inhibitors (SSRIs; e.g., fluoxetine, sertraline, paroxetine, citalopram, escitalopram, fluvoxamine), serotonin and norepinephrine reuptake inhibitors (SNRIs; e.g., venlafaxine, desvenlafaxine, duloxetine), and the "atypical" antidepressants (e.g., trazodone, bupropion, nefazodone, mirtazipine). In addition, antidepressants may occasionally be used in conjunction with a wide variety of additional agents including lithium carbonate, anticonvulsants such as valproic acid and lamotrigine, atypical antipsychotic medications (ziprasidone, risperidone, olanzipine, aripiprazole, quetiapine), thyroid agents (triiodothyronine), psychostimulants (dextroamphetamine and methylphenidate), and anxiolytic medications (buspirone). These and other combinations are based on a sometimes tenuous evidence base, in what are commonly referred to as "augmentation" strategies to optimize antidepressant response (Fava & Rush, 2006).

The common thread linking the various classes of currently available antidepressants is pharmacological activity that alters synaptic concentrations of monoamine neurotransmitters, primarily serotonin and norepinephrine, but also dopamine in some cases (Slattery et al., 2004). Mechanistically, this may occur through the inhibition of enzymes such as monoamine oxidase (MAOIs), which degrade neurotransmitters within the synapse following their release, or the inhibition (TCAs, SSRIs, and SNRIs) of cellular transport proteins, such as the serotonin and norepinephrine transporters that physically remove (the process of reuptake) serotonin or norepinephrine from the synapse. Like conventional antidepressants, some atypical antidepressants have dose-dependent effects on reuptake inhibition, but they also appear to have complex effects on individual subtypes of serotonin and norepinephrine receptors. It is important to remember that the effects on monoamine neurotransmission represent the most proximal pharmacological effects of antidepressant medications and that their downstream physiological and genomic effects, both within individual neurons and at the level of neural ensembles and systems, which result in a clinical antidepressant response, remain obscure.

The key advances that have been made with respect to antidepressant pharmacology have been in substantial improvements in the safety and tolerability of antidepressants (Schatzberg, 2007), as opposed to their clinical efficacy. For example, the use of MAOIs requires particular dietary restrictions (e.g., certain types of cheese, dark chocolate, and other foods that contain tyramine) that, if disregarded, may result in a potentially life-threatening elevation of blood pressure known as a hypertensive crisis. TCAs as a drug class and lithium carbonate are both dose-dependently lethal in overdose, and particular TCAs as well as lithium carbonate have significant dose-dependent side-effect profiles as well. Despite these issues, MAOIs, TCAs, and lithium (in the case of bipolar depression) may produce remission of depressive symptoms when many other agents do not, and they accordingly remain core elements of the antidepressant armamentarium.

As with any medication, close monitoring of patient mental status and any side effects is central to effective treatment. It is very challenging to accomplish this monitoring in the absence of a strong therapeutic alliance with the patient and detailed appreciation of psychosocial stressors that may be impacting the response (or more often the lack of response) to medication. Inadequate duration of medication trials and insufficient drug dosing are additional common sources of perceived antidepressant treatment failure.

A major current focus of clinical trials research in depression is the derivation of treatment algorithms to guide effective implementation of antidepressant therapy, such as with the Sequenced Treatment Alternatives to Relieve Depression (STAR*D) trial (Trivedi, Rush, Wisniewski, Nierenberg, Warden, Ritz et al., 2006) and the integration of psychological and pharmacological treatments for depression. In addition, the discovery of biological predictors of treatment response and treatment-emergent symptoms, such as suicidal ideation and adverse effect burden, are additional major areas of investigation that will eventually allow clinicians to individualize antidepressant selection at the outset of treatment.

REFERENCES

Fava, M., & Rush, A. J. (2006). Current status of augmentation and combination treatments for major depressive disorder: A literature review and a proposal for a novel approach to improve practice. *Psychotherapy and Psychosomatics*, *75*, 139–153.

Fink, M. (2001). Convulsive therapy: A review of the first 55 years. *Journal of Affective Disorders*, *63*, 1–15.

Nemeroff, C. B. (2007). The burden of severe depression: A review of diagnostic challenges and treatment alternatives. *Journal of Psychiatric Research*, *41*, 189–206.

Schatzberg, A. F. (2007). Safety and tolerability of antidepressants: Weighing the impact on treatment decisions. *The Journal of Clinical Psychiatry*, *68*, Suppl. 8, 26–34.

Slattery, D. A., Hudson, A. L., & Nutt, D. J. (2004). Invited review: The evolution of antidepressant mechanisms. *Fundamental & Clinical Pharmacology*, *18*, 1–21.

Trivedi, M. H., Rush, A. J., Wisniewski, S. R., Nierenberg, A. A., Warden, D., & Ritz, L., et al. (2006). Evaluation of outcomes with citalopram for depression using measurement-based care in STAR*D: Implications for clinical practice. *The American Journal of Psychiatry*, *163*, 28–40.

CHARLES F. GILLESPIE
OLIVIA Y. HUNG
KRISTEN A. BURGESS
Emory University School of Medicine

See also: **Antianxiety Medications; Antipsychotic Medications; Mood Stabilizing Medications**

ANTIMANIC MEDICATIONS (See Mood Stabilizing Medications)

ANTIPSYCHOTIC MEDICATIONS

The initial observations of the tranquilizing effects of chlorpromazine on surgical patients were first described in the 1950s by the French surgeon Henri Laborit and the French anesthesiologist Paul Huguenard. At the time, Laborit and Huguenard, in collaboration with the French chemical company Rhone-Poulenc, were experimenting with pharmaceutical adjuncts to use with standard general anesthesia to reduce the prevalence of postsurgical shock. Struck by the relative calmness of surgical patients treated with chlorpromazine, Laborit and psychiatrist J. Hamon, of Val de Grace Hospital, administered a cocktail of chlorpromazine and barbiturates to a manic patient, resulting in a dramatic reduction of manic behavior. Intrigued by the results obtained by Laborit and Hamon, psychiatrists Jean Delay and Pierre Deniker treated a group of psychiatric inpatients with chlorpromazine alone, and they also observed a similarly impressive reduction in agitated behavior.

The serendipitous discovery of the antipsychotic properties of chlorpromazine, the first widely utilized antipsychotic medication, revolutionized the treatment of chronically psychotic patients within asylums around the world; this ushered in the era of modern psychopharmacology in clinical medicine. Antipsychotic medications are the primary pharmacological agents employed for the specific treatment of psychosis (hallucinations and delusional thinking) in thought and mood disorders. In addition, they are also used to manage the behavioral agitation observed in schizophrenia, bipolar disorder, developmental disorders, drug intoxications, and delirium, as well as to augment the effects of antidepressant medications.

The common thread linking the various classes of currently available antipsychotics is pharmacological activity that results in the blockade (also called antagonism) of the type 2 dopamine receptor (D_2). The first generation of antipsychotic medications, the so-called typical antipsychotics, are usefully divided into low-, mid-, and high-potency classes on the basis of their effectiveness (potency) at blocking the D_2 receptor, and they are further subclassified on the basis of chemical structure. For example, high-potency drugs, such as the butyrophenone haloperidol, are able to effectively block D_2 receptors at a lower total dose of medication than do low-potency antipsychotics, such as the phenothiazine chlorpromazine. The second generation of antipsychotics, known as the atypical antipsychotics (clozapine, olanzapine, risperidone, ziprasidone, quetiapine, aripiprazole), are further distinguished by their capacity to antagonize type 2 serotonin receptors ($5-HT_2$) as well as D_2 receptors. (Aripiprazole is a technical exception in that it is a partial agonist and not an antagonist of the D_2 receptor.) Like the typical antipsychotics, there are medication-specific potency differences with respect to blockade of D_2 receptors within the atypical antipsychotic class as well, with quetiapine and clozapine being low-potency agents and risperidone being a high-potency agent.

The D_2 receptors are found in regions of the brain that participate in the regulation of cognition, learning, and emotion (cerebral cortex, hippocampus, amygdala), movement (caudate nucleus, putamen), emesis (area postrema), and prolactin secretion (anterior pituitary gland). In addition to blockade of D_2 receptors, certain antipsychotic medications also antagonize histaminic, muscarinic cholinergic, serotonergic, and alpha-adrenergic receptors. As a consequence, the side effect profile of antipsychotic medications is variable, and it reflects the heterogeneous pharmacology of individual compounds. Side effects may include sedation (histamine-H_1 receptor blockade); extrapyramidal motor symptoms (EPS), including Parkinsonism (tremor, bradykinesia) and dystonia (D_2 receptor blockade); weight gain (unknown, possibly involving H_1 receptor blockade); dry mouth (muscarinic cholinergic receptor blockade); constipation (muscarinic cholinergic receptor blockade); inappropriate production and discharge of breast milk, called galactorrhea (D_2 receptor blockade); and postural hypotension (alpha$_2$ adrenergic receptor blockade). This is illustrated by the contrasting side effect profiles of low- and high-potency typical and atypical antipsychotics that result from their specific pharmacology.

Dose-dependent induction of EPS as a consequence of progressive D_2 receptor occupancy is observed with all antipsychotics, though high-potency agents carry a higher risk for causing EPS than do low-potency agents. Sedation, postural hypotension, dry mouth, and constipation are more common with the low-potency typical and atypical antipsychotics, whereas galactorrhea is observed at a greater rate with high-potency typical and atypical agents. Weight gain has been observed with high-, mid-, and low-potency agents, though olanzapine and clozapine are also especially problematic in this regard. Adverse events associated with exposure to antipsychotic medications include tardive dyskinesia, neuroleptic malignant syndrome, seizures, arrhythmias, and agranulocytosis.

A major current focus of clinical trials research in schizophrenia research is the derivation of treatment algorithms to guide effective implementation of antipsychotic therapy, as well as the integration of psychological and pharmacological treatments for psychosis. Medication tolerability, as it impacts treatment compliance, is the most significant barrier to effective treatment with currently available antipsychotic medications. The discovery of biological predictors of treatment response, treatment-emergent symptoms, and side effect burden will eventually allow clinicians to individualize antipsychotic selection at the outset of treatment on the basis of genomic and clinical variables to optimize treatment compliance and clinical response.

SUGGESTED READINGS

Lieberman, J. A., Bymaster, F. P., Meltzer, H. Y., Deutch, A. Y., Duncan, G. E., et al. (2008). Antipsychotic drugs: Comparison in animal models of efficacy, neurotransmitter regulation, and neuroprotection. *Pharmacology Reviews, 60,* 358–403.

Smith, M., Hopkins, D., Peveler, R. C., Holt, R. I., Woodward, M., & Ismail, K. (2008). First- v. second-generation antipsychotics and risk for diabetes in schizophrenia: Systematic review. *British Journal of Psychiatry, 192,* 406–411.

CHARLES F. GILLESPIE
Emory University School of Medicine

See also: Antianxiety Medications; Antidepressant Medications; Mood Stabilizing Medications

ANTISOCIAL BEHAVIOR

Antisocial behavior (ASB) is generally defined as conduct and deportment that interferes with society. The essential characteristic of ASB is a repetitive and persistent pattern of behavior in which the basic rights of others or major societal norms or rules are repeatedly violated, beginning in childhood or adolescence and often continuing into adulthood. These behaviors generally fall into several main groupings: aggressive behaviors that cause harm to or threaten harm to others, nonaggressive property destruction, covert aggressive behaviors of lying, deceitfulness, or theft, and rule or legal violations. Included are antisocial behaviors committed by persons of high standing in society and involving fraud and financial violations in business and industry (so-called white-collar crime) (Lewis, 2005). Antisocial behavior is pervasive. It is found in children, adolescents, and adults at all stages of life, with the exception of infancy, and in all cultures around the world. Although males traditionally express more ASB, over the last 30 years rates of antisocial problems in females appear to be rising.

Prevalence

Prevalence rates vary by gender, by setting, and by population. Data from population-based studies of youngsters less than age 18 years using the *Diagnostic and Statistical Manual of Mental Disorders* (DSM-IV-TR, American Psychiatric Association, 2000) indicate a prevalence of juvenile antisocial behaviors meeting criteria for conduct disorder ranging between 2% and 16% for boys and 1.5% to 15.8% for girls. For adults older than 18 years the estimated lifetime prevalence of antisocial behavior meeting diagnostic criteria for conduct disorder in the United States is 9.5%, including 12.0% for males and 7.1% for females (Kessler et al., 2005). Studies assessing lifetime prevalence rates using retrospective recall methodologies of adults suggest that the median age-of-onset of antisocial behaviors meeting a diagnosis of conduct disorder in the United States is 11.6 years (Kessler et al., 2005).

Documentation from The Office of Juvenile Justice and Delinquency Prevention illustrates rising rates of juvenile court appearances for antisocial behaviors and delinquency in both adolescent males and females. Female case rates have increased more sharply than male case rates since 1985. In males, ASB peaks between the ages of 15 years and 40 years and declines as individuals age. Urban settings generally report more ASB than rural communities.

Risk Factors

Research into risk factors for ASB has generally focused on correlates of antisocial behaviors, delinquency, and conduct problems. Correlational research has usually emphasized single variable and main effects models. Causal mechanisms for antisocial behaviors, however, are multifaceted, complex, and transactional (i.e., multiple risk and protective factors that feed forward and backward to influence one another over the course of an individual's lifetime). The ASB risk field is rapidly moving away from main effects perspectives towards viewpoints that attempt to integrate person factors, parenting and family factors, biological factors, and sociological factors into longitudinal and more ecologically valid models of etiology.

Person Factors

ASB is associated with several cognitive and learning styles. First, psychological testing of youth with conduct problems generally reveals lower scores on intelligence tests than found for nonconduct disordered youths. This is particularly true for verbal intelligence tests relative to performance intelligence tests. Second, individuals with ASB generally show a learning style that appears to be more sensitive to rewards than to the threat of punishment. This reward-dominant response style may explain why individuals with ASB tend to persist in maladaptive behaviors despite the threat of consequences. Third, deficits in social cognition are frequently found in youth with ASB. This may bias them to make more hostile attributional errors concerning relevant social cues, have deficiencies in the generation of varied solutions to social conflict situations, and see positive outcomes from engaging in aggressive behaviors (McMahon & Frick, 2007).

In both boys and girls, the co-occurrence of childhood onset hyperactivity and antisocial behaviors also appears to increase the risk for early adulthood ASB (Fontaine et al., 2008).

Callous Unemotional Personality Factors

Personality traits may identify a subgroup of conduct-disordered youth who possess callous unemotional personality characteristics, but who do not have information processing deficits such as low verbal intelligence. These personality characteristics include shallow emotions, inability to feel guilt or remorse, superficial charm, low anxiety, and increased sensation seeking. Adolescents with psychopathy and conduct disorder have been found to be more aggressive, violent, and self-centered. They also demonstrate decreased interpersonal attachments to others and less anxiety than conduct-disordered adolescents without psychopathic traits (Frick & White, 2008).

Age of Onset

Research has shown substantial differences in children who develop severe ASB in childhood as compared to those who first begin antisocial behaviors in adolescence or adulthood. Antisocial behaviors developing before the age of 10 years portend a particularly onerous prognosis. Early starters are at risk to develop more varied and severe antisocial behaviors, substance abuse, legal difficulties, and persistence of ASB across the lifespan than those who are later starters (McMahon & Frick, 2007).

Parenting and Family Factors

Many studies find that poor parenting practices are related to disruptive behaviors in offspring. Aspects of childrearing that have been consistently associated with children's antisocial behaviors include the degree of parental involvement with the child, poor monitoring of the child's whereabouts, not knowing what peers the child is associating with, coercive family process, and harsh and inconsistent discipline practices. Physically aggressive punishment of the child has been linked to child aggression. Low parental warmth and lack of involvement with the child has been linked to child oppositional and defiant behaviors. Parent psychopathology, including maternal depression, paternal ASB and parental alcohol and substance abuse, is a known risk factor for youth ASB (Connor, 2002).

Developmental Traumatic Stress

Childhood physical abuse may be a particular risk factor for the later development of conduct problems and aggressive behavior. This association is found for both community and clinically referred youth. Investigations of the effects of different forms of early abuse on later development of crime and violence in nonreferred community samples found that physical abuse and neglect early in childhood are significantly associated with arrest for violent crime in adulthood. This association retains its statistical significance even after studies control for the confounding effects of age, gender, and race. Childhood physical abuse, childhood neglect, or the combination of childhood physical abuse and neglect, appears to be particularly associated with increased arrest rates for violent offenses in adolescence and adulthood.

Biological Factors/Heritable Factors

Research has recognized that antisocial, aggressive, and conduct problems cluster in families to a greater extent than pure chance would suggest. Shared environmental factors include growing up in a family with antisocial parents, having a father with ASB, parental psychological distress (including maternal depression), and exposure to paternal alcoholism. Studies are consistent in finding a genetic influence for antisocial behavior, aggression, and adult crime. Weighted concordance rates for adult criminality range between 13% and 22% for fraternal twins and between 26% and 51% for identical twin pairs (Rutter, Giller, & Hagell, 1998).

Approximately 50% of the difference between measures of antisocial and nonantisocial behaviors is found attributable to genetic effects (Mason & Frick, 1994). Significantly larger estimates of genetic effects are found for more severe conduct and antisocial problems, as opposed to less severe behaviors, for antisocial behavior using clinic referred samples, as opposed to community samples, and for overt antisocial behaviors, as opposed to covert antisocial behaviors. Research into gene X environmental risk factor models in the genesis of early-onset ASB and conduct problems finds that in boys who experienced sexual and/or physical abuse during development, polymorphisms in the MAOA gene explained variance in the eventual development of conduct disorder (Caspi et al., 2002).

Physiological Factors

Studies have shown that individuals with conduct problems, antisocial behaviors, and aggression often demonstrate many signs of physiological hypo-arousal and decreased sensitivity to stress. Research has shown low resting heart rates and heart rate reactivity to stressful situations in fearless individuals. A lack of fear and anxiety in childhood to cues of social punishment may contribute to disturbed fear conditioning, the preferential use of aggression to solve interpersonal conflicts, and a lack of moral and conscience development in antisocial individuals.

Neuroendocrinologic Factors

The hypothalamic pituitary adrenal (HPA) axis is a major stress regulating system in the body. The final product of the HPA axis is the release of the hormone cortisol into the bloodstream. Cortisol has many effects on arousal systems preparing the organism to respond to environmental threats. Consistent with arousal theory, some studies have found low basal cortisol levels to be correlated with conduct problems and antisocial behaviors in clinically referred, at-risk, and nonreferred community samples of children and adolescents. Studies have also reported blunted cortisol reactivity in response to stress in antisocial youngsters (Connor, 2002).

Neuroanatomic Factors

Findings from imaging studies suggest that frontal lobe dysfunction may be associated with generalized antisocial and violent behavior. Findings from clinical case studies involving brain injury implicate the ventromedial and orbitofrontal subregions of the frontal cortex. Imaging studies of impulsively violent offenders with executive cognitive functioning deficits suggest involvement of the dorsolateral prefrontal cortex. Other studies have examined subcortical regions of interest. Emerging evidence implicates amygdala underfunctioning with psychopathic personality traits (Blair, 2004; Raine, 2002).

Sociological Factors

Extra familial risk factors for ASB include those that occur in the neighborhood or community, or in association with a deviant peer group. Larger trends in society, such as poverty, the easy availability of firearms, and the effects of media violence, are also important.

Peer Factors

The association between peer factors and aggression encompasses two distinct yet interrelated phenomena; early rejection of the aggressive child by peers and later association with a deviant peer group. In the early school years, aggression towards peers is highly associated with peer social rejection and peer social group victimization of the aggressive child. The aggressive child is disliked and singled out by the social peer group and then excluded from participation in the peer group's activities. The antisocial child then begins to associate with a deviant peer group. Both rejection and victimization appear to be associated with increased risk for subsequent conduct problems, aggression, and antisocial behaviors in the aggressive child and adolescent.

Social Factors

General social deprivation includes such factors as individual poverty, low socioeconomic class, unemployment, poor housing, location in violent neighborhoods, and overcrowded living conditions. There exists a relationship between indices of general social deprivation and increased rates of aggression, crime, and antisocial behavior in individuals. Low social class and poverty may be related to serious criminal offenses. On the level of the individual family and child, the effects of general environmental social deprivation on youth conduct problems may be mediated by individual parenting factors discussed above. As the number of stressors grows in an individual family, and as economic resources become increasingly constrained, the ability of parents to supervise and monitor their offspring in a manner conducive to the promotion of prosocial behavior may become increasingly strained and limited.

Cumulative Risk Factors

The importance of a cumulative risk model for onset and maintenance of ASB in persons across the lifespan is widely supported. Risk factors do not occur in isolation from one another, are frequently interactive and reciprocal, and are often multiple and chronic in an individual's life. Since most biological, psychological, and sociological risk factors are nonspecific and exert their effects on risk indirectly, the specific type of risk factor appears less important for the development of antisocial behaviors than the total number of risk factors present and their interactions across individual development (Connor, 2002; Rutter et al., 1998).

REFERENCES

American Psychiatric Association. (2000). *Diagnostic and statistical manual of mental disorders* (4th ed., text rev.). Washington, DC: Author.

Blair, R. J. (2004). The roles of orbital frontal cortex in the modulation of antisocial behavior. *Brain and Cognition, 55*(1), 198–208.

Caspi, A., McClay, J., Moffitt, T. E., Mill, J., Martin, J., Craig, I. W., et al. (2002). Role of genotype in the cycle of violence in maltreated children. *Science, 297*(5582), 851–854.

Connor, D. F. (2002). *Aggression and antisocial behavior in children and adolescents: Research and treatment.* New York: Guilford Press.

Fontaine, N., Carbonneau, R., Barker, E. D., Vitaro, F., Hebert, M., Cote, S. M., et al. (2008). Girls' hyperactivity and physical aggression during childhood and adjustment problems in early adulthood: A 15-year longitudinal study. *Archives of General Psychiatry, 65*(3), 320–328.

Frick, P. J., & White, S. F. (2008). The importance of callous-unemotional traits for developmental models of aggressive and antisocial behavior. *Journal of Child Psychology & Psychiatry.*

Kessler, R. C., Berglund, P., Demler, O., Jin, R., Merikangas, K. R., & Walters, E. E. (2005). Lifetime prevalence and age-of-onset distributions of DSM-IV disorders in the National Comorbidity Survey Replication. *Archives of General Psychiatry, 62*(6), 593–602.

Lewis, D. O. (2005). Adult antisocial behavior, criminality, and violence. In B. J. Sadock & V. A. Sadock (Eds.), *Kaplan &*

Sadock's comprehensive textbook of psychiatry (8th ed., Vol. II, pp. 2258–2272). Philadelphia: Lippincott Williams & Wilkins.

Mason, D. A., & Frick, P. J. (1994). The heritability of antisocial behavior: A meta-analysis of twin and adoption studies. *Journal of Psychopathology and Behavioral Assessment, 16,* 301–323.

McMahon, R. J., & Frick, P. J. (2007). Conduct and oppositional disorders. In E. J. Mash & R. A. Barkley (Eds.), *Assessment of Childhood Disorders* (4th ed., pp. 132–183). New York: Guilford Press.

Raine, A. (2002). Biosocial studies of antisocial and violent behavior in children and adults: A review. *Journal of Abnormal Child Psychology, 30*(4), 311–326.

Rutter, M., Giller, H., & Hagell, A. (1998). *Antisocial behavior by young people.* Cambridge, UK: Cambridge University Press.

SUGGESTED READINGS

Connor, D. F. (2002). Aggression and antisocial behavior in children and adolescents: Research and treatment. New York: Guilford Press.

Lewis, D. O. (2005). Adult antisocial behavior, criminality, and violence. In B. J. Sadock & V. A. Sadock (Eds.), Kaplan & Sadock's comprehensive textbook of psychiatry (Vol. II, 8th ed., pp. 2258–2272). Philadelphia: Lippincott Williams & Wilkins.

Rutter, M., Giller, H., & Hagell, A. (1998). Antisocial behavior by young people. Cambridge, UK: Cambridge University Press.

Daniel F. Connor
Lisa A. Fraleigh
University of Connecticut Health Center

See also: Antisocial Personality Disorder; Conduct Disorder

ANTISOCIAL PERSONALITY DISORDER

Antisocial personality disorder (ASPD) is characterized by a pattern of socially irresponsible, exploitative, and guiltless behavior that begins in early childhood or early adolescence. Typical behaviors include criminality and failure to conform to the law, failure to sustain consistent employment, manipulation of others for personal gain, frequent deception of others, and a lack of empathy for others.

Antisocial behavior has been described throughout recorded history. Formal descriptions date to the early nineteenth century when Philippe Pinel, founding father of modern psychiatry, used the term *manie sans delire* to describe persons who were not insane but had irrational outbursts of rage and violence. In the late nineteenth century German psychiatrists used the term *psychopathy* to describe a broad range of deviant behaviors and eccentricities. The term was later popularized by British psychiatrist David Henderson and American psychiatrist Hervey Cleckley. In Cleckley's *Mask of Sanity,* originally published in 1941 (1941/1976), psychopathy was portrayed as a syndrome of emotional aloofness, callousness, self-serving attitudes, and impulsive antisocial behavior.

The term Sociopathic Personality Disturbance was introduced in the first edition of the *Diagnostic and Statistical Manual of Mental Disorders* (DSM-I), published in 1952, and was replaced in 1968 in the second edition of the DSM (DSM-II) by Antisocial Personality Disorder, a term that has continued into the fourth edition of the DSM (DSM-IV) (American Psychiatric Association, 2000). Diagnostic criteria were first enumerated in 1980 with DSM-III, based in part on research conducted by sociologist Lee Robins (1966). The term "antisocial" implies that the disturbance is directed against society.

Clinical Findings

Antisocial persons typically report a history of childhood behavioral problems such as fights with peers, conflicts with adults, lying, cheating, stealing, vandalism, fire setting, running away from home, and cruelty to animals or other children. As the antisocial youth achieves adult status, additional problems develop such as unlawful behavior, poor job performance, domestic abuse, physical aggression, general irresponsibility, and disregard for the safety of others. Criminal behavior, pathological lying, and the use of aliases are characteristic.

Psychopathy is generally considered a distinct clinical construct that has much in common with Cleckley's depiction in *Mask of Sanity,* which emphasizes lack of emotional connectedness with others and incapacity for guilt or remorse. Evidence suggests that psychopathic persons have a particularly poor prognosis. The DSM–IV criteria for ASPD focus on observable behavioral manifestations. Most psychopathic persons meet criteria for ASPD, but the reverse is not true. Psychopathy may constitute a subtype of ASPD.

Survey data show that from 2% to 5% of men and 0.5% to 2% of women in the United States have ASPD. The percentages are much higher in prisons, in psychiatric hospitals and clinics, in homeless persons, and in alcohol and drug addicted persons. The disorder is more prevalent in younger than older persons, in persons with low incomes and low levels of education, and among those living in urban areas.

Natural History

ASPD has its origins in childhood, where the syndrome if sufficiently severe is diagnosed as conduct disorder; ASPD is reserved for those 18 years and older. Most children with conduct disorder do not develop ASPD, but they are at risk for doing so. ASPD tends to be chronic, and it is worse early in its course. Antisocial symptoms tend to abate as the person ages. In a 30-year follow-up study, Robins (1966) reported that of 82 antisocial subjects, 12% were in remission and another 20% were improved; the remaining subjects were considered as disturbed, or more so, than at the onset of the study. The median age at which improvement was noted was 35 years.

Co-occurring psychiatric disorders are common in ASPD, and many antisocial persons have comorbid alcohol or drug disorders, mood and anxiety disorders, or an attention deficit hyperactivity disorder. Risk of death from suicide, accidents, or homicide is greater than in the general population.

Etiology and Pathophysiology

Evidence suggests that ASPD is a neuropsychiatric syndrome with multiple causes. Family, twin, and adoption studies support a genetic diathesis. Not only does ASPD run in families, but ASPD is more commonly concordant in identical twins than nonidentical twins. Offspring of antisocial parents adopted in childhood are more likely to develop ASPD than adoptees who do not have an antisocial biologic parent.

Neurobiological theories of causation have been proposed. Autonomic nervous system under-arousal is thought by some to underlie ASPD. This theory is supported by evidence that antisocial persons have low resting pulse rates, low skin conductance, and increased amplitude on event-related potentials. One possibility is that persons with low levels of arousal seek out dangerous or risky situations to raise their arousal to more optimal level in order to satisfy their craving for excitement.

Abnormal brain structure and function have been associated with antisocial behavior. Positron emission tomography scans of criminals who either committed or attempted murder showed abnormal function in the prefrontal cortex. A study that used structural magnetic resonance imaging found that antisocial men had a reduction in prefrontal gray matter volume (Raine, Lencz, Birle, LaCasse, & Colleti, 2000). Because these brain regions help to regulate mood and behavior, impulsive or poorly controlled behavior could stem from functional abnormalities in these areas.

The central nervous system neurotransmitter serotonin has been linked with impulsive and aggressive behavior. Low levels of cerebrospinal fluid 5-hydroxyindoleacetic acid (5-HIAA), a serotonin metabolite, have been found in men who killed with unusual cruelty or committed arson, and in newborns with a family history of ASPD. Serotonin may help to dampen impulsive and violent behavior, and for this reason low levels of this neurotransmitter may play a role in the development of antisocial behavior.

The social and home environment also contributes to the development of antisocial behavior. Parents of troubled children show a high level of antisocial behavior themselves, and their homes are frequently broken by domestic abuse, divorce, separation, or parental absence. Antisocial persons often have a history of childhood abuse. Another important factor that may influence the development of ASPD is the presence of deviant peers. Antisocial children tend to choose similar children as playmates; these relationships can reward and encourage deviant behavior.

Both environmental and genetic factors may work together in the development of ASPD. In one study, men severely maltreated in childhood who had a polymorphism associated with low levels of monoamine A (MAOA) activity (an enzyme that metabolizes norepinephrine, serotonin, and dopamine) were more likely to engage in antisocial behaviors than men with a version of the gene associated with higher levels of MAOA who had been similarly maltreated. This finding suggests that a functional polymorphism of the MAOA genotype moderates the impact of early childhood abuse in the development of antisocial behavior (Caspi et al., 2002).

Assessing the Antisocial Person

The patient's history forms the most important basis for diagnosing ASPD. Family members and other informants can help fill in the gaps. Records of previous clinic or hospital visits or correctional records can provide diagnostic clues. A review of the medical history is important because antisocial persons are at risk for acquiring HIV and other sexually transmitted diseases, and they are predisposed to traumatic injuries and substance misuse.

Psychological testing is generally unnecessary, but it may be helpful when patients refuse to allow interviews with relatives or have no other informants available. Diagnostic interviews and questionnaires are available for this purpose, such as the Structured Interview for DSM-IV Personality, but these are mainly used in research settings. The Minnesota Multiphasic Personality Inventory yields a broad profile of personality functioning, and a particular pattern of results has been linked to ASPD. The Psychopathy Checklist has been used to measure the severity of psychopathy in criminal populations, in which it predicts both recidivism and parole violation. Tests of intelligence and educational achievement may provide useful information; learning disorders are common, and the IQs of antisocial persons are about 10 points lower than those of their nonantisocial peers. This information may be helpful in gaining a better understanding of the person's strengths and limitations and may help in treatment planning.

Managing ASPD

Antisocial patients rarely seek mental health care for treatment of their condition, but those who do can be evaluated in an outpatient setting. A clinical interview supplemented by information from informants is the best way to assess ASPD, because there are no diagnostic tests. Cognitive therapy has been used to treat mild cases of ASPD and involves helping patients to recognize and correct situations in which their distorted beliefs and attitudes interfere with functioning. Antisocial patients can be very difficult to treat, because they often blame others for their problems, have a low tolerance for frustration, and have difficulty forming trusting relationships.

Several drugs have been shown to reduce aggression, the chief problem of many antisocial individuals, but no medications are routinely used or specifically approved to treat ASPD. Lithium carbonate and phenytoin have been found to reduce anger, threatening behavior, and assaultiveness in prison inmates. Other drugs have been used to treat aggression in brain-injured or mentally challenged patients, including carbamazepine, valproate, propranolol, buspirone, trazodone, and antipsychotic medications. Tranquilizers from the benzodiazepine class are not recommended, because they may lead to behavioral dyscontrol in some persons and are potentially habit-forming. Medication targeted at comorbid mood or anxiety disorders or at attention deficit hyperactivity disorder may help to curb antisocial behavior. When concurrent substance use disorders are treated, antisocial persons are less likely to engage in antisocial or criminal behaviors and will have fewer family conflicts and emotional problems.

Antisocial persons with spouses and families may benefit from marriage and family counseling. Bringing family members into the counseling process may help ASPD patients recognize the impact of their disorder on others. Therapists who specialize in family counseling may be helpful in addressing antisocial persons' trouble in maintaining enduring attachments to their spouse or partner, their inability to be an affective parent, their trouble with honesty and irresponsibility, and the anger and hostility that can lead to domestic violence.

Prevention of ASPD

Preventive measures should focus on teaching children to recognize and reject bad behavior, to make acceptable judgments between right and wrong, and to connect actions with their consequences. Parents of troubled children may benefit from training to show them how to identify and correct antisocial misbehavior as it occurs and how to steer their children away from negative influences like delinquent peers. Antiviolence programs that have been implemented in some public schools may help children find alternatives to lashing out.

REFERENCES

American Psychiatric Association (2000). *Diagnostic and statistical manual of mental disorders* (4th ed., text rev.). Washington, DC: Author.

Caspi, A., McClay, J., Moffitt, T. E., Mill, J., Martin, J., Craig, I. W., et al. (2002). Role of genotype in the cycle of violence in maltreated children. *Science 297*:851–854.

Cleckley, H. (1976). *The mask of sanity: An attempt to clarify some issues about the so-called psychopathic personality* (5th ed.). St. Louis: Mosby. (Original work published 1941).

Raine, A., Lencz, T., Birle, S., LaCasse, L., Colleti, P. (2000). Reduced prefrontal gray matter volume and reduced autonomic activity in antisocial personality disorder. *Archives of General Psychiatry, 57*, 119–127.

Robins, L. (1966). *Deviant children grown up*. Baltimore: Williams and Wilkins.

SUGGESTED READINGS

Black, D. W. (1999). *Bad boys, bad men: Confronting antisocial personality disorder*. New York: Oxford University Press.

Hare, R. D. (1993). *Without conscience: The disturbing world of the psychopaths among us*. New York: Academic Press.

DONALD W. BLACK
*University of Iowa Roy J. and Lucille A.
Carver College of Medicine*

See also: **Conduct Disorder; Psychopathic Personality**

ANXIETY

Anxiety is a future-oriented emotional state characterized by a sense of apprehension, worry, and lack of control of one's own affective response. Anxiety should be differentiated from fear, a distinct and basic emotion that is best conceptualized as a primitive alarm in response to present danger. In contrast, anxiety is concerned with future threat, and although feelings of apprehension predominate, the emotional state of anxiety may be accompanied by a diffuse mix of shame, guilt, excitement, anger, or sadness. Anxiety tends to be a motivating force. It leads people to both intensify and narrow the focus of their attention to the perceived source of threat. If channeled into constructive activity, anxiety can be the source of motivation for problem solving, creativity, or other forms of adaptive change. However, anxiety may also interfere with performance. This is especially true for stronger feelings of anxiety and for more complex tasks where less-aroused states may be required for careful evaluation or problem solving.

Both anxiety and fear are accompanied by a wide range of somatic sensations associated with autonomic arousal, which at times can become a focus of apprehension in their own right. These symptoms include muscle tension, dry mouth, rapid heartbeat, trembling, dizziness, and shortness of breath. Associated symptoms to an anxious state also include sleeping difficulties, exaggerated startle response, and irritability. Because anxiety also tends to direct attention toward the perception and evaluation of threat as well as toward monitoring of the self, anxiety can be heightened by a self-perpetuating cycle of increasing attention toward the presence of symptoms and expectations of harm.

Both anxiety and fear motivate escape and avoidance behaviors, and it is avoidance in particular that underlies much of the disability associated with pathological anxiety. The distress and disability resulting from recurrent pathological anxiety has been classified into 12 distinct anxiety disorders in adults (American Psychiatric Association, 2000). These disorders are largely defined by the topography of the anxiety response as well as the focus of the anxious apprehension. *Generalized anxiety disorder* (GAD) and *obsessive-compulsive disorder* (OCD) are both defined by recurrent, anxiety-laden thoughts. Uncontrolled worries about a variety of topics characterizes GAD, whereas OCD is characterized by more focused, idiosyncratic, and repetitive obsessions that are accompanied by compulsive behaviors aimed at neutralizing anxious apprehension. Although acute anxiety may reach panic proportions in any of the anxiety disorders, *panic disorder* is defined by fear of and persistent concern about the anxiety response itself; whereas *social anxiety disorder* is defined by fears of humiliation or embarrassment related to social scrutiny. When panic disorder is accompanied by fear and avoidance of a variety of situations where a panic attack may occur, *panic disorder with agoraphobic avoidance* is defined, though *agoraphobia* may also occur in the absence of panic disorder. When anxiety and avoidance are the result of exposure to specific situations (e.g., heights or dogs), *specific phobia* may be the most appropriate label. *Posttraumatic stress disorder* (PTSD) is characterized by chronic anxiety and avoidance in response to the horror and helplessness that sometimes accompany exposure to a traumatic event. In contrast, when these symptoms (in response to a trauma) are more acute and are accompanied by dissociative experiences, *acute stress disorder* is considered for a diagnosis. Finally, three additional categories are used to define diagnoses from specific etiologies or less distinct conditions; pathological anxiety judged to be direct physiological consequence of a medical condition (*anxiety disorder due to general medical condition*); pathological anxiety judged to be the direct physiological consequence of a drug abuse, medication, or toxin (*substance-induced anxiety disorder*); and a residual category (*anxiety disorder not otherwise specified*).

Although they may begin at any time, most of these anxiety disorders tend to emerge in adolescence or early adulthood. Social anxiety disorder is the most prevalent anxiety disorder and is thought to occur at a lifetime rate of 13% in adults. Specific phobias have an approximate 12% lifetime prevalence in adults. Panic disorder and GAD disorders occur in approximately 5% of adults; OCD and Agoraphobia occur in approximately 1% of adults (Kessler et al., 2005). PTSD is linked to trauma onset and has been found to occur in the range of 21% for physical assault, 49% for rape in particular, and approximate 7%

in the adult population more generally (Breslau, Kessler, Chilcoat, Schultz, Davis, & Andreski, 1996). Anxiety disorders are more prevalent in women than men, with this difference between the sexes emerging in childhood. Anxiety disorders are also common across cultures, although the form that anxiety disorders take (e.g., the degree to which they are described in terms of somatic versus cognitive symptoms) and the focus and explanation for these symptoms can be culture-specific.

Family and genetic studies have shown that anxiety has a substantial heritable component; however, the greatest evidence points to an inherited vulnerability to develop an anxiety disorder, rather than a direct genetic causal relationship (Barlow, 2002). Fears of somatic symptoms of anxiety, as well as attentional biases toward perceiving threat have received support as potential causal agents for anxiety disorders (e.g., McNally, 2002). Indeed, conceptual models of panic disorder focusing on fears of anxiety sensations have been used as part of early prevention efforts, where early treatment of the fears of anxiety sensations appears to prevent the onset of panic disorder in prone individuals. Also, attempts to avoid or neutralize feared situations is thought to maintain anxiety disorders, thus insulating individuals from corrective experiences with the feared events.

In research studies, anxiety is often measured through interviews as well as self-report questionnaires, although physiological monitoring—of heart rate, breathing rate, muscle tension, or skin conductance—is also used to provide an objective index of anxious arousal. In the case of interview and self-report measures, the most widely accepted anxiety scales include a focus on both somatic and cognitive symptoms. For example, the Hamilton Rating Scale for Anxiety (HAMA) is an interview commonly used to assess anxiety symptoms in studies of pharmacologic treatment. Symptoms are rated on a variety of dimensions such as mood, intellectual functioning, and a variety of physical symptoms, such as muscular tension and respiratory difficulties. One of the most common self-report measures of anxiety is the Beck Anxiety Inventory (BAI), which encompasses nonphysical symptoms such as fear of dying or doing something uncontrolled as well as many physical symptoms such as racing heart and feeling faint.

For treatment, the available evidence supports the efficacy of cognitive-behavioral therapy (CBT) and pharmacotherapy (medication treatment). CBT for anxiety disorders most frequently utilizes informational, cognitive restructuring, and exposure interventions. Informational interventions teach patients about common patterns in their disorder, and cognitive restructuring is designed to correct thinking patterns (such as overestimations of the probability of feared outcomes or the degree of catastrophe assumed should those outcomes occur) that are thought to maintain anxiety disorders. Exposure interventions are designed to provide patients with the opportunity to relearn a sense of safety with feared situations and events by using the experience from a stepwise re-entry into these situations (Barlow, 2001). Successful pharmacotherapy of the anxiety disorders is most prominently characterized by the use of antidepressants, benzodiazepines, or a combination of these agents (Vasile, Bruce, Goisman, Pagano, & Keller, 2005). Newer antidepressants (e.g., the selective serotonin reuptake inhibitors [SSRIs]) have approximately the same efficacy as older agents (e.g., tricyclics such as imipramine) but offer a different side effect profile and are much safer in case of overdose.

CBT and pharmacotherapy offer similar efficacy for most anxiety disorders, although CBT appears to offer stronger efficacy for PTSD, and it may be a more cost-effective treatment in the long term for many of the anxiety disorders (Otto, Smits, & Reese, 2005). The greater cost-effectiveness of CBT is based largely on the long-term maintenance of treatment gains as patients learn strategies for undoing the cognitive, emotional, and behavioral responses that maintain anxiety disorders. In contrast, relapse is common when medication treatment of anxiety disorders is stopped. Despite the hope that the combination of pharmacotherapy and cognitive-behavior therapy might comprise an especially powerful treatment, these hopes have not been realized to date; combination treatment offers only a subtle and inconsistent treatment advantage over CBT alone (Otto et al., 2005). However, new combination treatment strategies are now being considered; for example, the use of medication (e.g., D-cycloserine) to strengthen the memory of CBT interventions rather than medication treatment in its own right. Early data on this approach is promising (Norberg, Krystal, & Tolin, 2009).

REFERENCES

American Psychiatric Association. (2000). *Diagnostic and statistical manual of mental disorders* (4th ed., text rev.). Washington, DC: Author.

Barlow, D. H. (2001). *Clinical handbook of psychological disorders* (4th ed.). New York: Guilford Press.

Barlow, D. H. (2002). Anxiety and its disorders: The nature and treatment of anxiety and panic. New York: Guilford Press.

Breslau, N., Kessler, R. C., Chilcoat, H. D., Schultz, L. R., Davis, G. C., & Andreski, P. (1996). Trauma and posttraumatic stress disorder in the community: The 1996 Detroit area survey of trauma. *Archives of General Psychiatry, 55,* 626–632.

Kessler, R. C., Berglund, P., Demler, O., Jin, R., Merikangas, K. R., & Walters, E. E. (2005). Lifetime prevalence and age-of-onset distributions of DSM-IV disorders in the National Comorbidity Survey replication. *Archives of General Psychiatry, 62,* 593–602.

McNally, R. J. (2002). Anxiety sensitivity and panic disorder. *Biological Psychiatry, 52,* 938–946.

Norberg, M. M., Krystal, J. H., & Tolin, D. F. (2008). A meta-analysis of D-cycloserine and the facilitation of fear extinction and exposure therapy. *Biological Psychiatry*. Retrieved

February 10, 2009, from http://209.85.173.132/search?q=cache:EOwqj3f1f7IJ:www.journals.elsevierhealth.com/periodicals/bps/article/PIIS0006322308001066/abstract.

Otto, M. W., Smits, J. A. J., & Reese, H. E. (2005). Combined psychotherapy and pharmacotherapy for mood and anxiety disorders in adults: Review and analysis. *Clinical Psychology: Science and Practice, 12,* 72–86.

Vasile, R. G., Bruce, S. E., Goisman, R. M., Pagano, M., & Keller, M. B. (2005). Results of a naturalistic longitudinal study of benzodiazepine and SSRI use in the treatment of generalized anxiety disorder and social phobia. *Depression and Anxiety, 22,* 59–67.

MICHAEL W. OTTO
AMANDA W. CALKINS
BRIDGET A. HEARON
Boston University

See also: **Anxiety Disorders**

ANXIETY DISORDERS

Anxiety Disorders are among the most prevalent of psychological disorders, affecting up to 20% of the population. The key features shared by anxiety disorders include excessive or unrealistic fear and anxiety, avoidance of feared objects and situations, and excessive attempts to reduce discomfort or to protect oneself from potential threat. In addition, for an anxiety disorder to be diagnosed, the person has to report clinically significant distress over having the anxiety symptoms, or the symptoms have to cause significant interference in the individual's life. Indeed in severe cases, people with anxiety disorders may be unable to work, develop relationships, or even leave their homes. Anxiety disorders often pose an enormous burden on society. For example, they often lead to lower work productivity and considerable increases in health care utilization (Kessler, Ruscio, Shear, & Wittchen, 2009).

Types of Anxiety Disorders

The most recent edition of the American Psychiatric Association's *Diagnostic and Statistical Manual of Mental Disorders* (DSM-IV-TR; American Psychiatric Association, 2000) describes 11 different anxiety disorders. Each of these is listed in Table 1, along with its most important defining feature. Although other psychological problems may be associated with extreme fear or anxiety (e.g., eating disorders are associated with a fear of gaining weight), only the conditions listed in Table 1 are officially classified as anxiety disorders in the DSM-IV-TR.

Table 1. Key Features of the Anxiety Disorders

Anxiety Disorder	Key Features
Panic Disorder with or without Agoraphobia	The presence of unexpected or uncued *panic attacks* (a panic attack is a rush of fear or discomfort that peaks quickly and is accompanied by four or more associated symptoms, such as racing heart, dizziness, breathlessness, and others).
	The presence of anxiety over the panic attacks, worry about the possible consequences of attacks (e.g., dying, losing control, "going crazy"), or a change in behavior related to the attacks.
	Agoraphobia often occurs with panic disorder. This refers to anxiety about, or avoidance of, situations in which escape might be difficult or help unavailable in the event of a panic attack or panic-like symptoms. Feared situations may include crowded places, travel, driving, enclosed places, and others.
Agoraphobia without History of Panic Disorder	The presence of agoraphobia, without ever having met the full diagnostic criteria for panic disorder.
Specific Phobia	An excessive or unrealistic fear of a specific object or situation, such as an animal, heights, blood, needles, elevators, or flying.
Social Anxiety Disorder (Social Phobia)	An excessive or unrealistic fear of one or more social or performance situations, such as public speaking, conversations, or meeting new people. The fear is of being embarrassed, humiliated, or judged by others.
Obsessive-Compulsive Disorder (OCD)	The presence of *obsessions* (i.e., thoughts, images, or impulses that are perceived as intrusive and distressing), such as fears of being contaminated, doubts about one's actions, or irrational fears of hurting others).
	The presence of *compulsions* (i.e., repetitive behaviors, such as checking, washing, or counting, that are used to reduce anxiety or to prevent something bad from happening).
Posttraumatic Stress Disorder (PTSD)	The experience of a trauma in which an individual has been confronted with a threat to his or her physical well-being, or the physical well-being of another individual (e.g., experiencing a rape, assault, or accident; witnessing an act of violence).
	One month or more, in which the individual experiences recurrent recollections of the trauma, avoidance of situations that remind him or her of the trauma, emotional numbing, symptoms of arousal and hypervigilance.
Acute Stress Disorder	Similar to PTSD, except with a duration of between two days and four weeks.
Generalized Anxiety Disorder (GAD)	Frequent worry about a number of different areas (e.g., work, family, health), with difficulty controlling the worry and a number of associated symptoms (e.g., muscle tension, sleep problems, poor concentration).
Anxiety Disorder Due to a General Medical Condition	Significant problems with anxiety that are directly caused by a medical condition (e.g., panic attack symptoms triggered by hyperthyroidism).
Substance-Induced Anxiety Disorder	Significant problems with anxiety that are directly caused by a substance (e.g., panic attack symptoms triggered by cocaine use, caffeine, or alcohol withdrawal).
Anxiety Disorder Not Otherwise Specified	Significant problems with anxiety that do not meet the diagnostic criteria for another anxiety disorder, nor for some other psychological disorder.

Demographic Features of the Anxiety Disorders

Anxiety disorders can occur across a wide range of cultures, ages, sexes, and income levels. In most cases, anxiety disorders are more common in women than in men. The more frequent occurrence in women is most pronounced for panic disorder with agoraphobia and certain specific phobias (particularly animals and storms). For other anxiety disorders, such as social anxiety disorder, blood and needle phobias, and obsessive-compulsive disorder (OCD), the differences between men and women are smaller. The typical onset of anxiety disorders varies, with some tending to begin in early childhood (e.g., animal phobias), others beginning during the teen years (e.g., social anxiety disorder, OCD), and others tending to begin

in early adulthood (e.g., panic disorder) (Kessler et al., 2009).

Causes of Anxiety Disorders

Although there are still many unanswered questions about how anxiety disorders begin, a number of contributing factors have been identified (for a review, see Antony & Stein, 2009). From a biological perspective, there is mounting evidence supporting the role of genetics. Certain neurotransmitters in the brain also appear to play a role. For example, OCD appears to be associated with abnormal levels of serotonin, whereas panic disorder appears to be associated with abnormalities in the norepinephrine system, as well as others. Differences have also been found when comparing the patterns of blood flow in the brains of individuals with and without anxiety disorders. A number of studies have found that these patterns may normalize following treatment, either with medication or with psychological treatment.

From a psychological perspective, life experiences appear to play a role in the onset and exacerbation of anxiety disorders. For example, life stress can contribute to the development of panic disorder and other anxiety disorders. In addition, traumatic events in particular situations likely trigger the onset of posttraumatic stress disorder (PTSD), a specific phobia, or another anxiety-related problem.

In addition to the role of life events, there is significant evidence that anxious biases in a person's beliefs, assumptions, and predictions can contribute to anxiety symptoms (McNally & Reese, 2009). For example, individuals with social anxiety disorder tend to be overly concerned that others will judge them in a negative way. Likewise, individuals with panic disorder tend to misinterpret normal physical sensations, such as dizziness or breathlessness, as being dangerous.

Treatment of Anxiety Disorders

Anxiety disorders are among the most treatable of psychological problems. Most individuals who receive appropriate treatment experience a significant reduction in symptoms. For substance-induced anxiety disorders and anxiety disorders resulting from a general medical condition, the focus is generally on reducing the substance use or on treating the medical condition that is causing the problem. However, for the other anxiety disorders, evidence-based treatments include primarily medications, cognitive behavioral therapy (CBT), or a combination of these approaches (Antony, Federici, & Stein, 2009).

The selective serotonin reuptake inhibitors (SSRIs) such as paroxetine, fluoxetine, and sertraline have been shown to be useful for treating most of the anxiety disorders. Other antidepressants (e.g., venlafaxine, mirtazapine) are also useful for particular anxiety disorders. Anxiolytic medications (especially the benzodiazepines, such as alprazolam and diazepam), are also effective for reducing anxiety, although they are usually prescribed with caution due to the potential for abuse and the difficulty that some people have discontinuing these drugs. All of the anxiety disorders, except perhaps specific phobias, have been shown to improve following treatment with medications.

CBT includes a number of components. First, patients are encouraged to expose themselves to the situations they fear until their fear subsides. For example, individuals with social anxiety disorder may practice meeting new people, engaging in conversations, or purposely making minor mistakes in social situations. Individuals with panic disorder are encouraged to expose themselves to the physical feelings they fear (e.g., running on the spot until their fear of a racing heart decreases), in addition to the feared agoraphobic situations. In the case of OCD, the exposure is combined with prevention of the compulsive rituals (e.g., touching "contaminated" objects without washing one's hands).

Cognitive therapy is often used to help individuals to replace their anxious beliefs with more balanced, realistic thoughts, after considering relevant evidence. For example, an individual with generalized anxiety disorder (GAD) who worries whenever his or her spouse is late would be encouraged to consider all of the possible factors that may contribute to the lateness, rather than assuming the worst.

Treatment may also include teaching the individual other relevant skills. For example, people with GAD often benefit from relaxation or meditation-based treatments. Individuals with social anxiety disorder may benefit from learning to communicate more effectively.

Treatment often includes a combination of medication and CBT. Generally, CBT, medications, and combined treatments are equally effective, on average, although some individuals respond better to one approach over another. In the long term, after treatment has been discontinued, symptoms are more likely to return following treatment with medications than they are following treatment with CBT.

REFERENCES

American Psychiatric Association. (2000). *Diagnostic and statistical manual of mental disorders* (4th ed. Text rev.). Washington, DC: Author.

Antony, M. M., Federici, A., & Stein, M. B. (in press). Overview and introduction to anxiety disorders. In M. M. Antony & M. B. Stein (Eds.), *Oxford handbook of anxiety and related disorders* (pp. 3–15). New York: Oxford University Press.

Antony, M. M., & Stein, M. B. (Eds.). (2009). *Oxford handbook of anxiety and related disorders*. New York: Oxford University Press.

Kessler, R. C., Ruscio, A. M., Shear, K., & Wittchen, H. U. (2009). Epidemiology of anxiety disorders. In M. M. Antony & M. B. Stein (Eds.), *Oxford handbook of anxiety and related disorders* (pp. 17–33). New York: Oxford University Press.

McNally, R. J., & Reese, H. E. (2009). Information-processing approaches to understanding anxiety disorders. In M. M. Antony & M. B. Stein (Eds.), *Oxford handbook of anxiety and related disorders* (pp. 136–152). New York: Oxford University Press.

SUGGESTED READINGS

Antony, M. M., & Norton, P. J. (2009). *The anti-anxiety workbook: Proven strategies to overcome worry, panic, phobias, and obsessions.* New York: Guilford Press.

Barlow, D. H. (2002). *Anxiety and its disorders: The nature and treatment of anxiety and panic* (2nd ed.). New York: Guilford Press.

Martin M. Antony
Ryerson University, Toronto, Ontario, Canada

See also: **Generalized Anxiety Disorder; Obsessive-Compulsive Disorder; Panic Disorder; Phobic Disorder; Posttraumatic Stress Disorder**

APPLIED BEHAVIOR ANALYSIS

Applied behavior analysis (ABA) refers to the application of the science of behavior whereby observable behavior is studied and operantly modified. Data are continually collected and evaluated during baseline and intervention phases, and guide all decisions regarding intervention modifications. The roots of applied behavior analysis can be tracked back to the field of experimental behavior analysis in which animal behaviors were modified through systematic manipulation of environmental events, such as the repeated presentation and removal of antecedents (events that immediately precede behavior) and consequences (events that immediately follow behavior).

B.F. Skinner (1904–1990) first coined the term "operant behavior" to denote operational responses. Although Skinner is revered as the founder of operant conditioning and behavior analysis, the classification of this field of study was influenced by his analysis of the work of scientists before him such as Ivan Pavlov (1849–1936) and Edward L. Thorndike (1874–1949), who unknowingly demonstrated both operant and classical conditioning.

As Ivan Pavlov struggled to eliminate the experimental variables confounding his research into qualitative and quantitative aspects of saliva in canines, his subjects exhibited behaviors that were, in retrospect, operant in nature. For example, the dogs were inclined to approach and lick the light bulbs when illuminated, perhaps to hasten superstitiously the delivery of the food pellet. Pavlov eventually shifted his dissertation research to examine related learned phenomena, now known as classical conditioning effects, but he did not identify those effects known as operants.

Edward L. Thorndike also appeared to have demonstrated operant conditioning with his puzzle box. In this study, a hungry cat was placed in a box after seeing food placed outside the box. The cat's successful physical struggle to get out of the box accidentally resulted in the opening of the box and subsequent access to food. After repeated trials with the puzzle box, the cat came to discriminate which responses resulted in escape from the box and access to food, and which did not.

Unfortunately, Pavlov and Thorndike both failed to recognize the importance of these patterns. However, Skinner described this systematic manipulation of antecedents and consequences to increase or decrease behavior as a three-term contingency (A → B → C), or operant conditioning. This three-term contingency is the guiding principle behind the science known today as applied behavior analysis.

Three-Term Contingency

The three-term contingency and guiding principle of ABA consists of the antecedent, the behavior, and the consequence. Once a behavior is operationally defined (in observable and measurable terms), one can manipulate the events that occur immediately prior to behavior (antecedents) and the events that occur immediately following behavior (consequences) (A → B → C) to maintain, increase, or decrease behavior. This interrelation is also documented as

$$S^d \rightarrow R \rightarrow S^r/S^p$$

where the S^d is an antecedent stimulus in the presence of which a response is reinforced, R is the response (or behavior), and S^r is a stimulus presented or removed resulting in the response increasing (reinforcement), or S^p is a stimulus presented or removed resulting in the response decreasing (punishment).

Reinforcement versus Punishment

Through this systematic manipulation of environmental events pre- and postbehavior, one may influence the future probability of behavior. The process of increasing behavior is known as reinforcement. The process of decreasing behavior is known as punishment. Reinforcement and punishment can be broken down even further into positive or negative reinforcement, and positive and negative punishment. It is important to note that the terms "positive" and "negative" do not refer to the quality of stimuli, but rather the presentation (+) or removal (−) of stimuli.

Positive Reinforcement ($S^d \rightarrow R \rightarrow S^{r+}$; behavior increases)

The observable increase in behavior over time following the consistent presentation of a stimulus, contingent on a response, is known as positive reinforcement. For example, upon completion of chores (response), a child receives a dollar allowance (stimulus presented). If this allowance is consistently delivered following the completion of chores *and* completion of chores increases or maintains, this is referred to as positive reinforcement.

Negative Reinforcement ($S^d \rightarrow R \rightarrow S^{r-}$; behavior increases)

If, on completion of chores, instead of the presentation of allowance, the consequence is simply removal of additional chores, *and* chore completion is observed to increase over time, this is known as negative reinforcement. Although commonly misunderstood, negative reinforcement is *not* punishment. Negative reinforcement is the removal of an aversive stimulus (additional chores), contingent on a response (completion of chores), which increases the future probability of the response (completion of chores more often).

Positive Punishment ($S^d \rightarrow R \rightarrow S^{p+}$; behavior decreases)

On the contrary, any procedure that results in a decrease in behavior is known as punishment. If, when asked to do his chores, the child says "no" (response), and the consequence is a verbal reprimand (stimulus presented), and in the future, the child is observed to say "no" less often, then this is referred to as positive punishment. Positive punishment is the presentation of a stimulus (verbal reprimand), contingent on a response (child saying "no"), which decreases the future probability of the response (child says "no" less often).

Negative Punishment ($S^d \rightarrow R \rightarrow S^{p-}$; behavior decreases)

If the child is asked to do his chores, and he says "no," and the consequence is the removal of previously earned allowance, which results in an observed decrease in the child's saying "no" when asked to do his chores, this is known as negative punishment. Negative punishment is the removal of stimulus (previously earned allowance), contingent on a response (child saying "no"), which decreases the future probability of the response (child says "no" less often).

Behavior Analysis Application

Although grounded in experimental studies, the application of the principles of behavior analysis has expanded to enhance the lives of different populations. The effects of ABA are far-reaching and are utilized in many settings, with many populations, with and without knowledge of its use. The principles of ABA first evolved from the experimental analysis of animal behavior to applied settings such as zoos and aquariums, as well as to dog training programs commonly used today. The ABA principles have also extended into the workplace, known today as performance improvement or organizational behavior management (OBM). ABA has been used successfully in the workplace to influence employee behaviors resulting in increased productivity, safety, performance, and time-management, which results in higher profits and less turnover for organizations.

The practice of ABA in institutional settings also evolved from treating mental health patients by modifying behaviors associated with mental illness. It has been utilized with the developmental disability population with whom ABA has been hugely successful in increasing functional language and independence skills and decreasing maladaptive behaviors and physical aggression.

ABA continues to be successfully used in institutional settings, and it is also now commonly practiced in clinical, educational, and medical settings. More specifically, it is used to teach socially appropriate behavior to mental health and juvenile justice populations in an outpatient clinical model in order to prevent institutionalization. It is also practiced in the medical field to increase medical compliance, teach pain management, and increase functional, socially appropriate behavior and decrease addictions as well as the impulsive and aggressive behaviors typical among brain injury patients.

ABA is now frequently used in the educational system. Often the principles of ABA are referred to within this system as positive behavior support (PBS), which is a specific methodology within the field of ABA. Teachers use these principles in their general classroom management to increase academic performance and reduce disruptive behaviors. The use of individual, classroom-, and school-wide contingencies, token systems and response cost procedures, and time-out are all examples of the use of positive and negative reinforcement and punishment used in the schools today. Regular and special education classrooms often use data analysis to create individualized skill acquisition and behavior reduction interventions for students who are gifted, at-risk, or have a variety of disabilities. This is done by simply setting intervention goals and measuring behavioral increases or decreases related to the classroom interventions.

The use of ABA is perhaps most commonly identified with the autism community. Specific ABA technologies employed with this population include discrete trial teaching (DDT), natural environment teaching (NET), and verbal behavior (VB). These teaching procedures are often used in home programs, but are also common in center-based, school, and community programs. However, it should be noted that, although widely used with this population, these procedures are not specific only to the autism community. They are simply different methodologies derived from ABA. As Skinner identified that the principles of Applied Behavior Analysis are effective with all organisms, so too are those specific methodologies.

SUGGESTED READINGS

Ellis, J. (1993). Security officer's role in reducing inmate problem behaviors: A program based on contingency management. *Journal of Offender Rehabilitation, 20,* 61–72.

Fox, D. K., Hopkins, B. L., & Anger, W. K. (1987). The long-term effects of token economy on safety performance in open-pit mining. *Journal of Applied Behavior Analysis, 20*, 215–224.

Kazdin, A. E. (2001). *Behavior modification in applied settings* (6th ed.). Belmont, CA: Wadsworth.

Lovaas, O. I., & Smith, T. (2003). Early and intensive behavioral intervention in autism. In A. E. Kazdin & J. R. Weisz (eds.), *Evidence-based psychotherapies for children and adolescents* (pp. 325–340). New York: Guilford Press.

O'Hara, K., Johnson, C. M., & Beehr, T. A. (1985). Organizational behavior management in the private sector: A review of empirical research and recommendations for further investigation. *Academy of Management Review, 10*, 848–864.

Skinner, B. F. (1953). *Science and human behavior*. New York: Macmillan.

Sundberg, M. L., & Partington, J. W. (1999). The need for both discrete trial and natural environment language training for children with autism. In P. M. Ghezzi, W. L. Williams, & J. E. Carr (Eds.), *Autism: Behavior analytic perspectives* (pp. 139–156). Reno, NV: Context Press.

Tate, D. F., Wing, R. F., & Winett, R. A. (2001). Using Internet technology to deliver a behavioral weight loss program. *Journal of the American Medical Association, 285*, 1172–1177.

STEPHANIE K. MEADOR
DAVID B. HATFIELD
Developmental Behavioral Health, Inc.,
Colorado Springs, CO

See also: **Behavior Modification; Operant Conditioning**

APPROACH-AVOIDANCE CONFLICT

When meeting a group of strangers, or being asked to speak in public, we can experience concurrent approach and withdrawal tendencies—both stick and carrot. When approach and avoidance are both strong, the conflict can be experienced as social, or performance, or some other form of anxiety. It can also bias our economic behavior making us risk averse. If chronic, conflict results in stress.

Conflict can involve approach-approach, avoidance-avoidance, and other tendencies, but "approach-avoidance conflict is by far the most important and the most common form of conflict in animal behavior" (McFarland, 1987). Approach and avoidance can each result from stimuli that do so in a particular species without previous experience, or from previously neutral stimuli after learning. Approach-avoidance conflict is currently important for discovering antianxiety drugs (McNaughton & Zangrossi, in press) and for analyzing the brain areas involved in human anxiety disorders (Gray & McNaughton, 2000).

Conflict in the wild elicits complex patterns of behavior. Suppose food is close to danger. Animals will approach while they are far from the food (and danger) but will move away again when too close to the danger (and food). They will usually finish up in an ambivalent "dithering" posture at some intermediate distance (see, e.g., McFarland, 1987). The problem is how to get your lunch without becoming lunch for someone else, which has forced the evolution of distinctive conflict-resolving behavior. In a simple robot a balance of approach and avoidance would result in unending dithering at an intermediate distance. But animals tend to produce "risk assessment" behavior that can resolve the conflict by providing new information. When this fails, "conflict behavior is [also] often replaced by other seemingly irrelevant, behaviour ... termed displacement activity" (McFarland, 1987)—such as biting your finger nails.

Laboratory experiments provide some explanation of dithering. In 1944, Miller (Gray, 1987; Miller, 1944) described how both the tendency to approach a desired object and the tendency to avoid a feared object increase as the object gets closer to the animal. This has been measured in terms of the strength with which the animal will pull toward or away from the object. The avoidance gradient is often, but not always, steeper than the approach gradient (Gray, 1987). Thus, at large distances, the animal approaches, while at short distances it avoids; so it moves to an equilibrium point at which conflict behavior is observed.

Recently, observations of relatively natural behaviors in a laboratory setting show this pattern extends to time as well as spatial distance (Blanchard & Blanchard, 1989). When a cat is present, rats avoid an arena containing food. When there is no sign of a cat, rats enter the arena and eat the food. When a cat has recently been present or when the smell of a cat is present, the rats engage in an approach-avoidance oscillation accompanied by "risk analysis" behavior that cautiously gathers new information.

Blanchard and Blanchard (1989) ascribe pure avoidance to fear and distinguish this from risk analysis in the presence of threat, which they ascribe to anxiety. As predicted by this, the former are sensitive to antipanic agents and the latter to antianxiety agents (Blanchard, Griebel, Henrie, & Blanchard, 1997); and, in learning experiments involving either fear or frustration, conflict is sensitive to antianxiety drugs but pure avoidance is not (Gray & McNaughton, 2000). As with the ethological analysis, this suggests that approach-avoidance conflict involves more than a simple balance between approach and avoidance. It produces risk assessment behavior, displacement activity, and, importantly, increases avoidance tendencies—animals have a more "safety-first" or "risk averse" attitude than if approach and avoidance were simply allowed to sum arithmetically.

This effect of the antianxiety drugs appears to be mediated by "limbic" areas of the brain such as the hippocampus and amygdala. These areas receive information about approach and avoidance tendencies, detect conflicts, and (particularly with approach-avoidance conflict) increase avoidance tendencies (Gray & McNaughton, 2000). On this view, generalized anxiety disorder (but not simple phobia or panic) can involve hyperactivity of the septo-hippocampal system.

Risk aversion is also important in economic choices. Neoclassical economics can almost be defined as the study of the rational resolution of conflict. But risk aversion, in particular, produces failures of neoclassical economic theory (Glimcher & Rustichini, 2004). Neuroeconomists, therefore, are now attempting to correct neoclassical economics with neuroscience. The hope is that "economics, psychology, and neuroscience are converging today into a single, ... general theory of human behavior." (Glimcher & Rustichini, 2004).

Approach-avoidance conflict, then, has been under detailed investigation for many decades with a clear picture now emerging of its structure, function, and psychological properties. Dysfunction of the mechanisms controlling approach-avoidance conflict appears fundamental to anxiety disorders. Detailed neural mechanisms and sites of action of therapeutic drugs on those neural mechanisms are now being discovered as substrates of the psychological processes involved. Of particular cause for optimism, ethology, behavior analysis, cognitive psychology, psychopharmacology, behavioral neuroscience, and now perhaps even economics appear to be combining to produce a single, coherent, integrated, story in this area.

REFERENCES

Blanchard, R. J., & Blanchard, D. C. (1989). Antipredator defensive behaviors in a visible burrow system. *Journal of Comparative Psychology, 103*(1), 70–82.

Blanchard, R. J., Griebel, G., Henrie, J. A., & Blanchard, D. C. (1997). Differentiation of anxiolytic and panicolytic drugs by effects on rat and mouse defense test batteries. *Neuroscience and Biobehavioral Reviews, 21*(6), 783–789.

Glimcher, P. W., & Rustichini, A. (2004). Neuroeconomics: The consilience of brain and decision. *Science, 306*, 447–452.

Gray, J. A., & McNaughton, N. (2000). *The neuropsychology of anxiety: An enquiry into the functions of the septo-hippocampal system.* Oxford: Oxford University Press.

McNaughton, N., & Zangrossi, H. (in press). Theoretical approaches to the modeling of anxiety in animals. In R. J. Blanchard, D. C. Blanchard, G. Griebel, & D. J. Nutt (Eds.), *Handbook of anxiety and fear* (Vol. 17, pp. 11–27): Elsevier B.V.

Miller, N. E. (1944). Experimental studies of conflict. In J. M. Hunt (Ed.), *Personality and the behavioural disorders.* New York: Ronald.

SUGGESTED READINGS

Gray, J. A. (1987). *The psychology of fear and stress.* London: Cambridge University Press.

McFarland, D. (1987). *The oxford companion to animal behaviour.* Oxford: Oxford University Press.

NEIL MCNAUGHTON
University of Otago, Dunedin, New Zealand

See also: Fight/Flight Reaction

APTITUDE TESTING

Aptitude testing has been difficult to understand because this topic has been plagued by definitional ambiguity. This is complicated further because there have been two general types of assessment: achievement testing and ability testing. The distinction between achievement tests and aptitude tests historically has been demarcated by their intended use. Aptitude tests are typically used to predict future performance, such as the likelihood of success in training or on the job. Achievement tests are typically used as summative assessments of the candidate's knowledge after formal learning through education or training. However, the intended use of a test is a highly imprecise criterion to make differentiations among types of tests, as any test score could be used for prospective or retrospective purposes.

The blurring between ability testing and aptitude testing is even more acute. A traditional distinction is that "abilities" are innate (e.g., physical coordination) while "aptitudes" represent a confluence of abilities and the effects of learning under relatively uncontrolled, unknown conditions. The seeming synonymous nature of these terms is further evidenced by descriptions of classic tests. For example, the Bennett Mechanical Comprehension Test (BMCT; Bennett 1980) is variously described as measuring "mechanical ability" and "mechanical aptitude." The test currently used to select U.S. military personnel is the Armed Services Vocational Aptitude Battery (ASVAB). The ASVAB produces several composite scores, one of which is termed "academic ability."

Such definitional inconsistency does not influence the value and diagnosticity of the constructs measured by these tests; however, even the mildly discerning reader could legitimately be confused by what is measured with tests of achievement, aptitude, and ability. Perhaps the safest and most reasonable conclusion is that psychologists have come to understand (primarily through factor analytic research), that there are other attributes not highly correlated with intelligence (or general mental ability) that add to our understanding of human behavior. Although there is variability in what these tests are labeled as measuring, they do add predictive value in our repertoire of psychological assessments.

Substantive Issues

Five substantive issues are worthy of mention in a discussion of aptitude testing.

1. *Uses:* In the history of psychological assessment, aptitude testing has been directed toward making judgments about individuals in the vocational or occupational arenas of life. Aptitude tests are used in helping individuals make vocational choices; individuals are told that their aptitudes are consistent with members of particular vocational groups. Successful performance within any occupation is due to the possession of the requisite abilities plus the interest to engage in activities associated with such occupations. In more restricted contexts apart from vocational guidance, aptitude tests are used to assess a candidate's suitability for employment. Examples include assessments of mechanical, clerical, and artistic aptitudes. In short, aptitude testing was developed for the purpose of facilitating judgments about individuals' suitability for occupational membership.

2. *Validity:* The criterion-related validity of aptitude tests has been assessed for over 80 years (Hull, 1928). The validity of aptitude tests depends upon both the particular aptitude being assessed and the criterion in question. Historically, the validity of mechanical aptitude tests has been impressive (i.e., coefficients in the .30–.50 range are typical) when used to predict success in mechanical training programs or on-the-job performance (Muchinsky, 2004). The validity of clerical aptitude tests is not as high, typically in the range of .20–.35. Finally, the validity of musical and artistic aptitude tests is typically so low as to warrant questioning their practical value in making personnel decisions. However, the lack of validity of musical and artistic aptitude tests may well be more attributable to the choice and relevance of the criteria selected as measures of musical and artistic accomplishment.

3. *Incremental validity:* The current prevailing opinion regarding tests for personnel selection is that assessments of general mental ability (g) are superior to any other type of assessment. The superior predictive power of g has been well established across a variety of jobs. However, in reality, a given organization offers employment not "across a wide range of jobs," but within a narrow range consistent with its business strategy. Thus, in a practical sense, it is specious to state that tests of general mental ability have higher predictive power over aptitude tests. Such a statement is patently true across all jobs as evidenced by empirical research, and patently irrelevant given the particular staffing needs of individual organizations. In jobs requiring mechanical aptitude, for example, tests of mechanical aptitude have exhibited superior predictability over tests of general mental ability (Muchinsky, 1993). Aptitude tests were developed to assess a very narrow range of human attributes, although multiple tests can be combined to create a battery (e.g., ASVAB). When the prediction context is broad-based (e.g., performance as a student) tests of general mental ability are demonstrably superior. When the prediction context is narrow and specific (e.g., performance as a mechanic), aptitude tests exhibit validity that exceed tests of general mental ability.

4. *Alternative assessment methods:* If the goal of aptitude testing is to facilitate the judgment of a candidate's suitability for entrance into a training program or job, what alternatives to paper-and-pencil assessments are available? The only practical alternative to aptitude testing would be a work sample or performance test. Thus, the rationale of measurement would switch from construct assessment to behavioral sampling (Muchinsky, 2009). The long-standing attendant problems associated with these two assessment strategies would be highly evident. Performance tests (e.g., removing and repairing a gear box as a measure of mechanical aptitude) are individual assessments, inefficient in terms of time and cost, especially with a large applicant pool, and are limited to the generalizability of the behavior sampled. Additionally, performance tests measure what an individual can do at the time of assessment and are not necessarily predictive of the individual's capacity for skill acquisition after a period of training. However, in other capacities, a performance measure (e.g., a musical recital) may well be far more diagnostic of a candidate's potential for accomplishment than a paper-and-pencil test of musical aptitude.

5. *Adverse impact:* Aptitude tests, like ability tests, have demonstrated adverse impact. That is, test scores for one subgroup of candidates are substantially lower than tests scores for another subgroup. Within the domain of aptitude testing, the most frequent object of such research is mechanical aptitude, and the most strongly affected subgroup is gender.

There are two classical strategies for addressing issues of adverse impact of test scores. The first is founded on assessments of criterion-related validity that indicate women perform lower than men on tests of mechanical aptitude, and women also perform lower than men in mechanical training programs or mechanical jobs. As such, the mean difference in tests scores between the genders is not evidence of test bias against women, but the validity (i.e., accuracy) of the assessment. Women have scored lower than men on the Bennett Mechanical Comprehension Test (BMCT) since its initial development in

1940, and a gender difference in test score performance has persisted over decades marked by societal change, including the decline in occupational gender segregation.

Despite the criterion-related validity of the BMCT, there is legitimate concern that many test items are derived from life experiences more typically encountered by men than women. However, the underlying principles of physics measured by BMCT (such as heat conductance, velocity, force, pressure, etc.) are universal and timeless. A relatively new test of mechanical aptitude, the Wiesen Test of Mechanical Aptitude (Wiesen, 1999), measures these same principles, but presents some test items in contexts more typically encountered by women (e.g., the amount of pressure exerted on the floor by a flat-heeled versus a high-heeled shoe). Although the amount of psychometric data on the Wiesen test is sparse compared to the Bennett test, the existing evidence indicates the specific test items used to reflect the principles of physics do influence mechanical aptitude test scores. In short, the magnitude of the male-female difference in mechanical aptitude test scores can be reduced by item content, but to date there is insufficient psychometric evidence to compare to the two tests for predictive accuracy. Gender differences in mechanical aptitude testing are a prime exemplar of the dilemma of simultaneously trying to maximize test validity and social fairness in assessment (e.g., Sackett, Schmitt, Ellingson, & Kabin, 2001).

REFERENCES

Bennett, G. K. (1980). *Test of mechanical comprehension.* New York: The Psychological Corporation.

Hull, C. L. (1928). *Aptitude testing.* Yonkers-on-Hudson, NY: World Book.

Muchinsky, P. M. (1993). Validation of intelligence and mechanical aptitude tests in selecting employees for manufacturing jobs. *Journal of Business and Psychology, 7,* 373–382.

Muchinsky, P. M. (2004). Mechanical aptitude and spatial ability testing. In J. C. Thomas & M. Hersen (Eds.), *Comprehensive handbook of psychological assessment, Vol. 4: Individual and organizational assessment* (pp. 21–34). Hoboken, NJ: John Wiley & Sons.

Muchinsky, P. M. (2009). *Psychology applied to work* (9th ed.). Summerfield, NC: Hypergraphic Press.

Sackett, P. R., Schmitt, N., Ellingson, J. E., & Kabin, M. B. (2001). High-stakes testing in employment, credentialing, and higher education: Prospects in a post-affirmative-action world. *American Psychologist, 56,* 302–318.

Wiesen, J. P. (1999). *WTMA: Wiesen test of mechanical aptitude.* Odessa, FL: Psychological Assessment Resources.

SUGGESTED READINGS

Anastasi, A., & Urbina, S. (1999). *Psychological testing* (7th ed.). Upper Saddle River, NJ: Prentice-Hall.

Doverspike, D., Cober, A. B., & Arthur, W., Jr. (2004). Multi-aptitude test batteries. In J. C. Thomas & M. Hersen (Eds.), *Comprehensive handbook of psychological assessment,* Vol. 4: *Individual and organizational assessment* (pp. 35–55). Hoboken, NJ: John Wiley & Sons.

PAUL M. MUCHINSKY
University of North Carolina at Greensboro

ARCHETYPES

Carl Gustav Jung introduced the concept of *archetype* to the discipline of psychology to represent the contents of the psyche called the *collective unconscious* in his theory of the mind. Jung identified this part of the unconscious to be universal, with contents and modes of behavior that are more or less the same in all individuals. Jung (1969) observed that the personal unconscious consists for the most part of complexes, and the content of the collective unconscious is made up essentially of archetypes. Archetype is one of the most popular concepts in Jung's theory. In his theory, he presented the ego as the organization of the conscious mind. He then offered terms for other areas of the psyche (Latin for "spirit" or "soul") such as the personal unconscious, which adjoins the ego and contains psychic activities and content incongruous with conscious functions—repressed or disregarded for various reasons, such as stressful thoughts.

Jung (1969) suggested that the collective unconscious functions as a container full of inherited images from an ancestral past (primordial types), which are predispositions and potentialities for experiencing and responding to the world in the ways of our ancestors. Jung described archetypes as the contents of the collective unconscious not dependent on personal experiences. He believed this part of the unconscious to be universal, in contrast to the personal unconscious. Moreover, he suggested that archetypes function instinctively as universally distributed and inherited ideas that form motive forces, which long to be expressed through the human experience. Jung observed that the number of archetypal images is limitless, and he identified and described many of them, such as mother, God, spirit, angel, wise old man, hero, the child, the trickster, rebirth, and natural objects such as the sun, the moon, trees, wind, rivers, fire, and animals, to name a few. These archetypal images are recognizable in many contemporary ideas about inner mysteries and life's thresholds of passage, such as stages of life span or grief and loss.

Idea of Archetype

Jung resurrected the term *archetype* from philosophical ideas of ancient times. In the earliest periods of ancient Egyptian thought, there were notions that there was a distinct area of the psyche inherently interconnected with conscious ideas. Jung found that what was myth in Greece was actual ritual in Egypt. In his widely known translated essays on archetypes and the collective unconscious, Jung (1969) noted that the term *archetype* occurs as early as Philo Judaeus, Iraenaeus, and Dionysius the Areopagite. He also noted that in early Greek philosophy, the term originally served to reference the God-image in man, archetypal light, and ideas not yet formed contained in the divine understanding (*ideae principales*).

The concept of archetype resonates with the philosophy of Plato, Romanticism, and idealism. However, these views were silenced in the realm of intellect by the rise of empiricism; they were left to the realm of the humanities such as art, poetry, and literature. Jung (1965) viewed his approach as a natural science, but also conceded its limitations, especially the personal bias of the observer. He suggested that an observer gain some understanding of the historical and literary parallels of observations to avoid at least the simplest errors in judgment.

Jung's early years in psychiatric work at Burghölzli Mental Hospital in Zurich served as a foundation for his scholarly inquiry. There he analyzed his own and his patients' dreams and visions and observed patterns while working with psychotic patients who described experiences of universal religious imagery and mythological symbols they could not have possibly known about. Combining his knowledge of philosophy with the patterns he observed, and influenced by esotericism, occultism, and questions raised by Gnostic spiritual philosophy, Jung was led to form his archetype theory.

Arguably, Jung's travels and ethnological study in such places as Africa, China, and Mexico influenced his ideas about how archetypes were expressed in traditional knowledge systems. Jung (1965) observed that traditional knowledge systems hold the wisdom of the human experience from ancient times. He was especially interested in describing archetype expression in human experience (i.e., visible manifestation of the life of the psyche). He observed sacred rituals and ceremonies, oral traditions, and material culture. Jung believed archetype imagery appears in dreams and in cultural symbols such as anima or trickster images as expressions of positive and negative aspects of human qualities. Archetypes are also found in myths, fairy tales, and legends as symbols of inner forces and human aspirations such as beauty, sexuality, wisdom, and moral virtue, as well as prophetic wisdom.

Archetype Theory in Modern Psychology

Jung presented the idea that the psyche embraces all thought, feeling, and behavior and acts as a guide that regulates and adapts individuals to their social and physical environment. He believed that people are born whole and healthy and spend their life span developing this inherent wholeness to its greatest potential. There is the personal

unconscious or private side of psyche life, but archetype refers to contents of the collective unconscious that influence individual personality and character. The archetype is universal representation of psychic content that has not been submitted to conscious expression. In other words, the idea is pre-existent to the phenomenon. Archetype is the form, but many other factors influence the conscious experience. Archetype invites human consciousness into its depths as symbolism that has cultural significance.

Jung believed conscious expression of these basic patterns may be found and taught according to tradition in myths, fairy tales, and legends and cultural products such as works of art, literature, and religious, social, and political ideas. In modern psychology, archetype belongs to the realm of ideas impossible to substantiate using empirical reasoning. Thoughts of metaphysical conjecture, superstition, faith, and subjective reasoning immediately come to mind. While we can no longer deny that thinking, understanding, and reasoning cannot be independent of subjective processes, we tend to accept as valid psychological science only phenomenon that can be confirmed from the outside.

REFERENCES

Jung, C. G. (1969). *The archetypes and the collective unconscious. The collected works of C. G. Jung, Vol. 9, Pt. I* (2nd ed.). Princeton, NJ: Princeton University Press.

Jung, C. G. (1965). *Memories, dreams, reflections.* New York: Vintage Books.

SUGGESTED READINGS

Adams, M. (1996). *The multicultural imagination: Race, color, and the unconscious.* London: Routledge.

Campbell, J.C. (1993). *Myths to live by.* New York: Viking Penguin. (Original work published 1972)

Singer, J. (1994). *Boundaries of the soul.* New York: Anchor Books. (Original work published 1972)

Waddell, T. (2006). *Mistakes: Archetype, myth, and identity in screen fiction.* London: Routledge.

FAYTH M. PARKS
Georgia Southern University

See also: Collective Unconscious

ARGENTINA, PSYCHOLOGY IN

Scientific psychology started developing in Argentina soon after Wundt's 1879 establishment of the first laboratory for experimental research in psychology. In 1891, Víctor

Mercante (1870–1934) founded the first psychology laboratory in the city of San Juan, Argentina. Horacio Piñero (1869–1919) also created an experimental psychology laboratory at the Colegio Nacional de Buenos Aires in 1898, and a psychophysiology laboratory at the University of Buenos Aires in 1901 (Papini, 1976). In 1906, two other research laboratories were created: Félix Krueger, disciple of Wundt, founded a short-lived center at the Instituto Nacional de Profesorado Secundario (National Institute of Secondary Teaching), and Víctor Mercante set up a laboratory at the Department of Education within the School of Law and Social Sciences, at the University of La Plata (Talak & García, 2004). Scientific research in psychology took its first steps in Argentina almost hand in hand with the psychological scientific activity in the world's most important academic centers in Europe and the United States.

Before the year 1930, however, the reaction against positivism represented by Korn, Romero, and Alberini led to the closing of most psychological research laboratories in Argentina (Beebe-Center & McFarland, 1941). Moreover, political instability in the country also negatively affected the development of psychology. From the overthrow of Yrigoyen by the military coup of 1930, through approximately 1945, a "religious integralism" prevailed, which discouraged even the slightest idea of scientific research of the human mind. In turn, the teaching of experimental psychology was prohibited during Perón's first term in office in 1949 (Vilanova, 1994). It was the beginning of a period in which Argentine psychology was isolated from the developments that were taking place in the most prestigious academic centers of the world. In the following years, Argentine psychology gradually became a more service-oriented discipline and, as a result, research was assigned a minor role.

The Programs of Study in Argentina

The various degrees in psychology that are well established today in most public Argentine universities started developing 1950. Most professors of these newly developed programs of study were psychiatrists, educators, philosophers, or theologians, and many among them were clinicians trained in psychoanalysis who lacked research experience (Ardila, 1986). This period of the history of psychology in Argentina is often referred to as the "professional period" or "professional psychology stage" (Klappenbach, 1995; Alonso & Nicenboim, 1997). During the 1950s the development of psychological research in Argentina slowed down. At present, governmental bodies, such as the *Comisión Nacional de Evaluación y Acreditación Universitaria* (National Commission for University Evaluation and Accreditation), the National Board of Education and Culture, and the Board of Health and Environment, and university bodies, such as the *Asociación de Unidades Académicas de Psicología* (AUAPsi; Association of Psychology Academic Units), have underscored the need for a critical revision of the scientific training of future psychology graduates.

Scientific training in psychology became a priority after the degree was incorporated under the provisions of section 43 of the National Act of Higher Education No 24.521; that is, since the study of psychology became regulated by the government because of its status as a high-risk and public service profession. Recently, the AUAPsi and the *Federación de Psicólogos de la República Argentina* (FEPRA) submitted a document to the National Board of Education and Culture outlining national standards for awarding of graduate psychology degrees, a proposal for a core curriculum, and a description of the activities associated with a plan of study for a degree in psychology. Both entities have now started working on a similar outline for postgraduate studies in Psychology.

Institutional Affiliation of Psychologists in Argentina

In Argentina, professional psychologists consider themselves best represented by psychologists' associations that can be found in all the provinces or by national bodies such as FEPRA. In turn, Argentine research psychologists, in addition to the psychologists' associations, group together in national organizations that support research more actively, such as the *Asociación Argentina de Ciencias del Comportamiento* (Argentine Association of Behavioral Sciences), or international associations, such as the American Psychological Association, the *Sociedad Interamericana de Psicología* (Interamerican Society of Psychology), the International Union of Psychological Science, the *Asociación Iberoamericana de Diagnóstico y Evaluación Psicológica* (Ibero-American Association of Psychological Diagnosis and Assessment), and the Research Society on Alcoholism, to name a few.

Psychological Research in Argentina

There are different psychological research groups in Argentina, some of which are well established and internationally recognized, such as the Centro Interdisciplinario de Investigaciones en Psicología Matemática y Experimental in the city of Buenos Aires; the laboratory of Alcohol, Learning and Early Ontogeny at the Instituto de Investigaciones Médicas Mercedes y Martín Ferreyra in the city of Córdoba; the laboratory of Experimental and Applied Psychology at the Instituto Lanari in the city of Buenos Aires; the Comparative and Experimental Psychology group at the Instituto de Ciencias Humanas, Sociales y Ambientales, Centro Regional de Investigaciones Científicas y Tecnológicas, Mendoza; the History of Psychology group in the School of Human Sciences at the National University of San Luis; and the group of Sociocognitive Learning Processes at the Instituto Rosario de Investigación en Ciencias de la Educación, among others.

Furthermore, there are other psychological research groups at private universities and research institutes all over the country. However, research activities have never received significant financial support from the national governments, or from universities. A brief review shows that psychological research in Argentina assessed by related scientific bodies is varied, basic, and applied. It correlates with research activities carried out in other parts of the world, tries to respond to social demands, is partially financed, and is subject to the evaluation of national and international scientific communities through publications in the field, presentations at national and international meetings, and national and international grant proposal applications.

Publications in Psychology Edited in Argentina

There are refereed periodic publications that are edited mainly by Argentine public universities and are included in international databases. Among the most important journals in Argentina include the following: *Revista de Investigaciones en Psicología* of the University of Buenos Aires; *Perspectivas en Psicología* of the National University of Mar del Plata; *Evaluar* of the National University of Córdoba; and *Investigando en Psicología* of the National University of Tucumán. In addition, the following journals are edited by other organizations and also indexed in well-known databases: *Acta Psiquiátrica y Psicológica de América Latina* (Fundación Acta), *Interdisciplinaria*, *Revista IRICE*, and *Revista Argentina de Clínica Psicológica* (Fundación Aiglé).

REFERENCES

Alonso, M., & Nicenboim, E. (1997). La psicología en la República Argentina. Aspectos académicos y profesionales. *Papeles del psicólogo*, 67, 71–75.

Ardila, R. (1986). *La psicología en América Latina. Pasado, presente y futuro* México: Siglo Veintiuno Editores.

Beebe-Center, J. G., & McFarland, R. A. (1941). Psychology in South America. *Psychological Bulletin*, Vol. 38, N°8, 627–667.

Klappenbach, H. (1995). Antecedentes de la carrera de psicología en Universidades Argentinas. *Acta Psiquiátrica y Psicológica de América Latina*, 40, 237–243.

Papini, M. (1976). Datos para una historia de la psicología experimental Argentina, hasta 1930. *Revista Latinoamericana de Psicología*, 8, 319–335.

Talak, A. M., & García, P. (2004). Las mediciones estadísticas en la producción de conocimiento psicológico en Argentina (1900–1930) y sus vinculaciones con las investigaciones psicológicas en Europa y Estados Unidos. In: Martins, R. A. et al. (Eds.) *Filosofía e história da ciencia no Cone Sul: Tercero Encontro*. Campinas: AFHIC, 36–46.

Vilanova, A. (1994). La investigación psicológica en la Argentina. *Nexos, Año 1, Vol. 1*. Secretaría de Ciencia y Técnica de la Universidad Nacional de Mar del Plata. Reimpressed in: Vilanova, A. (2003). *Discusión por la Psicología*. 44–47. Departamento de Servicios Gráficos: Universidad Nacional de Mar del Plata.

JUAN CARLOS GODOY
SILVINA BRUSSINO
National University of Cordoba,
Cordoba, Argentina

ART THERAPY

"'I could draw it,' a dreamer often says to us, 'but I don't know how to say it.'" So said Sigmund Freud (1963, p. 90). Considering that Freud regarded dreams to be "the royal road to the unconscious," it is surprising that he did not ask his patients to do so.

Put another way, Irvin Yalom discusses the difficulty in communication between client and therapist, preventing a real knowing of one another:

> A series of distorting prisms block the knowing of another.... First, there is the barrier between image and language. Mind thinks in images, but, to communicate with another, must transform image into thought and then thought into language. That march, from image to thought to language, is treacherous. Casualties occur: the rich, fleecy texture of image, its extraordinary plasticity and flexibility, its private nostalgic emotional hues—all are lost when image is crammed into language. (Yalom, 1989, p. 180)

In art therapy, work with images is at the core of treatment.

Although art therapy is a relatively young and small profession, it is very broad, with art used in a number of different ways with varying populations. Most art therapy sessions, whether individual, group, couple, family, or community work, include a period of art-making followed by discussion, in which the art therapist encourages verbal reflection about the image(s) created. Although in the early days of the profession art therapists may have thought in terms of interpretations of the images and sometimes provided these interpretations to the client, for the most part art therapists today urge clients to do their own self-exploration. Many art therapists assure their clients that artistic excellence or even talent is not expected. The purpose of art therapy is self-expression and self-exploration.

Figure 1 is a plaster casting made by Debra Paskind, ATR-BC, LCPC, now an experienced art therapist and art

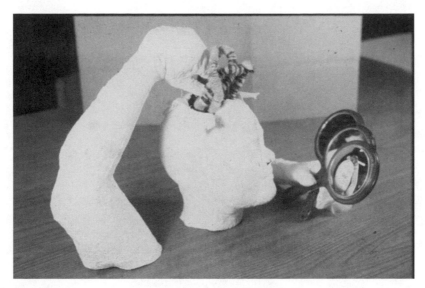

Figure 1. An impression of art therapy.

therapy educator. She made this art piece while still an art therapy student, showing her impression of art therapy, in which she is looking into multiple mirrors and pulling material out of her head to explore.

To give a brief overview of the variety in this work, the venues in which art therapists work with their diversity of populations may suggest how the goals and conditions of treatment may differ widely as the therapists determine the nature of the work. Traditionally, art therapists worked in psychiatric settings, such as hospitals and clinics. As the profession has grown, art therapy has expanded to use in schools, especially those for emotionally and behaviorally disturbed children; in facilities for the elderly, both day centers and nursing homes; in substance abuse programs; in hospital units for medical illnesses, especially cancer; in facilities for survivors of sexual and physical abuse, both children and adults, as well as perpetrators; in shelters for the homeless; in immigration centers, including programs for victims of torture; in penal facilities such as jails and prisons; in after-care programs; in community relief programs; and in many more.

Although art is used with many populations to promote insight, with many others it is more an activity for socialization and the enhancement of self-esteem, particularly in centers where clients stay for long periods of time, such as after-care facilities, shelters for the homeless, facilities for the elderly, and community centers. As is evident from these many venues, the art is likely to be used very differently with specific populations and treatment facilities, with respect both to the art materials used and the kind of art projects encouraged. Nevertheless, there are advantages to using art that would apply to many treatment conditions.

Advantages of Art Therapy Imagery

As stated by Freud and Yalom, we think in images. We thought in images before we had words, knowing our mother's face before we could think or say, "Mama." Because we had images before words, it is likely that imagery forms a significant foundation layer in personality development. Moreover, psychotherapy clients often have had experiences that cannot be expressed in words, especially aspects of trauma. These experiences, embedded in deeper layers than the verbal, often surface in drawings and paintings.

People diagnosed with acute schizophrenia have been able to depict hallucinations and delusions readily in their artwork. Given the idiosyncratic nature of hallucinations and delusions, these people often live in an envelope of isolation. Depicting these phenomena in their art expressions allowed for communication that bridged the moats of isolation that surrounded them.

Decreased Defenses

Because most clients are much less familiar with making art than with talking, surprising and unexpected things often come out in the artwork that would have been repressed in verbal communication alone. These unintended characteristics can form the leading edge of increased insight; for example, when a client drew a face that looked angry while denying such feelings, she was able to identify the feelings in the drawing and eventually came to own them.

The frequent misconception that artistic ability is necessary for self-expression in art may actually work in reverse. Those experienced in art-making may actually be better able to defend themselves in art expression. For example, an elderly man diagnosed with agitated

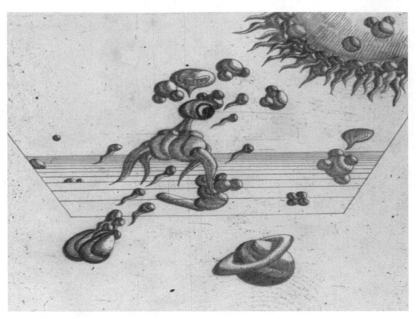

Figure 2. Drawing by a man with paranoid delusions.

depression, who had been a draftsman, created peaceful landscapes, denying that his pictures had any meaning. Eventually, however, he depicted himself as a smoldering volcano.

Catharsis

Catharsis is an especially important aspect of art-making. Clients can do whatever they want to the paper. One middle-aged woman who had made two serious suicide attempts murdered her husband many times on the paper over the course of her treatment before eventually settling into relative contentment in her marriage.

Craig, an adolescent diagnosed with paranoid schizophrenia, whom his parents feared would harm his little sister, was dragged into the National Institutes of Health Clinical Center by seven police officers. Since the research protocol for the schizophrenia project there kept the patients free of medication, most of them regressed on admission. The staff was fearful of potential violence in Craig, but he was one of the few patients who did not decompensate. The reason? He loved to draw. He spent many hours, both in art therapy sessions and on his own, drawing intricate pictures of the Judgment Day, the Mother of the Universe, and various delusions, discharging his feelings in this more productive way. Despite his elaborate paranoid delusional system, he even came to trust me with his "secrets." In Figure 2, he has drawn sperm cells and scrota being pulled into the sun-ovum (upper right). He is riding in the central object with the eye for protection. He said that anyone looking at this picture would become psychotic. Wadeson (1980) gives a more detailed account of work with this patient.

Permanence

Unique to art therapy is the permanence of the art product, which can provide some interesting possibilities. It is not subject to the distortion of memory, as ephemeral words may be, and cannot be denied. Sometimes clients look back on an earlier drawing and are surprised to discover how they felt at that time. New insights may emerge as a result. Most important, looking at the artwork over time allows both the client and the art therapist to discern patterns that may not be recognized when the art pieces are viewed singly. Also, the art is evidence of significant milestones in the ongoing development of the therapeutic process and in this way may be very encouraging.

The art product can also serve as interesting data for research and for communicating about a patient's status to other staff members. For example, with some suicidal patients, the art was often the first expression of renewed suicidal ideation, which could then be shared with staff for the patient's protection.

Spatial Matrix

Whereas speaking is a sequential form of communication, an art piece displays a spatial matrix, which is more often the way a situation is experienced. For example, if a client is exploring family relationships, instead of sequentially describing each family member and their relationships with one another, a picture can show the family dynamics all at once, which of course is the way the client experiences it. A woman can show her mother in an angry fit but close to her brother, her father removed from the other family members, herself small and sad, neglected by the others, and so forth. In family art therapy it is especially productive to ask each family member to make a picture of the family. When family members share these drawings, there are often surprises about perceptions that have never been communicated. If the father appears on the periphery of every picture, it is difficult for him to deny that his family sees him as removed from them, for example.

Another interesting way to explore family dynamics is with the use of clay. After clients have reflected on their figures and the relationships among them, I often ask them to change the clay tableau to the way they would like the family to be. This activity usually arouses very strong feelings.

Creative and Physical Energy

Some groups, particularly those that meet in the evening, started out sluggishly with a check-in, proceeded to the art-making phase, and afterward miraculously came to life. The change in energy level became activated by art-making. This change is thought to be the result of stimulating creative energy. It may be related to the release of physical energy as well, which is very different from the more passive sitting and talking that is characteristic of verbal therapy.

There is also the particularly interesting contagion in group art therapy, in which the members are stimulated in their own art-making by the creative expression of the others. In a group, they come to know one another by their images and artistic styles.

Brief History of Art Therapy

In a sense, the roots of art therapy can be said to reach back to prehistory, when our ancestors painted animals in the caves of Lascaux, France, 17,000 years ago, or Australian Aboriginals made rock paintings that date back 40,000 years. Since before recorded time, humans used images to make their mark. In the early twentieth century there was much interest in the art of the insane, most notably as exhibited in the Heidelberg Collection that gathered works from the major mental hospitals of Europe. The mother of art therapy was Margaret Naumburg, an educator trained in both Freudian and Jungian analysis, who asked her clients to draw and "free associate" to their art. Working in New York, Naumburg began training other art therapists in the 1950s. Her contemporary was Edith Kramer, an artist who worked with children, also in New York. Whereas Naumburg utilized a more analytical approach, Kramer believed that the art-making process was healing in and of itself, and she based her work on the concept of sublimation.

In the 1960s, Elinor Ulman, a Washington, DC, art therapist, founded an art therapy journal that served to unite the handful of art therapists practicing around the country, and in 1969 the American Art Therapy Association was formed. University training programs were developed, and books and papers on art therapy proliferated (see Junge & Wadeson, 2006).

Art Therapy Today

Currently, there are approximately 5,000 members in the American Art Therapy Association. Art therapy has also been established in other countries, but in most of these countries it is not as developed as it is in the United States. The American Art Therapy Association publishes a newsletter and a journal and holds an annual conference. There are many regional conferences as well. The terminal degree in art therapy is the master's, and there are between 20 and 30 university training programs throughout the country. Some art therapy educators hold a PhD, often in a related area.

In most states, art therapy numbers are too small for licensure, so many art therapists are licensed as counselors or social workers. The art therapy credential is the ATR, Art Therapist Registered, available to those graduating from an approved master's degree program and completing a specified amount of supervised experience. There is also Board Certification, ATR-BC, which ATRs may receive after passing an examination.

Current Trends

Art therapy studies are showing effectiveness in pain management, especially among cancer patients, and links with neurophysiology in examining art-making's influence on the brain. Art therapists are working more and more with trauma victims, utilizing art therapy for social action, and working in areas of community crisis. Art therapists were called on to work with families of those killed on 9/11. In New York, many were involved in helping those affected to create memorials and to deal with their grief and fears. Art therapists from all over the country traveled to Louisiana and Mississippi to work with victims of Hurricane Katrina. Many traveled there over several years to work with displaced persons. The profession of art therapy is a dynamic one, continuing to expand into many areas of individual and social need, often in collaboration with other mental health professionals and in association with numerous societal facilities.

REFERENCES

Freud, S. (1963). *New introductory lectures on psychoanalysis* (ed. James Strachey). *Part II: Dreams*. Vol. XV. London: Hogarth Press.

Junge, M. B., & Wadeson, H., Eds. (2006). *Architects of art therapy*. Springfield, IL: Charles C. Thomas.

Wadeson, H. (1980). *Art psychotherapy*. New York: John Wiley & Sons.

Yalom, I. (1989). *Love's executioner and other tales of psychotherapy.*
New York: HarperCollins.

HARRIET WADESON
University of Illinois at Chicago

See also: Catharsis

ASIAN PSYCHOLOGIES

Until recently, most Western mental health professionals
usually assumed that their own psychologies and therapies were the only ones worthy of serious consideration,
but fortunately this ethnocentric attitude is changing
rapidly. Here we will limit discussion to four Asian
psychologies—the yogic and Buddhist psychologies of
India, and the Taoist and neo-Confucian systems of
China—which despite their differences, also display
significant commonalities.

Personality

Asian psychologies reflect ideas about human nature,
health, pathology, and potential that, in certain ways,
differ significantly from traditional Western views. We
can summarize the Asian claims under the six headings
of consciousness, development, identity, motivation, psychopathology, and health.

Consciousness

In *The Varieties of Religious Experience* William James
concluded:

> Our normal waking consciousness ... is but one special type
> of consciousness, whilst all about it, parted from it by the
> filmiest of screens, there lie potential forms of consciousness
> entirely different.... No account of the universe in its totality
> can be final which leaves these other forms of consciousness
> quite disregarded.

Asian psychologies agree completely. They recognize
multiple states of consciousness (SOCs), and that some
states may be associated with specific functions and abilities unavailable in our usual state. Perceptual sensitivity,
attention, and the sense of identity, as well as affective,
cognitive, and perceptual processes may all vary with the
SOC in precise ways.

"Higher" states possess the effective functions of the
usual states, plus heightened perceptions, insights or
affects outside the realm of day-to-day experience. If higher
states exist, then our usual state must be suboptimal. This

is exactly the claim of Asian psychologies. They argue that
our usual state of consciousness is underdeveloped, constricted, and distorted—even dreamlike—to a remarkable
but usually unrecognized degree. Thus "normal" people
who are unaware of their mental limitations are seen as
"asleep" or "dreaming."

When this "dream" is especially painful or disruptive,
it becomes a nightmare, and is then recognized as psychopathology. However, since the vast majority of the
population "dreams," our true state of affairs goes unrecognized. When individuals heal these dysfunctions and
mature, and thereby permanently "awaken" from their
"dreams," they are able to recognize the nature and
limitation of both their former state and that of the population. This awakening—known variously as *wu, moksha,*
liberation, or enlightenment—is a central aim of Asian
psychologies.

Development

The nature of Asian systems, and their relationship to
Western ones, can be better understood if research on
development is considered. Western researchers describe
development as proceeding through three major stages:
preconventional, conventional, and postconventional; or
prepersonal, personal, and transpersonal. Analogously,
psychotherapies address three degrees of pathology-
health: pathology reduction, existential and adjustment
issues, and transpersonal concerns.

Western psychologies have developed sophisticated
maps of prepersonal and personal development, and
effective therapies for many pathologies. However, until
recently, they offered very little for fostering postconventional development, nor therapies for addressing
existential or transpersonal concerns. By contrast,
Asian psychologies focus on fostering postconventional
development—for example, postconventional stages
of emotional, moral, and cognitive development—and
on addressing existential and transpersonal concerns.
However, they offer little on early development or severe
psychopathology.

This relates to the previous discussion of states of
consciousness. SOCs are transient. Asian psychologies and
disciplines therefore aim to transform temporary higher
states into enduring higher stages of development.

These Asian goals are, in part, an extension of traditional Western psychology. For example, the West has long
recognized that normal individuals suffer unrecognized
perceptual distortions. In addition, Western researchers
have recently identified postconventional developmental
stages beyond those formerly considered to be the upper
reaches of conventional normality.

However, Asian psychologies extend these findings.
They assert that "normal" perceptual distortions are far
more pervasive and harmful than usually recognized.

Likewise, they suggest that "normal" conventional development falls far short of our potentials.

Fortunately, Asian psychologies also offer good news. They suggest that many of our "normal" conventional psychological limitations can be reduced, and normal capacities can be enhanced by specific mental training. For example, they claim (and research supports) that meditation can enhance perceptual sensitivity and reduce perception distortions. Likewise, they claim (and research again supports) that meditation, yoga, and related trainings foster psychological development to healthier postconventional levels.

Identity

Western psychologists usually assume that our natural and optimal identity is "egoic," implying a sense of self that is inextricably separated, even alienated, from other people and the world. Asian psychologies suggest that our usual egoic identity is unnecessarily constricted, resulting in a sense of egocentricity, alienation, and angst. These psychologists also suggest that a more mature, expansive, or transpersonal identity is possible, and that this claim is directly testable by anyone willing to undertake meditative-yogic practices.

A transpersonal identity is one in which the sense of self "extends beyond (trans) the individual person or personality to encompass wider aspects of humankind, life, psyche, and cosmos" (Walsh & Vaughan, 1993, p. 3). Western psychologists periodically rediscover some of these transpersonal experiences and shifts of identity. Better known examples include Jung's *numinous* experience, Maslow's *peak* and *plateau* experiences, Fromm's *atonement*, Grof's *holotropic* experience, and James' *cosmic consciousness*. These shifts to a transpersonal sense of self can occur spontaneously, especially in exceptionally healthy people, or by mental training. In either case, they may confer significant psychological benefits (Alexander, Rainforth, & Gelderloos, 1991).

Asian disciplines offer methods to systematically induce transpersonal experiences and their benefits. By contrast, until recently, Western psychology was unaware of such methods. Transpersonal experiences and senses of identity were therefore disregarded at best, or even confused with regression to prepersonal pathology—a diagnostic error now known as the pre/post or pre/trans fallacy (Wilber, 2000)

Motivation

Asian psychologies, especially yogic psychology, tend to see motives as hierarchically organized analogously to suggestions by Abraham Maslow and Ken Wilber. However, Eastern psychologies emphasize the importance of "higher motives" such as self-transcendence and selfless service, which are rarely recognized in Western psychology.

One motivational factor that is given great emphasis and viewed as a major determinant of pathology is craving or addiction. Western psychology recognizes addiction to a limited number of things such as drugs, food, and sex. However, Asian psychologies argue that craving is far more pervasive and pathogenic, can occur to almost anything, and that it plays a major role in human suffering and psychopathology. From this perspective, psychologically based suffering is a feedback signal, indicating the existence of addictions and the need to release them.

Addiction/craving invariably gives rise to its mirror image: aversion. Whereas addiction says "I must have something in order to be happy," aversion says "I must avoid something in order to be happy." Aversion is said to underlie anger, aggression, and many psychological and spiritual dysfunctions. Not surprisingly, the reduction of craving and aversion is a major goal of Asian disciplines. They offer an array of practices for this, that Western therapists are beginning to draw on.

Psychopathology

Asian views of psychopathology center around three ideas: (1) immaturity, (2) unhealthy mental qualities, and (3) the "three poisons" of greed, hatred, and delusion.

Asian psychologies regard our usual adult state as a problematic form of arrested development. As such, they would agree with Abraham Maslow's (1968, p. 16) provocative claim that "it seems more and more clear that what we call 'normal' in psychology is really a psychopathology of the average, so undramatic and so widely spread that we don't even notice it ordinarily." From this perspective, development has proceeded from preconventional to conventional, but has then faltered and ground to a premature halt far short of our full potentials. At this stage the mind operates suboptimally, capacities remain unrealized, many unhealthy mental qualities flourish, while healthy ones remain underdeveloped.

These unhealthy qualities include, for example, attentional difficulties such as distractibility and agitation, cognitive deficits such as mindlessness, disruptive emotions such as anger and jealousy, and problematic motives such as craving and selfishness. The most fundamental pathogenic factors are described, especially in Buddhism, as the "three poisons" of (cognitive) delusion and (motivational) craving and aversion.

Asian psychologies agree in significant ways with existentialism about our usual human condition. For example, they agree about the inevitability of existential conflicts and issues—such as finitude, meaning, isolation, and suffering—at the conventional egoic level of development. Indeed, existentialists might be said to have rediscovered part of the Buddha's First Noble Truth: that unsatisfactoriness is part of (unenlightened) life, and (for the untrained mind) is accompanied by angst. However, existentialists' major recommendations are a specific *attitude* toward these conflicts (such as Tillich's *courage*, Heidegger's *resoluteness*, or Yalom's *heroism*), and a *lifestyle* of *authenticity* and *engagement*.

Asian psychologies agree completely with the importance of such attitudes and lifestyles. However, they also offer more. For example, Buddhism's remaining three Noble Truth's point to the possibility of cultivating qualities such as ethics, attention, awareness, and wisdom. These qualities in turn foster maturation to postconventional stages in which existential conflicts may find a transpersonal resolution (Wilber, 2000).

Mental Health

The Asian ideal of psychological health extends beyond pathology reduction to encompass postconventional development and potentials. Health is defined primarily in terms of three changes: (1) reduction of unhealthy mental qualities, (2) cultivation of healthy qualities, and (3) maturation to postconventional states and stages of development.

Asian psychologies emphasize that specific healthy mental qualities must be deliberately cultivated to ensure psychological and spiritual health and maturity. Valued qualities encompass multiple mental domains. For example, attentional virtues include heightened concentration and focus, while desired modulations of arousal include calm and equanimity. Cultivated emotions include love, compassion, and joy. Cognitive refinements encompass insight and wisdom. Likewise, refinements of awareness include perceptual sensitivity, empathy, and mindfulness. Mindfulness is usually understood in the West as precise and ongoing awareness of the nature of the stimuli being observed. As such, it can be regarded as a highly developed form of the Freudian "observing ego."

Psychological health also includes maturation to postconventional stages and capacities. These include, for example, postformal operational cognition and wisdom, postconventional morality, transpersonal emotions such as encompassing love and compassion, and metamotives such as self-transcendence and selfless service. Research suggests that meditation does foster psychological development on multiple dimensions, including measures of ego, moral, and cognitive development, self-actualization, defenses and coping skills, and states and stages of consciousness (Alexander & Langer, 1990).

Asian Disciplines and Therapies

The applied side of Asian psychologies focuses on disciplines designed to foster psychological and spiritual development and well-being. The best known such disciplines are meditation and yoga. Meditation refers to a family of techniques that train awareness and attention in order to bring mental processes under greater voluntary control. This control is used to reduce destructive mental qualities, to cultivate beneficial qualities such as concentration, compassion, and insight, and to enhance psychological and spiritual growth and well-being. Yogas are more inclusive disciplines that encompass meditation, ethics, lifestyle modification, body postures, breath control, and intellectual study (Shear, 2006; Wallace, 2007).

In addition to specific meditative and yogic techniques, Asian systems, like contemplative traditions around the world, emphasize seven central practices and goals. These comprise (1) redirecting motivation, especially by reducing attachment and aversion and moving up the hierarchy of needs; (2) transforming emotions, especially reducing problematic affects such as anger and fear, and cultivating beneficial emotions such as love and compassion; (3) living ethically, so as to reduce destructive mental qualities such as greed and aversion, and to foster helpful qualities such as empathy and generosity; (4) developing concentration; (5) refining awareness; (6) fostering wisdom; and (7) increasing generosity and altruism (Walsh, 1999, 2008).

To give just two examples of Asian techniques and resultant capacities—which until recently Western psychologists considered impossible—consider the cultivation of love and lucid dreaming. Several meditations specifically cultivate the unconditional, encompassing love and compassion known in the East as *bhakti*, *metta*, or *jen*, and in the West as *agape*. Electroencephalographic (EEG) studies provide experimental support.

Dream yoga is a 2,000-year-old discipline for developing lucid dreaming: the ability to know one is dreaming while still asleep. Advanced practitioners claim to maintain awareness and continue meditation throughout both dream and nondream sleep, a claim now supported by EEG studies. Advanced meditators have now demonstrated at least 12 distinct capacities formerly considered impossible by Western psychologists (Walsh & Shapiro, 2006).

These capacities hint at the remarkable abilities, developmental possibilities, and powers of mind—some still largely unrecognized by Western psychologists—that Asian psychologies have discovered in their 3,000-year-long exploration of our inner universe. The Swiss psychiatrist Medard Boss, one of the first Westerners to examine Asian practices, suggested that compared with the extent of yogic self-exploration, "even the best Western training analysis is not much more than an introductory course." However, even modest amounts of practice can produce significant psychological, physiological, and therapeutic changes, as several hundred experiments and clinical studies have shown (Walsh & Shapiro, 2006).

Integrations

Because of their different foci, Asian and Western psychologies may be partly complimentary. Each has much to learn from the other, and some of the twenty-first-century's major advances may include syntheses between both systems. Three kinds of integrations across different

Western psychologies and therapies are recognized: (1) theoretical integration, (2) recognizing underlying common factors, and (3) technical eclecticism combining techniques.

Theoretical integrations already include the fields of psychosynthesis, Diamond/Ridhwan, transpersonal, and integral psychologies, of which Ken Wilber's (2000) integral psychology is the most encompassing. Underlying common factors that mediate Western psychotherapeutic and Asian meditative-yogic benefits include heightened awareness (mindfulness), insight, and social support (Walsh & Shapiro, 2006).

Technical eclecticism is proceeding rapidly. Meditation is now popular in both the culture at large, and also in psychotherapy where it is often used in conjunction with traditional Western therapies. "Mindfulness-based" therapies—such as *mindfulness-based stress reduction*—that add mindfulness training to traditional therapeutic packages are proliferating, and proving effective for a widening array of disorders.

Experimental studies have found meditation and yoga to be effective therapeutic strategies for a variety of psychological and psychosomatic disorders, especially those that are stressed based. For example, meditation has proved helpful with psychological disorders such as anxiety, phobic, sleep, and eating disorders. Psychosomatic applications include cardiovascular disorders such as hypertension and hypercholesterolemia, as well as asthma, chronic pain, and premenstrual dysphoria. Meditation also appears beneficial for enhancing psychological performance and well-being in normal people.

However, as yet there have been few studies that test the kind of benefits that meditation and yoga were intended for—namely postconventional and spiritual maturation and well-being, let alone the highest reaches of "enlightenment." The deeper potentials of Asian psychologies and what Maslow called "the farther reaches of human nature" that they point to, remain largely untapped.

REFERENCES

Alexander, C. & Langer, E. (Eds.). (1990). *Higher stages of human development*. New York: Oxford University Press.

Alexander, C. N., Rainforth, M. V., & Gelderloos, P. (1991). Transcendental meditation, self-actualization, and psychological health. *Journal of Social Behavior and Personality*, 6, 189–247.

Marsella, A. (1998). Toward a "global community psychology": Meeting the needs of a changing world. *American Psychologist*, 43, 1282–1291.

Shear, J. (2006). *The Experience of meditation: Experts introduce the major traditions*. St. Paul, MN: Paragon House.

Wallace, A. (2007). *Contemplative science: Where Buddhism and neuroscience converge*. New York: Columbia University Press.

Walsh, R. (1999). *Essential spirituality: The seven central practices*. New York: John Wiley & Sons.

Walsh, R. (2008). Contemplative psychotherapies. In R. Corsini & D. Weddingame (Eds.), *Current Psychotherapies* (8th ed., pp. 437–480). Itasca, IL: Wadsworth Publishing.

Walsh, R. & Shapiro, S. (2006). The meeting of meditative disciplines and Western psychology: A mutually enriching dialogue. *American Psychologist*, 61(3), 227–239.

Walsh, R. & Vaughan, F. (Eds.). (1993). *Paths beyond ego: The transpersonal vision*. New York: Tarcher/Putnam.

Wilber, K. (2000). *Integral psychology*. Boston: Shambhala.

ROGER WALSH
University of California College of Medicine, Irvine

ASPERGER SYNDROME

Asperger syndrome (AS; also identified as Asperger's disorder) is a pervasive developmental disorder thought to be closely related to autism. Although first conceptualized in 1944 by Austrian pediatrician Hans Asperger, one year after the independent description of autism by Leo Kanner, AS did not gain wide recognition diagnostically until the early 1980s (Wing, 1981). It has since come to be accepted as a specific neurodevelopmental disorder in its own right within the psychiatric, psychological, and developmental fields (American Psychiatric Association [APA], 2000). AS is generally conceptualized as one endpoint along the autism disorder spectrum; however, there remains significant debate about where AS falls along the continuum of autism spectrum disorders, and more specifically about its relationship to high-functioning autism (HFA), with which it is often compared and contrasted (Ghaziuddin, 2008).

Currently, diagnostic criteria specified for AS in the DSM-IV-TR (APA, 2000) require identification of impairments in social interaction and a history of restricted or repetitive behaviors or interests, but no delays in the acquisition of language. Therefore, when considering just formal diagnostic criteria, the primary difference between AS and autism is the requirement that early speech and language be acquired at a typically expected time developmentally in individuals with AS, whereas individuals with autism have delayed speech and language development (Volkmar & Klin, 2000). Additionally, diagnosis of AS typically occurs later in childhood than does that of autism, although the age of diagnosis of AS is declining, likely because of increased awareness and knowledge of the syndrome among medical professionals and the general public (Cederlund & Gillberg, 2004).

Characteristics

Social impairments

The impairments in social interaction observed in AS may take many forms, such as difficulty with nonverbal behaviors, failure to form developmentally appropriate peer relationships, and a lack of social reciprocity (APA, 2000). Although individuals with AS may have a good understanding of social conventions, this knowledge may not translate well to spontaneous interactions (Volkmar & Klin, 2000). Individuals with AS often show little regard for the reactions and emotions of others, either within a conversation (Ozonoff, Dawson, & McPartland, 2002) or when relating an interaction with others. Persons with AS may also talk at length without ever realizing that the other person is trying to end or redirect the conversation. They may additionally share socially inappropriate information. A frequent hallmark symptom is that persons with AS may not effectively or appropriately engage or maintain eye contact (Volkmar & Klin, 2000).

Although the diagnostic criteria for social impairment are identical between autism and AS, there are also several important qualitative differences (Ghaziudin, 2008). Unlike with autism, individuals with AS are not seemingly unaware of or disinterested in social interaction (Volkmar & Klin, 2000); instead, they are frequently frustrated by their social failures and may share their frustrations verbally and, at times, behaviorally. Individuals with AS frequently share that they want friends and romantic relationships. Notably, persons with AS may be best able to engage with others who have the same types of intense interests; these individuals often become strong peers of children with AS. Lastly, children with AS are often teased or bullied and may become socially isolated; however, they often have little awareness that their behavior may be a contributing factor to their social failure (Ozonoff et al., 2002).

Repetitive Behaviors and Interests

Individuals with AS exhibit restricted or repetitive behaviors and interests (Volkmar & Klim, 2000). It is common for individuals to ask repetitive questions, talk incessantly about one topic, and to amass information on a specific subject or small number of subjects (Ozonoff et al., 2002). Individuals with AS often gravitate toward subjects about which they can accumulate vast amounts of factual information, such as transportation, music, sports, and video games, and they may pursue their interests intensely, to the exclusion of all other topics. Persons with AS may focus on specific details, but in turn will be unable to differentiate the important information from the trivial. This often means being unable to apply this vast knowledge to decision making. For many individuals with AS, the specific subject of interest is integrally related to their sense of self, such that they experience disinterest in the topic as rejection. Many individuals with AS continue to have subjects of intense focus throughout their lives. As a result of this symptom, some educators have encouraged the integration of the subject of a person with AS's focused interest into person's school curriculum on an individual

basis, to help motivate and engage a student who might otherwise be disinterested (Ozonoff et al., 2002).

Speech and Language

Unlike children with autism, individuals with AS develop basic aspects of language; however, their language skills may be quite qualitatively different from those of children without AS (Ozonoff et al., 2002). There are commonly noted impairments in the social use of language and in pragmatic understanding, although these may remediate somewhat as children get older. Conversations are typically associative, rather than goal-oriented; they are also tangential, egocentric, and frequently focused on the individual's topic of interest to the exclusion of other's interests or needs (Volkmar & Klin, 2000). Difficulties interpreting nonverbal cues may contribute to these conversational problems (Ozonoff et al., 2002; Volkmar & Klin, 2000). While listening during conversations, individuals with AS may misinterpret the meaning of statements because of a lack of understanding of nonverbal cues (e.g., sarcasm; Ozonoff et al., 2002).

It is important to note that the appropriate acquisition of language is typically determined during an evaluation through parent report. This retrospective assessment may take place well after the critical age when language is first emerging, with the result that language development may be recalled as having been more typical than was truly the case. This can complicate differentiating AS from high-functioning autism (HFA; Gillberg, 1998) and has led to some debate about what constitutes a language delay. Specifically, if language acquisition is on time, but is qualitatively different from that of children without AS, is it possible to say that language development was typical? This question remains a specific area of ongoing controversy in the literature (Gillberg, 1998).

Motor Skills

There is also ongoing debate as to whether motor deficits should be included in the criteria for diagnosis of AS, as it was one of the original characteristics that Asperger (1944) noted and might further differentiate AS from autism. Studies have found that motor clumsiness is common among individuals with AS, but it is as yet unclear whether there are actual significant differences in dexterity between individuals with AS and those with autism (Smith, 2000). Research is further complicated by the large variety of measures used to ascertain dexterity, making comparisons across studies difficult.

Epidemiology and Etiology

AS is a relatively rare disorder affecting from 0.25 to 7 people per 1000 and more males than females (Fombonne, 2005). The origins of AS are still unclear, although there is a growing body of research indicating that genetic and environmental factors may together play a role (Volkmar & Klin, 2000; Fombonne, 2005). Studies examining the incidence of AS and autism among families have indicated that there is a strong genetic component and that AS may be particularly common among individuals with fathers or other male relatives with AS or AS-like traits (Volkmar & Klin, 2000). This high incidence of both AS and autism within families reinforces the belief that they are closely related disorders (Fombonne, 2005; Ghaziuddin, 2008). There has been some research into the specific chromosomal abnormalities that may play a role in the development of AS (Cederlund & Gillberg, 2004), including the identification of genes or sets of genes involved in neuronal development that might be particularly significant in AS (Ghaziuddin, 2008; Ozonoff, et al., 2002).

Research into the environmental factors that may lead to the development of AS has been extremely limited, but has considered such prenatal and perinatal risk factors as preeclampsia, prematurity, post maturity neonatal concerns (Cederlund & Gillberg, 2004), and newborn encephalopathy. Results have thus far been inconclusive, but have provided some support for the hypothesis that early neurological insult may be a contributing factor in the development of autism spectrum disorders (Volkmar & Klin, 2000).

Neuropsychological Functioning

Research regarding specific neuropsychological deficits related to AS has focused on general cognitive and executive functioning. Some studies have indicated that individuals with AS may be more likely to have higher verbal than nonverbal IQs (Ghaziuddin & Mountain-Kimchi, 2004), with some individuals meeting criteria for a nonverbal learning disability (Cederlund & Gillberg, 2004). There is evidence, however, that this pattern is reversed for some individuals with AS (Ghaziuddin & Mountain-Kimchi, 2004). Investigations into associated executive functioning deficits have revealed significant impairments in cognitive flexibility, word generation, set shifting, and response selection/monitoring among individuals with AS. These are in fact believed to be common neurocognitive difficulties in individuals with AS that affect their learning and social success (Ozonoff et al., 2002).

Neurological Functioning

Studies of functional and structural neurological abnormalities associated with AS have highlighted dysfunction in the medial temporal lobes and the amygdala-hippocampus region. Other studies have considered differences such as volume of gray matter and connectivity. As yet, no universal pattern of neurological dysfunction has been identified among individuals with AS (Ozonoff et al., 2002; Volkmar & Klin, 2000).

Comorbidity

Many individuals with AS are also diagnosed with other psychological disorders, including most commonly, attention deficit/hyperactivity disorder (ADHD), obsessive-compulsive disorder (OCD), depression, and anxiety (Ozonoff et al., 2002). ADHD is typically seen in younger children, whereas mood disorders (depression in particular) are more common in adolescents and adults (Ghaziuddin, 2008). It is common for there to be a familial history of depression among individuals diagnosed with AS (Ghaziuddin, 2008). Comorbid disorders are often the more difficult behavioral and psychosocial concerns addressed clinically as individuals with AS mature and move toward independence, given the potential of independence to intensify and complicate already existing social and communication difficulties.

Treatment

Research regarding the treatment of individuals with AS has emphasized that intervention should be tailored to the individual's strengths and weaknesses and should address not only AS-related deficits, but also other areas of impairment and co-occurring psychological disorders (Volkmar & Klin, 2000). Most children with AS do not wish to be socially isolated, and they may become depressed if they are unable to form desired social relationships (Ozonoff et al., 2002). The primary treatment for the interpersonal impairments associated with AS is social skills training. The goal of social skills training is to utilize the individual's intact verbal skills to teach learning strategies, coping techniques, and awareness of social norms (Volkmar & Klin, 2000). It teaches strategies for dealing with commonly occurring social situations (e.g., meeting someone for the first time) and for dealing with novel situations as well. The ultimate goal of social skills training is to increase conversational skills, interpersonal skills, and employability, so that the person can enjoy greater personal and professional efficacy. This is often provided best through a collaborative approach between speech, language, occupational, and mental health therapists; implementation of social skills training interventions should also occur across environments in which the individual with AS participates (Ozonoff et al., 2002).

Repetitive behaviors and focused interests may respond well to behavioral intervention, including such approaches as response prevention, redirection, and substitution. Development of an intervention approach may require conducting a functional behavioral analysis, in order to better understand the role the behavior or interest plays in the individual's daily life. Again, effective management requires cross-environment collaboration.

Psychotherapy is another commonly used intervention among individuals with AS, and it can be useful in addressing problems related to vocational planning, family functioning, social adjustment, and mood variations.

Some individuals with AS also benefit from involvement in support groups in which they can socialize with others with AS. Long-term planning regarding potential supports and guidance in terms of life goals is often required, to obtain positive outcomes for individuals with AS (Ozonoff et al., 2000).

Remediation of cognitive concerns, particularly attentional and executive functioning difficulties, often requires accommodation within the learning environment, together with structured tutoring interventions regarding problem solving and task management. Individuals with AS who present with significant difficulties with organization, flexibility, and engagement may require more specialized educational approaches. Similar to some children with autism, children with AS may respond well to structured behavioral programming and classroom predictability.

Long-Term Outcomes

Research on the long-term outcomes for individuals with AS has been extremely limited, but a recent study by Cederlund et al. (2008) provides some much needed preliminary information. They found that outcomes for individuals with AS are generally better than for individuals with autism, although not as positive as had been predicted. Outcome ratings were based on employment, appropriate school enrollment, independent living, and having friends or a steady relationship. Twenty-seven percent of AS subjects had a good outcome, 47% had a fair outcome, 23% had a restricted outcome, and 3% had a poor outcome. The authors conclude that, although outcomes are better in AS than in autism, they are "suboptimal" when considered in light of the AS individual's intact intellectual skills. Ongoing research is attempting to outline best practices for supporting individuals with AS as they prepare to move into adulthood.

REFERENCES

American Psychiatric Association (2000). *Diagnostic and statistical manual of mental disorders* (4th ed., *text rev.*). Washington, DC: Author.

Asperger, H. (1944). Die "Autistischen Psychopathen" im kindersalter. *Archiv fur Psychiatrie und Nervenkrankheiten, 117*, 76–136.

Cederlund, M., & Gillberg, C. (2004). One hundred males with Asperger syndrome: A clinical study of background and associated factors. *Developmental Medicine and Child Neurology, 46*, 652–660.

Cederlund, M., Hagberg, B., Billstedt, E., Gillberg, I., & Gillberg, C. (2008). Asperger syndrome and autism: A comparative longitudinal follow-up study more than five years after original diagnosis. *Journal of Autism and Developmental Disorders, 38*, 72–85.

Fombonne, E. (2005). The changing epidemiology of Autism. *Journal of Applied Research in Intellectual Disabilities, 18*, 281–294.

Ghaziuddin, M., & Mountain-Kimchi, K. (2004). Defining the intellectual profile of Asperger syndrome: Comparison with high-functioning Autism. *Journal of Autism and Developmental Disorders, 34*(3), 279–284.

Ghaziuddin, M. (2008). Defining the behavioral phenotype of Asperger syndrome. *Journal of Autism and Developmental Disorders, 38*, 138–142.

Gillberg, C. (1998). Asperger syndrome and high-functioning Autism. *The British Journal of Psychiatry 172*(3), 200–209.

Ozonoff, S., Dawson, G., & McPartland, J. (2002). *A parent's guide to Asperger syndrome and high-functioning Autism.* New York: Guilford Press.

Smith, I. (2000). Motor functioning in Asperger syndrome. In A. Klin, F. Volkmar & S. Sparrow (Eds.). *Asperger Syndrome.* (pp. 97–124). New York: Guilford Press.

Volkmar, F., & Klin, A. (2000). Diagnostic issues in Asperger syndrome. In A. Klin, F. Volkmar & S. Sparrow (Eds.). *Asperger Syndrome.* (pp. 25–71). New York: Guilford Press.

Wing, L. (1981). Asperger's syndrome: A clinical account. *Psychological Medicine, 11*, 115–129.

SCOTT J. HUNTER
VALERIE MALZER
University of Chicago

See also: **Autistic Disorder**

ASSESSMENT PSYCHOLOGY

Assessment psychology is a field of behavioral science concerned with methods of identifying similarities and differences among people in their mental and emotional characteristics, their functioning capacities, and their dispositions to behave in certain ways. To this end, assessment methods are designed to provide information about individuals' intellectual abilities, their personality features, their neuropsychological status, and their attitudes, interests, and attainments. This article reviews the history of assessment psychology, its primary areas of inquiry, its commonly employed measures, and its present position as a field of psychological science and practice.

History

Assessment psychology emerged from scientific and professional interests in assessing individual differences, the roots of which reach back to the very beginnings of scientific psychology. The generally acknowledged "father" of individual psychology is the British scholar Sir Francis Galton, who was intrigued by Darwin's notions of evolution and heredity and was particularly interested in the origins of genius. Galton proposed that differences among people in their intellectual ability could be measured by their performance on various psychomotor tasks, such as grip strength and visual acuity (Galton, 1869, 1983). In assessment psychology, the honorific of "father" belongs to James McKean Cattell. While working as an assistant in Wilhelm Wundt's Leipzig laboratory, the establishment of which in 1879 is considered to mark the inception of psychology as a scientific discipline, Cattell did his doctoral research on individual differences in reaction time. Subsequently, as head of the Columbia University Psychology Laboratory, Cattell generated widespread interest in psychological tests, pioneered in the development of mental testing, and introduced the term *mental test* to the psychological literature (Cattell, 1890).

In the twentieth century wake of Cattell's generativity, the formal pursuit of methods of identifying similarities and differences among people was often stirred by some practical purpose that needed to be served, as illustrated in the discussion that follows. Advances in assessment methods were psychology's main avenue of response to community and national needs during the first half of the twentieth century, and applied psychology was largely defined during this time by assessment conducted in clinical and educational settings. Students interested in practicing or studying aspects of applied psychology were routinely trained in assessment methods of various kinds, and being a competent assessor was generally considered an integral part of being a competent psychological practitioner.

However, the place of assessment in applied psychology changed markedly in the second half of the twentieth century. Practicing psychologists embraced many new roles as therapists and consultants, and they expanded their primary work settings from a narrow range of clinical and educational facilities to include a broad array of agencies and institutions in forensic, health care, organizational, and government settings. Consonant with these new directions in practice, assessment came to play a lesser part than before in the activities of applied psychologists, and many practitioners chose not to include assessment among the services they offer. Nevertheless, as indicated in the last section of this article, the reduced preeminence of assessment has not marked a decline in the vigor and value of assessment psychology, which more than at any time in its history is currently a scientifically productive and professionally thriving endeavor.

Areas and Measures

Assessment psychology addresses four primary areas of inquiry within applied psychology: (1) the determination of intellectual ability; (2) the identification of personality characteristics and psychopathological conditions; (3) the evaluation of neuropsychological status; and (4) the examination of aptitudes, achievement, and interests. In each of these areas, numerous formal assessment measures have been developed and proved dependable sources of useful information.

Determining Intellectual Ability

Formal assessment of intellectual ability had its beginnings in 1904, when the Minister of Public Instruction in Paris asked Alfred Binet, a distinguished experimental psychologist of his day, to assist him in identifying "subnormal" elementary school children who needed special educational services not available in regular classrooms. In collaboration with a colleague, Theodore Simon, Binet designed a series of verbal and perceptual-motor tasks for measuring whether students' mental abilities were substantially below expectation for their age. Arranged to provide an index of mental age, these tasks were published as the Binet-Simon method of diagnosing abnormal intellectual level, which served its intended purpose well in the Parisian schools. The Binet-Simon scale was translated into English by Lewis Terman at Stanford University and published as the Stanford-Binet Intelligence Scale in 1916. Terman added to this translation a formula by which assessed mental age could be divided by chronological age to yield what he called an "intelligence quotient"—thereby introducing the term *IQ* into the language of psychology and common parlance as well. The kinds of tasks designed by Binet have continued to the present day to provide the foundation on which most other tests of intelligence have been based. The Stanford-Binet itself is currently in its fourth edition and remains frequently used in the assessment of children's intellectual functioning.

The most widely used measure of intellectual testing and the most frequently used of all psychological tests in clinical settings are two scales developed by David Wechsler: the Wechsler Adult Intelligence Scale (WAIS), which was first published in 1939 as the Wechsler-Bellevue, while Wechsler was chief psychologist at Bellevue Hospital in New York City; and the Wechsler Intelligence Scale for Children (WISC), which was first published in 1949 (Hogan, 2005). Wechsler had reservations about the utility of Binet's mental age concept in assessing intelligence, especially in adults. Instead, he proposed determining intellectual level by comparing an individual's test score with the normative distribution of tests scores among large samples of people in general. Proceeding in this way, he formulated the IQ in statistical terms as having a mean of 100 and a standard deviation of 15, which led to a widely accepted convention of translating IQ scores into percentile ranks. For example, approximately two-thirds of the population can be expected to have IQs between 85 (16th percentile) and 115 (84th percentile).

Like the Stanford-Binet, the Wechsler scales comprise a variety of tasks measuring different kinds of verbal, perceptual-motor, and cognitive abilities. Beyond using performance on these subtests to generate a single overall IQ score, Wechsler postulated that a person's pattern of relative strengths and weaknesses across subtests measuring different kinds of mental abilities could be used to identify normal and abnormal variations in numerous cognitive characteristics and coping capacities. The potential for such meaningful interpretation of profiles of subtest scores has resulted in the Wechsler scales being widely used in clinical health settings as a measure not only of intellectual ability but also of features of neuropsychological impairment and disordered thinking. Both the WAIS and the WISC are in their fourth edition, and there is a Wechsler scale for young children as well, the Wechsler Preschool and Primary Scale of Intelligence.

Identifying Personality Characteristics and Psychopathological Conditions

Formal assessment of personality characteristics and pathological conditions involves some combination of three procedures: self-report inventories, performance-based measures, and interviews. Self-report inventories are relatively structured tests in which respondents reply to specific questions by selecting their answer from a list of alternatives (e.g., Question: "Do you feel unhappy?" Alternative answers: "Most of the time," "Occasionally," "Hardly ever"). Like formal assessment of intelligence with the Stanford-Binet, self-report assessment of personality and psychopathology originated in response to a government request for help in meeting a public need. During World War I, Robert Woodworth, a prominent experimental psychologist who had studied with Cattell, was asked to assist the military in identifying psychologically fragile draftees who would be at risk for nervous breakdown if exposed to the stress of combat. For this purpose, Woodworth designed a list of "Yes" or "No" questions related to emotional stability. Published after the war as the Personal Data Sheet, Woodworth's questionnaire was the first generally available formal self-report personality assessment inventory.

Spurred by Woodworth's initial effort, subsequent generations of psychologists developed numerous longer and more complex self-report personality inventories notable for their breadth and dimensionality. Well beyond Woodworth's original intent merely to classify respondents as emotionally stable or unstable, contemporary self-report inventories help to identify an extensive array of pathological conditions and a broad range of personality characteristics, and they include as well scales that can help indicate whether a person has responded honestly. The currently best known of these inventories is the Minnesota Multiphasic Personality Inventory (MMPI), which is the second most frequently used test in clinical settings, after the WAIS (Hogan, 2005). Other commonly used and extensively researched self-report inventories include the Millon Clinical Mulitaxial Inventory, the Personality Assessment Inventory, the NEO-PI, and the Sixteen Personality Factor Questionnaire.

Performance-based personality assessment measures are relatively unstructured methods in which respondents are presented with somewhat ambiguous test stimuli and given only minimal instructions concerning what they should say about or do with these stimuli (e.g., asked to make up stories about a series of pictures they are shown). Measures of this kind have traditionally been called "projective" tests, because they encourage people to attribute and thereby reveal some of their own characteristics in formulating their responses. However, because most of these relatively unstructured tests have some clearly defined as well as ambiguous aspects, they are becoming more appropriately referred to as performance-based measures. By contrast with self-report data, the data obtained by performance-based measures consist not of what people say about themselves, but of the manner in which they respond to the various tasks that are set for them.

The best known and most widely used of these performance-based personality assessment measures is the Rorschach Inkblot Method (RIM), which is the second most frequently used personality test in clinical settings, after the MMPI (Hogan, 2005). Hermann Rorschach was a Swiss psychiatrist who, in the years just preceding 1920, had the idea that he could learn something about his patients' personality characteristics and adaptive difficulties by studying their perceptual style when they were asked to say what some inkblots might be. Acting on this idea, he developed specific procedures for deriving such information from responses to a standard set of inkblots. Although Rorschach's scoring system procedures and interpretive principles have been substantially expanded and refined in the ensuing 90 years, the 10 inkblots he published in 1921 remain the same standard set that is used today in the U.S. and around the world. Another well-known performance-based personality measure that has stood the test of time is the Thematic Apperception Test (TAT), which was developed in the mid-1930s by Henry Murray, a psychoanalytically trained physician who was then director of the Harvard Psychological Clinic. The TAT consists of a series of pictures of people and scenes about which respondents are asked to make up a story. Like the RIM, the TAT remains in its original form, and it is the second most frequently used performance-based personality assessment measure in clinical practice (Hogan, 2005). Two other frequently used measures of this kind are figure drawing tests, which require drawing people and other objects and answering questions about what has been drawn (e.g., "What is this person like?"), and sentence completion tests, in which the task consists of expressing one's feelings by extending brief phrases (e.g., "I regret . . . ") into full sentences.

Although discussed here in relation to identifying assessing personality characteristics and psychopathological conditions, interview methods are also commonly employed in assessing neuropsychological functioning and aptitudes, achievement, and interests. Of further note, interview methods include both self-report and performance-based components; interviewers typically base their impressions on not only what respondents say about themselves, but also on how they say it and how they conduct themselves while being interviewed. Clinical interviews vary in their degree of structure, depending on the purposes and preferences of the interviewer. Unstructured interviews consist largely of open-ended requests for information that may give interviewees some idea of what to talk about but little notion of what they should say, as in "Tell me about your family." An unstructured interview format allows considerable flexibility in adapting to how interviewees present themselves, and it is usually a rich source of information about a person's problems and preferences that is useful in planning psychotherapy. On the other hand, unstructured interviews lack sufficiently standardized procedures to ensure reliable and replicable data collection.

By contrast, structured interviews consist of specific and narrowly focused questions that often can be answered "Yes" or "No" (e.g., "Are you having trouble sleeping?"). Several standardized formats for conducting structured interviews have been developed, primarily for purposes of arriving at a formal clinical diagnosis or for classifying participants in research studies. The most comprehensive of these instruments are the Diagnostic Interview Schedule (DIS) and the Structured Clinical Interview for DSM (SCID). In practice, many clinicians combine open-ended and narrowly focused questions to conduct a semistructured interview that allows for both flexible inquiry and the formulation of a reliable diagnosis for clinical and research purposes.

Monitoring Neuropsychological Status

Neuropsychology is a discipline concerned with studying relationships between brain functions and behavior. In applied practice, clinical neuropsychology consists primarily of using various assessment procedures to measure the development and decline of brain functions and their impairment as a consequence of head injury, cerebrovascular accidents (stroke), neoplastic disease (tumors), and other illnesses affecting the central nervous system, of which Alzheimer's disease is the most prevalent. Best known among the earliest psychological methods constructed to measure brain functions is the Bender Visual Motor Gestalt Test (BVMGT), which was developed in the late 1930s by Lauretta Bender, a psychiatrist at New York's Bellevue Hospital. The BVMGT consists of nine cards, each of which has on it a geometric design that respondents are asked to copy. Difficulty in copying these designs is likely to reflect impairments in visual organization and perceptual-motor coordination, which in turn can be helpful in identifying brain damage or dysfunction.

Its long history and still common use notwithstanding, the BVMGT is not as sensitive to neuropsychological dysfunction as more extensive measurements of cognitive functions provided by the previously mentioned Wechsler intelligence scales and by multifaceted neuropsychological test batteries comprising measures of a broad range of these functions. Currently, the most prominent neuropsychological test batteries are the Halstead Reitan Neuropsychological Test Battery, which was first developed in the 1950s, and the Luria-Nebraska Neuropsychological Battery, which was first published in 1985. Other specific measures commonly used by contemporary neuropsychologists include the Wechsler Memory Scale, the Wide Range Assessment of Memory and Learning, the Boston Naming Test, the Stroop Neuropsychological Screening Test, and the Trail Making Test.

Measurement of Aptitudes, Achievement, and Interests

As mentioned earlier, intellectual assessment and personality assessment emerged largely out of a perceived necessity for administrators to make decisions about people, namely, the Parisian schoolchildren and the World War I U.S. draftees. By contrast, methods of assessing achievement, aptitudes, and interests were developed primarily to help people make decisions about themselves. These measures are typically used to assist people in planning their educational and vocational future on the basis of what appear to be their abilities and interests. With respect to assessing abilities, achievement tests identify a person's currently attained performance level in various areas of knowledge or skill, whereas aptitude tests provide an index of a person's potential for increasing knowledge or gaining skill in response to education or training. Illustrative and widely used tests of these kinds include the Woodcock-Johnson Tests of Achievement and Cognitive Abilities, the Wide Range Achievement Test, and the Strong Interest Inventory.

Present Position

As stated previously, assessment psychology is currently a thriving field of endeavor. The utilization of assessment psychology has extended far beyond its original base in clinical and educational settings and become widely applied in the newer and growing areas of forensic psychology, health psychology, and industrial and organizational psychology. Whenever decisions by or about people are based at least in part on psychological considerations, the information provided by formal and standardized psychological assessment can facilitate the decision-making process. In addition to these practical applications, interest in the nature of psychological assessment methods and their psychometric foundations has generated extensive research over the years and a vast body of published literature. There are more quality journals and current textbooks and handbooks concerned with assessment psychology available now than at any time in the past, and this literature includes an international array of publications.

Assessment psychology is also well-represented in prospering scientific and professional organizations that embrace an international community of assessment psychologists. Within the American Psychological Association, Division 40 is devoted to Clinical Neuropsychology and Divisions 5 (Evaluation, Measurement, and Statistics) and 12 (Clinical Psychology) have sections on assessment. Other prominent assessment organizations include the National Academy of Neuropsychology, the Society for Personality Assessment, the European Association of Psychological Assessment, the International Test Commission, and the Division of Psychological Assessment and Evaluation within the International Association of Applied Psychology.

REFERENCE

Hogan, T. P. (2005). Fifty widely used psychological tests. In G. P. Koocher, J. C. Norcross, & S. S. Hill III (Eds.), *Psychologists' desk reference* (2nd ed., pp. 101–104). New York: Oxford University Press.

SUGGESTED READINGS

Goldstein, G., & Beers, S. R. (Eds.). (2004). *Intellectual and neuropsychological assessment*. Vol. 1 in M. Hersen (Ed.-in-Chief), *Comprehensive handbook of psychological assessment*. Hoboken, NJ: John Wiley & Sons.

Graham, J. R., & Naglieri, J. A. (Eds.) (2003). *Assessment psychology*. Vol. 10 in I. B. Weiner (Ed.-in-Chief), *Handbook of psychology*. Hoboken, NJ: John Wiley & Sons.

Groth-Marnat, G. (2003). *Handbook of psychological assessment* (3rd ed.). Hoboken, NJ: John Wiley & Sons.

Weiner, I. B. (2003). Assessment psychology. In D. K. Freedheim (Ed.), *History of psychology* (pp. 279–302). Vol. 1 in I. B. Weiner (Ed.-in-Chief), *Handbook of psychology*. Hoboken, NJ: John Wiley & Sons.

Weiner, I. B., & Greene, R. L. (2008). *Handbook of personality assessment*. Hoboken, NJ: John Wiley & Sons.

IRVING B. WEINER
University of South Florida

See also: Intelligence Testing; Interview Assessment; Neuropsychology; Personality Assessment; Psychological Assessment

ASSISTIVE TECHNOLOGY

As all areas of society continue to become more technologically advanced, individuals who have disabilities and chronic medical conditions are benefiting through the use of assistive technology and becoming more mainstreamed into American society. As they become more independent in all areas of life and are less reliant on public services,

society benefits as well. Many of these persons have been able to find employment or return to work. Therefore, the income for individuals with disabilities increases, as does their purchasing power to buy goods and services. Assistive technology offers an effective and viable means to increase or restore functioning, enhance quality of life, and diminish barriers, physical as well as attitudinal.

Definitions

Assistive technology is defined in the Technology-Related Assistance for Individuals with Disabilities Act of 1988 as any item, piece of equipment, or product system, whether acquired commercially off the shelf, modified, or customized, that is used to increase, maintain, or improve functional capabilities of people with disabilities. A technology service is any service that directly assists an individual with a disability in the selection, acquisition, and use of an assistive technology device. At present, approximately 20 million Americans with disabilities are using some form of assistive devices, equipment, computers, and other apparatus (Brodwin, Swett, Lane, & Star, 2005). People benefit from assistive technology at the workplace, in school, at home, and in leisure activities.

Use of Technology

Through understanding technology as applied to people with disabilities, practitioners can provide more meaningful, practical, and realistic clinical counseling and services to clients. Technology has a profound impact on improving all aspects of the lives of people with disabilities. As noted by Scherer (2007), technology is significantly changing the lives of individuals who have disabilities. Assistive technology has enhanced the quality of life and extended the life span of persons with congenital and developmental disabilities, as well as those who have acquired disabilities and chronic medical conditions. Devices and equipment may be low-tech (mechanical) or high-tech (electromechanical or computer-related) and can compensate for sensory and functional loss. Assistive technology provides the means to move (e.g., adaptive equipment on automobiles and vans, wheelchairs, powered wheelchairs, scooters, lifts), speak (e.g., augmentative and alternative communication devices), read (e.g., Braille input, voice recognition devices), hear (telecommunication devices for the deaf or TDD, hearing aids, audio loops), and manage self-care tasks (e.g., remote environmental control systems, prosthetic and orthotic devices, devices to aid in eating and in other activities of daily life).

Examples of Technology

Robotics

An example of advanced technology is the continuing development of robotic controls. Through the use of robotics, a person can manipulate objects, perform functions through prosthetic (e.g., artificial extremity) and orthotic (e.g., braces) applications, render movement in spinal cord injuries (e.g., persons with paralysis), and perform many work tasks that before were not possible (Rubin & Roessler, 2008). A robotic arm can be attached to a powered wheelchair and controlled by a direct selection and toggle interface. It provides assistance with such functions as drinking, removing items from shelves, desktop manipulation of objects, and recreation (e.g., games). Fixed workstation (desktop) robots assist with manipulation of objects. A desktop vocational robot assistant can perform activities of daily living (e.g., meal preparation and feeding, writing, retrieving books, keyboard operations, use of a telephone). It also may assist with hygiene activities by washing and drying the operator's face, brushing teeth, combing hair, and shaving, as well as providing access to video and other games and craft (leisure) activities and to work (Cook, Polgar, & Hussey, 2008; Scherer, 2007).

Sensory Technology

Accommodations for people with visual impairments include both optical and nonoptical devices for low vision. Examples of optical devices are magnifiers, specially coated lenses, and eyeglass telescopes. Nonoptical visual aids include talking clocks and watches, talking calculators, closed-circuit televisions that enlarge print electronically, and personal computers and peripherals with the capacity of print magnification, speech output, and optical scanning (Brodwin, Star, & Cardoso, 2007). Additionally, hearing aids, TDD, cochlear implants, electronic ears, amplified telephones, and audio loops are helpful technology devices for persons who are deaf or hard of hearing.

Eye-Tracking Technology

Eye-gaze technology can track the movement of one eye to activate a computer (Johnson, Beard, & Carpenter, 2007; Mann, 2005). The individual must have sufficient head control and the ability to gaze directly at a camera. Derived from military eye control systems, the camera is typically attached to the head. Current scientific research promises enhanced eyeglass systems. Researchers described innovative gaze technology that features virtual reality goggles with an integrated camera and viewing screen to provide communication through icon choice. The user chooses targets by gazing at icons on the computer screen; the camera, integrated within the goggles, tracks eye-gaze motion and relays information for instantaneous processing.

Benefits of Technology

Upward social mobility is more realistic for persons with disabilities because of increased educational and employment opportunities and a greater sense of personal well-being (adjustment to disability) (Scherer, 2007). Technological devices, equipment, and services have allowed many people with disabilities to (1) exert greater control over their own lives; (2) participate in and contribute more fully and readily to activities in their own homes, school, employment, and community; (3) interact to a far greater extent with nondisabled individuals; and (4) benefit from opportunities that are taken for granted by persons who do not have disabilities (Cook et al., 2008).

Technology Interface

An area often overlooked by practitioners involves the interface (that part of the assistive technology with which the user interacts) between the person and the technological devices and equipment. An appropriate and usable fit may provide the difference as to whether an individual with a disability will continue to use the assistive technology or discontinue its use. The rate at which these people discontinue using technologies ranges from a low of 8% to a high of 75%. A national survey on assistive technology abandonment, conducted by Riemer-Reiss and Wacker (2000), found that 29% of devices and equipment obtained were later discarded. The number one reason cited for discontinuance was a lack of "relative advantage." This concept encompasses the effectiveness of the product, its reliability, and its ease of use, comfort, and enhancement of the user's performance. To decrease nonuse, the user needs to be involved throughout the process. The reality that many forms of assistive technology for people with disabilities are expensive needs to be carefully taken into account before recommending a device. This is not to say that most devices and equipment are costly, because many are inexpensive and easy to find.

The major goal of assistive technology is to enhance functional independence for individuals who have disabilities. The focus, therefore, is not on the disability but on the remaining functional capabilities that people use to accomplish their chosen objectives. Expectations a person has concerning technology are individualized and influenced by the disability and the consequences of that particular disability (Scherer, 2007). Through exploration of the individual's capabilities, functional limitations, and feelings about technological devices, practitioners can most effectively provide rehabilitation services. When assistive technology systems are considered for use, practitioners need to evaluate the various characteristics of the person that affect successful adaptation. With this in mind, practitioners can be well prepared to offer recommendations in the area of technology.

REFERENCES

Brodwin, M. G., Star, T., & Cardoso, E. (2007). Users of assistive technology: The human component. In A. E. Dell Orto &

P. W. Power (Eds.), *The psychological and social impact of illness and disability* (5th ed., pp. 505–519). New York: Springer.

Brodwin, M. G., Swett, E. A., Lane, F. J., & Star, T. (2005). Technology in rehabilitation counseling. In R. M. Parker, E. M. Szymanski, & J. B. Patterson (Eds.), *Rehabilitation counseling: Basics and beyond* (4th ed., pp. 363–393). Athens, GA: Pro-Ed.

Cook, A. M., Polgar, J. M., & Hussey, S. M. (2008). *Cook and Hussey's assistive technologies: Principles and practices.* St. Louis, MO: Mosby Elsevier.

Johnson, L., Beard, L. A., & Carpenter, L. B. (2007). *Assistive technology: Assistive technology for all students.* Upper Saddle River, NJ: Pearson/Prentice Hall.

Mann, W. C. (Ed.). (2005). *Smart technology for aging, disability, and independence: The state of the science.* Hoboken, NJ: Wiley-Interscience.

Reimer-Reiss, M. L., & Wacker, R. R. (2000). Factors associated with assistive technology discontinuance among individuals with disabilities. *Journal of Rehabilitation, 66,* 44–50.

Rubin, S. E., & Roessler, R. T. (2008). *Foundations of the vocational rehabilitation process* (6th ed.). Austin, TX: Pro-Ed.

Scherer, M. J. (2007). *Living in the state of stuck: How assistive technology impacts the lives of people with disabilities.* Brookline, MA: Brookline Books.

SUGGESTED READING

De Jonge, D., Scherer, M. J., & Rodger, S. (2007). *Assistive technology in the workplace.* St. Louis, MO: Mosby Elsevier.

Martin G. Brodwin
California State University, Los Angeles

See also: **Rehabilitation Psychology**

ASSOCIATION FOR BEHAVIOR ANALYSIS INTERNATIONAL

The Association for Behavior Analysis International (ABAI) is a nonproft membership organization with the mission to develop, enhance, and support the growth and vitality of behavior analysis through research, education, and practice. Behavior analysis is an approach to the science of behavior that emphasizes behaviorist epistemologies and methods. ABAI was founded in 1974 as a result of concerns that this approach to behavior science did not receive adequate consideration from existing professional audiences. Similar concerns gave rise, at around the same time, to the founding of two major behavioral journals, *Journal of the Experimental Analysis of Behavior* and *Journal of Applied Behavior Analysis.*

Although according to some accounts the rise of cognitive science marked the end of behavior analysis, since the mid-1990s ABAI has approximately doubled in size. In 2008, ABAI had more than 5,000 members internationally and was parent organization to more than 60 affiliate groups that encompassed 12,000 members in more than 40 nations. ABAI sponsors an annual convention that attracts more than 4,000 registrants to more than 1,400 professional sessions. ABAI also stages regular specialty conferences and a biennial international conference. At the state and regional level, ABAI's affiliate groups sponsor approximately 40 additional annual meetings devoted to the science and practice of behavior analysis.

ABAI's members include basic researchers, applied researchers, and practitioners. Members' scholarly efforts, at both the basic and applied level, tend to focus on topics in, or that intersect with, operant learning. Topics that receive the attention of special interest groups within the association include, but are not limited to, applied animal behavior, autism, gerontology, behavioral medicine, behavioral pharmacology and toxicology, gambling, clinical issues, crime and delinquency, development, education, health and fitness, neuroscience, rehabilitation, sex therapy, and speech pathology.

ABAI publishes three scholarly journals. Its flagship journal, *The Behavior Analyst,* features review, theoretical, and discussion articles on a variety of topics related to the science and profession of behavior analysis. *Behavior Analysis in Practice* focuses on practical and scientific issues relevant to disseminating behavioral interventions to various field settings. *The Analysis of Verbal Behavior* is a specialty publication that examines the relevance of behavior analysis to understanding language and communication.

The Society for the Advancement of Behavior Analysis, ABAI's sister organization, solicits charitable contributions that support various grant and fellowship programs for students and professionals in behavior analysis. ABAI also is a member of the Federation of Behavioral, Psychological, and Cognitive Sciences. ABAI is based in Kalamazoo, MI, and its web site is http://www.abainternational.org.

Thomas S. Critchfield
Illinois State University

ASSOCIATION FOR BEHAVIORAL AND COGNITIVE THERAPIES

Founded in 1966, the Association for Behavioral and Cognitive Therapies (ABCT) is an interdisciplinary organization comprised of researchers, psychologists, psychiatrists, physicians, social workers, nurses, and other mental health practitioners and students (located nationally and internationally) who adhere to, develop, evaluate, and disseminate behavioral and cognitive approaches to the assessment and treatment of behavioral and mental health problems.

Mission Statement

The core mission of ABCT is to advance a scientific approach to the understanding and amelioration of problems of the human condition. To that end, ABCT supports the investigation and application of behavioral, cognitive, and other evidence-based principles to assessment, prevention, and treatment. While primarily an interest group, ABCT is also active in (1) encouraging the development, study, and dissemination of scientific approaches to behavioral health; (2) promoting the utilization, expansion, and dissemination of behavioral, cognitive, and other empirically derived practices; and (3) facilitating professional development, interaction, and networking among members.

Professional Activities

ABCT conducts a variety of activities to support and disseminate the behavioral and cognitive therapies. The organization produces two quarterly journals, *Behavior Therapy* (research-based) and *Cognitive and Behavioral Practice* (treatment focused), as well as its house periodical, the *Behavior Therapist* (eight times per year). The association's convention is held annually in November. ABCT also produces fact sheets, an assessment series, and training and archival videotapes. The association maintains a web site (http://www.abct.org) with features such as a "Find-a-Therapist" search engine for consumers, among other resources for the public and the mainstream media. Members receive the benefits of an online clinical directory, more than 30 special interest groups, a list serve, a job bank, and an awards and recognition program. Other offerings available on the web site include sample course syllabi, listings of funding sources, and a broad range of offerings of interest to mental health researchers.

History

The organization was originally founded in 1966 under the name Association for Advancement of Behavioral Therapies (AABT; Franks, 1997). In opposition to the then prevalent models of psychosocial treatment, "The seminal significance of behavior therapy was the commitment to apply the principles and procedures of experimental psychology to clinical problems, to rigorously evaluate the effects of therapy, and to ensure that clinical practice was guided by such objective evaluation" (Wilson, 1997).

The first president of the association, Cyril Franks, founded the organization's flagship journal *Behavior Therapy* and was the first editor of the AABT *Newsletter*. The first annual meeting of AABT took place in 1967, in Washington, DC. An article in the November 1967 issue of the *Newsletter*, entitled "Behavior Therapy and Not Behavior Therapies" (Wilson & Evans, 1967) influenced the association's first name change to the Association for Advancement of Behavior Therapy because, as the authors argued, "the various techniques of behavior therapy all derive from learning theory and should not be misinterpreted as different kinds of behavior therapy ..." (quoted in Franks, 1987). This issue remains a debate in the field and within the organization, particularly with the emergence of the term "cognitive behavioral therapies," which resulted in yet another name change in 2005 to the Association for Behavioral and Cognitive Therapies.

AABT/ABCT remains at the forefront of the professional, legal, social, and ethical controversies and dissemination efforts that have accompanied the field's evolution. The 1970s was perhaps the most explosive period of development. As noted by Gerald Davison (AABT's eighth president), "A major contribution of behavior therapy has been a profound commitment to full description of procedures and careful evaluation of their effects" (Davison & Stuart, 1974, p. 3). ABCT continues to play an instrumental role in the dissemination of empirically supported treatments.

The training of mental health professionals also remains a significant priority for the association. With continued concerns over quality control and standardization of practice, ABCT plays an active role in supporting the education and training of behavior therapists. As an example, ABCT supported the development of the American Academy of Cognitive and Behavioral Psychology, a specialty board of the American Board of Professional Psychology that provides board certification in Cognitive and Behavioral Psychology.

The governance of ABCT consists of elected officials with voting privileges along with nonvoting, appointed members who serve in volunteer positions. The executive committee (EC) consists of the elected offices of president, immediate past-president, president-elect, and secretary/treasurer. In addition to the EC, elected representatives-at-large and appointed members including chairs of publications, conventions, and membership committees, and a finance committee headed by the secretary/treasurer, form the main leadership positions of ABCT. The organization maintains a central office in New York City. The current executive director of the ABCT is Mary Jane Eimer. For a wealth of historical specifics (governing bodies, lists of editors, past presidents, award winners, SIGs, and conventions from the past 40 years) see ABCT's 40th anniversary issue of *the Behavior Therapist* (Albano, 2006).

About Behavioral and Cognitive Therapies

Cognitive and behavioral therapists help people learn to actively cope with, confront, reformulate, and/or change the maladaptive cognitions, behaviors, and symptoms that limit their ability to function. Goal-oriented, time-limited, research-based, and focused on the present, the cognitive and behavioral approach is collaborative; it values feedback from the client, and encourages the client to play an active role in setting goals and the overall course and pace of treatment. Practitioners teach clients concrete skills and exercises—from breathing retraining to keeping thought records to behavioral activation—to practice at home and in sessions, with the overall goal of optimal functioning and the ability to engage in life fully.

Because CBT is based on broad principles of human learning and adaptation, it can be used to accomplish a wide variety of goals. CBT has been applied to issues ranging from depression and anxiety to the improvement of the quality of parenting, relationships, and personal effectiveness. A wealth of scientific study has documented the helpfulness of CBT for a wide range of concerns throughout the lifespan. Cognitive-behavioral treatments "have been subjected to more rigorous evaluation using RCTs [randomized controlled trials] than any of the other psychological therapies" (Wilson, 1997).

REFERENCES

Albano, A. M. (Guest Editor). (2006). Forty years of ABCT [Special issue]. *The Behavior Therapist, 29*(7).

Davison, G., & Stuart, R. (1974). Statement on behavior modification from the Association for Advancement of Behavior Therapy. *AABT Newsletter, 1*(2), 2–3.

Franks, C. M. (1987). Behavior Therapy and AABT: Personal recollections, conceptions, and misconceptions. *The Behavior Therapist, 10*, 171–174.

Franks, C. M. (1997). It was the best of times, it was the worst of times [Special issue: Thirty years of behavior therapy]. *Behavior Therapy, 28*, 389–396.

Wilson, G. T. (1997). Behavior therapy at century close. *Behavior Therapy, 28*, 449–457.

Wilson, G. T., & Evans, W. I. M. (1967). Behavior therapy and not the behavior therapies. *Newsletter of the Association for the Advancement of the Behavioral Therapies, 2*, 5–7.

STEPHANIE SCHWARTZ
Association for Behavioral and Cognitive Therapies,
New York, NY

GEORGE RONAN
Central Michigan University

ANNE MARIE ALBANO
Columbia University College of Physicians and Surgeons

ASSOCIATION FOR PSYCHOLOGICAL SCIENCE

The Association for Psychological Science (APS, http://www.psychologicalscience.org) is the leading international organization devoted solely to scientific psychology. Its mission is to promote, protect, and advance the interests of scientifically oriented psychology in research, application, and improvement of human welfare. APS has been a significant force in unifying and strengthening the science of psychology.

Overview

Established in 1988 as the American Psychological Society, APS was instantly embraced by psychology's scientific community, and its membership grew rapidly. By the end of its first year, APS opened an office in Washington DC and now has approximately 20,000 members from around the world. Members are engaged in scientific research or the application of scientifically grounded research spanning all areas of psychology. There are also student affiliates and organizational members. Distinguished contributions are recognized by Fellow status and awards. In 2006, the members of APS voted overwhelmingly in favor of changing the organization's name to Association for Psychological Science, to underscore both its scientific mission and its international scope. Today, APS is a vibrant and significant organization whose impact on national policy is well recognized and whose journals are among the best in the field of psychological science.

History

APS was created out of recognition that (1) the needs and interests of scientific and academic psychologists were distinct from those of members of the professional community primarily engaged in clinical practice, and (2) there was a strong need for an organization that would advance the interests of the discipline in ways that more specialized organizations were not intended to do. An interim group, the Assembly for Scientific and Applied Psychology (ASAP) had sought to reform the American Psychological Association from within, but their efforts were rejected by an APA membership-wide vote. APS then became the official embodiment of the ASAP reform effort, and the new organization was launched on August 12, 1988.

APS Publications

APS publishes four journals, all of which span the entire field of scientific psychology. *Psychological Science*, which is among the field's most highly ranked and prestigious journals, publishes authoritative articles of interest across all of scientific psychology's subdisciplines. *Current Directions in Psychological Science* offers concise invited reviews spanning all of scientific psychology and its applications. *Psychological Science in the Public Interest* is a unique journal that provides definitive assessments by panels of distinguished researchers on topics where psychological science has the potential to inform and improve the well-being of society. *Perspectives on Psychological Science* is a bimonthly journal that features longer integrative pieces and an eclectic mix of reviews, essays, and other formats. APS has taken the additional step of allowing much public access to these journals, including never charging copyright fees for use of any journal article in the classroom or other education use; this policy stems from APS's founding commitment to "give psychology away."

APS also publishes the following: the monthly *Observer*, featuring news and opinion pieces; a *Current Directions Readers* series in conjunction with Pearson Education; a book series "Modern Pioneers in Psychological Science" in conjunction with Psychology Press; and self-published books on the teaching of psychology.

Annual Convention

APS's annual meeting, generally held in late spring, showcases the best, cutting-edge research across the full range of scientific psychology. The program features presentations by distinguished researchers and educators in a variety of formats, including invited addresses and symposia, unique crosscutting theme programs, and submitted symposia and posters. The convention also includes workshops on specialized topics, and increasingly is the venue for meetings of researchers in emerging research areas.

APS Funds

The David and Carol Myers foundation has given $1,000,000 to APS for the creation of an endowment fund that aims "to enhance the teaching and public understanding of psychological science for students and the lay public, in the United States, Canada, and worldwide." This endowment led to the establishment of the APS Fund for Teaching and Public Understanding of Psychological Science, which supports a variety of initiatives, including a program of small grants for innovative teaching projects, the annual APS David Myers Lecture on the Science and Craft of Teaching Psychology, and a public affairs internship to develop a new generation of science writers in psychology. APS also administers the Fund for Advancing Psychological Science, which receives significant donations for the benefit of psychology; this fund is partnering with the Cattell Fund, which supports sabbatical extensions for outstanding scholars.

Achievement Awards

APS recognizes exceptional contributions to scientific psychology with two annual awards: the APS William James Fellow Award for significant intellectual contributions to the basic science of psychology, and the James McKeen Cattell Fellow Award for outstanding contributions to the area of applied psychological research.

Advocacy

APS is widely recognized as an active and effective leader in advancing the interests of basic and applied psychological research in the legislative arena and in the federal agencies that support these arenas of research. One of the primary reasons APS was established was to provide a distinct Washington presence for scientific psychology. From its earliest days, APS has shaped the federal science infrastructure to increase support for behavioral and social science research. APS was a driving force behind the creation of a separate directorate for these disciplines at the National Science Foundation and was organizer of several discipline-wide summit meetings that resulted in the development of research agendas in the broad areas of health and behavior, aging, violence, productivity, psychopathology, and basic research.

As a core constituent of the National Institutes of Health, APS has successfully advocated for greater support of behavioral science and research and training at NIH. APS has led the effort to establish an infrastructure for basic behavioral science research at NIH, resulting in strong Congressional encouragement for programs in this area. APS has also advocated for the translation of basic behavioral research into clinical applications, with particular emphasis on mental health treatment, health promotion, and disease prevention.

APS is also supporting an effort by the Academy of Psychological Clinical Science to develop an accreditation system for clinical science training programs, with the ultimate goal of ensuring that future clinicians deliver mental health treatments and clinical interventions.

Engaging the Public

As part of the Association's mission to increase public understanding and use of research findings in psychology, APS showcases the latest findings in psychological science directly through blogs, audio podcasts, and an interactive public information Web site, as well as through coverage in a wide variety of science and general news outlets. In one example of the scope and reach of these efforts, versions of Wray Herbert's blog, "We're Only Human," featuring research published in APS journals and other psychology journals, consistently are in the top 10 most popular items on *Newsweek.com*, which translates into millions of readers for each column. Herbert's blogs also appear in *Scientific American MIND*, with similarly positive impact.

By engaging the public with psychological science through modern technology and social networking, APS is restoring the image of psychology as a science-based discipline and providing people with interesting and important information in the areas of health, education, business, society, and virtually all other areas of human activity.

Detailed information on APS is available at http://www.psychologicalscience.org.

ALAN KRAUT
SARAH BROOKHART
*Association for Psychological
Science, Washington, D.C.*

ASSOCIATION OF PSYCHOLOGY POSTDOCTORAL AND INTERNSHIP CENTERS

Founded in 1968 and incorporated in 1982, the Association of Psychology Internship Centers (APIC) was originally constituted as an informal group of psychologists involved in internship training. These trainers banded together for the purpose of sharing information about mutual problems. Over time, the organization expanded its mission to include postdoctoral training as well as internship training, and in 1992 it was renamed the Association of Psychology Postdoctoral and Internship Centers (APPIC).

The overarching mission of APPIC is to enhance internship and postdoctoral training in professional psychology (Kaslow & Keilin, 2006) (http://www.appic.org). To accomplish this mission, APPIC (1) develops minimum standards for quality training programs at the internship and post-doctoral levels; (2) fosters the creation of new internship and postdoctoral programs; (3) devises selection policies and procedures to ensure a fair and orderly process of matching internship applicants and internship sites; (4) offers an online directory of internship and postdoctoral programs in professional psychology that fulfill APPIC membership criterion; (5) provides the APPIC Clearinghouse, which facilitates placing unmatched internship applicants to available positions; (6) encourages dialogue regarding salient selection and training issues for applicants, interns, and postdoctoral fellows; (7) facilitates, through both formal and informal mechanisms, management and resolution of challenges that emerge during selection or training of interns or fellows; (8) interacts with professional organizations and groups focused on doctoral and postdoctoral training and other aspects of professional psychology; (9) fosters the exchange of information between doctoral programs and agencies providing internship and/or postdoctoral training in professional psychology; (10) represents the views of internship and postdoctoral agencies to relevant groups and organizations in professional psychology; (11) shares with relevant stakeholders information on experiential training to members of the psychology community; and (12) encourages empirical investigations pertinent to psychology education, training, and supervision.

APPIC has a central office in Washington D.C. that includes a full-time executive director and two additional full-time staff. The APPIC board of directors includes seven psychologist members elected by APPIC-member internship and postdoctoral programs and one nonpsychologist public member chosen by the other board members. APPIC also has a number of committees focusing on membership at the internship and postdoctoral levels, the directory, universal application, and problem resolution.

APPIC is a membership and not an accrediting organization. To be accepted for APPIC membership, internship and postdoctoral residency programs must meet specific membership criteria related to the amount of training, the number and qualifications of supervisors, due process, and the payment of trainees. Membership is automatic for programs accredited by the American Psychological Association (APA) or the Canadian Psychological Association (CPA). To assist new and developing programs in meeting the criteria for membership, APPIC sponsors a mentoring program. In addition, doctoral-level academic programs in professional psychology may choose to become APPIC academic affiliates, a status that provides specific services to the program and its students.

APPIC offers a multitude of services. Beginning with the 1972–1973 training year, APPIC published a printed directory that contained descriptions of its member programs. In the summer of 2000, APPIC launched an online and more comprehensive version of the directory that can be updated at any time by training directors, and that permits users to search for programs using a variety of criteria. Effective 2008, the printed version of the directory will no longer be published. In the 1972–1973 directory, there were 90 internship programs listed and no postdoctoral programs. As of December 2007, in the 2008–2009 APPIC Directory Online, a total of 760 APPIC-member programs (650 internship and 110 postdoctoral residency programs) were listed.

Another major service is the facilitation of the internship placement process. For the 1972–1973 through 1998–1999 training years, APPIC conducted a standardized internship selection process, which utilized a uniform notification date to structure a previously unregulated process (Keilin, 1998). In 1999, APPIC instituted a computer-based internship matching program (called the APPIC Match) to place applicants into available positions (Keilin, 1998). Furthermore, APPIC has operated a postselection clearinghouse since 1986 to assist unplaced students and programs with unfilled positions.

In 1996, responding to concerns expressed by students about the variability among sites with regard to application formats and requirements, APPIC developed a standardized application form called the APPIC Application for Psychology Internships (AAPI). This form requires the applicant to describe his/her background and education, as well as his/her practicum experiences and hours. There also are five essay questions on the AAPI. APPIC is currently developing a Web-based centralized application service that will allow applicants to complete and submit their application materials via the internet.

APPIC offers formal and informal assistance with problem resolution. These mechanisms are available to address formal complaints, as well as to provide consultation and assistance to all constituency groups.

The provision of information is another key service offered by APPIC, and this occurs in multiple ways. The first APPIC newsletter was published in 1980, and it has served as a major communication method regarding internship and postdoctoral training issues for member and subscriber programs. The APPIC Web site (http://www.appic.org), along with a variety of e-mail news and discussion lists, also aids in the dissemination of information to member and subscriber programs, intern and postdoctoral applicants, interns, and postdoctoral residents. More in-depth sharing of information also occurs at biannual membership conferences. In addition, APPIC has played a major role in the collection and dissemination of data and perspectives related to the supply and demand imbalance (Baker, McCutcheon, & Keilin, 2007; Keilin, 2000; Keilin, Baker, McCutcheon, & Peranson, 2007), internship matching process (Keilin, 1998; Keilin, Thorn, Rodolfa, Constantine, & Kaslow, 2000), models of internship training (Rodolfa, Kaslow, Stewart, Keilin, & Baker, 2005), and competencies in professional psychology (Kaslow, 2004; Kaslow et al., 2004).

In 2007, in collaboration with the American Psychological Association (APA), APPIC launched a peer-reviewed journal, titled *Training and Education in Professional Psychology*, published quarterly. This journal is published quarterly and includes papers that advance professional psychology education and that pertain to such topics as supervision, training, and the process of education leading to licensure.

There are myriad ways in which APPIC has been involved actively in the larger national and multinational psychology education, training, and credentialing communities. APPIC has ongoing liaison relationships with doctoral, internship, and postdoctoral training councils, as well as credentialing organizations. APPIC participates actively in various interorganizational groups related to training, credentialing, and professional issues in psychology. APPIC is directly responsible for nominating candidates for three seats on the APA Commission on Accreditation of the APA. APPIC coordinates the nomination process for the two additional "other internship seats" and one additional "postdoctoral" seat in conjunction with the other internship and postdoctoral communities of interest.

APPIC has taken a leadership role in national and multinational psychology conferences. In 1992, APPIC hosted the National Conference on Postdoctoral Training in Professional Psychology in Ann Arbor (Belar et al., 1993), which helped to lay the groundwork for the accreditation of postdoctoral residencies. In response to the supply and demand crisis in psychology, related in part to the imbalance in the number of intern applicants and internship positions (Keilin, 2000; Keilin et al., 2000), in 1996 APPIC and APA cosponsored the National Working Conference on Supply and Demand: Training and Employment Opportunities in Professional Psychology (Pederson et al., 1997). This conference drew attention to the crisis and led to the development and implementation of multiple strategies designed to reduce this imbalance. In 2002, APPIC hosted, with multiple other sponsoring groups, Competencies 2002: Future Directions in Education and Credentialing in Professional Psychology in Scottsdale (Kaslow, 2004; Kaslow et al., 2004). This conference has resulted in greater attention by the profession to the identification and training of core competencies, as well as a competency-based focus on assessment and evaluation of interns and postdoctoral fellows.

APPIC remains committed to taking the lead in addressing many of the complex issues that pertain to internship and postdoctoral training. This includes, but is not limited to, the internship supply-demand imbalance, postdoctoral requirement and structures, quality control monitoring, competency-based approaches to education and training, training models, new roles and new settings, funding, and the conduct of meaningful research (Kaslow & Keilin, 2006; Stedman, 2007).

REFERENCES

Baker, J., McCutcheon, S., & Keilin, W. G. (2007). The internship supply-demand imbalance: The APPIC perspective. *Training and Education in Professional Psychology, 1*, 287–293.

Belar, C. D., Bieliauskas, L. A., Klepac, R. K., Larsen, K. G., Stigall, T. T., & Zimet, C. N. (1993). National Conference on Postdoctoral Training in Professional Psychology. *American Psychologist, 48*, 1284–1289.

Kaslow, N. J. (2004). Competencies in professional psychology. *American Psychologist, 59*, 774–781.

Kaslow, N. J., Borden, K. A., Collins, F. L., Forrest, L., Illfelder-Kaye, J., Nelson, P. D., Rallo, J. S., Vasquez, M. J. T., & Willmuth, M. E. (2004). Competencies Conference: Future directions in education and credentialing in professional psychology. *Journal of Clinical Psychology, 80*, 699–712.

Kaslow, N. J., & Keilin, W. G. (2006). Internship training in clinical psychology: Looking into our crystal ball. *Clinical Psychology: Science and Practice, 13*, 242–248.

Keilin, W. G. (1998). Internship selection 30 years later: An overview of the APPIC matching program. *Professional Psychology: Research and Practice, 29*, 599–603.

Keilin, W. G. (2000). Internship selection in 1999: Was the Association of Psychology Postdoctoral and Internship Centers' match a success? *Professional Psychology: Research and Practice, 31*, 281–287.

Keilin, W. G., Baker, J., McCutcheon, S., & Peranson, E. (2007). A growing bottleneck: The supply-demand imbalance in 2007 and its impact on psychology training. *Training and Education in Professional Psychology, 1*, 229–237.

Keilin, W. G., Thorn, B. E., Rodolfa, E. R., Constantine, M. G., & Kaslow, N. (2000). Examining the balance of internship supply and demand: 1999 Association of Psychology Postdoctoral and Internship Centers' Match implications. *Professional Psychology: Research and Practice, 31*, 288–294.

Pederson, S. L., DePiano, F., Kaslow, N. J., Klepac, R. K., Hargrove, D. S., & Vasquez, M. (1997). *Proceedings from the National Working Conference on Supply and Demand: Training and Employment Opportunities in Professional Psychology.* Paper presented at the National Working Conference on Supply and Demand: Training and Employment Opportunities in Professional Psychology, Orlando, Florida.

Rodolfa, E. R., Kaslow, N. J., Stewart, A. E., Keilin, W. G., & Baker, J. (2005). Internship training: Do models really matter? *Professional Psychology: Research and Practice, 36*, 25–31.

Stedman, J. M. (2007). What we know about predoctoral internship training: A 10-year update. *Training and Education in Professional Psychology, 1*, 74–88.

SUGGESTED READINGS

Kaslow, N. J., & Keilin, W. G. (2006). Internship training in clinical psychology: Looking into our crystal ball. *Clinical Psychology: Science and Practice, 13*, 242–248.

Kaslow, N. J., & Keilin, W. G. (in press). Postdoctoral education and training in professional psychology. In E. Altmaier and B. D. Johnson (Eds.), *Encyclopedia of counseling.*

Stedman, J. M. (2007). What we know about predoctoral internship training: A 10-year update. *Training and Education in Professional Psychology, 1*, 74–88.

NADINE J. KASLOW
Emory University School of Medicine

W. GREGORY KEILIN
University of Texas at Austin

JEANETTE HSU
Veterans Affairs Palo Alto Health Care System

See also: **Clinical Psychology; Clinical Psychology, Graduate Training in**

ASTHMA

Asthma is characterized by inflammation of the airways, leading to hyperresponsiveness and/or and obstruction, which result in cough, shortness of breath, wheezing, and other clinical symptoms. Asthma often begins in childhood and is the most common chronic illness of childhood. Host (e.g., genetic) and environmental (e.g., allergens, stress) factors appear to interact to produce altered immune system responses that result in inflammation. Asthma is more prevalent in children (8.5%) than in adults (6.7%), females than males, African Americans than whites, those of Puerto Rican than Mexican origin among Hispanics, and among impoverished persons versus those at or above the federal poverty level (Moorman et al., 2007).

Psychological Aspects

The role of stress in the initiation, persistence, and exacerbations of asthma has long been recognized. As such, asthma may be considered a psychosomatic illness: a physical disorder with demonstrable perturbation in physical function and structure that is associated with psychological factors. A stressful early family environment, perhaps especially maternal distress, seems to contribute to the onset of childhood asthma. While the pathophysiology of stress and asthma is complex, there are several pathways through which stress alters immune function, which may include inflammatory processes in the airways, resulting in asthma symptoms. Strong emotions and/or stress may be among patients' triggers for asthma, or impair appropriate asthma self-management.

Asthma warrants more attention from behavioral scientists (see Lehrer, Feldman, Giardino, Song, & Schmaling, 2002, for a review of psychological aspects of asthma). Successful asthma self-management depends on patients who are educated and engaged in their care. Every patient with asthma should have a self-management plan. In partnership with their healthcare providers, patients with asthma should identify personal triggers for asthma exacerbations (such as strong emotions, allergens) and learn how to control them or mitigate their effects; learn their typical patterns of symptoms; and learn how to recognize the need for additional treatment (e.g., when to self-administer more or different medications). However, a minority (less than 40%) of adults and children with asthma reported that they have ever had an asthma management plan (King & Rudd, 2007). Improved collaborations between patients (and for children with asthma, family members, and others with significant roles in children's lives such as teachers) and providers that emphasize education, communication, and empowerment, could lead to better management and less impairment secondary to asthma.

The self-monitoring and self-management of asthma present a number of potential psychological challenges including cognitive-perceptual, behavioral, and interpersonal challenges. Patients with asthma vary in their ability or willingness to monitor and interpret appropriate bodily sensations that might herald airway changes because of insensitivity to these sensations or due to denial, minimization, or rejection of the sensations (for example, because of not wanting to take more medications). In the most serious cases, underresponding to asthma symptoms and subsequent delays in seeking treatment can be fatal. There are a variety of feedback methods that can increase patients' abilities to recognize airways changes. For example, a peak-flow meter is a self-monitoring device that many patients with asthma use to check and monitor their breathing. Medication adherence is a challenge: adherence to an inflexible medication regimen should be easier to establish because of the ability to develop routine habits and prompts; an asthma self-management plan usually includes contingent and therefore changing medication use.

Management

The National Heart, Lung, and Blood Institute (NHLBI) of the National Institutes of Health has developed and disseminated comprehensive guidelines for the diagnosis and management of asthma since 1991 when the first Expert Panel Report (EPR) was published. The second EPR was published in 1997, and an update to the second EPR was published in 2002. The third and most recent EPR, EPR-3, was published in 2007 (NHLBI, 2007). The goals of asthma management are to help patients avoid diminution in quality of life or functional limitations because of asthma.

Health services researchers consider asthma to be an ambulatory care sensitive condition—a condition that should be managed on an outpatient basis and for which hospitalizations should be preventable. Hospitalizations for asthma may reflect poor access to primary care and/or the failure of the asthma self-management plan. As evidence of the former, nearly 30% of healthcare visits for asthma occurred in emergency departments among patients without health insurance whereas only 6% of healthcare visits for asthma occurred in emergency departments for patients with private health insurance (CDC, 2003). Regarding the latter, Flores, Abreu, Chaisson, & Sun (2003) found that providers tended to attribute avoidable hospitalizations for asthma among children to parent or patient self-management failures whereas parents tend to attribute them to provider failures. Increased access to primary care and better communication among providers, patients, and significant others should result in better disease management, few life disruptions, and significantly decreased healthcare costs.

The EPR-3 presented emerging evidence of comorbid conditions that complicate or interfere with asthma management; some of these conditions—such as depression and obesity—also have strong behavioral components. There is some evidence that weight reduction among obese persons with asthma is associated with less perceived breathing difficulty and improved pulmonary function based on physiological measures. Comorbid depression seems to be more strongly associated with patient perceptions of more asthma symptoms and poorer asthma self-management, such as medication adherence, than with objective measures of pulmonary function. Depression treatment may improve asthma medication adherence (including the treatment of depression for depressed mothers who have the primary responsibility to manage their children's asthma) and patients' perceptions of asthma symptoms.

Attending to the behavioral and perceptual issues associated with asthma is a best practice (per the EPR-3) and some studies have made psychological interventions the centerpiece rather than an adjuvant intervention. Written emotional expression and relaxation training are examples of such interventions (Lehrer et al., 2002; NHLBI, 2007). There is limited evidence regarding their efficacy: positive effects tend to be found for patients' perceptions of asthma symptoms, but there is less evidence for change in objective measures of pulmonary function. Further research to establish the efficacy of primary or adjuvant psychological interventions is indicated.

REFERENCES

CDC. Health-care visits for asthma, by medical setting and health-insurance status—United States, 2003. *Morbidity and Mortality Weekly Reports, 55*(14), 405.

Flores, G., Abreu, M., Chaisson, C. E., & Sun, D. (2003). Keeping children out of hospitals: Parents' and physicians' perspectives on how pediatric hospitalizations for ambulatory care sensitive conditions can be avoided. *Pediatrics, 112*(5), 1021–1030.

King, M. E., & Rudd, R. A. (2007). Asthma self-management education among youths and adults—United States, 2003. *Morbidity and Mortality Weekly Reports, 56*(35), 912–915.

Lehrer, P., Feldman, J., Giardino, N., Song, H. S., & Schmaling, K. (2002). Psychological aspects of asthma. *Journal of Consulting and Clinical Psychology, 70*(3), 691–711.

Moorman, J. E., Rudd, R. A., Johnson, C. A., King, M., Minor, P., Bailey, C., et al. National surveillance for asthma—United States, 1980–2004. (2007). *Morbidity and Mortality Weekly Reports, 56*(SS08), 1–14,18–54.

National Heart, Lung, and Blood Institute. (2007). Expert Panel Report 3: Guidelines for the diagnosis and management of asthma. Downloaded from http://www.nhlbi.nih.gov/guidelines/asthma/asthgdln.htm on March 9, 2008.

KAREN B. SCHMALING
University of North Carolina at Charlotte

See also: **Stress Consequences**

ATHLETIC COACHING

At all levels of sport, coaches function as educators, leaders, and strategists. In these roles, they can strongly influence the performance and personal development of the athletes with whom they come in contact. In the United States alone, an estimated 41 million children participate in nonschool programs, and another 6 to 7 million in interscholastic sports. Others participate at more elite levels, in intercollegiate, or professional sports. The teaching techniques coaches employ, the goal priorities they establish, the values they exhibit and reinforce, and the relationships they form with athletes in this important domain of athletic involvement have all been topics that have attracted the attention of psychological researchers.

One important area of research is coaching instructional techniques. Behavioral researchers have observed and analyzed the techniques employed by outstanding coaches at all levels of competition. They have found that such coaches tend to use approaches that have proven successful in enhancing performance in other performance domains, such as education and business. Systematic goal setting has proven to be a powerful technique for positive skill development (Gould, 2006). Coaches who employ this technique analyze the task requirements and current skills of the athlete, set specific behavioral (not outcome) goals, develop individualized action plans for developing the needed skills, set timelines for attainment, and closely monitor the targeted behaviors. This approach has proven effective from the youth to the professional levels.

Other research has shown that behavioral feedback and the use of positive reinforcement enhances the development of sport skills. In general, a "positive approach" to strengthening desired behaviors through encouragement, sound technical instruction, and positive reinforcement of desired behaviors is preferred by athletes to a negative one featuring criticism, punishment, and an emphasis on avoiding mistakes (Smith, Smoll, & Christensen, 1996). Athletes expect coaches to exert control over the situation and to establish and enforce discipline, but they prefer that it occur within the context of a basically positive coach-athlete relationship.

Increased research attention has been directed toward youth sports in recent years (Conroy & Coatsworth, 2006). Behavioral coding techniques have been developed, enabling researchers to observe coaches during practices and games, code their responses to particular classes of situations (e.g., positive and negative athlete behaviors, particular game situations), and generate behavioral profiles of the coaches based on thousands of their behaviors (Smith et al., 1996). They can also obtain athletes' and coaches' ratings of how often the coach engaged in the various behaviors that were coded. Such research has shown that even child athletes are more accurate perceivers of coaching behaviors than the coaches are, indicating that most coaches have limited awareness of their behavior.

Research has also shown that coaching behaviors are far more strongly related to athletes' attitudes toward the coach than are won-lost records. Although winning becomes more important in adolescence than at earlier ages, behaviors continue to be more powerful predictors of athletes' evaluations of coaches. In line with the "positive approach" described above, coaches who create a supportive environment through their use of encouragement, technical instruction, positive reinforcement of desired athlete behaviors (including compliance with team rules), and avoidance of punitive behaviors are best liked by athletes (Smith & Smoll, 1997). On teams coached by positive coaches, athletes also like their teammates more, possibly because of the socially supportive atmosphere encouraged and modeled by the coach.

Such findings have inspired a number of coach training programs designed to help coaches create an athletic environment that is enjoyable and fosters positive psychosocial outcomes (Conroy & Coatsworth, 2006; Smoll & Smith, 2006). Such programs give coaches specific behavioral guidelines, show them how to engage in the positive behaviors and find alternatives for punitive ones, and teach coaches how to monitor their own behavior so as to make them more self-aware.

In research assessing the effects of such training, behavioral observations and athletes' ratings of their coaches' behaviors indicated that, compared with untrained coaches, trained coaches behaved in a more supportive and encouraging manner. Although they were not more successful at a won-lost level, the trained coaches were evaluated more positively by their athletes and their athletes showed significant increases in self-esteem and decreases in performance anxiety by the end of the season. They also showed a lower rate of dropping out of sports the following season. Athletes who played for trained coaches showed only a 6% attrition rate compared with a 27% dropout rate among athletes who played for untrained coaches (Smith & Smoll, 1997). The latter finding is important because there is considerable evidence that children and adolescents who remain involved in sports are less likely to engage in delinquent and other self-defeating behaviors.

An important current focus of research is the "motivational climate" created by coaches. Analyses of achievement-related goals in children and adults have identified two important goal orientations, known as mastery and ego orientation. Mastery-oriented people feel successful and competent when they have learned something new, witnessed skill improvement in themselves, mastered the task at hand, or given their best effort. Their achievement strivings are described as self-referenced because they compare their effort and performance with their own internal standards.

In contrast, ego-oriented people's feelings of competence are other-referenced, relying more on comparison with others. They feel successful when they show their superiority over others or avoid feeling inferior to others. Although both orientations can lead to successful performance, research in both educational and sport settings indicate that mastery-oriented people are more likely to persist in the face of adversity or failure, place more emphasis on effort than outcome compared with ego-oriented individuals, and select more challenging goals. They can feel successful even when the desired outcome has not been attained if they believe that they gave maximum effort and learned important things from the experience. Ego-oriented individuals are more likely to experience distress and eventually to avoid settings in which they do not win out over others.

Most people have both task and ego orientations to varying degrees. The situational context or motivational climate that exists in achievement settings can differ in the extent to which task- or ego-involving goals are emphasized. A mastery-oriented motivational climate supports and strengthens task orientation, whereas an ego-oriented climate fosters other-referenced competitiveness with others. Much educational research has shown that mastery-oriented climates promote better academic performance and intrinsic motivation to learn, lower levels of fear of failure, and a positive orientation toward mastery, and the same is being found within sports (Duda & Balaguer, 2007).

These research results are now being applied within the athletic domain by coaches at all levels of sport. The principle is that if athletes are thoroughly oriented toward becoming as proficient as possible ("their" best rather than "the" best), are not shackled by fear of failure, and are prepared and well-coached, winning will take care of itself within the limits of their ability. Research shows that mastery-oriented sport environments provide more enjoyable and fulfilling settings for the majority of athletes. One recent study revealed that the extent to which coaches created a mastery environment was 10 times more important than was the team's won-lost record in accounting for variations in young athletes' liking for their coaches (Cumming, Smoll, Smith, & Grossbard, 2007).

Other research has shown that training coaches to create a mastery climate has notable positive effects on young athletes. In response to a decreased emphasis on winning, such athletes exhibited significant decreases in performance anxiety over the course of the season, whereas anxiety increased in a control condition whose coaches were not trained as competitive pressures increased over the course of the season (Smith, Smoll, & Cumming, 2007). Athletes also showed salutary changes in their achievement goal orientations, moving toward a mastery orientation and defining success in terms of personal improvement and effort rather than winning or besting others (Smoll, Smith, & Cumming, 2007). More importantly, the lessons learned in mastery environments may have salutary carryover to other achievement domains as well. In the latter study, children who played for the trained coaches exhibited stronger mastery achievement orientation in school as well by the end of the athletic season.

Recent years have witnessed an increasing awareness of the fact that coaches must not only be skilled teachers of technical skills and strategies, but also must attend to social-psychological aspects of the athletic environment. This awareness has been reflected in a burgeoning literature on psychological principles in peak performance, team cohesion, and athletes' sport commitment and enjoyment, as well as psychologically oriented coach training programs.

REFERENCES

Conroy, D. E., & Coatsworth, J. D. (2006). Coach training as a strategy for promoting youth social development. *The Sport Psychologist, 20,* 128–144.

Cumming, S. P., Smoll, F. L., Smith, R. E., & Grossbard, J. R. (2007). Is winning everything? The relative contributions of motivational climate and won-lost percentage in youth sports. *Journal of Applied Sport Psychology, 19,* 322–336.

Duda, J. L., & Balaguer, I. (2007). Coach-created motivational climate. In S. Jowett & D. Lavalee (Eds.), *Social psychology in sport* (pp. 117–130). Champaign, IL: Human Kinetics.

Gould, D. M. (2006). Goal-setting for peak performance. In J. M. Williams (Ed.), *Applied sport psychology: Personal growth to peak performance* (5th ed., pp. 240–259). Boston: McGraw-Hill.

Smith, R. E., & Smoll, F. L. (1997). Coaching the coaches: Youth sports as a scientific and applied behavioral setting. *Current Directions in Psychological Science, 6,* 16–21.

Smith, R. E., Smoll, F. L., & Christensen, D. S. (1996). Behavioral assessment and interventions in youth sports. *Behavior Modification, 20,* 3–44.

Smith, R. E., Smoll, F. L., & Cumming, S. P. (2007). Effects of a motivational climate intervention for coaches on children's sport performance anxiety. *Journal of Sport & Exercise Psychology, 29,* 39–59.

Smoll, F. L., & Smith, R. E. (2006). Development and implementation of coach-training programs: Cognitive-behavioral principles and techniques. In J. M. Williams (Ed.), *Applied sport psychology: Personal growth to peak performance* (5th ed., pp. 458–480). Boston: McGraw-Hill.

Smoll, F. L., Smith, R. E., & Cumming, S. P. (2007). Effects of a psychoeducational intervention for coaches on changes in child athletes' achievement goal orientations. *Journal of Clinical Sport Psychology, 1,* 23–46.

RONALD E. SMITH
FRANK L. SMOLL
University of Washington

See also: **Sport Performance Interventions; Sport Psychology**

ATTACHMENT AND BONDING

"Attachment and bonding" is a phrase that one now naturally thinks of in describing the early intimate interactions between parent and infant. "Attachment" is the more scientific term that originally referred to an infant's relationship with his or her parent. As attachment theory and research developed, it became applied to individuals of all ages when describing relationships in which they turn to another for safety and the felt-sense of safety. "Bonding" or "affectional bonds" is taken to refer to an ongoing relationship with a specific person that is emotionally meaningful and creates a desire to maintain mutual contact. Using the terms in this manner, a mother would not be considered to be "attached" to her infant, because she would not turn to her infant for safety. Seeking safety from the other may or may not be a feature in an "affectional bond," whereas it is always a central component of an attachment relationship. In the most important book in the attachment field, *Handbook of Attachment* (Cassidy & Shaver, 1999), "bonding" is not even listed in the subject index.

Attachment theory originated through the joint work of John Bowlby (1969), a British psychiatrist, and Mary Ainsworth, an American psychologist, in the 1950s and 1960s. Over the past 50 years, buttressed by a very large body of research, it has emerged as the dominant theory of child development. It is accepted as a central organizing principle of emotional, social, motivational, and cognitive development, not only in childhood, but throughout life. Attachment relationships become organized into comprehensive patterns of interactions that are quite comparable to, and influential in, the development of the personality. These attachment patterns, when functioning well (i.e., characterized by security), demonstrate a persistent and repetitive quality, but they are not rigid. The patterns are able to change over time in response to new attachment relationships. Thus, a boy's attachment characteristics may develop one way in response to his relationship with his parents and evolve in different directions in relationship to teachers, coaches, mentors, therapists, and partners. Attachment patterns develop—and remain important—from infancy and childhood to adulthood and old age (Grossmann, Grossmann, & Waters, 2005).

The experience of safety, the core of attachment relationships, is now seen as a crucial feature in the optimal functioning of the brain (Schore, 2001). Within conditions of safety, the entire brain functions in a unified and coherent manner to best understand the immediate situation and to respond in the best possible manner. For young children, their attachment figures become the focus of their early learning about themselves and the world. Their emerging experience of self and other and of objects and events is organized and deepened through the attuned and "meaning-making" relationship that they have with their attachment figures (Siegel, 2001).

The most common attachment classification (close to two thirds of the population) is known as "secure." Children (and adults, in which case the classification is called "autonomous") who manifest this pattern have a relationship with their attachment figure that is characterized by open and inclusive communications. When under stress, these children readily turn to their attachment figures for safety, including comfort and support. Once they feel safe, they are then free to explore the world, often with a good degree of interest and independence. Securely attached children are most definitely not "dependent" children. They are able to blend very adaptively the need to rely on an adult when necessary and to rely on self when able to do so. The securely attached—of all the classifications—are the most able to successfully combine their own need for autonomy with intimate relationships. They are aware of their own interests and values as well as those of others. They are able to address and understand differences and they have the skills needed to resolve conflicts (Sroufe, Egeland, Carlson, & Collins, 2005).

Parents of securely attached children are likely to be available, sensitive, and responsive to their child's needs along with his or her inner life of thoughts, feelings, and wishes. They are also willing and able to repair any breaks in the relationship when necessary, providing the child with a crucial sense of safety that the relationship will exist in spite of separations or conflicts. Most importantly, the parents of such children manifest attachment security in their own relationships. In fact, measures of their own attachment classification, which are based on their telling the story of their own attachment histories, are better predictors of their child's attachment classification than are their specific interactions with their child (Hesse, 1999).

"Avoidant" and "ambivalent" are the two other organized attachment patterns. In the former, the individual tends to minimize the importance of his attachment relationship while attempting, instead, to "go it alone." The "avoidant" individual tends to downplay the importance of both emotions and relationships in his life and adopts a more detached, self-reliant, and rational view of his situation. The "ambivalent" individual tends to overemphasize the importance of her relationships with attachment figures and downplay her own perspective and independence. She is likely to become immersed in the emotional immediacy of situations rather than taking a more distant and long-term perspective. This individual often compulsively, but unsatisfactorily, focuses on attachment relationships at the expense of developing her independence and more reflective skills.

There is a fourth attachment classification that does not represent an organized pattern of interactions and perceptions as do the other three. This classification is known as "disorganized" (or "unresolved" for the adult), which reflects the individual's lack of a predictable response to relationships, especially in situations of stress. Because of its unpredictable features, persons with these features were originally considered to fall in a "cannot classify" category. Children with this classification tend to attempt to control all events in their lives. They are at risk for problems of externalization (attention deficit/hyperactivity, oppositional-defiance, aggressive outbursts) as well as problems of internalization (anxiety, depression, dissociation) (Lyons-Ruth & Jacobvitz, 1999). Parents of these children tend to have difficulty in maintaining their own sense of safety when their child's attachment needs are the most active. The parents tend to become frightening to the child or show signs of being frightened by their child in those circumstances. In worst cases, they are at risk to abusing and/or neglecting their child.

Although attachment security is seen to be positively correlated to many important features of childhood development, one might emphasize now two central features. First, children with attachment security tend to manifest a high level of emotional development. They are likely to be quite able to identify, express, and regulate the full range of their emotional experiences. In doing so, they tend to be proficient in maintaining ongoing "affectional bonds" with family and friends and to have excellent social skills in most situations. Second, individuals with attachment security tend to be able to reflect on their experiences and to be aware of the features of their own inner lives as well as the inner lives of others. They are proficient at considering other perspectives and integrating their relationships with others into their own developing sense of organized values and interests. Being proficient in both their emotional and reflective abilities, they tend to be able to determine the "best possible" response in a given situation and then to respond in a flexible, adaptive, manner.

Although attachment theory is now firmly established in academic centers studying human development, it is only beginning to present applications of this theory and related research in the many fields where it most certainly is relevant. These include maternal care and childbirth, early childhood development, day care and preschool programs, education, social services, mental health and psychotherapy, health, parenting and family studies, child abuse and neglect, trauma and its treatment, life cycle, and aging.

REFERENCES

Bowlby, J. (1969). *Attachment and loss, Vol. 1: Attachment*. New York: Basic Books.

Cassidy, J., & Shaver, P. R. (Eds.). (1999). *Handbook of attachment*. New York: Guilford Press.

Grossman, K. E., Grossmann, K., & Waters, E. (Eds.). (2005). *Attachment from infancy to adulthood*. New York: Guilford Press.

Hesse, E. (1999). The adult attachment interview: Historical and current perspectives. In J. Cassidy & P. Shaver (Eds.), *Handbook of attachment*. New York: Guilford Press.

Lyons-Ruth, K., & Jacobvitz, D. (1999). Attachment disorganization: Unresolved loss, relational violence, and lapses in behavioral and attentional strategies. In J. Cassidy & P. Shaver (Eds,), *Handbook of attachment*. New York: Guilford Press.

Schore, A. N. (2001). Effects of a secure attachment on right brain development, affect regulation, and infant mental health. *Infant Mental Health Journal, 22*, 7–67.

Siegel, D. J. (2001). Toward an interpersonal neurobiology of the developing mind: Attachment relationships, "mindsight," and neural integration. *Infant Mental Health Journal, 22*, 67–94.

Sroufe, L. A., Egeland, B., Carlson, E., & Collins, W. A. (2005). *The development of the person*. New York: Guilford Press.

SUGGESTED READINGS

Bowlby, J. (1988). *A secure base*. New York: Basic Books.

Goldberg, S. (2000). *Attachment and development*. New York: Oxford University Press.

Siegel, D. J. (1999). *The developing mind*. New York: Guilford Press.

DANIEL H. HUGHES
Lebanon, PA

See also: **Attachment Styles; Attachment Theory**

ATTACHMENT DISORDERS

Attachment describes the human infant's tendency to seek comfort, support, nurturance, and protection from a relatively small number of preferred caregivers or attachment figures. The capacity to form an attachment is not present at birth, but develops over time. Although infants in the first 6 months are able to distinguish among different interactive partners, they do not express an obvious preference for one caregiver over another. All of this changes at around 7 to 9 months of age. At that point, infants begin to exhibit stranger wariness and separation protest, two behaviors that herald the onset of focused attachment. Stranger wariness varies from mild reticence to outright distress, but it contrasts with the infant's comfort with an attachment figure, from whom the infant seeks comfort, support, nurturance, and protection. Separation protest describes the infant's reaction to actual or anticipated separation from an attachment figure. After these two behaviors appear, infants are attached to one or more caregivers. Once infants have developed the cognitive capacity to exhibit separation protest and stranger wariness, they may form new attachments with any caregivers with whom they have significant interactive experiences.

Under species typical rearing conditions, the infant forms a small number of selective attachments to caregiving adults, based on having regular interactions with them. Although older children can sustain attachment relationships over time and space, in the first three years of life or so the young child needs actual interaction with caregivers in order to become attached to them. Behaviors of the young child that promote physical proximity to the caregiver are called attachment behaviors and are readily observed, especially when the child is frightened, frustrated, tired, or ill. These states tend to diminish the child's exploration of the physical or social world and intensify the child's seeking proximity from an attachment figure. Strangers, or even adults with whom the child is familiar and comfortable, cannot provide the child with needed comfort unless the child has formed an attachment to them.

For infants raised in species atypical rearing conditions, disturbed and developmentally inappropriate ways of relating may evolve. Examples of atypical rearing conditions include institutions (i.e., orphanages), frequent changes of caregivers (as sometimes happens in foster care), neglectful or abusive caregiving, losing a caregiver suddenly, and being raised by an inappropriately responsive or unresponsive caregiver.

The clinical entity describing serious attachment abnormalities is called reactive attachment disorder (RAD). RAD is rare, occurring only in conditions of severe neglect. According to the *Diagnostic and Statistical Manual of Mental Disorders* (DSM IV-TR; American Psychiatric Association [APA], 2000), RAD is a disorder in which specific behavioral abnormalities result from pathogenic care and appear before the age of five years. DSM IV-TR defines two subtypes of RAD, inhibited and disinhibited.

Inhibited RAD is characterized by "persistent failure to initiate or respond in a developmentally appropriate fashion to most social interactions as manifest by excessively inhibited, hypervigilant, or highly ambivalent and contradictory responses" (APA, 2000, p. 130). Children with this subtype have been severely neglected and become emotionally withdrawn and unresponsive, exhibit few positive expressions of emotion, and do not seek comfort when distressed (Zeanah & Smyke, 2008).

Disinhibited RAD is characterized by "indiscriminate sociability with marked inability to exhibit appropriate selective attachments" (APA, 2000, p. 130). Children with this RAD subtype also have been severely neglected, but they look quite different from children with the emotionally withdrawn/inhibited type. They express positive emotions, interact readily, are socially responsive, and may even seek comfort when distressed. Nevertheless, they are not selective in expressing these behaviors. What characterizes their behavior is lacking the expected reticence around strangers, approaching them without hesitation, and being willing to go off with them. They may lose track of their caregivers in public, wander away without concern, and seem socially comfortable with unfamiliar adults (Zeanah & Smyke, 2008).

Longitudinal data about the course of attachment disorders are limited. The criteria define a disorder of early childhood. At this time, there is no agreed upon method for diagnosing attachment disorders in older children or adults, although indiscriminate behavior has been described in adolescents (O'Connor & Zeanah, 2003).

Although some of the signs and symptoms of RAD are similar to those of other disorders, the diagnosis is clear because of its distinctive clinical subtypes and the history of neglect. The social impulsivity in attention-deficit-hyperactivity disorder, the unresponsiveness in pervasive developmental disorders and the marked inhibition in some anxiety disorders may pose diagnostic challenges. Other clinical problems associated with severe neglect, such as language and cognitive delays, may co-occur and sometimes complicate the clinical picture. In order to diagnose RAD, the American Academy of Child and Adolescent Psychiatry Practice Parameters for RAD (AACAP, 2005) recommend observing the child serially with all involved caregivers and with an unfamiliar adult, in addition to obtaining a thorough history of early caregiving environments from collateral sources.

The first priority of treatment is to establish a safe and stable caregiving environment with a warm and consistent caregiver. Treatment of RAD begins with addressing the relationship between the primary caregiver and child. Treatment may be conducted with the caregiver or with the caregiver and child, but it is essential for the relationship between the child and a primary caregiving adult to be the focus. The chief goal of the treatment is helping the child learn through repeated interactions with the adult caregiver and that the caregiver can be relied on to provide comfort, support, nurturance, and protection. Associated problems, such as cognitive and language delays, aggression, and posttraumatic symptoms, should also be addressed with appropriate therapeutic interventions.

The emotionally withdrawn/inhibited subtype of RAD seems to be especially responsive to introduction of a caring adult, although it is less clear whether the child remains at risk for subsequent interpersonal difficulties. The indiscriminate/disinhibited type of RAD, on the other hand, is less responsive to caregiving, particularly in children who experience neglect after they reach the age of 2 years. Children with the indiscriminate/disinhibited type of RAD do appear to be at increased risk for peer relational problems in adolescence (Zeanah & Smyke, 2008).

REFERENCE

AACAP Work Group on Quality Issues (N. W. Boris and C. H. Zeanah, principal authors) (2005). Practice parameters for the assessment and treatment of children and adolescents with reactive attachment disorder of infancy and early childhood. *Journal of the American Academy of Child and Adolescent Psychiatry*, *44*(11), 1206–1219.

American Psychiatric Association (2000). Diagnostic and statistical manual of mental disorders (4th ed., text rev.). Washington, DC: Author.

O'Connor, T., & Zeanah, C. H. (2003). Attachment disorders: Assessment strategies and treatment approaches. *Attachment and Human Development, 5*, 223–244.

Zeanah, C. H., & Smyke, A. T. (2008). Attachment disorders in family and social context. *Infant Mental Health Journal, 29*, 219–233.

SUGGESTED READINGS

Cassidy, J., & Shaver, P., (Eds). (2008) *Handbook of attachment: Theory, research, and clinical applications*, 2nd edition. New York: Guilford Press.

Chaffin, M., Hanson, R., Saunders, B., Nichols, T., Barnett, D., Zeanah, C., et al. (2006). Report of the APSAC task force on attachment therapy, reactive attachment disorder, and attachment problems. *Child Maltreatment, 11*, 76–89.

Zeanah, C. H., Keyes, A., & Settles, L. (2003). Attachment relationship experiences and child psychopathology. *Annals of the New York Academy of Sciences, 1008*, 1–9.

Zeanah, C. H., & Smyke, A. T. (2008). Attachment disorders and severe deprivation. In M. Rutter, D. Bishop, D. Pine, S. Scott, J. Stevenson, E. Taylor, et al. (Eds.), Rutter's *Child and Adolescent Psychiatry* (pp. 906–915). London: Blackwell.

CAROLINE CAMPION
CHARLES H. ZEANAH
Tulane University School of Medicine

See also: **Attachment Theory; Separation Anxiety Disorder**

ATTACHMENT STYLES

Unraveling the nature of the bonds that form between people and identifying the sources of variation in the relational characteristics observed across groups of people are prominent topics in the social sciences. One approach to explaining and predicting the variations in close personal relationships is to classify individuals based on consistent patterns of interpersonal behavior and emotional reactions to relational partners. A variety of typologies based on Bowlby's (1969) attachment theory have been proposed for classifying interpersonal tendencies according to prototypical categories known as attachment styles. Attachment styles have been classified categorically on the basis of observed behavioral differences in response to controlled situations, by inference from responses to structured interviews, and from scores derived from responses to multiple-choice questionnaires.

Dimensions of attachment that can be scored along a continuum, such as relational anxiety and avoidance of intimacy, have also been derived from categorical attachment styles to allow finer grained analyses of individual differences. Even a cursory understanding of the meaning and implications of attachment styles requires some familiarity with the underlying theory, the empirically derived typology of styles, the methods used at various ages to assess attachment styles, and the implications of individual difference in attachment styles across a variety of domains of human functioning.

Attachment Theory

Bowlby (1969) formulated his attachment theory based on the premise that many of the most primitive aspects of human relatedness evolved to support the survival of infants, who are born helpless and are thus highly vulnerable to predators and to fatal accidents. Because human infants must maintain close physical proximity to a responsive and protective caregiver, an attachment-maintaining behavioral system is thought to have developed as an adaptation to constrain infant mortality rates. Without such consistent protection and nurturance, children are unlikely to attain puberty and produce progeny of their own. Thus, children of nurturing and protective parents are endowed with an adaptational advantage that results in a greater likelihood of their familial genetic legacy enduring and influencing the characteristics of their species.

Given the propositions that compose this framework, attachment theory is clearly rooted in theories of evolutionary biology and child development. However, attachment-maintaining traits are not understood to be purely heritable but are instead attributed to experiential learning transmitted from parent to child in a manner consistent with social learning theory. Indeed, when Bowlby first presented the ideas that led him to formulate attachment theory, he was characterized by his detractors in the British psychoanalytic community as a behaviorist (Bretherton, 1997).

Attachment theory has been extended beyond its more circumscribed beginnings in child development and romantic bonding to explain the interpersonal regulation of affect (Diamond & Fagundes, 2008) and the cognitive representation of relational experiences and expectations (Baldwin, Keelan, Fehr, Enns, & Koh-Rangarajoo, 1996). Furthermore, what was once understood as a theory pertaining mainly to developmental psychology has been adopted by researchers in the domains of clinical and social psychology, as well as primatology and behavioral neuroscience. As attachment theory is applied across diverse cultures in manifold domains by researchers trained in disparate disciplines, there is some danger that its principles and meaning will be distorted to fit so many aims that a corresponding loss of coherency will result. For instance, Main (1999) raised the objection that attachment has been applied in such an overly general manner to pertain to all affectionate relationships that its unique relevance to enhancing children's safety under conditions of perceived threat is often lost.

Typology of Attachment Styles

Individual relational patterns, known as *attachment styles*, have been observed to emerge during infancy and are linked to the sensitivity, responsiveness, and consistency of children's caregivers (Ainsworth, Blehar, Waters, & Wall, 1978). These patterns are held to provide evidence of flexible but enduring cognitive structures termed *internal working models* (Bowlby, 1969), which in turn guide interpersonal expectations and relational behaviors while influencing the meanings attributed to interpersonal experiences throughout the lifespan.

Infants whose cries and other signals of distress consistently receive warm, sensitive, and nurturing care tend to develop a style of responding well to soothing behavior from others. Such children appear to expect nurturance and to thrive on it. These children demonstrate a balance of exploratory interest in their environment and reliance upon the caregiver as a secure base in times of insecurity or distress. The attachment style of children fitting this description is deemed to be a *secure* one. Adults who are comfortable with depending on others and having relational partners depend on them are considered to exhibit a secure adult attachment pattern. Patterns of attachment behavior at any age that deviate substantially from this model are characterized as *anxious* or *insecure*.

Anxious attachment styles have been defined by various terms, including ambivalent, avoidant, and disorganized/disoriented among children and preoccupied, dismissive, and fearful among adults. Children who seem reticent to seek parental care and who may even show somewhat more interest in the attention of adult strangers may be classified as avoidant. The corresponding style of adults who adopt an extremely self-reliant attitude and who express little desire for relationships with others is termed *dismissive*. If, however, an adult's pattern of devaluing relationships contains evidence of chronic interpersonal anxiety and concerns about how well they themselves can function in close relationships, the classification of a *fearful* attachment style is more fitting.

Some children heartily protest the absence of their caregivers, but are difficult to soothe when their signals of distress are responded to. This pattern has been attributed to inconsistencies in the sensitivity and responsiveness of the child's caregivers. Such inconsistent care undermines the child's ability to reliably predict the caregiver's behavior, thus raising the child's anxiety in anticipating that the caregiver's response may be delayed, inadequate, or unpleasant. This style of anxious attachment may be classified as *ambivalent*, because the child appears to relate to the parent as alternately desirable and aversive. When adults perceive relationships as highly desirable, but seem prone to anxious concerns about rejection and to require

excessive reassurance from their partners, they are likely to be classified as exhibiting a *preoccupied* attachment style.

The most recent classification of attachment in children, termed *disorganized* (Main & Solomon, 1986), was created to capture the behavior patterns of children who fit poorly in the other attachment categories. These children display idiosyncratic and contradictory sequences of attachment responses that may reflect the insensitive and erratic characteristics of their caregivers. Parent-child relationships in this group have sometimes been characterized as highly conflictual or hostile, and these children have been shown to be at elevated risk for disorders of conduct and defiance (Lyons-Ruth, 1996). The corresponding category on Main's Adult Attachment Interview (AAI; George, Kaplan, & Main, 1985) is termed *unresolved*, in reference to the frequent association between unresolved issues of loss and trauma in childhood and this attachment style. Members of this attachment category tend to experience fear in close personal relationships. When methods other than the AAI are employed to assess adult attachment, such individuals may be more likely to be classified with the previously noted fearful attachment style.

Methods of Assessing Attachment Style

Although attachment classification was pioneered by means of observing infants in the Strange Situation Test (Ainsworth et al., 1978), later studies examined attachment styles in adults by employing either interviews or self-report measures. The previously mentioned AAI is the most prominent example of the interview approach.

Researchers desiring measures that lend themselves to use with larger population samples have developed paper and pencil measures yielding various indices of self-reported attachment tendencies. Early samples of this method included the three-category approach of Hazan and Shaver (1987) and the four-category approach of Bartholomew and Horowitz (1991). Later developments of these measures have departed from categorical assignment and allowed individuals to rate the degree of correspondence between themselves and each of the attachment-style prototypes. These scores can then be combined to develop a more complex picture of individual differences in adult attachment styles. An alternative method has been to disassemble the attachment prototypes into their constituent statements, which can be rated on a Likert-type scale. The scores can then be combined to provide indices of various theoretical dimensions or subscales.

One such method (Bartholomew & Horowitz, 1991) yields scores along dimensions of anxiety about oneself in relationships (model of self) and one's appraisal of the reliability and desirability of others as attachment partners (model of other). These dimensions within attachment styles can then be used to make finer distinctions regarding linkages between attachment styles and other personal and interpersonal characteristics. This approach is congruent with the conceptualization of internal working models of the self and of the attachment figure described earlier as components of attachment theory.

Since Bartholomew first established a dimensional model for assessing attachment styles, much research has been conducted on the relative merits of categorical and dimensional models, as well as on comparisons between self-report questionnaires versus interviewing methods. Bartholomew and Shaver (1998) demonstrated varying degrees of convergence across a variety of methods, supporting the proposition that the underlying conceptual dimensions of attachment theory can be tapped by various means. A large and elaborate factor-analytic study comparing the results obtained from most of the established self-report measures of adult attachment (Brennan, Clark, & Shaver, 1998) found support for two independent factors corresponding to the theoretically formulated dimensions of relational avoidance and relational anxiety. A study contrasting the AAI with two prominent self-report measure of adult attachment (Shaver, Belsky, & Brennan, 2000) found further support for the existence of underlying dimensions that connect the otherwise different methods of assessing adult attachment and concluded that dimensional assessment of adult attachment provides results of greater precision when compared to methods employing categorical typologies.

REFERENCES

Ainsworth, M. D. S., Blehar, M. C., Waters, E., & Wall, S. (1978). *Patterns of attachment: Assessed in the strange situation and at home.* Hillsdale, NJ: Lawrence Erlbaum.

Baldwin, M. W., Keelan, J. P. R., Fehr, B., Enns, V., & Koh-Rangarajoo, E. (1996). Social cognitive conceptualization of attachment styles: Availability and accessibility effects. *Journal of Personality and Social Psychology, 71,* 94–109.

Bartholomew, K., & Horowitz, L. M. (1991). Attachment styles among young adults: A test of a four-category model. *Journal of Personality and Social Psychology, 61,* 226–244.

Bartholomew, K., & Shaver, P. R. (1998). Methods of assessing adult attachment: Do they converge? In J. A. Simpson & W. S. Rholes (Eds.), *Attachment theory and close relationships* (pp. 46–76). New York: Guilford Press.

Bowlby, J. (1969). *Attachment and loss: Vol. I. Attachment.* Middlesex, UK: Penguin Books.

Brennan, K. A., Clark, C. L., & Shaver, P. R. (1998). Self-report measurement of adult romantic attachment: An integrative overview. In J. A. Simpson & W. S. Rholes (Eds.), *Attachment theory and close relationships* (pp. 46–76). New York: Guilford Press.

Bretherton, I. (1997). The origins of attachment theory: John Bowlby and Mary Ainsworth. In S. Goldberg, R. Muir, & J. Kerr (Eds.), *Attachment theory: Social, developmental, and clinical perspectives* (pp. 45–84). Hillsdale, NJ: Analytic Press.

Diamond, L. M., & Fagundes, C. P. (2008). Developmental perspectives on links between attachment and affect regulation over the lifespan. In R. V. Kail (Ed.), *Advances in child development and behavior, 36,* 83–134. San Diego, CA: Elsevier Academic Press.

George, C., Kaplan, N., & Main, M. (1985). *The Adult Attachment Interview.* Unpublished manuscript, Department of Psychology, University of California, Berkeley.

Hazan, C., & Shaver, P. R. (1987). Romantic love conceptualized as an attachment process. *Journal of Personality and Social Psychology, 52,* 511–524.

Lyons-Ruth, K. (1996). Attachment relationships among children with aggressive behavior problems: The role of disorganized early attachment patterns. *Journal of Consulting and Clinical Psychology, 64,* 64–73.

Main, M. (1999). Epilogue: Attachment theory: Eighteen points with suggestions for future studies. In J. Cassidy & P. R. Shaver (Eds.), *Handbook of attachment: Theory, research, and clinical applications* (pp. 845–887). New York: Guilford Press.

Main, M., & Solomon, J. (1986). Discovery of a new, insecure-disorganized/disoriented attachment pattern. In M. Yogman & T. B. Brazelton (Eds.), *Affective development in infancy* (pp. 95–124). Norwood, NJ: Ablex.

Shaver, P. R., Belsky, J., & Brennan, K. A. (2000). Comparing measures of adult attachment: An examination of interview and self-report methods. *Personal Relationships, 7,* 25–43.

GILBERT REYES
*Fielding Graduate University,
Santa Barbara, CA*

See also: **Attachment and Bonding; Parental Approaches; Separation-Individuation**

ATTACHMENT THEORY

Attachment theory defines an evolutionary-based relationship between a child and a parent figure. Attachment is a biologically based behavioral system that evolved in ways that influence and organize human motivational, emotional, and cognitive and memory processes. The relationship is conceived to develop initially in infancy and contribute to development, other relationships, risk, and mental health throughout the life span (Bowlby, 1969/1982, 1973, 1980; Cassidy & Shaver, 2008). Attachment has become a shorthand term that connotes a complex set of interrelated patterns of behavior and thinking directed toward a parent figure that is wiser, protective, and caring.

Attachment is distinguished from other social relationships by the following constellation of behavior and processes: (1) proximity seeking; (2) distress when separation is not understandable; (3) happiness at reunion; (4) grief/sadness at loss; (5) secure base behavior, which is the capacity to explore when the attachment figure is present (Ainsworth, 1989); and (6) viewing the attachment figure as having an enduring commitment to being available when needed (Kobak, Cassidy, & Ziv, 2004). Children develop preferred attachment relationships with parents and other caring adults (e.g., foster parents, day-care providers). Attachment contributes to the development of an integrated self, confidence in self and others, and the ability to endure life's challenges and stressors (George & West, in press; Sroufe, Egeland, Carlson, & Collins, 2005).

Attachment behavior is adaptive, from both an evolutionary perspective and a proximate, immediate care perspective. It keeps children close to and cared for by attachment figures, thus improving the chances of survival and parent reproductive fitness. Attachment behavior is guided by a neurologically based mental representational system that has specific biological substrates and influences physiological homeostasis (Cassidy & Shaver, 2008). When the attachment system is activated by perceived stress or threat, individuals desire physical or psychological proximity or contact with attachment figures (Bowlby, 1969/1982, 1973). Both internal cues (e.g., illness, fatigue, hunger, pain) and external cues can activate attachment. Some of these cues are universal to humans through evolution, (e.g., peripheral movement; separation from attachment figures), and others are learned.

Childhood Attachment Patterns

The quality of the child's attachment reflects real experience with the parent. Attachment patterns, also termed "status" (Ainsworth, Blehar, Waters, & Wall, 1978), are influenced but not determined by temperament, genetics, parents' marital satisfaction, and culture. Attachment is dyad-specific; quality of attachment with one parent is independent of other attachment relationships. There are four major patterns of child attachment, originally identified in infants and later extended to older children. Three patterns are conceived as organized forms of attachment; secure, insecure-avoidant, insecure-ambivalent-resistant (Ainsworth et al., 1978). The fourth pattern is disorganized-controlling (Main & Cassidy, 1988; Main & Solomon, 1990). Several decades of research provide a lens for understanding these patterns, including cross-cultural naturalistic and laboratory studies (e.g., Strange Situation, Attachment Q-sort) and studies of attachment and caregiving representations (e.g., Attachment Doll Play, Separation Anxiety Test, interview) (Solomon & George, in press).

Children with organized attachments signal need and get close to their parents when they experience attachment distress. *Secure* children signal promptly and clearly and prefer care by their parents above all others. They are confident that their parents are accessible, sensitive, and responsive and will follow through promptly and completely. Their parents view them as deserving care. They work hard to juggle their own needs with their children's needs in a developmentally and contextually appropriate manner. The secure relationship is balanced, mutually satisfying and comfortable, and characterized by emotional sharing and the co-construction of plans and activities. The secure attachment relationship is conceived as a "goal-corrected partnership" (Bowlby, 1969/1982).

Children develop insecure attachments when parental accessibility and sensitivity are compromised. Insecure children are anxious and use defensive processes to manage distress (e.g., exclusion, transformation of attachment experience and affect) so as to achieve at least minimal parental care. Insecure-avoidant children maintain an independent facade. Defensive deactivation, the goal of which is to cool down distress, is their primary form of defense. Deactivation is not always 100% effective, and distress does leak through, for example, in the form of strong separation anxiety when separated from parents. Their parents contribute to attachment distance with mild rejection and behavior that shifts children's attention away from attachment. A goal-corrected balance is compromised by mutual emphasis away from comfort and intimacy to exploration, achievement, and activity.

Insecure-ambivalent-resistant children are overtly anxious, immature, and clingy. Their primary form of defense, cognitive disconnection, separates attachment affect from its source. As a result, attachment signals are unclear, contradictory (e.g., desire to be picked up and immediately put down), and often intense (to remind parents to keep them close by). Anger wells up in these children because their parents are inconsistently responsive. Parental actions are often not related to their children's needs. These parents are uncertain about what their children need and are distracted by worry, frustration, and guilt. A goal-corrected balance is compromised by a mutual emphasis on intimacy and over-involvement over autonomy.

Insecure-disorganized children are the most anxious children in the attachment nosology. They are called disorganized because organized attachment behavioral and defensive processes literally break down, leaving these children defenseless and overwhelmed. Disorganized infants appear disoriented (e.g., trance-like state), frightened (e.g., freezing, apprehensive), conflicted about proximity (e.g., approach with head uncomfortably averted), and hostile (e.g., aggression without apparent cause). Typically by age 6, children develop controlling strategies that direct the parents' attention and behavior such that children assume a role that is usually considered appropriate for a parent. Controlling children can be punitive (e.g., rude, vindictive) or caregiving (overly solicitous). The roles of child and parent are inverted, and disorganized-controlling relationships are completely out of balance.

Studies investigating parental contributions to disorganized-controlling attachment emphasize a range of processes and experiences carried from the parent's past or in the current relationship that include (1) extreme parental psychological or physical withdrawal and "invisibility" (e.g., dissociative behavior); (2) unresolved, contradictory, or unpredictable frightening experiences (e.g., rage, hostile-intrusive interaction), sometimes associated with certain forms of psychopathology (e.g., anxiety disorder, borderline personality disorder, depression), abuse, alcoholism, or parental conflict; (3) helplessness; (4) child empowerment/deference (e.g., glorification, in which the child is viewed as more capable of caring for others than the parent); and (5) dissolution of parent-child boundaries (the parent merges with the child, acts like a child, and treats the child like a spouse). The single underlying thread in this list is the fear generated by feelings of helplessness and isolation in both the parent and the child. Disorganized-controlling children become so overwhelmed by their parents' inaccessibility that organized attachment strategies are disrupted or blocked. Their parents are inaccessible and helpless to provide care and protection in those exact moments children need them the most. They are essentially alone and defenseless in a world that is dangerous and out of control (George & Solomon, 2008).

Attachment theory suggests that attachments should become increasingly stable and resistant to change during early childhood (infancy to age 5) as relationships become internalized through the development of representational skills. Continuity and discontinuity is lawfully connected to experiences with their parents; changes in attachment status occur when there are significant changes in parental sensitivity and responsiveness due to life events that can stabilize attachment security (e.g., infant mental health intervention) or threaten it (e.g., loss of a parent).

Secure attachment is the most common attachment for children around the world. The predominant forms of insecure attachment vary and are influenced by the degree to which families and cultures emphasize closeness. Avoidant insecurity is more predominant in groups that value independence; ambivalent-resistant insecurity is more predominant in groups that value closeness and enmeshment. The proportion of disorganized-controlling attachment ranges from 13% to 90%, depending on the family risk factors present (Cassidy & Shaver, 2008).

Attachment status contributes to and serves as a buffer or risk factor for social, cognitive, and emotional development, including autonomy, confidence, self-esteem, emotion regulation and stress, problem solving, abstract reasoning, mastery, ego resilience, sociability, peer and leadership skills, and the development of conscience. Security with father contributes to play and exploratory competence. Disorganized-controlling attachment is associated with developmental risk, including internalizing and externalizing problems; peer aggression, defiance, coercion, poor academic- and self-esteem, limited social competence, poor math and deductive reasoning skills, and fantasies of helplessness, destruction, and death. Disorganized attachment in infancy also predicts dissociative symptoms and high psychopathology ratings in adolescence.

Adolescent and Adult Attachment Patterns

The goal of attachment—proximity to attachment figures when distressed—is the same for adolescents and adults as for children. There are also important differences. The range of activating conditions, response intensities, and need for physical proximity to attachment figures decrease. Attachment relationships extend to peers and spouse/partner in addition to parents (Cassidy & Shaver, 2008; West & Sheldon-Keller, 1994).

Adult attachment status is conceived in terms of representation or "state of mind," which is one's current perspective on past attachment experiences. Adult attachment status is assessed using representational measures and reflects one's qualitative synthesis of memories and affects of past attachment experiences and emotions in light of current expectations and evaluations (e.g., Adult Attachment Interview; Adult Attachment Projective Picture System). Attachment status in adolescents and adults may differ from one's actual childhood patterns. Metacognitive and abstract thought that emerge beginning in adolescence can provide a lens of understanding that is not possible in childhood and can re-organize or disrupt childhood patterns.

There are four main adult attachment groups, three that are organized (secure/flexibly integrated, dismissing, preoccupied) and one that is unresolved. Adult attachment status is a generalized representation of attachment experience. It should not be confused with attachment style, which is a social-cognitive model of personality (Cassidy & Shaver, 2008).

Adults with organized attachment status use a range of strategies to manage feelings of need, closeness, and intimacy, to assuage attachment distress, and to maintain psychological closeness to attachment figures. Secure adults are flexibly integrated in thought and action. They fluidly reconsider and reevaluate attachment from new perspectives as an ongoing process in their lives. Secure adults value attachment figures as available and accessible to provide comfort when needed. They have internalized resources that promote constructive problem solving, integrity, and connectedness in relationships ("internalized secure base," George & West, in press).

Insecure-organized adults want closeness, but past and current attachment anxiety interferes with their ability to use personal and attachment resources to assuage distress. They manage anxiety with defensive processes that shift attention and behavior away from making bids to attachment figures they know will be ineffective and disappointing. Dismissing attachment, analogous to avoidant child attachment, is maintained by deactivating strategies that mute mistrust, distress, and anger. Individuals appear cool, neutralized, and detached. Attachment relationships are viewed as instrumental, in that they can provide basic care without intimacy or dependence. Representations of self and others emphasize personal strength, rules, achievement, intellect, problem-solving capabilities, and strict adherence to social scripts, all of which are characteristics that protect the self from feeling rejected. Preoccupied attachment, analogous to ambivalent-resistant child attachment, is maintained by disconnecting strategies that fosters closeness but does not effectively manage accompanying feelings of anger and sadness. Preoccupied individuals are confused about how to think about self, attachment figures, and contexts. Preoccupied individuals portray self and others as unable to solve problems, entangled, angry, withdrawn, emotionally withholding, distracted, and over-involved.

Unresolved adult attachment is analogous to disorganized child attachment. The etiology of unresolved attachment is trauma that is so painful and threatening that these adults cannot integrate experience and affects at the representational level. In essence, attachment trauma becomes repressed or "segregated" (Bowlby, 1980). Segregated memories and feelings are unleashed when attachment is activated, resulting in lapses in metacognitive monitoring and dissociation (Hesse & Main, 2006). Unresolved individuals are overcome by attachment trauma to an extent that flexible integration and organizing defenses break down; they are flooded and dysregulated by fear and feelings of isolation, abandonment, and helplessness (George & West, in press).

Attachment status in adolescence and adulthood is also lawfully related to attachment experience. In adolescence, the transition to psychological and relationship autonomy may account for a greater proportion of dismissing adolescents than avoidant children or adults in many studies. Population statistics for attachment group prevalence depends on the populations being studied (e.g., college students, parents, psychiatric patients). Proportions of security tend to be smaller in adolescent and adult samples than in child samples (Cassidy & Shaver, 2008).

Adolescent and adult attachment status is associated with self and relationship characteristics, including autonomy, reflective capacity, family/relationship interaction patterns (communication, relatedness, conflict), and adjustment. Attachment status is related to emotion regulation and stress responses (heart rate, skin conductance) and the interactions among cortical (thinking, planning, regulation) and limbic system (autobiographical and emotional memory) processes. Unresolved individuals are more likely to demonstrate dissociative tendencies, although typically not at the level of mental health risk. Participants in clinical as compared with community samples have higher rates of unresolved attachment, but unresolved attachment does not in itself predict any particular psychiatric diagnosis.

Attachment theory predicts interrelationship transmission of attachment to other intimate social relationships based on the template developed in childhood, including friendship, dating, partner selection, and parenting. Interrelationship transmission is robust for secure adults, but equivocal for insecure adults. Past attachment experience in childhood serves as an important foundation for other relationships, although current experience in new relationships has the potential to change appraisals of the past.

REFERENCES

Ainsworth, M. D. S. (1989). Attachment beyond infancy. *American Psychologist, 44*, 709–716.

Ainsworth, M. D. S., Blehar, M., Waters, E., & Wall, S. (1978). *Patterns of attachment: A psychological study of the strange situation.* Hillsdale, NJ: Lawrence Erlbaum.

Bowlby, J. (1969/1982). *Attachment and loss: Vol 1. Attachment.* New York: Basic Books.

Bowlby, J. (1973). *Attachment and loss: Vol. 2. Separation.* New York: Basic Books.

Bowlby, J. (1980). *Attachment and loss: Vol. 3. Loss.* New York: Basic Books.

Cassidy, J., & Shaver, P. R. (Eds.). (2008). *Handbook of attachment: Theory, research, and clinical application* (2nd ed.). New York: Guilford Press.

George, C., & Solomon, J. (2008). The caregiving system: A behavioral systems approach to parenting. In J. Cassidy & P. R. Shaver (Eds.), *Handbook of attachment: Theory, research, and clinical application* (2nd ed.). New York: Guilford Press.

George, C., & West, M. (in press). *The Adult Attachment Projective Picture System: A new assessment of adult attachment.* New York: Guilford Press.

Hesse, E., & Main, M. (2006). Frightened, threatening, and dissociative parental behavior in low-risk samples: Description, discussion, and interpretations. *Development and Psychopathology, 18*, 309–343.

Kobak, R., Cassidy, J., & Ziv, Y. (2004). Attachment-related trauma and posttraumatic stress disorder: Implications for adult adaptation. In W. S. Rholes & J. A. Simpson (Eds.), *Adult attachment: Theory, research, and clinical implication.* (pp. 388–407). New York: Guilford Press.

Main, M., & Cassidy, J. (1988). Categories of response to reunion with the parent at age 6: Predictable from infant attachment classifications and stable over a 1-month period. *Developmental Psychology, 24*, 1–12.

Main, M., & Solomon, J. (1990). Procedures for identifying infants as disorganized/disoriented during the Ainsworth strange situation. In M. T. Greenberg, D. Cicchetti, & E. M. Cummings (Eds.), *Attachment in the preschool years* (pp. 121–160). Chicago: University of Chicago Press.

Solomon, J., & George, C. (Eds.). (in press). *Disorganized attachment and caregiving*. New York: Guilford Press.

Sroufe, L. A., Egeland, B., Carlson, E. A., & Collins, A. W. (2005). *The development of the person*. New York: Guilford Press.

West, M., & Sheldon-Keller, A. E. (1994). *Patterns of relating: An adult attachment perspective*. New York: Guilford Press.

CAROL GEORGE
Mills College, Oakland, CA

See also: Attachment and Bonding; Attachment Disorders

ATTENTION (See Selective Attention)

ATTENTION LAPSES

Attention lapses are a frequently annoying fact-of-life with which we all have firsthand experience. Technically, attention lapses are taken to be failures of sustained attention. The lapses referred to are therefore usually defined as temporary and often brief shifts of conscious attention away from some primary task to unrelated internal information processing. This sort of definition of attention lapse has the advantage of specifying research paradigms as well as relating absentmindedness to the important practical issue of understanding cognitive and action failures during instrumental tasks (Reason & Mycielska, 1984).

On the other hand, such a negative definition may distract us from considering potential benefits of what also might be more neutrally defined as spontaneous redirections of attentional focus. Attention lapse–induced mind wandering may also be seen as a form of curiosity, a spontaneous toying with ideas, facilitating discovery and innovation. Cognitive activity during attention lapses often involves productive forward planning and problem solving, even though unrelated to the present task at hand. Moreover, although many cognitive errors and action slips can certainly be directly linked to absentmindedness, the observation that people often continue successfully to perform complex tasks without explicit conscious attention suggests that attention lapses may also have interesting implications for our understanding of intention, volition, and agency in human action.

Notwithstanding potential benefits of absentmindedness, research has almost exclusively focused on the costs of failures of sustained attention in terms of personal productivity and well-being. Real-world health and economic costs of absentmindedness have been extensively documented (e.g., Reason & Mycielska, 1984). Although attention lapses are often assessed using self-report measures, the development of the Sustained Attention to Response Task (SART; Robertson, Manly, Andrade, Baddeley,

& Yiend, 1997) provided an important behavioral tool enabling the investigation of cognitive and physiological processes underlying failures of attention. Different aspects of SART performance have been shown to be differentially associated with self-report measures of attention lapses, cognitive errors, and action slips in everyday life (Cheyne, Carrier, & Smilek, 2006). The development of the SART has undoubtedly contributed significantly to the reinvigoration of interest in attention lapses and has been employed in studies of cognitive, physiological, and phenomenological components of absentmindedness as well as in the investigation of such applied issues of attention deficit disorder and traumatic brain injury.

Although research has often focused on individual differences, persistence in achieving difficult goals is something that most people find difficult—especially when the task at hand is not under the control of basic biological imperatives (hunger, sex, and so on). A perhaps radical hypothesis about attention lapses is that they reflect the natural state of flux characterizing all biological systems: consciousness, behavior, and physiology alike. Cognitive systems appear often to be governed by a kind of pandemonium model, shunted here and there by cognitive demons and salient environmental events. Directed thinking and action, guided by an executive system with an overarching goal, monitoring automatic processing and environmental variations, may be a rare, hard-to-achieve anomaly rather than the norm.

REFERENCES

Cheyne, J. A., Carriere, J. S. A., & Smilek, D. (2006). Absentmindedness: Lapses in conscious awareness and everyday cognitive failures. *Consciousness and Cognition, 15*, 578–592.

Reason, J. T., & Mycielska, K. (1982). *Absent-minded? The psychology of mental lapses and everyday errors*. Englewood Cliffs, NJ: Prentice-Hall.

Robertson, I. H., Manly, T., Andrade, J., Baddeley, B. T., & Yiend, J. (1997). "Oops!": Performance correlates of everyday attentional failures in traumatic brain injured and normal subjects. *Neuropsychologia, 35*, 6, 747–758.

SUGGESTED READINGS

Reason, J. T. (1984). Lapses of attention in everyday life. In R. Parasuraman & D. R. Davies (Eds.), *Varieties of attention*. New York: Academic Press.

Robertson, I. H. (2003). The absent mind: Attention and error. *The Psychologist, 16*, 9, 476–479.

Smallwood, J. M., & Schooler, J. W. (2006). The restless mind. *Psychological Bulletin, 132*, 946–958.

ALLAN CHEYNE
University of Waterloo, Canada

See also: Attention-Deficit/Hyperactivity Disorder

ATTENTION-DEFICIT/HYPERACTIVITY DISORDER

Attention-Deficit/Hyperactivity Disorder (ADHD) is characterized by persistent and chronic inattention and/or excessive motor restlessness and impulsivity. Inattentive symptoms include poor organizational skills, making careless errors, forgetfulness, trouble listening, and distractibility. Hyperactive/impulsive symptoms include restlessness, excessive talking, and interrupting. For the purpose of diagnosis, symptom manifestation should be developmentally inappropriate and exhibited in two or more settings (e.g., home and school). Much of the research in the past decade has focused on deficits associated with the disorder in regard to executive function, response inhibition, cognitive control, and motivational dysfunction in response to delayed reinforcers.

The manifestation of ADHD and its associated core problems vary with development. ADHD in the combined subtype is characterized in the preschool and prepubescent period by high rates of gross motor activity, difficulty sitting in one's seat, academic difficulties, and peer-interaction problems. ADHD in adolescence is a period associated with high risk-taking behavior, and teenagers and young adults with ADHD are likely to have more traffic accidents, substance abuse, treatment for sexually transmitted diseases (Barkley et al., 2006), and earlier initiation of sexual activity and intercourse (Flory, Pelham, et al., 2006). ADHD in adulthood is recognized as a period with less observable gross motor hyperactivity. However, problems with sustaining attention and impulsive behavior continue to result in poor work performance, greater unemployment, higher divorce rates, and engagement in criminal behavior (Barkley, 2006).

According to the fourth edition of the *Diagnostic and Statistical Manual of Mental Disorders* (DSM-IV-TR, 2000), there are three ADHD subtypes: predominantly inattentive, predominantly hyperactive-impulsive, and a combined subtype that is the most prevalent. Individuals diagnosed with the combined subtype exhibit both inattentive and hyperactive/impulsive symptoms to a significant degree. Individuals identified with the inattentive or hyperactive/impulsive diagnoses present with predominant inattention or hyperactive and impulsive symptoms, respectively. There is also recent interest in a subset of the ADHD, inattentive, which is characterized by slow or sluggish cognitive tempo (McBurnett et al., 2001). Children with this inattentive type of ADHD appear hypoactive and seem to be in a fog or daydreaming.

There is evidence to suggest that there are differences in the genetic profile and treatment response among the ADHD subtypes. Consistent, robust differences on a neuropsychological level among the ADHD subtypes are difficult to identify, however. Neuropsychological studies that have found differences have been contradictory in nature or apply primarily to a subset of the subjects. In general, however, it appears that children with the ADHD combined subtype perform poorly on planning, cognitive flexibility, and response inhibition tasks, whereas children with the ADHD inattentive subtype display difficulty using cues to guide their behavior and demonstrate slowed motor output, impaired vigilance, and altered arousal effects.

ADHD is frequently comorbid with other disorders, most commonly with disruptive behavior disorders. From 42.7% to 56% of children meeting criteria for ADHD in community samples meet criteria for conduct disorder as well. It is the ADHD-type symptoms rather than the conduct disorder symptoms that are most likely to predict academic achievement, thus indicating that the attentional symptoms need to be addressed as robustly as the conduct problems in children who have both. Other frequently occurring comorbid disorders in childhood ADHD include learning disabilities and anxiety disorders. Children with ADHD are also more vulnerable than young people in general to develop a substance abuse disorder and smoke nicotine.

Prevalence

Prevalence rates of ADHD in the childhood population vary, with expert opinion most often citing an incidence of approximately 3%–7% (American Psychiatric Association, 2000). The majority of children with the disorder continue to exhibit some symptoms in adulthood. Prevalence rates in adults are estimated to be about 4.4% (Kessler et al., 2006). The disorder is more common in males, with 6:1 frequency among clinic-referred samples and a 3.4:1 frequency among nonclinic-referred samples for males to females (Barkley, 2006).

Etiology

There is considerable evidence to suggest a genetic basis for ADHD. The disorder is highly heritable, with a risk of 57% of occurrence from parents with ADHD to their children. Most of the genetic research has focused on candidate genes involved in dopaminergic transmission, although noradrenergic and serotonin systems are also studied. The most reliable findings in ADHD are associated with the DRD4 repeat polymorphism (Barkley, 2006). Other associations for candidate genes have included DAT1, DBH, DRD5, SNAP-25, 5HTT, and HTR1B. ADHD also has been associated with markers at several chromosomes including, but not limited to, regions 5p, 6q, 9q, 11q, 16q, and 17p. Additional factors thought to contribute to ADHD include low birth weight, environmental toxins such as prenatal exposure to maternal smoking and alcohol consumption, and postnatal exposure to lead.

Neuroimaging research into brain structure and function in ADHD repeatedly finds significant differences between ADHD and controls in frontal, anterior cingulate, basal ganglia, and cerebellar anatomy and function. Reviews of the literature from structural MRI methods (e.g., Krain & Castellanos, 2006) reveal perhaps the most consistent findings in regard to ADHD imaging studies. Comparisons in global brain volume between children with ADHD and healthy comparison children have repeatedly found evidence of significantly reduced total brain volume, frontal cortical volume, and reductions in frontal regions in ADHD using gray-white matter segmentation techniques. Measures of cortical thickness via a recent longitudinal study (Shaw et al., 2007) revealed a delay of approximately three years in an ADHD group compared to controls in attaining peak thickness throughout the cerebrum, with delays ranging from two to five years in the prefrontal regions. Interestingly, the ADHD group had slightly earlier peak thickness (about four months) in the primary motor cortex compared to the control group.

Studies that use a variety of functioning imaging techniques suggest decreased brain activation in the frontal cortex in ADHD, although a number of studies have also shown relative increased brain activation in ADHD (see Fassbender & Schweitzer, 2006). Accumulating evidence also suggests that the anterior cingulate cortex is implicated in ADHD and is often hypoactive in both child and adult participants. The basal ganglia are another structure of inherent interest in ADHD, given the functional attributes of this structure and the fact that it is a clear target of the most common treatment for ADHD, which is stimulant medication. Methylphenidate appears to increase dopamine levels in the basal ganglia via blocking its reuptake. Alterations are consistently found in the basal ganglia during functional brain-imaging studies, with the evidence mixed about whether the alterations in basal ganglia activation are increased or decreased (see Fassbender & Schweitzer, 2006). Stimulants appear to increase basal ganglia activation in children with ADHD.

Another subcortical structure, the cerebellum, also appears to be altered in structure and function in ADHD. The cerebellar vermis and hemispheres are smaller in children with ADHD than in comparison groups of healthy controls. Methylphenidate appears to increase cerebellar vermis activity, but only in a nontask-related fashion. Rates of hyperactivity and response to methylphenidate treatment also appear to be linked to the degree of activity in the cerebellar vermis (Fassbender & Schweitzer, 2006). Associations between the cerebellum, the basal ganglia, and the PFC suggest that abnormalities found in these regions may reflect a circuit-wide dysfunction in prefrontal-basal ganglia-cerebellar loops in ADHD. Ultimately, methods combining behavioral, imaging, and genetic techniques should help identify ADHD subgroups and potentially develop more targeted treatment efforts for the subgroups.

Diagnosis

Practice parameters for ADHD have been identified by several organizations including the American Academy of Pediatrics (AAP) and the American Academy of Child and Adolescent Psychiatry. These organizations include recommendations for the evaluation of ADHD and, via AAP, access to rating scales for evaluating ADHD and monitoring treatment response. A comprehensive evaluation of ADHD in adults or children should assess the presence or absence of symptomatology, differential diagnosis from other disorders that mimic ADHD, and the possibility of comorbid psychiatric disorders. At a minimum, the evaluation should include a clinical interview, a medical evaluation conducted within the past year, standardized behavior-rating scales from parents and teachers, and a direct observation of the patient. Evaluations for both children and adults also should include a family history as well as documentation regarding developmental, social, and academic functioning.

An evaluation for adults also ought to include information regarding childhood via academic records and retrospective-childhood ratings by the adult patient and a parent or another individual who knew the patient as a child. An assessment of intellectual, academic, neuropsychological, and attentional functioning is desirable for purposes of differential diagnosis, as well as for pointing out individual strengths and weaknesses. Psychoeducational testing can also be useful when a low level of intellectual functioning or a learning disability mimics or coexists with ADHD. Preferably, the evaluation should be individualized to address areas of concern for each patient.

Treatment

Although the evidence for the efficacy of pharmacological treatments for ADHD has strong empirical support (Jensen, 2002; MTA Cooperative Group, 1999; MTA Cooperative Group, 2004), there is also a role for behavioral interventions in the treatment of the disorder. Behavioral interventions are necessary for the 20%–30% of patients who do not respond to stimulants and for those who experience significant side effects from pharmacological agents. Perhaps most importantly, these interventions can also address comorbidity such as anxiety, academic performance, parent-child conflict, and stress in the parent (MTA Cooperative Group, 1999). Behavioral interventions for children include social skills training, school interventions, and parent training in contingency management. There is recent support for the use of behavioral and cognitive-behavioral treatments for adults with ADHD (e.g., Solanto et al., 2008) as well. The adult interventions teach compensatory strategies, organizational skills, planning, and the development of new habits to help resist distracters. Adults and adolescents may also benefit from "coaching" to monitor progress toward academic, career, and social goals.

The use of pharmacological interventions is warranted if the symptoms are interfering significantly with functioning. Most medications for ADHD appear to affect the dopaminergic and/or noradrenergic system. The majority of individuals (children and adults) are responsive to psychostimulant medications (e.g., methylphenidate and dextroamphetamine), and these compounds are considered safe and effective treatments for ADHD. Stimulants, typically considered the first line of defense, can produce improvements in impulse control, attention, on-task behavior, and social behavior. A number of fairly new delivery systems (including a pill and a transdermal "patch") for psychostimulant medications are commercially available, including several with long-acting or extended-release options, such as Concerta, Metadate, Ritalin SR, and Ritalin LA. A recently released drug, Vyvanse (lisdexamfetamine dimesylate and mixed amphetamine salts), is an extended-release formulation of *d*-amphetamine that becomes therapeutically active following oral ingestion. Thus, Vynase should be less likely to be abused than other stimulants. Atomoxetine, a nonstimulant compound that is a highly selective inhibitor of the presynaptic noradrenergic transporter, has FDA approval for treatment of ADHD in adults and children. Other pharmacological options include bupropion and tricyclic antidepressants, but these drugs are prescribed less frequently than the stimulants. The most common side effects for stimulants and atomoxetine include decreased appetite, mild stomachaches or headaches, insomnia, increased anxiety, and/or irritability. All medications need to be monitored on a frequent and regular basis, given that children's needs may change as they mature.

REFERENCES

American Psychiatric Association. (2000). *Diagnostic and statistical manual of mental disorders* (4th ed., text rev.). Washington, DC: Author.

Barkley, R. A. (2006). *Attention-deficit hyperactivity disorder: A handbook for diagnosis and treatment* (3rd ed.). New York: Guilford Press.

Fassbender, C. & Schweitzer, J. B. (2006). Is there evidence for neural compensation in attention deficit hyperactivity disorder? A review of the functional neuroimaging literature. *Clinical Psychology Review, 26*:445–465.

Flory, K., Molina, B., Pelham, G., Gnagy, E., & Smith, B. (2006). Childhood ADHD predicts risky sexual behavior in young adulthood. *Journal of Clinical Child & Adolescent Psychology, 35,* 571–577.

Jensen, P. (2002). Longer term effects of stimulant treatments for Attention-Deficit/Hyperactivity Disorder. *Journal of Attention Disorders; 6* Suppl 1:S45–56.

Kessler R. C., Adler L., Barkley R., Biederman J., Conners C. K., Demler O., Faraone S. V., Greenhill L. L., Howes M. J., Secnik K., Spencer T., Ustun T. B., Walters E. E., & Zaslavsky, A. M. (2006). The prevalence and correlates of adult ADHD in the United States: Results from the National Comorbidity Survey Replication. *American Journal of Psychiatry, 163*:716–723.

Krain, A. L., & Castellanos, F. X. (2006). Brain development and ADHD. *Clinical Psychology Review, 26,* 433–444.

MTA Cooperative Group. (1999). A 14-month randomized clinical trial of treatment strategies for attention-deficit/hyperactivity disorder. Multimodal Treatment Study of Children with ADHD. *Archives of General Psychiatry, 56*:1073–1086.

MTA Cooperative Group. (2004). National Institute of Mental Health Multimodal Treatment Study of ADHD follow-up: 24-month outcomes of treatment strategies for attention-deficit/hyperactivity disorder. *Pediatrics, 114,* 514.

McBurnett, K., Pfinner, L. J., & Frick, P. J. (2001). Symptom properties as a function of ADHD type: An argument for continued study of sluggish cognitive tempo. *Journal of Abnormal Child Psychology, 29,* 207–213.

Shaw, P. Eckstrand, K., Sharp, W., Blumenthal, J., Lerch, J. P., Greenstein, D., Clasen, L., Evans, A., Giedd, J., & Rapoport, J. L. (2007). Attention-deficit/hyperactivity disorder is characterized by a delay in cortical maturation. *PNAS, 104,* 19649–19654.

Solanto M. V., Marks D. J., Mitchell K. J., Wasserstein J., & Kofman, M. D. (2008). Development of a new psychosocial treatment for adult ADHD. *Journal of Attention Disorders, 11*:728–736.

SUGGESTED READING

Biederman J., & Spencer T. J. (2008). Psychopharmacological interventions. *Child and Adolescent Psychiatric Clinics of North America, 17*:439–458.

JULIE B. SCHWEITZER
University of California, Davis

See also: **Psychostimulant Treatment for Children**

ATTITUDES

Psychologists use the term *attitude* to refer to a general evaluation that an individual holds regarding a particular entity, such as an object, an issue, or a person. An individual may hold an extremely favorable attitude toward a particular political candidate, for example, and a mildly unfavorable attitude toward another candidate. Thus, attitudes vary in valence as well as extremity, and they reflect an individual's overall summary evaluation of an attitude object. Attitudes toward the countless objects that we encounter in our day-to-day lives are stored in memory, and they remain at least somewhat stable over time. In this way, attitudes are different from fleeting, momentary evaluative responses to an object. In addition, attitudes are specific to particular objects, unlike diffuse evaluative reactions like moods or dispositions.

How Are Attitudes Formed?

Attitudes can be formed in several different ways. Some attitudes are derived from our cognitions about an attitude object. We may hold a positive attitude toward a particular political candidate, for example, because we believe that the candidate will enact legislation that will bring about a set of desirable outcomes. Our beliefs about candidates and their policy positions may be organized in an elaborate interconnected cognitive structure containing an array of knowledge about these candidates, and from this set of cognitions we may derive a positive or negative overall evaluation of these candidates.

Other attitudes have little to do with our cognitions about an object and are instead based on our affective reactions to the object. Rather than basing our attitude toward political candidates on our thoughts and beliefs, for example, we may derive our attitude from the emotional response that they elicit. To the extent that candidates evoke feelings of optimism and pride, we may form a positive attitude toward them. But if instead candidates elicit feelings of contempt or anger, we may derive a negative attitude toward them. Such attitudes would be affectively based.

In addition to affect and cognition, attitudes can also be based on our behavior. We often infer others' attitudes from the behaviors that they perform, and in much the same way we sometimes look to our own behavior for insights regarding our attitudes (Bem, 1972). When contemplating our attitude toward a particular political candidate, for example, we may reflect on the behaviors that we have performed for insight into our attitude. We may recall, for example, that we recently signed a petition in favor of the candidate when a co-worker asked us to do so, or that we accepted a button from one of the candidate's campaign workers whom we encountered on our way to work. From these behaviors, we may infer that we hold a positive attitude toward the candidate.

Our behaviors can affect our attitudes in a second way as well. Rather than inferring our attitudes from our behaviors, we sometimes modify our attitudes so that they align more closely with the behaviors we have performed in the past. According to cognitive dissonance theory, we do this because we find it uncomfortable when we discover internal inconsistencies (e.g., Festinger, 1957). When we recognize, for example, that we have performed a behavior that is incongruent with our attitude, we experience an uncomfortable tension. To reduce this tension, we look for ways to eliminate the inconsistency. Of course, the behavior has already been performed, so the easiest way to restore consistency often involves changing the attitude so that it is more congruent with the behavior. And

indeed, there is evidence that people often do precisely this, revising their attitudes in light of their past behavior.

What Do Attitudes Do?

Attitudes play a critical role in our interactions with the world around us. Because they summarize the positive and negative outcomes or attributes associated with an object, attitudes help us to obtain rewards and avoid punishment, efficiently guiding our behavior toward the object. Without attitudes stored in memory, we would need to size up the evaluative implications of the people, places, and things in our social environment every time we encounter them. This slow and cognitively taxing process would leave us in a precarious situation when the circumstances call for swift action.

Instead, attitudes permit us to make sense of and react to the world around us quickly and efficiently. In fact, physiological evidence indicates that, as soon as we encounter an object, our attitudes are activated, enabling us to differentiate between things that we like and things that we do not like. Even when we are not explicitly intending to evaluate an object, our brains seem to do exactly that. Given the evolutionary significance of being able to swiftly approach things that are beneficial to us and even more swiftly avoid things that are detrimental, it should perhaps come as no surprise that our attitudes are spontaneously activated upon encountering an object.

But what happens when an attitude has been activated? A large literature attests the far-reaching consequences of attitudes for thought and behavior. There is evidence, for example, that attitudes can color our interpretations of events. When we watch a political debate, we often come away convinced that our preferred candidate was victorious, and we are mystified when we learn that others came to a different conclusion. In many cases, this is because our attitudes toward the candidates biased our perceptions of their respective performances. In this and many other ways, attitudes often influence information processing.

And when an attitude is activated, it often influences our behavior as well. We approach things that we like and we actively avoid things that we dislike. Whether we take the extra step to recycle yesterday's newspaper, for example, depends to a large degree on our attitudes toward recycling. In the same way, our attitudes toward consumer products have a big impact on how we spend our money. And of course, attitudes toward political candidates largely determine our electoral behavior. In countless domains, there is clear evidence that attitudes often motivate and guide behavior.

Attitude Strength

As we have seen, attitudes can be tremendously consequential, influencing virtually all of our interactions with the world around us. It is important to note, however, that this is not always the case. To the contrary, although some attitudes exert a powerful impact on thought and behavior, others are largely inconsequential. Similarly, whereas some attitudes are firm, resistant to even the strongest challenges, others are highly malleable and fluctuate greatly over time. Psychologists use the term "attitude strength" to capture this distinction. More formally, strong attitudes are those that (1) resist persuasion, (2) remain stable over time, (3) guide behavior, and (4) influence information processing (Krosnick & Petty, 1985).

Attitude strength provides important leverage for anticipating an attitude's cognitive and behavioral consequences. For example, knowing that an individual holds a positive attitude toward recycling can be quite useful in predicting his or her likelihood of participating in various recycling programs, but knowing the strength of that attitude vastly improves the precision of these predictions.

Not surprisingly, then, attitude strength has been the focus of sustained scholarly attention for more than two decades. Of particular interest has been the identification of specific features of strong attitudes that differentiate them from weak attitudes, and a large literature now exists that does precisely this (see Petty and Krosnick, 1995; Visser, Bizer, & Krosnick, 2006). For example, strong attitudes tend to be held with great certainty, and they tend to be supported by a good deal of information stored in memory. Strong attitudes also tend to be those to which people attach a great deal of psychological significance, considering them to be personally important. Given this, measures of attitude certainty, attitude-relevant knowledge, and attitude importance offer fundamental insights regarding the strength of an individual's attitude and therefore its likely impact on thought and behavior.

Ambivalence is also an indicator of attitude strength. Toward some attitude objects, we may experience a mix of positive and negative reactions, rendering us ambivalent about the object. Even if we support capital punishment, for example, we may nonetheless have a number of unfavorable thoughts and feelings about it as well. Ambivalent attitudes of this sort tend to be weaker than univalent attitudes, so measures of attitudinal ambivalence can provide useful leverage for differentiating strong attitudes from weak ones.

Finally, the speed and ease with which we can access and report our attitudes also yields valuable information about the strength of those attitudes. Strong attitudes tend to spring to mind quickly, whereas weaker attitudes often require more time and effort to retrieve from memory. Increasingly, then, researchers have relied on the latency with which individuals report their attitudes as an indicator of attitude strength.

Attitudes are overall evaluations of the people, places, and things around us. They can have cognitive, affective, or behavioral bases (or some combination of the three). Attitudes enable us to effectively navigate our social environment by efficiently summarizing the evaluative implications of the stimuli we encounter. They guide our behavior toward those objects that are beneficial to us and away from objects that may be deleterious, and they often influence the way we process information.

REFERENCES

Bem, D. J. (1972). Self Perception Theory. In L. Berkowitz (Ed.), *Advances in experimental social psychology*, (Vol. 6, pp. 1–62). New York: Academic Press.

Festinger, L. (1957). *A theory of cognitive dissonance*. Stanford, CA: Stanford University Press.

Krosnick, J. A., & Petty. R. E. (1985). Attitude strength: An overview. In R. E. Petty & J. A. Krosnick (Eds.), *Attitude strength: Antecedents and consequences* (pp. 215–245). Mahwah, NJ: Lawrence Erlbaum.

Petty, R. E., & Krosnick, J. A. (1995). *Attitude strength: Antecedents and consequences*. Mahwah, NJ: Lawrence Erlbaum.

Visser, P. S., Bizer, G. Y., & Krosnick, J. A. (2006). Exploring the latent structure of strength-related attitude attributes. In M. Zanna (Ed.), *Advances in experimental social psychology*. New York: Academic Press.

SUGGESTED READINGS

Eagly, A. H., & Chaiken, S. (1993). *The psychology of attitudes*. Fort Worth, TX: Harcourt, Brace, Janovich.

Eagly, A. H., & Chaiken, S. (1998). Attitude structure and function. In D. T. Gilbert, S. T. Fiske, & G. Lindzey (Eds.), *The handbook of social psychology* (4th ed., vol. 1, pp. 269–322). New York: McGraw-Hill.

Fazio, R. H., & Olson, M. A. (2003). Attitudes: Foundations, functions, and consequences. In M. Hogg & J. Cooper (Eds.), *Sage Handbook of Social Psychology*. London: Sage Publications.

PENNY S. VISSER
University of Chicago

See also: **Cognitive Dissonance**

ATTRIBUTION THEORY

Attribution theory refers to a field of study rather than to a specific scientific conception. The heart of this area of investigation includes assumptions, hypotheses, and theories regarding how laypersons arrive at answers to "why" questions such as: "Why did I fail my exam?" and "Why did Jim and Mary break up?" Note, then, that this approach grapples with both self- and other perception. In addition, there also is concern with the consequences of causal beliefs, including their emotional and motivational significance. Although attribution inquiry is typically included under the domain of social psychology, it has had impact in the areas of clinical, cognitive, developmental, educational, personality, and motivational psychology as well, thereby providing a general foundation for psychology.

Attribution thinking was introduced into psychology by Fritz Heider (1958). But his seminal book was relatively neglected prior to subsequent publications by Jones and Davis (1965) and Kelley (1967). In addition to these contributions, the book *Attribution: Perceiving the Causes of Behavior* (Jones, Kanouse, Kelley, Nisbett, Valins, & Weiner, 1972) also was responsible for ushering in nearly two decades (1970–1990) of dominance in social psychology. Attribution analyses, often associated with naïve or commonsense psychology, replaced the "noncommon sense" theory of cognitive dissonance in social psychology, and itself was subsequently supplanted within social psychology by a return to the irrational, this time with a focus on unconscious processes and "priming."

Reaching Causal Inferences

One goal of attribution research has been to identify the personal and situational determinants of causal understanding. It is assumed that humans want to attain a cognitive mastery of their world. Further, people are regarded as naïve scientists, logical and rational, albeit not infallible and subject to systematic biases and errors.

In the desire for understanding, it has been documented that causal search is not undertaken in all instances but is most likely given an important, unexpected, and negative event or outcome. This might be failure at a crucial exam, rejection of a marriage proposal, and the like. Principles found in covariation analyses regarding the presence and absence of causes and effects are important sources of causal information to help determine the answers to "why" questions. For example, failure at an exam is more likely to be self-attributed if there have been many prior personal failures and knowledge of the successes of others (see Kelley, 1967). In addition, causal rules are used such that, for example, if beliefs of multiple causality for achievement failure are elicited, then even in the presence of insufficient effort, there will be additional attributions to lack of ability or to some environmental factors as causes of the negative outcome. Further, the presence of some causes may result in other causes being discounted. One controversy associated with the latter process concerns the arguable hypothesis that rewarding pupils for successful achievement performance reduces their motivation because the extrinsic reward results in a discounting of their intrinsic interest.

It also has been reasoned (again with controversy) that the behavior of others tends to be ascribed to a stable disposition or trait inasmuch as explanations that capture enduring aspects of the world are preferred and the other is dominant in social perception. Underestimation of the situation as a perceived cause of the behavior of others and over-attribution to the person has been labeled "the

fundamental attribution error." However, this principle is being challenged in cross-cultural research, for it has been argued that situational attributions are more salient among Asians.

Another bias that has been examined in attribution research concerns beliefs about the causes of positive and negative events. Self-attributions tend to be given for positive outcomes ("I succeeded because I studied hard"), whereas negative outcomes elicit external attributions ("I failed because the exam was unfair"). This pattern of attribution is labeled the "hedonic bias" inasmuch as positive self-directed emotions and the maintenance of self-esteem are fostered. The postulation of a hedonic bias and the hypothesis that self-related attributions are made to environmental causes at times are conflicting. That is, if individuals tend to ascribe personal success to internal causes such as ability and effort, then this masks or supersedes the tendency to attribute personal outcomes to causes located in the environment (see Malle, 2006).

Consequences of Causal Beliefs

The research activity concerning the consequences of perceived causality is less voluminous than that associated with the reaching of causal inferences, but it nonetheless is very substantial, particularly in disciplines other than social psychology. Here again only a small sample of the research direction is presented.

A large body of research in the field of emotion documents that what is being thought, including causal beliefs, directly relates to emotional experience. For example, in educational contexts, failure due to lack of effort gives rise to guilt; failure because of low ability produces shame and embarrassment; success attributed to help from others elicits gratitude; and so on (see review in Weiner, 2006). These thinking-feeling relations have important implications in nonachievement-related contexts as well. For example, in the field of clinical psychology, it has been suggested that ascribing negative events to something about the self that is not subject to personal control, that is, a cause the individual can do nothing to alter, produces a state of "learned helplessness." This belief promotes and/or accompanies depression. Hence, for example, social or job failure ascribed to lack of aptitude may be an antecedent (or correlate) of depression (see Seligman, 1975).

Attribution-guided research within clinical psychology also has revealed that when the behavior of a mentally ill family member is ascribed by others to a cause under personal control, that is, when the cause implicates personal blame and "it could be otherwise" (e.g., "he is just lazy"), then negative emotions including anger are elicited among family members. This increases the likelihood of subsequent recidivism. The relation between causal beliefs in personal control, anger, and adverse mental-health consequences has been found among both schizophrenic and depressive persons (see Barrowclough & Hooley, 2003).

Assignment of responsibility and blame also are central in many other contexts, revealing that in addition to being naïve scientists, humans also act as naïve judges. Other-blame is one indicator of marital distress, is elicited by a variety of stigmas including alcoholism and obesity, and in general decreases help giving. Thus, for example, less charity aid is offered to persons obese due to overeating as opposed to having a thyroid problem, or to those with AIDS because of promiscuous sexuality as opposed to AIDS caused by an infected mother (see reviews in Weiner, 1995, 2006).

The anticipation of negative consequences due to being perceived as responsible for a negative outcome gives rise to a variety of impression management techniques to alter this inference. For example, students publicly claim lack of ability rather than low effort as the cause when explaining their failure to authority figures (but not when ascribing the cause of failure to peers). In addition to excuses (ex = from; cuse = cause), confessions also are an effective interpersonal technique because the cause of the transgression is altered from something stable about the person ("he is a bad seed") to something unstable and changeable ("he did a bad thing but is not a bad person and will not do it again").

Adaptive and maladaptive attributions also have been identified in studies of coping with stress. Following a negative life stressor, such as rape, individuals ascribing this event to their character ("I am a risk-taker") do not cope as well as those attributing the event to a particular behavior ("I accidentally was in the wrong place at the wrong time"). A trait is perceived to be a relatively stable and uncontrollable cause, whereas a behavioral causal ascription is temporary and subject to volitional change. For these reasons, attributional therapies have been devised that attempt to change causal beliefs so they are more adaptive. In educational contexts, these programs often alter beliefs about the cause of failure from lack of ability to the absence of effort or effective strategies (see Perry, Hechter, Menec, & Weinberg, 1993). These latter ascriptions again are more adaptive because behavioral change and instrumental activities are possible to alter the anticipated (and actual) consequences.

In sum, causal beliefs play an important role in self- and other- understanding and significantly influence emotions and subsequent actions. The study of causal attributions therefore provides one of the basic building blocks for social psychology and also has great relevance for other disciplines within psychology.

REFERENCES

Barrowclough, C., & Hooley, J. M. (2003). Attributions and expressed emotion: A review. *Clinical Psychology Review, 23,* 849–880.

Heider, F. (1958). *The psychology of interpersonal relations.* New York: Wiley & Sons.

Jones, E. E., & Davis, K. E. (1965). From acts to dispositions: The attribution process in person perception. In L. Berkowitz (Ed.), *Advances in experimental social psychology, Vol. 2.* (pp. 219–266). New York: Academic Press.

Jones, E. E., Kanouse, D. E., Kelley, H. H., Nisbett, R. E., Valins, S., & Weiner, B. (Eds.), (1972). *Attribution: Perceiving the causes of behavior.* Morristown, NJ: General Learning Press.

Kelley, H. H. (1967). Attribution theory in social psychology. In D. Levine (Ed.), *Nebraska symposium of motivation, Vol. 15* (pp. 192–238). Lincoln: University of Nebraska Press.

Malle, B. F. (2006). The actor-observer asymmetry in causal attributions: A (surprising) meta-analysis. *Psychological Bulletin, 132,* 895–919.

Perry, R. P., Hechter, F. J., Menec, V. H., & Weinberg, L. E. (1993). Enhancing achievement motivation and performance in college students: An attributional retraining perspective. *Research in Higher Education, 34,* 687–723.

Seligman, M. E. P. (1975). *On depression, development, and death.* San Francisco: Freeman.

Weiner, B. (1995). *Judgments of responsibility: A foundation for a theory of social conduct.* New York: Guilford Press.

Weiner, B. (2006). *Social motivation, justice, and the moral emotions.* Mahwah, NJ: Lawrence Erlbaum.

SUGGESTED READING

Försterling, F. (2001). *Attribution theory, research, and practice. Social psychology: A modular course.* New York: Psychology Press.

BERNARD WEINER
University of California, Los Angeles

See also: **Cognitive Development; Emotion Regulation; Self-Control**

AUDITORY PERCEPTION

The world is a noisy place. Almost all objects vibrate, and those vibrations can produce audible sound. Hearing allows an organism to process information about these sound sources. Hearing assists animals in navigation, seeking prey, avoiding predators, finding a mate, and in communication (e.g., speech and language). Sound can also add an aesthetic quality, as in music. The study of auditory perception seeks to understand the auditory system's ability to process the sound from sound sources. Such processing turns out to be a challenging task. The sound pressure wave that radiates from a vibrating object (e.g., the string of a violin) does not have physical parameters that directly indicate the physical dimensions of the source. Sound is defined by its frequency, amplitude, and temporal dimensions.

For instance, the sound pressure wave itself carries no information about where the sound source is located, yet most animals can locate the sources of sound. Thus, the auditory system must do the calculations that allow for sound source location. The problem of processing the sound from sources is even more complicated when there is more than one sound source producing sound at the same time, such as at a cocktail party. The sounds from all sources are combined into one complex sound that impinges upon the auditory system, so the auditory system must do the analysis that allows for the perceptual segregation of the various sound sources (Yost, Popper, & Fay, 2007). Bregman (1990) refers to this challenge as "auditory scene analysis."

The peripheral parts of the auditory system (outer, middle, and inner ears; auditory nerve) perform an eloquent analysis of the spectral (frequency), amplitude, and temporal dimensions of sound (Yost, 2007). The temporal-spectral neural code for the three physical dimensions of sound is sent to the brainstem via the auditory nerve and then to the auditory cortex for further processing. A great deal of what is known about auditory perception relates to the neural code provided by the auditory periphery (Yost, Fay, & Popper, 1993).

Many animals, including humans, can detect the presence of sound at remarkably low sound-pressure levels (20 micropascals—at this pressure the human eardrum moves a distance equal to approximately the diameter of a hydrogen atom). The auditory system can tolerate changes in sound pressure over a very large range (approximately 10^7 in humans). And, the auditory system processes frequency over a considerable range (approximately 10 octaves from 20 to 20,000 Hz for humans), although the frequencies at which sensitivity is best are in the middle of this frequency range (500 to 4000 Hz for humans).

The sound-pressure-level thresholds required to detect the presence of sound over the frequency range of 125 Hz to 8000 Hz have been standardized and are the reference for the basic measure of hearing loss, the audiogram. The audiogram measures a person's ability to detect the presence of sounds of different frequencies and compares this ability to standardized values based on the detection of these sounds by normal hearing young listeners.

Just as the auditory system is exquisitely sensitive to the absolute values of the physical properties of sound, so too is it able to discern very small changes in these properties. A change of about 0.5% in frequency is discriminable, as is a 7% (less than 1 dB) change in sound pressure level, and a 10% change in sound duration. When the sound pressure level changes over time (the sound is amplitude modulated), the auditory system remains sensitive to these sound-pressure level modulations up to about 50 modulations per second; above 50 modulations/second human listeners lose their sensitivity to the sound pressure fluctuations.

In the everyday world many different sound sources often produce sound at nearly the same time so that the sound from one source (the masker) could interfere with the ability to detect the presence of another sound (the signal). Sounds similar in frequency mask each other more than sounds of different frequencies. In detecting a signal of one frequency, there is a critical band of masker frequencies centered on the signal frequency that produces the most masking. Signal threshold is usually proportional to the power of the masker within this critical band. It is also the case that low-frequency maskers provide more masking of higher-frequency signals, than high-frequency maskers provide for lower-frequency signals (upward spread of masking) (Moore & Patterson, 1986).

Sound has no physical dimensions of space, yet humans and almost all other animals can locate the position of sound sources based on the interaction of sound with obstacles in the path of sound as it travels to the outer ears. A sound from a source off to one side of a listener will arrive at the ear closest to the sound source before the sound reaches the other ear, and because the head produces a sound shadow, the sound pressure level is greater at the near ear. These interaural (between ears) time and level differences covary with the location of the sound source in the horizontal plane around the listener (the azimuth plane). The auditory system uses microsecond variations in interaural time difference (ITD) and 0.5 to 1 dB variations in the interaural level difference (ILD) to process the azimuth location of sound sources (Blauert, 1997).

The ITDs and ILDs are not usable cues for localizing sounds in the vertical direction. For instance, consider sound sources located directly in front of a listener, directly above the listener, and directly behind the listener. Because each of these sources is located midway between the ears, the ILD and ITD are always both zero, yet human listeners can locate the position of each of these sound sources (i.e., ILDs and ITDs could not be cues for locating these source locations). Localization in the vertical plane appears to depend on the interaction of sound with the torso, head, and outer ear (pinna) of the listener as the sound travels from a source to the outer ear. These structures selectively alter the sound, especially the high-frequency content of the sound, that arrives at the outer ear. These transformations are called Head Related Transfer Functions (HRTF), and the form of the HRTF changes as a function of the relative location of a sound source. Thus, the form of the HRTF and a comparison of the HRTFs between the ears probably provide the information used by the auditory system to assist in the location of sound sources in the vertical plane (Blauert, 1997).

A masking sound that arrives from a sound-source location that differs from that of a signal sound source provides less masking of the signal than when the signal and masker are colocated. Thus, the ability of the auditory system to separate the position of sound sources (especially in the azimuth plane) aids in the ability to detect and attend to a sound from a source at one position when competing sounds sources are at other locations. These spatial effects are often studied as masking-level differences (MLDs) in which there are differences in the signal level required for signal detection when the spatial parameters of the signal differ from those of the masker.

In addition to the perception of the location of sound sources, the sound pressure waveform has the subjective attributes of loudness, pitch, temporal change, and timbre. Loudness is directly related to sound pressure, but a sound's frequency will also affect perceived loudness, in that two sounds of different frequency but of the same sound-pressure level can be perceived as different in loudness. Equal-loudness contours describe the sound-pressure level required to judge sounds of different frequencies to be equally loud and are the basis for the phon measure of loudness (ANSI, 1997).

One aspect of the nonlinearity of peripheral processing is a compressive transfer of input sound level to neural output in that for low-level (soft) sounds there is a linear relationship between sound level and neural output. At higher (loud) sound levels, the same increase in sound level that produced a large change in neural output at low sound levels produces a smaller change in neural output at this higher input sound level. This compressive nonlinearity influences loudness perception and masking (Bacon, Fay, & Popper, 2004).

For simple sounds, pitch can be directly related to frequency, but for complex sounds pitch is more likely related to the fine structure of the synchronous neural response to the sound's time-pressure waveform rather than to the sound's spectrum (Plack et al., 2005). For instance, a harmonic complex sound that has frequency components of 400, 500, 600, and 700 Hz will have a perceived pitch of 100 Hz, despite the fact that there is no energy in the sound at 100 Hz (100 Hz is the fundamental of the harmonic complex, and the fundamental is missing). The pitch of missing fundamental type stimuli can often be explained by the fine-structure timing of the neural discharge pattern to the sound-pressure waveform.

Timbre is defined as that perceptual quality of sound that allows a listener to differentiate the sound from two sources when each sound is judged to have the same pitch, loudness, and duration. Thus, a violin is discernable from a viola even when each instrument produces the same note (pitch), at the same loudness, and for the same duration. This difference in sound quality is a timbre difference. There is no clear relationship between timbre perception and the physical properties of sound, nor is there anything about the neural peripheral code for sound that has been usable to account for the wide variety of timbre differences that have been studied.

Sound sources produce sounds that are perceived as being different in pitch, loudness, temporal properties, timbre, and spatial location. All of these variables influence the ability to determine sound sources and to segregate sound sources when several exist together. But identifying and segregating sound sources involves other aspects of auditory perception as well. For instance, a masking sound of one frequency will not mask a signal sound of a very different frequency. But this result occurs in an experimental procedure in which the masker and signal are repeated many times to estimate signal threshold. As long as the masker frequencies are not similar (are outside the critical band) to the signal frequency, little masking occurs. However, if from trial to trial the masker frequency varies randomly so the listener receives no predictable repetition of the masker frequency, there can be considerable masking even when each of the individual masking frequencies provide very little masking when measured alone. This additional masking caused by the random presentation of the various masker frequencies is called informational masking. These results might be explained in terms of attention, in that when the masker frequency varies randomly from trial to trial the listener cannot attend to the pitch of the signal; the changing pitch of the masker distracts the listener (Kidd et al, 2007).

Informational masking along with masking that occurs as a function of the direct interaction of the sound from various sound sources (energetic masking) are both components of segregating the sound from one source from that of other sources. The ability to attend to one sound source over another and the storage and retrieval of acoustic information from memory are other variables that probably play a role in processing an auditory scene.

While speech and music have unique perceptual aspects, they are nonetheless sounds that travel through the same neural pathways as all other sounds. Thus, processes that determine the perception of speech and music are probably also based partially, or maybe largely, on those that process all sounds. There is an emerging view of auditory perception that attempts to incorporate an integrated perceptual-cognitive account for processing all sounds that enter the auditory system (Holt & Lotto, 2008).

REFERENCES

ANSI S3.4-1980. (R 1997). American National Standard Procedure for the Computation of Loudness of Noise. New York: American National Standards Institute.

Bacon, S. P., Fay, R .R., & Popper, A. N. (Eds.) (2004). *Compression: From the cochlea to cochlear implants*. New York: Springer.

Blauert, J. (1997). *Spatial hearing*. Cambridge, MA: MIT Press.

Bregman, A. S. (1990). *Auditory scene analysis: The perceptual organization of sound*. Cambridge: MIT Press.

Holt, L. L., & Lotto, A. J. (2008). Speech perception within an auditory cognitive science framework. *Current Directions in Psychological Science, 17*, 42–46.

Kidd, G. Jr., Mason, C. R., Richards, V. M., Frederick, J., Gallun, F. J., Nathaniel, I., & Durlach, N. I. (2007). Informational masking. In W. A. Yost, A. N. Popper, & R. R. Fay (Eds.), *Auditory perception of sound sources*. New York: Springer.

Moore, B. C. J., & Patterson, R. D. (Eds.). (1986). *Auditory frequency selectivity*. London: Plenum Press.

Plack, C. J., Oxenham, A. J., Fay, R. R., & Popper, A.N. (Eds.). (2005). *Pitch: Neural coding and perception*. New York: Springer.

Yost, W. A. (2007). *Fundamentals of hearing: An introduction* (5th ed.). San Diego: Academic Press.

Yost, W. A., Popper, A. N., & Fay, R. R. (Eds.). (1993). *Human psychoacoustics*. New York: Springer.

Yost, W. A., Popper, A. N., & Fay, R. R. (Eds.). (2007). *Auditory perception of sound sources*. New York: Springer.

SUGGESTED READING

Moore, B. C. J. (2003). *An introduction to the psychology of hearing* (5th ed.). San Diego: Academic Press.

WILLIAM A. YOST
Arizona State University

See also: **Deafness and Hearing Loss; Speech Perception**

AUSTRALIA, PSYCHOLOGY IN

The history of psychology in Australia is relatively well documented. It was highly influenced in its early years by British psychology, and indeed the early psychologists formed an Australian chapter of the British Psychological Society as their learned society and primary professional body. It was only in 1966 that the Australian Psychological Society, with its own charter, Code of Ethics, and accreditation and standards committees came into being, with a resounding vote from the Australian members to become independent. Since those early days, the Australian Psychological Society has grown into a strong peak professional and scientific body in Australia, with more than 17,000 members in 2008 (approximately 60% of all psychologists in the country). The Australian Psychological Society is consulted by government and nongovernment organizations and by the media on the broad range of issues affecting psychologists and the general community, and for expert comment and advice on various psychological issues that arise.

Psychologists in Australia must be registered to practice in their state or territory. Psychologist Registration Boards are appointed by the state or territory government and comprise senior psychologists, members of other professions, and community members. The Council of Australian Governments has determined that, by July of 2010, health professions will be subject to a national registration, and this includes psychologists, whether working in the health sector or not. In order to be registered as a psychologist currently, one must have followed a minimum course of study that includes four years of psychology.

Accreditation of university courses for the purpose of gaining professional standing as a psychologist is done through the Australian Psychology Accreditation Council (APAC), which was formed through agreement between the Australian Psychological Society and the Council of Psychologist Registration Boards and is wholly owned and operated by those two entities.

Psychology can be studied at 37 different Australian universities via APAC accredited courses. There are accredited postgraduate courses in at least nine different specialties that coincide with the specialist colleges of the Australian Psychological Society, namely, clinical psychology, clinical neuropsychology, community psychology, counseling psychology, developmental and educational psychology, forensic psychology, health psychology, organizational (industrial) psychology, and sports psychology.

Psychology as a profession has boomed in Australia since the beginning of the twenty-first century. With an increase in acknowledgement of the role of human behavior in the development and course of serious illnesses, and with the increased concern with the prevalence of mental illness, psychology has become a high-profile and well-thought-of profession. There is considerable competition for places in postgraduate programs, despite the recognition of a workforce shortage by the government and the subsequent release of scholarships to support students.

In 2006, after a 32-year battle for recognition, psychological services for the treatment of people with a mental illness were included in the schedule of items that are reimbursed under Medicare, the national health insurance scheme. This has changed the face of psychological practice in Australia, with members of the community having significantly increased access to psychological assistance when they need it. People are referred through their family doctor for up to 12 sessions in a calendar year with a psychologist or specialist clinical psychologist.

The Australian population is mainly centered in metropolitan areas, with about 30% of the population living outside the major cities. Even the indigenous population, 70% of whom live outside major centers, are nowadays largely urbanized. Psychologists reflect the general population, with a much higher proportion living and practicing in the major cities than in remote areas; only about 30% of psychologists practice outside the major cities. This distribution of psychologists has meant that, with Medicare, there are increased services for those people who live in areas not serviced by a psychiatrist. Entry into the Medicare scheme has also altered the relationship between psychology as a profession and many other health professions. In recent years, psychology, through the Australian Psychological Society, has become part of the Allied Health Professions Australia and the Mental Health Professions Association. These relationships with other professions have enhanced psychology's ability to advise the government and impact government policy.

There are many psychological scientists of world repute working in Australian universities and research centers. Australian research is published in both Australian and international journals. There has been an increasing effort in recent years to do translational research, so that the community can understand the contribution of psychology to human understanding and well-being.

The indigenous population is very small in Australia—probably only 2.5% of the total highly multicultural population. Until recently there was almost no acknowledgement of the specific needs of indigenous Australians and the particular nature of indigenous Australian psychology. In 2008 the Australian Indigenous Psychology Association was launched, under the auspices of the Australian Psychological Society. The goals of this association are to support the two dozen or so indigenous psychologists in Australia, as well as fostering the development of more indigenous psychologists. Some 400 additional indigenous psychologists will need to be trained in order to provide parity of service with the nonindigenous population. This association will work with the Bendi Lango ("cutting edge") Bursary Foundation, which was established by the Australian Psychological Society in 2006 to provide financial support bursaries for postgraduate indigenous psychology students.

National Psychology Week was established in 2003, following an inaugural National Psychology Day in 2002. Through media activities, a national research survey and a range of member events throughout Australia, National Psychology Week showcases the diverse ways in which psychologists enhance community well-being. The focus of the week, which encompasses all areas of psychology, is "Think well. Be well." In 2008 there were more than 400 member events around the country, with displays in public areas, public lectures, professional development activities, and the first National Oration by a highly esteemed psychologist.

Australian psychologists are represented internationally through membership of the International Union of Psychological Science and the International Association of Applied Psychology, as well as many other international organizations. Australian psychology plays a role regionally through the Asian Psychological Association, and the Australian Psychological Society has Memoranda of Understanding with various other national psychology associations, to ensure that Australian psychology remains international in its purview. Australian psychologists have also shown a willingness to engage with social issues, both locally and internationally, and have spoken up to enhance community and individual well-being whenever they can be supported by the psychological evidence. In recent years individuals have used their psychological knowledge to support community action in areas such as the health and well-being of refugees, asylum seekers, and victims of torture, trauma, natural disasters, racism, and terrorism. Being able to represent oneself as a psychologist in Australia is something of which one can be proud.

AMANDA GORDON
Sydney, Australia

AUTHORITARIANISM

Authoritarianism is one of the most studied and most controversial concepts in personality, social, and political psychology. It also has wide usage in political discourse, as, for example, in the distinction between authoritarian and totalitarian regimes. It has entered the general vocabulary: a Google search finds more than one-and-a-half million references to the word.

In psychology, the seminal discussion of the concept was *The Authoritarian Personality* (Adorno, Frenkel-Brunswik, Levinson, & Sanford, 1950). It was published soon after the end of a world war against fascism, and the authors hoped to identify an authoritarian personality (AP) trait that predisposes some people to support fascistic political philosophies, programs, and politicians.

Theory

Who are these people? Using in-depth interviews and questionnaires, and interpreting results following psychoanalytic and Marxist theories, Adorno et al. (1950) identified AP as the product of what would now be called a positive feedback loop between dictatorial, punitive child-rearing methods and an exploitive, oppressive, capitalist economic system. Authoritarians had parents who punished them harshly if they misbehaved or expressed disagreement with the rules of society and the family, especially in sensitive areas such as sexual mores. Components of the adult AP include prejudice against religious, ethnic, and other outgroups; the prominence of defense mechanisms such as repression, projection, and denial; rigid thinking; adherence to conventional values and aggressiveness toward those who violate them, particularly about sexual morality; submissiveness toward authorities; preoccupation with toughness and power; disdain for introspection and tender-mindedness; superstitious beliefs in unknown powers; general cynicism; and a belief that wild and dangerous things are going on.

Later theorists have neglected or ignored Adorno et al.'s psychoanalytic explanations and instead linked authoritarianism with cognitive styles marked by simplistic and black-and-white thinking, aversion to novel ideas, need for structure and closure, and rigid closed-mindedness. Cognitive styles are content-free; these ways of thinking characterize how the individual processes all information, whatever its nature or source. Whether there can actually be content-free authoritarianism is a moot point.

Current researchers often use the concept of right-wing authoritarianism (RWA) and the RWA Scale (Altemeyer, 1981). RWA focuses on three aspects of AP: (1) deference to traditional authorities, (2) adherence to conventional norms of the person's in-group, and (3) aggressiveness against those who reject or violate those authorities and norms. As a general measure of authoritarianism, it is an improvement over a Fascism (F) Scale developed by Adorno et al., but it has problems of its own. One problem is that it treats differences in degrees of authoritarianism (higher vs. lower) as differences in personality type (AP vs. non-AP); another problem is inattention to what a low score actually means. Martin (2001) presents an extended critique of RWA.

Measurement

Adorno et al.'s interpretations of their in-depth interview responses have been criticized as biased (Martin, 2001); this issue aside, more attention has been paid to their culminating questionnaire for measuring anti-democratic tendencies, the F Scale, which remains today widely known and used. The F Scale came under scientific attack for two major reasons. One was psychometric problems related to subject sampling, item wording, susceptibility to response bias (e.g., a high score on every item was pro-Fascistic), and the conflation of conservative and fascistic ideas. The other reason was ideological: in 1950, the Korean War and the Cold War loomed on the horizon, and critics argued that communists were just as prone as fascists to submission to authority, aggressiveness against those who disagreed with their moral code, focus on power, rejection of tender-mindedness, and the like (e.g., Eysenck, 1981–1982).

AP and Political Ideology

Revised scales corrected the most obvious technical errors in the F Scale (Christie & Jahoda, 1954), but the political criticism was less amenable to such a simple solution. Alternative scales (e.g., of dogmatism and rigid thinking) were developed to be ideologically balanced, and the RWA Scale labels all authoritarians as being right-wing—presumably including Mao's Red Guard, the Animal Liberation Front, eco-terrorists, and so on—thereby defining the problem out of existence. Studies administering authoritarianism scales to various samples have generally found AP all along the left-right political spectrum, but more prevalently on the right, as Adorno et al. had reported. However, the studies were conducted in European and North American democracies, where leftists by definition do not support the nation's traditional politics and economics and have professed ethnic tolerance. Had the studies been done in ethnocentric (and in some cases anti-Semitic) communist dictatorships, such as the Soviet Bloc, North Korea, and China, the findings might have been different. In post-communist Hungary, authoritarianism is associated with extremism across the political spectrum (Todosijeviç & Enyedi, 2008), and neither the moderate left nor the moderate right can be convincingly depicted as authoritarian. A recent Left-Wing Authoritarianism Scale, tapping submission to left-wing leaders and support for violence against "the Establishment," found a few high scorers in a Dutch voter sample but significantly high scores among extreme leftist political activists (Van Hiel et al., 2006).

Adorno et al. pointed out that content may change: a leader could move a conventionalistic person from communism to Catholicism (p. 230); many loyal Nazis turned into loyal communists in postwar Eastern Europe. Whether movement between being an AP or non-AP individual is possible needs to be established, as do relationships between AP and political behavior, other values and attitudes, and even genetics. Much remains for future research of both theoretical and applied political interest.

REFERENCES

Adorno, T. W., Frenkel-Brunswik, E., Levinson, D. J., & Sanford, R. N. (1950). *The authoritarian personality*. New York: Harper & Row.

Altemeyer, B. (1981). *Right-wing authoritarianism*. Winnipeg: University of Manitoba Press.

Christie, R., & Jahoda, M. (Eds.). (1954). *Studies in the scope and methods of "The Authoritarian Personality."* Glencoe, IL: Free Press.

Eysenck, H. J. (1981–1982). Left-wing authoritarianism: Myth or reality? *Political Psychology, 3*, 234–238.

Martin, J. L. (2001). *The Authoritarian Personality*, 50 years later: What lessons are there for political psychology? *Political Psychology, 22*, 1–26.

Todosijeviç, B., & Enyedi, Z. (2008). Authoritarianism without dominant ideology: Political manifestations of authoritarian attitudes in Hungary. *Political Psychology, 29*, 767–787.

Van Hiel, A., Duriez, B., & Kossowska, M. (2006). The presence of left-wing authoritarianism in Western Europe and its relationship with conservative ideology. *Political Psychology, 27*, 769–793.

SUGGESTED READINGS

Rokeach, M. (1960). *The open and closed mind: Investigations into the nature of belief systems and personality systems*. New York: Basic Books.

Samelson, F. (1993). The authoritarian character from Berlin to Berkeley and beyond: The odyssey of a problem. In W.F. Stone, G. Lederer, & R. Christie (Eds.), *Strength and weakness: The authoritarian personality today* (pp. 22–43). New York: Springer-Verlag.

Stone, W. F., Lederer, G., & Christie, R. (Eds.). (1993). *Strength and weakness: The authoritarian personality today*. New York: Springer-Verlag.

PETER SUEDFELD
University of British Columbia, Canada

See also: Attitudes; Political Psychology

AUTISTIC DISORDER

Autistic disorder is an Axis I clinical disorder in the *Diagnostic and Statistical Manual of Mental Disorders* (DSM-IV-TR; American Psychiatric Association [APA], 2000) and is one of three autism spectrum disorders (ASDs) in this diagnostic system. The current diagnostic criteria for ASDs are those listed in the DSM-IV-TR; however, it is likely that these criteria may undergo changes in the upcoming DSM V, based on a growing research literature suggesting that autistic disorder, Asperger's disorder, and pervasive developmental disorders-NOS (not otherwise specified) represent points on a severity continuum that run in the same families, rather than being qualitatively distinct conditions.

History

Although autism was first described by Itard in 1801 and later in the clinical literature in 1943 by Leo Kanner, in the 1952 DSM, children with autistic disorder (AD) symptoms received the schizophrenic reaction diagnosis. In the 1968 DSM-II, children with such symptoms were diagnosed schizophrenic, childhood type. The 1980 DSM-III explicitly listed the condition we now call autistic disorder, but it was called infantile autism; in 1987, the name was changed to autistic disorder. The DSM-IV includes AD among other pervasive developmental disorders (Asperger's disorder, Rett's disorder, childhood disintegrative disorder, and pervasive developmental disorder-NOS (PDD-NOS).

Prevalence

Until the middle to late 1980s, it was believed that 6 in 10,000 children had autism. Only children now diagnosed with more severe AD would then have been identified as having autism. Subsequent studies revealed that prevalence was approximately 1:1,000, if every child within a given catchment area was tested at regular intervals to the age of 5. Shortly after the introduction in 1968 of the first widely accepted diagnostic test, the Autism Diagnostic Observation Schedule (ADOS), ASD prevalence estimates abruptly rose, as more clinicians were trained to administer the test. The ADOS detected PDD-NOS and Asperger's disorder, as well as AD. Many parents sought early diagnoses, so their children could receive early intervention services. In 1991 the U.S. Department of Education created a new category of special education eligibility for ASDs. Over the past decade, the Center for Disease Control has reported prevalence figures as high as 1:150.

A combination of factors appears to account for most of the apparent increase in prevalence: (1) increased ascertainment; (2) broadened diagnostic criteria; (3) creation of an ASD special education category; (4) diagnostic substitution, as children formerly labeled learning disabled or mild intellectual disability and language problems were now diagnosed with an ASD; and (5) questionable diagnoses by some community providers. Although actual prevalence may have risen, it is more likely that most of the apparent increase is an artifact (Rutter, 2005). The best estimate at this time is that actual prevalence is, and probably always has been, approximately 1:170, with the use of modern diagnostic criteria. Approximately 1:454 have AD, and 1:272 are diagnosed with Asperger's disorder or PDD-NOS (Chakrabarti & Fombonne, 2005).

Etiology

The ASDs have multiple etiologies. Miles and colleagues (2005) reported that 20% of individuals with ASDs had small head size and/or unusual physical features (dysmorphology), or complex autism. The remaining 80% had normal or larger than normal head size and no dysmorphology, or essential autism. Complex autism is believed to result from early errors in embryonic development (morphogenesis) that affect various brain areas as well as causing other dysmorphic features. Essential autism appears to result from microdeletions, which are mutations or chromosomal rearrangements producing localized brain developmental differences. Essential autism appears to be a heritable disorder, with more relatives with ASDs within families (20% vs. 9%). Individuals with complex autism are likely to receive an autistic disorder diagnosis, rather than Asperger's disorder or PDD-NOS, because their symptoms are usually more severe. There has been widespread speculation about vaccines containing mercury causing autism, but more than 16 independent studies have failed to find an association between autism prevalence and vaccinations (Doja & Roberts, 2006).

Diagnostic Features

A total of 6 features from a list of 16 must be endorsed from three symptom categories to qualify for an AD diagnosis. The three categories are (1) social impairment, (2) communication impairment, and (3) repetitive fixed interests and routines. Delays in social interaction, language, or imaginative play must have been apparent prior to age 36 months (APA, 2000).

Social interaction impairments include such things as eye contact, gestures, appropriate facial expression, failure to develop peer relationships, lack of interest in showing enjoyment, and lack of social reciprocity. Communication impairments include delay in or total lack of spoken language, marked impairment in the ability to initiate or sustain a conversation, repetitive use idiosyncratic language (e.g., echolalia), and lack of make-believe play. Restricted repetitive and stereotyped behavior, interests, and activities include preoccupation with restricted patterns of interest that are excessive or highly focused (e.g., exclusive interest in weather or dinosaurs), rigidly following specific and nonfunctional routines (e.g., lining up objects), repetitive stereotyped motor mannerisms (e.g., rocking, flapping, twirling), and persistent preoccupation with parts of objects rather than the whole object and its function (e.g., the wheels of toy cars).

Screening and Diagnostic Assessment

Diagnosis of autism is made by a psychologist or physician with extensive experience with individuals having autism spectrum disorders within the chronological age range in question. A clinical psychologist, clinical neuropsychologist, school psychologist, or other licensed psychologist with specialization in autism typically conducts the diagnostic assessment. Medical specialists in developmental behavioral pediatrics, child psychiatry, or pediatric neurology are also often qualified to conduct diagnostic assessments. General pediatricians often conduct screening for possible autism and refer their patients to other specialists for full evaluation.

There is currently no biological test for autism. Combinations of history, an interview around current symptoms, and standardized psychological screening and diagnostic assessment instruments are used. Children with speech, language, and social behavioral developmental delays are screened beginning at age 1 year to 18 months. First-Signs is an excellent resource in planning screening for possible ASD. Screening determines whether a child has sufficient autism features to warrant thorough diagnostic evaluation. Screening instruments include the Checklist for Autism in Toddlers (CHAT), the Childhood Autism Rating Scale (CARS), the Gilliam Autism Rating Scale, (GARS), and the Social Communication Quotient (SCQ).

The Autism Diagnostic Observation Schedule-Generic (ADOS-G) is the gold standard in autism diagnostic assessments. The Autism Diagnostic Interview-Revised (ADI-R) is primarily a research tool and is used infrequently for routine clinical diagnosis because it is time consuming to administer. The Pervasive Developmental Disorder

Behavior Inventory (PDDBI) is a parent and teacher informant questionnaire that is used less frequently than the ADOS. It is often helpful to interview more than one informant in arriving at a diagnosis. Diagnostic assessments by experienced practitioners yield a high degree of agreement (more than 90%) if all three ASDs are included in a sample. However, agreement drops sharply in distinguishing between Asperger's disorder and PDD-NOS. People undergoing autism diagnostic assessment should also receive developmental and age-appropriate speech and language, intellectual, and adaptive behavior assessments.

Comorbid Conditions

Few studies have examined comorbidities differentially among the three ASD subtypes. There is a high degree of comorbidity between fragile X syndrome and ASDs (50% of boys and 20% of girls met ASD in one study). Nearly all individuals with Smith-Lemli-Opitz (SLO) syndrome exhibit autism spectrum disorder symptoms. Many individuals with Cornelia de Lange syndrome display autistic features. People with the maternal uniparental disomy (UPD) form of Prader Willi syndrome are at greater risk for autistic symptomatology than those with paternal deletions of 15q11-q13. There is overlap between symptoms of attention-deficit/hyperactivity disorder (ADHD) and ASDs, as well as shared genes. However, the DSM-IV-TR states that ADHD should not be diagnosed in an individual with autism, in that attention problems are considered part of autism spectrum disorders. Many professionals treat children and youth with autism for their ADHD symptoms if they meet diagnostic criteria for both conditions. Epilepsy is present in 20–60% of individuals with autistic disorder, depending on their age and the setting from which the sample is drawn (Thompson, 2007).

Differential Diagnosis

It is as important to rule out alternative diagnoses that could account for symptoms as it is to identify autistic features during a diagnostic assessment. Children who do not have an ASD but who have obsessive-compulsive traits, language disorder, attention problems, or Tourette's syndrome, in combination with borderline intellectual functioning, can appear to present some autistic features during standardized assessments. Such individuals may become upset when a preferred routine is changed, may have difficulty verbally responding to some questions, may flap their hands when excited, may appear shy and anxious, and may have difficulty in focusing on a task for more than a few seconds at a time. However, individual children may exhibit good eye contact, smile reciprocally, exhibit joint attention, exhibit imaginative play, display appropriate affect, and share their interests with the examiner. It is very unlikely that an individual with autism would display these behavior patterns, so a more appropriate diagnosis should be sought in such instances.

Treatment and Prognosis

Until the late 1980s, it was believed that there were no effective treatments for autistic disorder. At that time, approximately 80% of people receiving an autism diagnosis would test within the intellectual disability range (less than 70 IQ). Most youngsters diagnosed with AD were served in special education classrooms for the severely emotionally disturbed or had the label "moderate/severe mental retardation" (a term no longer used). In 1987, psychologist Ivar Lovaas published a landmark study showing that after 3 years of treatment, half of a group of children who had received intensive early behavior therapy for 40 hours per week functioned within the typical range intellectually and in their adaptive behavior and successfully attended regular education classrooms. Since then, there have been numerous replications of Lovaas's findings with similar outcomes.

Relatively fewer children with an AD diagnosis (as contrasted with Asperger's disorder and PDD-NOS) would be expected to achieve this level of functioning, because they have more severe symptoms at treatment entry. Nonetheless, many children with autistic disorder show high levels of achievement in intensive early behavior therapy. Lord and McGee's (2001) National Research Council panel, reviewing education for young children with ASDs, concluded that structured behavior therapies were the only interventions demonstrated to produce lasting cognitive, language, and social gains for young children with ASDs. A more recent review of all published early intervention research concluded that TEACCH and the Colorado Health Sciences interventions for children with ASDs were "probably effective" and that various behavioral interventions based on applied behavior analysis were the only interventions "well established" (Eikeseth, 2009).

Among older individuals with ASDs who display behavior challenges, the most effective interventions have been based on functional assessment of circumstances surrounding the behavior problem, including skill deficits. Within educational settings, positive behavioral support strategies are widely used with favorable outcomes (O'Neill et al., 1997).

Pharmacological, Dietary, and Complementary Alternative Medicine Interventions

Because of frequent tantrums, compulsive ritualistic behavior, hyperactivity, and aggression, many youth and adults with AD are treated with psychotropic medications. Selective serotonin reuptake inhibitors can reduce repetitive stereotyped behavior among individuals with AD. The atypical antipsychotic drug risperidone was approved by the FDA for treating irritability in autism (aggression and self-injury). Risperidone and other atypical antipsychotics cause weight gain and risk Type II diabetes (Posey & McDougle, 2000). The opiate antagonist naltrexone has reduced self-injury by 30–50% of individuals with severe intellectual disabilities, some of whom had AD (Symons, Thompson, & Rodriguez, 2004). Melatonin improves sleep onset among children and youth with ASDs (including autistic disorder), a very common problem.

A 1998 publication concluded that the pancreatic hormone, secretin, when administered to three children with autism, had curative properties. Since then, more than 15 double-blind placebo-controlled studies have failed to reveal any positive treatment effects of secretin in autism (Sturmey, 2005). Though diets without casein-gluten (CG) are very widely used by parents of children with autistic disorder, controlled blind studies have failed to reveal positive treatment effects from the CG diet. Two studies have suggested that high-dose vitamin B_6 and magnesium supplements may have improved symptoms of some children with autism spectrum disorders. Parents of children with autism use many other alternative medicine therapies, but in very few instances have controlled investigations been conducted (Thompson, 2007).

REFERENCES

American Psychiatric Association. (2000). *Diagnostic and statistical manual of mental disorders* (4th ed., text rev.). Washington, DC: Author.

Chakrabarti, S., & Fombonne, E. (2005). Pervasive developmental disorders in preschool children: Confirmation of high prevalence. *American Journal of Psychiatry, 162*, 1133–1141.

Doja, A., & Roberts, W. (2006). Immunization and autism: A review of the literature. *Canadian Journal of Neurological Sciences, 33*, 341–346.

Eikeseth, S. (2009). Outcome of comprehensive psychoeducational interventions for young children with autism. *Research in Developmental Disabilities, 30*(1), 158–178.

First Signs. Retrieved April 27, 2008, from www.firstsigns.org.

Itard, J. M. G. (1962). *The wild boy of Aveyron* (G. Humphrey & M. Humphrey, Trans.). New York: Appleton-Century-Crofts. (Original works published 1801 and 1806)

Kanner, L. (1943). Autistic disturbances of affective contact. *Nervous Child, 2*, 217–250.

Lord, C. E., & McGee, J. G. (2001). *Educating children with autism.* Committee on Educational Interventions for Children with Autism, Division of Behavioral and Social Sciences and Education, National Research Council. Washington, DC: National Academies Press.

Lovaas, O. I. (1987). Behavioral treatment and normal educational and intellectual functioning in young autistic children. *Journal of Consulting and Clinical Psychology, 55*, 3–9.

Miles, J. H., Takahashi, T. N., Bagby, S., Sahota, P. K., Vaslow, D. F., Wang, C. H., et al. (2005). Essential versus complex autism: Definition of fundamental prognostic subtypes. *American Journal of Medical Genetics A, 135*(2), 171–180.

O'Neill, R. E., Horner, R. H., Albin, R. W., Sprague, J. R., Storey, K., & Newton, J. S. (1997). *Functional assessment and program development for problem behavior* (2nd ed.). Pacific Grove, CA: Brooks/Cole.

Posey, D. J., & McDougle, C. J. (2000). The pharmacotherapy of target symptoms associated with autistic disorder and other pervasive developmental disorders. *Harvard Review of Psychiatry, 8,* 45–63.

Rutter, M. (2005). Incidence of autism spectrum disorders: Changes over time and their meaning. *Acta Paediatrica, 94,* 2–15.

Sturmey, P. (2005). Secretin is an ineffective treatment for pervasive developmental disabilities: A review of 15 double-blind randomized controlled trials. *Research in Developmental Disabilities, 26,* 87–97.

Symons, F. J., Thompson, A., & Rodriguez, M. R. (2004). Self-injurious behavior and the efficacy of naltrexone treatment: A quantitative review. *Mental Retardation and Developmental Disabilities Research Reviews, 10,* 193–200.

Thompson, T. (2007). *Making sense of autism.* Baltimore: Paul H. Brookes.

SUGGESTED READING

Volkmar, F. (2007). *Autism and developmental disorders.* Cambridge, England: Cambridge University Press.

TRAVIS THOMPSON
University of Minnesota School of Medicine

See also: **Asperger Syndrome**

AUTONOMIC NERVOUS SYSTEM (See Parasympathetic Nervous System; Sympathetic Nervous System)

AUTOSHAPING

Autoshaping typically occurs when biologically primed stimulus-response relations interact with and occasionally override operantly learned, potentially incompatible response-reinforcer relations. It may also be referred to as "misbehavior of organisms." The name is derived from quick operant shaping that occurred without apparent reinforcement of successive approximations. Typically, the behavior observed depends on object or goal received; for example, food appears to release eating behavior and water to release drinking behavior. Although initially thought to manifest only among simpler mammals, autoshaping may occur in different animals including humans (Siegel, 1978). Consensus regarding etiology is lacking, although this is not a result of irregularities in data; the phenomenon of autoshaping is valid and reliable. As an example of autoshaping, pigeons quickly learn key pecking responses when a key is illuminated and provides a reliable and salient cue for the delivery of food (Brown & Jenkins, 1968). However, attempts to operantly extinguish or negatively punish pecking generally fail, which leaves open the question of whether the behavior was acquired through operant training or some other modality.

Theories of Autoshaping

As with most behavior, autoshaping resides in the gap between nature and nurture. It represents an interaction between organism and environment, phylogeny and ontogeny, and respondent and instrumental processes. Each of these explanations represents a different level of analysis to the puzzle of autoshaping.

Although the formal study of autoshaping largely began in the late 1960s, the existence of the phenomenon may have been foreshadowed by Darwin's theory of evolution (1859), which posited natural selection as the mechanism whereby species-specific morphogenesis and behavior would need to show environmental adaptation (i.e., functionality) with regard to subsistence and reproduction. At worse, the new structure or behavior could not impair the animal's relative ability to compete for basic resources. Influenced by Darwin's work, William James (1890) implied the existence of autoshaping in discussions of instinct. James defined instinct as "the faculty of acting in such a way as to produce certain ends, without foresight of the ends, and without previous education in the performance" (p. 383). However, instincts were not to be considered immutable stimulus-response relations; they were to be considered "blind" to the resultant consequences of the action only on the first occurrence of the behavior, after which they could be "disguised or modified." Hence, fixed action patterns, an interchangeable term for instinct used by ethologists, may be more or less fixed depending on the effect of the behavior, as well as on the species under consideration. James implicated the existence of a process whereby innate, hard-wired behavior might interact with and be modified by resultant environmental stimuli.

Lorenz (1957), an early ethologist, posited the more widely held view that, due to the simplicity of the nervous system of lower animals, constraints on stimulus perception and response are more likely than in humans, and that those responses would be adaptive to the survival of the animal. This view of instinct proposed a mechanism whereby the animal perceived a stimulus that *released* a species-specific response (e.g., pecking) designed to provide a specific consequence (e.g., food). This paradigm also adhered to the assumption that instinctive responses were unlearned, yet were modifiable, although the modification would only be found in the offspring. Lorenz postulated that the fixed-action pattern released by a specific stimulus should be referred to as an instinct; all supporting, orienting, or learned behaviors maintaining or modifying an instinct are to be considered appetitive responses. In practice, however, the line between instinctive and appetitive behaviors remained blurred, perhaps because the etiology of instincts, or phylogenically predisposed fixed-action patterns, was not well understood.

Better understood are ontogenic models for acquiring behavior within the life of the animal. Two specific forms of learning, classical and operant conditioning, appear relevant to autoshaping. In the aforementioned example with autoshaped pecking in pigeons, it was originally thought that innate aspects of the bird provided for, or predisposed the bird for, rapid shaping via reinforcement of successive approximations of pecking. However, introducing terms like "innate aspect" or "predisposition" weakened the scientific explanation, as those terms were not operationally defined, did little to advance the understanding of the data, and were usually tautological (i.e., based in circular reasoning). Brown and Jenkins (1968) were the first to report that noncontingent food presentation temporally contiguous with key illumination resulted in pigeon pecking. Furthermore, Williams and Williams (1969) conducted the first example of omission training with pigeons, whereby the presentation of food was contingent upon the nonoccurrence of pecking. Under an omission-training model, behavior under operant control would cease or become greatly reduced. However, the pigeons continued to exhibit pecking over many trials without food. This study underscored the implausibility that autoshaping was maintained by contingent reinforcement with food, even if intermittently or superstitiously. This prompted researchers to investigate the possibility that key pecking was classically conditioned.

The rationale for considering classical conditioning as the mechanism of action for autoshaping stems from the fact that within each operant there resides the potential for simultaneous classical conditioning (for in-depth discussion, refer to texts by Davis & Hurwitz, 1977; Honig & Staddon, 1977; Rachlin, 1976; Schwartz, 1989). Due to the stimulus properties of consequences, particularly primary consequences, neutral stimuli that reliably precede and predict delivery may become conditioned. In other words, reinforcers and punishers may also serve as unconditioned stimuli-unconditioned response (US-UR) pairs, inadvertently creating conditioned stimuli (CS) and responses (CR). In the example with pigeons, the food pellet was contingently delivered upon pecking at the key when illuminated. This food pellet, both a potential reinforcer and paired US-UR, might allow the light inside the key to become a CS that elicits a key pecking response (CR) that closely approximates a normal unconditioned eating response (UR). This model fits the data well, as autoshaped behaviors closely approximate the normal phylogenic response released by the "goal" stimulus. In a further testing of this model, noncontingent delivery of the food maintained key pecking as long as the illumination preceded and was temporally contiguous to the food delivery, that is, CS continued to evoke the CR when it reliably predicted the US → UR delivery (Brown & Jenkins, 1968). Later, Jenkins (1977) altered the predictability of the CS so that it no longer preceded the food delivery. Classical conditioning extinction curves were noted, as were spontaneous remission curves when contiguity was reestablished. Jenkins also noted that maintenance of the pecking response was best when both contiguity and contingency were in place; in other words, that classical and operant conditioning may be additive processes.

In summary, autoshaping appears to be primarily a function of classical conditioning in that underlying US-UR relations are a requisite condition. However, operant consequences may also serve as US-UR pairs, allowing the occurrence of classical conditioning. Autoshaping per se only manifests when operant training appears to be overriding US-UR patterns, or in the terms of James and Lorenz, attempting to modify instinctive fixed-action patterns for obtaining goals. Hence, behaviors exhibited during autoshaping continue to defy simple categorization and precise etiologic explanation.

REFERENCES

Brown, P., & Jenkins, H. (1968). Auto-shaping of the pigeon's key peck. *Journal of the Experimental Analysis of Behavior, 11,* 1–8.

Darwin, C. A. (1859). *The origin of species by means of natural selection.*

Davis, H., & Hurwitz, H. M. B. (1977). *Operant-Pavlovian interactions.* NY: John Wiley & Sons.

Hergenhahn, B. R., & Olson, M. H. (1997). *An introduction to theories of learning* (5th ed.). Upper Saddle River, NJ: Prentice-Hall.

Honig, W. K., & Staddon, J. E. R. (1977). *Handbook of operant behavior.* Englewood Cliffs, NJ: Prentice-Hall.

James, W. (1890). *Principles of psychology* (Vols. 1–2). NY: Holt.

Jenkins, H. (1977). Sensitivity to different response systems to stimulus-reinforcer and response-reinforcer relations. In H. Davis & H. M. B. Hurwitz (Eds.), *Operant-Pavlovian interactions* (pp. 47–66). NY: John Wiley & Sons.

Lorenz, K. (1957). Companions in the life of birds, reprint. In C. Schiller (Ed.), *Instinctive behavior.* NY: International Universities Press.

Rachlin, H. (1976). *Behavior and learning.* San Francisco: W.H. Freeman & Company.

Schwartz, B. (1989). *Psychology of learning and behavior* (3rd ed.). NY: W.W. Norton & Company.

Siegel, R. K. (1978). Stimulus selection and tracking during urination: Autoshaping directed behavior with toilet targets. *Journal of Applied Behavior Analysis, 10*(2), 255–265.

Williams, D., & Williams, H. (1969). Auto-maintenance in the pigeon: Sustained pecking despite contingent non-reinforcement.

Journal of the Experimental Analysis of Behavior, 12, 511–520.

STEPHANIE K. MEADOR
DAVID B. HATFIELD
*Developmental Behavioral Health,
Colorado Springs, CO*

See also: Comparative Psychology; Operant Conditioning

AVOIDANCE LEARNING

Avoidance learning occurs when an individual's behavior prevents exposure to an unpleasant consequence. This arrangement, or contingency, is pervasive in everyday life. For example, in writing a mortgage check each month, the homeowner does so not because this behavior is immediately pleasurable, but rather because it avoids conflict with, and possible foreclosure by, a financial lender. Or, consider the motorist who is traveling above the speed limit posted on a highway. On seeing the blinking light of a police vehicle ahead, the driver slows down to avoid a negative encounter with law enforcement. It might be said, in fact, that learning by avoidance is what motivates most people, most of the time.

Avoidance learning has its roots in experimental psychology and conditioning theory. This article describes theoretical basis of avoidance learning, reviews conceptual issues, and discusses the role of avoidance learning in clinical psychology.

Theory

B. F. Skinner was a psychologist who, among other things, studied the effects of behavior consequences on animal and human learning (Skinner, 1953). Although he wrote extensively about many topics, he is most commonly associated with operant conditioning and the principles of positive and negative reinforcement. Positive reinforcement is the presentation of a pleasurable consequence following a behavior, which produces an increase in the future probability of that behavior. By contrast, negative reinforcement is the behavior-contingent removal or postponement of a nonpleasurable experience, which also produces an increase in responding.

As noted, negative reinforcement can operate in two ways. When a person's behavior stops or reduces ongoing contact with an unpleasant experience, it functions as "escape." To illustrate, turning up the thermostat at home during winter months will terminate the cold temperature in a room. With the second operation, a person is not confronted with a contemporaneous unpleasant situation,

but behaves to prevent or "avoid" its occurrence. Escape responding, therefore, requires that behavior be demonstrated in the presence of the nonpreferred (negative) situation, whereas avoidance responding occurs in the absence of the nonpreferred (negative) situation.

Avoidance learning can be traced to the study of "discriminated avoidance" that emerged from animal research (Hoffman, 1966). A neutral stimulus such as a light or tone was presented to a rat in an experimental chamber preceding the delivery of electric shock through a grid floor. If the rat pressed a lever during a preset interval between onset of the stimulus and the noxious stimulation, the electric shock would be prevented. The behavior of lever pressing is "discriminated" because it does not occur in the absence of the light or tone, which has become a "warning signal."

Other Considerations in Avoidance Learning

As revealed in the preceding example with lower organisms, avoidance learning is predicated on exposure to aversive stimulation that subsequently can be predicted by an exteroceptive cue or "signal." Among humans, however, similar learning can be promoted without direct contact with an unpleasant situation. On one hand, an individual's behavior may adhere to the avoidance paradigm by observing other people behaving. Avoiding interpersonal difficulties with a supervisor on the job, for instance, might be the outcome for a worker who sees colleagues being chastised, rebuked, or receiving similar harsh consequences when they interact with that individual.

Learning through avoidance without actually experiencing negative situations also can be the result of giving an individual verbal instructions, directions, or explanations. Such is the case when a parent informs a young child, "Don't touch the stove," in order to prevent injury. Similarly, the visibility of "do" and "don't" signs abundant in our environment provides explicit warnings for the purpose of avoiding untoward (and possibly fatal) consequences. Verbal and written language is said to mediate or control behavior through rule governance (Skinner, 1957).

Avoidance Learning in Clinical Psychology

Within clinical psychology avoidance learning is pertinent in both understanding the causes of maladaptive behaviors and formulating methods to intervene therapeutically. Relative to etiology, psychologists have long posited that experiential avoidance is at the heart of many clinical disorders. Thus, a person who struggles to cope effectively may abuse alcohol or use illicit drugs to avoid confronting sources of stress and discomfort. Our internal language, or "self-talk," also contributes to avoidance behavior (Hayes, Follette, & Linehan, 2004).

When implemented for therapeutic purposes, avoidance learning follows a five-step process: (1) identifying a problem behavior to be reduced or eliminated, (2) selecting a response to serve as replacement for the problem behavior, (3) choosing a negative consequence, (4) pairing the negative consequence with the problem behavior, and (5) allowing the person receiving treatment to avoid the negative consequence. Although this step-wise progression looks like a straightforward process, it is not without complications. First, there are ethical concerns when proposing or using negative and distressing events with individuals who already have adjustment difficulties. Second, even if an avoidance learning approach to treatment seems appropriate, it can be an arduous task arranging behavior and unpleasant conditions contiguously. And third, negative reinforcement generally would not be considered the sole basis of treatment but instead would be combined with other therapeutic procedures to prompt and maintain compensatory skills.

Avoidance learning for therapeutic purposes is employed typically by professionals from the disciplines of behavior therapy and behavior modification. Beginning in the early 1960s, several research reports by behavioral psychologists described examples of avoidance conditioning that incorporated extremely aversive stimulation. In one demonstration, children who had autism and were unresponsive to social interaction learned to avoid electric shock by approaching a therapist who called to them, "Come here" (Lovaas, Schaeffer, & Simmons, 1965). Faradic and other noxious stimuli such as foul odors and tastes also were programmed with individuals to condition avoidance of cues and situations associated with alcohol ingestion, drug use, and "deviant" sexual orientation (Hallam & Rachman, 1976). By contemporary standards these approaches would be unacceptable and viewed by some as "de-humanizing." In fact, the majority of behavioral practitioners have essentially abandoned invasive treatment procedures in favor of positively oriented and skill-building strategies.

Although avoidance learning is still included in many current therapies, the types of negative experiences are more benign than those found in the historical record. Notably, when contrasted to other behavior-change procedures, avoidance learning and training is used less frequently in clinical practice. Again, because teaching avoidance requires exposure (real or threatened) to unpleasant conditions, it should be considered cautiously and applied with great care on those occasions where it can be justified clinically (Iwata, 1987). Having children or adults relieved from performing mildly effortful tasks or activities when they refrain from problem behavior is one way avoidance learning can motivate desirable change with low risk (Luiselli, 2007).

Avoidance learning is a powerful influence on human behavior. It is generated by encountering a negative situation, observing other people in similar circumstances, or being informed about the consequences of behavior. Verbal and written language serve frequently as "warning stimuli" that occasion avoidance-maintained responding. In a clinical context, avoidance learning has been incorporated to overcome problems and teach compensatory skills.

REFERENCES

Hallam, R. S., & Rachman, S. (1976). Current status of aversion therapy. In M. Hersen, R. M. Eisler, & P. M. Miller (Eds.), *Progress in behavior modification* (Vol. 2, pp. 179–222). New York: Academic Press.

Hayes, S. C., Follette, V. M., & Linehan, M. M. (2004). *Mindfulness and acceptance: Expanding the cognitive-behavioral tradition.* New York: Guilford Press.

Hoffman, H. S. (1966). The analysis of discriminated avoidance. In W. K. Honig (Ed.), *Operant behavior: Areas of research and application.* New York: Appleton-Century-Crofts.

Iwata, B. A. (1987). Negative reinforcement and applied behavior analysis: An emerging technology. *Journal of Applied Behavior Analysis, 20,* 361–378.

Luiselli, J. K. (2007). Single-case evaluation of a negative reinforcement toilet training intervention. *Child & Family Behavior Therapy, 29,* 59–69.

Skinner, B. F. (1953). *Science and human behavior.* New York: Macmillan.

Skinner, B. F. (1957). *Verbal behavior.* New York: Appleton-Century-Crofts.

SUGGESTED READING

Catania, A. C. (1998). *Learning* (4th ed.). Upper Saddle River, NJ: Prentice-Hall.

JAMES K. LUISELLI
May Institute, Randolph, MA

See also: **Behavior Modification**

AVOIDANT PERSONALITY DISORDER

At the core of avoidant personality disorder (APD) as defined by the *Diagnostic and Statistical Manual of Mental Disorders* (DSM) is an extreme sensitivity to negative evaluation that, coupled with a view of self as incompetent and inferior to others, leads to pervasive avoidance in a number of social situations (American Psychiatric Association, 2000). People with this disorder may, for example, refrain from trying new activities for fear of failure. They are also likely to be inhibited in relationships, even with family members, for fear of shame and ridicule. This leads to isolation and a lack of close relationships, and often to secondary disorders such as major depressive disorder. This negative cycle is not a function of disinterest in intimate relationships. Rather, the fear of negative evaluation is so intense as to outweigh the deep-seated longing to interact with others.

The DSM-IV-TR (American Psychiatric Association, 2000) estimates the prevalence of APD to be between 0.5% and 1%. Features of this disorder start as early as infancy or childhood. There is a lack of longitudinal studies of APD, but there is evidence to suggest that without intervention it runs a chronic course. Some symptoms may be more stable than others, however, and one longitudinal study suggests that the personality trait of feeling socially inept and inadequate is stable over time, but that dysfunctional behaviors such as avoiding jobs with interpersonal contact is less stable (Skodol, Gunderson, Shea, McGlashan, Morey, et al., 2005).

Different theories of APD all hold that a behaviorally inhibitive temperament (which is conceptualized as genetic, biological, or psychological depending on the theory) interacts with early experiences of ridicule or shame in creating APD (Alden, Laposa, Taylor, & Ryder, 2002). In many cases, parents of people with APD were overly critical of them and their performance in social situations. These individuals learned that social situations are dangerous and that it is devastating if others do not think highly of them. At an early age, these experiences created a negative view of self and a hypersensitivity to negative evaluation. Cognitive approaches to intervention stress how people with APD process information; they are always scanning every social situation for clues of negative evaluation. Because they resort to avoidance rather than testing out what cognitive theorists call *schemas* (Beck & Freeman, 1990), there is a tendency to overestimate how dangerous the social situations are, and avoidance becomes a lifestyle.

Although there are many descriptions of avoidant individuals since at least the early twentieth century, the category of avoidant personality disorder was not formally introduced into the DSM until the third edition, published in 1980, in large part due to the work of Theodore Millon (1981). The conceptualization and history of APD must be tied to social phobia (SP), which was also brought into the DSM for the first time in the third edition. There was a distinction made between Axis I clinical disorders and Axis II personality disorders in the DSM-III, and SP was categorized as a clinical disorder and APD as a personality disorder. There were clear similarities between the two disorders, and social phobia was defined as the fear of being humiliated or embarrassed in a social situation. Initially, social phobia would only be diagnosed when the individual feared one social situation. If there were more than one social situation, APD would be assigned. However, in the revision of the third edition of the DSM (American Psychiatric Association, 1987), both disorders could be assigned to the same person if he or she met criteria for them. In addition, the subtype of "generalized" social phobia was created to refer to those individuals who feared "most" situations. It seems that SP, like APD, follows a chronic and unremitting course if left untreated (Heimberg & Becker, 2002).

What is the difference between SP and APD? This question has been the subject of considerable debate and has not been completely resolved. Some theorists have argued that the research findings are biased, in that they are for the most part based on studies of participants who meet criteria for SP (Arntz, 1999). The majority view, however, is that there is not a *qualitative* but a *quantitative* difference between the two disorders. More specifically, there are some additional symptoms in APD, such as not seeking involvement with people unless being certain of being liked, that indicate a more severe condition than SP. However, it is not accurate to say that a person who meets criteria for both generalized SP and APD has two disorders, but rather that he has a severe form of this condition (see Heimberg & Becker, 2002). The distinction between the two disorders in different editions of the DSM was not based on empirical data (Reich, 2000). In conclusion, the best way to make sense of the empirical literature is to think of APD and SP as referring to the same general condition, with APD capturing a more severe form of generalized SP.

APD is not only found to be frequently comorbid with clinical disorders such as major depressive disorder. Its comorbidity with other personality disorders is quite high, in particular with dependent personality disorder (DPD). There is some evidence to suggest that only the symptom of social withdrawal reliably discriminates between these two personality disorders (Alden et al., 2002).

APD is seldom the sole focus of empirical studies (Alden et al., 2002). As an example, there is just one published paper in existence reporting on an outcome study comparing different forms of therapy for APD (Emmelkamp, Benner, Kuippers, Geiertag, Coster, et al., 2006). This is probably in large part due to the close ties between APD and SP. Thus, there are many studies that study the association between SP and APD, and whether APD predicts response to treatment of SP, rather than studying APD in its own right. These studies seem to suggest, in general, that rates of improvement for participants with APD in addition to generalized SP are similar to participants without APD. Limitations of these studies with regard to outcome for APD are that the outcome measures assess SP rather than APD. In the only study involving solely participants with APD, cognitive-behavioral treatment (CBT) outperformed brief dynamic therapy (BDT), and only 9% of the CBT participants compared to 36% of the BDT participants met criteria for APD at a 6-month follow-up (Emmelkamp et al., 2006). Although much more research needs to be done on the treatment of APD, this work extends the finding that CBT is effective for APD in addition to SP, and that a personality disorder such as APD, which by definition is resistant to change, is treatable.

In addition to specific techniques based on the CBT model, the relationship between therapist and client may be a crucial vehicle of change. The APD client is commonly distrustful of the therapist and fears negative evaluation and even embarrassment in the treatment setting. Therapists aim to build trust between themselves and the client and to teach clients that they can be assertive without losing the bond with their therapist. If the therapist is successful in creating that trust, the next step in treatment becomes to generalize that experience to other relationships in the client's life, and to creating new relationships.

REFERENCES

Alden, L. E., Laposa, J. M., Taylor, C. T., & Ryder, A. G. (2002). Avoidant personality disorder: Current status and future directions. *Journal of Personality Disorders, 16*, 1–29.

American Psychiatric Association (2000). *Diagnostic and statistical manual of mental disorders* (4th ed.). Washington: Author.

Arntz, A. (1999). Do personality disorders exist? On the validity of the concept and its cognitive-behavioral formulation and treatment. *Behaviour Research and Therapy, 37*, 97–134.

Beck, A. T., & Freeman, M. D. (1990). *Cognitive therapy of personality disorders*. New York: Guilford Press.

Emmelkamp, P. M. G., Benner, A., Kuipers, A., Feiertag, G. A., Koster H. C., & van Apeldoorn, F. J. (2006). Comparison of brief dynamic and cognitive-behavioural therapies in avoidant personality disorder. *British Journal of Psychiatry, 189*, 60–64.

Heimberg, R. G. & Becker, R. E. (2002). *Cognitive-behavioral group therapy for social phobia*. New York: Guilford Press.

Millon, T. (1981). *Disorders of personality. DSM-III: Axis II*. New York: Wiley & Sons.

Reich, J. (2000). The relationship of social phobia to avoidant personality disorder: A proposal to reclassify avoidant personality disorder based on clinical empirical findings. *European Psychiatry, 15*, 151–159.

Skodol, A. E., Gunderson, J. G., Shea, M. T., McGlashan, T. H., Morey, L. C., Sanislow, C. A., Bender, D. S., et al. (2005). The Collaborative Lngitudinal Personality Dsorders Study (CLPS): Overview and implications. *Journal of Personality Disorders, 19*, 487–504.

SUGGESTED READING

Millon, T., Grossman, S., Millon, C., Meagher, S., & Ramnath, R. (2004). *Personality disorders in modern life* (2nd ed.) [See especially the chapter on "The Avoidant Personality," pp. 187–222]. New Jersey: John Wiley & Sons.

ANDRI S. BJORNSSON
University of Colorado at Boulder

See also: **Shyness; Social Phobia**

B

BABINSKI SIGN

In 1896, Joseph Jules François Félix Babinski (1857–1932) reported a clinical sign that now famously bears his name (Babinski, 1896). In point of fact, Babinski described several signs of importance in neurology, but the one under consideration here (and the one usually referred to as *the* Babinski sign) denotes the extension, rather than the expected flexion, of the great toe upon mildly noxious stimulation of the soles of the feet in patients who have lesions of the pyramidal tracts. Others had seen this reflex response, but Babinski was the first to call attention to its diagnostic importance (for example, in differentiating structural from hysterical paralysis) (Babinski, 1898). He later pointed out that fanning of the lateral toes may accompany extension of the great toe (Babinski, 1903), but this is not an essential component of the sign.

The sign is best elicited by having the patient lie supine with the leg uncovered and supported by the examiner. After informing the patient about what is to happen, a stimulus (ranging from light touch to moderately firm and slightly noxious pressure from a blunt object like a key or a wooden applicator stick) is applied to the lateral plantar surface of the foot in a gently sweeping motion from heel to ball (van Gijn, 1995). The hallmark positive (extensor) response is mediated by contraction of the long extensor of the great toe, and careful palpation to confirm tightening of the *extensor hallucis longus* tendon may resolve doubts about whether the sign is present or not. Extensor responses can be evoked by stimuli applied to a number of other loci on the foot or leg, but the interpretation of the response is the same no matter how the response is elicited. Extension of the toe (away from the noxious stimulus on the sole) is accompanied by a generalized flexion response of the stimulated limb, so there may be visible flexion of thigh on hip, leg on knee, and foot on ankle, brought about by contraction of the *tibialis anterior*, hamstrings, *tensor fasciae latae* and iliopsoas muscles, respectively (Bassetti, 1995).

The clinical significance of the Babinski sign is found by reviewing its developmental course. A positive, and sometimes unilateral, response has been reported in a large preponderance of normal newborns (Jaynes, 1997; Gupta & Gupta, 2003). The pyramidal tracts of the central nervous system, carrying neurons from the motor cortex into the spinal cord, subserve voluntary muscle function throughout the body. As these tracts mature during the first six months of life, the toe response changes from extensor to flexor, and by the age of 9–12 months the entire flexion response of the lower extremity is extinguished along with Babinski response (van Gijn, 1995). Since maturation of the pyramidal tracts underlies the developmental disappearance of the Babinski response, it is not surprising that persistence of the response after the first year of life—or its later reappearance, especially if laterally asymmetrical—indicates disease affecting the pyramidal tract. As Babinski knew, the sign often accompanies destructive lesions of the motor fibers innervating the foot, and careful testing may reveal weakness of the affected limb or at least disturbances of fine motor function (Bassetti, 1995; Miller & Clairborne Johnston, 2005).

Now, more than a century after its initial description, the extensor response of the great toe remains one of the best-known and clinically useful eponymic signs in clinical medicine, although some continue to doubt its value. For instance, Miller and Clairborne Johnston (2005), testing a group of clinicians, found that their test subjects rarely agreed with each other about whether Babinski's sign was present or not. Miller and Clairborne Johnston suggested that testing for the sign be excluded from the routine neurological examination, a recommendation that brought forth a flurry of responses claiming that the fault lies not in the sign but in the skill with which it is elicited (see, for example, Landau, 2005). In any case, at this juncture more than 100 years after its enunciation, it seems safe to say that the presence of Babinski's sign in an adult almost always indicates serious structural abnormalities of the upper motor neurons serving the affected limb. The finding of a positive Babinski response after the first year of life should be considered abnormal, and appropriate neurological investigation undertaken to identify the nature and location of the abnormal process.

REFERENCES

Babinski, J. (1896). Sur le réflexe cutané plantaire dans certains affections organiques du système nerveux central. *Comptes Rendus de la Société de Biologie, 48*, 207–208.

Babinski, J. (1898). Du phénomène des orteils et de sa valeur sémiologique. *Semaine Médicale, 18*, 321–322.

Babinski, J. (1903). De l'abduction des ortreils. *Revue Neurologique (Paris), 11*, 728–729.

Bassetti, C. (1995). Babinski and Babinski's sign. *SPINE*, 20:2591–2594.

Gupta, A., & Gupta, P. (2003). Neonatal plantar response revisited. *Journal of Paediatrics and Child Health, 39*, 349–351.

Jaynes, M. E., Gingold, M. K., Hupp, A., Mullett, M. D., & Bodensteiner, J. B. (1997). The plantar response in normal newborn infants. *Clinical Pediatrics, 36*, 649–651.

Landau, W. M. (2005). Plantar reflex amusement: Misuse, ruse, disuse, and abuse. *Neurology, 65*, 1150–1151.

Miller, T. M., & Johnston, C. (2005). Should the Babinski sign be part of the routine neurologic examination? *Neurology, 65*, 1165–1168.

van Gijn, J. (1995). The Babinski reflex. *Postgraduate Medical Journal, 71*, 645–648.

SUGGESTED READINGS

Lance, J. W. (2002). The Babinski sign. *Journal of Neurology, Neurosurgery & Psychiatry*, 70:360–362.

Skalski, J. H. (2007). Joseph Jules François Félix Babinski (1857–1932). *Journal of Neurology*, 254:1140–1141.

van Gijn, J. (1995). The Babinski reflex. *Postgraduate Medical Journal*, 71:645–648.

Francis A. Neelon
Rice Diet Program, Durham, North Carolina

BANDURA, ALBERT (1925–)

Albert Bandura is David Starr Jordan Professor of Social Sciences in Psychology at Stanford University. He received his bachelor's degree from the University of British Columbia in 1949 and his Ph.D. degree from the University of Iowa in 1952. After completing his doctorate, Bandura joined the faculty at Stanford University, where he has remained throughout his career.

Bandura has been a proponent of social cognitive theory. This theory accords a central role to cognitive, vicarious, self-regulatory, and self-reflective processes in human adaptation and change. In this view, people are self-organizing, proactive, self-reflecting, and self-regulating, not just reactive organisms shaped and shepherded by environmental forces or driven by concealed inner impulses. Human functioning is the product of a dynamic interplay of personal, behavioral, and environmental influences. In this model of triadic reciprocal causation, people are producers as well as products of their environment. His book *Social Foundations of Thought and Action: A Social Cognitive Theory* provides the conceptual framework and analyzes the large body of knowledge bearing on his theory.

Bandura's initial program of research centered on the prominent role of social modeling in human motivation, thought, and action. At the time, psychologists focused almost exclusively on learning through the consequences of one's actions. Bandura showed that the tedious and hazardous process of trial-and-error learning can be shortcut through social modeling of knowledge and competence exhibited by a rich variety of models. He rightfully pointed out that modeling was not simply response mimicry. By extracting the rules underlying the modeled styles of behavior, people generate new behavior patterns in a similar style but go beyond what they have seen or heard. He further showed that, in addition to cultivating new competencies, modeling influences alter motivation by instilling behavioral outcome expectations, and create emotional proclivities and value systems through the emotional expression of others toward given persons, places, or things. Bandura also noted that a lot of modeling goes on in creativity. By novel synthesis of existing innovations or adding new elements to them, something new is created. Modeling influences can promote creativeness by exemplifying diversity for novel synthesis and fresh perspectives that weaken conventional mind sets.

The revolutionary advances in the technology of telecommunications have made symbolic modeling a key vehicle in the social diffusion of ideas, values, and styles of behavior worldwide. Recognizing the growing power of the symbolic environment in people's lives, Bandura extended his theorizing and research to the mechanisms through which symbolic modes of modeling produce their widespread social effects.

Another major focus of Bandura's theorizing addressed the extraordinary symbolizing capacity of humans. By drawing on their symbolic capabilities, people can comprehend their environment construct guides for action, gain new knowledge by reflective thought, and communicate with others at any distance in time and space. By symbolizing their experiences, people give structure, meaning, and continuity to their lives.

A further distinctive feature of social cognitive theory that Bandura singled out for special attention was the capacity for self-directedness. People plan courses of action, anticipate their likely consequences, and set goals and challenges for themselves to motivate, guide, and regulate their activities. After adopting personal standards, people regulate their own motivation and behavior by the positive and negative consequences they produce for themselves. The human capacity for self-management is an aspect of the theory that makes it particularly apt to the changing times. The accelerated pace of informational, social, and technological changes has placed a premium on people's capabilities to exert a strong hand in their own self-renewal and functioning through the course of life.

The capability for self-reflection concerning one's functioning and personal efficacy to produce effects is another human attribute that is featured prominently in social cognitive theory. Bandura regards the self-efficacy belief as the foundation of human motivation, well-being, and personal accomplishments. Unless people believe that they can bring about desired outcomes by their actions, they have little incentive to act or to persevere in the face of difficulties. A wealth of empirical evidence documents that beliefs or personal efficacy touch virtually every aspect of people's lives—whether they think productively, self-debilitatingly, pessimistically, or optimistically; how well they motivate themselves and persevere in the face of adversities; their vulnerability to stress and depression; and, the life choices they make.

Human lives are not lived in isolation. Bandura, therefore, expanded the conception of human agency to include collective agency. People work together on shared beliefs about their capabililties and common aspirations to better their lives. This conceptual extension makes the theory applicable to human adaptation and change in collectivistically-oriented societies as well as individualistically-oriented ones. In his book *Self-Efficacy: The Exercise of Control*, Bandura set forth at length the basic tenets of his theory on self-efficacy and its fruitful applications to the fields of life-course development, education, health, psychopathology, athletics, business, and international affairs.

Viewed from the social cognitive perspective, the major distinguishing mark of humans is their endowed plasticity and learnability. Their specialized neurophysiological structures and systems provide a vast potentiality that can be fashioned by direct and vicarious experiences into diverse forms within biological constraints. Bandura cites the remarkable cultural diversity of behavior patterns and the rapid pace of social change as testimony that biology permits a wide range of possibilities.

Bandura's contributions to psychology have been recognized in the many honors and awards that he has received. He was elected to the presidencies of the American Psychological Association and the Western Psychological Association and was appointed Honorary President of the Canadian Psychological Association. Some of the awards he has received include the Distinguished Scientist Award, Division 12 of the American Psychological Association; the William James Award of the American Psychological Association for Outstanding Achievements in Psychological Science; the Distinguished Contribution Award from the International Society for Research in Aggression; a Guggenheim Fellowship; the Distinguished Scientist Award of the Society of Behavioral Medicine; and the Robert Thorndike Award for Distinguished Contribution of Psychology Education, American Psychological Association. He has been elected to the American Academy of Arts and Sciences and the Institute of Medicine in the National Academy of Sciences. He is the recipient of many honorary degrees.

REFERENCES

Bandura, A. & Walters, R. H. (1963). *Social learning and personality development*. New York: Holt, Rinehart, & Winston.

Bandura, A. (1969). *Principles of behavior modification*. New York: Holt, Rinehart, & Winston.

Bandura, A. (1977). *Social learning theory*. Englewood Cliffs, NJ: Prentice Hall.

Bandura, A. (1997). *Self-efficacy: The exercise of control*. New York: W. H. Freeman.

STAFF

BARBITURATES (See Antianxiety Medications)

BARNUM EFFECT

The Barnum Effect refers to the tendency of people to accept vague, generally positive statements about their personality as unique to them even though feedback is likely to be true of most people. Bertram Forer (1949) first systematically documented this phenomenon by presenting to students a clinical personality inventory followed by statements from horoscopes that purported to describe each student as "You have a great deal of unused capacity which you have not turned to your advantage." Even though all students received identical feedback, they rated the description as highly relevant to them as individuals. Many students failed to accept a number of the individual feedback statements as highly accurate in describing them, but they still gave high ratings of the overall validity of the feedback.

Psychologists refer to the tendency to accept such vaguely accurate feedback as personal validation. The purpose of Forer's exercise was to demonstrate the problem of personal validation in clinical psychology; for example, feedback to a client might be true but not provide information that is useful for understanding the individual or for generating a clinical diagnosis.

Psychologists have linked the Barnum Effect to various cognitive phenomena. For example, according to the self-serving bias, people accept positive statements but tend to reject negative statements. This tendency appears in the Barnum Effect.

Another relevant cognitive distortion is confirmation bias, which is the label for the tendency to search only for cases that support a belief, while ignoring evidence countering that belief. In accepting bogus feedback, individuals may recall actual experiences matching the feedback, but they do not search for disconfirming evidence.

In addition, selective memory for a few highly accurate feedback statements may overshadow the statements that are only marginally relevant to the individual. This possibility could explain why lower acceptance of a few statements may not diminish a person's overall sense that feedback is highly valid.

Since Forer's original study, numerous researchers have documented a wide spectrum of variables associated with the acceptance of Barnum statements, including type of feedback (e.g., favorable; apparently unique to research participants), the type of assessment that leads to the bogus feedback (projective tests), and characteristics of people who are likely to accept or reject the feedback (e.g., high in authoritarianism; high in external locus of control; high in need for social approval). Furthermore, Forer and subsequent psychologists have noted that the apparent success of horoscopes, handwriting analysis, and other pseudosciences relies on the phenomenon of personal validation.

REFERENCE

Forer, B. R. (1949). The fallacy of personal validation: A classroom demonstration of gullibility. *Journal of Abnormal and Social Psychology, 44,* 118–123.

SUGGESTED READING

Dickson, D. H., & Kelly, I. W. (1985). The "Barnum Effect" in personality assessment: A review of literature. *Psychological Reports, 57,* 367–382.

Bernard C. Beins
Ithaca College

BASE RATES

Base rates refer to the relative frequencies with which certain states or conditions occur in a population. The concept denotes the same as *prevalence*, a term often used by epidemiologists. A base rate is defined for and restricted to a specified population. In other words, a base rate is the *a priori* chance or prior odds that a member of a specified population will have a certain characteristic, assuming that we know nothing else about this person other than that he or she is a member of the population we are examining (Kamphuis & Finn, 2002). For example, the base rate of suicide in the general population is less than 1%, whereas the base rate of suicide for a more restricted population, for example, among patients with borderline personality disorder, may be as high as 10%.

Base rates have important implications for the prediction of behaviors, the interpretation of test data, and the making of diagnostic decisions according to their interplay with cut-off scores or cut-off points. The interpretation

of a wide variety of assessment instruments relies on cut-off scores: critical scores beyond which membership of a certain category is indicated. For example, on the Minnesota Multiphasic Personality Inventory-2 (MMPI-2) clinical scales, a T-score greater than 65 is used to demarcate clinically significant problems or dysfunction. In a similar vein, prevailing psychiatric diagnostic systems (e.g., the *Diagnostic and Statistical Manual of Mental Disorders, DSM*) specify cut-offs for the minimum number of diagnostic criteria a patient must meet in order to satisfy a diagnostic category. Cut-offs, however, are imperfect heuristic rules, and it is important to realize that most often these cut-off scores were selected as to minimize total error. Faulty classificatory decisions fall in two categories (see the contingency table, Table 1): one may incorrectly assign a condition to a person who does not have that condition (Cell B, False Positive), or one may fail to detect a condition that is in fact present (Cell C, False Negative). The distribution of these errors and their complement, called hit-rates, are quite sensitive to base rate effects. This can be readily understood from inspecting the contingency table.

The base rate of the condition in this sample is a + b divided by the total sample size (i. e., n, or a + b + c + d). Two questions are of particular interest to most practitioners when facing decisions regarding placement, selection, or categorization: (1) if the test score exceeds the cut-off point and thus predicts condition A, what are the chances that A is indeed present?; and conversely, (2) if the test predicts A is absent, what are the chances that A is indeed absent? The answers to these questions are reflected in the hit rates called Positive Predictive Power (PPP, or a/a+b in the contingency table) and Negative Predictive Power (NPP, or d/c+d), respectively. It can be readily seen from the contingency table that, when the base rate (a +c/n) decreases, false positives increase, in turn causing a drop in PPP. Inspection of this table also reveals that there is a necessary trade-off between the two types of errors.

A procedure that has predictive power beyond the base rate accuracy is called *efficient*. In the case of extreme (high or low) base rates, it will be hard for a single test to outperform the base rate prediction or, in other words, to

Table 1. Contingency Table, Crossing States of Nature (Columns) and Test Predictions (Rows)

	Condition A present	Condition A absent
Test score > cut-off Prediction: condition A present	Cell A: True Positive (a)	Cell B: False Positive (b)
Test score <= cut-off Prediction: condition A absent	Cell C: False Negative (c)	Cell D: True Negative (d)

be efficient. A typical example is the prediction of suicide. Suicide in a given population may be well below 5%. If this is the case, anyone consistently predicting "no suicide" regardless of available test data will be correct more than 95% of the time. Even moderately strong signs do not add much to the predictive accuracy. What if one nevertheless wanted to predict low base rate phenomena anyway, as one may want to do with such consequential events as suicide or rare serious diseases? A two-step procedure may work, as explicated by Streiner (2003). First, one might use a highly sensitive screening test to boost the base rate. The resulting "at risk" subgroup will have a base rate closer to the optimal .50, at which a diagnostic test is more likely to be efficient in ruling individuals in or out.

Hence, the diagnostic efficiency of any test greatly depends on the base rate of the phenomenon it is trying to predict. Conversely, without knowing the base rate, it is impossible to evaluate the diagnostic accuracy of a given cut-off point. It can also be shown that reliability estimates are similarly sensitive to base rate effects. As do the hit-rates, reliability coefficients vary with base rates and there is not a single reliability but a whole series of reliabilities, one for each base rate.

Of practical importance is also the related notion that, when the base rate in a given practice—the so-called local base rate—is notably different from the base rate operative in the research that underlies the reported indices, one cannot expect to achieve similar proportions of correct decisions. Hence, for a practitioner using tests or other assessment instruments, knowledge of the local base rate as well as the base rate underlying the cut-off point is essential to optimal decision making. Ideally, one would like to use tests (and accompanying cut-offs) that were designed for similar settings (i.e., base rates), or that have documented hit-rates for different settings and samples. When this information is not available and use of the instrument seems nevertheless indicated, one may consider adjusting the cut-off score, in ways that seem consistent with the local base rate, and match one's aims (e.g., selection/specificity or screening/sensitivity). For example, when working with a restricted population of gifted students, increasing the minimal cut-off for achievement ratings based on general students may optimize allocation.

REFERENCES

Kamphuis, J. H., & Finn, S. E. (2002). Implementing base rates in daily clinical decision making. In James N. Butcher, *Clinical Personality Assessment,* (2nd ed. pp.257–268). New York: Oxford University Press.

Meehl, P. E., & Rosen, A. (1955). Antecedent probability and the efficiency of psychometric signs, patterns, or cutting scores. *Psychological Bulletin, 52,* 194–216.

Streiner, D. L. (2003). Diagnosing tests: Using and misusing diagnostic and screening tests. *Journal of Personality Assessment, 81,* 209–219.

JAN H. KAMPHUIS
University of Amsterdam, The Netherlands

See also: Errors, Type I and Type II

BATTERED WOMAN SYNDROME

Twenty-five percent of women are physically or sexually abused, and in nearly all instances psychologically abused, by intimate partners during the course of a relationship. Walker (1979) identified Battered Woman Syndrome (BWS) as a predictable pattern of psychological response to domestic violence. During the same time period, Post-Traumatic Stress Disorder (PTSD) was identified by the American Psychiatric Association (1980) to describe the predictable effects of traumatic events. It became increasingly clear that different types of terrifying experiences, including combat, rape, torture, and childhood physical and sexual abuse, all resulted in the same basic psychological response (Herman, 1992). Nearly two-thirds of battered women experienced symptom patterns that met the diagnostic criteria for PTSD (Goodman & Epstein, 2008). By the 1990s, it became apparent that PTSD in battered women and BWS were explaining the same condition.

Walker (1979) reported that battering occurs in a three-stage cycle, which begins with tension-building, and eventually results in an acute battering episode, with periods of normal, nonviolent, loving behavior occurring between episodes of abuse. Psychological and behavioral patterns associated with being battered involve a predictable process that is rooted in sustained fear. The profound fears exhibited by battered women may seem exaggerated to those who view these violent relationships from the outside, but is based in reality; these fears typically represent the actual dangerousness of the situation.

Beyond the terror inherent in being battered, the pattern of features associated with BWS/PTSD include: extraordinarily high levels of anxiety, anger, helplessness, horror and/or shame; reexperiencing overwhelming, intrusive memories and intense emotions; emotional constriction and avoidance of painful memories and reminders, which offer psychological protection from painful thoughts and feelings, and allow necessary, everyday tasks to be accomplished; heightened sense of danger, including hyperarousal and hypervigilance; dissociation or a sense of detachment or disconnection from relationships and surroundings; and disturbances in normal eating, sleeping, and interpersonal functioning. Battered women also experience additional psychological difficulties associated with PTSD, including substance abuse, depression, and suicidality.

Batterers' coercive, controlling behaviors, such as economic control, isolating women from sources of support, using children for manipulative purposes, and threats of harm or death, are terrifying and can thwart the capacity to escape. Battered women often tell no one, do not seek medical attention, do not call the police, and do not contact shelters (Kaser-Boyd, 2004). Escaping or stopping violence often seems overwhelming or impossible when trying to negotiate the Byzantine networks in the law enforcement and legal systems.

Battered women experience an additional dimension of psychological trauma that is not present for victims of other forms of trauma. Other forms of violence are typically perpetrated by strangers or individuals who are not well known to the victim (e.g., combat), while domestic violence is perpetrated by a relational partner who is intimately known, cared about, trusted, believed to be safe, and who has become dangerous (Goodman & Epstein, 2008). Based on this crucial distinction between domestic violence and other forms of traumatic stress, Herman (1992) posited a new diagnosis, Complex PTSD, which accounts for the profound, and potentially irrevocable, personality and interpersonal changes that occur in victims of chronic partner abuse. While not an official diagnosis at this time, Complex PTSD has become widely integrated into a full understanding of domestic violence and BWS.

Although PTSD has generally been viewed as a non-blaming framework for understanding and treating domestic violence, some concerns exist about the potential for stigmatizing battered women who receive a diagnostic label, creating the mistaken impression that battered women are mentally ill and therefore not credible in their reports of relational violence (Goodman & Epstein, 2008). While this controversy continues, the conceptualizations of PTSD have largely served to reduce the stigma for battered women by accurately explaining seemingly counterintuitive behaviors. For instance, when battered women stay with their batterers, this counterintuitive act is understood in the context of an external, damaging environment (i.e., comparable to combat or being taken hostage), rather than an internal psychological weakness.

Victims typically know the very real dangers of living with a batterer and act in ways to survive, including self-protective or retaliatory behaviors. Women who have killed their batterers typically experience sustained domestic violence that is extremely severe, with a greater number of threats and injuries, than women who have not killed their batterers (Kaser-Boyd, 2004).

In a report released by the U.S. Department of Justice, the U.S. Department of Health and Human Services,

and the National Institute of Mental Health (U.S. Department of Justice, 1996), a survey of judges and attorneys revealed the view that the term Battered Woman Syndrome "is not adequate to encompass the scientific and clinical knowledge about battering and its effects" (p. vii) and that the term "portrays a stereotypic image of battered women as helpless, passive, or psychologically impaired" (p. viii). Nevertheless, significant consensus exists in the judicial system supporting the admissibility of Battered Woman Syndrome in the trials of battered women or their batterers. Based on BWS, expert witness testimony has served to interpret and explain domestic violence and its effects (U.S. Department of Justice, 1996).

Forensic testing to assess for BWS in criminal, civil, or family court proceedings typically involves a review of relevant police and legal documentation, clinical interviews, and psychosocial histories. The Battered Woman Syndrome Questionnaire is a structured, eight-hour, clinical interview that can be used for forensic evaluations by trained interviewers; however, the length makes the measure impractical for clinical use, though it can be used as a model for assessing BWS.

Serving as expert witnesses, psychologists will often conduct formal psychological testing for purposes of consultation and testimony on BWS/PTSD. Traditional personality assessments, such as the MMPI-2, the MCMI-III, and the Rorschach, aid in psychologists' ability to describe accurately the psychological functioning of battered women and to diagnose BWS/PTSD (Kaser-Boyd, 2004). Psychologists who assess battered women must be cautious not to apply biased, inaccurate, and inflexible interpretations to assessment profiles. Battered women generate unique profiles, which require specialized knowledge on the part of expert witnesses to discriminate accurately between battered women with and without PTSD (Morrell & Rubin, 2001). The traumatic effects associated with relational violence must inform a full understanding of BWS and PTSD.

REFERENCES

Goodman, L. A., & Epstein, D. (2008). *Listening to battered women: A survivor-centered approach to advocacy, mental health, and justice.* Washington, DC: American Psychological Association.

Herman, J. (1992). *Trauma and recovery.* New York: Basic Books.

Kaser-Boyd, N. (2004). Battered woman syndrome: Clinical features, evaluation, and expert testimony. In B. J. Cling (Ed.), *Sexualized violence against women and children: A psychology and law perspective* (pp. 41–70). New York: Guilford Press.

Morrell, J. S., & Rubin, L. J. (2001). The Minnesota Multiphasic Personality Inventory-2, Posttraumatic stress disorder, and women domestic violence survivors. *Professional Psychology: Research and Practice, 32,* 151–156.

U. S. Department of Justice. (1996). The validity and use of evidence concerning battering and its effects in criminal trials: Report responding to Section 40507 of the Violence Against

Women Act. Washington, DC: U.S. Department of Justice, Office of Justice Programs, National Institute of Justice.

Walker, L. E. (1979). *The battered woman*. New York: Harper & Row.

SUGGESTED READINGS

Herman, J. (1992). *Trauma and recovery*. New York: Basic Books.

Kaser-Boyd, N. (2004). Battered woman syndrome: Clinical features, evaluation, and expert testimony. In B. J. Cling (Ed.), *Sexualized violence against women and children: A psychology and law perspective* (pp. 41–70). New York: Guilford Press.

Walker, L. E. A. (2006). Battered woman syndrome: Empirical findings. In F. L. Denmark, H. H. Krauss, E. Halpern, & J. A. Sechzer (Eds.), *Violence and exploitation against women and girls* (pp. 142–157). Boston: Blackwell Publishing on behalf of the New York Academy of Sciences.

LINDA RUBIN
Texas Women's University

See also: **Posttraumatic Stress Disorder**

BAYLEY SCALES OF INFANT AND TODDLER DEVELOPMENT

The Bayley Scales are carefully constructed norm-referenced measures for assessing the development of infants and toddlers, ages 1 month to 3 years 6 months. Originally developed by Dr. Nancy Bayley and published in 1969, the Second Edition of the Bayley Scales (BSID-II) was published in 1993, and a third edition (Bayley-III) was released in 2006. The description that follows focuses on the Bayley-III, developed by the staff of the Psychological Corporation with advice from a panel of outside experts, consultants, and reviewers. The administration manual states that Bayley-III "maintains the original nature and purpose of the Bayley Scales as envisioned by its author, Nancy Bayley" (Bayley, 2006a, p.1).

The scope of Bayley-III has expanded considerably from that of BSID-II, which was composed of only two separate scales, the Mental Scale and the Motor Scale. Five content domains are now assessed by Bayley-III: Cognitive, Language, Motor, Socio-Emotional, and Adaptive Behavior. Three of these content domains—Cognitive, Language, and Motor—are assessed by items administered to the child, whereas the Social-Emotional and Adaptive Behavior domains are based on information supplied by the primary caregiver to items contained in a separate questionnaire.

In addition, a Behavior Observation Inventory, designed to be completed by both the examiner and caregiver, provides valuable information based on observations made during testing. These various components yield a comprehensive assessment of the child essential for effective use of the Bayley-III in various applications, such as identifying children with developmental delay and planning appropriate interventions, monitoring progress following intervention, and developmental research. Caveats provided in the administration manual caution that the Bayley-III should not be viewed as an intelligence test or as a predictor of future academic achievement (Bayley, 2006a, p. 7).

Materials needed to administer, score, and interpret the Bayley-III are packaged in a test kit, which contains the manipulatives and printed stimulus material needed to administer the test items, a record form designed to facilitate summarizing, scoring, and presentation of the test results, the Social-Emotional and Adaptive Behavior response form, and two separate manuals: the administration manual and the technical manual.

The Bayley-III content represents a refinement and extension of that contained in the BSID-II Mental and Motor scales. The Bayley-III Cognitive scale contains 91 items that measure sensorimotor development, exploration and manipulation, object relatedness, concept formation, memory, and other aspects of cognitive processing. In addition, certain BSID-II Mental Scale items relying more on language and fine motor skills were moved to the separate Language and Motor scales in Bayley-III. The Language Scale contains 97 items divided into two subtests: Receptive Communication (49 items) and Expressive Communication (48 items); the Motor Scale contains 138 items divided into two subtests: Fine Motor (66 items) and Gross Motor (72 items).

The Social-Emotional Scale (35 items), completed by the caregiver, is an adaptation of the *Greenspan Social-Emotional Growth Chart: A Screening Questionnaire for Infants and Young Children* (Greenspan, 2004) and assesses acquisition of certain social and emotional milestones in young children, such as the child's mastery of functional emotional skills, including self-regulation and interest in the world; communicating needs; engaging others and establishing relationships; using emotions in an interactive, purposeful manner; and using emotional signals or gestures to solve problems (Bayley, 2006a, p. 4). The Adaptive Behavior Scale (241 items in 10 skill areas) is composed of items from the Parent/Primary Caregiver Form of the *Adaptive Behavior Assessment System—Second Edition* (ABAS-II; Harrison & Oakland, 2003), a comprehensive assessment of adaptive behavior functioning (Bayley, 2006a, p. 4). The Behavior Observation Inventory (13 items) is used by the examiner and the caregiver to report qualitative information observed during the child's responses to the test items.

Standardization of the Bayley-III used stratified quota sampling with proportionate allocation to obtain a representative sample of U.S. children aged 1–42 months. The sample consisted of 1,700 children in 17 age groups, each with 100 children (50 males and 50 females) stratified by parent education, race/ethnicity, and geographic region. Special care was taken to ensure that each child selected for the sample was born without medical complications at 36–42 weeks of gestation. In addition, each child was included only if there were no medical complications after birth, meaning that the child did not have a history of medical complications and was not currently diagnosed or receiving treatment (including medication) at the time of testing.

Special studies were also undertaken by including children diagnosed with Down syndrome, cerebral palsy, pervasive developmental disorder, premature birth, language impairment, and (children) at risk for developmental delay. The children in these special studies constituted about 10% of the normative sample and were included to represent the population of infants and toddlers more accurately (Bayley, 2006b, p. 34). Standardization of the *Greenspan Social-Emotional Growth Chart* was done by administering the scale to 456 children aged 15 days to 42 months throughout the United States (Bayley, 2006b, p. 41). As stated previously, the Adaptive Behavior Scale is the Parent/Primary Caregiver Form of the ABAS-II; norms for the Bayley-III were generated from the ABAS-II standardization sample, along with the reliability estimates, standard errors of measurement, and validity evidence for the Bayley-III Adaptive Behavior Scale.

The following types of derived scores were developed from the Bayley-III standardization data: Scaled Scores (mean=10; s.d.=3, range 1–19), Composite Scores (mean=100, s.d.=15, range 40–160), Percentile Ranks (median=50, range 1–99), Confidence Intervals (90% and 95%), and Growth Scores (generated from Item Response Theory with mean=500, s.d.=100, range 200–800). The Scaled Scores and Composite Scores are both normalized standard scores similar to those used with other tests published by the Psychological Corporation, such as WISC and WAIS, and will be familiar to users of those and other tests using these reporting scales.

Both internal consistency reliability and test-retest stability coefficients are reported in the Technical Manual (Bayley, 2006b). Average internal consistency reliabilities for the 17 age groups were .91 for the Cognitive Scale; .93 for the Language Scale, and .92 for the Motor Scale. For the Social-Emotional Scale, the average internal consistency for the eight standardization age groups was .90. For the Adaptive Behavior Scale composite score (GAC), the average internal consistency reliability for the 10 standardization age groups was .97. The manual also contains extensive validity data, such as intercorrelations among all subtest and composite scores, factor structure of the Bayley-III, correlations of Bayley-III with

other measures, such as BSID-II, WPPSI-III, Preschool Language Scale-4, Peabody Developmental Motor Scale-2, and Adaptive Behavior Assessment System-II Parent/Primary Caregiver Form. For each of the special studies groups mentioned above in connection with their inclusion in the standardization sample, data are presented comparing mean Bayley-III performance for each group with that of a matched control group. Performance of the special studies groups on the Social-Emotional Scale and the ABAS-II are also provided.

REFERENCES

Bayley, N. (2006a). *Bayley scales of infant and toddler development—Third edition: Administration manual.* San Antonio, TX: Harcourt Assessment.

Bayley, N. (2006b). *Bayley scales of infant and toddler development—Third edition: Technical manual.* San Antonio, TX: Harcourt Assessment.

Greenspan, S. I. (2004). *Greenspan social-emotional growth chart: A screening questionnaire for infants and young children.* San Antonio, TX: Harcourt Assessment.

Harrison, P. L. & Oakland, T. (2003). *Adaptive behavior assessment system—Second edition.* San Antonio, TX: Psychological Corporation.

GARY J. ROBERTSON
Tampa, Florida

See also: Cognitive Development; Emotional Development

BECK, AARON T. (1921–)

A native of Providence, Rhode Island, Aaron T. Beck has had an interest in psychiatry and psychology as far back as he can remember. At Brown University he was associate editor for the Brown *Daily Herald* and received a number of honors and awards, including Phi Beta Kappa, the Francis Wayland Scholarship, the Bennett Essay Award, and the Gaston Prize for Oratory. After graduating magna cum laude in 1942, he embarked on a career in medicine at Yale Medical School, receiving his M.D. in 1946. He participated in rotating internship, followed by a residency in pathology at Rhode Island Hospital.

Although initially interested in psychiatry, he found the then-current approaches to be nihilistic and unrewarding and decided on a career in neurology, attracted by the high degree of precision that characterizes this discipline. During his residency in neurology at the Cushing Veteran Administration (VA) Hospital, he rotated through psychiatry and was intrigued by the dynamic psychoanalysts F. Deutsch and E. Semrad. When he complained to his colleagues that psychoanalytic theories seemed very farfetched, they explained that they had once felt the same but had discovered that this attitude was simply an indication of their resistance. He concluded that the only way he could validly evaluate the psychoanalytic concepts was to follow their advice and undergo personal analysis.

Beck spent two years as a fellow at the Austen Riggs Center at Stockbridge, where he became impressed with modified psychoanalytic approaches as powerful tools for treating sicker patients. He was particularly influenced by the clinical approaches of R. Knight, M. Brenman, E. Erickson, D. Rapaport, and R. Schafer. Interest in cognition, derived from Rapaport's ego psychology, was stimulated at this time.

The Korean War shifted Beck's area of work to the Valley Forge Army Hospital, where he was assistant chief of neuropsychiatry. Following his graduation from the Philadelphia Psychoanalytic Institute in 1956, he was most influenced by his contacts with L. J. Saul, a progressive and empirically oriented psychoanalyst in the tradition of Alexander and French. Convinced that psychoanalysis offered important insights into psychological disorders, Beck decided to use accepted research methodology to "validate" psychoanalytic hypotheses and, thus, to convince the skeptical that psychoanalysis is a valid theory and therapy.

Beck's first research study involved the testing of the psychoanalytic hypothesis that depression was caused by hostility turned against the self. The findings from his experimental work on dreams and other ideational data, combined with his clinical observations, led Beck to discard psychoanalytic theory to formulate his cognitive theory and therapy of depression and other psychiatric disorders. To his surprise, he found that by teaching depressed patients to examine and test their negative ideas, they were able to correct their dichotomous thinking, overgeneralizations, arbitrary inferences, and so on, and their depression would start to improve (Beck later learned that A. Ellis had made similar observations several years earlier). The important concepts that he developed include cognitive specificity (i.e., each disorder has a specific cognitive content), cognitive bias, and cognitive vulnerability, the idea that patients with a particular cognitive constellation were predisposed to develop a disorder when their experiences impinged on this vulnerability (which consisted, to a large extent, of a cluster of dysfunctional beliefs).

Beck joined the University of Pennsylvania in 1954 and is currently a University Professor Emeritus of Psychiatry. Faculty appointments have included visiting professorships at Harvard University (1982) and Oxford University. Since 1994, he has been president of the Beck Foundation for Cognitive Therapy and Research.

In order to implement his successive research projects, Beck developed a number of instruments, including among others, the Beck Depression Inventory, the Beck Hopelessness Scale, the Beck Anxiety Inventory, the Self-Concept Test, the Sociotropy-Autonomy Scale, the Suicide Intent Scale, and the Scale for Suicide Ideation. His various inventories are among the most widely used psychological assessment instruments. In a long-term study, Beck found that hopelessness, as measured by the Beck Hopelessness Scale at the time of the patient's index admission to a hospital, predicted ultimate suicide within 10 years. This finding was later confirmed with psychiatric outpatients.

Since 1959, Beck has directly funded research investigations of the psychopathology of depression, suicide, anxiety disorders, panic disorders, alcoholism, drug abuse, and personality disorders, and cognitive therapies of these disorders. His work has been consistently supported by the National Institute of Mental Health and the Center for Disease Control and Prevention.

Beck has received numerous awards and honorary degrees including a Doctor of Medical Science honorary degree from Brown University and a Doctor of Humane Letters degree from Assumption College. He is the only psychiatrist to receive research awards from the American Psychological Association and the American Psychiatric Association. He has also received the PSYCHE Award and awards from the Society for Psychopathology Research, Society for Psychotherapy Research, the New York Academy of Medicine, Brown University, and the California Psychological Association. In 2006, he was named the winner of the prestigious Lasker Award for clinical medical research. He is also a senior member of the Institute of Medicine of the National Academy of Sciences. He has authored and co-authored over 400 publications, including 14 books.

Since completing his recent volume, *Prisoners of Hate: The Cognitive Basis of Anger, Hostility, and Violence*, Beck has begun work on the cognitive therapy of schizophrenia. His research and clinical work has stimulated a vast amount of research by other investigators. Cognitive therapy has been recognized as the fastest growing psychotherapy in the world.

REFERENCES

Beck, A. T. (1976). *Cognitive therapy and the emotional disorders*. New York: International Universities Press.

Beck, A. T., Rush, A. J., Shaw, B. F., & Emery, G. (1979). *Cognitive therapy of depression*. New York: Guilford Press.

Beck, A. T., Freeman, A., Davis, D. D., & Associates. (2003). *Cognitive therapy of personality disorders*. New York: Guilford Press.

STAFF

BECK DEPRESSION INVENTORY-II

The Beck Depression Inventory-II (BDI-II) is a 21-item self-administered inventory designed to measure the intensity of depressive symptoms in adults and adolescents (Beck, Steer, & Brown, 1996). Respondents are instructed to indicate which statement best describes how they felt during the past two weeks including today. Items are rated on a 4-point (0 to 3) scale, with total scores obtained by summing the ratings for all items. Scores ranging between 0 and 13 are indicative of minimal depression; scores that fall between 14 and 19 are considered to reflect a mild level of depression; scores of 20 to 28 are considered moderate; and a score ranging from 29 to 63 is labeled severe. The BDI-II requires approximately 5–10 minutes to complete and is appropriate for individuals 13 to 80 years of age.

Test Development

The BDI-II items were selected specifically to evaluate the symptoms and attitudes characteristic of the phenomenology of depression rather than to adhere to any particular theory (Beck et al., 1996). In addition, although the BDI-II's items are congruent with the inclusionary criteria outlined in the fourth edition of the *Diagnostic and Statistical Manual of Mental Disorders* (DSM-IV; American Psychiatric Association, 1994), this measure is intended to identify the severity of symptoms rather than nosological depression. Thus, the BDI-II should be supplemented with other information for a comprehensive assessment and diagnosis of depression.

The BDI-II represents an updated version of the amended Beck Depression Inventory (BDI-IA; Beck, Rush, Shaw, & Emery, 1979), which itself had replaced the original BDI (Beck, Ward, Mendelson, Mock, Erbaugh, 1961). Several changes were made in the BDI-II to increase its compatibility with DSM-IV: four items were eliminated, 17 response options were reworded, 2 items were relocated, 4 new items were constructed (i.e., agitation, worthlessness, loss of energy, and concentration difficulty), item labels were provided to make the intention of each item more explicit, and the time frame was extended to 2 weeks (see Beck et al., 1996).

Reliability and Validity

A number of studies have documented the high internal consistency of the BDI-II. The average coefficient alpha is .91 (see Dozois & Covin, 2004). Regardless of the population investigated, the internal reliability of the BDI-II appears to excellent. Less information is available on the test-retest reliability of the BDI-II, although a reliability coefficient of .93 was reported in the test manual (Beck et al., 1996) and previous versions of this instrument have yielded an average test-retest reliability coefficient of .72 (Yin & Fan, 2000).

The content validity of the BDI-II appears to be excellent. The BDI-II covers the major content domains of depression, including sadness, anhedonia, pessimism, beliefs of being a failure, feelings of guilt, punishment feelings, self-dislike, self-criticalness, suicidal ideation, experiences of crying, agitation, indecisiveness, feelings of worthlessness, lack of energy, altered sleep patterns, irritability, changes in appetite or weight, concentration difficulties, fatigue, and loss of interest in sex.

The convergent and divergent validity of the BDI-II also appears to be well supported. The BDI-II correlates significantly with other indices of depression and depression-related constructs, including the BDI-IA ($r = .93$; Beck et al., 1996), the Hamilton Rating Scale for Depression ($r = .71$), and the Beck Hopelessness Scale ($r = .63-.68$; Beck et al., 1996; Osman, Barrios, Gutierrez, Williams, Bailey, 2008). BDI-II scores also correlate more highly with measures of depression than with measures of anxious symptomatology. The divergent validity of the BDI-II is also upheld by low correlations with age, sex, ethnicity, and social desirability (e.g., Segal, Coolidge, Cahill, & O'Riley, 2008). The BDI-II appears to differentiate well between depressed and nondepressed persons and distinguish among varying levels of depressive severity (Beck et al., 1996). Evidence for the construct validity of the BDI-II also stems from factor-analytic studies. With few exceptions, two main factors (somatic-affective and cognitive aspects of depression) appear to emerge consistently in the literature (see Dozois & Covin, 2004).

Applications

The BDI-II and its predecessors have been used extensively in research and practice and are among the most frequently used psychological tests to date. A number of populations have been studied over the years using the BDI scales, including different psychiatric groups, nonclinical (analogue, undergraduate, and community) samples, ethnic groups, medical populations, and age groups. The BDI scales have been translated into several languages, including Spanish, French, Chinese, Portuguese, Dutch, Persian, Arabic and Hmong. In general, these translated versions show psychometric properties that are comparable to the untranslated version (see Dozois & Covin, 2004). This instrument is an extremely useful research tool and is also a clinically sensitive instrument that may be used for determining a baseline level of severity, formulating clinical hypotheses, deriving a case conceptualization, monitoring session-by-session treatment change, and determining treatment outcome.

The BDI-II has numerous assets that make it an excellent choice for both research and practice. These strengths include the BDI-II's consistency with DSM-IV criteria, its excellent psychometric properties, the ease of administration and scoring, its sensitivity to treatment change, and its large empirical database with which to compare results. Some of the limitations of the BDI-II include its inability to provide conclusive diagnostic evidence, the potentially inaccurate weighting of some item statements (as identified via item characteristic curves), the instability of scores over time even among nonclinical samples and inadequate normative data for different ethnic groups (see Dozois & Covin, 2004). Many of these limitations are not uncommon among self-report instruments, however, and have to do more with the *use* of the BDI-II than with the instrument per se. As such, this inventory will likely remain among the most commonly utilized psychological tests.

REFERENCES

Beck, A. T., Rush, A. J., Shaw, B. F., & Emery, G. (1979). *Cognitive therapy of depression.* New York: Guilford Press.

Beck, A. T., Steer, R. A., & Brown, G. K. (1996). *Beck depression inventory manual* (2nd ed.). San Antonio, TX: Psychological Corporation.

Beck, A. T., Ward, C. H., Mendelson, M., Mock, J., & Erbaugh, J. (1961). An inventory for measuring depression. *Archives of General Psychiatry, 4,* 561–571.

Dozois, D. J. A., & Covin, R. (2004). The Beck Depression Inventory-II (BDI-II), Beck Hopelessness Scale (BHS), and Beck Scale for Suicide Ideation (BSS). In M. Hersen (Series Ed.), D. L. Segal & M. Hilsenroth (Vol. Eds.), *Comprehensive handbook of psychological assessment: Vol. 2. Personality assessment and psychopathology* (pp. 50–69). Hoboken, NJ: John Wiley & Sons.

Osman, A., Barrios, F. X., Gutierrez, P. M., Williams, J. E., & Bailey, J. (2008). Psychometric properties of the Beck Depression Inventory-II in nonclinical adolescent samples. *Journal of Clinical Psychology, 64,* 83–102.

Segal, D. L., Coolidge, F. L., Cahill, B. S., & O'Riley, A. A. (2008). Psychometric properties of the Beck Depression Inventory-II (BDI-II) among community-dwelling older adults. *Behavior Modification, 32,* 3–20.

Yin, P. & Fan, X. (2000). Assessing the reliability of Beck Depression Inventory scores: Reliability generalization across studies. *Educational and Psychological Measurement, 60,* 201–223.

DAVID J. A. DOZOIS
University of Western Ontario

See also: Depression

BEHAVIOR ASSESSMENT SYSTEM FOR CHILDREN

The Behavior Assessment System for Children, Second Edition (BASC–2; Reynolds & Kamphaus, 2004) is a multimethod, multidimensional system used to evaluate the behavior and self-perceptions of children, adolescents, and young adults aged 2 through 25 years. The BASC–2 is multimethod in that it has the following components, which may be used individually or in any combination: (1) two rating scales, one for teachers (Teacher Rating Scales, or TRS) and one for parents (Parent Rating Scales, or PRS), which gather descriptions of the child's observable behavior, each divided into age-appropriate forms; (2) a self-report scale (Self-Report of Personality, or SRP), on which the child or young adult can describe his or her emotions and self-perceptions; (3) a Structured Developmental History (SDH) form; (4) a form for recording and classifying directly observed classroom behavior (Student Observation System, or SOS), which is also available for PDA applications as an electronic version known as the BASC–2 POP or Portable Observation Program; and (5) a self-report for parents of children ages 2–18 years, designed to capture a parent's perspective on the parent-child relationship in such domains as communication, disciplinary styles, attachment, involvement, and others.

The BASC–2 is multidimensional in that it measures numerous aspects of behavior and personality, including positive (adaptive) as well as negative (clinical) dimensions. The BASC–2 is a revision of the Behavior Assessment System for Children (BASC; Reynolds & Kamphaus, 1994). Users of the original BASC can shift easily to using the BASC–2. The BASC–2 retains all of the key features of the BASC and makes numerous improvements, including improved reliabilities and additional scales (Functional Communication, TRS and PRS; Activities of Daily Living, PRS; and Adaptability, TRS–A and PRS–A; Attention Problems and Hyperactivity on SRP) without lengthening the forms; a standardization sample matched to recent U.S. population figures (Current Population Survey, 2001); greater similarity of item content across levels and between the TRS and PRS; a reduction in the length of the TRS; newly devised content scales that can be used as an aid in interpreting the primary scales and to broaden the coverage of the behavior areas assessed by BASC–2; a mixed item-response format on the SRP, which improves both scale reliability and the ability to measure at the extremes of the score ranges; expanded age range for assessing students through age 21 years who are still attending secondary school and, on the SRP, students aged 18 through 25 attending postsecondary institutions; and more detailed clinical norms.

Scoring and interpretive software programs are available for the BASC–2 that make actuarial as well as content matches to the educational classification of emotional disturbance and also to various clinical diagnoses. The most popular and useful of the programs is the BASC–2 Plus program, which also scores and interprets the Content Scales, which other programs do not do.

The BASC–2 was designed to facilitate the differential diagnosis and educational classification of a variety of emotional and behavioral disorders of children and to aid in the design of treatment plans. When used individually, the BASC–2 components are reliable and psychometrically sophisticated instruments that provide an array of beneficial data. When used as a total system, the BASC–2 provides information about a child from a variety of sources and provides the clinician with a coordinated set of tools for evaluation, diagnosis, and treatment planning.

As a system, the BASC–2 components afford a triangulated view of the child's behavioral problems by (1) examining behavior in multiple settings (at home and school); (2) evaluating the child's emotions, personality, and perceptions of self; (3) providing important background information useful when making educational classifications or clinical diagnoses, an area commonly shortchanged in educational settings; and (4) including software that provides a sophisticated means for evaluating change or progress of individuals over time in response to interventions.

Key Features of the BASC–2

The BASC–2 has numerous features that make it a sophisticated and reliable system of behavior assessment. The BASC–2 assesses a wide range of distinctive dimensions. In addition to evaluating personality and behavioral problems and emotional disturbance, the BASC–2 identifies positive attributes that can be capitalized on in the treatment process, attributes that are valuable but too often ignored in clinical assessment.

The range of dimensions assessed helps in making differential diagnosis of specific categories of disorder, such as those denoted in the *Diagnostic and Statistical Manual of Mental Disorders* (DSM–IV–TR; American Psychiatric Association, 2000), as well as general categories of problems, such as those addressed by The Individuals with Disabilities Education Act. The BASC–2 is highly relevant to federal regulations concerning the diagnosis of severe emotional disturbance in the schools and also is sensitive enough to detect even mild behavior problems among children in other disability categories, including learning disabilities and mental retardation.

The BASC–2 allows information from multiple sources to be compared using instruments with overlapping norms to help achieve reliable and accurate diagnoses. The software programs available for the BASC–2 also will compare data from each of the BASC–2 components and assess them for similarities and differences statistically and graphically. Each BASC–2 component is designed for a specific setting or type of respondent because some constructs or behaviors are more important or measurable in some settings than in others. This also gives clinicians a clear view of the generalizability of the individual's behavior as well as the setting-specific nature of any behavior problems that occur principally in one type of surrounding.

The BASC–2 scales were designed to be highly interpretable and are built around clearly specified constructs with matching item content, developed through a balance of theory and empirical data. Experienced clinicians wrote the initial items, and they were assigned initially to scales using expert methods but refined iteratively using an empirical approach based on the responses of nearly 50,000 individuals. Scales are consistent not only across sex and age levels but also between the teacher and parent forms. This provides a basis for consistent interpretation of scales and for meaningful across-source and across-time score comparisons. BASC–2 norms are based on large, U.S. Census Bureau representative samples and are differentiated according to the age, sex, and clinical status of the child. Clinicians have a choice of sex-based norms or combined-sex norms when deriving standard scores for the various subscales and composites. The BASC–2 covers the full age range, 2 through 21 years, of students in preschool through high school settings, while maintaining developmental sensitivity and continuity of constructs. The BASC–2 also offers a version of the SRP for ages 18 through 25 for use in technical schools, colleges, and universities.

The BASC–2 scales and composites have high internal consistency and test-retest reliability. Most alpha coefficients for the BASC–2 subscales and composites exceed .80 and are sufficiently reliable for application to diagnostic and treatment issues. Additionally, the BASC–2 offers various types of validity checks to help the clinician detect careless or untruthful responding, misunderstanding, or other threats to validity.

The BASC–2 PRS, SRP, and SDH are available in Spanish as well as English and are also available on audio for nonreaders. The BASC–2 can be either hand-scored or computer-scored (manual or scanable item entry).

The BASC–2 has been widely used and is available throughout the English-speaking world from Pearson Assessments of Bloomington MN and throughout the Spanish-speaking world from TEA Ediciones in Madrid. Versions in several other languages are also available and updated information on these versions can be obtained by contacting Pearson Assessments (http://www .pearsonassessments.com). Estimates from sales figures indicate that the BASC–2 is one of, if not the most, frequently administered individual psychological tests in the public schools of the United States.

REFERENCES

American Psychiatric Association. (2000). *Diagnostic and statistical manual of mental disorders* (4th ed., text rev.). Washington DC: Author.

Reynolds, C. R., & Kamphaus, R. W. (2004). *Behavior assessment system for children* (2nd ed.). Bloomington, MN: Pearson Assessments.

Reynolds, C. R., & Kamphaus, R. W. (1994). *Behavior assessment system for children.* Bloomington, MN: Pearson Assessments.

SUGGESTED READINGS

Ramsay, M., Reynolds, C. R., & Kamphaus, R. W. (2002). *Essentials of behavioral assessment.* Hoboken, NJ: John Wiley & Sons.

Reynolds, C. R., & Kamphaus, R. W. (2002). *The clinician's guide to the Behavior Assessment System for Children.* New York: Guilford Press.

CECIL R. REYNOLDS
Texas A&M University

See also: Behavioral Assessment; Psychological Assessment

BEHAVIOR MODIFICATION

Behavior modification is the field of study that focuses on using principles of learning and cognition to understand and change people's behavior (Sarafino, 2001). Although not all experts in this field would include cognitive processes in the definition (see Lee, 1992; Sweet & Loizeaux, 1991; Wolpe, 1993), these processes have been widely adopted and applied by behavior modification professionals since the early 1970s (Dobson, 1988; Kazdin, 1978; Mahoney, 1993; Williams, Watts, MacLeod, & Mathews, 1988).

Defining Characteristics of Behavior Modification

The field of behavior modification has several characteristics that make its approach unique (Kazdin, 1978; Wixted, Bellack, & Hersen, 1990). First, professionals in this field focus on people's *behavior,* which can be *overt,* such as motor or verbal acts, or *covert,* such as feelings, thoughts, or physiological changes. As a result, their approach typically involves (1) defining people's current status and progress in terms of behavior rather than traits or other broad features, (2) measuring the behavior in some way, and (3) whenever possible, assessing covert behaviors, such as fear, in terms of overt actions. Efforts to improve behavior can be directed at a *behavioral deficit*—that is, the behavior occurs with insufficient frequency, strength, or quality—or a *behavioral excess*—that is, it occurs too frequently or strongly. The behavior to be changed is called the *target behavior.*

Second, although behavior modification professionals recognize that injury and heredity can limit the abilities of an individual, they assume that human behavior is, for the most part, *learned* and influenced by the environment. The most basic types of learning are *respondent (classical) conditioning*—in which a stimulus gains the ability to elicit a particular response by being paired with an unconditioned stimulus that already elicits that response—and *operant conditioning*—in which behavior is changed by its consequences. The methods applied in behavior modification generally involve altering the *antecedents* and *consequences* of the target behavior.

Third, behavior modification has a strong scientific orientation. As a result, there is a major focus on carefully gathering empirical data, analyzing and interpreting the data, and specifying the precise methods used to gather and analyze the data. The field is also quite pragmatic, emphasizing the need to find and use techniques that work, as indicated by carefully conducted research. Fourth, behavior modification techniques for changing behavior often have clients or subjects become active participants, such as by performing "homework" and "self-management" activities, in the process of modifying their behavior.

History of Behavior Modification

Behavior modification developed from the perspective called *behaviorism,* which emerged with the work of John B. Watson (1913, 1930) and B. F. Skinner (1938, 1953). This perspective emphasizes the study of observable and measurable behavior and proposes that nearly all behavior is the product of learning, particularly operant and respondent conditioning. Three lines of research laid the foundation for behaviorism. Ivan Pavlov (1927) demonstrated the process of respondent conditioning. John Watson and Rosalie Rayner (1920) showed that an infant, "Little Albert," learned to fear a white rat through respondent conditioning. And Edward Thorndike (1898, 1931) studied how "satisfying" and "annoying" consequences—which we now call *reinforcement* and *punishment*—affect learning. Other studies formed the basis for applying the ideas of behaviorism by showing that conditioning techniques could effectively reduce fears (Jones, 1924) and improve problem behaviors of psychiatric patients (Ayllon & Michael, 1959; Lindsley, 1956). The field of behavior modification now includes the areas of the *experimental analysis of behavior,* which examines basic theoretical processes in learning, *applied behavior analysis,* which emphasizes application to socially important problems in various settings, and *behavior therapy,* which focuses on application in psychotherapy settings.

Application and Techniques of Behavior Modification

Behavior modification techniques have been applied successfully in a wide variety of settings and with many types of behaviors and populations (Sarafino, 2001). They have been used to improve general parenting skills, help parents correct children's problem behaviors, enhance instructional methods in schools, improve classroom conduct, train developmentally disabled children in self-help skills, reduce substance abuse, reduce depression and anxiety, promote people's health and prevent illness, and improve worker productivity and safety.

The techniques used in modifying behavior are quite varied. Operant techniques include some that deal with the consequences of behavior. In *reinforcement,* consequences strengthen the target behavior. *Positive reinforcement* involves introducing a desirable event after the target behavior, and *negative reinforcement* involves removing or reducing an aversive circumstance if the target behavior occurs. *Extinction* is a procedure whereby eliminating the reinforcers of a target behavior weakens that behavior. When *punishment* is used as a consequence, it suppresses the target behavior. Operant techniques also address the antecedents of the target behavior. For instance, *prompting* involves using a stimulus to remind individuals to perform a behavior they know how to do or help them perform a behavior they do not do well. Other operant methods concentrate on the behavior itself. *Shaping* improves a target behavior by requiring better and better performance to receive reinforcement, and *chaining* is used to develop complex motor behaviors by organizing simple responses into a sequence.

Respondent techniques are usually applied to reduce conditioned emotional responses, such as fear or anger. One technique is *extinction,* in which a conditioned response is weakened by repeatedly presenting the conditioned stimulus without the unconditioned stimulus. Another method is *systematic desensitization,* whereby a conditioned emotional response is reduced by having the person experience increasingly strong conditioned stimuli while maintaining a relaxation response. The conditioned stimuli are arranged in a hierarchy from a very weak stimulus to a very intense one.

Other behavior modification techniques include *modeling,* a vicarious process in which individuals learn a behavior by watching someone else perform it; biofeedback; and various cognitive methods, such as relaxation training, thought-stopping, and covert sensitization. *Biofeedback* is a technique that teaches people to regulate physiological functioning by presenting moment-by-moment information about the status of the body system. The form of relaxation that is most commonly applied in behavior modification is *progressive muscle relaxation,* which has the person alternately tense and relax separate muscle groups. Once the relaxation response is mastered, the procedure can be used by itself or as part of systematic desensitization. *Thought stopping* is a technique in which individuals interrupt distressing thoughts by saying "Stop" emphatically, either aloud or covertly. *Covert sensitization* is a method that is used to teach a person to dislike a liked event, such as drinking alcohol, by pairing it repeatedly with an aversive event in an imagined situation.

Applying behavior modification is a creative enterprise that organizes techniques into programs that are tailored to meet the needs of specific clients in particular circumstances.

REFERENCES

Ayllon, T., & Michael, J. (1959). The psychiatric nurse as a behavioral engineer. *Journal of the Experimental Analysis of Behavior, 2,* 323–334.

Dobson, K. S. (Ed.) (1988). *Handbook of cognitive-behavioral therapies.* New York: Guilford Press.

Jones, M. C. (1924). The elimination of children's fears. *Journal of Experimental Psychology, 7,* 382–390.

Kazdin, A. E. (1978). *History of behavior modification: Experimental foundations of contemporary research.* Baltimore: University Park Press.

Lee, C. (1992). On cognitive theories and causation in human behavior. *Journal of Behavior Therapy and Experimental Psychiatry, 23,* 257–268.

Lindsley, O. R. (1956). Operant conditioning methods applied to research in chronic schizophrenia. *Psychiatric Research Reports, 5,* 118–139.

Mahoney, M. J. (1993). Introduction to special section: Theoretical developments in the cognitive psychotherapies. *Journal of Consulting and Clinical Psychology, 61,* 187–193.

Pavlov, I. P. (1927). *Conditioned reflexes.* (G. V. Anrep, Trans.). New York: Oxford University Press.

Sarafino, E. P. (2001). *Behavior modification: Principles of behavior change* (2nd ed.). Mountain View, CA: Mayfield.

Skinner, B. F. (1938). *The behavior of organisms.* New York: Appleton-Century-Crofts.

Skinner, B. F. (1953). *Science and human behavior.* New York: Macmillan.

Sweet, A. A., & Loizeaux, A. L. (1991). Behavioral and cognitive treatment methods: A critical comparative review. *Journal of Behavior Therapy and Experimental Psychiatry, 22,* 159–185.

Thorndike, E. L. (1898). Animal intelligence: An experimental study of the associative processes in animals. *Psychological Review Monograph Supplements, 2,* No. 8.

Thorndike, E. L. (1931). *Human learning.* New York: Century.

Watson, J. B. (1913). Psychology as the behaviorist views it. *Psychological Review, 20,* 158–177.

Watson, J. B. (1930). *Behaviorism.* New York: Norton.

Watson, J. B., & Rayner, R. (1920). Conditioned emotional reactions. *Journal of Experimental Psychology, 3,* 1–14.

Williams, J. M. G., Watts, F. N., MacLeod, C., & Mathews, A. (1988). *Cognitive psychology and emotional disorders.* New York: John Wiley & Sons.

Wixted, J. T., Bellack, A. S., & Hersen, M. (1990). Behavior therapy. In A. S. Bellack & M. Hersen (Eds.), *Handbook of comparative treatments for adult disorders.* New York: John Wiley & Sons.

Wolpe, J. (1993). Commentary: The cognitivist oversell and comments on symposium contributions. *Journal of Behavior Therapy and Experimental Psychiatry, 24,* 141–147.

EDWARD P. SARAFINO
The College of New Jersey

See also: **Dialectical Behavior Therapy; Rational Emotive Behavior Therapy**

BEHAVIOR PROBLEMS OF CHILDHOOD AND ADOLESCENCE

During the long process of maturation, nearly all youth have transitory problems of adjustment, behavior, and emotion. Parents of preschoolers often lament their children's tantrums, shyness, and unruliness; families of teenagers worry about rebellion, lack of academic motivation, and temptation for drugs and alcohol. Although such problems typically resolve with further development, when issues related to impulse control, emotion regulation, or behavioral deportment are quite extreme for the child's age and when they interfere with schooling and academic achievement, family life, or the attainment of independence, referrals may be made for diagnosis of a psychological or psychiatric condition. In fact, serious levels of problem behavior are usually not short-lived. The subject of this entry is the nature, etiology, and treatment of such clinical-range problems.

How can we organize and classify the many potential behavior problems that youth may exhibit? For several decades a major distinction has been made between what are termed *externalizing* behaviors (related to defiance, impulsivity, aggression, and antisocial actions; sometimes termed "behavior problems" or "disruptive behaviors") and those that comprise the *internalizing* spectrum (e.g., anxiety, depression, somatic concerns, social withdrawal, and the like; sometimes called "emotional problems" or "overcontrolled" behaviors). A potentially confusing point of terminology is evident: The label "behavior problems" can refer specifically to the externalizing spectrum or more generally to all behavioral and emotional problems of youth. This entry refers to both internalizing and externalizing problems, but the key information focuses on differences between these two classes of behavior.

This distinction emerged when investigators began to subject the wide variety of problem behaviors to statistical techniques like factor analysis, with the aim of uncovering a smaller number of underlying dimensions. Indeed, across the hundreds of specific problems a child may exhibit, a finite number of problem dimensions usually emerges including overtly aggressive actions, delinquent behaviors, impulsivity and attention problems, disturbances in thinking, difficulties in social interactions, excessive somatic concerns, social isolation, anxiety, and depression (Achenbach, 1991). When this set of problem dimensions is itself factor analyzed, two overarching factors usually emerge, and are categorized as externalizing and internalizing.

In passing, clear parallels with classification of mental abilities can be noted. Herein, a number of cognitive abilities in youth can be subdivided into discrete subtests (e.g., verbal analogies, vocabulary skills, understanding of part-whole relations, spatial rotations), which themselves form factors comprising the major components of intelligence, known as Verbal versus Performance IQ. General intelligence comprises the combination of these two

meta-domains in the way that overall problem behavior represents the summation of internalizing and externalizing actions.

A key question is whether internalizing and externalizing problems are distributed continuously or whether there are distinct clusters of youth who either do or do not exhibit such problems. The debate regarding the continuous/quantitative versus categorical nature of psychopathology is long-standing and contentious (Pickles & Angold, 2003). Across a host of research investigations, there is extremely limited evidence for pure "types" or categories of child behavioral disturbance; nearly all such problems are continuously distributed across the population. Thus, designations of clinical disorders are somewhat arbitrary, parallel to the cutoff point in medicine distinguishing normal blood pressure from hypertension. Yet, there are practical reasons for designating a certain subset of the population as falling within the clinical range, chiefly related to decisions to engage in treatment. Current systems for making diagnostic decisions are concerned with ensuring that those above the diagnostic thresholds have demonstrable impairments beyond their symptoms per se (American Psychiatric Association, 2000). In other words, one would diagnose a child as having attention-deficit/hyperactivity disorder (ADHD), depression, autistic disorder, or any other classification only if the symptoms yield major problems in daily life.

Three key issues are salient regarding the classification of child and adolescent problem behavior. First, behavior patterns with rare frequency in the population (such as those related to autism or extreme restrictions of caloric intake, signifying anorexia nervosa) sometimes do not even make it into the lists of items to be factor analyzed. At the same time, cognitive and learning problems are evaluated on the basis of tests of mental ability or academic achievement rather than evaluations of problematic behavior. As a result, listings of internalizing and externalizing conditions often omit relatively rare conditions like autistic disorder and must be augmented by cognitive assessment to incorporate diagnoses of mental retardation or learning disorders.

Second, because all behavior patterns of children are shaped by contextual factors (e.g., socioeconomic status, quality of schooling, family characteristics, childrearing styles, neighborhood characteristics), comprehensive evaluations of children and adolescents must transcend assessment of problematic behavioral and emotional functioning and appraise strengths and weaknesses in the child's environmental settings. In other words, because problem behavior does not exist in a vacuum, identification of contextual factors is crucial for distinguishing truly disordered functioning from responses to environmental adversity and for forging treatment plans, which may well involve alteration of family practices, classroom structure, and the like.

Third, although internalizing and externalizing behaviors might appear to be quite distinct, statistical association between these dimensions is surprisingly high, even in normative samples (Achenbach, 1991). Similarly, comorbidity—a term signifying the presence of two or more conditions in the same child or adolescent—is more likely than the presence of single disorders in isolation (Angold, Costello, & Erkanli, 1999). Indeed, not only are rates of comorbidity high *within* the internalizing spectrum (e.g., anxiety and depression) or the externalizing spectrum (e.g., ADHD and aggressive conduct disorder), but comorbidity exists *across* internalizing and externalizing conditions. For instance, nearly a third of youth with conduct disorders also display significant depression. Such patterns raise the point that common risk factors may well exist across internalizing and externalizing problems, and treatments for a given condition are often incomplete unless comorbid diagnoses are taken into account.

Still, differences do exist between externalizing and internalizing problems. Broadly speaking, externalizing behavior patterns show more stability, or persistence across time, than internalizing problems. Thus, on average, a child with significant aggression is more likely to show such behavior patterns persistently than is a child with anxiety symptoms. It is a mistake, however, to dismiss internalizing problems as transitory or ephemeral. Severe, focused anxiety (in the form of obsessive-compulsive disorder or panic disorder) is typically *not* transitory, and major depression is highly likely to recur at later points in an individual's lifespan (Rudolph, Hammen, & Daley, 2006). Investigators are just beginning to understand the continuities and discontinuities of both externalizing and internalizing problems from childhood through adolescence and adulthood (Hinshaw, 2008).

In terms of the origins of these types of problem behaviors, there is great interest in the topic of *temperament*. Briefly put, temperament involves particular constellations of behavioral and emotional tendencies, which are present from the earliest months of life and presumably based in early biology, these tendencies then provide the "building blocks" of later personality. Among the dimensions of temperament are activity level, emotional intensity, the ability to be soothed, and behavioral inhibition. Although early manifestations of such temperamental traits are not destiny, given the ways in which environment and context can promote malleability, there is significant predictability from extremes of temperament to significant behavior problems in childhood and adolescence (Caspi, Moffitt, Newman, & Silva, 1996).

Temperament is but one of many influences on child and adolescent behavior. Indeed, no single factor (i.e., genes, temperament, attachment to caregivers, general childrearing style) is sufficient to predict outcome with much certainty. Fascinating findings reveal the ways in which "nature" (i.e., genes) and "nurture" (i.e., environmental influences) work together to predict

behavioral disturbance. For instance, to predict those at risk for violent behavior, it is the confluence of early biological risk (i.e., prenatal factors and birth complications) plus severe psychosocial rejection during the first year of life that yields the strongest predictive power (Raine, Brennan, & Mednick, 1994). Furthermore, in terms of depression, the presence of a particular "risk gene" related to the neurotransmitter serotonin plus key psychosocial factors during development (either maltreatment in childhood or high levels of negative life events in adolescence or early adulthood) maximize the risk for this significant internalizing disorder (Caspi et al., 2003); neither genes nor environments alone are strong predictors. Indeed, emerging from recent, sophisticated research is the knowledge that interactions and transactions (i.e., repeated cycles of the interactions of biology and environment over time) are far more influential in causing and maintaining problem behavior than are main effects of either source alone. The discipline of developmental psychopathology emphasizes that interactive influences work together in reciprocal ways akin to cascading, symphonic causation (Boyce, 2006).

Do boys and girls display the same types of problem behavior? A key rule of thumb is as follows: for the types of behavioral disorders that have their onset in childhood (e.g., autistic disorder, early-onset aggression, ADHD), boys outnumber girls; but for the categories that tend to emerge during adolescence (e.g., internalizing conditions such as anxiety disorders, depression, and eating disorders), girls reveal higher prevalence. Intriguingly, the very factors that protect girls from exhibiting externalizing problems during childhood, such as verbal skills, empathy, and compliance—which girls display, on average, at higher rates than boys—may actually serve as risk factors for the display of internalizing problems in girls during and after puberty, particularly in the presence of additional family risk factors such as a depressed parent (see Hinshaw, 2009). It is clear, therefore, that deciding whether a certain variable is harmful or helpful (i.e., whether it serves as a risk or protective factor) depends on a child's age and sex, as well as contextual factors.

In conclusion, how do clinicians go about treating such problem behaviors? The research base, with respect to both medication and psychological interventions for child and adolescent disorders, is a fast-growing enterprise (Silverman & Hinshaw, 2008). Indeed, there are a number of evidence-based treatment strategies for both externalizing and internalizing conditions that show considerable promise for reducing symptoms and alleviating impairment. For some conditions, like ADHD and depression, pharmacologic treatment is quite effective, at least for as long as it is given, and adding individual, family, or school-based behavioral/cognitive treatments typically enhances clinical benefits. For other disorders (e.g., autism, most forms of aggression, and many child anxiety disorders), medications are *not* the primary treatment;

rather, individual or family approaches, if applied diligently, can provide clinical headway and provide effective coping strategies.

The overall clinical picture, however, is far from rosy. First, definitive information on risk and causal factors for child and adolescent behavior disorders is still lacking, meaning that treatments are directed largely at symptoms (and accompanying impairments) rather than known causal mechanisms. Second, there is far greater evidence for treating single disorders than comorbid conditions; the most complex cases usually prove the hardest to treat. Third, research-based interventions in controlled university trials typically produce far larger benefits than do clinic-based treatments in community settings. In other words, there is a large gap between what are termed "efficacy" studies (i.e., tightly controlled experimental interventions for single disorders) and what are called "effectiveness" studies (i.e., examination of outcome in real-world settings with youth who display complex problems).

A huge need exists to bridge the gap between (1) research on basic mechanisms that can explain the development and maintenance of problem behavior and (2) the kinds of therapeutic processes that can provide lasting, meaningful benefit. The clear majority of adult forms of mental disturbance have their origins in childhood, and given that longitudinal research now reveals the distressingly persistent nature of most forms of child disorders; it is therefore imperative that basic research on relevant psychological and contextual mechanisms can synergize with clinical investigations of efficacy and effectiveness, in order to develop more effective treatments as well as viable prevention strategies. The long-term consequences of child and adolescent behavior disorders are sufficiently severe that such clinical and research efforts are mandatory at the levels of individuals, families, communities, and society at large.

REFERENCES

Achenbach, T. M. (1991). *Integrative guide for the 1991 CBCL/4-18, YSR, and TRF profile*. Burlington, VT: University of Vermont Department of Psychiatry.

American Psychiatric Association. (2000). *Diagnostic and statistical manual of mental disorders* (4th ed., text rev.). Washington, DC: Author.

Angold, A., Costello, E. J., & Erkanli, A. (1999). Comorbidity. *Journal of Child Psychology and Psychiatry, 40*, 57–88.

Boyce, W. T. (2006). Symphonic causation and the origins of childhood psychopathology. In D. Cicchetti & D. J. Cohen (Eds.), *Developmental psychopathology* (2nd ed., Vol. 2: Developmental neuroscience, pp. 797–817). Hoboken, NJ: John Wiley & Sons.

Caspi, A., Moffitt, T. E., Newman, D. L., & Silva, P. A. (1996). Behavioral observations at age 3 predict adult psychiatric disorders: Longitudinal evidence from a birth cohort. *Archives of General Psychiatry, 53*, 1033–1039.

Caspi, A., Sugden, K., Moffitt, T. E., Taylor, A., Craig, I. W., Harrington, H., McClay, J., Mill, J., Martin, J., Braithwaite, A., & Poulton, R. (2003). Influence of life stress on depression: Moderation by a polymorphism in the 5-HTT gene. *Science, 301*, 386–389.

Hinshaw, S. P. (2008). Developmental psychopathology as a scientific discipline: Relevance to behavioral and emotional disorders of childhood and adolescence. In T. P. Beauchaine & S. P. Hinshaw (Eds.), *Child and adolescent psychopathology* (pp. 3–26). Hoboken, NJ: John Wiley & Sons.

Hinshaw, S. P., with Kranz, R. (2009). *The triple bind: The hidden crisis among today's teenage girls*. New York: Random House.

Pickles, A., & Angold, A. (2003). Natural categories or fundamental dimensions: On carving nature at its joints and the rearticulation of psychopathology. *Development and Psychopathology, 15*, 529–555.

Raine, A., Brennan, P., & Mednick, S. A. (1994). Birth complications combined with early maternal rejection at age 1 year predispose to violent crime at age 18 years. *Archives of General Psychiatry, 51*, 984–988.

Rudolph, K. D., Hammen, C., & Daley, S. E. (2006). Mood disorders. In D. A. Wolfe & E. J. Mash (Eds.), *Behavioral and emotional disorders in adolescents: Nature, assessment, and treatment*. New York: Guilford Press.

Silverman, W., & Hinshaw, S. P. (Eds.). (2008). Evidence-based psychosocial treatments for children and adolescents: The ten year update. *Journal of Clinical Child and Adolescent Psychology* (Special Issue), 37.

SUGGESTED READINGS

Beauchaine, T. P., & Hinshaw, S. P. (Eds.). (2008). *Child and adolescent psychopathology*. Hoboken, NJ: John Wiley & Sons.

Cicchetti, D., & Cohen, D. J. (Eds.). (2006). Developmental psychopathology (2nd ed.; three volumes). Hoboken, NJ: John Wiley & Sons.

Mash, E. J., & Barkley, R. A. (Eds.). (2003). *Child psychopathology* (2nd ed.). New York: Guilford Press.

STEPHEN P. HINSHAW
University of California, Berkeley

See also: Conduct Disorder; Emotional Disturbances; Psychopathology

BEHAVIOR THERAPY (See Behavior Modification)

BEHAVIORAL ACTIVATION

Behavioral activation (BA) is a structured psychosocial treatment for depression based on the assumption that people with depression develop maladaptive patterns of behavioral responses to life's problems that reduce their ability to experience positive reward in their environments and impair effective problem solving. It is suggested both that such patterns can maintain depression over time and that interrupting such patterns can alleviate depression and reduce subsequent risk for relapse. Thus, BA is aimed at helping depressed clients activate and reengage in their environments in ways that maximize contact with positive reward and facilitate effective problem solving.

History and Evidence Base

BA is rooted in the work of early behavioral pioneers like Charles Ferster and Peter Lewinsohn. Ferster (1973) argued that individuals develop depression when their behavior does not result in positive reward from their environments or when avoidance of unpleasant situations inadvertently negatively reinforces their behavior. Ferster emphasized the importance of conducting a functional analysis to identify patterns of avoidant behavior than can lead to limited positive reinforcement. Lewinsohn's model of depression (1974) also highlighted the behavior-environment contingency and the lack of pleasant events and excess of aversive events in understanding depression. The BA model also is convergent with prior research on problem solving therapy for depression (e.g., Nezu, 1989).

Interest in the value of such approaches for the treatment of depression was largely eclipsed by a focus on cognitive therapy (CT), which integrated behavioral treatment strategies into a larger cognitive framework, until Jacobson and colleagues conducted a dismantling study of CT. This study suggested that the BA component of CT and the full CT package performed comparably in both the acute treatment of depression and the prevention of relapse (Jacobson et al., 1996; Gortner et al., 1998). These results galvanized interest in BA as a standalone treatment with a clearly defined conceptualization of depression and specified interventions.

Dimidjian and colleagues (2006) tested this standalone BA model in a comparison with CT and antidepressant medication (ADM) in a randomized placebo-controlled trial. Results of this study suggested that, among severely depressed patients, BA was comparable in efficacy to ADM, and both outperformed CT. Additionally, attrition was significantly lower in the BA condition than in the ADM condition. There were no significant differences among any of the treatments for the less severely depressed patients. This study suggested that BA has significant promise in the treatment of depression. Furthermore, a related brief behavioral activation treatment has shown promise in studies with depressed inpatients and depressed cancer patients (Hopko et al, 2003; Hopko et al., 2005). Also, other activation-oriented approaches, including exercise-based interventions (Stathopoulou et al.

2006) and problem-solving therapy for depression have been widely investigated (i.e., Unutzer et al. 2002).

Case Conceptualization

The BA model emphasizes contextual events and circumstances as proximal precipitants to depression. According to this model, depression is an understandable result of an environment that provides too little reward and too much aversive control. One's behavioral responses to such contexts are emphasized heavily in BA, particularly the tendency toward inactivity, withdrawal, and avoidance. Such patterns tend to maintain depression over time by inhibiting access to positive reinforcement and exacerbating life stressors. Although patterns of inactivity, withdrawal, and avoidance can provide immediate relief in that they permit escape from aversive stimuli, they often preclude contact with natural sources of potentially rewarding experiences and keep individuals stuck in depression over time.

Treatment Strategies

Although highly structured, BA is an idiographic approach that is optimally tailored to each individual. The following describes the general course of BA and should be used to guide and not dictate to the reader.

Orienting

In the first session, the therapist presents the BA model of depression and orients the client to treatment procedures. Presenting the model involves collaboratively identifying specific ways in which the model applies to the client. Orienting to treatment includes discussing the specific treatment interventions and clarifying both the therapist and client's roles. Throughout the initial orientating process, and treatment in general, therapists encourage clients to ask questions and express concerns they may have about the treatment model and interventions.

Assessment Strategies

Assessment procedures are used throughout the course of BA. The primary goals of assessment in BA include defining problems, assessing consequences of behavior, identifying behavioral patterns, and developing treatment goals. The process of assessment involves the therapist and client working together to define problems in the client's life that will likely become targets of intervention. Once clear problems have been identified, the therapist assesses the context and consequences of such problems to understand not only the form of a given behavior, but more importantly, its function. Similarly, the therapist and client of how behavior influences mood and vice-versa across time and settings.

Developing goals usually involves identifying avoidance behaviors and short- and long-term goals. Frequently, a focus on short-term goals involves addressing avoidance patterns that interfere with activation and replacing them with active coping behaviors. After the therapist and client address short-term goals, they consider larger goals that have the potential to improve life context (e.g., finding a new job, moving). A primary tool for conducting such functional analyses involves having clients monitor their activity between sessions by completing daily activity and mood charts. When examining activity charts, BA therapists are attentive to the relationships between activity and mood, contextual triggers for mood shifts, and the client's responses to such triggers.

Activation Strategies

BA does not simply encourage clients to become more active. Rather, the therapist and client work closely together to identify mutually agreed upon activities that will likely have antidepressant effects. The idiographic nature of BA implies that the course of treatment can vary significantly from client to client. However, the following strategies are hallmarks of BA and are likely to be heavily utilized in any course of treatment, albeit aimed at individualized treatment targets.

Activity scheduling. Most of the therapeutic work in BA occurs outside of therapy and scheduling activities is an essential strategy to this end. It is especially useful for the therapist and client to designate specific days and times for the client to complete the agreed-upon activities. Such specificity may increase the likelihood of the client following through with activation assignments.

Activity structuring. The BA model assumes that initiating new behavior when depressed is a challenging endeavor and that success will be maximized by grading tasks. Typically, depressed individuals experience taking action as overwhelming. Thus, breaking complex behaviors down into more manageable units is a core strategy of BA. A key feature of graded task assignment is emphasizing initiation of activities and not necessarily accomplishing all parts of the activity. Accomplishing subcomponents of tasks can prime motivation to tackle progressively larger components of the overall task.

Solving problems and modifying avoidance. As individuals avoid different experiences for different reasons, avoidance modification takes on many forms in BA. In targeting avoidance behaviors, it is essential that the therapist convey empathy for the difficulties clients experience that lead subsequently to avoidance. In this context, therapists also can highlight how avoidance may serve an adaptive function in that it provides immediate relief, but in the long run often is incompatible with activation and overcoming depression. Since avoidance behavior typically involves a response to problematic situations, the therapist adopts a problem-solving stance and helps the client generate and evaluate a range of solutions to approach and solve problems (e.g., exercising, looking for a job, asking for a raise, grieving over a loss).

Targeting rumination. The BA model views ruminative thinking as a private behavior that can be targeted for change in the same way as other overt behaviors. Rumination is often conceptualized as a form of avoidance. Rumination can prevent people from fully participating in their activities and environments and can prevent effective problem solving. Therapists encourage clients to interrupt ruminative patterns by attending to the direct and immediate experience of their current activity and surroundings and by directing their attention to specific tasks and goals.

Relapse Prevention

Given that depression is often a recurring disorder, acute treatment models must also include specific plans for relapse prevention. Throughout BA, therapists help clients reduce risk for relapse by changing their context and teaching them activation skills. Near the end of treatment, the therapist and client work together to anticipate environmental triggers that previously caused depression and develop plans to cope with such situations.

BA employs a parsimonious set of strategies to help clients overcome depression in a structured and systematic fashion. These strategies include common factors such as orienting the client to treatment, structuring therapy sessions, and assigning homework, and specific factors, such as functional analysis, activity scheduling and structuring, and avoidance modification. BA has shown promise in a number of clinical trials, although additional research is required to evaluate its outcomes across an array of settings and patients. Moreover, initial interest in BA derived in part from the speculation that, with its easy-to-grasp model of depression and straightforward interventions, BA may lend itself particularly well to dissemination. Whether or not BA can help bridge the clinical practice-research gap awaits further research.

REFERENCES

Dimidjian, S., Hollon, S. D., Dobson, K. S., Schmaling, K. B., Kohlenberg, R. J., Addis, M. E., et al. (2006). Randomized trial of behavioral activation, cognitive therapy, and antidepressant medication in the acute treatment of adults with major depression. *Journal of Consulting and Clinical Psychology, 74*(4), 658–670.

Ferster, C. B. (1973). A functional analysis of depression. *American Psychologist, 28*(10), 857–870.

Gortner, E. T., Gollan, J. K., Dobson, K. S., & Jacobson, N. S. (1998). Cognitive-behavioral treatment for depression: Relapse prevention. *Journal of Consulting and Clinical Psychology, 66*(2), 377–384.

Hopko, D. R., Armento, M. E., Hunt, M. K., Bell, J. L., & Lejuez, C. W. (2005). Behavior therapy for depressed cancer patients in primary care. *Psychotherapy: Theory, Research, Practice, Training,* *42*(2), 236–243.

Hopko, D. R., Lejuez, C. W., LePage, J. P., Hopko, S. D., & McNeil, D. W. (2003). A brief behavioral activation treatment for depression: A randomized pilot trial within an inpatient psychiatric hospital. *Behavior Modification, 27*(4), 458–469.

Jacobson, N. S., Dobson, K. S., Truax, P. A., Addis, M. E., Koerner, K., Gollan, J. K., et al. (1996). A component analysis of cognitive-behavioral treatment for depression. *Journal of Consulting and Clinical Psychology, 64*(2), 295–304.

Lewinsohn, P. M. (1974). A behavioral approach to depression. In R. M. Friedman & M. M. Katz (Eds.), *The psychology of depression: Contemporary theory and research* (pp. 157–185). New York: John Wiley & Sons.

Nezu, A. M. (1989). A problem solving formulation of depression: A literature review and proposal of a pluralistic model. *Clinical Psychology Review, 7,* 121–144.

Stathopoulou, G., Powers, M. B., Berry, A. C., Smits, J. A. J., & Otto, M. W. (2006). Exercise interventions for mental health: A quantitative and qualitative review. *Clinical Psychology: Science and Practice, 14,* 358–371.

Unutzer, J., Katon, W., Callahan, C. M., Williams, J. W., Jr., Hunkeler, E., Harpole, L., et al. (2002). Collaborative care management of late-life depression in the primary care setting: A randomized controlled trial. *Journal of the American Medical Association, 288*(22), 2836–2845.

SAMUEL HUBLEY
SONA DIMIDJIAN
University of Colorado, Boulder

See also: Cognitive Behavioral Analysis System of Psychotherapy; Cognitive Therapy

BEHAVIORAL ASSESSMENT

Behavioral assessment is an approach to the measurement and understanding of human behavior that is founded on several fundamental assumptions. These assumptions also differentiate behavioral assessment from other assessment approaches such as personality assessment and projective assessment. The first and most important assumption is functional contextualism (Hayes, 2004; Haynes & O'Brien, 2000; O'Brien & Schwetschenau, 2008). This assumption posits that target behaviors (cognitive, emotional, and overt-motor responses that are the focus of treatment) are not randomly emitted, but occur as a function of context variables that can be thought of as a collection of causal influences. Some of these causal influences arise from internal experiences (e.g., thoughts and feelings) while other causal influences arise from external sources such as interpersonal interactions and nonsocial environmental events (e.g., temperature).

Functional contextualism also supports the belief that the fundamental unit of analysis in behavioral assessment is the relationship between target behaviors and the contexts within which they occur (Fletcher & Hayes, 2005). As a result, in behavioral assessment the focus is on how and why target behaviors occur within specific and well-defined intraindividual, interpersonal, and environmental contexts.

Empiricism is a second characteristic associated with behavioral assessment. From this framework, a primary goal for the assessor is to develop detailed, objective, and measurable operational definitions of target behaviors and contextual causal factors. The empirical assumption also supports the use of using quantitative methods to evaluate the form and function of target behaviors. Finally, the empirical assumption supports the use of hypothetico-deductive methods in the assessment process (O'Brien, Kaplar, & McGrath, 2004).

Because the form and function of target behaviors are thought to arise from the unique interaction of behaviors, person, and context, behavioral assessment emphasizes an idiographic approach to measurement (Haynes & O'Brien, 2000). Congruent with this perspective, behavioral assessment also emphasizes the use of methodological and statistical procedures that can evaluate data collected from an individual client or case study.

A fourth characteristic of behavioral assessment is a reliance on learning theories as a basis for understanding how and why target behaviors are acquired, maintained, and changed. Thus, in behavioral assessment, the use of psychodynamic models or personality theories to explain target behavior-context interactions is deemphasized. Instead, the behavioral assessor will seek to understand how target behavior-context interactions can be understood using principles derived from classical conditioning, operant conditioning, social learning theory, or relational frame theory.

The fifth characteristic of behavioral assessment is behavioral plasticity. This assumption implies that any target behavior can be modified through the careful analysis of its function and the application of learning principles. Therefore, for every target behavior encountered, there may be a unique combination of causal variables that can be understood and modified for the purposes of enhancing client functioning.

Finally, behavioral assessment endorses a multivariate assumption proposing that target behaviors are comprised of many components. As such, each target behavior is related to a many other behaviors. It is further assumed that most behaviors are controlled by more than one casual factor.

Behavioral assessment thus rests on several critical assumptions about why target behaviors occur, the favored manner for evaluating data, the preferred level of analysis, the possibility for change, and an assumption of multideterminism. At a practical level, these assumptions are evident in the use of specifically focused assessment procedures that are designed to yield data from carefully defined and well-validated measures of multiple target behaviors and causal events for an individual client.

The primary goal of behavioral assessment is to improve clinical decision making by providing reliable and valid information about the form and function of target behaviors. This primary goal is realized through two subordinate goals of behavioral assessment: (1) to objectively measure behavior and (2) to identify and evaluate relationships among target behaviors and causal contextual factors. These two goals are respectively referred to as the topographical analysis (i.e., specifying the form of target behaviors) and the functional analysis (i.e., determining the function of target behaviors).

Topographical Analysis

Target behaviors can be operationalized and measured in an infinite number of ways. In behavioral assessment the modes and parameters of target behaviors are of primary interest. The term *mode* refers to three classes of target behaviors: cognitive responses (e.g., thoughts), affective/physiological responses (e.g., emotional experiences), and overt-motor responses (e.g., observable actions). The term *parameter* refers to the ways that a target behavior can be quantified. In most cases, intensity, frequency, and duration are the main parameters of interest. In order to render a topographical analysis of target behaviors, the behavioral assessor uses a number of data gathering strategies. The most commonly used data gathering strategies are behavioral interviewing, behavioral questionnaire administration, systematic observation, self-monitoring, and psychophysiological recording (O'Brien, Kaplar, & McGrath, 2004).

Functional Analysis

After a topographical analysis is generated, the focus of behavioral assessment turns to learning about the function of target behaviors. This involves identifying key causal contextual factors and evaluating the degree of impact these casual factors exert on the target behaviors. Behavioral assessment focuses on causal contextual variables that are operating in the present (as opposed to historical events). Additionally, these causal contextual factors are thought to fall into three main categories: social/interpersonal factors (e.g., interactions with others), nonsocial environmental factors (e.g., settings, time of day), and intrapersonal factors (e.g., cognitive processes and structures, physiological capacities).

After causal contextual factors have been identified, the assessor attempts to evaluate the strength of relationships that exist among target behaviors, among causal contextual factors, and among causal contextual factors and target behaviors. This is a complex decision process that involves collecting detailed information about how behavior changes in relation to the presence or absence of specific causal contextual variables. Several behavioral assessment methods are used to evaluate the relationships between target behaviors and causal contextual variables. The initial method is behavioral interviewing. Here, the assessor asks questions about how the frequency, intensity, and duration of target behaviors change in response to interpersonal events, intrapersonal events, and environmental events. Behavioral interviewing has the advantage of being relatively convenient and inexpensive in terms of time investment. However, the reliability and validity of behavioral interviewing is uncertain (Haynes & O'Brien, 2000). Consequently, target behavior-causal contextual variable relationships identified in interviewing need to be evaluated using more rigorous empirical procedures. These follow-up procedures most commonly include naturalistic observation (where the client is observed in different naturally occurring contexts), self-monitoring (where the client self-observes and self-records the target behaviors and causal contextual variable occurrences), and laboratory observation (where the assessor manipulates the occurrence of a causal contextual variable and records how it affects target behavior occurrence).

Once the topographical and functional analysis is completed, the assessor generates a case conceptualization that summarizes the assessment information. Behavioral assessment case conceptualizations can be presented as causal models (Haynes & O'Brien, 2000), tables and flow charts (e.g., Persons, 2007), graphs (Hanley, Iwata, & McCord, 2003), or narratives that describe the relationships among target behaviors and causal contextual variables.

Future Directions

Behavioral assessment is a well-developed approach to evaluating human behavior, and the procedures used to conduct the topographical analysis have shown good reliability and validity. However, the reliability and validity of the functional analysis and behavioral case conceptualizations have not been rigorously evaluated. Further, the decisions that are imbedded in the functional analysis and case conceptualization have not been extensively studied. Finally, although the treatment utility of the functional analysis for developmentally disabled populations has been supported (Hanley, Iwata, & McCord, 2003), there exist no systematic evaluations of the treatment utility of the functional analysis in other settings and populations. Research that is designed to explore these gaps in the literature is needed so that we can better understand and enhance behavioral assessment processes and outcomes.

REFERENCES

Fletcher, L., & Hayes, S. C. (2005). Relational frame theory, acceptance and commitment therapy, and a functional analytic definition of mindfulness. *Journal of Rational-Emotive & Cognitive Behavior Therapy, 23,* 315–336.

Hanley, G., Iwata, B. A., & McCord, B. E. (2003). Functional analysis of problem behavior: A review. *Journal of Applied Behavior Analysis, 36,* 147–185.

Hayes, S. C. (2004). Acceptance and commitment therapy, relational frame theory, and the third wave of behavioral and cognitive therapies. *Behavior Therapy, 35,* 639–665.

Haynes, S. N., & O'Brien, W. H. (2000). *Principles and practice of behavioral assessment.* New York: Plenum.

O'Brien, W. H., Kaplar, M., & McGrath, J. J. (2004). Broadly-based causal models of behavior disorders. In M. Hersen, S. N. Haynes, & E. M. Heiby (Eds.), *The handbook of psychological assessment, Volume 3: Behavioral assessment* (pp. 69–93). Hoboken, NJ: John Wiley & Sons.

O'Brien, W. H., & Schwetschenau, H. (2008). Overview of Behavioral Treatments with Adults. In M. Hersen & J. Rosqvist (Eds.) *Handbook of psychological assessment, case conceptualization, and treatment, Volume 1: Adults* (pp. 76–94). Hoboken, NJ: John Wiley & Sons.

Persons, J. B. (2007). Case formulation driven psychotherapy. *Clinical Psychology: Science and Practice, 13,* 162–170.

William H. O'Brien
Carmen Oemig
Bowling Green State University

See also: **Computerized Behavioral Assessment; Functional Analysis; Psychological Assessment**

BEHAVIORAL INHIBITION

The term *behavioral inhibition* was introduced into learning theory by the 1904 Nobel Laureate in Physiology and Medicine, Ivan Pavlov (1927). Pavlov turned his attention to studies of salivary conditioning after completing his prize-winning research examining neural regulation of the circulatory organs. He found that an initially neutral conditioned stimulus (CS), such as the sound of a metronome, could acquire significance if it reliably signaled the delivery (excitatory conditioning) or omission (inhibitory conditioning) of a biologically relevant unconditioned stimulus (US), such as meat powder. Excitatory conditioning allowed a hungry dog to prepare for the US in advance of its arrival, supporting the development of a conditioned response (CR). Inhibitory conditioning permitted a learned CR to be suppressed on trials in which the otherwise expected US was omitted in the presence of another CS, such as a light.

In *Conditioned Reflex* (1927), Pavlov described four experimental procedures that he believed would produce behavioral inhibition: (1) withholding the US on trials in which an inhibitory CS occurs along with an excitatory CS (the latter being reinforced on its own); (2) omitting the US after previous CS-US pairings, which leads to experimental extinction; (3) randomly alternating unreinforced trials involving an inhibitory CS with reinforced trials involving an excitatory CS, called differential conditioning; and (4) nonreinforcing the early portion of a relatively long duration CS that signals a long delay until the arrival of the US.

Although the study of inhibitory conditioning is now viewed as important, Pavlov's work on the topic was initially poorly received. The problem was that inhibitory conditioning was hard to discern from other behavioral effects. For example, a putatively inhibitory stimulus might distract the animal or evoke a competing response, neither of which involves learning about the absence of the US. Of particular concern was B.F. Skinner's suggestion that reductions in responding could be a matter of less excitation rather than of more inhibition. If A is reinforced, and AB is not, the compound as a whole might simply have little excitatory strength.

Three events contributed to a revival in the study of inhibitory conditioning in the 1950s and 1960s. First, behavioral inhibition turned out to be a powerful and necessary concept for understanding a wide range of phenomena, including the persistence of phobic avoidance in the absence of further trauma. It is much easier to explain how avoidance behavior is maintained by invoking behavioral inhibition. The response inhibits the learned expectation that the aversive event will occur, so its subsequent omission is not surprising and does not cause fear to extinguish. On the other hand, it is exceedingly difficult to explain why the absence of a physical event should serve as a reinforcer in absence of behavioral inhibition. Second, the informational view of conditioning process was gaining popularity during this period. Calling for the learning of both negative and positive correlative relationships (Rescorla, 1969), it gave equal status to both types of learned connections and encouraged further experimentation on the topic. Third, and perhaps most importantly, a new consensus was forming about the kinds of behavioral tests necessary for certifying the inhibitory status of a CS (Williams, Overmier, & LoLordo, 1992). The concept of behavioral inhibition is now routinely used to explain simple forms of learning, such as Pavlovian and instrumental conditioning as well as other more complex forms of cognition.

Considerable interest has been directed at identifying the neural underpinnings of behavioral inhibition. One exciting finding is the discovery of dopamine neurons in the monkey brain that encode the surprising omission of an expected reward (Tobler, Dickinson, & Schultz, 2003). These neurons fire at the moment when an expected reward is first omitted and eventually stop firing after the omission of the reward is no longer novel. The critical point to appreciate is that neural activity is observed when a previously learned expectation of reward is disconfirmed, not because a physical reward has been presented or omitted. The same neuron also fires when the monkey receives a reward for the first time after making the desired response and then disappears with further training.

The last of the preceding observations confirms what behavioral research has suggested since the 1970s. Learning occurs when a subject's expectations are not matched by subsequent experience (Rescorla & Wagner, 1972). For example, if two distinctive CSs are paired on separate trials with the US, and these two CSs in combination with a third CS are reinforced as a triplet, the third CS will acquire inhibitory properties (Kremer, 1978). Why does the third CS become inhibitory even though the US occurred in its presence? The procedure itself suggests an answer. Unusually high levels of excitation are evoked—much higher than can be sustained by a single US—when two excitatory CSs are combined. Hence, the third CS acquires inhibitory properties because the US is overexpected in the presence of the two excitatory CSs.

One particularly interesting area of application for research concerning behavioral inhibition is experimental extinction. When a CS is extinguished it does not lose its excitatory power. Contrary to the dictionary meaning of the word "extinction," a new inhibitory CS-US association joins the previously acquired excitatory association, causing a temporary reduction in the probability of the CR (Bouton, 2002). It is abundantly clear that extinction has not erased previous learning; a rest period after extinction causes *spontaneous recovery* of the CR, which shows original CR had not been eliminated and was only temporarily suppressed. Additionally, if extinction takes place in a different physical context than acquisition, a return to the context of acquisition causes renewal *l* of the CR. Renewal is of obvious importance for our understanding of relapse. A recovered addict may experience severe withdrawal symptoms many years later when reexposed to cues associated with drug administration. These cues, CSs, may have been successfully extinguished in a treatment program, but the passage of time (spontaneous recovery) or a return to the context in which the addiction originated (renewal) might reawaken the old habit. This last example demonstrates that behavioral inhibition is a rich area for both application and theory (Redish, Jensen, Johnson, & Kurth-Nelson, 2007).

REFERENCES

Bouton, M. E. (2002). Context, ambiguity, and unlearning: Sources of relapse after behavioral extinction. *Biological Psychiatry, 52*, 976–986.

Kremer, E. J. (1978). The Rescorla-Wagner model: Losses in associative strength in compound conditioned stimuli. *Journal of Experimental Psychology: Animal Behavior Processes, 4*, 22–36.

Pavlov, I. P. (1927). *Conditioned reflexes.* Oxford, UK: Oxford University Press.

Redish, A. D., Jensen, S., Johnson, A., & Kurth-Nelson, Z. (2007). Reconciling reinforcement learning models with behavioral extinction and renewal: Implications for addiction, relapse, and problem gambling. *Psychological Review, 114*, 784–805.

Rescorla, R. A. (1969). Conditioned inhibition of fear resulting from negative CS-US contingencies. *Journal of Comparative & Physiological Psychology, 67*, 504–509.

Rescorla, R. A., & Wagner, A. R. (1972). A theory of Pavlovian conditioning: Variations in the effectiveness of reinforcement and nonreinforcement. In A. H. Black & W. F. Prokasy (Eds.), *Classical conditioning II* (pp. 64–99). New York: Appleton-Century-Crofts.

Tobler, P. N., Dickinson, A., & Schultz, W. (2003). Coding of predicted omission by dopamine neurons in a conditioned inhibition paradigm. *The Journal of Neuroscience, 23*, 10402–10410.

Williams, D. A., Overmier, J. B., & LoLordo, V. M. (1992). A reevaluation of Rescorla's early dictums about Pavlovian conditioned inhibition. *Psychological Bulletin, 111*, 275–290.

SUGGESTED READING

Denniston, J. C., & Miller, R. R. (2007). Timing of omitted events: An analysis of temporal control of inhibitory behavior. *Behavioural Processes, 22*, 274–285.

DOUGLAS A. WILLIAMS
University of Winnipeg

See also: **Pavlovian Conditioning**

BEHAVIORAL MODELING

Much human learning takes place sitting and watching or just happening to notice what someone else is doing. Indeed, more *social learning* occurs from observing others than from engaging in actual social interactions and the subsequent positive or negative outcomes. Observation provides information about what may be learned (alternative behaviors, potential consequences, etc.). Whereas such information may be ignored or misunderstood, observation under the right circumstances can result in rapid changes in learning and performance.

Modeling is defined as the process in which an individual (the model) serves to illustrate behavior that can be imitated or adapted in the behavior of another individual (the observer). The observed model may also influence thoughts and attitudes. The model may be live, filmed, described in any other medium (e.g., print) or even imagined. The term "behavioral modeling" is distinguished from mathematical modeling and so on. Otherwise the simpler term "modeling" is used. A person's appearance may imply certain behaviors, as a fashion model or simply seeing a person appealingly dressed implies purchasing and wearing similar clothing. However, it is procedurally important that modeling has focused on directly observed behavior (see Bandura, 1997).

When people observe themselves, there is potential for "self modeling" (Dowrick, 1999). Most of the research on this process has been in the video medium. One interpretation is that the basis of all modeling is self-modeling, as we need to see ourselves in the observed model to be likely to copy the behavior. Alternatively, we extract components of observed behavior and apply them to our own self-image in the context of the observed situation (Dowrick, 2006).

Applications

Modeling has been widely applied and evaluated in a variety of areas. Representative examples are described below under headings in seven broad categories.

Social skills and daily living. Modeling by in-vivo demonstration is widely used as part of social skills training. Video modeling is the staple of many standard programs; it has been the primary component in training programs as diverse as teaching young, isolated children to overcome their shyness, as well as providing alternatives to social behavior related to drug abuse, aggression, and other illicit or unhealthy activity. Videos in training packages geared toward resisting peer pressure, for example, continue to be popular, although they are seldom well researched. The superiority of positive behavioral modeling over observing outcomes of what *not* to do is illustrated by the effectiveness of videos that illustrate adaptive coping (e.g., resisting coercion without destroying friendships), versus the lack of effectiveness in showing negative consequences (e.g., early, gruesome death by cancer).

Parent and child issues. Different forms of modeling have been widely used in programs for parent training. Observing effective models is the best way to identify effective child-care skills, where real-life or *in vivo* practice and coaching are then usually necessary. Most parent training is requested because of the "child's problem." Therefore, children are taught communication and self-control skills as well. Modeling also proves effective for this purpose, using either peers or adults as models (Webster-Stratton, 2005).

Medical care and self-care. The need to prepare patients, especially children, for potentially invasive or scary treatment procedures has been extensively served by modeling strategies. Information (e.g., what steps are involved in the procedure) is important to emotional and long-term attitudes, but modeling is more essential to the immediate situation. An interesting new development is the use of videogames to teach adolescents and young adults with chronic illnesses, such as cancer, how to manage their health. Players are noted to view the avatar as "I"

and "me," indicating potential for a strong modeling effect (Beale, Kato, Marin-Bowling, Guthrie, & Cole, 2007).

Physical performance. Sport and other body coordination skills are widely taught using some form of demonstration by peers, coaches, and experts. Physical therapists also use modeling as the major component in rehabilitation through therapeutic exercises. The commercial video market is replete with mildly effective examples, in which experts serve as models for the development of individual skills (golf, tennis, aerobics, skiing, etc.). Participants in team sports watch videotapes of opponents, not just to find weaknesses, but to seek out and replicate superior playing strategies (McCullagh & Weiss, 2002). Special effects (e.g., slow motion, still frames) in video modeling are useful in motor performance applications.

Professional training. Modeling is often used in training human service personnel. For example, videotaped modeling has been used as a key component in training healthcare personnel to handle psychiatric emergencies and in the training of job coaches for individuals with disabilities. Other popular training areas range from counselors to military special services, where it accounts for larger gains in skill acquisition than role playing or feedback.

Diverse populations. Appropriately designed modeling has obvious application to individuals with disabilities and other diversity, who may lack suitable models in their natural environment. Well-documented examples exist in the teaching of daily living skills, such as shopping by young adults with autism. Other types of skills for which modeling-based training has been developed include social skills, recreation, communication (including sign language), vocational skills, and academics. Generally, live models have been found to be more effective than filmed models, but the reverse is found for some groups (e.g., children with autism; Charlop-Christy, Le, & Freeman, 2000). It would seem best to use peers as models, but in practice the models are often expert adults from the dominant culture. Such modeling must be carefully constructed to match the individuality of the intended trainees.

Community-level modeling. Television soap operas have been produced in several countries to address social issues affecting many people. For example, significant impact has been made on women's rights in China and Mexico and HIV in Tanzania (Bandura, 2004). Stories show people making decisions (birth control, fidelity, etc.) that empower viewers in their personal development.

General Principles

A modeling procedure focuses on the skill to be learned, its context, and sometimes its outcomes or consequences. The modeled event is effective if the observer (1) absorbs the skill and information and later (2) has the opportunity, motive, and self-belief to use it (cf. Bandura, 1997). Considerable research in the last 40 or so years has contributed to an understanding of these components.

Much research has focused on how the characteristics of the model contribute to the effectiveness of the procedure. The use of similar models, multiple models, and coping (versus "mastery") performances have been shown to assist effectiveness. These factors contribute to the ability of the viewer to absorb the skill information. They help to ensure that at least some of the skills demonstrated are attainable at an appropriate level of use by the observer. More important, some model characteristics enable the observer to construct an improved self-model image, in a manner of yes-I-can-do-that, that-could-be-me. Thus, model characteristics should be considered relative to characteristics of the observer, not in isolation.

When the model is similar, the observer will pay more attention and is more likely to be motivated to replicate the demonstrated behavior. Because the *activity* is important, behavioral similarity counts more than looks, social background, etc., and unusual models, such as clowns, can gain attention but backfire in the goal of that-could-be-me. The use of multiple models can work when different aspects of different models contribute value to the observer.

Coping (better called "struggling") models are usually more effective than mastery models who demonstrate only expert performance. High-status models can also be effective. These potentially contrary results are understood by considering how different aspects of the modeled activity are differentially relevant to the observer and how modeling may invite competition as well as imitation.

Sometimes observational learning must first be taught as a skill in itself; for example, young children with autism may not have learned to imitate others. Emphasizing a positive outcome or reward for the target behavior can enhance the effectiveness of a model. It's important, however, to note the frequent failure of "negative modeling" to act as a deterrent. The reverse is often the case, sometimes tragically. Multiple times, news reports or televised dramatizations of teenage suicides, intended as deterrents, have been followed by increases in suicides of young people.

Modeling is well documented as a powerful intervention in its own right, but it is mostly used along with other procedures, such as discussions and the opportunity to practice. It will normally take its place early in the learning sequence: basic information, modeling, practice, feedback, and feedforward. It can also be used as a sophisticated component in advanced learning applications.

REFERENCES

Bandura, A. (1997). *Self-efficacy: The exercise of control.* New York: Freeman.

Bandura, A. (2004). Health promotion by social cognitive means. *Health Education & Behavior, 31,* 143–164.

Beale, I. L., Kato, P. M., Marin-Bowling, V. M., Guthrie, N., & Cole, S. W. (2007). Improvement in cancer-related knowledge following use of a psychoeducational video game for adolescents and young adults with cancer. *Journal of Adolescent Health, 41,* 263–270.

Charlop-Christy, M. H., Le, L., & Freeman, K. (2000). A comparison of video modeling with in vivo modeling for teaching children with autism. *Journal of Autism & Developmental Disorders, 30,* 537–552.

Dowrick, P. W. (1999). A review of self modeling and related interventions. *Applied and Preventive Psychology, 8,* 23–39.

McCullagh, P., & Weiss, M. R. (2002). Observational learning: The forgotten psychological method in sport psychology. In J. L. Van Raalte & B. W. Brewer (Eds.). *Exploring sport and exercise psychology* (2nd ed.). (pp. 131–149). Washington, DC: American Psychological Association.

Webster-Stratton, C. (2005). The Incredible Years: A training series for the prevention and treatment of conduct problems in young children. In E. D. Hibbs & P. S. Jensen (Eds.), *Psychosocial treatments for child and adolescent disorders: Empirically based strategies for clinical practice* (2nd ed.). (pp. 507–555). Washington, DC: American Psychological Association.

SUGGESTED READING

Nikopoulos, C., & Keenan, M. (2006). *Video modelling and behaviour analysis.* London: Jessica Kingsley [Chapter 3].

PETER W. DOWRICK
University of Hawaii at Manoa

See also: Self-Efficacy; Video Applications

BEHAVIORAL OBSERVATION

This article provides a brief introduction to the methodology, applications, and analysis associated with behavioral observation and is accordingly divided into three sections.

Methodology

Behavioral observation and coding constitute categorical measurement. Hence, the nature and operational definition of the categories used is core and critical to what is being measured. Investigators must initially determine if they are interested in measuring specific behaviors or behavioral constructs. Specific behaviors might include the extent to which persons in a rehabilitation program use an arm that has been compromised by stroke. Behavioral measurement might be more appropriate for tracking such specific behaviors like limb movements in rehabilitation contexts, waist movements in hyperactive children, obese, and depressed adults, and sleep-related behaviors (cf. Tryon, 2006).

Behavioral coding requires a human observer to identify and record the behavioral code that best matches what the observer sees. Investigators commonly assess behavioral constructs that are composed of various behaviors that cohere in some important way. For example, there are various ways to praise someone and the behavioral construct "praise" consists of all of them. Considerable inference can be involved in behavioral observation. For example, people cannot directly observe attention, impulsivity, anxiety, depression, or other psychological states or traits but they can record whether the behaviors they observe qualify as instances of these behavioral constructs.

Heyman (2001) discussed 25 coding systems for couples and provided a primer on observational research with couples and then reviewed nearly 200 studies that used an observational coding system to study the behavior of couples. He discussed the psychometric properties of couples-observation constructs. The author reported that interobserver reliability appears to be adequate when all codes are considered as a group but that test-retest reliability has generally not been assessed. Validity is a construct that is conditional upon the purposes and objectives of the test and/or methods in question and therefore not easily answered. Predictive validity is possible for investigators interested in studying the relationship between behavioral observations and a relevant distal variable. Ideally the predictive model is developed on one sample, or a portion of one sample, and cross-validated on another sample, or the remainder of the one sample in order to control for sample specific overfitting. Observers tend to drift and therefore must be periodically retrained. The logistics and expense of obtaining behavioral observation is a limitation and impediment to their common clinical usage. Kerig and Baucom (2004) described 15 coding systems.

Applications

Clinic (Analogue) Assessment

The objective of analogue behavioral assessment is to obtain a standardized behavioral sample, much like psychological tests do, for the purpose of making inferences about the person's future behavior in their natural environment. Examples of analogue studies include the functional analysis of behavior, role playing, family and marital interaction tasks, and behavioral avoidance tests. Behavioral approach tests of children's fear of dogs, snakes, and water have been used. Three types of analogue assessments have been used to assess parent-child interactions: (1) free play, (2) parent-directed play, and (3) parent-directed chores. Surprisingly, positive parenting codes do not seem to consistently separate experimental from control groups. The free play analogue should be used to enhance positive parent-child interaction rather

than to identify and/or remediate problematic parent-child interactions. The parent-directed chore analogue appears to more accurately elicit oppositional child behaviors that occur at home than does the parent-directed play analogue and is recommended for clinical assessment.

Home Assessment

For more than 40 years Gerald Patterson, John Reid, and their colleagues at the Oregon Social Learning Center (http://www.oslc.org) have developed coding systems for family observation. Downloadable pdf documents describing the details of these behavioral observation systems are available at http://www.oslc.org/resources/codingsystems.html. They have developed microanalytic systems and dimensional rating systems for recording behavioral observations made at home. The Family Interaction Coding System is one example. It is composed of 29 code categories that include both child behaviors and parent reactions to those behaviors.

Additional time and expense is involved in sending observers to the home but is compensated for by observing what people actually do at home versus attempting with uncertainty to create situations that set the occasion for behaviors that occur at home. I am unaware of any studies that have observed people in analogue situations and at home and have empirically demonstrated that behaviors observed during analogue situations are the same as behaviors observed in the home.

School Assessment

Several systems of behavioral observation have been developed for schools. The BASC-2 Student Observation System (BASC-2, SOS; Reynolds & Kamphaus, 2004) defines 65 specific behaviors and groups them into 13 categories; four for positive behaviors and nine for problem behaviors. It requires only a 15-minute behavioral sample. The Achenbach System of Empirically Based Assessment (ASEBA: Achenbach & Rescorla, 2001) has a Direct Observation Form and is a revised version of the CBCL-DOF. It was designed to be used on three to six separate 10-minute behavioral samples to increase representativeness. This method consists of three parts. The first part is a written narrative of the child's behavior. The second part consists of observing for five seconds at the end of each minute and coding if the child is on- or off-task. The third part consists of rating the child on 96 behaviors using a four-point scale.

Data Analysis

Bakeman (2000) provided a good overview of data analysis for behavioral observations. Frequencies, rates, and bouts are common ways of summarizing behavioral data. Observer reliability concerns the extent to which different observers categorize the same behaviors in the same way; in other words, enter the same code for the same behavior. He discussed several ways to assess reliability. Some methods use point-by-point methods that ignore time while others require that observers agree at each time point. The percent agreement approach has been effectively replaced by the Cohen's Kappa, which corrects for chance agreement. Generalizability theory can be used to move from observer agreement to formal reliability analysis.

Observer validity reduces to reliability in the sense that the central issue is whether the indicated behavior was actually present when it was coded. The fact that at least two observers agree on the presence of the act at the designated time is evidence of existence and therefore evidence of validity. Whether observed rates of said behavior(s) are systematically related to the clinical condition of the person being observed or are useful in any way goes to clinical utility, which differs from validity. Multitrait-multimethod criteria can be used to demonstrate convergent validity of two or more observational methods.

Bakeman (2000) also discussed conditional measures of association such as conditional and transitional probabilities. Strength of association measures, odds ratios, Yules Q, and the phi coefficient can be calculated from a 2 x 2 table. Multiway frequency tables can be constructed to analyze far more complex relationships.

REFERENCES

Achenbach, T. M., & Rescorla, L. A. (2001). *Manual for the ASEBA School-age forms & profiles: An integrated system of multi-informant assessment*. Burlington: University of Vermont.

Bakeman, R. (2000). Behavioral observation and coding. In H. T. Reis, & C. M. Judd (Eds.), *Handbook of research methods in social and personality psychology* (pp. 138–159). Cambridge, UK: Cambridge University Press.

Heyman, R. E. (2001). Observation of couple conflicts: Clinical assessment applications, stubborn truths, and shaky foundations. *Psychological Assessment, 13*, 5–35.

Kerig, P. K., & Baucom, D. H. (Eds.). (2004). *Couple observational coding systems*. Mahwah, NJ: Erlbaum.

Reynolds, C. R., & Kamphaus, R. (2004). *BASC-2: Behavior assessment system for children* (2nd ed.). Circle Pines, MN: American Guidance Services.

Tryon, W. W. (2006). Activity Measurement. In M. Hersen (Ed.) *Clinician's handbook of adult behavioral assessment* (pp. 85–120). Boston: Elsevier.

SUGGESTED READINGS

Bakeman, R., & Gottman, J. M. (1997). *Observing interaction: An introduction to sequential analysis*. (2nd ed.). New York: Cambridge University Press.

Patterson, J. R. (1982). *Coercive family process*. Eugene, OR: Castalia.

Roberts, M. W. (2001). Clinic observations of structured parent-child interaction designed to evaluate externalizing disorders. *Psychological Assessment, 13*, 46–58.

WARREN W. TRYON
Fordham University

See also: **Participant Observation; Qualitative Research Methods**

BEHAVIORAL PEDIATRICS

Behavioral pediatrics is a multidisciplinary field whose focus is on psychosocial aspects of child and adolescent health. Because the topic is so broad, the field includes knowledge and skills from clinical and developmental psychology, education, environmental design, law, nursing, nutrition, pediatrics, physical education, psychiatry, and social work. Practically, however, most professionals with special expertise in behavioral pediatrics are pediatricians. For example, 79% of the members of the Society for Developmental and Behavioral Pediatrics are MDs (most of whom are pediatricians); the non-MD members are largely PhD psychologists but also include attorneys, educators, nurses, nutritionists, psychiatrists, and social workers (N. Ritchey, personal communication, April 11, 2008). Non-MDs also contribute disproportionately to the scientific basis for behavioral pediatric practice, as seen in a new textbook (Wolraich et al., 2008) in which 51% of the authors are not physicians (78% of these are psychologists).

Children's health care has always included psychosocial issues, but interest in psychosocial problems increased in the 1970s due to major changes in disease patterns that had occurred in the pediatric population. Successful treatment of infectious diseases and widespread immunization against previously severe illnesses greatly reduced the morbidity and mortality of traditional medical problems. At the same time, the increase in the prevalence of psychosocial (or behavioral) problems, and their impact on child and family function, led to their identification as "the new morbidity" (Haggerty, 1975). For example, of the 10 leading causes of death among American adolescents and youth (12 to 24 years), four are behavioral in origin: unintentional injury/accidents, homicide, HIV, and suicide (accidents, homicide, and suicide cause more than 80% of deaths in this age group) (Neinstein, 1996).

As the importance of behavioral aspects of health care gained increased recognition, the impetus to develop this field came from several concurrent activities (see Haggerty & Friedman, 2003). The American Academy of Pediatrics tasked a prestigious group to survey the current status of pediatric training, identify key gaps in training, and set priorities for the future. The Task Force Report, published in 1978, identified more training in child development and behavior as one of its highest priorities. Also, in 1979, the W.T. Grant Foundation funded 11 pediatric programs for five years to develop specific training in behavior for their pediatric residents, as well as funding a formal evaluation that compared these 11 programs with 13 others that did not have this specific training. These grants supported an annual two-day meeting of program directors and key faculty from the 11 core programs plus the evaluation group, which promoted the identification and development of a multidisciplinary faculty at each site, which then coalesced into a large group and provided leadership for the emerging field. This led to the formation of the Society for Behavioral Pediatrics in 1982, which later became the Society for Developmental and Behavioral Pediatrics and in 1985 adopted an official journal (the *Journal of Developmental and Behavioral Pediatrics*).

Research and clinical practice in behavioral pediatrics address a wide variety of topics and include primary and secondary prevention efforts as well as targeted intervention. At one end of the "biopsychosocial" continuum are psychosocial issues occasioned by physical illness or trauma (e.g., management of terminal illness, effects of burns or amputation); at the other end are the physical results of risky or maladaptive behavior (e.g., sexually transmitted diseases, teen pregnancy, drug overdose). In between are a host of mixed disorders that require attention to both behavioral and physical issues (e.g., management of diabetes in adolescents who decide that they want to eat and behave exactly like their "normal" peers and no longer do those special things required of diabetics).

For most of pediatric practice, the focus is on (1) "normal" developmental issues of concern to parents, anticipatory guidance, and counseling as children change developmental stages, (2) screening and recognition of significant behavioral and developmental problems, and (3) effective referral for further treatment when indicated. In addition, pediatric contact with mothers during well-child visits provides an opportunity to screen for parent and family problems such as maternal depression; given the negative impact on child well-being, detection and intervention should improve outcomes.

Good health is more than the absence of disease, and promoting healthy development is clearly a crucial focus of pediatric care for all children. In addition, however, it is important that any pediatrician be able to manage the psychosocial aspects of physical disease or chronic conditions (e.g., asthma) as well as less severe psychosocial problems such as learning disabilities or minor family conflict because there are simply not enough mental health professionals available to treat all learning, developmental, emotional, and behavioral problems evidenced by an estimated 25%–30% of American children and teenagers

(see Wolraich et al., 2008). For example, each child psychiatrist in the United States would have a caseload of 750 patients if she treated *only* the *most severe* mental health problems of children and teenagers (an estimated 5% of the population, see Kim, 2003).

Providing appropriate treatment for developmental and behavioral problems thus requires that as many of these as possible be managed by primary care providers (typically pediatricians or family medicine practitioners), who also are aware of and skilled at accessing specialized resources such as child psychiatrists, clinical child psychologists, developmental-behavioral pediatricians (Developmental-Behavioral Pediatrics was approved as a formal subspecialty by the American Board of Medical Specialties in 1999; see Haggerty & Friedman, 2003), neuro-developmental pediatricians (a different formal specialty of pediatrics), psychiatric nurses, or psychiatric social workers. The goal of including training in psychosocial issues as part of residency program in pediatrics is therefore to produce general pediatricians with the knowledge and skills to provide these services. Advanced training at the fellowship level provides both clinical specialists and the springboard for leadership, teaching, and research. Collaboration with professionals from other disciplines stimulates the development and dissemination of a rich knowledge base in the field of behavioral pediatrics.

REFERENCES

Haggerty, R. J., Roghman, K. J., & Pless, I. B. (1975). *Child health and the community*. (pp. 94–95). New York: John Wiley & Sons.

Haggerty, R. J., & Friedman, S. B. (2003). History of developmental-behavioral pediatrics. *Journal of Developmental & Behavioral Pediatrics*, 24, S1–S18.

Kim, W. J. (2003). Child and adolescent psychiatry workforce: A critical shortage and national challenge. *Academy Psychiatry*, 27, 277–282.

Neinstein, L. S. (1996). Vital statistics and injuries. In L. S. Neinstein (Ed.), *Adolescent health care: A practical guide* (3rd ed., pp. 110–138). Baltimore: Williams & Wilkins.

Ritchey, N. (April 11, 2008). Executive Assistant, Society for Developmental and Behavioral Pediatrics, Personal communication.

Wolraich, M. L., Drotar, D. D., Dworkin, P. H., & Perrin, E. C. (Eds.). (2008). *Developmental–behavioral pediatrics: Evidence and practice*. Philadelphia: Mosby.

SUGGESTED READINGS

Levine, M. D., Carey, W. B., & Crocker, A. C. (Eds.). 2008. *Developmental-behavioral pediatrics* (3rd ed.). Philadelphia: W.B. Sanders.

Olson, A. L., Dietrich, A. J., Prazar, G., & Hurley, J. (2006). Brief material depression screening at well-child visits. *Pediatrics*, 118, 207–216.

Phillips, S. (2003). Adolescent health. In A. M. Nezu, C. M. Nezu, & P. A. Geller (Eds.), Health psychology. Vol. 9. In I. B. Weiner (Ed.), *Handbook of psychology* (pp. 465–485). Hoboken: John Wiley & Sons.

SHERIDAN PHILLIPS
University of Maryland School of Medicine

See also: Pediatric Psychology

BEHAVIORISM (See Radical Behaviorism)

BEM SEX ROLE INVENTORY

In the early 1970s psychologists questioned the assumption that masculinity (i.e., agency) and femininity (i.e., communion) were opposite ends of a one-dimensional continuum. Rather, masculinity and femininity were conceptualized as independent dimensions; an individual could have a score on each. The Bem Sex Role Inventory (BSRI) is based on the theory that individuals differ in the extent to which masculinity and femininity are the basis for a cognitive schema that affects the processing of information and behavior.

The inventory, as originally developed by Sandra Bem (1974), includes 60 items: 20 masculine (e.g., Acts as a leader), 20 feminine (e.g., Affectionate), and 20 neutral (e.g., Adaptable) personality characteristics. Respondents indicate on a 7 point Likert type scale (1 = never or almost never true; 7 = always or almost always true) the extent to which each item is self-descriptive. The scale yields scores on two constructs, presumed to be independent and labeled masculinity and femininity, which index the extent to which sex-typed adjectives are reported as self-descriptive. A short form of the inventory has also been developed. Although different scoring methods have been used, these two scores are used to categorize one's sex role orientation.

A person may be classified as feminine (high on the femininity scale and low on the masculinity scale), as masculine (high on the masculinity scale and low on the femininity scale), as androgynous (high on both the masculinity and femininity scales), or as undifferentiated (low on both the masculinity and femininity scales). Theoretically, psychological androgyny represented the integration of both masculine and feminine characteristics in one's gender schema. Bem hypothesized that psychologically androgynous individuals should display greater behavioral flexibility across situations, because their responses would not be constrained by rigid gender schemas that guide behavior.

The introduction of the inventory prompted both theoretical and empirical debate. Conceptually, are the constructs being measured by the inventory masculinity and femininity, as proposed by Bem, or do the items quantify instrumentality and expressiveness, respectively, as proposed by Spence and Helmreich (1981)? A number of studies have focused on the factor structure of the BSRI. Pedhazur and Tatenbaum (1979) concluded that the masculine items form a single factor, whereas the feminine items and the neutral items are indistinguishable in that they form two subfactors ("emotional sensitivity" and "emotional immaturity"). Consequently, there has been concern with the validity of the basic constructs that has implications for the validity of the scores computed from these scales. An additional concern is the relevance of the masculine and feminine items of the scale, which were based on gender stereotypes of the time. In 2009, the masculinity and femininity items of the BSRI may be interpreted differently than they were in 1974, as there have been major changes in the roles of men and women in society during the intervening 35 years. The debate and research spurred by Bem's 1974 paper (cited 856 times as of August 20, 2008) has led to important theoretical and empirical advances in the understanding of gender and behavior.

REFERENCES

Bem, S. L. (1974). The measurement of psychological androgyny. *Journal of Consulting and Clinical Psychology, 42,* 155–162.

Pedhazur, E. J., & Tatenbaum, T. J. (1979). Bem Sex Role Inventory: A theoretical and methodological critique. *Journal of Personality and Social Psychology, 37,* 996–1016.

Spence, J. T., & Helmreich, R. L. (1981). Androgyny versus gender schema: A comment on Bem's gender schema theory. *Psychological Review, 88,* 365–368.

THOMAS E. MALLOY
Rhode Island College

See also: Gender Differences; Gender Roles

BENDER VISUAL-MOTOR GESTALT TEST

In 1938, Lauretta Bender published her groundbreaking monograph, *A Visual Motor Gestalt Test and Its Clinical Use.* Over time, the Visual-Motor Gestalt Test, more commonly referred to as the Bender-Gestalt Test, became a "mainstay in the assessment battery ... as an assessment tool in appraisal of intelligence ... as a screening technique for neuropsychological dysfunction, as a clinical tool for sampling visual-motor proficiency, and as a standard projective technique in the assessment of personality" (Piotrowski, 1995, p. 1272).

The Bender-Gestalt Test evolved from Max Wertheimer's (1923) early studies of the Gestalt theory of perception. He examined the principles of perceptual organization (e.g., similarity, proximity, good continuation) using a variety of geometric designs. He presented these designs to subjects and asked them to describe them. Bender, who was interested in the gestalt experiences of psychiatric patients, adapted nine of Wertheimer's designs, put them on cards, and asked subjects to draw them.

Bender also devised an elaborate scoring system that judged the overall quality of the reproduction of each design. Her monograph provided clinicians with normative data (from a small regional sample) on the maturation of the visual-motor-gestalt function in children from 4 to 11 years of age, as well as detailed descriptions of the performance of individuals with various pathological conditions (e.g., organic brain disorders, schizophrenias, psychoneuroses).

Bender's scoring system did not generate much research, but it did stimulate others to develop creative ways to administer and score the test to assess visual-motor functioning, psychopathology, and organic brain dysfunction in children and adults. Over its 70-year history, numerous variations in administration (e.g., a background interference procedure in which designs are drawn on paper containing random lines) and scoring (i.e., both holistic and error based systems) have emerged.

One of the more prominent developments was Max Hutt's inspection system, which blended an objective scoring system with clinical insight. His Psychopathology Scale, for example, examined 17 factors in three areas: organization of the drawings on the paper, changes in the gestalt of the drawings (e.g., the degree of angulation of a design), and distortion of the gestalt of the drawings (e.g., simplifying elements of a design). He also stressed the importance of incorporating the observation of behaviors accompanying drawing in his psychodiagnostic process. His work extended over 50 years (see Hutt, 1985) and provided clinicians with a comprehensive system for evaluating the test.

Another important development was Gerald Pascal and Barbara Suttell's (1951) quantitative scoring system, which was composed of 105 specific deviations (e.g., part of design missing, dashes for dots). The deviations were selected based on their ability to discriminate normal individuals from psychiatric patients. Although the system was designed mainly for the assessment of adults and generated considerable research, its greatest impact was actually on child-oriented assessment.

Elizabeth Koppitz recognized the need for a scoring system for children and for over a 20-year period developed and refined the Developmental Bender Scoring System (see Koppitz, 1975). The 30-item system, based heavily on the work of Pascal and Suttell (1951), focused on four types of errors in children's drawings: distortion, rotation, perseveration, and integration. Her Development Scoring System and her 12 Emotional Indicators (e.g., small size of drawings, overworked lines of drawings) were used widely, especially in the diagnosis of academic and emotional problems.

An alternative approach, developed over the past 20 years by Gary Brannigan and Nancy Brunner, was more consistent with Bender's philosophy because it utilized a holistic approach to scoring. Brannigan and Brunner devised the Qualitative Scoring System for judging the overall quality of each drawing. They also reduced the number of designs from nine to six, choosing only those that were most appropriate for their target population, preschool and early primary school children. Their modified Bender-Gestalt Test is used primarily for educational decision making for young children (see Brannigan and Brunner, 2002). Their work also provided the groundwork for the first major revision of the Bender-Gestalt Test.

The revised edition of the Bender Visual-Motor Gestalt Test (Bender-Gestalt II) was published by Gary Brannigan and Scott Decker in 2003. The most notable changes were the addition of seven new designs to the original nine and the development of the Global Scoring System to assess the overall quality of each design. The standard copy phase and a new, memory (recall) phase of the test were normed on a large, nationally representative sample of individuals ages 4 to 85+ years. Motor and Perception Supplementary tests were developed to aid the detection of specific problems in these areas, separate from the integrative processes required for reproduction of the Bender-Gestalt II designs.

Research on nonclinical and clinical (e.g., individuals with learning disabilities, mental retardation, attention deficit/hyperactivity disorder, Alzheimer's disease, autism) samples indicated that the test is a reliable and valid measure of visual-motor functioning. Brannigan and Decker (2006) concluded that the Bender-Gestalt II is a more dynamic assessment tool because of the innovations to the test. They added that further research should stress its role in various phases (i.e., from screening to comprehensive evaluation) of the process of diagnosing organic pathology, predicting school learning problems, and assessing personality dynamics and psychopathology.

REFERENCES

Bender, L. (1938). *A visual motor gestalt test and its clinical use.* American Orthopsychiatric Association, Research Monographs (No. 3). New York: American Orthopsychiatric Association.

Brannigan, G. G., & Brunner, N. A. (2002). *Guide to the qualitative scoring system for the Modified Version of the Bender-Gestalt Test.* Springfield, IL: Thomas.

Brannigan, G. G., & Decker, S. L. (2003). *Bender Visual-Motor Gestalt Test* (2nd ed.). Itasca, IL: Riverside.

Brannigan, G. G., & Decker, S. L. (2006). The Bender-Gestalt II. *American Journal of Orthopsychiatry, 76,* 10–12.

Hutt, M. L. (1985). *The Hutt Adaptation of the Bender-Gestalt Test* (4th ed.). New York: Grune & Stratton.

Koppitz, E. M. (1975). *The Bender-Gestalt Test for young children* (Vol. 2). New York: Grune & Stratton.

Pascal, G. R., & Suttell, B. J. (1951). *The Bender-Gestalt Test*. New York: Grune & Stratton.

Piotrowski, C. (1995). A review of the clinical and research use of the Bender-Gestalt Test. *Perceptual and Motor Skills, 81,* 1272–1274.

Wertheimer, M. (1923). Studies in the theory of Gestalt Psychology. *Psychologische Forschung, 4,* 301–350.

GARY G. BRANNIGAN
State University of New York—Plattsburgh

See also: Gestalt Psychology; Neuropsychology

BENZODIAZAPINES (See Antianxiety Medications)

BEREAVEMENT (See Grief)

BETA AND GAMMA RHYTHMS

Beta and gamma rhythms were first studied in the human electroencephalogram (EEG) recorded from the scalp. Beta waves of >13 Hz appear in the occipital EEG when the eyes are open, as first reported by Hans Berger who also named the 8–12 Hz alpha rhythm (Niedermeyer, 2005). As used by neuroscientists, beta typically designates 13 to ~30 Hz and gamma describes ~30 to 100 Hz, including the 40-Hz oscillations, while higher frequency activities are called ripples (~100–500 Hz). Beta, gamma, and ripple EEGs are of relatively low amplitude (<30 μV) in the EEG, and quantification normally requires computer analysis, with careful separation from muscle and 50–60 Hz electrical power artifacts. Other than in the EEG, gamma and beta activities can be found in the magnetoencephalogram (MEG), local field potentials, extracellular neuronal unit firings, and intracellularly recorded membrane potentials. Spontaneous (steady-state), evoked, and induced gamma rhythms are distinguished. Spontaneous rhythm occurs without stimulation, evoked gamma activity is time-locked to the stimulus, and induced gamma is increased by the stimulus but not time-locked to it.

Synchronization of neuronal activity appears to be more robust at the beta/gamma frequencies than any other frequencies. Thus, gamma synchronization has been proposed to form the temporal binding underlying perceptual grouping, object representation, and sensorimotor integration (Tallon-Baudry & Bertrand, 1999; Engel & Singer, 2001). Memory storage and retrieval and motor task execution may also be coordinated by gamma oscillations. In the visual cortex, microelectrode recordings reveal that single neurons may code for various features of a visual object, like size, form, and orientation. These features must be combined to yield an unambiguous representation of the object; this is commonly referred to as the binding problem.

It is proposed that the spatially distributed neurons that code for different features may synchronize through gamma oscillations, thus forming a dynamic assembly of neurons that represents an object uniquely. Gamma oscillations in other sensory cortices (auditory, somatosensory, olfactory) may serve in feature integration and perceptual grouping as well. Temporal binding is considered an active, top-down process instead of a bottom-up process that solely depends on stimulus properties. The active temporal binding depends on attention, contextual information, and motivation, which may involve the cortex interacting with subcortical structures, notably the thalamus, basal ganglia, and basal forebrain nuclei (Steriade & McCarley, 2005). Among all brain areas, the olfactory bulb and cortex show the most robust and dominant gamma rhythm, which helps to build a dynamic population neural code for smell (Freeman, 1991). In the limbic system, the entorhinal cortex and the hippocampus express beta and gamma activities that facilitate normal spatial behaviors (Leung, 1998; Buzsaki, 2006) and possibly incite schizophrenia-like behaviors under abnormal conditions.

Gamma and beta oscillations are present in many parts of the brain, possibly because of the multiple mechanisms that generate these oscillations. Single neurons may oscillate at the gamma frequency, while intrinsic membrane properties allow some neurons to respond preferentially (resonate) to gamma frequency driving (Traub et al., 2004; Steriade & McCarley, 2005). A network of purely inhibitory interneurons can generate 40-Hz oscillations, but normal beta and gamma activities in the brain are likely generated by neural networks involving excitatory principal neurons and inhibitory interneurons (Freeman, 1991; Leung, 1998; Traub et al., 2004; Buzsaki, 2006). The critical role of inhibition in generating beta/gamma activities is highlighted by the effect of sedative drugs, such as benzodiazepam and barbiturate, on enhancing beta and low-gamma frequency EEG. Inhibitory neurons typically use gamma-amino-butyric acid (GABA) as a neurotransmitter, and sedative drugs are GABA-A receptor agonists, while GABA-A receptor antagonists suppress gamma oscillations. Beta/gamma synchronization is in part enhanced by presynaptic facilitation that occurs >10 Hz (or within 100 ms interpulse intervals) and limited by the relative refractory period of action potentials (~5 ms or 200 Hz).

Gamma/beta rhythms have been associated with activation of the cerebral cortex or consciousness (Steriade

& McCarley, 2005). Surgical levels of general anesthetic tended to suppress high-frequency gamma activity. Altered gamma synchrony in the EEG has been reported in schizophrenic patients (Uhlhaas & Singer, 2006) and in animal models of schizophrenia. Other conditions with abnormal gamma synchrony include epileptic seizures, Alzheimer's and Parkinson's diseases (Uhlhaas & Singer, 2006).

REFERENCES

Freeman, W. J. (1991). The physiology of perception. *Scientific American, 264*, 78–85.

Leung, L. S. (1998). Generation of theta and gamma rhythms in the hippocampus. *Neuroscience Biobehavioral Reviews, 22*, 275–290.

Niedermeyer, E. (2005). The normal EEG of the waking adult. In E. Niedermeyer & F. H. Lopes da Silva (Eds.), *Electroencephalography* (5th ed., pp. 167–192). Philadelphia: Lippincott, Williams & Wilkins.

Steriade, M., & McCarley, R. W. (2005). *Brain control of wakefulness and sleep,* pp. 262–276. New York: Springer.

Traub, R. D., Bibbig, A., LeBeau, F. E., Buhl, E. H., & Whittington, M. A. (2004). Cellular mechanisms of neuronal population oscillations in the hippocampus in vitro. *Annual Review of Neuroscience, 27*, 247–278.

Uhlhaas, P. J., & Singer, W. (2006). Neural synchrony in brain disorders: Relevance for cognitive dysfunctions and pathophysiology. *Neuron, 52*, 155–168.

SUGGESTED READINGS

Buzsaki, G. (2006). *Rhythms of the brain,* pp. 231–261, Oxford: Oxford University Press.

Engel, A. K., & Singer, W. (2001). Temporal binding and the neural correlates of sensory awareness. *Trends in Cognitive Sciences, 5*, 16–25.

Tallon-Baudry, C., & Bertrand, O. (1999). Oscillatory gamma activity in humans and its role in object representation. *Trends in Cognitive Sciences, 3*(4), 151–162.

L. STAN LEUNG
University of Western Ontario

See also: **Electroencephalography**

BIAS (See Assessment Bias; Confirmatory Bias; Cultural Bias; Prejudice and Discrimination)

BIBLIOTHERAPY

Bibliotherapy is a self-help technique presented in the written format of a book or track. Although the term bibliotherapy can refer to the use of any literary work, including fiction and inspirational forms of literature, it typically involves the use of nonfiction books, manuals, or pamphlets that provide information while encouraging or guiding the person to make some type of change (Campbell & Scott, 2003). Bibliotherapy is currently the primary type of media-based (e.g., books, manuals, audiotapes, or some combination of these formats) self-help approach (Watkins, 2008).

Self-help books have a long history in American culture and can be traced back to the 1600s with the arrival of English colonists in the New World. More recently, the 1960s through the 1980s saw a proliferation in the publication of self-help books for a variety of problems (e.g., anxiety, depression, eating, smoking, drinking, relationships, enuresis, conduct problems). Part of the appeal of self-help books may likely be due to the belief that persons can improve their circumstances through individual effort (Watkins, 2008).

There are several types of bibliotherapy, and one way of categorizing them is as general self-help books, problem-focused self-help books, or technique-focused self-help books (Pantalon, 1998). General self-help books address a variety of emotional health and relationship issues, but not specific problems or disorders. Furthermore, general self-help books do not usually include systematic methods of assessment or treatment. Problem-focused self-help books, on the other hand, target a particular problem (e.g., panic attacks, depression, eating) and provide specific methods of assessment and treatment. Although based on a variety of theoretical models (e.g., gestalt, rational-emotive, transactional analysis), most recent problem-focused self-help books have been cognitive behavioral in nature. In addition, problem-focused approaches have been the most empirically tested. Finally, technique focused self-help books are similar to problem-focused books, but they discuss techniques (e.g., relaxation techniques) that can be applied across various problem areas (Watkins, 2008).

Bibliotherapy is used increasingly as an adjunctive treatment by mental health professionals. In a recent study, Adams and Pitre (2000) found that 68% of therapists whom they surveyed used bibliotherapy with their clients, a finding consistent with previous research. In addition, experienced therapists (i.e., 10 or more years of experience) were more likely to use self-help books than less experienced therapists. Furthermore, therapists reported recommending books to their clients to enhance traditional therapy, foster client independence, and as a response to increased requests for self-help materials from their clients (Adams & Pitre, 2000).

Empirical Status of Bibliotherapy

Empirical investigation of bibliotherapy in particular and self-help treatments in general has lagged greatly behind their use by professionals and the public (Watkins, 2008). Furthermore, only a relatively small number of books have received empirical support. The effectiveness of self-help programs has often been based on the subjective impressions of therapists or surveys of mental health professionals, rather than empirical data (Adams & Pitre, 2000).

Research into the effectiveness of bibliotherapy approaches has nevertheless increased in the past 30 years. Both original research and meta-analytic studies have found bibliotherapy to have moderate-to-large effect sizes, particularly in the treatment of anxiety disorders (e.g., Marrs, 1995). However, more research is needed to better determine the overall usefulness of bibliotherapy approaches, the problems that are particularly amenable to bibliotherapy, the degree of expectable improvement, and the permanency of change produced.

The majority of treatment outcome studies in the field have used group experimental designs. Although group experimental designs have many advantages, they also have their limitations. Therefore, research in this area may benefit by the use of other research designs, such as single-case designs and qualitative studies, in addition to group experimental designs. Finally, the inclusion of more diverse sample populations in future treatment outcome studies will be important in order to demonstrate the effectiveness of bibliotherapy with a wide range of individuals.

Level of Therapist Contact

An important finding to emerge from both narrative reviews (e.g., Newman, Erickson, Przeworski, & Dzus, 2003) and meta-analytic studies (e.g., Marrs, 1995) is that the amount of therapist contact is an important moderator of outcome for individuals using bibliotherapy approaches. The level of therapist contact can vary a great deal in self-help treatments. Glasgow and Rosen (1978) discussed four degrees of therapist/client contact: (1) self-administered therapy, which may include contact for assessment only; (2) predominantly self-help-treatment, including check-ins and an initial introduction to the materials; (3) minimal contact therapy with some active involvement of a therapist; and (4) therapist-administered treatments. The first three degrees of therapist/client contact reflect varying levels of bibliotherapy and self-help treatments in general, as the person is primarily responsible for carrying out the treatment (Watkins, 2008). Furthermore, the type of problem may also be a determining factor in the level of contact that is necessary. How much therapist contact is necessary to produce positive change remains an empirical question.

REFERENCES

Adams, S. J., & Pitre, N. L. (2000). Who uses bibliotherapy and why? A survey from an underserviced area. *Canadian Journal of Psychiatry, 45,* 645–650.

Campbell, L. F., & Smith, T. P. (2003). Integrating self-help books into psychotherapy. *Journal of Clinical Psychology/In Session: Psychotherapy in Practice, 59,* 177–186.

Glasgow, R. E., & Rosen, G. M. (1978). Behavioral bibliotherapy: A review of self-help behavior therapy manuals. *Psychological Bulletin, 85,* 1–23.

Marrs, R. W. (1995). A meta-analysis of bibliotherapy studies. *American Journal of Community Psychology, 23,* 843–870.

Newman, M. G., Erickson, T., Przeworski, A., & Dzus, E. (2003). Self-help and minimal contact therapies for anxiety disorders: Is human contact necessary for therapeutic efficacy? *Journal of Clinical Psychology/In session: Psychotherapy in Practice, 59,* 251–274.

Pantalon, M. V. (1998). Use of self-help books in the practice of clinical psychology. In A. S. Bellack & M. Hersen (Series Eds.) & P. Salkovskis (Vol. Ed.), *Comprehensive clinical psychology: Vol. 6. Adults: Clinical formulation and treatment* (pp. 265–276). New York: Elsevier Science.

Watkins, P. L. (2008). Self-help therapies: Past and present. In P. L. Watkins & G. A. Clum (Eds.), *Handbook of self-help therapies* (pp. 1–24). New York: Taylor & Francis.

SUGGESTED READINGS

Rosen, G. M., Glasgow, R. E., & Moore, T. E. (2003). Self-help therapy: The science and business of giving psychology away. In S. O. Lilienfeld, S. J. Lynn, & J. M. Lohr (Eds.), *Science and pseudoscience in clinical psychology* (pp. 399–424). New York: Guilford Press.

Watkins, P. L., & Clum, G. A. (2008). Handbook of self-help therapies. New York: Taylor & Francis.

GREG A. R. FEBBRARO
*Counseling for Growth and Change,
L.C., Windsor Heights, IA*

See also: **Self-Help Groups**

BINET, ALFRED (1857–1911)

Alfred Binet took his first degree in law in Paris. While in Paris he became acquainted with Jean Charcot and studied hypnosis under him. His interests changed to the natural sciences, in which he received his second degree. He became particularly interested in the higher mental processes of humans.

Binet soon became interested in abnormal psychology and wrote the *Alterations of Personality and Suggestibility.* In addition, he became concerned about the thinking process in children and much of his data was based on studying his own daughters. He gave them problems to solve and asked them to report to him the steps they went through in the process. All this led to his concept of intelligence.

He became aware that considerable individual differences existed in children. He realized that there were those who were slow, whom he identified as "feebleminded." He was sharply critical of the medical profession for considering mental deficiency a disease.

He was aware of the work of Ebbinghaus on memory and forgetting, as well as the research on sensory, perceptual, and motor measures, which included reaction time, sensory acuity, and the span of attention. In association with Victor Henri he discovered that there were different kinds of memory: visual memory, memory for numbers, musical memory, and memory for sentences. Together they developed tests to measure these different types of memory.

The preceding studies set the stage for the development of a scale of intelligence. In 1904 the Minister of Public Instruction appointed a committee to recommend what should be done about the education of "subnormal" children in the schools of Paris. The decision to place them in special schools depended on the development of some means of identifying them. Binet was called upon to develop a test that became the first scale for the measurement of intelligence. In 1905 this test appeared as a result of the collaboration of Binet and Theodore Simon. The scale consisted of a series of tasks increasing in difficulty. In 1908 the test was revised and the individual tasks were arranged, not only according to difficulty, but also according to the age at which the average child could complete them. It was called the Binet-Simon Scale

In the emergence of the tests, these tasks were arranged and rearranged so as to be appropriate for various age levels. If a test was too easy at the 8-year level, for example, it was then placed at an earlier level, say, at 7 years. The general rule was that if 60–90% of the children passed it at a given level, than that level was appropriate for the test. Thus, the "mentally retarded" child who performed appreciably below the norm for his or her age was considered a deviant from the norm and could be identified. In this way the mental age of the child could be computed, regardless of his or her actual chronological age. Binet identified labels for three levels of mental retardation: idiots (lowest), imbecile, and moron.

The last of Binet's revisions appeared in 1911, the year of his death. He added new tests, and he discarded old ones that he thought depended too much on school information. He also designated a given number of tests for a particular year, so mental age could be expressed in months. If there were six tests at a particular age level, each test passed could be given a score of two months at that level. The tests passed, regardless of the years at which they were passed, could be added together to give a total mental age. In 1916, the Binet-Simon Intelligence Test was translated and standardized by Lewis Terman at Stanford University, and it was called the "Stanford-Binet" scale.

Binet did not develop the concept of intelligence quotient, or IQ; this was developed by a German psychologist, William Stern.

SUGGESTED READINGS

Binet, A., & Simon, T. (1915). *A method of measuring the development of intelligence in young children.* Chicago: Chicago Medical Books.

Binet, A., & Simon, T. (1915). *The development of intelligence in children.* New York: Arno Press.

RALPH W. LUNDIN
Wheaton, IL

BINGE EATING (See Bulimia Nervosa)

BIOENERGETIC THERAPY

Bioenergetic therapy combines bodywork with psychoanalysis. Also known as bioenergetic analysis or simply bioenergetics, this therapeutic system was created by Alexander Lowen (2004), a protégé of Wilhelm Reich (see Sharaf, 1994), who in turn was Freud's student; as such, it stems from the Freudian psychoanalytic tradition. It is seen as a humanistic psychotherapy for its holistic mind-body approach and is also sometimes grouped with gestalt, orgonomy, and radix as a neo-Reichian therapy. Bioenergetics is a way to understand and therapeutically intervene both psychologically and physically. Diagnoses focus on both understanding psychological issues through traditional psychoanalytic concepts (e.g., defense mechanisms) and physical issues through observing bodily form (e.g., posture) and function (e.g., qualities of movement during respiration) stemming from Reich's (1980) insights into the role of chronic muscular tension patterns (body "armoring") in shaping "character."

The etymology of emotion refers to movement (i.e., e-"motion"), and muscles are the organs of movement, so armoring inhibits both emotional feelings and expressions (e.g., pelvic tightness related to sexual conflict blocks both sexual pleasure and performance). Although mind and body are discussed as if separate, they are assumed to be unctionally identical, differing only semantically: what happens mentally through "character"-istic ways of experiencing life (e.g., proneness to feeling panic) affects physical expression (e.g., causing chronically raised shoulders), as if anticipating being attacked), while what happens bodily (e.g., chronically raised shoulders) affects the mental (e.g., increasing the likelihood of breakthrough panic), in mutually reinforcing ways. Consequently, bioenergetics always involves both psychological and physical processes: the psychological work is similar to the search for meaning in psychoanalysis, while the bodywork focuses on increasing freedom of movement and energy available to the person.

A key tenet is that the level of energy available determines overall quality of life. For example, depression is seen as related to both lowered psychological experience of energy and literally "depressed" physical energy, such as caused by decreased respiration due to chronic muscular tensions in the chest, while bioenergetic treatment of depression may involve vigorous physical movements, such as kicking and stretching, to increase physical energy, and psychoanalytic explorations to regain emotional contact that was previously blocked by chronic muscular tensions and can only become reexperienced after physical release. Bioenergetics aims to relieve such chronic maladjusted patterns, both mental and physical, and is applicable to understanding and treating a variety of psychological conditions. It may be particularly helpful for diffuse, so-called negative, symptoms, such as a lack of feeling pleasure and aliveness.

In contrast to most bodywork, bioenergetics considers it essential that physical changes be processed in the context of psychodynamic understandings of character in order to result in permanent changes; in contrast to most psychotherapies, bioenergetics considers that psychological interventions without corresponding bodily changes result only in short-lasting effects that inevitably revert to characteristic ways of experiencing and behaving. The combination of psychological and bodily approaches allows bioenergetics to help clients resolve emotional problems and realize greater pleasure in life than would either approach alone, facilitating self-understanding grounded in body experience and continuously reinforced through freely expressed emotions.

REFERENCES

Lowen, A. (2004). *Honoring the body*. Alachua, FL: Bioenergetics Press.

Reich, W. (1980). *Character analysis* (3rd ed.). New York: Farrar, Straus & Giroux. (Originally published 1933.)

Sharaf, M. (1994). *Fury on earth: A biography of Wilhelm Reich*. Cambridge, MA: DaCapo Press.

SUGGESTED READINGS

Lowen, A. (1977). *Bioenergetics: The revolutionary therapy that uses the language of the body to heal the problems of the mind*. New York: Penguin.

Lowen, A. (2006). *Language of the body: Physical dynamics of character structure*. Alachua, FL: Bioenergetics Press.

Lowen, A., Lowen, L., & Skalecki, W. (2003). *The way to vibrant health*. Alachua, FL: Bioenergetics Press.

HARRIS FRIEDMAN
University of Florida

ROBERT GLAZER
Florida Society for Bioenergetic Analysis

BIOFEEDBACK

Biofeedback is best understood as a closed feedback loop consisting of a person or animal, a response, a means to detect the response, and a mechanism for displaying the response to the person or animal—the response is thus fed back. For example, a person can be instructed to increase his or her heart rate; the heart rate is displayed by a monitor and fed back to the person; a feedback loop is thereby established. Biological systems have numerous, reflexive feedback loops to maintain homeostatic integrity: body temperature, blood sugar, blood pressure, endocrine levels, etc. Fluctuations are kept within narrow limits by such feedback loops. However, biofeedback learning is not reflexive—it is more closely associated with higher-order learning processes.

One motive for development of biofeedback was to devise therapies for volitional control over processes considered automatic and reflexive. Processes like heart rate, blood pressure, and gastric secretion change along their respective dimensions, depending upon metabolic needs and emotional states. But when such processes move beyond certain limits, the health and proper functioning of the organism become compromised. Biofeedback self-regulation, as a therapy, can be viewed as a learning technique to help keep systems with proper limits with few, if any, side effects of more traditional medical therapies.

A second incentive for biofeedback development came from concern with disproving the hypothesis that responses innervated by the autonomic nervous system were not modifiable by reward learning (Kimmel, 1967). This position held that such responses were modifiable only through the conditional response techniques crafted by I. P. Pavlov (Pavlov, 1927).

A third reason for exploration came from interest in the self-control of conscious states. The fact that electroencephalographic (EEG) rhythms might be modifiable by providing feedback to the observer regarding EEG activity led to more biofeedback research.

Finally, the idea that self-regulation of neuromuscular function might help alleviate certain types of pain, such as headache, or lead to recovery of muscular function following trauma or disease, further helped the development of biofeedback.

Early experimental reports indicated that human subjects could control vasomotor responses, electrodermal activity, and heart rate. In the first of these studies a Russian investigator, Lisina (in Razran, 1961), reported that when individuals were allowed to view a polygraph displaying their vasomotor responses to electric shock, they learned to produce vasodilatation to escape the shock—the usual response to cutaneous electrical stimulation is vasoconstriction.

Following these early studies, a number of laboratories began publishing data claiming to have successfully used reward learning on a variety of autonomically mediated responses with both humans and animals. Besides the usual methodological objections, debate centered on the mechanisms responsible for the behavioral changes. A mediation mechanism was proposed that held that true reward learning was not occurring. Instead, it was argued, the subjects could be mediating the autonomic response through either cognition (i.e., thinking either calming or emotional thoughts) or covert striate muscular activity (either intended, with no movement, or actual movement). Although this issue remains unresolved, studies on subjects paralyzed by spinal lesions and plagued by hypotension indicated that neither cognitions, small muscular twitches, nor actual movement could account entirely for the biofeedback-produced changes (Miller, 1969).

Autonomic reward learning is also influenced by such variables as type of feedback, awareness, instructions, homeostatic restraints, and links between somatic and autonomic response systems.

Biofeedback has been applied for the amelioration of a variety of disorders. Table 1 lists some of these afflictions and response routes. The applications continue to expand, and biofeedback is, in fact, the preferred method for treating Raynaud's disease.

The application of biofeedback techniques to problems resulting from neuromuscular dysfunction has been validated on a wide array of disorders, ranging from headache to foot drop. Neuromuscular feedback has shown impressive specificity of control by successfully training subjects to either activate or inhabit single motor muscle units (Basmajian, 1962) as well as controlling fecal incontinence.

Electroencephalographic (EEG) activity has been modified by biofeedback. Results of these studies reported that biofeedback for alpha (8–12 Hz) increased alpha and was accompanied by changes in cognitive states. Increased alpha was paralleled by feelings of relaxed attention and absence of anxiety. Whether increased alpha produced changed psychological states or the psychological states were responsible for the changes in EEG became part of the mediation issue. However, evidence strongly implicates the role of eye movement in the production or suppression of alpha, and this oculomotor hypothesis is the salient explanation of alpha control. Convergence, divergence, and focusing of the eyes are related to the amount of alpha produced. In addition, correlated psychological states are at least partly due to expectations. Biofeedback has also been applied to theta EEG (4–7 Hz) in order to produce dreamlike imagery and creative insight. Finally, some research has focused on modification of the sensori-motor rhythm (12–14 Hz) to reduce epileptic seizures with some success.

Further information and recent publications on biofeedback can be found at the Web site of the Applied Psychophysiology and Biofeedback Society (http://www .aapb.org).

Table 1. Some Response Systems and Afflictions to Which Biofeedback Has Been Applied

Electroencephalographic	Electromyographic	Autonomic
Epilepsy, concentration, attention-deficit hyperactive disorder (ADHD), alcohol dependency	Self-awareness (SA), athletic performance, cardiac abnormalities, headache, functional diarrhea, temporomandibular disorder, ADHD, gait disorders, irritable bowel syndrome, tinnitus, asthma, systematic desensitization (SD)	SA, Raynaud's disease, cardiac abnormalities, headache, essential hypertension, urinary incontinence, anxiety, sexual arousal, SD

REFERENCES

Barclay, L., & Lie, D. (2007). Biofeedback reduces psychological burden in older women with urge UI. *Journal of the American Geriatric Society, 55,* 2010–2015.

Basmajian, J. V. (1962). Control and training of individual motor units. *Science, 141,* 440–441.

Kern-Buell, C. L., McGrady, A. V., Conran, P. B., & Nelson, L. A. (2000). Asthma severity, psychophysiological indicators of arousal, and immune function in asthma patients undergoing biofeedback-assisted relaxation. *Applied Psychophysiology and Biofeedback, 25,* 79–91.

Kimmel, H. D. (1967). Instrumental conditioning of autonomically mediated behavior. *Psychological Bulletin, 67,* 337–345.

Miller, N. E. (1969). Learning of visceral and glandular responses. *Science, 163,* 434–445.

Monastra, V. J., Monastra, D. M., & George, S. (2002). The effects of stimulant therapy, EEG biofeedback, and parenting style on the primary symptoms of attention-deficit/hyperactivity disorder. *Applied Psychophysiology and Biofeedback, 27,* 231–249.

Palsson O., Heymen S., & Whitehead W. (2004). Biofeedback treatment for functional anorectal disorders: A comprehensive efficacy review. *Applied Psychophysiology and Biofeedback 29,* 153–174.

Pavlov, I. P. (1927). *Conditioned reflexes: An investigation of the physiological activity of the cerebral cortex.* (Trans. and ed. by G. V. Anrep.) London: Oxford University Press.

Razran, G. (1961). The observable unconscious and the inferable conscious in current Soviet psychophysiology: Interoceptive conditioning, and the orienting reflex. *Psychological Review. 68,* 81–147.

Schneider, F., Elbert, T., Heimann, H., Welker, A., Stetter, F., Mattes, R., et. al. (1993). Self-regulation of slow cortical potentials in psychiatric patients: Alcohol dependency. *Biofeedback and Self-Regulation, 18.*

SUGGESTED READINGS

Gatchel, R. J. & Blanchard, E. B. (Eds.). (1993). *Psychophysiological disorders: Research and clinical applications*. Washington, DC: American Psychological Association.

Hatch, J. P. Fisher, J. G., & Ruch, J. D. (Eds.). (1987). *Biofeedback: Studies in clinical efficacy*. New York: Plenum Press.

Schwartz, M. S. (Ed.). (1998). *Biofeedback: A practitioner's guide*. (2nd ed.). New York: Guilford Press.

WILLIAM A. GREENE
Eastern Washington University, Spokane

See also: Operant Conditioning; Sympathetic Nervous System

BIOGRAPHICAL DATA

Biographical data of one sort or another are shared in most day-to-day social encounters. When meeting new people, for example, some exchange of biographical data often occurs (e.g., the disclosure of one's occupation or place of employment). Professionals who work with people in a variety of contexts (e.g., physicians, government workers, potential employers) frequently obtain histories of health-related events, education, and employment. In applied clinical settings, for example, therapists will often assess aspects of a client's life history (e.g., family history; school and occupational history; social history; health, medical, and psychiatric history), and evaluate the potential relevance of this information in relation to the client's stated reasons for entering into therapy and for the selection of appropriate therapies. Several methods or resources can be used for the collection of biographical data, including informal interviews, semi-structured interviews (von Zerssen, Pössl, Hecht, Black, Garczynski, & Barthelmes, 1998), "memory books" (Thomson & Holland, 2005), institutional records, documents, and specially designed biographical inventories and checklists.

One form of biographical data is referred to as "life narratives" or "life stories." These are autobiographical accounts offered by persons in their own words, and are sometimes used in the study of individual lives or personality. Such narratives often highlight major life events, significant life transitions, personal strivings, notable achievements, extraordinary challenges, periods of harmony or disarray in social relationships, and times of contentment and tranquility. Such stories also frequently include reports of personal appraisals, accounts of coping and resilience, and descriptions of guiding values.

Perhaps most importantly, such narratives reveal connections that bind together discrete elements of one's life, and in so doing, expose coherence and consistency in the manifestations of personality.

"Psychobiography" is a method used to study lives of individuals, usually historical figures, from the perspective of psychological theory. Biographical data have been used, for example, to infer the prevalence and nature of mental illness among U.S. presidents (Davidson, Connor, & Swartz, 2006). As illustrated by Runyan's (1981) review of psychological explanations for Van Gogh's cutting off his ear, however, psychobiographical inquiries into the motives, behavior, or personality of historical figures can result in a variety of interpretations, the validity of any single account being difficult to determine.

Biographical data (sometimes referred to as "biodata" in occupational settings and organizational psychology) are occasionally used in personnel selection. Examples of data used for this purpose include resumes, reference letters, and information provided by applicants on standard application forms (e.g., academic information, school-related awards and prizes, employment history, social activities, and community involvement). Data related to each of these areas might be weighted according to their ability to predict future job success, with final decisions concerning applicant selection informed by the sum of these weighted variables. Although there are several indications that biographical data can usefully predict future job performance (Bliesener, 1996), there are associated concerns about the accuracy and reliability of such data, the relevance of such information for hiring decisions, potential equal employment opportunity risks, and the possible invasion of privacy. There is also currently no clear consensus as to what constitutes appropriate biodata for personnel selection.

REFERENCES

Bliesener, T. (1996). Methodological moderators in validating biographical data in personnel selection. *Journal of Occupational and Organizational Psychology, 69,* 107–120.

Davidson, J. R. T., Connor, K. M., & Swartz, M. (2006). Mental illness in U.S. presidents between 1776 and 1974: A review of biographical sources. *Journal of Nervous and Mental Disease, 194,* 47–51.

Runyan, W. McK. (1981). Why did Van Gogh cut off his ear? The problem of alternative explanations in psychobiography. *Journal of Personality and Social Psychology, 40,* 1070–1077.

Thomson, R., & Holland, J. (2005). 'Thanks for the memory': Memory books as a methodological resource in biographical research. *Qualitative Research, 5,* 201–219.

von Zerssen, D., Pössl, J., Hecht, H., Black, C., Garczynski, E., & Barthelmes, H. (1998). The Biographical Personality Interview (BPI)–A new approach to the assessment of premorbid personality in psychiatric research. Part I: Development of the instrument. *Journal of Psychiatric Research, 32,* 19–35.

SUGGESTED READINGS

McAdams, D. P. (1999). Personal narratives and the life story. In L. A. Pervin & O. P. John (Eds.), *Handbook of personality: Theory and research* (2nd ed., pp. 478–500). New York: Guilford Press.

Runyan, W. McK. (1997). Studying lives: Psychobiography and the conceptual structure of personality psychology. In R. Hogan, J. Johnson, & S. Briggs (Eds.), *Handbook of personality psychology* (pp. 41–69). San Diego, CA: Academic Press.

Sundberg, N. D. (1977). *Assessment of persons* (pp. 84–109). Englewood Cliffs, NJ: Prentice-Hall.

RICHARD F. FARMER
Oregon Research Institute

NORMAN D. SUNDBERG
University of Oregon

BIPOLAR DISORDER

Bipolar disorder, previously referred to as manic-depressive illness, is a disorder affecting mood, behavior, and cognition. Individuals with bipolar disorder experience symptoms from two "poles": (1) depression, characterized by low mood, sadness, anhedonia, sleep and appetite disturbance, poor concentration, fatigue, feelings of guilt and worthlessness, and psychomotor slowing; and (2) mania, distinguished by euphoric, elevated and/or irritable mood, decreased need for sleep, increased energy and activity, hypersexuality, pressured speech, racing thoughts, grandiosity, and increased risk-taking.

Subtypes of bipolar disorder include bipolar I disorder, in which the individual experiences depressive episodes alternating with manic episodes. DSM-IV criteria for mania require elevated, expansive, or irritable mood lasting at least one week, or any period of time if hospitalization is required. Some individuals simultaneously experience symptoms of mania and depression, which is referred to as a mixed state. Bipolar II disorder is characterized by depressive episodes alternating with hypomanic episodes—that is, a less severe manic state that is not associated with psychosis, need for hospitalization, or marked functional impairment, yet is still noticeable by others and uncharacteristic of the individual when euthymic (in a stable mood). DSM-IV criteria for hypomania require elevated, expansive, or irritable mood lasting at least four days.

Epidemiology

Bipolar disorder is estimated to affect between 0.5% and 1.3% of the population. Bipolar I disorder is equally common among men and women, whereas rates of bipolar II disorder are higher among women. The disorder appears to be similarly distributed among social classes and education levels, although recent studies indicate that bipolar disorder is associated with lower family income—possibly as a consequence of illness. No associations with race or ethnicity have been supported.

Course and Outcome

There exists great interindividual variability in the course of bipolar illness. Three basic mood-cycling patterns have been identified among individuals with bipolar disorder: mania followed by depression followed by euthymia; depression followed by mania followed by euthymia; and continuous cycling between mood episodes. Individuals who experience four or more mood episodes within a one-year period are labeled "rapid cycling." Rapid cycling is equally common in bipolar I and II disorders and more common among women, and it is generally considered to be a more treatment-refractory variant of illness. Recent research indicates that more than half of individuals with bipolar disorder continue to experience subsyndromal symptoms that interfere with functioning during the interepisode period.

Depressive episodes and mixed episodes tend to last longer than pure manic episodes, with an overall mean episode length of approximately four months (Goodwin & Jamison, 2007a). Improvements in pharmacotherapy have resulted in a significant decrease in the duration of affective episodes in bipolar disorder. However, nearly three-fourths of individuals with bipolar disorder experience affective episode recurrences over five years even with adequate pharmacotherapy. Furthermore, treatment adherence is a significant clinical problem associated with bipolar disorder, with up to 50% of patients reporting nonadherence to their treatment regimen at any point in time.

Recent research indicates that the average age of bipolar illness onset is 22. This figure has steadily decreased since the 1990s, with various hypotheses having been set forth to account for this phenomenon. These hypotheses include genetic anticipation, improved diagnostic specificity, increased use of antidepressants and stimulants among youth (possibly hastening a bipolar diathesis in vulnerable individuals), and increasing recognition of bipolar disorder in children and teens. Studies consistently indicate that earlier age of onset is associated with poorer outcomes. A significant gap (on average, 6–8 years) between time of illness onset and time to first diagnosis and treatment is commonly reported.

Bipolar disorder currently ranks among the top 10 most disabling disorders. The illness can have an enduring negative impact on an individual's ability to function in occupational, interpersonal, and recreational domains. Up to 30% of patients with bipolar disorder cannot work, and nearly 75% fail to recover premorbid levels of functioning. Depressive, rather than manic, symptoms appear to be associated with the majority of the functional impairment in bipolar disorder. The illness is associated with high rates of divorce, legal problems, and substance use, and it is associated with annual direct health care costs exceeding $15,000 per individual (Dardennes, Thuile, Even, Friedman, & Guelfi, 2006).

Mortality rates up to six times the expected rate in the general population have been documented among individuals with bipolar disorder. Suicide accounts for a great burden of the mortality; up to 15% of individuals with bipolar disorder will die from suicide. However, other illness-related factors contribute to morbidity rates in this population, including increased burden of medical illness (particularly cardiovascular disease), substance abuse, and accidents.

Comorbid Conditions

Comorbid psychiatric conditions are the rule rather than the exception in bipolar disorder, wherein upward of 60% of patients meet criteria for at least one comorbid Axis I disorder (Bauer et al., 2005). The most common comorbid classes of psychiatric disorder include substance use disorders (42%) and anxiety disorders (42%; most commonly panic disorder) (Sasson, Chopra, Harrari, Amitai, & Zohar, 2003).

Bipolar patients also experience general medical conditions at a higher rate than the general public. The metabolic syndrome, characterized by obesity, glucose dysregulation, and dyslipidemia, is present among 30% of adult patients with bipolar disorder, placing bipolar patients at increased risk for cardiovascular disease (Fagiolini, Frank, Scott, Turkin, & Kupfer, 2005). Biological, behavioral, and treatment-related factors, including sedentary lifestyle, unhealthy eating habits, suboptimal medical care, and negative effects of psychotropic medications are believed to contribute to the development of comorbid medical illness in individuals with bipolar disorder.

Models of Bipolar Disorder

Biological Factors

Bipolar disorder is among the most heritable of psychiatric conditions. The most powerful evidence for the contribution of genetics to susceptibility for bipolar disorder is evidence from twin studies. Recent studies report a 63% concordance rate among monozygotic twins and a 13% rate among dizygotic twins, with an overall heritability of 0.78 (where 1.0 is complete heritability) (Goodwin & Jamison, 2007b). Genetic linkage studies have identified multiple regions of potential interest on several chromosomes, including 4 and 18. More recently, results from genetic association studies implicate the role of the serotonin transporter gene and the brain-derived neurotrophic factor

(BDNF) (Neves-Pereira et al., 2002), although attempts to replicate these findings have been mixed. Taken together, these findings overwhelmingly indicate that bipolar disorder is a complex disorder characterized by genetic heterogeneity, such that several genes differentially contribute to risk for bipolar disorder across families.

Research has also focused on understanding the physiological mechanisms underlying bipolar disorder. Alterations in three primary neurotransmitter systems— serotonin, dopamine, and norepinephrine— have been widely studied, and attempts have been made to link these neurotransmitter deficits to drug mechanisms of action. Structural neuroimaging studies have identified decreased volume in multiple brain areas of individuals with bipolar disorder including the prefrontal cortex, basal ganglia, hippocampus, and anterior cingulate; functional neuroimaging studies show hypoactivity in the prefrontal cortex and hippocampus, and hyperactivity in the amygdala (Phillips, Drevets, Rauch, & Lane, 2003). These findings converge on a model in which brain dysfunction in bipolar disorder is characterized by dysregulation in those brain regions associated with emotion and reward sensitivity. As technology continues to advance, the clinical relevance of these findings may contribute to improved methods for diagnosis and treatment.

Psychosocial Factors

The lack of complete (i.e., 100%) concordance for bipolar disorder among monozygotic twins, as well as the wide-ranging heterogeneity observed in the course and presentation of bipolar disorder, have been cited as evidence for a contribution of environmental factors to bipolar disorder. Research has identified several psychosocial factors that contribute to risk, primarily involving the family environment and stressful life events. It is believed that these environmental stressors interact with biology in individuals with a biological diathesis for the disorder. Specifically, research indicates that individuals with bipolar disorder who return to stressful family environments characterized by criticism, hostility, and/or emotional overinvolvement (operationalized as Expressed Emotion) following hospitalization for an acute affective episode have been shown to be at increased risk for relapse over one-year follow-up (Butzlaff & Hooley, 1998). However, the directionality of this relationship is not yet well understood. It is possible that the stress of the family environment evokes symptoms in vulnerable individuals, that the strain of caring for a psychiatrically ill relative contributes to increased tension in the family, or alternatively, the relationship may be mediated by a third variable.

Retrospective studies also link life stress to episode onset and course in bipolar disorder. More stressful life events have consistently been described in the month preceding affective relapse among bipolar patients (Hunt, Bruce-Jones, & Silverstone, 1992). Furthermore, recovery from mood episodes triggered by stressful life events is prolonged, up to threefold, over those episodes not associated with life events (Johnson & Miller, 1997). Substantial evidence indicates that bipolar disorder is strongly linked to circadian functioning; thus, those life events with a disruptive effect on sleep/wake cycles, including pregnancy and childbirth, are associated with a particularly elevated risk for relapse.

Research suggests that life events are more strongly associated with relapse early in the course of illness (Swann et al., 1990). Some studies suggest the mechanism whereby this occurs is through activating a preexisting biological vulnerability. This is in accord with the kindling hypothesis (Post, 1992), which posits that episodes increase in frequency and duration over time, with diminishing importance of psychosocial stressors in the onset and course of the illness.

Treatment

Guidelines for the treatment of bipolar disorder recognize pharmacotherapy as an essential cornerstone of optimal treatment. Psychotherapy is also strongly recommended as an adjunct to medication management for the illness.

Pharmacotherapy

Mood-stabilizing medications serve as the foundation of pharmacotherapy for individuals with bipolar disorder. Such medications moderate acute affective symptoms and prevent future mood episodes of both mania and depression. For many years, lithium was the only FDA-approved option for the treatment of bipolar disorder. Effective for approximately 50% of patients, lithium can also be associated with undesirable side effects, including problems with the kidney and thyroid, and lithium treatment therefore warrants regular blood tests. In the 1990s, anticonvulsants including divalproex (Depakote) and carbamazepine (Tegretol) were found to have mood-stabilizing properties and began to be widely used for individuals with bipolar disorder who had difficulty tolerating lithium, were lithium nonresponsive, or had certain illness profiles deemed to be less lithium responsive (e.g., rapid cycling). More recently, the atypical neuroleptics, including olanzapine (Zyprexa), aripiprazole (Abilify), and quetiapine (Seroquel) have become widely used as first-line mood-stabilizing agents in bipolar disorder.

Unfortunately, mood-stabilizing medications appear to be more efficacious in the treatment and prevention of mania than depression. Thus, adjunctive antidepressants, most often selective serotonin reuptake inhibitors (SSRIs) are added to a mood stabilizer as a means of treating depressive symptoms. Antidepressant treatment in bipolar disorder should be undertaken with caution, as antidepressants can precipitate manic symptoms as well as accelerate mood cycling in up to half of bipolar

patients (Ghaemi, Boiman, & Goodwin, 2000). There is also evidence to support the use of electroconvulsive therapy (ECT) in bipolar depression for patients with treatment refractory depression. Experimental procedures including transcranial magnetic stimulation (tms) and vagus nerve stimulation (vns) also may hold promise for treatment-resistant bipolar depression, but further research is needed to understand the appropriate parameters for these treatments. Other common adjunctive medications include antipsychotics for the treatment of psychosis, agitation, and sleep difficulties and anxiolytics for the treatment of comorbid anxiety.

Treatment adherence has long been identified as a major clinical problem associated with bipolar disorder—in fact, among psychiatric populations, individuals being treated for bipolar illness rank among the least treatment adherent of all diagnostic groups. Studies examining nonadherence rates in bipolar illness report poor adherence in nearly 60% of patients. A substantive body of work has identified risk factors for nonadherence in bipolar illness, with four categories of adherence-related factors (Jamison, Gerner, & Goodwin, 1979): (1) illness-specific factors including comorbid substance abuse; (2) patient factors like negative feelings about having mood controlled by medicine and missing the "highs" of mania; (3) treatment factors consisting largely of unpleasant medication side effects like weight gain, cognitive dulling, and gastrointestinal upset; and (4) physician factors, in particular the extent to which the patient feels his/her treatment is a collaborative effort with the treatment team.

Psychotherapy

Bipolar disorder can be a debilitating, unpredictable disorder with symptoms that can wreak havoc on the lives of those afflicted and those close to them. Symptoms can profoundly affect relationships, occupational functioning, and financial well-being. Psychotherapy can be a valuable means of aiding bipolar patients to monitor symptoms and triggers, manage stressors, improve relationships, and work toward acceptance of the illness. It is through these avenues that psychotherapy is believed to help delay manic and depressive relapses, improve psychosocial functioning, and enhance medication adherence.

Recent data from the large multisite Systematic Treatment Enhancement for Bipolar Disorder (STEP-BD) trial indicate that three empirically validated intensive psychotherapy approaches for bipolar disorder are equally effective in hastening recovery from depression, increasing amount of time well, and enhancing overall psychosocial functioning, relationship functioning, and life satisfaction over a brief (three-session) psychoeducational intervention. These approaches include Family-Focused Therapy (FFT) (Miklowitz, George, Richards, Simoneau, & Suddath, 2003), which is a treatment model delivered with the family unit that includes psychoeducation, communication, and problem-solving skills; Interpersonal and Social Rhythm Therapy (IPSRT) (Frank, 2005), primarily an individual treatment approach in which the aim is to help patients achieve stability in daily social routines and sleep/wake cycles, as well as improve interpersonal functioning; and Cognitive Behavioral Therapy (CBT), in which the focus is on the interrelationship between thoughts, feelings, and behaviors (Otto & Reilly-Harrington, 2002).

In summary, bipolar disorder is a severe mental disturbance affecting mood, cognition, and behavior. The illness can have a profound deleterious effect on occupational, economic, interpersonal, and social functioning. Psychosocial stress impacts the course of the illness. Treatments, both pharmacological and psychotherapeutic, have been shown to ameliorate the negative outcomes associated with this condition.

REFERENCES

Bauer, M. S., Altshuler, L., Evans, D. R., Beresford, T., Williford, W., & Hauger, R. (2005). Prevalence and distinct correlates of anxiety, substance, and combined comorbidity in a multi-site public sector sample with bipolar disorder. *Journal of Affective Disorders, 85,* 301–315.

Butzlaff, R. L., & Hooley, J. (1998). Expressed emotion and psychiatric relapse: A meta-analysis. *Archives of General Psychiatry, 55,* 547–552.

Dardennes, R., Thuile, J., Even, C., Friedman, S., & Guelfi, J. (2006). The costs of bipolar disorder. *L'Encephale, 32,* 18–25.

Fagiolini, A., Frank, E., Scott, J., Turkin, S., & Kupfer, D. J. (2005). Metabolic syndrome in bipolar disorder: findings from the Bipolar Disorder Center for Pennsylvanians. *Bipolar Disorders, 7,* 424–430.

Frank, E. (2005). *Treating bipolar disorder: A clinician's guide to interpersonal and social rhythm therapy.* New York: Guilford Press.

Ghaemi, S. N., Boiman, E. E., & Goodwin, F. K. (2000). Diagnosing bipolar disorder and the effects of antidepressants: A naturalistic study. *Journal of Clinical Psychiatry, 61,* 804–808.

Goodwin, F. K., & Jamison, K. R. (2007a). Course and outcome. In F. K. Goodwin & K. R. Jamison (Eds.), *Manic-depressive illness* (2nd ed., pp. 119–154). New York: Oxford University Press.

Goodwin, F. K., & Jamison, K. R. (2007b). Genetics. In *Manic-depressive illness* (2nd ed., pp. 411–462). New York: Oxford University Press.

Hunt, N., Bruce-Jones, W., & Silverstone, T. (1992). Life events and relapse in bipolar affective disorder. *Journal of Affective Disorders, 25,* 13–20.

Jamison, K. R., Gerner, R. H., & Goodwin, F. K. (1979) Patient and physician attitudes toward lithium: Relationship to compliance. *Archives of General Psychiatry, 36,* 866–869.

Johnson, S., & Miller, I. (1997). Negative life events and time to recovery from episodes of bipolar disorder. *Journal of Abnormal Psychology, 106,* 449–457.

Miklowitz, D. J., George, E. L., Richards, J. A., Simoneau, T. L., & Suddath, R. L. (2003). A randomized study of family-focused psychoeducation and pharmacotherapy in the outpatient management of bipolar disorder. *Archives of General Psychiatry, 60,* 904–912.

Neves-Pereira, M., Mundo, E., Muglia, P., King, N., Macciardi, F., & Kennedy, J. L. (2002). The brain-derived neurotrophic factor gene confers susceptibility to bipolar disorder. *American Journal of Human Genetics, 71,* 651–655.

Otto, M. W., & Reilly-Harrington, N. A. (2002). Cognitive-behavioral therapy for the management of bipolar disorder. In S. G. Hoffman & M. Tompson (Eds.), *Treating chronic and severe mental disorders: A handbook of empirically supported interventions* (pp. 116–130). New York: Guilford Press.

Phillips, M. L., Drevets, W. C., Rauch, S. L., & Lane, R. (2003). The neurobiology of emotion perception II: Implications for major psychiatric disorders. *Biological Psychiatry, 54,* 515–528.

Post, R. M. (1992). Transduction of psychosocial stress into the neurobiology of recurrent affective disorder. *American Journal of Psychiatry, 149,* 999–1010.

Sasson, Y., Chopra, M., Harrari, E., Amitai, K., & Zohar, J. (2003). Bipolar comorbidity: From diagnostic dilemmas to therapeutic challenge. *International Journal of Neuropsychopharmacology, 6,* 139–144.

Swann, A. C., Secunda, S. K., Stokes, P. E., Croughan, J., Davis, J. M., Koslow, S. H., et al. (1990). Stress, depression and mania: Relationship between perceived role of stressful events and clinical and biochemical characteristics. *Acta Psychiatrica Scandinavica, 81,* 389–397.

SUGGESTED READINGS

Fawcett, J., Golden, B., & Rosenfeld, N. (2000). *New hope for people with bipolar disorder.* New York: Three Rivers Press.

Goodwin, F. K., & Jamison, K. R. (Eds.). (2007). *Manic-depressive illness* (2nd ed.). New York: Oxford University Press.

Jamison, K. R. (1995). *An unquiet mind.* New York: A.A. Knopf.

TINA R. GOLDSTEIN
University of Pittsburgh

***See also:* Mood Disorders**

BIRTH ORDER

Birth order has often been viewed as an important determinant of personality. In the early 1900s, the psychoanalyst Alfred Adler argued that birth order influences parental care directed toward, and the dynamics among, siblings. According to Adler, firstborns receive a favoured position from parents. However, in multiple sibling households, firstborns must also contend with feelings of being "dethroned" as parental attention is diverted towards younger siblings. Middle-borns, particularly second-borns, may struggle with the feeling of inferiority as they compete with their older, stronger rivals. Last-borns may be pampered, spoiled, and may need to deal with constant upward comparisons. As a result, they may seek situations, including careers, where they try to forge a unique identity.

Early birth-order research, including those studies attempting to test Adler's theory, were often fraught with methodological problems (e.g., confounds such as family size) and the results were, at best, mixed. Indeed, influential literature reviews suggested that reliable birth order effects did not exist. By the early 1970s, birth order began to fall out of favor as an explanation of development of psychological variation.

There has been a resurgence of interest, however, in birth-order effects. This renewed interest is in part because better methodological techniques (e.g., meta-analysis) have recently been applied to old data, but also because new theories have been forwarded to explain birth-order effects. For example, Zajonc (e.g., 1976) theorized that firstborns develop higher IQs because they may have enriched intellectual environments stemming from their early formative years being spent primarily with adults, whereas later-borns may have a mixed intellectual environment with both adults and other children (other siblings) during their formative years. Zajonc's "confluence model" of sibling development has received some support (Kristensen & Bjerkedal, 2007; Rodgers, Cleveland, Van den Oord, & Rower, 2000). Sulloway (1996) has theorized that later-borns are less likely to receive favored parental resources and are prone to fulfill unconventional niches; thus, they are "born to rebel," which is also the title of his popular book on birth order. In support of his theory, Sulloway has provided historical evidence that later-born scientists (e.g., Charles Darwin) were more open to radical paradigm shifts in science. He has also re-analyzed a large amount of data collected in the 1960s and 1970s and found evidence for birth-order effects on personality. For example, there is evidence that later-borns score higher on the Big-Five factor of Openness to Experience but lower on Conscientiousness (the other factors are Extraversion, Agreeableness, and Neuroticisim).

Part of the recent resurgence of interest in birth order has occurred because there is evidence that sibling variables predict human variation beyond traditionally defined personality, including sexual orientation. Building on early work by Eliot Slater and others suggesting that birth order may predict men's sexual orientation, Blanchard and Bogaert (1996) have demonstrated that gay men have a higher number of older brothers (but not older sisters) than heterosexual men. This older brother (or Fraternal Birth Order) effect is not large and does not apply to women's sexual orientation, but it is a reliable effect, having been found in numerous samples from different time periods and in different countries. Recent evidence (Bogaert, 2006) suggests that

this effect is not likely to result from family or rearing dynamics, but instead results from gestational changes that occur in a mother's womb as a result of her carrying previous male fetuses. This evidence adds to other recent research suggesting that biological factors (e.g., prenatal influences) may play an important role in sexual orientation development.

Research on birth order is likely to continue, but one of the challenges is in detecting potentially declining effects in recent samples, as many modern societies continue to have very low birth rates. For example, in modern China, as a result of strict government intervention, most families have only one child. These demographic trends may have implications for the development of human personality and other psychological variations. This leads one to wonder if there will be any later-born children left to rebel.

REFERENCES

Blanchard, R., & Bogaert, A. F. (1996). Homosexuality in men and number of older brothers. *American Journal of Psychiatry, 153,* 27–31.

Bogaert, A. F. (2006). Biological versus nonbiological older brothers and men's sexual orientation. *Proceedings of the National Academy of Sciences (PNAS), 103,* 10771–10774.

Kristensen, P., & Bjerkedal, T. (2007). Explaining the relation between birth order and intelligence. *Science, 316,* 1717.

Rodgers, J. L., Cleveland, H. H., van den Oord, E., & Rowe, D. (2000). Resolving the debate over birth order, family size, and intelligence. *American Psychologist, 55,* 599–612.

Sulloway, F. J. (1996). *Born to rebel: Birth order, family dynamics, and creative lives.* New York: Pantheon Books.

Zajonc, R. B. (1976). Family configuration and intelligence. *Science, 19,* 227–236.

SUGGESTED READING

Puts, D. A., Jordan, C. L., & Breedlove, S. M. (2006). O brother, where art thou? The fraternal birth-order effect on male sexual orientation. *The Proceedings of the National Academy of Sciences, USA, 103,* 10531–10532.

ANTHONY F. BOGAERT
Brock University, St. Catharines, Canada

See also: Sibling Relationships

BISEXUALITY

Bisexuality is a sexual orientation characterized by attraction to members of more than one sex. Often, bisexuality is thought of as attraction to both men and women; however, neither sex (i.e., biological and chromosomal traits that determine whether a person is male or female) nor gender (i.e., socially constructed behaviors and traits associated with femininity and masculinity) are always dichotomous. As with other sexual orientations (i.e., heterosexual, lesbian, gay), a bisexual orientation is an enduring pattern of attraction, sexual behavior, emotional affection, social contacts, and personal identity oriented toward individuals of more than one sex.

Research on bisexual individuals lags behind research on lesbian women and gay men. Although the research base is small in comparison, there is a growing interest in bisexual issues, and the literature does provide insights into the unique issues faced by bisexual individuals. In general, the literature suggests that bisexual individuals are different from both lesbian/gay individuals and heterosexual individuals. One unique concern that bisexual individuals face is social disapproval and inaccurate stereotypes from both heterosexual and lesbian/gay communities.

Numerous stereotypes concerning bisexuality exist. Bisexuality is often thought of as not existing, the stereotype being that bisexuality is simply a stepping stone on the way to a gay or lesbian identity or a lapse in an otherwise heterosexual identity. As such, bisexual identity is seen as illegitimate and nonexistent. Another common stereotype is that bisexual individuals are incapable of maintaining monogamous relationships because of a need for sexual partners of more than one sex. Finally, as with lesbian/gay individuals, there exists a belief that bisexual individuals are mentally ill, deviant, and/or unhealthy. The psychological research refutes all these stereotypes. Early sexuality studies, such as those conducted by Kinsey and by Masters and Johnson, found that the prevalence of bisexuality was equal to or greater than the prevalence of homosexuality. More recent research has demonstrated similar findings. Regarding monogamy, research has revealed that bisexual individuals engage in monogamous relationships and that those relationships are long-lasting. Only small numbers of bisexual individuals report being romantically involved with both men and women simultaneously. However, Weinberg, Williams, and Pryor (1994) found that a higher proportion of bisexual individuals were engaged in nonmonogamous relationships than lesbian women, gay men, and heterosexual women and men. Finally, research has demonstrated healthy psychological functioning among bisexual individuals.

Erroneous stereotypes of bisexual individuals are held by both heterosexual and lesbian/gay individuals. Inaccurate views of and negative feelings and thoughts toward bisexual individuals are important components of biphobia. Biphobia, similar to homophobia, refers to fear, hatred, or intolerance of bisexual individuals. Because both heterosexual and lesbian/gay communities report biphobia, bisexual individuals are in the unique position of simultaneously residing in both communities but lacking acceptance by either. Because both communities hold biphobic attitudes, bisexual individuals may experience discrimination from not one, but two communities. This dual discrimination can serve as a unique stressor in the lives of bisexual individuals. Moreover, because of the widespread stereotype of the nonexistence of bisexuality, bisexual individuals may not have an identified community or visible role models from whom to receive support.

The unique societal standing of bisexual individuals and subsequent stressors can create challenges to the development of a healthy bisexual identity. Research on bisexual identity has suggested that bisexual individuals develop a bisexual identity by progressing through certain stages. Three models of bisexual identity development have been explicated in the literature (see Bradford, 2004; Brown, 2002; Weinberg et al., 1994). These three models overlap to some extent, and each contains a focus on the unique role that a lack of societal support for bisexual identity plays in development. Moreover, the authors of these theories note that bisexual identity development is unique from lesbian/gay identity development.

The Weinberg et al. (1994) model was developed first, followed by Brown (2002). Both are both presented in four stages. The first stage in both is *Initial Confusion*. In this stage, individuals feel conflict and anxiety about their attractions and may identify as either heterosexual or lesbian or gay, while feeling that neither is fully accurate. Individuals may inhibit acting upon same-sex attractions. Finally, individuals may be confused about or unaware of the concept of bisexuality. The second stage in both models is *Finding and Applying the Label*. In this stage, individuals discover the label of bisexual and realize that it is more appropriate than labels of lesbian/gay or heterosexual; they are then able to apply that label to themselves. The third stage in both models is *Settling into the Identity*. In this stage, individuals' acceptance of a bisexual identity is more salient and may be accompanied by seeking out social networks that are supportive of individuals' bisexual identity. In this stage, individuals begin to see their bisexual identity as stable rather than transitory.

The final stage of bisexual identity development differs between the Weinberg et al. (1994) and Brown (2002) models. The final stage in the Weinberg et al. model is *Continued Uncertainty*. This stage is characterized by lingering doubt concerning the validity and/or stability of a bisexual identity. Because of widespread societal disapproval of bisexuality, individuals in this stage may have confusion about their identity. Additionally, individuals may feel the need to diminish the importance of their attractions to one sex when they are involved in a monogamous relationship (e.g., an individual who is in a same-sex romantic relationship may diminish his or her other-sex attractions). The final stage in Brown's model is *Identity Maintenance*.

Individuals in this stage may still question their bisexual identity from time to time; however, most will continue to embrace the label of bisexual regardless of the sex of their partner. Bradford's (2004) model has many similarities to the other two but focuses on social advocacy and downplays uncertainty in the later stages.

Despite the presence of biphobia in bisexual individuals' lives, many such individuals are able to develop healthy and stable bisexual identities with healthy psychological functioning. In addition, bisexual individuals report strengths and challenges in their romantic relationships that are similar to those of lesbian, gay, and heterosexual individuals.

REFERENCES

Bradford, M. (2004). The bisexual experience: Living in a dichotomous culture. *Journal of Bisexuality, 4,* 7–23.

Brown, T. (2002). A proposed model of bisexual identity development that elaborates on experiential differences of women and men. *Journal of Bisexuality, 2,* 67–91.

Weinberg, M. S., Williams, C. J., & Pryor, D. W. (1994). *Dual attraction: Understanding bisexuality.* New York: Oxford University Press.

SUGGESTED READINGS

Firestein, B. A. (Ed.). (1996). *Bisexuality: The psychology and politics of an invisible minority.* Thousand Oaks, CA: Sage.

Fox, R. C. (1995). Bisexual identities. In A. R. D'Augelli & C. J. Patterson (Eds.), *Lesbian, gay, and bisexual identities over the lifespan: Psychological perspectives* (pp. 48–86). New York: Oxford University Press.

NATHAN GRANT SMITH
McGill University

See also: Homosexuality; Lesbianism; Sexual Orientation and Gender Identity; Sexual Orientation, Roots of

BODY DYSMORPHIC DISORDER

Body Dysmorphic Disorder (BDD) is characterized by extreme body image dissatisfaction. The disorder was first described in 1886 as dysmorphophobia in the European medical literature, but not officially included as a distinct diagnosis in the *Diagnostic and Statistical Manual* (DSM) of the American Psychiatric Association until 1987. According to the DSM-IV-R, diagnostic criteria include (1) a preoccupation with an imagined or slight appearance defect; if slight defect is apparent, the person's concern is extreme; (2) the preoccupation results in significant distress or impairment in social, occupational, or other areas of functioning; and (3) the preoccupation is not due to another psychiatric disorder (e.g., anorexia nervosa). A diagnosis of Delusional Disorder, Somatic Type can also be applied to persons who hold their distorted beliefs with delusional intensity. BDD is currently categorized as Somatoform Disorder, although it has been argued that it is more appropriately classified as an obsessive-compulsive spectrum disorder or an affective spectrum disorder.

Prevalence

BDD is estimated to affect 1%–2% of the general population. In community samples, rates range from 0.7% to 3%. Among high school and college students, 2%–5% meet criteria for BDD. Rates of BDD are higher in cosmetic surgery and dermatology populations; studies suggest that 5%–15% of those patients meet diagnostic criteria for BDD.

Etiological Factors

The development of BDD is likely influenced by many factors. Studies suggest that BDD may run in families, and the disorder appears to be more common in families of persons with OCD. Neurobiological abnormalities, such as deficits in verbal and nonverbal memory skills and organizational strategies and encoding abilities; abnormalities in the frontal-striatal and dopaminergic systems; and deficiencies in the parietal region of the brain have been noted in persons with BDD.

Cognitive, behavioral, and sociocultural factors are also thought to play a role in the etiology of BDD. Cognitive factors may include selective attention to "defects" and misinterpretations of others' facial expressions. Behavioral factors include positive or intermittent reinforcement of appearance features and social learning (e.g., observing the importance of appearance from peers). Sociocultural factors, such as being raised in a family that is neglectful or abusive, being the target of appearance-related teasing, and exposure to unrealistic images of physical beauty in the mass media have also been implicated.

Clinical and Demographic Features

BDD typically begins during adolescence. It appears to affect women and men with equal frequency. Persons with BDD typically report preoccupation with the skin, hair, and nose, although any body part can become a source of preoccupation. Concerns can be specific or vague, and they may shift from one body part to another. Body-part preoccupation varies by gender. Men commonly report concerns with their genitals, height, hair, and body-build, while women describe preoccupation with their weight, hips, legs, and breasts.

Symptoms of the disorder can develop gradually or suddenly. Symptom severity varies over time but is typically chronic. Most individuals with BDD experience obsessive thoughts about their appearance. Level of insight is typically poor; however, it can vary from good insight to delusional thinking over the course of the disorder. Persons with delusional BDD appear to have more severe symptoms and functional impairment compared to those with the nondelusional variant.

BDD is also characterized by compulsive behaviors that often consume inordinate amounts of time and impair functioning. These behaviors are performed in order to inspect or improve the "defect." Examples include excessive grooming; mirror-checking requests for reassurance about appearance; skin picking; and camouflaging "defects" with make-up, body positions, or clothing. Although intended to reduce stress, these behaviors actually increase preoccupation and in some instances can actually damage skin or other body parts over time.

BDD is typically associated with significant impairment and suffering. Self-esteem and quality of life tend to be poor. Some individuals with BDD become housebound. Up to 78% of persons with BDD experience suicidal ideation, and 17%–33% attempt suicide over the course of the disorder. Despite this suffering, most individuals with BDD do not seek treatment until their early thirties. Complete symptom remission is rare, even with treatment. Severe symptoms of long duration and comorbid personality disorders are associated with reduced likelihood of remission.

Comorbidity

Persons with BDD typically experience comorbid psychiatric disorders, most commonly, depression. Other common co-occurring disorders include obsessive-compulsive disorder, social phobia, substance use disorders, eating disorders, and personality disorders. Because of the high rates of comorbidity, BDD is frequently misdiagnosed. The reluctance of sufferers to share their concerns with others, namely because of fear that their concerns will be trivialized, also contributes to misdiagnosis.

Treatment of BDD

Because individuals with BDD believe that their appearance "defects" are responsible for their distress, many seek cosmetic treatments to address their problems. Studies that have examined cosmetic treatments in persons with BDD suggest that up to 76% seek and 66% receive such treatments, including cosmetic surgery (e.g., rhinoplasty) and dermatological treatments (e.g., acne medications). Unfortunately, these treatments rarely improve symptoms and typically lead to no change in symptom severity. In some cases, cosmetic treatments can exacerbate BDD symptoms. Despite the likelihood of poor outcomes, patients often engage in doctor shopping until they find a provider who will agree to treat them. Some even attempt to perform do-it-yourself cosmetic procedures. Patients with BDD have also threatened and/or enacted lawsuits and physical violence toward their treatment providers.

Psychological and psychiatric treatments are more appropriate and effective treatments for BDD. Cognitive behavior therapy has been found to be an effective treatment for BDD. Selective serotonin reuptake inhibitor (SSRI) antidepressants also appear to be effective. However, patients may require long trials or higher doses in order to obtain symptom improvements. Antipsychotic medications alone do not appear to be effective treatments for delusional or nondelusional BDD.

BDD is a relatively common disorder that can result in significant distress and impaired functioning. Neurobiological, cognitive, behavioral, and social factors appear to play a role in the onset and maintenance of this disorder. BDD typically co-occurs with other psychiatric disorders, particularly depression and anxiety disorders. Persons with BDD frequently pursue cosmetic treatments to correct their perceived defects; however, such treatments rarely improve symptoms. Cognitive-behavioral therapy and psychopharmacologic treatments appear to be more effective in reducing the obsessive appearance-related thoughts and compulsive behaviors that characterize this disorder.

SUGGESTED READINGS

Crerand, C. E., Franklin, M. E., & Sarwer, D. B. (2006). Body dysmorphic disorder and cosmetic surgery. *Plastic and Reconstructive Surgery, 118,* 167e–180e.

Crerand, C. E., Phillips, K. A., Menard, W., & Fay C. (2005). Non-psychiatric medical treatment of body dysmorphic disorder. *Psychosomatics, 46,* 549–555.

Phillips, K. A. (1996). *The broken mirror: Understanding and treating body dysmorphic disorder.* New York: Oxford University Press.

Phillips, K. A. (2004). Treating body dysmorphic disorder using medication. *Psychiatric Annals, 34,* 945–953.

Phillips, K. A., Menard, W., Fay, C., & Weisberg, R. (2005). Demographic characteristics, phenomenology, comorbidity, and family history in 200 individuals with body dysmorphic disorder. *Psychosomatics: Journal of Consultation Liaison Psychiatry, 46,* 317–325.

Sarwer, D. B., Crerand, C. E. (2008). Body dysmorphic disorder and appearance enhancing medical treatments. *Body Image, 5,* 50–58.

CANICE E. CRERAND
Children's Hospital of Philadelphia

DAVID B. SARWER
University of Pennsylvania School of Medicine

***See also:* Somatoform Disorders**

BOGARDUS SOCIAL DISTANCE SCALE

The Bogardus Social Distance Scale was an early technique for measuring attitudes toward racial and ethnic groups. The basic concept behind the Bogardus scale is that the more prejudiced an individual is against a particular group, the less that person will wish to interact with members of that group (R. M. Dawes, 1972). Thus, the items that compose a Bogardus scale describe relationships into which a respondent might be willing to enter with a member of the specified cultural group (e.g., spouse, friend, neighbor, co-worker, citizen, visitor to our country). Items are worded in terms of inclusion or exclusion. "Would you accept an 'X' as a spouse?" is an example of an inclusion question and "Would you keep all 'Ys' out of America?" is an example of an exclusion question. The attitude or esteem with which the respondent holds the specified group is defined as the closeness of relationship that the respondent reports as being willing to accept with a member of that group.

In Bogardus's (1928) early work, he found that White Americans maintained relatively small social distances to groups such as the British, Canadians, and Northern Europeans, but greater social distances to Southern Europeans. Groups that differed racially (e.g., Blacks and Asians) were subject to even larger social distances. Extending the use of the Bogardus scales, H. C. Triandis and L. M. Triandis (1960) used multifactor experimental designs to separate the independent effects of varying aspects of group membership (e.g., race, religion, and occupation). They later (1962) showed that various aspects of group membership of the respondents interact with the social distances they assign various other groups. Thus, Americans were found to consider race an important variable while Greeks considered religion to be more critical.

Personality factors such as dogmatism have also been shown to be related to one's proclivity to desire relatively large social distances with groups other than one's own. The Bogardus scale is a type of Guttman scale. Thus, someone willing to accept members of a certain group as friends would also be willing to accept them as neighbors, co-workers, fellow citizens, and all other more distant relationships. While the responses of some individuals do occasionally reverse the rank-ordered nature of the items, average responses of groups (e.g., cultural or racial groups) tend to maintain the order in a well-constructed Bogardus scale (H. C. Triandis & L. M. Triandis, 1965). Hence, the Bogardus approach to attitude measurement is an effective means of estimating the esteem with which one group is held by other distinct groups.

Although the Bogardus approach to measuring attitudes between and among groups is primarily of historical importance, it has continued to be used in recent years and is sometimes still employed to assess attitudes in the sense of social distances among both ethnic and racial groups as has been the case historically, and among various psychologically defined groups and groups representing those with various disabilities (see Eisenman, 1986 or Tolor & Geller, 1987).

REFERENCES

Bogardus, E. S. (1928). *Immigration and race attitudes*. Boston: Heath.

Dawes, R. M. (1972). *Fundamentals of attitude measurement*. New York: John Wiley & Sons.

Eisenman, R. (1986). Social distance ratings toward Blacks and the physically disabled. *College Student Journal, 20*, 189–190.

Kleg, M., & Yamamoto, K. (1998). As the world turns: Ethno-racial distances after 70 years. *Social Science Journal, 35*, 183–190.

Triandis, H. C., & Triandis, L. M. (1960). Race, social class, religion and nationality as determinants of social distance. *Journal of Abnormal and Social Psychology, 61*, 110–118.

Triandis, H. C., & Triandis. L. M. (1962). A cross-cultural study of social distance. *Psychological monographs, 76*, No. 540.

Triandis, H. C., & Triandis, L. M. (1965). Some studies of social distance. In Steiner, I. D. and Fishbein, M. (Eds.), *Current studies in social psychology*. New York: Holt, Rinehart and Winston.

SUGGESTED READINGS

Adler, L. L. (1985). Projected social distances as an indicator of attitudes. In Pedersen, P. (Ed.), *Handbook of cross-cultural counseling and therapy* (247–255). Westport, CT: Greenwood.

Law, S. G., & Lane, D. S. (1987). Multicultural acceptance by teacher education students: A survey of attitudes toward 12 ethnic and national groups and a comparison with 60 years of data. *Journal of Instructional Psychology, 14*, 3–9.

Tolor, A., & Geller, D. (1987). Psychologists' attitudes toward children having various disabilities. *Psychological Reports, 60*, 1177–1178.

KURT F. GEISINGER
University of Nebraska-Lincoln

See also: Attitudes; Prejudice and Discrimination

BONDING (See Attachment and Bonding)

BORDERLINE PERSONALITY DISORDER

Borderline Personality Disorder (BPD) is one of 10 personality disorders listed in the *Diagnostic and Statistical Manual-Text Revision* (DSM-IV-TR; American Psychiatric Association, 2000), the manual used by mental health professionals to diagnose mental disorders. BPD is considered a "cluster B" personality disorder. The cluster B identifier signifies a general pattern of behavior characterized by deficiencies in impulse control and affect regulation and is also known as the "dramatic-erratic" cluster. The diagnostic criteria listed in the DSM-IV-TR specific to BPD are as follows:

A pervasive pattern of instability of interpersonal relationships, self-image, and affects, and marked impulsivity beginning by early adulthood and present in a variety of contexts, as indicated by five (or more) of the following:

1. frantic efforts to avoid real or imagined abandonment

2. a pattern of unstable and intense interpersonal relationships characterized by alternating between extremes of idealization and devaluation

3. identity disturbance: markedly and persistently unstable self-image of sense of self

4. impulsivity in at least two areas that are potentially self-damaging (e.g., spending, sex, substance abuse, reckless driving, binge eating)

5. recurrent suicidal behaviors, gestures, or threats, or self-mutilating behavior

6. affective instability due to a marked reactivity of mood (e.g., intense episodic dysphoria, irritability, or anxiety usually lasting a few hours and only rarely more than a few days)

7. chronic feelings of emptiness

8. inappropriate, intense anger or difficulty controlling anger (e.g., frequent displays of temper, constant anger, recurrent physical fights)

9. transient, stress-related paranoid ideation or severe dissociative symptoms (American Psychiatric Association, 2000, p. 710)

BPD is the most prevalent personality disorder found in clinical settings. The prevalence of BPD is estimated to be 1–2% of the general population, with a 10% estimated prevalence in outpatient settings and a 15–20% estimated prevalence in inpatient settings (Trull, Stepp, & Durrett, 2003). The nature of the disorder, with its suicidal gestures, often intense emotional instability, unstable relationship patterns, frantic efforts to avoid abandonment, and transient psychotic symptoms, leads many clients with BPD to present for treatment to inpatient treatment facilities multiple times in a single year, even though they may be already receiving outpatient care. Compared to persons with other personality disorders, studies have shown that clients with BPD are significantly younger when they enter treatment, spend more time in individual therapy and psychiatric hospitals, and take psychotropic medications for a longer period of time. A higher percentage of BPD clients, compared to persons with other personality disorders, report a history of individual and group therapy, day and residential treatment, psychiatric hospitalization, participation in self-help groups, and use of psychotropic medications and use at higher volumes over a lifetime. Overall, these individuals use mental health services and inpatient services at a much higher rate than patients with other mental disorders (Zanarini, Frankenburg, Khera, & Bleichmar, 2001).

Theoretical conceptualizations of BPD have a rich history. The term "borderline" was originally introduced by Adolph Stern, who believed these individuals were on the "border" between neurosis and psychosis (Stern, 1938). Notions of this original conceptualization are often observed in clients with BPD, as they often function relatively well until confronted with a crisis or threat that results in a rapid breakdown of coping mechanisms. BPD conceptualizations also have roots in psychoanalytic theory, with the interest in the disorder gaining attention in the 1950s and solidifying in 1975 with Otto Kernberg's object relations approach to conceptualization. Kernberg's articulate use of developmental theory in explaining the etiology of BPD had a significant impact on how the disorder is conceptualized today. Early editions of the DSM drew from these developmental conceptualizations as diagnostic formulations of the disorder were created. As the DSM-IV-TR notes, personality disorders have a stable and persistent pattern that can be traced back to adolescence or early adulthood and that speaks to the developmental nature of these disorders. This is likely most applicable to BPD.

As a result of these early theoretical conceptualizations and ongoing clinical emphasis on development in BPD, research has often focused on developmental pathways that may influence the etiology of BPD. Of the 10 personality disorders, BPD has received the most attention in this regard. Conceptualizations of developmental pathways opened the door to risk factor research that helped support the notion that childhood development and experiences may have a significant impact on the development of the disorder. A number of researchers have investigated developmental antecedents to BPD and found that the childhood histories of clients with BPD are often characterized by inconsistent or neglectful parenting, disturbed or overinvolved parenting, early parental separation or loss, incest, and sexual, and/or physical abuse (Liotti & Pasquini, 2000; Paris, 1997, 1998; Zanarini, 2000).

Such histories provide the foundation for insecure attachment mechanisms that have been associated with a variety of dysfunctional behaviors and emotional states that arise in clients with BPD. As a result, some researchers have characterized BPD as a "disorder of attachment" (Bender, Farber, & Geller, 2001; Fonagy, Target, & Gergely, 2000; Nickell, Waudlby, & Trull, 2002). Although developmental theories have been the primary school of thought in understanding the disorder, the technological advances in genetic and biological mechanisms have recently contributed additional etiological conceptualizations. There is limited but promising evidence that suggests some role of genetic and biological markers in the development of the disorder. Genetic and biological contributions have the potential to provide a good balance to developmental conceptualizations, because there are always exceptions to the rule. Not all individuals with developmental deprivation develop the disorder, and there are some instances in which the disorder develops in the absence of such backgrounds or history.

Due to its prevalence in clinical populations and scholarly research, BPD is not without its controversy. As the DSM-IV-TR states, the substantial majority (75%) of clients diagnosed with BPD are women, and other research has indicated that the diagnosis is applied disproportionately in nonwhite racial groups. This has led multicultural and feminist scholars to question whether or not the diagnosis, in some cases, may reflect bias in either the conceptualization of the disorder or the application of the criteria to clients. Such scholars argue that symptoms of BPD are actually signs of traumatic stress related to repeated and prolonged experiences of oppression and victimization (Herman, 1992) and that, accordingly, the stigma of the BPD diagnosis (or any diagnosis that disregards cultural nuances) contributes an additional layer of oppression to such groups.

Treatment efficacy and effectiveness with BPD clients have been mixed. As noted earlier, clients with BPD utilize mental health services at a higher rate than persons with other disorders, which suggests that in many cases BPD clients relapse more frequently and severely than other clients and that BPD is difficult to treat. Pharmaceutical treatments like mood stabilizers, antidepressants, and antipsychotics have been somewhat effective in treating affective instability, anger, hostility, and some symptoms of depression. However, such treatments are often complicated by medication noncompliance and the frequency of crisis states common in BPD clients.

Behavioral treatments have also shown some promise in efficacy and effectiveness studies. Most notably, dialectical-behavior therapy (DBT; Linehan, 1993) was the first treatment approach to document sustained improvement in BPD symptoms in controlled studies. The treatment follows a largely cognitive-behavioral framework, utilizing homework assignments and psychoeducational interventions within the context of an accepting, validating therapeutic stance. However, despite treatment advances, more than persons with other personality disorders, clients with BPD present a tremendous treatment challenge for mental health professionals. They are typically characterized as treatment resistant and difficult to work with. As a result, some mental health professionals avoid working with these clients because of the time and emotional investment that is perceived to be required. Others may provide only minimal support to them in treatment settings in order to manage emotional boundary violations common with the disorder. Unfortunately, these practices often compete with the client's overwhelming need for treatment and likely perpetuate the likelihood they will require more treatment in the future.

REFERENCES

American Psychiatric Association. (2000). *Diagnostic and statistical manual of mental disorders* (4th ed., text rev.). Washington, DC: Author.

Bender, D. S., Farber, B. A., and Geller, J. D. (2001). Cluster B personality traits and attachment. *Journal of the American Academy of Psychoanalysis, 29*, 551–563.

Fonagy, P., Target, M., & Gergely, G. (2000). *Attachment and borderline personality disorder: A theory and some evidence.* The Psychiatric Clinics of North America, 23, 103–122.

Herman, J. L. (1992). *Trauma and recovery.* New York: Basic Books.

Kernberg, O. F. (1975). *Borderline conditions and pathological narcissism.* New York: Jason Aronson.

Linehan, M. M. (1993). *Skills training manual for treating borderline personality disorder.* New York: Guilford Press.

Liotti, G., & Pasquini, P. (2000). Predictive factors for borderline personality disorder: Patients' early traumatic experiences and losses suffered by the attachment figure. *Acta Psychiatrica Scandinavia, 102*, 282–289.

Nickel, A. D., Waudby, C. J., & Trull, T. J. (2002). Attachment, parental bonding, and borderline personality disorder features in young adults. *Journal of Personality Disorders, 16*, 148–159.

Paris, J. (1998). Does childhood trauma cause personality disorders in adults? *Canadian Journal of Psychiatry, 43*, 148–153.

Paris, J. P. (1997). Childhood trauma as an etiological factor in the personality disorders. *Journal of Personality Disorders, 11*, 34–49.

Stern, A. (1938). Psychoanalytic investigation of and therapy in the borderline group of neuroses. *Psychoanalytic Quarterly, 7*, 467–489.

Trull, T. J. (1995). Borderline personality disorder features in nonclinical young adults: 1. Identification and validation. *Psychological Assessment, 7*, 33–41.

Trull, T. J., Stepp, S. D., & Durrett, C. A. (2003). Research on borderline personality disorder: An update. *Current Opinion in Psychiatry, 16*, 77–82.

Zanarini, M. C. (2000). Childhood experiences associated with the development of borderline personality disorder. *Psychiatric Clinics of North America, 23*, 89–101.

Zanarini, M. C., Frankenburg, F. R., Khera, G. S., & Bleichmar, J. (2001). Treatment histories of borderline patients. *Comprehensive Psychiatry, 42*, 144–150.

SUGGESTED READING

Sherry, A., & Whilde, M. (2008). Borderline personality disorder. In M. Hersen & J. Rosqvist (Eds.), *Handbook of assessment, conceptualization, and treatment.* Hoboken, NJ: John Wiley & Sons.

ALISSA SHERRY
University of Texas at Austin

See also: **Attachment Disorders; Personality Disorders**

BOREDOM AND BOREDOM PRONENESS

Boredom is a state most people experience at one time or another. Many cultures have words that refer to experiences consistent with boredom: "ennui" (French), "Langeweile" (German), "malal" and "dajira" (Arabic), "khaali" (Hindi), "bosan" (Indonesian), "na buwa" (Taiwanese), "taikutsu" (Japanese), "jidooham (Korean), and "wuliau" (Chinese). Whereas terms such as *boring, bored, or boredom* refer to a state or temporary conditions, *boredom proneness* refers to a trait-like condition or frequently reoccurring experience.

When used to describe a state condition, boredom is typically regarded as an unpleasant experience. States of boredom often arise in settings experienced as monotonous, repetitive, nonstimulating, or tiresome. Emotional, cognitive, and motivational components of boredom frequently consist of experiences such as dissatisfaction, disinterest, alienation, fatigue, apathy, tedium, weariness, emptiness, meaninglessness, deadness, or nothingness. Behavioral manifestations of boredom often include frequent yawning, glassy eyes, slumped posture, inactivity, passivity, distractibility, and facial expressions that convey a disconnection from one's environment. When bored, time is often experienced as passing slowly, and even relatively simple actions are perceived as requiring considerable effort. Impatience, fidgetiness, or agitation might accompany feelings of boredom, perhaps signaling an inclination to flee or escape from situations where boredom occurs. Boredom, however, is often associated with an uncertainty about what to do, perhaps contributing to a perception when bored of being trapped or "at loose ends." Physiologically, individuals who are bored frequently report being under-aroused, not alert, and cognitively dull.

Boredom proneness has been defined as "a tendency to experience tedium and lack of personal involvement and enthusiasm, to have a general or frequent lack of sufficient interest in one's life surroundings and future" (Sundberg, Latkin, Farmer, & Saoud, 1991, p. 210). This trait-like experience of boredom has been associated with a number of concerns, such as depressed mood, loneliness, hopelessness, irritability, anger, insecurity, procrastination, low persistence, impulsivity, pathological gambling, substance abuse, truancy, binge eating, social dependency, social skills deficits, narcissism, dissatisfaction in many spheres of life, low motivation, and an absence of goal- or value-directed behavior (e.g., Dahlen, Martin, Ragan, & Kuhlman, 2004; Farmer & Sundberg, 1986; Vodanovich, 2003). Chronic boredom associated with institutional settings has also been hypothesized to increase psychiatric symptomatology among persons with severe and persistent mental disorders (Todman, 2003). Others, such as Zuckerman (1979), have suggested that the unpleasant experience of boredom motivates some persons to seek out stimulation or highly arousing experiences as ways to terminate or decrease the intensity of this aversive condition.

There is some indication that boredom proneness is multidimensional, whereby facets of this construct share different associations with major dimensions of personality (Culp, 2006; Vodanovich, 2003). Two facets of boredom proneness that frequently emerge in factor analytic studies relate to internal stimulation (e.g., inability to generate interesting activities) and external stimulation (e.g., perception of low environmental stimulation) (Vodanovich, Wallace, & Kass, 2005). There is also an indication, in need of further study, that boredom proneness reaches its peak in adolescent and early adult years, and is comparatively low during advanced adulthood.

Theories of boredom and boredom proneness generally emphasize either external conditions or internal predispositions or characteristics. Boredom, for example, has been characterized as situation-dependent or situation-independent (Todman, 2003). Situation-dependent boredom is more strongly influenced by environmental features or conditions (e.g., repetitive or nonstimulating situations). Examples of environments regarded as high-risk for such forms of boredom include assembly lines or air traffic control centers. Situation-independent boredom, on the other hand, is regarded as a more chronic manifestation of boredom that is comparatively uninfluenced or unmodified by environmental contexts. Other theoretical models emphasize the interaction of environmental and personal variables in the influence of boredom. From an interactional perspective, boredom can be regarded as a motivational concept that links inner experiences with external environmental conditions. Csikszentmihalyi (1975) has proposed that boredom frequently arises in contexts where personal competencies exceed situational challenges or opportunities.

Whereas boredom and boredom proneness were little researched prior to 1985, research on these constructs has increased significantly in the last 25 years. This increased interest perhaps reflects growing awareness of the social and personal problems that frequently accompany boredom. The most frequently used full-scale measure of boredom proneness in research investigations is the Boredom Proneness (BP) scale (Farmer & Sundberg, 1986; see also Vodanovich, 2003). A shorter version of the BP scale includes items that perform similarly across diverse cultures (Sundberg et al., 1991). Examples of items from these measures include, "I am often trapped in situations where I have meaningless things to do" and "Unless I am doing something exciting, even dangerous, I feel half-dead and dull." These measures demonstrate satisfactory levels of reliability, and validity is supported by dozens of studies that demonstrate associations with variables hypothesized to be related to boredom proneness. Among the more frequent findings is the observation that men tend to score higher on boredom proneness measures than women (Sundberg et al., 1991), whereas the converse is generally true with measures of depressed mood.

Boredom and boredom proneness are incompatible with a number of experiences people frequently regard as pleasant or desirable, such as interest, enthusiasm, involvement, engagement, "flow," and optimal stimulation. Future research on boredom and boredom proneness might seek to integrate research findings specific to these experiences into larger theories of emotions.

REFERENCES

Csikszentmihalyi, M. (1975). *Beyond boredom and anxiety*. San Francisco: Jossey-Bass.

Culp, N. A. (2006). The relations of two facets of boredom proneness with the major dimensions of personality. *Personality and Individual Differences, 41,* 999–1007.

Dahlen, E. R., Martin, R. C., Ragan, K., & Kuhlman, M. M. (2004). Boredom proneness in anger and aggression: Effects of impulsiveness and sensation seeking. *Personality and Individual Differences, 37,* 1615–1627.

Farmer, R., & Sundberg, N. D. (1986). Boredom proneness—The development and correlates of a new scale. *Journal of Personality Assessment, 50,* 4–17.

Sundberg, N. D., Latkin, C. A., Farmer, R. F., & Saoud, J. (1991). Boredom in young adults: Gender and cultural comparisons. *Journal of Cross-Cultural Psychology, 22,* 209–223.

Todman, McW. (2003). Boredom and psychotic disorders: Cognitive and motivational issues. *Psychiatry, 66,* 146–167.

Vodanovich, S. J. (2003). Psychometric measures of boredom: A review of the literature. *Journal of Psychology, 137,* 569–595.

Vodanovich, S. J., Wallace, J. C., & Kass, S. J. (2005). A confirmatory approach to the factor structure of the Boredom Proneness Scale: Evidence for a two-factor short form. *Journal of Personality Assessment, 85,* 295–303.

Zuckerman, M. (1979). *Sensation seeking: Beyond the optimal level of arousal*. Hillsdale, NJ: Lawrence Erlbaum.

RICHARD F. FARMER
Oregon Research Institute

NORMAN D. SUNDBERG
University of Oregon

See also: **Depression**

BORING, EDWIN G. (1886–1968)

Edwin G. Boring studied psychology at Cornell University under the Structuralist, E. B. Titchener, and he received his doctorate in 1914. He went to Clark University in 1919 and moved to Harvard in 1922; he remained there for the rest of his career as a general experimental psychologist. He influenced many generations of students through his teaching of the introductory course in psychology at Harvard.

Although Boring accomplished some classical research on his own, most of his publications were theoretical. He served as Editor of *American Journal of Psychology* from 1920 until his death; he wrote many papers and editorials. Boring is best known for his histories of psychology. His *History of Experimental Psychology* was first published in 1929; the 1950 edition, a widely accepted classic, is still considered by many to be the outstanding history of psychology. The book's theme brought together the individual creative scientist and the *Zeitgeist*, or spirit of the times, and explained how interaction of the two influenced the direction of psychology.

One of Boring's early books, *The Physical Dimensions of Consciousness*, defined the basic psychological terms such as sensation, consciousness, and body-mind dualism. He theorized that the body-mind split was not necessary for psychology. In effect, Boring began to move away from Titchener's dualism towards monism, the belief that there is basically only one kind of reality.

Because of his long and distinguished career at Harvard and his general service to psychology through its organizations and institutions, Boring was popularly referred to as "Mr. Psychology."

SUGGESTED READINGS

Boring, E. G. (1933). *The physical dimensions of consciousness*. New York: Dover.

Boring, E. G. (1950). *A history of experimental psychology*. (2nd ed.). Englewood Cliffs, NJ: Prentice-Hall.

STAFF

BOSTON NAMING TEST

Although in clinical use for approximately 30 years (Kaplan, Goodglass, & Weintraub, 1978, 1983), the Boston Naming Test (BNT) continues to enjoy wide appeal and wide acceptance as the premier visual confrontational naming test for use in clinical (i.e., Alzheimer's Disease, stroke) and nonclinical populations (i.e., children, young adults). The BNT assesses visual naming ability via the use of black and white line drawings, and its appeal is reflected in translations into several languages (e.g., Chinese, Jamaican, Korean, Spanish, and French) and the development of various short forms of the original 85 item test (e.g., 60-, 30- and 15-item versions) that retain its original validity and reliability and continued ease of use, scoring, and interpretation of various neuropsychological processes related to language usage and language ability. As with other neuropsychological tests that have endured for so many years, the BNT enjoys a rich database of the effects of various demographic variables as well as extensive normative data across a wide age range (Strauss, Sherman, & Spreen, 2006).

Recently, one area of interest regarding the BNT is its use in issues related to ethnicity and acculturation (e.g., Ferraro, Bercier, Holm, & McDonald, 2002). The topic of cross-cultural neuropsychological assessment has taken center stage in discussions related to appropriate use of such tests as part of initial neuropsychological screening batteries in populations where no normative data exist. The rich history of the use of the BNT across regional, cultural, and ethnic boundaries is adding significantly to this discussion by showing the applicability, as well as the possible problems, in the use and adaptation of a standard neuropsychological test to various populations. At the same time, the construction, validation, and reliability of normative data from these various regional, cultural, and ethnic boundaries will be a central issue in the continued use of the BNT.

REFERENCES

Ferraro, F. R., Bercier, B., Holm, J., & McDonald, J. (2002). Preliminary normative data from a brief neuropsychological test battery in a sample of Native American elderly. In F. R. Ferraro (Ed.), *Minority and cross cultural aspects of neuropsychological assessment*. Bristol, PA: Swets & Zeitlinger.

Kaplan, E. F., Goodglass, H., & Weintraub, S. (1978, 1983). *The Boston Naming Test: Experimental edition (1978)*. Boston, MA: Kaplan & Goodglass. (2nd ed., Philadelphia, PA: Lea & Febiger).

Strauss, E., Sherman, E. M. S., & Spreen, O. (2006). Boston Naming Test-2 (BNT-2). In Strauss et al., (Eds.), *A compendium of neuropsychological tests: Administration, norms and commentary* (3rd Ed.). New York: Oxford University Press.

SUGGESTED READINGS

Gollan, T., Fenneman-Notestine, C., Montoya, R. I., & Jernigan, T. L. (2007). The bilingual effect on Boston Naming Test performance. *Journal of the International Neuropsychological Society, 13*, 197–208.

Tallberg, I. M. (2005). The Boston Naming Test in Swedish: Normative data. *Brain & Language, 94*, 19–31.

F. Richard Ferraro
Kristen Lowell
University of North Dakota

See also: Neuropsychology

BOWLBY, JOHN (1907–1990)

John Bowlby is known for his work on the ill effects of maternal deprivation on personality development and for formulating attachment theory as a way of conceptualizing a child's tie to the mother. The son of a London surgeon, he studied medicine and psychology at Cambridge, completed his medical training in London (1933), and specialized in child psychiatry and psychoanalysis. After five years as an Army psychiatrist, he joined the Tavistock Clinic and Tavistock Institute of Human Relations, where he worked full time (1946–1972) as a clinician, teacher, and researcher in child and family psychiatry.

Believing that the influence of children's real experiences with their parents has been greatly underestimated in accounting for personality disorders and neuroses, he selected the responses of very young children to brief or long separation from parents as a focus of research. Early publications included "Forty-four juvenile thieves" and *Maternal Care and Mental Health*, the latter contributing to radical changes in the care of children in hospitals and institutions.

In 1951, dissatisfied with existing psychological and psychoanalytic theorizing as a way of understanding children's social and emotional development, he began developing a new conceptual framework drawing on ethology, control theory, and, later, cognitive psychology, as well as psychoanalysis. Preliminary papers appeared in 1958–1963, followed by the trilogy, *Attachment and Loss* (1973, 1980). He worked with several influential colleagues including Robert A. Hinde and Mary D. S. Ainsworth.

SUGGESTED READINGS

Bowlby, J. (1950). *Maternal care and mental health*. New York: Schocken Books.

Bowlby, J. (1969). *Attachment and loss* (2nd Ed.). New York: Basic Books.

Bowlby, J. (1989). *The making and breaking of affectional bonds*. London & New York: Routledge.

Staff

BRAIN

The human brain is a complex aggregate of billions of cells working together to process stimuli, to monitor needs, and to direct behavior. Developmentally, the brain begins at the most rostral extension of the neural tube; it bends over and convolutes as it expands within the confines of the skull (cranium). The brain's expansion is disproportionate

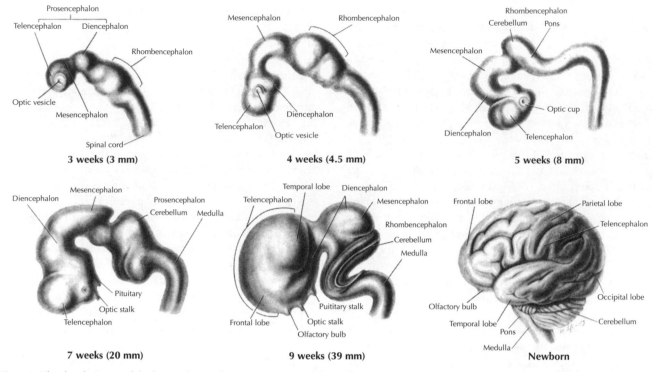

Figure 1. The development of the human brain, showing its major subdivisions.

relative to the growth of the spinal cord, the most caudal extension of the central nervous system. Figure 1 illustrates the development of the human brain, showing its major subdivisions.

There are three major sections of the brain: the prosencephalon or forebrain, the mesencephalon or midbrain, and the rhombencephalon or hindbrain. The forebrain is the largest and most expansive and is made up of two subdivisions: the telencephalon (endbrain) and the diencephalon (interbrain). Telencephalic structures account for about 75% of the weight of the entire human central nervous system. These structures include the two cerebral hemispheres that are connected by a mass of crossing of fiber tracts (called the corpus callosum). Smaller white matter bundles that form connections between the hemispheres include the anterior and posterior commissures. The surface of the hemispheres is a multicellular layer of brain tissue called the cerebral cortex, which varies in thickness from 1.5 millimeters to 4.5 millimeters. The cortex is divided into subregions according to gross neuroanatomical landmarks called sulci and gyri. The largest subregions are called lobes, of which there are four in each hemisphere: occipital, temporal, parietal, and frontal. The location of the four lobes and other major brain structures can be seen in Figures 1 and 2.

The occipital lobes have visual functions and can be divided into subregions based on the portions of visual space to which neurons contained in those subareas respond. The lateral surface of the temporal lobes is important for audition, and on the left side of the brain for understanding language. Medial regions of the temporal lobes are crucial for learning and memory functions, and ventral regions of the temporal lobes contribute to visual object recognition (including faces and words). The parietal lobes control somatosensory and visuospatial functions, and have been implicated in multimodal spatial integration, sensorimotor coordination, and more recently, in attentional switching and visual short-term memory. At the junction with the temporal lobe, the left parietal cortex is important for language comprehension. Frontal cortex is polysensory. It controls movement, and on the left side it controls language expression. The most anterior portion of the frontal lobes (prefrontal cortex) is considered to be the brain's "executive," and is important in social cognition, self-awareness, impulse control, emotional behavior, problem solving, attentional selection, and working memory.

In the cerebral hemispheres, the cortex has a laminar architecture with different neuronal cell types organized in layers. From an evolutionary standpoint, the layered cortical areas have changed in complexity across the phylogenetic scale. The most recently evolved brain areas (neocortex) typically have six defined neuronal layers, while phylogenetically older regions such as the hippocampus have fewer. In addition to neurons, the brain is composed of different types of supporting cells called neuroglia, including oligodendrocytes, microglia, and astrocytes. Oligodendrocytes are responsible for the myelination of nerve fibers (axons), which allows for faster transmission between neurons.

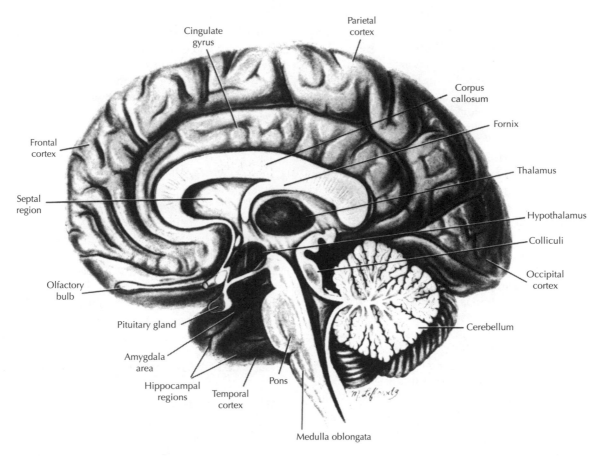

Figure 2. The location of the four lobes and other major brain structures of the adult brain.

Microglia have many functions including serving as macrophages. As such, microglia are thought to play a role in brain development following programmed cell death of neurons and to become activated following brain injury. Astrocytes, while initially thought only to provide neuronal scaffolding and to monitor homeostatis, more recently have been shown to have bidirectional signaling with neurons, demonstrating their important role in signal transmission throughout the brain (Squire et al., 2003; Allen & Barres, 2005).

Cortical nerve cell bodies collectively appear gray, thus accounting for the fact that cerebral cortex is commonly called "gray matter." Likewise, nerve fibers emanating from the cell bodies, because of their collective white appearance subcortically, have been referred to as "white matter." These fibers connect with other nerve cells that are aggregated in clusters often referred to as subcortical nuclei. In the telencephalon, these subcortical nuclei include the limbic system (including the septum, the amygdaloid complex, and the hippocampus) and nuclei of the basal ganglia (caudate, putamen, and globus pallidus). Septal and amygdala regions are intimately connected to each other and are important in emotional and motivational functions. The hippocampal region, which can be divided into the dentate gyrus, the hippocampus proper, and the subiculum, is important for memory formation and consolidation. The basal ganglia are concerned largely with various aspects of motor control, and have also been implicated in a number of other functions, including procedural learning and habit formation.

The cerebral hemispheres are attached to the diencephalon by massive fiber bundles known as the corona radiata. Major structural components present in the diencephalon include the thalamus, the subthalamus, the hypothalamus, and the epithalamus. The thalamus is the largest component of the diencephalon, and is considered a relay station for projections to cortical neurons from subcortical sensory nuclei. The subthalamus is located below the thalamus and is a way station between the thalamus and the cortex. The hypothalamus (literally, "under the thalamus") is made up of several subnuclei that play critical roles in autonomic, endocrine, and emotional regulation. The epithalamus, which contains the pineal body and the habenular complex, plays a role in endocrine function and the regulation of circadian rhythms (Nolte, 2002).

The middle section of the developing brain is called the mesencephalon or midbrain. At maturity, the mesencephalon resembles its early embryonic form more closely than do either the prosencephalon or the rhombencephalon. The mesencephalon is made up of three main parts, the tectum (containing auditory and visual relay stations called the inferior and superior colliculi), the tegmentum (containing the midbrain reticular formation that activates attention, the substantia nigra that subserves motor functions, and numerous other nuclear groups), and the crus cerebri (a descending bundle of fibers).

The third major section of the brain, part of which eventually exits into the spinal cord at the base of the skull, is the rhombencephalon or hindbrain. It is composed of two subparts, the metencephalon (consisting of the pons and cerebellum) and the myelencephalon (the medulla oblongata). The cerebellum (Latin for "little brain") is a prominent eminence containing more neurons than all other areas of the brain combined. It is subdivided into the vermis, the intermediate zones, and the cerebellar hemispheres. The cerebellum is the center for motor skills and postural adjustments, and it also is involved in certain types of cognitive and emotional activities (Schutter & van Honk, 2005; Schmahmann, 1997). The pons and medulla oblongata contain clusters of cranial nerve nuclei that connect the nerves going to and from the face and head. Because of the shape and position of the pons and medulla at the base of the brain, they often are referred to as the brain stem, although this term usually includes structures in the midbrain and lower diencephalon as well.

Embedded within the brain are four fluid-filled ventricles: two lateral ventricles (one in each hemisphere), the third ventricle, and the fourth ventricle. The lateral ventricles each reside in one of the cerebral hemispheres. The third ventricle is located near the diencephalon, and the fourth ventricle is near the pons and medulla. Cells within the lining of the ventricles produce cerebrospinal fluid (CSF), the clear liquid that fills these cavities. The CSF serves many functions in the brain, including protection from damage by providing a buffer during impact injuries, and removal of waste products from the brain. CSF is also contained within the meninges—the three protective coverings of the brain known as the dura mater, arachnoid, and pia mater.

The various components of the brain are interconnected through a very complicated network of neuronal pathways (Schmahmann & Pandya, 2006), and neurons are in continuous communication (through specialized chemicals called neurotransmitters). Nuclei within the brain seldom act autonomously. Instead, several nuclei and their fiber tracts may act together to organize and modulate complex behaviors, and through their interaction, form the basis for life. The functions subserved by these many diverse structures and systems are generally similar in all normal, healthy adults. Sensory systems regulate information coming from outside and inside the body; attentional systems not only keep us alert, but also allow us to ignore stimulus information that may be irrelevant, and to rest when we need to; motor systems regulate how we respond and move about; and emotional/motivational systems monitor drives, needs, and homeostasis. Other systems help us to learn and to remember or forget. Together, the functioning brain is essential to every aspect of life and consciousness.

REFERENCES

Allen, N. J., & Barres, B. A. (2005). Signaling between glia and neurons: Focus on synaptic plasticity. *Current Opinion in Neurobiology, 15*, 542–548.

Nolte, J. (2002). *The human brain: An introduction to its functional anatomy* (5th ed.). St. Louis: Mosby.

Schmahmann, J. D. (Ed.). (1997). *The cerebellum and cognition.* San Diego, CA: Academic Press.

Schmahmann, J. D., & Pandya, D. N. (2006). *Fiber pathways of the brain.* New York: Oxford University Press.

Schutter, D. J., & van Honk, J. (2005). The cerebellum on the rise in human emotion. *Cerebellum, 4*(4), 290–294.

Squire, L. R., Bloom, F. E., McConnell, S. K., Roberts, J. L., Spitzer, N. C., & Zigmond, M. J. (Eds.). (2003). *Fundamental neuroscience* (2nd ed.). San Diego, CA: Academic Press.

SUGGESTED READINGS

Haines, D. E. (2008). *Neuroanatomy: An atlas of structures, sections, and systems* (7th ed.). Philadelphia: Wolters Kluwer Health/Lippincott Williams & Wilkins.

Nolte, J. (2002). *The human brain: An introduction to its functional anatomy* (5th ed.). St. Louis: Mosby.

Ramachandran, V. S. (Ed.). (2002). *Encyclopedia of the human brain.* San Diego, CA: Academic Press.

Marlene Oscar-Berman
Susan M. Mosher
*Boston University School of Medicine,
and Department of Veterans Affairs
Healthcare System, Boston Campus*

See also: **Central Nervous System; Neocortex; Primary Motor Cortex**

BRAIN DEVELOPMENT

Unlike the predominant conceptions from a few decades back, brain development is currently understood to be an active, dynamic process, involving complex interactions between a person's biological predispositions, physical environment, and social nurturance. Rather than a hard-wired, purely genetically programmed system, children's experiences actively organize their brain over time, in accordance with biological principles and constraints (Johnson, 2001). In turn, children's own neuropsychological profiles of strengths and weaknesses shapes the way they perceive and behave in the world. As they grow and develop, physiological and sociocultural processes work together in intricate, nuanced patterns to sculpt their brain's development.

From the beginning, the brain grows as a dynamic system, with prolific growth of neurons that organize themselves into multiple, interconnected structures that form networks for action in the world and regulation of the body. For example, during prenatal growth a layer of growth cells creates huge numbers of neurons, which organize themselves into six layers of the cortex of the brain. As children live, act, and grow, their experiences shape the structure and function of complex networks of brain areas, creating cognitive, social, and emotional skills for understanding and acting in the world. The development of these skills is dynamic, with characteristic fluctuations in skill level depending on the emotional, social, cognitive and physical context in which the person is acting.

For example, as a baby learns to crawl, neural networks connecting the frontal, parietal, and occipital brain areas responsible for coordinating motor, somatosensory, and visual information show a large spurt in coherence of the electroencephalogram (EEG), a measure of connection between components (Bell & Fox, 1996). That is, as the child grapples to master the skill of crawling, electrical activity produced by the neurons in these distant brain regions becomes increasingly synchronized, a process that is thought to reflect the growth of a neural network by which neurons in motor and sensory cortices can connect with and influence each other in order for the infant to crawl. Once the baby becomes skilled at crawling, the degree of intra-hemispheric coherence decreases again, as extra connections are pruned. Repeatedly in development, the brain grows in such dynamic cycles to facilitate the organization of people's behaviors. These growth cycles mark periods of brain reorganization, during which neural networks reshape themselves to produce newly emerging capacities. There seem to be approximately 10 periods between birth and 30 years of age when many reorganizations occur, such as the emergence of crawling at about 8 months of age (Fischer & Bidell, 2006).

Brain Development Involves Building Distributed Neural Networks to Support Skills

As children grow and develop, they build skills for understanding and acting on the world and successively reorganize those skills for more complex actions and goals. The cognitive functions that come together to make these skills, for example for crawling, for phonological decoding in reading, or for persuading your father to give you one more cookie before bed, are instantiated in the brain, and involve the recruitment of many processing areas distributed in many parts of the brain. As learners build more complex neural networks to support functional skills, different people recruit different neuropsychological systems. Even when they build a common skill, such as crawling, they may do it in different ways.

This modern view is quite different from the traditional localizationist account of brain function, in which cognitive functions were mapped in one-to-one correspondence onto specific locations in the brain, with the young brain composed of distinct, preformed modules or faculties. Learning is now understood to involve the formation of connections of networks in various regions of the brain. Although specific brain areas do carry out particular types of processing in each individual, real-world skills are embodied in the networks they recruit, rather than in any one neural location. For example, there is no language, emotion, or mathematics area of the brain that is not also involved in processing many other domains of knowledge.

Because of the constructive, neurally distributed nature of learning, there are various routes to effective skill development, especially in the case of complex skills such as reading, math, or social processing. Children are resourceful in recruiting their neuropsychological strengths to build the skills they need to act, and although many common skills are similar across people with similar developmental experiences, good evidence shows that people can adapt their neuropsychological capacities to learn skills in diverse ways. For example, Immordino-Yang (2007) studied compensation for basic skills in two adolescent boys who had recovered from the surgical removal of an entire cortical hemisphere to control intractable seizures. She found that each boy had compensated for neuropsychological weaknesses by transforming important skills into new ones that accommodated his remaining neural strengths. In a similar vein, whereas most children learn to read by developing a particular sequence of educationally-relevant skills such as rhyming and phoneme-grapheme matching, many children learn to read by following alternate pathways, with more or less success (Knight & Fischer, 1992).

Brain Development Is Shaped by Both Emotional and Cognitive Processing

In this way, the development of neuropsychological skills involves recruiting and connecting functional networks across the brain into organized systems that underlie complex and varied behavior—a process that occurs repeatedly during learning and development. Of necessity, for these complex skills to be appropriately and adaptively engaged involves not only cognitive but also emotional brain systems (Immordino-Yang & Damasio, 2007). For example, think again of the infant learning to crawl. The skill of crawling involves coordinating networks for motor planning and control, somatosensation, and vision, distributed within the frontal, parietal and occipital lobes of the brain. However, in addition to these networks, we must consider that the infant's skill is constructed within an emotional and social context—for example, a baby sees something out of reach that he wants to play with, or a baby's father calls her over to climb up on his lap, and the baby uses the newly developing skill for crawling to get the interesting toy or to go to her father. In this way, the development of babies' skill for crawling is driven by goals—babies crawl because they want to, or because they need something or someone, or to move away from something they fear. In each of these cases, the neural systems supporting emotion and attention work together with those supporting cognition to shape the development of the neural networks underlying the skill.

Studies of Brain Development Can Inform Developmental Psychological Theories

The modern study of brain development is coming increasingly to inform and constrain theories of cognitive and emotional development, most notably in the fields of developmental psychology and education. Key questions include how experience serves to organize specialized brain networks for complex tasks such as crawling, reading, or social perspective-taking and how people coordinate the behaviors and neural systems underlying such a skill during learning and development. For example, in learning to read, Knight & Fischer (1992) found that while a majority of children follow a normative developmental pathway in which they coordinate skills for letter identification and for rhyming into a more general skill for reading, other children follow less common and less efficient pathways in which the skill for rhyming develops separately from the skills for recognizing letters and reading. Since this early study, there has been an explosion of work on the neural systems underlying each of these components of reading, as well as significant progress in relating the development of these systems to literacy acquisition (Katzir & Pare-Blagoev, 2006), with the aim of helping dyslexic and normal children become more effective readers.

A New Approach: Human Nature and Nurture Are Intertwined in Brain Development

In recent years, the advent of new tools and technologies for studying brain development (e.g., functional Magnetic Resonance Imaging to analyze brain functioning) has precipitated the establishment of a new interdisciplinary approach that integrates neuroscientific with developmental psychological methods and practical applications, including education. This approach, known as Mind, Brain and Education, presents a complex landscape in which to study brain development—in which social nurturance, culture, and other experiences shape the mind and brain in a dynamic interaction with a person's genes (Fischer et al., 2007). As in the crawling example, mental skills and their underlying brain networks act as dynamic systems, continually changing to reflect the situation, wants, and needs of people as the live and learn in context. Children are born with a propensity for different types of neural processing, and brain development involves the active construction and specialization of neural networks to handle cognitive and emotional skills for thought and action in that child's physical and social world.

REFERENCES

Bell, M. A., & Fox, N. (1996). Crawling experience is related to changes in cortical organization during infancy: Evidence from EEG coherence. *Developmental Psychobiology, 29*(7), 551–561.

Fischer, K. W., & Bidell, T. (2006). Dynamic development of action and thought. In W. Damon & R. Lerner (Eds.), *Handbook of child psychology, Vol. 1: Theoretical models of human development* (6th ed., pp. 313–399). Hoboken, NJ: John Wiley & Sons.

Fischer, K. W., Daniel, D. B., Immordino-Yang, M. H., Stern, E., Battro, A., & Koizumi, H. (2007). Why *Mind, Brain, and Education?* Why now? *Mind, Brain and Education, 1*(1), 1–2.

Immordino-Yang, M. H. (2007). A tale of two cases: Lessons for education from the study of two boys living with half their brains. *Mind, Brain, and Education, 1*(2), 66–83.

Immordino-Yang, M. H., & Damasio, A. R. (2007). We feel, therefore we learn: The relevance of affective and social neuroscience to education. *Mind, Brain and Education, 1*(1), 3–10.

Johnson, M. H. (2001). Functional brain development in humans. *Nature Reviews: Neuroscience, 2*(7), 475–483.

Katzir, T., & Pare-Blagoev, J. (2006). Applying cognitive neuroscience research to education: The case of literacy. *Educational Psychologist, 41*(1), 53–74.

Knight, C., & Fischer, K. W. (1992). Learning to read words: Individual differences in developmental sequences. *Journal of Applied Developmental Psychology, 13*, 377–404.

SUGGESTED READINGS

Fischer, K. W., & Bidell, T. (2006). Dynamic development of action and thought. In W. Damon & R. Lerner (Eds.), *Handbook of child psychology, Vol. 1: Theoretical models of human development* (6th ed., pp. 313–399). Hoboken, NJ: John Wiley & Sons.

Johnson, M. H. (2001). Functional brain development in humans. *Nature Reviews Neuroscience, 2*(7), 475–483.

Immordino-Yang, M. H. & Damasio, A. R. (2007). We feel, therefore we learn: The relevance of affective and social neuroscience to education. *Mind, Brain, and Education, 1*(1), 3–10.

MARY HELEN IMMORDINO-YANG
University of Southern California

KURT W. FISCHER
Harvard University

BRAIN IMAGING (See Neuroimaging)

BRAIN INJURIES

The brain can suffer injury in diverse ways: metabolic or structural abnormalities that are genetically inherited or perinatally induced; trauma from civilian accidents or military combat; toxicity from drugs, heavy metals, or poisonous gases; malnutrition; infections or diseases; tumors; cerebrovascular accidents (stroke); surgical removal of brain tissue for relief of epilepsy, intractable pain, or serious psychiatric symptomatology; and aging-related disorders (e.g., Alzheimer's disease).

Early perinatal brain lesions tend to be more extensive and diffuse than those incurred later in life. Early lesions often are detected by abnormalities in behavior observed during later development, and the time of onset of the damage can only be approximated in relation to presumed prenatal events. By contrast, lesions incurred beyond infancy often can be linked to a specific event or to an approximate onset in the symptomatology, and premorbid behavior can be compared with post-injury behavior. Some injuries in adulthood produce clearer abnormalities than others. For example, destruction of an area of the cerebral cortex in the anterior region of the right frontal lobe may produce subtle changes in emotional functions and personality, whereas a lesion in the analogous area in the left frontal lobe may cause a noticeable disruption in normal speech. Similarly, a lesion in the left frontal lobe near the junction with the parietal lobe can result in loss of language comprehension, but no such problem occurs after an analogous lesion on the right side of the brain.

Brain damage may have divergent effects, depending upon the locus and extent of the damage. For example, clinically, it has been noted that lesions in distinctly different areas of the brain will disrupt visual perception at different levels of processing. Damage in the optic nerves, superior colliculi, lateral geniculate nuclei of the thalamus, and cortex of the occipital lobes will interfere with visual functioning at the level of stimulus input, or processing of stimulus features. Damage in the temporal lobes adjacent to the occipital lobes will disrupt visual perception at a higher level of analysis, such as evaluating the importance or meaningfulness of stimuli, or remembering what the stimuli are. If the damage is in the left temporal lobe, verbal comprehension of written material (e.g., reading) is impaired. Additionally, damage to the parietal cortex adjacent to the occipital lobes can impair spatial localization of perceived objects. Finally, damage in the frontal lobes may interfere with the level of expression of responses to the stimulus. Not surprisingly, left frontal damage can interfere with language expression (e.g., speaking or writing words).

Because brain damage does not always result in immediately apparent symptoms, localization of the site and extent of damage may be difficult. For example, while an analysis of a specific sensory function, such as the integrity of the visual fields, can reveal basic sensory defects, more subtle cognitive and intellectual defects may require careful scrutiny. Functions involved in attention, motivation, emotion, and language often must be measured through the skillful administration and interpretation of tests specifically designed to elucidate organically based impairments. Descriptions of many of these tests may be found in books by Lezak, Howieson, and Loring (2004) and Strauss, Sherman, and Spreen (2006), as well as in a chapter by Oscar-Berman and Bardenhagen (1998).

Accidental head trauma, generally called traumatic brain injury or TBI, is a common yet severely disabling disorder. Because of the shape of the skull and the way the brain rests inside this bony case, violent blows to the head often seriously impact the prefrontal cortex and its connections with other brain regions. Severe frontal dysfunction leads to relaxed inhibitory control over appetitive and sexual drives and thus to inappropriate social behaviors that can prevent the TBI patient from returning to full functional independence. In TBI, brain injury occurs due to both the initial accident, as well as to resulting ischemia—a loss of blood supply to neurons. A lack of oxygen in ischemia can lead to cerebral infarcts, or regions of the brain where neurons are dead or dying. TBI can also lead to intracerebral hemorrhaging, or the rupturing of a blood vessel within the brain.

Neurologists rely on a variety of imaging and recording techniques for visualizing brain abnormalities in their patients. The techniques are used to measure parameters such as cerebral blood-flow patterns and obstructions, ventricular size, regional glucose and oxygen utilization, the presence of abnormal tissue masses, and seizure activity. Such techniques include angiography, X-ray computerized tomography (CT scans), structural and functional magnetic resonance imaging (MRI and fMRI scans), positron emission tomography (PET scans), single photon emission computed tomography (SPECT scans), electroencephalography (EEG), evoked potentials (EP), and magnetoencephalography (MEG). Each technique provides the neurologist and neuroscientist with a particular type of information about the structure or function of the brain.

Some techniques use X-rays to reveal images of abnormal blood flow through cerebral arteries (carotid angiography), or lesions produced by stroke or brain tumors (CT scans). MRI scans provide images of the brain without X-rays, and because of the nature of the signal that produces MR images, the scans can easily visualize small tumors, multiple sclerosis plaques, and infarctions. Other imaging techniques such as PET, SPECT, and fMRI provide images of regional cerebral blood flow, blood volume, or glucose metabolism, all of which are closely coupled under normal conditions and correlate with neuronal activity, and are thus indirect measures of brain functioning.

Electrical changes in the brain can be measured with another set of techniques, which include EEG, EP, and MEG. These procedures generally entail the attachment of electrodes to the scalp (or magnetic field detectors near the scalp, in the case of MEG) at standard locations in order to pick up electrical and magnetic signals from the brain within milliseconds. The signals are amplified and interpreted for the presence of abnormalities. For a summary of various neuroimaging techniques, see reviews by Toga and Mazziotta (2002); Bremner (2005); Huettel, Song, and McCarthy (2004); Preissl (2005); Bailey, Townsend, Valk, and Maisey (2005); and Cabeza and Kingstone (2006).

REFERENCES

Bailey, D. L., Townsend, D. W., Valk, P. E., & Maisey, M. N. (Eds.). (2005). *Positron emission tomography: Basic sciences*. New York: Springer.

Bremner, J. D. (2005). *Brain imaging handbook*. New York: W.W. Norton & Company.

Cabeza, R., & Kingstone, A. (Eds.). (2006). *Handbook of functional neuroimaging of cognition* (2nd ed.). Cambridge, MA: MIT Press.

Huettel, S. A., Song, A. W., & McCarthy, G. (2004). *Functional magnetic resonance imaging*. Sunderland, MA: Sinauer Associates.

Lezak, M. D., Howieson, D. B., & Loring, D. W. (2004). *Neuropsychological assessment* (4th ed.). New York: Oxford University Press.

Oscar-Berman, M., & Bardenhagen, F. (1998). Nonhuman primate models of memory dysfunction in neurodegenerative disease: Contributions from Comparative Neuropsychology. In A. Tröster (Ed.), *Memory in neurodegenerative disease* (pp. 3–20). New York: Cambridge University Press.

Preissl, H. (Ed.). (2005). *Magnetoencephalography, vol. 68 (International Review of Neurobiology)*. San Diego, CA: Academic Press.

Strauss, E., Sherman, E. M. S., & Spreen, O. (2006). *A compendium of neuropsychological tests: Administration, norms, and commentary*. (3rd ed.). New York: Oxford University Press.

Toga, A. W., & Mazziotta, J. C. (2002). *Brain Mapping: The methods* (2nd ed.). New York: Academic Press.

SUGGESTED READINGS

Elbaum, J., & Benson, D. (Eds). (2007). *Acquired brain injury: An integrative neuro-rehabilitation approach*. New York: Springer.

Ogden, J. A. (2005). *Fractured minds: A case-study approach to clinical neuropsychology* (2nd ed.). New York: Oxford University Press.

Ponsford, J. (2004). *Cognitive and behavioral rehabilitation: From neurobiology to clinical practice*. New York: Guilford Press.

MARLENE OSCAR-BERMAN
SUSAN M. MOSHER
*Boston University School of Medicine,
and Department of Veterans Affairs
Healthcare System, Boston Campus*

See also: Neuroimaging; Neuropsychology

BRAIN STEM

The brain stem, which consists of the midbrain, pons, and medulla oblongata, connects the cerebrum above to the spinal cord below. It is a highly organized structure that, in addition to conveying ascending and descending tracts, contains the nuclei of the cranial nerves III to XII and is responsible for a number of complex functions, including control of respiratory and cardiovascular activity and regulation of the level of consciousness.

The midbrain is the shortest segment of the brainstem. It consists of a ventral and a dorsal portion separated by the ventricular space. The dorsal or posterior portion is called the tectum and consists of four rounded swellings, the paired superior and inferior colliculi. The ventral or anterior portion is called the tegmentum and contains the reticular formation, the nuclei of cranial nerves III and IV, and ascending and descending pathways.

The pons is readily identified from the midbrain above and from the medulla oblongata below as a bulge on the ventral surface of the brainstem lying on the dorsum sellae of the sphenoid bone. The dorsal or posterior surface of the pons is taken up superiorly by the superior cerebellar peduncles, while inferiorly it forms the upper part of the floor of the fourth ventricle. The pons contains ascending and descending tracts and connections with the cerebellum, as well as the nuclei of cranial nerves V to VIII.

The medulla oblongata extends from the lower limit of the pons to a level just above the first pair of cervical nerves, where it is continuous with the spinal cord. It is pyriform in shape, larger superiorly than inferiorly. The cephalad half of the dorsal surface of the medulla oblongata forms the lower part of the floor of the fourth ventricle. The ventral surface is made up of the pyramids containing the corticospinal tracts. The medulla oblongata contains the nuclei of cranial nerves IX through XII, which exit along its lateral aspects. The caudal half of the medulla oblongata represents a transition to the spinal cord, with cross-sectional organization and a central canal similar to the cord.

Given the complexity of the structure of the brainstem and the proximity of the motor and sensory tracts and cranial nerve nuclei, it is not surprising that disturbances in brain stem function can be seen with small lesions. Until the advent of computerized tomography (CT) in the late 1970s, the brain stem could be imaged only by indirect means. However, even CT is not very useful, primarily because of distortions of the images caused by the surrounding bone. Magnetic resonance imaging (MRI) is therefore now the imaging modality of choice for any patient in whom a lesion in the brain stem is suspected. Indeed, the increasing incidence of brain stem tumors over the past two decades has been considered to be in large part due to better detection using MRI of lesions that in the past may have gone undiagnosed.

Lesions that may affect the brain stem include vascular malformations such as angiomas, which may be a cause of spontaneous hemorrhage, infectious diseases such as tuberculosis (although this is rare in developed countries), demyelinating diseases such as multiple sclerosis, and tumors.

Tumors in the brain stem are rare in adults but account for as many as 10–15% of all brain tumors seen in the pediatric age group. There are several types of brain stem tumors, each characterized by a distinct clinical presentation and MRI appearance. These include focal tumors, most often seen in the midbrain, dorsal exophytic tumors that grow from the dorsal aspect of the medulla into the fourth ventricle, and cervicomedullary tumors that originate in the upper cervical cord or medulla and grow posteriorly to project into the fourth ventricle. These types collectively account for at least 20% of all brain stem tumors. Some, notably focal tumors arising in the tectum, may do well without any therapeutic intervention. Others may do very well treated with surgery alone or, if this is not possible or if the tumor progresses or recurs after surgery, with radiotherapy.

In contrast, 70–80% of all brain stem tumors are of the so-called diffuse intrinsic kind that typically arise in the pons. These are very aggressive tumors that grow very rapidly and cause multiple neurological deficits and a rapid clinical deterioration. Biopsy, even though associated with less risk now than in the past, is considered unnecessary in the context of typical clinical and imaging findings. The only known effective treatment is radiotherapy, but, even despite a satisfactory early response to treatment, outcome is very poor. The median time to progression after treatment with radiotherapy is only of the order of 6 months, and the median survival time is less than one year. Fewer than 10% of patients will be alive 2 years after treatment. Current research studies are testing various types and combinations of chemotherapy and biological agents given along with radiotherapy in the hope of achieving an improved outcome for children with these tumors.

SUGGESTED READINGS

Freeman, C. R. & Farmer, J-P. (1998). Pediatric brain stem gliomas: A review. *International Journal of Radiation Oncology: Biology, 40*, 265–271.

Schumacher, M., Schulte-Mönting, J., Stoeter, P., Warmuth-Metz, M., & Solymosi, L. (2007). Magnetic resonance imaging compared with biopsy in the diagnosis of brainstem diseases of childhood: a multicenter review. *Journal of Neurosurgery (2 Suppl. Pediatrics), 106*, 111–119.

CAROLYN R. FREEMAN
McGill University, Montreal, Quebec, Canada

See also: **Brain; Brain Development**

BRAIN SURGERY (See Psychosurgery)

BRAINWAVES (See Electroencephalography)

BRIEF PSYCHOTHERAPY (See Short-Term Psychotherapy)

BUFFERING HYPOTHESIS

The buffering hypothesis suggests that under some conditions social support protects (or "buffers") individuals from the harmful effects of stressful situations. Two important conditions must be satisfied to demonstrate the buffering effect: (1) individuals must experience relatively high levels of stress in response to a stressful situation, and (2) social support is defined in terms of the availability of interpersonal resources that can potentially offset needs occasioned by the stressful event. This specific type of social support is sometimes referred to as "instrumental support" (Cohen, 1988; Cohen & Wills, 1985), examples of which include financial aid, material resources, and needed services. The buffering hypothesis has been evaluated in a variety of areas of human functioning (e.g., depression, substance abuse, physical health) and in studies of immune response functioning among monkeys.

The buffering hypothesis is often contrasted with the "main effects model," whereby social support is thought to have a beneficial and direct impact on physical and psychological well-being regardless of the levels of stress individuals experience. These two models, main effects and buffering, are not mutually exclusive, and are frequently evaluated simultaneously in the same statistical analysis, usually with hierarchical multiple regression or two-way analysis of variance. Support for the main effects model would be evident when the amount or level of social support accounts for significant variance in the dependent measure (e.g., a specific indicator of physiological health or psychological well-being). Support for the buffering hypothesis would be evident by a stress support interaction, whereby the level or degree of social support moderates the association of stress on well-being, specifically when the level of perceived stress is high (but not when stress levels are comparatively low). Cohen and Wills (1985, p. 319) go on to suggest that a "pure buffering effect" would be evident when mean scores on a measure of well-being are similar under conditions of low stress for low- and high-support subjects, but differ significantly under conditions of high stress whereby those high in social support demonstrate greater well-being (or less pathogenic symptomatology) than those low in social support.

These two models suggest different processes through which social support influences well-being. The main effects model suggests that the number of persons in one's social network or the degree of social closeness one experiences directly promotes well-being. The buffering hypothesis, in contrast, suggests that social support counters the effects of high levels of stress by altering one's perception of threat from stressors (e.g., close friends are perceived as potentially offering resources that counter the negative effects of a stressor, such as temporary financial aid following the loss of one's job), or by modifying one's stress response to a highly stressful event (e.g., through the provision of physical comfort, emotional support, or advice by others). Instrumental social support might also have stress-buffering effects under high-stress conditions by bolstering one's self-esteem or self-confidence.

The buffering hypothesis has received mixed support in a number of health-related areas, such as overall mental health, cardiovascular reactivity, and emotional adjustment among women with advanced breast cancer. The buffering hypothesis has also received equivocal support in the area of substance abuse. Social support, for example, has been observed to moderate the association between stressful life events and drug cravings (Ames & Roitzsch, 2000) and alcohol involvement (Peirce, Frone, Russell, & Cooper, 1996) in some studies but not in others (e.g., Baer, Garmezy, McLaughlin, Pokorny, & Wernick, 1987). The buffering hypothesis has frequently not been supported in relation to depression (Burton, Stice, & Seeley, 2004).

Failures to support the buffering hypothesis might be the result of how social support is measured. As noted previously, measures of social integration or the breadth of one's social network are more likely to produce outcomes consistent with the main effects model. Social support measures that are more likely to demonstrate buffering effects are those that evaluate the degree to which social support is instrumental in addressing the functional needs occasioned by the stressor.

REFERENCES

Ames, S. C., & Roitzsch, J. C. (2000). The impact of minor stressful life events and social support on cravings: A study of inpatients receiving treatment or substance dependence. *Addictive Behaviors, 25,* 539–547.

Baer, P. E., Garmezy, L. B., McLaughlin, R. J. Pokorny, A. D., & Wernick, M. J. (1987). Stress, coping, family conflict, and adolescent alcohol use. *Journal of Behavioral Medicine, 10,* 449–466.

Burton, E., Stice, E., & Seeley, J. R. (2004). A prospective test of the stress-buffering model of depression in adolescent girls: No support once again. *Journal of Consulting and Clinical Psychology, 72,* 689–697.

Cohen, S. (1988). Psychosocial models of the role of social support in the etiology of physical disease. *Health Psychology, 7,* 269–297.

Cohen, S., & Wills, T. A. (1985). Stress, social support, and the buffering hypothesis. *Psychological Bulletin, 98,* 310–357.

Peirce, R. S., Frone, M. R., Russell, M., & Cooper, M. L (1996). Financial stress, social support and alcohol involvement: A longitudinal test of the buffering hypothesis in a general population survey. *Health Psychology, 15,* 38–47.

RICHARD F. FARMER
Oregon Research Institute

NORMAN D. SUNDBERG
University of Oregon

See also: **Psychological Health; Resilience; Social Support**

BULIMIA NERVOSA

Bulimia nervosa is an eating disorder characterized by three primary symptoms: recurrent episodes of binge eating, inappropriate compensatory behaviors, and extreme concern about body weight and shape. Binge eating involves the consumption of a large amount of food in a relatively short period of time along with a perception of loss of control over eating. Binge eating may be triggered by a number of factors including hunger, negative mood, interpersonal stressors, and thoughts about weight and shape. Inappropriate compensatory behaviors are strategies aimed at controlling body weight and shape, including self-induced vomiting, misuse of laxatives and/or diuretics, excessive exercising, and fasting.

The *Diagnostic and Statistical Manual of Mental Disorders* (DSM-IV) divides bulimia nervosa into two subtypes. The "purging" subtype is distinguished by the presence of purging compensatory behaviors such as self-induced vomiting or laxative misuse. The "nonpurging" subtype is diagnosed in presence of only nonpurging compensatory behaviors (e.g., excessive exercise). Individuals with bulimia nervosa also exhibit overconcern about their body weight and shape and usually engage in extreme dietary restriction outside of binge-eating episodes in order to control weight and shape. The dysfunctional concerns about weight and shape typically are conceptualized as the central feature or core psychopathology of bulimia nervosa.

Bulimia nervosa usually begins with rigid and unhealthy dieting that is motivated by the desire to be "thin" and lose weight. Individuals with bulimia nervosa attempt to limit the amount and type of food that they consume, particularly during the early stages of the disorder. Over time, they become increasingly preoccupied with thoughts of food, and episodes of binge eating alternate with periods of restriction. Vomiting, laxative misuse, and other inappropriate compensatory behaviors usually follow the onset of binge eating.

Bulimia nervosa most commonly occurs in women and usually begins in adolescence or early adulthood. Approximately 1%–2% of young women meet criteria for the disorder. A greater number of young women, however, appear to meet criteria for subthreshold bulimia nervosa (van Hoken, Seidell, & Hoek, 2003). In contrast to anorexia nervosa, individuals with bulimia nervosa maintain normal weight. As a result, bulimia nervosa is more difficult to detect than anorexia nervosa as physical signs are not readily apparent to the casual observer. Bulimia is often a secretive disorder, and individuals with bulimia nervosa typically experience guilt and shame about their behavior. Individuals with bulimia nervosa display rigid patterns of thinking and tend to view the world and their experiences from an "all or nothing" perspective. For example, bulimics often describe eating as either being "in control" or "out of control" and weight or appearance as either "thin" or "fat."

Although the medical complications associated with bulimia nervosa are generally regarded as less severe than those associated with the low body weight of anorexia nervosa, it is important to recognize that bulimia nervosa can be associated with significant and life-threatening medical complications (see Mitchell, 1995 for further discussion). Medical complications in bulimia nervosa are often, but not always, a result of purging or compensatory behaviors. Electrolyte disturbances represent one of the most serious complications and may lead to cardiac irregularities and, in some cases, heart failure. Electrolyte disturbances typically result from purging; for instance, individuals who use diuretics may lose significant amounts of potassium in their urine, which can result in hypokalemia.

Inflammation and esophageal tears are another serious potential complication resulting from repeated vomiting. Laxative abuse also may result in constipation and, in rare cases, permanent damage to the colon. An additional complication is gastric dilatation, which usually occurs after binge eating. Gastric dilatation can be fatal if it results in gastric rupture. Other medical complications include fatigue, enlargement of salivary glands leading to puffy cheeks, headaches, dry skin, abrasions to fingers from inducing vomiting, and dental erosion. Athletes or individuals who exercise extensively also may experience stress fractures, repeated injuries, and prolonged recovery periods. The Female Athlete Triad (Nattiv, Agostini, & Yeager, 1994), which consists of disturbed eating, menstrual disorders, and osteoporosis, should be investigated in female athletes given the long-term effects of low bone density. Type-I diabetics who have bulimia nervosa may intentionally engage in the dangerous practice of omitting or underdosing insulin to reduce their weight.

Numerous causal factors have been proposed as being related to the development of bulimia nervosa.

Disturbances in such neurotransmitter systems as those of serotonin and dopamine have been observed, but it remains unclear whether these biological irregularities cause bulimia nervosa or result from the disturbed eating behaviors that characterize the disorder. Findings from several studies suggest that bulimia nervosa may result, in part, from dieting-based changes in serotonin functioning in vulnerable individuals. Neurochemical abnormalities appear to persist after recovery. A genetic basis for bulimia nervosa is supported by family studies, which examine the clustering of disorders within families, and by twin studies, which compare the similarity between genetically identical and genetically nonidentical twin pairs. Family studies find increased rates of eating disorders in the families of individuals with bulimia nervosa as compared to the families of individuals without bulimia nervosa. Twin studies have yielded a heritability range from 31% to 83% (Bulik et al., 2000). Currently, the exact role genetic factors play in the development of bulimia nervosa remains unclear, and environmental factors clearly influence the development of the disorder.

Although it is widely believed that childhood sexual abuse causes eating disorders, there is little evidence for a specific relationship between a history of sexual abuse and the development of these disorders in that childhood sexual abuse appears to increase one's risk for psychological disorders in general, not eating disorders specifically. Trauma, however, has been found to be more closely associated with bulimia nervosa as compared to the restricting subtype of anorexia nervosa. Trauma frequency, but not severity, also appears to increase the risk of developing bulimia nervosa or an eating disorder with bulimic features. In addition, research suggests that individuals who have been traumatized and who subsequently develop posttraumatic stress disorder (PTSD) may be at increased risk for bulimia nervosa or bulimic-like eating disorders (see Brewerton, 2007 for further discussion).

Cultural factors do appear to play a role in the development of bulimia nervosa. The ideal female weight in Western society, often referred to as the thin-ideal, has continued to decrease even as the average female weight increases. As a result, more and more women experience normative body dissatisfaction secondary to a discrepancy between their "ideal" and actual weight. Body dissatisfaction is widespread among adolescent girls, and research links body dissatisfaction, along with acceptance of the thin-ideal, to the development of bulimia nervosa. Prospective research has also found a strong relationship between dieting and the later development of an eating disorder.

The dual pathway model of bulimia nervosa (Stice, 1994) proposes that internalization of the thin-ideal contributes to body dissatisfaction, which then leads to elevated dieting and negative affect. Dieting and negative affect are posited to increase the risk of developing binge eating and bulimia nervosa. Other potential risk factors include early onset of menstruation, a personal and/or parental history of obesity, parental dieting, and personality traits such as perfectionism. Bulimia nervosa often co-occurs with other psychological disorders including depression, anxiety disorders, substance abuse disorders, and/or some personality disorders such as borderline personality disorder.

According to the DSM-IV, bulimia nervosa is typically either intermittent, with binge eating and/or purging alternating with periods of remission, or chronic. Treatment, however, can significantly affect outcome. Cognitive behavioral therapy (CBT), a psychological treatment, is widely viewed as the treatment of choice for bulimia nervosa. The National Institute for Clinical Excellence has given CBT for bulimia nervosa a grade of "A," indicating strong empirical support. CBT for bulimia nervosa includes education about bulimia nervosa, self-monitoring of eating behaviors, establishing a regular pattern of eating, strategies to reduce binge eating and compensatory behaviors (e.g., vomiting), problem solving, and cognitive restructuring.

Cognitive restructuring is a strategy designed to help patients identify and challenge their patterns of thinking. Numerous studies have demonstrated that the majority of patients treated with CBT benefit from treatment and that improvement is maintained over time. Between 40% and 50% of patients treated with CBT remit. Overall CBT produces between 60% and 70% symptom reduction (see Waller & Kennerly, 2003, for discussion). Interpersonal psychotherapy (IPT) is another psychological treatment that is supported by research, although fewer studies have examined this form of psychotherapy. Research indicates that IPT may take longer to achieve comparable results to CBT. Increasingly, clinicians also are utilizing modified variants of dialectical behavior therapy, particularly when treating complex patients who have significant comorbidity (Wisniewski & Kelly, 2003). Additionally, antidepressant medications appear to reduce bulimic symptoms, at least initially. Data supporting the long-term efficacy of antidepressants are lacking (Wilson, Grilo, & Vitousek, 2007).

REFERENCES

Brewerton, T. (2007, July). Eating disorders, trauma, and comorbidity: Focus on PTSD. *Eating Disorders: The Journal of Treatment & Prevention, 15*(4), 285–304.

Bulik, C. M., Sullivan, P. F., Wade, T. D., & Kendler, K. S. (2000). Twin studies of eating disorders: A review. *International Journal of Eating Disorders, 27*, 1–20.

Mitchell, J. E. (1995). Medical Complications of Bulimia nervosa. In K. D. Brownell & C. G. Fairburn (Eds.), *Eating disorders and obesity: A comprehensive handbook*. New York: Guilford Press.

Nattiv, A., Agostini, R., & Yeager, K. K. (1994). The female athlete triad: The inter-relatedness of disordered eating, amenorrhea, and osteoporosis. *Clinical Sports Medicine, 13*, 405–418.

Stice, E. (1994). A review of the evidence for a sociocultural model of bulimia nervosa and an exploration of the mechanisms of action. *Clinical Psychology Review, 14*, 633–661.

van Hoken, D., Seidell, J., & Hoek, H. W. (2003). Epidemiology. In J. Treasure, E. van Furth, & U. Schmidt (Eds.), *Handbook of eating disorders*, (2nd ed.). Chichester, UK: John Wiley & Sons.

Waller, G., & Kennerley, H. (2003) Cognitive behavioural treatments. In J. Treasure, E. van Furth, & U. Schmidt (Eds.), *Handbook of eating disorders*, (2nd ed.). Chichester, UK: John Wiley & Sons.

Wilson, G., Grilo, C., & Vitousek, K. (2007). Psychological treatment of eating disorders. *American Psychologist, 62*(3), 199–216.

Wisniewski, L., & Kelly, E. (2003). The application of dialectical behavior therapy to the treatment of eating disorders. *Cognitive and Behavioral Practice, 10*(2), 131–138.

SUGGESTED READINGS

Brewerton, T. D (Ed.). (2004). *Clinical handbook of eating disorders: An integrated approach*. New York: Marcel Dekker.

Treasure, J., van Furth, E., & Schmidt, U. (Eds.). (2003). *Handbook of eating disorders* (2nd ed.). Chichester, UK: John Wiley & Sons.

CAROLYN BLACK BECKER
Trinity University

See also: Anorexia Nervosa; Eating Disorders

BULLYING

Bullying is quite distinct from normal child interaction, which may seem rough to some observers but is mutual, enjoyable, and friendly. By contrast, bullying is always repeated, intentionally harmful, and imposed on someone weaker. Taken together, these three characteristics make bullying not only unfair, but also destructive. Bullying harms the victims (who may become depressed lifelong), the bullies (who risk serious injury or prison if they do not change their behavior), and everyone else. Severe bullying was once thought to be rare, only physical, and confined to schools. Research has found each of these assumptions to be false.

The first of these assumptions was toppled first. Three Norwegian boys killed themselves in the early 1970s, each after being bullied. The government asked a researcher, Dan Olweus, to assess how common bullying was. In a nationwide survey, Olweus (1993) found that about 11% of the boys and 4% of the girls were self-acknowledged bullies. Soon researchers in other nations reported similar or higher rates. A United Nations survey confirmed the findings of national surveys: high prevalence and wide variation. Overall, almost a third of all children said they had been bullies, victims, or both "two or three times or more in the past months" (Currie, Roberts, Morgan, Smith, Settertobulte, Samdal, et al., 2004).

The second assumption is also false. Physical bullying—kicking, punching, beating—is only one type. Another type is verbal bullying—repeated derogatory remarks or names—which often echo for years to come. A third type, called relational bullying, is designed to shame or isolate someone, as when children deliberately ignore a classmate, or adults repeat humiliating gossip, or a supervisor sneers with evident disapproval. Relational bullying becomes increasingly prevalent as children become more socially skilled and is favored by girls, although boys do it, too (Underwood, 2003). The most recently identified form of bullying is cyber bullying, in which a covert photo or nasty rumor is transmitted via computers or cell phones.

Bullying occurs in every social setting. Although research has focused on schools, bullying is evident in families, not just parent-to-child but among siblings; in prisons, among inmates as well as from guards to inmates; in hospitals, from staff to patients and from doctors to interns and nurses; and in colleges, among students as well as from professors and deans. Indeed, every social grouping may spawn bullying. The form changes with maturity: young children hit more than talk, whereas adults more often use cutting remarks or social shunning. When only physical bullying is considered, it becomes less frequent with age, but other forms may increase. Social bullying in particular increases when children enter middle school. The impact is similar at every age: victims feel lonely and depressed and function less well than they might.

It is a myth that bullies are deeply insecure, lonely, or mentally deficient. Most bullies, by early adolescence, enjoy "high social status" (Juvonen, Graham, & Schuster, 2003, p. 1233) with friends who encourage them, onlookers who relish a fight, and peers who laugh at victims. As time goes on, some bullies become bosses and political leaders, with a reputation for being tough, and feared as well as admired. Others overstep, losing respect and affection.

Victims are defenseless and friendless, sometimes because they are different in some way (homosexual teenagers are often victims) and sometimes because they are unusually anxious, hostile, socially inept, or hypersensitive. Most are passive sufferers, but a few become bully-victims and turn on others to harm them. As an example in families, children who are bullied by a parent have an increased likelihood of becoming a bully at school. Most children and adults who observe bullying are afraid to stop the aggression they see. They suffer as well. On days when students observe bullying, they dislike school more (Nishina & Juvonen, 2005). Children and adults who live or work among bullies are more stressed and less healthy themselves.

What can be done? The first step is to recognize the problem. Some adults say "boys will be boys" or "names will never hurt me" or "mind your own business." These ideas are all destructive. The research on bullying in schools finds that bullying in some schools is up to six times more frequent than in other schools similar in size, community setting, and religious composition (Rigby, 2002). Obviously something in adult behavior must affect the school context in ways that account for this difference.

Unfortunately, although reducing bullying is possible, many interventions have not worked. Putting bullies together to teach them respect and sympathy sometimes increases bullying. Many educators have used psychological theories to design interventions (Rigby, 2004). The outcome has often been disappointing, not only in the United States but in dozens of other nations as well. However, researchers have discovered some aspects of intervention that seem pivotal. Changing the entire social climate is needed, including befriending victims and stopping bullying at an early age. This is stressed by most European experts (Smith, 2003), unlike in North America, where "bullying and victimization are often considered as personal problems of individual youth rather than problems requiring a collective response" (Juvonen et al., 2003, p. 1236).

When an entire school, workplace, or family undertakes a concerted effort to halt bullying, some success is reported. One example comes from Kempele, Finland, where the entire community reduced bullying. The number of children victimized "fairly often" declined about 1% a year over eight years (from 9% to 3%) (Koivisto, 2004). Since Olweus's original studies, people in many nations recognize bullying as common, harmful, and affected by the social context, which is a major advance. Bullying is now seen as the root of school violence (e.g., Columbine). The next major advance will be to reduce it.

REFERENCES

Benbenishty, R., & Astor, R. A. (2005). *School violence in context.* New York: Oxford University Press.

Crick, N. R., & Grotpeter, J. K. (1995). Relational aggression, gender and social-psychological adjustment. *Child Development, 66,* 710–722.

Currie, C., Roberts, C., Morgan, A., Smith, R., Settertobulte, W., Samdal, O., et al. (Eds.). Young people's health in context. *Health Behaviour in School-aged Children (HBSC) study: International report from the 2001/2002 survey.* WHO Policy Series Health Policy for Children and Adolescents. Copenhagen: World Health Organization.

Juvonen, J., Graham, S., & Schuster, M. A. (2003). Bullying among young adolescents: The strong, the weak, and the troubled. *Pediatrics, 112,* 1231–1237.

Koivisto, M. (2004). A follow-up survey of anti-bullying interventions in the comprehensive schools of Kempele in 1990–1998. In P. K. Smith, D. Pepler, & K. Rigby (Eds.), *Bullying in schools:*

How successful can interventions be? (pp. 235–249). Cambridge, UK: Cambridge University Press.

Nishina, A. & Juvonen, J. (2005). Daily reports of witnessing and experiencing peer harassment in middle school. Child Development, *76*, 345–450.

Olweus, D. (1993). *Bullying at school: What we know and what we can do.* Oxford, UK: Blackwell.

Rigby, K. (2002). *New perspectives on bullying.* London: Jessica Kingsley.

Rigby, L. (2004) Addressing bullying in schools: Theoretical perspectives and their implications. *School Psychology International*, *25*, 287–300.

Smith, P. K. (Ed.). (2003). *Violence in schools: The response in Europe.* London: Routledge.

Underwood, M. K. (2003). *Social aggression among girls.* New York: Guilford Press.

SUGGESTED READINGS

Ladd, G. W. (2005). *Children's peer relations and social competence.* New Haven: Yale University Press.

Zins, J. E., Elias, M. J., & Maher, C. A. (Eds.). (2007). *Bullying, victimization, and peer harassment: A handbook of prevention and intervention.* Binghamton, NY: Haworth Press.

KATHLEEN STASSEN BERGER
Bronx Community College, City University of New York

See also: **Aggression; Interpersonal Relationships**

BURNOUT

Burnout is a chronic syndrome describing a dysfunctional relationship with work. People experiencing burnout are tired, uninvolved, and ineffective. The concept has been the focus of extensive research and consulting work since it was introduced in the mid-1970s.

Burnout was originally a colloquial term that human service providers used to describe colleagues who became overwhelmed with the demands of care giving. At first, the burnout concept was defined exclusively as a problem for "helping" professionals. Early theories proposed that the demands of the therapeutic relationship were at the root of the syndrome. Researchers and practitioners soon challenged this notion by identifying burnout among working people in other occupations. At present, burnout is seen as a potential hazard in any occupation that requires intense participation. This perspective leads to defining burnout as a syndrome of exhaustion, cynicism, and low professional efficacy.

Theoretical perspectives on burnout have developed in response to an impressive body of applied research (see Halbesleben & Buckley, 2004; Maslach, Schaufeli, & Leiter, 2001). Research has confirmed that exhaustion is at the core of burnout. Chronic work overload depletes employees' capacity to sustain an energetic approach to their work. Work overload fundamentally constitutes an imbalance of demands over available resources.

The relevant work demands may arise from employers' directives, or they may reflect employees' personal aspirations for their work. The relevant resources may be personal strength, sophisticated equipment, support staff, or expertise. Most often, the major resource gap is time: there is simply not enough time for people to complete what needs to be done. Insufficient time results in work invading on employees' personal time. The breakdown of the boundary between work and personal life is disruptive in itself, but it also interferes with employees' capacity to regenerate energy between workdays.

Chronic exhaustion undermines employees' capacity to become deeply involved in their work because dedicated involvement requires energy. Over time, employees develop a cynical perspective on their work. Experiencing chronic exhaustion and cynicism at work, employees become discouraged and lose confidence in their professional efficacy.

The definition of burnout as a three-part syndrome is generally accepted, although burnout first and foremost has also been viewed as an exhaustion problem. This perspective acknowledges that the association of exhaustion with cynicism and low efficacy is a casual sequence, but it does not represent an integrated syndrome. Another perspective views burnout as an integrated syndrome of exhaustion and cynicism, as reflected in the strong, consistent association between these two components. Low professional efficacy, which has a weaker and less consistent connection to the other two constructs, is seen as incidental.

The various perspectives on burnout maintain the syndrome as a consistently productive research focus. The concept appeals to individuals and to professional groups who perceive widespread distress at work as a reflection of problems in the work environment rather than individual failings. The close interconnections among these three qualities support defining burnout as a syndrome.

Work Engagement

Work engagement defines a positive alternative to burnout. When first introduced by Maslach and Leiter, (1997), work engagement as a polar opposite to burnout was defined as an energetic involvement with work that builds professional efficacy. Subsequent approaches have considered work engagement as a positive contrast to burnout, but have operationalized it on several dimensions.

The first dimension refers to the subjective experience of energy. When experiencing burnout, people experience exhaustion that prevents people from becoming avidly involved in their work. The second dimension is involvement. In contrast to cynicism or depersonalization, involvement is the capacity to become absorbed in an activity or a challenge work. It is the process of focusing intently on work with an emotional investment. An energetic and involved approach to work supports confidence in professional efficacy.

Consequences of Burnout

The experience of burnout is unpleasant in itself and has broader implications for health and performance difficulties. The health implications follow an energy process, which begins with an unmanageable workload. People vary considerably in the amount or intensity of demands they can comfortably manage. A defining issue is the balance of work resources to demands. When resources, such as time, materials, equipment, or support staff, are in short supply, employees invest more of their personal energy into maintaining a level of performance. In high-demand situations, people lose the capacity to replenish their personal energy, which leads to chronic exhaustion. The experience of chronic exhaustion prompts a variety of health complaints, including hypertension, gastro-intestinal upsets, sleeplessness, and anxiety. These health problems initiate a vicious cycle as they further inhibit employees' capacity to maintain sufficient energy for work.

Measurement

The most widely used measure of burnout is the Maslach Burnout Inventory (MBI; Maslach, Jackson, & Leiter, 1996). The original MBI Human Services Scale (MBI-HSS) comprised 22 items representing three subscales: emotional exhaustion, depersonalization, and personal accomplishment. Burnout is indicated by high scores on exhaustion and depersonalization in conjunction with low scores on personal accomplishment. To accommodate a growing body of research attempting to apply the burnout construct to other occupational groups, the MBI-General Scale (MBI-GS; Schaufeli, Leiter, Maslach, & Jackson, 1996) was developed. It parallels the original three dimensions, relabeling them as exhaustion, cynicism, and professional efficacy. A large body of theoretical and empirical writing has confirmed the relevance of these three dimensions, their factor structure, and their validity (Maslach, Schaufeli, & Leiter, 2001).

In recent years, researchers have developed more streamlined burnout inventories, such as the Oldenburg Burnout Inventory (OLBI; Demerouti, 1999); which measures burnout on two dimensions: exhaustion and disengagement. The Copenhagen Burnout Inventory concentrates solely on exhaustion, considering it in various life domains, not only work life (Kristensen, Borritz, Villadsen, & Christensen, 2005).

The MBI and the other inventories were developed in a research context as instruments to assess burnout on the level of the workgroup or the organization; they were not developed as individual diagnostic instruments. As people increasingly cite burnout or related experiences as rationales for their inability to work, governments and disability insurance companies have sought a method for establishing a definitive diagnosis of job burnout. In some countries, most notably the Netherlands, negative scores on the MBI exhaustion scale in conjunction with clinical indicators of neurasthenia provide the basis for diagnosing burnout for disability coverage (Schaufeli, Bakker, Schaap, Kladler, & Hoogduin, 2001).

Action

Alleviating and preventing burnout have presented challenges to researchers and practitioners. The qualities underlying burnout—exhaustion, cynicism, and inefficacy—persist, showing remarkable consistency over months or even years. Intervention approaches have targeted individuals, improving their coping skills or enhancing their overall health. The strength of these approaches is that they empower individuals to take charge of important aspects of their work life. The weakness is that these approaches are limited to the range of individual employees' discretion: They do not have an impact on the broader work context.

Management interventions address this limitation by focusing primarily on the procedures, structures, and roles that contribute to employees' experience of burnout. These interventions begin with employee surveys to identify areas of work life that are closely associated with the burnout experience in a specific organization. Management draws upon this information to develop strategies to address persistent problems. These may include redesigning jobs to address work overload or increasing the transparency of consequential workplace decisions to enhance employees' perception of organizational justice.

The most effective interventions encompass both approaches: management interventions to enhance the work environment and individual training to encourage employees to make effective use of their changed work situation. These approaches build upon a thorough assessment of the organizational context through staff surveys, analysis to identify factors associated with burnout, planning that elicits broad participation in the project, and action that implements new policies or programs. Ideally, organizations integrate these initiatives and their performance indictors into their ongoing information flow.

In summary, job burnout has been the focus of an international research effort since the late 1970s. The work to date indicates that the syndrome involves energy, involvement, and efficacy, personal qualities that are central to employees' experience of their work lives. While this research has thoroughly mapped the syndrome's causes and consequences, considerable work is required to demonstrate effective intervention strategies to alleviate or prevent the syndrome. Organizations reduce their vulnerability to burnout through effective human resource management practices. Alleviating burnout requires more assertive approaches that encourage active participation from employees throughout the organization.

REFERENCES

Demerouti, E. (1999). *Burnout: Eine Folge konkreter Arbeitsbedingungen bei Dienstleistungs- und Produktionstatigkeiten.* [Burnout: A consequence of specific working conditions among human service, and production tasks]. Frankfurt/Main: Lang.

Halbesleben, J. R. B., & Buckley, M. R. (2004). Burnout in organizational life. *Journal of Management, 30,* 859–879.

Kristensen, T. S., Borritz, M., Villadsen, E., & Christensen, K. B. (2005). The Copenhagen burnout inventory: A new tool for the assessment of burnout. *Work & Stress, 19,* 192–207.

Leiter, M. P., & Maslach, C. (2005). *Banishing burnout: Six strategies for improving your relationship with work.* San Francisco: Jossey-Bass.

Maslach, C., Jackson, S. E., & Leiter, M. P. (1996). *Maslach burnout inventory manual* (3rd ed.). Palo Alto, CA: Consulting Psychologists Press.

Maslach, C., & Leiter, M. P. (1997). *The truth about burnout.* San Francisco: Jossey-Bass.

Maslach, C., Schaufeli, W. B., & Leiter, M. P. (2001). Job burnout. *Annual Review of Psychology, 52,* 397–422.

Schaufeli, W. B., Bakker, A., Schaap, C., Kladler, A., & Hoogduin, C. A. L. (2001). On the clinical validity of the Maslach Burnout Inventory and the Burnout Measure. *Psychology & Health, 16,* 565–582.

MICHAEL P. LEITER
Acadia University, Nova Scotia, Canada

See also: Job Stress Survey

BUROS MENTAL MEASUREMENTS YEARBOOK

As a new professor of measurement and statistics at Rutgers University in the early 1930s, Oscar Krisen Buros recognized the increasing importance of standardized testing to industrialized societies. In order to insure greater public accountability for tests and to evaluate the many claims being made by test authors and publishers, Buros created the *Mental Measurements Yearbook* (MMY) series. During an editorship that would last over 40 years, Buros recruited a cadre of skilled professionals to write "candidly critical" test reviews that would serve a variety of public interests. For test users, the series would allow valuable access to the expertise of scholars and professionals. Buros believed that knowledgeable test users would gradually become informed consumers of testing products and would select tests that met or exceeded minimal standards of psychometric adequacy. For test writers and publishers, Buros maintained that the publication of critical reviews would "cause authors and publishers to publish fewer but better tests" (Buros, 1938).

Buros was undaunted by pressures brought by some in the testing community to curtail publication of the MMY series. Occasionally, Buros was threatened with lawsuits over critical reviews. In addition, the logistics of recruiting qualified professionals and editing their reviews for a large number of testing instruments promised to be (and has remained) an enormous undertaking. To sustain him in this endeavor, Buros enlisted the considerable talents of his wife, Luella, and small group of devoted staff. Funding to create a "Consumer's Research Bureau," whereby specially trained teams of psychometricians would independently evaluate tests did not materialize. Instead, Buros continued to rely upon large numbers of academics and specialized professionals to serve in the role of test reviewers.

Despite the name "The Mental Measurements Yearbook" and the desire of its editor to publish new volumes annually, the exacting standards of Buros and the size of the undertaking mandated a production schedule for the MMY averaging once every five years. Besides the publication of the MMY, Buros also edited special monographs on testing in distinct subject areas (e.g., vocations, personality) and initiated production of the *Tests in Print* (TIP) series. TIP was designed to serve the testing community as a compendium of all currently available tests and to provide a quick reference to test reviews published in the MMY series. Whereas each new edition of the MMY provides a description and review of new or revised commercial tests, new editions of the TIP series contain descriptive entries of all known commercial tests currently available in the English language.

Buros began his publication series with *Educational, Psychological, and Personality Tests of 1936* and *The Nineteen Thirty Eight Mental Measurements Yearbook* and continued through *The Eighth Mental Measurements Yearbook* (1978), during which he passed away. After a nationwide search to determine a successor location, Luella Buros selected the University of Nebraska–Lincoln to continue the work begun by her late husband. The world's largest collection of tests and testing material was subsequently crated and shipped, and publication recommenced in 1983 with *Tests in Print III* and in 1985 by *The Ninth Mental Measurements Yearbook*.

The dream of Oscar Buros for fewer, better quality tests has been partially realized in several ways. A current count of in-print tests suggests a small reduction in the number of commercially available instruments being offered for sale since 1983. In addition, many of the sophisticated methodological strategies designed to insure test reliability, validity, and appropriate standardization had not been developed or even imagined in the days when Buros made his initial proclamation about the state of testing. With the advent of testing standards first articulated in 1954 (and most recently in 1999) by the American Educational Research Association, the American Psychological Association, and the National Council on Measurement in Education, test authors and publishers alike have greater guidance by which to judge the adequacy of their products.

Shortly before her death in 1995, Luella Buros funded the Buros Center for Testing. Mrs. Buros believed that, in order to speed advances in the field of testing and measurement, it was essential to create a consultation service that would share its test development expertise with both public and private sectors. Working as the umbrella organization, the Center combines the historic publishing objectives of the Buros Institute of Mental Measurements to improve testing products with consultation services from the newly created Buros Institute for Assessment Consultation and Outreach.

In response to continual requests to make test reviews more accessible to the public, Test Reviews Online was launched in September 2001. This Internet service (www.unl.edu/buros) provides, for a modest fee, immediate access to over 2,500 testing instruments across a wide variety of subject areas. Additional test reviews are added on a regular basis as new reviews are submitted. The Buros Center for Testing continues the work of improving tests and assessments first articulated by Oscar Buros over 70 years ago.

Brief History of the Buros Institute of Mental Measurements

1938: *The 1938 Mental Measurements Yearbook*; Oscar K. Buros (Editor)

1940: *The 1940 Mental Measurements Yearbook*; Oscar K. Buros (Editor)

1949 to 1978: *The Third through Eighth Mental Measurements Yearbooks*, and *Tests in Print* and *Tests in Print II*; Oscar K. Buros (Editor)

1978: Oscar K. Buros passes away. Luella Gubrud Buros relocates the Buros Institute of Mental Measurements to the University of Nebraska–Lincoln

1983 to 1985: *Tests in Print III* and *The Ninth Mental Measurements Yearbook*; James V. Mitchell, Jr. (Editor)

1989: *The Tenth Mental Measurements Yearbook*; Jane Close Conoley & Jack J. Kramer (Editors)

1992: *The Eleventh Mental Measurements Yearbook*; Jack J. Kramer & Jane Close Conoley (Editors)

1994: The Oscar and Luella Buros Center for Testing is created as a parent organization, adding the Buros Institute for Assessment Consultation and Outreach to the Buros Institute of Mental Measurements. *Tests in Print IV*; Linda L. Murphy, Jane Close Conoley, & James C. Impara (Editors)

1995: *The Twelfth Mental Measurements Yearbook*; Jane Close Conoley & James C. Impara (Editors)

1998: *The Thirteenth Mental Measurements Yearbook*; James C. Impara & Barbara S. Plake (Editors)

1999: *Tests in Print V*; Linda L. Murphy, James C. Impara, & Barbara S. Plake (Editors)

2001: *The Fourteenth Mental Measurements Yearbook*; Barbara S. Plake & James C. Impara (Editors). Test Reviews Online (a collection of over 2,000 recent test descriptions and reviews from *The Mental Measurements Yearbook* and *Tests in Print* series) becomes available via the Internet.

2002: *Tests in Print VI*; Linda L. Murphy, Barbara S. Plake, James C. Impara, & Robert A. Spies (Editors)

2003: *The Fifteenth Mental Measurements Yearbook*; Barbara S. Plake, James C. Impara, & Robert A. Spies (Editors)

2005: *The Sixteenth Mental Measurements Yearbook*; Robert A. Spies and Barbara S. Plake (Editors)

2006: *Tests in Print VII*; Linda L. Murphy, Robert A. Spies, and Barbara S. Plake (Editors)

2007: *The Seventeenth Mental Measurements Yearbook*; Kurt F. Geisinger, Robert A. Spies, Janet F. Carlson, and Barbara S. Plake (Editors)

REFERENCES

American Educational Research Association, American Psychological Association, & National Council on Measurement in Education. (1999). *Standards for educational and psychological testing*. Washington, DC: American Educational Research Association.

Buros, Oscar K. (Ed). (1938). *The 1938 mental measurements yearbook*. New Brunswick, NJ: Rutgers University Press.

Test Reviews Online. Available from www.unl.edu/buros

ROBERT SPIES
Buros Institute of Mental Measurements

BYSTANDER INVOLVEMENT

In March 1964, Kitty Genovese was brutally murdered in New York while 38 of her neighbors watched from their apartment windows. Even though the attack lasted over a half hour, no one called the police until it was over. As a direct result of this incident, a great deal of empirical and theoretical knowledge has been generated on the topic of bystander involvement.

According to the model developed by Latane and Darley (1970), the decision to intervene consists of a series of decisions. First, the bystander must notice that something is happening. Second, the bystander must interpret or label what has been noticed as an emergency. Third, the bystander must decide that she has a responsibility to become involved. Fourth, the bystander must decide what form of assistance to render. And fifth, a decision must be made regarding how to implement the previous decision.

Research supporting this model attests the important role played by social influence factors at two stages of the model: labeling the event as an emergency, and feeling responsible for becoming involved. Bystanders may use the actions of others in the situation to help them interpret the event. If a group of people are all unsure about what is happening and hesitate to take action, each person may use this seeming passivity of others to label the event as a nonemergency. Even when a bystander is certain that the event is an emergency, the presence of others may diffuse responsibility for taking action. As a result, bystanders are less likely to aid the victim. The "diffusion of responsibility" explanation of bystander involvement is supported by a wide range of empirical findings showing that the greater the number of bystanders present, the less likely a victim is to receive aid.

Another model of bystander involvement for which there is considerable empirical support is the arousal/cost-reward model first proposed by I. Piliavin, Rodin, and J. Piliavin (1969). This model consists of two components: an arousal component and a cost/reward component. The components are conceptually distinct but functionally related. This model proposes that bystanders are aversively aroused by the victim's distress, that they are motivated to reduce their arousal, and that helping the victim is one way to accomplish this. According to the model, "arousal is a function of the clarity and severity of the crisis and of the psychological and physical closeness of the bystander to the victim" (Dovidio, Piliavin, Gaertner, Schroeder, & Clark, 1991, p. 89). In their search for ways to reduce arousal, bystanders are guided by their assessment of the rewards and costs of each option. The model proposes that they will prefer responses that most rapidly and completely reduce arousal and that yield the most favorable costs to benefits ratio. Successive versions of the model have added to its breadth and it has become increasingly complex (the current version has 8 boxes and 17 arrows) making causal analysis more difficult.

Batson has challenged this model, claiming that it assumes bystanders are egotistically motivated (Batson, 1987). That is according to the above model, bystanders' primary concern is to reduce their own distress and helping the victim is a means for achieving this goal. In contrast, Batson proposes a model of helping based on empathic concern. According to his empathy-altruism hypothesis, witnessing another individual in distress can lead to empathic concern, involving feelings of sympathy, compassion, and tenderness. Such emotions can "evoke motivation with an ultimate goal of benefiting the person for whom the empathy is felt—that is, altruistic motivation" (Batson, 1998, p. 300). In a series of experiments that controlled for alternative egoistic motivation, Batson (1987) demonstrated strong support for altruistically motivated helping. The research thus suggests there can be multiple motives for bystanders' reactions and their helping behavior can best be viewed as a weighted function of egoistic and altruistic motives.

Two important moderators of bystander reactions are attributions and type of relationship. The types of attributions bystanders make about the victim and about themselves (e.g., their arousal) can influence their helping behavior. For example, bystanders have been found less likely to aid victims if they view the victims as being responsible for their fate. The type of relationship that the bystander has with the victim can also moderate helping. Bystanders who feel a sense of "we-ness" with the victim or who are in a communal relationship with the victim may feel more empathy for the victim, and thus, they experience greater arousal and distress than bystanders who perceive the victim as being different or as being a member of an out-group.

Personality factors have been found to provide a poorer accounting of bystander involvement than have features of the situation. Although there has been some recent success in identifying dispositional predictors of helping, correlations rarely exceed .30 to .40 (Batson, 1998).

REFERENCES

Batson, C. D. (1987). Prosocial motivation: Is it ever truly altruistic? In L. Berkowitz (Ed.), *Advances in experimental social psychology* (Vol. 20, pp. 65–122). New York: Academic Press.

Batson, C. D. (1998). Altruism and prosocial behavior. In D. T. Gilbert, S. T. Fiske, & G. Lindzey (Eds.), *The handbook of social psychology* (Vol. 2, pp. 282–316). New York: McGraw-Hill.

Dovidio, J. F., Piliavin, J. A., Gaertner, S. L., Schroeder, D. A., & Clark, R. D., III. (1991). The arousal: Cost-reward model and the process of intervention: A review of the evidence. *Prosocial behavior* (pp. 86–118). Newbury Park, CA: Sage.

Latane, B., & Darley, J. M. (1970). *The unresponsive bystander: Why doesn't he help?* New York: Appleton-Century-Crofts.

Piliavin, I. M., Rodin, J., & Piliavin, J. A. (1969). Good Samaritanism: An underground phenomenon. *Journal of Personality and Social Psychology, 13,* 289–299.

SUGGESTED READINGS

Batson, C. D., Van Lange, P. A., Ahmad, N., & Lishner, D. A. (2003). Altruism and helping behavior. In M. A. Hogg & J. Cooper (Eds.), *The Sage handbook of social psychology* (pp. 279–295). Thousand Oaks, CA: Sage.

Latane, B., & Nida, S. A. (1981). Ten years of group size and helping. *Psychological Bulletin, 89,* 308–324.

MARTIN S. GREENBERG
University of Pittsburgh

See also: **Altruism; Prosocial Behavior**

C

CAFFEINE-RELATED DISORDERS

The widespread consumption of caffeine is a relatively recent phenomenon in human history. European colonization in the sixteenth and seventeenth centuries led to coffee and tea being transported around the world, and this process of dissemination proved to be extraordinarily successful. Caffeine has come to be the most widely used psychoactive substance in history, with more than 80% of people worldwide now consuming the drug daily (James, 1997).

Globally, coffee is the main source of caffeine. Tea is consumed more widely, but qualifies as the second main source because its caffeine content is generally lower than that of coffee. In many countries, per capita intake varies from about 200 to 400 mg of caffeine per day, the approximate equivalent of two to six cups of coffee or tea per day. Caffeine soft drinks (e.g., cola) represent an increasingly important source of the drug and are often the main source for children. The more recently developed so-called "energy" drinks are also an increasingly important source of caffeine for young people.

The presence of caffeine in coffee and tea beverages is due to its presence in the plants (as a defense against being eaten by predators) from which these beverages are derived. The caffeine in sodas and energy drinks may also partly derive from plants (e.g., cacao, cola nut, guarana), although most of the caffeine in such drinks is added in the refined form. Indeed, there is increasing concern about the success of the marketing of caffeine to children, for whom it may be serve as a gateway to the use of nicotine, alcohol, and other drugs.

Caffeine exerts diverse pharmacological actions believed to be mostly due to antagonism of endogenous adenosine, a neuromodulator with diverse actions in the body, especially the central nervous system. Having a similar molecular structure to adenosine, caffeine occupies adenosine receptor sites, with A_1 and A_{2A} receptors appearing to be the primary targets. It is believed that adenosine generally functions to inhibit physiological activity. It is involved in the regulation of sleep and wakefulness, dilates cerebral and coronary blood vessels, acts as an antidiuretic, induces bronchoconstriction, and inhibits acid secretion in the gastrointestinal tract. By blocking adenosine receptors, caffeine has effects broadly opposite to those of adenosine.

Caffeine-related disorders are recognized instances of physical and psychological dysfunction in major systems of diagnostic classification, including the *International Statistical Classification of Diseases and Related Health Problems* (ICD-10; (World Health Organization, 2007) and the *Diagnostic and Statistical Manual of Mental Disorders* (DSM-IV-TR; (American Psychiatric Association, 2000). ICD-10 has a specific classification of mental and behavioral disorders due to use of other stimulants, including caffeine, which includes subcategories of *acute intoxication, dependence syndrome*, and *withdrawal state*. Similarly, under the rubric of caffeine-related disorders (within the broader category of substance-related disorders), DSM-IV-TR has classifications for *caffeine intoxication, caffeine-induced anxiety disorder*, and *caffeine-induced sleep disorder*.

The essential features of caffeine intoxication, as specified in DSM-IV-TR, are (1) recent consumption of caffeine, usually in excess of 250 mg (two–three cups of coffee), but potentially involving as little as 100 mg of caffeine per day, and (2) five or more symptoms that develop during, or shortly after, caffeine use. Symptoms include restlessness, nervousness, excitement, insomnia, flushed face, diuresis, and gastrointestinal complaints. With higher levels of consumption (e.g., 1000 mg per day), more pronounced symptoms may appear, including muscle twitching, rambling flow of thought and speech, tachycardia or cardiac arrhythmia, periods of inexhaustibility, and psychomotor agitation.

As the name implies, the classification of caffeine-induced anxiety disorder refers to the occurrence of symptoms of anxiety (e.g., nervousness, worry, apprehension) associated with, and believed to be precipitated by, the consumption of caffeine. Caffeine-induced sleep disorder typically refers to insomnia (e.g., increased sleep latency, decreased sleep time, fragmented sleep) provoked by caffeine consumption. However, periods of reduced caffeine intake or abstinence can also lead to bouts of sleepiness (hypersomnia). That is, additional to nighttime insomnia, caffeine-induced sleep disorder may refer to the occurrence of withdrawal-induced daytime sleepiness due to caffeine abstinence or reduced caffeine intake.

The acute effects of caffeine and the physical dependence associated with dietary use have commonplace implications. For example, caffeine-induced hand tremor has been found to undermine surgical precision, withdrawal-induced headache may disrupt pre-surgical preparation in hospital patients, and withdrawal-induced sleepiness associated with dietary use may contribute to traffic accidents. Furthermore, although caffeine is widely believed to be beneficial to mental performance and mood, controlled studies show that these perceived benefits are largely illusory. Considerable scientific effort has gone into clarifying to what extent benefits generally attributed to caffeine represent genuine net effects of the drug or reversal of withdrawal effects. Studies show that decrements in psychomotor performance and mood are detectable after as little as six–eight hours since caffeine was last ingested (Heatherley et al., 2005), and that improvements in performance and mood, widely perceived to be net psychostimulant effects, are primarily attributable to reversal of the withdrawal effects that accompany even short periods of abstinence (James & Rogers, 2005).

The process of caffeine withdrawal (identified in DSM-IV-TR as a syndrome under consideration but not yet a formal diagnosis) is central to understanding many of the implications of the dietary caffeine habits of the majority of people. Daily use commonly leads to physical dependence, characterized by the appearance of a withdrawal syndrome of behavioral, physiological, and subjective disruption (including, most prominently, headache, sleepiness, and lethargy) when plasma caffeine levels are depleted (Juliano & Griffiths, 2004). Withdrawal symptoms typically peak between 24–48 hours after caffeine was last consumed, and may persist for up to one week. In contrast to caffeine physical dependence, which is comparatively well established, caffeine tolerance in humans is considerably less well characterized. Although repeated exposure to caffeine probably leads to a degree of tolerance to some of its effects, it is doubtful whether complete tolerance occurs in the context of dietary use. For this reason, there is concern that specific acute effects of caffeine (e.g., increased blood pressure, feelings of anxiety or "stress") may have long-term adverse consequences.

REFERENCES

American Psychiatric Association. (2000). *Diagnostic and statistical manual of mental disorders* (4th ed., text rev.). Washington, DC: Author.

Heatherley, S. V., Hayward, R. C., Seers, H. E., & Rogers, P. J. (2005) Cognitive and psychomotor performance, mood, and pressor effects of caffeine after 4, 6, and 8 h caffeine abstinence. *Psychopharmacology, 178*, 461–470.

James, J. E. (1997). *Understanding caffeine: A biobehavioral analysis.* Thousand Oaks, CA: Sage.

James, J. E., & Rogers, P. J. (2005). Effects of caffeine on performance and mood: Withdrawal reversal is the most plausible explanation. *Psychopharmacology, 182*, 1–8.

Juliano, L. M., & Griffiths, R. R. (2004). A critical review of caffeine withdrawal: Empirical validation of symptoms and signs, incidence, severity, and associated features. *Psychopharmacology, 176*, 1–29.

World Health Organization (2007). *International Statistical Classification of Diseases and Related Health Problems* (10th rev.). Geneva, Switzerland: Author.

SUGGESTED READINGS

Heatherley, S. V., Hancock, K. M. F., & Rogers, P. J. (2006). Psychostimulant and other effects of caffeine in 9- to 11-year-old children. *Journal of Child Psychology and Psychiatry, 47*, 135–142.

James, J. E. (2004). A critical review of dietary caffeine and blood pressure: A relationship that should be taken more seriously. *Psychosomatic Medicine, 66*, 63–71.

James, J. E., Gregg, M. E., Kane, M., & Harte, F. (2005). Dietary caffeine, performance, and mood: Enhancing and restorative effects after controlling for withdrawal relief. *Neuropsychobiology, 52*, 1–10.

JACK E. JAMES
National University of Ireland, Galway, Ireland

See also: **Drug Addiction**

CALIFORNIA PSYCHOLOGICAL INVENTORY

The California Psychological Inventory (CPI) is a self-report, paper and pencil test comprised of 434 True-False items. There is also a 260-item short form. Questions relate to a person's typical behaviors, opinions, feelings, and attitudes regarding family, ethical, and social matters. It can be administered to individuals between the ages of 12 and 70 having a minimum of a fourth grade education. Results of the test are presented as a profile comprised of 20 scales, 3 vectors (or factors), and a variety of special purpose scales. It is typically used within normal populations to help understand vocational preferences, interpersonal behavior, intrapersonal function, and orientation toward normative values.

One of the noteworthy features of the CPI is its use of familiar, everyday constructs that have been referred to as "folk concepts." These include dominance, self-control, self-acceptance, and responsibility. As a result, the test is fairly easy to interpret and readily used in cross-cultural contexts, and feedback concerning its results is readily understood by examinees.

The original version of the CPI was derived from an item pool of 3,500 questions. Of the 468 items originally selected, 178 were identical to Minnesota Multiphasic Personality Inventory (MMPI) items, 35 were very similar, and the remaining 255 were developed specifically for the CPI. An empirical criterion keying method was utilized to generate the majority of questions, while a conceptual approach was used to generate a subset that assessed the characteristics the scales were trying to measure. The specific sample question pool items were either accepted or rejected based on the extent of interitem correlation, and they were cross-validated with other populations to determine their validity and reliability.

The original 18 scales of the CPI were first published as the CPI 480 in 1957 using a normative sample of 6,000 males and 7,000 females with a wide range in age, socioeconomic status, and geographic area. In 1987, the instrument underwent a substantial revision with the addition of new scales for Empathy and Independence (see Table 1). The CPI also utilizes three validity scales that assess test-taking attitudes including "faking bad," "faking good," and the extent to which common responses are given. Research on the CPI continued, and the inventory was again revised in 1996 to conform to the 1990 Americans with Disabilities Act. The 1996 revision was based on 3,000 participants of each sex selected from the CPI archives to represent the U.S. population in terms of age, education, status, and other relevant variables. (Gough, 1996/2002). A short form, the CPI 260, was published in 2002 (Gough & Bradley, 2005).

Psychometric evaluation of the CPI has found that it is comparable to other well-developed personality inventories (see Groth-Marnat, 2009). Test-retest reliability for the long form (CPI-434) has ranged from .51 to .84 (median = .76), and internal consistency has ranged from .43 to .85 (median = .76; Gough, 1996). Research on validity indicates that it is capable of making accurate predictions related to a wide range of areas including academic performance, teaching effectiveness, parole success, and leadership. Factor analyses have indicated that it measures core aspects of personality. The two major factors that have emerged relate to introversion-extraversion and norm-favoring versus norm-doubting.

A number of predictive studies have been conducted and several useful regression equations have been developed as aids in predicting behavior. However, extremely few studies have tested the validity of predictions made by clinicians in actual practice (Gynther, 1978). It may be that clinical judgments based on the CPI are generally accurate, but, at this point, further empirical studies are needed for verification. It is somewhat of a contradiction that a test with an emphasis on practical usefulness has not been sufficiently evaluated in the clinical context.

Interpretation of the CPI often relies on noticing how patterns of scales relate to one another. A first step is to note that the CPI scales are clustered around scales that measure interpersonal style, how people orient themselves to and relate to social norms, modes of cognitive achievement, and sensitivity and level of insight (see Table 1). This allows the interpreter to note how examinees orient themselves to others or the extent to which they value achievement in their lives. Interpreters can also develop more nuanced understandings by observing how the various scales interact with one another. For example, a person who is high in Dominance but low in Empathy can be expected to have a fairly cold, impersonal leadership

Table 1. CPI scale clusters, individual scales, and abbreviations.

Cluster	Abbreviation	Name
Interpersonal style and orientation	Do	Dominance
	Cs	Capacity for Status
	Sy	Sociability
	Sp	Social Presence
	Sa	Self Acceptance
	In	Independence
	Em	Empathy
Normative orientation and values	Re	Responsibility
	So	Socialization (Social Conformity)*
	Sc	Self-Control
	Gi	Good Impression
	Cm	Communality
	Wb	Well-Being
	To	Tolerance
Cognitive and intellectual function	Ac	Achievement via Conformance
	Ai	Achievement via Independence
	Ie	Intellectual Efficiency (Conceptual Fluency)
Role and personal style	Py	Psychological Mindedness (Insightfulness)
	Fx	Flexibility
	F/M	Femininity/Masculinity (Sensitivity)
Vector/factor scales	v1	Externality/Internality
	v2	Norm favoring vs. norm questioning
	v3	Ego integration

*Scale names in parentheses represent the names used in the CPI short form (CPI 260).

style. The vector factor scales also help to "color" various interpretations. For example, the previously stated Dominance/Empathy pattern would take on more negative characteristics if the person were both norm-questioning and extraverted (high Externality). A final aspect of interpretation is the inclusion of the Special Purpose Scales. These scales use everyday language and include such scales as Managerial Potential, Creative Temperament, Tough Mindedness, and Narcissism. The short form of the CPI (260) uses these same scales, but in some cases the names have been slightly altered (e.g., Psychological Mindedness has been renamed Insightfulness); however, the principles of interpretation remain essentially the same.

The preceding information clearly highlights a number of assets of the CPI. It has become one of the most popular and widely utilized instruments for the assessment of specific personality characteristics within normal populations. Unlike many other tests, it focuses on assessing levels of functioning in the realm of interpersonal relationships by predicting stable behavioral dimensions in both short- and long-term circumstances. It has also been used with a wide range of age groups (high school and beyond) and across a large cross-section of society. It is widely used in determining leadership and management styles and in determining fitness for service in high-risk occupations such as police and fire protection. With younger populations, it has been used to predict the likelihood of high school and college graduation, as well as the potential for juvenile delinquency and criminal behavior. Because the instrument has generally proven to be a useful tool in the area of behavioral prediction, it has been particularly useful with high school and college students as well as with personnel selection. Perhaps one of the strongest assets of the CPI is its use of simple, everyday descriptors for each of the instrument's concepts and scales. Because the CPI's basic concepts were developed within the framework of interpersonal relationships, the CPI interpretations are more likely to be relevant, useful, and have a greater impact on the client receiving feedback.

Despite these many assets, the CPI has a number of limitations. A frequently noted difficulty is that many of the scales correlate highly with one another, which is consistent with the fact that they typically share many of the same items. However, this can be defended in that there is a natural overlap and blending of characteristics in the actual functioning of examinees. For example, a person who is highly self-controlled might also be quite responsible, but these are still somewhat different constructs. Thus it would be natural that they would be moderately correlated on a test such as the CPI. Despite this, little research has been done to understand more fully the meanings of combinations of scales (so called "code types"). In addition, more research could be done to understand the clinical applications and implications of the CPI. Several of the CPI scales have relatively weak psychometric properties, including Psychological Mindedness/Sensitivity, Communality, and Flexibility. As a result, these properties should be interpreted with caution. A final weakness of the CPI is that more research needs to be done to establish the equivalence of the long form (CPI 434) and the more recently developed short form (CPI 260).

REFERENCES

Gough, H. G. (2002). *California Psychological Inventory*. (3rd ed.). Palo Alto, CA: Consulting Psychologists Press.

Gough, H. G., & Bradley, P. (2005). *CPI 260 manual*. Mountain View, CA: Consulting Psychologists Press.

Groth-Marnat, G. (2009). *Handbook of psychological assessment* (5th ed.). Hoboken, NJ: John Wiley & Sons.

Gynther, M. D. (1978) The California Psychological Inventory: A review. In O. K. Buros (Ed.), *The eighth mental measurements yearbook* (Vol. 1, pp. 733–737). Hihgland Park, NJ: Gryphon Press.

SUGGESTED READINGS

Donnay, D., & Elliott, T. R. (2003). The California Psychological Inventory. In L. E. Beutler & G. Groth-Marnat (Eds.). *Integrative assessment of adult personality* (2nd ed.). (pp. 227–261). New York: Guilford Press.

Megargee, E. I. (2002). *The California Psychological Inventory Handbook* (2nd ed.). San Francisco: Jossey-Bass.

GARY GROTH-MARNAT
MICHAEL J. MULLARD
Pacifica Graduate Institute, Carpinteria, CA

See also: **Personality Assessment; Self-Report Inventories; Vocational Counseling**

CALKINS, MARY WHITON (1863–1930)

Mary W. Calkins attended Smith College where she studied classics and philosophy. After graduating in 1884, she worked with William James. When Hugo Munsterberg came to Harvard, Calkins worked for three years in his laboratory. Despite the fact that Calkins successfully defended her dissertation to a distinguished committee including William James, Hugo Munsterberg, and Josiah Royce, because of her gender the university records show that the successful examination was noted but that the PhD was never awarded. She later rejected the offer of a PhD from Radcliffe. At Wellesley College, where she taught, she established a psychological laboratory that she directed for 10 years. During this period she invented the method of paired associates for the study of memory.

As Calkins's interests shifted toward philosophy, she became increasingly dissatisfied with the Wundt-Titchener experimental structuralist tradition. She supported her self-psychology, which recognized the self as an integrating agent in conscious life. Having worked as an introspectionist, she appealed to the direct experience of the person. Her revised textbook, *A First Book in Psychology* (1909), presents her mature position. Calkins argued that the various schools of psychology might unite in a personalistic psychology.

Calkins served as the first female president of the American Psychological Association in 1905 and she was also president of the American Philosophical Association in 1918. She has been ranked in the second 10 of psychologists starred in the first edition of *American Men of Science*.

SUGGESTED READINGS

Calkins, M. W. (1907). *The persistent problems of philosophy: An introduction to metaphysics through the study of modern systems* (5th ed.). New York: Macmillan.

Calkins, M. W. (1910). *A first book in psychology*. New York: Macmillan.

Calkins, M. W. (1918). *The good and the good man: An introduction to ethics*. New York: Macmillan.

P. E. LICHTENSTEIN

CANADIAN PSYCHOLOGICAL ASSOCIATION

The Canadian Psychological Association (CPA), founded in 1939 and incorporated as a not-for-profit corporation in 1950, is Canada's national association of psychologists. It is a voluntary association for the profession and discipline of psychology. As such, it serves as an advocacy body; meeting the needs of its members as well as contributing psychological knowledge and expertise for the welfare of Canadians and Canadian society. The CPA is not a regulatory body for the practice of psychology—this latter activity is the responsibility of provincial and territorial regulatory bodies for each of the health professions.

As stated on CPA's web site, its mandate is to:

- Improve the health and welfare of all Canadians
- Promote excellence and innovation in psychological research, education, and practice
- Promote the advancement, development, dissemination, and application of psychological knowledge
- Provide high-quality services to members (http://www.cpa.ca/aboutcpa/)

In 2008, CPA's 6,300 members included psychologists employed in diverse settings across Canada as well as students. CPA hosts 30 sections on a diversity of sub-specialties of psychology and one interest group. The membership elects a Board of Directors whose members are responsible for portfolios (e.g., Science, Professional Affairs, Education, and Training), standing committees (e.g., Ethics, Publications), and ad hoc committees (e.g., Task Force on Supply and Demand for Psychologists). The Board sets policy for CPA, the implementation of which is the responsibility of its Executive Director, who is employed by and responsible to the Board. Head Office staff members report to the Executive Director and fulfill roles and responsibilities that reflect the mandates of the CPA (e.g., communications and publication, membership services including continuing education, accreditation).

CPA published its first journal, the *Bulletin of the Canadian Psychological Association*, in 1940. Over the following decades, two more journals were added. CPA's three peer-reviewed journals have operated under the following titles for several decades: *Canadian Psychology,* the *Canadian Journal of Behavioural Science*, and the *Canadian Journal of Experimental Psychology*. The journals are owned and copyrighted by the CPA and, since 2008, a quarterly newsletter, *Psynopsis,* has been published. CPA has recently launched a new initiative, the Canadian Psychological Association Press.

In response to the growth of professional psychology training throughout Canada, accreditation standards and processes were established by the CPA in 1984. CPA currently accredits 28 doctoral programs and 27 internships in professional psychology (clinical, counseling, school, and neuropsychology) throughout Canada. The Canadian Code of Ethics for Psychologists is internationally recognized for addressing issues to be considered by psychologists in various roles, but also for providing a framework for ethical decision making.

Over the past several decades, CPA has promoted psychology through diverse activities and partnerships related to the science and practice of psychology. These have included alliances, activities, and initiatives with other health care and research organizations, government grants and appointments to advisory groups, and the preparation of briefs to Standing Senate and House of Commons Committees. CPA has prepared a number of position statements and papers that inform social and health policy in Canada.

CPA's annual conventions attract up to 1,800 delegates, bringing together basic scientists and scientist-practitioners. Its continuing education activities allow members to stay current on advances in the ever-changing field.

Information about the CPA, its organization, officers, and activities can be found at http://www.cpa.ca.

KAREN R. COHEN
Canadian Psychological Association

CANCER (See Psychooncology)

CANNABIS-RELATED DISORDERS

In 2007, 3.9 million persons in the United States aged 12 or older (1.6% of the population) met DSM criteria for cannabis dependence or abuse. The numbers of those who had used marijuana ever, in the past year, and in the past month in 2007 were 100.5 million, 25.1 million, and 14.5 million, respectively (Substance Abuse and Mental Health Services Administration [CSAT], 2008). Approximately 4.3% of Americans have been dependent on cannabis.

The risk of become cannabis dependent is estimated as 9% among those who have used the drug at least once. Among more frequent users, as many as 50% may meet criteria for the cannabis dependence diagnosis (Swift, Hall, & Copeland, 2000). Initiation of use early in adolescence appears to elevate the risk. In 2007, 12.9% of those who had first used cannabis before age 15 met cannabis abuse or dependence criteria, while the comparable figure for those who had first used the drug at age 18 or older was 2.7%.

Among adults entering treatment for cannabis dependence, most have been smoking the drug regularly for 15 or more years, have made an average of six serious attempts at quitting, and have been aware that they have been experiencing problems related to their use for 8 to 10 years (Stephens, Roffman, & Simpson, 1993). The most common reasons for wishing to overcome cannabis dependence are loss of self-control, negative self-image, lowered productivity, relationship and family problems, sleep and memory difficulties, and low life-satisfaction.

Studies of the endogenous cannabinoid system in the central nervous system have pointed to biological mechanisms involved with cannabis withdrawal, a syndrome that includes elevated levels of anger, irritability, and depression as well as sleeping difficulty, decreased appetite, and craving. Most symptoms abate within three weeks, with peak effects occurring between four and six days after cessation of use (Budney & Hughes, 2006).

At least 11 controlled trials of cannabis dependence counseling interventions with adults have been conducted, with most evaluating motivational enhancement therapy (MET), cognitive-behavioral therapy (CBT), and contingency management (CM), either alone or in combination (Budney, Roffman, Stephens, & Walker, 2007; Roffman & Stephens, 2006). The state of the science at this time appears to favor combining these three approaches, although the successful attainment of durable abstinence has been modest. A substantial subset of cannabis dependent adults in treatment shifts from the goal of becoming abstinent to achieving moderation. Although it appears that some are successful in reducing their cannabis use as well as related problems, the illegal status of cannabis has thus far prevented treatment researchers from evaluating the efficacy of a moderation-focused intervention. Following a multisite trial of brief MET and CBT cannabis dependence interventions, CSAT published a therapist's manual (Brief Counseling for Marijuana Dependence) that can be downloaded from http://www.kap.samhsa.gov/products/brochures/pdfs/bmdc.pdf.

Interventions tailored for adolescent cannabis users have included MET, CBT, and CM, as well as various family-focused therapies such as functional family therapy, multidimensional family therapy, multisystemic therapy, family support network intervention, and brief strategic family therapy. Five therapist manuals, each offering a protocol for an alternate approach to treating adolescent cannabis users, can be accessed at http://www.kap.samhsa.gov/products/manuals/cyt/index.htm. These protocols were developed for the CSAT-funded Cannabis Youth Treatment multisite trial, which reported modestly successful outcomes across conditions.

The "marijuana check-up," a motivational enhancement intervention tailored for the concerned cannabis user who is neither seeking treatment nor self-initiating change, has been studied with both adult and adolescent users. Publicized as an unpressured opportunity to take stock of one's experiences and think through one's options, the check-up studies have shown promise in eliciting voluntary participation among ambivalent users and promoting greater readiness for change (Walker, Roffman, Picciano, & Stephens, 2007).

Research on pharmacotherapy for cannabis dependence is at an early stage, with most studies examining medications targeting the withdrawal syndrome. Orally administered THC has shown promise, much as have nicotine patches with nicotine dependence and methadone with opiate dependence, in reducing craving and other cannabis withdrawal symptoms. Another approach being examined involves using a cannabinoid receptor antagonist (rimonabant) to block the subjective and physiological effects of cannabis.

Finally, one of the challenges faced when discussing cannabis use disorders is misinformation. For more than 40 years, cannabis control policy has been the focus of considerable debate in the U.S. Both prohibitionists and those promoting policy reform have commonly supported their positions with a selective and sometimes inaccurate set of assertions. The polarized positions presented to the public have contributed to widely disparate views as to whether cannabis use disorders exist and their relative harm.

REFERENCES

Budney, A. J., & Hughes, J. R. (2006). The cannabis withdrawal syndrome. *Current Opinion in Psychiatry, 19*(3), 233–238.

Budney, A. J., Roffman, R., Stephens, R. S., & Walker, D. D. (2007). Marijuana dependence and its treatment. *Addiction Science and Clinical Practice, 4*, 4–16.

Roffman, R. A., & Stephens, R. S. (Eds.). (2006). *Cannabis dependence: Its nature, consequences, and treatment.* Cambridge: Cambridge University Press.

Stephens, R. S., Roffman, R. A., & Simpson, E. E. (1993). Adult marijuana users seeking treatment. *Journal of Consulting and Clinical Psychology, 61,* 1100–1104.

Substance Abuse and Mental Health Services Administration. (2008). Results from the 2007 national survey on drug use and health: National findings (Office of Applied Studies, NSDUH Series H-34, DHHS Publication No. SMA 08–4343), Rockville, MD.

Swift, W., Hall, W., & Copeland, J. (2000). One year follow-up of cannabis dependence among long-term users in Sydney, Australia. *Drug and Alcohol Dependence, 59,* 309–318.

Walker, D. D., Roffman, R. A., Picciano, J., & Stephens, R. S. (2007). The check-up: In-person, computerized, and telephone adaptations of motivational enhancement treatment to elicit voluntary participation by the contemplator. *Substance Abuse Treatment, Prevention, and Policy, 2*(2), http://www.substanceabusepolicy.com/content/2/1/2.

ROGER ROFFMAN
University of Washington

See also: **Drug Addiction**

CAREER COUNSELING

Career counseling can be thought of in at least three ways: one, as a single intervention that can assist clients with career behavior, issues, and problems; second, as a process that is overarching and includes various interventions that can be combined in different configurations to support the career counseling process and the needs of a given client; and third, as a continuum of career counseling and related interventions that make up a subspecialty within the general class of counseling (Gysbers, Heppner, & Johnston, 2003). This continuum responds to a wide-range of content that clients bring to career counselors, such as situational and personal dilemmas, unemployment, underemployment, job dissatisfaction, relationship problems with co-workers or supervisors, inadequate work skills, and family conflicts related to work.

Although the third way of viewing career counseling tends to be the most contemporary, there is no one model of career counseling that fits all clients. Rather, various interventions subsumed by the career counseling process are employed in a systematic way as they are relevant to the needs of a particular individual. Such interventions might include individual counseling, group counseling, personal and emotional support, assessment and testing, job shadowing, explorations of career options on the Internet, preparation for interviewing, anger management, examining personal narratives or life themes related to work, or gaining skills in decision-making (Herr, Cramer, & Niles, 2004).

Historically, career counseling has been treated as separate from psychotherapy or personal counseling. However, career development and work-related issues as the content of career counseling have come to be seen as complex behaviors. As such, they often involve emotional distress, stress, conflicts in work and other life roles, relationship issues, the exploration and choice of work roles and preparation for work, and the ability to adapt to rapid change in work organizations and in the ways work is done. Emerging perspectives include extending the conceptions of career counseling in new and more comprehensive ways: to the unique needs of particular populations (immigrants, women, persons with disabilities, racial and ethical minorities), to a widening range of problems addressed by it, and to the settings in which it should be offered.

Within such contexts, it has become accepted that work adjustment and personal adjustment exist in a symbiotic relationship. One affects the other and often needs to be addressed in career counseling by working with clients in a holistic and interactive manner, engaging content that is at once both situational and personal. Whereas traditional models of career counseling have tended to focus on career exploration, matching persons with jobs, clarification of life and career goals, and improvement in decision-making skills, recent applications of career counseling tend to address many concerns that require a fusion of career and personal counseling (Herr, 1997).

Definitions of Career Counseling

As the psychological and sociological influences on individual career development, the complexity of career information, and the globalization of work have expanded and become more complex, new definitions have emerged. These definitions have shifted from viewing career problems as rational, objective, and unaffected by emotional crises outside of the workplace to a growing emphasis on the interaction of work-related or career problems with those of personal identity, family concerns, interpersonal issues, adaptation to change, and related issues.

These latter dimensions add a strong emotional component to what had earlier been viewed as primarily a cognitive or information problem. As an example, emotional issues associated with an involuntary transition (e.g. unemployment, major illness) frequently have to be addressed before the counselor and client can focus on the next steps the client might consider in exploring new job options or other relevant actions. Such a circumstance often occurs in working with clients who have recently experienced being "fired." In such cases, the first need will be to help the client deal with the anger caused by his or her termination. Other emphases may relate to "What happened?" "Why was I fired?" "Why me?" These are emotional questions that need to be examined before the counselor and the client can turn effectively to exploring what alternatives are available, what content needs to be explored, what skills the client has that are transferable to other jobs or settings, or how to identify and interview potential employers.

Several authors have incorporated the elements of career counseling discussed here into definitions of career counseling. One of the classic definitions was offered by Brown and Brooks (1991, p. 5):

> Career counseling is an interpersonal process designed to assist individuals with career development problems. Career development is that process of choosing, entering, adjusting to and advancing in an occupation. It is a life-long psychological process that interacts dynamically with other life roles. Career problems include but are not limited to career indecisions and undecidedness, work performance, stress and adjustment, incongruence of the person and the work environment, and inadequate or unsatisfactory integration of life roles (e.g., parent, friend, or citizen).

In addition to the integrative characteristics of the Brown and Brooks definition, Herr, Cramer, and Niles (2004, p. 540) provided a definition that reduced the career counseling process to its essential elements:

> Career counseling is a largely verbal process in which a professional counselor and counselee(s) are in a dynamic and collaborative relationship, focused on identifying and acting on the counselee's goals, in which the counselor employs a repertoire of diverse techniques or processes, to help bring about self-understanding, understanding of the career concerns involved and behavioral options available as well as informed decision making in the counselee, who has the responsibility for his or her own actions.

In essence, the combination of these two definitions indicates that career counseling is used with individuals and with groups, represents a continuum of approaches tailored to the career concerns and needs of individual clients, and is likely to be part of a program of interventions that include career assessments, self-directed activities, assistance with skill development, and related functions.

Approaches to Career Counseling

The actual implementation of career counseling is frequently described in cyclical, sequential, or phased terms. Wise decision-making and positive action are frequently expected outcomes of career counseling, but the methods of arriving at such outcomes vary somewhat from model to model. A typical portrayal of the stages in career counseling might include the following: (1) Greeting the client and beginning to establish a working alliance, that is, a rapport that facilitates counselor-client collaboration; (2) Defining the problem that brought the client to the career counselor; (3) Providing assessments and their interpretations, if relevant to the client's concerns; (4) Formulating alternative actions or solutions to the client's problem; (5) Gathering information on the possible options relevant to changing the client's problem; (6) Applying information seeking skills; (7) Processing information collected; (8) Making plans and selecting goals; and (9) Implementing and evaluating the plan of action decided on by the client with the assistance of the counselor.

Such a model of the career counseling process is only one of many that might be used to characterize this process. By whatever terminology they are labeled, career counseling processes are intended to assist individuals in filtering objective data through subjective perceptions of risk-taking, self-efficacy, utility, and emotionality as a stimulus to action in constructing a career plan.

Evaluation of Career Counseling

Career counseling has been the focus of many research studies using a variety of methodological approaches. In general, these studies have reported positive effects for career interventions on diverse career outcomes (Sexton, Whiston, Blever, & Walz, 1997). Using meta-analysis, Whiston, Sexton, and Lasoff (1998) compared the effectiveness of several types of career interventions (e.g., workshops, career classes, computer programs, and individual counseling). Individual career counseling was found to be the most effective of these interventions. Oliver and Spokane (1988), also using meta-analysis, compared several career interventions and found that individual career counseling demonstrated the greatest amount of gain for clients in the shortest amount of time, per hour or session. These researchers, as well as Whiston et al., have reported that significant predictors of career counseling were the "dosage" or treatment intensity of career counseling and the comprehensiveness of the career counseling provided to clients. It is also possible that interventions included in the career counseling process may influence the effectiveness of the outcomes attained. For example, clients who receive test interpretations provided on an individual rather than a group basis had larger gains in counseling than those who did not receive test interpretations or who received them on a group rather than individual basis (Goodyear, 1990).

In sum, the many studies comparing different approaches to career counseling, career guidance, and career education indicate that each of these types of career intervention have yielded positive results. Their general effectiveness is no longer at issue, and these studies have provided important insights into the elements comprising an effective intervention. Such studies have become the foundation for the on-going research into evidence-based approaches to career counseling interventions. Such insights continue to advance the science on which career counseling is based, its costs and its benefits, and the changing content that it addresses.

REFERENCES

Brown, D., & Brooks, L. (1991). *Career counseling techniques*. Boston: Allyn and Bacon.

Goodyear, R. K. (1990). Research on the effects of test interpretation: A review. *The Counseling Psychologist, 18*, 240–257.

Gysbers, N. C., Heppner, M. J., & Johnston, J. A. (2003). *Career counseling: Process, issues, and techniques* (2nd ed.). Boston: Allyn and Bacon.

Herr, E. L. (1997). Career counseling: A process in process. *British Journal of Guidance and Counseling 25*, 81–93.

Herr, E. L., Cramer, S. H., & Niles, S. G. (2004). *Career guidance and counseling through the lifespan: Systematic approaches* (6th ed.) Boston: Allyn and Bacon.

Oliver, L. W., & Spokane, A. R. (1988). Career intervention outcome: What contributes to client gain? *Journal of Counseling Psychology, 35*(4), 447–462.

Sexton, T. L., Whiston, S. C., Blever, J. C., & Walz, G. R. (1997). *Integrating outcome research into counseling practice and training*. Alexandria, VA: American Counseling Association.

Whiston, S. C., Sexton, T. L., & Lasolf, D. L. (1998). Career intervention outcome: A replication and extension of Oliver and Spokane (1988). *Journal of Counseling Psychology, 45*(2), 150–165.

EDWIN L. HERR
Pennsylvania State University

See also: Career Development; Counseling; Vocational Counseling

CAREER DEVELOPMENT

The term *career development* has several meanings. At one level it is the term used to describe the large body of theory and research that serves as the knowledge base for career counselors and psychologists. This knowledge base identifies the factors, both internal to the individual and external in the environment, that interact across the life span as individuals forge their personal career identity, acquire work-related behaviors, anticipate and explore career options, adjust to the settings in which their work-related behavior is implemented, and manage the interaction of career and family roles.

There is no one theory of career development that captures the totality of career behavior. Instead, there are multiple theories that provide important insights into different facets of career behavior at different life stages, across settings, and in relation to different career development tasks such as exploration and decision-making. Some theories describe major factors affecting career behavior and, in turn, educational, job, occupational, and career choices. Some career theories emphasize the role of decision-making as the process by which an individual expresses positive or negative perceptions about self and work opportunities. Other theories talk about the centrality or meaning of work in individual career behavior, how people are inducted into work and adjust to the workplace, how individual career paths change overtime, and how career behaviors unfold in different life stages from growth to retirement.

Career Defined

To understand career development from a theoretical perspective, it is useful to consider the meaning of career. *Career* is different from either *job* or *occupation*. Although these three terms are often used interchangeably, they do not have the same meaning. Jobs or occupations describe sets of tasks that exist in a firm, an office, a factory, or a store, whether or not people are employed in them. Jobs can be vacant or filled, but they are still present in workplaces. Jobs and occupations can be described and listed as available in directories, newspaper advertisements, and information from employment services as methods of recruiting people to apply for and do such work. But the word career means more than the work performance of a set of tasks embodied in a job or an occupation.

Careers are different. Careers are not independent of the person who creates and pursues them. In this sense, one does not select a career as one selects a job or occupation; one creates or constructs a career by the decisions made or avoided with regard to such examples as education level chosen, amount of risk-taking the individual is willing to engage in, geographical mobility, the balance of work roles, and other life roles which the individual decides to pursue. Thus, the term career is comprehensive and includes within it jobs, occupations, the integration of work roles with those of family and community roles, lifestyle choices, education obtained, and decision-making processes.

Perspectives on Career Development

Career development can be understood as one of the many elements of socialization that combine to create human development. In psychological terms, the individual acquires motivation to explore, prepare for, and choose particular career paths related to, among other factors, his or her beliefs about personal self-efficacy, the ability to perform effectively or not in particular work options, and whether or not such work would yield valued outcomes. Thus the individual learns through influences from parents, teachers, role models, and exploratory activities or media that certain outcomes will likely result from some choices and not others and how the salience of work contributes to his or her personal identity.

In sociological terms, individual career development can be considered a product of the existing constraints or barriers on choices to be made or on access to particular options that arise from political or economic circumstances. Sociological effects on choice also can be seen in family or cultural influences. Families with differing educational or socioeconomic backgrounds tend to reinforce different educational and occupational goals and belief systems related to career development. Nations and cultural groups also differ in how particular types of education, work, or family roles are valued, and these perceptions tend to be internalized by group members and reflected in their choices.

Career development can be thought of in both structural and developmental terms. The structure of career development refers to the elements that comprise concepts like career maturity, career adaptability, career planfulness, and person-job congruence. As an example, research on career maturity in adolescence and career adaptability in adulthood tends to include five factors: planfulness or time perspective, exploration, information, decision-making, and reality orientation. These five factors are seen as structural components of career maturity and career adaptability, and each factor has its own structural sub-elements (Herr, Cramer, & Niles, 2004).

Career development, in addition to its structural elements, is also viewed by researchers in developmental terms. From this perspective, a different set of issues exists. These issues include the following: Does career maturity change over time? Is behavior described as career maturity at age 18 the same as career adaptability at age 40 or later? What are the factors that influence individual career behavior at the different life stages of childhood, adolescence, young adulthood, mid-career adulthood, and older adulthood? Do decision-making principles remain the same at any age even though the content of decisions and the life stage differ?

Other perspectives view career development as a continuous search for meaning by each individual, an attempt to construct a career path that is not simply a passive processing of information but a life-long narrative of meaning-making by which individuals construct their realities through the choices they make (Savickas, 2005). Other theorists view career development as a lifestyle concept. In this perspective, the work roles that one implements throughout the lifespan are not independent of other life roles, but may instead complement or be in conflict with them.

Theories of Career Development

Career behavior is complex. As a result, it is the object of attention in a wide-ranging set of theories of career development that are broad and interdisciplinary. These theories encompass perspectives that address career behavior using many different disciplines. Super (1990) provided insight into this matter when he discussed the pioneers of career development. He stated that they are "differential psychologists interested in work and occupations, developmental psychologists concerned with the 'life course,' sociologists focusing on occupational mobility as a function of social class, and personality theorists who view individuals as organizers of experience" (p. 197). To these theorists of different aspects of career development, one can add the growing attention of political scientists, economists, and organizational theorists as persons concerned with career behavior.

In a collective sense, theorists representing the disciplines identified have broadened the theoretical interests that have relevance for career development. In an earlier treatise, Super (1983) suggested that the three original categories of career theories were "Those that match people and occupations, those that describe development leading to matching, and those that focus on decision making" (p. 8). As suggested earlier in this article, there are now other emphases in career theories that have evolved over the past 25 years or so and have led to an increasingly comprehensive view of career development.

Emerging Issues

Although career development theories represent major approaches to hypothesizing about and summarizing the nature of career behavior and its evolution through the life span, there are other issues still to be analyzed, factors studied, and predictions made. For example, as the nature of contextual factors changes because of political, economic, or social events, the theories that include such content may need to amend selected propositions. Among the emerging major issues are the changing nature of work, the rapidity of this change, and the new career paths evolving in the twenty-first century (Littleton, Arthur, & Rosseau, 2000). These changes have altered some of the assumptions made by theorists in the twentieth century and suggest the need for new or modified theories. For example, in some of the career development theories of the twentieth century it was assumed that progression of individuals through their work life was age-related and linear. Thus, persons would be expected to move in predictable sequences from growth, to exploration, to preparation, to induction into the work force, to adjustment to work place dynamics, to consolidation of their advancement, and to retirement. Such a model is currently in jeopardy in various industries and occupations. It is now assumed that career development in the future will be more fragmented and interrupted than previously thought and that there will likely be a widening diversity of career patterns and expectations, more frequent career transitions, increased expectations that workers will need to be responsible for their career development and employability and will need to be personally flexible in order to cope with rapid and constant change (Hall, 2004). Such dynamics are still to be fully studied and captured in available career development theories.

REFERENCES

Hall, D. T. (2004). The protean career: A quarter-century journey. *Journal of Vocational Behavior, 65*, 1–13.

Herr, E. L., Cramer, S. H., & Niles, S. G. (2004). *Career guidance and counseling through the life-span* (6th Ed). Boston: Allyn & Bacon.

Littleton, S. M., Arthur, M. B., & Rousseau, D. M. (2000). The future of boundaryless careers. In A. Collin & R. Young, *The future of careers* (pp. 101–114). Cambridge, UK: Cambridge University Press.

Savickas, M. L. (2005). The theory and practice of career construction. In S. D. Brown & R. W. Lent (Eds.), *Career development and counseling: Putting theory and research to work* (pp. 42–70). Hoboken, NJ: John Wiley & Sons.

Super, D. E. (1983). Assessment in career guidance: Toward truly developmental counseling. *Personnel and Guidance Journal, 61*, 555–562.

Super, D. E. (1990). A life-span, life-space approach to career development. In D. Brown & L. Brook (Eds.), *Career choice and development: Applying contemporary theories to practice* (pp. 197–261). San Francisco: Jossey-Bass.

SUGGESTED READINGS

Chartrand, J. M. (1991). The evolution of trait-and-factor career counseling: A person x environment fit approach. *Journal of Counseling and Development, 69*, 518–524.

Davenport, T. O. (1999). *Human capital: What it is and why people invest in it*. San Francisco: Jossey-Bass.

Gordon, E. E. (2000). Help wanted: Creating tomorrow's work force. *The Futurist, 34*, 48–67.

Herr, E. L. (1998). *Counseling in a dynamic society . . . Contexts and practices for the 21st century* (2nd Ed.). Alexandria, VA: American Counseling Association.

EDWIN L. HERR
Pennsylvania State University

See also: **Career Counseling; Occupational Interests**

CATHARSIS

The concept of catharsis is the source of considerable controversy in the psychological literature. From the standpoint of mental health and social adjustment, cathartic procedures have been shown to have negligible or destructive effects while there is also evidence attesting to their psychological utility. Although the controversy and conflicting claims cannot be fully resolved, much of the difference in judgment regarding the utility of catharsis is due to the different meanings and mechanisms ascribed to catharsis.

The concept of catharsis has its origins in Aristotle's theoretical account of the impact on the audience of Greek drama, particularly the tragedies. In the words of one author, it referred to "the state of feeling produced by the dramatic tragedy. It meant the stillness at the center of one's being which came after pity or fear had been burned out, the soul is purified and calmed, freed from the violent passions" (Schaar, 1961, p. 520).

There are significant changes in the properties and meaning of catharsis as it has been applied in both clinical and social psychology. From a clinical standpoint, the possibility arose that the expression of particular feelings in a clinical session, like the expression of feeling that takes place in witnessing a Greek drama, may have positive mental health effects. It was at the inception of psychoanalysis, in the work of Freud's mentor, Josef Breuer, that the therapeutic utility of expressing suppressed feelings was discovered. This process has been labeled as abreaction as well as catharsis. Freud eventually felt that the therapeutic utility of abreaction was limited and stressed the importance of insight achieved through free association and the relationship between the therapist and client.

The similarity between the dramatic and clinical use of the concept of catharsis lies in the expression of affect. In the case of dramatic presentations, the expression is accomplished through a vicarious experience while, in the clinical situation, it is mediated by direct recall of an affect-arousing event. The utility of both the dramatic and clinical models of catharsis, however, remains a matter of empirical and theoretical debate.

There are a number of psychotherapies for which emotional discharge is a central process, such as primal therapy, psychodrama, bioenergetics, Gestalt therapy, and Eastern meditation and expressive approaches (D'Andrea, 2007). Nevertheless, serious objections have been raised to the proposition that emotional expression, in and of itself, can reduce tension and be therapeutic. Bohart (2001) has stressed the importance of an empathic listener and of cognitive reframing in determining the therapeutic efficacy of emotional expression. Bloom-Feshbach and Bloom-Feshbach (2001) also describe circumstances in which emotional expression, in this instance anger, can be therapeutic. For the client who has been unable to acknowledge anger, the experience of anger and understanding of its antecedents in a supportive, empathic therapeutic environment, can result in the constructive expression of ordinarily destructive feelings. Objections to the clinical use of cathartic expressions of affect, notably anger, arise from concerns regarding the often limited role of cognitive understanding in that process. Rather than having a cathartic outcome, expressing anger or engaging in fantasy aggression (e.g., by pounding pillows with lightweight rubber bats [batacas] or hitting a punching bag) can result in strengthening the propensity to feel angry and act aggressively.

The clinical use of catharsis has not been limited to the affect of anger. A number of studies have demonstrated that when individuals simply write about a range of emotional experiences, significant physical and mental health improvements ensue and several studies have demonstrated the cathartic value of crying. Most importantly, the concept of catharsis is not restricted to the expression of emotions. Psychoanalytic theory has also suggested that when direct satisfaction of a motivation or drive is not possible, indirect or substitute actions may have a cathartic function; in other words, these substitute behaviors may serve to reduce the intensity of the drive. Catharsis, as used in this context, relates to substitute or fantasy acts rather than to emotional expression.

A. A. Brill, the psychiatrist who introduced Freud's psychoanalytic method to the United States, recommended attendance at a prizefight once a month. The purpose of the recommendation was to provide a situation that would help drain off into harmless channels biologically rooted aggressive impulses or anger and aggression that ensues as a result of the inevitable frustrations of everyday life. Other body contact sports such as football, hockey, and wrestling are alleged to have a similar function. It is this application of the concept of catharsis that has been the object of extensive research and that is the major source of controversy. Issues regarding the cathartic utility of substitute behaviors arise in regard to motivations other than aggression (e.g., whether pornography stimulates or helps reduce and regulate sexual impulses). However, by far the great bulk of the research bearing on this form of catharsis addresses the question of whether engaging in substitute aggressive activities, most notably, witnessing aggressive content on television or cinema, serves to modulate aggressive behavior.

The prevailing evidence, from both laboratory studies in which children are exposed to television aggression and from field studies in which the amount of TV violence viewed is correlated with degree of aggressive behavior, indicates that exposure to TV violence is likely to stimulate aggressive behavior rather than have a cathartic effect (Bushman, 2002; Geen, 1990). However, there have also been conflicting findings reflecting cathartic-like effects. In general, there has been relatively little research addressed to the broader issue of the conditions under which exposure to media violence is likely to stimulate, reduce, or have negligible effects on aggressive behavior. Thus several studies have shown that the less realistic the TV aggressive content, the less likely is exposure to result in increased aggression. Also, there is little resemblance between modern TV fare and Greek drama.

In summary, the clinical and social utility of catharsis and effects of the process of catharsis vary substantially; they depend upon several known parameters and others that have yet to be ascertained.

REFERENCES

Bloom-Feshbach, J., & Bloom-Feshbach, S. (2001). Catharsis as a constructive expression of destructive affect: Developmental and clinical perspectives. In A. C. Bohart & D. J. Stipek (Eds.). *Constructive and destructive behavior: Implications for family, school and society* (pp. 317–335). Washington, DC: American Psychological Association.

Bohart, A. C. (2001). How can expression in psychotherapy be constructive? In A. C. Bohart & D. J. Stipek (Eds.). *Constructive and destructive behavior: Implications for family, school and society* (pp. 337–364). Washington, DC: American Psychological Association.

Bushman, B. J. (2002). Does venting anger feed or extinguish the flame? Catharsis, rumination, distraction, anger and aggressive responding. *Personality and Social Psychology Bulletin, 28,* 724–731.

D'Andrea, A. (2007). An anthropological analysis of sannyasin therapies and the Rajneesh legacy. *Journal of Humanistic Psychology, 47,* 91–116.

Geen, R. G. (1990). The influence of the mass media. In R. G. Geen, *Human aggression* (pp. 83–112). Belmont, CA: Thomson Brooks/Cole Publishing Co.

Schaar, J. H. (1961). *Escape from authority.* New York: Basic Books.

SUGGESTED READING

Scheff, T. J. (2007). Catharsis and other heresies: A theory of emotion. *Journal of Social, Evolutionary and Cultural Psychology, 1,* 98–113.

SEYMOUR FESHBACH
University of California, Los Angeles

CATTELL, JAMES MCKEEN (1860–1944)

James McKeen Cattell attended Lafayette College for his undergraduate work. He traveled to Europe and studied at Gottingen and then in Leipzig under Wilhelm Wundt. He received a fellowship to return to Johns Hopkins in 1882 and study philosophy. While at Johns Hopkins, Cattell attended the lectures on psychology by G. Stanley Hall and began research on mental activities. He returned to work with Wundt in 1883 to study individual differences, which was characterized as a typically American project by Germans. Cattell received his PhD degree in 1886 in psychology. His dissertation was the first in psychology by an American.

Cattell lectured at Bryn Mawr and at the University of Pennsylvania. He went to England to lecture at Cambridge University where he met Sir Francis Galton, who shared

Cattell's interest in individual differences. From Galton, he learned measurement and statistics and then became the first psychologist to teach and emphasize statistical analysis of experimental results. In 1888, Cattell was appointed professor of psychology at the University of Pennsylvania, the first psychology professorship in the world.

In 1891, Cattell went to Columbia University as professor of psychology and head of the department, where he remained for 26 years. During these years, more doctorates in psychology were awarded by Columbia than by any other graduate school in the United States. Cattell's students were encouraged and, indeed, required to do independent research and to work on their own. Many of them became prominent in the field.

He served as president of the American Psychological Association in 1895. Cattell was one of the most prominent figures in psychology at the end of the nineteenth century and early twentieth century. He was cofounder and editor of *Psychological Review*, and he played a major role in the development of other scientific journals and organizations, including the American Academy of Nurse Practitioners (AANP).

As the years passed, Cattell's personal and professional independence strained his relationship with the administration at Columbia. An ardent pacifist, he opposed the entry of the United States into World War I, and he was dismissed from the university on the grounds of being disloyal to his country. Cattell sued Columbia for libel and won his case, but he was not reinstated to his professorship.

In 1921, Cattell organized the Psychological Corporation to provide applied psychological services to industry, the professional community, and the public. As a spokesman and editor, he was an active supporter of psychological organizations and societies.

The theme of all of Cattell's research was mental tests and individual differences, a feature of American as opposed to German psychology. His mental tests were different from later intelligence tests, because he measured elementary bodily or sensory-motor responses. Correlations between tests and the student's academic performances were low. Although tests of this kind were not valid predictors of intellectual ability (Alfred Binet developed a test of higher mental abilities that was an effective measure of intelligence), Cattell's influence was strong, particularly through his student E. L. Thorndike. Columbia University was the center of the testing movement, and Cattell's work contributed to the practical and applied psychology that was uniquely American and functional.

SUGGESTED READINGS

Baldwin, J. M., Cattell, J. M., & Jastrow, J. (1898). Physical and mental tests. *Psychological Review, 5*, 172–179.

Cattell, J. M. (1890). Mental tests and measurements. *Mind, 15*, 373–380.

N. A. Haynie

CENTRAL LIMIT THEOREM

Many statistical inferential procedures such as hypothesis testing and the estimation of confidence intervals are based on the assumption that the distribution of a sample statistic is normal. The Central Limit Theorem (CLT) often justifies the assumption that the distribution of a sample statistic (e.g., mean, sum score, and test statistic) is normal. The Central Limit Theorem states that, for a large sample of n observations from a population with a finite mean and variance, the sampling distribution of the sum or mean of samples of size n is approximately normal.

For all practical purposes and applications, the conditions for the population are always met (i.e., a mean and variance exist). The population can have any shape and the measurements need not even be continuous. For example, measurements could be integers that correspond to ordered discrete responses on a survey item (e.g., strongly agree, agree, disagree, strongly disagree) or they could be binary (e.g., 1 for correct and 0 for incorrect responses to items on a test). If the number of items is large enough, then the sampling distribution of the mean score would be approximately normal. Alternatively, the mean on a single item over a large number of respondents would be approximately normal.

As a demonstration of the CLT, consider the population depicted in Figure 1(A). In this example, the probabilities of integers 1 through 5 each equal .20. The distribution of means for all possible random samples of size $n = 2$ taken from this population is depicted by the histogram in Figure 1(B). Although there are only nine possible values for the mean, the sampling distribution of the mean is uni-modal and symmetric. A normal distribution is drawn in Figure 1(B) to show the similarity between the actual sampling distribution and the normal distribution. With a sample size of 30, which is depicted in Figure 1(C), the sampling distribution of means (the histogram) is nearly indistinguishable from the normal distribution.

As sample sizes increase, the distribution of means (sums) becomes uni-modal and symmetric. As an illustration, consider the skewed population distribution given in Figure 1(D) for a variable with values 1 through 5 (see Hayes, 1994, for an example of a skewed population for a continuous variables). For samples with $n = 2$ observations, the sampling distribution of the means (i.e., the histogram in Figure 1(E)), is still noticeably skewed but not as skewed as the population. For random samples of n

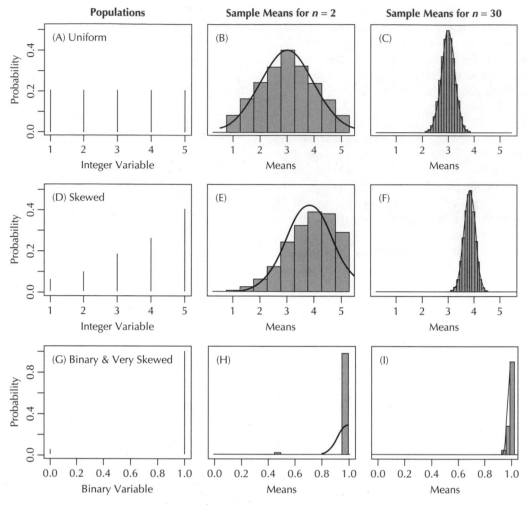

Figure 1. The first row contains figures for (A) a uniform population distribution with corresponding sampling distributions of the mean for (B) *n=2* and (C) *n=30*; the second row contains (D) a skewed population with sampling distributions for (E) *n=2* and (F) *n=30*; and the third row contains (G) a very skewed population with sampling distributions for (H) *n=2* and (I) *n=30*.

= 30, the distribution of the means as seen in Figure 1(F) is well approximated by a normal distribution.

A rule of thumb for how large is "large" is a sample size of 30. Agresti (1997) provides more examples of population distributions for continuous variables where a sample size of 30 leads to a distribution well approximated by a normal distribution. For populations that are uni-modal and roughly symmetric, a sample size less than 30 could be large enough to argue that the sampling distribution of the mean is approximately normal. When population distributions are very skewed, as in our next example, 30 may not be nearly large enough. Consider the probability distribution of a binary variable in Figures 1(H) and 1(I) where the probability of obtaining a 0 equals .01 and the probability for 1.0 equals .99. With samples of size 2, there are only three possible values of the mean (i.e., 0.0, 0.5, and 1.0), and as shown in Figure 1(G), the distribution of the means is extremely skewed. Even with samples of size

30, the sampling distribution of the mean is still extremely skewed. For this binary variable, the sample would need to be at least 500 for distribution of the sample means to be approximately normal.

The CLT does not require that the observations within samples be independent. Provided that observations within a sample are not too strongly related, the CLT will still apply. This fact if often used to explain why many populations of variables are approximately normal, including attributes of people that are the sum of many genetic and environmental components (e.g., height or ability).

The CLT, which was originally proven in the 1700s (see Tamhane & Dunlop, 2000, for a proof), should not be confused with the "The Law of Large Numbers." The latter states that as sample sizes get larger, sample means get closer to the population mean. When *n* is so large that it includes the entire population, the sample mean sample equals the population mean. The Law of Large Numbers gives us the mean of the sampling distribution of means and the CLT gives us the shape.

The importance of the CLT cannot be overstated. In practice, a single sample of data is collected, and based on this one sample, statistical inferences are made about the population. To make such inferences requires knowing the distribution of sample means (or sums) that would result if all possible samples from the population of the same size were taken. The CLT tells us the distribution of sample means or sums is approximately normal for large samples.

REFERENCES

Agresti, A. (1997). *Statistical methods for the social sciences* (3rd ed.). Upper Saddle River, NJ: Prentice Hall.

Hayes, W.L. (1994). *Statistics* (5th ed.). Orlando, FL: Harcourt Brace.

Tamhane, A. H., & Dunlop, D. D. (2000). *Statistics and data analysis*. Upper Saddle River, NJ: Prentice Hall.

CAROLYN J. ANDERSON
University of Illinois, Urbana-Champaign

See also: **Probability**

CENTRAL NERVOUS SYSTEM

The central nervous system (CNS) refers to the portion of the nervous system that lies within the skull and spinal column and receives nervous impulses from sense receptors throughout the organism, regulates bodily processes, and organizes and directs behavior. Anatomically, the CNS comprises the brain and spinal cord, which float within the cranial cavity of the skull and the vertebral canal of the spinal column in a liquid matrix called *cerebrospinal fluid*; this fluid also fills hollow space and serves as a protective cushion against damage. CNS tissue is further protected by three enfolding membranes called the meninges. The outer and toughest of the three, the *dura mater*, attaches to skull and spine, encasing the spongy *arachnoid membrane* within which the cerebrospinal fluid circulates. The soft *pia mater* is contiguous with the outer layer of brain and cord.

The basic structural unit of nervous tissue is the nerve cell or neuron, a specialized body cell within elongated shape (from a few microns to feet in length), whose enhanced reactivity and conductivity permit it to propagate or conduct an electrical impulse along its length. It also can chemically stimulate adjacent neurons to do likewise at specialized junctions called synapses. The nervous system is made up of billions of neurons that interconnect every part of the organism to monitor and regulate it. Receptor neurons lead, like the twigs of a tree, inward to branches and thence to great trunks, called nerves, which enter the CNS and ascend into the brain. There also, effector neurons originate and descend to exit the CNS as nerves branching repeatedly out to regulate all muscle tissue and therefore all bodily activity. Twelve bilateral pairs of cranial nerves enter the brain directly. The cord is the origin of 31 bilateral pairs of *spinal* nerves, which exit the CNS through openings between adjacent vertebrae. Each spinal nerve contains both entering receptor fibers and departing effector fibers, but divides on reaching the cord; sensory fibers enter on the back and motor fibers exit on the front.

The spinal cord is thus a great pathway for ascending and descending nerve tracts, but interconnectedness is a property of the CNS, within which a third type of neuron, the interneuron, is found. Interneurons connect effector and receptor neurons, and by repeated branchings of their tips may synapse at either end with many hundreds of other neurons. Their interconnectedness underlies and permits the remarkable complexity of the neural activities of the CNS and is present even at the spinal level. The functional unit of the nervous system is the reflex arc, which so links receptor and effector neurons that a stimulus at a sense receptor capable of causing its nerve to conduct will automatically trigger an effector neuron to produce a response in a muscle or gland. Some reflexes are extremely simple, but most are not. The CNS is hierarchically organized, with higher centers being stimulated by and acting upon lower centers, so that progressively more complex reflexes are organized progressively higher in the CNS. Certain muscle stretch reflexes operate spinally, for the most part. Respiratory reflexes are largely centered in the brain stem, that part of the brain which is contiguous to the spinal cord. Homeostatic reactions depend upon reflexes organized higher yet, in the hypothalamus, which may give rise to motivational states such as hunger and thirst, it is thought that, by means of progressively more complex reflexes (some inborn, but most acquired through learning), all functions of the CNS are conducted, including higher mental functions, the seat of which is the brain. The CNS is also symmetrically organized. Midline structures, like the cord, have two symmetrical halves. Other structures are duplicated, like the two cerebral hemispheres. Most fibers cross the midline (e.g., the left brain controls the right hand).

The brain is an organ of unparalleled complexity of parts and function, a reality, which may be obscured by summary description. Nevertheless, a great deal has been learned about the pathways followed by ascending and descending nerve tracts. Much of the CNS is white matter, being the encased processes or extensions of nerve cells, bundles of which indicate pathways called tracts. The nerve bodies are not encased and are present in gray matter, clusters of which indicate centers of activity called *nuclei*. Evolutionary influences have given characteristic shapes to the complex arrangements of neurons in the CNS, permitting them to be named and located on charts or in living tissue.

The gross anatomy of the brain, in very greatly oversimplified summary, may be divided into three regions: (1) the brain stem, the parts of which (medulla, pons, mesencephalon) contain the nuclei of the brain stem reticular formation, which is vital in consciousness and the level of arousal of the brain above; (2) the cerebellum, a center for the smooth regulation of motor behavior; and (3) the cerebrum, which is of greatest interest to psychology for its organizing role in the higher mental functions and emotion. Between brain stem and cerebrum are the thalamus and hypothalamus, which some authorities argue are within one and some maintain are in the other. Thalamic nuclei largely integrate and relay sensory impulses upward to the cerebrum. Hypothalamic nuclei, however, are vital in the regulation of homeostatic reactions and in integrating the reflexes of the nuclei of the limbic system, structures embedded deep within the cerebrum that give rise to emotional experience and expression.

The cerebrum's deeply fissured gray outer surface, the hemispheres of its cerebral cortex, are the terminus of sensory processes and the origin of motor processes. Much of the area is given over to association areas of interneurons, whose complex interconnections give rise to memory, speech, purposive behavior, and the higher mental functions.

The pathways, relays, and sensory and motor areas of the brain have been mapped by largely physical and physiological methods. Still, the nature of the higher mental processes of humans remains elusive because the structure and function of nervous tissue are so interrelated that they must be studied together. At some levels of the CNS, the appropriate units of function are physiological. Other levels are best studied through discrete behaviors. Even more complex functions of the brain, however, require scrutiny of complex patterns or styles of behavior, and the highest levels of brain function shade into issues of intelligence, logic, purpose, and consciousness, issues that are as little understood as the brain.

The study of the CNS in humans is thus the study of brain-behavior and brain-mind relationships, fields in which psychology is heavily involved. The relationship between brain and mind has long been observed. C. J. Golden (1980) noted that Pythagoras, in 500 BC, linked brain and human reasoning. Modern concepts regarding brain functions did not begin to develop until the 1800s (Golden, 1980), when a more scientific and reductionistic view of both brain and behavior emerged. Ramon y Cajal forwarded neuron theory in the late 1800s and received a Nobel Prize in physiology in 1906, the same year that Sherrington, who developed the concept of the reflex arc,

published on integrative mechanisms of the nervous system. Galton's work with the behavioral measurement of individual differences contributed greatly to the emerging science of *psychometrics* or mental measurements (Galton, 1879). J. B. Watson (1913) moved psychology toward the study of behavior rather than mental states. He and B. F. Skinner (1938) both contributed to a science and technology of behavior that has meshed well with biology in permitting brain behavior studies. But the complexities of mind, behavior, and brain are such that the more we learn, the more there remains to be learned. G. Sommerhoff (1974) put it thus: "The peculiar fascination of the brain lies in the fact that there is probably no other object of scientific enquiry about which we know so much and yet understand so little" (p. 3).

At the heart of the problem lies the fact that the nervous system, so simple in basic elements, is so complex in arrangements. As J. I. Hubbard (1975) observed, it is easy to just imagine neuronal arrangements capable of causing muscles to contract or glands to empty, but difficult to imagine such arrangements permitting the aging Beethoven to compose work he could no longer hear. The sheer complexity of interconnections sufficient to permit such complex behaviors virtually defies understanding. Some 5 million neurons, for example, may lie beneath a single square centimeter of brain surface, each of which synapses with hundreds of other neurons. Virtually the entire depth and surface of the brain may be involved in any given behavior; "although very basic skills can be localized, all observable behavior is a complex interaction of numerous basic skills so that the brain as a whole is involved in most actual behavior" (Golden, 1980, p. 225).

To be understood, the CNS must be understood a whole. Yet, owing to the limits in theory, knowledge, and perhaps capacity, we must approach the whole through study of the parts, viewed at many levels and from many perspectives. Full understanding of the CNS therefore lies beyond any one discipline. Psychology, however, contributes in many ways to the expanding interdisciplinary study of the CNS called neuroscience. Psychologists have put forward or contributed to models of the mind compatible with known facts of brain function (Miller, Galanter, & Pribram, 1960) and have helped develop new models of neural function drawing on and contributing to computer modeling (Parks, Levine, & Long, 1998). They have also used neuroscientific findings to develop models of human behavior (Somers, 1999) and to consider such fundamental issues as free will and responsibility (Rees & Rose, 2004). Psychologists commonly contribute directly to knowledge of brain-behavior relationships through experimental and clinical neuropsychology.

Experimental neuropsychologists have long studied such things as the behavioral derangements caused by known lesions and other disturbances of CNS tissue in animals. Clinical neuropsychologists study qualitative and quantitative aspects of behavior on special tasks to deduce or infer the probable locus and nature of brain tissue impairments in humans, and behavioral mappings of individual patient strengths and deficits help guide the person's specific treatment and rehabilitation efforts.

In recent decades, a remarkable proliferation of methods and tools has led to an explosion of information from interdisciplinary brain research but has not yet unified neuroscientific knowledge of the CNS. Neuroscience, however, begets neurotechnologies capable of altering both our understanding and capacities. Technologies, such as stem cell repair of brain damage, by which repairing the brain might help heal the mind, offer both benefit and risk. Each new capacity poses increasingly urgent questions, ethical issues, and choices for society. Yet, due to the inexhaustible complexity of the human brain, despite what may be learned and accomplished, we are always at the beginning: "With its hundred billion nerve cells, with their hundred trillion interconnections, the human brain is the most complex phenomenon in the known universe—always of course excepting the interactions of some 6 billion of such brains and their owners within the socio-technological culture of our planetary ecosystem" (Rose, 2004, p. 3).

As ongoing developments in knowledge and methodology continue to require new connections among the disciplines that comprise neuroscience, psychology remains a key participant in this evolution. N. E. Miller (1995) summarized the excitement for psychology of CNS research at all levels; Miller stated that the range of functions studied "... have relevance to all aspects of psychology, and all aspects of psychology have contributions to make to understanding them" (p. 901).

REFERENCES

Galton, F. (1879). Psychometric experiments. *Brain, 2,* 149–162.

Golden, C. J. (1980). Organic brain syndromes. In R. H. Woody (Ed.), *Encyclopedia of clinical assessment* (Vol. 1). San Francisco: Jossey-Bass.

Hubbard, J. I. (1975). *The biological basis of mental activity.* Reading, MA: Addison-Wesley.

Miller, G. A., Galanter, E., & Pribram, K. (1960). *Plans and the structure of behavior.* New York: Holt.

Miller, N. E. (1995). Clinical-experimental interactions in the development of neuroscience: A primer for nonspecialists and lessons for young scientists. *American Psychologist, 50*(11), 901–911.

Parks, R. W., Levine, D. S., & Long, D. L. (Eds.). (1998). *Fundamentals of neural network modeling: Neuropsychology and cognitive neuroscience.* Cambridge: MIT Press.

Rees, D., & Rose, S. (Eds.). (2004). *The new brain sciences: Perils and prospects.* Cambridge: Cambridge University Press.

Rose, S., (2004). Introduction, the new brain sciences, in D. Rees & S. Rose (Eds.), *The new brain sciences: Perils and prospects,* (pp. 3–14). Cambridge: Cambridge University Press.

Sherrington, C. S. (1906). *The integrative action of the nervous system.* New Haven, CT: Yale University Press.

Skinner, B. F. (1938). *The behavior of organisms: An experimental analysis.* New York: Appleton-Century.

Somers, M. J. (1999). Applications of two neural network paradigms to the study of voluntary employee turnover. *Journal of Applied Psychology, 34*(2), 177–185.

Summerhoff, G. (1974). *Logic of the living brain.* New York: Putnam.

Watson, J. B. (1913). Psychology as the behaviorist views it. *Psychological Review, 20,* 158–177.

SUGGESTED READINGS

Gellhorn, E. (Ed.). (1963). *Biological foundations of emotion.* Glenview, IL: Scott-Foresman.

Luria, A. R. (1973). *The working brain.* New York: Basic Books.

ROGER E. ENFIELD
West Central Georgia Regional Hospital,
Columbus

See also: **Brain; Neuroscience; Parasympathetic Nervous System; Sympathetic Nervous System**

CENTRAL NERVOUS SYSTEM DISORDERS

The central nervous system (CNS) is comprised of the brain and the spinal cord. The spinal cord controls movement and feeling of body regions located below the brain. Because the brain and the spinal cord are connected, the brain also plays a role in movement and feeling. However, the brain controls complex psychological processes such as attention, perception, motivation, emotion, language, cognition, and action. Central nervous system disorders may arise due to brain injury, or may occur as the result of congenital or degenerative neurological conditions.

When certain parts of the brain are damaged through accident or disease, specific functions may be lost. The type and extent of functional loss depends upon the location of the brain damage and the amount of brain tissue that is compromised. For example, damage to a strip of cortex in the posterior part of the frontal lobes controlling movement of parts of the body will result in paralysis of those body parts. Lesions within relay stations along the visual sensory system—from the optic nerves to the occipital lobes—will result in visual field defects such as scotomas ("blind spots"). Lesions deep in the hypothalamus may produce hunger, uncontrolled eating, and obesity. A destruction of areas involved in arousal may result in a permanent comatose state.

Damage to specific regions of the brain usually produces behavioral abnormalities that can be measured quantitatively and qualitatively by employing sensitive tests of impaired or lost functions. For example, an analysis of specific sensory functions can reveal basic sensory defects. Cognitive and intellectual defects can be measured through the skillful administration and interpretation of tests specifically designed to elucidate organically based impairments. Descriptions of many of these tests may be found in books on neuropsychological assessments (e.g., Strauss, Sherman, & Spreen, 2006), as well as in a chapter by Oscar-Berman and Bardenhagen (1998).

Disorders of the CNS usually are classified according to lesion location (e.g., abnormalities occurring after frontal lobe damage) or according to symptomatology and functional loss (e.g., amnesia and aphasia). The following discussion focuses on specific exemplars of CNS disorders. The first, frontal system disorders, exemplifies some possible consequences of damage to the anterior regions of the frontal lobes. The others exemplify disorders recognized by their presenting symptoms and functional abnormalities: Amnesia refers to disorders of memory, including memory for recent events (anterograde amnesia) and memory for events long ago (retrograde amnesia); and aphasia refers to language disturbances. Keep in mind, however, that the distinction between structure and function is not meant to be a mutually exclusive one. The brain has many highly interconnected parts, and when one part is damaged, other parts will be affected as well.

Frontal System Dysfunction

The frontal lobes are connected with all of the other lobes of the brain, and they receive and send fibers to numerous subcortical structures as well. While control of motor function takes place in the posterior region of the frontal lobes, the anterior region of the frontal lobes (prefrontal cortex) plays a kind of executive regulatory role within the CNS, inhibiting the occurrence of unnecessary or unwanted behaviors. Disruptions of normal inhibitory functions of frontal lobe neuronal networks often will have the interesting effect of releasing previously inhibited behaviors from frontal control. The resultant aberrant conduct of a frontal patient may be due to the freely unregulated functioning of the released brain region rather than a direct effect of a lesion within the frontal lobes, and as such may be referred to as a disinhibition syndrome (Starkstein & Kremer, 2001).

Early evidence for a role of the frontal lobes in supporting the ability to inhibit impulsivity came from the 1868 report of a physician on his patient Phineas Gage. Gage, a railway workman, survived an explosion that blasted an iron bar (about four feet long and an inch wide) through his frontal lobes. After recovering from the accident, Gage's personality changed. He became irascible, impatient, impulsive, unruly, and inappropriate. The damage had mostly been in the orbital frontal region of Gage's frontal lobes (Damasio, Grabowski, Frank, Galaburda, & Damasio, 1994).

Damage to frontal brain systems occurs in a number of CNS disorders, including stroke, brain tumors, dementing diseases (e.g., Alzheimer's), and head trauma. Patients with bilateral frontal disorders often display a pull to nearby objects (e.g., grabbing at doorknobs), as well as a remarkable tendency to imitate the actions of people nearby (echopraxia). The behaviors of frontal patients appear not to be based on rational decisions, but rather are under the control of salient objects around them, that is, objects that capture their attention. In other words, the patient's behaviors are environmentally driven rather than personally chosen. Environmental dependency and imitation behaviors can also be associated with "utilization behavior" (Archibald, Mateer, & Kerns, 2001). That is, if the examiner places a set of everyday objects in front of the patient with instructions neither to use them nor to pick them up, the patient nonetheless will do just that! If one of the objects were a comb, the patient would likely pick it up and begin combing his/her hair. Utilization behavior may even extend to dangerous objects such as hypodermic needles, with patients attempting to give themselves injections.

Brain Mechanisms in Memory

Amnesia, especially anterograde amnesia, is an intriguing but serious disorder. When amnesia occurs as a consequence of long-term alcoholism, it is referred to as alcoholic Korsakoff's syndrome (also Alcohol-Induced Persisting Amnestic Disorder). Patients with Korsakoff's syndrome are permanently unable to remember new information for more than a few seconds. However, old memories, which were formed prior to the onset of alcohol-related brain damage, are relatively well preserved. Because new events are forgotten a few seconds after they occur, virtually nothing new is learned, and the patient with Korsakoff's syndrome lives in the past.

George Talland in his classic book, *Deranged Memory* (Talland, 1965) linked the etiology of Korsakoff's disease most frequently with the polyneuropathy of chronic alcoholism and associated malnutrition. The critical brain lesions are thought to include the mammillary bodies of the hypothalamus and/or medial thalamic nuclei. Damage to these or to other regions of the brain (hippocampus, fornix, anterior thalamus) identified with the classic interconnected circuit described by Papez (1937) has been associated with memory impairments. The impairments include severe anterograde amnesia for recent events, and some retrograde amnesia for events prior to the appearance of obvious symptomatology.

Although anterograde amnesia is the most obvious presenting symptom in Korsakoff patients, it has been suggested that, in addition to having severe memory problems, these individuals have other cognitive impairments as well. Like patients with bilateral prefrontal cortical lesions, Korsakoff patients are abnormally sensitive to distractions (proactive interference). This sensitivity may be due to prefrontal dysfunction, which impairs the ability to counteract the effects of cognitive interruptions. Memory encoding requires the ability to resist displacement of the to-be-remembered information from ongoing memory processing. Similarly, memory retrieval requires the ability to screen out irrelevant contextual cues in order to focus on relevant cues and thus to select the target memory. In addition to their memory problems, perseverative behaviors, and distractibility, Korsakoff patients also have restricted attention, retarded perceptual processing abilities, and decreased sensitivity to reward contingencies (Oscar-Berman & Marinkovic, 2007). These additional abnormalities probably reflect widespread cerebral atrophy accompanying sustained alcohol abuse.

Aphasia

The term aphasia literally means "no language." More realistically, aphasic patients suffer from impairment in their previous level of ability to use language expressively or receptively, or both. For that reason, the term dysphasia (impairment in language) sometimes is used. There are many different forms of aphasia, and classification schemes can be found in Harold Goodglass's book, *Understanding aphasia* (Goodglass, 1993). Pathology is almost always within the left hemisphere of right-handers, as well as in a majority of left-handers. Frequently the location of the brain damage is in the frontal lobe (Broca's aphasia) or the temporal lobe (Wernicke's aphasia), and usually the damage is the result of a cerebrovascular accident (stroke), tumor, or trauma.

There are components of aphasia that can be considered language-specific amnesias (e.g., the anomias). If a lesion is in the neighborhood of a cortical sensory projection zone, the resulting disorder may involve one or another of the sensory modalities (audition or vision). If a lesion is in a polysensory integration zone, it will cause a disorder of more highly elaborate functions (e.g., spatial recognition, language, and/or voluntary movement). It has been argued that aphasia is a mere loss of certain linguistic abilities, and that the "intellect" remains intact. Others, however, regard aphasia either as the manifestation of a primary intellectual loss or as the loss of a restricted aspect of intellect. As cautioned earlier, this problem can be oversimplified by regarding either aphasia or intellectual impairment as unitary deficits. Both are known to vary with locus and extent of lesion, and any overlap in symptoms may result from overlapping neuroanatomical representation rather than from the nature of the disorder.

REFERENCES

Archibald, S. J., Mateer, C. A., & Kerns, K. A. (2001). Utilization behavior: Clinical manifestations and neurological mechanisms. *Neuropsychology Review, 11*(3), 1573–6660.

Damasio, H., Grabowski, T., Frank, R., Galaburda, A. M., & Damasio, A. R. (1994). The return of Phineas Gage: Clues about the brain from the skull of a famous patient. *Science, 264,* 1102–1105.

Goodglass, H. (1993). *Understanding aphasia.* San Diego, CA: Academic Press.

Oscar-Berman, M., & Bardenhagen, F. (1998). Nonhuman primate models of memory dysfunction in neurodegenerative disease: Contributions from comparative neuropsychology. In A. Tröster (Ed.), *Memory in neurodegenerative disease* (pp. 3–20). New York: Cambridge University Press.

Oscar-Berman, M., & Marinkovic, K. (2007). Alcohol: Effects on neurobehavioral functions and the brain. *Neuropsychology Review, 17*(3), 239–257.

Papez, J. W. (1937). A proposed mechanism of emotion. *Archives of Neurology and Psychiatry, 38,* 725–743.

Starkstein, S. E., & Kremer, J. (2001). The disinhibition syndrome and frontal-subcortical circuits. In D. G. Lichter and J. L. Cummings (Eds.), *Frontal-subcortical circuits in psychiatric and neurological disorders.* New York: Guilford Press.

Strauss, E., Sherman, E. M. S., & Spreen, O. (2006). *A compendium of neuropsychological tests: Administration, norms, and commentary* (3rd ed.). New York: Oxford University Press.

Talland, G. A. (1965). *Deranged memory: A psychonomic study of the amnesic syndrome.* San Diego, CA: Academic Press.

SUGGESTED READINGS

Clark, C. M., & Trojanowski, J. Q. (Eds). (2000). *Neurodegenerative dementias: Clinical features and pathological mechanisms.* New York: McGraw-Hill.

Hains, B. C. (2006). *Brain disorders.* New York: Chelsea House Publishers.

MARLENE OSCAR-BERMAN
SUSAN M. MOSHER
Boston University School of Medicine and Department of Veterans Affairs Healthcare System, Boston Campus

See also: **Brain; Parasympathetic Nervous System; Sympathetic Nervous System**

CENTRAL TENDENCY MEASURES

This article defines three different measures of central tendency: the mean, the median, and the mode. Each measure serves the same purpose, which is to describe the central tendency of data. We begin by defining what central tendency is, and then we explain how each measure of central tendency contributes to our understanding of a particular dataset.

Central tendency is a term that is used to describe the middle or center of a frequency or probability distribution.

Central tendency is often displayed in a frequency or probability distribution, where the x axis represents the variable of interest, and the y axis represents the frequency or probability of occurrence. Say, for example, that someone is trying to estimate how much money he or she will make if choosing to be a high school teacher. This individual might ask what the average high school teacher makes, or the majority of teachers tend to make. These are questions of central tendency.

The hypothetical frequency distribution in Figure 1 shows that a large percentage of teachers make between $23,000 and $27,000.

Central tendency is best understood in relation to the frequency or probability distribution we are trying to describe. Perhaps the easiest distribution to describe is one in which (1) the peak of the distribution is located in the middle, and (2) the distribution is symmetrical about the middle. When the data are symmetrical about the middle, the distribution is said to be "unimodal." Figure 1 illustrates such a symmetrical, unimodal distribution. In this case the mean, median, and mode will all be the same value.

When the distribution is not symmetrical, or the distribution is not unimodal, the mean, median, and mode will have different values. Say, for example, someone was interested in estimating the annual income of a salesperson. The hypothetical frequency distribution shown in Figure 2 tells us that most salespeople make between $45,000 and $60,000, but some make as much as $115,000.

Under this situation, it is more difficult to describe "typical annual income" because the mean, median, and mode have different values. Because not all frequency distributions are unimodal and symmetric, we need more than one measure of central tendency.

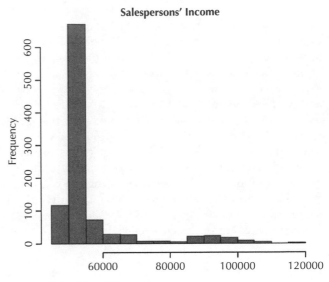

Figure 2. Salesperson's Income

The Mean

The mean, also called the arithmetic average, is the balancing point of the distribution. The mean is calculated by summing all of the scores and then dividing by the number of scores. The mean is often considered the most "democratic" measure of central tendency, because it takes every single value into consideration. Consider the following sample of 10 teachers' salaries:

$24,888.70
$29,665.49
$23,503.99
$28,100.14
$26,841.88
$25,538.42
$25,331.75
$25,107.02
$27,677.72
$24,888.24

The mean for these data is (24,888.70 + 29,665.49 + 23,503.99 + 28,100.14 + 26,841.88 + 25,538.42 + 25,331.75 + 25,107.02 + 27,677.72 + 24,888.24)/10 = $26,154.33. Note that each score is equally represented by the mean. However, equal representation may be a disadvantage when the data are not symmetrical. Consider the salesperson data:

$ 47,159.38
$ 47,583.71
$ 48,872.42
$ 49,046.00
$ 49,653.64

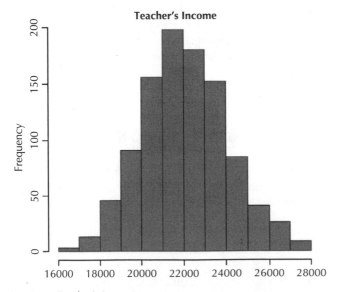

Figure 1. Teacher's Income

$ 50,463.73

$ 50,978.93

$ 52,377.81

$ 54,298.29

$139,209.46

The mean of this dataset is $58,964.34. However, this value does not represent the majority of our scores; in fact, none of our scores is close to this value. What has happened is that our extreme value of $139,209.46 has pulled the mean in an extreme direction so that it no longer represents a central tendency. In this type of situation, where the distribution is skewed, other measures of central tendency may provide a better representation of the data.

The Median

The median is the score that is the exact middle point of a distribution In order to calculate the median, we must (1) order all of the values from largest to smallest (or vice versa); (2) obtain the position of the median using the following formula:

$$\frac{N+1}{2}$$

where N represents the total number of values in the dataset; and (3) obtain the value of the median by counting from the largest value down to the smallest value (or vice versa) until we reach the value that is found in the position we obtained. For each of our datasets, we have 10 total values. Therefore, the score that falls in the middle position is in position $(10 + 1) / 2 = 5.5$. In other words, the median is the number that is halfway between our fifth and sixth position.

Unlike the mean, the median has the advantage of not being pulled by extreme scores. For the salesman data, after rank ordering the scores, the median is $50,058.69 (which is halfway between $49,653.64 and $50,463.73). Clearly this value is more representative of what someone is likely to make as a salesman than $58,964.34.

The Mode

The mode is simply the most frequently occurring value in a distribution. With respect to our illustrative datasets, the likelihood of even two people obtaining the exact same annual income is very slim. In these instances, then, we do not have a mode. There nevertheless are two advantages to using the mode when there is one. First, like the median, the mode has the advantage of not being swayed by extreme values. Second, the mode is the only measure of central tendency that is capable of measuring categorical, or non-numeric, data. For example, it makes no sense to calculate the average eye color in a group. Because eye color is non-numeric, we cannot calculate the mean or the median eye color. Instead, we resort to using the mode to describe eye color; we may, for example, end up saying that the majority of people in our sample have blue eyes.

In short, the mean, median, and mode each seek to describe a typical score in a distribution. Each measure of central tendency has some advantages and disadvantages, and each contributes to our understanding of a distribution.

DUSTIN FIFE
JORGE MENDOZA
University of Oklahoma

CHARACTER (See Personality Development)

CHARACTER DISORDERS (See Personality Disorders)

CHILD ABUSE

The problem of child abuse and neglect did not receive serious attention until C. Henry Kempe and his colleagues published their research in the mid-1960s on the "battered child syndrome," a pattern of unexplained physical injuries in children, purportedly inflicted by parents or caregivers. This work helped to initiate a movement in the United States to protect children from child abuse and neglect. The 1974 Child Abuse Prevention and Treatment Act (P.L. 93-247) mandated reporting laws as well as procedures for investigating suspected cases of child abuse and neglect. In addition, the act provided for research in child abuse and neglect and established the Center for Child Abuse and Neglect within the Children's Bureau of the Department of Health and Human Services. Since the 1960s and 1970s, progress in the field has been rapid, expanding our understanding about the definition and magnitude of child abuse and neglect, the emotional and physical sequelae of abuse, and potential treatment interventions to address the needs of child maltreatment victims and their families.

Defining and Estimating Child Abuse

Definitions of child abuse and neglect vary from state to state, and although not all experts agree on the specific behaviors or events that constitute the various forms of child maltreatment, progress has been made in broadly defining them. Physical abuse is the use of inappropriate physical strategies (e.g., punching, hitting, or kicking a child; striking a child with an object; burning a child) that result in substantial risk of physical or emotional harm to a child. Sexual abuse refers to activities between an adult and a child in which the child is used for the sexual stimulation of the perpetrator or another person (e.g., intrusion such as oral/anal/genital penetration; genital contact involving touching; and other unspecified acts not involving genital contact such as kissing and child pornography). Child neglect generally refers to acts of omissions that lead to deficits in the provision of a child's basic needs (e.g., failure to provide for a child's health care needs; inadequate supervision; inadequate nutrition, clothing, or hygiene). Psychological maltreatment, also referred to as emotional abuse, most often refers to "serious mental injury" and generally includes both emotionally neglectful behaviors (e.g., inadequate nurturance or affection; permitted drug or alcohol abuse; refusal or delay in psychological care) and emotionally abusive behaviors (e.g., verbally belittling, denigrating, threatening, or rejecting a child; tying or binding a child).

Prevalence rates for child abuse and neglect are difficult to determine because the abuse of children is a crime that tends to be underreported. According to the most recent figures reported by the National Child Abuse and Neglect Data system (NCANDS) (U.S. DHHS, 2007), however, Child Protective Services agencies across the United States received approximately 3 million reports of child maltreatment in 2005. Of these reports, approximately 899,000 were substantiated. Of these cases, child neglect was the most common form of maltreatment (62.8%), followed by physical abuse (16.6%), sexual abuse (9.3%), and psychological or emotional abuse (7.1%).

Negative Effects Associated with Abuse

A wide range of physical, social, and emotional difficulties has been associated with child abuse and neglect in both children and adults who report childhood histories of abuse and neglect. Behaviors and problems that represent the most common potential signs and symptoms of child maltreatment include physical complications (e.g., physical injury, sleep disturbances; somatic complaints), affective-behavioral problems (e.g., low self-esteem; aggression; anger, anxiety, depression; conduct problems; substance abuse), cognitive deficits (e.g., language deficits; academic and learning problems; intellectual delays; poor attention and concentration), and social deficits (e.g., disturbed parent child attachment and interactions; deficits in prosocial behavior; social withdrawal and isolation) (Miller-Perrin & Perrin, 2007).

The current research literature does not suggest that any one symptom or difficulty is experienced by all, or most, children who experience abuse and neglect in childhood, although one frequently cited problem among abused children and adults is posttraumatic stress symptoms (Widom, 1999). In addition, a significant minority of children with abuse histories report no mental health

problems (Kendall-Tackett, Williams, & Finkelhor, 1993). Whether a child experiences negative effects of abuse and neglect is likely related to several different factors associated with the abuse such as the severity and duration of the abuse, the relationship between the child and offender, the age at onset and/or disclosure of the abuse, the child's attributions of the event, and the number of subtypes of abuse experienced by the child (Miller-Perrin & Perrin, 2007).

Possible Causes of Child Abuse

The complex nature of child abuse helps to explain why most attempts to understand the cause of child abuse revolve around combinations of multiple factors believed to contribute to abuse. Various theoretical formulations of child abuse emphasize a number of factors such as child characteristics, characteristics of adult offenders, the family environment, and the role of society and culture (Miller-Perrin & Perrin, 2007). Certain predisposing characteristics of children, for example, can increase the likelihood of physical abuse such as a child's young age or special needs status (U.S. DHHS, 2007). In addition, physically abusive and neglectful parents are found disproportionately among economically disadvantaged groups and their environments tend to include a number of stressors such as having children at a young age, single parenthood, and various psychological and behavioral issues (e.g., depression, parenting difficulties, substance abuse) (Miller-Perrin & Perrin, 2007). Theories of sexual abuse, on the other hand, tend to focus on various forms of offender dysfunction, such as deviant sexual arousal or intergenerational theories of transmission centering on offenders' childhood histories of abuse (Marshall & Marshall, 2000). Because of the complex nature of the various forms of child maltreatment, developing one unified theory to explain the diversity of characteristics in question may not be feasible or desirable.

Treatment Approaches

Victims and offenders of child maltreatment represent diverse groups both in terms of symptom presentation and treatment response. Therefore, there is no canned "one-size-fits-all" treatment approach appropriate or effective for everyone. Although the amount of research examining treatment efficacy is limited, available studies suggest several approaches to intervening in cases of child maltreatment.

One of the most common forms of intervention for child and adult victims of child abuse is individual therapy. One major goal of such treatment is to help the victim of abuse manage the negative thoughts and emotions that are often associated with child maltreatment such as guilt, shame, stigmatization, anger, stress, and fear. It is necessary to allow victims to confront their negative feelings within a therapeutic environment and learn strategies for managing these feelings, such as relaxation training, anger management, problem-solving skills, positive coping statements, gradual exposure, stress inoculation, and the use of imagery (see Berliner & Saunders, 1996). Another treatment objective is to help victims confront and correct cognitions and beliefs that might lead to negative self-attributions. Cognitive-behavioral approaches are frequently used, for example, to help victims change their perceptions about being "different" as well as the beliefs that they are somehow to blame for the abuse.

In treating cases of child maltreatment, professionals also frequently include parent-focused interventions that target the parents of maltreated children. Most parent ·interventions have been developed for physically abusive and neglectful parents and include the following components: (1) education about normal child developmental processes to address misperceptions and unrealistic expectations of children, (2) education about the importance of disciplinary consistency and the appropriate use of reinforcement and punishment in shaping child behavior, (3) anger control techniques to enhance coping skills and reduce negative emotional responses and thoughts, and (4) stress management techniques such as relaxation training, stress reduction, and coping with stressful parent-child interactions (Schellenbach, 1998). Treatment programs for sexually abusive parents include a variety of approaches but most often incorporate cognitive and behavioral components to reduce deviant sexual arousal and cognitive distortions associated with abuse (Marshall & Marshall, 2000).

Treatment programs for child abuse also include various adjuncts to victim-oriented and parent-oriented approaches that include a broad range of services that not only address individual needs but also strengthen the functioning of the family, which is embedded within a community. Because maltreating families are also characterized by a lack of social and economic resources, for example, interventions to enhance both social and economic support are included, such as strengthening informal support networks through support groups (e.g., Parents Anonymous), linking parents with community volunteers, employing neighborhood helpers, training parents in social skills, and providing employment or economic assistance through local service organizations or the family's caseworker (Miller-Perrin & Perrin, 2007). In addition, given the high incidence of substance abuse and marital distress that occurs in maltreating families, alcohol or drug abuse treatment and marital counseling are also possible adjuncts to treatment.

REFERENCES

Berliner, L., & Saunders, B. E. (1996). Treating fear and anxiety in sexually abused children: Results of a controlled 2-year follow-up study. *Child Maltreatment, 1,* 294–309.

Kendall-Tackett, K. A., Williams, L. M., & Finkelhor, D. (1993). Impact of sexual abuse on children: A review and synthesis of recent empirical studies. *Psychological Bulletin, 113,* 164–180.

Marshall, W. L., & Marshall, L. E. (2000). The origins of sexual offending. *Trauma, Violence, & Abuse, 1,* 250–263.

Miller-Perrin, C. L., & Perrin, R. D. (2007). *Child maltreatment* (2nd ed.). Thousand Oaks, CA: Sage.

Schellenbach, C. J. (1998). Child maltreatment: A critical review of research on treatment for physically abusive parents. In P. K. Trickett & C. J. Schellenbach (Eds.), *Violence against children in the family and the community* (pp. 251–268). Washington, DC: American Psychological Association.

U.S. Department of Health and Human Services, Administration on Children, Youth, and Families. (2007). *Child maltreatment 2005.* Washington, DC: U.S. Government Printing Office.

Widom, C. S. (1999). Posttraumatic stress disorder in abused and neglected children grown up. *American Journal of Psychiatry, 156,* 1223–1229.

SUGGESTED READINGS

Kendall-Tackett, K. A., & Giacomoni, S. M. (Eds.). (2005). *Child victimization.* Kingston, NJ: Civic Research Institute.

Myers, J. E. B., Berliner, L., Briere, J., Hendrix, C. T., Jenny, C., & Reid, T. A. (Eds.). (2002). *The APSAC handbook on child maltreatment* (2nd ed.). Thousand Oaks, CA: Sage.

CINDY MILLER-PERRIN
Pepperdine University

See also: **Child Maltreatment; Child Neglect; Child Sexual Abuse**

CHILD BEHAVIOR CHECKLIST

The Child Behavior Checklist (CBCL), which is part of the broader Achenbach System of Empirically Based Assessment (ASEBA) tools, was first published in 1983 and has undergone several revisions since then. The CBCL assesses behavioral and emotional problems as well as social competencies of children and adolescents, ages $1\frac{1}{2}$–19 years, as reported by their parents and/or other caregivers. Caregivers rate the presence of 99 behaviors in very young children (CBCL/$1\frac{1}{2}$–5/LDS) or 118 behaviors in older children and teens (CBCL/6–18) during the past 6 months. Twenty additional items assess school performance, social relationships, and activities.

Nationally representative norms for the CBCL, based on socioeconomic status, ethnicity, and place of residence, are available for both normative and clinically referred children. Factor analysis of parent ratings consistently reveals two broadband domains, internalizing versus externalizing problems, with slightly different subscales for the very young versus older children. For children under age 3, the CBCL scales include Emotionally Reactive, Anxious/Depressed, Withdrawn, Somatic Complaints, Aggressive Behavior, Attention Problems, and Sleep Problems. For older children and teens, the subscales are Anxious/Depressed, Somatic Complaints, Withdrawn, Aggressive Behavior, Delinquent Behavior, and Social, Thought, and Attention Problems. A Total Problems score is also available for both young and older children. The CBCL scoring profile provides raw scores, T scores, and percentiles for all subscales and broad-based scales and three competency scales (School, Social, and Activities).

In addition, scores are available on several DSM-IV related scales: Affective Problems, Anxiety Problems, Attention Deficit/Hyperactivity Problems, and Oppositional Defiant Problems. For young children, there is also a scale for Pervasive Developmental Problems; for older children and teenagers, additional scales tap Somatic Problems and Conduct Problems.

The CBCL items have not changed since 2001; however, the scoring system has been expanded in several ways. Achenbach and Rescorla (2007) introduced a culturally sensitive scoring system that provides scoring against three sets of norms based on samples in which problem scores were relatively low (e.g., China, Germany), moderate (e.g., Australia, France), or high (e.g., Algeria, Portugal). Clinicians choose the norms most appropriate for each child based on his or her country of origin or immigration status. The 2007 revision of the scoring system for 6–18 year olds was expanded to assess additional DSM-IV based syndromes, such as Posttraumatic Stress Problems and Obsessive-Compulsive Problems as well as processes such as Sluggish Cognitive Tempo (e.g., McBurnett, Pfiffner, & Frick, 2001).

The CBCL has been translated into more than 80 languages, and there are established national norms in 33 countries across Asia, Africa, Australia, the Caribbean, Europe, and the Middle East. Its psychometric properties are excellent, and cross-cultural comparisons of the CBCL show a consistent factor structure across cultures (Ivanova et al., 2007). Along with the related ASEBA measures, the CBCL is one of the most widely researched and clinically used behavioral rating scales. It is particularly well suited to estimating DSM diagnostic profiles and dimensional ratings of psychopathology.

Although it is an exceptional measure of child and adolescent psychopathology, the CBCL has been criticized for its deficit-focused orientation and lack of attention to strength-based competencies. This has prompted new measures that assess both deficits and competencies, such as the Behavioral Assessment System for Children (Reynolds & Kamphaus, 2004).

REFERENCES

Doss, A. J., & Weisz, J. R. (2006). Syndrome co-occurrence and treatment outcomes in youth mental health clinics. *Journal of Consulting and Clinical Psychology, 74*, 416–425.

Ivanova, M. Y., Achenbach, T. M., Dumenci, L., Rescorla, L. A., Almqvist, F., Bilenberg, N., et al. (2007). Testing the 8-syndrome structure of the Child Behavior Checklist in 30 societies. *Journal of Clinical Child and Adolescent Psychology, 36*, 405–417.

McBurnett, K., Pfiffner, L. J., & Frick, P. J. (2001). Symptom properties as a function of ADHD type: An argument for a study of sluggish cognitive tempo. *Journal of Abnormal Child Psychology, 29*, 207–213.

Reynolds, C. R., & Kamphaus, R. W. (2004). Behavioral Assessment System for Children, *Behavior Assessment System for Children – Second Edition manual*. Circle Pines, MN: American Guidance Service Publishing.

SUGGESTED READINGS

Achenbach, T. M., & Rescorla, L. A. (2007). *Multicultural understanding of child and adolescent psychopathology: Implications for mental health assessment*. New York: Guilford Press.

Petty, C. R., Rosenbaum, J. F., Hirshfeld-Becker, D. R., Henin, A., Hubley, S., LaCasse, S., et al. (2008). The child behavior checklist broad-band scales predict subsequent psychopathology: A 5-year follow-up. *Journal of Anxiety Disorders, 22*(3), 532–539.

Marlene M. Moretti
Ingrid Obsuth
Simon Fraser University, Canada

See also: **Behavior Assessment System for Children; Behavior Problems of Childhood and Adolescence**

CHILD CUSTODY

History has witnessed a variety of trends in custody determination. Prior to the 1920s children were considered property of the father, who was almost always awarded custody. The Tender Years Doctrine, advanced in the 1920s, assumed that young children were better off in their mother's care. This resulted in a strong preference for awarding custody to the mother, a preference that continued until 1970 when the focus shifted to the best interests of the child.

In 1979, Congress adopted the best interests standard in the Uniform Marriage and Divorce Act. Individual states also developed specific criteria for determining custody. Some common criteria include parenting capacity; mental and physical status of the parents; wishes of the parents and children regarding custody; home, school, and community adjustment of the children; and the willingness of each parent to facilitate the children's relationship with the other parent.

The two major types of custody are legal and physical. Legal custody refers to decision-making power. With sole legal custody one parent retains all legal rights to decision making regarding the children, including physical placement. In the case of joint legal custody, both parents have equal legal rights and responsibilities for the children. Many states have a presumption for joint legal custody unless clear and convincing evidence suggests that it would be detrimental. This position is advocated because it maintains both parents' active involvement in major decision making for their children.

Physical custody refers to the physical placement of the children. Shared placement or joint physical custody indicates an equal or nearly equal distribution of time spent with the children. This is a workable plan when the parents live in close proximity, conflict between the parents is minimal, children are able to deal with transition, and the children's age/developmental needs support such a plan. Some common joint physical custody plans involve alternating weeks and the 2-2-5-5 schedule (Monday and Tuesday with one parent, Wednesday and Thursday with the other parent, and alternating weekends).

However, in the majority of cases the children reside predominately with one parent and have designated parenting time (e.g., visitation) with the other parent. Parenting time plans vary widely and must be developed to meet the individual needs of the parties. Some factors for consideration are work schedule(s) and availability of the parents, geographic distance between the parents, age/developmental needs of the children, special needs of the parents and children, degree of cooperation between the parents, and desires of the parents and children. With very young children frequent contact with the noncustodial parent is recommended, on a schedule that avoids a gap of more than three or four days between contacts (Kelly & Lamb, 2000).

The suitability of overnight parenting time for this age group is an area of ongoing controversy (Gould & Martindale, 2007). For children ages five and older, some common arrangements include (1) the noncustodial parent having parenting time with the children every Wednesday evening and every other weekend (Friday through Sunday evening or Monday morning) and (2) the noncustodial parent having parenting time with the children every weekend, or three of the four weekends per month with one evening or overnight before and after the non-weekend. During the summer, the parenting plan may continue or the time may be equally divided between the parents. Holidays and vacation breaks are usually divided or alternated between the parents.

In the overwhelming majority of child custody cases, the parents can successfully reach an agreement regarding legal and physical custody. However, in about 10% of cases the process becomes contentious. In these situations, the court sometimes orders a child custody evaluation. This type of forensic evaluation may be performed by a clinic affiliated with the court or by a private practice mental health professional with specialized training and experience in the child custody field.

Evaluations performed by a court clinic are typically brief, taking four to six hours to complete with a two- to five-page report presented to the court. The cost is usually minimal or determined according to a sliding scale. In contrast, evaluations performed by private mental health professionals are often comprehensive and costly. Doctoral-level psychologists working privately usually spend 24–28 hours completing the evaluation (Bow, 2006). Reports to the court are typically about 20 pages but may vary, depending on the complexity of the case (Bow, 2006).

The child custody evaluator should be appointed by the court, so that the professional may function in an independent, objective, and impartial role. The evaluator should not have a prior relationship with the family, in other words, as therapist (American Psychological Association [APA], 1994). The evaluation focuses on establishing the best interests of the children, and the evaluator must address the specific best interest criteria established by state law. All parties should be involved in the evaluation process because the evaluator needs to critically evaluate both sides of the dispute. Also, an evaluator should not provide an opinion about a person who has not participated in the evaluation (APA, 1994). In contrast to therapy, court-ordered evaluations have limited confidentiality, meaning that all information gathered during the evaluation may be reported to the court.

Guidelines for performing child custody evaluations are provided by professional organizations. For example, the American Psychological Association (1994) published the *Guidelines for Child Custody Evaluations in Divorce Proceedings*. These guidelines are aspirational and outline parameters for professional practice in this area. The Association for Family and Conciliation Courts (AFFCC) has also published model standards of practice for child custody evaluations (AFCC, 2007).

Child custody evaluations employ multiple methods of data collection. The following components are critical in the evaluation process: (1) interviews with each parent to gather a comprehensive psychosocial history and explore the marital history/dispute, (2) interviews with each child, (3) parent-child observations, (4) psychological testing of the parents, and children if needed, (5) collateral contacts with important individuals, such as new partners, therapists, teachers, and/or baby-sitters, and (6) review of pertinent documents and court records (Bow, 2006; Gould, 2006; Gould & Martindale, 2007).

Psychological testing of the parents frequently includes personality measures to assess personality traits and characteristics, along with signs of mental illness. The most popular tests for these evaluations are the Minnesota Multiphasic Personality Inventory-2, Millon Multiaxial Personality Inventory-III, and Rorschach Inkblot Method (Bow, 2006). Also, parenting inventories such as the Parenting Stress Index and Parent-Child Relationship Inventory are increasingly being used to assess parenting attitudes and beliefs (Quinnell & Bow, 2001).

These contentious cases frequently include an allegation of sexual abuse, domestic violence, substance abuse, or parent alienation. These allegations may be motivated by a variety of factors. Sometimes the parent is expressing a genuine concern for the children's welfare; however, in other instances the allegation is being used in a vengeful, vindictive way to gain leverage in the dispute. These allegations require much investigation and a high level of expertise on the evaluator's part (Gould & Martindale, 2007).

On average, a private child custody evaluation takes about two months to complete (Bow, 2006). The evaluator provides the court with a report of the findings and recommendations. Judges consider the report, along with other data, in making the ultimate decisions regarding custody and parenting time.

REFERENCES

American Psychological Association. (1994). Guidelines for child custody evaluations in divorce proceedings. *American Psychologist, 49*, 677–680.

Association of Family and Conciliation Courts. (2007). Model standards of practice for child custody evaluations. *Family Court Review, 45*, 70–91.

Bow, J. N. (2006). Review of empirical research on child custody practice. *Journal of Child Custody, 3*(1), 23–50.

Bow, J. N., & Quinnell, F. A. (2001). Psychologists' current practices and procedures in child custody evaluations: Five years post American Psychological Association guidelines. *Professional Psychology: Research and Practice, 32*, 261–268.

Gould, J. W. (2006). *Conducting scientifically crafted child custody evaluations* (2nd ed.). Sarasota, FL: Professional Resource Press.

Gould, J. W., & Martindale, D. A. (2007). *The art and science of child custody evaluations.* New York: John Wiley & Sons.

Kelly, J. B., Lamb, M. E. (2000). Using child development research to make appropriate custody and access decisions for young children. *Family and Conciliation Court Reviews, 38*, 297–311.

Quinnell, F. A., & Bow, J. N. (2001). Psychological tests used in child custody evaluations. *Behavioral Sciences and the Law, 19*, 491–501.

SUGGESTED READINGS

Martindale, D. A., & Gould, J. W. (2004). The forensic model: Ethics and scientific Methodology applied to child custody evaluations. *Journal of Child Custody, 1*(2), 1–22.

Otto, R. K., Buffington-Vollum, J., Edens, J. F. (2003). Child custody evaluation. In A. M. Goldstein (Ed.), *Handbook of psychology: Vol. 11: Forensic psychology* (pp. 179–208). New York: John Wiley & Sons.

JAMES N. BOW
Hawthorn Center, Northville, MI

See also: Expert Testimony; Forensic Psychology; Psychology and the Law

CHILD GUIDANCE CLINICS

The National Committee for Mental Hygiene marshaled the child guidance clinic movement, which spanned the decades of the 1920s to 1940s. Child guidance clinics (CGCs) were established for the psychiatric study, treatment, and prevention of juvenile delinquency and conduct and personality disorders in 3- to 17-year-old non-mentally retarded children. The CGC approach to children's mental health represented a shift from traditional treatment models, which were largely individual psychoanalytically oriented play therapy conducted by a psychiatrist or psychologist, toward more innovative modes of intervention. Further, the era of CGCs represented the first time that the mental health of children was considered an independently important focus for treatment.

CGCs were the first treatment facilities to consider family influence on the mental health of children. Their comprehensive, community-based approach to children's mental health service was carried our by multidisciplinary teams of psychologists, educational psychologists, psychiatrists, psychiatric social workers, speech therapists, and psychiatric occupational therapists. Owned by the local educational authority, CGCs represented a reallocation of responsibility for the mental health of children from individuals and families to the community as a whole.

At the close of the 1940s, the mental health focus again shifted away from children in order to respond to immediate World War II–related mental health needs. There were not any more substantial gains in children's mental health services until the Community Mental Health Centers (CMHCs) Act of 1963. Like child guidance clinics, CMHCs sought to address both the treatment and prevention of mental illness within communities. However, unlike child guidance clinics, CMHCs were not solely child focused; rather, they addressed mental health issues across development. CMHCs were responsible for a comprehensive menu of services including outpatient treatment, primary and secondary prevention efforts,

24-hour crisis response, and consultation with schools for early child risk evaluation.

Continuing the focus on community prevention that began with CGCs, current treatment approaches generally emphasize child-centered, family-focused, community-based efforts in the planning and implementation of treatment. Current post-CGC services available to children within the mental health system include inpatient and outpatient psychiatric and psychological treatment facilities, partial programs, mobile therapy, crisis teams, foster care, juvenile justice, education, social welfare, primary healthcare, emergency shelter, wraparound services, and home-based interventions. The role of case managers, whose job it is to coordinate children's mental health services within this complex system, has emerged to ensure that services are not fragmented and work in an interactive therapeutic manner to meet children's mental health needs.

In the past decade, School-Based Health Care Centers (SBHCs) represent the field's answer to the inaccessibility of mental health services for two-thirds of those children needing services. These centers address the currently understood biopsychosocial nature of mental illness. Though originally developed to serve the inner city, SBHCs have expanded to serve children in urban, suburban, and rural areas. Half of the current programs are implemented in high schools, though elementary schools and middle schools now have services available also.

The most significant change in this variety of services has been in the foundations underlying their approaches to intervention. Professionals are using developmental and clinical research to inform prevention and intervention programming. With the influence of the field of developmental psychopathology, research with normative, at-risk, and mentally ill populations is used to promote holistic health in children rather than simply the absence of illness. Additionally, mental health services strive to be both culturally competent and responsive to the cultural, racial, and ethnic differences within varied service populations. Undoubtedly, the mental health service system will continue to evolve in an effort to meet increasingly diverse generations of children's ever-changing physical, emotional, social, and educational needs.

SUGGESTED READINGS

Horn, M (1989). *Before it's too late: The child guidance movement in the United States, 1922–1945.* Philadelphia: Temple University Press.

Smuts, A. B. (2006). *Science in the service of children, 1893–1935.* New Haven: Yale University Press.

J. BROOKE WRIGHT
KELLY S. FLANAGAN
Wheaton College

CHILD MALTREATMENT

Each year, nearly 3 million suspected cases of child maltreatment are reported in the United States (Wekerle, Miller, Wolfe, & Spindel, 2006). Nearly 1 million cases are substantiated, although the true incidence is likely far greater than these estimates suggest. Abuse or neglect can fundamentally alter a child's developmental trajectory with long-term detrimental effects on physical, emotional, social/interpersonal, and behavioral health outcomes. Research studies find, however, that with appropriate and timely interventions, maltreated children can grow up to experience healthy and productive lives.

Child Maltreatment Terminology and Definitions

Broadly defined, child maltreatment refers to caregiver acts of commission or omission that result in physical and/or psychological injury to a child. The World Health Organization and International Society for Prevention of Child Abuse and Neglect (WHO & ISPCAN, 2006) identify four major types of child maltreatment: physical abuse, sexual abuse, emotional abuse, and neglect. Physical abuse is the deliberate use of physical force against a child that results in or has the potential to result in harm to the child's health, survival, development, or dignity. Often, it is confused with child discipline and inflicted as child punishment. Sexual abuse refers to "the involvement of a child in sexual activity that he or she does not fully comprehend, is unable to give informed consent to, or for which the child is not developmentally prepared, or else that violates the laws or social taboos of society" (WHO & ISPCAN, 2006). It includes any sexual experience between a child and someone at least 5 years older, or an adolescent and someone at least 10 years older (Wolfe, 1998). Emotional abuse includes isolated as well as repeated caregiver acts or omissions that result in a failure over time to provide a developmentally appropriate and supportive environment. Lastly, neglect refers to the "failure to provide care in accordance with expected societal standards for food, shelter, protection, affection" (Wekerle et al., 2006, p. 2). Although neglect is the most common form of child maltreatment, simultaneous or sequential occurrences of abuse *and* neglect are widespread.

Families in which child maltreatment exists often experience other difficulties, including substance abuse, domestic violence, and overall diminished parental capacity and skills, leaving many children chronically vulnerable to witnessing and/or experiencing other stressful and oftentimes traumatic life events (Osofsky, 2003). In addition, communities, especially those that are low-income and inner city, may also provide the context for youth to be further exposed to various forms of interpersonal violence and trauma.

Complex trauma is a relatively new construct created to characterize those individuals who experience chronic exposure to traumatic experiences and who often develop a broader constellation of symptoms and difficulties than those who experience more acute traumatic experiences (National Child Traumatic Stress Network, 2003). The symptoms associated with complex trauma have been categorized into six domains of impairment: Affect, impulse control, attention, cognitive processing, self-perception, and interpersonal relationships. Whether the outcomes associated with complex trauma require interventions different from those targeting the sequelae associated with more acute child maltreatment remains an empirical question.

Theories and Models of the Effects of Child Maltreatment

It is important to note that not all children suffer psychological consequences related to earlier abuse or neglect. Several factors may affect whether and how psychological symptoms are manifest, including the child's age and developmental status at the time of abuse or neglect, the type of maltreatment, the frequency and severity of maltreatment, the relationship between the victim and the perpetrator, the family environment, and family psychiatric history. Risk for functional impairment increases if the abuse has an early onset; is severe, violent, and lengthy in duration; involves multiple perpetrators; and if limited family support is available (Wekerle et al., 2006). Although some children are resilient in the face of maltreatment, many others do suffer negative consequences that last into adulthood. The impact of maltreatment on the developing child includes a complex range of outcomes that reflect the transactional nature of biological, psychological, and psychosocial processes (Wekerle et al., 2006).

The posttraumatic stress disorder (PTSD) symptomatology model suggests exposure to severe environmental stress adversely affects neurobiological systems, including the immune, neurotransmitter, and sympathetic nervous systems as well as the hypothalamic-pituitary-adrenal (HPA) axis, and this stress also produces significant structural and functional alterations in brain development (Wekerle et al., 2006). Accordingly, PTSD symptoms arise in response to changes in the neurobiological stress system which, in turn, increases the risk for subsequent chronic PTSD, compromised cognitive and psychosocial functioning, and negative health outcomes.

Social learning and information processing theories suggest that maltreatment affects the way children perceive and respond to environmental stimuli (Wekerle et al., 2006). Although these perceptual biases may produce responses that are adaptive in maltreatment contexts (e.g., early recognition and reaction to threat stimuli), they may also lead to misattribution of intent (e.g., hostile attributional bias), cognitive interference (e.g., inattention and poor working memory), and maladaptive behavioral responses (e.g., aggression or social withdrawal) in nonmaltreatment contexts (Wekerle et al., 2006).

Diagnosis and Treatment Indications

Childhood maltreatment is associated with heightened risk for a wide range of psychological and behavioral difficulties, including PTSD and other problems with mood, anxiety, behavior, and personality. PTSD is the most common DSM-IV-TR diagnosis assigned to maltreated children, with estimates ranging from 21% to 55% in physically and/or sexually abused children (Wekerle et al., 2006). The diagnosis is made after a person reacts with intense fear or disorganized behavior in response to one or more direct or indirect traumatic events and then shows impairment in each of the following three symptoms clusters for at least one month: (1) intrusive re-experiencing of the trauma(s) (e.g., flashbacks and nightmares), (2) persistent avoidance of trauma-related cues and emotional numbing, and (3) increased physiological arousal (e.g., sleep difficulties and hypervigilance).

Maltreated children are also two to three times more likely than nonmaltreated youth to develop mood disorders, including dysthymia and major depressive disorder, and they are also at significantly higher risk for suicidal and nonsuicidal self-injurious behavior. In addition to PTSD symptomatology, general symptoms of anxiety, nightmares, inappropriate fears of certain places, and clinging to parents are commonly found among child victims of maltreatment and may warrant diagnoses of generalized anxiety disorder and separation anxiety disorder. Aggression, delinquency (e.g., shoplifting), and risk-taking behaviors also are more common among maltreated youth, who also show elevated rates of oppositional defiant, conduct, and substance use disorders.

Child maltreatment, especially that which is more chronic and complex, may directly impact personality development (Wekerle et al., 2006). Individuals with a history of childhood abuse and/or neglect are four times more likely to have a personality disorder during young adulthood than those without a history of maltreatment. Furthermore, physically abused youth show an increased likelihood of exhibiting antisocial personality disorder, whereas sexually abused youth show an increased likelihood of exhibiting borderline personality disorder.

Evidence-Based Treatment Options

All clinicians are advised to conduct a comprehensive assessment before initiating treatment. A structured diagnostic interview is useful for assessing the presence of diagnosable mental disorders, traumatic events, and relevant histories (e.g., developmental, medical, and family). The purpose of treatment for child maltreatment is to provide children (and sometimes families) with the skills necessary to understand and cope with their abuse experience, to interact successfully with others, and to prevent any future risk of abuse. Cognitive-behaviorally based interventions show the greatest efficacy for the treatment of childhood maltreatment and contain elements of the following: psychoeducation, cognitive restructuring, exposure-based work, stress inoculation, and anxiety management training. Treatment studies of maltreated youth have found that the majority of children who receive treatment function better at posttreatment compared with their nontreated counterparts (Skowron & Reinemann, 2005).

Trauma-focused cognitive behavior therapy (TF-CBT; Cohen, Mannarino, & Deblinger, 2006) is one of the hallmark evidence-based treatments for maltreated youth and their caregivers who have experienced both discrete traumatic events as well as multiple chronic traumas. TF-CBT has been recognized by the American Academy of Child and Adolescent Psychiatry as the first line treatment for childhood PTSD. TF-CBT is a 12-week structured treatment comprised of three components: psychoeducation, coping skills, and exposure. The intervention is designed for children between the ages of 5 and 18 and their caregivers. Psychoeducation provides the child and caregiver with information about common trauma-related reactions and symptoms and reviews of personal safety skills (e.g., "good" versus "bad" touch). Coping skills training includes emotional expression skills, cognitive coping skills, relaxation techniques, and cognitive processing strategies (e.g., challenging automatic inaccurate thoughts). Lastly, exposure-based work includes prolonged exposure to the trauma narrative (i.e., what happened, how it felt, and what it meant). Through various partnerships, a free Web-based learning course in TF-CBT is offered at the following web site: http://tfcbt.musc.edu/.

For complex clinical cases, TF-CBT may be necessary but not sufficient to address the breadth and severity of the pathology (Wekerle et al., 2006). Some traumatized youth present with significant emotional and behavioral problems, including suicidal and self-injurious behaviors, substance abuse, and eating disordered behavior, to name a few. Before treating the abuse, therapy should first help the child or adolescent establish safety and behavioral control (Wekerle et al., 2006). To accomplish this goal, other evidenced-based treatments may be appropriate to use in addition to or prior to initiating TF-CBT.

Dialectical behavior therapy (DBT) may be useful for maltreated adolescents exhibiting suicidal and/or self-injurious behavior and borderline personality disorder features. DBT has shown promise in reducing suicidal behavior, depression, anxiety, borderline personality symptoms, and inpatient hospitalizations among multiproblem adolescents (Miller, Rathus, & Linehan, 2007). DBT blends cognitive-behavior therapy with dialectical philosophy and Zen practice, and it is organized into four treatment stages that parallel the stages of disorder:

Stage 1 focuses on establishing safety and behavioral control; Stage 2 aims to decrease posttraumatic stress and help process emotions; Stage 3 focuses on increasing respect for self and work on individual goals; and Stage 4 looks to increase ones capacity for experiencing pleasure.

Most treatment studies of traumatized youth have examined individual and family interventions. However, structured psychotherapy for adolescents responding to chronic stress (SPARCS; DeRosa et al., 2006) is a group treatment designed to help chronically traumatized youth, many of whom have complex trauma symptomatology, manage anxiety and mood changes more effectively, enhance self-efficacy, connect with others in more appropriate and healthy ways, establish supportive relationships, cultivate awareness, and create meaning in their lives.

Despite a growing number of effective interventions, abusive and neglectful families often have difficulty with treatment engagement and compliance and exhibit high rates of treatment dropout (Wekerle et al., 2006). Barriers to treatment may include, but are not limited to, perceived cultural mismatches, ease-of-access issues, and psychological barriers. Furthermore, systemic issues, such as the involvement of child welfare and legal services, can inadvertently delay treatment services. Ultimately, successful interventions must emphasize collaboration across systems, including individuals, families, and associated agencies.

REFERENCES

Cohen, J. A., Mannarino, A. P., & Deblinger, E. (2006). *Treating trauma and traumatic grief in children and adolescents.* New York: Guilford Press.

DeRosa, R., Habib, M., Pelcovitz, D., Rathus, J., Sonnenklar, J., Ford, J., et al. (2006). *Structured psychotherapy for adolescents responding to chronic stress.* Unpublished Manual.

Miller, A. L., Rathus, J. H., & Linehan, M. M. (2007). *Dialectical behavior therapy with suicidal adolescents.* New York: Guilford Press.

National Child Traumatic Stress Network. (2003). *Complex trauma in children and adolescents.* Retrieved March 15, 2008, from http://www.nctsnet.org/nctsn_assets/pdfs/edu_materials/ComplexTrauma_All.pdf.

Osofsky, J. D. (2003). Prevalence of children's exposure to domestic violence and child maltreatment: Implications for prevention and intervention. *Clinical Child and Family Psychology Review, 6*(3), 161–170.

Skowron, E., & Reinemann, D. (2005). Effectiveness of psychological interventions for child maltreatment: A meta-analysis. *Psychotherapy: Theory, Research, Practice, Training, 42*(1), 52–71.

Wekerle, C., Miller, A. L., Wolfe, D. A., & Spindel, C. B. (2006). *Childhood maltreatment.* Cambridge, MA: Hogrefe & Huber.

Wolfe, V. V. (1998). Child sexual abuse. In Mash, E. J. & R. A. Barkley (Eds.), *Treatment of childhood disorders* (2nd ed., pp. 545–597). New York: Guilford Press.

World Health Organization (WHO) and International Society for Prevention of Child Abuse and Neglect (ISPCAN). (2006). *Preventing child maltreatment: A guide to taking action and generating evidence.* Retrieved March 15, 2008, from http://whqlibdoc.who.int/publications/2006/9241594365_eng.pdf.

ALEC L. MILLER
DENA A. KLEIN
Albert Einstein College of Medicine

See also: **Child Abuse; Child Neglect; Child Sexual Abuse**

CHILD NEGLECT

Child abuse and child neglect are the two forms of child maltreatment. Both hurt children: abuse through deliberate action and neglect through omission of necessary action. Because of the pioneering work of thousands of professionals and lay people over the past half century, child abuse is now often (but not always) recognized and reported. As a result, children who are physically beaten, sexually exploited, and otherwise harmed are noticed and sometimes rescued.

However, because of "neglect of neglect" (Garbarino & Collins, 1999, p. 1), child neglect is often not noticed or reported until a child is starving, or wanders barefoot in the snow at midnight, or dies in a fire when no adults are home. Neglect is far more common than abuse, as well as more often deadly. It may be more crippling to psychological health as well. For example, some adults who were abused but not neglected recount their experiences with a smile. They seem to have overcome the trauma and to have normal adult lives. By comparison, those who were chronically neglected are often depressed and ashamed lifelong, unable to establish loving relationships or even to love themselves (Tyler, Allison, & Winsler, 2006).

Such an outcome is especially tragic, because child neglect, if it is recognized and remediated early in life, need not permanently damage the child. Humans are born with impulses to grow and develop well, to learn whatever language they hear, to love whoever cares for them, and to remedy whatever is amiss in their early development (called *self-righting*). For this reason it is crucial that everyone who cares about children recognize signs of neglect and help parents and children before it is too late.

One problem is that perfect parents do not exist. Every parent sometimes is late to secure preventive medical care, or feeds the child food that is not nutritionally ideal, or ignores a child's question. All of these actions are neglect. In some poor nations, almost all children are neglected, in that very few go to the dentist, eat three meals a day, or graduate from high school.

Because none of us is perfect, people hesitate to intervene. At what point does neglect become maltreatment? It could be argued that every child in the world should be as well cared for as the typical child in a nation with excellent child care, such as Sweden or Japan. However, a more contextual standard is usually applied. Essentially, parents and societies are expected to provide at least as much nurturance and guidance as that given the average child in their community. For example, almost all nations immunize their children. The groups of Northern Nigeria who did not provide polio immunization (and therefore caused a mini-epidemic two years later) could be considered neglectful, as could parents in developed nations who risk their child catching measles, mumps, and so on.

The crucial standard is whether the neglect harmed the children. In the United States examples would include children who are socially rejected because they never had opportunities to play with others, or slow to talk because they did not hear enough language, or overweight because their parents did not provide nutritious food, and so on. Descriptions of some specific forms of neglect follow next.

Physical Neglect

Failure to meet basic needs for food, rest, and shelter is physical neglect, which is the most commonly reported type of neglect. If an infant grows very slowly, such as a 4-month-old who weighs less than 10 pounds, the child may be showing failure-to-thrive. Such undernourishment is a very serious problem, as the brain develops rapidly during infancy, and malnutrition slows down neurological as well as physical growth. If older children are malnourished, they may be stunted (too short) and vulnerable to childhood diseases. One reason for stunting is that children have too little to eat, and another reason is that their growth is reduced because they are stressed and anxious, especially at night when growth hormones are most active. Inadequate and disturbed rest is evidence of neglect.

Exposure to hazards—motor vehicles, open water (drowning is the most common cause of death in some parts of the United States), fires, poisons, and the like—is neglect. Accidents are by far the leading cause of child death in the United States, accounting for more deaths than the top five diseases combined. Almost always, neglect is a factor in hazardous exposure, not only by virtue of inadequate supervision but also by lack of community attention. For example, some communities have safe play spaces, ample sidewalks, and school-crossing guards, but others do not, and children are injured as a consequence. A very specific example of social neglect is deteriorated housing. Fatal fires, for instance, occur five times more often in run-down dwellings in crowded neighborhoods than overall.

Emotional Neglect

From a psychological perspective, emotional neglect is even worse than physical neglect, because a child who grows up emotionally stunted is unable to experience the joy, love, and intimacy that make life worth living. If babies cannot establish normal attachments, perhaps because their caregivers are severely depressed or drug-addicted, the brain itself may never connect social interaction and positive emotions (Howe, 2005). Emotionally neglected children never learn emotional regulation, which is how and when to express fear, anger, love, and other feelings.

As a result, emotionally neglected children are overwhelmed by their impulses. They become bullies or victims, unable to distinguish hostility from unintentional mistakes and genuine warmth from superficial friendliness. As adolescents and adults, they may befriend people who exploit them or become antisocial, bitter, lonely, and a danger to others and themselves.

Educational, Medical, and Sexual Neglect

All children are eager to learn. Educational neglect begins long before entry into school, when young children learn to talk, to recognize letters, and to play with other children. Neglectful parents put their toddlers in front of the television for hours on end, never reading to them or taking them out to play with other young children. Educational neglect becomes apparent in first grade, when a child is obviously behind in talking and playing. This developmental arrest typically gets worse as time goes on, leading to a child who repeats grades and drops out of school.

Medical neglect occurs when a child's health needs are ignored. Some children never see a doctor or dentist. Sadly, when children are so severely abused that they are hospitalized, it is not unusual for x-rays to reveal bones that had been broken but never set. As in this example, neglect and abuse often occur together, which is another reason why early signs of neglect should be noticed.

Sexual neglect occurs when children do not develop the respect for their own bodies. Before puberty, children should know much more than how to avoid sexual diseases and unwanted pregnancy; they should know that humans love each other. Explicit sexual interaction need not be taught; indeed it is considered neglect if a child is not shielded from naked adult passion. However, having parents who love each other speaks volumes about healthy sexuality.

Prevention

Parents are directly responsible for their children, but parents are not alone. Many factors in the child's home increase the likelihood of neglect, including a family with two or more children under age 6, a father being unemployed or absent, a mother who did not complete high school, an impoverished or high-crime neighborhood, and a low family income. Each of these factors correlates with less attention to the child and make neglect more likely, although some families that experience all of these stresses nonetheless take good care of their children. In extreme cases, authorities intervene, either to help the parents or remove the child from the home. For children removed from their home, a foster or adoptive family provide love and nurture until they reach adulthood. Unfortunately, however, social neglect is often added to family neglect. Foster children average three placements before finding a permanent home (Pew Commission on Foster Care, 2004), with each move adding to the risk of a poor outcome (Oosterman, Schuengel, & Slot, 2007).

Parents' dedication is the best defense against child neglect. Almost all parents want their children to become strong, smart, and happy. Despite this, many parents have trouble providing proper care, especially the kind emotional and educational care just described. At that point, every doctor, nurse, teacher, psychologist, relative, and neighbor needs to notice the baby or child who is slow to talk, explore, or grow. The signs of neglect are obvious to those who look for them, the consequences are serious, and the solution is simple—if people want to help.

REFERENCES

Garbarino, J., & Collins, C. C. (1999). Child neglect: The family with a hole in the middle. In H. Dubowitz (Ed.), *Neglected children: Research, practice, and policy* (pp.1–23). Thousand Oaks, CA: Sage.

Howe, D. (2005). *Child abuse and neglect: Attachment, development and intervention*. New York: Macmillan.

Oosterman, M., Schuengel, C., & Slot, N. W. (2007). Disruptions in foster care: A review and meta-analysis. *Children and Youth Services Review, 29*, 53–76.

Pew Commission on Children in Foster Care. (2004). *Fostering the future: Safety, permanence, and well-being for children in foster care.* Philadelphia: Pew Charitable Trusts.

Tyler, S., Allison, K., & Winsler, A. (2006). Child neglect: Developmental consequences, intervention, and policy implications. *Child and Youth Care Forum, 35*, 1–20.

SUGGESTED READING

Dubowitz, H. (Ed.). (1999). *Neglected children: Research, practice, and policy*. Thousand Oaks, CA: Sage.

KATHLEEN STASSEN BERGER
Bronx Community College, City University of New York

***See also:* Child Abuse; Child Maltreatment; Child Sexual Abuse**

CHILD PSYCHOLOGY

Child psychology deals with the personality and behavior of children, typically from conception to puberty. Child psychology has referred in the past to both normal and abnormal behavior, to both theory and research, and also to the psychotherapy or counseling of disturbed children. Current usage, however, limits the term to a branch of the science of developmental psychology, while specifying "child clinical" when referring to the professional practice of child psychology.

Childhood can be divided into substages: prenatal, infancy, toddlerhood, preschool, middle childhood, and later childhood. Some researchers, however, argue that development is best understood in the context of the total span of life and propose a "life-span developmental psychology." Additionally, current research has focused on the contexts that influence development, including the family, school, and peers (see Bronfenbrenner, 1989, 1993).

History

Four sorts of history can be considered. Ontogenetic history, the history of the organism from conception to death, is the basic material of human development. Phylogenetic history refers to the evolutionary development of the species. According to one theory—proposed by G. Stanley Hall in his treatise on *Adolescence* (1904), but now largely discounted—the ontogenetic history of individuals represented a "recapitulation" or repeating of the species' phylogenetic history.

A third sort of history refers to changes over time in the concept of childhood, corresponding to the sociocultural history of the family. Philippe Müller (1969) identified four periods in the cultural history of the family that corresponded to changing conceptions of the child.

A fourth kind of history in child psychology is the history of the field, itself. Early Greek writers were concerned with stages of development, the socialization process, and the proper education of children. The origins of child psychology as a science, however, can be traced to the careful observations recorded in early "baby biographies," such as those written by Tiedemann (1787), Darwin (1877), and Preyer (1882). Despite their shortcomings as scientific data, these biographies paved the way for more careful observation, for attention to psychological processes, and finally for experiments dealing with child behavior.

More recent influences on child psychology have been the testing movement and the development of child guidance clinics and major university centers for research on child behavior. Current literature emphasizes developmentally appropriate guidance, that is, optimal ways to work with and parent children.

Theories

Early theories of child psychology were largely implicit, children being thought of as miniature adults. Not until the late nineteenth century and the emergence of a formal discipline of psychology did theories about child behavior become prominent. An early psychologist, G. Stanley Hall, proposed a biogenetic theory emphasizing biological growth and genetic predispositions.

Freud, the father of psychoanalysis, emphasized environmental and especially social factors in the development of child behavior and personality. One of the first to stress the influence of early experience on later behavior, Freud assigned a major role to the unconscious. He postulated a series of psychosexual stages that are defined by the characteristic way in which libido, or mental sexual energy, gets expressed.

Jean Piaget developed a major theory of cognitive development. For Piaget, the stages of development concern the increasingly complex way in which the individual can incorporate and process information and assimilate it into his or her own previously developed mental structures.

Learning theorists tended to view children's behavior as based on environmental rather than organismic factors and, like Freud, saw the organism as passive rather than active in its own development. The emergence of social learning theory was in some respects a combination of psychoanalytic and learning theory concepts.

Research Methods

Since the days of the baby biographies, child psychology has progressed in methodology as well as theory. Using a longitudinal approach, investigators follow the same subjects over the years of interest and observe age changes. With a cross-sectional approach, the researcher tests subjects of different ages. A combination of the two procedures has been suggested (Schaie, 1970) as a more powerful approach.

Research methods have included questionnaires; ratings and rankings by teachers, peers, parents, and oneself; interviews; observation; projective tests; personality and intelligence tests; and direct experimentation on a wide variety of topics, including personality, emotion, intelligence, perception, neurology, linguistics, culture, and social groups. A good source for understanding the basic information on research methods in child psychology is *Research Methods in Human Development* (Brown, Cozby, Kee, & Worden, 1999).

Issues in Developmental Psychology

The contrasting view of the child as an active agent or a recipient remains a salient issue in child psychology. The relative influence of environmental factors, contrasted with genetic predispositions, is also an important dimension to child psychologists. Finally, child psychologists differ in the importance they place on stages in development: Whereas some theorists perceive development as proceeding by discrete stages, others assume a more continuous unfolding of personality and behavior.

One measure of the growth of child psychology in the past 75 years might be the increase in the number of books and journals devoted to this field or the rapidly increasing number of research studies that deal with child development. The first edition of the *Handbook of Child Psychology* (Murchison, 1931) contained 711 pages. The sixth edition (Damon & Lerner, 2006) contains four volumes, each more than 1,000 pages.

REFERENCES

Bronfenbrenner, U. (1989). Ecological systems theory. In R. Vasta (Ed.), *Six theories of child development. Annals of Child Development,* 6, 187–249. Greenwich, CT: JAI Press.

Bronfenbrenner, U. (1993). The ecology of cognitive development: Research models and fuguitive findings. In R. H. Wozniak & K. W. Fischer (Eds.), *Development in context: Acting and thinking in specific environments* (pp. 3–44). Hillsdale, NJ: Lawrence Erlbaum.

Brown, K. W., Cozby, P. C., Kee, D. W., & Worden, P. E. (1999). *Research methods in human development* (2nd ed.). Mountain View, CA: Mayfield Publishing.

Damon, W., & Lerner, R.M. (Eds.). (2006). *Handbook of child psychology* (Vols. 1–4). Hoboken, NJ: John Wiley & Sons.

Darwin, C. A. (1877). A biographical sketch of an infant. *Merid, 2,* 285–294.

Hall, G. S. (1904). *Adolescence: Its psychology and its relations to physiology, anthropology, sociology, sex, crime, religion, and education,* Vol. I. Englewood Cliffs, NJ: Prentice-Hall.

Müller, P. (1969). *The tasks of childhood.* New York: McGraw-Hill.

Murchison, C. (Ed.). (1931). *A handbook of child psychology.* Worcester, MA: Clark University Press.

Preyer, W. (1882/1888). *The mind of the child.* New York: Appleton-Century.

Rousseau, J. J. (1738/1762). *Emile, or concerning education.* New York: Dutton.

Schaie, K. W. (1970). A reinterpretation of age-related changes in cognitive structure and functioning. In L. R. Goulet & P. B. Baltes (Eds.), *Life-span developmental psychology: Research and theory.* New York: Academic Press.

Tiedemann, D. (1787). *Beobachtungen über die Entwicklung der Seelenfähigkeiten bei Kindern.* Altenburg: Bonde.

JOHN PAUL MCKINNEY
Michigan State University

KATHLEEN MCKINNEY
University of Wyoming

See also: **Cognitive Development; Developmental Psychology; Psychosexual Stages**

CHILD REARING (See Parental Approaches)

CHILD SEXUAL ABUSE

Child sexual abuse (CSA) is defined as the involvement of a child in sexual activity to provide sexual gratification or financial benefit to the perpetrator, including contacts for sexual purposes, prostitution, pornography, and other sexually exploitive activities. CSA allegations are addressed in a variety of psycholegal contexts, including, but not limited to, child custody evaluations in a family court, child protection proceedings in dependency court, personal injury cases in civil proceedings, and prosecution of legal charges in criminal and military courts. Few areas of psychological evaluation involve such a variety of complex evaluation issues and potentially serious consequences for faulty conclusions.

Problems Identifying Sexually Abused Children

Research consistently shows that only a minority of victimized children disclose their sexual abuse during childhood (see London, Bruck, Ceci, & Shuman, 2000). A review of retrospective CSA disclosure studies from 1990 forward indicates that two-thirds of the adults alleging CSA did not make a disclosure during childhood. The disclosure rates were similar for studies that specifically recruited adults with childhood histories of CSA and for studies that recruited adults from the general population. Furthermore, findings from studies using sexually abused child subjects were consistent with the retrospective findings showing significant delays in disclosure by the majority of children.

A review of research by London and her colleagues (2005) examined not only the rate of CSA disclosure during childhood, but also the characteristics of abuse that were associated with nondisclosure and the issue of recantation. Although a number of experts assert that a substantial percentage of sexually abused children do not disclose abuse because of the method of coercion used by the perpetrator and fear of physical harm, London et al. found little empirical evidence to support these conjectures. Conversely, the majority of current research suggests that threats of physical harm are associated with higher rates of children's disclosures. The researchers also found little scientific support for the assertion that a high percentage of sexually abused children recant their disclosure. However, further research is needed on these issues of disclosure and recantation due to the problems in the research methodology in many of the studies examining these issues.

Unreliable information obtained from children through inadequate interviews also confounds the identification and protection of sexually victimized children. Issues raised about the testimony of children whose reliability was determined to be compromised by suggestive interview techniques (e.g., *State v. Michaels*, 1993) led to several appellate courts overturning the convictions of persons found guilty of child sexual abuse. In a number of these cases, the children's memories and statements were so significantly contaminated by improper interviewing that it was determined that the truth of the matter was unattainable (see Bruck & Ceci, 1995).

Children's Testimonial Competency

The legal test of a child's competency to testify in most jurisdictions declares that children of any age may testify if they possess the capacities to (1) appreciate the difference between truth and falsehoods, (2) understand the obligation to tell the truth, (3) accurately perceive and recall the events witnessed, and (4) relate facts accurately (Kuehnle, 2003). Although the legal test to determine whether a child is competent to testify is based on well-defined and observable behaviors, rather than on subjective perceptions of the child's believability, not all judges, juries, and forensic experts appreciate the complexity of factors underlying the reliability of children's testimony, including an understanding of the complex interaction of a child's age with the type of interview questions asked, the structure of the questioning, the demeanor of the interviewer, the number of formal and informal interviews experienced by the child, and the delay between the alleged event and a forensic interview (Buck & Warren, in press).

The interaction of these factors influences the accuracy of the information provided by a child and increases or decreases the risk of false positive or false negative findings. Research consistently shows that, when certain conditions are met (e.g., neutral interviewer, open-ended questioning, absence of repeated suggestive interviewing), children's recall is highly accurate, because they have not been influenced by the presentation of potentially misleading information. Open-ended questions, however, can also elicit inaccurate reports if a child has incorporated misinformation into his or her memory from previous questioning (see Kuehnle, 2003).

The legal test of a child's competency to testify, as just identified, may not serve its intended purpose. This is because children are unaware when their memories have been altered through suggestive and misleading questioning, and they may believe that the inaccurate information they report from their tainted memory is the truth. Despite children's motivation to be truthful, if their memories are contaminated with false information, their demonstrated knowledge of truthfulness and falsehoods to the court may have little meaning regarding their ability to provide accurate testimony. As a result, erroneous conclusions may be drawn by mental health professionals, judges, and juries regarding the abuse status of a child.

Memory for Traumatic and Nontraumatic Events

Infants show the capacity for auditory, olfactory, and visual memory, but explicit verbal memories of nontraumatic or traumatic experiences from birth through the early toddler years are not retained by older children, adolescents, and adults. This absence of early memory is commonly referred to as infantile amnesia. Although there are individual differences in the age for first memories, as well as cultural differences in the average age of first memory, it is rare for individuals to remember events that occurred prior to the preschool years. Many children exposed to trauma after about 3 years of age continue to remember their experiences over time, often in vivid detail, but a subset do forget or fail to report such experiences after long delays (Greenhoot & Tsethlikai, in press). It is important to remember that, although many experiences of sexual abuse are traumatic, not all experiences of sexual abuse are distressing or traumatic to a child.

Researchers continue to argue over whether memories for traumatically stressful events are processed in a substantially different way than for nontraumatic stressful events. Proponents of the traumatic amnesia mode assert that, when children are confronted with trauma they are unable to process, they employ the defense mechanism of dissociation to compartmentalize the unintegrated memory, which consists mainly of sensory perceptions and affective states. Current research, however, does not provide evidence that traumatized children experience amnesia for large periods of childhood, although they may tend to avoid thinking or talking about the details of past experiences, which could reduce memory accessibility over long delays.

Children and adolescents are found to forget traumatic events such as child abuse, and some evidence suggests that they might later remember these events in spite of earlier periods of forgetting. However, there is little evidence to suggest that this forgetting is driven by forces like repression and dissociation that result in the formation of unconscious, indelible memories that can later be recovered. Rather, research indicates that the predictors of forgetting and remembering are generally consistent with research findings on memory for nontraumatic events and memory development. Children are most likely to forget traumatic experiences when they are very young at the time of occurrence, are not re-exposed to the trauma or reminders of the event, and have autobiographical memory skills that are below average (Greenhoot & Tsethlikai, in press).

Diagnosis versus an Event

Child sexual abuse is not a psychiatric diagnosis. Rather, it is an event with psychological consequences associated with multiple factors including, but not limited to, the relationship between the child victim and perpetrator, sexual acts experienced, violence accompanying the sexual acts, co-occurring family violence, nonoffending parent(s) response(s) to the child's disclosure, and resiliency of the child.

One of the most important findings from research addressing the effects of sexual victimization of a child is that no single sign or symptom, including sexualized behavior, characterizes the majority of sexually abused children. Problems with sleeping, wetting, soiling, eating, physical symptoms, and sexual behaviors do not discriminate sexually abused from nonabused children. Specifically, sleep complaints are common throughout development and many factors can contribute to enuresis (wetting problem) or encopresis (soiling problems), including a family history of wetting, numerous medical conditions, constipation, and life stressors. Headaches, abdominal discomfort, and fatigue are common among preschool and school-aged children and do not differentiate between sexually abused and nonabused children (Poole & Wolfe, in press). Because one-fourth to one-half of sexually abused children are asymptomatic, the absence of symptoms is not an indicator that a child has not been abused.

Despite the absence of discriminating markers for identification of sexually abused children, research is robust in showing that child sexual abuse is a significant risk factor in children's development of mental health disorders and serious emotional and behavioral difficulties. Children who live in abusive family environments and experience multiple forms of child maltreatment, such as sexual abuse and physical abuse and/or domestic violence, are at the greatest risk for long-term psychopathology. Individuals sexually abused as children are vulnerable to substantial long-term effects because of the formative nature of the neurological system, attachments to other humans, personality structure, and sexuality (see Kuehnle, 2004).

Child Prostitution and Pornography

The exploitation of children as prostitutes and the photographically documented sexual victimization of children are significant problems in the United States. Child prostitution or creation of child pornography may accompany the sexual abuse of a child within the family, but they are more likely to be orchestrated by individuals outside of the victim's family. Runaway and homeless children may be exploited by pimps, drug dealers may use addicted juveniles for prostitution to pay for their drugs, and parents may sell their children's sexual services.

The trafficking of children for prostitution is also an immense problem in our society. The number of children trafficked to the United States varies across countries and international regions. Children are trafficked for prostitution in the United States from all parts of the world and are used primarily to service members of their own linguistic, cultural, or ethnic group (the National Incidence Based Reporting System). Prostituted children often suffer irreparable damage to their physical and mental health. They face pregnancy by their johns or pimps and are at high risk for sexually transmitted diseases, particularly AIDS.

The photographic documentation of a sexual predator sexually abusing a child and the sharing of these illegal materials through the Internet is also a widespread and increasing problem in the United States and other countries. It is estimated that as much as 20% of all pornographic activity on the Internet may involve child pornography. However, accurate estimates are difficult to produce, since reliable data collection has yet to be developed. National incident data indicates that approximately two-thirds of juvenile victims identified with pornography crimes are female and typically are not a member of the pornographer's family. Minors used in pornographic films range in age from several months to 17 years old. Some data sources indicate that juveniles age 12 to 17 are most frequently exploited for child pornography, and other data sources indicate that children age 6 to 12 are the most vulnerable. Pornographic material may be used by pornographers to blackmail children into continued sexual exploitation (the National Incidence Based Reporting System; National Center for Missing and Exploited Children).

In summary, CSA is a category of behaviors involving the sexual exploitation of children. Identifying sexually abused children is a complex problem, given that the majority of child victims will not disclose their abuse and cannot be identified by emotional or behavioral symptoms. Further complicating identification of sexually abused from nonabused children are the informal or formal interviews that taint children's memories for the event of interest. Although many sexually exploited children suffer significant damage to their physical and mental health, others do not. The variability in the psychological consequences of sexual abuse are associated with multiple factors including, but not limited to, the identity and number of offenders, types of sexual acts perpetrated, and violence accompanying the sexual acts. It is unknown what psychological damage children may suffer when they falsely believe they are a victim of sexual abuse perpetrated by a parent.

REFERENCES

Buck, J. A., & Warren, A. R. (in press). Jurors and professionals in the legal system: What do they know and what should they know about interviewing child witnesses? In K. Kuehnle & M. Connell (Eds.), *The evaluation of child sexual abuse allegations: A comprehensive guide to assessment and testimony*. Hoboken, NJ: Wiley & Sons.

Bruck, M., & Ceci, S. J. (1995). *Amicus* brief for the case of *State of New Jersey v. Michaels* presented by committee on concerned social scientists. *Psychology, Public Policy, & Law, 1*, 272–322.

Greenhoot, A. F., & Tsethlikai, M. (in press). Recollections of childhood trauma: Evidence concerning the repression and recovery of memories during childhood and adolescence. In K.

Kuehnle & M. Connell (Eds.), *The evaluation of child sexual abuse allegations: A comprehensive guide to assessment and testimony.* Hoboken, NJ: Wiley & Sons.

Kuehnle, K. (2003). Child sexual abuse evaluations. In A. M. Goldstein & I. B. Weiner (Eds.), *Handbook of psychology, volume eleven: Forensic psychology* (pp. 437–460). Hoboken, NJ: John Wiley & Sons.

Kuehnle, K. F. (2004). Child sexual abuse: Treatment issues. In. G. P. Koocher, J. C. Norcross, S. S. Hill, III (Eds.), *The psychologist's desk reference: Second edition.* Boston, MA: Oxford University Press.

London, K., Bruck, M., Ceci, S., & Shuman, D. (2005). Disclosure of child sexual abuse: What does the research tell us about the ways that children tell? *Psychology, Public Policy, and Law, 11,* 194–226.

National Center for Missing and Exploited Children, http://www.cybertipline.com.

National Incidence Based Reporting System, http://www.fbi.gov/ucr/ucr.htm.

Poole, D. A., & Wolfe, M. A. (in press). Child development: Normative sexual and non-sexual behaviors that may be confused with symptoms of sexual abuse. In K. Kuehnle & M. Connell (Eds.), *The evaluation of child sexual abuse allegations: A comprehensive guide to assessment and testimony.* Hoboken, NJ: John Wiley & Sons.

State of New Jersey v. Margaret Kelly Michaels, (1993) 264 N.J. Super., 579.

SUGGESTED READINGS

Bottoms, B. L., Goodman, G. S., & Najdowski, C. J. (Eds., in press). *Child victims, child offenders: Psychology and law.* New York: Guilford Press.

Kuehnle, K. F., & Connell, M. (Eds., in press). *The evaluation of child sexual abuse allegations: A comprehensive guide to assessment and testimony.* Hoboken, NJ: John Wiley & Sons.

KATHRYN KUEHNLE
University of South Florida

See also: **Pedophilia; Recovered Memories; Sex Offenders**

CHILDHOOD PSYCHOSIS

Psychotic symptoms are rather uncommon in the overall psychopathology presenting in childhood and adolescence. However, affective psychoses (psychosis associated with mood disorders), dissociative psychoses (psychosis associated with PTSD or dissociative identity disorder), and psychoses associated with or secondary to substance abuse are commonly seen in clinical practice. Although the existence of childhood schizophrenia has been recognized since the early twentieth century (Kraepelin, 1919), the term "childhood psychosis" before the 1960s was used to refer to a heterogeneous group of pervasive developmental disorders without hallucinations and delusions. It was not until the 1980s that childhood-onset schizophrenia (COS) was formally differentiated from autistic disorder, and that was after evidence was established that the clinical picture, family history, age of onset, and course of the two disorders were different. Even today, high rates of misdiagnosis remain, because transient psychotic symptoms can occur in healthy children, and fleeting hallucinations are not uncommon in nonpsychotic children, especially in the face of severe stress and anxiety. There is an increasing focus on COS as a neurodevelopmental disorder that is associated with deficits in cognition, affect, and social functioning (American Academy of Child and Adolescent Psychiatry [AACAP], 2001).

Epidemiology

Very early-onset schizophrenia (defined as onset before the age of 12 years) is an uncommon illness in preadolescence and is probably 25 to 50 times less common than early-onset schizophrenia in adolescence. Onset of the illness occurs rarely before the age of 12 years, but initial onset increases steadily during adolescence. The true incidence of COS is unknown, but population studies have suggested that the prevalence may be less than in 10,000 (Werry, 1979). With respect to sex ratio in COS, most studies have shown a higher male-to-female ratio estimated at about 1.67 boys to 1 girl, but as age increases, the ratio tends to even out. The symptoms usually emerge insidiously, and the diagnostic criteria are met gradually over time. The prevalence of schizophrenia among parents of children with schizophrenia is about 8%.

Etiology

The etiology of COS is unknown, and the relative roles of genetic, neurobiological, environmental, and psychosocial influences remain controversial. More recent research studies have indicated a pathophysiological role for certain brain regions including the limbic system, the frontal cortex, and the basal ganglia. Although the pathophysiology of schizophrenia remains unclear, it has been hypothesized that increased dopaminergic neurotransmission in the mesolimbic pathways produces the positive symptoms of the disease. Based on this working hypothesis, it is thought that antipsychotic medications work by blocking dopamine D2 receptors, thus reducing psychotic symptoms. Neuroimaging studies have shown structural abnormalities in children with COS when compared to normal children; these abnormalities include smaller total cerebral volume and a greater rate of cortical gray matter loss, especially in the frontal and temporal regions (Rapport, Giedd, & Blumenthal, 1999). Children with COS also tend to have a higher genetic loading for schizophrenia, a more treatment refractory course, and a poor prognosis.

Diagnosis and Assessment

Accurate diagnosis and treatment require familiarity with the clinical presentation, phenomenology, and course of the disorder while also incorporating an understanding of the youth's developmental, social, educational, and psychological needs. A review of the phenomenology of psychotic illnesses in children and adolescents shows that the same symptoms are present in these children and adolescents as are present in adults with schizophrenia; however, establishing the diagnosis may be more difficult among youth. Children and adolescents with schizophrenia have been described as having two broad sets of symptom clusters: positive and negative. Positive symptoms consist of hallucinations and thought disorder of which hallucinations are the most frequently reported. In children, delusions and hallucinations are usually less elaborate and visual hallucinations are more common. Negative symptoms are deficit symptoms, such as flattened affect, amotivation, and alogia (American Psychiatric Association [APA], 1997).

The diagnosis of schizophrenia in children and adolescents is currently made by using the criteria outlined in the *Diagnostic and Statistical Manual of Mental Disorders* (DSM-IV-TR; APA, 2000). The active phase of the illness is characterized by the presence of at least two of the following symptoms, each of which must be present for a significant proportion of time during a one month period: (1) delusions, (2) hallucinations, (3) disorganized speech, (4) grossly disorganized or catatonic behavior, and (5) negative symptoms. Only one symptom is needed if the delusions are bizarre or if the hallucinations involve either a voice giving a running commentary on the person's behavior or thinking or two or more voices conversing. In addition to these symptoms, there must also be a marked deterioration in social or occupational functioning that is present for a significant amount of time since the onset of the disturbance, or there must be a failure to achieve expected levels of interpersonal, academic, or occupational achievement (APA, 2000). DSM-IV-TR diagnostic criteria require continuous signs of disorder for a six-month period, during which there is at least one month of active-phase symptoms. Schizophrenia is considered to be a phasic disorder with the following phases:

1. *Prodrome.* Prior to developing overt psychotic symptoms, most individuals will experience some period of deteriorating function with nonspecific symptoms (increased anxiety and mood symptoms), idiosyncratic or bizarre preoccupations, unusual behaviors, academic problems, social isolation, and/or deteriorating self-care skills.
2. *Acute Phase.* This is the phase in which patients often present, and it is dominated by positive psychotic symptoms and functional deterioration.
3. *Recovery Phase.* This follows the acute phase and often has some ongoing psychotic symptoms; this phase may also be associated with confusion, disorganization, and/or dysphoria.
4. *Residual Phase.* During this phase, positive psychotic symptoms are minimal, but patients will still generally have ongoing problems with "negative symptoms," that is, social withdrawal, apathy, amotivation, and/or flat affect.
5. *Chronic Impairment.* Some patients remain chronically impaired by persistent symptoms that have not responded adequately to treatment.

Schizophrenia is associated with cognitive deficits that produce functional impairment (AACAP, 2001). It is sometimes difficult to determine whether delays are due to impact of the illness or cognitive functioning or whether they existed premorbidly, because premorbid test results are often not available. Language and communication deficits as well as information processing problems have been observed in COS (Caplan, Guthrie, Tang, Komo, & Asarnow, 2005). A comprehensive patient assessment is required; this entails interviews with family and collaborative sources as well as endocrine, metabolic, neurologic, infectious, and toxicologic laboratory evaluations that are used to rule out other medical disorders (AACAP, 2001).

Differential Diagnosis

The differential diagnosis of psychoses in children and adolescents encompasses a wide range of disorders. The interpretation of psychotic symptoms in these patients must consider age, developmental level, symptomatology, and etiology for an appropriate DSM-IV diagnosis. The differential diagnosis of childhood psychosis includes a schizophrenia spectrum disorder, autism, Asperger's syndrome, affective psychoses, anxiety disorder (e.g., post-traumatic stress disorder or obsessive compulsive disorder), drug-induced psychosis, schizotypal personality disorder, and psychotic states caused by organic disorders (e.g., seizure disorders, infectious diseases, metabolic and endocrine disorders, central nervous system lesions).

Treatment and Outcome

Treatment involves interventions aimed at all spheres of the child or adolescent's life. Therapeutic recommendations are primarily based on the adult literature, since there is a lack of treatment research for youth with schizophrenia. A multimodal approach is required with the combination of therapeutic services including comprehensive outpatient and community programs that have pharmacotherapy, psychotherapeutic, psychoeducational, and case management services; family support, vocational, and rehabilitative assistance; specialized educational programs; inpatient/day patient psychiatric units with developmentally appropriate psychiatric, neurological, and medical services; and in some cases, longer-term residential programs depending on the severity of the illness. Interventions may vary depending on the individual characteristics of the patient and the stage of the disorder.

The introduction of atypical antipsychotic agents, including clozapine, risperidone, olanzapine, quetiapine, ziprasidone, and aripiprazole has been a major advance in the pharmacotherapy of schizophrenia. These medications are the first-line treatment among youths with psychotic illnesses. These agents are considered atypical because they work as both dopaminergic and serotonergic antagonists, and they have fewer incidences of extrapyramidal side effects than the traditional neuroleptics (i.e., haloperidol). The traditional neuroleptics are all dopamine antagonists (especially D2), which is the mechanism responsible for their antipsychotic properties and characteristic side-effect profile (Ernst et al., 1998). A trial of an atypical antipsychotic should be implemented for a period of at least four to six weeks, using an adequate therapeutic dosage, before determining the efficacy of the medication. The most common immediate but transient side effect of the atypical antipsychotic is sedation, with the antipsychotic effects becoming more evident after the first or second week. If there is no improvement after four to six weeks on a therapeutic dosage, of if side effects are unmanageable, then the recommendation is to switch to a trial of a second atypical antipsychotic (APA, 1997; AACAP, 2001).

The long-term course of childhood and adolescent-onset schizophrenia is worse than in adult schizophrenia, and the prognosis for patients who present with manifestations of the disorder before the age of 14 is very poor and complicated by comorbidities. Further longitudinal studies in childhood psychotic illnesses are warranted to better investigate the neurobiological basis and effective treatment strategies for this complex neurodevelopmental disorder.

REFERENCES

American Academy of Child and Adolescent Psychiatry. (2001). Practice parameters for the assessment and treatment of children and adolescents with schizophrenia. *Journal of the American Academy of Child and Adolescent Psychiatry*, *40*(suppl.), 4S–23S.

American Psychiatric Association. (1994). *Diagnostic and statistical manual of mental disorders*, (4th ed.). *(DSM-IV)*. Washington, DC: Author.

American Psychiatric Association. (1997). Practice guideline for the treatment of patients with schizophrenia. *American Journal of Psychiatry*, *154*(4, suppl.), 1–63.

American Psychiatric Association. (2000). *Diagnostic and statistical manual of mental disorders*, (4th ed., text rev.). Washington, DC: Author.

Caplan, R., Guthrie, D., Tang, B., Komo, S., and Asarnow, R. F. (2000). Thought disorder in childhood schizophrenia: Replication and update of concept. *Journal of the American Academy of Child Adolescent Psychiatry*, *39*, 771–778.

Ernst, M., Malone, R. P., Rowan, A. B., George, R., Gonzalez, N. M., and Silva, R. R. (1998). Antipsychotics (neuroleptics). In: *Practitioner's guide to psychoactive drugs for children and adolescents*, (2nd ed.). Werry, J. S., & Aman, M. G., (Eds.). New York: Plenum, 297–328.

Kraepelin, E. (1919). *Dementia praecox and paraphrenia*. Huntington, NY: Robert E Krieger.

Rapport, J. L., Giedd, J. N., & Blumenthal, J. (1999). Progressive cortical change during adolescence in childhood-onset schizophrenia: A longitudinal magnetic resonance imaging study. *Archives of General Psychiatry*, *56*, 649–654.

Werry, J. S. (1979). The childhood psychoses, in *Psychopathological Disorders of Childhood*, (2nd ed.). Ed. by H. C. Quay & J. S. Werry (pp. 41–89). New York: John Wiley & Sons.

SUGGESTED READING

American Academy of Child and Adolescent Psychiatry. (2000). Summary of the practice parameters for the assessment and treatment of children and adolescents with schizophrenia. *Journal of the American Academy of Child and Adolescent Psychiatry*, *39*, 1580–1582.

MELITA DALEY
TYRONE CANNON
University of California, Los Angeles

See also: Psychotic Disorders; Schizophrenia; Schizophrenia, Childhood and Adolescent

CHINA, PSYCHOLOGY IN

Modern Chinese psychology was founded in the early years of the twentieth century. The Chinese reformer and educator Yuanpei Cai studied in Wilhelm Wundt's Leipzig laboratory between the years 1908 and 1911, returned to China, and became President of Peking University in 1917. In the same year, Daqi Chen, with Cai's support, established the first psychological laboratory in China. This marked the beginning of modern Chinese psychology. In the ensuing years many departments of psychology were established in various universities in China. The Chinese Psychological Society was founded in 1921, and in 1922 the first journal, *Psychology*, was published. The Institute of Psychology under Academia Sinica was established in 1929. The outbreak of the Sino-Japanese war in 1937 caused a major setback to progress of psychology until the end of World War II.

After the founding of the People's Republic of China in 1949, Chinese psychology was reconstructed after the model in the Soviet Union. A new Institute of Psychology under the Chinese Academy of Sciences was established in 1951. Educational reform and industrial development in the early days of the People's Republic promoted the progress of educational and industrial psychology. Developmental psychology was a major field of basic research to understand the teaching and learning processes. In the early 1960s, Chinese psychologists, as in the West, also took ideas from cybernetics, information theory, and computer science in their study of mental processes, while at the same time they conducted research in the fields of industrial and military applications. Some research contributions from China reached a level comparable to international standards at that time. The Chinese Psychological Society also expanded to include 24 provincial organizations with a total of 1,056 members. With the onset of the Cultural Revolution in 1966, psychology was proclaimed a pseudoscience, and the development of psychology came to a halt for almost 10 years.

With the end of the Cultural Revolution and the launching of China's reform and opening-up policy, psychology was rehabilitated and formally recognized as a scientific discipline. Since 1980, Chinese psychology witnessed a rapid and steady development. The first Department of Psychology in Peking University was established in 1978, and departments of psychology and schools of psychology have now been established in almost 200 universities across the country.

Research and Application

The fields of study of Chinese psychology cover almost all branches of modern psychology. The following are recent developments in several fields of study.

Cognitive Psychology and Cognitive Neuroscience

In this field, psychologists have made contributions in perception, attention, memory, thinking, emotion, and language. Two national level laboratories, called State Key Laboratories, in China were established in this field in 2005. One of these laboratories, the Lab of Brain and Cognitive Science, mainly studies the cognitive processes and neurological bases of visual perception. Another laboratory is the Lab of Cognitive Neuroscience and Learning, which is dedicated to issues related to learning and teaching. In the coming years we expect to see further support from the Chinese government in this field.

Developmental and Educational Psychology

In this field, psychologists have studied various aspects of human development, including cognition, language, and social behavior, not only for average children but for the

mentally retarded and gifted children as well. The theory of mind is another topic of study. Additionally, problems raised in educational reform and practice, such as learning and teaching, as well as intelligence and creativity, have attracted the attention of educational psychologists.

Biopsychology

Biopsychologists are concerned with how the brain generates behavior, and conversely, how behavior modulates the functions of the brain and body. Early studies in biopsychology in China were conducted under the name of physiological psychology and comparative psychology, and a wide range of studies have been carried out in this field. The current major research areas in animal and human behavior are behavioral and physiological studies of stress; depression and immunity; memory and learning; and drug addiction.

Psychotherapy and Psychological Counseling

Clinical psychologists conduct their research and practice at four levels: (1) general practice, (2) mental hospitals, (3) universities and schools, and (4) the community level. In the process of social-economic reform and in recent natural disasters, psychologists are playing an increasingly important role in helping people who have mental health problems. The Chinese clinician's methodological approach is under the influence of both Western therapeutic theories and Chinese traditional medicine. Its therapeutic orientations include (1) directive orientation, using didactic and instructional methods in the therapeutic process; (2) integrative orientation, analyzing the causes of mental problems and disorders from holistic and integrative points of view in accordance with traditional Chinese philosophy; and (3) natural orientation, following the Chinese traditional principle that encourages a person to "acclimate the natural laws" in therapeutic practice.

Economic Psychology

The field of economic psychology is mostly concerned with the human and social phenomena in business enterprises from behavioral perspectives. As an emergent discipline, the topics of study in this field consist of behavioral decision making, human factors in economic and financial interactions, methodological issues relating to experimental observation, and survey research strategies used to better understand the social and economic behavior of the workforce, and how they affect the market and society at large. Moving beyond the traditional topics of risk perception, Bayesian reasoning, consumer behavior, social dilemmas, and group decision making, Chinese psychologists are involved in the emerging fields of neuroeconomics, the study of human and social cognitive bias study, and the study of overall economic changes in a country.

Forensic Psychology

In this field, topics of study include the causes leading to criminal acts, the classification of crimes, and theories of criminal acts. Some psychologists have studied the psychological formation of witness testimony and laid out the principles and methods of evidence collection. Other researchers study psychological principles in the judicial review system and the process of psychological correction in prisons.

Education and Training

Education and training in psychology are being carried out in universities, research institutions, correspondence schools, vocational schools, and continuing education systems. The number of students majoring in psychology has increased dramatically in recent years; in 2007, the total enrollment for undergraduate students in psychology reached 43,976 with another 6,430 studying for a master's degree and another 929 students studying for the PhD degrees. Correspondence schools and continuing education institutions offer psychology courses to people who wish to update their knowledge or obtain higher education certificates, such as an MBA. Vocational schools train young students and adults for licenses in psychology. All these schools have contributed to expanding the training of psychologists and psychological practitioners to meet the needs of society.

Organizations

The Chinese Psychological Society (CPS), which is under the Chinese Association of Science and Technology, is a national organization for Chinese psychologists. It has more than 7,000 members, and currently publishes two journals: *Acta Psychologica Sinica* and *Psychological Science*. All provinces and autonomous regions, including Tibet, have their own local psychological societies, which are affiliated with CPS. In addition to CPS there are three other psychology organizations: the Chinese Associations of Mental Health (12,000 members), the Chinese Society of Social Psychology (2,000 members), and the Chinese Ergonomic Society (500 members). CPS became a national member of the International Union of Psychological Science in 1981. In 2004, the Chinese Psychological Society hosted the 28th International Congress of Psychology in Beijing.

Challenge and Prospects

The developments of Chinese psychology in the last century has paved the way for its future development both as a science and as a profession. With the economic boom taking place in China, the rapid social and economic transitions in a modern society produce both challenges and problems for psychological science. The fields most readily affected are population, education, mental health, social stability, and the solution of conflicts between a global culture and China's traditional culture. Recently, the Chinese government called for building a harmonious society; this policy has made the development of human well-being a major task for psychologists. These challenges have also provided psychology with new opportunities for its development and opened up a broad scope for its utilization. The coming years will see an increasing number of young Chinese psychologists and many new achievements in psychological science. As evidenced by China's modernization process, Chinese psychologists will incorporate traditions and culture, thus making distinctive Chinese contributions to world psychology in the twenty-first century.

REFERENCES

Chinese Psychological Society. (2008). *Report on Advances in Psychology (2006–2007)*. Beijing: Chinese Science and Technology Press.

Yufang Yang (2004). Advances in Psychology in China. In M. J. Stevens and D. Wedding (Eds.), *Handbook of International Psychology* (2nd ed.). (pp.179–192). New York: Hove, Taylor, & Brunner-Routledge, Francis Group.

YUFANG YANG
Chinese Academy of Sciences, Beijing, China

CHI-SQUARE TEST

The chi-square (χ^2) test was developed by Karl Pearson in 1900; this is often regarded as a seminal event in the history of statistics. The test and the statistical distribution on which it is based have wide application not only in psychology and the behavioral sciences but also in numerous related disciplines. Its two principal uses are to test the independence of two variables and to assess how well a theoretical model or set of a priori probabilities fits a set of data (goodness of fit). In both cases the test is typically thought of as a nonparametric procedure involving observed (O) and expected (E) frequencies. The expected frequencies may be determined either theoretically or empirically. The basic formula for calculating χ^2 is

$$\chi^2 = \Sigma[(O - E)^2/E].$$

It is commonly applied to a wide variety of designs, including $k \times 1$ groups, $2 \times k$ groups, 2×2 contingency tables, and $R \times C$ contingency tables. It is used most appropriately with nominal (categorical) data, but it is also used frequently with ordinal data. The χ^2 statistic is related to several measures of association, including the phi coefficient (ϕ), contingency coefficient (C), and Cramer's phi (ϕ' or ϕ_C). $\phi^2 = \chi^2/N$ is used frequently as a measure of effect size for 2×2 tables.

Historically, there has been concern over the use of the χ^2 test when any E was small (e.g., < 5), because the underlying χ^2 distribution is continuous whereas the distribution of observations is discrete. For 2×2 tables this led to the development of the widely used and recommended Yates' correction for continuity. Most recent evidence, however, seems to suggest that the use of Yates' correction is unnecessary even with small sample sizes.

The χ^2 distribution is related to the normal distribution, such that the square of a standard normal deviate (z^2) is distributed as a χ^2 with one degree of freedom. The χ^2 distribution also describes the sampling distribution of the variance, s^2, such that $\chi^2 = (N-1) \, s^2/\sigma^2$ with $N-1$ degrees of freedom. These relationships form the basis for many tests of statistical significance, including the analysis of variance F statistic, which may be thought of as the ratio of two χ^2 statistics.

The χ^2 statistic and distribution has wide application in many multivariate statistical procedures, such as logistic regression and multivariate analysis of variance, and in calculating multinomial probabilities, especially for log-linear models. Multivariate statistics that use both generalized least squares and maximum likelihood procedures also rely on χ^2. For example, in structural equation modeling, the χ^2 statistic forms the basis for many goodness-of-fit tests and for alternative model comparisons. In the 1930s, Fisher developed a procedure using the χ^2 test to combine the results of several independent tests of the same hypothesis, an early version of meta-analysis. The χ^2 test continues to be used in meta-analytic applications, such as the Q test for assessing the homogeneity of the distribution of effect sizes.

SUGGESTED READINGS

Meyers, J. L., & Well, A. D. (2004). *Research design and statistical analysis* (2nd ed.). Mahwah, NJ: Lawrence Erlbaum.

Tabachnick, B. G., & Fidell, L. S. (2007). *Using multivariate statistics* (5th ed.). Boston: Pearson Education.

Zar, J. H. (1999). *Biostatistical analysis* (4th ed.). Upper Saddle River, NJ: Prentice-Hall.

JOSEPH S. ROSSI
University of Rhode Island

See also: **Contingency Tables; Multivariate Methods; Nonparametric Statistical Tests**

CHOMSKY, A. NOAM (1928–)

A. Noam Chomsky is a controversial figure in psycholinguistics and probably the foremost theorist in the field. For his achievements, he has received numerous honorary doctorates. Chomsky was educated at the University of Pennsylvania, where he received the BA, MA, and PhD (1955) degrees. From the time he received his PhD he has been on the faculty of the Massachusetts Institute of Technology, although he has offered courses and lectured throughout the world, including Oxford and Berkeley Universities.

Chomsky's books include *Syntactic Structures, Current Issues in Linguistic Theory, Aspects of the Theory of Syntax, Cartesian Linguistics, Topics in the Theory of Generative Grammar, The Sound Pattern of English* (with Morris Halle), *Language and the Mind, Studies on Semantics in Generative Grammar, Reflections on Language,* and *Language and Responsibility.*

Chomsky views the understanding of language as genetically determined and developing comparably to other bodily organs. Because the human brain is preprogrammed by a "language acquisition device," humans generate sentences with grammar ("generative grammar") that is universal. Chomsky argues that humans have an innate capacity for grasping language. Learning a language is both species-specific and species-uniform: only humans have the capacity for language acquisition, and all languages share a common underlying logical structure. Thus, the logic (or logical syntax) of all language is the same. Terming the logical structure *deep structure,* Chomsky holds that it is not learned. Language that human beings must learn is a *surface structure*—phonetic sounds or sentences that are uttered. Chomsky's psycholinguistics has been labeled *generative transformational grammar,* a system that integrates both surface and deep structure.

Chomsky's psycholinguistics is diametrically opposed to B. F. Skinner's verbal learning theory. One of the great events in U.S. history of psychology was the debate regarding origins of language, a debate between Chomsky and Skinner conducted in 1959. Chomsky is also widely known for his political activism, especially during the Vietnam War.

SUGGESTED READINGS

Chomsky, A. N. (1975). *Reflections on language.* New York: Pantheon Books.

Chomsky, A. N. (2002). *Syntactic structures* (2nd ed.). Berlin & New York: Mouton de Gruyer.

Chomsky, A. N. (2006). *Language and mind* (3rd ed.). Cambridge, U.K., & New York: Cambridge University Press.

STAFF

CHRONIC FATIGUE SYNDROME

Although diseases similar to chronic fatigue syndrome (CFS) have been recognized for centuries under various rubrics, strict diagnostic criteria for conditions dominated by medically unexplained chronic fatigue were first proposed in 1988. Current diagnostic criteria were originally crafted in 1994 by an International Chronic Fatigue Syndrome Study Group as an attempt to standardize patient populations included in research studies. The International CFS Research Case Definition requires chronic fatigue of at least six-months duration; this fatigue cannot be substantially alleviated by rest, is not the result of ongoing exertion, and is associated with substantial reductions in occupational, social, and personal activities. In addition, at least four out of the following eight symptoms must occur with fatigue in a six-month period: prolonged extraordinary postexertional fatigue, impaired memory or concentration, unrefreshing sleep, aching or stiff muscles, multijoint pain, sore throat, tender glands, and new headaches (Fukuda et al., 1994). Importantly, the research case definition precludes classification as CFS if a patient has an identifiable medical cause of being fatigued. Similarly, individuals with certain psychiatric conditions cannot be classified as CFS in research studies. Exclusionary psychiatric conditions include schizophrenia, bipolar disorder, and melancholic major depression. Notably, comorbidity with psychiatric disorders is relatively high. Recent data indicate that almost 60% of CFS cases in the population suffer from at least one comorbid psychiatric condition, with affective disorders being the most prevalent ones.

In 2003, following a series of annual workshops from 2000 to 2002, the International Chronic Fatigue Syndrome Study Group published recommendations concerning standardized application of the 1994 case definition (Reeves et al., 2003). The Group recommended the use of validated instruments to obtain standardized measures of the major symptom domains of the illness. It is important to realize that the CFS case definition was devised for research purposes, and the concept of exclusionary conditions is critical to avoid confounding CFS with other medical disorders. In clinical settings the list of exclusionary conditions is most useful as a list of differential diagnoses. In clinical practice, patients with various exclusionary conditions may also be diagnosed and managed as having CFS based on the physician's medical opinion.

Prevalence and Prognosis

Fatigue is a common complaint. Community-based epidemiological studies suggest that at any given time approximately 10% of women and 5% of men suffer from fatigue of greater than six-month duration. However, because CFS requires severe, medically unexplained fatigue that is not resolved by rest, cannot be explained by medical or psychiatric illness, and is accompanied by specific symptoms, CFS itself is far less common. Prevalence rates vary significantly across studies, probably as a result of differences in diagnostic criteria and experimental design. Nevertheless, it appears that 0.1 to 2.5% of the population meet criteria for CFS (Reeves et al., 2007).

It has traditionally been believed the prevalence rates for CFS are highest in middle- and upper-middle class white females. It is now clear that this belief reflects a bias in early studies that recruited from medical practices. Large community-based epidemiological studies in the U.S. indicate that CFS is equally or more common in African Americans, Hispanics, and Native Americans and in individuals who make less than $40,000 per year. However, in all these groups women are two to four times more likely than men to have CFS.

CFS is a chronic illness that waxes and wanes over time, and, although patients report significant improvement, it is unclear whether the illness ever resolves completely. Patients with CFS are strikingly disabled: between 40% and 70% are unable to work or attend school, and 93% report severe impairment in their ability to perform daily life activities. Some evidence suggests that patients who develop CFS suddenly may have a better outcome than those who develop the illness insidiously over time.

Etiology

Despite several decades of research and virtually thousands of published articles, the etiology of CFS remains unclear. In any potential etiological domain, studies reporting positive findings are nearly always counterbalanced by studies that are negative. Nonetheless, tentative conclusions can be drawn concerning physiological systems that may be abnormal in at least some patients with CFS. It is important to remember, however, that it remains unknown whether any given abnormality represents a cause or a consequence of CFS.

Early etiological theories of the disorder focused on the immune system and infection with Epstein Barr and other latent viruses. Although cases of CFS may follow such infections, it is clear that specific viral infections are not a primary cause for the disorder. A variety of immune system abnormalities have also been reported, including decreases in natural killer cell activity and increases in proinflammatory cytokines, especially in patients with sudden-onset CFS. A recent meta-analysis found no evidence for clear immune abnormalities in CFS. The authors came to the conclusion that the better the study design employed, the less likely positive findings were to emerge (Lyall, Peakman, & Wessely, 2003).

Patients with CFS also may have decreased functioning of the hypothalamic-pituitary-adrenal (HPA) axis, one of the body's primary stress response systems, which is also contributing to the peripheral and central causes of chronic pain and fatigue. Several studies report decreased levels of circulating cortisol and decreased adrenocortical reserve. In addition to decreased functioning, the HPA axis has also been reported to lose its normal circadian rhythm in CFS patients (Nater et al., 2008). Clinical improvement has been associated with normalization of this circadian rhythm. The overall picture may be summarized as a relative hypoactivity of the HPA axis in CFS patients (Cleare, 2003).

Other physiological abnormalities have been reported in patients with CFS. It has been reported that abnormal autonomic nervous system (ANS) functioning may be common in patients with CFS, based on the facts that CFS includes typical autonomic symptoms, such as disabling fatigue, dizziness, diminished concentration, tremulousness, and nausea, and that at least some CFS patients demonstrate orthostatic intolerance when subjected to tilt table testing. Conversely, patients with postural orthostatic intolerance syndrome often manifest symptoms similar to those seen in CFS. Whereas there is some evidence for involvement of altered ANS functioning, it needs to be noted that some CFS symptoms, such as sore throat, myalgias, and cognitive alterations cannot be attributed to dysautonomia.

Also, studies of the central nervous system (CNS) in CFS have examined both structural and functional alterations. Various studies have pointed to subtle morphological changes in CFS, although these changes might not be specific for CFS. Functional studies have found potential explanations for some of the motor and cognitive dysfunctions typically described in CFS.

Finally, psychological and stress-related factors have been associated with CFS. By some authors, CFS is seen as the consequence of dysfunctional cognitive styles and maladaptive coping strategies. According to this notion, inadequate treatment efforts and maladaptation to challenge results in persistent fatigue and other related symptoms. Many patients report an increase in life stress in the year prior to disease development, especially when the illness develops slowly. Recent findings from a prospective study indicated that stress levels prior to manifestation of CFS predicted the risk for developing CFS (Kato, Sullivan, Evengard, & Pedersen, 2006). In addition, adverse experiences early in life increased risk of developing CFS in adulthood, as another recent study showed (Heim et al., 2006). Stressful experiences seem to play an important role in triggering CFS symptoms. However, it is likely that stress interacts with other vulnerability factors. Ongoing or acute stressors might elicit physiological changes in the predisposed body, ultimately leading to pathophysiological changes associated with CFS.

Treatment

Numerous treatments have been applied to CFS patients with various results. Those with the best experimental data to support their efficacy include graded exercise training and cognitive behavioral therapy (CBT). CBT strategies for CFS typically involve organizing activity and rest cycles, initiating graded increases in activity, establishing a consistent sleep regimen, and attempting to restructure beliefs around self, as well as disease attributions (Malouff, Thorsteinsson, Rooke, Bhullar, & Schutte, 2008). Low dose corticosteroids have been reported to improve symptoms in two studies. Trials of antidepressants have yielded a confusing mix of positive and negative results, but in general these agents appear to be significantly less effective for CFS than for depressive or anxiety disorders. Other CFS treatments with at least one positive study to their credit include growth hormone, selegiline, immunoglobulin, ampligen, nicotinamide adenine dinucleotide (NADH), and omega-3 fatty acids. Taken together, treatments may ameliorate symptoms, but none is known to resolve the disorder.

REFERENCES

Cleare, A. J. (2003). The neuroendocrinology of chronic fatigue syndrome. *Endocrine Reviews, 24*(2), 236–252.

Fukuda, K., Straus, S. E., Hickie, I., Sharpe, M. C., Dobbins, J. G., & Komaroff, A. (1994). The chronic fatigue syndrome: A comprehensive approach to its definition and study. International Chronic Fatigue Syndrome Study Group. *Annals of Internal Medicine, 121*(12), 953–959.

Heim, C., Wagner, D., Maloney, E., Papanicolaou, D. A., Solomon, L., Jones, J. F., et al. (2006). Early adverse experience and risk for chronic fatigue syndrome: Results from a population-based study. *Archives of General Psychiatry, 63*(11), 1258–1266.

Kato, K., Sullivan, P. F., Evengard, B., & Pedersen, N. L. (2006). Premorbid predictors of chronic fatigue. *Archives of General Psychiatry, 63*(11), 1267–1272.

Lyall, M., Peakman, M., & Wessely, S. (2003). A systematic review and critical evaluation of the immunology of chronic fatigue syndrome. *Journal of Psychosomatic Research, 55*(2), 79–90.

Malouff, J. M., Thorsteinsson, E. B., Rooke, S. E., Bhullar, N., & Schutte, N. S. (2008). Efficacy of cognitive behavioral therapy for chronic fatigue syndrome: A meta-analysis. *Clinical Psychology Review, 28*, 736–745.

Nater, U. M., Youngblood, L. S., Jones, J. F., Unger, E. R., Miller, A. H., Reeves, W. C., et al. (2008). Alterations in diurnal salivary cortisol rhythm in a population-based sample of cases with chronic fatigue syndrome. *Psychosomatic Medicine, 70*, 298–305.

Reeves, W. C., Jones, J. F., Maloney, E., Heim, C., Hoaglin, D. C., Boneva, R. S., et al. (2007). Prevalence of chronic fatigue syndrome in metropolitan, urban, and rural Georgia. *Population Health Metrics, 5*(1), 5.

Reeves, W. C., Lloyd, A., Vernon, S. D., Klimas, N., Jason, L. A., Bleijenberg, G., et al. (2003). Identification of ambiguities in the 1994 chronic fatigue syndrome research case definition and recommendations for resolution. *BMC Health Services Research, 3*(1), 25.

SUGGESTED READINGS

Afari, N., & Buchwald, D. (2003). Chronic fatigue syndrome: A review. *American Journal of Psychiatry, 160*(2), 221–236.

Prins, J. B., van der Meer, J. W., & Bleijenberg, G. (2006). Chronic fatigue syndrome. *Lancet, 367*(9507), 346–355.

URS M. NATER
University of Zurich, Switzerland

ANDREW H. MILLER
Emory University School of Medicine

WILLIAM C. REEVES
Centers for Disease Control and Prevention, Atlanta, GA

CHARLES RAISON
Emory University School of Medicine

CHRONIC PAIN, PSYCHOLOGICAL FACTORS IN

Psychology has long been a topic addressed in the etiology of chronic pain; however, the hypothesized role these factors play has varied greatly. Psychological factors were traditionally considered to account for pain that could not be attributed to any physiological abnormalities. Pain was viewed as a dichotomy: it was either of physiological origin (somatogenic) or due to psychological issues (psychogenic). Thus, pain severity that was not linearly related to the amount of pathological abnormality was considered psychogenic, or "all in the patient's head."

The current view of pain experience is multidimensional and dynamic rather than linear. Psychological, social, cognitive, physiological, and behavioral factors are hypothesized to all interact and result in individual pain experience (i.e., Flor, Birbaumer, & Turk, 1990; Melzack & Casey, 1968; Turk, Meichenbaum, & Genest, 1983). Thus, two people who endure identical stress fractures may vary greatly in the intensity, duration, and degree of impact their injury has on their life. Additionally, the impact and duration of a headache may vary day to day for the same person, based on psychological and environmental circumstances at any given time. Consideration of major psychological variables associated with pain helps to account for this large degree of variability both within and between individuals in pain experience. The major psychological factors thought to play a primary role in pain etiology and maintenance include affective-motivational processes, behavioral processes, and cognitive processes. Each of these will be addressed in the sections that follow.

Pain and Affect

Pain is ultimately a subjective perception described in terms of sensory and affective properties. As defined by the International Association for the Study of Pain: "[Pain] is unquestionably a sensation in a part or parts of the body but it is also always unpleasant and therefore also an *emotional experience*" (Merskey, 1986; emphasis added). The affective component of pain incorporates many different emotions. Depression, anxiety, and anger have been shown to play an important role in the perception, experience, and response to pain (Fernandez, 2002).

Emotional distress is commonly observed in people with chronic pain. They often feel rejected by the medical system, believing that they are blamed or labeled as whiners and complainers by their physicians, family members, and employers when their symptoms do not respond to treatment. As treatments expected to alleviate pain are proven ineffective, people with pain may lose faith and become frustrated and irritated with the healthcare system. As their pain persists, they may be unable to work, have financial difficulties, and have adverse reactions to treatment. They may become fearful and have inadequate or maladaptive support systems and limited coping resources on which to draw. These consequences of chronic pain can result in self-preoccupation, isolation, depression, anger, and anxiety—an overall sense of demoralization.

The majority of chronic pain research has focused on the role of negative affect, such as anxiety, depression, and anger. Anxiety is common for patients with symptoms of pain, particularly when symptoms are unexplained, as is often the case for chronic pain syndromes. For example, in a large scale, multicentered study of fibromyalgia patients, between 44% and 51% of patients acknowledged that they were anxious (Wolfe, Smythe, Yunus, Bennett, Bombardier, et al., 1990). Feelings of anxiety may be related to unknown etiology of symptoms, fear of reinjury, fear that people will not believe their pain condition, and about the potential lifestyle impact they will experience due to their pain condition. Reduction in pain-related anxiety predicts improvement in functioning, affective distress, pain, and pain-related interference with activity (McCracken & Gross, 1998). Levels of anxiety have been shown to influence not only pain severity but complications following surgery and number of days of hospitalization (e.g., Pavlin, Rapp, & Pollisar, 1998).

Research suggests that 40% to 50% of chronic pain patients suffer from depression (Banks & Kerns, 1996). Level of depression has been shown to affect treatment completion rates (Kerns & Haythornthwaite, 1988) and has been hypothesized to play a modulating role on pain through the effect of decreased quality of life (Penacoba-Puente, Fernandez-de-las-Penas, Gonzalez-Gutierrez, Miangolarra-Page, & Pareha, 2008).

Anger expression has also been recognized to have a key influence on the experience of pain. Bruehl, Chung, and Burns (2006) reviewed the literature surrounding anger and pain and suggest the majority of literature supports a positive relationship between chronic pain severity and dysfunction and anger expression (Bruehl et al., 2006). The precise mechanisms by which anger and frustration exacerbate pain are not known, however it has been hypothesized that anger exacerbates pain by increasing autonomic arousal (Burns, 1997; Cacioppo, Bernston, Klein, & Poehlmann, 1997).

Cognitive Factors

Appraisal and Beliefs

Pain appraisal refers to the meaning ascribed to symptoms by an individual (Sharp, 2001). Beliefs refer to assumptions about reality that shape how one interprets events and can thus be considered as determinants of appraisal. Pain beliefs develop during the lifetime as a result of an individual's learning history and cover all aspects of the pain experience (e.g., the causes of pain, its prognosis, suitable treatments).

Appraisal and beliefs about pain can have a strong impact on an individual's response to pain. If a pain signal is interpreted as a threat, it may be perceived as more intense and unpleasant and evoke more escape or avoidance behavior. Pain appraisal and pain beliefs are also prominent determinants of adjustment to chronic pain (Turner, Jensen, & Romano, 2000).

Personality Characteristics. Temperamental or personality factors based on genetics and life experiences may predispose some people to make certain kinds of appraisals and to be more susceptible to some beliefs than to others. Temperament and personality can be a vulnerability factor that predisposes toward catastrophic misinterpretation of pain sensations and maladaptive pain beliefs, or they can be a resilience factor protecting against maladaptive cognitions and promoting self-efficacy beliefs.

One personality trait that has received attention in chronic pain is anxiety sensitivity (AS). AS is defined as the fear of anxiety-related sensations (Reiss, Peterson, Gursky, & McNally, 1986). Individuals with high AS interpret unpleasant physical sensations (like rapid heart beating) more often as a sign of danger. AS is associated with distress, analgesic use, and physical and social functioning in chronic pain patients, and it may be a risk factor associated with prolonged pain and disability (Keogh & Asmundson, 2004).

Only a few studies have been looking at the role of dispositional optimism or hope in adaptation to chronic pain (Affleck, Tennen, & Apter, 2001; Treharna, Kitas, Lyons, & Booth, 2005). In general, pessimists turn to avoidant coping strategies and denial more often, whereas optimists employ more problem-focused coping strategies. It may not be the use of specific coping strategies, but optimism

(Snyder, Rand, & Sigmond, 2005) and flexibility of coping that protects against disability and distress (Carver & Scheier, 2005).

Catastrophizing and Fear-Avoidance Beliefs. Pain "catastrophizing" can be defined as an exaggerated negative orientation toward actual or anticipated pain experiences. Cross-sectional studies have demonstrated that catastrophizing is associated with increased pain, illness behavior, and physical and psychological dysfunction across numerous clinical and nonclinical populations. Prospective studies indicated that catastrophizing might be predictive of more intense pain and slower recovery after surgical intervention (Granot & Ferber, 2005) and the inception of chronic musculoskeletal pain (Picavet, Vlaeyen, & Schouten, 2002).

Perceived Control

Perceived control refers to the belief that one can exert influence on the duration, frequency, intensity, or unpleasantness of pain. Perceived controllability may modify the meaning of this stimulus and directly affect threat appraisal (Arntz & Schmidt, 1989). As a consequence, pain may be rated as less intense or less unpleasant, and pain tolerance may increase. The belief that one has control over pain has a strong influence on disability in patients with chronic pain complaints (e.g., Turner et al., 2000), and an increase in this belief after pain rehabilitation may predict pain reduction and decreases in disability (e.g., Jensen, Turner, Romano, & Lawler, 2001).

Self-Efficacy

Self-efficacy is the conviction that one can successfully perform a task or produce a desirable outcome (Bandura, 1977). Self-efficacy influences the prognosis after acute physical interventions like surgery (e.g., Dohnke, Knauper, & Muller-Fahrnow, 2005), affects physical and psychological functioning of chronic pain patients (e.g., Woby, Watson, Roach, & Urmston, 2005), is associated with improvements in pain, functional status, and psychological adjustment following rehabilitation (Keefe, Rumble, Scipio, Giordano, & Perri, 2004), and has a direct effect on opioid and immune systems (Weisenberg, 1998).

Pain and Behavior

Classical Conditioning

According to the principles of classical or respondent conditioning, if a painful stimulus is repeatedly paired with a neutral stimulus, the neutral stimulus will elicit a pain response. For example, a person who experienced pain after performing a treadmill exercise may become conditioned to experience a negative emotional response to the presence of the treadmill. The negative emotional reaction may instigate muscle tensing, thereby exacerbating pain, and further reinforcing the association between the stimulus and pain. Based on this, people with chronic pain may avoid activities previously associated with pain onset or exacerbation.

Operant Conditioning

The operant conditioning model proposes that acute pain behaviors (such as avoidance of activity to protect a painful area from additional pain) may come under the control of reinforcement contingencies (responses increase or decrease as a function of their consequences) and evolve into chronic pain (Fordyce, 1976). According to this model, since there is no objective way to measure pain, the only way we can know of peoples' pain is by their behavior. "Pain behaviors" include verbal reports, vocalizations (e.g., sighs, moans), motor activity, facial expressions, body postures, and gesturing (e.g., limping, grimacing), functional limitations (e.g., inactivity), and behaviors designed to reduce pain (e.g., taking medication).

Pain behaviors have two important features: sources of communication and observable. Observable behaviors are capable of eliciting a response and the consequences of behavior will influence subsequent behavior. Responses that receive positive consequences will more likely be maintained; whereas behaviors that fail to activate positive consequences, or that receive negative consequences will be less likely. Pain behaviors may be positively reinforced directly (e.g., attention from a spouse, financial compensation, avoidance of undesirable activity). Pain behaviors may also be maintained by the escape from noxious stimulation through the use of drugs or rest or the avoidance of undesirable activities such as work. In addition, "well behaviors" (e.g., performing household chores) may not be positively reinforcing and the more rewarding pain behaviors may, therefore, be maintained.

The operant conditioning model considers pain an internal subjective experience that can be directly assessed and may be maintained even after an initial physical basis of pain has been resolved rather than the initial causes. The pain behavior originally elicited by organic factors caused by injury or disease may later occur, totally or in part, in response to reinforcing environmental events.

Social Learning

The social learning model emphasizes that behavior can be learned not only by actual reinforcement but also by observation of others. Expectancies and actual behavioral responses to nociceptive stimulation are based, at least partially, on prior social learning history. Models can influence the expression, localization, and methods of coping with pain. A central construct of the social learning perspective is that of self-efficacy expectations described above (Bandura, 1977).

An Integrated Perspective

As evidenced by the extensive discussion of the key role of psychological, behavioral, and social factors in pain experience, a model focusing on only one of these factors will inevitably be incomplete. Several integrated theories of pain processing have been proposed (e.g. Melzack & Casey, 1968; Melzack & Wall, 1965; Turk et al., 1983; Flor et al., 1990). Each of these theories varies somewhat in their focus, but all view pain as a multidimensional experience that involves the interaction among psychological and physiological factors. The clinical implications of a multidimensional theory are to incorporate cognitive, behavioral, and affective components both diagnostically and in treatment.

REFERENCES

Affleck, G., Tennen, H., & Apter, A. (2001). Optimism, pessimism, and daily life with chronic illness. In E. C. Chang (Ed.), *Optimism & pessimism: Implications for theory, research, and practice* (pp. 147–168). Washington, DC: American Psychological Association.

Arntz, A., & Schmidt, A. J. M. (1989). Perceived control and the experience of pain intensity. In A. Steptoe & A. Appels (Eds.), *Stress, personal control and health* (pp. 20–25). Oxford, UK: John Wiley & Sons.

Bandura, A. (1977). Self-efficacy: Toward a unifying theory of behavioral change. *Psychological Review, 84*, 191–215.

Banks, S. M., & Kerns, R. D. (1996). Explaining high rates of depression in chronic pain: A diathesis-stress framework. *Psychological Bulletin, 119*, 95–110.

Bruehl, S., Chung, O. Y., Burns, J. W. (2006). Anger expression and pain: An overview of findings and possible mechanisms. *Journal of Behavioral Medicine, 29*, 593–606.

Burns, J. W. (1997). Anger management style and hostility: Predicting symptom-specific physiological reactivity among chronic low back pain patients. *Journal of Behavioral Medicine, 20*, 505–522.

Cacioppo, J. T., Bernston, G. G., Klein, D. J., & Poehlmann, K. M. (1997). The psychophysiology of emotion across the lifespan. *Annual Review of Gerontology and Geriatrics, 17*, 27–74.

Carver, C. S., & Scheier, M. F. (2005). Optimism. In C. R. Snyder & S. J. Lopez (Eds.), *Handbook of positive psychology* (pp. 231–243). Oxford, UK: Oxford University Press.

Dohnke, B., Knauper, B., & Muller-Fahrnow, W. (2005). Perceived self-efficacy gained from, and health effects of, a rehabilitation program after hip joint replacement. *Arthritis and Rheumatism, 53*, 585–592.

Fernandez, E. (2002). *Anxiety, depression, and anger in pain: Research implications.* Dallas, TX: Advanced Psychology Resources.

Flor, H., Birbaumer, N., & Turk, D. C. (1990). The psychobiology of chronic pain. *Advances in Behaviour Research and Therapy, 12*, 47–84.

Fordyce, W. E. (1976). *Behavioral methods for chronic pain and illness,* St. Louis: Mosby.

Granot, M., & Ferber, S. G. (2005). The roles of pain catastrophizing and anxiety in the prediction of postoperative pain intensity: A prospective study. *Clinical Journal of Pain*, 21, 439–445.

Jensen, M. P., Turner, J. A., Romano, J. M., & Lawler, B. K. (1994). Relationship of pain-specific beliefs to chronic pain adjustment. *Pain*, 57, 301–309.

Keefe, F. J., Rumble, M. E., Scipio, C. D., Giordano, L. A., & Perri, L. M. (2004). Psychological aspects of persistent pain: Current state of the science. *Journal of Pain*, 5, 195–211.

Keogh, E., & Asmundson, G. J. G. (2004). Negative affectivity, catastrophizing and anxiety sensitivity. In G. J. G. Asmundson, J. W. S. Vlaeyen, & G. Crombez (Eds.), *Understanding and treating fear of pain* (pp. 91–115). Oxford: Oxford University Press.

Kerns, R. D., & Haythornthwaite, J. A. (1988). Depression among chronic pain patients: Cognitive-behavioral analysis and effect on rehabilitation outcome. *Journal of Consulting and Clinical Psychology*, 56, 870–876.

McCracken, L. M., & Gross, R. T. (1998). The role of pain-related anxiety reduction in the outcome of multidisciplinary treatment for chronic low back pain: Preliminary results. *Journal of Occupational Rehabilitation*, 8, 179–189.

Melzack, R., & Casey, K. L. (1968). Sensory, motivational, and central control determinants of pain: A new conceptual model. In D. Kenshalo (Ed.), *The skin senses* (pp. 423–443). Springfield, IL: Charles C. Thomas.

Melzack, R., & Wall, P. D. (1965). Pain mechanisms: A new theory. *Science*, 150, 971–979.

Merskey, H. International Association for the Study of Pain (1986). Classification of chronic pain: Descriptions of chronic pain syndromes and definitions of pain terms. *Pain*, 3, S1–226.

Pavlin, D. J., Rapp, S. E., & Pollisar, N. (1998). Factors affecting discharge time in adult outpatients. *Anesthesia and Analgesia*, 87, 816–826.

Penacoba-Puente, C., Fernandez-de-las-Penas, C., Gonzalez-Gutierrez, J. L., Miangolarra-Page, J. C., & Pareja, J. A. (in press). Interaction between anxiety, depression, quality of life and clinical parameters in chronic tension-type headache. *European Journal of Pain*.

Picavet, H. S., Vlaeyen, J. W. S., & Schouten, J. S. (2002). Pain catastrophizing and kinesiophobia: Predictors of chronic low back pain. *American Journal of Epidemiology*, 156, 1028–1034.

Reiss, S., Peterson, R. A., Gursky, D. M., & McNally, R. J. (1986). Anxiety sensitivity, anxiety frequency and the predictions of fearfulness. *Behavior Research & Therapy*, 24, 1–8.

Sharp, T. J. (2001). Chronic pain: A reformulation of the cognitive behavioural model. *Behaviour Research and Therapy*, 39, 787–800.

Snyder, C. R., Rand, K. L., & Sigmond D. R. (2005). Hope theory: A member of the positive psychology family, In: C. R. Snyder, S. J. Lopez (Eds.) *Handbook of positive psychology*. Oxford: Oxford University Press.

Treharne, G. J., Kitas, G. D., Lyons, A. C., & Booth, D. A. (2005). Well-being in rheumatoid arthritis: The effects of disease duration and psychosocial factors. *Journal of Health Psychology*, 10, 457–474.

Turk, D. C., Meichenbaum D., Genest, M. (1983). *Pain and behavioral medicine: A cognitive-behavioral perspective*. New York: Guilford Press.

Turner, J. A., Jensen, M. P., & Romano, J. M. (2000). Do beliefs, coping, and catastrophizing independently predict functioning in patients with chronic pain? *Pain*, 85, 115–125.

Weisenberg, M. (1998). Cognitive aspects of pain and pain control. *International Journal of Clinical & Experimental Hypnosis*, 46, 44–61.

Woby, S. R., Watson, P. J., Roach, N. K, & Urmston, M. (2005). Coping strategy use: Does it predict adjustment to chronic back pain after controlling for catastrophic thinking and self-efficacy for pain control? *Journal of Rehabilitation Medicine*, 37, 100–107.

Wolfe, F., Smythe, H. A., Yunus, M. B., Bennett, R. M., Bombardier, C., Goldenberg, D. L., et al. (1990). The American College of Rheumatology 1990 criteria for the classification of fibromyalgia: Report of the Multicenter Criteria Committee. *Arthritis and Rheumatism*, 33, 160–172.

DENNIS C. TURK
HILARY D. WILSON
University of Washington

See also: **Pain Disorder**

CIRCADIAN RHYTHMS

Circadian rhythms are endogenously generated daily cycles in physiology and behavior. In this context, the term *endogenous* means that circadian rhythms are dependent on internal biological timing mechanisms, referred to as circadian "clocks," "pacemakers," or "oscillators." As implied by the combined *circa* and *dian*, these timing mechanisms produce biological rhythms with period lengths of approximately 24 hours. When exposed to the precise 24-hour periodicity of the environment—for example, to daily 24-hour light-dark cycles—endogenous circadian clocks become synchronized or *entrained* to those environmental cycles. In contrast, when maintained in experimental isolation from daily time-cues, circadian clocks express their endogenous "free-running" periodicity, which only approximates 24 hours. Researchers generally consider the free-running period as expressed in constant darkness to best reflect the period of the endogenous circadian clock.

Although this parameter generally varies between about 22 and 26 hours across species and individuals, a wide variety of environmental (e.g., light, temperature) and physiological (e.g., hormones, metabolic state) variables are known to modulate free-running period. Thus, entrainment requires a daily correction in the endogenous cycle length that results in an exact match to the cycle length of the environmental synchronizer. The dynamics of this process have been described in an influential nonparametric theory of entrainment that predicts quantitatively the period and phase of entrained circadian rhythms under both standard and nonstandard light-dark cycles. In essence, the nonparametric theory proposes that entrainment is effected by near-instantaneous phase shifts of the circadian clock induced by the light-to-dark and dark-to-light transitions associated with dusk and dawn, respectively.

Origin and Molecular Mechanism

Circadian rhythms are expressed at all levels of phylogeny, from unicells to plants and animals, including humans. This phylogenetic ubiquity undoubtedly reflects the pervasive selection pressure exerted by daily environmental cycles of light, temperature, nutrient availability, and other factors. Circadian rhythms are also physiologically ubiquitous and are manifest at all levels of biological organization, from basic genomic and cellular processes to complex behavioral and cognitive functions. Indeed, it would be remarkable to find any biological process that fails to display circadian timing. The basic mechanism of circadian timing at the cellular level is thought to involve a number of so-called circadian "clock genes" that are transcribed rhythmically under negative feedback regulation by their own protein products. The basic logic of this molecular feedback loop is very similar in all organisms that have been examined, and in fact, homologous genes and proteins appear to regulate the cellular circadian clock in animals ranging from flies to humans. Beyond the core molecular feedback loop, gene expression profiling studies have revealed that about 10% of the genome is expressed rhythmically in any given tissue from complex multicellular organisms. Such "clock-controlled genes" (CCGs) are then responsible for conveying the circadian timing signal from the core clock loop to other cellular processes.

Role of Behavior in Circadian Rhythm Research

Behavioral experiments have been critical in elucidating the complex phenomenology of circadian rhythms. This is because measures of spontaneous locomotor activity, such as perch-hopping in birds and wheel-running in rodents, can be conveniently and noninvasively monitored over long periods of time in individual animals. In contrast, studies of circadian rhythms in hormone secretion, body temperature, or other physiological parameters generally require invasive measurements, or even the sacrifice of separate groups of animals at different points in time. Obviously, researchers interested specifically in the circadian timing of hormone secretion must measure hormone secretion, but, in contrast, researchers focused on the circadian clock

itself have generally assayed locomotor activity or other easily monitored spontaneous behaviors.

Of course, this strategy carries the implicit assumption that a single circadian clock regulates all circadian rhythms, such that one overt rhythm is as good as another for making inferences about the underlying clock. Although this assumption is not always justified, studies of locomotor activity have nevertheless revealed the basic processes of entrainment by light and other factors, the diversity of variables influencing free-running period, and the frequent dissociation of circadian rhythms under constant light. More recently, behavioral experiments have shown that mutation of specific circadian clock genes results in specific alterations in circadian phenotype at the behavioral level, thus facilitating a nuanced understanding of the underlying molecular processes.

Neurobiology of the Mammalian Circadian Clock

In mammals, circadian clock cells expressing the molecular feedback loop are broadly distributed in the brain and body. Nevertheless, the overall circadian timing system is hierarchically organized, and includes a circadian pacemaker found in the suprachiasmatic nucleus (SCN) of the anterior hypothalamus. Studies conducted in the 1970s showed that surgical destruction of the SCN results in a widespread loss of circadian rhythms in a multitude of physiological and behavioral processes, showing that the SCN plays a critical role in generating circadian timing at the organismic level. Subsequently it was shown that transplantation of fetal SCN tissue into arrhythmic SCN-ablated hosts results in transference of the donor's free-running circadian period, effectively ruling out the hypothesis that the SCN simply secretes a permissive factor allowing circadian pacemaker function to be expressed elsewhere in the brain. Other classic studies of the same era showed that the SCN pacemaker is entrained by environmental light-dark cycles via direct retinal projections to the SCN known as the retinohypothalamic tract (RHT), and that the RHT is both necessary and sufficient for light entrainment. The RHT releases the excitatory neurotransmitter, glutamate, as well as a number of peptide cotransmitters, and glutamate acts to initiate intracellular signaling cascades in SCN clock neurons that ultimately alter the expression of specific clock genes.

Remarkably, it is now known that circadian entrainment (and other non-image-forming visual functions) is mediated in part by a set of photoreceptive retinal ganglion cells, as well as by classical retinal photoreceptors, and that neither the classical or novel photoreceptive systems are necessary or sufficient for light entrainment. Cultured SCN neurons express circadian rhythms that differ in circadian phase and period across individual cells in the same culture, confirming that circadian timing is essentially a cellular-level rather than a neural network phenomenon. In contrast, individual SCN clock cells show strongly coupled rhythms when studied in organotypic brain slice cultures, or, of course, *in vivo*. The mechanisms of intercellular oscillator coupling are not fully understood, but appear to include both synaptic and extrasynaptic interactions.

Other than the RHT, major SCN inputs arise from the intergeniculate leaflet of the thalamus (IGL), a retinorecipient component of the lateral geniculate complex, and from the midbrain serotonergic raphe nuclei. These projections serve to modulate light entrainment of the SCN pacemaker. Although the precise role of the IGL in light entrainment has not been defined, IGL projections to the SCN release the inhibitory neurotransmitter GABA as well as neuropeptide Y (NPY), and both GABA and NPY antagonize the effects of light and glutamate on the SCN. Similarly, raphe projections release serotonin at the SCN (and the IGL), and serotonin also generally antagonizes the effects of light on the SCN. In addition to modulation of light entrainment, the IGL and raphe also appear to mediate the entrainment of the SCN pacemaker by nonphotic, arousal-related cues. Thus, under certain conditions and in at least some mammalian species, stimuli related to arousal, locomotor activity, and sleep-wake state are capable of entraining free-running circadian rhythms, and these effects are eliminated or attenuated after surgical or pharmacological disruption of IGL and raphe inputs to the SCN.

A Multioscillatory Clockshop

As previously mentioned, circadian clock cells are found outside the SCN, in other brain regions and in many tissues and organs throughout the body. Cultured tissue from several brain regions and from a multiplicity of peripheral organs show at least damped circadian rhythms. Although these non-SCN cells generally show less robust and less persistent rhythms than do SCN cultures, it appears that this difference may reflect weaker intercellular oscillator coupling in non-SCN relative to SCN tissue. Thus, individual cellular-level rhythms may be sustained, but uncoupled, while tissue-level rhythms are simultaneously lost. According to this view, non-SCN clock cells are highly dependent on rhythmic signals emerging from the SCN pacemaker to sustain coherent, tissue-level rhythmicity. The relevant SCN signals appear to be distributed within the central nervous system by both neural projections and paracrine secretions, while SCN signals reach peripheral tissues via the autonomic nervous system and pituitary hormone secretions.

In addition, SCN signals may influence peripheral clock cells indirectly, via SCN-dependent changes in body temperature, metabolism, and behavior. Circadian clocks in non-SCN tissues are almost certainly responsible for the local regulation of tissue-specific physiological processes, and one may presume that such local temporal regulation is critical for normal homeostatic function. This view has led to a recent explosion in research linking the regulation and dysregulation of tissue-specific circadian rhythms to health and disease. Thus, environmental, physiological and genetic manipulation of the circadian clock has now been associated with psychiatric and sleep disorders, diabetes and obesity, and cancer, among other illnesses. Eventually, this avenue of research should lead to the broad acceptance of circadian-based therapies and treatments for a diversity of medical conditions.

SUGGESTED READINGS

Allada, R., Emery, P., Takahashi, J. S., & Rosbash, M. (2001). Stopping time: The genetics of fly and mouse circadian clocks. *Annual Review of Neuroscience, 24*, 1091–1119.

Aschoff, J. (Ed.). (1981). *Handbook of behavioral neurobiology, Vol. 4: Biological rhythms*. New York: Plenum Press.

Hastings, M. H., Reddy, A. B., & Maywood, E. S. (2003). A clockwork web: Circadian timing in brain and periphery, in health and disease. *Nature Reviews Neuroscience, 4*, 649–661.

Lowrey, P. L., & Takahashi, J. S. (2004). Mammalian circadian biology: Elucidating genome-wide levels of temporal organization. *Annual Review of Genomics and Human Genetics, 5*, 407–441.

Morin, L. P., & Allen, C.N. (2006). The circadian visual system, 2005. *Brain Research Reviews, 51*, 1–60.

Rosenwasser, A. M., & Adler, N. T. (1986). Structure and function in circadian timing systems: Evidence for multiple coupled circadian oscillators. *Neuroscience and Biobehavioral Reviews, 10*, 431–448.

ALAN M. ROSENWASSER
University of Maine

CIVIL COMPETENCE

Competence, in civil legal matters, refers to the capacity to make independent decisions and conduct legal and financial transactions on one's own behalf. Adults are generally presumed to be competent to handle their own affairs, but when there is compelling evidence to the contrary, an individual may be found, by law, to be incompetent. Either the state or a private party, usually a family member, may raise the issue. Legal determinations of competence are important to fair execution of justice. A just outcome in any matter requires that parties are fully able to understand and participate in the decision making that is required for the matter; if they are not, that accommodation is arranged so that they can participate by representation from someone who has their interests in mind. If the court declares a person to be incompetent, a guardian may be appointed and legally empowered to make decisions on behalf of the person. This may be a family member of other close relation, or it may be the court itself, in which case the person becomes a "ward of the court." This reflects the notion of *parent patriae*, or the state's interest in assuring care for those who cannot care for themselves.

Different Competencies

The law may be interested in an individual's competence to execute wills, trusts, and estates; competence to issue medical directives for long-term care, assign a power of attorney, or open a trust account; competence to enter into contracts; competence to make decisions in domestic relations matters; and competence in "guardianship of property." Competence to make medical decisions, including consenting to treatment or refusing treatment, may arise as part of a tort action against a medical provider or as part of a determination of an individual's capacity to make independent decisions in general.

In mental health court, questions of certain civil competencies may arise in relation to a criminal proceeding. Individuals may be remanded to civil commitment when they are unable to manage independent living without violating the law (or to put it differently, when a violation of the law springs from severe mental illness). During involuntary commitment, a person's competence to refuse treatment may be at question and may be decided by a mental health judge based on expert testimony from forensic evaluators and treatment personnel. These are only a few of the many circumstances under which an individual's competence may be of interest to the court; there are dozens of civil law contexts in which competency concerns may arise.

Variability of Competence

There is not always an evident distinction between the state of competence and that of incompetence. With progressive disorders such as Alzheimer's, for example, people may be intermittently impaired and make irresponsible decisions but at other times function competently. An individual may have sufficient competence to take care of basic needs, such as self-care, but become confused when faced with higher cognitive challenges such as managing finances.

Further, incompetence may not be a stable or permanent state. Some conditions that render an individual incompetent, such as severe mental retardation or massive brain injury, may cause permanent incompetence. Some conditions, such as schizophrenia, may only be debilitating when left untreated; with appropriate medication, the person may be competent. Other conditions, such as impairment that may follow stroke or some closed head injuries, may be acute and short-lived and any lost competence may be fully regained within weeks or months.

Challenging Competence

Because adults are presumed to be competent, when there is a question of competence the burden of proof generally falls to the party challenging the individual's competency. The definition of competency may differ according to the circumstances (competent to make medical decisions, to write a will, or to enter a complex contract, for example). In addition the definition of competency may vary according to the statue or case law in the jurisdiction, which may define the elements of a particular competency. It may also vary according to the fact of the particular case.

When an individual's competence is challenged, such as when a natural heir challenges the testamentary competence of the will writer at the time of the creation of the will, the law may presume competence and demand that the challenger offer evidence of lack of competence. Evidence may be presented of impaired cognitive functioning, memory capacity, or reasoning ability, all factors potentially relevant in determining whether an individual is (or was) competent to execute a will. Evidence may be offered in the form of expert testimony or testimony from lay or fact witnesses who describe behaviors suggestive of the absence of "knowing" or "understanding" decision making. In the case of a challenge to testamentary capacity, for example, there may be no evident basis for the decisions the testator made; for example, natural heirs may have been omitted from the will but recent superficial acquaintances were included. Or alternatively, perhaps the law called for knowledge of the extent of one's estate, but the will revealed that the testator had a gross misunderstanding of the estate.

When competence is regained, the person who seeks to be relieved of the legal status that ensued with the loss of competency (such as guardianship) may have the burden of proof show that competence has been restored.

Mental Health Experts and Competence Determination

Because competence may be defined in terms of certain cognitive capacities, forensic mental health professionals are often called upon to assess it. The specific focus of the evaluation depends on the legal definition of the competency at question. To be useful in court, evaluators must understand the underlying concept and convert it to functional capacities that can be assessed (Grisso, 2003). The results of the assessment must then be contextualized to take account of the questions under the consideration in the law.

Operationalizing the Competency

When the law requires a competence determination, the legal question must be operationalized or defined in a way that allows for an assessment. The law may pose the question, "Does this individual possess the competence to make a treatment decision?" The functional elements of this competence are the specific abilities, knowledge, or understanding the individual must possess in order to be competent (Grisso, 2003). Treatment competency, for example, may be functionally defined as the ability to make a knowing and intelligent decision to receive, or refuse, medical or mental health treatment. Knowing or intelligent decision making must be further defined and might be operationalized as the ability to understand the nature of the illness embodied in a diagnosis, the treatment options available, the benefits and risks of each treatment option, and the ability to reasonably consider those benefits and risks in terms of one's own circumstances, means, and preferences.

Evaluating Competency

The evaluator conducts this assessment by reviewing records, interviewing family members or others who may have pertinent knowledge of the individual's functional abilities, and, if the individual is living, interviewing and administering a number of psychological or neuropsychological tests (Heilbrun, 2001). The examiner may assess general intellectual ability, attention, concentration, reality orientation, memory, reasoning, or judgment. Of specific relevance may be the individual's knowledge and appreciation of the nature and purposes of the decisions that are the subject of the competency action (e.g., understanding the purpose of real estate contracts) and the ability to carry them out (e.g., being able to read and comprehend the contents of contracts, understand the methods by which property value is established, and understand the tax implications of a decision to buy or sell property).

Objective measures of memory functions, cognitive reasoning ability, and judgment may be helpful to address the question before the court. Specific instruments have been developed to guide or aid in some kinds of competency assessment (see Parry & Drogin, 2007, for a review). Whether a formal instrument is used, the evaluator directly explores the functional areas at question. Additionally, as is true for all forensic assessments, any assessment of competency should include a measure of the individual's openness, cooperativeness, and tendency to over- or under-report cognitive difficulties (Heilbrun, 2001; Rogers, 1997). This is important because the outcome of the evaluation may have a profound impact on the examinee's life, thus raising the possibility of deliberate or unintentional misrepresentation.

Through this process of data collection and synthesis, the evaluator develops an expert opinion regarding the functional components at question and may develop an opinion regarding whether the person possesses the legal competency that is being evaluated. Generally the latter determination, often a moral or value-laden issue, is considered to be the exclusive province of the fact finder. The expert generally has no special knowledge to make the final determination, but the expert's opinions may be of invaluable assistance to the trier of fact, who considers those opinions along with other evidence to reach a finding (Melton, Petrila, Poythress, & Sloogin, 2007).

When necessary, this evaluative process is undertaken retroactively and the determination of competency is focused upon some former time when the individual entered in a contract, for example, executed a will. In such cases, the evaluator relies on records and interviews with people who may have relevant information, or when available, audio or video recordings of the individual around the time of the action about which there is question of competency. Much more accurate assessment of current competency of a living individual can be made, of course, than of a prior competency and especially one possessed by a now deceased individual who cannot be examined directly (Simon & Shuman, 2002).

REFERENCES

Grisso, T. (2003). *Evaluating competencies: Forensic assessments and instruments*, (2nd ed.). New York: Kluwer Academic/Plenum.

Heilbrun, K. (2001). *Principles of forensic mental health assessment*. New York: Kluwer Academic/Plenum.

Melton, G. B., Petrila, J., Poythress, N. G., & Slobogin, C. (2007). *Psychological evaluations for the courts*, (3rd ed.). New York: Guilford Press.

Parry, J., & Drogin, E. Y. (2007). *Mental disability law, evidence, and testimony*. Washington, DC: American Bar Association.

Rogers, R. (Ed). (1997). *Clinical assessment of malingering and deception*, (2nd ed.). New York: Guilford Press.

Simon, R. I., & Shuman D. W. (Eds). (2002). *Retrospective assessments of mental states in litigation: Predicting the past*. Arlington, VA: American Psychiatric Publishing.

SUGGESTED READINGS

Perlin, M. L., Champine, P. R., Dlugacz, H. A., & Connell, M. A. (2008). *Competence in the law: From legal theory to clinical application*. Hoboken, NJ: John Wiley & Sons.

Perlin, M. L., Morton, C., & Ellis, H. (2006). *Mental disability law: Civil and criminal*, (18th ed.). Durham, NC: Carolina Academic Press.

MARY CONNELL
Fort Worth, Texas

See also: Competency to Stand Trial; Expert Testimony; Forensic Assessment Instruments and Techniques

CLARK, KENNETH B. (1914–2005)

Kenneth B. Clark was brought to New York City by his mother when he was four. He attended schools in Harlem and graduated from George Washington High School in 1931. He received the BS and MA from Howard University and the PhD degree in psychology from Columbia University in 1940.

As a social psychologist, Clark worked with lawyers in the series of cases on equality of educational opportunity that led to the historic 1964 *Brown v. Board of Education of Topeka, Kansas* decision. His studies on the effects of segregation on the personality development of children were cited by the U.S. Supreme Court in footnote 11 of the decision.

In 1946, Clark and his wife, Dr. Mamie Phipps Clark, founded the interracial Northside Center for Child Development for the treatment of children with personality and learning problems. In 1964, he became a founder and director of Harlem Youth Opportunities (HARYOU), a prototype community development program that sought to increase the participation of low-income groups in decisions on education, housing, employment and training, and economic development.

A member of the faculty at City College of the City University of New York from 1942 to 1975, he was named Distinguished Professor of Psychology in 1971. He was a member of the New York Board of Regents from 1966 until 1986.

A member of Phi Beta Kappa and Sigma Xi, Clark served as president of the American Psychological Association (1970), of the Society Psychological Studies of Social Issues (1959), and of the Metropolitan Applied Research Center (1967–1975). From 1975 until his death in 2005, he served as President of Clark, Phipps, Clark, & Harris, Inc., a human-relations consulting firm.

SUGGESTED READINGS

Clark, K. (1983). *The art of humanism.* London: John Murray.

Clark, K. (1988). *Prejudice and your child.* Middleton, CT: Wesleyan University Press.

Clark, K. (1989). *Dark ghetto: Dilemmas of social power.* Middleton, CT: Wesleyan University Press.

STAFF

CLASSICAL CONDITIONING (See Pavlovian Conditioning)

CLASSROOM BEHAVIOR

Classroom behavior has been studied most often as a form of social competency that contributes to a student's overall adjustment to school. Typically, classroom behavior is defined with respect to negative or maladaptive behavioral styles (e.g., aggressive, inattentive, or disruptive behavior) or to prosocial and socially responsible competencies such as cooperative and prosocial interactions and self-regulated behavior. These behavioral styles are manifest in the degree to which students adhere to social rules and expectations reflecting cooperation, respect for others, and positive forms of group participation that govern social interactions with teachers and peers in the classroom.

The relevance of classroom behavior for understanding school success is two-fold. First, positive forms of classroom behavior are valued outcomes in and of themselves. Social behavior in the form of moral character, conformity to social rules and norms, cooperation, and positive styles of social interaction is promoted consistently within schools as a goal for students to achieve. Second, classroom behavior is a consistent and strong predictor of academic achievement. Students who are socially competent also tend to be academically successful.

This entry describes the types of classroom behavior that are a valued part of students' functioning at school and their relation to academic outcomes. Pathways of influence that describe how classroom behavior develops and, in turn, how classroom behavior might lead to positive academic outcomes are also discussed.

Classroom Behavior and School Adjustment

The importance of classroom behavior for understanding students' success at school is reflected in the educational goals for students held by policy makers as well as school personnel. A review of the history of American education reveals that at the policy level, educational objectives have included the development of social competencies as well as scholastic achievements for producing model citizens as well as scholars. Character development and social responsibility have been stated as explicit objectives for public schools in almost every educational policy statement since 1848 and have been promoted with the same frequency as the development of academic skills (Wentzel, 1991).

At the classroom level, teachers express clear opinions concerning the behavioral characteristics of well-adjusted and successful students (for a review, see Wentzel, 2003). Elementary-school teachers have consistently reported preferences for students who are cooperative, conforming, cautious, and responsible; they also tend to report antisocial and aggressive behavior as most detrimental to classroom order. When describing "ideal" students, middle school teachers also mention social behavioral outcomes such as sharing, being helpful to others, and being responsive to rules as desirable forms of student behavior.

Of additional importance is that these behavioral competencies have been related consistently and strongly to academic accomplishments (Wentzel, 2003). Correlational studies indicate that tendencies to be prosocial and empathic, prosocial interactions with peers, appropriate classroom conduct, and compliance have been related positively to intellectual outcomes in the elementary years. Positive social interactions of preschool children also predict engagement and positive motivational orientations in the classroom. Similarly, socially responsible decision making in adolescents has been related positively to academic outcomes. Young adolescents' prosocial behavior also has been related positively to classroom grades and standardized test scores.

Longitudinal studies also have linked behavioral competence to academic achievements. Specifically, elementary-grade retention is related to conduct as well as academic problems, whereas recurring nonpromotion at the junior high level is related primarily to classroom misconduct and other behavioral problems. Adaptive classroom behavior in elementary school predicts later grades and test scores in elementary school and in high school, over and above early achievement and IQ. Similarly, aggressive and disruptive behavior in the elementary grades is a strong negative predictor of academic grades in middle school and high school after taking into account IQ, sex, grade level, and other demographic factors. Antisocial and aggressive behavior in the early grades also appears to place children at risk for dropping out of high school.

Pathways of Influence

There are several theoretical issues relevant to understanding the development of positive behavioral styles at school and the role of classroom behavior in student achievement. With respect to factors that support the development and maintenance of classroom behavior, parents and teachers appear to play important roles. The literature on parenting suggests that specific dimensions of parent-child interactions can predict reliably children's social behavioral competencies. As described by Baumrind (1971), these dimensions reflect consistent enforcement of rules, expectations for self-reliance and self-control, solicitation of children's opinions and feelings, and expressions of warmth and approval. Appropriate monitoring and contingent feedback also appear to contribute to children's positive behavioral styles, as do specific disciplinary techniques such as induction and reasoning (Hoffman, 2000).

Teachers also spend an enormous amount of time teaching their students how to behave and act responsibly in class (Wentzel, 1991). In this regard, teachers tend to have a core set of behavioral expectations for their students reflecting appropriate responses to academic requests and tasks, impulse control, mature problem solving, cooperative and courteous interaction with peers, involvement in class activities, and recognition of appropriate contexts for different types of behavior. Teachers also communicate expectations for students' interactions with each other. High school teachers tend to promote adherence to interpersonal rules concerning aggression, manners, stealing, and loyalty, and elementary school teachers tend to focus on peer norms for sharing resources, being nice to each other, working well with others, and harmonious problem solving. Moreover, teachers actively communicate these expectations to their students, regardless of their instructional goals, teaching styles, and ethnicity.

In addition to communicating to students what they should be trying to achieve, teachers also can create classroom contexts that have the potential to either support or discourage the demonstration of positive forms of behavior (see Pianta, Hamre, & Stuhlman, 2003). For instance, young children's healthy behavioral adjustment to school has been related to teacher-student relationships characterized by warmth and the absence of conflict as well as open communication. In contrast, kindergartners' relationships with teachers marked by conflict and dependency predict less-than-adaptive academic and behavioral outcomes through eighth grade, especially for boys. When teachers are taught to provide students with warmth and support, clear expectations for behavior, and developmentally appropriate autonomy, their students develop a stronger sense of community and increase displays of socially competent behavior.

In addition to identifying antecedents of classroom behavior, researchers also have studied processes by which behavioral styles and interactions can influence academic outcomes. There are at least two mechanisms that can explain the contribution of students' classroom behavior to their academic accomplishments at school. First, prosocial and responsible behavior can contribute to academic achievement by creating a context conducive to learning. Quite simply, students' adherence to classroom rules and displays of socially competent behavior allow teachers to focus their efforts on teaching rather than classroom management. Presumably, all students will learn more when this occurs. In addition, constructivist theories of development (Piaget, 1965) propose that positive social interactions (e.g., cooperative and collaborative problem solving) can create cognitive conflict that hastens the development of higher-order thinking skills and cognitive structures. Empirical research supports this notion in that learning cooperatively with peers results in greatest gains when interactive questioning and explanation are an explicit part of the learning task (Gauvain & Perez, 2007).

An important issue with respect to these models, however, concerns the direction of effects. Assuming that causal relations do exist, do socialization influences cause the development of certain behavioral styles or does a child's behavior elicit specific socialization practices and reactions from parents, teachers, and peers? Similarly, is it that behavioral competence influences learning and achievement or that academic success promotes behavioral competence? It is clear that bidirectional influences exist. For instance, whereas irresponsible and antisocial behavior can lead to lost opportunities to learn, negative academic feedback can lead to acting out, noncompliance, and other forms of irresponsible behavior on the part of students. As noted earlier, however, antisocial behavior and a lack of prosocial skills tend to have their roots in poor family relationships. Therefore, how children are taught to behave before they enter school should have at least an initial impact on how they behave and subsequently learn in classroom settings. In addition, interventions that teach children appropriate social responses to instruction, such as paying attention and volunteering answers, have led to significant and stable gains in academic achievement, whereas interventions designed to increase academic skills do not necessarily lead to decreases in antisocial behavior, nor do they enhance social skills typically associated with academic achievement (see Wentzel, 2003). Therefore, it is reasonable to assume that at least to some degree, behavioral competence precedes academic competence at school.

REFERENCES

Baumrind, D. (1971). Current patterns of parental authority. *Developmental Psychology Monograph, 4*(1, Pt. 2).

Gauvain, M., & Perez, S. M. (2007). The socialization of cognition. In J. E. Grusec & P. Hastings (Eds.), *Handbook of socialization: Theory and research* (pp. 588–613). New York: Guilford Press.

Hoffman, M. L. (2000). *Empathy and moral development: Implications for caring and justice.* Cambridge, MA: Cambridge University Press.

Piaget, J. (1965). *The moral judgment of the child.* New York: Free Press. (Original published work in 1932)

Pianta, R. C., Hamre, B., & Stuhlman, M. (2003). Relationships between teachers and children. In W. Reynolds & G. Miller (Eds.), *Handbook of psychology, Vol. 7: Educational Psychology* (pp. 199–234). Hoboken, NJ: John Wiley & Sons.

Wentzel, K. R. (1991). Social competence at school: Relations between social responsibility and academic achievement. *Review of Educational Research, 61*, 1–24.

Wentzel, K. R. (2003). School adjustment. In W. Reynolds & G. Miller (Eds.), *Handbook of psychology, Vol. 7: Educational Psychology* (pp. 235–258). Hoboken, NJ: John Wiley & Sons.

Wentzel, K. R. (2005). Peer relationships, motivation, and academic performance at school. In A. Elliot & C. Dweck (Eds.), *Handbook of competence and motivation* (pp. 279–296). New York: Guilford Press.

SUGGESTED READINGS

Evertson, C., & Weinstein, C. (Eds.). (2007). *Handbook of classroom management: Research, practice, and contemporary issues.* Mahwah, NJ: Lawrence Erlbaum.

Reynolds, W., & Miller, G. (2003). *Handbook of psychology, Vol. 7: Educational psychology,* edited by I. B. Weiner, Editor-in-Chief. Hoboken, NJ: John Wiley & Sons.

KATHRYN R. WENTZEL
University of Maryland, College Park

See also: **Prosocial Behavior; School Learning**

CLIENT-CENTERED THERAPY

Client-centered therapy—also referred to as person-centered therapy and Rogerian therapy—is a major approach to counseling and psychotherapy developed by Carl R. Rogers. A fundamental clinical framework informing the humanistic psychology movement, client-centered therapy and its theoretical basis stand in stark contrast to theories and psychotherapies that reduce human beings to components. The client-centered approach maintains that human beings can only be understood as wholes, through their individual subjective experiences. Another difference between client-centered therapy and most approaches to psychotherapy is that client-centered therapy "definitely rejects the medical model which involves looking for pathology and developing a specific diagnosis, or thinking of treatment in terms of cure" (Rogers, 2007, p. 1). Client-centered therapy posits specific attributes of a "good life" beyond the relative absence of psychopathology; it was designed to provide the conditions that encourage natural human growth and development toward the realization of the individual's potentials. Throughout his lengthy career, Rogers contributed numerous theoretical constructs and propositions that marked the evolution of his perspective. However, the central concept that serves as the core of his approach is the *actualizing tendency.*

Actualizing Tendency

Rogers (1980) hypothesized an omnipresent formative tendency (Rogers, 1980, pp. 124–126), asserting that everything in the universe tends toward greater differentiation and integration. Living things express this formative principle as an actualizing tendency, that is, a tendency toward maintaining and enhancing themselves. The actualizing tendency, biological in nature, is the primary motivating force in life and, in humans, is manifested through inexorable movement toward growth and adaptation. This actualizing tendency, according to Rogers, is the essential restorative factor in psychotherapy; thus, the focus of client-centered therapy is to provide the relational conditions by through which the tendency can be most fully experienced and expressed by the individual client.

The Self and the Self-Actualizing Tendency

A human being's experience consists of "all that is going on within the envelope of the organism at any given moment which is potentially available to awareness" (Rogers, 1959, p. 197). For Rogers, human experience is the moment-to-moment, inward sense of living and includes one's physical sensations, sensory information, thoughts, images, and memories, that is, everything that is available to consciousness.

As human beings develop during childhood, they differentiate a portion of ongoing experience as the *self,* an ever-changing conceptual and organizational "map" that defines the individual to herself and includes the individual's personal awareness and agency. The self-actualizing tendency, therefore, is a subprocess of the actualizing tendency, and it is revealed through an individual's efforts to maintain and enhance the concept of the self. It is when the actualizing and self-actualizing tendencies operate at cross-purposes that human psychological problems develop, a condition that Rogers referred to as *incongruence*.

Psychological Maladjustment

According to Rogers' theory, psychological distress and maladjustment develop as a result of an individual denying or distorting experience, thus disrupting the natural tendency to process experience, to integrate it into one's self-structure, and to actualize potential. This often occurs because of the human's inherent need for social affiliation and acceptance, leading to the introjection of what Rogers called *conditions of worth*. Conditions of worth are messages that communicate to the individual receiving them that he or she is positively regarded only if possessing certain values, characteristics, or behaviors. Introjection of conditions of worth leads individuals to judge themselves based upon these conditions, which can require them to distort or deny experience. For example, if an individual introjects the message, "You are lovable only if you are patient," this individual will have difficulty if encountering a situation that leads to feelings of impatience. The person must either ignore the feeling or distort the experience to make it consistent with the introject (e.g., "I feel this way because I'm coming down with a cold."). In Rogers' words, therefore, "Psychological maladjustment exists when the organism denies to awareness significant sensory and visceral experiences, which consequently are not symbolized and organized into the gestalt of the self-structure" (Rogers, 1951, p. 510).

Accumulation of conditions of worth leads individuals to assess their self-worth based upon adherence to these conditions rather than their own life experiences. With significant discrepancy between an individual's conditions of worth and ongoing experience, psychological distress and maladjustment are the inevitable result.

Psychotherapy and the Necessary and Sufficient Conditions

In a classic 1957 article, Rogers hypothesized that, given specific conditions of the psychotherapist's attitude and behavior that are perceived by the client, the process of growth and the movement toward actualization will become increasingly manifested in the client. The client will become freer to remain aware of, process, and evaluate personal experience, thereby becoming more congruent. Thus, the theory and its attendant approach to therapy predict that its application will accomplish more than

assisting the client in solving life problems and becoming free of troubling symptoms; it will have a direct effect on the client's process of living more fully. The three therapist-offered "necessary and sufficient conditions," as Rogers referred to them, are *unconditional positive regard*, *congruence*, and *accurate empathy*. More than techniques, these essential conditions specify therapist attitudes and resultant behaviors, and are not effective unless the client perceives them. It is important to note that the three therapist-offered conditions dovetail, each enhancing the presence of the other two.

Unconditional Positive Regard

Central to the therapeutic relationship in client-centered therapy is the therapist's genuine caring for the client in the moment. Unconditional positive regard means that the therapist prizes the client and the client's experience without judgment, specific conditions, or expectations. This contrasts with what is hypothesized to have contributed to the client's difficulties; that is, conditional caring depending upon the client conforming to certain guidelines or conditions.

The presence of unconditional positive regard does not indicate that the therapist agrees with or supports everything the client says or does; rather, it means that the therapist accepts and respects the client's ongoing experience of life. This relational stance toward the client encourages the client to become more open to his or her own ongoing experience, while also providing a necessary foundation for the therapist to experience and express empathy.

Empathy

Rogers defined empathy as perceiving "the internal frame of reference of another with accuracy, and with the emotional components and meaning which pertain thereto, as if one were the other person, and without ever losing the 'as if' quality" (1959, p. 210). This concept can be easily misunderstood and, in fact, has been reduced by some to mean that a therapist needs only to parrot the client's expressed thoughts. Empathy is significantly more than that; it is the assumption of an attitude of sincere curiosity toward and persisting attention on the client's experiencing of the world, and it is expressing that understanding to the client as clearly as possible. It also is distinct from sympathy; that is, feeling whatever the client feels. At all times the therapist recognizes his or her distinction from the client, while using attention and imagination to enter the client's world as much as possible and revealing to the client what is found. Empathic statements are at least tacitly tentative, in that the therapist is not expressing judgment or a confident understanding of the client's life. Through the expression of empathic understanding, the therapist is inviting the client to actively engage in attending to experience, to carry experience forward, and to more clearly feel and articulate ongoing attempts at sensing and understanding the world.

Congruence

To be an effective therapist, Rogers believed that, as much as possible, the therapist must live in the moment, consistently aware of his or her own ongoing experience and remaining genuine in the relationship with the client. Rogers called this therapist genuineness "congruence," defining it as "an accurate matching of experience and awareness" (1961, p. 282). This does not suggest that a therapist freely shares whatever thoughts or feelings are present in the moment, only that he or she remains aware of them. More importantly, congruence aids the therapist—and therefore the client—by reducing the interpersonal distance between psychotherapy participants, making the relationship one marked by respect and free exploration, rather than professional formality and power imbalance.

The Fully Functioning Person

The implicit goal of client-centered therapy—beyond addressing clients' presenting complaints, distress, and maladjustment—is to more generally enhance the client's individual functioning and to assist the client to become more effectively actualizing. Actualization in Rogers' theory is not a definable end-state, but rather a process of living that can never be complete. Rogers used the term "the fully functioning person" to indicate the characteristics of living ideally, of the actualization tendency as it is evidenced in individuals' lives.

According to Rogers, the fully functioning person remains open to ongoing experience—not denying or distorting it—and participates fully in each moment as the individual makes ongoing efforts to integrate experience into his or her self. The result is more responsible living that leads to increasing fulfillment of the person's potential.

Legacy

The legacy of client-centered therapy is secure and impressive, remaining an important perspective in our attempts at understanding human psychology, maladjustment, growth, and possibility. The theory and basic approach of client-centered therapy has been found to have significant applications beyond the provision of therapy. For that reason, the basic approach has come to be known as "person-centered." Among the applications of a person-centered approach are education, organizational psychology, encounter groups, multicultural therapy, and the pursuit of international diplomacy and peacemaking.

Client-centered therapy has inspired numerous specific developments in psychotherapy, two of which are experiential therapy (Gendlin, 1996) and the process-experiential approach (Elliott & Greenberg, 2001). Work continues on further elucidating many of Rogers' perspectives, including empathy (Bohart & Greenberg, 1997) and the often-unacknowledged importance of the client's contribution to the therapy process (Bohart & Tallman, 1999). Client-centered therapy seems uniquely suited to addressing multicultural therapy issues; some authors (e.g., Toukmanian & Brouwers, 1998) have suggested that humanistic-existential approaches to psychotherapy, including client-centered therapy, are compatible with the values and orientations of many cultural groups in North America, whereas the psychoanalytic and cognitive-behavioral approaches are more narrowly consistent with the values of Anglo-American culture.

Although differentially acknowledged, Carl Rogers' insights regarding the qualities of the effective therapeutic relationship have become integrated into most approaches to psychotherapy, consistent with the finding that the nature of the therapeutic relationship, rather than the delivery of techniques, tends to be the best predictor of successful psychotherapy. With the emphasis on human possibilities, faith in the change process, and Rogers' lucid theoretical writings, client-centered therapy will likely maintain its status as a formidable influence in psychology and the helping professions.

REFERENCES

Bohart, A. C., & Greenberg, L. S. (Eds.). (1997). *Empathy reconsidered: New directions in psychotherapy*. Washington, DC: American Psychological Association.

Bohart, A. C., & Tallman, K. (1999). *How clients make therapy work: The process of active self-healing*. Washington, DC: American Psychological Association.

Elliott, R. F., & Greenberg, L. S. (2001). Process-experiential psychotherapy. In D. J. Cain & J. Seeman (Eds.), *Humanistic psychotherapies: Handbook of research and practice* (pp. 279–306). Washington, DC: American Psychological Association.

Gendlin, E. T. (1996). *Focusing-oriented psychotherapy: A manual of the experiential method*. New York: Guilford Press.

Rogers, C. R. (1951). *Client-centered therapy*. Boston: Houghton Mifflin.

Rogers, C. (1957). The necessary and sufficient conditions of therapeutic personality change. *Journal of Consulting Psychology, 21*, 95–103.

Rogers, C. R. (1959). A theory of therapy, personality, and interpersonal relationships as developed in the client-centered framework. In S. Koch (Ed.), *Psychology: A study of science* (Vol. 3, pp. 184–256). New York: McGraw Hill.

Rogers, C. R. (1961). *On becoming a person*. Boston: Houghton Mifflin.

Rogers, C. R. (1980). *A way of being*. Boston: Houghton Mifflin.

Rogers, C. R. (2007). The basic conditions of the facilitative therapeutic relationship. In M. Cooper, M. O'Hara, P. F. Schmid,

& G. Wyatt (Eds.), *The handbook of person-centred psychotherapy and counselling* (pp. 1–5). New York: Palgrave Macmillan.

Toukmanian, S. G., & Brouwers, M. C. (1998). Cultural aspects of self-disclosure and psychotherapy. In S. S. Kazarian & D. R. Evans (Eds.), *Cultural clinical psychology* (pp. 106–126). New York: Oxford University Press.

SUGGESTED READING

Cooper, M., O'Hara, M., Schmid, P. F., & Wyatt, G. (Eds.) (2007). *The handbook of person-centred psychotherapy and counselling.* New York: Palgrave Macmillan.

TRACY A. KNIGHT
Western Illinois University

See also: **Actualization; Experiential Psychotherapy; Humanistic Psychotherapies**

CLINICAL JUDGMENT

Clinical judgment is the cognitive process by which a clinician estimates a clinically relevant parameter for an individual patient or client. The product of that process (the parameter itself) may also be referred to as "a clinical judgment." Although there are many parameters that a clinician might estimate, the two most important classes of parameters are, broadly speaking, probabilities of a clinical event and values for clinical states.

Clinical probability judgment comprises judgments of probabilities in the absence of individuating information and judgments of probabilities conditional on individuating information. In several clinical fields, the clinical judgment of the probability of an outcome is referred to as the "index of suspicion" associated with the outcome. In medicine, clinical probability judgment forms the basis of the process of differential diagnosis, by which a physician establishes a list of possible causes for a patient's symptoms, ordered by their judged likelihood, in order to guide further diagnostic workup.

In the judgment of probabilities absent individuating information, clinicians must estimate the likelihood of some outcome on the basis of their knowledge and previous experience with the outcome (e.g., that a new patient will be schizophrenic, or allergic to penicillin). In principle, the novice clinician ought to do this by retrieving information about the frequency of the outcome that they have learned during their clinical education or from epidemiological studies, while the more experienced clinician is likely to treat the judgment as a pattern-matching task, and assess the likelihood of outcomes on the basis of their similarity to prototypical outcomes with which

the clinician has familiarity and knows the relative frequency. In medicine, Geoff Norman, Georges Bordage, Larry Gruppen, and their colleagues have been influential in the description of the semantic and cognitive structures underlying these pattern-matching judgments.

The psychological literature, particularly the work of Daniel Kahneman and Amos Tversky in the 1970s and 1980s, suggests that probability judgments are often subject to systematic biases as a consequence of the dual processes of the human judgment system, in which one process, termed *System 1*, produces a fast intuitive judgment, while the other, *System 2*, may be invoked simultaneously or thereafter to produce a reasoned, deliberative judgment. To produce its fast judgments, System 1 relies on a set of associative judgmental heuristics, such as the availability heuristic, in which cognitively more available (recent, memorable) events are judged to be more likely than less available events. For example, if a rare disease has recently been discussed in a medical conference or the mainstream media, physicians may overestimate the likelihood that their next patient has the disease. In medicine, students are often given maxims like "when you hear hoofbeats, think of a horse, not a zebra" to encourage them to consider common diseases before rare ones.

In the second case, clinicians attempt to revise their belief about the patient's status on the basis of individuating information, such as patient history, physical examination, or diagnostic testing. For example, a clinical psychologist may wish to estimate the probability that a client is schizophrenic, conditional on the score of the client's MMPI. Bayes' theorem is the normative model for revision of probability judgments on the basis of new evidence, but formal Bayesian calculations require the clinician to specify not only their prior belief about the patient's status (and in some cases, a complete prior probability distribution for the possible statuses) but also the likelihood ratio associated with the individuating information. Moreover, Bayes' theorem makes independent assumptions about the combination of multiple predictors that can be difficult to meet in clinical practice. Hal Arkes and several other psychological researchers have characterized clinical judgment as insufficiently Bayesian, and reported both inappropriate conservatism in judgments (failure to revise beliefs sufficiently) and inappropriate disregard for prior probabilities (resulting in too much revision).

The use of pattern-matching strategies can also lead to systematic biases, notably those resulting from the so-called representativeness heuristic, in which the likelihood of an event is judged by how representative the case is to the prototypical event. For example, the representativeness heuristic may result in a fallacious belief that events even out over the short run (the gambler's fallacy) or that representative combinations of events are more likely to occur than any component event alone (the conjunction fallacy). However, it is unclear how frequently these biases impact clinical judgments in the real world, and how important their impact is.

Probability judgments alone are rarely sufficient to make a clinical decision, because the values of a correct diagnosis, a correctly rejected misdiagnosis, a missed diagnosis (a false negative), and a false positive diagnosis are often different. Accordingly, the other major class of clinical judgment is estimations of the value that patients or clients will place on an outcome. Although clinicians can often directly ask their patients to evaluate the impact of outcomes on their quality of life, in many circumstances, clinicians find themselves acting as surrogate judges of value as well as probability.

As with probability judgments, clinical value judgments have been shown to be susceptible to several systematic biases. Arthur Elstein and his colleagues have documented several of these biases since their research program began in the late 1960s. Although many of these biases are also at work in patients or clients making their own value judgments, some specific studies of clinician value judgments on patients' behalves have also revealed discrepancies. For example, the Elstein et al. 2004 study of 120 prostate cancer patients and their physicians compared patient values for three hypothetical future states and for their own current health with each physician's estimates of the same values for her patient. Although physicians were reasonably accurate in predicting the preference order in which patients would place the four health states, there was no correlation between the utilities provided by the patient and his or her physician within each health state. On the other hand, other studies have found good correspondence between surrogate and personal values in particular aspects of value judgment, such as the rate at which future events are discounted in evaluations.

Accuracy in clinical judgment is presumed to be acquired through experience and to be associated with expertise. Several approaches to the measurement of the quality of clinical judgment have been suggested. The most common is to measure calibration of probability judgments. In a well-calibrated clinician, events judged to have a given probability actually occur with that relative frequency. For example, events that the clinician considers 70% likely should actually occur 70% of the time that the clinician makes the judgment. However, calibration over events alone does not provide information about whether the clinician can distinguish which individual cases are more or less likely to have experienced the event. Accordingly, calibration must be examined across a large number of patients and situations.

Neal Dawson has reviewed three more sophisticated approaches: (1) receiver-operating characteristic curves, (2) mean probability scores, and (3) Brunswickian lens model analyses. The quality of clinical value judgments must usually be assessed by their association with direct judgments of outcome values by the patients or clients involved. Multiattribute utility approaches can also be

applied to attempt to determine if the clinician places the same relative weights on the dimensions of the outcome that their patient or client does.

Because unaided clinical judgment may be subject to several systematic biases, many clinical areas rely on guidelines, scoring rules, or other algorithms as judgmental aids. These aids may call attention to important cues or dimensions to consider in the judgment, warn against the use of irrelevant cues, or even prescribe a formula for combining observed cues and prior beliefs to provide an estimate of the object of judgment. Research by Paul Meehl, Robyn Dawes, and other psychologists has repeatedly demonstrated that even simplified statistical prediction rules, such as simple averages of cue values, can outperform clinical prediction in a variety of situations. Such rules may also be incorporated in computerized decision support systems. Although some guidelines and decision support systems have been successfully introduced in clinical fields, many are applied inconsistently or run afoul of practitioners' beliefs that their clinical judgment is likely to be superior to an algorithm or rule.

SUGGESTED READINGS

Dowie, J. A., & Elstein, A. S. (Eds.). (1988). *Professional judgment: A reader in clinical decision making*. Cambridge, UK: Cambridge University Press.

Hastie, R., & Dawes, R. M. (2001). *Rational choice in an uncertain world: The psychology of judgment and decision making*. Thousand Oaks, CA: Sage Publications.

Kahneman, D. (2003). Maps of bounded rationality: A perspective on intuitive judgment and choice. In T. Fransmyr (Ed.), *Les Prix Nobel. The Nobel Prizes 2002*. Stockholm: Almqvist & Wiksell.

ALAN SCHWARTZ
University of Illinois at Chicago

See also: **Statistical Prediction**

CLINICAL PSYCHOLOGY

For decades clinical psychology has been the most popular specialty area within psychology at the graduate, postgraduate, and professional levels (American Psychological Association, 2001; Mayne, Norcross, & Sayette, 2006). The remarkable amount of public attention that clinical psychologists such as Phillip McGraw (aka Dr. Phil) receive, as well as the frequency with which clinical psychologists are portrayed in movies, television programs, novels, and other media outlets is a testament to the popularity and intrigue of clinical psychology among the general population. This article overviews the field of clinical psychology and provides information about definitions, training, employment settings, activities, subspecialties, and current and future trends.

Definitions

Clinical psychology draws on quality research about human behavior, cognitive processing, emotional functioning, and interpersonal relationships to assist people as individuals, couples, families, and various groups in their struggles with psychological, behavioral, and emotional difficulties to live better quality lives. Thus, clinical psychology applies the knowledge obtained about human functioning to help people better manage, cope, and understand whatever distress they may experience. Clinical psychology integrates biological, psychological, and social influences on behavior to help others in need. Clinical psychology has accordingly been defined as "the aspect of psychological science and practice concerned with the analysis, treatment, and prevention of human psychological disabilities and with the enhancing of personal adjustment and effectiveness" (Rodnick, 1985, p. 1929).

There are of course many professional and paraprofessional fields and disciplines that are focused on helping people with emotional, behavioral, and relational troubles and concerns. Counselors, nurses, psychiatrists, social workers, marriage counselors, peer helpers, and clergy members are just a few of the many professionals, paraprofessionals, and volunteers who use principles of psychology to help others. What makes clinical psychology unique or different? It is primarily the training approach and emphasis in clinical psychology that make these professionals unique relative to others in related fields.

Professional Training

Although many different professionals, paraprofessionals, and volunteers work to help people with their emotional distress and both behavioral and relational problems, clinical psychologists go through a unique training process that equips them well to employ the skills needed to help others. The American Psychological Association (APA) has developed policies and procedures to accredit graduate training programs at the doctoral level to best ensure that students of clinical psychology have the training that is needed to offer state-of-the-art quality services as a professional clinical psychologist. Students interested in becoming clinical psychologists must complete a doctoral program that generally takes at least five years after college to complete. One of the years of training consists of a full year clinical internship usually offered at a major hospital, clinic, or other professional health care or educational setting that allows for rigorous clinical experience with patients as well as intensive supervision by clinical psychologists and other mental health professionals.

Students can apply to PhD (Doctor of Philosophy) clinical psychology programs or the newer PsyD (Doctor of Psychology) graduate training programs. The PhD programs usually focus on more research activities than the PsyD programs, which tend to focus more on clinical experiences and training. However, graduate training and degree programs can differ a great deal from school to school. While most graduate training programs are located in major universities across the United States, Canada, and around the world, in recent decades accredited doctoral programs in clinical psychology have emerged in freestanding professional schools that are not affiliated with any universities.

Graduate training in clinical psychology includes course work in the diagnosis, assessment, and treatment of psychological disorders and troubles as well as courses in multiculturalism, personality, cognition, and the biological, psychological, and social bases of behavior. Courses in research methods and statistics and in history and systems of psychology, as well as a variety of supervised clinical practicum placement activities, round out the training program. Finally, a master's degree thesis and doctoral dissertation are completed on some research or clinical issue. In PhD programs, the thesis and dissertation usually involve an independent research investigation of a clinical psychology topic of interest to the student and the student's advisors.

After graduating from the doctoral program, the aspiring professional clinical psychologist must then complete a postdoctoral fellowship to become license eligible. Some states require one year of postdoctoral training prior to licensing, and other states require two years of study. The postdoctoral fellowship year(s) usually takes place in a major hospital, clinic, or university environment where students complete supervised clinical, research, or other professional activities before they are eligible to become licensed as a clinical psychologist in their respective state or province. The licensing examination process is managed by each state and usually consists of a nationally used written multiple choice examination and a separate examination on the ethical and legal issues that professionals must know to practice clinical psychology in a particular state. Often an oral or essay examination administered by the state is included as well. Once doctoral-level psychologists have completed and passed these tests, they obtain a license to practice as a psychologist in their respective state or province.

In reviewing the training process for clinical psychologists, it is clear that the many years of rigorous study and supervised clinical practice experiences all seek to help students get the education and experience that they need to be able to provide state-of-the-art and high-quality competent professional clinical services to the public. These services might include psychological testing, psychotherapy, and consultation, provided in an ethical, professional, and competent manner. Clinical psychologists' education and training allow them to evaluate and treat clients with a wide range of concerns and diagnoses and to draw on both research findings and clinical best practices that are well established and empirically supported.

Professional Activities

Clinical psychologist are well trained to provide psychotherapy, psychological assessment, including the use of a wide variety of psychological tests, and consultation with other professionals, a broad range of agencies and institutions, and the general public about the science, practice, and utilization of clinical psychology. Psychotherapy may be conducted using a variety of theoretical perspectives, including psychodynamic or psychoanalytic, behavioral, cognitive, humanistic, and family systems approaches. Most contemporary clinical psychologists use a combination of theoretical perspectives and embrace a biopsychosocial view (Engel, 1977). This perspective suggests that most emotional, behavioral, cognitive, and relational problems and issues may have biological, psychological, and social influences that interact in contributing to the manifestation of symptoms, and that these interacting influences need to be taken into consideration when planning and implementing intervention strategies.

Additionally, clinical psychologists must be highly attentive to research results and best practices in professional clinical services to ensure that their clients receive the highest quality professional care. In recent years, empirically supported treatments (Task Force on Promotion and Dissemination of Psychological Procedures, 1995) have become more popular in the form of research supported manualized treatment protocols for helping people with particular psychological and behavioral diagnoses. These might include conditions such as panic disorder, major depression, attention deficit hyperactivity disorder, bulimia, and so forth. Whereas most clinical researchers fully embrace empirically supported treatments, many clinicians have been skeptical of their exclusive use, since many feel that it is impossible to fully manualize treatment services and that most people whom they treat experience a wide range of complex and comorbid problems within the context of a unique set of life circumstances that manualized treatment protocols cannot fully appreciate.

Psychological testing may include diagnostic testing to determine how a confluence of patient symptoms may be understood and appreciated in terms of a particular diagnosis. Behavioral rating scales, questionnaires, structured clinical interviews, symptom checklists, and other measures may be employed to fine-tune one's understanding of the particular disorder or disorders the person is experiencing. Cognitive testing such as neuropsychological and IQ testing may also be used by clinical psychologists to evaluate intellectual and other cognitive processing abilities. Personality and psychological testing using both objective and projective tests may also be administered to more fully understand a person's psychological and personality functioning. These tests may include pencil and paper measures that compare individual scores to national norms, such as the Minnesota Multiphasic Personality Inventory-2 (MMPI-2), or they might include projective instruments in which clients are asked to respond to a series of ambiguous stimuli, such as the famous ink blot test, the Rorschach. There are hundreds of tests available for clinical psychologists to use, and thus professionals must be sure that they are competent and up-to-date on the administration, scoring, and interpretation of the tests that they choose to use in their professional practices. No one can be an expert on all of these available tests, and psychologists must choose selectively which tests they can use competently in their professional activities.

Psychological consultation might include working with other professionals, such as physicians, school teachers and guidance counselors, clergy members, and police officers, among others, to help them best understand the role that psychological functioning and psychopathology might play among those with whom they work or interact. Consultation also occurs with the general public in the form of helping people from all walks of life to better understand the principles of psychology as they apply to their behavioral, emotional, cognitive, and relational questions, concerns, and conflicts.

Professional Employment Settings

Most people may assume that clinical psychologists generally work in private practice environments treating psychotherapy patients. While 35% of clinical psychologists do in fact work in either solo or group practices (Norcross, Karpiak, & Santoro, 2005), 65% do not. About 20% work in academic environments such as colleges and universities (Mayne et al., 2006). Most clinical psychologists in university or college settings are often professors who may actually not treat clients but instead teach courses, conduct independent and collaborative research, and perhaps supervise student research projects and activities. Some clinical psychologists working in academic environments work in university counseling centers that offer brief assessment, treatment, and consultation services to students, faculty, and staff. Other clinical psychologists work in hospitals, medical schools, outpatient clinics, and prisons, in the military, and in business and industry. Some even work for professional sport teams. Therefore, there are a wide variety of employment settings for the contemporary clinical psychologist in addition to independent clinical practice.

Professional Subspecialties

As clinical psychology research and practice has evolved over many years, more and more clinical psychologists have found it necessary to subspecialize in order to provide quality professional services and activities and are thus less likely to be generalists. For example, many clinical psychologists specialize in concerns that are based on age ranges (e.g., young children, teenagers, adults, elderly), while many specialize based on diagnosis (e.g., depression, anxiety, schizophrenia, sexual disorders, personality disorders). Still other clinical psychologists specialize in treatment modalities (e.g., individual, couples, group, or family services). Some focus on health related problems, such as obesity, diabetes, brain injury, or cardiovascular disease, in which lifestyle and stress management services often prove beneficial. Others focus on legal issues such as child custody evaluations, assessment of dangerousness to self and others, and criminal behavior. The professional skills of clinical psychologists can thus be used in a variety of settings with a variety of populations, and, as the field evolves, professionals find themselves specializing and subspecializing in areas of focus where they can fully concentrate their efforts.

Current and Future Trends

Multiculturalism

Multiculturalism and diversity is an important contemporary trend not only in the United States and elsewhere, but specifically for clinical psychologists as well. In fact, it is estimated that half of the American population will consist of ethnic minorities by the year 2050 (U.S. Bureau of the Census, 2000). Psychologists now are required to have at least minimal training in multiculturalism and, depending on their work setting and geographic location, attention to particular differences in cultural background, ethnicity, race, language, and religious differences as well as other aspects of diversity is needed in order to provide quality contemporary clinical psychology services. Furthermore, attention to both gender and sexual orientation differences is also important for contemporary clinical psychologists. As communities continue to become more diverse, clinical psychologists must find ways to provide high quality services that are appropriate to these various diverse populations.

Technological Advances

Technological advances, such as e-mail, cell phones, and Internet products and services, and medical advances in areas such as psychopharmacology, imaging techniques, and human genome and DNA testing, all have an impact on clinical psychology. For example, increasing amounts of psychotropic medication are being used with persons experiencing a wide range of psychological, behavioral, and emotional troubles such as anxiety, depression, attention deficit disorder, eating disorders, psychotic disorders, and so forth. Imaging techniques as well as genetic testing can be effectively used to better diagnose, treat, and

even prevent psychiatric and psychological problems from emerging. Virtual reality treatment has been used to treat a variety of disorders such as phobias and panic (e.g., Annesi, 2001). Clinical psychologists must keep abreast of advances in technology and determine how their clients can be better served using the most updated advances.

Prescription Privileges

Historically, clinical psychologists have not been involved with medication management for their patients. However, in recent years some states have passed legislation allowing appropriately trained clinical psychologists to prescribe psychotropic medications for their patients. These locations currently include Louisiana, New Mexico, and Guam and also the Department of Defense in the United States military. Legislation to allow psychologists to prescribe medication is pending in additional states as well. The APA has developed and endorsed a rigorous training program for psychologists, intended to ensure competence in using psychotropic medications with their patients, and the future is likely to see an increasing number of psychologists in additional states become trained and legally certified to provide these services (American Psychological Association, 1996).

Empirically Supported Treatments

Empirically supported treatments are, by definition, manualized treatments that have adequate research basis for their use (Task Force on Promotion and Dissemination of Psychological Procedures, 1995). In recent years, these treatment protocols as previously noted have received a great deal of attention, and most students in clinical psychology are now being trained to use these manualized treatments. During contemporary times, when more standardized and research supported services are being demanded by health care facilities, insurance carriers, and patients themselves, it is important to offer quality psychological services that are well established with quality research support. As also previously noted, however, many clinicians are skeptical of these empirically supported treatments, because they generally do not take into consideration the highly unique nature of individual clients and their unique life circumstances (Plante, Boccaccini, & Andersen, 1998).

REFERENCES

American Psychological Association (1996). *Recommended postdoctoral training in psychopharmacology for prescription privileges.* Washington, DC: Author.

American Psychological Association. (2001). *Directory of the American Psychological Association, 2001 edition.* Washington, DC: Author.

Annesi, J. J. (2001). Effects of music, television, and combination entertainment systems on distraction, exercise adherence, and physical output in adults. *Canadian Journal of Behavioural Science, 33,* 193–202.

Engel, G. L. (1977). The need for a new medical model: A challenge for biomedicine. *Science, 196,* 129–136.

Mayne, T. J., Norcross, J. C., & Sayette, M. A. (2006). *Insider's guide to graduate programs in clinical and counseling psychology: 2006/2007 edition.* New York: Guilford Press.

Norcross, J. C., Karpiak, C. P., & Santoro, S. M. (2005). Clinical psychologists across the years: The division of clinical psychology from 1960– 2003. *Journal of Clinical Psychology, 61,* 1467–1483.

Plante, T. G., Boccaccini, M., & Andersen, E. (1998). Attitudes concerning professional issues impacting psychotherapy practice among members of the American Board of Professional Psychology. *Psychotherapy, 35,* 34–42.

Rodnick, E. H. (1985). Clinical psychology. In H. I. Kaplan & B. J. Sadock. *Comprehensive textbook of psychiatry,* (4th ed.). (pp. 1929–1935). Baltimore, MD: Williams & Wilkins.

Task Force on Promotion and Dissemination of Psychological Procedures (1995). Training in and dissemination of empirically validated psychological treatments: Report and recommendations. *Clinical Psychologist, 48,* 3–23.

U.S. Bureau of the Census (2000). *Census of population and housing summary* (Tape File 1C, CD-ROM). Washington, DC: Government Printing Office.

SUGGESTED READINGS

Hall, J., & Llewelyn, S. (2006). *What is clinical psychology?* London: Oxford University Press.

Plante, T. G. (2005). *Contemporary clinical psychology* (2nd ed.). Hoboken, NJ: John Wiley & Sons.

Routh, D. K., & deRubeis, R. J. (Eds.). (1998). *The science of clinical psychology: Accomplishment and future directions.* Washington, DC: American Psychological Association.

Stricker, G., Widiger, T. A., & Weiner, I. B. (2003). *Handbook of Psychology, Vol. 8, Clinical Psychology.* Hoboken, NJ: John Wiley & Sons.

THOMAS G. PLANTE
Santa Clara University and
Stanford University School of Medicine

See also: Clinical Psychology, Graduate Training in; Clinical Psychology, Historical Roots of

CLINICAL PSYCHOLOGY, GRADUATE TRAINING IN

Graduate training in clinical psychology is based on the science of psychology. To that end, all programs provide education in the broad and general foundational areas of psychology, which include the social, biological, cognitive, and affective aspects of behavior as well as human development. Specific training in the area of clinical psychology centers on diagnosing and defining problems through psychological assessment and measurement, implementing intervention strategies, providing consultation and supervision, and evaluating the efficacy of interventions.

Although less common, individuals may pursue graduate training resulting in a master's degree in clinical psychology. Such programs award either the MA (usually when no thesis is required) or the MS (a thesis is typically required). In either case, graduates are prepared for practice-oriented settings, via coursework and practicum experiences, but in most states such individuals are prohibited from using the title of psychologist. The term psychologist is usually protected by legislation to refer to an individual with a doctoral degree, either PhD or PsyD, in psychology.

More typically, training in clinical psychology is at the doctoral level. Preparation for doctoral training in psychology generally involves earning an undergraduate degree in psychology. Students are also expected to have a strong grade-point average, good scores on the Graduate Record Examination, relevant research and/or applied experiences, and excellent letters of recommendation. A master's degree in psychology is rarely a prerequisite for admission to a doctoral program. Programs vary in their emphasis on different aspects of the undergraduate record, but nearly all will look at these basic areas. For more information about admission criteria and processes, the interested reader is encouraged to read "A Guide to Getting Into Graduate School," which is posted on the website of the Education Directorate of the American Psychological Association (APA) (http://www.apa.org/ed/getin.html).

Doctoral programs in clinical psychology are eligible for consideration of accreditation by the APA. Accreditation ensures that graduates of accredited programs will meet the minimal standards of training required for entry-level practice in most states. A list of currently accredited programs is maintained by the Office of Program Consultation and Accreditation of the APA (http://www.apa.org/ed/accreditation/).

Historical Traditions within Doctoral Training

The oldest tradition is frequently referred to as the "Boulder Model," whose name derives from a conference held in Boulder, Colorado, in 1949. Participants at that conference asserted that doctoral training in psychology should only be done at university settings and not in professional schools, as had already been done in training related to medicine and dentistry. They established the expectation that all graduates earn a Doctor of Philosophy (PhD) with a focus on clinical psychology. The Boulder Model emphasized that equal weight should be given to training in psychological research and training in clinical practice.

In 1973, an alternative training approach was proposed at a conference held in Vail, Colorado. What became known as the "Vail Model" encouraged the development of schools of professional psychology, which would offer a doctoral degree in psychology (PsyD) and in which the focus of training would be primarily on clinical practice, with less emphasis on psychological research. In the years that followed, numerous professional schools were developed in this tradition.

The 1980s and 1990s saw a growth of both Boulder-style, university-based programs and Vail-style, freestanding professional schools. This made it more difficult to distinguish between training programs. For example, some Vail tradition programs were established in university settings, and most freestanding professional schools developed PhD programs alongside their already established PsyD programs. Many of these professional school PhD programs were more practice focused than research focused, and some university programs became more science based than practice based. The difference between the PhD and PsyD degrees became less meaningful as a result.

Contemporary Models of Training

As a function of this confusion, training programs today are not easily distinguished from one another based on degree offered (PhD or PsyD) or setting (university based or professional school). Today, programs typically define themselves around one of three training models that are not necessarily linked to degree or setting: scholar-practitioner, scientist-practitioner, and clinical-scientist.

The scholar-practitioner model is more consistent with the Vail history, but it can be seen in both PsyD and PhD programs. There is a greater emphasis in these training programs on clinical practice as informed by the science of psychology. Students are trained to become quality consumers of research. The training council most closely associated with scholar-practitioner programs is the National Council of Schools and Programs of Professional Psychology (NCSPP; http://www.ncspp.info/index.html).

The scientist-practitioner model is most closely derived from the Boulder history, but there is an important distinction. The Boulder model stated that students should be trained in both the science of psychology and the practice of psychology, but it allowed for such training to be distinct, one from the other. The contemporary scientist-practitioner model requires that training in these two areas be fully integrated with one another, so that science and practice are truly interdependent. Scientist-practitioner programs are represented by the Council of University Directors of Clinical Psychology (CUDCP; http://www.cudcp.org).

The clinical-scientist model places greater emphasis on the development of research skills designed to prepare students for careers in clinical research settings. Students in these programs are trained in practice skills, but the emphasis is on the development of scientists rather than practitioners. Clinical science programs are represented by the Academy of Psychological Clinical Science (APCS; http://psych.arizona.edu/apcs/index.php).

Training Experiences

Training is accomplished via two primary mechanisms: didactic instruction (e.g., coursework, colloquia) and practica (e.g., clinical, research), totaling approximately 90 credit hours completed over five to seven years.

With respect to didactic instruction, students in training can expect to complete approximately 90 credit hours (i.e., about 30 courses) focusing on the broad and general areas of psychology, coursework specific to clinical psychology, and specialty electives. The specific coursework offerings vary by program. There is more agreement among programs with respect to the broad and general areas and greater diversity in offerings with respect to specialty training (e.g., clinical child, clinical health, forensic psychology, neuropsychology, and so on).

Coursework in doctoral training is only a portion of the degree requirements, as required practica (i.e., clinical and, possibly, research) comprise a significant portion of the doctoral training experience. One might expect to spend two to three years in clinical practicum settings on a part-time basis (10 to 20 hours per week) accruing face-to-face client contact hours under supervision.

Research practica vary substantially based on the program model. Some offer a "mentor model" in which students are admitted to doctoral training to work with a specific faculty member for the duration of their doctoral research training. Other programs admit students without consideration of who will mentor the student's research training. Such programs may encourage students to become involved with research teams, work with multiple faculty members on projects, or engage in supervised independent research projects.

Following completion of coursework and practica, two remaining requirements must be met to earn the doctoral degree. One is the completion of a doctoral project, often a dissertation, and the other is completion of an internship. The dissertation is frequently characterized as an independent, but supervised, research project that provides a contribution to the literature on the science of psychology. The format of such a document varies across, and sometimes within, programs. It is commonly expected that the dissertation be underway prior to the start of the clinical internship.

The clinical internship usually occupies the final year of training, regardless of program model, and is typically a full-time, one-year practice-focused experience. Internship training is not usually provided by the degree granting institution and requires a separate competitive application process. Internship programs are separately accredited by APA, and the most sought after internships are members of the Association of Psychology Postdoctoral and Internship Centers (APPIC; http://www.appic.org).

Future Directions in Clinical Training

The above information provides an overview of what is typical in clinical training; however, there exists much diversity in training, and exceptions to any of these general training practices can be found among existing training programs. It is difficult to predict which of the current practices will persist and which will be modified in the coming years. There are a few areas in which debate about best training practices appears to be growing, and we mention three of them here as areas worth watching.

First, at present there is little consensus on distance education and online degree programs; although large numbers of these programs exist, few are accredited, and their outcomes are uncertain. Second, the optimal structure and timing of the internship experience is also an area of considerable attention, with a range of alternative models recently proposed. Third, the role of specialty training within clinical psychology is unclear, with some advocating for specialty training within the doctoral program (e.g., clinical child) and others indicating that it should occur predominantly at the post-doctoral level (e.g., clinical neuropsychology).

SUGGESTED READINGS

Appleby, D., Keenan, J., & Mauer, B. (1999). Applicant characteristics valued by graduate programs in psychology. *Eye on Psi Chi, 3,* 39.

Benjamin, L. T. Jr. (2001). American psychology's struggles with its curriculum: Should a thousand flowers bloom? *American Psychologist, 56,* 735–742.

Landrum, R. E., Jeglum, E. B., & Cashin, J. R. (1994). The decision-making processes of graduate admissions committees in psychology. *Journal of Social Behavior & Personality, 9,* 239–248.

FRANK L. COLLINS, JR.
JENNIFER L. CALLAHAN
University of North Texas

See also: **Association of Psychology Postdoctoral and Internship Centers; Clinical Psychology, Historical Roots of**

CLINICAL PSYCHOLOGY, HISTORICAL ROOTS OF

Clinical psychology is probably the most common specialty within psychology around the world today (Lunt & Portinga, 1996). Its principal aims include the study of psychopathology and its assessment and treatment. Many clinical psychologists are also concerned with the psychological aspects of physical health problems as well. This same territory is shared by a number of other professional disciplines, including psychiatry, social work, mental health nursing, and various types of counseling and psychotherapy. Compared to professionals in these neighboring fields, present-day clinical psychologists are distinctive in the quality of their training in research, behavior therapy, and objective assessment methods.

The earliest influential concepts of what is now considered psychopathology are found in the writings of the Greek physician Hippocrates (circa 460–377 BCE), who was notable for his naturalistic approach to disease. He viewed madness as being like fever, simply a symptom of illness. For example, Hippocrates identified the condition called melancholia as being due to an excess of black bile produced by the pancreas (the very word *melancholia* means "black bile"). Such an imbalance of the internal fluids, or "humors," was treated by administering purgatives, whereas a furious manic state was more likely to be treated by bleeding the patient. Other symptoms of illness mentioned by Hippocrates included ordinary depression (Greek "dysthymia"), phrenitis (fever of the brain), and delirium (irrational talk) associated with acute illness (Hippocrates, 1923).

The specialty of psychiatry did not develop until the eighteenth century, and it did so simultaneously in a number of countries, including England, Italy, France, and the new United States of America. The most famous figure of this era was the physician Philippe Pinel (1745–1826), who was in Paris at the time of the French Revolution. He elaborated the principles of moral treatment of mental patients. The basic idea was that it was not necessary to chain a mental patient to the wall. Instead, one should treat the individual in a kind and considerate way, without coercion. It was during this time that asylums began to be considered as a way of treating the insane and not simply a way of confining them to protect society. In 1838, a French law was passed creating a secular national system of asylums. Soon afterward, formal organizations of "alienists" or psychiatrists developed and began to publish scholarly journals. For example, the organization that became the American Psychiatric Association was founded in 1844.

During the later nineteenth century, modern experimental psychology emerged in Germany, with the founding of Wilhelm Wundt's laboratory in 1879. Psychology in England, including the work of Frances Galton, focused on individual differences. In France, psychology was concerned mainly with psychopathology. It emerged from philosophy but its early practitioners obtained scientific grounding by also taking courses and sometimes degrees from the Faculty of Medicine at the University of Paris.

The first such pioneer was philosopher Hippolyte Taine (1828–1893), who published a treatise on "Intelligence" in 1870 but was unable to obtain an academic post as a psychologist. The philosopher Theodule Ribot (1839–1916) succeed in 1888 in becoming Professor of Experimental and Comparative Psychology at the prestigious College de France. He is considered the founder of modern psychology in France and is remembered for "Ribot's Law," stating that in cases of amnesia, the most recent memories are the ones most likely to be lost. Ribot did no experiments of his own but was known as a synthesizer of the findings of others, mostly physicians and psychiatrists (Brooks, 1998).

Ribot's successor at the College de France was Pierre Janet (1859–1947), who had doctoral degrees in both philosophy and medicine, studying under the famous Paris neurologist, Jean Martin Charcot. Janet had established a psychology laboratory under Charcot at the Salpetriere Hospital. Janet treated thousands of patients during his career and established his own approach known as "psychological analysis." He developed the concept of "dissociation" that is still important in understanding such conditions as hysteria, posttraumatic stress disorder, and multiple personality disorder. Finally, the French experimental psychologist Alfred Binet (1857–1911) developed the first successful intelligence test. Thus, French psychology was probably more important than that in any other country as background for the emergence of the field of clinical psychology in the United States.

In 1896, a psychological clinic was founded at the University of Pennsylvania by Lightner Witmer (1867–1956), a professor there. This event is generally regarded as the origin of the field of clinical psychology. Witmer, who had obtained his doctorate under Wundt, was especially interested in children with learning problems, including those in language, reading, and spelling as well as general academic retardation. What was especially new was his suggestion that psychologists with no formal medical training not only study people but also attempt to help them. He used the techniques being developed by experimental psychologists to study children and worked with teachers, physicians, and others to try to remediate such problems. Witmer trained psychology doctoral students at the University of Pennsylvania in these activities and in 1907 founded a journal, the *Psychological Clinic*, in which he outlined his ideas concerning the new field (Witmer, 1907).

The intelligence test developed by Binet in France in 1905 was quickly translated into English and imported to the United States, where it soon underwent various technical modifications by Lewis M. Terman (1877–1956) and became the Stanford-Binet (Terman, 1916). Administering Binet tests became the most characteristic activity of the first generation of clinical psychologists in the United States. For example, psychologists were incorporated into the clinical teams of the first child guidance clinics primarily as intelligence testers. In 1908, psychologist Henry Goddard founded the first psychology internship program at the Vineland School in New Jersey; the program mainly provided extensive experience in such mental testing. The first organization of clinical psychologists, the American

Association of Clinical Psychologists, founded in Pittsburgh in 1917, had as one of its purposes the staking out of individual mental testing as the professional domain of clinical psychologists (Routh, 1994).

Meanwhile, psychologists at Harvard University and in the Boston area were much influenced by the work of Pierre Janet in France. A physician named Morton Prince founded the *Journal of Abnormal Psychology* in 1906 to publish research in psychopathology and later endowed the Harvard Psychology Clinic to train doctoral students for research in psychopathology. Sigmund Freud visited the United States for the first and only time in 1909, lecturing at Clark University in nearby Worcester, Massachusetts, and the psychoanalytic movement began its rapid growth in the United States. However, clinical training in psychoanalysis in this country was mostly restricted to physicians, and there were many barriers that clinical psychologists had to overcome to occupy such roles.

Before World War II, clinical psychology was a small field. However, even before 1945, the repertoire of clinical psychologists in the area of mental testing expanded greatly, establishing its pattern for the remainder of the century. Herman Rorschach (1884–1922), a Swiss psychiatrist, developed the Rorschach inkblot test. In 1943, psychologist Starke R. Hathaway (1903–1984) and psychiatrist J. C. McKinley published the first edition of the Minnesota Multiphasic Personality Inventory. The *Journal of Consulting Psychology*, now one of the premier journals in clinical psychology, was established in 1937; during its first decade, it was devoted largely to professional issues and to advances in mental testing.

After World War II, clinical psychology was newly supported by government funds and expanded enormously. In the United States, the Veterans Administration and the National Institute of Mental Health requested information about which universities provided adequate training in clinical psychology. The American Psychological Association responded by setting up an official system for accrediting training in clinical psychology. In 1949, the Boulder Conference set the pattern for such programs, which sought to train "scientist-practitioners." In Britain and in the Scandinavian countries, clinical psychologists began to be incorporated into the national health systems.

In this era, clinical psychologists have generally expanded their scope of practice well beyond mental testing to include various intervention activities. In the postwar United States, the most influential clinical psychologist involved in psychotherapy was no doubt Carl R. Rogers (1902–1987). Other psychologists, such as Hans Eysenck (1916–1997) in Britain, launched the behavior therapy movement.

In conclusion, clinical psychology has emerged from its first century of existence as a large psychological specialty, beginning with a focus on the study, assessment, and treatment of psychopathology and later expanding to the psychological aspects of physical health problems.

REFERENCES

Brooks, J. I. III. (1998). *The eclectic legacy: Academic philosophy and the human sciences in nineteenth century France.* Newark: University of Delaware Press.

Hippocrates. (1923). With an English trans. by W. H. S. Jones. 4 vols. London: Heinemann.

Lunt, I., & Portinga, H. (1996). Internationalizing psychology. *American Psychologist, 51,* 504–508.

Routh, D. K. (1994). *Clinical psychology since 1917: Science, practice, and organization.* New York: Plenum.

Terman, L. M. (1916). *The measurement of intelligence.* Boston: Houghton Mifflin.

Witmer, L. (1907). Clinical psychology. *Psychological Clinic, 1,* 1–9.

DONALD K. ROUTH
Florida Gulf Coast University

See also: **Clinical Psychology, Graduate Training in; Clinical Psychology, Historical Roots of**

CLUSTER ANALYSIS

Cluster analysis refers to a family of related techniques that are used to create groups of objects that, in some sense, minimize the distance between the objects within a cluster (Arabie, Hubert, & DeSoete, 1996; Hartigan, 1975). It is generally viewed as a type of exploratory data analysis in which the clusters emerge from the analytical procedures. Cluster analysis has been used extensively since the 1970s by social scientists, market researchers, numerical taxonomists, and many others. Cluster analysis is also at the heart of many current approaches in machine learning, pattern recognition, and data mining.

Clustering algorithms can be divided into *hierarchical* methods and *partitional* methods. Hierarchical methods result in a dendrogram in which the entire family of nested clusters is represented by the clustering solution. Such methods are typically agglomerative, in which items are combined together into larger sets, as opposed to divisive methods, which iteratively split clusters into smaller sets, or optimization methods, which fit an optimal tree structure directly through least-squares, branch-and-bound, or a related optimization method. In contrast to hierarchical methods, partitional clustering algorithms find a single optimal partition of the data. The most commonly used partitional method is called *k*-means, in which the number of clusters (*k*) is specified ahead of time. Partitional methods are generally more efficient than hierarchical methods and have been adapted to run with extremely large datasets in data mining, image analysis, and other data-intensive applications.

The use of cluster analysis requires a number of steps, each of which has numerous options, adding to the complexity of choosing the optimal method for any specific clustering problem. These steps include selecting the dataset, selecting the variables from the dataset, weighting or standardizing the variables chosen, selecting the number of clusters, and validating the clustering results. The data are typically in the form of a dissimilarity matrix, which is either collected directly (i.e., *two-way, one-mode* data) or derived from a rectangular matrix (i.e., *two-way, two-mode* data). In the latter case, the data must first be transformed into two-way, one-mode data through a chosen distance function. Various methods exist in assisting with variable selection and weighting, variable standardization, if any, and selection of the number of clusters (Milligan & Hirtle, 2003). Validation typically occurs through either internal analysis, using bootstrapping or other sampling methods, or external analysis, using additional variables not part of the initial cluster analysis.

Cluster analysis has also been used in the field of psychology as model of proximity relationships rather than simply an algorithm for fitting data (Arabie, Hubert, & DeSoete, 1996; Milligan & Hirtle, 2003). This approach based on the use of additive trees and has been used successfully in cognitive psychology to account for mental structures that are best described through feature-based knowledge representations. Additive trees are governed by the additive inequality, in contrast to the ultrametric inequality that governs dendrograms, and thus are less restrictive data structure.

REFERENCES

Arabie, P., Hubert, L. J., & De Soete, G. (Eds.). (1996). *Clustering and classification.* River Edge, NJ: World Scientific.

Hartigan, J. A. (1975). *Clustering algorithms.* New York: John Wiley & Sons.

Milligan, G. W., & Hirtle, S. C. (2003). Clustering and classification methods. In J. A. Schinka & W. F. Velicer, (Eds.), I. B. Weiner (Ed.-in-Chief), *Handbook of Psychology, Vol. 2: Research Methods in Psychology* (pp. 165–186). Hoboken: John Wiley & Sons.

STEPHEN C. HIRTLE
University of Pittsburgh

See also: **Factor Analysis; Principal Component Analysis**

COACHING

Before 1990, coaching as a profession was recognized only in connection with mentoring corporate executives (Williams & Menendez, 2007). Within the last 15 years, however, coaching has come to be considered one of the fastest growing trends in the areas of health and well-being (Williams & Anderson, 2006). At present coaching encompasses a growing number of specialties as diverse as getting adolescents to do their homework and assisting those leaving the workplace to create meaningful retirements.

Coaching is a solution-focused enterprise in which a coaching professional partners with a client to design the client's future. It is not what the coach perceives to be in the client's best interest, but the client's own goals for the future that are the sole focus. Utilizing basic coaching skills such as a belief in the brilliance of the client, establishing a relationship based on trust, active listening, powerful questioning, reframing, creating awareness, and designing action plans, coaches elicit commitments from clients, who are held accountable for follow-through.

The International Coach Federation (ICF) was formally organized in 1995 to establish coaching as a profession distinct from any other helping profession. ICF has become the largest and most recognized organization in coaching. The ICF Code of Ethics defines coaching in the following way:

Professional Coaching is an ongoing relationship that helps people produce extraordinary results in their lives, careers, businesses and organizations. Through the process of coaching, clients deepen their learning, improve their performance, and enhance their quality of life. In each meeting, the client chooses the focus of the conversation, while the coach listens and contributes observations and questions. This interaction creates clarity and moves the client into action. Coaching accelerates the client's progress by providing greater focus and awareness of choice. Coaching concentrates on where clients are now and what they are willing to do to get where they want to be in the future ... (http://www.coachfederation.org/ICF/For+Current=Members/Ethical+Guidelines/).

Clients considered suitable for coaching must be considered *whole* in the sense of being psychologically healthy (Williams & Davis, 2002), and referrals for therapy are ethically required if psychological problems are detected (ICF Code of Ethics, Standard 20). Despite the firm distinction drawn between coaching and psychotherapy, coaching owes much to psychological theorists in its foundation and practice.. Not only the theories of Sigmund Freud, but his discovery of the "talking cure" provided the professional world with the unique idea that two people, one a professional and the other in need of assistance, could engage in an ongoing dialogue to initiate significant and beneficial change. The change, not unlike coaching today, involved creating self-awareness. Carl Jung's symbolism and more holistic, spiritual understanding also contribute substantially to what coaches are taught and how they practice, as does Jung's focus on the individual's innate potential for positive growth and the power of an active, focused

relationship between the therapist and patient (Sollod & Monte, 2009, chap. 5; Williams & Anderson, 2006).

William James, the father of psychological theory in America, proposed the notion that people often mask or bury their brilliance (Williams & Anderson, 2006, p. 5). Professional coaching also begins with a belief in the brilliance of the client. Whereas James referred to as people burying their brilliance, coaches use terms such as *gremlins* to refer to beliefs and behaviors that clients must move beyond (Carson, 2003). Alfred Adler viewed ubiquitous early feelings of inferiority as giving rise to feelings of weakness and helplessness in adults that must be overcome in order for individuals not to engage in maladaptive patterns of behavior (Sollod & Monte, 2009, chap. 4). Adler also advocated the clinician taking an active problem-solving role in working with patients, which is akin not only to current day counseling, but to professional coaching as well. Likewise, in measuring the skill of coaches, ICF identifies four categories of core competencies, actions in which the coach must demonstrate proficiency. The core competency headings are (1) setting the foundation, (2) co-creating the relationship, (3) communicating effectively, and (4) facilitating learning and results. (http://coachfederation.com/ICF/For+Current+Members/Credentialing/Why+a+Credential/).

The behaviorism of B. F. Skinner and John Watson added the important notion that change can be measured and brought about with specific methods (Peltier, 2001). Abraham Maslow and Carl Rogers turned from the mechanistic approach of behaviorism to the phenomenological aspects of the human experience, the former identifying a hierarchy of people's needs and values and the proclivity of humans to pursue self-actualization, and the latter initiating a client-centered approach and unconditional positive regard (Williams & Anderson, 2006; Williams & Menendez, 2007). These tenets are considered basic to coaching theory and technique. In fact, the work of Maslow and Rogers provided the foundation for humanistic psychology and the human potential movement from which coaching is a more direct outgrowth. As in coaching, Maslow looked at the whole person rather than fragmented parts and studied healthy personality, moving away from the notion of pathology. In addition, Martin Seligman's promotion of positive psychology is an important contribution to current day coaching (Williams & Menendez, 2007).

Is coaching a fad, or is it here to stay? Indications are that coaching has created a permanent niche among the helping professions. The ICF currently has approximately 15,000 individual members in more than 80 countries. It certifies individual coaches and more than 50 independent coaching institutes, as well as certificate and degree granting programs in colleges and universities (Williams & Menendez, 2007). Coaching will never obviate the need for practitioners who work with diagnosable mental conditions. It does add an important service to those who are psychologically healthy, yet want to create more possibilities in their lives.

REFERENCES

Carson, R. (2003). (Rev. ed.). *Taming your gremlin.* New York: HarperCollins.

Peltier, B. (2001). *The psychology of executive coaching: Theory and application.* New York: Brunner-Routledge.

Sollod, R. N., & Monte, C. F. (2009). *Beneath the mask: An introduction to theories of personality* (8th ed.). Hoboken, NJ: John Wiley & Sons.

Williams, P., & Anderson, S. K. (Eds.). (2006). *Law & ethics in coaching: How to solve and avoid difficult problems in your practice.* Hoboken, NJ: John Wiley & Sons.

Williams, P., & Davis, D. C. (2002). *Therapist as life coach.* New York: W.W. Norton & Co.

Williams, P., & Menendez, D. S. (2007). *Becoming a professional life coach.* New York: W.W. Norton & Co.

KAREN COLBY WEINER
Southfield, MI

See also: Positive Psychology; Quality of Life

COCAINE-RELATED DISORDERS

Cocaine, produced from the coca plant, is self-administered as a reinforcing substance in various preparations (e.g., coca leaves, coca paste, cocaine hydrochloride, and cocaine alkaloid). These preparations differ in potency due to varying levels of purity and route of administration. Chewing coca leaves or smoking of coca paste in combination with tobacco and marijuana is common among native populations in Central and South America, where coca is grown. Cocaine hydrochloride powder is usually "snorted" through the nostrils or dissolved in water and injected intravenously, and it is sometimes mixed with heroin, which is called a "speedball." "Crack" is cocaine alkaloid that is extracted from its powdered salt by processing it into small "rocks." Crack is easily vaporized and inhaled, and its effects have a rapid onset. Crack also can be broken down with citrus juice and injected, but it is most commonly smoked. Cocaine mixed with alcohol results in the production by the liver of a potent stimulant, Cocaethylene.

Cocaine-related disorders are defined in the *Diagnostic and Statistical Manual of Mental Disorders* (DSM-IV-TR; American Psychiatric Association, 2000). They manifest as a cluster of cognitive, behavioral, and physical symptoms resulting from continued use despite negative consequences. Two categories of symptoms are cocaine-use disorders (cocaine dependence and abuse) and cocaine-induced disorders (cocaine intoxication and withdrawal; cocaine-induced delirium; psychotic, mood, anxiety, sexual, and sleep disorders). Cocaine intoxication includes one or more of the following: euphoria with enhanced vigor, gregariousness, hyperactivity, restlessness, hypervigilance, talkativeness, anxiety, tension, grandiosity, stereotyped and repetitive behavior, and impaired judgment. These behavioral manifestations are accompanied by two or more of the following physical symptoms: tachycardia or bradycardia, papillary dilation, elevated or lowered blood pressure, perspiration or chills, nausea or vomiting, psychomotor agitation or retardation, weight loss, respiratory depression, chest pain, cardiac arrhythmias, confusion, or seizures. Tolerance and withdrawal are characteristics of cocaine dependency; overdose and premature death have been documented among users of cocaine.

In 2006, 6 million Americans age 12 and older abused cocaine in any form and 1.5 million abused crack at least once in the year prior to being surveyed (SAMHSA Office of Applied Studies, 2007). Although the prevalence of addictive drug use among youth has fallen recently, one stimulant drug that did not show a decline in 2006 was cocaine. Cocaine use reached a recent peak among teens in the late 1990s, declined for a year or two, and has held relatively level in recent years. Currently, the annual prevalence ranges between 2% and 5% in grades 8, 10, and 12 (Monitoring the Future, 2007, 2008). Among adults, crack is the predominant form of cocaine used across the United States, as judged by the proportions of primary treatment admissions who smoked the drug (Community Epidemiology Work Group, 2007). High proportions of the heroin abusers admitted to drug abuse treatment programs also reported cocaine/crack as their secondary drug of abuse. Crack-cocaine has been associated with homelessness, HIV risk, mental disorders, crime and arrests, sex trade, drug-exposed neonates, and overdose. Cocaine is often implicated, along with other drugs/alcohol, in emergency room deaths.

Treatment for cocaine disorders was initially adopted, unsuccessfully, from existing residential outpatient addiction treatment models primarily for alcoholism. Targeted efforts then were launched to discover a medication to treat cocaine disorders and more effective psychosocial approaches. To date, the most empirically supported cocaine abuse intervention demonstrating reliable efficacy in rigorous randomized trials conducted over a 15-year period is voucher-based reinforcement treatment or contingency management (Higgins, Silverman, & Heil, 2008). Contingency management has been found to be effective not only alone, but also in combination with other intensive counseling, narcotic substitution, and mental health interventions in community drug-free and methadone maintenance clinics. Voucher-based reinforcement approaches also have been successful with special populations, including homeless persons (Schumacher et al., 2007).

As of the time of this writing, no medications are approved by the Food and Drug Administration for treatment of cocaine dependence. However, several medications have shown promise in double-blind, placebo-controlled clinical trials, including abstinence initiation medications (GABA Enhancers, Disulfran, and TA-CD Vaccine) (Kampman, 2008). Current evidence-based behavioral interventions are projected to be the best courses of action for the treatment of cocaine dependence.

Research into cocaine dependence is supported in large part by the National Institutes of Health, National Institute on Drug Abuse (NIDA). Studies funded by NIDA's Division of Basic Neuroscience and Behavioral Research, for example, address the following areas: genetic (loci of genetic variations among addicted individuals); developmental (effect of drugs on prenatal development and developing brains of children and adolescents); behavioral (consequences of drug abuse on behavior and cognition for treatment and prevention); and neurobiological (processes and mechanisms in the brain and nervous system underlying addiction). Recent research in the area of cocaine and cue-induced brain activity found that when cocaine-addicted patients watched a drug-related videotape, activation of the posterior cingulate cortex (highlighted by fMRI imaging) occurred more quickly in those who subsequently relapsed (Kosten et al., 2006). In the future, patients' brain scans may help clinicians tailor treatment to improve therapeutic outcomes.

REFERENCES

American Psychiatric Association. (2000). *Diagnostic and statistical manual* (4th ed., text rev.). Washington, DC: Author.

Community Epidemiology Work Group. (2007). *Epidemiologic trends in drug abuse: Highlights and executive summary, proceedings of the community epidemiology work group* (Vol. 1). Bethesda, MD: U.S. Department of Health and Human Services.

Higgins, S. T., Silverman, K., & Heil, S. H. (2008). *Contingency management in substance abuse treatment*. New York: Guilford Press.

Kampman, K. M. (2008). The search for medications to treat stimulant dependence. *Addiction Science and Clinical Practice, 4*(2), 28–35.

Kosten, T. R., Scanley, B. E., Tucker, K. A., Oliveto, A., Prince, C., Sinha, R., et al. (2006). Cue-induced brain activity changes and relapse in cocaine-dependent patients. *Neuropsychopharmacology, 31*(3), 644–650.

Monitoring the Future 2007. (2008). Retrieved April 10, 2008, from http://monitoringthefuture.org/data/07data.html#2007data-drugs.

SAMHSA Office of Applied Studies. (2007). National survey on drug use and health 2006 (Publication. Retrieved March 20, 2008, from Substance Abuse and Mental Health Services Administration Office of Applied Studies: http://www.oas.samhsa.gov/prescription/LOF.htm.)

Schumacher, J. E., Milby, J. B., Wallace, D., Meehan, D. C., Kertesz, S., & Vuchinich, R., et al. (2007). Meta-analysis of day treatment and contingency-management dismantling research: Birmingham homeless cocaine studies (1990–2006). *Journal of Consulting and Clinical Psychology, 75*(5), 823–828.

JOSEPH E. SCHUMACHER
University of Alabama School of Medicine

JESSE B. MILBY
University of Alabama at Birmingham

DAVID S. BATEY
University of Alabama School of Medicine

See also: **Addiction; Drug Addiction**

COEFFICIENT ALPHA

Because test scores are known to contain errors, test developers and administrators must concern themselves with test score consistency (or reliability). Such concerns are commonly investigated using coefficient alpha, an internal consistency reliability coefficient that is computed as follows:

$$\frac{k}{k-1}\left(1 - \frac{\sum_i s_i^2}{s_t^2}\right)$$

where k is the number of test items, s_i^2 is the variance of scores on item i, and s_t^2 is the variance of total test scores. Alpha is generally applicable for studying reliability on a single test at one point in time from multiple observations on individuals (e.g., scores on test items, task-performance ratings from multiple judges).

In the mid-twentieth century, dissatisfaction with split-half reliability coefficients, which depend on the particular splitting used to compute them (e.g., first and second half, odds and evens), stimulated efforts to develop alternative reliability coefficients that could be computed using data from a single test administration. In his landmark publication "Coefficient Alpha and the Internal Structure of Tests," Cronbach (1951) established alpha as preeminent among internal consistency reliability coefficients. Cronbach demonstrated that alpha is the mean of all possible split-half reliability coefficients and showed that the Kuder-Richardson formula 20, which preceded alpha, was a special case of alpha for dichotomous data. Alpha estimates the lower bound of the proportion of variance in test scores attributable to all common factors underlying item responses. Thus, alpha does not require the assumption that all items in a test be unidimensional (i.e., measuring only one aspect of individual differences), so it is applicable to common educational tests that measure multiple abilities across items.

Alpha is sometimes misinterpreted as a coefficient of precision, which reflects the correlation between scores from one administration with a hypothetical second administration of the same test when no changes in the examinees have occurred. Instead, alpha is a coefficient of equivalence, because it represents the correlation between two different tests. In this case, the two tests consist of k items randomly drawn from a universe of items like those in the test and administered at the same time. However, alpha is a lower bound to the coefficient of precision, because the correlation between a test and itself would always be higher than the correlation between two different tests. Alpha does not provide any indication of test score inconsistency that might result if repeated testings were separate in time.

In a 2004 article published posthumously, "My Current Thoughts on Coefficient Alpha and Successor Procedures," Cronbach (2004) expressed doubt that alpha was the best way to study reliability. Instead, alpha should be viewed as part of a larger system of reliability analysis known as *generalizability theory*, which affords analyses of complex measurement data using random-effects analysis of variance in order to estimate variance components arising from measurement facets (e.g., items, occasions, raters) and their interactions in order to explain observed score variance. Further, results from such studies may be used to compute alpha-like reliability coefficients and investigate the effects of changing the number of items (or raters or occasions).

REFERENCES

Cronbach, L. J. (1951). Coefficient alpha and the internal structure of tests. *Psychometrika, 16*(3), 297–334.

Cronbach, L. J., & Shavelson, R. J. (2004). My current thoughts on coefficient alpha and successor procedures. *Educational and Psychological Measurement, 64*(3), 391–418.

SUGGESTED READINGS

Haertel, E. H. (2006). Reliability. In R. L. Brennan (Ed.), *Educational Measurement* (pp. 65–110). Westport, CT: Praeger.

Shavelson, R. J., & Webb, N. M. (1991). *Generalizability theory: A primer*. Newbury Park, CA: Sage.

JEFFREY T. STEEDLE
Council for Aid to Education, New York, NY

RICHARD J. SHAVELSON
Stanford University

See also: **Psychometrics; Reliability**

COEFFICIENT OF AGREEMENT (See Kappa Coefficient)

COGNITIVE BEHAVIORAL ANALYSIS SYSTEM OF PSYCHOTHERAPY

The Cognitive Behavioral Analysis System of Psychotherapy (CBASP; Keller, McCullough, Klein, Arnow, Dunner, Gelenberg et al., 2000; McCullough, 1984, 2000, 2006) is a psychological treatment program developed specifically for chronically depressed patients (Klein, in press; McCullough, Klein, Borian, Howland, Riso, Keller, et al., 2003). In the *Diagnostic and Statistical Manual of Mental Disorders* (DSM-IV-TR; American Psychiatric Association, 2000), chronic depression is a unipolar affective disorder lasting a minimum of two years; without adequate treatment, and the patient more often than not faces a lifetime of psychosocial disability. Early (prior to age 21) and late-onset are the diagnostic descriptors indicating when the disorder began. The clinical course among chronically depressed patients includes several types of profiles. Two of the more common ones are (1) an early-onset of dysthymia beginning at 12–13 years of age followed by a continuing course that includes one or more episodes of major depression—a clinical profile labeled "double depression"; and (2) a late-onset course exacerbated at age 25–26 with a major depressive episode that almost never fully remits. Approximately 23% of late-onset adults who have their first episode do not recover, and the course becomes chronic. Without adequate regimes of medication and psychotherapy, prognosis for recovery for both types is poor, and even with treatment, the ever-present danger of relapse and recurrence remains a serious threat throughout the lifespan.

The longstanding course of chronic depression, often coupled with a developmental history characterized by maltreatment at the hands of significant others, results in clinicians facing entrenched and refractory emotional-cognitive-behavioral habit patterns. This means that the CBASP psychotherapist must address issues that denote more than just a cognitive or thinking disorder. Emotional abuse and trauma characterize the patient whose mood state is highly resistant to change (Klein, Shankman, & Rose, 2006). Refractory emotional patterns have to be resolved in addition to the individual's cognitive and behavioral patterns; thus, a broadband attack that tackles multiple intrapersonal and interpersonal problems is required (Howland, 1996). CBASP offers a broadband treatment approach addressing the developmental-intrapersonal issues concomitantly with the interpersonal ones.

Chronically depressed patients enter treatment demoralized and with prominent helplessness and hopelessness symptoms. Both demoralization and the helplessness-hopelessness dilemma point to a core issue. Pervasive and chronic interpersonal avoidance patterns and a failure to perceive that one's behavior has predictable interpersonal consequences render these individuals socially isolated and perceptually alone. The interpersonal ripple effects of this lifestyle are catastrophic and leave family members, caring friends, spouses, and work colleagues helpless to aid the individual. Patients begin therapy entrapped in an egocentric circle of helplessness and hopelessness with no exit.

Motivation to change at treatment outset is inhibited by generalized outlook of despair which patients frequently express with such statements as, "It doesn't matter what I do, I stay depressed." The social skill deficits originating from a chronic history of interpersonal avoidance coupled with the fact that patients are unable to recognize that the way they behave literally pushes others away make their despairing statement a valid self-diagnosis!

Three CBASP Techniques

CBASP psychotherapy seeks to accomplish two overarching goals. The first goal is to teach patients to recognize and identify the interpersonal consequences of their behavior. Situational analysis (SA; McCullough, 2000) is the technique used for this purpose. In SA, patients learn through repeated practice to focus on specific and problematic interpersonal encounters. Approaching interpersonal conflicts in this specific manner helps clinicians counter-condition the patient's tendency to talk in a general, global matter (e.g., "No one could ever care for me," "Nothing will ever work out," "I'll always fail," and so on). SA also makes explicit how one contributes directly to negative interpersonal problems. Over time, the consistent message of SA finally gets through to the patient: If you tire of interpersonal outcomes that you describe in SA, then you must change your behavior! Achieving a perceived functionality perspective denotes that patients understand that the negative interpersonal consequences they report are self-productions. Recognizing that one's behavior affects others in malevolent ways has another positive outcome—it motivates persons to behave differently. Reacting to others in more positive ways predictably results in more desirable situational outcomes, and best of all, it leads to patients feeling better.

The second overarching goal of CBASP is to socialize the patient through therapist disciplined personal involvement (McCullough, 2000, 2006), which usually results in persons experiencing more positive outcomes. The rationale for this goal arises from the severe social isolation and the trauma and abuse history many chronically depressed patients describe. Disciplined personal involvement is a novel therapeutic role used in CBASP to deal with the person's idiosyncratic problems. An extensive description of the personal involvement role is found in McCullough's 2006 book.

As noted earlier, achieving the second therapy goal requires CBASP practitioners to engage patients on a disciplined personal involvement level (McCullough, 2000, 2006). This means that therapists become proactive and nonneutral participants in the treatment process. For example, patients are taught to discriminate between the consequences received at the hands of maltreating significant others (caregivers) and the salubrious ones they experience with the CBASP psychotherapist. The Interpersonal discrimination exercise (IDE; McCullough, 2000, 2006) is the technique used to accomplish this goal. IDE does three things: (1) it ensures that the patients learn to discriminate between the person of the therapist and others who have hurt them; (2) it heals early emotional trauma through the salubrious responsivity of the practitioner; and (3) it makes explicit the fact that growth possibilities are now possible because of the absence of the earlier toxic interactions that were so damaging. All of these outcomes lead patients to feel better about themselves and others.

CBASP practitioners utilize a second disciplined personal involvement technique called contingent personal responsivity (CPR; McCullough, 2006). In many cases patients' interpersonal behavior in the early sessions precludes clinicians from conducting CBASP therapy. Many patients come to treatment with interpersonal habits that compete with the work of therapy. For example, some persons make blatantly hostile comments about the practitioner's competence, the therapy model, the therapy setting itself, the clinic staff, or the therapist's integrity. Other patients make overt sexual comments or overtures that are intended to detour the direction of treatment. Withdrawn or disassociating patients often refuse to make eye contact. Patients often "talk over" the clinician, disregarding his or her comments, some patients are patently rude and inattentive, while some actively refuse to answer questions they are asked and change the subject at every opportunity. All of these behaviors inhibit the administration of CBASP therapy and require that the clinician personally address the problem—thus, CPR is administered.

CBASP psychotherapists require two basic cognitive-behavioral skills from patients if they do their work: (1) therapists must be able to achieve some degree of verbal stimulus control over patient talk (e.g., patients must be able and willing to listen and answer the therapist's questions; and (2) the patient must be able to focus and concentrate on the subject matter or task-at-hand. Individuals who cannot generate these behaviors must be taught to do so before psychotherapy begins. CPR provides consequences for and shapes up these "pre-therapy behaviors," utilizing the personal reactions of the therapist as a direct interpersonal consequence for such prohibitive patterns.

The chronically depressed adult is challenging. CBASP has been developed to deal specifically with an idiosyncratic and refractory lifestyle, and to date, it has achieved notable success (e.g., Keller et al., 2000).

REFERENCES

American Psychiatric Association (2000). *Diagnostic and statistical manual of mental disorders* (4th ed., text rev.). Washington, DC: Author.

Howland, R. H. (1996). Psychosocial therapies for dysthymia. In J. Lonsdale (Ed.), *The Hatherleigh guide to managing depression* (pp. 225–241). New York: Hatherleigh Press.

Keller, M. B., McCullough, Jr., J. P., Klein, D. N., Arnow, B. A., Dunner, D. L., Gelenberg, A. J., et al. (2000). A comparison of nefazodone, the cognitive behavioral analysis system of psychotherapy, and their combination for the treatment of chronic depression. *New England Journal of Medicine, 342*, 1462–1470.

Klein, D. N. (in press). Classification of Depressive Disorders in DSM-V: Proposal for a two-dimensional system. *Journal of Abnormal Psychology*.

Klein, D. N., Shankman, S. A., & Rose, S. (2006). Ten-year prospective follow-up study of the naturalistic course of dysthymic disorder and double depression. *American Journal of Psychiatry, 163*, 872–880.

McCullough, Jr., J. P. (1984). Cognitive-behavioral analysis system of psychotherapy. *Psychiatry, 47*, 234–240.

McCullough, Jr., J. P. (2000). *Treatment for chronic depression: Cognitive behavioral analysis system of psychotherapy (CBASP)*. New York: Guilford Press.

McCullough, Jr., J. P. (2006). *Treating chronic depression with disciplined personal involvement: CBASP*. New York: Springer.

McCullough, Jr., J. P., Klein, D. N., Borian, F. E., Howland, R. W., Riso, L. P., Keller, M. B., & Banks, P. L. C. (2003). Group comparisons of DSM-IV subtypes of chronic depression: Validity of the distinctions. Part 2. *Journal of Abnormal Psychology, 112*, 614–622.

SUGGESTED READING

McCullough, Jr., J. P. (2005). Cognitive behavioral analysis system of psychotherapy: Treatment for chronic depression. In J. C. Norcross & M. R. Goldfried (Eds.), *Handbook of psychotherapy integration* (2nd ed.; pp. 281–298). London: Oxford University Press.

JAMES P. MCCULLOUGH, JR.
Virginia Commonwealth University

See also: Behavioral Activation; Behavior Modification; Cognitive Therapy

COGNITIVE DEVELOPMENT

The term *cognitive development* refers to age changes in the ability to acquire, manipulate, or reason about information in particular contexts. When the intellectual capacities of at least two age groups are compared and the oldest group has not yet reached middle age, changes in performance are usually for the better, in the sense that they reflect improvements of one kind or another (e.g., those in the older group recall more information; those in the older group draw more appropriate inferences). It is not possible to summarize all of the details of what is known about cognitive development in a single brief article. Readers interested in more comprehensive treatments should consult sources such as Byrnes (2008), Bjorklund (2004), or Siegler and Alibali (2004). In the present overview, some general age trends in the structural and functional aspects of cognition are presented in order to provide a sense of the kinds of important and influential changes that occur.

Changes in Structural Aspects of Cognition

In a structural analysis of some physical or mental system, the focus is on the component parts of the system and how these parts are organized and interrelated. In a functional analysis, on the other hand, the emphasis is on the activity or operation of the system to achieve certain goals. These two perspectives are intrinsically related to each other because the component parts both determine and place constraints on the way the system can carry out tasks or operations. For example, the fact that the human heart has several kinds of chambers arranged in a particular way (a structural analysis) determines how blood can circulate through the body (a functional analysis). In the case of cognition, there are two structural features that both subtend and constrain the performance of mental processes: knowledge and processing capacity. When people have more knowledge and more processing capacity, they can perform a wider array of mental tasks and do so more accurately and efficiently. In what follows, age changes in these two structural aspects are summarized.

Knowledge Changes

The term *knowledge* refers to three kinds of information structures that are stored in long-term memory: declarative knowledge, procedural knowledge, and conceptual knowledge (Byrnes, 1999). Declarative knowledge, or "knowing that," is a compilation of all of the facts that a person knows in various domains (e.g., George Washington was the first U.S. President; the answer to the problem "3 + 2" is "5"). In contrast, procedural knowledge, or "knowing how to," is a compilation of all of the procedures that a person knows how to perform (e.g., knowing how to ride a bicycle, knowing how to solve math problems). Conceptual knowledge, or "knowing why," pertains to a person's understanding of facts, procedures, and systems (e.g., knowing why humans are classified as mammals; knowing why 7/12 is the answer to 1/3 + 1/4).

Across a variety of domains, numerous studies have shown that declarative, procedural, and conceptual knowledge increase between infancy and adulthood (Byrnes, 2008). For example, consider the large-scale national assessments that are regularly conducted by the federal government (i.e., the National Assessment of Educational Progress or NAEP). About every two years, the NAEP studies measure the school-related competencies of thousands of 4th, 8th, and 12th graders in subject areas such as reading, writing, math, science, history, geography, and civics. Regardless of the domain, there is clear evidence of knowledge accumulation with age on any given NAEP. However, the largest increases are for declarative and procedural knowledge. Even among 12th graders, the majority of children fail to demonstrate a deep conceptual understanding of the core topics. When grouped into levels of performance such as "basic," "proficient," and "advanced," most children are categorized or placed into the "basic" level.

One reason for the low level of conceptual knowledge evident in 12th graders is the abstract, multidimensional, and counterintuitive nature of the most advanced concepts in each domain. Even when teachers try their best to explain topics such as scarcity, civil rights, diffusion, limit, and conservation of energy, many children have difficulty understanding these topics. Compounding the relative lack of conceptual knowledge is the fact that children often develop misconceptions as well. For example, the scientific concept of force that is presented in physics courses is very different from children's everyday concept of force; in addition, their everyday concepts tend to be very resistant to change.

This is not to say, however, that one cannot find the rudiments of sophisticated ideas even in very young children. A number of scholars argue that children come into the world equipped with the ability to acquire foundational notions in domains such as physics, mathematics, biology, and psychology (Gelman, 1998). Using very clever experimental techniques, preschoolers have been found to possess surprising insight into psychological concepts (e.g., that human behavior can be predicted from a person's beliefs and desires) and biological concepts (e.g., that invisible germs are the cause of illness). Nevertheless, these rudimentary conceptions are a far cry from the sophisticated ideas children will need, but often fail, to master in their courses as middle school, high school, and college students.

Capacity Changes

In addition to knowledge, the second structural feature that influences the ability to perform mental tasks is processing capacity which is usually characterized in the form of working memory. When engaged in some mental task (e.g., performing a math calculation, evaluating several career options), an individual has to hold a certain amount of information in mind until the task is completed (e.g., the answer is derived, a career is decided upon). Complex problems require more processing capacity because more items of information need to be considered simultaneously

and sequentially over time. Similar to what was reported above for knowledge, developmental studies of working memory show that there are monotonic increases in the ability to hold and attend to items in memory as children progress through the preschool, elementary school, and high school periods (e.g., Swanson, 1999).

Changes in Functional Aspects of Cognition

Functional aspects of cognition include any mental processes that alter, operate on, or extend incoming or existing information. Examples include learning (getting new information into memory), retrieval (getting existing information out of long-term memory), reasoning (drawing inferences from single or multiple premises), and decision making (generating, evaluating, and selecting courses of action). Given the intrinsic connection between structural and functional aspects of cognition, it is expected that older children would show better performance on learning, memory, reasoning, and decision-making tasks than younger children because knowledge and processing capacity increase with age. As detailed next, many studies have confirmed this expectation.

Learning and Retrieval

The primary method used to show that an individual has learned something is to show that he or she can recall the information on some kind of test. Hence, learning and retrieval are inherently interconnected (Anderson, 2004). As such, it makes sense to discuss age trends for both processes in the same section.

The literature on expertise shows how experts recall considerably more from a domain-relevant situation than novices because the former can use their extensive knowledge to encode the situation as a meaningful whole (Ericsson, Charness, Feltovich, & Hoffman, 2006). Thus, it is to be expected that older children would naturally recall more than younger children in most situations since older children have more knowledge than younger children. Numerous studies show this to be the case. In addition, older children, adolescents, and adults are more likely than younger children to use effective memory strategies to recall information (Bjorklund, 2004). Finally, older children can devote more of their attentional resources to a situation because (1) older children process information more quickly than younger children; (2) older children have greater working memory capacity than younger children; and (3) skills are more likely to be automated in older children than in younger children (due to differences in the amount of practice). Differences in knowledge, strategy use, speed of processing, and working memory capacity all contribute to substantial differences in learning and memory performance between older and younger children (Bjorklund, 2004; Siegler & Alibali, 2004).

Reasoning

Whenever individuals draw inferences from one or more items of information, they engage in reasoning. Scientists have investigated age differences in both domain-general categories of reasoning those that can be applied to multiple domains (e.g., deductive and inductive reasoning), and domain-specific forms of reasoning (e.g., mathematical reasoning, scientific reasoning, historical reasoning). Deductive reasoning consists of reasoning from a set of initial premises to a conclusion that logically follows from the premises (e.g., Premise 1 = John is taller than Bill. Premise 2 = Bill is taller than Mary. Conclusion: Therefore, John is taller than Mary). Inductive reasoning, in contrast, involves generating a general conclusion or rule from specific instances (e.g., speakers put "-s" on the end of "dog" to make it plural and at the end of "cat" to make it plural; therefore the rule is to put "-s" onto any noun to make it plural). Reasoning within domains reflects specific forms that may not have analogous counterparts in other domains. For example, the ways in which students reason from knowns to unknowns on a math problem is not exactly comparable to the ways in which students engage in scientific reasoning to set up experiments that reveal the cause of some outcome. Similarly, the ways in which scientists reason from evidence to causes is not exactly comparable to the ways in which historians reason about documentary evidence to conjecture about the events that may have transpired on a particular date.

Studies have shown improvements in all forms of reasoning between the preschool and adulthood periods (Byrnes, 2008; Markovits & Barrouillet, 2004). For example, whereas young children can draw some kinds of deductive inferences when given considerable scaffolding from adults, older adolescents and adults can draw a broader range of deductive inferences on their own. In the content areas, children progress from relatively primitive forms of scientific and historical reasoning in elementary school, to more sophisticated kinds of reasoning by the end of adolescence (Byrnes, 2008). Nevertheless, a number of studies have shown that even adults fall prey to a variety of reasoning fallacies. Thus, while reasoning performance improves with age, it is far from perfect in adulthood.

Decision Making

Decision making involves the generation, evaluation, and selection of options that can be used to attain goals (e.g., reading college guides to decide which schools to apply to). Although relatively few studies have examined the decision-making skills of children and adolescents, enough studies have been conducted to draw the following tentative conclusions: Older adolescents and adults seem to be more likely than younger adolescents or children to (1) understand the difference between options that are likely to satisfy multiple goals (e.g., a car that gets both good gas mileage and has a good repair record) and options that are likely to satisfy only a single goal; (2) anticipate a wider range of consequences of their actions; and (3) learn from their decision-making successes and failures (Byrnes, 2002). Nevertheless, as was noted above for reasoning studies, there are quite a large number of studies that show the various limitations of decision-making skills in adults (Jacobs & Klaczynski, 2005).

Metacognition

One further development that occurs during the childhood and adolescent periods is an increased ability to reflect upon one's own thought processes and treat thinking as an object of thought (Bjorklund, 2004). This metacognitive ability can help older adolescents and adults see the errors of their ways and possibly avoid reasoning problems in the future. Collectively, the changes in structural aspects, functional aspects, and metacognition transform children into adults who have most of the skills they will need to be successful. Some adults are more successful than others, so the task remains to understand how individual differences in cognitive abilities emerge so that interventions can be created to help all individuals be successful.

REFERENCES

Anderson, J. R. (2004). *Cognitive psychology and its implications* (6th ed.). New York: Worth Publishers.

Bjorklund, D. F. (2004). *Children's thinking: Cognitive development and individual differences* (4th ed.). Belmont, CA: Wadsworth Publishing.

Byrnes, J. P. (1999). On the nature and development of representation: A synthesis of competing perspectives. In I. Sigel (Ed.), *Theoretical perspectives on the concept of representation*. Mahwah, NJ: Lawrence Erlbaum.

Byrnes, J. P. (2002). The development of decision-making. *Journal of Adolescent Health, 31*, 208–215.

Byrnes, J. P. (2008). *Cognitive development and learning in instructional contexts* (3rd ed.). Needham Heights, MA: Allyn & Bacon.

Ericsson, K. A., Charness, N., Feltovich, P. J., & Hoffman, R. R. (2006). *The Cambridge handbook of expertise and expert performance*. Cambridge, UK: Cambridge University Press.

Gelman, R. (1998) Domain specificity in cognitive development: Universals and nonuniversals. In M. Sabourin, F. Craik, & M Robert (Eds.), *Advances in psychological science: Vol. 2. Biological and cognitive aspects* (pp. 557–579). East Sussex, UK: Psychology Press.

Jacobs, J. E., & Klaczynski, P. A. (2005). *The development of judgment and decision-making in children and adolescents*. Mahwah, NJ: Lawrence Erlbaum.

Markovits, H., & Barrouillet, P. (2004). Introduction: Why is understanding the development of reasoning important? *Thinking and Reasoning, 10*, 113–121.

Moshman, D. (2004). From inference to reasoning: The construction of rationality. *Thinking and Reasoning, 10*, 221–239.

Siegler, R. S., & Alibali, M. A. (2004). *Children's thinking* (4th ed.). Englewood Cliffs, NJ: Prentice Hall.

Swanson, H. L. (1999). What develops in working memory: A life span perspective. *Developmental Psychology, 35*, 986–1000.

JAMES P. BYRNES
Temple University

See also: Child Psychology; Emotional Development; Social Cognitive Development

COGNITIVE DISSONANCE

Few constructs within social psychology have generated more research and controversy than cognitive dissonance. Cognitive dissonance describes a state in which two or more cognitions (including attitudes, beliefs, values, and behaviors) conflict such that the inverse of one follows from another. When Festinger first introduced the concept of cognitive dissonance in 1957, he used the example of a smoker encountering information that smoking was bad for his health. Festinger proposed that such a dissonant state is aversive and motivates cognitive change, just as the aversive state of hunger motivates eating. The more important and the greater the difference between the cognitions, the greater the need to reduce dissonance will be. Festinger argued that dissonance may be reduced through a variety of means. For instance, the individual in this example might reduce dissonance by (1) ceasing to smoke; (2) questioning the evidence that smoking is bad for his respiratory health; or (3) deciding that, perhaps, it is true that smoking is bad for his health, but that it keeps his weight down and the dangers of being overweight are worse than the dangers of respiratory illness.

Various paradigms have been employed to explore the impact of cognitive dissonance on cognition. Brehm (1956) first introduced the free choice paradigm in which individuals rate the attractiveness of various alternatives, choose between two alternatives, and then rerate the attractiveness of all the alternatives. When the options are originally equally attractive to individuals, they typically later rate the chosen option as more attractive than they did originally and the rejected option as less attractive. This "spreading of alternatives" is thought to result from individuals' needs to resolve their knowledge of the unattractive features of the chosen alternative and the attractive attributes of the rejected option with the choice they have made.

In induced compliance paradigms, individuals typically espouse a view they do not hold; in Festinger and Carlsmith's landmark 1959 study this was exemplified by a male participant lying about his enjoyment of a boring task to an alleged peer. In this study, individuals who received insufficient justification for lying ($1) later reported that, in fact, they enjoyed the task. Those who received sufficient justification for lying ($20) do not seem to undergo a parallel shift in attitudes. It was thought that those who have received only $1 for their lie reconciled the dissonance between their negative attitudes toward lying and their actual attitude toward the boring task, while those who have received $20 easily justified their lie through their compensation. On the flip side of this finding, individuals who incurred a large cost for something liked it more than individuals who incurred a smaller cost for the same thing. Importantly, such results are only obtained when participants have the illusion of freely engaging in the target behaviors.

Although Festinger's (1957) proposal that dissonance constitutes an aversive motivational state has been supported, various alternative theories have been proposed to account for dissonance results. Some of these postulate that cognitive inconsistency does not drive such effects. According to Bem's (1967) self-perception explanation of cognitive dissonance, individuals infer their own attitudes from their own behaviors in the absence of external pressures. Impression-management theorists maintain, on the other hand, that individuals shift their attitudes in order to appear consistent to observers rather than the self. Proponents of the New Look model argue that evidence of cognitive dissonance is only observed when individuals feel that they are responsible for external, aversive consequences that violate norms for behavior (Cooper & Fazio, 1984). They propose that individuals revise their attitudes in order to justify their non-normative behavior.

Other models have postulated that cognitive dissonance effects arise from inconsistencies between behavior and individuals' sense of self. According to self-consistency theory (Aronson, 1968), people's sense that they have failed to behave consistently with their standards of morality or competence is responsible for observed shifts in attitudes. This theory predicts that individuals with high self-esteem should exhibit more dissonance-induced attitude change. In his self-affirmation theory of cognitive dissonance, Steele (1988) proposes that cognitive dissonance produces cognitive change because dissonance is perceived as a threat to one's sense of moral and adaptive integrity; he also proposes that individuals with high self-esteem are protected from dissonance-induced attitude change. The self-standards model (Stone & Cooper, 2001) attempts to reconcile these perspectives by proposing that the self will only mediate dissonance effects when self-constructs are activated, and context dictates whether the self will act as an expectancy (along the lines of self-consistency theory) or as a resource (consistent with self-affirmation theory). When self-constructs are not active, dissonance may be found when individuals feel that they have violated societal norms.

Current directions in cognitive dissonance research include further work into the role of the self in dissonance phenomena, the formulation of connectionist models that may account for dissonance results, the minimal requirements of a system in order for dissonance reduction to come online.

REFERENCES

Aronson, E. (1968). Dissonance theory: Progress and problems. In R. P. Abelson, E. Aronson, W. J. McGuire, T. M. Newcomb, M. J. Rosenberg, & P. H. Tannenbaum, (Eds.), *Theories of cognitive consistency: A sourcebook*. Chicago: Rand McNally.

Bem, D. J. (1967). Self-perception: An alternative interpretation of cognitive dissonance phenomena. *Psychological Review, 74,* 183–200.

Brehm, J. W. (1956). Postdecision changes in the desirability of alternatives. *Journal of. Abnormal and Social Psychology, 36,* 384–389.

Cooper, J., & Fazio, R. H. (1984). A new look at dissonance theory. *Advances in Experimental Psychology, 17,* 229–262.

Festinger, L. (1957). *A theory of cognitive dissonance*. Stanford, CA: Stanford University Press.

Steele, C. M. (1988). The psychology of self-affirmation: Sustaining the integrity of the self. In L. Berkowitz (Ed.) *Advances in experimental social psychology, Volume 22,* 261–301. San Diego, CA: Academic Press.

Stone, J., & Cooper, J. (2001). A self-standards model of cognitive dissonance. *Journal of Experimental Social Psychology, 37,* 228–243.

SUGGESTED READINGS

Elliot, A. J., & Devine, P. G. (1994). On the motivational nature of cognitive dissonance: Dissonance as psychological discomfort. *Journal of Personality and Social Psychology, 67*(3), 382–394.

Festinger, L., & Carlsmith, J. M. (1959). Cognitive consequences of forced compliance. *Journal of Abnormal and Social Psychology, 58,* 203–211.

Lieberman, M. D., Ochsner, K. N., Gilbert, D. T., & Schacter, D. L. (2001). Do amnesiacs exhibit cognitive dissonance reduction? The role of explicit memory and attention in attitude change. *Psychological Science, 12,* 135–140.

LOUISA EGAN
Yale University

See also: **Attitudes; Cognitive Development; Social Cognitive Development**

COGNITIVE MAPS

Cognitive mapping is the process of encoding sensed data and storing, decoding, representing, and internally manipulating these data in working memory for use in completing tasks or solving problems. A *cognitive map* is a hypothetical concept constructed from one's experiences in the real world. The concept is hypothetical because, as yet, there is no evidence that environmental information is stored in memory in a cartographic-like fashion, but it does appear that, on an as-needed basis, an individual can draw on these encoded data and create a working image to assist in performing certain spatial tasks or solving spatial problems. To do this requires knowledge of location, place, environmental objects, and spatial relations.

Tolman (1948), first introduced the concept of cognitive maps; they since have been interpreted as metaphors or as cartographic-like representations. Although Tolman clearly indicated that the cognitive map was internal to the brain and was a construct of mind, the term has been used in various contexts to describe the externalization of stored spatial information (*spatial products*).

Lynch (1960) pioneered the use of sketch maps to produce urban images. Since then, other procedures have been developed to allow individual flexibility of the form of such representations (e.g., text speech, gestures, graphics, and various art forms). The cognitive map, therefore, refers to a level of spatial information that can be organized in the mind as a system of interconnected locations, places, and spatial relations, thus lending some credence to the use of the term "map." It is generally accepted that cognitive maps incorporate a series of transformation rules and include a combination of declarative and procedural knowledge.

The extent to which a spatial product reflects accurately that part of the world it intends to represent depends on personal spatial abilities. A spatial product contains the biases, levels of fuzziness, distortion, and incompleteness that are contained in the cognitive map.

Methods of Obtaining Spatial Products for Cognitive Maps

Perhaps the most frequently used procedure is Lynch's sketch-mapping procedure. Sketches are not maps in the cartographic sense, for they usually lack scale, orientation, and common reference frames. Lynch's urban images were derived by counting the frequencies with which particular objects, places, and connectivities were represented on the sketches. While one may be able to extract and externally represent information about sequencing, order, perceived location, and proximity, and linkage from the sketches, these concepts are usually relative and cannot be measured in a direct metric fashion.

Although sketch mapping is perhaps the most frequently used method for compiling a spatial product, the creation of text or auditory descriptions using a mix of common and technical language is widespread. In text and speech, frequent use is made of relative spatial relations as indicated by prepositions such as near, on, before, after, close to, far, and many others. It is usually very difficult to translate these into metric information. At the very least, individual differences may account for dramatically different interpretations of such prepositions: near to one person may be next door while to another it may be half a mile.

In addition to sketching and verbalizing or creating text descriptions, other methods for obtaining spatial products include (1) reproducing stored spatial information from memory, by walking distances or turning angles; (2) using scaled proximity judgments and multidimensional scaling techniques to create latent configurations embedded in the scaled responses; (3) using simple pointing activities from a set of real or imagined places, either to establish the direction of other objects or, via a process of projective convergence, to give estimates of the location of such places; (4) performance of spatial updating after location translation; (5) creating allocentric configurations that remain the same (or are similar), regardless of perspective viewing or location of the viewer; (6) exploring spatial relations in virtual environments; and (7) building tabletop models.

Why Spatial Products?

An externalization of one's internal representation of the world is always incomplete, distorted, and usually fuzzy, because one's senses cannot absorb all possible relational information embedded in an environment. Externalizing cognitive maps is one of a set of useful ways for comprehending the actions and behaviors of humans. Geographers, in particular, have sought to obtain spatial products and then examine them to explain human actions and activities or behaviors in space. Planners, architects, and designers have used the concept to identify structural, functional, and symbolic legibility of particular objects, features, and places. Because spatial information can be expressed in graphic, verbal, text, or gesture modes, the spatial products that represent these externalizations can be quite varied.

Experimental Procedures

Included among the many experimental procedures designed to produce valid and reliable spatial products are wayfinding, direction giving, pointing, interpoint distance estimation, configurational or layout representation of settings, neural net modeling, computational process modeling, revealed place preference analysis, and protocol analysis of verbalizations.

It must be remembered that a spatial product is a cross section representing what is known about a scenario or setting at a particular time. Continued interaction with the outside world requires ongoing encoding and adding data to that already stored in long-term memory. The cognitive map, thus, is a dynamic concept and may constantly be in the process of updating and change. With increasing familiarity, spatial relations become better known and estimated and, eventually, facilitate developmental of

spatial products that are much closer to the equivalent spatial arrays of external reality.

Given that humans learn about environments from different locations, different perspectives, and with different reasons, there must be substantial individual differences in nature, complexity, and accuracy of cognitive maps and spatial products. The human need to communicate about their environments suggests there must be common elements in any set of cognitive maps. Recall Lynch's ability to create images of urban places by looking for landmarks, nodes, paths, boundaries, and districts. Given such communication needs, there should be a minimal set of features (anchorpoints) that would facilitate communication. This implies that cognitive maps must consist of common and idiosyncratic materials. Common features may be equivalent to Lynch's landmarks, but they may also be in the form of points, line segments, or districts. They represent anchorpoints in the person's cognitive map and are the quickest and easiest forms of reference when communicating about environments. In addition to common features, the bulk of information in cognitive maps is idiosyncratic (i.e., based on personal experience). For most people, their own home becomes a significant anchorpoint, equivalent to the most familiar local landmark. But that home base may not even occur as a minor order node in another person's cognitive map.

Defining what may be known about an environment is one aspect of cognitive maps. Determining if what is known bears an accurate, or even definable, relationship to what exists in objective reality is usually a concern. These concerns have been primary in encouraging research into cognitive maps. A specific but unanswered question is how to best match spatial products with the real world. In neurosciences, more attention has been given to determining how, when, and where bits of sensed information are stored in the brain, how they are accessed by recall processes, and how they are manipulated in working memory. Methods of analyzing verbal reports or text based on externalizations are stimulating considerable interest (e.g., in the development of concept maps and different types of content analysis). Cognitive maps, therefore, are essentially a repository for personalized information as mediated by an array of social, cultural, ethical, moral, and other constraints. What is in the cognitive map must also be mediated by the power of an individual's sensing organism; to the extent that these are damaged, missing, or incomplete, the reliability and validity of their encoding and manipulation capabilities will also vary. While most research has focused on the metric accuracy of cognitive maps and spatial products, comprehensive studies involving the totality of all relevant dimensions remain to be developed.

REFERENCES

Lynch, K. (1960). *The image of the city*. Cambridge, MA: MIT Press.

Tolman, E. C. (1948). Cognitive maps in rats and men. *Psychological Review, 55*, 189–208.

SUGGESTED READINGS

Blades, M. (1990). The reliability of data collected from sketch maps. *Journal of Environmental Psychology, 10*(4), 327–339.

Golledge, R. G. (2005). Cognitive maps. In K. Kempf-Leonard (Eds.), *Encyclopedia of Social Measurement, Vol. 1* (pp. 329–339). San Diego, CA: Elsevier.

Kitchin, R. & Freundschuh, S. (Eds.). (2000). *Cognitive mapping: Past, present, and future*. London and New York: Routledge.

REGINALD GOLLEDGE
University of California Santa Barbara

COGNITIVE NEUROSCIENCE

The study of the neural basis of cognition, or cognitive neuroscience, has evolved rapidly in the last 15 years. In large part this has resulted from the parallel advances in imaging technology and raw computing power. Indeed, the exponential growth and concomitant movement of extraordinarily powerful computers to the desktop has made routine the analysis of large complex datasets. Cognitive neuroscience is an enterprise that depends heavily on the use of modern imaging technologies like positron emission tomography (PET) and functional magnetic resonance imaging (fMRI), and because of this reliance on technology, the ability to look noninvasively at the functionings of the human brain has only become possible very recently.

The fundamental goal of the cognitive neuroscientist is to understand the neural basis of the human mind. Historically, the mind had been thought to be separate from the body. Rene Descartes, the eighteenth-century French philosopher/mathematician was perhaps the most vociferous advocate of mind-body dualism. The question of where the human mind, perhaps even the soul, resides has plagued humanity for at least as long as written records exist. Until recently, there was no reason to suspect that the mind might have components that were tied to the body. After all, this notion might be discordant with the belief of the immortality of the soul—if the body dies, then so does the mind. Descartes circumvented the problem by separating the mind from the body, and therefore the brain.

Mind-body dualism did not last long. Neurologists of the nineteenth century began to notice that patients with specific brain injuries, either from stroke or trauma, displayed consistent behavioral deficits. Pierre Paul Broca, a French neurologist, systematically described the effect of lesions in the left frontal cortex on language. Insightfully, he was the first to state that language was localized to the left cerebral hemisphere. This opened the door for an explosion of cognitive localization in the brain. In its extreme form, phrenology, every function of the human mind could be localized to some bump or valley in the brain (and skull). The use of brain lesions to deduce brain function subsequently became the predominate method for exploring the mind/brain for the next 100 years.

The lesion method truly was the first cognitive neuroscience technique. Its growth paralleled the recognition of other types of deficiency syndromes in medicine. The lesion method relied solely on the power of observation and a ready supply of patients with various types of brain injury. The history of the field is full of references to famous patients whose unfortunate circumstances led to some insight about the functioning of some particular brain region. Phineas Gage, perhaps the first famous patient, was a nineteenth-century railroad worker who had an iron rod accidentally driven upwards from just below his left eye out through the top of his skull. Remarkably, he lived for another decade, and his subsequent change in personality from a reliable steady worker to a profane, erratic, and irascible man was aptly characterized by his physician at the time, "Gage was no longer Gage." Lesion studies remain important for the field of cognitive neuroscience not only because the development of novel neurotoxins has enabled experimenters to produce precisely localized lesions to specific regions of the animal brain and observe subsequent changes in behavior and cognition, but, importantly, they provide complementary data to correlational noninvasive methods such as PET and fMRI.

The father of modern psychology, William James, was attuned to these advancements in understanding the brain in the late nineteenth century. Further evidence linking brain function to cognitive processing continued to amass. The observation that regional changes in cerebral blood flow were tied to mental function can be traced to the fortuitous discovery in a patient with an arteriovenous malformation in his frontal lobe. This patient (and his physician) noticed an increase in audible blood pulsation when performing mental calculation. This observation, that local changes in cerebral blood flow are linked to neural activity, underlies all of modern functional imaging techniques.

The parallel development of new imaging technologies with increased computational power in the late twentieth century resulted in the development of two new methods to study human brain function. Positron emission tomography (PET) developed as an outgrowth of autoradiography. Unlike its predecessor, PET could be performed without the requirement of sacrificing the animal. PET takes advantage of the fact that when a positron, that is, a positively charged electron, encounters an electron, the two particles annihilate each other, and two high-energy gamma rays are emitted in exactly opposite directions. By arranging a series of gamma-ray detectors in a ring, the origin of the particle can be computed. Positron emitters can be synthesized into common molecules, like water or 2-deoxyglucose, and when injected into a subject can be used to map cerebral blood flow or metabolism respectively. Similarly, fMRI relies on the coupling of neural activity to local cerebral blood flow. Current thinking suggests that transient increases in neural activity result in a hyperemic blood flow response. Oxygenated hemoglobin and deoxygenated hemoglobin have different magnetic properties, and because the increase in blood flow results in a transient increase in the oxy- to deoxy-ratio, this can be detected with MRI. By rapidly acquiring MRIs while a subject is performing a cognitive task in the scanner, the changes in blood flow can be correlated to what the subject is doing.

Although PET and fMRI typically measure only relative changes in brain activity, through careful experimental design it is possible to isolate the neural circuits associated with specific cognitive processes. The basis for this is called subtractive design. By designing an experiment with at least two cognitive conditions, one of which is a control state, the brain activity maps obtained during the control state can be subtracted from the brain activity during the condition of interest. In actual practice, a statistical test is usually performed instead of a simple subtraction, but the assumption is that whatever brain regions show different activity between the conditions represent the circuit associated with processing the extra information. It is critical that the control state be chosen appropriately. Otherwise, one might be subtracting cognitive states that are so different from one another that the assumptions of this method are violated. In particular, subtraction assumes that cognitive processes behave linearly, i.e., that processes can be added and subtracted without interacting with each other. This has been demonstrated to be true under some circumstances, but not all (Dale & Buckner, 1997).

In general, the subtractive approach to imaging has confirmed what was known from the lesion method, but recent advances in fMRI have allowed the description of more subtle processes. By presenting subjects with very brief stimuli, the cerebral blood flow response can be measured and correlated with individual events. This goes beyond the subtractive approach, which often employs blocked designs that require the subject to maintain a cognitive state for tens of seconds to minutes. Event-related fMRI measures the brain response to discrete events that are often shorter than a second, which is much closer to the timescale at which the brain operates. By using principles from electroencephalography (EEG), namely time-locking the fMR signal to the onset of the event and averaging this signal across many trials in the same experimental condition, it is possible to extract small (typically <1%) but significant changes in the amplitude of the fMR signal.

Event-related designs have enabled observations of brain activity during more complex cognitive tasks constituted of event sequences. To avoid the presence of confounding variables, these paradigms require experimental conditions to be presented to the subject in random order and at unexpected time intervals. In recent years, a multitude of such tasks have been employed in conjunction with event-related fMRI to investigate the neural correlates of various cognitive domains including memory (e.g., n-back and delayed match-to-sample tasks), attention (e.g., cued target detection tasks), executive function (e.g., Tower of London tasks) and general decision-making.

A prototypical finding from fMRI investigations of the neural correlates of cognition suggests significant activation of regions within a fronto-parietal network during top-down attentional control when subjects perform the cued target detection task (Kastner & Ungerleider, 2000). A single trial of this task, which is widely used to examine various aspects of attention and its neural correlates, consists of a number of events that need to occur in a particular order: at the beginning of a typical trial, a brief instructive cue is presented to guide spatial attention covertly to peripheral target locations. The subject is required to maintain attention at the cued location throughout a delay period, called the interstimulus interval, after which a target stimulus is presented. Most commonly, a trial ends with detection of the target stimulus, which is indicated via button press, but modified versions of this task have asked subjects to discriminate target from distracter stimuli, or to track a target's movement. The sequential nature of this task, and many similar behavioral paradigms, prevents the use of a blocked design. Furthermore, to control for alternative explanations, it is essential that the location and timing of both cue and target be unpredictable to the subject. These issues can only be addressed with event-related designs.

A recurring finding from fMRI studies employing such behavioral paradigms is documented in the cognitive neuroscience literature, suggesting that the brain recruits widely distributed cortical networks during performance of such tasks regardless of the underlying cognitive domain examined by the experiment. This is due to the fact that multiple perceptual, cognitive and motor processes can be simultaneously evoked following the presentation of a single trial. Recent fMRI studies have employed event-related designs to uncouple signals associated with cognitive processes occurring during specific time periods of a given task. This can be achieved via separating events that follow each other in time, typically via randomly varied interstimulus and intertrial intervals and/or via extracting the time course of the hemodynamic response to discrete events. A study by Hopfinger et al. (2000), which employed a version of the cued target detection task outlined above, made use of the experimental flexibility of event-related fMRI and introduced relatively long and randomly varied intervals between the cue and target phases. Thus the authors were able to reveal that separate neural networks are engaged during top-down attentional control and target detection.

More recently, experimenters have succeeded in establishing a closer link between behavior and brain activations. A simple approach that accomplishes this task is based on sorting trials according to subjects' responses, for instance into those trials during which a correct versus an incorrect response was produced. This approach allows for investigating performance-related brain activity and even predicting subjects' responses based on brain activation patterns. Using this method, Pessoa et al. (2002) were able to isolate a network of structures that showed greater fMRI amplitude during the encoding, maintenance, and retrieval phases of a standard working memory task on trials that resulted in success compared to failure. Logistic regression was then used to quantify the relationship between fMRI amplitude and behavioral performance. The authors were able to show that signal amplitude within a frontoparietal network during the maintenance period was predictive of successful task performance on a trial-by-trial basis.

More recent experiments have made use of the multivariate nature of fMRI data using similar principles in conjunction with statistical pattern recognition algorithms to predict conscious states, percepts and behavior based on distributed brain activation patterns (Haynes and Rees, 2006). These new computational algorithms are revealing the complex correlations that occur between different brain regions and begin to uncover the choreography of brain activity that must be the hallmark of cognition.

REFERENCES

Dale, A. M., & Buckner, R. L. (1997). Selective averaging of rapidly presented individual trials using fMRI. *Human Brain Mapping, 5,* 329–340.

Damasio, A. R. (1994). *Descartes' error: Emotion, reason and the human brain.* New York: G. P. Putnam's Sons.

Frackowiak, R. S. J., Friston, K. J., Frith, C. D., Dolan, R. J., & Maziotta, J. C. (1997). *Human brain function.* San Diego: Academic Press.

Haynes, J. D., & Rees, G. (2006). Decoding mental states from brain activity in humans. *Nature Reviews Neuroscience, 7,* 523–534.

Hopfinger, J. B., Buoncore, M. H., & Mangun, G. R. (2000). The neural mechanisms of top-down attentional control. *Nature Neuroscience, 3,* 284–291.

Huettel, S. A., Song, A. W., & McCarthy, G. (2004). *Functional magnetic resonance imaging.* Sunderland, MA: Sinauer Associates.

Kastner, S., & Ungerleider, L. G. (2000) Mechanisms of visual attention in the human cortex. *Annual Review of Neuroscience, 23,* 315–341.

Kwong, K. K., Belliveau, J. W., Chesler, D. A., Goldberg, I. E., Weisskopf, R. M., Poncelet, B. P., Kennedy, D. N., Hoppel, B. E., Cohen, M. S., Turner, R., Cheng, H. M., Brady, T. J., &

Rosen, B. R. (1992). Dynamic magnetic resonance imaging of human brain activity during primary sensory stimulation. *Proceedings of the National Academy of Sciences, USA, 89,* 5675–5679.

Ogawa, S., Tank, D. W., Menon, R., Ellerman, J. M., Kim, S. G., Merkle, H. & Ugurbil, K. (1992). Intrinsic signal changes accompanying sensory stimulation: Functional brain mapping with magnetic resonance imaging. *Proceedings of the National Academy of Sciences, USA, 89,* 5951–5955.

Pessoa, L., Gutierrez, E., Bandettini, P., & Ungerleider, L. (2002). Neural correlates of visual working memory: fMRI amplitude predicts task performance. *Neuron, 35,* 975–987.

SUGGESTED READINGS

Gazzaniga, M. S. (2004). *The cognitive neurosciences III.* Cambridge, MA: The MIT Press.

LeDoux, J. (2002). *Synaptic self: How our brains become who we are.* New York: Viking.

JAN B. ENGELMANN
GREGORY S. BERNS
Emory University School of Medicine

See also: **Magnetic Resonance Imaging; Neuroimaging; Neuroscience**

COGNITIVE THEORIES OF AFFECT

One of the greatest puzzles about human nature concerns the still poorly understood relationship between thinking and feeling, cognition and affect. Emotions represent a ubiquitous and powerful phenomenon in our lives, yet psychological research on emotions has remained a relatively neglected field until recently. Contemporary research linking cognition and affect has examined both (1) the role of antecedent cognitive processes in affective reactions and (2) the cognitive consequences of affect. This article reviews both orientations.

Historical and Theoretical Background

Cognition and affect were first proposed as distinct faculties of the human mind in eighteenth-century philosophy. In subsequent psychological research these faculties were often seen as sovereign domains that can be studied in isolation. Emotions were also long regarded in Western thought as dangerous and incompatible with reason. The apparent inability of humans to exert direct cognitive control over their emotions is often considered a defining characteristic of our species.

Recent research suggests, however, that affect is often a useful and even essential input to effective cognition

(Damasio, 1994). Evolutionary theories also see affect as adaptive in recruiting appropriate cognitive strategies to deal with environmental challenges (Bless & Fiedler, 2006, Forgas, 2002). Neural structures of emotion processing, such as the amygdala and medial prefrontal cortex, are also implicated in social cognition. Conversely, neural structures of social cognition, such as the orbitofrontal and medial prefrontal cortex, fusiform gyrus, and inferior frontal gyrus, are also involved in emotional processing. Thus, emotion regions tend to be involved in the cognitive processing of social stimuli, and the social-cognitive regions are also involved in affective processing. It may be that it was adaptive evolutionary pressures to deal flexibly with significant environmental stimuli that first resulted in the linking of structure and function in the social and emotional brain areas. The hierarchical and modular organization of the brain also allows for unconscious affective states (such as moods) to have a direct influence on cognition.

Early psychological ideas linking cognition and affect were shaped by theories such as psychoanalysis and behaviorism. Psychoanalytic accounts saw affect as located within the id and exerting pressure against the countervailing forces of rational, cognitive ego mechanisms. Radical behaviorism suggested a direct link between emotion and cognition through the mechanism of conditioned blind associations. According to this view, the full repertoire of human emotions can be explained in terms of cumulative conditioning experiences superimposed on just a few fundamental wired-in emotions.

The emerging cognitive paradigm in the 1960s initially also focused on cold, affect-less cognition. By the early 1980s, however, it was recognized that cognition and emotion are inseparable. Cognitive theories such as Gordon Bower's associative network model specified how affective states may have an impact on cognition through selectively priming affect-consistent associations (Bower, 1981).

The Cognitive Antecedents of Affect: The Appraisal Approach

How do people know what is the right emotional reaction in a given situation? As early as in the 1960s, Schachter and Singer suggested that unexplained arousal becomes an experienced emotion only after cognitive processes are employed to infer what sort of emotional response is appropriate. Following this tradition, *appraisal theories* seek to explain the cognitive genesis and functions of the entire repertoire of human emotions. Emotional appraisal requires that situational and personal information is combined to determine the appropriate emotional response. Emotion appraisals have deep adaptive significance, as emotions represent different modes of action readiness in a given situation.

Emotion appraisal rules can take the logical form of if–then statements. Different antecedent conditions such as personal relevance, causal origins, and ability to cope produce different emotions. Acceptance or rejection by others appears to be a particularly potent cause of emotional reactions. Forecasting future emotional reactions represents a special case of emotional appraisal, and people seem to make many systematic cognitive mistakes when they are forecasting future emotional reactions (Wilson & Gilbert, 2003). Past emotional states are also interpreted through cognitive processes; for example, the peak intensity and the last three minutes of pain during a medical procedure have a disproportionate influence on the way the episode is appraised and remembered.

Recent appraisal models focus on the cognitive mechanisms of how situational information and memory-based information are combined to produce an emotional reaction through processes such as priming and spreading activation (Smith & Kirby, 2000). Spontaneous appraisals may subsequently be modified by analytical reasoning that provides a more finely tuned emotional response, allowing the emotion system to "learn" new interpretations. Whereas appraisal theory focuses on the cognitive antecedents of emotions, complementary approach analyses the cognitive consequences of affective states.

The Cognitive Consequences of Affect

Affect can influence cognition in two ways: (1) by exerting an informational function, influencing the content and valence of memories and thinking, and (2) by exerting a processing effect, influencing the information processing strategies employed to perform a task.

Informational Effects

Affect can inform cognition (usually producing affect congruency) as a result of memory processes (such as affect priming) and inferential processes (the affect-as-information model; see Clore & Storbeck, 2006). According to the associative network model (Bower, 1981), affect may selectively prime in memory affect-congruent information. Affectively primed ideas in turn are more likely to be used in constructive cognitive tasks, such as recall, social judgments, and inferences (Bower, 1981, Forgas, 2002). Affect priming is most likely to occur when the affective state is strong, salient, and self-relevant and when the cognitive task calls for open and constructive information processing, promoting the use of memory-based information (Forgas, 1995, 2002).

Alternatively, individuals may sometimes misattribute their affective state and use it directly as information (Clore & Storbeck, 2006). The "how-do-I-feel-about-it" heuristic suggests that affective influences on cognition are caused by an inferential error, the misattribution of affect to an unrelated cause. This theory, just like earlier conditioning models, posits an incidental and mistaken association between affect and a cognitive target. Using affect as information is at best a partial explanation of affect congruence, and this use is most likely when people lack motivation or capacity to compute a more thorough response. The informational value of a prevailing affective state is often also unclear and depends on the circumstances. The model fails to explain how informational cues other than affect, such as stimulus details, memories, and the like, are combined to produce a response. Personally relevant and realistic tasks typically call for more elaborate memory-based processing.

Processing Effects

In addition to information effects, affect also influences the process of cognition, that is, how people think (Bless & Fiedler, 2006). Positive and negative affect trigger qualitatively different processing styles. Positive affect promotes a more assimilative, schema-based, top-down processing style in which preexisting ideas, attitudes, and representations dominate information processing. In contrast, negative affect produces a more accommodative, bottom-up, and externally focused processing strategy in which attention to situational information drives thinking. The assimilative-accommodative processing dichotomy captures well the adaptive, functional influence of positive and negative affective states on cognition. Consistent with this theory, numerous experiments show that negative affect often results in superior cognitive outcomes when careful attention to situational details is required (Forgas, 2007).

Integrative theories such as the Affect Infusion Model (AIM; Forgas, 2002) link the informational and processing consequences of affect and attempt to specify the circumstances that facilitate or inhibit affect infusion into cognition. The AIM predicts that affective influences on cognition depend on the processing styles used that can differ in terms of two features: the degree of, and the degree of openness of the information processing strategy. By combining processing quantity (effort) and quality (openness, constructiveness), the model identifies four distinct processing styles: direct access processing (low effort, closed, not constructive), motivated processing (high effort, closed, not constructive), heuristic processing (low effort, open, constructive), and substantive processing (high effort, open, constructive).

This model predicts that affect priming should be most reliably observed when cognitive tasks call for highly constructive processing that necessitates the use of memory-based information. Similarly, the affect-as-information model is most likely in circumstances that promote heuristic processing. In contrast, affect should not infuse thinking when motivated or direct access processing is used. The AIM also recognizes that affect itself has a significant influence on information processing strategies, consistent with the assimilative/accommodative distinctions proposed by Bless and Fiedler (2006).

It appears then that there are close neural links and a complex, multifaceted, and bidirectional relationship between affect and cognition. Cognitive processes determine emotional reactions, and, in turn, affective states influence how people remember, perceive, and interpret information. These effects are highly context sensitive and depend on the kind of information processing strategies adopted. However, significant problems remain. The various research areas linking emotion and cognition remain poorly integrated. An important task for future work is to better integrate research on the cognitive antecedents of emotion with the study of the cognitive and behavioral consequences of affect. A better understanding of the interface of affect and cognition is of vital importance in a variety of applied fields and is likely to yield important new insights into the emotional and cognitive domains of human life.

REFERENCES

Bless, H., & Fiedler, K. (2006). Mood and the regulation of information processing. In J. P. Forgas (Ed.), *Affect in social cognition and behavior*. New York: Psychology Press.

Bower, G. H. (1981). Mood and memory. *American Psychologist, 36*, 129–148.

Clore, G. L., & Storbeck, J. (2006). Affect as information about liking, efficacy, and importance. In J. P. Forgas (Ed.), *Affect in social thinking and behavior* (pp. 123–143). New York: Psychology Press.

Damasio, A. R. (1994). *Descartes' error*. New York: Grosset/Putnam.

Forgas, J. P. (1995). Mood and judgment: The affect infusion model (AIM). *Psychological Bulletin, 117*, 39–66.

Forgas, J. P. (2002). Feeling and doing: Affective influences on interpersonal behavior. *Psychological Inquiry, 13*, 1–28.

Forgas, J. P. (2007). When sad is better than happy: Negative affect can improve the quality and effectiveness of persuasive messages and social influence strategies. *Journal of Experimental Social Psychology, 43*, 513–528.

Gilbert, D. T., Wilson, T. D. (2007). Prospection: Experiencing the future. *Science, 317*(5843), 1351–1354.

Schachter, S. & Singer, J. E. (1962). Cognitive, social and physiological determinants of emotional state. *Psychological Review, 69*, 379–399.

Schwarz, N. (1990). Feelings as information: Informational and motivational functions of affective states. In E. T. Higgins & R. Sorrentino (Eds.), *Handbook of motivation and cognition: Foundations of social behaviour* (Vol. 2, pp. 527–561). New York: Guilford Press.

Smith, C. A., & Kirby, L. D. (2000). Consequences require antecedents: Toward a process model of emotion elicitation. In J. Forgas (Ed.), *Feeling and thinking: The role of affect in social cognition* (pp. 83–106). New York: Cambridge University Press.

SUGGESTED READINGS

Forgas, J. P. (Ed.). (2006). *Affect in social thinking and behavior*. New York: Psychology Press.

Forgas, J. P., & Smith, C. A. (2007). Affect and emotion. In: M. Hogg & J. Cooper (Eds.). *The SAGE handbook of social psychology: Concise student edition.* (pp. 146–175). Thousand Oaks: Sage.

JOSEPH P. FORGAS
University of New South Wales, Australia

See also: **Cognitive Development; Emotions**

COGNITIVE THERAPY

Cognitive therapy (CT), a system of psychotherapy with an operationalized treatment, is based on an elaborated theory of psychopathology and personality. The theory has been empirically validated in hundreds of cognitive science studies, and the therapy itself has been demonstrated to be effective in hundreds of randomized controlled trials for a wide variety of psychiatric disorders, psychological problems, and medical conditions with psychological components (Beck, 2005). Research has shown that CT is highly effective in helping patients not only overcome their disorders but also in preventing relapse (Hollon et al., 2005).

CT treatment is goal-oriented, time-sensitive, educative, and collaborative, and it is based on an information-processing model. The cognitive model posits that the way people perceive their experiences influences their emotional, behavioral, and physiological reactions. Correcting misperceptions and modifying unhelpful thinking and behavior brings about improved reactions (Beck, 1964).

CT was developed in the early 1960s by Aaron T. Beck, a psychiatrist. Trained as a psychoanalyst, Beck conducted a series of experiments in the 1950s that he believed would provide scientific validation of the psychoanalytic concepts of depression. When his research failed to validate the notion that depression was a result of retroflected hostility, he began further investigations into the nature of this psychiatric disorder. He discovered that depressed patients displayed a characteristic negative bias in their thinking. They continually had spontaneously occurring negative cognitions ("automatic thoughts" that were verbal or imaginal in nature) about themselves, their worlds, and their future. Beck found that his depressed patients rapidly improved when he moved from free association to a more directive style of treatment in which he and his patients focused on solving current problems and engaged in collaborative empiricism, jointly investigating the accuracy and utility of the patients' automatic thoughts. When patients solved their problems, modified their dysfunctional behavior, and corrected the distortions in their thinking, they quickly experienced enduring improvement

in their mood, symptoms, functioning, and relationships (Beck, 1979).

After developing the cognitive theory and therapy of depression, Beck and colleagues turned their attention to developing cognitive formulations and treatments for other disorders. They found, for example, that anxious patients were pre-occupied with fearful automatic thoughts about danger, risk, vulnerability, and their inability to cope effectively to prevent or handle adverse circumstances. The thinking of substance-abusing patients was characterized by an underestimation of the risks of using drugs or alcohol and by permission-giving cognitions. By the early years of the twenty-first century, researchers throughout the world had found empirical validation for the theory and treatment of a myriad of disorders, including various forms of depression, the range of anxiety disorders, eating disorders, body dysmorphic disorder, somatization disorder, substance abuse, personality disorders, and, in conjunction with medication, severe mental illnesses such as bipolar disorder and schizophrenia. CT has also been shown to be effective in the treatment of medical conditions such as insomnia, infertility, fibromyalgia, chronic pain, irritable bowel syndrome, erectile dysfunction, obesity, premenstrual syndrome, and migraine headaches. The therapy has been adapted and its efficacy demonstrated in individual and group treatment, for children and adolescents, for adults and older adults, and for couples and families.

The theory of CT was influenced by Greek Stoic philosophers and by a number of contemporary theorists such as Adler, Alexander, Horney, Sullivan, Kelly, Arnold, Ellis, Lazarus, Bandura, Lewinsohn, and Meichenbaum. Breaking with psychoanalytic models of theory and practice, Beck incorporated behavioral approaches as espoused by social learning, stress inoculation training, problem solving training, and self-control therapy, with a primary emphasis on changing cognition as well as behavior.

CT treatment is based on a cognitive formulation that varies from disorder to disorder (Beck, 1967). In panic disorder, for example, therapy focuses on the catastrophic misinterpretation of symptoms and extinction of avoidance behaviors. CT treatment is also based on a specific cognitive conceptualization of the individual. One patient, for example, thought, "I'm having a heart attack," whenever she perceived that her heart was beating rapidly. Her specific safety behaviors were to avoid physical exertion and to leave situations when she started to feel anxious. The cognitive formulation of avoidant personality disorder involves negative beliefs about the self and others, and cognitive, behavioral, social, and emotional avoidance. One such patient had automatic thoughts such as "No one likes me," "I can't stand feeling this way," and "If I go to the party, people will reject me." He avoided most social occasions, and, when he did attend an event, he avoided making eye contact, conversing with others, and drawing attention to himself. He tried to avoid even thinking about things that led to his feeling anxious and thereby distracted himself whenever he experienced a negative emotion.

The cognitive formulation of patients' disorders focuses not only on their most superficial level of thinking (their automatic thoughts), but also on deeper level cognitions (their basic assumptions and core beliefs) and patterns of dysfunctional behavior. A man with paranoia may think, "My neighbors are plotting against me," which is a specific reflection of his general core beliefs, "I am vulnerable" and "People are likely to hurt me." He displays characteristic behaviors, or coping strategies, of guardedness and vigilance for interpersonal harm, related to his basic assumptions, "If I trust others, I'll be harmed" and "If I'm always on guard, I can protect myself."

The current emotional and behavioral reactions of patients are understandable once their perceptions of situations are elicited; these perceptions make sense once the basic way they view themselves, their worlds, and other people, together with their characteristic ways of coping with their experiences, are identified. The treatment of patients with personality disorders (as compared with symptomatic disorders like depression and anxiety) generally requires a greater emphasis on understanding the meaning to patients of their adverse childhood experiences; how these experiences led to the development and maintenance of extremely strong, rigid, global beliefs about the self, world, and others; how these beliefs shape their interpretations of current experiences; how these beliefs could be faulty (despite the very strong sense patients have that these ideas are true); and how, over time, these beliefs can be modified (Beck et al, 2004; Beck, 2005).

When conceptualizing and treating individual patients, the therapist is informed by the general cognitive formulation of the patient's disorder(s) and collects data to develop an individualized cognitive conceptualization. Treatment is modified to suit the individual's preferences, and the therapist takes into consideration relevant factors such as the patient's age, gender, developmental level, ethnicity, culture, religious beliefs, and childhood, family, social, educational, vocational, medical, and psychiatric history.

Therapists initially conduct an intensive evaluation to diagnose patients on the five axes of DSM-IV, including an emphasis on current functioning and a review of pertinent aspects of the patient's history. Based on this evaluation and on the cognitive formulation of patients' disorder(s), therapists present a general treatment plan. Using examples from patients' recent distressing experiences, therapists conceptualize and help patients understand how their thinking has influenced their emotions, behavior, and sometimes physiology as well. They emphasize that patients get better by making small, daily changes in their thinking and behavior and that the overall goal of treatment is to teach patients to become their own therapist. Therapists elicit feedback from the patient about the treatment plan and modify it, if needed. They then elicit specific behavioral goals that the patient wishes to accomplish as a result of treatment.

CT sessions are structured to make maximal use of time to help patients solve their problems, feel better by the end of the session, and develop a plan to improve their experience in the coming week(s). At the beginning of sessions, therapists reestablish rapport with patients and collect data to organize the session. They conduct a mood check to ensure that patients' symptoms are diminishing over time. They elicit important experiences, both negative and positive, from the past week that might bear further discussion, they review homework, and they inquire whether important events or problems might arise in the coming week and should be discussed. To set a collaborative agenda, therapists summarize this information and ask patients which problems they most want help in solving. Together they prioritize the problems and plan how to divide the session time.

In the context of solving specific problems, therapists collect data, plan a strategy, and determine needed techniques. They provide a rationale for their interventions, elicit feedback, and modify their approach as needed. They primarily use Socratic questioning and guided discovery to help patients identify, evaluate, and modify key cognitions. They directly teach patients skills to solve their own problems; to test their thinking through a process of realistic appraisal and/or behavioral experiments; to develop new core beliefs; to alter maladaptive behavior; to improve daily functioning and relationships; and to regulate emotion. They continually elicit feedback to ensure that patients find interventions useful. After discussing a problem and devising a plan of action for patients to carry out at home, therapists ask patients to summarize key points of their discussion, which the therapist or patient then writes down. They also record what the patient has decided to do about the problem in the coming week, for example, by instituting solutions to problems, reading therapy notes, testing the validity and utility of automatic thoughts and beliefs, responding to predicted and novel cognitions, and trying new behavioral skills.

Toward the end of the session, therapists and patients review the follow-up tasks (homework) and, if needed, modify the tasks or the patient's maladaptive thinking about the tasks, to ensure that the patient is highly likely to accomplish them. Therapists then elicit feedback on the session as a whole, asking whether patients felt accurately understood, whether they found the session helpful, and whether they would like to make changes in the next treatment session (Beck, 1995).

A number of studies have demonstrated that the degree to which therapists follow these principles of treatment is associated with the degree of improvement their patients display. The Cognitive Therapy Rating Scale (available from http://www.academyofct.org, along with an instructional manual) provides a summary of these skills and is an essential tool to ensure treatment fidelity and efficacy. It measures general therapeutic skills in setting agendas, eliciting feedback, accurate understanding, interpersonal effectiveness, collaboration, and pacing and making efficient use of time. It also emphasizes conceptualization, strategy, and technique, through an assessment of the expertise therapists display in guided discovery, focusing on key cognitions and behaviors, strategy for change, application of techniques, and homework design and review (Young & Beck, 1980).

The field of cognitive therapy is likely to expand as it continues to gain credibility, not only through the overwhelming evidence of outcome research but also newly demonstrated changes in the neurobiology of patients treated with CT (Beck, 2008). The number of cognitive scientists, researchers, and practitioners worldwide continues to grow exponentially, and new discoveries serve to continually help clinicians refine their understanding and treatment of psychiatric disorders, psychological problems, and medical problems with psychological components.

REFERENCES

Beck, A. T. (1964). Thinking and depression: Theory and therapy. *Archives of General Psychiatry, 10*, 561–571.

Beck, A. T. (1976). *Cognitive therapy and the emotional disorders*. New York: International Universities Press.

Beck, A. T. (2005). The current state of cognitive therapy: A 40-year retrospective. *Archives of General Psychiatry, 63*, 953–959.

Beck, A. T. (2008). The evolution of the cognitive model of depression and its neurobiological correlates. *American Journal of Psychiatry, 165*, 969–977.

Beck, A. T., Freeman, A., Davis, D. D., Pretzer, J., Fleming, B., Beck, J. S., et al. (2004). *Cognitive therapy of personality disorders* (2nd ed.). New York: Guilford Press.

Beck, A. T., Rush, A. J., Shaw, B. F., & Emery G. (1979). *Cognitive therapy of depression*. New York: Guilford Press.

Beck, J. S. (1995). *Cognitive therapy: Basics and beyond*. New York: Guilford Press.

Beck, J. S. (2005). *Cognitive therapy for challenging problems*. New York: Guilford Press.

Hollon, S. D., DeRubeis, R. J., Shelton, R. C., Amsterdam, J. D., Salomon, R. M., O'Reardon, J. P., et al. (2005). Prevention of relapse following cognitive therapy versus medications on moderate to severe depression. *Archives of General Psychiatry, 62*, 417–422.

Young, J. E., & Beck, A. T. (1980). *Cognitive therapy scale: Rating manual*. Bala Cynwyd, PA: Beck Institute for Cognitive Therapy and Research.

JUDITH S. BECK
Beck Institute for Cognitive Therapy and Research and University of Pennsylvania

See also: **Behavior Modification; Cognitive Behavioral Analysis System of Psychotherapy**

COHEN'S *d*

Cohen's (1988) *d* is one of several statistics used to examine differences between means, as in the case of the difference in mean outcome between participants who received treatment X and participants who received treatment Y. This difference score, calculated in standard deviation units, falls under the broader category of effect sizes. Effect sizes provide an important complement to traditional null hypothesis statistical significance testing. The traditional *p* value indicates the likelihood of obtaining the observed results if the null hypothesis is true (Cohen, 1988). It does not, however, offer any information about the magnitude of the research findings (e.g., how much of a difference it makes if someone receives treatment X vs. treatment Y; Rosenthal & Rosnow, 2008). Cohen's *d* offers an effective way of obtaining this information from means and standard deviations calculated in primary research.

Cohen (1988) offered tentative benchmarks for interpreting *d* as small, medium, or large in behavioral science research. He defined a *d* of 0.2 as small, a *d* of 0.5 as medium, and a *d* of 0.8 as large. Many researchers have adopted these benchmarks to contextualize and interpret their effect sizes. Cohen's *d* also has important applications for power analysis, that is, determining the probability of rejecting the null hypothesis when it is in fact false. When combined with other relevant study information, a researcher can use Cohen's *d* to determine the power of a given study. This information is helpful in deciding a priori whether to conduct the study or what sample size would be needed in order to yield sufficient power (Cohen, 1988).

In addition to its utility in effect size calculation for primary research and power analysis, Cohen's *d* has valuable applications for meta-analysis. Cohen's *d* is particularly well suited for meta-analytic research on differences between two treatments or between a treatment and a control group. By standardizing the differences between groups, Cohen's *d* offers researchers the opportunity to aggregate findings across studies that may not have utilized the same measure of the dependent variable (Lipsey & Wilson, 2001).

REFERENCES

Cohen, J. (1988). *Statistical power analysis for the behavioral sciences* (2nd ed.). Hillsdale, NJ: Lawrence Erlbaum.

Lipsey, M. W., & Wilson, D. B. (2001). *Practical meta-analysis.* Thousand Oaks, CA: Sage.

Rosenthal, R., & Rosnow, R. L. (2008). *Essentials of behavioral research: Methods and data analysis* (3rd ed.). New York: McGraw-Hill.

SUGGESTED READINGS

McGrath, R. E., & Meyer, G. J. (2006). When effect sizes disagree: The case of *r* and *d*. *Psychological Methods, 11*, 386–401.

Thompson, B. (2007). Effect sizes, confidence intervals, and confidence intervals for effect sizes. *Psychology in the Schools, 44*, 423–432.

Marc J. Diener
Argosy University, Washington, DC

See also: Effect Size; Statistical Power

COLLABORATIVE ASSESSMENT (See Therapeutic Assessment)

COLLECTIVE UNCONSCIOUS

In the early days of psychoanalysis, Sigmund Freud and Carl Gustav Jung collaborated and explored unconscious aspects of the mind as they observed and experienced it clinically and personally. Archaeological and geological metaphors proved useful in describing the apparent layering of psyche seen in their patients and in themselves. Both men recognized what they saw as two main strata to the unconscious, correspondingly composed of ontogenetic and phylogenetic factors. Although Freud focused more attention on the ontogenetic factor in the development of psychopathology (the infantile neuroses), he did retain a view throughout his life that these phylogenetic contributions were acquired traits and were inherited; in other words, he held to a Lamarckian hypothesis, despite protest from his followers (Hoffer, 1992).

Jung on other hand, while sustaining a belief in a phylogenetic component in the organization of the mind, distinguished the potential to form phylogenetically based images—his Kantian "archetype-as-such"—from the actual contents, the archetypal images. The archetypes are understood as the human equivalent of instincts, that is, primal and universal patterns that operate at the deepest levels shaping human thought, behavior, and affect. These patterns are psychosomatic entities characterized by autonomy from consciousness, numinosity, and profound unconsciousness, never having been conscious thus unlike the repressed material of the ontological unconscious.

The personal dimension of the unconscious was seen by Jung as composed of complexes from the individual's history, but even these complexes are seen as having archetypal cores. Maladaptive complexes lead to neuroses and aspects of character disorders. The archetypal potentials are neutral sources of psychological energy and can be a wellspring of creativity, but when activated in problematic ways, they can manifest in psychotic processes. The entire field of archetypes taken as whole is what makes up and defines the collective unconscious, also referred to as the "objective psyche."

As the theory of archetypes developed, Jung gave considerable attention to articulating their major forms and the ways in which they operate in the psyche at the individual and collective levels. He devoted an entire volume to these signature concepts (Jung, 1969), and most of his later works are filled with references to them. Culturally, archetypes are frequently expressed in mythopoetic forms. Hence, the importance of myths, legends, fairy tales, and the like in detecting these patterns. The clinical methods for working with archetypal material differ from those focused solely on ontological aspects of the unconscious. Jung evolved the tools of amplification and active imagination to augment the type of dream analysis he used to explore this realm for its scientific and transformative potentials. A series of layers then emerges spanning the individual, familial, tribal, sociocultural, and universal strata of the psyche.

In recent years an important revision of archetypal theory has developed from the application of complexity and emergence theories. Archetypes have been shown to be emergent properties of the dynamic interactions of the psyche-soma with the environment in a narrative field. The collective unconscious then in turn can readily be modeled as a scale-free network of archetypes with links of varying strengths between the elements. These networks are known to have self-organizing properties that tend to give rise to the sense of autonomy and numinosity first identified by Jung as characteristic of archetypes (see Cambray & Carter, 2004). The structural model of the psyche founded on a network system, the collective unconscious, can thereby be brought into accord with some of the latest findings in science.

REFERENCES

Cambray, J., and Carter, L. (Eds.). (2004). *Analytical psychology: Contemporary perspectives in Jungian analysis.* Hove and New York: Brunner-Routledge.

Hoffer, Peter T. (1992). The concept of phylogenetic inheritance in Freud and Jung. *Journal American Psychoanalytic Association, 10,* 517–530.

Jung, C. G. (1969). *The archetypes and the collective unconscious* (R. F. C. Hull, Trans.; 2nd ed.). *The collected works of C. G. Jung,* vol. 9, part 1. Princeton: Princeton University Press.

SUGGESTED READINGS

Stein, M., (Ed.). (2008). *Jungian psychoanalysis.* Chicago: Open Court.

Von Franz, M.-L. (1999). *Archetypal dimensions of the psyche.* Boston and London: Shambhala.

JOSEPH CAMBRAY
Massachusetts General Hospital,
Harvard Medical School

See also: Analytical Psychology; Archetypes

COLOMBIA, PSYCHOLOGY IN

This article presents a brief synthesis of the antecedents and current state of psychology in Colombia. First, historical information about early authors, events, and practices in the development of the discipline is presented. Then, information on the state of psychology as a discipline and as a profession is organized around indicators of development suggested by the International Union of Psychological Science: development of training programs, scientific research, professional associations, and legal recognition of the profession.

The emergence of psychology in Colombia has been associated with some events that constituted the bases for the development of the discipline and the consolidation of a psychological community. Some of the main events include the foundation of the Institute of Applied Psychology and the opening of the first psychology program at National University in 1948; the publication of the first volume of the *Revista de Psicología* in 1956, and the *Revista Latinoamericana de Psicología* in 1969; and the organization of the XV Interamerican Congress of Psychology in 1974 and the first Latin American Meeting on Psychology Training in 1979, among others (Giraldo & Rodríguez, 2000; Mankeliunas, 1993).

The consolidation of the first psychology programs in Colombia was accompanied by a significant growth in the quality of teaching, research, and applied work. During the 1970s and 1980s a concern for the ways in which psychological knowledge could be applied to social problems and an interest in transforming research questions into structured research programs influenced important discussions

and reviews of the psychology curriculum. As a result, early research and intervention programs were developed in areas such as learning, motivation, development, social, and educational and clinical psychology.

Colombia is considered a leader in the quality of psychology training in Latin America (Ardila, 1986). An undergraduate program lasts five years on average. The curriculum includes disciplinary formation in the areas of history, epistemology, and methods in psychology, biological and sociocultural foundations of behavior, behavioral processes, developmental, individual, and social psychology. It also includes training in clinical, educational, organizational, and (recently) forensic psychology. In addition to courses related to these areas, students take a one-year practicum. In a few institutions, they also write a thesis in order to obtain the degree. There are 130 undergraduate and 57 graduate programs. The first graduate programs were created in the mid-1980s; currently, three doctoral programs (one more is currently being approved), 18 master degree programs, and about 36 specializations are offered around the country. The Ministry of Education estimates that 50,000 people hold an undergraduate or graduate degree in psychology. In Colombia, psychology has traditionally been a major chosen mostly by women; although an increasing number of men are now selecting this field of study, nearly 70% of students continue to be women.

Starting in 1992, the Colombian government has been developing a strategy to implement evaluation mechanisms to guarantee minimal requirements to create new training programs and to certify high-quality programs. In order to be certified, the offering institution has to pass a demanding evaluation process coordinated by the National Council of Accreditation. To date, 15 psychology programs have received a high-quality certification.

Two main features characterize psychology training in Colombia: a multiparadigmatic conception of the discipline at the level of training and professional work, and a defined profile that includes academic and professional activities in a wide spectrum of psychological fields.

During the last decade there has been an important consolidation of the research activity in Colombian psychology. The definition of policies promoting the development of science and technology has included strategies to promote and regulate research. One of these strategies is the formalization, productivity measurement, ranking, and strategic planning of research groups. This process has resulted in 79 research groups in different areas of psychology. Among the groups, 30% have been classified in category A, assigned to high-quality and internationally competitive research groups. Some of the areas of research by these groups are: animal learning and behavior, behavioral neuroscience, social psychology, health psychology, and developmental psychology. Historically, most of the research done in the country has been published in local or regional journals. In the last decade, however, a growing number of researchers have begun to publish their work in international journals, published in English. This has increased the impact of Colombian research production on the discipline at large.

Sixteen internationally recognized psychology journals are published in Colombia. One third of them, including the *Revista Latinoamericana de Psicología, Universitas Psychologica*, and *Acta Colombiana de Psicología* and *Avances en Psicología Latinoamericana*, have a growing impact on the psychology literature and are included in the main international indexes for scientific publications such as *ISI, Scopus, PsycInfo, Scielo*, and *Redalyc*, among others.

The first professional organization of psychologists was the Colombian Federation of Psychologists founded in the 1960s. Although a number of small organizations have played a role in the development of certain areas of psychology, the most general and representative associations are the Sociedad Colombiana de Psicología (founded in 1978), and the Colegio Colombiano de Psicólogos (founded in 1999). The Asociación Colombiana de Facultades de Psicología (founded in 1986) has played a key role in the improvement of quality standards of professional training. These organizations have contributed in an important way to the legal recognition and regulation of the profession by the Colombian government.

REFERENCES

Ardila, R. (1986). *La Psicología en América Latina. Pasado, presente y futuro*. México: Siglo XXI.

Giraldo, B., & Rodríguez, O. R. (2000). Eventos significativos de la Psicología colombiana en el siglo XX. *Suma Psicológica, 7*, 275–294.

Mankeliunas, M. (1993). *Desarrollo histórico*. En R. Ardila (Comp.), *Psicología en Colombia: Contexto social e histórico* (pp. 43–66). Bogotá: TM Editores.

Peña-Correal, T. (2007). 60 años de la Psicología en Colombia. *Revista Latinoamericana de Psicología, 39*, 675–676.

JULIO EDUARDO CRUZ
SONIA CARRILLO
University of the Andes, Bogotá, Colombia

COMMUNICATION DISORDERS

Communication disorders limit or disrupt any of the processes of human communication, including language, voice, speech, and hearing. The major types of communication disorder are considered in this article; more detailed information is provided by Anderson and Shames (2006) and Owens, Metz, and Haas (2007).

Prevalence

Hearing loss affects millions of children and adults. Some estimates of hearing loss in children run as high as 15%, and it is believed that about 30% of adults over the age of 60 years have a hearing loss. Disorders of voice, speech, and language also affect a large part of the population (Kent, in press). Most conservative estimates of prevalence range from 6% to 10%, but there is considerable variance in reported figures, owing to differing criteria used for diagnosis, different methodologies, and heterogeneity in the demographic characteristics of the sampled population. In general, communication disorders affect males more than they do females, with sex ratios as high as 3:1 or 5:1. Hearing loss also occurs more frequently in males. The origin of these sex imbalances is not completely understood, but biological factors unquestionably play a major role in them.

Basic Concepts

It is important to distinguish among speech, voice, and language, which are separate aspects of human communication and are associated with distinct disorders. Language is a complex system that involves the comprehension, manipulation, and expression of symbols to communicate ideas, feelings, and observations. Human language can be studied as several components: (1) syntax, or grammar, which refers to the rules that specify how words are put together to form phrases and sentences; (2) semantics, which deals with the meaning of words; (3) phonology, which concerns the assembly of sounds into words; and (4) pragmatics, which addresses the function of language in socially acceptable ways. Spoken language is produced through the coordinated actions of the respiratory system (lungs and associated structures), the larynx (voicebox), and the articulatory system (consisting principally of the jaw, lips, tongue, and soft palate). Voice is often subsumed in the production of speech, given that vibration of the vocal folds within the larynx is a primary energy source for speech sounds. Because speech is central to the everyday expression of language, hearing is critically important to human communication.

Speech Sound Disorders

Children gain proficiency with speech over several years, beginning with babbling in infancy and progressing through a mastery of speech sounds at the age of about 8 years. Some children have persistent difficulties correctly producing speech sounds. These developmental speech sound disorders are also known as phonological, articulatory, or phonological-articulatory disorders. There are multiple causes of these disorders, including hearing impairment, psychosocial factors, and neurological conditions, but in the great majority of affected children, the etiology is unknown.

Stuttering

This condition, usually diagnosed when a child is between 3 and 5 years of age, is a disruption in the flow or fluency of speech and takes the form of sound or syllable repetition, prolongations of sounds, or hesitations or blocks. It is entirely normal for children to experience some degree of disfluency in early language learning, but the majority overcome these episodes to develop normally fluent speech. What sets apart children who stutter is the severity and persistence of their disfluencies. The worldwide prevalence of stuttering is estimated to be about 1%, and the prevalence in children is thought to be about 5%. Frequently, stuttering co-occurs with other speech-language disorders, especially speech sound disorders. Although the etiology of stuttering is not completely clear, evidence points to neurological abnormalities based on genetic predisposition and a vulnerability to environmental stressors.

Structurally Based Speech Disorders

These disorders are related to a physical abnormality of the speech production system. The abnormality can be congenital, as in the case of a cleft palate, or acquired, as in the case of physical trauma or surgical ablation of tissues (for example, to treat cancer). The effects on speech and voice depend on the nature and extent of damage. The most common orofacial anomaly in humans is clefting (cleft lip, cleft palate, or both), which has a worldwide incidence of 1 in 700 births. Although the etiology of clefting remains under study, evidence indicates that both genetic and environmental factors are involved. Surgical repair of the cleft is typically accomplished early in the child's life, and speech-language therapy usually is needed to ensure effective speech production.

Neurogenic Speech Disorders: Dysarthria and Apraxia of Speech

A neurogenic speech disorder results from neural damage that disrupts the normal control of the muscles of speech production. Dysarthria is an impairment of the muscles of speech production owing to damage or disease affecting the nervous system. The speech impairment is related to weakness, slowness, or incoordination of the speech musculature. The nature of the speech disorder varies with the type of neural damage. Dysarthria can be associated with neurological disorders that have increased prevalence in older individuals (e.g., stroke and Parkinson's disease), but it also occurs in children who have conditions such as cerebral palsy. Apraxia of speech disturbs primarily the programming or sequencing of speech movements, and, unlike dysarthria, it is not associated with obvious muscular impairments. The responsible neural damage usually is in the cerebral cortex.

Developmental Language Delay

Several different terms have been used for a delayed or deviant language development in children that is not related to conditions such as deafness, autism, or mental retardation. The most prevalent subtype is specific language impairment (SLI), which refers to language difficulties that are not attributable to emotional disorder, cognitive delay, sensory impairment, or language difference. This disorder can affect any or all of the domains of language discussed earlier in this article. SLI can interfere with a child's educational and social activities and may contribute to difficulties in reading and writing. The etiology of SLI is not well understood, but much of current research focuses on genetic factors and neurological abnormalities.

Aphasia

The most common acquired language disorder in adults is aphasia, which results from damage to the brain that disrupts one or more of the processes of language formulation, expression, and reception. In the early history of aphasia, two primary types of aphasia were recognized. Expressive aphasia is a disorder of language output and has been linked especially with damage to the front (anterior) regions of the brain. Receptive aphasia is a disorder of language comprehension and has been associated primarily with damage to the posterior regions of the brain. A number of other types of aphasia were subsequently described, depending on their effects on various aspects of language processing. Across all types, the most frequent cause of aphasia is a stroke or cerebrovascular accident.

Hearing Disorders

These disorders are the third major cause of disability in the United States. The three major types are conductive (relating to the mechanical function of the middle ear), sensorineural (relating to damage to the neural pathway), and mixed (a combination of conductive and sensorineural). Hearing disorders can be congenital or acquired. Acquired disorders have multiple etiologies, including exposure to intense sounds, ototoxic drugs, and otologic diseases. In population studies, hearing loss increases with age, more so in men than in women. The loss can be on one side only (unilateral) or both sides (bilateral).

The audiogram is a chart that shows loudness (or hearing loss) as a function of the frequency (the main physical correlate of pitch) of pure tones (sinusoids). Hearing testing usually samples the frequency range of 250 Hz to 8,000 Hz. The frequency range of human hearing actually extends up to about 20,000 Hz, but most of the energy in speech is contained in a smaller frequency band that reaches only to about 4,000 Hz. The audiogram shows both the degree and pattern of hearing loss. Degree of loss is measured as loss in decibels (dB), a logarithmic unit. The pattern of hearing loss is the configuration of loss across the frequency range. Some hearing losses are flat (nearly the same loss across different frequencies), some are high-frequency losses (affecting especially the high frequencies), and others are low frequency (affecting primarily the low frequencies) (Bess & Humes, 2008).

Hearing disorders sometimes entail complications such as loudness recruitment (an abnormal increase in loudness sensation), tinnitus (subjective noises unrelated to physical stimuli), and difficulties in speech discrimination. Making sounds louder can provide some benefit to persons with hearing loss, but there are limits to amplification, and making sounds louder does not necessarily resolve the other problems that can occur. A number of treatments are used to correct or reduce hearing loss, depending on the underlying factors. Surgery can be used to correct some physical causes. The most common treatment is amplification by hearing aids, but other treatments include assistive listening devices and cochlear implants. The cochlear implant is the most successful neural prosthesis. It uses implanted electrodes to transmit sound energy to the individual's auditory neural pathway. Cochlear implants are being used with increasing success and allow implanted individuals to participate in an oral/aural world.

REFERENCES

Anderson, N. B., & Shames, G. H. (Eds.) (2006) *Human communication disorders: An introduction* (7th ed.). Boston: Pearson.

Bess, F. H., & Humes, L. E. (2008). *Audiology: The fundamentals* (4th ed.). Philadelphia: Lippincott Williams & Wilkins.

Kent, R. D. (in press). Disorders of speech and language. In J. Snow & G. Woodson (Eds.), *Ballenger's otolaryngology head and neck surgery* (17th ed.). Hamilton, Ontario: B C Decker.

Owens, R. E. Jr., Metz, D. E., and Haas, A. (2007). *Introduction to communicative disorders: A life span perspective.* Boston: Allyn & Bacon.

RAY D. KENT
University of Wisconsin

See also: **Deafness and Hearing Loss; Speech Production**

COMMUNICATION SKILLS TRAINING

Communication skills training has developed over the past 50 years and has been applied to training a range of professionals and paraprofessionals, other occupational groups, patients, and students. The range of health professionals exposed to communication skills training is extensive, including physicians, dentists, nurses, psychologists, and pharmacists. There are several meta-analytical studies showing that the impact of training with these health professional groups is positive, enhancing professional–patient communication and patient satisfaction (Smith et al., 2007). Other professional and paraprofessional groups, for whom communication skills training is a key element of their education, are counselors, social workers, helpline workers, aviation personnel, and insurance company employees, to name but a few.

Therapists of diverse theoretical positions have long realized that numerous patients with a variety of complaints are deficient in interpersonal or communication skills. Persons diagnosed as having psychiatric disorders or serious behavior, drinking, marital, or child management problems have all been identified as having difficulties in interpersonal communication. Three major trends have led to increased emphasis on communication skills training as an important therapeutic and preventive tool. First, an increasing number of therapists have turned to a different set of assumptions from those of the medical model. Basic to this approach is the assumption that the client is suffering from a skill performance deficit and that the role of the therapist is to teach or train the client to perform the requisite set of skills.

A second trend has been the increasing application of behavioral strategies to the treatment of a diversity of problems. It was quickly recognized that some clients would have to learn an extensive array of communication skills, such as conversational skills, assertiveness, and job acquisition skills. A third trend was the application of the microcounseling method, used to train counselors and psychotherapists to train psychiatric patients, parents, marital partners, and families in communication skills.

Communication skills training is focused usually on two broad sets of interpersonal skills: skills in simply interacting with one or more persons and skills involving interpersonal or shared problem solving. Conversational skill training is directed toward the enhancement of an individual's ability to initiate and maintain conversations with other people. This form of training has been employed with schizophrenic patients (Ku et al., 2007), fibromyalgia patients (Stillman, 2006), and elderly persons with Alzheimer's disease (Gentry & Fisher, 2007). Date initiation and heterosexual interaction skills are another set of communication skills training procedures developed for those having difficulty with these spheres of life. Communication skills training is a central component of most assertiveness-training procedures, because effective communication is seen as an important precursor to assertive behavior.

Another specific form of communication skills training is job interview training directed toward chronically unemployed persons and people about to enter or reenter the job market. Most premarital, marital, and parenting programs, whether developed for therapeutic, preventive, or educational purposes, include communication skills training in both interactional and shared problem-solving skills. Many organizational development programs directed toward increasing the quality of working life include communication skills training as a critical component. Programs concerned to facilitate interpersonal communication and/or shared problem solving have been developed for managers, supervisors, and coworkers. With the increasing realization that primary prevention programs are best directed at the younger members of our society, communication skills training programs have been developed for use from prekindergarten to high school (Godfrey, 2005).

The elements of a communication skills training program are determined by the group to be trained and the range of skills to be included. The range of skills runs from highly specific skills (question asking in a school population) to a more general group of skills (counseling skills). The first step is to carry out a task analysis to identify the skills to be trained and the characteristics associated with them. There are many examples of such analyses, including the Kalamazoo Consensus Statement on the elements of communication in medical encounters (Participants in the Bayer-Fetzer Conference, 2001), the review of communication skills training in social work programs in England (Dinham, 2006), and the counseling skills delineated by Kuntze, van der Molen, and Born (2007).

Most programs use a variant of the microteaching or microcounseling approach, in which single skills are trained and then integrated (Evans, Hearn, Uhlemann, & Ivey, 2008). When training single skills or integrating skills, the first step involves a didactic segment that may be delivered by using a variety of media, such as a manual, a video, or a computer-based program. Simply learning about the skills is not sufficient; some form of practice element is required. The most popular form of practice is role-play practice with feedback. Again this element of the program may involve small groups of trainees (each assuming different roles), simulated patients, or virtual reality. Less frequent but important in programs are procedures designed to enhance maintenance of the skills learned.

Initial research in this area involved the demonstration that communication skills training methods produced significant increments in performance during and following training. A second wave of research involved the demonstration that increments in communication skills performance led to changes in other behaviors, such as decreased delinquency, improved marital and parent–child relations, and increased academic performance. A subsequent concern of researchers was the demonstration that educationally based methods of communication skills training

are superior to methods based on other assumptions, such as sensitivity training. Yet another focus of research has been the specification of the skills that should be included in communication skills training programs and the best methods of training the constituent skills. It can be concluded that communication skills training programs are effective; however, considerable research is required to develop programs that enhance the generalization of the skills to different situations and over time.

REFERENCES

Dinham, A. (2006). A review of practice of teaching and learning of communication skills in social work education in England. *Social Work Education, 25*, 838–850.

Evans, D. R., Hearn, M. T., Uhlemann, M. R., & Ivey, A. E. (2008). *Essential interviewing: A programmed approach to effective communication.* Belmont, CA: Brooks/Cole.

Gentry, R. A., & Fisher, J. E. (2007). Facilitating conversation in elderly persons with Alzheimer's disease. *Clinical Gerontologist, 31*, 77–98.

Godfrey, J. (2005). Developing children's conversational skills in mainstream schools: An evaluation of group therapy. *Child Language Teaching and Therapy, 21*, 251–262.

Ku, J., Han, K., Lee, H. R., Jang, H. J., Kim, K. U., Park, S. H., et al. (2007). VR-based conversation training program for patients with schizophrenia: A preliminary clinical trial. *Cyber Psychology & Behavior, 10*, 567–574.

Kuntze, J., van der Molen, H. T., & Born, M. P. (2007). Progress in mastery of counseling communication skills: Development and evaluation of a new instrument for the assessment of counseling communication skills. *European Psychologist, 12*, 301–313.

Participants in the Bayer-Fetzer Conference on Physician–Patient Communication in Medical School. (2001). Essential elements of communication in medical encounters: The Kalamazoo consensus statement. *Academic Medicine, 76*, 390–393.

Smith, S., Hanson, J. L., Tewksbury, L. R., Christy, C., Talib, N. J., Harris, M. A., et al. (2007). Teaching patient communication skills to medical students. *Evaluation & the Health Professions, 30*, 3–21.

Stillman, A. M. (2006). The effect of anger management and communication training on functional and quality of life status in fibromyalgia patients. *Dissertation Abstracts International: Section B, 67*, 1177.

SUGGESTED READINGS

Bull, P. (2002). *Communication under the microscope: The theory and practice of microanalysis.* New York: Routledge.

Farmer, R. F., & Chapman, A. L. (2008). Changing behavior by building skills. In R. F. Farmer & A. L. Chapman (Eds.), *Behavioral interventions in cognitive behavior therapy: Practical guidance for putting theory into action* (pp. 177–201). Washington, DC: American Psychological Association.

Hargie, O. (2006). Training in communication skills: Research, theory and practice. In O. Hargie (Ed.), *The handbook of communication skills* (3rd ed., pp. 553–565). New York: Routledge.

DAVID R. EVANS
University of Western Ontario, Canada

See also: Anger Management; Coping Skills Training; Social Skills Training

COMMUNITY PSYCHOLOGY

Community psychology is the study of the interaction between individuals and all of the levels of their environment (Dalton, Elias, & Wandersman, 2007). Community psychologists are interested in examining and improving the quality of life of individuals, communities, and society through collaborative research and action (Jason & Glenwick, 2002). Duffy and Wong (2000) characterized this field as emphasizing prevention over treatment; underscoring strengths and competencies over weaknesses; adopting an ecological perspective that examines the relationships among people and their environment; valuing and respecting diversity and differences; stressing empowerment, which involves enhancing the processes by which people gain control over their lives; emphasizing action research and social change, which provide more alternatives; stressing collaboration with other disciplines; examining how social support can act as a buffer against stress; and focusing on interventions that build a sense of community.

The field grew out of concern for the social and community problems confronting the United States during the 1960s and 1970s (Tolan, Keys, Chertok, & Jason, 1990). It was formally founded in 1965 at a conference in Swampscott, Massachusetts (Levine & Perkins, 1997), where psychologists stressed the need to emphasize prevention and the importance of targeting the social environment. A core belief of this approach was that the flow of human casualties could be reduced by modifying social systems to make them more responsive and health inducing or teaching persons how to live behaviorally healthy lifestyles (Cowen, 1973). Thus, through community-based prevention and promotion, it was hoped that cost-effective services could be implemented with fewer resources ultimately devoted to remediating hard-to-cure, entrenched problems. To understand human behavior in context, we should actively work to develop an understanding of the social institutions and forces in which individual humans are enmeshed, which also directly points to employing complex, dynamic systems theories.

From a more theoretical perspective, several models of prevention have been advanced, the principal ones being social competence, empowerment, and an ecological approach. Some theorists focus on a social competence model, where the goal is to prevent disorders by enhancing individuals' competencies (Duffy & Wong, 2000). Favored by many behaviorally oriented psychologists because of its emphasis on explicit skills, this approach can assist persons in gaining more resources and increasing their competence and independence (Bogat & Jason, 2000; Glenwick & Jason, 1980).

Another approach is the empowerment model, which attempts to enhance people's sense of control over their own destinies and ability to create change (Rappaport, 1981). Empowerment is action-oriented and goes beyond the individual level as emphasized in the social competence model to include social and public policies. Individuals, organizations, and communities can be empowered, and in the process, they gain greater access, power, and influence over decisions and resources (Zimmerman, 2000). One difficulty for practitioners of the empowerment model involves deciding which groups to help empower. In many communities, there are opposing groups, with each regarding its perspective as correct.

Another paradigm that has captured the attention of many prevention practitioners and community psychologists is the use of the ecological model (Kelly, 1985, 1990), which was adapted from the biological field of ecology. Kelly's theory includes four ecological principles that describe characteristics of settings and systems. For example, various components of a system are interdependent, in that change in one part influences change in another. Dynamic systems theory applied to psychology delves into the embedded contexts, which are central to the ecological approach, and acknowledges the reciprocal interactions among observer, observed, and the larger social systems (Kelly, 2006). In such a relationship, the systemic interrelationships among the individual, the community, and the larger social context must be considered in each treatment intervention. Also, including community members in the research, intervention, and the social policy process enables them to receive support, learn to identify resources, and become better problem-solvers.

Community psychologists agree on working collaboratively with communities, involving them as active participants, in efforts to strengthen the mental and physical health of community members (Jason et al., 2004). These psychologists rely on strategies that are less individualistic in nature (Rappaport, 1981). It is common for interventions to target systemic second-order change that amounts to long-term improvements for a larger number of individuals. This is often done through creating and using research to influence public policy, directly changing the social organization and shaping the systems in which people live.

There are many significant problems that our planet is facing, including poverty, excessive waste of resources, and environmental degradation. The field of community psychology is committed to finding ways to focus on improving the quality of life through research and action (Jason, 1997). As Albee (1986) argued, in the absence of social change, psychopathology will continue to exist as long as there is excessive concentration of economic power, nationalism, and institutions that perpetuate powerlessness, poverty, sexism, racism, ageism, and other forms of oppression.

REFERENCES

Albee, G. W. (1986). Toward a just society. *American Psychologist, 41*, 891–898.

Bogat, G. A., & Jason, L. A. (2000). Towards an integration of behaviorism and community psychology: Dogs bark at those they do not recognize. In J. Rappaport & E. Seidman (Eds.), *Handbook of community psychology* (pp. 101–114). New York: Plenum.

Cowen, E. L. (1973). Social and community interventions. In P. Mussen & M. Rosenzweig (Eds.), *Annual review of psychology* (Vol. 24, pp. 423–472). Palo Alto, CA: Annual Reviews.

Dalton, J. H., Elias, M. J., & Wandersman, A. (2007). *Community psychology: Linking individuals and communities* (2nd ed.). Belmont, CA: Wadsworth.

Duffy, K. G., & Wong, F. Y. (2000). *Community psychology* (2nd ed.). Boston: Allyn and Bacon.

Glenwick, D. S., & Jason, L. A. (Eds.). (1980). *Behavioral community psychology: Progress and prospects*. New York: Praeger.

Jason, L. A. (1997). *Community building: Values for a sustainable future*. Westport, CT: Praeger.

Jason, L. A., & Glenwick, D. S. (Eds.). (2002). *Innovative strategies for promoting health and mental health across the lifespan*. New York: Springer.

Jason, L. A., Keys, C. B., Suarez-Balcazar, Y., Taylor, R. R., Davis, M., Durlak, J., Isenberg, D. (Eds.). (2004). *Participatory community research: Theories and methods in action*. Washington, DC: American Psychological Association.

Kelly, J. G. (1985). The concept of primary prevention: Creating new paradigms. *Journal of Primary Prevention, 5*, 269–272.

Kelly, J. G. (1990). Changing contexts and the field of community psychology. *American Journal of Community Psychology, 18*, 769–792.

Kelly, J. G. (2006). *Becoming ecological. An expedition into community psychology*. New York: Oxford University Press.

Levine, M., & Perkins, D. V. (1997). *Principles of community psychology: Perspectives and applications* (2nd ed.). New York: Oxford University Press.

Rappaport, J. (1981). In praise of paradox: A social policy of empowerment over prevention. *American Journal of Community Psychology, 9*, 1–25.

Tolan, P., Keys, C., Chertok, F., & Jason, L. (Eds.). (1990). *Researching community psychology: Issues of theories and methods*. Washington, DC: American Psychological Association.

Zimmerman, M. (2000). Empowerment theory: Psychological, organizational and community levels of analysis. In J. Rappaport & E. Seidman (Eds.), *Handbook of community psychology* (pp. 43–63). New York: Plenum.

LEONARD A. JASON
NICOLE PORTER
DePaul University

See also: **Prevention of Mental Disorders; Social Support**

COMORBIDITY

Individuals seeking healthcare commonly present with more than one problem. Psychologists typically describe these individuals as having comorbid conditions. Professionals note this status because conditions may interact. In fact, comorbidity is present in approximately half of the individuals presenting in clinical settings.

Although the basic concept of comorbidity is relatively simple, professionals vary in how they define it. As such, it is important to anticipate potential differences in professional conceptualizations of comorbidity and strive to understand them fully when engaging in discussions on comorbidity.

Issues to Consider in Defining Comorbidity

The word *comorbid* is composed of *co* and *morbid*. *Co* implies that something is in combination with something else. *Morbid* implies that something is diseased or of a disease. By bringing these word fragments together, the term implies more than one pathological condition in the same person.

Implicit in this expression is that there are multiple conditions occurring. This is important because diseases are, by definition, unique. As such, when conditions are comorbid, no one condition is merely a consequence of another. The conditions are self-sustaining pathological processes. Thus, when considering how professionals define comorbidity, one must understand how professionals recognize individual conditions.

For example, some professionals may only recognize conditions if they meet formal diagnostic criteria, such as those in the *Diagnostic and Statistical Manual of Mental Disorders* (DSM-IV-TR; American Psychiatric Association, 2000). Others may acknowledge problem behaviors that interact with diagnosable conditions, but do not meet formal diagnostic criteria. To illustrate, imagine an individual presenting with depression and alcohol problems. One professional might see these as comorbid conditions if both problems met formal diagnostic criteria, while another might do so if one met the criteria, but the other did not. In clinical practice, this may determine the treatment approach used (integrated or not). In research, this could determine whether a participant was included or excluded from a study.

Another consideration is how many conditions comorbidity includes. Certainly two conditions defines the most basic kind—but professionals also may study special constellations of conditions presenting together, such that they may include three, four, or even more conditions. From a practical perspective, it is important to understand parameters related to the number of conditions considered, as they may vary from case to case, article to article.

Related to this is the nature of the conditions included. Comorbidity is a term used inside and outside of psychology. In education, it is learning problems combined with other disorders. In medicine, medical problems plus other disorders occurring together define comorbidity. Psychologists discuss comorbidity as varied combinations of conditions from anxiety with depression, depression with dementia, and conditions like posttraumatic stress disorder and substance use, as well as others.

In clinical practice for substance-use problems, for example, there are at least four ways to discuss comorbidity, or what is more commonly called dual diagnosis in this area. These include a substance-induced disorder combined with substance abuse or dependence, substance-use disorder and another mental health disorder on Axis II or Axis I of the DSM, and the latter combined with a physical condition on Axis III of the DSM. This latter combination, also known as triple diagnosis, often involves human immunodeficiency virus or acquired immunodeficiency syndrome (HIV/AIDS), but any health condition on Axis III would be appropriate. This latter combination reflects the increasingly common practice of examining physical health, substance use, and other mental health disorders in combination (Piotrowski, 2007). Note, however, that it is not common to discuss more than one abuse or dependence diagnosis involving different substances as comorbid because use of multiple drugs is relatively common among individuals presenting in clinical settings. As such, special designations cease to be practically meaningful in this regard.

Different Terms Related to Comorbidity

Comorbidity has many names. One variant is co-occurring disorders, often implying simultaneous presentation of multiple diagnosable conditions. Co-occurring sometimes also implies lifetime, as opposed to simultaneous, co-occurrence; the term co-existing disorders is more common with regard to lifetime co-occurrence. Dual diagnosis, referring to the presence of two disorders, also is a common practice describing a specific number of conditions, such as triple diagnosis as mentioned previously. There also have been efforts to specify distinctions based on patterns of how disorders present temporally. Concurrent and successive are two such specifiers (Angold, Costello, &

Erkanli, 1999). Concurrent implies conditions occurring in some overlapping fashion; successive means they may never have occurred simultaneously and substantial time may separate their occurrence.

Similarly, in substance-use treatment there are discussions of dually diagnosed conditions as primary or secondary. Sometimes this denotes greater or lesser problem severity for the substance use or other mental health disorder, as each may vary on its own severity continuum. "Primary" and "secondary" also have been used to distinguish the sequence in which problems developed. For instance, maybe one problem developed in adolescence and the other followed in early adulthood. Names of such dual diagnosis pairs in the clinical literature reflect such distinctions in severity emphasis and/or timing. These include mentally ill–chemically addicted (MICA); –substance abuser (MISA); –substance user (MISU); psychiatrically ill–substance abuser (PISA); –chemically addicted (PICA); medically compromised–substance using (MCSU); and substance using–mentally ill (SUMI). Interchangeable use of these terms is common. Thus it is imperative to know whether the communicator is referencing severity, timing, or something else (Piotrowski, 2007).

The Evolving Nature of Comorbidity

Future advances in epidemiology examining relationships among conditions will adjust our understanding of comorbidity trends. Conditions identified as unique but comorbid with other pathology today may be complex singular conditions tomorrow; issues such as culture, development, gender, and other demographic characteristics may further frame its recognition; and multiple models of interaction among conditions, even within the same individual, may apply (Piotrowski, 2007). Future recognition, discussion, and management of comorbidity will require keen understanding of contemporary definitions of this phenomenon.

REFERENCES

American Psychiatric Association. (2000). *Diagnostic and statistical manual of mental disorders* (4th ed., text rev.). Washington, DC: Author.

Angold, A. E., Costello, J., & Erkanli, A. (1999). Comorbidity. *Journal of Child Psychology and Psychiatry, 40,* 57–87.

Piotrowski, N. A. (2007). Comorbidity and psychological science: Does one size fit all? *Clinical Psychology: Science & Practice, 14,* 16–19.

SUGGESTED READINGS

Kessler, R. C., & Merikangas, K. R. (2004). The National Comorbidity Survey Replication (NCS-R): Background and aims. *The International Journal of Methods in Psychiatric Research, 13,* 60–68.

Mueser, K. T., Drake, R. E., Noordsy, D. L., & Fox, L. (2003). *Integrated treatment for dual disorders: A guide to effective practice.* New York: Guilford Press.

NANCY A. PIOTROWSKI
Capella University

See also: **Diagnostic Classification; Epidemiology of Mental Disorders**

COMPARATIVE NEUROPSYCHOLOGY

Results of nonhuman animal research can provide new information that human experimentation does not permit, usually for ethical considerations, or because of limited control over complex environmental influences. The new knowledge can then be used to help understand human disorders. One approach to understanding interspecies brain functions, comparative neuropsychology, involves the direct evaluation of human clinical populations by employing experimental paradigms originally developed for nonhuman animals (Oscar-Berman & Bardenhagen, 1998). Of particular applicability has been the study of nonhuman primates, our closest genetic relatives.

Over many decades of animal research in behavioral neuroscience, the paradigms were perfected to study the effects of well-defined brain lesions on specific behaviors, and later the tasks were modified for human use. Generally the modifications involve changing the reward from food to money, but standard administration of the tasks in humans still involves minimal instructions, thus necessitating a degree of procedural learning in humans as in nonhuman animals alike. Currently, comparative neuropsychological paradigms are used with neurological patients to link specific deficits with localized areas of neuropathology (see Fuster, 2003; Oscar-Berman & Bardenhagen, 1998).

The comparative neuropsychological approach employs simple tasks that can be mastered without relying upon language skills, making them suitable for administering to nonhuman animals. Precisely because these simple paradigms do not require linguistic strategies for solution, they are especially useful for working with patients whose language skills are compromised, or whose cognitive skills may be minimal. Comparative neuropsychology contrasts with the traditional approach of using tasks that rely upon linguistic skills, and that were designed to study human cognition (e.g., Lezak, Howieson, & Loring, 2004; Strauss, Sherman, & Spreen, 2006). Because important ambiguities about its heuristic value had not been addressed empirically, only recently has comparative neuropsychology become popular for implementation with brain-damaged patients (see Oscar-Berman &

Bardenhagen, 1998), and it has had prevalent use as a framework for comparing and contrasting the performances of disparate neurobehavioral populations on similar tasks.

Among the paradigms that have been employed are classical delayed reaction tasks such as delayed response (DR) and delayed alternation (DA). Both tasks measure a person's ability to bridge a time gap. This ability has been termed *working memory*, which is a transient form of memory. Working memory is multimodal in nature and serves to keep newly incoming information available online; it acts much like a mental clipboard for use in problem solving and planning. In the classical DR task, the experimenter places a small reward into a reinforcement-well under one of two identical stimuli. The subject is able to see the experimenter put a reward there, but cannot reach it. After the experimenter covers the reinforcement-wells with the stimuli, s/he lowers a screen, obscuring the stimulus tray. After a delay period, usually between 0 and 60 seconds, the experimenter raises the screen to allow the subject to make a choice. The subject then pushes one of the stimuli away and, with a correct choice, takes the reward; attentional and spatial memory skills are needed to do this.

DA shares important features in common with DR. Both are spatial tasks, and both have a delay between stimulus-presentation and the opportunity to make a response. In DA, however, subjects must learn to alternate responding from left to right. On each trial, the side not previously chosen is rewarded, and a brief delay (usually 5 seconds) is interposed between trials. Instead of having to notice and remember the location of a reward placed there by the experimenter (in DR), subjects must remember the side last chosen, and whether a reward had been available. Subjects must also learn to inhibit, on each trial, the previously rewarded response (i.e., they must not perseverate with consecutive responses to one side only). Rankings of the performance levels of a wide range of mammals, including children, on delayed reaction tasks have been reported to parallel the phylogenetic scale.

Comparative neuropsychological tasks such as DR and DA are simple to administer and do not rely on intact language abilities. Both tasks also are sensitive to abnormalities after damage to frontal brain systems. Furthermore, successful performance on DR and DA tasks is known to rely upon different underlying neuroanatomical and neuropsychological mechanisms. Thus, prefrontal cortex is host to at least two subsystems: dorsolateral and orbitofrontal (on the ventral surface). While the dorsolateral system contains intimate connections with other neocortical sites, its connections with limbic sites are less striking than the orbitofrontal system's.

The dorsolateral system, although important for successful performance on both DR and DA, is especially important for DR performance, in which visuospatial, mnemonic, and attentional functions are considered critical. By contrast, functions involved in response inhibition have been linked to the orbitofrontal system. With an inability to inhibit unintended responses comes abnormal perseverative responding, a salient characteristic of orbitofrontal damage. The orbitofrontal system is intimately connected with the basal forebrain and limbic structures; its connections with other neocortical regions are not as extensive as the dorsolateral system's. The orbitofrontal system, like the dorsolateral system, supports successful performance on both DA and DR, but it is especially important for DA performance.

Comparative neuropsychological research has provided a framework that is helpful for understanding memory dysfunction in neurodegenerative disorders. In some neurodegenerative diseases (e.g., Parkinson's disease and progressive supranuclear palsy), patients may have working-memory and attentional impairments resulting from prefrontal system damage. In other disorders (e.g., Korsakoff's syndrome and herpes encephalopathy), there may be new learning impairments suggestive of limbic system damage (Oscar-Berman & Bardenhagen, 1998).

Implicit in nonhuman research models of human brain functioning is the assumption of homologous structural-functional relationships among the species (e.g., Wasserman, 1993). A number of different factors can be taken into account when attempting to establish homologies between brain regions in humans and other animals, including neuroanatomical location, connectivity, cyto- and myeloarchitecture, and functional response characteristics. The majority of homologous regions that have been identified between humans and nonhuman primates are in lower-order sensory regions. Clearly inferred homologies for regions involved in higher order cognitive functioning (e.g., attention and working memory) are less well established (Orban, Van Essen, & Vanduffel, 2004).

The integration of basic research on animals with clinical research in human patients is the goal of translational research and translational medicine. In recent years, there has been new weight placed on the importance of integrating laboratory and clinical research in this manner. Broadly considered, translational medicine is an approach that attempts to connect basic research to patient care, with an emphasis on the linkage between the laboratory and the patient's bedside. Such research often requires collaboration across laboratories that study humans and other animals. In the realm of behavioral neuroscience, for example, translational research might involve comparisons of performance patterns of rats and humans—both groups having sustained damage to the hippocampus—while learning similar types of memory tasks (Kesner & Hopkins, 2006). Other examples of this kind of work include investigating the role of prefrontal cortex stimulation in post-traumatic stress disorder by looking at fear conditioning responses in rats (Milad, Rauch, Pitman, & Quirk, 2006) or developing tests of frontal-striatal function in humans, rats, and monkeys to better understand the effects of damage to this circuitry in Parkinson's disease (Chudasama & Robbins, 2006).

Research on brain mechanisms underlying behaviors across species contributes to the discovery of common and divergent principles of brain-behavior relationships. Ultimately this helps neuroscientists to understand how the brain functions. With understanding, comes the potential for assessment and treatment of human neurobehavioral disorders.

REFERENCES

Chudasama, Y., & Robbins, T. W. (2006). Functions of frontostriatal systems in cognition: Comparative neuropsychopharmacological studies in rats, monkeys and humans. *Biological Psychology*, 73(1), 19–38.

Fuster, J. M. (2003). *Cortex and mind*. New York: Oxford University Press.

Kesner, R. P., & Hopkins, R. O. (2006). Mnemonic functions of the hippocampus: A comparison between animals and humans. *Biological Psychology*, 73(1), 3–18.

Lezak, M. D., Howieson, D. B., & Loring, D. W. (2004). *Neuropsychological assessment* (4th ed.). New York: Oxford University Press.

Milad, M. R., Rauch, S. L., Pitman, R. K., & Quirk, G. J. (2006). Fear extinction in rats: Implications for human brain imaging and anxiety disorders. *Biological Psychology*, 73(1), 61–71.

Orban, G. A., Van Essen, D., & Vanduffel, W. (2004). Comparative mapping of higher visual areas in monkeys and humans. *Trends in Cognitive Sciences*, 8(7), 315–324.

Oscar-Berman, M., & Bardenhagen, F. (1998). Nonhuman primate models of memory dysfunction in neurodegenerative disease: Contributions from comparative neuropsychology. In A. Tröster (Ed.), *Memory in neurodegenerative disease* (pp. 3–20). New York: Cambridge University Press.

Strauss, E., Sherman, E. M. S., & Spreen, O. (2006). *A compendium of neuropsychological tests: Administration, norms, and commentary* (3rd ed.). New York: Oxford University Press.

Wasserman, E. A. (1993). Comparative cognition: Beginning the second century of the study of animal intelligence. *Psychological Bulletin*, 113, 211–228.

SUGGESTED READINGS

Butler, A. B. (2005). *Comparative vertebrate neuroanatomy: Evolution and adaptation*. Hoboken, NJ: Wiley-Interscience.

Milner, A. D. (Ed.). (1998). *Comparative neuropsychology*. New York: Oxford University Press.

MARLENE OSCAR-BERMAN
Boston University School of Medicine and Department of Veterans Affairs Healthcare System, Boston Campus

See also: **Comparative Psychology; Neuropsychology**

COMPARATIVE PSYCHOLOGY

Comparative psychology involves the study of the evolution and development of behavior. Comparative psychology is a branch of science that lies in the intersection between psychology and biology. Thus, it is not surprising that comparative psychologists recognize as part of their foundational tradition the works and ideas of a diverse group of scientists, including Charles Darwin (founder of modern evolutionary theory), Ivan P. Pavlov (discoverer of conditioning), John B. Watson (founder of behaviorism and a pioneer of field experiments), and Edward L. Thorndike (proponent of one of the first theories of behavior based on experimental research), among many others (Boakes, 1984). Comparative psychologists are interested in providing answers to questions such as:

- What is the evolutionary origin of behavioral patterns observed in animals?
- Does behavior contribute to individual reproductive success?
- What external and internal factors determine animal behavior?
- What factors regulate the development of behavior?

The first two questions are concerned with the ultimate causes of behavior, whereas the last two questions are concerned with the proximate causes of behavior (Tinbergen, 1963). Although these types of questions can be asked somewhat independently, the knowledge derived from one usually has important implications for the way we study the others. One way to view the complementary nature of these questions is to think that, on the one hand, ultimate causes are responsible for the evolution of the mechanisms and developmental trajectories explored in studies of proximate causation, whereas, on the other, proximate mechanisms provide limits within which evolutionary forces shape behavior (Papini, 2008).

Evolutionary Principles

Modern evolutionary theory starts with Charles Darwin (1823–1913) and Alfred Russell Wallace (1809–1882), who first proposed an explanation of evolution in terms of natural selection. Evolution can be briefly defined as descent with modification (Darwin, 1993/1859, Chapter IV). Descent with modification refers to the fact that offspring are usually not identical to their parents, at least in sexually reproducing organisms (asexual reproduction can also lead to descent with modification via, e.g., mutations). Darwin posited that character variations in individual animals accumulate in a population of animals, across generations, in relation to the extent to which they promote individual reproductive success. With a sufficient number of generations, descendant individuals may exhibit modified versions of the character (modified with respect to the ancestral character). To the extent that subpopulations adapt to different aspects of their physical and social environment, and interbreeding is disrupted, these subpopulations may evolve into new species over many generations. This so-called Darwinian view of evolution is based on three major prerequisites: (1) characters must vary in individuals within a population; (2) alternative characters must be correlated with differential reproductive success; and (3) characters must have a hereditary basis.

For example, social behavior is currently being favored in male lions, as demonstrated by an assessment of individual reproductive success as a function of number of males in a coalition (Packer et al., 1988). Thus, traits that promote social affiliation among males are positively selected relative to traits that promote a solitary life. Because most large carnivores live solitary lives, it may be argued that over the course of many generations in African lion populations, social affiliation among males has been favored by natural selection, causing this favored phenotype to spread in the population, relative to the alternative phenotype.

This natural process is mimicked by human intervention through selective breeding—a process called *artificial selection*. Artificial selection is responsible for the domestication of animals and plants over the last 10,000–20,000 years, and it is currently being applied under more controlled conditions in field and laboratory experiments. In one long-term experiment (Ricker & Hirsch, 1985), fruit flies of the Genus *Drosophila* were selectively bred for either a tendency to move up (called *negative geotaxis*) or down (*positive geotaxis*) in a vertical maze. After thousands of generations, flies showed extreme versions of either character and displayed partial reproductive isolation when interbreeding was allowed. Thus, flies in the negative geotaxis strain placed in a flat dish with both negative and positive geotaxis flies tended to mate with members of their strain, and vice versa for flies in the positive geotaxis strain. Such partial reproductive isolation is interpreted as incipient speciation.

In the laboratory, these behavioral changes are the result of selective pressures induced by researchers favoring one set of behavioral traits over another when they allow only some individuals to mate with each other. For the fruit flies in the artificial selection study just described, the reproductive success correlated with the alternative characters of negative and positive geotaxis was determined by the experimenter. Similarly, field experiments suggest that natural ecological pressures can lead to character changes across many generations.

Examples of Comparative Psychology

Many comparative psychologists have contributed to understanding the evolution and development of behavior from a variety of perspectives and combining different procedures. Here are some relevant examples. Consider the behavior of many birds that cache food during the summer and later retrieve the food during the winter, when food is scarce. To be successful, food hoarding requires that an animal remember the locations where it had stored food at the time of food recovery. In turn, this implies an efficient set of memory storage and retrieval mechanisms. It has been estimated that Clark's nutcrackers, for example, stored tens of thousands of seeds, sometimes up to 20 kilometers from the site where they found the seeds, to recover them months later with significant accuracy.

Several studies show that a brain area concerned with spatial learning and memory, the hippocampus, is enlarged in food-hoarding birds relative to closely related species that do not store food (Sherry, Jacobs, & Gaulin, 1992). Similar results have been reported in other species solving other types of problems that require spatial learning and memory. For example, homing pigeons (which have been selectively bred for navigational ability) display increased hippocampal size relative to other strains of domestic pigeon. Similarly, meadow vole males (which are polygynous and defend large territories) exhibit a larger hippocampus than females of the same species and than males and females of monogamous pine voles, all of which defend small territories. Selective pressures have resulted in an increase in the size of the hippocampus in different species that each use spatial abilities to solve ecologically important problems.

Another example involves the study of successive negative contrast (SNC), a phenomenon that appears to be unique to mammals, among the vertebrates. Most mammals actively search for food and water, and given their high metabolic rate, are bound to a minimum average daily intake to avoid starvation. Thus, when sites that used to provide these resources no longer do so, mammals need a mechanism that can break the attachment to the location and redirect behavior in a novel path. SNC may reflect such a basic foraging mechanism. Under laboratory conditions, SNC occurs when an animal is trained to expect a large incentive, but instead receives a small one. Compared to unshifted controls that always receive the small incentive, downshifted animals abruptly decrease goal-directed and consummatory activities related to the smaller incentive. The fact that SNC is reduced or even eliminated by antianxiety pharmacological treatments and that it is accompanied by an increase in stress hormones suggests that the incentive downshift triggers an emotionally aversive reaction. Comparative research indicates that SNC occurs in several mammalian species, but not in nonmammalian vertebrates, such as pigeons, turtles, toads, and teleost fish (Papini, 2003). Thus, mammalian evolution may have included the emergence of brain mechanisms that support emotional detachment from sites that no longer produce needed resources.

Methodological Issues

Comparative psychologists must address methodological limitations inherent in the task of comparing animals of different species in a variety of situations. After considering the examples given above, some readers may wonder how species differences in specific behavioral capacities can be determined. For example, drawing broad conclusions about spatial learning or adjustment to incentive downshifts requires comparative research across difference species in analogous tasks. But how can one be certain that task requirements are equivalent across species?

It is reasonable to surmise that differences in locomotor behavior, sensory abilities, and motivational tendencies can affect behavioral measurement independently of (or in addition to) the learning and memory capacities that are under study in these two examples. These factors, known as contextual variables, greatly complicate data interpretation. For example, searching for food may involve different sensory-motor skills in, say, turtles and rats. To deal with the problems of direct comparisons across species, comparative psychologists focus on functional relationships between variables that affect behavior in any given situation. For example, instead of asking whether a reduction from 20 to 2 pellets affects the behavior of turtles and rats similarly, they ask whether various magnitudes of incentive downshift affect the behavior of turtles and rats similarly (Bitterman, 1975).

Using the framework provided by evolutionary principles, comparative psychologists conceptualize species differences and similarities in behavioral capacities as resulting from the homology, homoplasy, or divergence of underlying mechanisms. Similar behavioral outcomes across species suggest continuity based on homology of underlying mechanisms or on the operation of independently evolved mechanisms by homoplasy. By contrast, different behavioral outcomes suggest evolutionary divergence based on different underlying mechanisms. Demonstrations of homology, homoplasy, and divergence in behavioral capacities like those mentioned above require not only an analysis of behavioral outcomes, but also an understanding of the brain circuits (neurobiological level), synaptic properties (neurochemical level), and cellular mechanisms (cell-molecular level) underlying the behavioral capacities in question. Mechanistic homology in a behavioral capacity across two or more species occurs when the phenomenon requires the same mechanisms at these four levels of analysis in all the species being compared. Homoplasy occurs when behavioral similarities can be attributed to different underlying mechanisms. Finally, divergence occurs when different mechanisms can be demonstrated to lead to different behaviors.

Comparative psychology is thus a branch of scientific psychology that interfaces with the biological sciences and is concerned with the study of the evolution and development of behavior. In addition to drawing from traditional areas within psychology, including learning theory, cognitive psychology, behavioral neuroscience, and evolutionary psychology, comparative psychology connects with evolutionary biology, behavioral ecology, sociobiology, ethology, neuroscience, and anthropology to contribute to an understanding of behavior. Fruitful for its integrative and multidisciplinary nature, comparative psychology provides a coherent narrative that sometimes is lacking in modern psychological research.

REFERENCES

Bitterman, M. E. (1975). The comparative analysis of learning. *Science, 188*, 699–709.

Boakes, R. (1984). *From Darwin to behaviourism. Psychology and the minds of animals.* Cambridge, UK: Cambridge University Press.

Darwin, C. (1993/1859). *The origin of species.* New York: Random House.

Packer, C., Herbst, L., Pusey, A. E., Bygott, J. D., Hanby, J. P., Cairns, S. J., & Mulder, M. B. (1988). Reproductive success of lions. In T. H. Clutton-Brock (Ed.), *Reproductive success* (pp. 363–383). Chicago: University of Chicago Press.

Papini, M. R. (2003). Comparative psychology of surprising non-reward. *Brain, Behavior and Evolution, 62*, 83–95.

Papini, M. R. (2008). *Comparative psychology: Evolution and development of behavior.* (2nd ed.). New York: Psychology Press.

Ricker, J. P., & Hirsch, J. (1985). Evolution of an instinct under long-term divergent selection for geotaxis in domesticated populations of *Drosophila melanogaster. Journal of Comparative Psychology, 99*, 380–390.

Sherry, D. F., Jacobs, L. F., & Gaulin, S. J. C. (1992). Spatial memory and adaptive specialization of the hippocampus. *Trends in Neuroscience, 15*, 298–303.

Tinbergen, N. (1963). On aims and methods of ethology. *Zeitschrift für Tierpsychologie, 20*, 410–433.

SUGGESTED READINGS

Domjan, M. (2003). *Principles of learning and behavior* (5th ed.). Belmont, CA: Thomson/Wadsworth.

Krebs, J. R., & Davies, N. B. (1993). *An introduction to behavioral ecology* (3rd ed.). London: Blackwell Science.

Papini, M. R. (2002). Pattern and process in the evolution of learning mechanisms. *Psychological Review, 109*, 186–201.

Trut, L. N. (1999). Early canid domestication: The farm-fox experiment. *American Scientist, 87*, 160–169.

JACOB N. NORRIS
MAURICIO R. PAPINI
Texas Christian University

See also: **Animal Learning and Behavior; Comparative Neuropsychology; Evolutionary Psychology**

COMPETENCY TO STAND TRIAL

Defendants can be found incompetent to stand trial, under provisions in criminal law, if they are unable to understand their legal circumstances and participate adequately in their defense. If they are found incompetent, further judicial proceedings are suspended until their competency has been restored. The purposes behind this procedure are to ensure that defendants receive a fair trial and to preserve the dignity of the adversarial process (Melton, Petrila, Poythress, & Slogobin, 2007). The competency standard that is currently recognized by the courts was established in *Dusky v. United States* (362 U.S. 402, 1960), which holds that defendants must be able to consult with an attorney and have a rational and factual understanding of the proceedings.

Competency and criminal responsibility are often confused. Whereas competency is concerned with a defendant's present ability to participate in the defense, criminal responsibility refers to a defendant's mental state at the time of the alleged crime. It is quite possible that a defendant could be found to be competent to stand trial and then later successfully raise the insanity defense. Indeed, if the competency issue had been raised, a defendant would have to be considered competent before being allowed to proceed with an insanity defense.

Based on a thorough review of case law, Bonnie (1992) outlined two types of competence: competence to assist counsel, and decisional competence. Competency to assist counsel refers to the minimum capacities defendants would need to assist their defense, such as the capacity to understand the criminal charges they are facing and the role of defense counsel. These capacities are different from those capacities that may be needed to make decisions that arise in a particular case. Decisional competency refers to the ability to understand and choose among alternative courses of action. In Bonnie's view, it is possible that some defendants could be considered competent to assist their attorney but incompetent to make certain decisions that arise during the course of the defense, such as whether to enter a guilty plea, to waive constitutional rights, or to employ an insanity defense. However, the United .States Supreme Court held in Godinez v. Moran (309 U.S. 389, 1993) that the standards for various types of criminal competency should be the same.

Given that most criminal cases are dealt with through plea bargaining, the term *adjudicative competence* has been suggested as a more appropriate descriptive term, as it encompasses legal competencies in various stages of legal proceedings, such as waiver of appeals, waiver of counsel, and plea bargaining (Poythress, Bonnie, Monahan, Otto, & Hoge, 2002).

Both defense and prosecution can raise the issue of competence. The courts have historically used mental health professionals, including psychologists and psychiatrists, to evaluate competency. Since competency is a legal issue, a judge makes the final determination, but evaluators have considerable influence (Zapf & Roesch, 2005). Competency evaluations are the most common type of forensic assessment, but only a small proportion of defendants referred for fitness evaluations is found incompetent, usually about 10% to 25%.

Competency evaluations may be intentionally misused by attorneys to delay the trial, investigate the feasibility of an insanity plea, or discover new information about the defendant (Roesch & Golding, 1980). Competency evaluations may also be used as a "back door" to the hospital when a mentally ill individual does not meet the dangerousness criteria for civil commitment.

A number of forensic assessment instruments are available to assist evaluators (Zapf & Roesch, 2005). These include the Competency Screening Test, the Competency Assessment Instrument, the Evaluation of Competency to Stand Trial—Revised, the Georgia Court Competency Test-R, the Interdisciplinary Fitness Interview, the Competency Assessment for Standing Trial with Mental Retardation, the Fitness Interview Test-Revised, and the MacArthur Competency Assessment Tool—Criminal Adjudication.

Psychosis, and to a lesser extent mental retardation, are the basis for an incompetency determination. It is important that evaluators are aware that the presence of a mental disorder is a necessary but not sufficient basis for a finding of incompetency. Once the presence of a mental disorder is established, evaluators must specify how this disorder affects a defendant's functioning in the legal process. Research has shown that many individuals with major mental disorders are competent (Zapf & Roesch, 2005), so determining a causal connection between mental disorder and legal abilities is essential.

Treatment of competency is generally successful, with estimates suggesting restoration rates ranging from 90% to 95% (Zapf & Roesch, 2005). However, Mossman (2007) found that individuals with certain characteristics, such as a long-standing psychotic disorder, prior lengthy hospitalizations, or irremediable cognitive deficits, were well below average in terms of their chances of successful restoration. In cases where competence can not be restored, alternative dispositions, including dismissal of charges or civil commitment, are considered.

The most common form of treatment for incompetent defendants is psychotropic medication (Zapf & Roesch, 2005). However, although psychotropic medication may alleviate a defendant's mental disorder, it does not address the person's psycholegal impairments. Some jurisdictions have established competency restoration programs designed specifically to reduce or eliminate psycholegal impairments (e.g., focusing on such topics as courtroom procedures and the roles of the key players in them) as well as other factors that are limiting a defendant's ability to participate in his or her defense (Zapf & Roesch, 2005).

REFERENCES

Bonnie, R. (1992). The competence of criminal defendants: A theoretical reformulation. *Behavioral Sciences and the Law, 10,* 291–316.

Melton, G. B., Petrila, J., Poythress, N. G., & Slobogin, C. (2007). *Psychological evaluations for the courts: A handbook for mental health professionals and lawyers* (3rd ed.). New York: Guilford Press.

Mossman, D. (2007). Predicting restorability of incompetent criminal defendants. *Journal of the American Academy of Psychiatry and the Law, 35,* 34–43.

Poythress, N. G., Bonnie, R. J., Monahan, J., Otto, R. K., & Hoge, S. K. (2002). *Adjudicative competence: The MacArthur studies.* New York: Kluwer Academic/Plenum.

Roesch, R., & Golding, S. L. (1980). *Competency to stand trial.* Urbana: University of Illinois Press.

Zapf, P. A., & Roesch, R. (2005). Competency to stand trial: A guide for evaluators. In I. B. Weiner & A. K. Hess (Eds.), *Handbook of forensic psychology* (3rd ed., pp. 305–331). Hoboken: John Wiley & Sons.

SUGGESTED READINGS

Grisso, T. (2003). *Evaluating competencies: Forensic assessment and instruments* (2nd ed.). New York: Kluwer Academic/Plenum.

Roesch, R., Zapf, P. A., & Eaves, D. (2006). *Fitness interview test–revised: A structured interview for assessing competency to stand trial.* Sarasota, FL: Professional Resource Press.

Skeem, J., Golding, S. L., & Emke-Francis, P. (2004). Assessing adjudicative competency: Using legal and empirical principles to inform practice. In W. O'Donohue & E. Levensky (Eds.), *Handbook of forensic psychology: Resource for mental health and legal professionals* (pp. 175–211). New York: Academic Press.

RONALD ROESCH
KAITLYN MCLACHLAN
Simon Fraser University

See also: Civil Competence; Criminal Responsibility; Expert Testimony

COMPULSIONS

Compulsions, along with obsessions, are a hallmark feature of obsessive-compulsive disorder (OCD). According to *DSM-IV-TR* (American Psychiatric Association, 2000), compulsions are "repetitive behaviors ... or mental acts ... the goal of which is to prevent or reduce anxiety or distress" (p. 418). Although behaviors resembling compulsions occur at a range of frequencies in the normal population, in order to be considered pathological the compulsions must be associated with either intense distress or functional impairment. Impairment from compulsions can be quite severe, with some individuals spending several hours per day performing rituals, feeling unable to stop and attend to their daily responsibilities. The label "compulsion" has been applied to a broad range of repetitive behaviors, including excessive drinking, gambling, and shopping, but, these behaviors are differentiated from true compulsions by the function they serve. This function is described in detail in this article.

Types of Compulsions

Compulsive behaviors vary on a continuum from normal to extreme. Factor-analytic studies using standardized symptom checklists have suggested the following dimensions of compulsive behavior:

Checking. Compulsive checking behaviors can include repeatedly checking external stimuli such as making sure the door is locked, the oven is turned off, or work was completed perfectly. Checking behaviors have been linked to an inflated sense of responsibility, overprediction of danger, and intolerance of uncertainty. Although some individuals check in response to poor memory confidence (e.g., "Did I really lock the door, or do I just think I did?"), experimental studies have shown that repeated checking paradoxically decreases memory confidence by creating additional confusion (van den Hout & Kindt, 2003).

Washing and Cleaning. Repetitive washing (e.g., handwashing, showering) and cleaning of one's environment are frequently associated with exaggerated beliefs about the likelihood of contamination, although washing may also be performed in response to an internal feeling of dirtiness that has been termed "mental pollution." In some cases, washing compulsions may arise from a feeling of disgust, rather than fear.

Ordering and Repeating Compulsions. Many compulsive behaviors take the form of ordering and arranging objects until they are perceived to be perfect, symmetrical, or just right. For example, an individual might spend hours lining up the cans on his/her pantry shelf. Other compulsions involve the repetition of routine behaviors, such as turning a light switch on and off over and over again. Unlike many other compulsions, which appear primarily motivated by fear of disastrous consequences, these behaviors may be driven by a sense of things being not just right.

Mental Compulsions. Early definitions of OCD maintained that obsessions were mental events, and compulsions were overt behaviors. Under this definition, some OCD patients without overt rituals were labeled "pure obsessives." However, current theories recognize that compulsions can be either actions or thoughts; nearly 80% of OCD patients describe mental compulsions. Mental compulsions are differentiated from obsessions according to their function, that is, whether they elicit distress or reduce it. Whereas obsessions elicit anxiety or distress, compulsions are defined as overt (behavioral) or covert (mental) actions that reduce or prevent distress elicited by obsessions. Examples of mental compulsions include attempting to think good thoughts, counting objects or counting up to a certain number, saying certain prayers in a rigid, repetitive manner, and mentally reviewing past actions or conversations to hunt for mistakes or other infractions.

Hoarding. Compulsive hoarding is defined as the acquisition of and subsequent failure to discard a large number of possessions, resulting in clutter that precludes activities for which living spaces were designed. At this time, the relationship between hoarding and other forms of compulsive behavior is unclear, as individuals with hoarding behaviors frequently do not exhibit other compulsions and hoarding behavior has been reported in the context of not only OCD but also a wide variety of disorders including schizophrenia, social phobia, organic mental disorders, eating disorders, depression, and dementia (see Steketee & Frost, 2003, for a review).

Association between Obsessions and Compulsions

For most patients with OCD, obsessions are followed by compulsions. Usually, the compulsions are thematically related to the obsessions; however, there is a broad range of logical coherence of this connection. Washing rituals, for example, are usually motivated by fears of contamination or illness. Checking rituals are usually prompted by worries that an action (e.g., turning off the stove) was performed incorrectly and that some catastrophic event (e.g., fire) will occur as a result. Other connections are less logical: for example, turning a light switch off and on several times in order to prevent one's family from dying in a car accident.

Current Theoretical Models of Compulsions

Behavioral models of OCD emphasize the functional significance of compulsions. Such models posit that compulsions are a form of active avoidance, which are cued by obsessive fears. When the individual performs a compulsion, fear is reduced. Thus, compulsions are negatively reinforced, and obsessive fear is increased. Studies have supported the anxiety-reduction hypothesis of compulsions: exposure to feared stimuli increased participants' anxiety, while performing compulsions led to decreased anxiety (Hodgson & Rachman, 1972). One problem with a two-factor model of compulsions is the fact that some individuals with OCD (e.g., some patients with checking compulsions) report that compulsions are associated with increased, rather than decreased, fear. Cases such as these might be better explained by Herrnstein's (1969) learning theory, which suggests that mildly anxiety-evoking behaviors might be considered avoidant if they serve to prevent the occurrence of strong anxiety. Thus, while checking may elicit anxiety in some patients, refraining from checking is perceived as even more aversive.

Cognitive models posit that compulsive behaviors are the result of maladaptive and erroneous beliefs.

Factor-analytic research has identified three major themes of OCD-related beliefs: (1) exaggerated sense of responsibility (e.g., "not preventing harm is as bad as causing harm" and exaggerated prediction of threat; e.g., "Harmful events will happen unless I am very careful"); (2) perfectionism (e.g., "things are not right if they are not perfect") and intolerance of uncertainty (e.g., "If I'm not absolutely sure of something, I'm bound to make a mistake"); and (3) importance of thoughts (e.g., "Having a bad thought is morally no different than doing a bad deed") and need to control thoughts (e.g., "To avoid disasters, I need to control all the thoughts or images that pop into my mind"). Although OCD patients endorse these beliefs to a greater extent than do patients with other anxiety disorders, a subset of OCD patients do not endorse obsessional beliefs (Taylor et al., 2006).

Biological models link compulsions to excessive activity in frontal-striatal circuits of the brain, in which mutually excitatory signals between the frontal cortex and thalamus go unchecked by the usual negative feedback loop from cortex to striatum to thalamus. This cortico-striato-thalamo-cortical (CSTC) model has been generally supported by functional neuroimaging research (e.g., Baxter et al., 1988), although results may differ for individuals with hoarding behaviors (Saxena et al., 2004). Additional research suggests that hyperactive error signals generated by the anterior cingulate cortex may be associated with OCD patients' subjective sense that something is wrong and that a behavioral change is needed to correct the problem (Maltby, Tolin, Worhunsky, O'Keefe, & Kiehl, 2005).

Differentiating Compulsions from Other Repetitive Behaviors

Attention to the function of compulsions may help with the differential diagnosis of OCD. Many *DSM-IV-TR* impulse control disorders have been classified as part of an "OCD spectrum." These disorders include "compulsive" overeating, gambling, and sex. However, these problems tend to be functionally distinct from compulsions, that is, they are not triggered by obsessions or fears and are not negatively reinforced by fear reduction. On the contrary, disinhibited behaviors are more likely to be triggered by feelings of tension or boredom, and because the behaviors are satisfying, they are positively, rather than negatively, reinforced. Although this distinction may not apply to every patient, until more convincing data are produced, the term "compulsion" is best reserved to indicate a specific functional relationship between behavior and fear.

REFERENCES

American Psychiatric Association. (2000). *Diagnostic and statistical manual of mental disorders* (4th ed., text rev.). Washington, DC: Author.

Baxter, L. R., Jr., Schwartz, J. M., Mazziotta, J. C., Phelps, M. E., Pahl, J. J., Guze, B. H., & Fairbanks, L. (1988). Cerebral glucose metabolic rates in nondepressed patients with obsessive-compulsive disorder. *American Journal of Psychiatry, 145*, 1560–1563.

Herrnstein, R. J. (1969). Method and theory in the study of avoidance. *Psychological Review, 76*, 49–69.

Hodgson, R. J., & Rachman, S. (1972). The effects of contamination and washing in obsessional patients. *Behaviour Research and Therapy, 10*, 111–117.

Maltby, N., Tolin, D. F., Worhunsky, P., O'Keefe, T. M., & Kiehl, K. A. (2005). Dysfunctional action monitoring hyperactivates frontal-striatal circuits in obsessive-compulsive disorder: An event-related fMRI study. *NeuroImage, 24*, 495–503.

Saxena, S., Brody, A. L., Maidment, K. M., Smith, E. C., Zohrabi, N., Katz, E., Baker, S. K., & Baxter, L. R., Jr. (2004). Cerebral glucose metabolism in obsessive-compulsive hoarding. *American Journal of Psychiatry, 161*, 1038–1048.

Steketee, G., & Frost, R. O. (2003). Compulsive hoarding: Current status of the research. *Clinical Psychology Review, 23*, 905–927.

Taylor, S., Abramowitz, J. S., McKay, D., Calamari, J. E., Sookman, D., Kyrios, M., Wilhelm, S., & Carmin, C. (2006). Do dysfunctional beliefs play a role in all types of obsessive-compulsive disorder? *Journal of Anxiety Disorders, 20*, 85–97.

van den Hout, M., & Kindt, M. (2003). Repeated checking causes memory distrust. *Behaviour Research and Therapy, 41*, 301–316.

SUGGESTED READINGS

Foa, E. B., Kozak, M. J., Goodman, W. K., Hollander, E., Jenike, M. A., & Rasmussen, S. A. (1995). DSM-IV field trial: Obsessive-compulsive disorder. *American Journal of Psychiatry, 152*, 90–96.

Rasmussen, S. A., & Eisen, J. L. (1992). The epidemiology and clinical features of obsessive compulsive disorder. *Psychiatric Clinics of North America, 15*, 743–758.

Rauch, S. L., & Savage, C. R. (2000). Investigating cortico-striatal pathophysiology in obsessive-compulsive disorders: Procedural learning and imaging probes. In W. K. Goodman, M. V. Rudorfer, & J. D. Maser (Eds.), *Obsessive-compulsive disorder: Contemporary issues in treatment* (pp. 133–154). Mahwah, NJ: Lawrence Erlbaum Associates.

DAVID F. TOLIN
The Institute of Living, Hartford, CT and Yale University School of Medicine

See also: **Hoarding; Obsessions; Obsessive-Compulsive Disorder**

COMPUTER-ASSISTED PSYCHOTHERAPY

Computer-assisted psychotherapy (CAT) can be defined as psychotherapy that utilizes a computer program to deliver a significant part of the treatment or uses computer tools to assist the work of the therapist. Clinician involvement usually includes screening, supervision, and support of program uses, and it may, in some applications, involve an integrated human-computer "team" method of delivery. The amount of therapist time spent in CAT has varied in different studies, but is typically reduced considerably from the amounts used in standard psychotherapy.

Some of the goals of CAT are to reduce the cost of treatment, increase psychotherapy efficiency, promote skill acquisition, and provide innovative and helpful tools to augment the work of therapists. Other possible benefits include the following: improved access to psychotherapy; effective provision of psychoeducation; ability to store, analyze, and display data; systematic feedback to the user; and promotion of the self-monitoring, homework, and self-help components of treatment (Wright, 2004).

One of the concerns raised about computer-assisted psychotherapy is that patients could experience therapy via a computer as a "dehumanizing" experience. However, research with therapeutic software has demonstrated that patients usually report high levels of satisfaction with their experiences in using a computer as part of treatment (Wright, 2004). Another concern is that computer programs cannot be programmed to have the empathy, wisdom, or creativity of a human therapist. Contemporary developers of computer-assisted therapy programs agree with this observation, and thus they do not attempt to simulate the traditional therapeutic interview.

Computers, unlike human therapists, do not have inherent values or ethical standards. However, developers convey their theoretical orientation, values, and ethics in writing software for computer programs. Sampson and Pyle (1983) have offered ethical guidelines for computerized psychotherapy programs including the following: (1) adequate protection of confidentiality; (2) up-to-date and accurate information; (3) well-functioning hardware and software; and (4) supervision of the treatment process by a clinician. Some developers of therapeutic software have produced professional and self-help editions. The professional edition is intended for use in clinician-directed computer-assisted therapy, whereas, the self-help edition is designed to be utilized in a manner similar to a self-help books.

Computer programs for psychotherapy have been based most commonly on cognitive and behavioral models, because these forms of treatment use specific interventions, emphasize psychoeducation, and employ self-help as a primary ingredient of therapy. An example of a cognitive behavior therapy (CBT)-oriented computer program is the software developed in the 1980s by Selmi and coworkers (1990). This program relied completely on written text to communicate with users and is no longer produced. However, Selmi and colleagues demonstrated that computerized CBT could be as effective a standard CBT.

More recent computer programs for psychotherapy have incorporated new technology geared to heightening the power of learning experiences and improving ease of use. Wright and his colleagues (1995) designed and tested the first multimedia program for computer-assisted CBT. Research with this software demonstrated high acceptance ratings by patients, significant increases in learning of cognitive therapy, and efficacy that was not different from standard CBT. Video, audio, and other multimedia elements are used to engage the user and stimulate affect. Users participate in a variety of interactive self-help exercises and are assigned homework to encourage use of CBT in real-life situations. A revised DVD-ROM version of this software (*Good Days Ahead: The Multimedia Program for Cognitive Therapy*) is available for clinical use. Another multimedia program, *Beating the Blues*, has been shown to be helpful in augmenting treatment as usual in primary care patients and is being used in clinical settings in the United Kingdom (Proudfoot et al., 2004).

Rothbaum, Anderson, Hodges, Price, and Smith (2002) have pioneered virtual reality technology applications for fear of heights, fear of flying, and posttraumatic stress disorders (PTSD). Many other virtual reality programs have been developed and tested. For example, Difede and colleagues (2007) have demonstrated that a program that creates a virtual reality environment of the World Trade Center attacks on September 11, 2001, was useful in reducing symptoms of PTSD. Although controlled trials have found evidence for the efficacy of virtual reality based on exposure therapy, the need for specialized equipment has limited the use of these methods. Reductions in cost of hardware and software for virtual reality exposure therapy may lead to increased utilization. A more conventional computer program, *Fear Fighter*, was developed in the United Kingdom (Kenwright, Liness, & Marks, 2001). This software utilizes text, graphics, and audio to help users plan self-exposure to feared situations and to endure anxiety until it diminishes. Preliminary research suggests that it can significantly lower the amount of clinician time required for effective treatment anxiety-based disorders.

Internet-based therapy has also been explored. The usefulness of Internet-delivered therapy may be influenced in a large way by the amount of clinician involvement in treatment. A meta-analysis of Internet-delivered CAT found that effect sizes for programs with no significant clinician participation in screening or in treatment delivery were small, and typical completion rates for program material were low (Speck et al., 2007). When a clinician provides either face-to-face or telephone-administered treatment along with the computerized component of Internet-delivered CAT, treatment outcomes and completion rates have been considerably better (Speck et al., 2007).

Handheld computers have also been shown to be effective for computer-assisted psychotherapy. Newman, Kenardy, Herman, and Taylor (1997) found that long-term outcome of computer-assisted CBT for panic disorder was equal to standard CBT even though clinician contact time was reduced to four sessions in those who received the computer adjunct. Computer-controlled, interactive voice response systems are another possible application of computer technology to perform psychotherapy functions. These systems use a conventional telephone to connect to a computer. Interactive voice response programs for Obsessive Compulsive Disorder and depression have been developed and tested (Wright, 2004).

Currently, computer programs are not widely used for delivery of psychotherapy. Due to ongoing technological advances and the ubiquitous nature of computers in society, it is reasonable to forecast the growth of research in this area and the increased utilization of computer-assisted therapy in clinical practice.

REFERENCES

Difede, J., Cukor, J., Jayasinge, N., Patt, I., Jedel, S., & Spielman, L., et al. (2007). Virtual reality exposure therapy for the treatment of posttraumatic stress disorder following September 11, 2001. *Journal of Clinical Psychiatry, 68*(11), 1639–1647.

Kenwright, M., Liness, S., & Marks, I. (2001). Reducing demands on clinicians by offering computer-aided self-help for phobia-panic: Feasibility study. *The British Journal of Psychiatry, 11*, 456–459.

Newman, M. G., Kenardy, J., Herman, S., & Taylor, C. B. (1997). Comparison of palmtop-computer-assisted brief cognitive-behavioral treatment for panic disorder. *Journal of Consulting and Clinical Psychology, 65*, 178–183.

Proudfoot, J., Ryden, C., Everitt, B., Shapiro, D. A., Goldberg, D., Mann, A., et al. (2004). Clinical efficacy of computerised cognitive-behavioural therapy for anxiety and depression in primary care: Randomised controlled trial. *The British Journal of Psychiatry, 185*, 46–54.

Rothbaum, B., Anderson, P., Hodges, L., Price, L., & Smith, S. (2002). Twelve-month follow-up of virtual reality and standard exposure therapies for the fear of flying. *Journal of Consulting and Clinical Psychology, 70*(2), 428–432.

Sampson, J. P., & Pyle, K. R. (1983). Ethical issues involved with the use of computer assisted counseling, testing and guidance systems. *Personnel and Guidance Journal, 61*, 283–287.

Selmi, P. M., Klein, M. H., & Greist, J. H. (1990). Computer-administered cognitive-behavioral therapy for depression. *American Journal of Psychiatry, 147*, 51–56.

Spek, V., Cuijpers, P., Nyklicek, I., Riper, H., Keyzer, J., & Pop, V. (2007). Internet-based cognitive behavior therapy for symptoms of depression and anxiety: A meta-analysis. *Psychological Medicine, 37*, 319–328.

Wright, J. H. (2004). Computer-assisted cognitive-behavior therapy. In J. H. Wright (Ed.), *Cognitive-behavior therapy* (pp. 55–82). Washington, DC: American Psychiatric Publishing.

Wright, J. H., Wright, A. S., Albano, A. M., Basco, M. R., Goldsmith, L. J., Raffield, T., et al. (2005). Computer-assisted cognitive therapy for depression: Maintaining efficacy while

reducing therapist time. *American Journal of Psychiatry, 162*, 1158–1164.

JESSE H. WRIGHT
University of Louisville School of Medicine

MARINA KATZ
San Diego, CA

REBECCA L. TAMAS
University of Louisville School of Medicine

See also: **Computerized Adaptive Testing; Computerized Behavioral Assessment**

COMPUTER-BASED TEST INTERPRETATION

Personality assessment has become an integral component in clinical and forensic psychological practice. Moreover, practitioners have increasingly come to rely on computers in conducting personality assessments by using them to assist in conducting clinical interviews; obtaining self-reports of symptoms, attitudes, and behavior; summarizing and integrating test correlates; and developing psychological reports to summarize test results (Atlis, Hahn, & Butcher, 2006).

There is a long history of using mechanical means to score psychological tests. The first data-scoring computer applications were developed in the 1950s to score responses to tests completed by paper and pencil. In the 1960s, the possibility that computers could assist in the more complex task of interpreting the test results emerged as well. The use of mechanical means for objective assessment of personality was influenced by Paul Meehl's call for more objective clinical decision making and for the use of actuarial prediction methods in assessment (see Meehl, 1954).

The first computer-assisted program to actually interpret test results was developed at the Mayo Clinic in Rochester, Minnesota (Rome et al., 1962), for the original MMPI. Patients who were being seen for a medical evaluation were administered the MMPI. Their responses were scored, and a brief summary of the test results was provided to assist the staff in ruling out any psychological problems that might have been present. This automated procedure enabled large numbers of patients to be screened quickly and economically, which allowed the small staff of psychology personnel to serve many individuals who otherwise might never have received an evaluation (Fowler, 1985). The success of the Mayo program, although somewhat rudimentary in output and limited in the information provided, stimulated the development of a number of other

MMPI interpretation systems. Other MMPI narrative reports were developed by Finney (1966), Caldwell (1971), and Lachar (1974). Butcher (1987) provided a description of the expanding programs that broadened the utility of the existing technology and focused on creating clinically useful narrative reports, with the continuing goal of helping psychiatrists and psychologists arrive at diagnoses.

Following the pioneering developments in computer-based assessment at the Mayo Clinic with the MMPI, computer interpretation programs for other tests emerged; for example, a scoring program was developed for the Sixteen Personality Factor Questionnaire (16PF; Eber, 1964). This program evolved over time, incorporating additional personality measures as well as intelligence and achievement testing that allowed combined reports to be generated for use in various settings (Fowler, 1985). In the 1970s, Karson developed a clinical interpretation report for the 16PF (Karson & O'Dell, 1987). Even some tests that were typically more subjective in interpretation began to be interpreted by computer. For example, the Rorschach Inkblot Test was first computer-processed in the 1960s (Piotrowski, 1964).

A more comprehensive system was developed by Exner (1987) to aid in the interpretation of the Rorschach, although a full interpretation was not provided at the time. Exner went on to develop a more widely used empirically based interpretive system in 1974, although he typically argued against the idea that computer technology can truly replicate the complex process of integrating protocol data in a manner that replicates the thought process of an experienced clinician (Exner, 1987). The Exner Rorschach Interpretation Assistance Program (RIAP) was revised by Exner and Weiner in (2003) to provide a more comprehensive analysis of the Rorschach. Fowler (1985) pointed out that some test authors have developed computer interpretation systems for their tests as they were being developed, for example, the MCMI (Millon, 1977).

The use of computers in processing psychological test results has expanded beyond their initial use in the United States, particularly for the MMPI and MMPI-2. There are now more than 33 translations of the MMPI-2 that are used in dozens of countries. Computer interpretation of test translations has also been evaluated in several countries. Butcher and his colleagues (1998) summarized the results of a study comparing the use of computer-based MMPI-2 reports in Australia, France, and Norway and concluded that the computerized interpretations generalized appropriately to patients in those settings, with 66% of computer-based reports being judged as 80% to 100% accurate and 87% of reports being judged as 60% accurate or more. More recently, Cheung and Butcher (2008) provided an extensive case evaluation of a number of Chinese patients who were given the MMPI-2, which was processed by computer using the Minnesota Reports, a computer-based interpretation system (Butcher, 2005). Clients were scored on both U.S. and Chinese norms, and extensive case information was provided. The computer-derived reports, based on American norms, were shown to be highly sensitive to the problems and symptoms shown by the patients' case analyses.

Limitations or Criticisms of Computer-Based Test Interpretation

From the beginning of computer-based test interpretation, some authorities have questioned its usefulness, its applicability in clinical practice, or even the ethics of its implementation in making human decisions. The question of whether computers dehumanize the assessment process and serve to work against the client's best interest has been posed and has been answered in part by noting that computer analysis is no more impersonal than are procedures such as paper-and-pencil administration methods (Fowler, 1985).

Butcher (1987) pointed out that computer reports are designed to serve as consultations to qualified professionals who are knowledgeable about how the particular test operates. The computer-based report is recommended to be used as adjunct or to augment clinical data obtained via other means, rather than serving as a replacement for them or as a substitute for clinical judgment. The computer-based interpretation system is designed to function as a test resource, analogous to an electronic resource book. The report should be considered by the practitioner as a likely summary of the client's personality and symptoms that need to be incorporated into the clinical picture and verified by other information. It is not considered to be a stand-alone report or one that is provided to the client as a take-home summary of his or her case. In addition, Butcher (1987) outlined the importance of ensuring that computerized narratives are internally consistent and focused on empirical data, such that they factor in specific demographic and other characteristics as appropriate.

Although psychologists have made great strides in developing computer-based test interpretation reports for use with traditional measures, the available technology has not been fully utilized in several areas, such as the development of virtual reality (lifelike) test stimuli, maximal data-processing methods, and complex interpretation strategies that account for the complexities of the real world (Atlis et al., 2006).

The current wide availability of the Internet has created new prospects for providing broadly accessible psychological assessment. Internet-based assessment, however, is faced with problems as well as opportunities (Naglieri et al., 2004). The development and validation of Internet-based assessment resources has not kept pace with technological developments, and there has been relatively limited research on the equivalence in testing conditions, equivalence of normative databases, and other considerations that are important to reliable and valid test use (Buchanan, 2002). Moreover, more research needs to be conducted on the similarity in test-taking attitudes for Internet-based tests compared with traditional testing approaches.

In conclusion, most assessment psychologists incorporate computer assessment technology in the evaluation at present. Over time, there has been a call for computers to provide more assistance with personality assessment, not less. This has been the case particularly as clinicians and resources become increasingly stretched, and the technology has improved. Greene recently concluded that "computer scoring and computer interpretation of all psychological assessment techniques should become the basis for the psychological report" and that "psychological assessment should become a computer-based field" (2005, p. 6). Although some dissent is likely to persist among practitioners who are approaching this debate from different perspectives, computer-based psychological assessment provides an effective and timely means of processing and integrating test results for inclusion in a clinical assessment.

REFERENCES

Atlis, M. M., Hahn, J., & Butcher, J. N. (2006). Computer-based assessment with the MMPI-2. In J. N. Butcher (Ed.), *MMPI-2: A practitioner's guide* (pp. 445–476). Washington, DC: American Psychological Association.

Buchanan, T. (2002). Online assessment: Desirable or dangerous? *Professional Psychology: Research and Practice, 33*(2), 148–154.

Butcher, J. N. (Ed.). (1987). *Computerized psychological assessment: A practitioner's guide.* New York: Basic Books.

Butcher, J. N. (2005). *User's guide for the Minnesota Clinical Report* (4th ed.). Minneapolis, MN: Pearson Assessments.

Butcher, J. N., Berah, E., Ellertsen, B., Miach, P., Lim, J., Nezami, E., et al. (1998). Objective personality assessment: Computer-based Minnesota Multiphasic Personality Inventory–2 interpretation in international clinical settings. In C. Belar (Ed.), *Comprehensive clinical psychology: Sociocultural and individual differences.* New York: Elsevier.

Caldwell, A. B. (1971, April). *Recent advances in automated interpretation of the MMPI.* Paper presented at the sixth annual MMPI Symposium, Minneapolis, MN.

Cheung, F. M., & Butcher, J. N. (2008). *Comparability of computer-based interpretive reports in Hong Kong.* Hong Kong: Chinese University of Hong Kong Press.

Eber, H. W. (1964, September). *Automated personality description with 16-PF data.* Paper presented at the meeting of the American Psychological Association, Los Angeles.

Exner, J. E., Jr. (1987). Computer assistance in Rorschach interpretation. In J. N. Butcher (Ed.), *Computerized psychological assessment: A practitioner's guide* (pp. 218–235). New York: Basic Books.

Exner, J. E., Jr., & Weiner, I. B. (2003). Rorschach interpretation assistance program: Version 5 (RIAP5™). Lutz, FL: Psychological Assessment Resources.

Finney, J. C. (1966). Programmed interpretation of the MMPI and CPI. *Archives of General Psychiatry, 15,* 75–81.

Fowler, R. D. (1985). Landmarks in computer-assisted psychological assessment. *Journal of Consulting and Clinical Psychology, 53,* 748–759.

Greene, R. L. (2005). Computer scoring and interpretation in psychological report writing. *SPA Exchange, 17,* 6.

Karson, S., & O'Dell, J. W. (1987). Computer-based interpretation of the 16PF: The Karson Clinical Report in contemporary practice. In J. N. Butcher (Ed.), *Computerized psychological assessment: A practitioner's guide* (pp. 198–217). New York: Basic Books.

Lachar, D. (1974). *The MMPI: Clinical assessment and automated interpretation.* Los Angeles: Western Psychological Services.

Meehl, P. E. (1954). *Clinical versus statistical prediction: A theoretical analysis and a review of the evidence.* Minneapolis: University of Minnesota Press.

Millon, T. (1977). *Millon clinical multiaxial inventory.* Minneapolis, MN: National Computer Systems.

Naglieri, J. A., Drasgow, F., Schmit, M., Handler, L., Prifitera, A., Margolis, A., et al. (2004). Psychological testing on the Internet: New problems, old issues. *American Psychologist, 59*(3), 150–162.

Piotrowski, Z. A. (1964). A digital computer administration of inkblot test data. *Psychiatric Quarterly, 38,* 1–26.

Rome, H. P., Swenson, W. M., Mataya, P., McCarthy, C. E., Pearson, J. S., Keating, F.R., et al. (1962). Symposium on automation techniques in personality assessment. *Proceedings of the Staff Meeting of the Mayo Clinic, 37,* 61–82.

SUGGESTED READINGS

Bartram, D., & Hambleton, R. K. (2006). *Computer-based testing and the Internet.* Hoboken, NJ: John Wiley & Sons.

Garb, H. N. (2007). Computer-administered interviews and rating scales. *Psychological Assessment, 19,* 4–13.

JAMES N. BUTCHER
University of Minnesota

See also: **Computer-Assisted Psychotherapy; Computerized Adaptive Testing; Psychological Assessment**

COMPUTERIZED ADAPTIVE TESTING

The Bible in the book of Judges (12:4–6) records an early example of testing with a one-item test that had very high stakes:

> Jephthah then called together the men of Gilead and fought against Ephraim. The Gileadites struck them down because the Ephraimites had said, "You Gileadites are renegades from Ephraim and Manasseh."

The Gileadites captured the fords of the Jordan leading to Ephraim, and whenever a survivor of Ephraim said, "Let me cross over," the men of Gilead asked him, "Are you an Ephraimite?" If he replied, "No," they said, "All right, say 'Shibboleth.'" He said, "Sibboleth," because he could not pronounce the word correctly, they seized him and killed him at the fords of the Jordan.

No validity or reliability studies were reported in support of this test's conclusions. The author of Judges did not record what proportion of those slain were in fact Ephraimites, and how many were unfortunate Gileadites with a speech impediment. Happily the science of testing has advanced considerably in the 3,000-odd years since Jephthah's struggle with Ephraim.

The formal practice of mental testing goes back at least 4,000 years, predating the Chan dynasty in China. During a significant portion of that time there has been a tension between individually administered and group administered tests. Individually administered tests have at least three advantages:

1. The items are focused on the topic of principal concern—the exam can be narrowly focused on the specific areas of the examiner's concern, and if weaknesses show up, the test can be shifted to explore those weaknesses in great depth. This is of special importance if the test is for diagnostic purposes and some sort of remediation/instruction is planned in its wake.

2. They are of an appropriate difficulty—items that are too easy or too difficult tell us nothing about the examinee's ability any more than having someone jump over a 2-inch or a 10-foot obstacle tells us about a person's hurdling ability. The examiner can easily tell when some questions are clearly beyond the examinee and shifts back to others more suitable. This avoids the boredom of too easy items and the frustration of too many hard ones.

3. Any unusual testing circumstances can be accommodated. If an examinee doesn't understand the instructions for the exam, or passes out from the heat, or breaks a pencil, an examiner can spot it easily and remediate the problem. This is less easily done in a large hall with hundreds of examinees.

Without extraordinary precautions, however, individual administrations are not standardized, and there is enormous difficulty doing any sort of rigorous and precise comparison among candidates. Group-administered exams, on the other hand, suffer and benefit from standardization. They suffer in that they cannot adapt themselves to the characteristics of the individual examinee, but, because of their standardized nature, they do allow accurate comparisons among examinees. Also, because group-administered items are to be used for testing many examinees, they can be pretested for quality and fairness in a much more rigorous way than is economically possible for items that are part of an individually administered exam.

Test theory, until the 1960s, was focused on the entire test as the fundamental unit of any examination. But in the 1960s, with Georg Rasch's simple model and Allan Birnbaum's more complex ones, test theories were developed that had the individual item as the fungible unit from which tests were constructed. The development of these item response theories made it possible to simultaneously individualize tests to suit each examinee and still to yield scores that were rigorously comparable across examinees; in short, mass-administered tests could be built that adapted to the ability of the person taking them.

Item response theory has a parameter that characterizes the difficulty of an item. To make a test adaptive one merely constructs a large pool of items whose difficulty varies from very easy to very hard. Then one begins a test by choosing an item of middling difficulty. If the examinee gets it right another item is chosen that is more difficult. If the first item is answered incorrectly the next one is easier. In this way the test quickly zeros in on items that most accurately match the ability of the examinee. The examinee's score is then a function of the difficulty of the items that were answered correctly.

Choosing the appropriate next item involves updating the current estimate of the examinee's ability and then finding that item in the pool that provides the most information about the examinee. These calculations are typically onerous, and could not be done by an unaided human examiner fast enough for the test to flow smoothly; thus the task of finding the next item to administer falls to a computer. Hence such tests are called computerized adaptive tests, or CATs for short.

Of course it is not as simple as I have sketched. The item choice algorithm does not just consider the difficulty of the next item to be chosen, but also its content, so that the test administered spans the content specifications for the test. It also keeps track of how often various items have already been administered and tries to balance out usage so that the items of the test are kept as secure as possible.

Eight years into the twenty-first century CATs are an important part of the commercial testing business with hundreds of thousands of them administered each year. The experience gained from these has taught us that (1) CATs are a viable way to test, (2) they typically yield about the same accuracy as a fixed length test with almost double the number of items, and (3) they are always more expensive than is anticipated because of the costs of building a large enough item pool so that the continuous exposure, the *sine qua non* of CAT, does not threaten its security, and a computer for each examinee is more expensive than an answer sheet and a #2 pencil.

REFERENCES

Birnbaum, A. (1968). Some latent trait models and their use in inferring an examinee's ability. In F. M. Lord and M. R. Novick, *Statistical theories of mental test scores* (chap. 17–20). Reading, MA: Addison-Wesley.

Lord, F. M. (1980). *Applications of item response theory to practical testing problems*. Hillsdale, NJ: Lawrence Erlbaum.

Lord, F. M., & Novick, M. R. (1968). *Statistical theories of mental test scores*. Reading, MA: Addison-Wesley.

Rasch, G. (1960). *Probabilistic models for some intelligence and attainment tests*. Copenhagen: Denmarks Paedagogiske Institut. (Republished in 1980 by the University of Chicago Press of Chicago.)

Wainer, H., Bradlow, E. T., & Wang, X. (2007). *Testlet response theory and its applications*. New York: Cambridge University Press.

Wainer, H., Dorans, N., Eignor, D., Flaugher, R., Green, B., Mislevy, R., Steinberg, L., & Thissen, D. (2000). *Computerized adaptive testing: A primer* (2nd ed.). Hillsdale, NJ: Lawrence Erlbaum.

HOWARD WAINER
National Board of Medical Examiners

See also: **Computerized Behavioral Assessment; Psychological Assessment**

COMPUTERIZED BEHAVIORAL ASSESSMENT

Behavioral assessment is a methodology characterized by direct or indirect observation of low-level (i.e., minimally inferential) phenomena by either a participant or observer. It is distinguished from other forms of assessment in that behavior is considered a function of proximal and distal antecedents and consequences, the modification of which should lead to changes in the frequency, duration, or magnitude of a selected behavior. As such, behavioral assessment is a critical component of behavior therapy as both an assessment and monitoring tool to gauge the effects of an intervention on behavior and the variables hypothesized to control behavior (Haynes & O'Brien, 2000).

The methods of behavioral assessment are rich and varied and possess unique strengths and weaknesses in their ability to contribute to the validity of clinical inferences regarding sources of variation in behavior. Direct observation techniques involve directly observing an individual over a period of time and (usually) coding a dimension of a selected behavior. Direct observation is often used in controlled environments through direct observation of individuals as they engage in natural behavior (e.g., direct observation of a schizophrenic patient on a hospital ward) or in an analogue condition designed to evoke the behavior of interest (e.g., observation of marital interactions using a challenge task; observation of a learning-disabled child attempting to complete several mathematics questions). Indirect observation involves techniques that do not involve a trained rater directly observing behavior. Self-monitoring tasks (e.g., recording one's own behavior over time), all forms of self-report, collection of behavioral byproducts (e.g., number of cigarette butts produced on smoke breaks), and psychophysiological measurement (e.g., heart rate) are considered forms of indirect measurement, because the behavior of interest is never directly observed by an independent observer.

Unlike other forms of assessment, behavioral assessment has always been conceptualized as an ongoing activity that should occur multiple times over the course of treatment. Multiple points of measurement permit a therapist to both monitor change in a client and draw inferences regarding sources of variability in a selected behavior. What precisely is monitored depends on the clinician's initial case formulation and identification of salient antecedents and consequences.

Technology Integration into Behavioral Assessment

Multiple measurement periods imply a large amount of data that does not lend itself to easy analysis. Further, because behavioral assessment does not emphasize norm-based assessment the way other assessment paradigms do, clinicians are ill-advised to use parametric statistical procedures when analyzing behavioral assessment data. Researchers should keep in mind that using parametric statistical procedures on data that may be autocorrelated (i.e., serially dependent; the value of an observation may depend on the value of a previous observation) can lead to serious violations of statistical assumptions of independence and inflate Type I error rates. As such, management and interpretation of large amounts of data collected from the single individual require sophisticated computer programs both for the data collection and the subsequent analysis (see Collins & Sayer, 2001).

Types of Computerized Behavioral Assessment Applications

Observational Software

Observational software has been developed to assist clinicians and researchers in the real-time coding of behavior. Handheld computers make ideal data collection tools given their small size and computing power. For example, Sarkar and colleagues (2006) developed BASIS (Behavior and Social Interaction Software), which runs on a handheld Palm computer and is designed to assist investigators in recording observations of complex interactions between children and various socializing agents (e.g., parents, teachers, etc.). Using the graphical BASIS interface, users can easily and rapidly code child behavior in terms of the setting, the situation, the general behavioral state of the child, the person with whom the child interacted, and twelve other behavioral categories. Because data are recorded immediately to the Palm's internal database, analysis is greatly speeded.

Researchers have found that, relative to more traditional paper-pencil methods, behavioral observation software improves both the efficiency and accuracy of data collection (Tapp, Ticha, Kryzer, Gustafson, Gunnar, & Symons, 2006). Other observational software tools include Observer 5.0 (Noldus Information Technology, 2003) and Interval Manager (INTMAN; Tapp et al., 2006).

Ecological Momentary Assessment

The term *ambulatory assessment* refers to the use of computer-assisted methodology to assess behavior as participants engage in their normal daily activities (Fahrenberg, Myrtek, Pawlik, & Perrez, 2007). Within the past few years, numerous reports have appeared in the scientific literature utilizing a form of ambulatory assessment called ecological momentary assessment (EMA). EMA is a sampling methodology utilizing handheld computers in which participants either make a data entry when a behavior occurs (i.e., event contingent recording) or do so contingent upon a signal from the computer at a scheduled time (i.e., signal contingent recording). Typically, questions delivered by the computer query for some dimension of the individual's current state or ask the individual to estimate behavioral dimensions within a specified time interval prior to the scheduled assessment (e.g., within the past four hours).

A tremendous advantage of EMA methodology is that assessment occurs in the person's natural environment. Thus, natural memory distortions that occur with the passage of time are minimized, although no assessment method is ever completely free of measurement error. Another advantage is that the multiple observations inherent in an EMA study permit researchers to identify proximal antecedents of behavior.

For example, in a recent study by Smyth and colleagues (2007), female bulimic patients carried a palmtop computer for two weeks using a signal-contingent protocol in which the computer prompted for a response six times per day. Participants rated their mood and reported any binge events. Results showed that on days in which bingeing occurred, participants reported higher negative affect, anger, hostility, and stress. Thus, dysphoric mood was predictive of disordered eating and purging. Further, the data also showed that bingeing was associated with rapid decreases in negative affect and hostility and corresponding increases in positive affect. Thus, the function of bingeing may be regulatory in that it permits both escape from an aversive dysphoric state while fostering an increase in positive affect.

EMA studies have examined other clinically-relevant phenomena as well, especially maintenance of gains following inpatient substance use or outpatient smoking cessation programs. For example, Cooney and colleagues (2007) gave outpatient graduates of a substance abuse program a handheld computer for 14 days. Participants responded to a variety of computer questions immediately prior to smoking a cigarette, five minutes after onset of cigarette smoking, and at random points unrelated to smoking. Using the EMA methodology, the researchers were able to show that, consistent with a cue reactivity model, the urge to drink alcohol was positively related to smoking a cigarette. In another EMA study, Twaltney, Shiffman, and Sayette (2005) had 214 smokers use palmtop computers to record momentary self-efficacy ratings during smoking urges. They found that smoking urges were highest when affect was negative and self-efficacy was reduced. Thus, self-efficacy was shown to be related, or reactive, to one's affective-motivational state, suggesting a mediated path to relapse.

Virtual Reality

Virtual reality environments have been used for both assessment and therapeutic purposes. Typically, participants in a virtual reality session wear a head-mounted visual display that synchronizes a computer-generated image with the participant's head movements. Scores of virtual worlds have been created and described in the scientific literature with the most common therapeutic interventions involving fear of flying, fear of heights, fear of spiders, posttraumatic stress, and social interactions with avatars. There is compelling evidence at this point that virtual reality exposure therapy is at least as effective as imaginal exposure therapy (see Bouchard, Côté, & Richard, 2006).

Virtual reality as an assessment tool has been discussed somewhat less. For example, Gutiérrez-Mandonado and colleagues (2006) exposed eating-disordered participants to several virtual environments (e.g., a kitchen, a restaurant, a swimming pool, and a neutral living room condition). They found higher levels of measured state anxiety in all of the first three conditions compared to the living-room condition. Further, virtual environments in which participants were required to virtually eat high-calorie food produced the greatest anxiety. Thus, there appears to be some potential for virtual environments to address the construct validity of psychiatric diagnoses, provide information about functional relations, and monitor treatment outcome.

Issues in Computerized Behavioral Assessment

In this section, we briefly consider issues related to the use of computerized behavioral assessment as well as obstacles to incorporating computerized behavioral assessment into routine clinical practice.

Reactivity. A measurement instrument is reactive if a dimension of a person's behavior changes by virtue of knowing that observation is occurring. Reactivity may be reduced by habituating participants to recording devices or making the devices unobtrusive. In self-monitoring contexts like EMA, however, reactivity is a significant concern because the observer is also the research participant. Recommendations have included having individuals use the handheld computer for a couple of days prior to collecting actual data for a study in order to avoid reactivity effects due to novelty. The degree to which participants are reactive to EMA technology is some matter of debate. Hufford, Shields, Shiffman, Paty, and Balabanis (2002) found only a small amount of behavioral and emotional reactivity in male and female undergraduate drinkers who completed a two-week monitoring protocol. Similarly, Gloster and colleagues (in press) found that most reactivity occurred when obsessive-compulsive patients were instructed to informally self-monitor their symptoms with very little reactivity occurring to subsequent EMA self-monitoring. Thus, it could well be that the instruction to attend to one's behavior accounts for most reactivity effects rather than the actual use of the handheld computer.

Computerized behavioral assessment and ethics. Standard 4.01 of the American Psychological Associations Code of Ethics notes that psychologists should take "reasonable precautions to protect confidential information through or stored in any medium." With regard to computerized behavioral assessment, steps should be taken to ensure that data cannot be meaningfully interpreted by individuals outside the research context. For example, handheld computers can be locked with a password or database files can be constructed in a way to make it impossible to associate the data with a particular person. Although we are not aware of any instance in which a person's identity was compromised this way, and paper-pencil diaries certainly carry risks as well with regard to confidentiality, researchers would be well advised to take steps to ensure confidentiality of responses.

Technology issues. Handheld computers do have their limitations. Their small size makes them easy to misplace, and they require daily battery recharging. Virtually all investigators who have used handheld devices have a power outage and data-loss story to tell. Further, the audio capabilities of handheld computers remain suboptimal and it is often difficult for individuals to hear the computer signal the start of an assessment session.

Barriers to clinical adoption. Technology can be expensive, and although researchers have been quick to discern the merits of computerized behavioral assessment, the advantages that accrue to researchers are significantly greater than those accruing to the average clinician. Barriers to clinical adoption include the cost of software and equipment, the time required to learn a computer system, and

the low likelihood that clinicians of alternative therapeutic orientations would embrace technology designed to facilitate behavioral assessment. Currently, clinicians spend less than five hours per week on assessment-related activities (Camara et al., 2000), most likely because assessment activities are not easily reimbursed by third parties (for a recent discussion, see Piasecki, Hufford, Solhan, & Trull, 2007).

Computerized behavioral assessment is a rapidly developing field utilizing the very latest computer technologies. In the future, one can expect applications to utilize cell phone technology in order for data entry to be made through one's phone to a remote web site or database. In fact, initial reports using cellular phone technology are beginning to appear with one research group using cell phones to track drug craving and using episodes in a homeless population (see Freedman, Lester, McNamara, Milby, & Schumacher, 2006). Although technology integration in behavioral assessment has been a boon to research investigators, whether computer technology will be embraced in routine clinical practice remains an open question.

REFERENCES

Bouchard, S., Côté, S., & Richard, D. C. S. (2007). Virtual reality applications for exposure. In D. C. S. Richard and D. Lauterbach (Eds.), *Handbook of exposure therapies* (pp. 347–388). New York: Academic Press/Elsevier.

Camara, W. J., Nathan, J. S., & Puente, A. E. (2000). Psychological test usage: Implications in professional psychology. *Professional Psychology: Research and Practice, 31,* 141–154.

Collins, L. M., & Sayer, A. G. (2001). *New methods for the analysis of change.* Washington, DC: American Psychological Association.

Cooney, N. L., Litt, M. D., Cooney, J. L., Pilkey, D. T., Steinberg, H. R., & Oncken, C. A. (2007). Alcohol and tobacco cessation in alcohol-dependent smokers: Analysis of real-time reports. *Psychology of Addictive Behaviors, 21,* 277–286.

Freedman, M. J., Lester, K. M., McNamara, C., Milby, J. B., & Schumacher, J. E. (2006). Cell phones for ecological momentary assessment with cocaine-addicted homeless patients in treatment. *Journal of Substance Abuse Treatment, 30,* 105–111.

Gloster, A., Richard, D. C. S., Himle, J., Koch, E., & Thornton, J. (In press). An ecological momentary assessment of recall accuracy of patients' obsessive-compulsive symptoms and estimation of functional relations. *Journal of Behaviour Research and Therapy.*

Gutiérrez-Maldonado, J., Ferrer-García, M., Caqueo-Urízar, A., & Letosa-Porta, A. (2006). Assessment of emotional reactivity produced by exposure to virtual environments in patients with eating disorders. *Cyberpsychology and Behavior, 9,* 507–513.

Gwaltney, C. J., Shiffman, S., & Sayette, M. A. (2005). Situational correlates of abstinence self-efficacy. *Journal of Abnormal Psychology, 114,* 649–660.

Haynes, S. N., & O'Brien, W. H. (2000). *Principles and practice of behavioral assessment.* Dordrecht, The Netherlands: Kluwer Academic Publishers.

Hufford, M. R., Shields, A. L., Shiffman, S., Paty, J., & Balabanis, M. (2002). Reactivity to ecological momentary assessment: An example using undergraduate problem drinkers. *Psychology of Addictive Behaviors, 16*, 205–211.

Noldus Information Technology (2003). *The Observer (Version 5): Professional system for collection, analysis, presentation, and management of observational data.* Wageningen: Noldus Information Technology.

Piasecki, T. M., Hufford, M. R., Solhan, M., & Trull, T. J. (2007). Assessing clients in their natural environments with electronic diaries: Rationale, benefits, limitations, and barriers. *Psychological Assessment, 19*, 25–43.

Sarkar, A. (2006). Development and use of behavior and social interaction software installed on Palm handheld for observation of a child's social interactions with the environment. *Behavior Research Methods, 38*, 407–415.

Smyth, J. M., Wonderlich, S. A., Heron, K. E., Sliwinski, M. J., Crosby, R. D., Mitchell, J. E., & Engel, S. G. (2007). Daily and momentary mood and stress are associated with binge eating and vomiting in bulimia nervosa patients in the natural environment. *Journal of Consulting and Clinical Psychology, 75*, 629–638.

Tapp, J., Ticha, R., Kryzer, E., Gustafson, M., Gunnar, M. R., & Symons, F. J. (2006). Comparing observational software with paper and pencil for time-sampled data: A field test of Interval Manager (INTMAN). *Behavior Research Methods, 38*, 165–169.

DAVID C. S. RICHARD
Rollins College

See also: **Behavioral Assessment; Computerized Adaptive Testing; Psychological Assessment**

CONCEPT FORMATION

A concept is a mentally possessed idea or notions that can be used to categorize information or objects. Over the course of each person's lifetime, thousands of concepts are learned for nouns like corkscrew, justice, and doorknob; for adjectives like green, symmetric, and beautiful; and for verbs like kick, climb, and eschew. Although some philosophers have maintained that we do not genuinely learn new concepts through induction (Fodor, 1998), most psychologists believe that concepts can be learned and that the representational capacity of learners increases as they acquire new concepts. Most efforts have been spent developing accounts of how people acquire and represent concepts, including models based on rules, exemplars, boundaries, and theories.

According to rule-based models of concept formation, to acquire a concept is to learn the rule that allows one to determine whether the concept applies to an entity. The most influential rule-based approach to concepts may be Bruner, Goodnow, and Austin's (1956) hypothesis testing approach. In a typical experiment, their subjects were shown flash cards that had different shapes, colors, quantities, and borders. The subjects' task was to discover the rule for categorizing the flash cards by selecting cards to be tested and by receiving feedback from the experimenter indicating whether the selected card fit the categorizing rule. However, at least three criticisms have been levied against this rule-based approach.

First, it has been proven to be very difficult to specify the defining rules for most concepts. Even a seemingly well-defined concept such as *bachelor* seems to involve more than its simple definition of "unmarried male." The counter-example of a five-year-old child (who does not really seem to be a bachelor) may be fixed by adding in an "adult" precondition, but an indefinite number of other preconditions are required to exclude a man in a long-term but unmarried relationship, the pope, and an 80-year-old widower with four grandchildren. Second, the category membership for many objects is not clear. People disagree with each other (and even themselves) from one occasion to the next on whether a starfish is a fish, a camel is a vehicle, a hammer is a weapon, and a stroke is a disease. Third, even when a person shows consistency in placing objects in a category, people do not treat the objects as equally good instances of the concept. When asked to rate the typicality of animals like robin and eagle for the concept *bird*, or chair and hammock for the concept *furniture*, subjects reliably give different typicality ratings for each different object.

In response to the preceding criticisms, a prototype model of concept formation was developed. Central to Eleanor Rosch's development of prototype theory is the notion that concepts are organized around family resemblance rather than rules (Rosch, 1975). The prototype for a concept consists of the most common attribute or shared feature values associated with the instances of the concept. Once prototypes for a set of concepts have been determined, categorizations can be predicted by determining how similar an object is to each of the prototypes. An empirical result consistent with the prototype view is that never-before-seen prototypes are often categorized as accurately as previously seen distortions of the prototype and with higher accuracy than new distortions. One interpretation of these results is that prototypes are extracted from resemblances among distortions and they are used as a basis for determining categorizations.

A third approach, exemplar modeling, denies that prototypes are explicitly extracted from individual cases. Instead, in exemplar models, to learn a concept is simply to store the actual individual cases that have been observed. An exemplar model forms the concept "bird" by representing all of the instances (exemplars) that belong to this category, including robins, eagles, and penguins. The exemplar approach assumes that categorization decisions are based on the similarity of the object to be categorized to all of the exemplars of each relevant concept (Nosofsky, 1986). Consistent with an exemplar account, evidence suggests that people show good categorization of new stimuli just to the extent that the new stimuli resemble previously learned members of the category. Instead of viewing rote memorization of exemplars as evidence of human stupidity or laziness, exemplar accounts argue that preserving the entire stimulus in its full richness of detail provides the most flexibility for future categorization and reasoning.

A fourth approach claims that a concept is formed when its category boundary has been established (Ashby & Townsend, 1986). Whereas the prototype model represents a concept by its center—its most typical member—a category boundary model represents the concept by its perimeter. Frequently, a category boundary models are constrained by assuming that the boundary that a person constructs to characterize a concept is the one that maximizes the likelihood of correctly categorizing an object into the concept. To learn a categorization is to learn the parameters that define the lines or curves that act as the boundaries between two or more categories. One problem with this account is that the boundary between two categories depends on several contextual factors that make some prototypes or exemplars more influential. In many cases, it is more parsimonious to hypothesize representations for the concept considered by itself and view category boundaries as side effects of the competition between neighboring categories. A fifth approach, theory-based concept formation, begins with the observation that the four preceding approaches all operate without regard to the actual meaning of the concepts. By contrast, many researchers have argued that the use of purely data-driven, inductive methods for concept formation is strongly limited and modulated by one's background knowledge. It has been observed developmentally that children choose a toy monkey over a worm as being more similar to a human, but that when told that humans have spleens, they are likely to infer that the worm has a spleen than that the toy monkey does. One conclusion is that inferences are driven by the theories that even young children have about living things and their rich internal organizations. The general claim is that concepts are formed around theories—organized systems of knowledge (Murphy & Medin, 1985). This claim is supported by evidence that concepts are more easily learned when a learner has appropriate background knowledge, suggesting that more than "brute" statistical regularities underlie our concepts.

It seems most likely that people use combinations of these representational strategies and can deploy them flexibly based upon the categories to be learned. There is growing consensus that at least two independent kinds of representational strategy operate in concept formation—rule-based and similarity-based processes (Sloman, 1996).

Even if one holds out hope for a unified model of all concept formation, these different representational strategies must be accommodated by that model.

Much of the most exciting current work in concept formation dispenses with the fiction that concepts are isolated, independent knowledge structures and focuses instead on how concepts are related to each other. For example, the concept *hammer* seems to be inherently connected to *nails* given that one of its most commonly listed features is "used to strike nails." In semantic networks, concepts are represented by nodes in a network and they gain their functionality by their links to other concept nodes. The meaning of a given concept is then derived from how it connects with other conceptual information.

If concepts are connected to each other, they are also importantly connected to at least two other cognitive processes: perception and language. According to Lawrence Barsalou's (1999) theory of Perceptual Symbol Systems, sensorimotor areas of the brain that are activated during the initial perception of an event are reactivated at a later time by association areas, serving as a representation of one's prior perceptual experience. Because these reactivated aspects of experience may be common to a number of different events, they may be thought of as symbols, representing an entire class of events. Because they are formed around perceptual experience, they are perceptual symbols, unlike the amodal symbols typically employed in symbolic theories of cognition. Consistent with this theory, perceptual and conceptual information influence one another. For example, in cases of acquired categorical perception, people are faster at discriminating between objects that belong to different categories rather than the same category, even when those categories are arbitrarily imposed through training.

The connection between concepts and language is similarly bidirectional. In particular, one's repertoire of concepts influences the types of word meanings that one learns, whereas the language that one speaks arguably influences the type of concepts that one forms. The former, less controversial influence is well documented by developmental evidence suggesting that word meanings are relatively easily acquired to the extent that the words map onto existing concepts that capture the correlational structure of the world. There is growing evidence amassing for the latter influence (Gentner & Goldin-Meadow, 2003) that demonstrates that words can selectively direct attention to particular dimensions, facilitate certain thought patterns (by increasing their likelihood of being triggered or creating tokens for complex ideas), and structure otherwise chaotic cognitive domains. Overall, the connections between concepts and perception on the one hand and between concepts and language on the other hand reveal an important dual nature of concepts. Concepts are used both to recognize objects and to ground word meanings. Working out the details of this dual nature will go a long way toward understanding how human thinking can be both concrete and symbolic.

REFERENCES

Ashby, F. G., & Townsend, J. T. (1986). Varieties of perceptual independence. *Psychological Review, 93*, 154–179.

Barsalou, L. W. (1999). Perceptual symbol systems. *Behavioral and Brain Sciences, 22*, 577–660.

Bruner, J. S., Goodnow, J. J., & Austin, G. A. (1956). *A study of thinking.* New York: John Wiley & Sons.

Fodor, J. A. (1998). *Concepts: Where cognitive science went wrong.* Oxford: Oxford University Press.

Gentner, D., & Goldin-Meadow, S. (Eds.). (2003). *Language in mind: Advances in the study of language and thought.* Cambridge, MA: MIT Press.

Murphy, G. L., & Medlin, D. L. (1985). The role of theories in conceptual coherence. *Psychological Review, 92*, 289–316.

Nosofsky, R. M. (1986). Attention, similarity, and the identification-categorization relationship. *Journal of Experimental Psychology: General, 115*, 39–57.

Rosch, E. (1975). Cognitive representations of semantic categories. *Journal of Experimental Psychology: General, 104*, 192–232.

Sloman, S. A. (1996). The empirical case for two systems of reasoning. *Psychological Bulletin, 119*, 3–22.

SUGGESTED READINGS

Estes, W. K. (1994). *Classification and cognition.* New York: Oxford University Press.

Margolis, E., & Laurence, S. (Eds.). (1999). *Concepts: Core readings.* Cambridge, MA: MIT Press.

Murphy, G. L. (2002). *The big book of concepts.* Cambridge, MA: MIT Press.

ROBERT L. GOLDSTONE
THOMAS T. HILL
SAMUEL B. DAY
Indiana University

See also: **Learning Theories; Problem Solving**

CONDITIONING (See Instrumental Conditioning; Operant Conditioning; Pavlovian Conditioning)

CONDUCT DISORDER

Within the framework of the *Diagnostic and Statistical Manual of Mental Disorders* (DSM-IV-TR; American Psychiatric Association [APA], 2000), conduct disorder is one of the Disruptive Behavior Disorders that are usually first diagnosed in childhood or adolescence. Conduct disorder (CD) is a repetitive and persistent pattern of behavior that violates societal norms or the basic rights of others (APA, 2000) and that consists of (1) aggressive behavior that threatens or causes physical harm to other people or animals (e.g., bullies, threatens, or intimidates others); (2) nonaggressive conduct that causes property loss or damage (e.g., fire-setting); (3) deceitfulness or theft (e.g., breaking into someone's house or car); and (4) serious violation of rules (e.g., truancy). To be diagnosed, at least 3 of 15 possible symptoms must have been displayed during the past 12 months. Childhood-onset CD is differentiated from adolescent onset when at least one of the behavioral characteristics is evident before age 10.

Although some forms of aggressive behaviors are relatively common in mild forms during early childhood years, such behaviors become clinically significant if the instances are highly intense, high in frequency, or characterized by notably violent elements in later years. Estimated rates of CD are 6% to 16% for boys and 2% to 9% for girls (APA, 2000), with boys outnumbering girls about three-to-one (Kazdin, 1998; Lochman, 2003). Loeber (1990) hypothesized that aggressive behavior in elementary school years is part of a developmental trajectory that can lead to adolescent delinquency and CD. Similarly, the DSM-IV indicates that oppositional defiant disorder (ODD) can evolve into childhood-onset CD and then into antisocial personality disorder in adults. Longitudinal research has documented that aggressive behavior and rejection by children's peers can be additive risk markers for subsequent maladjusted behavior in the middle school years, and substance use, overt delinquency, and police arrests add risk in later adolescent years. Children are more at risk for continued aggressive and antisocial behavior if they display aggressive behavior in multiple settings and if they develop "versatile" forms of antisocial behavior, including both overt and covert behaviors, by early to mid-adolescence (Lochman, 2003).

Children and adolescents with conduct disorders often have a number of co-occurring conditions that can affect the course of the disorder and can complicate treatment (Lochman, 2003). Attention deficit hyperactivity disorder (ADHD) is the most common comorbid diagnosis in children with conduct disorders, with rates ranging from 65% to 90% in clinic-referred children. Children with comorbid ADHD and CD have more conduct problem symptoms, an earlier onset of severe conduct problems, more aggressive conduct problems, and earlier and greater substance use than non-ADHD children with conduct disorders. Other common comorbid conditions are anxiety disorders, which occur in 60%–75% of clinic-referred CD children, depressive disorders which occur in 15%–31% of CD children, and substance use. Children and adolescents with both CD and substance use have an earlier onset of substance use and are more likely to abuse multiple substances.

The developmental trajectory leading to childhood-onset CD may start very early among inflexible infants with irritable temperaments (Loeber, 1990). These temperamentally difficult children are at risk for failing to develop positive attachments with caregivers, displaying high rates of hyperactivity and inattention in the preschool years, and becoming involved in increasingly coercive interchanges with parents and significant adults, such as teachers. Moffitt (1993) has suggested that life-course-persistent delinquents ("early starters") are at risk because of combined biological and family factors. In some children, family dysfunction may be sufficient to initiate this sequence of escalating aggressive behavior. Parents of aggressive conduct problem children often display high rates of harsh, inconsistent discipline, have unclear rules and expectations, and have low rates of positive involvement, adaptive discipline strategies, and problem-solving skills. Living in poor, crime-ridden neighborhoods also adds to the environmental risk factors leading to seriously aggressive problematic behavior.

Loeber (1990) hypothesized that children begin to generalize their use of coercive behaviors to other social interactions, leading to increasingly aggressive behavior with peers and adults and to dysfunctional social-cognitive processes, which in turn serve to maintain problem behavior sequences. For example, aggressive children tend to have hostile attributional biases and problem-solving strategies that rely on forceful direct action rather than verbal, negotiation strategies, and they expect that aggressive solutions will work. These information-processing difficulties are made worse for aggressive children because of their dominance-oriented social goals, pervasive schema-based expectations for others' behavior, and strong physiological reactivity in response to provocation (Lochman, 2003), as well as their poor verbal fluency and abstract reasoning abilities (Kazdin, 1998). Furthermore, children displaying aggressive behavior are often socially rejected by their peer group and can become increasingly withdrawn and isolated. By early to middle adolescence, they are prone to meeting their affiliation needs by gravitating toward deviant peer groups, which can become an additional proximal cause for delinquent behavior.

Historically, psychosocial treatment of antisocial, conduct-disordered youth has been perceived to be difficult and not very productive. However, in recent years randomized clinical research trials have identified empirically supported treatments for ODD and CD. Eyberg, Nelson, and Boggs (2008) have identified 16 parent-training and cognitive-behavioral intervention programs with well-established ●positive effects and nine other programs as possibly efficacious for treating disruptive behaviors. Kazdin (1998) has similarly identified several positive treatment approaches for CD, including parent management training, functional family therapy, cognitive problem-solving skills training, and multisystemic therapy.

Parent management training and functional family therapy are directed at dysfunctional parenting processes and have produced significant improvements in parenting practices and reductions in children's aggressive, conduct problem behavior. Cognitive-behavioral treatments designed to assist children's anger management, perspective-taking, and problem-solving skills have produced improvements in children's abilities to accurately perceive others' intentions and to generate more competent problem solutions and have led to reductions in problem behaviors. Multisystemic treatment relies on individualized assessments of antisocial youth and the impaired systems around them (e.g., parents, peer groups, school bonding) and uses intense, individualized treatment plans to impact these systems, producing significant reductions in antisocial behavior among seriously delinquent youth.

In recent years, there has been a focus on developing and evaluating effective multicomponent interventions that target both the social-cognitive and parenting skill deficits evident in conduct-disordered youth and their families. Intensive, comprehensive prevention programs have also been developed and evaluated with high-risk children starting as early as first grade, and the results indicate that aggressive behavior and CD can be reduced through early intervention (Lochman & Wells, 2004; Vitaro, Brendgen, Pagani, Tremblay, & McDuff, 1999).

REFERENCES

American Psychiatric Association. (2000). *Diagnostic and statistical manual of mental disorders* (4th ed., text rev.). Washington, DC: Author.

Eyberg, S. M., Nelson, M. M., & Boggs, S. R. (2008). Evidence-based psychosocial treatments for children and adolescents with disruptive behavior. *Journal of Clinical Child and Adolescent Psychology, 37*, 215–237.

Fite, P. J., Colder, C. R., Lochman, J. E., & Wells, K. C. (in press). Developmental trajectories of proactive and reactive aggression from 5th to 9th grade. *Journal of Clinical Child and Adolescent Psychology.*

Kazdin, A. E. (1998). Conduct disorder. In R. J. Morris & T. R. Kratochwill (Eds.), *The practice of child therapy* (3rd ed.) (pp. 199–230). Boston: Allyn and Bacon.

Lochman, J. E. (2003). Preventive intervention targeting precursors. In W. J. Bukoski & Z. Sloboda (Eds.), *Handbook of drug abuse prevention: Theory, science, and practice* (pp. 307–326). New York: Plenum Press.

Lochman, J. E., & Wells, K. C. (2004). The Coping Power program for preadolescent aggressive boys and their parents: Outcome effects at the one-year follow-up. *Journal of Consulting and Clinical Psychology, 72*, 571–578.

Loeber, R. (1990). Development and risk factors of juvenile anti-social behavior and delinquency. *Clinical Psychology Review, 10,* 1–42.

Moffitt, T. E. (1993). Adolescence-limited and life-course persistent antisocial behavior: A developmental taxonomy. *Psychology Review, 100,* 674–701.

Vitaro, F., Brendgen, M., Pagani, L., Tremblay, R. E., & McDuff, P. (1999). Disruptive behavior, peer association, and conduct disorder: Testing the developmental links through early intervention. *Development and Psychopathology, 11,* 287–304.

SUGGESTED READINGS

Crick, N. R., & Dodge, K. A. (1994). A review and reformulation of social information-processing mechanisms in children's social adjustment. *Psychological Bulletin, 115,* 74–101.

Lochman, J. E., Powell, N. R., Whidby, J. M., & FitzGerald, D. P. (2006). Cognitive-behavioral assessment and treatment with aggressive children. In P.C. Kendall (Ed.), *Child and adolescent therapy: Cognitive-behavioral procedures,* (3rd ed.) (pp. 33–81). New York: Guilford Press.

Lochman, J. E., & Wells, K. C. (2002). Contextual social-cognitive mediators and child outcome: A test of the theoretical model in the Coping Power Program. *Development and Psychopathology, 14,* 971–993.

JOHN E. LOCHMAN
TAMMY D. BARRY
University of Alabama

See also: **Antisocial Personality Disorder; Juvenile Delinquency; Oppositional Defiant Disorder**

CONDUCTION APHASIA

Conduction aphasia is a specific language deficit that consists of impaired repetition that is disproportionate to any defects in fluency or comprehension. Literal paraphasias—errors in which incorrect syllables are substituted within words for correct ones—are frequent and are exacerbated by attempts at repetition. In contrast to Wernicke's aphasia, patients are aware of their deficit and have no difficulty in comprehension. Ideomotor apraxias—inability to perform a manual task despite comprehending its goal—can also be present. To neurologists, conduction aphasia is an important clinical finding because it reliably indicates a brain lesion involving the dominant posterior perisylvian regions. To cognitive neuroscientists, conduction aphasia stands at the center of a long-standing debate on whether complex behaviors are created from the joining of simple cortical regions or are mediated by more specialized cortex.

Localization

Classically, conduction aphasia results from lesions of the arcuate fasciculus that disconnect receptive from expressive language regions. The arcuate fasciculus is a white matter tract that runs from Wernicke's area in the posterior superior temporal gyrus, arches around the Sylvian fissure, passes under the supramarginal and angular gyri, and runs anterioroly to the inferior front lobe of Broca's region.

Many lesions that cause conduction aphasia involve not only the arcuate fasciculus but also the supramarginal gyrus and sometimes the posterior temporal gyrus, left auditory complex, and portions of the insula. Most cases of conduction aphasia follow cerebral infarcts of the dominant hemisphere involving thromboembolic occlusion of a posterior branch of the middle cerebral artery. It is relatively rare in comparison to other major aphasias (global, expressive, and receptive) because thromboemboli usually lodge more proximally causing more anterior or widespread infarcts.

Carl Wernicke postulated that a lesion of the arcuate fasciculus that disconnected receptive from expressive centers would produce a deficit in repetition, or "conduction aphasia." Others proposed that a single cortical center was responsible for integration of receptive and expressive regions yet was independent of them (Goldstein, 1948). This hypothesis led to the adoption of the alternative term "central aphasia" because the specific cortical region mediated central or inner speech.

Evidence Supporting Disconnection

Evidence from subjects with conduction aphasia usually supports the concept of disconnection. In these studies (usually patients with strokes examined at autopsy or by neuroimaging), disruption of the arcuate fasciculus is obligated with variable involvement of adjacent regions of supra—or subsylvian cortex (Benson et al., 1973; Damasio & Damasio, 1980). Studies of cortical strokes, however, in determinations of cortical versus subcortical mechanisms can be misleading because regions of destruction involve both cortex and the arcuate fasciculus.

Circumscribed lesions of the arcuate fasciculus that spare overlying cortex also support disconnection (Tanabe et al., 1987; Aihara et al., 1995; Arnett et al., 1996), but with white matter lesions (caused by multiple sclerosis for example) it is not possible to differentiate between the relative importance of disruption of the arcuate fasciculus versus disconnections of overlying neurons along its course.

Physiological findings have also supported disconnection as the mechanism of conduction aphasia. Regional blood, determined by xenon CT-scan, was absent in Broca's region in stroke patients with conduction aphasia, suggesting functional disconnection (Demeurisse & Capon, 1991).

Electrical stimulation, compared with clinical-pathological correlations in stroke, can more selectively separate cortical from white matter dysfunction. Electrical stimulation of the eloquent cortex produces both Broca's and Wernicke's but not conduction aphasia (Schaffler, Lunders, & Beck, 1996) suggesting that conduction aphasia is not cortically mediated. Notably, in this series of patients with implanted subdural electrodes, the testing paradigm involved mainly reading aloud, and repetition may not have been tested (Schaffler et al., 1996).

Finally, recent studies with the use of diffusion tensor magnetic resonance imaging tractography provide important refinements in imaging of the arcuate fasciculus (Catani & Ffytche, 2005). Instead of a monolithic tract, white matter connections of language form a direct pathway (the classical arcuate fasciculus) and a parallel, indirect pathway that interconnects Broca's and Wernicke's regions with the supramarginal and angular gyri. Clinical sequelae of lesions of these specialized tracts have yet to be well-defined but have been hypothesized to account for common language deficits.

Evidence Supporting Cortical Specialization

Other studies suggest that disconnection may not be the only mechanism of conduction aphasia. Some cases of conduction aphasia were caused by lesions that clearly spared the arcuate fasciculus (Mendez & Benson, 1985; Marshall et al., 1996). Similarly, lesions confined to the arcuate fasciculus have not always resulted in conduction aphasia (Shuren et al., 1995).

Physiologic data provided by PET imaging does not clearly support the disconnection theory. In one study of stroke and conduction aphasia, cerebral metabolic patterns had no clear correlation to clinical findings (Kempler et al., 1988), suggesting that functional disconnection is not necessary to produce conduction aphasia.

PET studies are correlated by independent reports of cortical mapping using electrical stimulation of implanted electrodes. In these cases, impaired repetition, with other features of conduction aphasia, was transiently elicited by stimulations of the posterior superior temporal gyrus (Anderson et al., 1999; Quigg & Fountain, 1999; Quigg, Geldmacher, & Elias, 2006). The selective and reversible impairment of a specific region of cortex suggests that conduction aphasia is mediated by regions of specialized cortex. Similarly, functional MRI of normal subjects tested with a paradigm intended to demonstrate regions of speech perception and production show activation of the posterior superior temporal gyrus (Hickok et al., 2000). These physiological methods of isolating cortical function, therefore, support the mediation of conduction aphasia by regions of specialized cortex.

Conduction aphasia provides an important model by which to study the functional organization of the brain. Although the classic Wernicke model is insufficient to account for all cases of conduction aphasia, it remains a clinically useful means by which to organize deficits in language.

REFERENCES

Aihara, M., Oba, H., Ohtomo, K., Uchiyama, G., Hayashibe, H., & Nakazawa, S. (1995). MRI of white matter changes in the Sjogren-Larsson syndrome. *Neuroradiology, 37,* 576–577.

Anderson, J. M., Gilmore, R., Roper, S., Crosson, B., Bauer, R. M., Nadeau, S. S., et al. (1999). Conduction aphasia and the arcuate fasciculus: A re-examination of the Wernicke-Geschwind model. *Brain and Language, 70,* 1–12.

Arnett, P. A., Rao, S. M., Hussain, M., Swanson, S. J., Hammeke, T. A. (1996). Conduction aphasia in multiple sclerosis: A case report with MRI findings. *Neurology, 47,* 576–578.

Benson, D. F., Sheremata, W. A., Bouchard, R., Segarra, J. M., Price, D., & Geschwind, N. (1973). Conduction aphasia: A clinicopathological study. *Archives of Neurology, 28,* 339–346.

Catani, M., Jones, D. K., & Ffytche, D. H. (2005). Perisylvian language networks of the human brain. *Annals of Neurology, 57,* 8–16.

Damasio, H., & Damasio, A. (1980). The anatomic basis of conduction aphasia. *Brain, 103,* 337–350.

Demeurisse, G., & Capon, A. (1991). Brain activation during a linguistic task in conduction aphasia. *Cortex, 27,* 285–294.

Goldstein, K. (1948). *Language and language disturbances.* New York: Grune.

Hickok, G., Erhard, P., Kassubek, J., Helms-Tillery, A. K., Naeve-Velguth, S., Strupp, J. P., Strick, P. L., & Ugurbil, K. (2000). A functional magnetic resonance imaging study of the role left posterior superior temporal gyrus in speech production: Implications for explanation of conduction aphasia. *Neuroscience Letters, 287,* 156–160.

Kempler, D., Metter, E., Jackson, C., Hanson, W., Riege, W., Mazziotta, J., Phelps, M. (1988). Disconnection and cerebral metabolism. The case of conduction aphasia. *Archives of Neurology, 45,* 275–279.

Marshall, R., Lazar, R., Mohr, J., Van Heertum, R., & Mast, H. (1996). Semantic conduction aphasia from a posterior insular cortex infarction. *Journal of Neuroimaging, 6,* 189–191.

Mendez, M., & Benson, D. (1985). Atypical conduction aphasia: A disconnection syndrome. *Archives of Neurology, 42,* 886–891.

Quigg, M., & Fountain, N. B. (1999). Conduction aphasia elicited by cortical stimulation of the posterior superior temporal gyrus. *Journal of Neurology, Neurosurgery Psychiatry, 66,* 393–396.

Quigg, M., Geldmacher, D. S., & Elias, W. J. (2006). Conduction aphasia as a function of the dominant posterior perisylvian cortex. Report of two cases. *Journal of Neurosurgery, 104,* 845–848.

Schaffler, L., Luders, H., & Beck, G. (1996). Quantitative comparison of language deficits produce by extraoperative electrical stimulation of Broca's, Wernicke's, and basal temporal language areas. *Epilepsia, 37,* 463–475.

Shuren, J., Schefft, B., Yeh, H., Privitera, M., Cahill, W., & Houston, W. (1995). Repetition and the arcuate fasciculus. *Journal of Neurology, 242,* 596–598.

Tanabe, H., Sawada, T., Inoue, N., Ogawa, M., Kuriyama, Y, & Shiraishi, J. (1987). Conduction apahsia and arcuate fasciculus. *Acta Neurologica Scandinavica, 76,* 422–427.

MARK QUIGG
University of Virginia

See also: Anomic Aphasia; Language Comprehension; Speech Production

CONFIDENCE INTERVAL

The concept of the confidence interval was introduced and developed theoretically by Jerzy Neyman in the 1930s. The confidence interval indicates the degree of certainty that a specified range of values around a parameter estimate contains the true value of the population parameter. The upper and lower boundaries of the range are the confidence limits. The width of the confidence interval indicates the degree of precision associated with the parameter estimate. Wider intervals indicate less precision, and narrower intervals indicate greater precision. The width of the interval can never be zero, because there will always be some sampling error associated with estimating a population parameter from sample data. Sampling error may be due to measurement unreliability or other chance factors that cause fluctuations from sample to sample. The result is that, no matter how carefully a sample is drawn or how large it is, one can never be certain that the sample estimate is exactly equal to the parameter (population) value.

The calculation of the confidence interval for any parameter is based on the standard error of the relevant sampling distribution. For a simple observation, X, assuming an underlying normal distribution with mean μ and standard deviation σ, the confidence limits on the observation can be stated simply as: $X = \mu \pm z\sigma$, where z represents the standard normal deviate associated with any particular level of confidence. Although confidence level may be specified, in practice the most commonly used intervals are the 95%, 99%, and 99.9% levels:

$$95\% \text{ confidence limits: } -1.96\sigma \leq X - \mu \leq +1.96\sigma$$
$$99\% \text{ confidence limits: } -2.58\sigma \leq X - \mu \leq +2.58\sigma$$
$$99.9\% \text{ confidence limits: } -3.29\sigma \leq X - \mu \leq +3.29\sigma$$

During the early decades of research in experimental psychology, confidence intervals of 50% were commonly reported, based on the concept of the probable error ($\mu \pm 0.6745\sigma$). It is now seldom used and generally considered obsolete in psychology, but is used occasionally in other disciplines.

Confidence limits can be computed for any sample statistic for which the sampling distribution is known. For example, for the mean (M), the standard error of the mean (σ_m) is used so that: $M = \mu \pm z\sigma_m$. If the population mean and standard error are not known, which is often the case, estimates of the mean and standard error based on observed samples may be substituted. In this situation, unless the sample size is fairly large (e.g., $N > 30$), the confidence limits are set using the t distribution with $N{-}1$ degrees of freedom rather than the normal (z) distribution. When sampling distributions are unknown or seriously depart from the normal distribution, various procedures can be employed to estimate the standard error from observed data, such as bootstrapping, jackknifing, and computer simulation.

As an example of the use of confidence intervals, consider an incoming class of 750 college freshman with an average Scholastic Aptitude Test (SAT) score of 550 and a standard deviation (s) of 100, resulting is a standard error of the mean of $s_m = s/\sqrt{N} = 3.65$. The resulting 95% confidence interval around the class mean of 550 is 543–557. This interval is interpreted as meaning there is a 95% chance that the interval 543–557 contains the true value of the freshman class SAT score. However, since any specific interval either does or does not contain the true score, it is probably fairer to say that if a very large (in principle, an infinite) number of such group means were sampled, 95% of the resulting confidence intervals would contain the true population mean.

Confidence intervals are reported most commonly for well-known statistics such as sample means, proportions, correlation and regression coefficients, odds ratios, and predicted scores, but they should also be determined for less commonly used statistics, such as measures of effect size and goodness-of-fit indexes. In particular, estimating confidence intervals for the effect size index Cohen's d is becoming increasingly popular, especially in conjunction with its use in meta-analysis.

The use of confidence intervals is increasingly being recommended as a substitute for statistical significance testing. This position received its first major explication by William Rozeboom in 1960, and since then it has been elaborated by others, especially Jacob Cohen. This position holds that null hypothesis significance testing is a barrier to progress in behavioral science, especially with respect to the accumulation of knowledge across studies. The use of confidence intervals, in conjunction with other techniques such as effect sizes and meta-analysis, is proposed to replace traditional significance testing. By employing an interval estimate of the location of a parameter rather than a simple "point" estimate, confidence intervals can provide all of the information present in a significance test while yielding important additional information as well.

SUGGESTED READINGS

Agresti, A., & Finlay, B. (2009). *Statistical methods for the social sciences* (4th ed.). Upper Saddle River, NJ: Pearson Prentice Hall.

Cumming, G., & Finch, S. (2005). Inference by eye: Confidence intervals and how to read pictures of data. *American Psychologist, 60*, 170–180.

Harlow, L. L., Mulaik, S. A., & Steiger, J. H. (Eds.). (1997). *What if there were no significance tests?* Hillsdale, NJ: Lawrence Erlbaum.

Kline, R. B. (2004). *Beyond significance testing: Reforming data analysis methods in behavioral research.* Washington, DC: American Psychological Association.

Maxwell, S. E., & Delaney, H. D. (2004). *Designing experiments and analyzing data: A model comparison perspective* (2nd ed.). Mahwah, NJ: Lawrence Erlbaum.

Meyers, J. L., & Well, A. D. (2003). *Research design and statistical analysis* (2nd ed.). Mahwah, NJ: Lawrence Erlbaum.

Tabachnick, B. G., & Fidell, L. S. (2007). *Using multivariate statistics* (5th ed.). Boston: Pearson Education.

JOSEPH S. ROSSI
University of Rhode Island

See also: Cohen's *d*; Probability; Standard Error of Measurement

CONFIDENTIALITY AND LEGAL PRIVILEGE

The duty of health care professionals to protect the privacy of health care information is a bedrock legal and ethical principle. Two types of laws provide such protection. One concerns confidentiality, and the other concerns privilege. The two are related but discrete. *Confidentiality* is the legal and ethical obligation of health care professionals not to disclose information about an individual obtained in the course of providing diagnostic or treatment services. *Privilege* is the law's recognition of confidentiality in legal proceedings in which confidential material otherwise would be subject to disclosure as part of that proceeding. This article discusses the values that underlie confidentiality, the various sources of confidentiality law, and significant exceptions to it. The note concludes with a brief discussion of legal privilege.

Values that Underlie Confidentiality

There are three primary reasons for the ethical and legal principle of confidentiality. First, some illnesses, including mental illnesses, carry a degree of social stigma that in the most severe cases can be manifest as illegal discrimination. Permitting people to obtain treatment confidentially helps shield them from such consequences. Second, confidentiality is essential to the establishment of trust in a clinical relationship. The United States Supreme Court, in establishing a federal psychotherapeutic privilege, put the

matter succinctly: " ... the mere possibility of disclosure may impede the development of the confidential relationship necessary for treatment" (Jaffee v. Redmond, 1995 at 10). Finally, there is empirical evidence that people are more likely to seek health care if they believe that their doing so will be kept confidential (Jensen et al., 1991).

Sources of Confidentiality Law

Confidentiality law is shaped by many things, including statutory and case law, the latter being made by judicial decisions. There are several different types of state and federal confidentiality statutes. These include state public health laws, which define the confidentiality of general health information, both written and oral, in the particular state of origin. They also include state mental health and substance use treatment laws, which contain special rules for the confidentiality of information obtained when treating or evaluating a person for a mental illness or substance abuse disorder, as well as state laws concerning the protection and disclosure of information that someone is HIV positive or has AIDS.

There are also federal laws on the confidentiality of health care information. The most important of these laws is the regulation enacted pursuant to the Health Insurance Portability and Accountability Act (HIPAA). Other relevant federal laws include the statute and implementing regulations that protect the confidentiality of information that would identify someone as a patient in a substance abuse or alcohol treatment program (42 U.S.C. § 290dd-2; 42 CFR Part 2); and the Family Educational and Privacy Rights Act (FERPA), which governs the confidentiality of educational records.

Judicial decisions can also have a dramatic impact on confidentiality law. In one of the most famous decisions in the psychology and law field, the California Supreme Court ruled that a psychologist who had reason to believe his client posed a danger to an identifiable third party had a legal duty to take steps to protect the third party (Tarasoff v. Regents of the University of California, 1976). Prior to that decision, such an obligation imposed by the court—generally referred to as a "duty to warn"—did not exist.

The different sources of law can cause confusion, and a few points with respect to the manner in which federal and state law interact are especially worth noting. First, the federal HIPAA regulation creates a baseline for confidentiality law that state laws must at least meet. However, if a state law provides more protection of confidentiality than a similar provision of HIPAA, the state law must be followed. In nearly all circumstances involving mental health treatment, state laws will go further than HIPAA in protecting confidentiality; hence, as a general rule it is fair to assume that state law will apply in most circumstances. Second, the federal substance abuse and alcohol treatment regulations provide the most strict confidentiality law. Therefore, drug and alcohol treatment programs will always refer to these regulations as a primary source of law.

Third, a state legislature may override judicial decisions in some circumstances. It cannot be assumed that a judicial decision, once announced, establishes a legal principle for all time. An example is the Tarasoff case noted above. Even in California, the ruling of that case has been substantially changed by the California legislature. Therefore, it is important to determine whether even the most famous court decisions continue to be applicable law in the state in which they were decided or whether they have been adopted in other states.

Exceptions to Confidentiality

Although confidentiality is a very important legal and ethical principle, it is not absolute in application. There are many exceptions, some mandatory and some discretionary. These exceptions occur in situations in which other values are considered to take precedence over maintaining confidentiality. For example, because it is the patient's information that is confidential, the most common exceptions to confidentiality are instances in which the patient or client consents to disclosure. Many state statutes and federal regulations describe as well certain elements that must be present for a valid consent to disclosure to occur. An example of these elements is the age at which an adolescent may unilaterally consent to a waiver of confidentiality, on which state laws vary.

There are also situations in which health care professionals are required by law to breach confidentiality. For example, all confidentiality laws mandate that designated licensed professionals must report suspicions of child abuse. In many jurisdictions, this obligation includes suspicions of elder abuse as well. This duty is absolute and is generally not context specific. That is, if mandated reporters suspect abuse outside of their office, the obligation to report still applies. In other circumstances, the breach of confidentiality may be discretionary and depend on the judgment of the health care professional.

For example, in all jurisdictions health care professionals may take steps, including breaching confidentiality, to protect an individual who in their view may be at risk from a patient they are seeing. In the context of mental health care, most states make it discretionary on the part of the professional whether such steps are taken. In a handful of states, however, the obligation is mandatory, and professionals must know the rules of the jurisdiction in which they practice. In other contexts—for example, reporting an individual's identified sexual partner that the person is HIV positive—state health laws establish a clear and precise process by which such notification may occur. More recently, the discussion of a duty to warn has extended to consideration of whether there is an obligation to disclose genetic risks to the family of a patient (Offit et al., 2004).

Privilege

The exceptions to confidentiality just discussed, while not exhaustive, serve to illustrate the types of situations in which confidentiality may give way. Another common circumstance in which confidential information is sought arises when a court subpoenas confidential information relevant to legal proceedings. This circumstance raises the question whether information should be subject do discovery by the court or should instead be privileged.

There are many types of court cases in which a person's mental status may be at issue or in which mental health records might be considered relevant by one party or another. In a child custody proceeding, for example, one parent may wish to show through the other parent's mental health treatment records that the parent is unfit for having custody. In such a case, the court may issues a subpoena that requires mental health professionals and facilities to produce their records and perhaps to provide testimony as well. Courts have broad power to compel the production of material, including confidential information. However, the party in possession of that information may claim that the information is "privileged" by law and therefore can be exempted from disclosure, thereby maintaining the confidentiality of the material.

All states recognize some types of privileges, including non-disclosure of mental health and substance abuse treatment records. In addition, the United States Supreme Court has created a federal psychotherapeutic privilege in its Jaffee v. Redmond decision (1995). It is for mental health professionals, or for clients through their lawyers, or through lawyers in the proceedings to raise the question of privilege. It is then up to the judge to decide whether privilege applies. Health care professionals need to recognize that state and federal law create many different types of privileges. When confidential health care information is subpoenaed or otherwise demanded for use in a legal proceeding, it is incumbent on the professional to at least inquire whether privilege might apply.

REFERENCES

Jaffee v. Redmond, 518 U.S. 1 (1996).

Jensen, J. A., McNamara, J. R., & Gustafson, K. E. (1991). Parents' and clinicians' attitudes toward the risks and benefits of child psychotherapy: A study of informed-consent content. *Professional Psychology, Research and Practice, 22*, 161–170.

Offit, K., Groeger, E., Turner, S., Wadsworth, E., & Weiser, M. (2004). The "duty to warn" a patient's family about hereditary disease risks. *Journal of the American Medical Association 2004, 292*: 1469–1473.

Tarasoff v Regents of the University of California, 551 P. 2d 334 (Cal. 1976).

SUGGESTED READINGS

American Psychological Association. (1992). Ethical principles of psychologists and code of conduct. *American Psychologist, 47,* 1597–1611.

Beaver, K., & Herold, R. (2003). *The Practical Guide to HIPAA Privacy and Security Compliance.* Auebach.

Office of the Surgeon General (1999). Confidentiality of mental health information: Ethical, legal, and policy issues, in *Mental Health: A Report of the Surgeon General* (1999).

JOHN PETRILA
University of South Florida

See also: Admissibility of Expert Testimony; Ethical Issues in Psychology; Forensic Psychology

CONFLICT RESOLUTION

Conflict occurs in situations in which two or more interdependent parties (either individuals or groups) have interests, outcomes, and/or goals that are incompatible in some way (Deutsch, 1973; Deutsch & Coleman, 2000; Kelley et al., 2003; Schelling, 1980). If the parties are completely independent, or if their interests, outcomes, and goals are completely compatible, then no conflict can exist, because, to put it colloquially, there is nothing to fight about. Conflict can occur in both cooperative and competitive contexts (Deutsch, 1973), as well as in "mixed-motive" contexts that are marked by a combination of competitive and cooperative features. When the parties' interests are generally compatible or positively correlated, then resolving the conflict requires coordination (Kelley et al., 2003; Schelling, 1980).

Coordination involves working together to find a solution to a common problem. Consider a situation in which a husband and wife must decide how to spend their evening. The husband would prefer to go to a baseball game, while the wife would prefer to go to the movies, but both would rather be accompanied by their spouse than attend either event alone. One possible solution to a conflict of this sort would be coordinated alternation, such that on one evening both go to the husband's preferred destination, but on the next evening both go to the wife's preferred destination. Communication, assuming it is trusted, is extremely helpful in resolving coordination conflicts because it allows the parties to work out mutually beneficial agreements (Fisher & Ury, 1981; Schelling, 1980).

Unfortunately, not all conflicts are marked by compatible interests. Difficult and destructive conflicts generally occur when interests and outcomes are incompatible or negatively correlated, and the parties perceive them as such. One effective way of resolving conflicts of this sort is to reframe the situation into one that is marked by compatible rather than incompatible interests (Cohen & Insko, 2008; Deutsch & Coleman, 2000; Fisher & Ury, 1981). Consider the 1978 conflict between Israel and Egypt regarding which country would control the Sinai Peninsula. At the outset, Israel and Egypt's positions were in complete opposition, because only one country could control the disputed territory. As discussed by Fisher and Ury (1981), this conflict was ultimately resolved through a creative solution that reconciled the two sides' compatible underlying interests rather than their incompatible stated positions. Israel's underlying interest was safety—they did not want tanks close to their border. Egypt's underlying interest was sovereignty—they wanted to maintain the integrity of centuries-old borders. The eventual peace accord allowed Egypt to retain control of the Sinai, but required them to demilitarize it. This resolution to the conflict involved reframing the situation from one characterized by a competitive conflict of interests in which only one side could "win" to a situation characterized by compatible interests in which both sides could obtain mutually beneficial outcomes.

As illustrated by the Sinai Peninsula example, reframing a conflict such that cooperation is seen as more attractive than competition is one possible conflict resolution strategy. The difficulty with this strategy is conceptualizing how to transform the situation into one in which cooperation is valued. Making parties aware of their similarities and shared goals is one method for enacting a cooperative transformation (Cohen & Insko, 2008). Once Israel and Egypt realized that they both shared the overarching goal of a peaceful coexistence, they could focus on developing a solution to their mutual problem of deciding who should control the Sinai.

What are other methods for promoting cooperation? Cohen and Insko (2008) discussed three additional conflict resolution strategies that are particularly effective at promoting cooperation between groups: future-oriented thinking, empathy, and independent leadership. Encouraging groups to consider future consequences of competitive behavior increases intergroup cooperation. A simple strategy for inducing future-oriented thinking is to ask each side to consider how their own competitive actions will likely affect the other side's future actions. Future-oriented thinking can also be promoted by using a tit-for-tat strategy to interact with opponents and making it salient that there will be multiple interactions with the other side, as opposed to just one. Future-oriented thinking is effective at reducing conflict because it makes group members realize that the long-term costs of competition are often far greater than any short-term benefits. This realization tends to reduce distrust of the other side, and cooperation is promoted by reductions in distrust.

As for fostering feelings of empathy as a potential conflict-resolution strategy, Cohen and Insko (2008) note that individuals who feel empathy for other individuals are less likely to behave aggressively toward them and are more likely to behave prosocially and cooperatively. Although empathy for opposing groups is sometimes difficult to generate, it can be helpful for reducing conflict. One way to promote empathy for opposing groups is through intergroup contact. Studies of intergroup contact between the Protestants and Catholics in Northern Ireland and the Tamils and the Sinhalese in Sri Lanka have revealed that empathy generated by intergroup contact can help promote positive relations between groups with long histories of conflict.

Can strong leaders make peace? Research suggests that they can (Cohen & Insko, 2008; Deutsch & Coleman, 2000). However, leaders who wish to foster intergroup cooperation must be given some independence from their constituency so that they have the freedom to cooperate with those with whom their more extreme base might prefer to compete. Of course, not all leaders will be swayed to act cooperatively by virtue of being given independence. Reduced accountability allows less ethical leaders to pursue their own selfish goals. But, if a group's leader is a moral or ethical person, a certain degree of independence is likely to be quite helpful for negotiating cooperative deals with other groups.

Although conflict can at times be constructive, more often than not it is destructive (Deutsch, 1973; Deutsch & Coleman, 2000). Resolving or managing conflict effectively requires implementing strategies that promote cooperation. Cooperatively reframing the conflict, encouraging future-oriented thinking, fostering empathy for the opposing side, and giving group leaders a measure of independence in their decision making are several strategies that can be used to promote cooperation. Hopefully, future research will shed light on additional conflict resolution strategies so that interpersonal and intergroup conflicts throughout the world do not take a destructive course.

REFERENCES

Cohen, T. R., & Insko, C. A. (2008). War and peace: Possible approaches to reducing intergroup conflict. *Perspectives on Psychological Science, 3,* 87–93.

Deutsch, M. (1973). *The resolution of conflict: Constructive and destructive processes.* New Haven: Yale University Press.

Deutsch, M., & Coleman, P. T. (Eds.). (2000). *The handbook of conflict resolution: Theory and practice.* San Francisco: Jossey-Bass.

Fisher, R., & Ury, W. (1981). *Getting to yes.* Boston: Houghton Mifflin.

Kelley, H. H., Holmes, J. G., Kerr, N. L., Reis, H. T., Rusbult, C. E., & Van Lange, P. A. M. (2003). *An atlas of interpersonal situations.* New York: Cambridge University Press.

Schelling, T. C. (1980). *The strategy of conflict.* Cambridge, MA: Harvard University Press.

SUGGESTED READING

Deutsch, M. (1990). Sixty years of conflict. *International Journal of Conflict Management, 1,* 237–263.

TAYA R. COHEN
Northwestern University

***See also:* Group Cohesiveness; Interpersonal Perception**

CONFORMITY

Are people generally conformists who are easily influenced by their peers? Or are they independent thinkers who stick to their individual beliefs? In the 1950s, experimental psychologist Solomon Asch was becoming increasingly discontented as accruing evidence indicated that people were highly suggestible. Critical of this perspective, Asch (1956) began a line of research that he expected would invalidate and dispel the notion that humans are "like sheep."

Asch brought together groups of eight college students for a study on visual perception. Seated around a table, the group was shown a picture of a standard line. Their task was to indicate which one of three comparison lines matched the standard line in length. This was an intentionally easy and obvious task, given that only one of the comparison lines was clearly the same length as the line in question. The catch was that each group actually had only one real participant. The other seven were confederates who had been instructed to give unanimous, incorrect answers. One by one, each confederate publicly announced what appeared to be an obviously wrong response until, finally, the participant was asked to respond. When asked to respond in private, participants gave the accurate response in more than 99% of the trials. But when asked to respond in front of the group, only 24% of people answered correctly on all trials. Contrary to expectations, Asch's research on the objective judgments of line length became compelling evidence of human conformity to group pressure (see Cialdini & Goldstein, 2004).

Conformity, then, is the changing of a behavior or an attitude to match the beliefs, expectations, or behaviors of real or imagined others. Conformity can occur when there is group pressure for an individual to behave in a certain way, but it can also occur when a group has no explicit desire to influence one's actions or beliefs. Indeed, the tendency to conform or mimic others can be so swift and mindless that it is almost automatic.

Why Do People Conform

People generally conform for one of two underlying reasons. First, following others can often lead to better and more accurate decisions. For example, if all of your friends like a restaurant, you will probably like it, too. This kind of conformity is known as informational influence (Deutsch & Gerard, 1955), and it serves the underlying goal of accuracy. Informational influence has deep evolutionary roots. For both human and nonhuman animals, when a situation is uncertain and time is precious, following the majority of others is often the most efficient and effective way to behave.

The second reason people conform is because going along with another person tends to produce liking. This kind of approval-based conformity is known as normative influence (Deutsch & Gerard, 1955), and it serves the underlying goal of affiliation. Normative influence is especially potent, because people who deviate from the group are more likely to be punished, ridiculed, and even rejected by other group members. In the classic Asch (1956) line length studies, for example, participants tended to conform to the group not necessarily because they believed the group consensus reflected the correct response, but because it was easier to go with the crowd than to face the social consequences of going against it.

The Prevalence and Underestimation of Conformity

Because the desire to choose correctly and the desire to be accepted are powerful, the tendency to follow the crowd is both strong and widespread. Countless historical examples document instances of mass conformity, which can result in panics, hysteria, or speculative financial bubbles (MacKay, 1841). Many well-designed and highly controlled studies have confirmed the power of peer influence. For example, based on evidence of what their peers are doing, bystanders decide whether to help in an emergency, citizens decide whether to pay their taxes fully, spouses decide whether to cheat sexually, juveniles decide whether to commit a wide range of crimes, homeowners decide whether to recycle their trash, and hotel guests decide whether to reuse their towels (e.g., Goldstein, Cialdini, & Griskevicius, 2008).

What is surprising, given the ubiquity and strength of the evidence, is how little note we take of the potency of peer influence. Evidence suggests that people are not only poor at recognizing why they behave as they do, but are also particularly clueless at identifying the similar actions of others as the causes of their own behavior (see Nolan et al., 2008). Indeed, it may be the strong belief of being invulnerable to conformity that leads peer influence to have such powerful effects on our behavior.

Factors that Increase or Decrease Conformity

Several factors are known to increase the tendency to conform. Related to the goal of accuracy, people are especially likely to turn to others when they are uncertain about how to act in a situation. The tendency to follow a group also depends on the size of the group: The more group members are in agreement with each other, the more likely the tendency to conform. We are also more likely to follow the actions of those who are similar to ourselves and those who have been in similar situations.

Related to the goal of affiliation, people are much more likely to go along with the group when their actions are public, especially when the group is desirable and the person is new to the group. Conformity is also more likely when a group is working toward a common goal. People working for a common goal might fear that deviance from the group will be seen as a threat. Similarly, people are also more likely to go along with the group when they are in a state of fear, because it is especially risky to stick out from the crowd in times of danger. Some factors can also increase the ability to resist conformity (Levine & Russo, 1987). People are less likely to follow the group when there is a social supporter who has publicly opposed the group. In the Asch line length studies, for example, the presence of only one dissenter dramatically reduced conformity. Not only does the presence of a dissenter reduce the confidence that the group has the right answer, but having just one supporter can lower people's fear that they will be punished for deviance.

Although the tendency to conform is powerful, people are also sometimes motivated to nonconform either by showing independence (resisting influence) or anticonformity (rebelling against influence) (see Nail, MacDonald, & Levy, 2000). Both types of nonconformity tend to be effective in differentiating people from others, which can satisfy a need for individuation or uniqueness. For example, when a person's uniqueness is threatened by an encounter with a highly similar individual, such a situation increases the tendency to nonconform.

Individual Differences in Conformity

Although multiple attempts have been made to create valid measures of a conforming personality, none has proved to be very useful as a general measure of one's tendency to conform. Part of this difficulty stems from the fact that the same person often behaves rather differently from one situation to another. For example, a person might be a conformist when it comes to choosing wine, but a nonconformist when it to comes to choosing beer.

Nevertheless, some individual differences have been documented. For example, when it comes to public conformity, men are generally less conforming than women. This sex difference does not indicate that women are somehow less capable of resisting conformity. Instead, it reflects the fact that men generally have more to gain than women by putting on a public show of disagreement. For example, men who are motivated to impress a potential romantic partner are especially likely to go against the group to assert their uniqueness and dominance (Griskevicius et al., 2006).

Is Conformity Good or Bad?

The term "conformity" often carries a negative connotation in Western culture. Yet conformity is often an ecologically rational and adaptive response, particularly when it serves the purposes of a person who desires to respond accurately to a complex and uncertain environment. Similarly, a person who desires to be liked and accepted by a group will often find that agreeing with others is a useful tactic. Nevertheless, conformity can have negative consequences. Sometimes following the crowd leads to poor decisions, such as when crowd behavior is based on erroneous or sinister beliefs. Similarly, although people generally like those who agree with them, being overly agreeable can lead one to be seen as subservient and spineless. Indeed, when groups are charged with goals that can benefit from creative thinking, groups are often more successful and creative when the group includes individuals who explicitly challenge group norms and force the group to think outside the box.

Although the question of whether conformity is good or bad is complex, few people would want to live in a world in which everyone conforms all the time or no one ever conforms. Both conformity and nonconformity serve underlying evolutionary goals that help us effectively and efficiently navigate the complex milieu of life.

REFERENCES

Asch, S. E. (1956). Studies of independence and submission to group pressure: I. A minority of one against a unanimous majority. *Psychological Monographs, 70,* (9, Whole Issue).

Cialdini, R. B., & Goldstein, N. J. (2004). Social influence: Compliance and conformity. *Annual Review of Psychology, 55,* 591–621.

Deutsch, M., & Gerard, H. B. (1955). A study of normative and informational social influences upon individual judgment. *Journal of Abnormal and Social Psychology, 51,* 629–636.

Goldstein, N. J., Cialdini, R. B., & Griskevicius, V. (2008). A room with a viewpoint: Using social norms to motivate environmental conservation in hotels. *Journal of Consumer Research, 35.*

Griskevicius, V., Goldstein, N. J., Mortensen, C. R., Cialdini, R. B., & Kenrick, D. T. (2006). Going along versus going alone: When fundamental motives facilitate strategic (non)conformity. *Journal of Personality and Social Psychology, 91*(2), 281–294.

Levine, J. M., & Russo, E. (1987). Majority and minority influence. In C. Hendrick (Ed.), *Review of personality and social psychology: Group processes* (Vol. 8, pp. 13–54), Newberry Park, CA: Sage.

MacKay, C. (1841/1932). *Extraordinary popular delusions & the madness of crowds.* New York: Farrar, Straus, and Giroux.

Nail, P. R., MacDonald, G., & Levy, D. A. (2000). Proposal of a four-dimensional model of social response. *Psychological Bulletin, 126,* 106–116.

Nolan, J. P., Schultz, P. W., Cialdini, R. B., Goldstein, N. J., & Griskevicius, V. (2008). Normative social influence is underdetected. *Personality and Social Psychology Bulletin, 34,* 913–923.

VLADAS GRISKEVICIUS
University of Minnesota

See also: Mob Psychology; Peer Influences

CONSTANCY

An object's physical attributes (its size, shape, reflectance, location, and so on) are distal stimuli; our sense organs are activated by patterns of proximal stimulus energies, which change with distance, illumination, and so on. Things do not generally seem to expand when approached or to become darker (less reflective) when moved from light to shade. Such stabilities are termed size constancy, lightness constancy, shape constancy, position constancy, and the like.

Understanding how constancies occur and their implications and limitations is highly important to any approach to perception and its related disciplines, and it should also concern those technologies that substitute devices for people (as in computer vision) or provide displays for whatever needs representation (as in computer simulation, virtual realities, and the pictorial arts quite generally). A persistent rubric, initially offered by Hermann von Helmholtz more than a century ago, runs this way: One perceives that state of affairs in the world that would, under normal conditions, most likely have given rise to the pattern of sensations that arise from the proximal stimulation that one's sense organs receive.

Theories and Implications of Constancy

Classical Theory of Constancy

In Helmholtz's classical theory of perception, we apply (usually unconsciously) what we have learned from our experiences in the world, and thereby infer (also unconsciously) what the distal situation must be. Thus, we use information about the distances ($d1$, $d2$) implied by the *perspective* in Figure 1A to deduce the disks' distal sizes, given their proximal sizes. Similarly, we use estimates about illuminations and our knowledge about how light bounces off surfaces to infer the object's reflectance in cases of color or lightness constancy (see Figure 2A, B). And we take the information about slants and viewpoints to arrive at perceived shapes. Perhaps least noted, when our viewpoints change—whether by our own movements, through transportation, or in a moving picture—we obtain layout constancy (Figure 3) by correctly compensating for the movements.

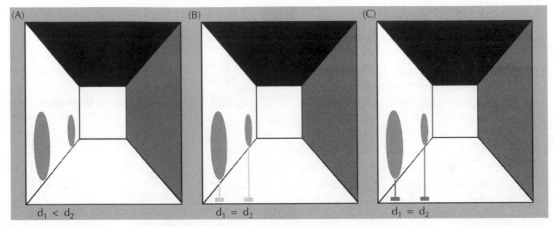

Figure 1. Size constancy and distance. (A) Taking perspective-conveyed depths into account, both discs should appear to represent approximately equal sizes. (B) Attention to the two bases conveys their equal distances so the right disc should look smaller, which should be more mandatory in C.

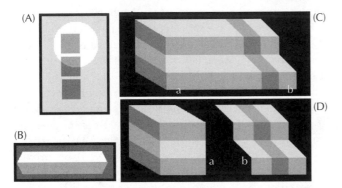

Figure 2. Lightness constancy and illumination. (A) The squares appear of equal reflectance (lightness), while providing different amounts of light (brightness) to the eye, presumably with different illuminations (a spotlight) inferred. (B) Mach's folder: Although stimulation remains unchanged, the top and bottom appear equally light if seen as 3D and illuminated from above, but with the bottom as darker if seen as equally illuminated. If an invariant ratio of a region to its surround determines perceive lightness, such should not happen. (C) Adelson's impossible staircase: the perceived lightness of *a* and *b* depend on which one is attended. (D) The differences in 3D orientation and illumination, not explicitly emphasized in C; as analyzed by Sinha & Adelson (1993).

In the specific details of this theory, the sensory information and its accompanying muscular actions (shifting gaze, reaching hand) consist of aggregates of simple sensations; in vision, these are responses of myriad point-by-point retinal rods and cones. In most approaches, conscious experience was neither discussed nor implied, and sensations were presumed to come from psychophysical consistencies, not from introspection. Analysis of visual displays to achieve point-by-point similarities is of course similar to what various graphic artists had approximated for centuries, and it is essentially what digital video technologies now accomplish in their own way when representing scenes. In this classical theory of human perception, after such sensory analyses, sensations are mutually bonded through associative learning to form our

perceptions. Memories of eye movements, of head turning, of reaching, and the like, also mediated by associative learning, contribute what we perceive of layout and distances.

In this theory, viewers need knowledge beyond the information in the proximal stimulation, and they need to have learned the ecological likelihoods involved. In exchange, it does plausibly explain other perceptual phenomena besides the constancies, including contrast and other illusions, and even some of the Gestalt organizational phenomena of organization.

Years of quantitative theorizing and research targeted the response characteristics of the supposedly independent sensory receptors (e.g., using carefully isolated dots, in vision), and explored what were taken to be the characteristic laws of associative learning (usually using lists of nonsense-syllables). After this theory lost its foundations, and independent sensory receptors and simple associations between them had to be abandoned as analytic tools, new ways to observe and measure the underlying processes in eye and brain, to manipulate stimuli, and to analyze the relevant ecological statistics, have changed the goals of perceptual research.

Direct Theories of Constancy

With the distal stimulus invariant, some aspects of proximal stimulation may remain invariant, even as viewing conditions change other proximal attributes (image sizes, luminances, and so on) of the retinal image. This argument forms the core of two different classes of direct theories of constancy.

Physiological Theories of Constancy

The first class comprises physiological theories of constancy. Hering and Mach, Helmholz's contemporaries, had proposed that innate networks of lateral connections

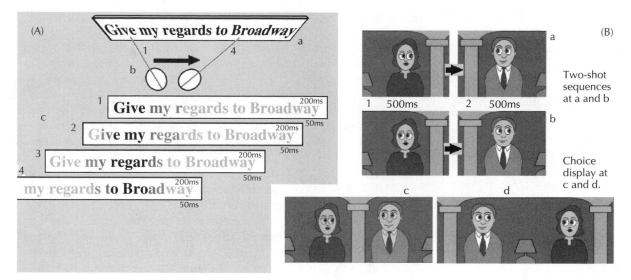

Figure 3. (A) The text remains and appears notably constant (despite awareness of the saccades, 1–4). (B) Which room (*c* or *d*) appears to remain constant across a two-view sequence (like those as in *a, b*) depends on where attention is directed within those shots.

between the receptors might contribute to some perceptual constancies, particularly lightness constancy. Interneural interconnections have now in fact been robustly demonstrated and measured, and they surely affect how we perceive. In the simplest example, a more strongly illuminated region in the retinal image reduces the response of adjacent regions of the retina through a process of lateral inhibition. Thus, when the illumination on an object and on its more reflective surroundings increases (e.g., Figure 2A), inhibition from the latter reduces response to the former, and the perceived lightness of the object should therefore remain constant if the objects' and surroundings' reflectances remain constant. Several illusions are addressed by the same type of explanation, contrast being the most obvious example, as when a brighter surround makes a gray object look darker.

Ecological Approaches to the Constancies

Aside from testing perceptual theories and exploring neurophysiological functions, there is growing technological need to study the constancies and to specify what perceptions will occur under different circumstances. For example, mathematical algorithms in the fields of color science and computer vision (e.g., B. Wandell and colleagues), aim at separately estimating surfaces' colors and illuminations in pictures of natural scenes. Such attempts to treat constancies as direct responses to stimulus invariances allow one to defer questions both about neural mechanisms, which have only recently became measurable, and about Helmholtzian inference, which remains difficult to investigate, although brain-imaging promises to help.

Earlier, J. J. Gibson had argued that, for things in the natural ecosystem in which we have evolved, the changing proximal stimulus pattern received by a perceiver who is moving naturally in a normal environment must offer invariants that reflect the structure of the physical world and that therefore make any inference-like processes wholly unnecessary. Earlier still, and more generally, E. Brunswik had long argued that perceptual experience teaches the learner about such invariances in the world, as close examination of photographs should show: In 1953, he and J. Kamiya used *Life* magazine photographs to argue that the Gestalt laws of organization have ecological validity. In recent years, numerous quantitative approaches have used photographs, arguing that what we perceive agrees with measurable ecological probabilities, primarily using Bayesian decision theory (for an early compendium, see D. Knill; for comprehensive review, see Geisler, 2008), but with an increasing use of a conceptually simpler analysis, empirical ranking (for comparison, see Howe et al., 2006). However, these direct approaches omit important and revealing contributions made at the viewer's choice.

Inference, Attention, and Anticipation in Constancy

Although the direct approaches are potentially highly useful, there is no evidence that most constancies are direct reponses to invariances. Moreover, many examples of attention-dependent context-selective processes remain, and these need to take the viewer's intentions and expectations into account. In Figure 2C, devised by E. Adelson, *a* and *b* are identical as printed, but *a* looks like a dark (paint-striped) surface and *b* looks like a light but shadowed surface, depending on where one attends; such attention-dependent examples are easy to find when judging portrayed distal size, shape, and the like. In Figure 1B, the right disk looks smaller than or equal to the left one, depending on whether you attend to its stand. And as the sequences sketched in Figure 3 suggest, layout-constancy across views depends on how you attend the landmarks and on what you infer about them. Whether reading, guiding your hand, or watching the movie cuts, it is important to remember that looking activity, which is the rapid ongoing behavior underlying much of perception, is itself a directed and anticipatory behavior. Because one's glance is directed by one's perceptual goals, which are not themselves clearly (if at all) visible when the action starts, attention and inference remain involved in assembling the perceived world and in understanding the process.

REFERENCES

Brunswik E, & Kamiya, J. (1953). Ecological cue-validity of "proximity" and other Gestalt factors. *American Journal of Psychology*, 66, 20–32.

Geisler, W. S. (2008), Visual perception and the statistical properties of natural scenes. *Annual Review of Psychology*, 59, 10.1–10.26.

Hochberg, J. (1998). *Perception and cognition at century's end*. San Diego: Academic Press. Chs.1, 9.

Hochberg, J. (In press). Perceptual prosody and perceived personality: Physiognomics precede perspective. In E. Morsella (Ed.), *Expressing oneself: Communication, language, cognition, and identity*. London: Taylor & Francis.

Howe, C. Q., Lotto, R. B., & Purves, D. (2006). Comparison of Bayesian and empirical ranking approaches to visual perception. *Journal of Theoretical Biology*, 241, 866–875.

Knill, D., & Richards W. (Eds). (1996). *Perception as Bayesian inference*. Cambridge, MA: Cambridge University Press.

Sinha, P., & Adelson, E. (1993) Recovering reflectance and illumination in a world of painted polyhedra. In *Fourth International Conference on Computer Vision* (pp. 156–163). Berlin.

JULIAN HOCHBERG
Columbia University

See also: **Perception; Visual Illusions**

CONSTRUCTIVIST PSYCHOTHERAPY

Constructivism refers to a group of theories (originally stemming from Kelly's personal construct theory [1955]) holding the philosophical position that so-called reality is, in some ways, created by persons. Rather than imposing some objective truth on persons seeking help, constructivist therapists attempt experientially to grasp the lived reality of each client. This relationship is more egalitarian and client-empowering than approaches in which the more powerful therapist imposes diagnostic and treatment "realities" on the less powerful client. Constructivist

psychotherapy can be seen as a part of the broader group of humanistic, existential, and postmodern therapies.

Although all constructivists agree that reality cannot be known directly, different theoretical groups disagree on the exact nature of the relationship between the person and the world. Radical constructivists argue that one cannot even speak of a reality outside of the meanings the person has created. Social constructionists might argue that we are saturated with meanings created by cultures and imposed upon us. Occupying a middle ground, critical constructivists believe that meanings are cocreated in the dynamic interaction between the person and the world (see Leitner et al., 2005).

Although there are numerous specific approaches, constructivist therapies generally share certain attitudes about therapy. Most constructivists will listen to clients with the assumption that everything the client says is true in the sense of revealing important aspects of the client's experiential meaning system (Kelly's credulous approach). There is a respect for contrast, oppositionality, or the dialectic in meaning making. Most constructivists also are attuned to making therapy a safe place for clients to experience life, and they emphasize seeing the client as a process of meaning creation rather than a static entity composed of specific meanings. The client's process of construction is seen as active, in contrast to reactive, and underscores the agency of the person, again emphasizing the humanistic and existential roots of the approach.

Different constructivist therapists employ these attitudes in different therapeutic approaches. In Kelly's fixed-role therapy, for example, the client first writes a character sketch that is open, revealing, yet sympathetic. This sketch is written in the third person, from the perspective of a friend who might know the client most intimately. The therapist and client then cocreate an alternate sketch for the client to enact, typically for a two-week period. Fixed-role therapy is viewed as a failure if the client sees it as a behavioral prescription; it is designed to free the client to experiment with alternative ways of experiencing life.

Experiential personal construct psychotherapy (EPCP; Leitner et al., 2005) construes persons as simultaneously needing and being terrified of emotional closeness. On the one hand, such intimate relationships can affirm the meanings that have formed the foundation of our existence. On the other hand, we can experience devastating disconfirmation in intimate relationships. Clients then struggle with needing to connect with others, risking terror to gain profound richness, versus retreating from intimacy, buying safety at the cost of the empty objectification of self and others. Therapeutic growth can occur if the therapist experiences optimal therapeutic distance, a blending of profound connection and separateness, when the therapist is close enough to feel the client's experience yet distant enough to recognize those feelings as the client's and not the therapist's own.

Other constructivist therapists employ narrative approaches to therapy. These therapists believe that narratives give meaning and continuity to the lived experience of clients. Gaps, incompleteness, and incoherence in the client's life story may indicate struggles in creating an integrated experience of self-in-the-world. Goncalves (Goncalves, Korman, & Angus, 2000) illustrates constructivist narrative therapy with his "moviola" technique, in which the therapist's attention scans the setting of a client's life, much like a camera in a movie. The therapist can zoom in on a detail or back off and get a more panoramic view. For example, a therapist might start by having the client describe the entire room in which he or she was abused. Eventually, the therapist might help the client see in detail his or her face, filled with fear and horror, while the abuse occurred. Because people innately create meanings to understand their experiences, the experience of re-viewing the abuse with an empathic therapist allows for new constructions to be created. These newer meanings, in turn, allow for newer experiences as clients' lives move into the future.

Depth-oriented brief therapy (DOBT; Ecker & Hulley, 2000) applies constructivist principles to help clients understand and engage in radical change in a very short-term treatment. DOBT understands the symptom as painful because of the ways it invalidates important aspects of our experience. At the same time, there are other constructions, often at a lower level of consciousness, making the symptom absolutely necessary for the client. DOBT uses specific experiential techniques to help the client gain access to these deeper meanings. The client then can more consciously decide whether to keep or abandon these more unconscious meanings.

Constructivist therapy has been used with a wide range of problems, from mild adjustment issues to the most severely disturbed clients. It has been used with specific symptoms (e.g., stuttering, obesity, bulimia, posttraumatic flashbacks) as well as more general life distress. It also has been useful with young children as well as elderly clients. Specific constructivist techniques have been developed for family therapy (e.g., systematic bow-ties to help each client understand how their actions, based upon their deepest fears, confirm the deepest fears of other family members).

There have been numerous methodologically sound studies exploring the effectiveness of constructivist therapies across different countries, ages, and types of problems. Effect sizes for client change in these studies rival those reported in the cognitive-behavioral and psychoanalytic literature. In other words, good constructivist therapy respects the lived experiences of persons and has been empirically supported by studies that meet the most rigorous of experimental criteria (Holland, Neimeyer, Currier, & Berman, 2007; Metcalfe, Winter, & Viney, 2007).

REFERENCES

Ecker, B., & Hulley, L. (2000). The order in clinical "disorder": Symptom coherence in Depth-Oriented Brief Therapy. In R. A. Neimeyer & J. D. Raskin (Eds.), *Constructions of disorder: Meaning-making frameworks for psychotherapy* (pp. 63–89). Washington, DC: American Psychological Association.

Goncalves, O. F., Korman, Y., & Angus, L. (2000). Constructing psychopathology from a cognitive narrative perspective. In R. A. Neimeyer & J. D. Raskin (Eds.), *Constructions of disorder: Meaning-making frameworks for psychotherapy* (pp. 265–284). Washington, DC: American Psychological Association.

Holland, J. M., Neimeyer, R. A., Currier, J. M., & Berman, J. S. (2007). The efficacy of personal construct therapy: A comprehensive review. *Journal of Clinical Psychology, 63*(1), 93–107.

Kelly, G. A. (1955) *The psychology of personal constructs.* New York: Norton.

Leitner, L. M., Faidley, A. J., Domenici, D., Humphreys, C., Loeffler, V., Schlutsmeyer, M., et al. (2005). Encountering an other: Experiential personal construct psychotherapy. In D. Winter & L. Viney (Eds.), *Advances in personal construct psychotherapy* (pp. 54–68). London: John Wiley & Sons.

Metcalfe, C., Winter, D., & Viney, L. (2007). The effectiveness of personal construct psychotherapy in clinical practice: A systematic review and meta-analysis. *Psychotherapy Research, 17,* 431–442.

SUGGESTED READINGS

Fransella, F. (Ed.). (2005). *The essential practitioner's handbook of personal construct psychology.* Chichester, UK: John Wiley & Sons.

Winter, D. A., & Viney, L. A. (Eds.). (2005). *Personal construct psychotherapy: Advances in theory, practice, and research.* London: Whurr.

LARRY M. LEITNER
JULIE R. LONOFF
Miami University

See also: **Personal Construct Theory**

CONSUMER PSYCHOLOGY

As a discipline, consumer psychology employs distinctively psychological concepts and methods to study consumer behavior. Consumer behavior refers to the decisions and overt behavior involving the acquisition, consumption, and disposal of time and offerings (goods, services, and ideas) by decision-making units. Consumer behavior is pervasive, universal, and all encompassing. It involves choices made during every waking moment of virtually all human beings in all societies and cultures.

The pervasive nature of consumer behavior is reflected by a number of key elements from this definition. First, consumer behavior involves more than just buying tangible products. It also includes a wide variety of services, activities, and ideas (such as visiting a dentist, taking a vacation, or hiring a consultant). Second, it involves more than buying. Consumer researchers are very interested in the many ways in which people acquire, use, and dispose of an offering. For example, in addition to buying, consumers can acquire an offering by trading, renting or leasing, bartering, gift giving, or finding. The variety of ways consumers consume and dispose of offerings is also of interest. The symbolic implications of consumption, for example, have provided many important academic as well as practical implications. The study of disposal behaviors has also provided key insights for recycling and conservation efforts.

Third, consumer behavior involves many different types of decisions. These include understanding whether, why, when, where, how, how much, how often, and for how long consumers will buy, use, or dispose of an offering. Finally, consumer behavior does not necessarily reflect the action on a single individual (such as a housewife). It can involve many people including a family, a work group, or a group of friends, to name just a few.

The field of consumer behavior/psychology is relatively young compared to many other areas of psychology. Nevertheless, the field has experienced an explosion of research in a wide variety of areas. Although there is a tremendous diversity in terms of topics studied, the research streams can be divided into four broad areas: (1) the psychological core, (2) the consumer decision-making process, (3) the consumer's culture, and (4) consumer behavior outcomes. Although covering the vast number of studies conducted and knowledge generated is well beyond the scope of this article, some highlights are discussed next. For more detailed information, see Hoyer and MacInnis (2007) or Haugtvedt, Herr, and Kardes (2008) For a psychologically oriented perspective integrating these elements, see Jacoby (2002).

The Psychological Core

Before consumers can make a decision regarding the acquisition, use, or disposition of an offering, they must have some knowledge and the capability of making this decision. The psychological core refers to internal knowledge structures and processes that the consumer brings to the situation. Influenced by advances in cognitive and social psychology, consumer researchers have been vitally interested in exploring a variety of topics in this area including (but not limited to) consumer memory, learning and expertise, motivation and goals, and consumer information processing (e.g., attention, comprehension, and inference making).

In terms of memory, researchers have investigated the content and structure of consumers' memory and how memory processes impact on the consumer-decision process. Key topics have included the types of associations contained in memory and how they are integrated to form larger structures such as *schemas* (knowledge about objects or things) and *scripts* (knowledge about a sequence of events such as a grocery shopping trip). Researchers have been interested in how schemas can be created, developed, changed, and protected. A variety of important consumer-related schemas have been studied including brand image and brand personality. Also of interest is the topic of *categorization,* or how consumers organize knowledge by grouping similar concepts into the same category. Studies have examined the processes by which consumers make these categorizations and how they are organized into a hierarchical structure (i.e., superordinate, basic, and subordinate levels).

A related area is consumer learning and expertise. Some consumers have developed more extensive and complex knowledge structures than others. Research has examined how these experts make quantitatively and qualitatively different decisions than other consumers (especially novices). Also of interest has been the process by which consumers learn consumer-related information. Information is acquired through processes such as information search, exposure to marketing communications (advertising, packaging, and so on), and observation of others' behavior. A significant amount of learning occurs through actual experience with products and services, involving a process of hypothesis testing. Consumers form hypotheses and then test these hypotheses through consumption experiences, thereby receiving feedback to confirm or disconfirm the hypotheses. As discussed next, these outcomes lead to such things as satisfaction or dissatisfaction with one's acquisition.

Motivation is critical. One of the key motivational constructs studied has been that of involvement (or personal relevance). When involvement is high, consumers are motivated to engage in information search, process information, and make a more detailed decision in an effort to achieve a specific goal (e.g., buy the best car for me). More recently, researchers have been quite interested in certain types of goal-directed behaviors such as promotion or approach goals (attaining positive outcomes) versus protection or avoidance goals (avoid bad ones). In other decision-making contexts, involvement can be low, in which case consumers have the goal of minimizing cognitive effort, thereby engaging in little information processing and a very simple decision process. Recent research has investigated nonconscious behavior and "thin slice" judgments (e.g., Ambady et al., 2006).

Finally, researchers have investigated how consumers process information, especially from advertising and other types of marketing communications. First, in the very cluttered marketing communication environment of today, it is very difficult to get the consumer's attention. Studies have investigated a variety of ways to capture the consumer's attention, such as making the communication personally relevant, pleasant, surprising, or easy to process. Researchers have also been very interested in comprehension, that is, whether consumers understand the meanings, direct and indirect, being conveyed by these communications. Studies have found that the miscomprehension rate is unexpectedly high for such simple communications as advertising, pointing out the need to better understand how to improve comprehension for these stimuli.

Relatedly, consumers make inferences about marketing stimuli—new meanings generated by consumers based on an interaction between a stimulus and prior knowledge that can either be correct or incorrect. They can occur in response to any marketing stimulus including brand names and symbols, product features, packaging, price, distribution, or promotions.

The Consumer Decision-Making Process

For obvious reasons, consumer researchers have been vitally interested in the consumer decision-making process. Although thousands of studies have been conducted on this topic, for the sake of simplicity, three broad research areas can be identified: Multi-attribute attitude models, behavioral decision theory, and emotional decision making.

Research on multi-attribute models dominated much of the 1960s and 70s. Investigators were interested in determining how beliefs about product features or benefits were combined to form an overall evaluation or attitude. Many studies focused on ways to identify the most important or determinant beliefs as well as the combinatorial rule used to form an attitude. A variety of different models were proposed and tested in two major categories: compensatory and noncompensatory models. Subsequent research introduced the notions of attitude specificity and normative influences to focus on behavioral intentions as a predictor of choice and behavior (e.g., the Theory of Reasoned Action; see Fishbein & Azjen, 1980).

Related to these efforts and paralleling research in social psychology, consumer researchers have been interested in determining how to influence consumer decision making or attitude change through marketing efforts. Researchers investigated how elements of the communication source, message, receiver, or channel influence this process. Later work employed the Elaboration Likelihood Model (Petty & Cacioppo, 1986) to understand how persuasion operates differently when motivation to process or involvement is high (central route processing) relative to when it is low (peripheral route processing).

In the 1980s (and continuing today), consumer researchers became interested in the emerging area of behavioral decision theory, which includes decision making

under uncertainty or risk and the types of heuristics employed in these situations. Theories such as prospect theory (Novemsky & Kahneman, 2005) have been influential in guiding these efforts. Also studied have been a variety of heuristics and processing biases such as the confirmation bias, the attraction effect, extremeness aversion, anchoring and adjustment, and framing, as well as how goals impact on these processes.

Last, researchers now recognize the key role of emotions and affect in the decision-making process. Emotions such as love, joy, and pride can and often do affect the decision. Emotions are particularly critical for products/services that are hedonic (i.e., involving pleasure or aesthetics) or are high in symbolic value. Interestingly, emotions can sometimes overwhelm rational thought, leading consumers to make choices inconsistent with their rational preferences.

The Consumer's Sociological and Cultural Context

Many aspects of the consumer's culture can greatly influence consumers' acquisition, consumption, and disposition decisions. Over the years, consumer researchers have investigated a variety of cultural influences such as demographics, social class, households, and the social environment. All these variables have a strong influence on consumers' values, personality, and life styles, which in turn have an impact on consumers' decisions.

Research on demographics is based on the notion that consumers sharing certain demographic characteristics such as age, gender, country of origin or ethnicity share common experiences and values, and this can influence their consumer behavior. Similar values are also shared between members of a social class. Consumer researchers have studied a variety of topics related to social class such as upward/downward mobility, conspicuous consumption and status symbols, compensatory consumption, and the meaning of money.

Many consumer decisions are made in the context of households rather than as individuals and consumer researchers have investigated topics such as the family life cycle, changes in household structure (delayed marriage, divorce, cohabitation, and dual-career families), household decision roles (i.e., gatekeeper, influencer, decider, buyer), spousal decision roles, and the roles of children. Research on social influences has examined how information or pressure from other individuals, groups, and various media affect consumer behavior. These sources can exert normative as well as informational influence.

Last, researchers have investigated the role of values, personality, and life styles on consumer behavior. Key values that have been investigated include: materialism, the family and children, health, hedonism, and the environment. Personality has been investigated from a variety of angles and theories, but the most influential have been trait theories. Key personality traits in a consumer context have included: need for cognition, creativity, need for uniqueness, self-monitoring, and susceptibility to persuasion. Lifestyles, a conglomeration of the consumers' activities, interests, and opinions (AIOs), have also been well researched.

The Outcomes of Consumer Behavior

Researchers have investigated a variety of outcomes emanating from the consumer decision process, including satisfaction/dissatisfaction, regret, word-of-mouth communications, the adoption and diffusion of innovations, symbolic consumer behavior, the "dark side" of the consumer, and public policy-related issues. Recent research has focused on symbolic aspects such as the symbolic meaning of products/services, special possessions, sacred meaning, and gift giving. The "dark side" includes topics such as compulsive buying, theft, black markets, addictive consumption (e.g., smoking, drinking), and compulsive consumption. Finally, consumer researchers have made important contributions to understanding and influencing public policy issues and regulations, including those regarding deceptive advertising and labeling, deceptive selling practices, advertising to children, and privacy on the Internet.

Whereas the majority of research conducted in the field of consumer behavior has applied psychological theories and methods, the field has experienced important shifts in research methodology. Early nonpsychological research placed great reliance on surveys. As psychological factors assumed greater prominence in the field's models, experimentation became the dominant methodological approach. Since the 1990s, there has been a gradual acceptance of qualitative research methods of various sorts (i.e., ethnographic, interpretivistic, introspective). It is expected that consumer researchers will exhibit greater use of qualitative and improved quantitative methods to capture the dynamic nature of the behavior and underlying psychological processes.

REFERENCES

Ambady, N., Krabbenhoft, M. A., & Hogan, D. (2006). The 30-sec sale: Using thin-slice judgments to evaluate sales effectiveness. *Journal of Consumer Psychology, 16*(1), 4–13.

Fishbein, M., & Azjen, I. (1975). *Belief, attitude, intention, and behavior: An introduction to theory and research*, Reading, MA: Addison-Wesley.

Haugtvedt, C. P., Herr, P., & Kardes, F. (2008). *Handbook of consumer psychology*. New York: Psychology Press.

Hoyer, W. D., & MacInnis, D. (2007). *Consumer behavior* (4th ed.). Boston: Houghton-Mifflin.

Jacoby, J. (2002). Stimulus-organism-response reconsidered: An evolutionary step in modeling (consumer) behavior. *Journal of Consumer Psychology, 12*(1), 51–57.

Novemsky, N., & Kahneman, D. (2005). The boundaries of loss aversion. *Journal of Marketing Research, 62*, 119–128.

Petty, R. E., & Caccioppo, J. T. (1986). *Communication and persuasion*. New York: Springer-Verlag.

WAYNE D. HOYER
University of Texas, Austin

JACOB JACOBY
New York University

See also: Advertising Psychology; Consumer Research

CONSUMER RESEARCH

Every one of us is a consumer. Daily we are bombarded with many product messages ranging from cars to homes to beauty products to cat food to services. The exposure we experience is not accidental. Much careful research has gone into discovering what we view, what we listen to, what we read, and what we do. Current highly-sophisticated technologies have made this an ever-more-exacting "science" in learning who each one of us is, developing our individual portrait, and sending us the messages tailored to our portrait.

Consumer research takes many forms. It is the person who stops you in the mall to ask you product questions and, perhaps, invite you into a room equipped with different choice samples and features. It is the uninvited cookie in your computer that traces where you go on the Internet and what you purchase there. It is the focus group of teens, young adults, or senior citizens that are invited to a gathering aimed at learning their preferences for a specific product or service. It is the "play supermarket" for young children to determine the toys, cereal products, candies, wrappers, colors, shapes, and designs that appeal to them. It is also the laboratory where very young children are exposed to different stimuli and features while being monitored for GSR, pupil dilation, and the like. Each of these—and a wide range of variations within them—constitute the current landscape of consumer research.

Early "product advertising" is as old as recorded history. It took the form of a sign on a wall telling citizens the way to the central bath or a comparable service and place within the community. It was not until the 1920s that consumer research began to focus on two-way communication – gathering information from consumers to prepare more effectively-targeted advertising and sales strategies. Still later, attention was given to consumer attitudes and opinions prior to product design. As this consumer focus steadily grew, it marked the appearance of a newly independent member of the advertising family–consumer psychology.

This new arrival gained its own identity in 1960, when the Division of Consumer Psychology was formed within the American Psychological Association.

With the formal recognition of consumer psychology came a shift from looking strictly at the consumer's purchasing role to the more global perspective of the consumer. No longer was the point-of-purchase the central interest. The approach now broadened dramatically to the events that preceded the purchase decision and the events that followed. The consumer's thoughts, feelings, and perspectives took on major importance. In combination with highly sophisticated technological research, this shift in focus characterizes current consumer research.

The question of what consumers want represents a significant step beyond the question of how to assure that consumers purchase products already on retail shelves. Now greater attention is given to questions such as why a specific choice is made, how satisfied the consumer is with the choice, and what changes in design or features will make the product more desirable and user friendly. Questions such as these constitute the two-way, direct-feedback connection to the consumer.

Several aspects of the feedback loop are not transparent to the consumer, nor are they intended to be. A child may go online and hit on a given website. If it is, for example, a dog food website, that information will be stored along with the child's contact information. In all likelihood the child will be asked a few additional questions. This inquiry aspect will fill out more of the family profile (e.g., perhaps how many children and their ages, occupation of parents, other household pets, et al.). Though the Children's Online Privacy Protection Act (1998) was designed to safeguard children younger than age 13, marketers have developed a variety of innovative approaches to reach children. Online clubs, newsletter-sign-ups, and advergames are but a few of the many approaches directed to children. Though it is highly likely that a child's address will become known within the Internet interaction, it is not essential. The research data-collection contact already has been made.

Research Techniques and Procedures

With its broad, interdisciplinary scope, consumer research taps an equally broad and diverse set of research tools and techniques. In addition to Internet "mining", credit card and grocery store purchasing patterns and preferences, and the techniques directed to children, consumer opinions and attitudes, for example, rely heavily upon attitude scales and polling techniques. The more general the consumer research approach (e.g., consumer attitudes, thoughts, and feelings), the more likely that the research tool emphasis will be upon scales or surveys.

Ad and Product Testing

In *ad testing,* interest centers upon the attention-getting capacities of different advertising features and their effectiveness in communicating the product or service message. Sophisticated laboratory techniques make it possible to *camera-monitor* and *computer-record* where an individual is looking on a page or screen. This digital record can be carefully studied to determine whether the aspects considered important in basic ad design have had their desired attentional effect.

Product testing addresses brand distinctiveness and consumer response to product characteristics. Distinctiveness investigations frequently use the classic "blindfold" test to determine whether nonvisual characteristics of the product itself will be brand distinctive. Product improvement and the development of new products rely heavily upon information gathered from consumers through product testing.

Consumer Surveys, Focus Groups, and Advisory Panels

Consumer surveys span a broad range in inquiry. The panoramic spectrum may target general attitudes, personality characteristics, likes, and dislikes whereas the more focused approach may seek response to an existing product or service. Malls, labs, Internet, mail, or phone surveys are among the channels used to gather consumer responses.

Focus groups provide an excellent venue for tapping consumer attitudes in the formative stages of a product or service. A bank may want to know what services senior citizens prefer and need. Select groups of senior citizens in different parts of the bank service area will be contacted and invited to an evening meeting with a trained focus-group leader. Through the course of the evening both general attitudes and specific recommendations will be invited and shared. Frequently, the discoveries made within these groups differ markedly from what the bank may have assumed or designed.

Advisory panels take the focus group concept one step further. In this instance, a select group of individuals is online-invited to serve as a product/preference response panel for the corporation. Supermarkets frequently use the panel approach, and this group–unlike the focus group–is ongoing and advisory over a period of time.

Academic Consumer Research

Universities and an array of academic disciplines within them conduct consumer research. The approach is both basic (knowledge-seeking) and applied (specific context-oriented). An industrial/organizational psychologist or a professor in a school of business or marketing may serve as a consultant to a given corporation. Frequently, these consultants apply current academic research to a corporation's consumer-product-related issue. Though basic research does not begin from the starting point of addressing applied setting issues, the findings of a given research study can be quite informative. For example, a department store would welcome the finding that cookie-scented candles can enhance the likelihood of a consumer making an "out of domain" purchase such as a sweater, a coat, or a dress.

The field, however, is not without its problems and growing pains. In her Presidential Address to the 2007 Conference of the Association of Consumer Research, Brucks made the point that researchers by work ethic and temperament tend to be insular from the general public.

In addition, they tend to pursue research questions of strong personal interest to them. This lends itself to a patchwork knowledge base and a potential disconnect from issues most germane to the general public. Recommendations were made for increasing breadth, diversity, and connectedness to the general public.

Consumer research as an independent identity is relatively young within scholarly disciplines. The Association and *Journal of Consumer Research* date from 1974. Since its inception, the field has grown dramatically, and its youthfulness and growth have carried both potentials and problems. With many academicians and professionals coming to it from several different disciplines, the field lacks a uniformity of approach. Continued rapid growth seems assured. Coherence in research priorities and their systematic pursuit will constitute the greater challenge.

Organizations and Journals Related to Consumer Research

The *Journal of Consumer Research,* the *Journal of Consumer Psychology,* and the *Journal of Marketing* are three major scholarly journals in the field. The professional organization most central to this topic is the Association for Consumer Research.

REFERENCES

Brucks, M. (2007, October 26). Choices in consumer research: Unintended consequences. *Presidential Address to the Association for Consumer Research Conference*, Memphis, Tennessee. Retrieved March 1, 2008, from http://www.acrwebsite.org/topic.asp?artid=413.

Kinney, L. (2006). Sports sponsorship. In A. L. Raney & J. Bryant (Eds.), *Handbook of sports and the media*. Special attention to pp. 300–304. Mahwah, New Jersey: Erlbaum.

Montgomery, K. C. (2001). Digital kids: The new online children's consumer culture. In D. G. Singer & J. L. Singer (Eds.), *Handbook of children and the media*. pp. 635–650.

Palmer, E. L. & C. F. Carpenter. (2006). Food and beverage marketing to children and youth: Trends and issues. *Media Psychology, 8*, 165–190.

Roedder John, D. (1999, December). Consumer socialization of children: A retrospective look at twenty-five years of research. *Journal of Consumer Research, 26*, 183–213.

Zandl, I. & Leonard, R. (1992). Targeting the trendsetting consumer: *How to market your product or service to influential buyers*. Homewood, Illinois: Business One Irwin.

Zollo, P. (1995). *Wise up to teens: Insights into marketing and advertising to teenagers*. Ithaca, New York: New Strategist.

EDWARD L. PALMER
Davidson College

CONTEXTUALISM

Contextualism is a philosophy of science based on modern variants of American pragmatism. The core analytic unit of contextualism or pragmatism is the ongoing act in context: the common sense situated action. It is doing as it is being done, such as in hunting, shopping, or making love. This has sometimes been termed the "historical act," but not in the sense of a thing done in the past. Rather, the term "historical act" recognizes that acts occur not just in a current situational context, but also as part of a stream of purposive acts in an individual's life. In practical terms, contextualists (1) focus on the whole behavioral event, (2) are continuously sensitive to the role of context in understanding the nature and function of this event, and (3) maintain a firm grasp on a pragmatic truth criterion. Contextualism is commonly distinguished from mechanism, formism, teleological perspectives, organicism, and other broad philosophical approaches.

To contextualistic psychologists, a psychological act incontext cannot be explained by an appeal to actions of various parts of the organism, such as its brain or muscles. Legs do not go shopping, brains do not go hunting, and penises do not make love. People do these things, and people are integrated organisms. This does not mean that information about the operation of the brain or other parts of the organism are not relevant, but that the whole event is always primary, and reductionism and expansionism are rejected. Contextualism is applicable at all levels of analysis. If one were to become interested in the action of a part of the organism (say, the brain), then this would become the new whole, and all else would be context at this new level of analysis. What is learned at one level of organization will not fully explain events at other levels of organization, however.

Each participant in a whole event defines the qualities of the other participants, much as the front of a coin implies a back and vice versa. For example, going shopping implies a place to go from and to, a reason to go, a method of going, and future events that shopping will enable.

All of these facets working together are the whole event, and none of them can be examined out of context and be fully understood. The legs may move in a particular fashion as one goes to the store, but moving legs are not "shopping," and the same leg movements may participate in completely different acts in other contexts (e.g., dancing, exercising). To a contextualist, the whole behavioral event cannot be built up from its components, because qualities of the whole event exist only in the totality.

What creates the "whole event" is the purpose of the behaving organism and, at another level, the purpose of the person doing the analysis. In other words, units of action are entirely functional. It is not assumed that there are "true" units, only useful ones. The universe is the ultimate context, but the universe is not something that can be described, so all units are taken to be convenient analytic fictions. The specific contextual or behavioral features to be abstracted are those that contribute to the achievement of the goals of the therapist or scientist in doing an analysis.

The truth criterion of contextualism emerges from the core analytic unit itself, which is successful working. Going shopping implies a place to shop, and, when that place has been reached and shopping has occurred, the act is complete. Similarly, a pragmatic truth criterion implies a goal to be reached, and, when that goal is reached, the analysis is complete. Since successful working is the means by which contextualists evaluate events, and goals allow this criterion to be applied, analytic goals themselves cannot ultimately be evaluated or justified. They can only be stated. To evaluate a goal via successful working would require yet another goal, but then that second goal could not be evaluated, and so on *ad infinitum*.

When dealing with science and treatment, these same ideas are applied to clinicians and scientists alike. The analytic work of the scientist is also an act in context. It too needs to be understood with regard to its purpose in order to know if the analysis is successful. That means that contextualists must state their goals in advance and that there may be many truths possible in a given context if there are many different purposes. In psychology we can organize contextualists into two rough groups. Descriptive contextualists seek a full and personal appreciation of the participating factors in a whole event. They are like historians, wanting to appreciate a unique historical event by examining closely all the strands that make up the whole story. Dramaturgy, hermeneutics, narrative psychology, interbehaviorism, feminist psychology, and social constructionism are all examples of this type of contextualism. The second group, functional contextualists, seek the prediction and influence of events as an integrated goal. Contextualistic behavior analysis, some forms of Marxist psychology, and some forms of psychobiological thinking are examples.

The choice of a goal in contextualism is pre-analytic. It is a means of analysis, not the result of analysis. Thus, neither descriptive nor functional contextualists can claim that their goal is the right goal. However, we can examine what happens when these different goals are adopted.

Consider, for example, the environmentalism that is so characteristic of behavior analysis. Initially this focus seems dogmatic, since obviously behavior influences the environment as much as environment influences behavior. The dogmatism is removed when one realizes that the contextual features to be abstracted in any contextualistic analysis are those that contribute to the achievement of the goals of the analysis. Functional contextualists want analyses that achieve prediction and influence as an integrated goal. Only contextual features that are external to the behavior of the individual being studied and that are manipulable, at least in principle, could possibly lead directly to behavioral influence as an outcome. Verbal analyses generate rules for people, not rules for the world. To accomplish prediction and influence, rules must start with the environment, in the sense of the "world outside of the behavior," because that is where the consumers of these rules are. The environmentalism in behavior analysis is thus made more coherent (and non-dogmatic) by seeing it as part of a particular contextualistic system.

One of the more disconcerting aspects of contextualism is that it undermines a realist ontology—indeed, any ontology at all. If what is true is what works and what works is with regard to a goal, absolutely nothing of practical utility is added by the claim "and the reason it works is that it is true in the sense that the world is really pre-arranged in this way." That does not mean that contextualism is idealistic, but that is it both monistic and focused on a psychological epistemology, so much so that it becomes completely silent and uninterested in ontological claims, preferring to stick to the situated actions of scientists, clinicians, and clients living in and with the one world. In clinical work this leads to an emphasis on the values of clients and what their direct experience says about the success of steps taken to achieve these goals.

In the hands of a contextualist, mundane clinical statements can lead to unusual outcomes. For example, suppose a client says "I can't leave my home or I will have an anxiety attack." A mechanistic therapist would wonder why the person is anxious, or how the panic can be alleviated. Among several other steps, a contextualistic clinician might (1) look for the larger contexts that are implied by this formulation (e.g., that anxiety is bad), (2) examine the context in which the client would say such a thing (e.g., what is the person accomplishing in therapy by this speech act—is the person asking for support, explaining dependence, or whatever), (3) look for contexts that exist or could be created in which panic and staying home are unrelated events (e.g., if anxiety were no longer avoided, would anxiety still lead to staying inside), or (4) see if there are parts of this statement that could be supported therapeutically. Several new forms of intervention in the behavioral and cognitive therapies (e.g., Acceptance and

Commitment Therapy; Functional Analytic Psychotherapy) are contextualistic and take advantage of the new light contextualism casts on old issues.

STEVEN C. HAYES
University of Nevada

See also: **Functional Analysis**

CONTINGENCY TABLES

A contingency table is an array of counts or frequencies arranged in a two-way table usually consisting of $r \geq 2$ rows and $c \geq 2$ columns. The name comes about from the statistical test used to determine if the relative frequency for a cell in the table is contingent on the marginal frequencies for the row and column in which it's found. Hence, the null hypothesis is one of independence, $H_0 : p_{ij} = p_{i.}p_{.j}$, and the alternative is association, $H_a : p_{ij} \neq p_{i.}p_{.j}$. The test of significance is called "contingency chi square" and is computed with the following formula:

$$\chi^2 = \sum_{i=1}^{r} \sum_{j=1}^{c} \frac{(n_{ij} - n_{i.}n_{.j}/n_{..})^2}{n_{i.}n_{.j}/n_{..}},$$

Although x^2 is used as the symbol for the test statistic, under the null hypothesis, it is only approximately distributed as a chi square random variable with $(r - 1)(c - 1)$ degrees of freedom.

Contingency tables arise frequently in research involving categorical data. Such would be the case in a study to determine whether certain kinds of compulsive behavior tend to be gender specific. The researcher may have random samples of $r = 3$ different types of compulsive behavior of interest along with the number of men and women in each sample. Under the null hypothesis, the gender ratio would be essentially the same for each sample, but if the test statistic is significant, there is compelling evidence that certain kinds of behavior are more likely to be displayed by one gender than the other. However, it does not test whether all these behaviors are more common for one gender; to answer this question, a test procedure other than contingency chi square is needed.

The cell frequencies (n_{ij}) are often called *observed values* and symbolized as o_{ij} and the product of the marginal relative frequencies ($n_{i.}n_{.j}/n_{..}$) called *expected values* (e_{ij}). The test statistic given as follows:

$$\chi^2 = \sum_{i=1}^{r} \sum_{j=1}^{c} (o_{ij} - e_{ij})^2/e_{ij}$$

In this form it can be seen that the difference between observed and expected values is squared and divided by the expected value. Thus, it is understandable how squared differences of the same magnitude, say $(o_{ij} - e_{ij})^2 = 2^2 = 4$, will not have the same contribution to the numerical value of the test statistic when e_{ij} is as large as it was when the expected value is small. William G. Cochran, in two seminal papers, published in 1952 and 1954, respectively, discussed this and other concerns associated with chi square tests. As a consequence of the large values of the test statistic arising solely due to small expected values in the equation, a "rule of thumb" is that a chi square test be used only if all expected values are greater than 1.0 and not more than 20% of the $e_{ij} < 5.0$ (Dowdy et al., 2004).

Because contingency chi square is so frequently used in the analysis of research data, theoretical and applied statisticians have done extensive research on the test procedure itself, and there is now a rich lode of useful publications going nearly unmined. A review of the older literature on this procedure was published by Conover (1999).

REFERENCES

Cochran, W. G. (1952). The χ^2 goodness of fit. *Annals of Mathematical Statistics, 23*, 315–345.

Cochran, W. G. (1954). Some methods for strengthening the common chi-square tests. *Biometrics, 10*, 417–451.

Conover, W. J. (1999). *Practical nonparametric statistics* (3rd ed.). New York: John Wiley & Sons.

Dowdy, S. M., Wearden, S., & Chilko, D. (2004). *Statistics for research* (3rd ed.). Hoboken: John Wiley & Sons.

SUGGESTED READINGS

Agresti, A. (2002). *Categorical data analysis*. New York: John Wiley & Sons.

Haberman, S. J. (1978). *Analysis of qualitative data*. New York: Academic Press.

Hollander, M., & Wolfe, D. A. (1999). *Nonparametric statistical methods* (2nd ed.). New York: John Wiley & Sons.

STANLEY WEARDEN
West Virginia University

See also: **Chi-square Test**

CONTROL THERAPY

Control Therapy is an integrated approach to psychotherapy and health care that combines theory, research, and practice. Its theory, test construction, and interventions have been developed and empirically tested over a 25-year period involving research and clinical work with thousands of individuals in more than a dozen countries.

Control Therapy rests on the premise that issues of personal control (e.g., desire for control, fear of losing control, power struggles) underlie most concerns brought to therapy (e.g., Strupp, 1970; Frank, 1982; Shapiro, Schwartz, & Astin, 1996); that there are individual differences in people's Control Profiles in terms of their preferred modes for facing this central issue of gaining and maintaining a sense of control; and that for a specific clinical problem, matching clinical control-enhancing interventions to the individual's Control Profile maximizes the opportunity for therapeutic success (Shapiro & Astin, 1998).

This therapeutic approach incorporates the use of a reliable and valid standardized multidimensional psychological assessment tool, the Shapiro Control Inventory (SCI), to provide a Control Profile for the client, showing sense of control in the general domain, in specific life areas, and in regard to motivation for change, desire for change, and preferred style for gaining control: that is, an assertive/change mode of control; a yielding/accepting mode of control; and agency of control (self and/or other) (Shapiro, 1994). An updated *Control Therapy Training Manual* (Soucar, Astin, Shapiro, & Shapiro, 2008) provides standardized procedures useful for both replicating treatment research and for training clinicians. Both the SCI and the *Control Therapy Training Manual* are available online at no charge to licensed health care professionals (http://controlresearch.net).

A Unifying Theory of Control

The theoretical basis of Control Therapy builds upon and integrates several psychological theories and concepts, including Bandura's self-efficacy; Seligman's learned helplessness and optimism; White's concept of competence; Menninger's psychodynamic dyscontrol; Brehm's reactance; Frankl's will to meaning; Adler's will to superiority; Rotter and Wallstons' internal and external locus of control; Schwartz's cybernetic feedback models and disregulation; and Mischel's self-control/delay of gratification. Shapiro and Astin (1998) have reviewed these theoretical foundations of Control Therapy. Essentially, control theory rests upon a unifying biopsychosocial foundation and has three postulates: (1) all individuals desire a sense of control in their lives; (2) there are healthy and unhealthy ways by which individuals attempt to gain or regain that sense of control; and (3) there are individual differences in people's Control Profiles; therefore it is important to match clinical control strategies to the person to help individuals maintain a healthy sense of control in their lives.

Developing a Client Control Profile: Assessing the Theory

A client Control Profile is based on clinical assessment with the SCI, which has undergone extensive reliability and validity testing, including an investigation of neurobiological correlates of control using positron emission tomography (Shapiro, Wu, et al., 1993). The 187-item, nine-scale SCI is a clinically reliable and valid multidimensional instrument that measures four primary and interrelated components of clients' sense of control: (1) desire for control (i.e., where they want control and why they want it); (2) current sense of control in both general and specific domains; (3) the modes by which clients seek control (assertive/change and yielding/accepting); and (4) use of both self and other agencies in gaining control. Research shows that this method of assessing client Control Profiles is the most sensitive inventory yet devised to differentiate among clinical disorders and between clinical and normative populations (Shapiro, Potkin, Jin, Brown, & Carreon, 1993).

Control Therapy also includes methods for listening to clients' speech, including client narratives (their "control stories"), control-related beliefs and assumptions, and assaults to their sense of control, and for identifying and monitoring domains where clients feel a lack of control.

Control-Based Interventions

Control Therapy consists of an 8- to 12-week step-by-step treatment program that involves defining the client's area of concern, performing initial and ongoing assessment, monitoring, goal setting, determining appropriate strategies/skills needed for change, teaching the strategies/skills, and evaluating progress. Therapeutic interventions involve detailed and well-defined clinical instructions for matching treatment strategy to the client's Control Profile, thus offering both standardized, replicable techniques while providing flexibility and sensitivity to each client's individual needs and style.

Based on the goal selected, individually tailored cognitive and behavioral strategies are utilized to help clients regain a sense of control through one or both of the positive modes of control. Fostering the assertive/change mode of control, which historically has been emphasized in Western scientific psychology, involves having individuals learn to identify, monitor, and gain active control of those aspects of their lives that are, or should be, amenable to change.

Fostering use of the yielding, accepting mode, which derive primarily from non-Western philosophical and spiritual traditions, means helping clients learn the value of surrendering, accepting, and letting go with serenity (i.e., without feelings of helplessness or resignation) of those aspects of their lives that are not under personal control. Yielding can mean letting go of inappropriate or excessive active control efforts. Practical instructions in each mode are explained, as well as ways to integrate and achieve balance between the two positive modes.

A Control-Based View of Psychological Health: Suboptimal, Normal, and Optimal

Traditional Western psychology argues that loss of control and learned helplessness are unhealthy and suboptimal. Normal control is defined as gaining control (which even includes an illusion of control) and is equated with mental health. This traditional view argues that instrumental control is good, and that the more control one has, the better (e.g., Thompson, 1981), even if this means an illusory, over-inflated perception of control (Taylor & Brown, 1994); or the use of defense mechanisms such as making external attributions for failure (Seligman, 1991).

The theory, research, and practice of Control Therapy agree that normal control is better than suboptimal control. However, some normal control strategies (e.g., external attributions for failure, over-inflated sense of control) can also be problematic. They can keep individuals from being aware of the unconscious, reflexive, and reactive nature of many of their control desires and efforts; they are often insular and self-serving; and they can inhibit people from learning from their mistakes.

Therefore, a concept of optimal control is needed. Optimal control, according to Control Therapy, involves:

- Increased conscious awareness of one's control dynamics, including affective, cognitive, and somatic experiences, in order to learn when and how desire and efforts for control are expressed; when control beliefs, goals, desires, and strategies are reflexive, limiting, and potentially destructive; and when they should be increased, decreased, or channeled in more constructive directions.

- A balanced and integrated use of assertive/change and yielding/accepting modes of control matched to the situation and goals, desires, and temperament of the individual.

- The ability to gain a sense of control from both self (self-regulation of cognitions, affect, and behavior) and from a benevolent other/Other, (e.g., whether from a doctor [cf. Taylor, 1983] or from one's view of the nature of the universe, including religious and spiritual beliefs [Smith, 1983]).

Benefits of Control Therapy

Control Therapy has been shown to be effective in both assessment (sensitivity and specificity) and treatment (clinical outcome) with a wide range of mental disorder diagnoses and health-related concerns. Clinical areas investigated include Generalized Anxiety Disorder, panic attack, depression, borderline personality, eating disorders, and adult children of alcoholics. Control issues have also been investigated in Type-A individuals with myocardial infarction, women with breast cancer, and individuals at high cardiovascular risk (See Astin et al, 1999; Soucar, 2006; and an updated listing of published articles on Control Therapy and the SCI at http://controlresearch.net).

There are several advantages to Control Therapy and the unifying theory upon which it is based. First, a unifying theory helps clinicians understand control as a central component underlying all schools of therapy: the analytic view that humans are governed by unknown and uncontrolled forces; the cognitive-behavioral schools' emphasis on self-control; and the humanistic or existential focus on personal choice, individual freedom, and self-determination.

Second, in addition to the theory's universality and parsimony, it also can be operationalized, thereby providing an empirical foundation for assessing a client's Control Profile. Based on individual variations in Control Profiles, specific techniques can be matched to client needs and clinical problem (Evans et al., 1993). Drawing from both Eastern and Western psychological traditions, Control Therapy involves specific assertive/change and yielding/accepting modes of control intervention techniques, and the matching of these techniques to a client's Control Profile, goals, and clinical problem.

Finally, Control Therapy articulates a control-based vision of mental, physical, and interpersonal health involving suboptimal, normal, and optimal Control Profiles. Thus, although Control Therapy was designed to specifically address individual mental and physical health problems, it can also be used as a means to help promote growth in many contexts, including intrapersonal, interpersonal, and even societal health and well-being.

Future Directions

Further research on the clinical effectiveness of Control Therapy needs to be replicated and extended and compared to other treatment interventions, including behavioral "third wave" approaches such as Hayes's Acceptance and Commitment Therapy, Linehan's Dialectical Behavior Therapy, and Segal's Mindfulness Based Cognitive Therapy to demonstrate its effectiveness as a treatment of choice for specific clinical populations.

Control Therapy has been built upon and owes an enormous debt to other approaches. Thus, it is neither a final ultimate panacea, nor a closed system. Therapists from other theoretical orientations may find Control Therapy provides useful insights into how control processes may be relevant to their own therapeutic work with clients. The Control Profile and control stories may help clinicians think about their clients in new, control-based ways. The modes of control may be valuable as a tool for conceptualizing how a sense of control can be achieved (i.e., emphasizing the two positive modes of control). Finally, specific control-based interventions may prove of use as part of the clinical armamentarium.

As a final note it may be helpful to remember as a context for therapy—and life itself—that we live on a small planet in a small solar system in a small galaxy. On the one hand, we humans are amazingly complex and resilient with vast worlds within each of us. On the other hand, we are also small, fragile, and impermanent physical beings. There is suffering in this world that is part of the life experience, and no amount of control efforts can ever completely ameliorate that. We are all fellow travelers on a temporary journey. This perspective can help us remember that compassion, empathy, and kindness are wise attitudes as a context for our gallant, even noble efforts to teach, learn, and practice positive control in our lives.

REFERENCES

Astin, J. A., Anton-Culver, H., Schwartz, C. E., Shapiro, D. H., McQuade, J., Breuer, A. M., Taylor, T., Lee, H., & Kurosaki, T. (1999). Sense of control and adjustment to breast cancer: The importance of balancing control coping styles. *Behavioral Medicine, 25,* 3, 101–109.

Evans, G. E., Shapiro, D. H., & Lewis, M. (1993). Specifying dysfunctional mismatches between different control dimensions. *British Journal of Psychology, 84,* 255–273. *Series* (Vol. 1, pp. 9–37). Washington, DC: American Psychological Association.

Seligman, M. E. P. (1991). *Learned optimism.* New York: Knopf.

Shapiro, D. H. (1994). *Manual for the Shapiro Control Inventory (SCI).* San Jose, CA: Behavior data. Also available online at http://controlresearch.net.

Shapiro, D. H., Potkin, S., Jin, Y., Brown, B., & Carreon, D. (1993). Measuring the psychological construct of control: Discriminant, divergent, and incremental validity of the Shapiro Control Inventory and Rotter's and Wallston's Locus of Control Scales. *International Journal of Psychosomatics, 40*(1–4), 35–46.

Shapiro, D. H., Schwartz, C. E., & Astin, J. A. (1996). Controlling ourselves, controlling our world: Psychology's role in understanding positive and negative consequences of seeking and gaining control. *American Psychologist, 51*(12), 1213–1230.

Shapiro, D. H., Wu, L., Buchsbaum, M., Hong, C., Elderkin-Thompson, V., & Hillard, D. (1995). Exploring the relationship between having control and losing control to functional neuroanatomy within the sleeping state. *Psychologia, 38*(3), 133–145.

Smith, H (1983). Spiritual discipline in Zen and comparative religion. *The Eastern Buddhist, 16*(2), 9–25

Soucar, E. A. (2006). Establishing culturally competent practice: Effects of control-enhancing psychotherapy on depression and anxiety for African American outpatients. *Dissertation Abstracts International, 67*(3-A), 849 . (UMI No. AAI3211907.)

Soucar, E. A., Astin, J. A., Shapiro, S. L., Shapiro, D. H. (2008). *Control therapy training manual.* From http://controlresearch.net.

Taylor, S. (1983). Adjustment to threatening events: A theory of cognitive adaptation. *American Psychologist, 38,* 1161–1173.

Taylor, S., & Brown, I. D. (1994). Illusion and well-being revisited: Separating fact from fiction. *Psychological Bulletin, 116,* 21–27.

Thompson, S. (1981). Will it hurt less if I can control it? A complex answer to a simple question. *Psychological Bulletin, 90,* 89–101.

SUGGESTED READINGS

Frank, J. (1982). Therapeutic components shared by all psychotherapies. In J. J. Harvey & M. M. Parks (Eds.), *Psychotherapy research and behavior change.* Master lecture. Washington, DC: American Psychological Association.

Shapiro, D. H., & Astin, J. A. (1998). *Control Therapy: An integrated approach to psychotherapy, health, and healing.* New York: John Wiley & Sons.

Strupp, H. (1970). Specific versus non-specific factors in psychotherapy and the problem of control. *Archives of General Psychiatry, 23,* 393–401.

DEANE H. SHAPIRO
University of California, Irvine, School of Medicine

JOHN A. ASTIN
California Pacific Medical Center

SHAUNA L. SHAPIRO
Santa Clara University

ELIZABETH SOUCAR
Penndel Mental Health Center, Penndel, CA

CRAIG SANTREE
VA Puget Sound Health Care System,
Seattle Division

See also: **Behavioral Modeling; Perceptual Control Theory; Self-Control**

CONVERSION DISORDER

Conversion disorder is a mental disturbance in which patients present with neurological symptoms such as paralysis, numbness, or blindness, but for which no neurological or other organic explanation can be identified. Instead, psychological mechanisms are believed to cause the symptoms. Conversion symptoms were initially described in the context of hysteria. The term "conversion disorder" was originated by the physicians Josef Breuer and Sigmund Freud, who suggested that negative emotions were repressed and "converted" into physical symptoms. Other adjectives frequently used to describe conversion symptoms are "psychogenic," "pseudoneurological," or "medically unexplained" bodily symptoms. Known for millennia, this disorder has always been subject to debate and conceptual confusion. This is reflected, for example, in the manner in which the disorder is currently classified within the two major current nosologies. In the *International Statistical Classification of Diseases and Related Health Problems* (ICD-10: WHO, 1992) conversion disorder is a dissociative disorder; in the *Diagnostic and Statistical Manual of Mental Disorders* (DSM-IV-TR: APA, 2000) it is a type of somatoform disorder.

Characteristics

Definition

The diagnostic criteria for conversion disorder according to the DSM-IV-TR are as follows:

- The patient has one or more symptoms or deficits affecting voluntary motor or sensory function suggesting a neurological or other general medical condition.
- Psychological factors are judged to be associated with the symptoms because conflicts or other stressors precede the initiation or exacerbation of the symptoms.
- The symptom is not intentionally produced or feigned (as in factitious disorder or malingering).
- The symptom, after appropriate investigation, cannot be fully explained by a medical condition, substance intake, or as a culturally sanctioned behavior.
- The symptom causes clinically significant distress or impairment in social, occupational, or other important areas of functioning or warrants medical evaluation.
- The symptom is not limited to pain or sexual dysfunction, does not occur exclusively in the context of somatization disorder, and is not better accounted for by another mental disorder.

Symptom Presentation

The presentation of conversion symptoms mimics a broad spectrum of neurological disorders. The most common conversion symptoms are motor symptoms, such as paralysis, weakness, gait disturbances, and tremor. The second most common symptom cluster consists of sensory symptoms that may involve loss of sensation, blindness, and sometimes deafness. Another cluster of symptoms involve psychogenic non-epileptic insults. There can also be a mixed presentation in which there are motor, sensory, and seizure-like symptoms.

Demographics

The lifetime prevalence rates of conversion disorder in the general U.S. population are estimated to fall between 11 and 300 per 100,000 people. In clinical populations, the rates vary between 5% and 14% of general hospital patients; 1%–3% of outpatient referrals to psychiatrists; and 5%–25% of psychiatric outpatients. However, in neurological settings, up to 30% of the patients present with symptoms that are only somewhat or not at all explained by disease (Carson et al., 2000). Because only a few of these patients are referred for additional psychiatric evaluation, it remains unknown how many of these patients meet the diagnostic criteria for conversion disorder. Prevalence rates are higher in rural and lower socio-economic groups, and conversion disorder is more common in females than males, with a female-to-male ratio varying between 6:1 and 2:1. Although conversion disorder may present at any age, symptom onset is most frequently between age 30 and 40.

Psychiatric and Neurological Comorbidity

Psychiatric comorbidity is common in conversion disorder. Depression and anxiety disorders are present in 22%–75% of the patients. Personality disorders are observed in 37–59% of the patients. Although histrionic personality disorders have been observed, other types of disorders such as avoidant and dependent personality disorder are far more common. Conversion symptoms are, by definition, not attributable to a neurological or other organic pathology. Nevertheless, neurological comorbidity is common, with rates varying between 3% of the patients in psychiatric settings and up to 50% in neurological settings.

Diagnostic Issues

Major difficulties in diagnosing conversion disorder are (1) the exclusion of neurological disease, (2) the exclusion of feigning, and (3) the identification of psychological mechanisms. With respect to excluding neurological disease, Slater and Glithero (1965) published an alarming report that at follow-up one third of their patients appeared to have developed neurological disease. Later authors argued that this study was biased and published studies reporting rates around 4%, which is comparable to the rate of neurological disorders in general. Some signs like the Hoover's sign (the involuntary extension of a paralyzed leg when the "good" leg is flexing against resistance) may be beneficial in discriminating conversion from neurological disorder (Ziv et al., 1998). However, signs formerly taken as indicative of conversion disorder, such as *"la belle indifference"* (a relative lack of concern about the nature or implications of the symptoms), appear to be unreliable and equally common in neurological disorder.

Feigning or malingering is difficult to detect in persons with physical complaints, and clinicians should be suspicious when patients are involved in legal or insurance procedures. An increasing number of neurophysiological studies have shown that, at least in a research setting, feigning can be differentiated from conversion disorder, as evidenced by discrete brain activation in cases of motor and sensory conversion disorder (e.g., Spence et al., 2000). In clinical settings video observations may be helpful.

Despite the difficulties of excluding neurological disorder and feigning, experts state that conversion disorder can be diagnosed with a fair amount of reliability provided that standard diagnostic protocols are carefully followed (Halligan, Bass, & Marshall, 2001).

The third and perhaps most controversial step in diagnosing conversion disorder is the identification of a psychological stress factor that, according to the DSM-IV, should precede the onset or exacerbation of the symptoms. Childhood trauma and subsequent life-events have indeed been linked to conversion and somatization symptoms. Nevertheless, several authors have questioned the necessity of identifying psychosocial precipitants in order to make a firm diagnosis of conversion disorder. Although clear environmental precursors are often found, they can be absent in some cases (see Roelofs & Spinhoven, 2007, for a review).

History and Theoretical Models

In the nineteenth century, Jean-Martin Charcot and Paul Briquet in France and Josef Breuer in Vienna were investigating what was then called hysteria, a disorder primarily affecting women (the term "hysteria" comes from the Greek word for uterus or womb). Women diagnosed with hysteria had frequent emotional outbursts and presented with a variety of pseudo-neurological symptoms. Descriptions of *arc-de-cercle* (a bizarre posture in which patients arched their body backwardly) stem from this time. Pierre Janet, a French psychiatrist and student of Charcot, suggested that hysteria resulted from psychological trauma and proposed that patients suffering from hysteria presented with an altered state of consciousness, described as a state of dissociation (Janet, 1907).

Despite the variety of manifestations of conversion symptoms, the symptoms share one important feature, that is, the patient's symptom presentation is characterized by marked dissociation between voluntary (more conscious or explicit) and automatic (more unconscious or implicit) functions, whereby the voluntary motor and sensory processes fail and the automatic more unconscious processes remain intact (Kihlstrom, 1992). Systematic investigations have shown, for example, that patients with conversion blindness could modify their behavior in response to visual information they deny seeing. In the case of conversion paralysis, the patient is unable to intentionally move one or more parts of the body, whereas under less controlled or intentional circumstances, such as during sleep, hypnosis, or during tests like the Hoover's test, the patient may show some movement in the affected area (Ziv et al, 1998). These discrepancies between voluntary and automatic motor as well as sensory functions have raised considerable confusion in clinical practice. The question of what accounts for these contradictory phenomena has intrigued and preoccupied philosophers, psychiatrists, and neurologists throughout history. Roughly, three categories of explanatory models can be distinguished (Roelofs & Spinhoven, 2007).

Psychodynamic Models

According to psychodynamic models stemming from Freud's theories, conversion symptoms reflect repressed emotions that have been converted to bodily symptoms. Freud later argued that the repressed experiences were sexual or aggressive in nature. In his view, the primary gain from conversion symptoms is the negative emotions associated with these experiences becoming unconscious and no longer felt. However, high comorbidity of anxious and depressed mood in conversion disorder question the validity of this theory by indicating that patients with conversion symptoms may continue feeling distressed.

Dissociation Models

Dissociation theory, initially developed by Pierre Janet (1859–1947), assumes that under the influence of overwhelming psychological stress, individuals experience a spontaneous narrowing of attention. This attentional narrowing limits the number of sensory channels that can be attended to simultaneously and results in the loss of deliberate attentional control over unattended channels. However, information in the unattended channel is still processed outside of awareness and leads to so-called negative dissociative symptoms (e.g., loss of motor control or somatosensory awareness). Moreover, attentional narrowing precludes full awareness of aspects of the traumatic event and prevents integration of new memories with existing autobiographical memories. However, trauma reminders can trigger these dissociated traumatic memories (also described as fixed ideas) and produce so-called positive dissociative symptoms (e.g., sensory distortions or pain). More recent dissociation models (Kihlstrom, 1992) are still influential in explaining conversion disorder, but they cannot adequately specify when, why, and at what level information processing will fail.

Cognitive Integrative Models

More recently cognitive theories have been developed that build on dissociation theory but regard dissociation as a non-pathological "normal" psychological process. In these models, the term dissociation is used descriptively rather than mechanistically, and traumatic experiences are no longer incorporated as a necessary causal factor in the development of dissociative symptoms. Brown (2004), for example, emphasizes the role of illness-related cognitive representations that may develop and become increasingly activated under the influence of a variety of cognitive and environmental factors, including psychological stress, self-suggestion, and self-focused attention. Cognitive models can adequately account for the fact that conversion symptoms are experienced as non-volitional, but they lack integration with current neurophysiological findings.

Neurophysiological Findings

Several neurophysiological and neuropsychological studies support the view that higher-level voluntary motor and sensory control functions are disturbed in conversion disorder, while elementary stages of sensory or motor processing remain intact. Using a variety of brain imaging techniques, these studies have attempted to identify specific neural correlates associated with conversion symptoms. In an exhaustive review, Vuilleumier (2005) concluded that striato-thalamo-cortical circuits controlling sensorimotor function and voluntary behavior may play an important role in the manifestation of conversion symptoms. Most of the findings fit theories proposing that the sensorimotor representations may be modulated by stress-related factors, perhaps involving primitive reflexive defense mechanisms and hyperalertness that are partly independent of conscious control (Vuilleumier, 2005). However, the variability in results, methods, and populations in these studies prohibit definite conclusions on the neurophysiological correlates of conversion symptoms. Moreover it remains a question whether the neurophysiological and neuropsychological alterations reflect causative, maintaining, or consequential factors of conversion symptoms.

Treatment

Controlled single case studies suggest that various treatments, including cognitive-behavioral, operant, cue conditioning, and symptom-focused approaches, may be effective in treating conversion disorder. However, controlled clinical group trials providing information on the successful treatment of longstanding conversion disorders and long-term treatment outcome are very few in number. Only two randomized-controlled group studies on the treatment of conversion disorder have been published, both demonstrating the efficacy of an eclectic multi-modal approach that includes hypnotic techniques in both inpatients and outpatients with conversion disorder (Moene et al., 2002). Important elements of the treatment are a clear explanation, application of symptom-reduction techniques, physiotherapy where appropriate, treatment of comorbid depression or anxiety if present, and teaching learning to cope with stressful events if applicable. The explanation should emphasize that the symptoms are genuine, common, and potentially reversible. Giving a rational for the symptoms that is acceptable for the patient as well as the environment of the patient is helpful in preventing the patient from losing face. In addition, symptom-reduction techniques using indirect suggestions, such as hypnosis and imagery, are thought to be helpful by virtue of by-passing the voluntary (impaired) functions (Moene et al., 2002).

REFERENCES

American Psychiatric Association (2000). *Diagnostic and statistical manual of mental disorders* (DSM-IV-TR). (4th ed., text rev.) Washington DC, Author.

Brown, R.J. (2004). Psychological mechanisms of medically unexplained symptoms: An integrative conceptual model. *Psychological Bulletin, 130,* 793–812.

Carson, A. J., Ringbauer, B., Stone, J., McKenzie, L., Warlow, C., & Sharpe, M.. (2000). Do medically unexplained symptoms matter? A prospective cohort study of 300 new referrals to neurology outpatient clinics. *Journal of Neurology, Neurosurgery and Psychiatry, 68,* 207–210.

Halligan, P.W., Bass, C., & Marshall, J. (2001). *Contemporary approaches to the study of hysteria: Clinical and theoretical perspectives.* Oxford: Oxford University Press.

Janet, P. (1907). *The major symptoms of hysteria.* New York: MacMillan.

Kihlstrom, J.F. (1992). Dissociative and conversion disorders. In D.J. Stein & J.E. Young (Eds.). *Cognitive science and clinical disorders* (pp. 247–270). San Diego: Academic Press.

Moene, F.C., Spinhoven, P., Hoogduin, C.A.L., & Van Dyck, R. (2002). A randomized controlled clinical trial on the additional effect of hypnosis in a comprehensive treatment programme in patients with conversion disorder of the motor type. *Psychotherapy and Psychosomatics, 71,* 66–76.

Roelofs, K., & Spinhoven, P. (2007). Trauma and medically unexplained Symptoms: Towards an integration of cognitive and neuro-biological accounts. *Clinical Psychology Review 27,* 798–820.

Slater E.T., & Glithero, E. (1965). A follow-up of patients diagnosed as suffering from "hysteria." *Journal of Psychosomatic Research, 9,* 9–13.

Spence, S.A., Crimlisk, H.L., Cope, H., Ron, M.A., & Grasby, P.M. (2000). Discrete neurophysiological correlates in prefrontal cortex during hysterical and feigned disorder of movement. *Lancet, 355,* 1243–1244.

Vuilleumier, P. (2005). Hysterical conversion and brain function. *Progress in Brain Research, 150,* 309–329.

World Health Organization (W.H.O., ICD 10, 1992). *International classification of disorders.* Clinical descriptions and diagnostic guidelines. Chapter 5: Mental and Behavioral Disorders, Diagnostic Criteria and Diagnostic Guidelines. Geneva: World Health Organization, Division of Mental Health.

Ziv, I., Djaldetti, R., Zoldan, Y., Avraham, M., & Melamed, E. (1998). Diagnosis of "non-organic" limb paresis by a novel objective motor assessment: The quantitative Hoover's test. *Journal of Neurology, 245,* 797–802.

KARIN ROELOFS
PHILIP SPINHOVEN
Leiden University, The Netherlands

CONVULSANTS

Convulsants are substances that induce seizure-like paroxysmal behaviors by producing patterns of electrical activity in the brain that resemble those seen in human epilepsy. Epilepsy is characterized by recurring episodes in which the electrical activity of many thousands of neurons becomes abnormally elevated and pathologically synchronized. This discharge interrupts normal brain function and leads, in some forms of epilepsy, to alterations in behavior (seizures). Seizures come in many varieties, ranging from brief, barely detectable losses of consciousness in what are called *absence* or *petit mal epilepsies*, to uncontrollable tonic-clonic contractions of large muscle groups in the so-called *grand mal epilepsies*. The behavioral manifestations and severity of the seizure reflect primarily the size and localization of the abnormal electrical discharge.

One remarkable aspect of the human epilepsies in the diversity of underlying etiological factors, including perinatal trauma, brain infection, drug and alcohol withdrawal, tumors, and stroke. Our current understanding of epilepsy is that epileptiform brain activity and the behavioral seizures produced by that activity arise as the symptom of some underlying brain pathology. Perhaps it is not surprising, therefore, that an incredibly diverse group of chemical substances can produce convulsions when given centrally or applied directly to brain tissue.

The study of the mechanism of action of convulsants has led to the formulation of one of the more enduring hypotheses of the generation of epilepsy (Traub & Miles, 1991). There seems to be a delicate balance between the strength of inhibitory and excitatory synaptic transmission in the brain. Any disturbance in this balance that favors excitation will lead to the uncontrolled spread of excitation between cells so that their discharge become rapidly synchronous. In this sense, epilepsy is a disease of population of cells, rather than individual cells.

In fact, not all brain regions are equally likely to be identified as sites of epileptiform discharge in patients, and not all brain regions are equally sensitive to convulsants. It is thought that the ability of a convulsant to trigger seizures in a given brain region depends on a number of factors. First, the convulsant's appropriate target must be present. The convulsant strychnine, for example, will be inactive in nuclei lacking glycinergic inhibition. Second, the necessary neuronal circuitry must be present. In particular, there must be local excitatory axon collaterals so that excitation can spread between cells. These connections are particularly prominent between pyramidal cells in the hippocampal formation and neocortex—two regions that are highly sensitive to most convulsants and in which epileptic discharge is typically initiated in human epilepsy patients. Finally, some output connections capable of influencing behavior and/or consciousness must be present.

Several of the most widely used and better understood convulsants are listed in Table 1 (for reviews see Fister, 1989; Loscher & Schmidt, 1988), and they have been classified by their actions on the balance of excitatory and inhibitory synaptic transmission, when known. It should be noted that the patterns of seizures and electrical abnormalities are not the same for all convulsants and may vary for any one convulsant depending on where and how the substance is applied.

Convulsants That Decrease Inhibition

Much of our understanding of the cellular basis of epilepsy comes from the application of convulsants to the brain, in whole animal experiments and, more recently, to isolated slices of brain tissue maintained *ex vivo*. Penicillin, the first widely used convulsant, is a weak antagonist of the receptors for the predominant brain inhibitory neurotransmitter Υ-aminobutyric acid (GABA). More potent antagonists, such as bicuculline and the ion channel-block picrotoxin, are now more typically used. Seizures and epileptiform discharge can also be elicited by blocking the synthesis or release of GABA. In addition, substances active at modulatory sites on GABA receptors can also exert convulsant activity, such as inverse agonists of the benzodiazepine receptor.

Convulsants That Increase Excitation

Substances that directly or indirectly increase excitation are powerful convulsants. For example, application of saline containing a lower than physiological concentration of $Mg2+$ relieves the normal block of the ion channels gated by N-methyl-D-aspartate (NMDA) – preferring excitatory amino acid receptors, and thus considerably enhances the synaptic excitation of cells. Application of kainic acid, an agonist of non-NMDA excitatory amino acid receptors, is also widely used to trigger seizures in whole animals, by injection either into the cerebral vesicles or directly into the tissue. The release of endogenous excitatory amino acids can also be triggered by increasing the excitability of neurons with substances that block repolarizing $K+$ conductances. Neurons have perhaps hundreds of such $K+$ conductances, and numerous antagonists of these channels are effective convulsants, including tetraethylammonium, 4-amminopyridine, and various naturally occurring peptide toxins. Finally, modulators of central cholinergic synaptic function are also employed as convulsants, including direct agonists such as pilocarpine as well as acetylcholinesterase inhibitors, and are believed to act by increasing neuronal excitability.

Other Convulsants

Although the mechanism of action of these convulsants fits well with the hypothesized balance of synaptic

Table 1. Widely Used Convulsants and Their Mechanism of Action

Class of Action	Target System	Mechanism of Action	Examples
Decrease inhibition	1. g-Aminobutyric acid 2. Glycine	a. receptor antagonists b. Synthesis inhibitors c. Benzodiazepine receptor d. Release inhibitors a. Receptor antagonists	penicillin, bicuculline, picrotoxin, methoxypyridoxine, isoniazid, 3-mecaptoproioncin acid inverse agnoists opioid peptides strychnine
Enhance excitation	1. Excitatory amino acids (e.g., glutamate) 2. Acetylcholine	a. NMDA receptors b. non-NMDA receptors c. Potassium channel blockers a. Receptor agonists b. Cholinesterase inhibitors	Magnesium-free saline Kainic acid Tetraethylammonium, 4-aminopyridine, various peptide toxins piolcarpine soman
Unknown		a. Neurotoxins b. Injury/Trauma c. CNS Stimulant	cholera toxin, tetanus toxin alumina hydroxide, cobalt p entylenetetrazol

excitation and inhibition in epilepsy-prone brain regions, it is less well understood how other important convulsants exert their effects. Cholera toxins is an activator of adenylate cyclase and may therefore trigger seizures by mimicking any of the many cellular actions of cAMP and cAMP-dependent protein kinase, including reduction of K+ conductances and facilitation of transmitter release. Tetanus toxin inhibits the release of both excitatory and inhibitory neurotransmitters. Epileptiform activity elicited by focal application of alumina hydroxide or cobalt has been used as a model for posttraumatic epilepsy, although the mechanisms underlying seizure generation remain unclear. Pentylenetetrazol is a powerful and widely used convulsant whose mechanism of action is also unknown.

REFERENCES

Fischer, R. S. (1989). Animal models of the epilepsies. *Brain Research Reviews, 14*, 245–278.

Loscher, W., & Schmidt, D. (1988). Which animal models should be used in the search for new antiepileptic drugs? A proposal based on experimental and clinical observations. *Epilepsy Research, 2*, 145–181.

Traub, R. D., & Miles, R. (1991). *Neuronal networks of the hippocampus.* New York: Cambridge University Press.

SCOTT M. THOMPSON
University of Maryland

See also: **Anticonvulsant Medications; Epilepsy**

CONVULSIVE THERAPY (See Electroconvulsive Therapy)

COPING BEHAVIOR

Coping refers to the thoughts and behaviors people use to deal with stressful situations. Although most psychologists limit the concept of coping to conscious and intentional efforts to manage stressful encounters, some theorists have argued that more automatic and unintentional ways of dealing with stressful circumstances should also be included within the coping rubric.

The concept of coping plays an important role in theories of human vulnerability and resilience: Why does adversity lead some people to become depressed, whereas others seem to weather the same adversity or perhaps even thrive in its aftermath? Coping is also intimately related to theories of emotion. Since one goal of coping efforts is to ameliorate negative emotions and promote positive emotions in the face of stress, this aspect of coping can be thought of as emotion regulation in stressful circumstances. Some psychologists have suggested that both coping and emotion regulation are components of self-regulation.

The numerous theoretical frameworks advanced to explain coping processes are for the most part variants of two broad coping models. One model is Lazarus and Folkman's (1984) distinction between efforts to resolve or reduce the threat, called problem-focused coping, and efforts to modulate event-related emotional distress, referred to as emotion-focused coping. The other model distinguishes coping efforts that are directed toward the perceived source of stress, which is approach coping, and those efforts that are intended to distance the person from the source of stress, which is avoidance coping (Moos, Brennan, Fondacaro, & Moos, 1990).

Although problem-focused versus emotion-focused and approach versus avoidance are the most widely accepted coping categories, not all coping theorists agree that they represent the best guiding frameworks for understanding the structure of coping. For example, Skinner, Edge, Altman, and Sherwood (2003) concluded a review of the coping literature by arguing that single function models, such as problem-focused versus emotion-focused, miss the fact that any particular way of coping typically serves many functions, and topological models such as approach versus avoidance fail to capture coping's multidimensional nature. Instead, Skinner and colleagues urged investigators to consider multidimensional, multifunctional coping categories like accommodation, which includes cognitive efforts to adapt to the situation through such strategies as positive reframing and distraction.

Although the preponderance of coping research has focused on adults, there has been increased interest in the importance of developmental transitions for understanding the coping process of children and adolescents. Skinner and Zimmer-Gembeck (2007), for example, note that cognitive coping does not emerge until middle childhood, as evidenced by the appearance of distraction and problem solving. Adolescents add to their coping armamentarium the ability to guide their coping strategies on the basis of long-term goals rather than immediate needs.

Coping Resources and Coping Strategies

Taylor and Stanton (2007) identified four coping resources—optimism, mastery, self-esteem, and social support—that are antecedents of specific coping strategies and also have direct effects on psychological and physical health. These coping resources appear to predispose the person to appraise stressful circumstances as less threatening and more controllable through personal action, which in turn initiates approach-related coping.

Although coping resources are associated with approach-oriented coping strategies such as positive reappraisal of the stressor, coping strategies are not simply proxies for coping resources. Rather, as Taylor and Stanton (2007) note, the available evidence suggests that coping mediates the link between coping resources and adaptational outcomes during a stressful encounter. There is also some prospective evidence suggesting that avoidance coping may actually generate life stressors, which in turn places individuals using these strategies at risk for physical and emotional distress (Hammen, 2006; Holahan, Moos, Holahan, Brennan, & Schutte, 2005).

Fit between Situational Demands and Coping Strategy Selection

Both Lazarus's (Lazarus & Folkman, 1984) transactional model of coping and social-cognitive theories of personality (e.g., Mischel, 1973) underscore the adaptive value of flexible thought and action in response to changing situational demands. Indeed, a cornerstone of the transactional model is that coping is a dynamic process that requires adaptation of coping efforts across stressful situations (Tennen, Affleck, Armeli, & Carney, 2000). One important indicator of coping flexibility is a person's ability to ensure a "fit" between the demands of a stressful circumstance and her/his coping response. Thus, problem-focused coping should be more effective in more controllable situations in which the situation can actually be altered, whereas emotion-focused coping should be more effective in situations that cannot be changed. This connection between types of coping and types of situations has been referred to as the goodness-of-fit hypothesis (Terry & Hynes, 1998).

Drinking to Cope: An Example of Maladaptive Avoidance Coping

Several theoretical frameworks posit that, for some people, alcohol consumption is involved in the process of coping with stressful encounters. Negative reinforcement models view alcohol use as a coping strategy that allows the individual immediate escape from an aversive emotional state. On the other hand, Volpicelli's (1987) endorphin compensation hypothesis (ECH) predicts that drinking should actually decrease during stressful periods and increase only after the stress is resolved. According to the ECH, coping with aversive situations results at first in short-term increases followed by deficits in endorphin after the stressful situation has subsided. Individuals learn to compensate for this reduced endorphinergic activity by consuming alcohol to stimulate opiate receptor activity. Muraven and Baumeister's (2000) self-regulation model posits that the demands of coping can deplete self-control resources, resulting in a lack of self-control that leaves people vulnerable to drinking beyond their normal limits. These competing models capture the complexities of studying coping and emotional regulation as they unfold in daily life.

Stress, Coping, and Positive Emotions

Coping theory and research have focused primarily on coping in relation to negative emotional states. Recently, however, psychologists have discovered that certain coping strategies may help individuals maintain positive emotions during a prolonged stressful encounter. Studies of individuals with debilitating illnesses, people who have recently lost a loved one, and caregivers of chronically ill partners or family members reveal that despite the experience of painful negative emotions, positive emotions actually prevail, and certain coping strategies, such as reframing the threat, appear to be more closely related to positive emotions than to negative emotions (Folkman & Moskowitz, 2000).

Creating Positive Meaning as a Way of Coping

Several longitudinal studies demonstrate that people who cope with major life challenges by creating positive meaning or construing benefits from the threatening situation go on to have more positive health outcomes. In one such study acutely ill newborns went on to achieve higher developmental test scores as toddlers if their mothers had coped with the child's initial hospitalization by finding benefits in it (Affleck, Tennen, & Rowe, 1991). In another study, men who coped with their first heart attack by finding benefits in the situation were in better cardiac health eight years later and were less likely to suffer a second heart attack (Affleck, Tennen, Croog, & Levine, 1987). Similarly, individuals who coped with a disaster by deriving something positive from the incident fared better than those who did not (McMillen, Smith, & Fisher, 1997). It remains for investigators to distinguish positive meaning and benefit finding as a spontaneous response from the more intentional efforts most theorists view as the hallmark of coping.

Sex Differences in Coping

Several theories in areas of biological development, sex-role socialization, and role theory address how women and men cope differently with stressful encounters. Although popular conceptions of gender-based coping differences assert that men engage in more problem-focused and avoidant coping than women, a meta-analytic review by Tames, Janicki, and Helgeson's (2002) provided no evidence of sex differences in problem-focused coping and only modest evidence that men rely more than women on avoidant strategies. The sex difference that emerged most clearly was that women seek emotional social support more than men. For most other coping strategies, the effect sizes varied across studies, indicating the need to evaluate potential effect moderators. Indeed, across the studies reviewed, Tames and colleagues found that the nature of the stressor was clearly a moderator of sex differences in coping.

As Yet Unfulfilled Promises in the Study of Coping

Although coping is among the most widely studied topics in psychology, the yield from this vast area of inquiry has been somewhat disappointing. For example, we still do not really know how coping operates, and for quite a few coping strategies we do not know if or when coping is helpful. In part, the relatively meager yield from

coping research reflects the field's excessive reliance on coping questionnaires, which require individuals to recall how they coped with a particular stressor (Coyne & Gottlieb, 1996). It is now clear that recalled coping bears only a modest resemblance to coping as it actually occurs (Ptacek, Smith, Espe, & Raffety, 1994). Another problem is that relatively few research investigations have examined coping repeatedly over time. And coping as it is now studied involves people's efforts to deal with events that have already occurred or that are now occurring. With few exceptions (e.g., Aspinwall & Taylor, 1997), the coping literature has been silent regarding people's proactive coping efforts to prevent or anticipate stressors. Despite this rather slow progress, psychologists retain a continued fascination with the concept of coping.

REFERENCES

Affleck, G., Tennen, H., Croog, S., & Levine, S. (1987). Causal attributions, perceived benefits, and morbidity following a heart attack: An eight-year study. *Journal of Consulting and Clinical Psychology, 55,* 29–35.

Affleck, G., Tennen, H., Rowe, J. (1991). *Infants in crisis: How parents cope with newborn intensive care and its aftermath.* New York: Springer-Verlag.

Aspinwall, L. G., & Taylor, S. E. (1997). A stitch in time: Self-regulation and proactive coping. *Psychological Bulletin, 121,* 417–436.

Coyne, J. C., & Gottlieb, B. H. (1996). The mismeasure of coping by checklist. *Journal of Personality, 64,* 959–992.

Folkman, S., & Moskowitz, J. T. (2000). Positive affect and the other side of coping. *American Psychologist, 55,* 647–654.

Hammen, C. (2006). Stress generation in depression: Reflections on origins, research, and future directions. *Journal of Clinical Psychology, 62,* 1065–1082.

Holahan, C. J., Moos, R. H., Holahan, C. K., Brennan, P. L., & Schutte, K. K. (2005). Stress generation, avoidance coping, and depressive symptoms: A 10-year model. *Journal of Consulting and Clinical Psychology, 73,* 658–666.

Lazarus, R. S., & Folkman, S. (1984). *Stress, appraisal and coping.* New York: Springer.

McMillen, J. C., Smith, E. M., & Fisher, R. (1997). Perceived benefit and mental health after three types of disaster. *Journal of Consulting and Clinical Psychology, 65,* 733–739.

Mischel, W. (1973). Toward a cognitive social learning reconceptualization of personality. *Psychological Review, 80,* 252–283.

Moos, R. H., Brennan, P. L., Fondacaro, M. R., & Moos, B. S. (1990). Approach and avoidance coping responses among older problem and nonproblem drinkers. *Psychology and Aging, 5,* 31–40.

Muraven, M., & Baumeister, R. F. (2000). Self-regulation and depletion of limited resources: Does self-control resemble a muscle? *Psychological Bulletin, 126,* 247–259.

Ptacek, J. T., Smith, R. E., Espe, K., & Raffety, B. (1994). Limited correspondence between daily coping reports and retrospective coping recall. *Psychological Assessment, 6,* 41–49.

Skinner, E. A., Edge, K., Altman, J., & Sherwood, H. (2003). Searching for the structure of coping: A review and critique of category systems for classifying ways of coping. *Psychological Bulletin, 129*, 216–269.

Skinner, E. A., & Zimmer-Gembeck, M. J. (2007). The development of coping. *Annual Review of Psychology, 58*, 119–144.

Tames, L. K., Janicki, D., & Helgeson, V. S. (2002). Sex differences in coping behavior: A meta-analytic review and an examination of relative coping. *Personality and Social Psychology Review, 6*, 2–30.

Taylor, S. E., & Stanton, A. L. (2007). Coping resources, coping processes, and mental health. *Annual Review of Clinical Psychology, 3*, 377–401.

Tennen, H., Affleck, G., Armeli, S., & Carney, M. A. (2000). A daily process approach to coping: Linking theory, research and practice. *American Psychologist, 55*, 626–636.

Terry, D., & Hynes, G. J. (1998). Adjustment to a low-control situation: Re-examining the role of coping responses. *Journal of Personality and Social Psychology, 74*, 1078–1092.

Volpicelli, J. (1987). Uncontrollable events and alcohol drinking. *British Journal of Addiction, 82*, 381–392.

SUGGESTED READINGS

Aldwin, C. M. (2007). *Stress, coping, and development: An integrative perspective* (2nd ed.). New York: Guilford Press.

Austenfeld, J. L., & Stanton, A. L. (2004). Coping through emotional approach: A new look at emotion, coping, and health outcomes. *Journal of Personality, 72*, 1335–1364.

Carver, C. S., Scheier, M. F., & Weintraub, J. K. (1989). Assessing coping strategies: A theoretically based approach. *Journal of Personality and Social Psychology, 56*, 267–283.

Folkman, S., & Moskowitz, J. T. (2004). Coping: Pitfalls and promise. *Annual Review of Psychology, 55*, 745–774.

HOWARD TENNEN
MARK D. LITT
University of Connecticut

See also: Emotion Regulation; Stress Consequences

COPING SKILLS TRAINING

Cognitive-behavioral therapy is among the most influential theories in psychology today. The foundation of this theory is the idea that the person plays a key role in controlling his or her own emotional well-being and health. According to cognitive behavioral theory, adaptational outcomes are in part a function of thoughts, feelings, and behaviors that ameliorate or exacerbate psychological distress. To the extent that maladaptive thoughts, feelings, and behaviors are learned, they can also be unlearned or replaced.

A significant determinant of psychological health is stress. Sources of stress may be physical, such as illness or injury, or psychological, the result of interpersonal or intrapersonal tensions. It is well documented, for example, that stress may heighten anxiety and can even exacerbate chronic illnesses like diabetes and hypertension. Lazarus and Folkman (1984) argued, however, that one's efforts to cope with stressful encounters help determine the impact of stress on emotional well-being and physical health. Coping refers to the cognitive and behavioral efforts that are made to manage physical and psychological stress. Coping often involves the use of specific skills, that is, adaptive thoughts and behaviors that are brought to bear in response to stress. Many of the interventions developed in the field of cognitive-behavioral psychology involve helping individuals develop new coping skills to manage threats to their well-being. Examples include the teaching of relaxation or meditation to help control anxiety and cognitive reappraisal strategies to help manage depression (Beck, Rush, Shaw, & Emory, 1979).

Assessment of Coping Skills

Different coping skills are called for in different circumstances. A program of coping skills training should, therefore, begin with an assessment of the circumstances under which the distressing symptoms occur and the responses typically made by the patient to manage the distress. An evaluation is then conducted to determine what skills the patient needs to acquire and what maladaptive cognitive and behavioral habits need to be replaced.

General Coping Questionnaires

One way to assess a person's coping abilities is through the use of questionnaires that assess a person's responses in a general way. Individuals are asked, for example, how they typically respond when confronting difficult or stressful events in their lives. They are then presented with a list of possible actions they might take, and they are asked to indicate how frequently they might take a given action in that situation. Both effective and ineffective responses may be endorsed, highlighting the patient's strength and weaknesses. A number of these questionnaires (e.g., the COPE; Carver, Scheier, & Weintraub, 1989) are currently in use.

Problem Specific Checklists

The general coping questionnaires have a number of limitations for clinical use. They tend to be long and tedious to complete, and their general nature limits their utility for assessing responses to specific problems. Problem-specific coping inventories are therefore used more often in clinical situations. The *Coping Strategies Scale* (Litt, Kadde, Cooney, & Kabela, 2003), for instance, was developed to assess coping with relapse situations in treated alcoholics. Because the coping abilities assessed are specific to the problems at hand, these checklists are clinically useful.

In-Vivo Assessment of Coping

Despite the improved specificity offered by problem-specific coping checklists, they still require the patient to make generalizations about his or her responses to stressful situations. These generalizations may be affected by quirk of memory, or they may be biased toward more active or adaptive responses. In order to determine more precisely what patients are thinking and doing in response to stressful situations, clinicians may turn to assessment methods that are more closely tied to the situation of interest. One way this is done is through self-monitoring (Hollon & Kendall, 1981). In this procedure, a patient is asked to complete a worksheet one or more times per day or per week and make a record of instances of the thoughts, feelings, or behaviors or interest. The record includes the day, time, and location when the incident occurred as well as what the person thought, felt, and did at the time. Depending on the nature of the problem, self-monitoring may be carried out very frequently (e.g., multiple times per day for the patients with some types of anxiety disorders). In recent years the self-monitoring process has become increasingly automated and more accurate through the use of handheld computers and cell phones that prompt the person to self-monitor and record the responses.

Training Coping Skills

The assessment process should indicate to both the therapist and the patient what situations are most likely to elicit distress and the adaptive and maladaptive responses the patient makes in those situations. The purpose of coping skills training is to further develop adaptive responses and replace maladaptive ones.

Problem Solving

Problem solving is both a coping skill and a coping skills training method. Problem solving not only provides a way to determine what specific coping skills one needs in order to function more effectively, but it also provides a template for approaching new and different problems in the future. This systematic approach to problem solving started with the work of D'Zurilla and Goldfried (1971), who noted that "our daily lives are replete with situational problems which we must solve in order to maintain an adequate level of effective functioning" (p. 107). Their approach involved five stages: (1) general orientation or "self," (2) problem

definition and formulation, (3) generation of alternatives, (4) decision making, and (5) verification. The first step involves emphasizing that stress-related problems are manageable by the patient. Problem definition stresses identification of the problem and stating it in terms of specific situations or behaviors. Alternative solutions are generated through the use of techniques such as "brainstorming" in which multiple solutions are entertained regardless of their apparent practicality. Possible solutions are generated and ranked, and a decision is made as to which one(s) to try. Once an approach has been tried, the therapist and patient evaluate its effectiveness. Effective solutions may be enhanced, and ineffective ones are discarded in favor of other possibilities to be tried and evaluated. If all alternatives fail, the problem solving process is repeated.

Imaginal Coping Skills Training

Imaginal techniques allow the patient and therapist to test, or rehearse, skills in a controlled setting prior to attempting them in real life (Cautela, 1973). A typical example involves preparing a patient who has a fear of flying to take a trip on an airplane. Coping skills such as cognitive reconceptualization (i.e., efforts to view the stressful situation in a way that allows some control), meditation, or relaxation are tried while the patient is under the supervision of the therapist. As the therapist describes a stress-evoking scene to the patient, he may be instructed to imagine relaxing and asserting personal control. This process may be repeated over several sessions until the patient is proficient.

In-Vivo Coping Skills Training

In-vivo skills training, or behavioral rehearsal, involves taking the patient through all aspects of a stressful situation during training sessions in the actual stress-evoking setting. In the patient with a fear of flying, a tour of an airplane might be conducted in order to help the person develop coping resources (e.g., relaxation skills and cognitive reappraisal) in a realistic context. In-vivo skills training may follow imaginal skills training, or may be conducted independently.

Role-Playing

Role-playing is a type of behavioral rehearsal technique that involves the patient and the therapist assuming roles for the purpose of generating and practicing coping skills to be used later in real-world settings. Role-playing may be used for two purposes. First, the patient and therapist may assume each other's role. As the therapist discusses the problem at hand, the patient works to generate coping solutions. Because the patient is the one generating these solutions, they are more likely to be acceptable and practiced. Alternatively, the patient may act as himself while the therapist may act as someone else in the patient's life with whom the patient must associate. The therapist and patient then act out a stressful situation and the patient generates ways to manage it. This process is especially useful when the situation involves conflicts with another person that exacerbate a symptom such as anxiety. The roles can be reversed and the therapist may model adaptive coping behaviors for the patient to emulate.

Motivational Interviewing

Motivational interviewing is a directive counseling approach intended to help individuals resolve ambivalence about making behavioral changes (Miller & Rollnick, 2002). The process involves having the patient think carefully about his or her motivations for adopting or not adopting behavior change and to encourage the patient to value the benefits of change. Motivational interviewing is based upon four principles: (1) express empathy to create a climate for change by building a bond of trust; (2) develop discrepancies between the patient's goals and her behaviors; (3) acknowledge the patient's reluctance to change; and (4) support the patient's sense of personal competence or ability to change. Although no explicit coping skills training takes place in such a procedure, motivational interviewing is intended to set the stage for the patient to employ previously developed skills and competencies.

Homework and Enactive Learning

Coping skills practice assignments that are completed outside the treatment setting, in the patient's own work, social, and home environments, are essential to the development of effective coping skills. Skills practice assignments, commonly referred to as "homework," provide a means to extend the therapy session into the patient's real world and to practice the skills developed in therapy. Additionally, by practicing coping skills in real settings, the patient is given a chance to discover what works and what does not work and then discuss the experience with the therapist. This opportunity for active learning should build skills more quickly and efficiently than would be the case if skills were only discussed in the therapy session.

The development of improved coping skills forms the basis for improved adaptation to stressful circumstances and better control over symptoms such as depression or anxiety. A challenge for the field will be to improve the individualized assessment of coping skills and to train those skills most needed by the individual.

REFERENCES

Beck, A. T., Rush, A. J., Shaw, B. F. & Emery, G. (1979). *Cognitive therapy of depression*. New York: Guilford Press.

Carver, C. S., Scheier, M. F., & Weintraub, J. K. (1989). Assessing coping strategies: A theoretically based approach. *Journal of Personality and Social Psychology, 56*, 267–283.

Cautela, J. R. (1973). Covert processes and behavior modification. *Journal of Nervous & Mental Disease, 157*, 27–36.

D'Zurilla, T. J., & Goldfried, M. R. (1971). Problem solving and behavior modification. *Journal of Abnormal Psychology, 78*, 107–126.

Folkman, S., & Lazarus, R. S. (1980). An analysis of coping in a middle-aged community sample. *Journal of Health and Social Behavior, 21*, 219–239.

Hollon, S. D., & Kendall, P. C. (1981). In-vivo assessment techniques for cognitive-behavioral processes. In P. C. Kendall & S. D. Hollon (Eds.), *Assessment strategies of cognitive-behavioral interventions* (pp. 319–362). New York: Academic Press.

Lazarus, R. S., & Folkman, S. (1984). *Stress, appraisal, and coping*. New York: Springer.

Litt, M. D., Kadden, R. M., Cooney, N. L., & Kabela, E. (2003). Coping skills and treatment outcomes in cognitive-behavioral and interactional group therapy for alcoholism. *Journal of Consulting and Clinical Psychology, 71*, 118–128.

Miller, W. R., & Rollnick, S. (2002). *Motivational interviewing: Preparing people to change* (2nd ed.). New York: Guilford Press.

SUGGESTED READINGS

Beck, J. S. (1995). *Cognitive therapy: Basics and beyond*. New York: Guilford Press.

Hollon, S. D., & Beck, A. T. (2004). Cognitive and cognitive behavioral therapies. In M. J. Lambert (Ed.), *Bergin and Garfield's handbook of psychotherapy and behavior change* (5th ed. pp. 447–492). Hoboken, NJ: John Wiley & Sons.

Monti, P. M., Kadden, R. M., Rohsenow, D. J., Cooney, N. L., & Abrams, D. B. (2002). *Treating alcohol dependence: A coping skills training guide* (2nd ed.). New York: Guilford Press.

MARK D. LITT
HOWARD TENNEN
University of Connecticut

See also: **Coping Behavior; Problem Solving**

CORRECTIONAL PSYCHOLOGY

Psychologists have a long and storied history within American corrections. Although psychologists' roles were originally aimed at institutional management and correctional rehabilitation, over the course of time services have increasingly focused on treatment of serious mental illness (SMI) and emotional crises. For many years, correctional mental health services were often limited to psychopharmacological treatments; however, this is no longer the case, and psychologists are now in significant demand. With their versatile skill set (e.g., assessment, treatment, behavioral programming, and research), psychologists are the most frequently employed mental health professionals in correctional settings (Camp & Camp, 1999). Psychologists have become so essential to correctional facilities that the field has become a leading employer of clinical and counseling psychologists.

For the last several decades, constitutional litigation has required a focus on treatment of "serious medical needs" that were typically defined as SMI. Services for inmates with serious psychiatric needs have typically included the following: universal screening for suicide risk; mental health evaluations; specialized housing; suicide prevention services including, for example, crisis intervention and special watches; special housing for offenders who are unable to tolerate general population; group and/or individual psychotherapies; and other productive out-of-cell time such as activities therapies. These services are necessarily available to most inmates and can be referred to as "basic mental health services" (Morgan, 2003). The primary force driving this shift in focus was a constitutional mandate that correctional systems (including jails, prisons, and juvenile institutions) may not be "deliberately indifferent to serious medical needs," specifically including mental health needs. Generally, these serious mental health needs included serious mental illnesses such as schizophrenia, bipolar disorder, and major depression (frequently referred to as "priority populations" in mental health systems), and also suicide prevention. Resulting policy necessitated the general availability of basic mental health services for treating these serious problems (Cohen & Dvoskin, 1992).

In addition to constitutionally mandated roles, psychologists employ and help develop good public policy aimed at cost-effectively attending to public safety. Increasingly and most importantly, these activities include correctional rehabilitation (i.e., rehabilitative services; Morgan, 2003) aimed at reducing recidivism and increasing offenders' desistance from crime. Foremost among rehabilitative services are psychosocial treatment programs aimed at reducing criminogenic risk factors (i.e., dynamic factors that are significantly correlated with increased risk for future criminal activity; Andrews & Bonta, 2006) to include: drug and alcohol abuse treatment programs; cognitive change programs (i.e., programs aimed at reducing criminal cognitions); and programs aimed at reducing associations with criminal others. Many states have also developed specialized, psychologically based treatment programs for special needs offenders (e.g., sex offenders, violent offenders, offenders with SMI), as well as community reentry and prerelease treatment programs. Because of their specialized skill set, including program evaluation, psychologists remain in high demand to manage these programs.

It is important to note that drug and alcohol disorders were historically treated as unrelated to SMI; however, that is no longer the case. Research has clearly demonstrated that a high percentage of offenders with SMI have co-occurring substance use disorders (Peters, Matthews, & Dvoskin, 2005). Although drug and alcohol treatment programs have not been constitutionally mandated, when these disorders coexist with SMI, services are no longer optional. Finally, integrated treatment of substance abuse and SMI will soon become the standard of practice for inmates with serious co-occurring mental health and substance use disorders.

In addition, as more is learned about correctional psychology, it is becoming increasingly clear that more attention must be paid to the treatment of aftereffects of trauma among offenders. Originally aimed at female offenders and juveniles, these efforts now include all offenders, regardless of gender or age.

In addition to providing services to inmates, psychologists typically assume roles that are essential to the safe and efficient running of the jail or prison facility (Dvoskin, Spiers, & Pitt, 2003). Often, these roles include service on various committees. Classification committees make important decisions about levels of security or custody, assignment of offenders to various correctional programs, and in some cases, assignment to segregated housing. This latter function should include attention to the possible psychologically deleterious effects of segregation upon some inmates, especially inmates with SMI and those who have been in segregation for long periods of time. Disciplinary committees, which are responsible for determining punishments when institutional rules and regulations are violated, may also include psychologists as members or occasional consultants. Psychologists are also frequently requested to serve or consult with personnel screening and selection. Finally, with training in research methodologies and data analytic skills, psychologists' expertise is often requested for program development and evaluation committees, especially when specialized accreditation is sought.

Correctional Mental Health Treatment Programs and Services

Universal Screening

It is now considered a mandate to screen every new admission to determine if he or she presents an imminent risk of suicide (see, for example, Steadman, Robbins, Islam, & Osher, 2007), especially in jails, because of their notoriously high rate of suicide. Originally instituted on a statewide basis in New York, these screening programs, in conjunction with a comprehensive suicide prevention plan for each institution, have been shown to reduce jail suicides by about two-thirds (Cox & Morschauser, 1997). Recently, this screening has been expanded to serve a second purpose, to identify SMI offenders who are likely to need basic mental health services during their period of incarceration. Offenders who screen positive for suicide risk are typically placed on suicide watch, often with special precautions based on initial risk level (e.g., provided limited property) to ensure their safety until they can be examined and assessed by a qualified mental health professional, often a psychologist.

Crisis Response and Post-Admission Referral

Inmates may develop mental illness or suicidal crises at any time during their incarceration, or these risks may have been missed during the initial screening. It is, therefore, equally important to have a system for timely referral to mental health services. Correctional psychologists often take the lead in teaching correctional officers how to identify (at a basic level) inmates who may pose a possible risk of suicide or require mental health services so that they can be assessed and, if necessary, treated by mental health professionals.

"Outpatient" Treatment

Many inmates with SMI are able to live in the general population, as long as they are afforded access to basic mental health services. Specifically, these inmates will require the basic mental health services already summarized, as well as specialized services targeting SMI such as medication management, supportive case management, and targeted psychosocial interventions (e.g., mental illness awareness).

Residential Treatment

Of course, some inmates are so disabled by mental illness that they are simply unable to live safely among the general population. Studies have shown that inmates with SMI are at risk for institutional disciplinary offenses (James & Glaze, 2006), as well as assault at the hands of predatory inmates (Abramsky & Fellner, 2003). In some cases, special housing is required for relatively brief periods to address crises. In other cases, offenders may be so persistently disabled that they will need special mental health housing for long periods of time, or perhaps even for the duration of their sentence.

Discharge Planning

For many years, correctional administrators believed their duties to inmates with mental illness began and ended at the institution's door. Recent case law suggests that courts are increasingly likely to view discharge planning as part of the service that is owed to offenders who are in custody. The breadth and extent of this duty are not yet clear, but it will undoubtedly include some means to obtain necessary medication until an offender can reasonably be expected to obtain it through community resources. In many cases, continuity of services will be attained through referral and/or formally developed liaisons with community mental health agencies; however, some states now include mental health services to parolees as a state-run service.

In conclusion, psychologists play an important role in the daily operation of correctional institutions. Whether providing assessment, treatment, intervention development, institutional consultation, or program evaluation needs, psychologists are uniquely qualified and highly coveted service providers. In fact, with high rates of SMI and policy mandates for effective services (to include both rehabilitative and basic mental health services), psychologist's are the preferred mental health professional to serve the offender and the correctional system (Camp & Camp, 1999).

REFERENCES

Abramsky, S., & Fellner, J. (2003). *Ill equipped: U.S. prisons and offenders with mental illness*. New York: Human Rights Watch.

Andrews, D. A., & Bonta, J. (2006). *The psychology of criminal conduct* (3rd ed.). Cincinnati, OH: Anderson Publishing.

Camp, C. G., & Camp, G. M. (1999). *The corrections yearbook 1999: Adult corrections*. Middletown, CT: Criminal Justice Institute.

Cohen, F., & Dvoskin, J. A. (1992). Inmates with mental disorders: A guide to law and practice. *Mental & Physical Disability Law Reporter, 16*, 3 and 4.

Cox, J. F., & Morschauser, P. C. (1997). A solution to the problem of jail suicide. *Journal of Crisis Intervention and Suicide Prevention, 18*(4), 178–84.

Dvoskin, J. A., Spiers, E. M., & Pitt, S. E. (2003). Mental health professionals as institutional consultants and problem-solvers. In T. Fagan & R. K. Ax (Eds.), *Correctional mental health handbook* (pp. 251–271). Thousand Oaks, CA: Sage.

James, D. J., & Glaze, L. E. (2006). *Mental health problems of prison and jail inmates* (Bureau of Justice Statistics Special Report, NCJ 213600). Washington, DC: Department of Justice.

Morgan, R. D. (2003). Basic mental health services: Services and issues. In T. Fagan & R. K. Ax (Eds.), *Correctional mental health handbook* (pp. 59–71). Thousand Oaks, CA: Sage.

Peters, R. H., Matthews, C. O., & Dvoskin, J. A. (2005). Treatment in prisons and jails. In J. H. Lowinson, P. Ruiz, R. B., Millman, & J. G. Langrod (Eds.), *Substance abuse: A comprehensive textbook* (3rd ed.). (pp. 707–722). Baltimore, MD: Williams & Wilkins.

Steadman, H. J., Scott, J. E., Osher, F. C., Agnese, T. K., & Robbins, P. C. (2007). Validation of the brief jail mental health screen. *Psychiatric Services, 56*, 816–822.

SUGGESTED READINGS

Ax, R. K., & Fagan, T. J. (2007). *Corrections, mental health, and social policy: International perspectives*. Springfield, IL: Charles C. Thomas.

Dvoskin J. A., Spiers E. M., & Brodsky S. L. (in press.). Correctional psychology: Law, ethics, and practice. In A. M. Goldstein, (Ed.), *Forensic psychology: Emerging topics and expanding roles*. Hoboken, NJ: John Wiley & Sons.

JOEL A. DVOSKIN
University of Arizona College of Medicine

ROBERT D. MORGAN
Texas Tech University

See also: Forensic Psychologists, Roles and Activities of; Police Psychology

CORRELATION METHODS (See Linear Regression; Multiple Correlation; Phi Coefficient; Rank Order Correlation)

COUNSELING

In an early attempt to define counseling, the Society of Counseling Psychology, which is Division 17 of the American Psychological Association, described counseling as a process of "helping individuals toward overcoming obstacles to personal growth, wherever these may be encountered, and toward achieving optimum development of personal resources" (Committee on Definition, Division of Counseling Psychology, 1956, p. 283). A more recent definition, offered by the American Counseling Association (ACA), is more specific: "... a process in which clients learn how to make decisions and formulate new ways of behaving, feeling, and thinking ... [and] involves both choice and change, evolving through distinct stages such as exploration, goal setting, and action" (American Counseling Association, 2007). The ACA further elaborates that counseling is "the application of mental health, psychological, or human development principles, through cognitive, affective, behavioral or systemic intervention strategies, that address wellness, personal growth, or career development, as well as pathology" (ACA, 2008).

According to the American Counseling Association, the profession of counseling grew out of the guidance movement. Guidance involves helping a person make a choice that is in line with his or her values, whereas counseling involves helping a person learn to make changes and learn new ways of thinking, behaving, or feeling. Guidance is also provided by someone in a position of power or authority; in contrast, many models of counseling endorse an attitude of equality between counselor and client (ACA, 2007).

Professionals disagree on the use of the closely related terms counseling and psychotherapy. Counseling, by tradition, deals with individuals who are functioning within the "normal" range, whereas psychotherapy is thought to address more severe psychopathology. Another distinction drawn between psychotherapy and counseling is in length of treatment. For example, psychotherapy typically lasts between six months and two years, whereas counseling is generally more short term, typically consisting of 8 to 12 sessions over the course of less than six months. Additionally, psychotherapy is provided in both inpatient and outpatient settings, whereas counseling is generally restricted to outpatient settings such as schools or community mental health centers and focuses on vocational, empowerment, educational, personal, or social issues (ACA, 2007).

Traditional definitions of counseling and psychotherapy thus point to differences between the two forms of helping. However, other opinions exist. For example, major models of intervention that are generally considered to be psychotherapy (e.g., cognitive behavioral therapy) are short-term in nature. Further, those who provide counseling often encounter clients who express high levels of distress. Most textbooks on theories of intervention are titled "theories of counseling and psychotherapy" suggesting blurred boundaries between the two activities. These kinds of observations lead some professionals to discount the distinctions traditionally drawn between these terms (Murdock, 2009).

Over the years, many general outlines of the process of counseling have been formulated. One current model that is widely accepted is that of Hill (2004), who proposes three stages of counseling: exploration, insight, and action. In the exploration stage of counseling, counselors focus on developing a therapeutic relationship with the client and learning about their clients by facilitating an examination of the client's thoughts, emotions, and behavior (Hill, 2004). Additionally, counselors help clients to set goals for counseling, clarify the presenting concern, and formulate treatment plans (Nugent & Jones, 2005). Carl Rogers' Person Centered Therapy informs, to a large degree, the role of the counselor in the exploration stage of counseling (Hill, 2004; Rogers, 1957).

The second stage of counseling is the insight stage. This stage is focused on helping clients gain an understanding and make connections between their thoughts, feelings, and actions. The role of the counselor is a collaborative one, in which he or she works with clients to discover " ... inner dynamics and attain new awareness of [clients'] role in perpetuating their own problems" (Hill, 2004, p. 30). This is an important stage in counseling, because insight and understanding are considered fundamental to client change. The counselor works with the client to reframe experiences and make meaning and sometimes challenges the client to see things in a new way. Additionally, the counselor may provide clients feedback about their behaviors in sessions and how the counselor perceives these behaviors. Because to some degree the counseling relationship parallels the types of relationships clients have outside of counseling, clients' understanding how their behaviors are perceived by the counselor may allow them to be better able to understand the reactions other people have to them (Hill, 2004).

In the action stage, counselor and client decide what action to take based on the exploration and insight stages of counseling (Hill, 2004; Nugent & Jones, 2005). The role of the counselor in this stage is in "... guid[ing] clients toward making decisions and changes that reflect their new understanding of themselves" and together with the client "... determin[ing] whether clients want to change and explor[ing] the meaning of change in clients' lives" (Hill, 2004, p. 32).

Rogers (1957) identified the essential elements of counseling, and most within the profession today would acknowledge these same elements, even if slightly different terminology is used. These elements are (1) the therapeutic relationship (also called the working alliance), (2) empathic understanding, (3) unconditional positive regard, and (4) counselor congruence. The therapeutic relationship refers to the "... part of the relationship focused on the therapeutic work" (Hill, 2004, p. 44). Counselors deliberately build the therapeutic relationship and encourage the client to explore thoughts and feelings by attending nonverbally, listening carefully to what clients say, reflecting feelings, and asking open-ended questions (Hill, 2004). Nugent and Jones (2005) describe the relationship as one that allows the client to feel empowered to solve his or her problem as a result of building "... trusting, dynamic, interactive relationship ... " with the counselor (p. 207). According to Gelso and Fretz (2001), the outcomes of counseling are directly related to the strength of the working alliance in the first few sessions: early positive alliances produce good results. Wampold (2001) also speaks to the importance of the alliance between counselor and client and includes aspects such as the motivation and ability of the client to work collaboratively with the therapist, client and therapist agreement about the goals of counseling, the client's emotional relationship with the counselor, and the therapist's "... empathic responding to and involvement with the client" (p. 149–150).

Good therapeutic relationships also involve congruence, which refers to the ability of both the counselor and client to be authentic, open, and honest in sessions, allowing counselor and client to perceive one another in a realistic way (Gelso & Fretz, 2001). Congruence on the part of the therapist is considered particularly critical, so it is often highlighted as a specific element required for successful counseling, following Rogers' early formulations (Gelso & Fretz, 2001). In fact, Rogers further defined congruence as the ability of counselors to fully experience and convey their thoughts and feelings in the counseling relationship

(Rogers, 1957). More generally, counselors are urged to attend to their own mental health and personal growth, and often those who educate counselors recommend that students engage in personal counseling while in training.

Empathic understanding occurs when the counselor experiences the client's world as if it was his or her own and expresses this to the client, but without passing judgment. Conveying this understanding to clients builds the therapeutic relationship and helps clients develop insight into their thoughts, behavior, and experiences (Rogers, 1957).

Rogers (1957) described unconditional positive regard as "... a warm acceptance of each aspect of the client's experience as being part of that client ... there are no conditions of acceptance ... " (p. 249). Gelso and Fretz (2001) point out that unconditional positive regard refers to a counselor's "... basic attitude toward the client [that] does not fluctuate according to the client's emotions or behavior" (p. 251).

Counseling can be conducted with individuals, couples, families, or groups. Many models or theories of counseling have been offered throughout the years, and the general consensus among professionals is that the major approaches to counseling generally produce positive outcomes (Lambert & Ogles, 2004; Wampold, 2001). All of these theories emphasize the importance of the therapeutic relationship, and most would acknowledge the significant effects of unconditional positive regard, empathy, and congruence. The stated goals offered by different theories of counseling span a wide range of objectives, from simply achieving goals identified by the client, to decreasing or eliminating distressing thoughts, emotions, and behaviors and fostering personal growth, authenticity, and improved personal relationships.

REFERENCES

American Counseling Association. (2007). Counseling fact sheets. Retrieved July 7, 2008, from http://www.counseling.org/Resources/ConsumersMedia.aspx?AGuid=97592202-75c2-079-b854-2cd22c47be3f.

Division of Counseling Psychology, Committee on Definition (1956). Counseling psychology as a specialty. *American Psychologist, 11,* 282–285.

Gelso, C., & Fretz, B. (2001). *Counseling psychology* (2nd ed.). Belmont, CA: Wadsworth.

Hill, C. E. (2004). *Helping skills: Facilitating exploration, insight, and action.* Washington, DC: American Psychological Association.

Lambert, M. J., & Ogles, B. M. (2004). The efficacy and effectiveness of psychotherapy. In M. J. Lambert (Ed.) *Bergin and Garfield's handbook of psychotherapy and behavior change* (5th ed. pp. 139–193) Hoboken, NJ: John Wiley & Sons.

Murdock, N. L. (2009). *Theories of counseling and psychotherapy: A case approach* (2nd ed.). Upper Saddle River, NJ: Pearson/Merril.

Nugent, F. A., & Jones, K. D. (2005). *Introduction to the profession of counseling*. Upper Saddle River, NJ: Pearson.

Rogers, C. R. (1957). The necessary and sufficient conditions of therapeutic personality change. *Journal of Consulting Psychology*, *21*, 95–103.

Wampold, B. E. (2001). *The great psychotherapy debate: Models, methods, and findings*. Mahwah, NJ: Lawrence Erlbaum.

SUGGESTED READING

American Psychological Association, Division 17 Student Section. (n.d.). *About counseling psychologists*. Retrieved August 5, 2008, from http://www.div17.org/students_defining.html.

NANCY L. MURDOCK
ROMANA C. KRYCAK
University of Missouri-Kansas City

See also: **Career Counseling; Psychotherapy; Vocational Counseling**

COUNTERTRANSFERENCE

The topic of the therapist's countertransference to the client and the client's verbal and nonverbal behavior has been around since the very earliest days of the "talking cure" in the early twentieth century. This concept, however, has had a complex and unsteady history. For many years, it was viewed as something to be done away with, and its presence marked a treatment that was not going well. Perhaps because of this negative view, countertransference was avoided as a topic of study in the early years of psychotherapy and psychoanalysis. During the past 25 years, however, there has been an upsurge of interest, and many studies have been conducted on countertransference. This increase has coincided with a broadened conception of countertransference as a process that may be highly beneficial to therapy or highly detrimental, depending on how and what the therapist does with his or her countertransference reactions. Epstein and Feiner (1979) maintain that these two themes, countertransference as a hinderance and countertransference as an aid to understanding, have been intertwined like a double helix throughout much of the history of therapy.

Definition of Countertransference

Over the years, there has been considerable debate about how countertransference might be best defined, with a range of definitions being advanced (Epstein & Feiner, 1979; Gelso & Hayes, 2007). Perhaps the two most prominent definitions are the classical psychoanalytic one and the totalistic one. In the former, countertransference is seen as comprising the therapist's largely unconscious, conflict-based reactions to the patient's transference. This definition focuses on the problematic nature of countertransference, and it came to be seen by many over the years as too narrow and restrictive. Partly as a reaction to the classical view, the totalistic conception saw countertransference as virtually all of the therapist's emotionally based reactions to the client. As Gelso and Hayes (2007) have noted, this definition makes countertransference so broad as to include essentially everything. A concept that is this broad has little scientific or clinical merit. Gelso and Hayes have provided the following definition that seeks to integrate the most prominent views: Countertransference may be defined as "the therapist's internal and external reactions that are shaped by the therapist's past or present emotional vulnerabilities and conflicts" (p. 25).

Internal countertransference involves the therapist's feelings, attitudes, and cognitions; whereas external reactions are usually seen as behavioral manifestations in response to the client. Generally, internal reactions are not seen as injurious to the therapy relationship, and if the therapist gains insight into these reactions, they may be of great help in understanding and helping the client. Countertransference that is manifested behaviorally, however, is seen as unhelpful and perhaps harmful. Such reactions often take the form of hostility toward the client, rejection of the client and his or her feelings, or avoidance of the client's feelings. Thus, one fact that has been substantially verified over many years by empirical research is that countertransference reactions that are unmanaged by the therapist have a negative effect on the therapeutic relationship and treatment outcome (Gelso & Hayes, 2007).

Origins and Triggers of Countertransference

Although the client's verbal and nonverbal behaviors are usually seen as the triggers for countertransference, it is generally agreed that the origin of countertransference resides within the therapist and reflects unresolved inner conflicts from his or her past. At times, countertransference is triggered not by the client; rather it represents internal conflicts the therapist carries within him- or herself that become manifested with all clients. Such reactions are called chronic countertransference.

Researchers have sought to uncover the client triggers, investigating whether behaviors that are systematically linked to countertransference. Few, if any, such client factors have been found. Instead, research has begun to uncover how the actual triggers are client behaviors interacting with particular therapist vulnerabilities. For example, one study found that the greatest amount of countertransference occurred when certain client relationship attachment patterns were combined with particular therapist relationship attachment patterns (Mohr, Gelso,

& Hill, 2005). Gelso and Hayes (2007) have proposed a countertransference reaction hypothesis as a guide to exploring how the interaction of client and therapist behaviors serves to trigger therapist countertransference more than either client or therapist behaviors alone.

Frequency of Countertransference

By virtue of being human, all therapists have unresolved issues and vulnerabilities. Because of this, many see countertransference as occurring in all psychotherapies despite theoretical orientation, therapist experience level, or any other factors (Gabbard, 2001; Kiesler, 2001). Regardless of the definition that is used, research supports the idea that countertransference occurs in all therapy. For example, in a qualitative study of eight expert psychotherapists of differing orientations, each working with a single client in brief therapy, Hayes and colleagues (1998) used a definition of countertransference similar to the integrative one noted earlier, and they found that countertransference occurred in 80% of these expert therapists' sessions. However, the number of instances of countertransference occurring within individual sessions was quite small. Thus, countertransference reactions (internal or external) appear to occur in most sessions but are infrequent within these sessions. Still, there is evidence to suggest that even when countertransference is exhibited infrequently it affects the treatment (Gelso & Hayes, 2007).

Countertransference Management

One of the most important ingredients of effective psychotherapy may be the therapist's ability to understand, contain, and process countertransference reactions so that they are not acted out with the client (Gabbard, 2001). The term that is often used for such activity (i.e., understanding, containing, processing) is countertransference management, and much writing has occurred in recent years on this topic (Gelso & Hayes, 2007). Countertransference management may be useful in preventing the countertransference during treatment, in minimizing the adverse impact once countertransference has been enacted in treatment, and in helping the therapist use internal countertransference reactions to better understand the client and facilitate the treatment.

What factors go into or constitute countertransference management? Gelso, Hayes, and their collaborators (e.g., Gelso & Hayes, 2007; VanWagoner, Gelso, Hayes, & Diemer, 1991) have offered a conceptualization that has been empirically supported in recent years. According to these authors, there are five main factors associated with effective countertransference management.

The first factor is therapist self-insight. Robertiello and Schoenewolf (1987) underscore this factor nicely when they suggest that therapists' knowledge of their propensities tend to keep them from falling too deeply into countertransference reactions, at least, help them to deal with such reactions more swiftly before they have done significant harm. Therapist self-insight may be the most fundamental constituent of countertransference management.

A second constituent of countertransference management is self-integration. This ingredient involves the therapist's possession of a unified, healthy character structure, which includes interpersonal boundaries that allow her to maintain differentiation from the client. At the same time, these boundaries are not so rigid that the therapist is prevented from temporarily putting the self aside and entering the client's emotional world. Some leading therapists have suggested that the good therapist is a "wounded healer" who by virtue of having experienced emotional conflicts, is better able to understand the client. The second factor implies that, although this may be true, the therapist's wounds must be sufficiently healed for her to be effective.

The third constituent of effective countertransference management is empathy. This ingredient allows the therapist to "walk in the client's shoes," cognitively and emotionally, in order to understand deeply what the client experiences. Empathy also allows the therapist to maintain the focus on the client's experience rather than being absorbed or overwhelmed by his own feelings. Therapist empathy has been one of the most extensively studied constructs in psychotherapy, and the empirical evidence strongly supports its importance to the success of diverse treatments (Bohart, Eliott, Greenberg, & Watson, 2002).

The fourth constituent, anxiety management, is a key constituent of effective countertransference management. Rather than eliminating one's anxiety, anxiety management involves recognizing, tolerating, and learning from one's anxiety. The good therapist, in a sense, embraces his anxiety and seeks to understand what it is about. If the therapist's anxiety is stirred by the client's behavior and the therapist then understands his own anxiety, this often results in better understanding the client and his impact of others.

Finally, conceptualizing skill is the last key constituent of countertransference management. This constituent involves conceptually and theoretically grasping the client's dynamics and the dynamics of the therapeutic relationship. Therapists who use theory (regardless of the particular theory) to help understand what is happening in the treatment hour are expected to do a better job of dealing with their own vulnerabilities that are inevitably exposed during psychotherapy.

Direct and indirect empirical evidence supports this five-factor conception of countertransference management as related to effective therapy process and outcome in diverse treatments (Gelso & Hayes, 2007). Such management appears to be a key part of the positive stance of Epstein and Feiner's (1979) double helix—countertransference as an aid to effective treatment. Thus, the evidence supports that counter-transference can be for better or worse, depending on how it is managed by the therapist.

REFERENCES

Bohart, A. C., Elliott, R., Greenberg, L. S., & Watson, J. C. (2002). Empathy. In J. C. Norcross (Ed.), *Psychotherapy relationships that work* (pp. 89–108). New York: Oxford.

Epstein, L., & Feiner, A. H. (1979). *Countertransference*. New York: Jason Aronson.

Gabbard, G. (2001). A contemporary model of countertransference. *Journal of Clinical Psychology/In Session, 58*, 861–867.

Gelso, C. J., & Hayes, J. A. (2007). *Countertransference and the therapist's inner experience: Perils and possibilities*. Mahwah, NJ: Lawrence Erlbaum.

Hayes, J. A., McCracken, J. E., McClanahan, M. K., Hill, C. E., Harp, J. S., & Carozzoni, P. (1998). Therapist perspectives on countertransference: Qualitative data in search of a theory. *Journal of Counseling Psychology, 45*, 468–482.

Kiesler, D. J. (2001). Therapist countertransference: In search of common themes. *Journal of Clinical Psychology/In Session, 57*, 1053–1063.

Mohr, J. J., Gelso, C. J., & Hill, C. E. (2005). Client and counselor trainee attachment as predictors of session evaluation and countertransference behavior in first counseling sessions, *Journal of Counseling Psychology, 52*, 298–309.

Robertiello, R. C., & Schoenewolf, G. (1987). *101 common therapeutic blunders: Countertransference and counterresistance in psychotherapy*. Northvale, NJ: Jason Aronson.

VanWagoner, S. L., Gelso, C. J., Hayes, J. A., & Diemer, R. A. (1991). Countertransference and the reputedly excellent therapy. *Psychotherapy, 28*, 411–421.

CHARLES J. GELSO
University of Maryland, College Park

See also: **Therapeutic Alliance; Transference**

COUPLES THERAPY

Couples therapy is a form of psychotherapy targeting problems within a couple (e.g., two individuals in a committed romantic relationship). Whereas individual psychotherapy focuses on one person and that person's problem areas, couples therapy targets the problems of the couple, whether married or unmarried, heterosexual or homosexual. Couples therapy has emerged as a crucial intervention in mental health due to the growing need for treating couple problems.

Approximately 20% of the population experience marital distress. Further, half of all marriages end in divorce, and only 70% of marriages make it through the first decade of marriage. Marital distress has a significant impact on society, in such forms as increased physical health problems, decreased work productivity, and increased child adjustment problems for children living in conflictual marriages. Given the negative impact marital distress has on our society, it is no surprise that marital distress is the most frequent problem for which people seek psychotherapy. In fact, 40% of psychotherapy clients report marital distress as the reason they sought treatment

There are many different types of couples therapy developed from different theoretical models. Across these different theoretical forms of couples therapy, there exist common factors or techniques common to all forms of couples therapy. These common techniques or foci include assessment, the therapeutic alliance, and managing resistance. Assessment is usually the first phase of couples therapy regardless of the theoretical orientation. The purpose of the assessment phase is to develop an understanding of the couple's presenting problems, develop goals for treatment, and develop an understanding of the factors maintaining the couples presenting problems.

Assessment typically examines the couple's relationship across a number of broad levels, such as the couple's view of their relationship (e.g., how unhappy are the partners, and on what do they agree and disagree?), commitment (e.g., how close is the couple to divorce or separation?), couple behavior (e.g., observing important variables within the session such as hostility, withdrawal, and the ratio of positive behaviors to negative behaviors), couple cognition (e.g., the dysfunctional beliefs or unrealistic beliefs about the relationship or partner), couple affect (e.g., the amount of emotional closeness between the partners), and couple dynamic processes (e.g., what are the couple's internal and family of origin related struggles that may contribute to their current problems?). The assessment phase of treatment is crucial in the development of treatment goals. However, assessment continues throughout therapy as a necessary way of continuing to develop an understanding of the couple's problems and possible solutions. Assessment is enabled by a number of well-validated measures of couple distress and functioning, such as the Marital Satisfaction Inventory, the Dyadic Assessment Scale, the Conflict Tactics Scale, and the Systemic Therapy Inventory of Change.

The therapeutic alliance is the relationship between the couple and the couple's therapist. Building a strong therapeutic alliance is a vital task at the beginning of couple therapy. If a strong alliance is not developed at the beginning of therapy, the couple may become dissatisfied with therapy and terminate therapy prematurely before they can receive a sufficient amount of the therapy to impact their relationship distress. Developing a strong therapeutic alliance in couples therapy is more complex than in individual therapy. Each partner has an alliance with the therapist, but the couple also has an alliance with one another, and the couple has a shared alliance as a couple with the therapist that differs from their individual connections. Thus, it is important for the couples therapist to build and monitor all of these forms of alliance in order to avoid a split alliance in which one partner has a positive alliance with the therapist and the other does not. In order to navigate this difficult task, the therapist must communicate fairness and balance while maintaining control over the process, not letting too much conflict spill into the therapy session, and creating a sense of safety for the couple.

Regardless of the particular type of couples therapy being used, all couples therapists must find ways of reducing resistance and noncompliance in therapy. There are numerous approaches to responding to noncompliance, including discussing the noncompliance in therapy, directly targeting the noncompliance, and increasing the couple's motivation to change. The type of technique used to target resistance and noncompliance in couples therapy may differ across different models of couples therapy, but it is always is necessary to target the noncompliance rather than ignore the elephant in the room.

There exist many different couples therapy models, the most prominent treatments used in the field being cognitive behavioral therapy, emotion focused therapy, and integrative methods integrating more than one theoretical model. Several different cognitive behavioral couple therapy models have been developed, including behavioral couple therapy (BCT), cognitive behavioral couple therapy (CBCT), and integrative behavioral couple therapy (IBCT). BCT is the oldest of these models and was developed based on social exchange theory. The goal of BCT is to increase the frequency of positive behaviors between each partner. There are two core techniques at the center of BCT, behavior exchange and communication/problem solving. Behavioral exchange techniques increase positive behaviors and decrease negative behaviors in the couple's daily life. The therapist asks each partner to increase specific positive behaviors that are reinforcing for the other partner (e.g., taking out the garbage, giving a back rub). Communication/problem solving techniques teach the couple specific skills such as communication skills (e.g., reflective listening), and problem solving techniques. However, BCT does not target affective or cognitive functioning within couples.

CBCT was developed based on BCT and includes behavioral techniques, behavioral exchange, and skills training, as well as cognitive techniques. CBCT uses cognitive restructuring in order to target couples dysfunctional ways of thinking about their relationship. The therapist helps identify dysfunctional beliefs that the couple has about each other and uses socratic questioning and guided discovery in order to help them change or modify their dysfunctional thinking styles.

The most recent adaptation of the behavioral model is ICBT, which utilizes change techniques from CBCT and BCT (i.e., behavioral exchange, skills training, and cognitive techniques) as well as acceptance strategies. The therapy attempts to change behaviors that are easily mutable and help the couple accept differences that are not easily changed through change techniques. Acceptance strategies include empathic joining, detachment from the problem, increased tolerance for the problem, and increasing self-care until the problem is ameliorated or changed.

Emotion Focused Couple Therapy (EFCT) is an experiential approach that focuses on couple emotion and attachment. A variety of techniques are used to engender positive attachment between the spouses, including heightening (repetition, images, or metaphors that help the couple reformulate an emotional experience) and softening ("hard" emotions like anger are explored and expressed as "softer" emotions such as fear, sadness, and shame).

There are several different forms of couple therapies that are integrative. Four of the most well known integrative couples therapy are Gurman's brief integrative marital therapy (BIMT), Snyder's affect-reconstruction therapy, Pinsof's integrative problem centered therapy (IPCT), and Gottman's Gottman method therapy. BIMT is brief in duration and problem focused, and it combines behavioral therapy and object relations therapy. Affect-reconstruction therapy combines insight oriented therapy and cognitive-behavioral therapy techniques. IPCT integrates individual, family, and biological therapies The therapist begins with the most direct therapy models (e.g. behavioral) and then proceeds to more complex, indirect methods of therapy (e.g., psychodynamic). The therapist moves to the next model (e.g., behavioral to cognitive or cognitive to object relations) based on failure. When couples' problems do not improve, the therapist moves to the next level in the model.

Gottman's method, which is based on his research, aims to build marital friendship, increase the ratio of positive to negative exchanges, increase good feeling (called positive sentiment override), learn and respond to each other's love maps as to what feels loving, and reduce the presence of the "four horsemen": criticism, defensiveness, contempt, and stonewalling. Gottman's method embraces arguing about differences, but also distinguishing arguments that can be resolved from those lifelong arguments that can only be improved by accepting and respecting difference.

Meta-analyses (which are mathematical combinations of the effect sizes of many research studies) have found that couples therapies are as effective as individual therapies (Lebow & Gurman, 1995; Sprenkle, 2002) and have a positive impact on three-fourths of couples treated. Several different models of couples therapy have solid research evidence for being effective, including BCT, ICBT, and EFCT. In the best of these studies, couples therapies have been demonstrated to ameliorate marital distress in a clinically significant way in even the most distressed couples. Couples therapy has also been found to be effective in ameliorating individual problems such as depression and to be a useful part of multimodal treatments for problems such as substance use disorders, panic disorder, bipolar disorder, and a wide range of child and adolescent adjustment difficulties.

REFERENCES

Lebow, J. L., & Gurman, A. S. (1995). Research assessing couple and family therapy. *Annual Review of Psychology, 46*, 27–57.

Sprenkle, D. H. (Ed.). (2002). *Effectiveness research in marriage and family therapy.* Alexandria, VA: American Association for Marriage and Family Therapy.

SUGGESTED READINGS

Gottman, J. M. (1999). *The marriage clinic: A scientifically based marital therapy.* New York: W. W. Norton.

Gurman, A. S., & Jacobson, N. S. (2003). Clinical handbook of couples therapy. (3rd ed.). *Journal of Marital & Family Therapy, 29*(2), 284–286.

JAY LEBOW
DANIELLE BLACK
Northwestern University

See also: **Marital Discord; Marriage Counseling**

CREATIVE THINKING

Creativity is among the most promising and optimistic aspects of the human experience; few constructs have the capacity to benefit people's experiences as comprehensively. This potential ranges from the very personal—arts-based therapeutic interventions, well-designed museum installations and programs—to the societal—educating more creative scientists, creating a national strategy to enhance the arts, producing unique solutions to diplomatic and military problems. Increasingly, our colleagues in other countries are seizing on the potential benefits of an increased focus on creativity, as are many of their ministries of education and culture (e.g., Kaufman & Sternberg, 2006). The question is not "In what areas can creativity be useful?" but rather "How does creativity apply in each and every area?"

What exactly is creativity? Plucker, Beghetto, and Dow (2004) proposed the following definition of creativity after conducting an exhaustive review of the literature: "Creativity is the interaction among aptitude, process, and environment by which an individual or group produces a perceptible product that is both novel and useful as defined within a social context" (p. 90).

Plucker et al. believe this definition applies to all types of creative endeavor and to the wide range of ways in which creativity manifests itself (e.g., a new thought that comes to you in the shower, a story you make up for your child, a popular song, a quicker way to travel to Mars). The definition also reflects the field's customary emphasis on originality and utility (broadly defined) as necessary components of creativity.

Creative thinking is a strong component of the creative process. One of the earliest theories of creativity was offered by Wallas (1926), who proposed a model of the cognitive creative process. According to his five-stage model, you first use preparation to begin work on a problem. Next, there is incubation, in which you may work on other things while your mind thinks about the problem. In intimation, you realize you are about to have a breakthrough (this phase is sometimes dropped from the model), and then you actually have the insight in the illumination phase. Finally, with verification, you actually test, develop, and use your ideas.

Another theory is Guilford's (1967) Structure of the Intellect model, which looked at all of cognition across three dimensions. The first dimension was called "operations," and simply meant the mental gymnastics needed for any kind of task (evaluation, cognition, memory, divergent production, convergent production). The second dimension, "content," referred to the general subject area (figural, symbolic, semantic, behavioral). The third dimension, "product," represented the actual products that might result from different kinds of thinking in different kinds of subject matters (units, classes, relations, systems, transformations, implications). With five operations, four contents, and six products, Guilford's model had an amazingly complex 120 different possible mental abilities.

Divergent production is a strong component of creativity, and Guilford (and many others) measured creativity according to the Structure of Intellect model. For example, people are asked to exhibit evidence of divergent production in several areas, including divergent production of semantic units (e.g., listing consequences of people no longer needing to sleep), of figural classes (finding as many classifications of sets of figures as is possible), and of figural units (taking a simple shape such as a circle and elaborating upon it as often as possible).

A more recent theory is the Geneplore model (Finke, Ward, & Smith, 1992). This framework has two phases—generative and exploratory. Generation, the "novel" part, is generating many different ideas. Exploration refers to evaluating these possible options and choosing the best one (or ones). In the generative phase, someone constructs a pre-inventive structure, or a mental representation of a possible creative solution (Finke, Ward, & Smith, 1992). For example, Elias Howe was working on his invention of the modern sewing machine. He couldn't quite get the needle correctly designed. Howe had an odd dream in which he was chased by savages who threw spears at him. The spears had a circle loop at their tips—and Howe realized that adding the circle (or an "eye") to the end of the needle was the solution he needed. The image of a spear with a circle at the end—the image that preceded Howe's insight—would be an example of one of these pre-inventive structures. They don't need to be as dramatic or sudden as Howe's story. Indeed, the generation of pre-inventive structures is only one part of the creative process according to the Geneplore model. The thinker must then explore these different pre-inventive structures within the constraints of the final goal. There may be several cycles before a creative work is produced.

REFERENCES

Finke, R. A., Ward, T. B., & Smith, S. M. (1992). *Creative cognition.* Cambridge, MA: MIT Press.

Guilford, J. P. (1967). *The nature of human intelligence.* New York: McGraw-Hill.

Kaufman, J. C., & Sternberg, R. J. (Eds). (2006). *The international handbook of creativity.* Cambridge, UK: Cambridge University Press

Plucker, J., Beghetto, R. A., & Dow, G. T. (2004). Why isn't creativity more important to educational psychologists? Potential, pitfalls, and future directions in creativity research. *Educational Psychologist, 39,* 83–96.

Wallas, G. (1926). *The art of thought.* New York: Harcourt, Brace, & World.

SUGGESTED READINGS

Amabile, T. M. (1996). *Creativity in context: Update to the social psychology of creativity.* Boulder, CO: Westview.

Finke, R. A., Ward, T. B., & Smith, S. M. (1996). Creative cognition: *Theory, research, and applications* (rev. ed). Boston: MIT Press.

Sternberg, R. J. (Ed.) (1999). *Handbook of creativity.* Cambridge, UK: Cambridge University Press.

Sternberg, R. J. (2003). *WICS: Wisdom, intelligence, and creativity, synthesized.* Cambridge, UK: Cambridge University Press.

Sternberg, R. J., Grigorenko, E. L., & Singer, J. L. (2004). *Creativity: From potential to realization.* Washington, DC: American Psychological Association.

JAMES C. KAUFMAN
California State University, San Bernardino

JONATHAN A. PLUCKER
Indiana University

See also: Giftedness; Intelligence

CREATIVITY

Most Asian, African, Native American, and other indigenous traditions used creative imagination to enrich and enhance everyday life; original contributions were typically seen as gifts from deities or spirits who used humans as their "channels." These insights would often come in nighttime dreams or daytime visions and were thought to re-create divine truth. In some of these societies, individuals who produced something unprecedented (such as a mask or weapon) would be hailed as heroes, but in others they would be censured for breaking with tradition. Women's creativity was undervalued for centuries, and they were given few educational opportunities or life circumstances on which creative productivity depends; this situation still characterizes many contemporary countries where innovations are suspect, especially if women are the innovators (Kaufman & Sternberg, 2006; Richards, 2007).

The English word "creativity" is a social construct that has been linked with the concept of origin itself (from the Latin *creare,* to make, and the ecclesiastical Latin *creator* or Creator). Some researchers and theorists focus on creative products, requiring that they be of social value or have attained some other type of consensual validation if they are to be called creative. Others emphasize the process by which the products (artwork, technology, concepts, and so forth) come into being or the milieu in which they emerge. Others conceptualize creativity as reflecting the unique achievement, ability, or attitude of a person or a consortium. In each of these perspectives, there can be levels of accomplishment, utility, or originality, implying that some persons or groups can be more or less creative than others.

The concept of *everyday creativity* (Richards, 2007) directs attention to creative outcomes in office management, child-rearing, home repairs, food preparation, or community service, as well as the "dark side of creativity" characterizing the all-too-frequent acts that are innovative but destructive. Thus, from a Western standpoint, creativity is a term that can be used to describe the process of bringing something new into being by becoming sensitive to gaps in human knowledge, identifying these deficiencies, searching for their solutions, making guesses as to a potential solution, testing one's hypotheses, and communicating the final results. However, the creative process is imperfectly understood; these steps may be linear or nonlinear (i.e., "chaotic"), may occur in a planned sequence or spontaneously, and/or may be intentional or largely unconscious.

Attempts to measure the creative *process* have led to the development of various tests and measures of "divergent thinking" and other cognitive skills. Biographical inventories and personality measures have been devised in an attempt to identify the creative person. The creative milieu has been assessed by various scales and questionnaires focusing on the classroom, studio, or workplace, while creative products have been rated through a variety of scales (Runco, 1999). Some of these attempts at assessment have been used to identify highly creative individuals in order to offer them special instruction; in the United States, entire programs—some of them statewide—have been based on pupils' test results and/or teachers' observations.

However, creativity measures have been criticized on the basis of content validity, construct validity, reliability, relevance to different populations, comprehensiveness, and the proclivity for their results to be influenced by situational or contextual factors. Some positive outcomes have resulted from assessing level or type of creativity through the use of such naturalistic assignments as writing a short story, assembling collages, or engaging in spontaneous problem solving. Despite their shortcomings, creativity tests have been utilized in many important research projects (Barron & Harrington, 1981).

Creative training programs assume that creative behavior can be enhanced, an assumption that has not gained acceptance among those psychologists for whom biological determinants and early learning are important variables. Some approaches admit that key creativity skills cannot be impacted within a short span of time, since these components include such elements as knowledge of the topic, technical skills, work history, and cognitive styles. As a result, these programs, both investigative and applied, emphasize task motivation through modeling, fantasy, and a deemphasis on evaluation. Other programs take a more optimistic view, focusing on cognitive rather than social psychological methods; for example, "brainstorming" and "creative problem solving" teach people how to generate unusual ideas. Some training programs for school children have been found effective in improving scores on standard creativity tests. Several elements converge to form creativity, for example, intelligence, accumulated knowledge, cognitive styles, personality traits, motivation, and environmental variables (Sternberg & Lubart, 1995); training programs need to address these elements in a systematic manner.

When personality characteristics of people identified as creative are observed, a common set of characteristics usually emerges, such as broad interests, high "energy" levels, attraction to complexity, independence of judgment, autonomy, use of intuition, ability to resolve paradoxes or to accommodate apparently opposite or conflicting aspects of one's self-concept, and a firm sense of one's self as creative (Barron & Harrington, 1981). However, there appear to be important differences among groups of creative people: artists have been described as more emotionally sensitive, tense, and impractical than scientists; many scientists grew up as intellectual rebels; musicians have suffered more problems with substance abuse, poets more mania and psychosis, and writers more biploar disorders (Ludwig, 1995).

Future research studies need to identify genetic predispositions for creative activity, reconcile personality and cognitive research data in creativity, pay more attention to genius level creativity, evaluate the role played by changed states of consciousness in creative ideation, determine the part played by mental illness in blocking or facilitating creative expression, and specify what environmental variables are critical factors in creative development (Kaufman & Sternberg, 2006; Richards, 2007). The need for creative solutions to the world's many social, economic, and environmental problems reflects the importance of this field, as well as the psychologists who dedicate themselves to studying it.

REFERENCES

Barron, F., & Harrington, D. M. (1981). Creativity, intelligence, and personality. *Annual Review of Psychology, 32*, 439–476.

Kaufman, J. C., & Sternberg, R. J. (Eds.). (2006). *The international handbook of creativity*. New York: Cambridge University Press.

Ludwig, A. (1995). *The price of greatness*. New York: Guilford Press.

Richards, R. (Ed.) (2007). *Everyday creativity and new views of human nature*. Washington, DC: American Psychological Association.

Runco, M. A. (1999). Tests of creativity. In M. A. Runco & S. R. Pritzker (Eds.), *Encyclopedia of creativity* (Vol. 2, pp. 189–202). San Diego, CA: Academic Press.

Sternberg, R. J., & Lubart, T. I. (1995). *Defying the crowd: Cultivating creativity in a culture of conformity*. New York: Free Press.

SUGGESTED READINGS

Gardner, H. (1993). *Creating minds*. New York: Basic Books.

Sternberg, R. J., Grigorenko, E. L., & Singer, J. L. (2004). *Creativity: From potential to realization*. Washington, DC: American Psychological Association.

STANLEY KRIPPNER
Saybrook Graduate School

See also: Intelligence

CRIMINAL PROFILING

Criminal profiling has received attention from the academic community and from the entertainment world since the FBI first published accounts of its profiling principles. It originally became popular through films such as *Silence of the Lambs* and the *X-Files* making headlines.

Since its emergence, criminal profiling has been labeled in several different ways, including psychological profiling, criminal profiling, criminal personality profiling, criminal investigative analysis, and behavioral evidence profiling.

Regardless of the descriptive label applied today, profiling as an investigative tool is based entirely on intuition and represents a less than educated attempt to provide law enforcement agencies with detailed information about the behavior of an unknown individual who has committed a crime (Holmes, 1996; Turvey, 1999).

Most published accounts of profiling that detail the methods employed by various individuals have taken the form of semi-autobiographical books and journalistic articles, rather than systematic academic work. They are, therefore, difficult to evaluate with respect to their accuracy or scientific basis. The major flaw of current profiling methods is that most profiles emphasize various psychological mechanisms and functions associated with a crime, especially murder, and presumed to characterize the offender. Consequently, these profiles make little distinction between the overt crime scene behaviors as they occur in murders and the psychodynamic processes that presumably produce the criminal behavior. Hence, there is little attempt by profilers to differentiate aspects of the offender's motivations and lifestyle from aspects of their offending behavior. Another problem with profiling is that many profilers view profiling as "crime scene reconstruction."

The Origin of the FBI's Criminal Profiling Project

The FBI's initial project on serial murder began in 1978 (Ressler, Burgess, & Douglas, 1988). The primary focus of the project was to conduct personal interviews with serial murderers about their crimes in order to find out how they attempted to avoid capture. The FBI serial murder project received added attention in Washington, DC, in the early 1980s due to public outcry after the murder of a six-year-old boy in Florida by a serial murderer (Ressler et al., 1988). Due to this public pressure, the FBI serial murder project was brought to the forefront and given U.S. Government funding, which eventually led to a unit being established in Quantico, Virginia, called the Behavioral Science Unit (BSU; Ressler et al., 1988). In 1995, a restructuring phase combined the BSU, the Violent Criminal Apprehension Program (VICAP), and the National Center for the Analysis of Violent Crime into one unit, calling it the Critical Incident Response Group (CIRG; Douglas & Olshaker, 1995).

The primary purpose of the serial murder project was to use interviews with convicted killers as a basis for constructing future classifications that could then be used to aid police investigations. A series of interviews with 36 incarcerated offenders, of whom 25 were defined as serial murderers (i.e., the killing of three or more individuals over time), took place between 1979 and 1983 in the United States. The interviews were guided by a checklist of relatively unstructured, open-ended questions. Prior to the interviews, other information about each of these offenders and their crimes was obtained by reviewing crime scene photos, physical reports, and psychiatric reports. No detailed analysis of this material has ever been publicly presented. Instead, a simple dichotomy was claimed to emerge from the project by which offenders could be classified either as organized or disorganized. The assignment of the offenders to either the organized or disorganized category was based on the appearance of the victims' attire or nudity, exposure of the victims' sexual parts, insertion of foreign objects into body cavities, or evidence of sexual intercourse.

As noted by Ressler and colleagues (1988), the FBI posited that the categorization (organized or disorganized) scheme could be used to classify a subgroup of serial murderers, namely, sex-related murders in which motive was often lacking. This supposition implies that, if a murderer is emotional and no organization can be deciphered from the murderer's actions at the crime scene, there is no motive. Because of the apparent lack of motive in cases such as these, FBI profilers decided to look for evidence of planning, irrationality, or some form of discord at these crime scenes to determine whether the offender was organized or disorganized. The organized and disorganized typology is then used to classify the murderer's personality, depending on the characteristics of the crime scene.

The distinction between organized and disorganized murders as inferred from crime scenes does seem to describe different levels of aggression in serial murders. However, whether this crime scene distinction can accurately classify a murderer's personality has yet to be demonstrated, and the literature does not provide any explanation of the differences between the organized and disorganized serial murderer.

Heuristics and Biases in Profiling Decision Making

The reliability, validity, and utility of criminal profiles generally provided in police investigations are questionable and have been the subject of considerable criticism over the years. For example, Godwin (1978) argued that profilers are playing a blindman's bluff, groping in all directions in the hope of touching a sleeve. Levin and Fox (1985) asserted that offender profiling is vague and general and of little use in identifying a killer. Blackburn (1993) echoed similar concerns and pointed out that profiling is more an art than a science and that evidence for its validity is limited. According to Snook, Cullen, Bennett, Taylor, and Gendreau (2008), "People may have been misled into believing that criminal profiling works, despite not sound theoretical grounding and no strong empirical support for this possibility" (p. 1257). Other criticisms of profiling have called attention to studies of conventional investigative approaches suggesting there is nothing special about detective work experience or clinical expertise (Elkman, 1991; Kohnken, 1987; Alison & Canter, 1997).

The Personality to Behavior Confusion in Profiling

The foundation of usual criminal profiling, as previously mentioned, is built on the notion that the crime scene reflects the offender's personality. In disagreement with this view, Godwin (2008) suggested that crime scene behavior reflects a person's life experiences. A behavioral approach to profiling looks at the behaviors of serial killers that can be observed rather than at their internal workings. As John B. Watson argued many years ago, "Only individuals can observe their perceptions and feelings, but someone else can observe your actions" (Hilgard, 1977). Consequently, it seems more reasonable to consider crime scene actions as experiences of behavior rather than as particular manifestations of intrinsic psychopathology. Thus the behavioral approach to profiling violent criminals suggests that an individual's actions are the result of an interaction between the offender's characteristics and the social and physical conditions of the situation. A behavioral approach to profiling sees behavior as being consistent across a number of situations rather than specific to a particular environmental context. By employing a behavioral approach, trends in how offenders behave from one crime to the next can be explored (Godwin, 2008).

Researchers often assume that personality traits are consistent, so that an offender can be characterized according to enduring personality characteristics. However, individuals are not uniformly rewarded across different crimes. Offenders may learn to discriminate between contexts in which certain behavior is appropriate and those in which it is not. Aggressive actions may be differentially rewarded, and learned discriminations are likely to determine the situations in which the individual will display a particular behavior. This suggests that diverse behaviors do not necessarily reflect variations of the same underlying motive, but instead are often discrete responses to different situations. Therefore, a behavioral profiling approach may generally be more representative of criminals than an approach focused on specifying personality traits.

On the whole, currently common criminal profiling methods are inherently flawed due to weak operational definitions and inferred deductive assumptions made about offender actions and characteristics. In its present form, this leads to empirically unsound and misleading profiles, and Snook and colleagues (2008) concluded that criminal profiling should not be used as an investigative tool, because it lacks scientific support. As Canter (2000) clearly points out, detectives and police investigators are particularly vulnerable to the creative fictions of profilers, because their task is very similar to that of a novelist. Investigators feel the need to invent a narrative that makes sense of all the facts and also indicates the psychological processes that give the plot its dynamics, usually rather ambiguously referred to as the "motive." If this invention adds weight to their own loosely formulated notions, it is even more attractive (Canter, 1994).

REFERENCES

Alison, L. J., & Canter, D. V. (1997). *Professional, legal and ethical issues in offender profiling.* London: Dartmouth Publishing.

Blackburn, R. (1993). *The psychology of criminal conduct: Theory, research and practice.* Chichester, UK: John Wiley & Sons.

Burgess, A. W., Hartman, C. R., Ressler, R. D., Douglas, J. E., & McCormack, A. (1986). Sexual homicide: A motivational model. *Journal of Interpersonal Violence, 1,* 251–272.

Canter, D. V. (2000). Offender profiling and criminal differentiation. *Legal and Criminological Psychology, 5,* 23–46.

Douglas, J. E., & Burgess, A. (1986). Criminal profiling: A viable investigative tool against violent crime. *FBI Law Enforcement Bulletin, 55,* 9–13.

Douglas. J. E., & Olshaker, M. (1995). *Mindhunter.* New York: Scribner.

Elkman, P. (1991). Who can catch a liar? *American Psychologist, 46,* 913–920.

Fox, J., & Levin, J. (1985, December). Serial killers: How statistics mislead us. *Boston Herald,* p. 45 .

Godwin, J. (1978). *Murder USA: The ways we kill each other.* New York: Ballantine Books.

Godwin, M. (2008). *Hunting serial predators* (2nd ed.). Sudbury, MA: Jones and Bartlett.

Hilgard, E. R. (1977). *Divide consciousness: Multiple controls in human thought and action.* New York: John Wiley & Sons.

Holmes, R. M., & Holmes, R. (1996). *Profiling violent crimes: An investigative tool,* (2nd ed.). Thousand Oaks, CA: Sage.

Kohnken, G. (1987). Training police officers to detect deceptive eyewitness statements: Does it work? *Social Behavior, 2,* 1–17.

Ressler, R., Burgess, A. W., & Douglas, J. (1988). *Sexual homicide: Patterns and motives.* Lexington, MA: Lexington Books.

Snook, B., Cullen, R. W., Bennett, C., Taylor, P. I., & Gendreau, P. (2008). The criminal profiling illusion: What's behind the smoke and mirrors? *Criminal Justice and Behavior, 35,* 1257–1276.

Turvey, B. (1999). *Criminal profiling: An introduction to behavioral evidence analysis.* London: Academic Press.

Maurice Godwin
St. Augustine's College, Raleigh, NC

See also: **Criminology**

CRIMINAL RESPONSIBILITY

The issue of criminal responsibility, or insanity, has to do with an individual's mental state at the time of the offense.

The basic philosophy—which stems back to the earliest recordings of Hebrew law and is still in effect throughout the United States, Canada, New Zealand, Australia, England, Wales, and other countries—is that to convict a person charged with a crime, he or she must be considered responsible for his or her criminal behavior. That is, the criminal behavior must have been a product of free will. If a defendant's behavior was not a product of free will, then he or she should not be held responsible for the crime.

Generally, two basic elements of the crime must be proved: the *actus reus*—Latin for "guilty act," which refers to the physical element or physical act of the crime—and *mens rea*—Latin for "guilty mind," which refers to the mental element of the crime, most often considered to be the intention to commit the crime. Insanity is a defense that generally contests the *mens rea* component of the crime, namely, that the individual, as a result of a mental disorder, was unable to formulate the requisite intention for the crime and thus should not be held responsible.

Legal Standards for Criminal Responsibility

In the United States, several varieties of insanity defense standards have been used across various jurisdictions and at various points in time including the M'Naghten test, the irresistible impulse standard, the Durham or product rule, the American Law Institute (ALI) standard or Brawner rule, and the insanity defense reform act standard. Currently, the two most common insanity defense standards used are a slightly restricted version of the traditional M'Naghten test and the ALI's formulation.

In the case of Daniel M'Naghten, which took place in England in 1843, the court established what has come to be known as the M'Naghten standard; also called the knowledge/right-wrong test of insanity. This standard requires that, in order to establish a defense on the grounds of insanity,

> it must be clearly proved that, at the time of the committing of the act, the party accused was labouring under such a defect of reason, from disease of the mind, as not to know the nature and quality of the act he was doing; or, if he did know it, that he did not know he was doing what was wrong. (M'Naghten's Case, 1843, p. 722)

Thus, the M'Naghten test requires that a defendant is suffering from a disease of the mind (interpreted as being a mental disorder) that causes impairment in terms of either (1) not understanding the nature and quality of his or her actions or (2) not knowing that those actions were wrong. The careful reader will note that there is a link between the mental disorder of the accused and the impairment in either knowledge of his or her actions (he or she did not know what he or she was doing) or in knowing right from wrong (he or she did not know that what he or she was doing was wrong) such that the mental disorder

must be directly related to one of these impairments. This standard is considered to be a cognitive standard, because it requires that a defect in knowledge or reason be linked to mental disorder.

The ALI standard was developed partially in an attempt to resolve the issue of the M'Naghten test being too cognitive in nature. The ALI standard established that an accused is not criminally responsible if, as a result of mental disease or defect, he lacks substantial capacity either to appreciate the criminality (wrongfulness) of his conduct or to conform his or her conduct to the requirements of the law (American Law Institute, 1962, p. 401). Thus, the ALI standard includes both a cognitive and a volitional component and appears to be more comprehensive than the M'Naghten test. The ALI standard is currently used in about half of the United States.

Use and Success of a Criminal Responsibility (Insanity) Defense

Public perceptions of the insanity defense are that it is frequently used, is frequently successful, and serves as a "loophole" guilty people use to go free; however, empirical research on whether these public perceptions are born out reveals that the public overestimates both the use and success of the insanity defense and underestimates the length of confinement of insanity acquittees (Silver, Cirincione, & Steadman, 1994).

Although the exact rates of use and success vary by jurisdiction, as a general statement, the insanity defense is rarely used and even more rarely successful. Silver, Cirincione, and Steadman (1994) compared public perceptions of the insanity defense with empirical data on its actual use and found that the public estimates the use of the insanity defense to be 37% (or 37 per 100 felony indictments), whereas the actual use is 0.9% (less than 1 per 100 felony indictments). Similarly, with respect to estimates regarding the success of the insanity defense, these authors report that the public estimates the success rate to be 44% (or 44 acquittals per 100 insanity pleas), whereas the actual rate of success is 26%. That is, there are nine insanity pleas for every 1,000 felony cases, about only two of which are successful.

Characteristics of Insanity Acquittees

Research examining the demographic characteristics of insanity acquittees in the United States (Cirincione, Steadman, & McGreevy, 1995) indicates that the typical insanity acquittee is male, between the ages of 20 and 29, single, unemployed, minimally educated, diagnosed with a major mental illness, has had prior contact with the criminal justice and mental health systems, and is acquitted for a violent offense. In terms of the types of mental illness that plague insanity acquittees, research has consistently demonstrated that the majority of insanity acquittees are diagnosed with psychotic disorders with schizophrenia being perhaps the most common.

Assessment of Criminal Responsibility

The assessment of criminal responsibility poses a special challenge to the mental health professional since this type of evaluation focuses narrowly on a specific period of time in the past and, thus, is retrospective in nature. In addition to interviewing the defendant, third party and collateral information sources are important resources for these evaluations since the mental health professional must attempt to reconstruct the thoughts, feelings, beliefs, and behaviors of the defendant for the time frame surrounding and including the commission of the criminal offense. A review of relevant records (including police reports and any available mental health records), interviews with individuals who know the defendant well or who were with the defendant at or around the time of the offense, and the administration of any relevant psychological tests or forensic assessment instruments make up the additional components of the evaluation process.

Although several forensic assessment instruments have been developed for use in other types of forensic assessments, there has only been one published instrument developed for use in the assessment of criminal responsibility—*Rogers Criminal Responsibility Assessment Scales* (R-CRAS; Rogers, 1984). The R-CRAS was developed as a way to standardize the collection of information for evaluations of criminal responsibility using the ALI standard but can also be adapted for use with the M'Naghten standard.

If defendants raise the issue of their mental state by using an insanity defense at trial (or by declaring his or her intention to pursue an insanity defense), the prosecution then has the right to have an evaluation of their mental state at the time of the offense conducted by an expert of the prosecution's choosing. If the case proceeds to trial (the vast majority of all cases are resolved by a guilty plea or a plea bargain), experts for both sides (prosecution and defense) may testify about the defendant's mental state, and the decision regarding whether defendants are to be held accountable for their actions rests with the legal decision maker in the case—the jury or, if there is no jury, the judge.

In many cases the issue of criminal responsibility is not disputed, and both sides agree that the defendant was insane at the time of the offense and should not be held criminally responsible. Cirincione (1996) examined the processing of insanity pleas and determined that the vast majority of insanity cases were handled through either plea bargain (42.9%) or bench trial (42.7%), with relatively few (14.4%) being handled via jury trial. Conviction rates were approximately 88% for plea bargain cases, 45% for bench trials, and 75% for jury trials.

REFERENCES

American Law Institute. (1962). *Model penal code.* Washington, DC: Author.

Cirincione, C. (1996). Revisiting the insanity defense: Contested or consensus? *Bulletin of the American Academy of Psychiatry and Law, 24,* 165–176.

Cirincione, C., Steadman, H. J., & McGreevy, M. A. (1995). Rates of insanity acquittals and the factors associated with successful insanity pleas. *Bulletin of the American Academy of Psychiatry and Law, 23,* 399–409.

M'Naghten's Case, 8 Eng. Rep. 718 (1843).

Rogers, R. (1984). *Rogers criminal responsibility assessment scales (RCRAS) and test manual.* Odessa, FL: Psychological Assessment Resources.

Silver, E., Cirincione, C., & Steadman, H. J. (1994). Demythologizing inaccurate perceptions of the insanity defense. *Law and Human Behavior, 18,* 63–70.

SUGGESTED READINGS

Perlin, M. (1994). *The jurisprudence of the insanity defense.* Durham, NC: Carolina Academic Press.

Rogers, R., & Shuman, D. W. (2000). *Conducting insanity evaluations.* New York: Guilford Press.

Zapf, P. A., Golding, S. L., & Roesch, R. (2006). Criminal responsibility and the insanity defense. In I. B. Weiner & A. K. Hess (Eds.), *Handbook of forensic psychology* (3rd ed., pp. 332–363). Hoboken, NJ: John Wiley & Sons.

PATRICIA A. ZAPF
*John Jay College of Criminal Justice—
The City University of New York*

See also: **Civil Competence; Expert Testimony; Forensic Psychology**

CRIMINOLOGY

Criminology is the scientific study of crime and criminal behavior. It encompasses criminal law, the measurement of crime, theories of criminal offending, types of offenders, and society's responses to offenders. Criminology is an interdisciplinary field, drawing from many disciplines including psychology, psychiatry, sociology, biology, public health, law, political science, criminal justice, economics, and geography.

Definition of Crime

Crimes are defined by law as offenses committed against society and punishable by the state according to statutorily defined limits. Punishment may include loss of freedom and, in many states, death in cases of murder. Many crimes are considered inherently wrong by most individuals and are labeled *mala in se* offenses, such as killing another person or sexually assaulting a child. In other instances, there is disagreement whether certain acts should be crimes. These acts, when criminalized, are referred to as *mala prohibita* offenses and include such activities as smoking marijuana and failure to pay income taxes (Gaines & Miller, 2008). Mala prohibita offenses, unlike mala in se offenses, are often construed as representing dominant and powerful interests groups in society.

Classification of Crime

Scholars and practitioners have found it useful to classify crime into different types. For many years, major crime subdivisions have focused on studying violent, property, public order, white collar, and organized crime (Gaines & Miller, 2008). Violent crimes include murder (killing of another person without lawful justification), robbery (taking of another's property by force or threat of force), rape/sexual assault (engaging in sexual relations with another by force or the use of force), and aggravated assault (hitting another with intent to cause serious injury, usually with a weapon likely to produce death or serious bodily harm).

Property crimes include burglary (breaking into a dwelling with intent to steal), auto theft (taking a car with intent to deprive the owner of the vehicle), larceny-theft (taking another's property without force or threat with intent to deprive the owner of the property), and arson (intentionally setting fire to property). Public order crimes are considered to offend social mores and often include prostitution, public drunkenness, gambling, and use of illegal drugs. These crimes are often considered victimless or consensual crimes because there is no identified victim in the traditional sense.

White collar crimes are broadly construed to include illegal activities committed without violence by individuals or business entities to secure some advantage. Examples include embezzlement (an employee uses his position to steal from his employer), insurance fraud (making a false claim to obtain money), consumer fraud (defrauding customers by making false promises or adding on hidden costs), and tax evasion (underreporting or ignoring tax liability). Organized crimes include acts committed by criminal enterprises usually involved in supplying illicit goods and services to the public.

Law and criminology are both dynamic fields. As the world has become more global, warfare more advanced, and technology more complex, more sophisticated crimes have emerged as a major focus of study. Terrorism uses symbolic acts of violence or the threat of violence to frighten the public at large to achieve political ends. Computer crimes consist of acts directed to harm computers, such as the spreading of viruses or worms, or using computers to commit white-collar crimes like fraud and embezzlement. Cyber crimes involve illegal acts committed by using the internet in the virtual world, such as cyber-stalking (stalking someone online), cyber fraud (fraud committed by use of misrepresentations made over the internet), and cyber theft (stealing information through the internet, such as identity theft). Predators who use the internet to solicit sex from minors and pedophiles who trade child pornography online are involved in cyber crime (Gaines & Miller, 2008).

Measurement of Crime

Measuring crime is often a difficult endeavor, as many crimes go unreported and some remain undetected. There are four major ways of measuring crime. Since 1930, the Federal Bureau of Investigation (FBI) has compiled national statistics on the frequency of specific crimes reported to police and the characteristics of individuals arrested for particular crimes analyzed by age, gender, race, and region. These analyses are published yearly in the *Uniform Crime Reports* and are known as official data (FBI, 2007).

Since 1973, the federal government has interviewed approximately 100,000 occupants in more than 40,000 households twice yearly about their crime experiences during the last six months as part of the *National Crime Victimization Survey*. Individuals are asked if they have been victims of rape, sexual assault, robbery, assault, theft, household burglary, or motor vehicle theft. Victimization rates are provided for the population and for specific groups such as the elderly, women, numbers of various racial groups, and urban dwellers (Bureau of Justice Statistics, 2008).

Self-report surveys ask respondents if they have ever committed specific crimes, such as robbery, assault, or teenage drinking. These surveys are typically given to juvenile lawbreakers, students in elementary and high schools, and students in college (Gaines & Miller, 2008).

The fourth type of crime measurement involves cohort studies. One of the classic studies in Criminology conducted by Marvin Wolfgang and his colleagues (1972) followed nearly 10,000 boys born in 1945 in Philadelphia to age 17 to analyze their involvement in delinquency. One of the key findings of this study was that 6.3% of the boys were chronic offenders defined as having five or more officially recorded police contacts. Together these 6.3% were responsible for 52% of all police contacts, and the majority of murders, robberies, rapes, and aggravated assaults. These findings were replicated in a study involving more than 13,000 boys born in Philadelphia in 1958 (Tracy, Wolfgang, & Figlio, 1990). In the second study, chronic offenders constituted 7.5% of the cohort and were responsible for 61% of all police contacts. Several cohort studies have been ongoing since the late 1980s in Rochester,

Denver, and Pittsburgh (Loeber, Wei, Stouthamer-Lober, Huizinga, & Thornberry, 1999).

Results of victimization surveys, self-report surveys, and cohort studies suggest that there is a large amount of hidden crime, crime that is not reported or known to police. Fortunately, many of the crimes that go unreported by victims and undetected by police are clustered in the less serious crime categories, such as larceny theft, simple assault, and underage drinking.

Theories of Crime Causation

A major focus that has dominated Criminology since its inception is crime causation. Theories have been developed to understand lawbreaking by juveniles, known as juvenile delinquency, as well as adult crime (Akers & Sellers, 2008). Most studies have focused on explaining crime committed by males because males are disproportionately represented in almost all crime categories.

Psychological and sociological explanations of crime predominated in the twentieth century. Psychological theories of crime examine why individuals commit specific crimes and look at factors such as trauma in early childhood, low intelligence, restricted personality development, traits such as psychopathy, and the presence of mental illness. They also include explanations that focus on the learning and maintaining of criminal behavior, cognitions that promote criminal behavior, and attempts to meet one's physical, social, and existential needs by committing crimes.

Sociological explanations of crime focus on structural factors and processes that push some groups more than others to commit crimes. Important sociological variables include poverty, declining and ineffective neighborhood institutions, family constellation, gang involvement, and peer associations. Theories suggest that people commit crimes because they lack legitimate opportunities to acquire societal goals (strain theory) or they are involved in deviant subcultures that value criminal behavior (subcultural theory). The poor are disproportionately represented in crime statistics because they are "labeled" criminals more than their affluent counterparts (labeling theory) and the laws passed by largely wealthy legislators tend to criminalize actions more common among the lower classes (radical criminology). Another sociological explanation (social control theory) maintains that certain individuals are free to commit crimes. These are people who lack the following: bonds to society as measured by attachment to parents, teachers, and conventional peers, commitment to school and work, involvement in prosocial activities, and law-abiding beliefs.

Biological theories of crimes were at the forefront when Criminology emerged as a discipline in the nineteenth century. Cesare Lombroso, an Italian physician (1835–1909) is considered "the father of Criminology." He initially hypothesized that criminals were born and were "atavistic" (less evolved human beings). Lombroso used cadavers of executed criminals to measure their physical characteristics (jaws, teeth, hairlines) in an attempt to find biological differences between offenders and nonoffenders.

Although many of the tenets Lombroso proposed have been discredited, biological explanations of crime are receiving renewed attention. These include investigation into the effects of brain injury and neurological impairment. Recent findings suggest an association between violent behavior and genetic influences, the neurotransmitter serotonin, and brain dysfunction (Heide, 1999). Advances in science, particularly those focusing on brain development and the effects of childhood trauma, suggest that biopsychological explanations will increasingly play a role in understanding violent behavior in the twenty-first century (Heide & Solomon, 2006).

Types of Offenders

Criminology often focuses on particular types of offenders. Groups studied include murders, sex offenders, arsonists, drug offenders, women offenders, and juvenile offenders. Investigations focus on within group differences with an aim to better understand offenders and to take appropriate actions regarding sentencing and prevention. For example, sex offenders are not a homogenous group. They include: a school teacher who has sex with her eighth-grade student, a man who breaks into a house and rapes the female occupant, a 40-year priest who prefers 8-year-olds as sexual partners, an 18-year-old boy who has consensual sex with his 15-year-old girlfriend, and a man who rapes, tortures, and kills a male prostitute he solicited for sex.

Society's Response to Offenders

Criminology systematically investigates offenders based on the factors that contributed to their lawbreaking behavior with an aim to early detection of aberrant behavior, appropriate intervention, and effective prevention. The discipline examines the effects of legislation that often fails to recognize the differences among particular types of offenders. Criminology critically evaluates treatment and intervention strategies to determine what works for what types of offenders under what type of circumstances. Research findings can be a powerful tool in influencing societal attitudes and informing public policy on dispositional alternatives for offenders.

REFERENCES

Akers, R., & Sellers, C. (2008). *Criminological theories: Introduction, evaluation, and application* (5th ed.). New York: Oxford University Press.

Bureau of Justice Statistics. (2008). *Crime and victim statistics*. U.S. Department of Justice. Retrieved July 10, 2008, from http://www.ojp.usdoj.gov/bjs/cvict.htm.

Federal Bureau of Investigation. (2007). *Crime in the United States 2006.* Washington, DC: Government Printing Office.

Gaines, L. K., & Miller, R. L. (2008). *Criminal justice in action: The core* (4th ed.). Belmont, CA: Thomson Wadsworth.

Heide, K. M. (1999). *Young killers: The challenge of juvenile homicide.* Thousand Oaks, CA: Sage.

Heide, K. M., & Solomon, E. P. (2006). Biology, childhood trauma, and murder: Rethinking justice. *International Journal of Law & Psychiatry, 29,* 220–233.

Loeber, R., Wei, E., Stouthamer-Loeber, M., Huizinga, D., & Thornberry, T. (1999). Behavioral antecedents to serious and violent juvenile offending: Joint analyses from the Denver Youth Survey, the Pittsburgh Youth Study, and the Rochester Development Study. *Studies in Crime and Crime Prevention, 8,* 245–263.

Tracy, P. E., Wolfgang, M. E., & Figlio, R. M. (1990). *Delinquency careers in two birth cohorts.* New York: Plenum Press.

Wolfgang, M. E., Figlio, R. M., & Sellin, T. (1972). *Delinquency in a birth cohort.* Chicago: University of Chicago Press, 1972.

SUGGESTED READING

Howell, J. C. (2003). *Preventing & reducing juvenile delinquency.* Thousand Oaks, CA: Sage.

KATHLEEN M. HEIDE
University of South Florida

See also: **Criminal Profiling**

CRISIS INTERVENTION

A crisis is a collapse in one's ability to solve problems or cope with a situation in which the person's existing strategies for coping do not work. Whether a crisis is situational or developmental, the person in crisis is not able to regain homeostasis or balance by the usual means of coping typically employed. The term crisis is easily misunderstood if one views it in terms of an event or situation. In mental health terms, a crisis is not the traumatic event, but rather a person's reaction to it. The same event could be devastating for one individual and not affect another.

The less psychologically stable a person is at the time of a precipitating crisis event, the more apt the person is to exhibit a crisis reaction. Minor stressors have a low probability of triggering a crisis response, unless the person is already experiencing a high level of turmoil. Major stressors have a higher probability of eliciting a crisis response than minor stressors. A person with strong resources is less likely to be in crisis than a person with poor coping abilities. A person is most apt to experience a

crisis response when he or she is currently nearing a state of disequilibrium.

A crisis differs from a problem by its level of severity. People who experience a crisis are in an emergency situation in which they may be dangerous to themselves or others or are gravely disabled (Parad & Parad, 1999). Someone in crisis usually can wait no longer than 24 to 72 hours for assistance that calls for specialized crisis-counseling techniques.

Many texts in crisis intervention refer to the Chinese word for the word crisis, which is formed with the characters for the word "danger" and the word for "opportunity." A person coming out of a crisis situation is changed by the event and will either grow or decline in a number of ways as a result of the crisis. Kanel (2003, p. 1) provides a good overall synopsis of other definitions of a crisis. Kanel states that a crisis has three parts: (1) a precipitating event occurs, (2) the perception of the event leads to subjective distress, and (3) usual coping methods fail. Thus, the person functions at a lower than usual level psychologically, emotionally, or behaviorally.

Risk Factors

Given the right circumstances, anyone can show crisis behavior. No one has unlimited resources that can prevent a state of disequilibrium from ever occurring. Individuals' resilience to stress varies, depending on a number of situational factors at a particular time in their life. People may be able to handle a given crisis situation or level of stress at one point in time, but not in another. Myers (1989) describes 12 types of risk factors for crisis reactions: (1) age and developmental phase, (2) health, (3) disability, (4) preexisting stresses, (5) previous traumatic life events, (6) strength of social supports, (7) coping skills, (8) expectation of self and others, (9) status of family members, (10) ethnic and cultural milieu, (11) interaction between the individual's occupation and event, and (12) perception and interpretation of the event. Disruptions in one or any combination of these factors decrease one's ability to cope with a crisis event, because these events can in themselves lower one's defenses.

Basis Assumptions of Crisis Intervention

Wiger and Harowski (2003) describe the following basic assumptions of crisis interventions:

1. Most crises are sudden and unpredictable. One of the reasons why crises affect a person so dramatically is that they are neither prepared for nor expected. A sudden crisis significantly disrupts any of a number of aspects of an individual's life. However, some predictable events, such as retirement, marriage, and graduation, still lead to a crisis response. Other crises may be the cumulative result of several built-up stressors or events.

2. Crises are temporary. Most crises last no more than a few weeks and average about 36 hours in duration. Humans cannot sustain the level of stress caused by a crisis. The level of stress can be so overwhelming that irrational decisions such as suicide might be viewed as the only option. Crisis interventions help in presenting immediate alternative behaviors.

3. A crisis results in a loss of psychological equilibrium in which a person's normal coping mechanisms are not sufficient to return to a homeostatic state. During this time, the person in crisis is atypically vulnerable to coping strategies (Puryear, 1979). This vulnerability may be adaptive (e.g., uncharacteristic openness to listening to others for help), or dysfunctional (e.g., suicidality or abuse of substances).

4. People in crisis are not necessarily mentally ill. Both people with and without mental illness can go through times of crisis. The related anxiety and depression resulting from a crisis are not, in themselves, indicators of mental illness. Diagnosing someone who is going through a situational crisis with a diagnosis of a chronic mental health disorder may be a significant error. Although the symptoms may appear identical to a mental health disorder, they could subside in a brief time period, unlike a chronic mental health disorder.

5. Knowledge of the cultural, ethnic, spiritual, and other biopsychosocial aspects of a person will help understand the specific effects a crisis will have on the person. Without such information, errors in assessment are bound to occur.

6. Crisis intervention is a crucial aspect of treatment. It has its place in mental health treatment. In fact, it has been referred to as the third of three revolutionary phases in the mental health field since 1900 (Hoff, 2001). These include discoveries of the unconscious by Freud, of psychotropic drugs in the 1950s, and of crisis interventions in the 1960s. However, crisis intervention does not take the place of psychotherapy. Not all people in crisis will need follow-up psychotherapy. If crisis intervention adequately helps a distressed person to cope with the crisis situation and return to premorbid functioning, psychotherapy may not be necessary.

History of Crisis Intervention

Soldiers in WWI and WWII receiving early interventions for severe distress fared better than those without early interventions. Holmes (1985) notes that soldiers who demonstrated significant stress reactions were often viewed as weak, insane, or even traitors. Soldiers treated immediately for what was early on called "shell shock" had a much better chance of returning to combat. In the 1930s,

New York's Mayor LaGuardia requested a study of police officers due to their proportionately high suicide rate. Hospital emergency personnel have historically suffered a high turnover rate due to job stressors. Stress management procedures developed by Marge Epperson-Sebour at the Shock Trauma Center in Baltimore in the mid-1970s have influenced crisis management problems today.

Erich Lindemann's (1944) classic study of a fire in Boston's Coconut Grove Melody Lounge, in which 493 people died, is often cited as the first significant study of crisis intervention. Lindemann and others from Massachusetts General Hospital, helping in the disaster, discovered that nonmedical personnel and clergy were effective in helping survivors who had lost loved ones. Their results identified five common reactions to acute trauma as somatic distress, preoccupation with images of the deceased, guilt for having survived, hostile reactions, and loss of patterns of conduct. Prognosis improves when people can go through a period of grieving and deal with the loss. Lindemann and his colleagues also found that those who later developed significant psychological symptoms had not gone go through a normal grieving process.

Lindemann and Gerard Caplan subsequently developed the Wellesley Project in Cambridge, Massachusetts, which focused on individuals reacting to traumatic events. This community mental health center became one of the first to emphasize preventive psychiatry within a short-term therapy model. Lindemann and Caplan are generally credited for initially developing contemporary crisis theory. Caplan continued his work in preventive psychiatry for the next few decades, focusing on early intervention and proposing theoretical concepts that are the foundations of modern crisis intervention theory. Virtually all writers in the field rely on or adapt Caplan's concepts of preventive psychiatry, which emphasized early interventions and incorporating community practitioners such as clergy, nurses, and teachers into efforts to help prepare people for predictable developmental crises like those defined by Erikson (1963) as requiring successful resolution for normal developmental growth to occur.

Throughout the 1960s the use of nonprofessionals and paraprofessionals in such contexts as suicide hotlines, walk-in centers, and community mental health centers (CMHC) expanded, and Caplan's model remained in the forefront. The community mental health movement was significantly aided by funding stemming from the Community Mental Health Centers Act of 1963. Rapoport (1967, p. 38) emphasized the need for immediate intervention for people in crisis, declaring "A little help, rationally directed and purposefully focused at a strategic time, is more effective than more extensive help given at a period of less emotional accessibility."

During the 1970s the research and knowledge base of crisis intervention techniques increased significantly. The rise in short-term therapy, and its lesser cost compared to long-term therapy, further increased the usage of crisis intervention services.

The 1980s led to a large increase in professional training of mental health workers. However, the combination of less public funds available and the requirement by insurance companies that mental health services be conducted by professionals with at least a master's degree led to a decrease in the crisis intervention models and an increase in long-term therapy (Kanel, 2003). Nevertheless, health maintenance organizations (HMOs) have demanded a short-term therapy mode of treatment, which once again turned the pendulum toward a crisis intervention model.

The 1990s and 2000s have seen widespread development of organized crisis intervention programs. The American Red Cross and critical incidents stress management (CISM) teams have developed national and training programs for group crisis interventions. Disasters such as the Oklahoma City Federal Building bombing, the 9/11 World Trade Center disaster, and other airline disasters have led to increased services for victims, families, and communities.

The field of community psychology has gradually developed to meet modern needs related to changes in family structure, an increasing geriatric population, and the integration of the mentally ill into society. Community health centers offer primary and secondary prevention services provided by multidisciplinary teams. Due to economic restraints, there has been an increase in the number of paraprofessionals who work in these centers under the supervision of professionals. Many people who would otherwise not obtain any mental health treatment receive crisis-counseling services over the telephone through 24-hour hotlines staffed by volunteers. The Internet also contains numerous sites offering free or paid mental health services.

Crisis Counseling

A team of crisis workers, who may include first-responders, family members, medical personnel, crisis counselors, mental health professionals, and after-care treatment providers, can affect the path a person in crisis takes to either grow or decline. When immediate and effective support is provided, the victim can learn the tools necessary to cope with the experience and be better prepared for future crises. Some people who do not receive timely help develop significant mental health problems. The primary purpose and goal of crisis intervention (also called psychological first-aid or emotional first-aid; see Neil, Oney, Difonso, Thacker, & Reichart, 1974) is to aid victims by helping them secure safety, obtain needed resources for stabilization, and return to normal functioning.

The first responders in crisis intervention are trained in specific techniques of psychological first aid. Greenstone and Leviton (2002) comment that, early in their careers, crisis workers learn established procedures in a logical and orderly process. They further note that actions are thoughtful, measured, and purposeful. Workers must learn specific and proven intervention methods, instead of using a hit and miss approach. Crisis workers providing psychological first aid should in particular take the necessary steps to offer immediate intervention, establish rapport, do an assessment, take action, utilize available resources, and see to aftercare.

Each goal of crisis intervention focuses on the current situation, not long-term planning or the pre-crisis situation. Like psychotherapy, crisis intervention involves assessment, treatment planning, and treatment. However, the specific interventions in a crisis situation involve different skills and treatment methods from those applied in traditional psychotherapy. Assessment in typical psychotherapy requires obtaining multiple details about a client's strengths, needs, abilities, and preferences ("SNAP's"); inquiring about past, present, and, often, future goals; and formulating a diagnosis (Wiger & Huntley, 2002). Crisis intervention assessment involves a brief assessment of the client's safety, immediate needs, and need for immediate services.

Crisis intervention planning is short-term and designed to restore people to a level equal to or above their functioning prior to the crisis. A primary focus of immediate crisis intervention is resources. Crisis intervention is narrowly focused and usually a few weeks or less in duration. It focuses on understanding, coping, and restoration. It is not designed to restructure the client's personality, as in traditional, long-term psychotherapy. Interventions in psychotherapy may involve a variety of therapeutic techniques, ranging from short-term to long-term therapy, and might focus on the past, present, or future.

Crisis workers can be categorized into three groups: frontline workers, paraprofessionals, and professionals. Frontline workers include such occupations as police officers, emergency medical personnel, and fire fighters. Frontline workers are present in emergency situations in which immediate help has been requested. In mental health situations, their primary purpose is to immediately assess the situation and deal with immediate concerns. Paraprofessionals are typically trained volunteers, undergraduate or graduate students in mental health, or others who receive specific, narrowly focused training in short-term crisis intervention. They usually work on hotlines or in centers for domestic violence, sexual assault, or crime. Professional mental health workers have at least an advanced degree in areas such as psychology, social work, counseling, psychiatric nursing, or psychiatry. Other professionals such as teachers and nurses might fit into more than one role. A large-scale situation, such as a trauma within a community, may require a multidisciplinary crisis intervention team.

REFERENCES

Erikson, E. H. (1963). *Childhood and society*. New York: W.W. Norton.

Greenstone, J. L., & Levitson, S. C. (1993). *Elements of crisis intervention: Crises and how to respond to them*. Pacific Grove, CA: Brooks/Cole.

Hoff, L. A. (2001). *People in crisis: Clinical and public health perspectives*. (5th ed.). San Francisco: Jossey-Bass.

Holmes, R. (1985). *Acts of War: The behavior of men in battle*. New York: Free Press.

Kanel, K. (2003). *A guide to crisis intervention*. (2nd ed.) Pacific Grove, PA: Brook/Cole.

Lindemann, E. (1944). Symptomology and management of acute grief. *American Review of Psychiatry, 101*, 101–148.

Myers, D. (1989). *Training manual for disaster mental health*. Sacramento, CA: California Department of Mental Health.

Neil, T., Oney, J., Difsons, L., Thacker, B., & Richart, W. (1974). *Emotional first aid*. Louisville, KY: Kempter-Behaviroral Sciences Associates.

Parad, H. J., & Parad L. G. (1999). *Crisis intervention: Book 2*. Canada: Manticore.

Puryear, D. A. (1979). *Helping people in crisis*. San Francisco: Jossey-Bass.

Rapoport, L. (1967). Crisis-oriented short-term casework. *Social Services Review, 41*(1), 31–43.

Wiger, D. E., & Harowski J. (2003). *Essentials of crisis counseling and intervention*. Hoboken, NJ: John Wiley & Sons.

Wiger, D. E., & Huntley, D. K. (2002). *Essentials of interviewing*. New York: John Wiley & Sons.

DONALD E. WIGER
Lake Elmo, MN

See also: **Disaster Psychology; Posttraumatic Growth; Posttraumatic Stress Disorder; Trauma Psychology**

CRONBACH, LEE J. (1916–2001)

Lee J. Cronbach received his BA from Fresno State College and the PhD from the University of Chicago in 1940. He taught at the Universities of Chicago, Illinois, and Stanford. He was Vida Jacks Professor of Education at Stanford. In 1957, he served as president of the American Psychological Association, and in 1974 received its Distinguished Scientific Contributions Award.

His most important books were *Essentials of Psychological Testing* and *Educational Psychology*. In his research, he was concerned with new approaches to the validation of psychological tests. His book on psychological testing emphasized general critical principles for test development and use.

This book and Anastasi's book on psychological testing were widely used as texts during the height of the historical period in which great advances were made in clinical assessment. Entire generations of assessment psychologists received their introduction to this area through these books. He chaired the 1951–1955 Committee on Test Standards (American Psychological Association); the mission was the development of the original code for maintaining quality tests of ability and personality. He developed a widely used measure of test reliability (internal consistency) called *Cronbach's Alpha*. Cronbach and Meehl's "Construct Validity in Psychological Tests" is considered one of psychology's classic papers.

In educational psychology, Cronbach has stressed the relationship between classroom practices and basic psychological principles, particularly those of generalization and the transfer of training.

SUGGESTED READINGS

Cronbach, L. J. (1977). *Educational psychology* (3rd ed.). New York: Harcourt Brace Jovanovich.

Cronbach, L. J., & Meehl, P. E. (1955). Construct validity in psychological tests. *Psychological Bulletin, 52*, 281–302.

STAFF

CROSS-CULTURAL AND CROSS-NATIONAL ASSESSMENT

Cross-cultural assessment refers to the practice of acquiring test data on persons who differ culturally. Such assessment practices originally were used somewhat exclusively by persons who specialized in cross-cultural psychology, a branch of psychology that studies similarities and variances in human behavior and psychological constructs across cultures (VandenBos, 2007). Cross-cultural scholarship has been described as growing from a whisper in the 1960s to a thriving enterprise in the twenty-first century (Segall, Lonner, & Berry, 1998). This growth is seen, in part, in an increase in the numbers of cross-cultural studies, going from an estimated 600 in 1978 to approximately 1,500 in 2003 (van de Vijver, 2006).

However, the greatest increase in cross-cultural assessment has occurred in its applied practices. Tests now are commonly used worldwide with individuals who differ culturally to describe current behavior and estimate future behaviors, assist guidance and counseling services, establish intervention methods, evaluate progress, screen for special needs, diagnose disabling disorders, help place persons in jobs or programs, facilitate administrative decisions, and assist in determining whether persons should be credentialed, admitted/employed, retained, or promoted. The widespread use of testing over the Internet (Bartram & Hambleton, 2006) as well as large scale international studies of education (e.g., Program for International Student Assessment and Trends in International Mathematics and Science Study) underscore the virtual explosion of cross-cultural assessment in applied practices.

Terminology

The term *cross-cultural psychology* is better understood if the terms *cross-cultural* and *cross-national* are used. Cross-cultural practices typically study and use knowledge of the means and variances both within and between two or more groups who differ by culture yet reside within one country. Test use with Native Americans and whites in the United States exemplifies cross-cultural practices. In contrast, cross-national practices typically study and use knowledge of the means and variances both within and between two or more groups within two or more countries. Test use with persons in the United States, France, and Greece exemplifies cross-national practices.

The use of the term *culture* also poses challenges, especially in its measurement. The term often refers to an integrated and shared pattern of human behavior that includes thought, language, action, and artifacts and depends on man's capacity for learning and transmitting knowledge to succeeding generations (*Merriam-Webster's New College Dictionary*, 1980). Given difficulties associated with measuring these qualities, psychology and other social sciences often rely on one or more of the following demographic qualities as a proxy for culture: race, ethnicity, language, social class, education level, religion, and geography. The use of these proxies does not provide knowledge of qualities that are likely to have a material impact on behavior, including shared values, goals, beliefs, attitudes, and resources. Thus, the absence of valid measures of culture limits the clarity of work cross-culturally and cross-nationally.

Early Efforts in Cross-Cultural and Cross-National Assessment

Cross-national studies often are interested in describing prevailing qualities within one country (e.g., an emic focus) and determining the extent one country's qualities are found elsewhere (e.g., an etic focus). For example, are gender differences in Thinking-Feeling temperament preferences found in the United States (an emic account) also found in most other countries (an etic account)?

Early efforts to engage in cross-cultural and cross-national assessment relied largely on tests developed in the United States and Western Europe and, if needed, translated for use in other locations. Efforts were made to select tests that minimize cultural differences by utilizing tests that focus on fluid abilities (e.g., those dependent on

neurological qualities such as memory and mental fluency) and that minimize crystallized abilities (e.g., those dependent on culturally acquired qualities such as academic achievement and language). Some tests were labeled *culture free* (a standard attainable only by some measures used in medicine) while others were labeled *culture fair* (a worthy yet often unattainable standard in the behavioral sciences). For example, the Raven's Progressive Matrices, introduced in 1938, often is cited as a culture-fair measure of intelligence. It utilizes visual abstract designs and a nonverbal administration.

The use of these measures often revealed mean score differences between persons from different cultures, thus leading some to conclude that the tests were biased and should not be used. However, others accepted mean score differences as possibly an accurate characterization and instead underscored test validity as the standard for judging test bias. Their work lead to a current definition of test bias as "the tendency of a test to systematically over- or underestimate the true score of individuals to whom the test is administered or those who are members of a particular group (e.g., ethnic minorities, sexes, etc.)" (VandenBos, 2007, p. 931). Among those who specialize in test development and use, a test's factor structure (e.g., examined through exploratory and confirmatory factor analysis) as well as concurrent and predictive validity generally have become the gold standard for judging test bias. A more complete discussion of the history of cross-cultural psychology is found in Segall et al., 1998 and on the Center for Cross-Cultural Research's web site (www.ac.wwu.edu/~culture/contents_complete.htm).

Three Critical Issues That Need to Be Addressed

Cross-cultural and cross-national assessment seemingly is poised to enter its next level of development by addressing three broad methodological issues. These include the need to take into account the hierarchical nature of cultural data, to address the assumption of equivalent psychological meaning and factorial structure of a test across cultural groups, and to recognize the importance of ethical issues governing test adaptation and use in diverse cultural settings (Byrne, Oakland, & Leong, in press). Each is summarized below.

Hierarchical Structure of Data

Data acquired in cross-cultural and cross-national studies are hierarchically structured. Individuals are nested in cultures. Thus, statistics need to analyze both aggregated (i.e., country level) data and well as disaggregated (individual level) data. Aggregated data allow one to examine differences in means and variance between groups. Disaggregated data allow one to examine the degree relationships among variables within culture are similarly related across cultures.

Structural and Measurement Equivalence

Persons engaged in cross-cultural and cross-national work may assume the psychological meaning of constructs and factor structures are equivalent for unaggregated and aggregated data. Equivalence may be evaluated in reference to the tests' functional impact, conceptual relationships, linguistic meaning, and statistical equivalence. Data on structural equivalence examine the extent to which the meaning and dimensional structure of a psychological construct are identical across cultural groups. Data on measurement equivalence examine the extent the item content and psychometric properties (e.g., reliability and validity) are similar across groups. Structural equation modeling (Byrne, 1998, 2001, 2006) provides the most rigorous test for cross-level equivalence. However, its need for large sample sizes often precludes its use. Similar information may be obtained by using exploratory analysis. Item response theory (Hambleton, Swaminathan, & Rogers, 1991) can be a useful strategy when testing for item equivalence across cultural groups.

Ethical Issues Associated with Cross-cultural and Cross-National Assessment

Professionals are expected to restrict their services to areas in which they are competent. However, the competence of professionals to engage in these assessment activities through research or applied practices may be meager. Most have not had formal training in cross-cultural psychology and few seek consultation from experts. In addition, few ethics codes from national psychological associations address issues pertaining to this work (Leach & Oakland, 2007). The two most prominent international psychological associations (e.g., International Association of Applied Psychology and the International Union of Psychological Science) do not have ethics codes.

International Test Commission

The International Test Commission (ITC, www.intestcom .org) provides leadership internationally for developing international guidelines for test development and use, including those for general test use (Bartram, 2001), computer-based testing and Internet (Coyne & Bartram, 2006; Bartram & Hambleton, 2007), and adapting tests (Hambleton, Merenda, & Spielberger, 2005; also see the ITC web site). Given the importance of test adaptation for cross-cultural and cross-national assessment, its test adaptation guidelines are summarized below.

Test Adaptations, Not Test Translations

Many countries do not have an infrastructure (e.g., adequate professional resources, a sufficiently large market, respect for copyright laws) needed for test development and use. Thus, they need to rely on transforming tests developed in other countries (i.e. the source test) for use in their country (i.e. the target test). This practice is acceptable provided target tests are adequately adapted and used.

Tests should be decentered by revising a test's source language leading to equivalent test content and language on the source and target tests. One of three translation methods typically are used: forward, backward, and consensus. Tests must use a suitable format (e.g., multiple choice, short answer, essay), consistent with the nature of the test and the prior experiences of those being tested. Tests should emphasize power (e.g., a person's mastery of the topic) rather than speed (e.g., the number of items one can complete in a predetermined time). The work of specialists in language, test content, and test development is critical to the success of this important initial process. Test data on a representative sample then are acquired and analyzed.

The equivalence of the source and target test's constructs initially is established through the use of judgmental strategies (e.g., interviewing and observing persons, literature reviews, consulting social anthropologists) and then through the use of classical (e.g., item difficulty, distractibility, and discrimination) and modern (e.g., item response theory) empirical methods. Proper test administration is promoted by insuring the directions minimize verbal interactions, are clearly understood, and are consistent between the source and target tests. Test administrators should be drawn from the target communities, familiar with the language and dialects, be experienced in administering tests, and recognize the importance of maintaining standardized methods. Ethical issues associated with test translation and adaptation are discussed elsewhere (Oakland, 2005).

REFERENCES

Bartram, D. (2001). International guidelines for test use. *International Journal of Testing, 1*, 93–114.

Bartram, D., & Hambleton, R. (Eds.). (2006). *Computer-based testing and the Internet.* West Sussex, UK: John Wiley & Sons.

Berry, J. W., Poortinga, Y. H., Segall, M. H., & Dasen, P. R. (1992). *Cross-cultural psychology: Research and applications.* Cambridge, UK: Cambridge University Press.

Byrne, B. M. (1998). *Structural equation modeling with LISREL, PRELIS, and SIMPLIS: Basic concepts, applications, and programming.* Mahwah, NJ: Lawrence Erlbaum.

Byrne, B. M. (2001). *Structural equation modeling with AMOS: Basic concepts, applications, and programming.* Mahwah, NJ: Lawrence Erlbaum.

Byrne, B. M. (2006). *Structural equation modeling with EQS* (2nd ed.): *Basic concepts, applications, and programming.* Mahwah, NJ: Lawrence Erlbaum.

Coyne, I., & Bartram, D. (Eds.). (2006). ITC guidelines on computer-based and Internet-delivered testing [Special issue]. *International Journal of Testing, 6*(2).

Hambleton, R. K., Merenda, P., & Spielberger, C. (Eds.). (2005). *Adapting educational and psychological tests for cross-cultural assessment*. Mahwah, NJ: Lawrence Erlbaum.

Hambleton, R. K., Swaminathan, H., & Rogers, H. J. (1991). *Fundamentals of item response theory*. Newbury Park, CA: Sage.

Leach, M., & Oakland, T. (2007). Ethics standards impacting test development and use: A review of 31 ethics codes impacting practices in 35 countries. *International Journal of Testing, 7,* 71–88.

Oakland, T. (2005). Selected ethical issues relevant to test adaptations. In R. K. Hambleton, P. F. Merenda, & C. D. Spielberger (Eds.), *Adapting educational and psychological tests for cross-cultural assessment* (pp. 65–92). Mahwah, NJ: Lawrence Erlbaum.

Segall, M. H., Lonner, W. J., & Berry, J. W. (1998). Cross-cultural psychology as a scholarly discipline: On the flowering of culture in behavioral research. *American Psychologist, 53,* 1101–1110.

VandenBos, G. (Ed). (2007). *APA dictionary of psychology*. Washington DC: American Psychological Association.

van de Vijver, F. J. R., & Watkins, D. (2006). Assessing similarity of meaning at the individual and country level: An investigation of a measure of independent and interdependent self. *European Journal of Psychological Assessment, 22,* 69–77.

THOMAS OAKLAND
University of Florida

See also: Cross-Cultural Psychology; International Test Commission; Multicultural Assessment

CROSS-CULTURAL PSYCHOLOGY

Cross-cultural psychology is the scientific study of human behavior across cultural or national boundaries (Adler & Gielen, 2002). It is based on the two premises that (1) our culture deeply impacts all aspects of our psyche, including perception, cognition, development, personality, abnormality, and social behavior; and (2) for scientific psychology to be accurate, it must study these cultural variations rather than overlook them.

Definitions

As psychology has moved toward cultural diversity in the past half-century, there have been four emerging terms for four evolving specialties. The earliest of these four was "Multicultural" and concerned cultural differences within a single nation. This specialty originated in the black civil rights movement of the 1950s, initially focused on racial differences, and gradually expanded to incorporate ethnic, linguistic, and gender differences in a single nation. The second emerging specialty was "Cross-cultural" psychology, which flowered quite separately beginning in the 1970s and led to the monumental five-volume *Handbook of Cross-Cultural Psychology* (Triandis & Berry, 1980) focused on differences across national groups (Berry et al., 1997). Then came "Cultural" (or indigenous) psychology, emerging in the 1990s with an emphasis on studying people in specific groups on their own terms, in the belief that "not only cross-cultural psychology, but the entire enterprise of scientific psychology is so flawed at its foundation that an entirely new discipline for the study of culture in mind must be formulated" (Cole, 1996, p. 3). Fourth and finally, "International" psychology has emerged in force since the 1990s, with a focus on the field of psychology across nations, particularly with respect to training, credentialing, and professional associations.

Cross-cultural psychology is best seen as a midpoint between two extremes. One is the "universal" extreme championed by Hans Eysenck (1995), for one, and maintaining that a century of scientific psychology has revealed universal truths about human perception, physiology, and social behavior that vary little across national boundaries. The other is the "cultural" extreme, which sees few if any truths independent of a person's cultural context. In the middle, cross-cultural psychology seeks to compare cultures scientifically, to gauge the balance of behavior that is culture-specific versus behavior that is universal across cultures. Whereas universal psychology minimizes cultural variations, and cultural psychology emphasizes these variations, cross-cultural psychology seeks to chart cultural variations through comparative research.

Importance

Since the 1980s in the United States, multicultural and cross-cultural psychology have been widely viewed as an overdue corrective for the field. For most of the century, experimental and psychometric psychologists collected data on convenience samples of white male college sophomores and published their findings as if they were universal truths that applied to all, with no attempt to replicate their findings across gender, ethnic, or national groups (Sears, 1986). As Robert Guthrie (1998) crisply noted, "Even the rat was white."

At the same time, psychology increasingly faces the unstated yet immense irony of cross-species research. An estimated 20 million nonhuman animals of all sorts are studied by U.S. researchers each year, particularly cats, dogs, rabbits, mice, and other primates (Mukerjee, 1997). This number of animal participants in psychological research far exceeds the number of human participants and is based on the premise that basic social as well as physiological processes transcend species (Zajonc et al., 1969). How much can findings on mice or dogs be generalized to humans? Psychology increasingly avers significant cultural differences separating people within the human species, but not separating humans from other species.

Development

In a way, cross-cultural psychology is as old as psychology itself. Although Wilhelm Wundt (1832–1920) is best known as the founder of the first psychology laboratory in 1879 at the University of Leipzig, it was decades later that Wundt (1916) authored his magnum opus, "*Volkerpsychologie*," or folk psychology, which is a series of 10 volumes analyzing the nature of language, art, mythology, and religion. This comparative study of cultural differences continued to flourish through the early twentieth century in the United States as well as parts of Europe, particularly Britain, France, and Germany. One key example of this flourishing was the a group of prolific Columbia University psychologists and anthropologists who surrounded Franz Boas (1858–1942) during his 40 years at Columbia from 1896 until 1936, including Ruth Benedict (1887–1949), Margaret Mead (1901–1978), Otto Klineberg (1899–1992), Abraham Kardiner (1891–1981), and Anne Anastasi (1908–2001). In 1937, Anastasi published the first of her three editions of *Differential Psychology*, a brilliant 700-page tome in which culture was one group difference considered among many others—race, gender, age, income, language, schooling, family, anatomy, biology, and heredity.

In the 1940s, psychologists' shock and disgust for the extreme "race science" of the Nazi era led them to avoid for a few decades any discussion of group differences in behavior. Differential psychology disappeared, only to resurface gradually with the civil rights movement in the 1950s, then feminism in the 1960s, and then ethnic pride in the 1970s.

Resources

A growing number of books, organizations, and resources are now available for the also-growing number of students and professionals interested in cross-cultural psychology (Takooshian & Stambaugh, 2007). The second edition of *The Handbook of Cross-Cultural Psychology* (Berry et al., 1997) offers a comprehensive reference of 1,400 pages in 32 chapters in three volumes. The interdisciplinary Society for Cross-Cultural Research (http://www.sccr.org) publishes its flagship journal, *Cross-Cultural Research*. The International Association of Cross Cultural Psychology (http://www.iaccp.org) publishes its *Journal of Cross-Cultural Psychology*, and its web site offers a compendium of dozens of course syllabi and suggested DVDs. The web site of the International Union of Psychological Science (http://www.iupsys.org) lists more than 100 organizations, many of them

focused on development, assessment, or other specific aspects of cross-cultural psychology. The American Psychological Association offers an Office of International Affairs (http://www.apa.org/international), as well as a division of international psychology (http://www.internationalpsychology.net), each of which offers a web-based bulletin. The International Test Commission (http://www.intestcom.org) offers guidelines on the use of assessments to study people across cultures.

REFERENCES

Anastasi, A. (1937). *Differential psychology*. New York: Macmillan.

Cole, M. (1996). *Cultural psychology: A once and future discipline*. Cambridge MA: Harvard.

Berry, J. W., Poortinga, Y. H., Pandey, J., Dasen, P. R., Saraswathi, T. S., Segall, M. H., et al. (1997). (Eds.). *Handbook of cross-cultural psychology* (2nd ed.). Needham Heights, MA: Allyn & Bacon.

Eysenck, H. J. (1995). Cross-cultural psychology and the unification of psychology. *World Psychology, 1,* 11–30.

Guthrie, R. V. (1998). *Even the rat was white: A historical view of psychology* (2nd ed.). Boston: Allyn & Bacon.

Mukerjee, M. (1997, February). Trends in animal research. *Scientific American,* 86–93.

Sears, D. O. (1986). College sophomores in the laboratory: Influences of a narrow data base on social psychology's view of human nature. *Journal of Personality & Social Psychology, 51,* 515–530.

Triandis, H. C., & Berry, J. W. (1980). *Handbook of cross-cultural psychology*. Boston MA: Allyn & Bacon. [5 volumes]

Wundt, W. (1916). *Elements of folk psychology: Outlines of a psychological history of the development of mankind*. (E. L. Schaub, Trans.). London: Allan and Unwin.

Zajonc, R. B., Heingartner, A., & Herman, E. M. (1969). Social enhancement and impairment of performance in the cockroach. *Journal of Personality & Social Psychology, 13,* 83–92.

SUGGESTED READINGS

Adler, L. L., & Gielen, U. P. (2002). (Eds.). *Cross-cultural topics in psychology*. (2nd ed.). Westport, CT: Praeger.

Eysenck, M. (2004). *Psychology: An international perspective*. London: Lawrence Erlbaum.

Takooshian, H., & Stambaugh, L. F. (2007). Getting involved in international psychology. Pp. 365–389 in M. J. Stevens & U. P. Gielen (Eds.), *Toward a global psychology: Theory, research, intervention, and pedagogy*. Mahwah, NJ: Lawrence Erlbaum.

HAROLD TAKOOSHIAN
Fordham University

See also: Culture and Psychotherapy; International Psychology; Multicultural Assessment; Multicultural Counseling

CROWD BEHAVIOR (See Mob Psychology)

CULTURAL BIAS IN PSYCHOLOGICAL TESTING

Cultural bias has no a priori definition. Instead, its presence is inferred from differential performance of socioracial (e.g., Blacks, Whites), ethnic (e.g., Latinos/Latinas, Anglos), or national groups (e.g., U.S. Americans, Japanese) on measures of psychological constructs such as cognitive abilities, knowledge or skills (CAKS), or symptoms of psychopathology (e.g., depression). Historically, the term grew out of efforts to explain between-group score differences on CAKS tests primarily of African American and Latino/Latina American test takers relative to their White American counterparts and concerns that test scores should not be interpreted in the same manner across these groups. Although the concept of cultural bias in testing and assessment also pertains to score differences and potential misdiagnoses with respect to a broader range of psychological concepts, particularly in applied psychology and other social and behavioral sciences, this aspect of cultural bias has received less attention in the relevant literature (Tyson, 2004). Therefore, cultural bias as it pertains to CAKS testing is the primary focus herein.

There have been three general philosophical perspectives that guide debates about potential cultural bias: (1) implicit, (2) psychometric, and (3) cultural equivalence. Each perspective implies a specific methodology for investigating cultural bias and takes a different posture with respect to what constitutes culture. Also, it should be noted that the term "cultural bias" has been used generically to pertain to a variety of sociodemographic comparison groups, including racial, ethnic-cultural, and socioeconomic groups, whose essences are presumed to be misrepresented by standard tests used for assessment or for decision-making purposes.

Implicit Perspective

More explicitly, with respect to the implicit perspective of cultural bias in CAKS tests, race and ethnic conscious theorists and test users argue that the reason why test scores of Black and Latino/Latina test takers have routinely been much lower than those of White test takers is because the tests used for assessment purposes carry the culture of White, middle-class, English-as-first language, U.S. Americans (WMEA) and, thereby, give White Americans an advantage over test takers whose socialization and life experiences are different (Hilliard, 1984). Consequently, cultural bias is situated in the test content or items and the testing process. Commonsense definitions of culture, whose organizing principles are usually not specified, guide this perspective. Advocates of the implicit perspective argue that by removing items from tests that favor WMEA over other cultures, it should be possible to eliminate cultural bias.

Thus, the primary methodology for demonstrating or eliminating potential cultural biases from this perspective is qualitative analyses in which cultural informants are asked to identify items that place the focal racial or cultural group of concern at a disadvantage. A more explicitly racial/cultural version of this perspective uses extant cultural theories to content analyze CAKS items (Banks, 2006). Group-level responses of test takers are statistically compared to determine whether mismatches between culturally contaminated item content and responses of different cultural groups might account for observed between-group differences in CAKS test scores.

Psychometric Perspective

To refute such interpretations, test developers and advocates of the cultural-bias psychometric perspective for explaining between-group differences define lack of cultural bias as the extent to which test items are related to each other in a similar manner (construct validity) or test scores are related equivalently across designated groups to nontest intended criteria (predictive validity). Investigations of why group-level differences occur are not a hallmark of this perspective. Psychometric theorists use culture and race/ethnic group ascriptions as interchangeable concepts. Nontest criteria typically are indices external to the test such as academic performance (e.g., grade point average) or job performance (e.g., supervisors' evaluations). Thus, for example, if the CAKS test scores of two samples of test takers, representing different racial groups, are each positively or meaningfully correlated with GPA, the relationships are interpreted as evidence that the test yields valid scores and, consequently, the test under investigation is not culturally biased (Brown, Reynolds, & Whitaker, 1999).

The Standards for Psychological and Educational Testing (American Educational Research Association, American Psychological Association, & National Council on Measurement in Education, 1999) recommend various psychometric strategies for examining the thesis of cultural test bias from a psychometric perspective. For example, evidence of construct validity may be inferred from factor analyses of groups' item or test responses, whereas evidence of predictive validity may be inferred from regression analyses in which test scores are used to predict the same nontest criteria for each group.

Comparison of the Implicit and Psychometric Perspectives

Given the greater sophistication of the psychometric statistical analytic strategies relative to the cultural-bias analytic strategies and the greater cultural sophistication of the implicit cultural bias perspective relative to the psychometric perspective, it is easy to overlook the difficulties inherent in explaining test score performance (i.e., potential cultural bias) from either the implicit or the psychometric perspective. In increasing order of conceptual meaningfulness, these perspectives share three difficulties:

1. Each perspective locates bias in test scores or items, the dependent or outcome variable in a research design in which mean scores of groups are compared.

2. Between-group differences in test scores are the catalysts for arousing suspicions that cultural bias has affected test scores in each perspective.

3. Each perspective imputes theoretical meaning to racial, ethnic, or cultural groups per se and assumes that such groups can serve in the role of conceptual independent, predictor, or moderating variables in a research design. Thus, when group differences in test scores are observed, psychometric proponents use racial groups to explain the differences. For example, Black test takers' lower CAKS test scores are interpreted as evidence that they are less intelligent or prepared than their White counterparts.

In psychology, an *independent variable* is defined as a representation of a psychological theoretical construct that can be operationally defined through manipulation, measurement, or creation. Obviously, none of these conditions pertains to racial, ethnic, or cultural groups because researchers (1) do not manipulate membership (i.e., cause a person to be a member of one group rather than another); or (2) measure the groups because, rather than being measures of individual differences, racial groups are nominal or dummy variables whereby everyone in a group is assigned the same numerical value. The reification of racial or ethnic groups as psychological constructs has been the impetus for theorists' attempts to define and assess constructs that might be associated with racial-group ascription and, therefore, are the source of cultural bias if it exists (Helms, Jernigan, & Mascher, 2005).

Cultural Equivalence Perspective

Advocates of this perspective locate culture in the person rather than the test or test items. Ethnic and racial cultures are presumed to result from group-determined socialization practices that lead individual test takers to internalize to some extent the customs or rituals, attitudes and values, language, and so forth that characterize their racial/cultural group(s) of origin rather than some other group (Helms, 1992). Members of every acknowledged group in the United States are presumed to have been socialized in some ethnic culture and some racial contexts. Accordingly, individual members of different groups may

perceive or react to the same item content or testing process differently because they have internalized different racial/cultural socialization experiences.

Thus, cultural bias exists when test scores unintentionally assess cultural/racial factors in a manner that advantages or disadvantages one group relative to others. For example, no societywide negative stereotypes about White Americans' intelligence exist, but such stereotypes about African Americans' intelligence are widely known (Steele & Aronson, 1995). If arousing fears of confirming negative stereotypes about their racial group's intelligence (i.e., stereotype threat) is associated with African Americans' lower test scores, then test scores are contaminated by "construct-irrelevant variance" using the terminology of advocates of the cultural-equivalence perspective and cultural bias using the terminology of the implicit culture perspective

The difference between the cultural equivalence and implicit bias perspectives is that the equivalence perspective requires measurement or manipulation of person-level constructs assumed to be cultural or racial, such as learning styles, racial attitudes, and acculturation, whereas the latter locates such factors in the test structure or content. Measurement of cultural/racial constructs permits the removal of their effects (i.e., bias) from group-level test scores by using various statistical approaches that are consistent with the psychometric perspective (AERA et al., 1999). Also, explicit measurement of cultural or racial factors as independent or predictor variables permits quantification of their effects on the scores of individual test takers (Helms, 2007). Detection of construct-irrelevant variance or cultural bias at the level of individuals rather than groups is important if test scores are used to make significant decisions about people's lives.

Although three discrete perspectives have guided inquiries about cultural bias in testing, advocates of each perspective agree that the possibility that cultural bias plays a role in testing is problematic. The perspectives differ in the extent to which proponents believe that the possibility is real. With the increased availability of cultural/racial theories and related measures for operationally defining racial/cultural constructs as true independent/predictor variables, this dispute may be resolved empirically in the future.

REFERENCES

American Educational Research Association, American Psychological Association, & National Council on Measurement in Education. (1999). *Standards for educational and psychological testing*. Washington, DC: American Psychological Association.

Banks, K. (2006). A comprehensive framework for evaluating hypotheses about cultural bias in educational testing. *Applied Measurement in Education, 19,* 115–132.

Brown, R. T., Reynolds, C. R., & Whitaker, J. S. (1999). Bias in mental testing since Jensen's *Bias in mental testing. School*

Psychology Quarterly. Special Issue: Straight talk about cognitive assessment and diversity, 14, 208–238.

Helms, J. E. (1992). Why is there no study of cultural equivalence in cognitive ability testing? American Psychologist, 47, 1083–1101. (Reprinted in N. R. Goldberger, & J. B. Veroff (Eds.), Culture and psychology reader, pp. 674–719. New York: New York University Press).

Helms, J. E. (2007). Fairness is not validity or cultural bias in racial-group assessment: A quantitative perspective. American Psychologist, 61, 845–859.

Helms, J. E., Jernigan, M., & Mascher, J. (2005). The meaning of race in psychology and how to change it. American Psychologist, 60, 27–36.

Hilliard, A. (1984). IQ testing as the emperor's new clothes: A critique of Jensen's Bias in Mental Testing. In C. R. Reynolds & R. T. Brown (Eds.), Perspectives on Bias in Mental Testing (pp. 139–170). New York: Plenum Press.

Steele, C. M., & Aronson, J. (1995). Stereotype threat and the intellectual test performance of African Americans. Journal of Personality and Social Psychology, 69, 797–811.

Tyson, E. H. (2004). Ethnic differences using behavior rating scales to assess the mental health of children: A conceptual and psychometric critique. Child Psychiatry & Human Development, 34, 167–201.

SUGGESTED READINGS

Freedle, R. O. (2003). Correcting the SAT's ethnic and social-class bias: A method for estimating SAT scores. Harvard Educational Review, 73, 1–43.

Steele, C. M. (1997). A threat in the air: How stereotypes shape intellectual identity and performance. American Psychologist, 52, 613–629.

JANET E. HELMS
Boston College

See also: Assessment Bias, Psychological Assessment; Psychological Measurement, Bias in

CULTURAL SENSITIVITY

Over the last four decades, psychologists have become gradually, and with some controversy, more focused on the importance of cultural sensitivity in applied psychology, in theory, and in research. The examination of culture as an important aspect of human experience and behavior began with a few scattered commentators decrying the incompleteness and potentially damaging character of a monocultural psychology. This early work on cultural sensitivity has expanded to encompass the accreditation standards, publication standards, practice standards, and governance of the major professional associations in psychology. Although there is far from complete consensus on what constitutes cultural sensitivity, it is now widely accepted that attending to the cultural sources of human experience and behavior is important.

Impediments to Cultural Sensitivity

In spite of this progress, there are powerful impediments to cultural sensitivity. Foremost among these impediments is the tendency toward ethnocentrism due to the natural attachment to the cultural heritage within which one is socialized. Cultural groups tend to operate tacitly, with little direct discussion of cultural mores, patterns, and beliefs. As individuals develop, they adopt culturally informed attitudes and behaviors unreflectively and therefore take their cultural heritage for granted. Cultural understandings provide a strong sense of identity and a powerful orientation toward what it is to live well. Although a natural outgrowth of enculturation, ethnocentrism fosters a strong, automatic in-group bias in perception, cognition, and affect. Members of one's group are viewed more favorably, differences in appearance and custom are regarded with suspicion, and negative attributions are frequently made about out-group individuals. In particular, members of the dominant culture often view people of Color with fear, mistrust, or bewilderment. In a complimentary manner, members of historically oppressed groups often respond with suspicion toward those outside of their racial/ethnic group, sometimes termed "healthy cultural paranoia."

In general, people report feeling most comfortable interacting with others who have similar interests, interpretations, and experiences. Even in the absence of questions of cultural preference and superiority, cultural differences can elicit discomfort, awkwardness, and mutual misinterpretation. The relative ease of interactions within one's cultural group engenders a preference for in-group interactions and impedes exploration and understanding of cultural differences.

Beyond immediate discomfort with cultural differences, developing cultural sensitivity requires the recognition that one's cultural heritage is one among many, without a privileged claim to truth or superiority. This recognition can lead to a disorienting loss of one's bearings and one's sense of what is worthwhile. For members of privileged groups, the dislocation of a sense of cultural superiority can be especially challenging because if one's cultural group has held a dominant position, one must address the responsibility for and personal benefits obtained from that dominant position.

There is also a strong leaning within the discipline of psychology to view the study of human behavior in universalist terms, with cultural factors playing a relatively minor role. An unreflective philosophical preference for universal conceptions of human behavior can impede the capacity to appreciate the role that cultural particulars play in individual and social life.

Approaches to Cultural Sensitivity

There are a number of approaches to cultivating cultural sensitivity, and this variation among perspectives and recommendations is an enduring feature of discussions about race and culture. Among the most noteworthy is the extended work by a dedicated group of thinkers that resulted in the Guidelines on Multicultural Education, Training, Research, Practice, and Organizational Change for Psychologists (APA, 2003). These guidelines go beyond cultural sensitivity to emphasize cultural competence. Indeed, those who identify with the multiculturalism movement would likely see cultural sensitivity as insufficient without the stronger capacity of being competent to work with culturally different others. The guidelines recommend the development of self-awareness regarding cultural matters, knowledge about one's own and others' cultures, and skills for addressing cultural issues.

Another approach to cultural sensitivity has been developed by racial identity theorists. Racial identity is "one's psychological response to one's race . . . the extent to which one identifies with a particular racial or cultural group and how that identification influences" responses "toward people from other groups" (Carter & Pieterse, 2005, p. 54). There are separate models of racial identity for Whites, Blacks, and people of color that are related to the distinct sociopolitical histories of each group. Racial identity theorists suggest that individuals vary in racial identity from "less differentiated, externally derived, and less mature status to a more internally based, complex, and differentiated mature status" (Carter & Pieterse, 2005, p. 54). Writers who focus on race (Carter & Pieterse, 2005; Helms & Cook, 1999) criticize terms such as cultural and multicultural as substitutes for race and for defusing the threat of discussing race and racism, thereby rendering discussion of race-based inequities more diffuse.

A recent contribution focused on personal transformation as the pathway to developing cultural sensitivity (Fowers & Davidov, 2006). From this viewpoint, cultural sensitivity requires one to overcome the natural stance of ethnocentrism and cultivate the character strength of openness to the other, which entails knowledge about cultural matters, a spontaneous interest in other viewpoints, a consistent pattern of open behavior toward those culturally different from oneself, and a willingness to allow one's cultural presuppositions to come into question in dialogue with others.

The focus on cultural sensitivity in the domain of psychotherapy has led to the development of culturally modified treatment approaches. These approaches seek to modify generally effective treatment methods to enhance their effectiveness with racial and ethnic minority populations as well as other communities of diversity.

In psychological theory and research, the two most prominent ways that cultural sensitivity are being explored and practiced are through the subdiscipline of cultural psychology and in attempts to examine cultural groupings as moderators of relationships among variables under study (e.g., Kitayama, Markus, & Kurokawa, 2000). Cultural psychologists study how psychological phenomena are co-constituted with sociocultural patterns. These thinkers see the psychological and the cultural as inseparable and most productively analyzed in tandem (Markus & Hamedani, 2007).

The viewpoints touched on here give a small sample of the multivocality on cultural diversity. Most thinkers recognize that culture is an extremely complex matter and that progress is possible only through exploring the contributions from many perspectives.

Elements of Cultural Sensitivity

The most basic requirement for understanding and practicing cultural sensitivity is to recognize the powerful influence of culture on human life. Human beings have been called the "incomplete animal" because humans are social beings with enormous mental flexibility. These two features of human nature necessitate the creation of shared cultural understandings and practices that allow social coordination and shared meaning. According to this viewpoint, culture "completes" the individual by providing the form and direction that is not available instinctively. This explains the power and persistence of cultural ties, and it suggests that cultural identity is a core aspect of human identity.

The recognition of cultural identity brings the powerful dialectic of identity and difference into focus. Cultural identity can only exist in contrast with culturally different others (Sacks, 2002). Therefore, cultural identity itself creates a tension between sameness and difference toward which individuals and groups must respond with cultural sensitivity or with cultural imperialism or alienation. Cultural sensitivity offers the possibility of appreciating the rich texture of human experience and difference, whereas cultural imperialism or alienation diminish the possibilities of human experience and dialogue.

Cultural sensitivity requires an ability to live with tensions that grow out of heartfelt differences without insisting that one perspective is right and the others are wrong. This suggests a kind of maturity in which culturally sensitive individuals are open to complexity, ambiguity, and dialectical rather than simplistic understandings. Cultural sensitivity also requires a self-reflexivity that allows one to take a step back from personal and cultural commitments to reflect on their sources and meanings. This reflexivity illuminates cultural understandings and practices as elements in a shared heritage that is to be honored, but not seen as universal truths about human beings. Reflexivity also facilitates the cultivation and monitoring of appropriate cultural sensitivity.

As one learns to manage tension and self-reflexivity, a posture of openness to the other becomes increasingly possible. Differences become interesting and illuminating rather than threatening or requiring resolution into agreement or consistency. This openness makes possible cultural dialogue, in which cultural beliefs and practices can be explored in contrast with those of other cultural perspectives. Dialogue can allow all parties to the conversation to learn about other cultural perspectives, increase their ability to interact with culturally different others, and gain greater clarity about their own deepest cultural commitments.

Cultivating cultural sensitivity is itself a dialectical process that involves encounter and reflection. One gains cultural sensitivity only through encountering culturally different others with an open mind, but one gains an open mind only through having one's cultural preconceptions challenged by other modes of life. Cultural sensitivity and knowledge about other cultures' history, beliefs, and practice are gained through repeated encounters through which the individual gradually increases his or her capacity to take in and appreciate cultural variety. As this capacity increases, individuals learn to recognize better when cultural sensitivity is called for and how to broach and explore cultural matters.

REFERENCES

American Psychological Association. (2003). Guidelines on multicultural education, training, research, practice, and organizational change for psychologists. *American Psychologist, 58,* 377–402.

Carter, R. T., & Pieterse, A. L. (2005). Race: A social and psychological analysis of the term and its meaning. In R. T. Carter (Ed.), *Handbook of racial-cultural psychology and counseling* (pp. 41–63). Hoboken, NJ: John Wiley & Sons.

Fowers, B. J., & Davidov, B. J. (2006). The virtue of multiculturalism: Personal transformation, character, and openness to the other. *American Psychologist, 61,* 581–594.

Helms, J. E., & Cook, D. A. (1999). *Using race and culture in counseling and psychotherapy.* Boston: Allyn & Bacon.

Kitayama, S., Markus, H. R., & Kurokawa, M. (2000). Culture, emotion, and well-being: Good feelings in Japan and the United States. *Cognition and Emotion, 14,* 93–124.

Markus, H. R., & Hamedani, M. G. (2007). Sociocultural psychology: The dynamic interdependence among self systems and social systems. In S. Kitayama & D. Cohen (Eds.), *Handbook of cultural psychology* (pp. 3–39). New York: Guilford Press.

Sacks, J. (2002). *The dignity of difference: How to avoid the clash of civilizations.* New York: Continuum International Publishing Group.

SUGGESTED READINGS

Carter, R. T. (Ed.). (2005). *Handbook of racial-cultural psychology and counseling.* Hoboken, NJ: John Wiley & Sons.

Kitayama, S., & Cohen, D. (Eds.). (2007). *Handbook of cultural psychology.* New York: Guilford Press.

BLAINE J. FOWERS
University of Miami

See also: **Multicultural Assessment; Multicultural Counseling**

CULTURE AND DEPRESSION

Understanding the relationship between culture and depression is crucial to effectively assessing and treating this disorder in all populations. Traditional conceptualizations of depression tend to minimize or totally ignore the role of cultural factors in the experience, expression, course, and treatment of depressive symptoms. As a result, most assessment techniques and therapeutic approaches lack empirical support in the treatment of cultural minorities. Therefore, it is important to realize and compensate for the limitations of such approaches with this population. This article identifies and discusses cultural factors that are particularly relevant in the assessment and treatment of depressive disorders. General guidelines for work with depressed individuals from cultural minority groups are also discussed.

A conceptualization of the interface between culture and depression must maintain the delicate balance between understanding cultural generalities and actively seeking to identify individual differences within groups. Failure to do this can result in stereotyping or, conversely, a complete disregard for the relevance of cultural factors in depressive illness.

Culture affects the nature and course of depressive symptoms. According to a recent comprehensive study by Riolo, Nguyen, Greden, and King (2005), African Americans and Mexican Americans had lower lifetime prevalence rates of depression compared to Caucasians (8.0%, 7.5%, and 10.4% respectively); minority groups also had fewer recurrences of depression. African Americans and Mexican Americans had higher rates of dysthymia than Caucasians. Another study among African Americans found that the severity of most somatic symptoms correlated with the overall severity of depressive mood, whereas the severity of cognitive symptoms generally did not correlate with the severity of the depressive episode (Ayalon & Young, 2003).

According to a recent study of treatment preferences, African Americans, Asian/Pacific Islanders, and Latino individuals were more likely than Caucasians to prefer counseling to antidepressant treatment and were less likely to construe their depression as being biological in nature (Givens, 2007). Also, individuals in such groups were more likely to view non-medical approaches, like prayer and counseling, as effective forms of treatment for depression. Native Americans had results consistent with the aforementioned minority groups, except that they were more likely to prefer antidepressant treatment to counseling.

African Americans and other minorities may be more likely to adhere to counseling than antidepressant treatment. A study by Brown and colleagues (1999) found that similar percentages of African Americans and Caucasians completed the acute phases of interpersonal therapy and pharmacotherapy. However, in the continuation phases of these treatments, 100% of African Americans adhered to interpersonal therapy, compared to only 76% of Caucasians. In contrast, 51% of African Americans did not adhere to the antidepressant regime, compared to 31% of Caucasians. African Americans also had higher prevalence of side effects from the medication.

Somatization of depressive symptoms is frequently associated with cultural minority status. It is important to understand the language of the client, as many cultures do not have language that is synonymous with the DSM-IV TR construal of depression. Kirmayer (2001) provides various cultural definitions of syndromes that are similar to depression. For instance, many Nigerians experience "heat in the head," a feeling of crawling on the skin, and somatic distress, and some Koreans experience hwa-byung, or "fire-illness," which is associated with gastrointestinal distress and interpersonal conflict. The DSM-IV TR also lists some culture-bound syndromes, which may serve as a useful starting point in determining syndromes similar to depression experienced by other cultures.

Many cultures associate treatment for depression as shameful or stigmatizing. Some individuals may construe their problems as spiritual or moral in nature and therefore may not regard psychological intervention as appropriate or necessary. Because clients may be reluctant to associate their difficulties with depression, one may need to take a more componential, symptom-based approach to treatment. Understanding the construal of symptoms from the client's cultural worldview (as opposed to the therapist's) is necessary for successful treatment. Also, particularly among African Americans, it is important to integrate spirituality into treatment.

Within-Group Differences

Degree of acculturation accounts for some differences within cultural minority groups. Acculturation is the process by which members of a minority group incorporate the behaviors, attitudes, beliefs, and cultural norms of the majority group. Unlike assimilation, in which the dominant culture completely replaces the minority culture, acculturation does not preclude retention of one's original culture. Depending on the individual's level of

acculturation, as well as the stress encountered while undergoing the process of acculturation (known as acculturative stress), depressive symptoms can vary. In general, those who are least acculturated tend to have higher rates of depression; this is likely due to more barriers encountered and reluctance to seek help (Gonzalez et al., 2001).

Cultural identity models also define some differences that exist within members of a cultural group. One of the most widely recognized models of cultural identity development, known as the Racial/Cultural Identity Development Model, was discussed by Sue and Sue (2003). In the first stage, that of conformity, minority individuals prefer aspects related to the dominant culture (a client in this stage may prefer a white therapist). In the second stage of dissonance, individuals, usually having an acute awareness of discrimination, begin to question their preference for the dominant culture, as well as the values associated with it. In the third stage of resistance and immersion, individuals become heavily involved with members of their own cultural group, rejecting and devaluing aspects of the dominant culture. In the fourth stage of introspection, individuals question their exclusive preference for their own cultural group and begin to construct a more flexible and integrated paradigm of cultural preferences. In the final stage of integrative awareness, individuals have an appreciation for their culture as well as other cultures, and will use criteria other than cultural membership in evaluating relationships.

One's stage of cultural identity may influence the preferences for treatment. Individuals who are in the stage of resistance and immersion may want to work exclusively with a therapist of their own race, using treatments that are culture specific. Conversely, individuals in the final stage of identity development may prefer a therapist with the same values that they hold, regardless of their race. The stage of cultural identity may contribute to depressive symptoms or, conversely, may serve as a protective factor. For instance, one who has experienced the harsh realities of discrimination in the stage of dissonance may experience increased levels of depression compared to an individual in the final stage of integrative awareness. Kibour (2001) found that Ethiopian immigrants whose stage of racial identity indicated preference for the majority culture were significantly more likely to be depressed than individuals in other stages of identity.

Biological Factors

Recent research has demonstrated that biological factors associated with culture affect the assessment and treatment of depression. For instance, cultural minorities tend to have different responses to the dexamethasone suppression test (DST), a measure of the hypothalamic-pituitary-adrenal (HPA) axis activity. Whereas depression has typically been associated with increased rates of a non-suppression response to DST, depressed individuals from cultural minority groups have significantly lower rates of this response or do not demonstrate it (Lin, 2006). Additionally, certain sleep patterns have traditionally been associated with depression, such as reduced REM latency (time between falling asleep and onset of REM) and increased REM density (frequency of eye movements during REM sleep). Lin (2001) cited various studies demonstrating that cultural minorities, such as African Americans and Latinos, who were diagnosed with depression demonstrated sleep patterns that differed from the typical profile associated with depression; such differences included increased REM latency and decreased REM density. This pattern occurred despite research demonstrating that sleep patterns are generally consistent across cultures.

Also, recent research has found that allelic variations in the CYP2D6 enzyme, which are associated with significantly reduced metabolism of antidepressants (mostly tricyclics), are present in higher frequencies among African Americans and Asians. CYP2D6 is involved in the metabolism of various antidepressant medications, and certain allelic variations are associated with reduced or nonexistent functioning of this enzyme. Such functioning is associated with increased sensitivity to the medication, higher prevalence of side effects, and higher metabolic ratios. In African Americans, median frequency of reduced functioning and nonfunctional alleles is approximately 50%. The median frequency of poor metabolizers among Asians and Pacific Islanders is approximately 41%. Furthermore, many individuals with normal genotypes in these groups are poor metabolizers of antidepressant medication (Bradford, 2002), suggesting that the rate of poor metabolism in these populations may be higher than the genotypic frequencies indicate. The results of this research indicate that lower doses of certain antidepressants may need to be considered in members of these populations.

To effectively assess and treat depression in cultural minorities, it is necessary to understand the cultural norms as well as determinants of individual differences within groups. An effective approach to understanding and treating depression will acknowledge and accommodate for the limitations of traditional diagnostic and therapeutic approaches. Culture affects the construal and expression of depressive symptoms, as well as course of symptoms, and preference for and response to treatment. Further research regarding the effect of culture on biological and sociocultural correlates of depression is necessary for an accurate conceptualization of this disorder in minority populations.

REFERENCES

Ayalon, L., & Young, M. (2003). A comparison of depressive symptoms in African Americans and Caucasian Americans. *Journal of Cross-Cultural Psychology, 34*, 111–124.

Bradford, L. D. (2002). CYP2D6 allele frequency in European Caucasians, Asians, Africans and their descendants. *Pharmacogenomics, 3*, 229–243.

Brown, C., Schulberg, H. C., Sacco, D., Perel, J. M., & Houck, P. R. (1999). Effectiveness of treatments for major depression in primary medical care practice: A post hoc analysis of outcomes for African American and White patients. *Journal of Affective Disorders, 53*, 185–192.

Gonzalez, H. M., Naan, M. N., & Hinton, L. (2001). Acculturation and the prevalence of depression in older Mexican Americans: Baseline results of the Sacramento area Latino study on aging. *Journal of the American Geriatric Society, 49*, 948–953.

Kibour, Y. (2001). Ethiopian immigrants' racial identity attitudes and depression symptomatology: An exploratory study. *Cultural Diversity and Ethnic Minority Psychology, 7*, 47–58.

Kirmayer, L. J. (2001). Cultural variations in the clinical presentations of depression and Anxiety: Implications for diagnosis and treatment. *Journal of Clinical Psychiatry, 62*(suppl. 13), 13–19.

Lin, K. (2001). Biological differences in depression and anxiety across races and ethnic groups. *Journal of Clinical Psychiatry, 62*(suppl. 13), 22–28.

Riolo, S. A., Nguyen, T. A., Greden, J. F., & King, C. A. (2005). Prevalence of depression by race/ethnicity: Findings from the National Health and Nutrition Examination Survey III. *American Journal of Public Health, 95*, 998–1000.

Sue, D. W., & Sue, D. (2003). *Counseling the culturally diverse: Theory and practice.* Hoboken, NJ: John Wiley & Sons.

SUGGESTED READINGS

Kleinman, A., & Good, B. J. (Eds.). (1986). *Culture and depression.* Berkeley: University of California Press.

Tseng, W. S., & Streltzer, J. (Eds.). (2001). *Culture and psychotherapy: A guide to clinical practice.* Arlington: American Psychiatric Publishing.

Williams Lawal-Solarin, F. M. (2008; manuscript in preparation). Depression in African American children and adolescents: Neurobiological and sociocultural factors as possible mechanisms for racial variation in depressive symptomatology.

FOLUSO M. WILLIAMS LAWAL-SOLARIN
Emory University School of Medicine

See also: **Cross-Cultural Psychology; Depression; Lifespan Depression**

CULTURE AND PSYCHOTHERAPY

In its broadest sense, culture refers to the sum of socially learned behaviors, attitudes, values, symbols, systems of thought, and concepts of the universe that distinguish one individual or group of people from another. Culture is both universal and particular; no individual is immune from the effects of culture or is totally dominated by it. A growing movement toward including multicultural perspectives in the development, evaluation, and provision of psychotherapy seeks to recognize the fundamental importance of culture in shaping the incidence, expression, and subjective interpretation of psychological distress, as well as remedy the significant deficits of established therapeutic methods and practices developed according to White European-American, middle-class norms and perspectives.

Therapy in a Multicultural Society

Researchers have outlined a number of reasons why an increasingly multicultural perspective is essential to the provision of just and efficacious psychotherapeutic services in the United States. According to the 2000 Census, ethnic minorities (Asian Americans, African Americans, Hispanics/Latino(a)s, and Native Americans) comprise approximately 30% of the population, and this number is projected to rise to 50% or more within the next 50 years. Established models, theories, tests, and practices of psychotherapy have been developed largely from the perspective of middle-class White American culture, which tends to be individualistic or idiocentric and as such have limited utility outside of this context.

Hall (2001) notes that empirically supported therapies (ESTs), if developed and validated without consideration for their appropriateness and efficacy with minority populations, are unlikely to be valid for ethnic minorities. He notes that extending psychotherapeutic research to include diverse populations serves an empirical purpose, as it can provide support for the external validity of current theories and approaches. In addition, ethnic minority groups may encounter unique and shared experiences, such as discrimination, systemic prejudice, and racism, which can act as stressors influencing the onset of psychological distress. Ethnic minority groups are also represented disproportionately in vulnerable populations, such as the poor and homeless, which are at greater risk for the development of psychological disorders and are profoundly underserved by mental health facilities.

Factors that have led to the underutilization of psychological services by ethnic minorities are also important to consider. Historically, the development of therapeutic models from Eurocentric, middle-class norms has led to the employment of a deficit model in addressing nonmajority therapeutic concerns, such that deviation from majority norms was largely interpreted as disorder on the part of the client. As Pedersen (2002) notes, further results of this scientific racism are the widespread perception by many members of minority groups that the institution of psychotherapy exists to perpetuate a majority viewpoint and a power differential and the consequential distrust and underutilization of psychological services by minority groups.

Developing Multicultural Competence: Research and Practice

An increasingly diverse population guarantees that service providers will encounter clients from unique and varied backgrounds, languages, religions, and traditions, and thus it is crucial that therapists gain multicultural competence in order to better serve their ethnically diverse clientele. From a position paper on cross-cultural counseling competencies prepared by its counseling division to a set of Guidelines on Multicultural Education, Training, Research, Practice and Organization Change, the American Psychological Association has devoted increasing attention to this aspect of psychotherapy over the last few decades. According to Leong and Gupta (2001), multicultural competence involves the development of greater cultural awareness and sensitivity, as well as recognition of the possible effects of a therapist's personal cultural biases on diagnosis and treatment. For example, a therapist who has not personally experienced systemic discrimination may be prone to interpret a client's discrimination-induced anxiety as a problem arising from the individual, rather than an adaptive response to a wider sociocultural context of majority group oppression and prejudice. As Leong and Gupta note, understanding the worldviews and personalities that clients bring into the therapeutic setting is essential, as they may influence their preferences for therapists and affect therapeutic outcomes.

Much of the research into multicultural issues of psychotherapy concerns the utility of mainstream approaches in assessment, intervention, and treatment. Researchers and practitioners continue to question the efficacy of established paradigms and methodology in working with minority clientele, and an ongoing debate in the field centers on the appropriateness of adapting established methods rather than developing indigenous frameworks for psychotherapy. Most research into the efficacy of established treatments has focused on the effect of client/therapist ethnic matching on therapeutic outcomes, as well as on considerations of therapist and client characteristics, client preferences, therapists' personal and training biases, and cultural competencies. However, given limited research as well as significant intersectionality between relevant considerations of class, gender, and sexual orientation, the interpretation of available data remains problematic. For example, although research suggests that many ethnic minority persons may prefer therapists of their own ethnicity, Leong and Gupta (2001) note that therapist preference is "a complex and interactive phenomenon" that may not be readily reduced to ethnicity alone. Zane and colleagues (2004) suggest that ethnic matching, although an imperfect measure of cultural match, has been found to be more strongly associated with positive therapeutic outcomes.

Vera, Vila, and Alegría (2002) have argued that an emphasis on client characteristics may encourage stereotyping on the part of therapists. Considerable within-group heterogeneity exists among racial and minority groups, and individuals vary greatly in their level of identification with cultural norms and practices. An individual's personality and cultural perspective can be influenced by numerous factors, including but not limited to age, gender, level of acculturation, language proficiencies, socioeconomic status, geographic location, and religion. As such, overgeneralization of group characteristics encourages stereotyping and serves to deprive individuals of their unique personal experiences. The authors propose the use of Falicov's multidimensional ecosystemic comparative approach (MECA), which establishes a framework by which practitioners interpret client behavior and cognition according to both universal (shared human experiences) and particular (both group and individual difference) considerations. In addition, MECA encourages practitioners to consider points of commonality and difference along a multitude of factors (such as education, socioeconomic status, ethnicity) between therapist and client in order to foster a culturally sensitive therapeutic relationship.

Another approach to multicultural research focuses on evaluating the applicability of theoretical models to diverse populations. The cultural accommodation model (CAM) developed by Leong and colleagues (2007) identifies cultural "blindspots" and gaps in an existing theory and works to accommodate these models to increase cross-cultural validity. One method of this approach examines the amount of cultural loading, or reliance on culture- and group-specific norms and expectations, in a given framework. It is assumed that clinical approaches consisting of a blend of culture-specific and culture-general elements can be more appropriately applied to racial or ethnic groups. At the same time, a measure of the cultural loading of a paradigm is indicative of the amount of cultural accommodation needed to improve the cross-cultural validity of a model. Once relevant changes have been made to an existing theory, CAM tests the culturally accommodated theory to determine whether it has incremental validity over the unaccommodated theory.

As the United States becomes increasingly diversified, and service providers encounter individuals from increasingly diverse backgrounds and perspectives, it is imperative that researchers and practitioners in psychotherapy develop culturally competent paradigms and practices to better serve the needs of all individuals in a multicultural society. Restricted samples, limited empirical research, and the continued cultural encapsulation of the field of psychology raise serious concerns about the generalizability of established models and the efficacy of mainstream treatments with minority populations. Continued development of culturally sensitive theoretical frameworks and greater empirical psychotherapy research is needed to redress the imbalances in therapeutic treatment between majority and minority groups.

REFERENCES

Hall, G. C. N. (2001). Psychotherapy research with ethnic minorities: Empirical, ethical, and conceptual issues. *Journal of Consulting and Clinical Psychology, 69*(3), 502–510.

Leong, F. T. L., & Gupta, A. (2008). Culture and race in counseling and psychotherapy: A critical review of the literature. In S. D. Brown & R. W. Lent (Eds.), *Handbook of counseling psychology* (4th ed.) (pp. 320–357). Hoboken, NJ: John Wiley & Sons.

Pedersen, P. B. (2002). Cross-cultural counseling: Developing culture-centered interactions. In G. Bernal, J. Trimble, A. Burlew, & F. Leong (Eds.), *Handbook of racial and ethnic minority psychology* (pp. 487–503). Thousand Oaks, CA: Sage.

Vera, M., Vila, D., & Alegría, M. (2002). Cognitive-behavioral therapy: Concepts, issues, and strategies for practice with racial/ethnic minorities. In G. Bernal, J. Trimble, A. Burlew, & F. Leong (Eds.), *Handbook of racial and ethnic minority psychology* (pp. 521–538). Thousand Oaks, CA: Sage.

SUGGESTED READINGS

American Psychological Association. (2003). Guidelines on multicultural education, training, research, practice and organization change for psychologist. *American Psychologist, 58*, 377–402.

Sue, D. W., Bernier, J. E., Durran, A., Feinberg, L., Pedersen, P., Smith, E., et al. (1982). Position paper: Cross-cultural counseling competencies. *The Counseling Psychologist, 10*, 45–52.

Zane, N., Hall, G. C. N., Sue, S., Young, K., & Nunez, J. (2004). Research on psychotherapy with culturally diverse populations. In M. J. Lambert (Ed.), *Handbook of psychotherapy and behavior change* (5th ed., pp. 767–804). Hoboken, NJ: John Wiley & Sons.

FREDERICK T. L. LEONG
BRITTANY K. LANNERT
Michigan State University

See also: **Cross-Cultural Psychology; Ethnocultural Psychotherapy**

CURRENT PSYCHOTHERAPIES

Psychotherapy cannot be defined with any precision, and it is not entirely clear when a supportive conversation becomes counseling or when counseling becomes psychotherapy. Raymond Corsini (1914–2008), until his recent death one of the world's leading psychotherapy scholars, defined psychotherapy as follows:

> Psychotherapy is a formal process of interaction between two parties, each party usually consisting of one person but with the possibility that there may be two or more people in each party, for the purpose of amelioration of distress in one of the two parties relative to any or all of the following areas

of disability or malfunction: cognitive functions (disorders of thinking), affective functions (suffering or emotional discomforts), or behavioral functions (inadequacy of behavior). The therapist who takes part in this interaction has some theory of personality's origins, development, maintenance, and change, applies some method of treatment logically related to the theory, and has professional and legal approval to act as a therapist. (Corsini, 2008, p. 1)

In a different book, the *Handbook of Innovative Psychotherapies*, Corsini (2001) identifies 250 different systems of psychotherapy, but estimates that there are at least 400 extant systems. Albert Ellis, one of the leading figures in psychotherapy in the twentieth century and the founder of his own system of therapy, notes that "[m]odern psychotherapy is an enormous field with an almost infinite number of methods" (Ellis, p. 23). However, only a handful of therapies have been widely adopted, and an even smaller number are taught in graduate programs in clinical and counseling psychology, social work, and related mental health professions.

Corsini and Wedding (2008) maintain that any truly established system of psychotherapy has to have core theoretical concepts, a history (i.e., sustained application by multiple practitioners and experience across diverse patient groups), at least a rudimentary theory, a defined process of psychotherapy, established mechanisms for effecting change, and some evidence of efficacy for the procedures, methods, and techniques promulgated by the system. They identify 13 systems that meet these criteria: psychoanalysis, Adlerian (individual) psychotherapy, analytical psychotherapy, client-centered psychotherapy, rational-emotive behavior therapy, behavior therapy, cognitive therapy, existential psychotherapy, gestalt therapy, multimodal therapy, family therapy, contemplative psychotherapies, and integrative psychotherapies.

Psychoanalysis

Although psychoanalysis is most closely associated with the work of Sigmund Freud (1856–1939), there are a number of different psychodynamic approaches to helping patients that would all be loosely included under the general rubric of psychoanalysis (Borden, 2009). However, they would all have certain features in common, which include a belief in and concern with the unconscious, appreciation for the way that inner conflict can influence behavior and interpersonal relationships, concern with the ways in which very early childhood experiences affect personality development, interest in the automatic ways of responding commonly referred to as defense mechanisms, and an appreciation for the important role of transference and countertransference in any psychotherapeutic relationship.

The interest in psychoanalysis and psychoanalytic approaches to treatment is underscored by the fact that the American Psychological Association (APA) Division of Psychoanalysis (Division 39) is one of the largest divisions in the association, with more than 4,000 members. The diverse interests of Division 39 members are reflected in the nine sections: (I) Psychologists-Psychoanalyst Practitioners, (II) Childhood and Adolescence, (III) Women, Gender, and Psychoanalysis, (IV) Local Chapters, (V) Psychologist-Psychoanalysts' Clinicians, (VI) Psychoanalytic Research Society, (VII) Psychoanalysis and Groups, (VIII) Section on Family Therapy, and (IX) Psychoanalysis of Social Responsibility.

Adlerian Psychotherapy

Alfred Adler referred to his approach to psychotherapy as "individual psychology." Although he is commonly identified as a student of Freud, he is more correctly identified as a contemporary and a colleague who frequently disagreed with Freud. Adler emphasized the social nature of most problems that individuals developed. He stressed the importance of *Gemeinschaftsgefühl*, a term that literally means "feeling for community" but that is generally translated as "social interest." Adler emphasized value and meaning as core elements of the human condition, and he believed that people's problems often relate to "basic mistakes" rather than unconscious conflict. Adlerian therapists often assess early recollections, and they emphasize the influence of birth order and the family constellation in shaping personality. Numerous specific techniques have been developed and are used by Adlerian therapists, many of which are described in *Tactics in Counseling and Psychotherapy* (Mosak & Maniacci, 1998).

Adlerian ideas have had a tremendous influence in educational settings, and the utility of Adlerian principles in school settings has been described by Corsini (2007), who developed a school system built around Adlerian principles. These schools are generally referred to as "Corsini 4R schools"; the 4 "R"s are responsibility, respect, resourcefulness, and responsiveness. The North American Society of Adlerian Psychology (NASAP) is the most influential organization in the world of Adlerian psychology; the Adler School of Professional Psychology in Chicago is the major Adlerian training institute in the United States.

Analytical Psychotherapy

Analytical psychotherapy is the system developed by Carl Jung (1875–1961). Jungians emphasize the collective unconscious, the importance of archetypes and complexes, and the significance of symbolism. Important Jungian concepts include the persona, the shadow, and Jung's ideas about the four basic ways of relating to the world (i.e., personality types): thinking, feeling, sensation, and intuition. Jung was also a contemporary of Freud's; however, like Adler, Jung had his own ideas and eventually broke free of the hegemony of thought associated with Freud's inner circle. Jungian therapists emphasize analysis of transference, the interpretation of dreams, and the analysis of the unconscious. Jung's ideas have influenced numerous approaches to treatment, including group therapy, family therapy, body/movement therapy, art therapy, and the use of sand tray therapy. Jung is often associated with mysticism and the occult, and his influence has in many ways been more significant outside of psychology than inside traditional academic psychology circles (Papadopoulos, 2006).

Client-Centered Therapy

Client-centered therapy, also known as person-centered therapy, is intimately linked to the life and work of Carl R. Rogers (1902–1987). Rogers was a prolific author (he published 16 books and more than 200 professional articles) and a committed teacher who personally trained hundreds of therapists and influenced tens of thousands of others through his writing. Rogers is regarded as one of the founders of humanistic psychology.

Rogers focused his attention on the relationship between the client and the therapist, and he believed that this relationship accounted for most of the variance in therapy outcomes. Rogers felt that three therapeutic attitudes were especially critical: congruence, unconditional positive regard, and empathic understanding. Congruence refers to integration between the therapist's behavior and his or her true beliefs. Unconditional positive regard refers to genuine positive feelings that the client feels regarding his or her client. Because of the therapist's unconditional positive regard, he or she is likely to develop empathic understanding and come to value and respect the client, even in those cases in which the client has done something reprehensible.

Rogers regarded congruence, unconditional positive regard, and empathic understanding as conditions that were both necessary and sufficient for change to occur in psychotherapy. When the therapist possesses these attributes, clients benefit and their lives improve. As a general rule, client-centered therapists devalue assessment and diagnosis, and they are likely to respond in a similar way with almost all clients; this tendency has resulted in an unfair caricature of the practice of client-centered therapy in which therapists frequently are shown simply repeating or paraphrasing whatever remarks the client makes. This caricature devalues the skills, timing, and talents of the client-centered therapist.

Rogers wrote about the "fully functioning person," the self-concept, locus of evaluation, and the importance of experiencing. Fully functioning people experience all of their feelings, are characterized by integrity, and have a generally positive self-concept. There are few therapists who have had more influence on the current generation of mental health care providers. Many therapists value the conditions Rogers articulated, and incorporate congruence, unconditional positive regard, and empathic understanding in their treatment approach without specifically regarding themselves as client-centered therapists.

Rational Emotive Therapy

Albert Ellis (1913–2007), initially trained as a psychoanalyst, went on to develop rational emotive therapy (RET), which he later renamed rational emotive behavior therapy (REBT) to acknowledge that the theory focused on cognitive, affective, and behavioral features of personality. Ellis developed a simple but compelling mnemonic for explaining the essential features of REBT: He maintained (1) that activating events trigger but do not cause emotional distress in people; (2) that people respond to these events with beliefs that are often irrational and self-defeating; (3) that these beliefs result in consequences such as neurotic behavior or feelings of inadequacy and inferiority; and (4) that it is the job of the therapist to dispute these irrational thoughts.

Albert Ellis had a unique personality and style that can be appreciated by anyone who attended any of the thousands of public presentations and lectures he gave during a long and productive career. In particular, Ellis is noted for the Friday night workshops he gave at the Albert Ellis Institute in New York City until the very last days of his life. The late period of his life was complicated by an ironic and well-publicized dispute between Ellis and the directors of the Albert Ellis Institute. This dispute resulted in the establishment of the Albert Ellis Foundation, an organization that continues to promulgate the work and ideas of its founder.

Ellis and other practitioners of REBT have little interest in early childhood experiences. They tend to be interested in the philosophical and scientific aspects of human behavior. They agree that change requires homework outside the therapy hour ("*only hard work and practice* will correct irrational beliefs—and keep them corrected" [Ellis, 2008, p. 189]).

When the members of the Division of Clinical Psychology (Division 12 of the American Psychological Association [APA]) and the Division Counseling Psychology (APA Division 17) were asked to name the most outstanding psychotherapists of all time, Carl Rogers was ranked first and Albert Ellis second. Sigmund Freud ranked as a distant third (Smith, 1982).

It will be interesting to see if REBT remains a viable system of therapy in the future. The theory and therapy are both closely linked to their charismatic founder, and many current REBT practitioners are confused and demoralized by the tension that existed near the end of his life between Ellis and the institute he founded.

Behavior Therapy

Behavior therapy has its roots in experimental psychology, and in particular in the work of Ivan Pavlov (1849–1936),

B. F. Skinner (1904–1990), Joseph Wolpe (1915–1997), and Albert Bandura. Over the past three decades, there has been a synthesis of behavior therapy and cognitive approaches to therapy. This change is reflected in the change in the name of the Association for the Advancement of Behavior Therapy (AABT), which is now the Association for Behavioral and Cognitive Therapies (ABCT).

Behavior therapists are deeply committed to the scientific method, and they believe that understanding the historical origins of a psychological problem may not be necessary for successful treatment of that problem. They believe that all behavior is learned, and they often employ a functional analysis of behavior, an approach that involves a detailed analysis of connections between behavior and its antecedents and consequences. Specific behavior therapy techniques include guided imagery, systematic desensitization, flooding, role-playing, and assertiveness and skills training. Critics of behavior therapy feel that it addresses symptom reduction at the expense of genuine understanding of clients and their problems; however, the shift in therapy toward evidence-supported treatments has generally favored behavioral and cognitive approaches.

Some writers have commented on the "third wave" in behavior therapy: The first wave consisted of a focus on the modification of overt behavior (e.g., the treatment of phobias); the second wave emphasized cognitive factors and is closely linked to the development of cognitive therapy; the third wave involves the development of new approaches to therapy that focus on acceptance and change, mindfulness, and commitment. Marsha Linehan's dialectical behavior therapy and Steve Hayes' acceptance and commitment therapy are two salient examples of this third wave.

Cognitive Therapy

Like many of the other current psychotherapies reviewed so far, cognitive therapy is closely linked to the work and seminal thinking of a single individual—Aaron T. Beck. Beck, a psychiatrist, emphasized the ways in which distorted thinking influenced the development and maintenance of psychopathology. Beck believes that people develop cognitive schemas that are often mistaken and inaccurate—but that still have tremendous impact because of their ability to influence how individuals receive and interpret new information.

Cognitive therapy has its roots in the research and writing of Alfred Adler, Karen Horney, and George Kelly. Much of the theoretical foundations of cognitive therapy was developed in the early 1960s when Beck was looking for effective treatment approaches for his depressed and suicidal patients. Like Ellis, Beck had originally been trained as a psychoanalyst, and, like Ellis, he found that analytic techniques and theories were inadequate to help him address the immediate needs of the patients he was treating.

Cognitive therapists look for evidence of systematic errors in thinking in troubled clients, which are generally referred to as cognitive distortions. Some of the most common cognitive distortions are arbitrary inference, selective abstraction, overgeneralization, magnification and minimization, personalization, and dichotomous thinking.

Existential Psychotherapy

Existential therapists are concerned with authenticity and what the philosopher Martin Heidegger referred to as "life in the ontological mode." These therapists tend to be erudite, widely read, and convinced that both literature and philosophy have much to contribute to psychotherapy. This approach to therapy has its roots in the existential movement in philosophy and especially in the work of Kierkegaard, Nietzsche, Heidegger, Camus, and Sartre.

Rollo May (1909–1994), a psychologist, was until his death the leading proponent of existential psychotherapy. May's writings drew heavily on his broad knowledge of philosophy and literature, and his books have made important contributions to the history of ideas. Three of May's students, Irvin Yalom, Ed Mendelowitz, and Kirk Schneider, are the leading proponents of existential psychotherapy today. Yalom, author of an influential book titled *Existential Psychotherapy* (Yalom, 1980), is frequently cited for his list of the four "givens" of human existence: death, freedom, isolation, and meaninglessness. Existential therapists help clients confront these realities and explore the ways their beliefs about them influence their behavior and interpersonal relations.

Other Current Psychotherapies

Corsini and Wedding (2008) include five other specific approaches to therapy in their book Current Psychotherapies: Gestalt therapy, multimodal therapy, family therapy, contemplative therapies, and integrative psychotherapies. The Gestalt therapy progenitor was Fritz Perls (1893–1970). Multimodal therapy is most closely associated with the work of Arnold A. Lazarus. Family therapy has multiple schools and several founders, including Murray Bowen (1913–1990), Salvador Minuchin, Virginia Satir (1916–1988), and Michael White. Contemplative therapies include a potpourri of approaches, many linked with Asian philosophy. Contemplative therapies have been influenced by transpersonal thinking and especially by the work of Ken Wilber. An integrative approach to psychotherapy is perhaps best reflected in the work of two psychologists, John Norcross and Larry Beutler. Norcross and Beutler have decried the ideological "cold war" that has separated the various school of psychotherapy, and they have called for integration and eclecticism, maintaining the very best of each of the approaches to therapy while rejecting those elements that systematic research shows to be unimportant or ineffectual. It seems likely that the future of psychology will move toward integration, and that there will be far less emphasis on competitive ideologies and more emphasis on identification of the core components that facilitate change in the clients that mental health professionals strive to help.

REFERENCES

Borden, W. (2009). *Contemporary psychodynamic theory and practice.* Chicago: Lyceum Books.

Corsini, R. J. (Ed.). (2001). *Handbook of innovative therapy* (2nd ed.). New York: John Wiley & Sons.

Corsini, R. J. (2007). What does Alfred Adler have to teach to contemporary psychologists? *PsycCRITIQUES, 52* (24), No pagination specified.

Corsini, R. J., & Wedding, D. (Eds.). (2008). *Current psychotherapies* (8th ed.). Belmont, CA: Thompson Brooks/Cole.

Ellis, A. (2003). Two views of *handbook of innovative therapy* (2nd ed.): Therapy, therapy, who has got the therapy. *PsycCRITIQUES, 48,* 23–24

Ellis, A. (2008). Rational emotive behavior therapy. In R. J. Corsini & D. Wedding, *Current psychotherapies* (pp. 187–222). Belmont, CA: Thompson Brooks/Cole.

Mosak, H. H., & Maniacci, M. P. (1998). *Tactics in counseling and psychotherapy.* Itasca, IL: F. E. Peacock.

Papadopoulos, R. K. (Ed.). (2006). *The handbook of Jungian psychology: Theory, practice and applications.* New York: Routledge.

Smith, D. (1982). Trends in counseling and psychotherapy. *American Psychologist, 37,* 802–809.

Wedding, D., & Corsini, R. J. (Eds.). (2008). *Case studies in psychotherapy* (5th ed.). Belmont, CA: Thompson Brooks/Cole.

Yalom, I. (1980). *Existential psychotherapy.* New York: Basic Books.

DANNY WEDDING
University of Missouri-Columbia School of Medicine

See also: Psychotherapy

CUTANEOUS SENSATION (See Haptic Perception; Tactile Sensation)

CYCLOTHYMIC DISORDER

Cyclothymic disorder is characterized by two or more years of recurrent and intermittent mood episodes in which the individual oscillates or "cycles" between periods of depression and hypomania, with or without normal periods interspersed between the depressive and hypomanic states. Cyclothymic depressions include symptoms such as sadness, anhedonia, low energy, pessimism, poor concentration, and sleep and appetite changes resembling those observed in episodes of major depression. Cyclothymic hypomanic periods involve symptoms such as euphoria, high energy/activity, talkativeness, high self-confidence and grandiosity, decreased sleep, and impulsive, reckless behaviors typically observed in mania. However, unlike major depression and mania, both types of cyclothymic mood episodes are of subsyndromal intensity and duration (two to three days on average). Cyclothymic disorder can present as predominantly depressed, predominantly hypomanic, or balanced with approximately equal proportions of high and low periods (Goodwin & Jamison, 1990).

Historically, controversy surrounded the issue of whether cyclothymia is best conceptualized as a personality temperament or a subsyndromal mood disorder (Goodwin & Jamison, 1990). Indeed, cyclothymic patients are often perceived as exhibiting features of personality disorder rather than mood disorder at first clinical presentation. Family members often describe them as "moody," "high-strung," "hyperactive," and "explosive" (Akiskal, Djenderedjian, Rosenthal, & Khani, 1977). Moreover, cyclothymic individuals exhibit social role impairment and considerable problems in interpersonal relations (Goodwin & Jamison, 1990). On the other hand, some individuals with cyclothymia exhibit high levels of achievement. An association between genetic liability for bipolar disorder and creativity has been reported, with an increased propensity for creativity being most strongly expressed in individuals with subsyndromal manifestations of the bipolar spectrum (i.e., cyclothymia; Richards, Kinney, Lunde, Benet, & Merz, 1988).

Cyclothymia is thought to be on a continuum with full-blown bipolar (manic-depressive) disorder and, indeed, may be a precursor to it. Four lines of evidence strongly support this continuum model and suggest that cyclothymia is an integral part of the bipolar disorder spectrum. First, the behavior of cyclothymic individuals is qualitatively similar to that of patients with full-blown bipolar disorder; cyclothymia merges imperceptibly with Bipolar II (individuals who exhibit major depressive and hypomanic episodes, but not manic episodes), and sometimes Bipolar I (individuals who exhibit both major depressive and manic episodes) disorder at the behavioral level (Akiskal et al., 1977; Depue et al., 1981).

Second, equivalent rates of bipolar disorder have been reported in the first- and second-degree relatives of cyclothymic and Bipolar I patients (Akiskal et al., 1977; Depue et al., 1981), and increased rates of cyclothymia are found in the first degree relatives of bipolar patients (Chiaroni, Hantouche, Gouvernet, Azorin, & Akiskal, 2005). In addition, among monozygotic twins, when one twin had bipolar disorder, the co-twin had elevated rates of both bipolar and cyclothymic disorders (Edvardsen et al., 2008). These findings suggest that cyclothymia shares a common genetic diathesis with bipolar disorder.

Third, cyclothymic individuals, like Bipolar I patients, often experience an induction of hypomanic episodes when treated with tricyclic antidepressants (Akiskal et al., 1977). In turn, lithium prophylaxis leads to clinical improvement in a significant proportion of cyclothymic persons, as it does in bipolar patients. Finally, individuals with cyclothymia are at increased risk for developing full-blown bipolar disorder. Among cyclothymic individuals followed from one to four years, 35%–50% have developed Bipolar II or I disorder (Akiskal et al., 1977; Shen, Alloy, Abramson, & Sylvia, 2008).

The onset of cyclothymia usually occurs in mid-adolescence (mean age 14 years; Akiskal et al., 1977), whereas the onset of Bipolar I or II disorder occurs around 24 years on average (Goodwin & Jamison, 1990). Thus, there is approximately a 10-year risk period in which cyclothymia could be identified prior to the onset of full-blown bipolar disorder. Both the General Behavior Inventory (GBI; Depue et al., 1981) and the Temperament Evaluation of Memphis, Pisa, Paris, and San Diego (TEMPS-A; Akiskal & Akiskal, 2005) have been developed as first-stage screening instruments for this purpose. Both questionnaires have been found to identify cyclothymic individuals reliably and validly, with high sensitivity and specificity.

Cyclothymia often presents a problem in differential diagnosis (Goodwin & Jamison, 1990). Symptoms such as hyperactivity and distractibility that are part of cyclothymic hypomanic periods are easily confused with attention deficit hyperactivity disorder (ADHD). The key difference is that when these symptoms are part of cyclothymia, they are more episodic and characterized by rapid swings in attention and activity level than when they are part of ADHD. The impulsive, reckless behaviors (e.g., shoplifting, speeding, substance abuse, hostility) seen in cyclothymic hypomanic periods can also be mistaken for antisocial personality disorder. Here, the association of these behaviors with elevated or irritable mood states is central to the differential diagnosis. In addition, the presence of symptoms of high energy despite little sleep and grandiosity are indicative of cyclothymic hypomanic periods rather than ADHD or antisocial personality.

Several personality characteristics and cognitive styles have been associated with cyclothymia. Recent evidence indicates that cyclothymic individuals exhibit stable cognitive styles as negative as those observed among unipolar depressed people (Alloy, Reilly-Harrington, Fresco, Whitehouse, & Zechmeister, 1999). Alloy and colleagues (1999) reported that cyclothymic individuals exhibited dysfunctional attitudes and attributional styles (styles for explaining the causes of negative life events) as negative as those of dysthymic individuals and that cyclothymics' dysfunctional attitudes and attributional styles remained stable across large changes in mood and symptomatology over time. However, although as negative as the cognitive styles of unipolar depressed individuals, cyclothymic individuals' cognitive styles have distinctive goal-striving characteristics, in which they exhibit high perfectionism, self-criticism, and achievement-orientation (Francis-Raniere, Alloy, & Abramson, 2006). Moreover, both a personality tendency to be hyper-responsive to goals and rewards and life events that are likely to induce goal striving predict the onset of hypomanic episodes among individuals with cyclothymia (Alloy et al., 2008; Nusslock, Abramson, Harmon-Jones, Alloy, & Hogan, 2007).

Some evidence suggests that the extreme mood swings observed among cyclothymic and other bipolar individuals may be attributable to both a behavioral and biological hypersensitivity to stress. For example, individuals with cyclothymia or Bipolar II disorder who exhibit little regularity in their daily activities have a shorter time to onset of both depressive and hypomanic episodes (Shen et al., 2008). Moreover, Francis-Raniere and colleagues (2006) and Reilly-Harrington, Alloy, Fresco, and Whitehouse (1999) found that cyclothymic and bipolar individuals' dysfunctional attitudes and negative attributional styles interacted with stressful life events to predict longitudinally depressive and hypomanic mood swings. Specifically, cyclothymic and bipolar participants with negative cognitive styles were the most likely to experience depressive and hypomanic mood swings in response to stressful events. Similarly, Depue and colleagues (Depue et al., 1981; Depue, Kleiman, Davis, Hutchinson, & Strauss, 1985) found that cyclothymic individuals showed slower behavioral recovery following a stressful life event and slower recovery of cortisol secretion following a laboratory stressor than did normal controls.

REFERENCES

Akiskal, H. S., & Akiskal, K. K. (2005). The theoretical underpinnings of affective temperaments: Implications for evolutionary foundations of bipolar disorder and human nature. *Journal of Affective Disorders, 85,* 231–239.

Akiskal, H. S., Djenderedjian, A. H., Rosenthal, R. H., & Khani, M. K. (1977). Cyclothymic disorder: Validating criteria for inclusion in the bipolar affective group. *American Journal of Psychiatry, 134,* 1227–1233.

Alloy, L. B., Abramson, L. Y., Walshaw, P. D., Cogswell, A., Hughes, M., Iacoviello, B. M., et al. (2008). Behavioral Approach System (BAS) and Behavioral Inhibition System (BIS) sensitivities and bipolar spectrum disorders: Prospective prediction of bipolar mood episodes. *Bipolar Disorders, 10,* 310–322.

Alloy, L. B., Reilly-Harrington, N., Fresco, D. M., Whitehouse, W. G., & Zechmeister, J. S. (1999). Cognitive styles and life events in subsyndromal unipolar and bipolar disorders: Stability and prospective prediction of depressive and hypomanic mood swings. *Journal of Cognitive Psychotherapy: An International Quarterly, 13,* 21–40.

Chiaroni, P., Hantouche, E., Gouvernet, J., Azorin, J., & Akiskal, H. S. (2005). The cyclothymic temperament in healthy controls and familially at risk individuals for mood disorder: Endophenotype for genetic studies? *Journal of Affective Disorders, 85*, 135–145.

Depue, R. A., Kleiman, R. M., Davis, P., Hutchinson, M., & Krauss, S. P. (1985). The behavioral high-risk paradigm and bipolar affective disorder: VIII. Serum free cortisol in nonpatient cyclothymic subjects selected by the General Behavior Inventory. *American Journal of Psychiatry, 142*, 175–181.

Depue, R. A., Slater, J., Wolfstetter-Kausch, H., Klein, D., Goplerud, E., & Farr, D. (1981). A behavioral paradigm for identifying persons at risk for bipolar depressive disorder: A conceptual framework and five validation studies (Monograph). *Journal of Abnormal Psychology, 90*, 381–437.

Edvardsen, J., Torgersen, S., Roysamb, E., Lygren, S., Skre, I., Onstad, S., & Oien, P. (2008). Heritability of bipolar spectrum disorders: Unity or heterogeneity. *Journal of Affective Disorders, 106*, 229–240.

Francis-Raniere, E., Alloy, L. B., & Abramson, L. Y. (2006). Depressive personality styles and bipolar spectrum disorders: Prospective tests of the event congruency hypothesis. *Bipolar Disorders, 8*, 382–399.

Goodwin, F. K., & Jamison, K. R. (1990). *Manic-depressive illness.* New York: Oxford University Press.

Nusslock, R., Abramson, L. Y., Harmon-Jones, E., Alloy, L. B., & Hogan, M. E. (2007). A goal-striving life event and the onset of bipolar episodes: Perspective from the Behavioral Approach System (BAS) dysregulation theory. *Journal of Abnormal Psychology, 116*, 105–115.

Reilly-Harrington, N. A., Alloy, L. B., Fresco, D. M., & Whitehouse, W. G. (1999). Cognitive styles and life events interact to predict bipolar and unipolar symptomatology. *Journal of Abnormal Psychology, 108*, 567–578.

Richards, R. L., Kinney, D. K., Lunde, I., Benet, M., & Merzel, A. (1988). Creativity in manic-depressives, cyclothymes, their normal relatives, and control subjects. *Journal of Abnormal Psychology, 97*, 281–288.

Shen, G. H. C., Alloy, L. B., Abramson, L. Y., & Sylvia, L. G. (2008). Social rhythm regularity and the onset of affective episodes in bipolar spectrum individuals. *Bipolar Disorders, 10*, 520–529.

Lauren B. Alloy
Temple University

Lyn Y. Abramson
University of Wisconsin-Madison

***See also:* Bipolar Disorder; Depression; Mood Disorders**